THE OXFORD HANDBOOK OF

JUVENILE CRIME AND JUVENILE JUSTICE

THE OXFORD HANDBOOKS IN CRIMINOLOGY AND CRIMINAL JUSTICE

General Editor: Michael Tonry, University of Minnesota

....

THE OXFORD HANDBOOKS IN CRIMINOLOGY AND CRIMINAL JUSTICE offer authoritative, comprehensive, and critical overviews of the state of the art of criminology and criminal justice. Each volume focuses on a major area of each discipline, is edited by a distinguished group of specialists, and contains specially commissioned, original essays from leading international scholars in their respective fields. Guided by the general editorship of Michael Tonry, the series will provide an invaluable reference for scholars, students, and policy makers seeking to understand a wide range of research and policies in criminology and criminal justice.

OTHER TITLES IN THIS SERIES:

Crime and Criminal Justice
Michael Tonry

Crime Prevention
Brandon C. Welsh & David P. Farrington

Sentencing and Corrections
Joan Petersilia & Kevin R. Reitz

Crime and Public Policy
Michael Tonry

THE OXFORD HANDBOOK OF

JUVENILE CRIME AND JUVENILE JUSTICE

Edited by

BARRY C. FELD

and

DONNA M. BISHOP

OXFORD
UNIVERSITY PRESS

OXFORD

UNIVERSITY PRESS

Oxford University Press is a department of the University of Oxford.
It furthers the University's objective of excellence in research, scholarship,
and education by publishing worldwide.

Oxford   New York
Auckland   Cape Town   Dar es Salaam   Hong Kong   Karachi
Kuala Lumpur   Madrid   Melbourne   Mexico City   Nairobi
New Delhi   Shanghai   Taipei   Toronto

With offices in
Argentina   Austria   Brazil   Chile   Czech Republic   France   Greece
Guatemala   Hungary   Italy   Japan   Poland   Portugal   Singapore
South Korea   Switzerland   Thailand   Turkey   Ukraine   Vietnam

Oxford is a registered trade mark of Oxford University Press
in the UK and certain other countries.

Published in the United States of America by
Oxford University Press
198 Madison Avenue, New York, NY 10016

© Oxford University Press 2012

First issued as an Oxford University Press paperback, 2013.

Library of Congress Cataloging-in-Publication Data
The Oxford handbook of juvenile delinquency and juvenile justice / Barry C.
Feld, Donna M. Bishop.
p.   cm.
Includes bibliographical references and index.
ISBN 978-0-19-538510-6 (cloth : alk. paper); 978-0-19-933827-6 (paperback)
1. Juvenile delinquency—United States.   2. Juvenile justice, Administration
of—United States.   I. Feld, Barry C.   II. Bishop, Donna M.
HV9104.O989 2011
364.360973—dc22   2011009505

Printed in the United States of America
on acid-free paper

For Ari and Julia, who embody the promise
and hope of the next generation.
BCF

I dedicate this book to my father, Joseph Francis Bishop,
and to the precious memory of my mother,
Dorothy Ann Bishop (1918–2010), with gratitude
for their unending love and support.
DMB

Acknowledgments

Barry Feld received outstanding research assistance from Ben Kaplan, University of Minnesota Class of 2010, during the writing of his chapters. He could not have completed this volume without the exceptional assistance of Julia Norsetter, Class of 2012, who shepherded the volume through the editorial process and helped compile the index.

Contents

PART IX. YOUTH IN CRIMINAL COURT

PART X. JUVENILE JUSTICE POLICY

PREFACE

Over the past quarter century, media depictions, public perceptions, and political calculations have pushed juvenile crime and juvenile justice systems' responses to it to the center of policy agendas. A sharp increase in urban youth homicide and gun violence between the mid-1980s and mid-1990s precipitated a spasmodic reaction of policies to get tough and crack down on youth crime. Cumulatively, these changes have significantly shifted the focus of the juvenile justice system from an emphasis on treatment of offenders to punishment for their offenses. These policies have affected every aspect of juvenile justice administration, from police practices at the front end to correctional operations at the back end. American juvenile justice policies—especially those associated with the transfer and punishment of youths in criminal courts—are much harsher than in other Western countries.

In a rational world, people would want public officials to adopt juvenile crime policies based on the most reliable knowledge about the causes of delinquency and the likely impact of alternative responses to it. While social science research cannot provide an unambiguous guide to policy makers, it can generate propositions about the relationships between two or more phenomena, for example, poverty and crime or delinquent peers and individual offending. And yet, most law makers adopt policies based on emotional responses and sound-bite politics, rather than a sound evidence base. For example, policies of transferring youths to criminal court persist even though research consistently demonstrates that such policies may be counterproductive and actually increase, rather than decrease, subsequent offending by youths.

Public officials and informed citizens should have ready access to what we do know, as well as what we don't know, about the scope and causes of youth crime, the effectiveness of prevention and intervention strategies, and potentials and pitfalls of juvenile justice administration. This volume provides comprehensive reviews of knowledge about the causes of juvenile crime and justice system responses. We divide the volume into two parts—juvenile crime and juvenile justice. We asked contributors to discuss the policy implications of the research they review for juvenile justice administration.

The section on juvenile crime examines trends and patterns of juvenile offending and the individual-level, micro-contextual level—family, peers, gangs, and schools—and macro-structural variables that affect youth crime. It examines how much delinquency occurs, who commits it, what causes some youths to commit crimes, what factors distinguish youths who persist or desist from criminal activities, what theories of delinquency best explain the phenomena, and the implications of criminological research for policies to prevent or reduce juvenile offending.

The section on juvenile justice administration examines the history of the juvenile court, the various stages of juvenile justice processing—police, intake, detention, adjudication, and disposition—the types of interventions employed—restorative justice, probation supervision, and institutional confinement—and the handling of special offender populations—girls and minority youths. It concludes by examining recent trends in juvenile justice administration and places the American practice in international perspective.

Books like this require a substantial commitment. Contributors worked to tight deadlines, prepared successive drafts to adhere to even tighter deadlines, and responded graciously to our numerous comments and requests. Even though, at times, we editors felt like we were "herding cats"—a consequence of soliciting the most esteemed and busy scholars—we are most grateful to them for their contributions, cooperation, and assistance in bring this volume to fruition.

We assembled an outstanding line-up of scholars to provide comprehensive overviews of every aspect of juvenile crime and juvenile justice administration. We asked contributors—each a leading authority on his or her topic—to present a readable and current review of the literature that would provide students, justice officials, interested citizens, and honest politicians with the best information available to make informed decisions. Each comprehensive chapter includes references and bibliographies to specialized literatures to enable readers to identify the most important sources and to further educate themselves. We asked contributors to provide accessible, nontechnical introductions to the subjects so that readers could quickly absorb the salient literature and the relationships among the topics. Readers will decide whether we have succeeded.

Barry C. Feld   Donna M. Bishop
Effie, MN   Boston, MA
June 2010   June 2010

LIST OF CONTRIBUTORS

ROBERT AGNEW is Samuel Candler Dobbs Professor of Sociology at Emory University.

RONALD L. AKERS is Professor of Criminology and Law at the University of Florida.

WILLIAM H. BARTON is Professor in the Indiana University School of Social Work at the Indiana University-Purdue University Indianapolis.

GORDON BAZEMORE is Professor and Chair in the School of Criminology and Criminal Justice and Director of the Community Justice Institute at Florida Atlantic University.

DONNA M. BISHOP is Professor of Criminology and Criminal Justice at Northeastern University.

SARAH L. BOONSTOPPEL is a PhD Candidate in the Department of Criminology and Criminal Justice at the University of Maryland, College Park.

JEFFREY A. BUTTS is Executive Director of the Research and Evaluation Center at John Jay College of Criminal Justice, City University of New York.

COLLEEN CHAMBERS is Research Assistant at the Institute on Crime and Public Policy at the University of Minnesota Law School.

DAVID P. FARRINGTON is Professor of Psychological Criminality at Cambridge University, England.

BARRY C. FELD is Centennial Professor of Law at the University of Minnesota.

RACHEL FREELAND is MA Candidate in the Department of Criminology and Criminal Justice at the University of Maryland, College Park.

YU GAO is Postdoctoral Research Associate in the Departments of Criminology, Psychology, and Psychiatry at the University of Pennsylvania.

ANDREA L. GLENN is PhD Candidate in Psychology at the University of Pennsylvania.

GARY D. GOTTFREDSON is Professor in the Department of Counseling and Personnel Services at the University of Maryland, College Park.

PETER W. GREENWOOD is Executive Director of the Association for the Advancement of Evidence-Based Practice at the University of Pennsylvania.

TAMARA M. HAEGERICH is PhD Candidate in Psychology at the University of Illinois, Chicago.

DONNA HANCOCK is a doctoral student in the Department of Child and Family Development at the University of Georgia.

KIMBERLY KEMPF-LEONARD is Professor and Chair in the Department of Criminology and Criminal Justice at the Southern Illinois University Carbondale.

BARRY KRISBERG is Distinguished Senior Fellow and Lecturer in Residence at the Berkeley Center for Criminal Justice.

CHARIS E. KUBRIN is Associate Professor of Sociology at the George Washington University.

JOHN H. LAUB is Distinguished University Professor in the Department of Criminology and Criminal Justice at the University of Maryland, College Park.

MICHAEL J. LEIBER Professor of Criminology, University of South Florida.

JIANGHONG LIU is Assistant Professor of Nursing at the University of Pennsylvania School of Nursing.

DORIS LAYTON MACKENZIE is Director of the Justice Center for Research and Professor in the Sociology Department at Pennsylvania State University.

JENNIFER LYNN-WHALEY is Senior Research Associate at the Berkeley Center for Criminal Justice.

KRISTY N. MATSUDA is Assistant Research Professor in the Department of Criminology and Criminal Justice at the University of Missouri, St. Louis.

CHERYL L. MAXSON is Associate Professor of Criminology, Law & Society at the University of California, Irvine.

EDMUND F. MCGARRELL is Director and Professor of the School of Criminal Justice at Michigan State University.

DANIEL P. MEARS is Professor in the Department of Criminology and Criminal Justice at Florida State University.

EDWARD P. MULVEY is Professor of Psychiatry and Director of the Law and Psychiatry Program at Western Psychiatry Institute and Clinic at the University of Pittsburgh School of Medicine.

ERIKA PENNER is PhD Candidate in Clinical Child Psychology at Simon Fraser University.

MELISSA PESKIN is PhD Candidate in Clinical Psychology at the University of Pennsylvania.

ALEX R. PIQUERO is Professor in the Program in Criminology, EPPS, University of Texas at Dallas, Adjunct Professor Key Centre for Ethics, Law, Justice, and Governance, Griffith University, Australia, Co-Editor, Journal of Quantitative Criminology.

ADRIAN RAINE is Chair of the Department of Psychology and Richard Perry University Professor in the Department of Criminology, Psychiatry, and Psychology at the University of Pennsylvania.

LINDSAY E. RANKIN is a doctoral student in the Department of Psychology at New York University.

RONALD ROESCH is Professor of Psychology at Simon Fraser University.

JOHN K. ROMAN is Senior Fellow in the Justice Policy Center at the Urban Institute.

CHRISTOPHER J. SCHRECK is Professor of Criminal Justice at the Rochester Institute of Technology.

CAROL A. SCHUBERT is Research Program Administrator in the Law and Psychiatry Program at Western Psychiatry Institute and Clinic at the University of Pittsburgh School of Medicine.

ROBERT A. SCHUG is Assistant Professor of Criminal Justice and Forensic Psychology at California State University, Long Beach.

CHRISTINE S. SELLERS is Associate Chair of the Department of Criminology at the University of South Florida.

LESLIE GORDON SIMONS is Associate Professor of Child and Family Development at the University of Georgia.

RONALD L. SIMONS is Professor of Sociology and Distinguished Research Fellow in the Institute for Behavioral Research at the University of Georgia.

ERIC A. STEWART is Professor in the Department of Criminology and Criminal Justice at Florida State University.

HOWARD N. SNYDER is Chief of Recidivism, Reentry and Special Projects at the Bureau of Justice Statistics within the U.S. Department of Justice.

DAVID S. TANENHAUS is Professor of History and the James E. Rogers Professor of History and Law at the William S. Boyd School of Law.

PATRICK H. TOLAN is Director of the Institute for Juvenile Research and Professor in the Department of Psychiatry at the University of Illinois at Chicago.

MICHAEL TONRY is Sonosky Professor of Law and Public Policy at the University of Minnesota Law School.

SUSAN F. TURNER is Professor of Criminology, Law & Society at the University of California, Irvine.

TOM R. TYLER is Professor and Chair in the Department of Psychology at New York University.

JODI VILJOEN is Assistant Professor of Clinical Psychology and Law-Forensic Psychology at Simon Fraser University.

MARK WARR is Professor of Sociology at the University of Texas, Austin.

DOUGLAS B. WEISS is PhD Candidate in the Department of Criminology and Criminal Justice at the University of Maryland.

BRANDON C. WELSH is Associate Professor in the College of Criminal Justice at Northeastern University and Senior Research Fellow at the Netherlands Institute for the study of Crime and Law Enforcement.

DEANNA L. WILKINSON is Associate Professor in the Department of Human Development and Family Science at Ohio State University.

JENNIFER L. WOOLARD is Associate Professor of Psychology at Georgetown University.

YALING YANG is Post-Graduate Researcher at the Laboratory of Neuro Imaging in the Department of Neurology at the University of California, Los Angeles School of Medicine.

THE OXFORD HANDBOOK OF

JUVENILE CRIME AND JUVENILE JUSTICE

PART I

NATURE AND PATTERNS OF JUVENILE OFFENDING

CHAPTER 1

JUVENILE DELINQUENTS AND JUVENILE JUSTICE CLIENTELE

TRENDS AND PATTERNS IN CRIME AND JUSTICE SYSTEM RESPONSE

HOWARD N. SNYDER[1]

In the United States, the legal definition of a juvenile varies from state to state. As a result, the United States does not have a unified juvenile justice system, and what constitutes a juvenile crime in one state may not be a juvenile crime in another. A person as young as seven in some states can be taken into custody (i.e., arrested) for a law-violating behavior. In most states the juvenile courts have original jurisdiction over youths up to the age of 18, while in other states youths ages 16 and/or 17 are always processed as adults in the criminal justice system. In fact, as we shall detail later, about two of every five 17-year-olds in the United States have no opportunity to be processed in a juvenile court. And all states have legislation that enables persons of juvenile age charged with a law-violating behavior to be tried as an adult in their criminal justice system. It is important to keep in mind these legal variations in the definition of *juvenile* when reviewing the statistical information that follows.

The goal of this chapter is to present an empirically based profile of the law-violating behavior of youth and the juvenile justice system's response to these behaviors over the last generation. First, trends in juvenile violent crime and drug abuse behavior will be documented using reports on or by victims and juvenile offender self-reports. Next, trends in these and other juvenile law-violating behaviors known to law enforcement will be described using arrest statistics. Then, using juvenile court caseload and juvenile corrections statistics, trends in the juvenile justice system's responses to these officially recognized behaviors will be explored. The statistical resources that will be used to build this picture have their own unique characteristics that need to be understood (at least to a minimum extent) to interpret their findings properly. When necessary, therefore, the relevant characteristics of the data systems will be briefly discussed.

I. Juvenile Offending

An understanding of trends in juvenile offending can be constructed through the use of several data resources. Trends in murders by juveniles can be inferred from the Supplementary Homicide Reports provided to the Federal Bureau of Investigation by law enforcement agencies. The Bureau of Justice Statistics' National Criminal Victimization Survey can be used to document trends in juvenile offending for crimes in which the victim sees the offender. For most other behaviors (e.g., burglary, shoplifting, drug selling, curfew violations), the only possible sources for incident and trending information on juvenile offending are self-reports from the juveniles themselves, and such data collection efforts are not common in the United States.

A. Lethal Violence

Annually the FBI's Supplementary Homicide Reports (SHR) collects information on about 90% of the estimated number of murders that occur in the United States. These data describe the demographic characteristics of homicide victims and the weapons used in the crimes. In addition, and when known, the SHR contains the demographics of the offenders and their relationships to the victims. Between 1985 and 2005, the SHR contained no information on offenders in 36% of reported murders. This proportion is composed of (1) those murders for which law enforcement was unable to identify an offender and (2) those murders for which an offender was identified but the information was not reported to the FBI. This large proportion of missing information presents a problem when attempting to describe juvenile offending trends. If it could be assumed that the offender characteristics in these murders were similar to those for which offender information was known, then it would be a simple process of extrapolating from the knowns to the unknowns. However, this assumption is likely to be false. As a result, we are left with trending the murders that are known to be caused by juvenile offenders (i.e., persons under age 18). This certainly undercounts the number of these murders; however, if the nature of the unknowns has remained constant over the time period, then the trend in murders caused by known juvenile offenders should be a good approximation for the trend in the actual number of murders with juvenile offenders.

Eleven percent (11%) of all murders that occurred between 1985 and 2005 for which an offender was known involved a juvenile offender (i.e., a person under age 18). This proportion grew from 7% in 1985 to its peak in 1994 at 16% and then fell there- after, reaching 9% by 2005. Over this period, about 30% of all murders involving a juvenile offender also involved an adult offender, with this proportion generally increasing across the time period (from 25% in 1985 to 38% in 2005). The annual number of murders attributed to juvenile offenders increased nearly 140% from 1985 to 1994 (see Figure 1.1). Following this sharp increase, the number of murders attributed to juvenile offenders fell as sharply through 2005, erasing all of the increase. In fact, the number of murders attributed to juvenile offenders in 2005 was 8% below the 1985 figure. If we take into account the fact that the SHR data contained

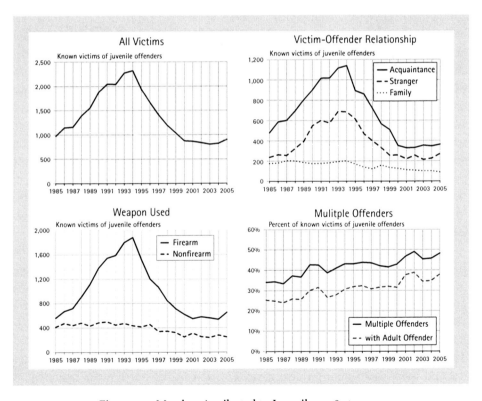

Figure 1.1. Murders Attributed to Juveniles: 1985 to 2005

Notes: Estimates were developed by the author using data reported to the FBI's Supplementary Homicide Reports Program. [United States Department of Justice, Federal Bureau of Investigation, Uniform Crime Reporting Program. Various years. *Supplementary Homicide Reports* for the years 1985 through 2005.]

a larger number of murders in 2005 than in 1985 for which no offender was identified, it is fair to say that the number of murders committed by juveniles in 2005 was roughly equal to the number committed in 1985.

To place the juvenile trend in context, it is useful to compare it to the trend in murders attributed to adult offenders. Murders attributable to adult offenders increased 13% between 1985 and its peak in 1991 (a few years prior to the juvenile peak). Between 1991 and 2005, the number of these murders fell 31%, so that by 2005, the number of murders attributable to adult offenders was below its 1985 level—even after taking into account larger numbers of murders for which no offender was identified. Finally, over this period, while adult offenders were involved in a substantial proportion of murders attributed to juvenile offenders (30%), juvenile offenders were involved in just 4% of murders attributable to adult offenders. In summary, over the period from 1985 through 2005, murders by both juveniles and adults increased into the early 1990s and then declined by 2005 to near their twenty-year lows; the difference was that the amplitude of the juvenile trend was far more pronounced than the adult trend.

With the SHR data it is possible to develop a better understanding of the nature of murders by juveniles and the factors related to the substantial changes in their annual counts over the twenty-year period. Over the period from 1985 to 2005 over half (55%) of all murder victims of juvenile offenders were classified as acquaintances of the offender, one-third (32%) were strangers, and the remainder (15%) were family members. During the period when the annual number of juvenile murders increased substantially, the number of murders of family members remained constant; and when the overall number of murders fell dramatically, murders of family members were cut in half. The sharp increase in juvenile murders between 1985 and 1994 was limited to murders of non-family members (i.e., acquaintances and strangers). However, by 2005 the numbers of these murders had declined to a point where murders of strangers had returned to their 1985 level and murders of acquaintances had fallen to below their 1985 level. Whatever factors were driving the increase in juvenile murders through the mid-1990s differentially affected the murder of family and non-family victims.

Another aspect of the juvenile murder trend is the relationship to firearms. Between 1985 and 1994, the annual number of murder victims killed by weapons other than a firearm (including hands, feet, and fists) remained constant. All of the growth in juvenile murders between 1985 and 1994 was limited to firearm-related crimes. Similarly, nearly the entire decline after 1994 was linked to the drop in firearm-related murders. The implication of this finding is interesting to consider. The speculation that juveniles became more violent from the mid-1980s through the mid-1990s was a common reason used by state legislators to revise laws making it easier to transfer juveniles to the adult criminal justice system. However, if juveniles had become more violent, it would be logical to predict that murders with and without firearms would have both increased. The fact that only firearm-related murders increased points not to a change in juveniles' propensity for violence but to a change in juveniles' access to (or willingness to use) firearms.

Another aspect of the trend in murders by juveniles is the growth in the proportion of these crimes that involved multiple offenders. From 1985 to 2005, the percentage of murders attributed to juveniles that involved at least two offenders generally increased from 34% to 48%. Over this period, an average of three-fourths (73%) of these multiple offender crimes involved an adult offender, with this proportion gradually increasing over the period.

In summary, while roughly the same in 1985 and 2005, the annual number of murders attributed to juvenile offenders spiked in the mid-1990s. This large increase was limited to crimes against non-family members and crimes involving firearms. Over the period, a large proportion of murders attributed to juvenile offenders involved multiple offenders. In most multiple offender murders, juveniles committed their crimes with adults.

B. Non-lethal Violent Crime

The National Criminal Victimization Survey (NCVS) is the primary source of information on the frequency, characteristics, and consequences of non-lethal criminal victimization in the United States. Each year a large sample of persons ages 12 and above are asked about the personal and property victimizations they have experienced. For serious violent crimes (i.e., sexual assault, aggravated assault, and robbery), the victims are asked for their perception of the age, sex, race, and Hispanic ethnicity of the offenders. Clearly, unless the offenders are known by the victims, the accuracy of victims' assessments of offenders' ages are questionable (i.e., it is difficult to distinguish between a 17-year-old and an 18-year-old). However, if there is a bias in the perception of offender age, it is likely that the bias has been constant over the years; so while the actual value of the incidence rate of juvenile offending within a year may be questioned, the NCVS trend in serious violent juvenile offending can be studied with greater confidence. Also it should be noted that, by not interviewing (or using surrogate responders for) persons under the age of 12, crimes against these persons are excluded from the NCVS, which may be a meaningful portion of the total amount of juvenile serious violent offending.

Based on victim reports to the NCVS, the period from the mid-1980s through the mid-1990s experienced a substantial growth in serious violent juvenile crime (Figure 1.2). Between 1985 and its peak in 1993, the rate of serious violent crimes committed by juvenile offenders increased 58%.[2] The growth was greater for aggravated assaults (65%) than for robberies (49%) and forcible rape (43%). To place these changes in perspective, victim reports indicate that the adult offending rate for serious violent crime increased just 2% between 1985 and 1993, with the rate of robbery by adults increasing 9%, adult aggravated assaults increasing 6%, and forcible rape by adults falling 28%.

After its peak in 1993, juvenile violence plummeted. Between 1993 and 2007, the rate of serious violent juvenile offending fell 74%. This decline wiped out all of the increase experienced between 1985 and 1993—and more. In 2007, the juvenile serious violent offending rate based on victim reports was 58% below what it was in 1985.

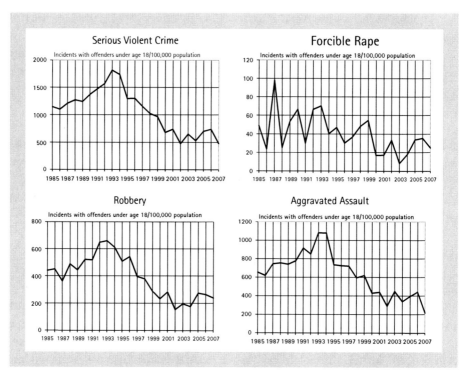

Figure 1.2. Juvenile Offending for Serious Violent Crimes: 1985 to 2007

Notes: Serious Violent Crime includes forcible rape, robbery and aggravated assault. Estimates were derived from victim reports of their violent juvenile offenders in BJS' National Crime Victimization Survey and reported by BJS in the machine readable data file *Age of offenders in serious violent crime, 1973–2007 by number of offenders* (BJS, 2009). Annual estimates of juvenile forcible rape offending are unstable due to the small number of such incidents reported to the NCVS.

Similar patterns were found in forcible rape, robbery, and aggravated assault, with their 2007 rates at least 45% below their 1985 levels. For whatever reasons, the overall decline in the rate of juvenile serious violent crime following its peak in 1993 drove the rate in the first decade of the twenty-first century to levels not seen since at least the beginning of the NCVS in 1973; in fact, the juvenile serious violent offending rate in 2007 was about one-third of the 1973 rate, so it is very likely the low rates in 2007 rivaled (or even surpassed) those of the 1950s and 1960s. It is important to note that the general trend from the mid-1980s into the early twenty-first century in juvenile non-lethal violent offending documented by the National Criminal Victimization Survey is remarkably similar to the trend in lethal juvenile offending documented by the Supplementary Homicide Report data. It is also important to consider that adult serious violent offending also fell markedly after the mid-1990s. By 2007, the adult serious violent offending rate was 64% below its 1985 level and just one-third of its 1973 level. Therefore, whatever the factors were that drove down the levels of serious violent offending in the United States after the mid-1990s, they had large effects on both juveniles and adults.

    Other NCVS analyses (e.g., Lynch and Snyder 2007) have compared juvenile violence trends for males and females and for whites and blacks over this period. This work found that serious violent offending by both juvenile males and juvenile females increased substantially from the mid-1980s through the mid-1990s and then dropped substantially through the mid-2000s; however, the juvenile female increase was greater than the juvenile male increase in the earlier period, and the juvenile female decline was less than the male decline in the latter period. Turning to race, the trends in white and black juvenile offending were similar over the period, with both rising from the mid-1980s through the mid-1990s and then declining sharply and equally through the mid-2000s. In all, the factors driving the trends in juvenile violence appear to have affected male and female youths and white and black youths similarly.

C. Self-Reported Drug Use

Another crime type for which available data provide a general understanding of trends in juvenile offending is the use of illicit drugs. One of these efforts (i.e., *Monitoring the Future*, or MTF) annually measures drug use in a national sample of high school students (Johnston et al. 2008). While MTF delves into many aspects of illicit drug use, for our purposes, it is sufficient to document the general trends for various population subgroups. Between 1985 and 1992, the proportion of twelfth graders who indicated they had used illicit drugs in the prior year fell from 46% to 27% (Figure 1.3).

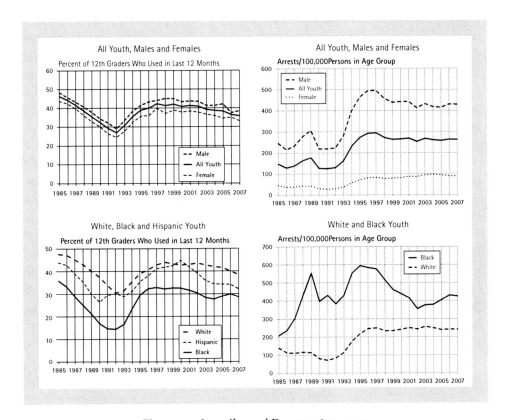

Figure 1.3. Juveniles and Drugs: 1985 to 2007

Notes: Self-reported illicit drug use prevalence percentages come from the Monitoring the Future Survey (Johnston et al. 2008). Arrest rate estimates were developed by the author from analysis of UCR arrest data (USDOJ, FBI UCRP, 2009) adjusted to reflect the FBI's national estimates of arrests.

Between 1992 and 1997, this proportion increased to 42%, and then gradually declined through 2007 to 36%.[3] The one-year prevalence trend was similar for males and females, with the male percentage marginally greater throughout the period. In contrast, the levels of white and black reported illicit drug use varied greatly over the period, while the general trend was similar for both. The reported annual rate of illicit drug use in 1985 was substantially higher for white (48%) than black (33%) youths. Both white and black rates declined to their relative low points in 1992 (30% versus 16%), then rose into the late 1990s (44% versus 33% respectively) before falling back somewhat through 2007 (39% versus 29%). Hispanic youths' reports of illicit drug use remained in between the white and black rates for most of the 1985 to 2007 period.[4]

II. Entry into the Justice System

Many crimes are never reported to law enforcement. For example, victim reports from the NCVS in 2005 indicate that only about 60% of all serious violent crimes were reported to law enforcement (Catalano 2006). This percentage falls to 42% for simple assault, a less serious person crime. In general, only about 40% of property crimes with person victims were reported to law enforcement in 2005. And while there is no national source of such information, it is highly likely that the proportion of "victimless" crimes known to law enforcement (e.g., drug use, drug selling, weapons possession, curfew violations) is much lower. Therefore the justice system is officially unaware of much of the crime that is committed, sometimes referred to as the *dark figure of crime*.

Information on crimes known to law enforcement, crimes cleared by arrest, and arrest trends can be found in the data reported by law enforcement agencies to the FBI's Uniform Crime Reporting (UCR) Program. From these data it is known that a large portion of crimes known to law enforcement is never cleared by arrest or other exceptional means (e.g., the death of the offender, the victim's refusal to cooperate). In 2007 the FBI reported that 45% of reported violent crimes and 16% of reported property crimes were cleared by arrest or other exceptional means. Murder had the highest clearance rate (61%), while just 12% of reported burglaries and 13% of reported motor vehicle thefts were cleared. Therefore, while it is likely that a large percentage of (especially repeat) offenders are eventually arrested for some crime, there is no guarantee that arrest trends reflect crime trends or offending behavior.

Arrest trends reflect a complex combination of crime trends, victims' willingness to report crime, police behavior, offenders' ability to elude arrest, and the public's demand for enforcement. Comparing victim reports and self-reports of delinquent behavior with law enforcement reports of clearances and juvenile arrests leads to an understanding of how these factors might interact, and how delinquent behavior results in entry into the justice system. The following table below provides

Table 1.1. What Percent of Violent Crimes were Committed by Juveniles in 2007?

Offense	Victim Reports		Law Enforcement Reports	
	Victim Report of Incidents with **All** Offenders Under Age 18	Victim Report of Incidents with **Any** Offender Under Age 18	Law Enforcement Reports of Offenses Cleared by Juvenile Arrest	Law Enforcement Reports of Juvenile Percent of All Arrests
Violent Crime	19%	22%	12%	16%
Rape/Sex Assault	13%	13%	11%	15%
Robbery	28%	29%	15%	27%
Aggravated Assault	15%	18%	12%	13%

Note: Author's analyses of NCVS and UCR data.

assessments of the relative volume of serious violent crime committed by juveniles (i.e., persons under age 18) in 2007 based on three separate data sources: victim reports, clearance statistics, and arrest statistics.

Victim reports in 2007 indicate that about one in five serious violent crimes was committed by juveniles. Law enforcement in 2007 reported that closer to one in ten serious violent crimes for which an offender was identified was cleared by the arrest of a juvenile. From these two statistics it appears that many crimes committed by juveniles are never reported to law enforcement (or juveniles are very good at avoiding detection). Some juvenile crimes (e.g., a fight between two neighborhood youths) may be handled informally by parents or school officials without reporting the incident to law enforcement, while many others may never be reported to any authority. Consequently, each year there is a large pool of serious violent juvenile crime that could be reported to law enforcement. Therefore, if the factors related to crime reporting were to change (e.g., victim's willingness to report increased, community's willingness to cooperate with law enforcement increased, mandatory reporting/arrest laws were implemented), the number of serious violent juvenile crimes reported to law enforcement and the number of juvenile arrests could increase without any actual increase in juvenile crime. Also note that the juvenile proportion of arrests for serious violent crime is much larger than the proportion of crimes cleared by juvenile arrests (e.g., for robbery 15% of crimes cleared and 27% of arrests). This difference reflects the well-known fact that juveniles are more likely than adults to commit crimes in groups; therefore, one juvenile robbery reported to law enforcement will result in multiple arrests more often than will one reported robbery committed by an adult. Consequently, if the proportion of juvenile crimes committed by groups of offenders increased (e.g., an increase in gang-related crimes), the juvenile proportion of arrests would increase, while the actual numbers of crimes committed by juveniles remained constant.

A clear example of the disconnect between juvenile offending and juvenile entry into the justice system via arrest is seen in the area of drug crimes. Self-reports of juvenile drug use find that juvenile males and females report similar levels and trends in drug use between 1985 and 2007 (Figure 1.3); however throughout that period, females accounted for only 14% of juvenile drug arrests. Throughout the period, white juveniles reported drug use in larger proportions than did black juveniles, while the arrest rate for black juveniles was substantially higher than the white juvenile arrest rate. In addition, while the reported use of drugs by black juveniles declined substantially between 1985 and 1989, the corresponding arrest rate soared. Obviously, arrest rates and arrest rate trends are not always good indicators of either the relative involvement of juveniles in crime or changes in prevalence/incidence of criminal behavior. However, while arrest statistics may not yield a good portrait of the crimes committed by juveniles, they are an excellent measure of the flow of youth into the juvenile justice system.

III. Juvenile Arrest Trends

In 2007 an estimated 2,171,200 arrests were made of youths under age 18. Half of all these juvenile arrests fell into five offense categories: larceny-theft, simple assault, disorderly conduct, drug abuse violations, and curfew/loitering violations (Table 1.2). If it can be assumed the FBI's *All Other Offense* category contains primarily public order offenses, then 15% of juvenile arrests in 2007 were for offenses against a person, 21% were for property offenses, 9% were for drug law violations, 43% were for public order offenses, and 12% were for status offenses (i.e., curfew and running away from home).

Between 1985 and 2007, the annual number of juvenile arrests controlling for variations in population (i.e., the juvenile arrest rate) peaked in 1996 (Figure 1.4). The juvenile arrest rate generally increased from 1985 to 1996, and then generally declined through 2007. The 24% increase between 1985 and 1996 was more than erased between 1996 and 2007, so that the juvenile arrest rate in 2007 was 10% below its 1985 level. Over the 1985 to 2007 period, the adult arrest rate followed a somewhat similar pattern of growth and decline, with the peak year being significantly earlier—in 1989. For adults. the 17% growth in the total arrest rate between 1985 and 1989 was also erased by its gradual decline between 1989 and 2007, falling to a level in 2007 7% below its 1985 level.

To understand the dynamics underlying the juvenile arrest rate trend, its offense-specific components must be explored. The period of the 1990s saw public attention focused on the issue of violent juvenile crime. Newspaper headlines

Table 1.2. Juvenile Arrests by Gender and Race in 2007

	Estimated Number	Percent of Total	Percent				
			Female	White	Black	Native American	Asian/Pacific Islander
All offenses	2,171,200	100.0%	29%	67%	30%	1%	2%
Murder	1,340	0.1%	8%	40%	57%	1%	1%
Forcible rape	3,580	0.2%	2%	62%	36%	1%	1%
Robbery	34,350	1.6%	10%	30%	68%	<1%	1%
Aggravated assault	57,230	2.6%	23%	57%	41%	1%	1%
Burglary	81,700	3.8%	11%	65%	33%	1%	1%
Larceny-theft	298,500	13.7%	43%	66%	31%	1%	2%
Motor vehicle theft	29,400	1.4%	17%	54%	42%	2%	2%
Arson	7,200	0.3%	12%	77%	21%	1%	2%
Other assaults	241,200	11.1%	34%	59%	39%	1%	1%
Forgery	3,100	0.1%	32%	72%	25%	1%	2%
Fraud	7,200	0.3%	36%	64%	33%	1%	1%
Embezzlement	1,700	0.1%	41%	58%	39%	1%	2%
Stolen property offenses	22,200	1.0%	18%	55%	43%	1%	1%
Vandalism	111,300	5.1%	13%	79%	19%	1%	1%
Weapons offense	43,600	2.0%	10%	61%	37%	1%	1%
Commercialized vice	1,500	0.1%	77%	41%	57%	1%	1%
Other sex offenses	15,500	0.7%	10%	70%	28%	1%	1%
Drug offense	195,400	9.0%	16%	69%	29%	1%	1%
Gambling	2,000	0.1%	2%	5%	95%	<1%	1%
Family offenses	5,800	0.3%	39%	73%	24%	2%	1%
Driving under the influence	18,100	0.8%	24%	93%	4%	2%	1%
Liquor law violations	139,100	6.4%	37%	91%	5%	3%	1%
Drunkenness	16,900	0.8%	26%	89%	8%	2%	1%
Disorderly conduct	203,000	9.3%	33%	58%	40%	1%	1%
Vagrancy	3,800	0.2%	29%	78%	21%	1%	<1%
Suspicion	400	<0.1%	25%	66%	33%	1%	<1%
Curfew/loitering	143,000	6.6%	31%	64%	34%	1%	1%
Runaways	108,900	5.0%	56%	67%	26%	2%	5%
All other offenses	374,200	17.2%	26%	70%	27%	1%	2%

Note: Estimates developed by author from data reported in *Crime in the United States, 2007*.

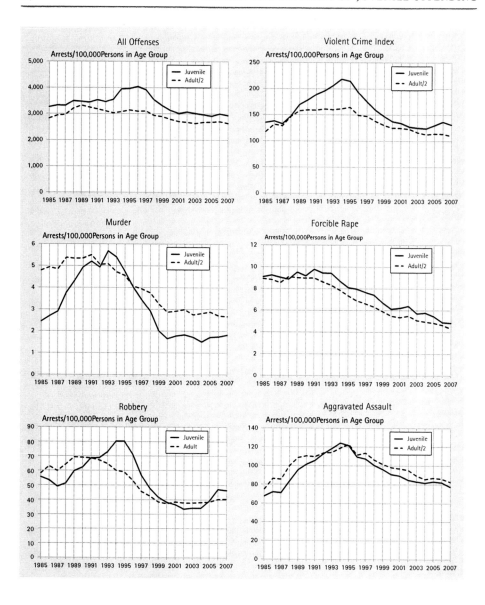

and magazine covers carried stories of incidents of juvenile violence, and commentators speculated about a new breed of juvenile offenders. The empirical support for this focus came in part from the substantial increases in juvenile violent crime arrests, especially arrests for murder and weapon law violations. It was common practice during this period to summarize violent crime patterns using the Violent Crime Index. The Violent Crime Index is the sum of four crimes (i.e., murder and non-negligent manslaughter, forcible rape, robbery, and

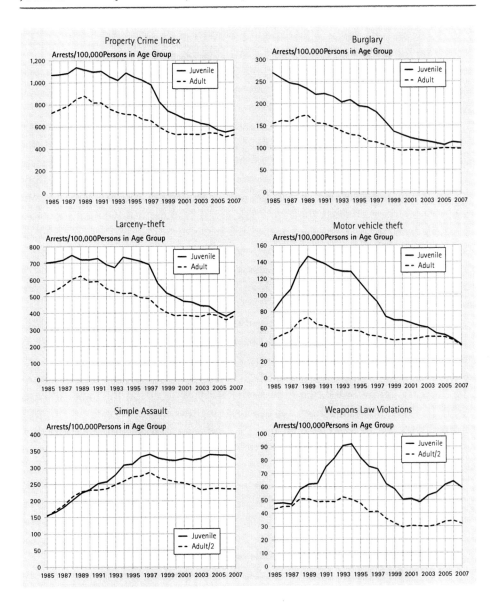

Figure 1.4. Juvenile and Adult Arrest Rates: 1985 to 2007

Notes: Arrest rate estimates were developed by the author from analysis of UCR arrest data (USDOJ, FBI UCRP, 2009) adjusted to reflect the FBI's national estimates of arrests. The Violent Crime Index includes murder and non-negligent manslaughter, forcible rape, robbery, and aggravated assault. The Property Crime Index includes arrests for burglary, larceny-theft, motor vehicle theft and arson. Juvenile arrest rate is 100,000 times the number of arrests of persons under age 18 divided by the population under age 18. Adult arrest rate is 100,000 times the number of arrests of persons age 18 and over divided by the population over age 17. For some graphs, the adult arrest rate is divided by two to improve the quality of the display.

aggravated assault) and was first used by the FBI in the late 1950s.[5] The juvenile arrest rate for crimes of murder and non-negligent manslaughter, forcible rape, robbery, and aggravated assault increased substantially (by 53%) between 1985 and their peak in 1993. More specifically, over this eight-year period, the juvenile arrest rate increased 31% for robbery, 74% for aggravated assault, and 133% for murder; in contrast, the juvenile arrest rate for forcible rape showed little change. The large increase in the juvenile violent crime arrest rate was in reality not that different from the increase in the adult violent crime arrest rate (i.e., 53% versus 36%). The juvenile and adult arrest trends were very similar for the high-volume violent crime of aggravated assault (as well as for simple assault). However, the public focused on the fact that the adult arrest rate for murder had increased very little (6%) in the eight-year period, while the juvenile arrest rate for murder had more than doubled. In addition, over this eight-year period, the increase in the juvenile arrest rate for weapon law violations (a violence-related crime to most persons) was more than four times the adult arrest rate increase (91% versus 21%).

The large increases in juvenile violent crime arrests were also in contrast to the relative stability of the juvenile arrest rate for property crimes over the period. In fact, the juvenile arrest rate for Property Crime Index offenses (i.e., burglary, larceny-theft, motor vehicle theft, and arson) actually declined 4% over the period. The Property Crime Index trend masks the differing trends in the major offenses within it. Over the period from 1985 to 1993, the juvenile arrest rate for burglary declined 25%, fell for larceny-theft just 4%, and increased for motor vehicle theft 59%—which is a perfect example of the major weakness of such broad crime indices.

To the public, juveniles in the 1990s had become more violent, so changes needed to be made. And changes were made. In the last half of the 1990s, most states modified their legislation to make it easier to process juveniles charged with a violent crime as adults. In the mid-1990s, the juvenile "superpredator" became the national caricature of the typical juvenile offender.

The juvenile violent crime arrest rate fell precipitously after its 1993 peak. By 2001, the juvenile arrest rate for Violent Crime Index offenses had fallen below its 1985 level. After its highly publicized peak in 1993, the juvenile arrest rate for murder fell to below its 1985 level in 1999 and remained near this low level through 2007. The juvenile arrest rate of robbery also fell in 1998 to its lowest level since 1985 and continued to decline for several years thereafter. By the early years of the twenty-first century, the juvenile arrest rates for murder, forcible rape, robbery, burglary, larceny-theft, and motor vehicle theft were all well below their 1985 levels, and the juvenile arrest rate for weapon law violations had returned to its 1985 level. By the early twenty-first century, juvenile law-violating behavior from the perspective of law enforcement had reached a generational low for most crime types, with the notable exceptions of drug abuse violations, aggravated assault, and simple assault.

A. Gender-Specific Arrest Trends

Between the mid-1980s and the mid-1990s, female arrest rates (though smaller in absolute terms) increased proportionately more than the corresponding male arrest rates (Figure 1.5). Both rates declined after reaching their peaks in the mid-1990s, but the male rate fell proportionately more than the female rate. Consequently, the juvenile male arrest rate in 2007 was 18% below its 1985 level, while the juvenile female arrest rate in 2007 was 20% above its 1985 level. Comparing these arrest rates

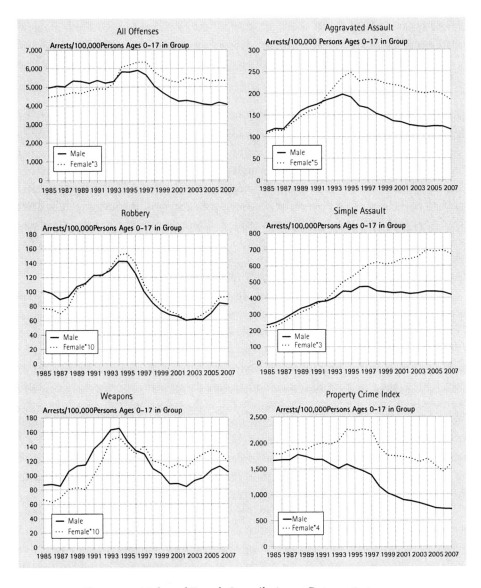

Figure 1.5. Male and Female Juvenile Arrest Rates: 1985 to 2007

Note: Arrest rate estimates were developed by the author from analysis of UCR arrest data (USDOJ, FBI UCRP, 2009) adjusted to reflect the FBI's national estimates of arrests. For some graphs, the female arrest rate is multiplied by a constant to improve the quality of the display.

directly, in 1985 the female arrest rate was 30% of the male rate; in 2007 it had grown to 44% of the male rate. The gender difference in arrests was narrowing.

Earlier we discussed factors other than juvenile law-violating behavior that have likely contributed to the juvenile drug arrest trends. It is likely that some of these factors are also involved in the narrowing of the gender difference in arrests. Victim reports from the National Criminal Victimization Survey show that assaults by juveniles peaked in 1993 and declined substantially through 2007; between 1993 and 2007, victims reported an 80% decline in the rate of aggravated assaults committed by juveniles. While the juvenile arrest rate for aggravated assault and victim reports between 1985 and 1993 both show substantial increases, the large decline in aggravated assaults reported by victims after 1993 was not seen in the juvenile arrest rate. A study of the juvenile male and female arrest rates provides insight into these differences.

A comparison of juvenile male and female arrest trends for robbery shows that between 1985 and 1993, the arrests rates followed a similar pattern of growth and decline—albeit the female rate averaged about one-tenth the male rate. Similar arrest rate trends were not found for aggravated assaults. While both juvenile male and female rates increased equally through the early 1990s, afterward they diverged. From 1991 through 1995, the juvenile female arrest rate increased proportionately more than the male rate. As a result, between 1985 and 1995, the juvenile male arrest rate for aggravated assault grew 70% while the female rate grew 129%. After 1995, both rates fell, but the male rate fell proportionately more (39% versus 26%). As a result, the male arrest rate for aggravated assault in 2007 was just 4% above its 1985 level, while the 2007 female rate was 70% above its 1985 level.

Why were there gender differences in the arrest trends for aggravated assault and not robbery? Some clues may be found in the arrest trend for simple assault. There was a similar increase in the female and the male arrest rates for aggravated and simple assault between 1985 and the early 1990s. Between 1991 and 1995, the juvenile female arrest rate increased more than the male rate for both offenses. Then, after 1995, the juvenile male and female arrest rates for aggravated assault both declined, but the female rate declined less. In stark contrast, after 1995, while the juvenile male arrest rate for simple assault held constant, the juvenile female arrest increased substantially. As a result, between 1985 and 2007, the simple assault arrest rate for juvenile males increased 78% and the female rate more than tripled. So what can explain these differing patterns of juvenile and female arrest rates for robbery, aggravated assault, and simple assault?

One cannot argue that the narrowing of the gender gap in juvenile arrest rates is because juvenile females became more violent, because that argument is not supported by (1) victim reports of declining violence by female offenders and (2) the fact the robbery arrest trends are nearly identical for males and females over the period. A clue to a possible explanation may be in the large divergence in male and female arrest rates for both aggravated and simple assault and not robbery arrests. Analyses of data from the FBI's National Incident-based Reporting System find that a greater portion of juvenile female than male violent crimes reported to law enforcement involves victims who are family members. Over the period we are considering, public policy and law enforcement agencies became more aware of the harm caused by domestic violence; as a result, intervention policies changed. Because of these changes, more of these incidents were likely to be reported to law enforcement, and more were likely to result in arrest. Even if juvenile males and females would be arrested equally in these domestic incidents, such a change in arrest policy would have a greater effect on the relatively low assault arrest rate of juvenile females than on the much higher arrest rate of juvenile males (Feld 2009; Snyder and Sickmund 2006). This explanation for these trends fits the data. Specifically, while the number of such domestic violence incidents had not increased (as evidenced by the NCVS data), a change in law enforcement's response to domestic violence incidents caused a disproportionate increase in the arrests of juvenile females for aggravated and simple assault (the most common charges in domestic violence incidents). At the same time, male and female arrest trends for robbery (a crime largely unrelated to domestic violence) was unaffected. This argument may help to explain the narrowing of the gender gap in juvenile violent crime arrest patterns, but it does not explain the narrowing gender gap in other crime types. That is, it does not explain why the juvenile male arrest rate for property offenses declined so much more after the mid-1990s than did the juvenile female arrest rate.

B. Race-Specific Arrest Trends

Between 1985 and 2007, the average total arrest rate for black youths (6,083) was twice the rate of white youth (3,130) and Native American youth (3,137) and four times the rate of Asian youth (1,411), where arrest rate is defined as the number of arrests per 100,000 youth ages 0 to 17 in the racial group. The arrest rate trends for each of the four racial groups followed a similar pattern over the period, with an increase from the mid-1980s through the mid-1990s, and then a decline thereafter (Figure 1.6). At its peak in the mid-1990s, the total arrest rate was 22% above its 1985 level for white youth, 36% above for black youth, 40% above for Native American youth, and 49% above for Asian youth. By 2007, the total arrest rates for black and Native American youth had returned to very near their 1985 levels (3% and 7% above their 1985 levels respectively), while white and Asian youth ended the period with arrest rates below their 1985 levels (14% and 26% respectively). As a result of their similar arrest trends, the relative size of the total arrest rates for each racial group changed little annually over the period.

As with arrests for all offenses, the black arrest rate for Property Crime Index offenses annually remained near twice the white arrest rate between 1985 and 2007. In contrast, over the period, the black arrest rate averaged five times the white rate for Violent Crime Index offenses, with the disparity in the rates declining for the Index (and for forcible rape, robbery, and aggravated assault) through most of the period. The disparity in the black and white arrest rates increased substantially and then declined during the period for murder, drug abuse violations, and weapon law violations. Changes in the ratio of black-to-white arrest rates over the period imply that the factors influencing the arrest of white and black youth differed, a topic which will be explored in more detail later in this volume.

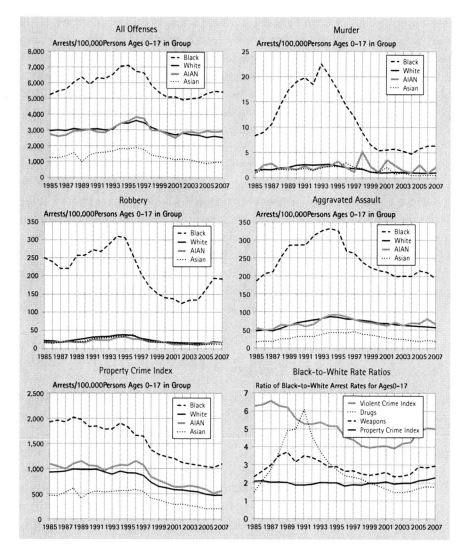

Figure 1.6. Juvenile Arrest Rates by Race: 1985 to 2007

Note. Arrest rate estimates were developed by the author from analysis of UCR arrest data (USDOJ, FBI UCRP, 2009) adjusted to reflect the FBI's national estimates of arrests.

IV. JUVENILE COURT REFERRAL TRENDS

Even though most delinquency cases are referred to juvenile court intake by law enforcement, juvenile court referral trends do not mirror juvenile arrest trends. The annual rate of delinquency cases disposed by juvenile courts increased from the mid-1980s to the mid-1990s (Figure 1.7). The rate increase from 1985 through 1996 was greater for juvenile court cases than for juvenile arrests (43% versus 24%). Then, after increasing more, juvenile court case rates decreased less than juvenile arrest rate from 1996 to 2005 (-15% versus -28%). As a result, while the juvenile arrest rate in 2005 was 10% below its 1985 level, the juvenile court case rate in 2005 was 22% above its 1985 level.

There are many reasons juvenile arrest and juvenile court case trends might differ. First, they cover somewhat different populations; that is, while juvenile arrests cover all arrests of persons under age 18, many of these youth are not handled in juvenile but in adult criminal courts due to the variations in state

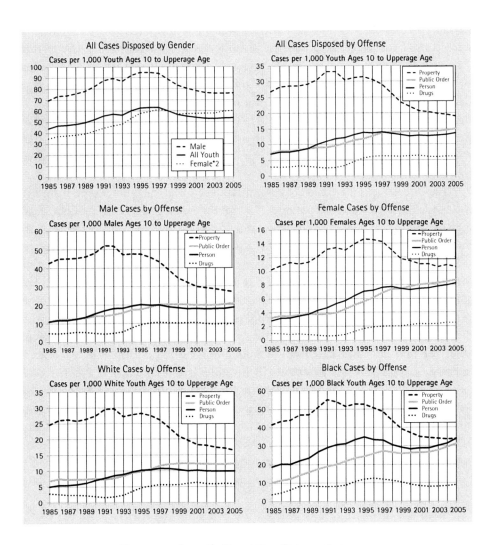

Figure 1.7. Juvenile Court Case Rates: 1985 to 2005

Notes: The unit of count is case disposed. A case is all of the offenses referred on a single day. A referral may be linked to one of more criminal incidents and/or one or more arrests. A referral may not be the result of an arrest and may be referred to juvenile court intake by other than law enforcement (e.g., a victim, a parent, a school official or a probation officer). Juvenile court case rate estimates were developed using data reported in Puzzanchera, C. and Kang, W. (2008). "Juvenile Court Statistics Databook."Online. Available: http://ojjdp.ncjrs.gov/ojstatbb/jcsdb/.

statutes described earlier in this chapter. To place these differences in perspective, it is helpful to know that in 2005, 10% of the 16-year-olds and 39% of the 17-year-olds in the United States lived in states in which any law-violating behaviors they allegedly committed were under the original jurisdiction of an adult criminal court (not a juvenile court). Another possible reason for the trend differences in juvenile arrest rates and juvenile court case rates is that about one in every six juvenile court cases is referred to the court by persons other than law enforcement (e.g., by victims, parents, school officials, and probation officers). However, even with these two differences, there is still substantial overlap in the juvenile arrest and juvenile court populations. So what could have caused the large difference in juvenile arrest and juvenile court trends? One possibility lies in the fact that a referral to juvenile court is a decision made by individuals. Over time, the likelihood of referral may vary with extra-legal factors such as community concerns about the threat of juvenile delinquency or the decision makers' perceptions of the effectiveness of juvenile court. Whatever the reason, it is fair to say that between 1985 and 2005, the juvenile justice system widened its net, bringing a greater proportion of arrested youth into the juvenile court system.

The offense-specific trends in juvenile court cases during the period from 1985 to 2005 fell into two general patterns. The juvenile court case rates increased from 1985 to 1995 in each of the four general delinquency offense categories, with the increases in person (95%), drugs (112%), and public order (73%) case rates substantially greater than the increase in the property case rate (14%). After its peak in the mid-1990s, the property offense case rate fell substantially, so that by 2005 it was 30% below its 1985 level. In contrast, between the mid-1990s and 2005, the other three case rates displayed a different pattern than the property case rate. Instead of declining, the juvenile court rates for person and drug cases held relatively constant while the juvenile court case rate for public order offenses displayed a moderate increase. Comparatively, the trends in juvenile arrests and juvenile court cases between 1985 to 2005 were roughly similar for person, property, and drug offenses, with the exception that the juvenile court case rates increased more or decreased less (i.e., demonstrating the effect of net widening). Given that a substantial portion of public order cases in juvenile court involve the crimes that are referred by sources other of law enforcement (e.g., obstruction of justice and probation/parole violations), there is no simple direct comparison in arrest statistics for public order cases in juvenile courts.

Juvenile court case trends differed for males and females as reflected by the increase in the proportion of females in the court caseloads (Puzzanchera and Kang 2008). Between 1985 and 2005, the female proportion of the juvenile court delinquency caseloads increased from 19% to 27%, with an increase in each case type: person (20% to 30%), property (19% to 27%), drug (17% to 20%), and public order (22% to 28%). These percent increases were the result of the female case rate increasing substantially more than the male case rate over the period for all delinquency cases and within specific offense categories.

	Change in case rates from 1985 to 2005	
Offense	Male	Female
All delinquency cases	9%	73%
Person offenses	70%	189%
Property offenses	−37%	3%
Drug offense	104%	143%
Public order offense	87%	167%

Juvenile court case trends differed for white and black youth between 1985 and 2005. Across the period, the overall delinquency case rate increased more for black youth than white youth, primarily because of larger increases in drug and public order cases and a smaller decline in property cases. As a result, the disparity in the ratio of the black-to-white case rates increased over the period. In 1985, the overall delinquency case rate for black youth was 1.9 times the white rate; by 2005, this ratio had increased to 2.4.

	Change in case rates from 1985 to 2005	
Offense	White	Black
All delinquency cases	12%	45%
Person offenses	97%	80%
Property offenses	−34%	−18%
Drug offense	108%	137%
Public order offense	76%	200%

V. Juvenile Court Case Processing Trends

The nature of juvenile court case processing varies across the country. However, in general, soon after a case is referred to juvenile court intake, two key decisions are made. One is whether the youth should be detained in a secure facility while awaiting case disposition. Over the period from 1985 to 2005, 20% of delinquency cases disposed by juvenile courts were securely detained for some time between referral to court intake and case disposition. This proportion changed relatively little over the period. However, given the large increase in juvenile court referrals between 1985 and 1998, the actual number of delinquency cases detained increased substantially (53%). Following this peak through 2005, the annual number of delinquency cases detained fell slightly, maintaining its relatively high levels of the late 1990s.

From 1985 to 2005, youth in 16% of property and 24% of person offense cases were securely detained, with this proportion changing little over the period. In contrast, the likelihood that a youth charged with a public order offense would be detained fell from 28% in 1985 to 20% in the mid-1990s and then increased to 24% in 2005. In comparison, the trend in the likelihood of detention in drug offense cases was unique. In 1985, the proportion of drug offense cases detained (22%) was lower than the proportion of person (24%) and public order offense (28%) cases detained. After 1985, as detention rates for the other three delinquency offense categories either held constant or declined, and the proportion of drug offense cases detained increased substantially. By 1990, a youth referred for a drug offense was far more likely to be detained (35%) than were youths referred to juvenile court for public order (25%), person (24%), or property (17%) offenses. However, this disparity in detention rates in drug offense cases was short-lived. By the mid-1990s, the likelihood of detention in drug offense cases had returned to its 1985 level, and by 2005, drug offense cases were once again less likely to be detained (18%) than person (25%) or public order (24%) cases.

The unique detention trend pattern in drug offense cases is linked to race. Over the period from 1985 to 2005, a black youth referred to juvenile court intake was far more likely to be detained than a white youth between referral and case disposition (26% versus 17%). This general disparity was found in person (28% versus 21%), property (21% versus 14%), drug (38% versus 17%), and public order (28% versus 22%) offense cases. Consistent with this pattern, black youths charged with a drug offense in 1985 were far more likely than white youths to be securely detained during the processing of their cases (33% versus 19% respectively). However, the unique growth in the likelihood of detention in drug cases during the late 1980s was disproportionately borne by black youth. More specifically, between 1985 and 1990, the drug case detention rate for white youth grew from 19% to 23%, while the black rate increased from 33% to 53%. By the mid-1990s, both the white and black detention rates in drug offense cases had returned to their (still disparate) 1985 levels, but these ten years saw an example of the juvenile justice system's race-specific response to crime.

The other decision made soon after intake is whether the case should be handled informally (i.e., without the filing of a petition) or formally (i.e., with the filing of a petition asking a judge to make a formal ruling in the case). In 1985, most (54%) delinquency cases disposed were handled informally, with informal processing less likely in person (46%) than in property (56%), drug (57%), and public order (54%) cases. The proportion of delinquency cases handled informally decreased from 54% in 1985 to 44% in 1996 and remained essentially constant through 2005. This general pattern held for all but drug offense cases, which saw a substantial decline in informal handling between 1985 and 1991 (from 57% to 34%), followed by an increase to 41% in 1994, and then stability thereafter. In other words, over this period, the juvenile justice decision makers decided that a smaller proportion of all delinquency cases should be handled informally.

The flip side of this trend is the growth during the same period in the formal processing of delinquency cases in juvenile court. Formal court caseloads doubled between 1985 and 1997. This increase in formally handled cases was greater for drug cases (242%), public order (169%), and person (149%) cases than for property (51%)

cases. Between 1997 and 2005, the number of formally processed cases changed little for all but property cases, which fell back to near the number of formally processed cases in 1985.

Nearly all delinquency petitions request that the court formally judge the youth to be a delinquent and, if the youth is adjudicated a delinquent, to order sanctions and/or treatment. During the period from 1985 to 2005, 63% of the cases in which a delinquency petition was filed resulted in a formal adjudication of delinquency. In general, the likelihood of adjudication declined from 1985 to 1995 (falling from 65% to 57%), and then quickly returned by 1998 to near its 1985 level and remained near there through 2005. Over that period, the likelihood that a youth would be adjudicated delinquent once a petitioned had been filed was similar for property, drug, and public order cases and lower for person offense case. A possible explanation for this latter finding is that court intake workers became less willing to informally process person offense cases and decided to pass the decision of how to handle these high-profile matters to judges in the formal court setting.

At disposition, a judge may order a youth to out-of-home placement or to a term of probation, or may order some other sanction (e.g., fine or restitution). Between 1985 and 2005, the number of cases in which youths were adjudicated delinquent increased 85%, undoubtedly placing a strain on service delivery within the juvenile justice system. The number of adjudicated delinquency cases that resulted in out-of-home placement increased about 30% over the period, while the number of cases placed on probation doubled and those given other formal sanction nearly tripled. This means that over this period, the probability that an adjudicated delinquent would be placed out of the home declined, from 32% in 1985 to 22% in 2005. So while out-of-home placements increased over the period, the increase (1) was due primarily to the growth in the court caseloads and (2) was not nearly as great as the increase in adjudicated delinquency cases.

Looking more closely, the number of adjudicated delinquency cases that resulted in out-of-home placement peaked in 1997, increasing from 1985 by about 70%, while adjudicated delinquency cases increased about 90%. Then, between 1997 and 2005, while adjudicated delinquency cases remained essentially constant, the number of adjudicated delinquency cases placed out of the home declined about 20%. The smaller increase in out-of-home placements between 1985 and 1997 might by itself reflect a lack of resources in which to place these youth; but the fact that the number of out-of-home placements declined between 1997 and 2005, while adjudicated delinquency caseloads were stable, indicates the juvenile justice system was seeking (and increasingly using) alternatives to placement during this twenty-year period.

In 2005, youth in 58% of the cases adjudicated and placed out of home were white, 39% were black, 2% were Native American, and 1% was Asian/Pacific Islander. These proportions had changed noticeably since 1985, when youth in 67% of adjudicated cases placed out of the home were white, 31% black, 2% Native American, and 1% Asian/Pacific Islander. One method to understand the nature of these changes is to compare the handling of white and black youth across the key stages of juvenile court processing. Over the 1985-to-2005 period, the black juvenile arrest rate averaged about twice the white rate (Figure 1.8). The ratio of the black-to-white arrest rates varied over the period and was mirrored very closely by the ratio of the black-to-white juvenile court case rates, with the court case ratio being somewhat larger (i.e., somewhat more racially disparate). In other words, black youth were arrested at about twice the rate of white youth and, once arrested, were somewhat more likely than white youth to be referred to juvenile court.

Once in juvenile court, the disparity in the processing of black and white youth increased when a decision was made to formally process the case, declined at the point of adjudication, and increased at the placement decision. Across the period from 1985 to 2005, delinquency cases referred to juvenile court with black youth were more likely to be processed formally than were those involving white youth. On average, over the period, 50% of white delinquency referrals were formally processed compared with 62% of black delinquency referrals—making it more likely that black youth would face a formal adjudication of delinquency and a formal court disposition. Once petitioned, however, the cases of white youth were more likely to result in

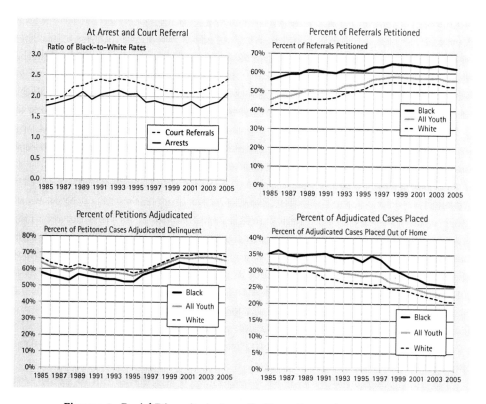

Figure 1.8. Racial Disparity in Juvenile Court Processing: 1985 to 2005
Notes: Arrest rate estimates were developed by the author from analysis of UCR arrest data (USDOJ, FBI UCRP, 2009) adjusted to reflect the FBI's national estimates of arrests. Juvenile court case rate estimates were developed using data reported in Puzzanchera, C. and Kang, W. (2008). "Juvenile Court Statistics Databook." Online. Available: http://ojjdp.ncjrs.gov/ojstatbb/jcsdb/.

an adjudication of delinquency, reducing the relative risk of black youth to receive a formal court disposition. In general, over the period, 64% of the formally processed delinquency cases involving white youth resulted in an adjudication of delinquency compared with just 58% of formally processed cases involving black youth. Finally, once adjudicated delinquent, black youth were more likely to be ordered to an out-of-home placement than were white youth (32% versus 26%).

In 2005, the population-based rate of juvenile court referral for black juveniles was 2.4 times the white referral rate, meaning that racial disparity existed upon entry to the juvenile court. There are many possible explanations for this disparity, ranging from differing levels of law-violating behavior by white and black youth to racial bias by decision makers prior to entry into the juvenile court. In 2005, the population-based rate of out-of-home placement for black youth was 3.2 times the white out-of-home placement rate, meaning that the level of racial disparity at the level of placement decision cannot be attributed entirely to the disparity at referral (2.4) and was enhanced during juvenile court processing. There are many possible reasons for this growth in disparity during juvenile court processing, an issue that will be discussed in more detail later in this book.

VI. Transfers to Criminal Court Trends

Arguably, the most severe sanction a juvenile court can impose is the transfer of the youth's case to criminal court for possible sanctioning as an adult. This is a rare event. In 2005, juvenile courts in the United States processed 1,697,900 delinquency cases, of which 6,900 (or 0.4%) were transferred by a juvenile court judge to a criminal court. The number of cases transferred to criminal court (or waived) increased 80% between 1985 and 1994, from 7,200 to 13,000. After this peak, the number of waived cases declined so that by 2005, the juvenile court waived an estimated 6,900 cases, equivalent to the number waived in 1985.

Much of this decline could arguably be attributed to changes in juvenile legislation that occurred during the mid-1990s. As mentioned earlier, these legislative changes increased the number of youth at risk for transfer to criminal court and the pathways these cases could follow. Younger youth were at risk of transfer. An expanded list of alleged crimes was made eligible for transfer. Many states increased the authority of the prosecutor to file some "juvenile" cases directly in criminal court, while other legislation required that a "juvenile" case be filed in criminal court. These latter two changes reduced the juvenile court's role in the process of placing juveniles in the criminal justice system. This is likely a primary reason juvenile court waivers declined so substantially after 1994. Why should prosecutors bring delinquency cases before juvenile court judges asking for the cases to be waived to criminal court when they could file the cases directly in criminal court, bypassing the juvenile courts completely? In addition, the increase in mandatory exclusions (i.e., the requirement that certain serious juvenile cases be filed directly in criminal court) skimmed off many cases that a juvenile court might have waived if given the opportunity. Therefore, it must be clearly understood that the decline in juvenile court waivers to criminal court does not mean that fewer youths were going into the criminal justice system; it just means that fewer youths were going to criminal court via the juvenile court.

There are no hard statistics on the number of juveniles whose age alone would place the law-violating behavior in the juvenile justice system but who are instead processed as adults in criminal court. The 6,900 cases waived in 2005 do not include those juvenile cases that ended up in criminal court that never passed through juvenile court. (i.e., those that state law requires to be handled in criminal court and those that were filed in criminal court at the discretion of the prosecutor). A very rough guess, based on personal experience alone, would be that these non-juvenile court pathways may process two to three times the cases waived by juvenile courts. Regardless, another "transfer" mechanism dwarfs all of these transfer mechanisms.

As noted earlier, many states in the United States give their criminal justice systems original jurisdiction over the law-violating behaviors of many youth below the age of 18. While these youth are not typically labeled as transfers to criminal court (since they never had the option of having their cases handled in a juvenile court), to many (especially those outside the United States), these youth are "juveniles handled in the criminal justice system." It is possible to develop an annual estimate of the number of criminal court cases there are involving these "age-excluded" juveniles. First, the annual number of youth ages 16 and 17 who live in states where they are under the sole jurisdiction of the criminal justice system is calculated. Then, if it can be assumed that they come to criminal court at the same rates as youth ages 16 and 17 come to juvenile court in states in which they are under the original jurisdiction of the juvenile justice system, an estimate can be produced. Using this method, it is estimated that in 2005, criminal courts in states with "age-excluded" youth processed 257,000 criminal cases involving persons under age 18. This figure increased by over 60% between 1985 and 2005. Clearly, this "transfer" mechanism contributes the greatest number of persons under age 18 to the U.S. criminal justice system.

VII. Conclusions

Juvenile crime trends do not always mirror juvenile arrest, juvenile court referral, and juvenile out-of-home placement trends. There are many decision makers along the way. Will the victim report the juvenile crime to law enforcement? Will the law enforcement officer arrest the youth? Will law enforcement refer the arrested youth to juvenile court intake? Will juvenile court intake recommend formal processing and will the prosecutor file formal charges? Will the judge adjudicate the youth a delinquent? Will probation recommend and/or the judge decide to place the adjudicated youth in an out-of-home facility? At each point, a decision is made that is influenced by a large number of legal and extra-legal factors. The relative importance of these factors can vary over time and with the decision maker. The juvenile justice system's response to law-violating behavior is not a mechanical process. This chapter has provided an empirical foundation of juvenile crime and juvenile justice trends. The validity of any explanation or insight found in the chapters that follow should be judged by how well its predictions match these trends.

NOTES

1. Howard N. Snyder is Chief of Recidivism, Reentry and Special Projects at the Bureau of Justice Statistics within U.S. Department of Justice. The findings, opinions, or points of view contained in this chapter do not necessarily represent the official position or policies of the U.S. Department of Justice.

2. The juvenile rate of serious violent crime is equal to the number of murder, forcible rape, robbery, and aggravated assault incidents involving juvenile offenders per 100,000 persons under age 18 in the U.S. population for that year. The corresponding adult rate is the number of such incidents per 100,000 persons over the age of 18 in the U.S. population.

3. A similar pattern was found when twelfth graders were asked about their illicit drug use in the prior thirty-day period, although the levels were understandably lower, ranging from 30% in 1985 to 22% in 2007.

4. If the white and Hispanic groups were combined, their joint rate would still be greater than the black rate throughout this time period. This point will be important when comparing self-report and arrest data; the FBI does not report arrest data for Hispanic youth, so most Hispanic youth are found in the white racial category.

5. Recently, questions have been raised about the utility and value of the Violent Crime Index, the Property Crime Index, and their combination, the Crime Index. The general problem with these indices is that all crimes are weighted equally and that they can mask important trends in their components. Currently, crime analysts are focusing more on the offense-specific trends rather than the indices.

REFERENCES

Bureau of Justice Statistics (2009). *Age of offenders in serious violent crime, 1973–2007 by number of offenders* [machine-readable data files]. Washington, DC: Bureau of Justice Statistics.

Catalano, S. 2006. *Criminal Victimization, 2005.* Washington, DC: Bureau of Justice Statistics.

Feld, B. 2009. "Violent Girls or Relabeled Status Offenders? An Alternative Interpretation of the Data." *Crime & Delinquency,* 55: 241–65.

Johnston, L. D., P. M. O'Malley, J. G. Bachman, and J. E. Schulenberg. 2008. *Monitoring the Future National Results on Adolescent Drug Use: Overview of Key Findings, 2007* (NIH Publication No. 08–6418). Bethesda, MD: National Institute on Drug Abuse.

Lynch, J., and Snyder, H. 2007. "Juvenile Crime Trends and their Implications for Understanding the Drop in Juvenile Violence." Unpublished manuscript.

Puzzanchera, C., and W. Kang. 2008. "Juvenile Court Statistics Databook." http://ojjdp. ncjrs.gov/ojstatbb/jcsdb/.

Snyder, H., and M. Sickmund. 2006. *Juvenile Offenders and Victims: 2006 National Report.* Washington, DC: U.S. Department of Justice, Office of Juvenile Justice and Delinquency Prevention.

U.S. Department of Justice, Federal Bureau of Investigation. 2008. *Crime in the United States, 2007.* http://www.fbi.gov/ucr/07cius.htm (retrieved 6/30/2009).

United States Department of Justice, Federal Bureau of Investigation, Uniform Crime Reporting Program. Various years. *Supplementary Homicide Reports* for the years 1985 through 2005 [machine-readable data files]. Washington, DC: FBI.

United States Department of Justice, Federal Bureau of Investigation, Uniform Crime Reporting Program. (2009). *Arrests by Age, Sex, and Race for 12-Month Complete Reporters for the Years 1985 through 2007* [machine-readable data files]. Clarksburg, West Virginia: FBI.

CHAPTER 2

HETEROGENEITY IN DELINQUENCY

ALEX R. PIQUERO AND

DOUGLAS B. WEISS

I. Introduction

BEGINNING with the early quantitative research by Quetelet (1841), transitioning to the qualitative life narratives documented by Shaw (1931) and most recently by Laub and Sampson (2003), and culminating in the first (Wolfgang, Figlio, and Sellin 1972) and second (Tracy, Wolfgang, and Figlio 1990; Tracy and Kempf-Leonard 1996) Philadelphia Birth Cohort Studies, research on criminal careers has generated an important amount of empirical knowledge about the longitudinal patterning of crime over the life course (see reviews in Blumstein et al. 1986; Piquero, Farrington, and Blumstein 2003). Collectively, these and other studies have revealed several facts about the heterogeneous nature of offenders and their criminal careers (see Farrington 2003), including: (1) some individuals offend, but others do not (prevalence); (2) among those that do offend, some begin offending early in the life course, while others start offending later in the life course (onset age); (3) some offend at low rates, while others offend at high rates (frequency, or λ); (4) some offenders engage in all types of crimes, while others specialize in a more narrow subset (crime type mix); (5) some offenders increase the severity of their crimes as they progress in their careers, while most others do not escalate (escalation); (6) some offend due to personal and familial characteristics such as poor self-control, neuropsychological problems, inept parenting, academic failure, and compromised socioeconomic environments, while others offend with the aid and comfort of peers; (7) most offenders commit crimes with other offenders (co-offending), while a handful offend by themselves; (8) most offenders desist from crime in early adulthood—sometimes as a result of some life event (marriage, job, child, incarceration), but a small select few persist throughout the life course (career length).

These are but just a few "facts" about the nature of delinquency and crime that underscore the heterogeneity evident within the offender population. Given that there is little ambiguity in the empiricism of these facts, what explains the above-referenced heterogeneity between offenders and offenses? In this chapter, we provide an overview of the heterogeneity that is often observed in delinquency and criminal careers. We begin with a discussion of the classic age–crime relationship, which has formed the basis for much of the theoretical, empirical, and policy discussion regarding crime and criminals. Following this introduction, we then turn our attention to the criminal career framework that parcels the longitudinal patterning of criminal offending into different dimensions, and then turn to an overview of the theories it helped to generate. Third, we then review some of the key empirical investigations that have assessed hypotheses emerging from these theories. Using the information generated from these investigations, the chapter then highlights several promising future research directions that should help fill some of the gaps in understanding the heterogeneity among offenders. Finally, the chapter presents a brief but poignant discussion regarding the policy implications emerging from theoretical and empirical literature surrounding offender heterogeneity.

II. AGE–CRIME CURVE

A classic criminological lesson begins with the relationship between age and crime. Commonly depicted at the aggregate level, this relationship rises from early adolescence to a peak in middle to late adolescence, and then begins a precipitous drop throughout the 20s and 30s. This age–crime curve has been observed in countless studies, from different locations throughout the world, and with a variety of different methods for measuring crime.

Yet, the age–crime relationship is one based on aggregate- and not individual-level offending information, thereby potentially obfuscating the variation that exists within criminal careers generally, and the clouding of distinct offender trajectories—each with their own patterning and etiology—in particular. In an effort to provide some clarity on these issues, the criminal career framework was developed to carefully describe the longitudinal patterning of criminal careers, including, in particular, the various dimensions of the criminal career. In the next section, we provide an overview of this framework and the career dimensions it attributes specific importance to.

III. CRIMINAL CAREER FRAMEWORK

Blumstein and his colleagues (1986) presented the first systemic overview of the criminal career concept and its encompassing dimensions in a two-volume report published by the National Academy of Sciences (NAS) entitled *Criminal Careers and "Career Criminals."* They define a criminal career as the "longitudinal sequence of crimes committed by an individual offender" (p. 12). The criminal career approach divides the aggregate offending rate into two primary components: participation, or the distinction between individuals who offend and those who do not; and frequency, or the level of activity of active offenders.

In addition to these primary components, the criminal career framework includes other dimensions such as career length, crime-type mix and seriousness, and desistance. Career length is defined as the interval between the initial offense and the termination of criminal offending. Crime-type mix and seriousness refers to the pattern of offenses committed during a criminal career. This dimension addresses issues of specialization, or the degree to which offenders concentrate their offending on one type of crime or a certain class of crimes, and escalation, whether offenders move on to commit more serious offenses as their career progresses. Despite its exclusion from the original NAS report, desistance is another key dimension of criminal careers (see Laub and Boonstoppel, Chapter 17 in this volume). Compared to the other criminal career dimensions, it has been considerably more difficult to measure and define desistance (Bushway et al. 2001).

Research on these criminal career dimensions has already produced a substantial body of knowledge regarding offending patterns and the demographic characteristics of age, gender, and race (Blumstein et al. 1986). While the results obtained depend in part on a number of methodological factors such as sample characteristics, reporting method (official records versus self-reports), crime type(s) under study, and study length, several consistent findings have emerged.

Regardless of methodological differences, studies consistently demonstrate that males are more likely to participate in serious crime than females at any age (Piquero, Farrington, and Blumstein 2003). Gender differences in participation are at their greatest for the most serious offenses and are relatively smaller for less serious offenses, and these gaps grow larger over time. Similar to the relationship between gender and participation, most studies suggest a strong association between race and participation and that the difference is greatest for the most serious offenses and also grows over time. Although most studies that have explored the relationship between race and participation have relied on official records, self-report studies also suggest that minorities (especially blacks) report greater involvement in violent crime than whites (Elliott 1994). However, rates of participation in minor delinquency tend to be similar among whites and blacks. Finally, there is a strong relationship between age and participation. Participation in criminal activity tends to be greatest between the age range of 13 and 18, on the low end for self-report studies and the higher end for official records (Moffitt et al. 2001). In addition, onset age varies by crime-type with participation in less serious crime tending to occur earlier than participation in more serious offenses (Loeber and Hay 1994; Piquero, Farrington, and Blumstein 2003).

Research on the frequency of offending has produced less consistent results than studies on participation due to differences in the definition and operationalization of offense rates (Spelman 1994). Differences in offending frequencies can be attributed to differences in the population sampled and the stage in the criminal justice system in which offenders are sampled (Canela-Cacho, Blumstein, and Cohen 1997). Nonetheless, research on the frequency of offending has provided evidence that many offenders go through periods of intermittent offending and that the distribution of offending frequencies is highly skewed, with a small group of offenders committing crimes at much higher rates. In his review of research on offending frequencies and with self-reports of offending from the Rand Inmate Survey, Spelman (1994) estimates that the average offender commits eight crimes per year, while those incarcerated at some point in their career commit between thirty and fifty crimes per year, and the average member of incoming prison cohort commits between sixty and one hundred offenses per year.

Research on criminal career duration is also greatly influenced by methodological differences between studies including whether self-reports or official records are used to measure initiation and termination; the types of crimes being measured (e.g., property, violent); the length of the study period; how career termination or desistance is defined; and different assumptions regarding the offender population. In their review of studies on career duration, Piquero and his colleagues (2003) found that most studies estimate criminal career duration to be between five and ten years. These estimates are likely to be biased downward, however, as the study period may end before offenders desist (Blumstein, Cohen, and Hsieh 1982). Studies on career duration and demographic characteristics have found that males have longer careers than females (Tarling 1993), non-whites have longer careers than whites (Piquero et al. 2002), and an earlier age of onset is associated with longer careers (Kazemian and Farrington 2006).

Other research on the criminal career paradigm has focused on patterns of offending in criminal careers such as the seriousness of the types of crimes committed and whether offenders specialize in committing certain types of crime. Most research on the severity of offending has been based on official records and suggests that the seriousness of offending increases somewhat throughout adolescence, stabilizes in early adulthood, and declines during the adult years (Piquero, Farrington, and Blumstein 2003). Studies of specialization in offending indicate that there is a small tendency for each successive crime to be similar to the one committed before, yet few criminal careers display patterns of specialization, and this is especially true among sex offenders (Zimring, Jennings, and Piquero 2007). Studies also suggest that specialization in offending increases as criminal careers progress (Blumstein et al. 1986), that it is greater among whites for some crime types such as fraud (Wolfgang, Figlio, and Sellin 1972; Blumstein et al. 1988), but not for others such as auto theft (Blumstein et al. 1988). Other research suggests that adult offenders and incarcerated juveniles are more likely to commit offenses within an offending cluster (e.g., violent, property, drug) than to switch to offenses outside a cluster (Cohen 1986; Visher 2000).

Having been described as a "watershed event" (Osgood 2005), the National Academy of Science's criminal career report spurred much debate and criticism (Gottfredson and Hirschi 1990) and led in part to the development of several criminological theories that took the criminal career dimensions and related research findings into account in articulating more formal crime-engendering processes and models. These theoretical models have done much to invigorate theoretical work in criminology and, as a result, have led to several empirical studies that have provided new information on life-course patterns of crime. The next section presents a brief overview of some of these theories, collected under the rubric of developmental/life-course criminology (Farrington 2003).

IV. THEORIES INFORMED BY THE CRIMINAL CAREER PARADIGM

The emergence of the criminal career paradigm steered the focus of criminological research on offending away from between-group differences and shifted it to the study of within-individual differences and changes in offending. Because early criminological theories were based on between-group differences in offending, this change in emphasis required the development of new theoretical explanations, aimed at the individual-level unit of analysis and with a focus on change.

Loeber and Le Blanc (1990) were among the first set of scholars to suggest that the field of criminology adopt a developmental approach to the study of offending. Building off the criminal career framework, Loeber and Le Blanc proposed three primary developmental processes to explain changes in offending over the life span: activation, aggravation, and desistance. Activation refers to the manner in which offending behavior is first initiated and consists of three sub-processes including acceleration (increased frequency of offending over time), stabilization (increased continuity in offending over time), and diversification (the propensity to become involved in different criminal activities). Aggravation refers to the developmental sequence in offending that escalates in seriousness over time. Desistance consists of four sub-processes that indicate the winding down of criminal activity including the deceleration in the frequency of offending, specialization, de-escalation, and reaching a ceiling.

While Loeber and Le Blanc view individuals as being arrayed along a developmental continuum of some sort of individual criminal propensity, other developmental theorists propose the idea that there are qualitatively distinct groups of offenders. Moffitt's (1993) taxonomy divides the offending population into two groups: life-course persisters and adolescent-limited offenders. Life-course persisters initiate antisocial behavior early in life, have a high offending frequency, commit many different types of crimes—including violence, and are unlikely to desist in adulthood. According to the taxonomy, individuals who follow this pattern of offending suffer from an interaction between neuropsychological deficits and family adversity early in life. These individuals demonstrate behaviors such as hyperactivity and conduct disorder in childhood, delinquency in adolescence, and criminal and related antisocial behavior in adulthood. Because this disposition is established early in life and such individuals have not developed important interpersonal skills, life-course persisters are unlikely to desist from crime.

Unlike their more serious counterparts, the second group—adolescent-limited offenders—initiate their foray into delinquency and crime in adolescence, offend at a lower rate, commit only certain types of offenses, and are likely to desist in early adulthood. The origins of offending for this group are found in the maturity gap and the peer social context. The maturity gap is a result of the disjunction between the adolescent's biological maturity and their limited access to adult privileges and responsibilities. For adolescent-limited offenders, delinquency is a way to assert their independence from parents and other authority figures and win peer approval. Among these individuals, offending is normative behavior and is restricted to instrumental offenses that provide money, goods, and adult-like status. Since the cause of their offending is not established early in life, and because they do not suffer the neuropsychological impairments and injurious childhoods that life-course persisters do, adolescent-limited offenders usually desist from crime when they enter young adulthood and take on adult roles. However, their offending careers can extend beyond adolescence because of snares, such as a criminal record or substance abuse problems, which encapsulate them into an antisocial trajectory and which make it difficult to make a successful transition into adulthood. (Note: Moffitt (2006) has recently revised her taxonomy to include a third group, low-level chronic offenders, who offend at stable but lower levels throughout adolescence and early adulthood.)

Patterson and colleagues' (1992) developmental theory is similar to that of Moffitt's (1993) in that there are two distinct groups of offenders—early starters and late starters—each of whom originate from two different causal processes. Early starters resemble Moffitt's life-course-persisters. These individuals display temper tantrums and aggression in childhood. In addition to these problem behaviors, poor interpersonal skills cause these individuals to form weak social bonds with parents, peers, and school. The poor (familial) socialization of these individuals early in the life course helps to develop a time stable propensity to offend throughout life. The second group of offenders in Patterson's typology—late starters—are similar to Moffitt's adolescent-limited offenders on two specific fronts: the principal cause of offending for this group is the deviant peer group rather than a "maturity gap," while their offending is constrained to the adolescent period and is relatively non-serious in nature.

The final developmental theory reviewed here is from Loeber and Hay (1994). These authors outline a three-pathway model beginning in childhood, in which individuals follow an orderly progression from less to more serious problem behaviors and delinquency from childhood to adolescence and for a small subset, into adulthood. The first group follows an "authority conflict pathway" prior to the age of 12 that begins with stubborn behavior, morphs into defiance at the second stage, and then progresses to authority avoidance (e.g., truancy) as a third stage. The second group follows a "covert pathway" prior to age 15 that starts with minor covert acts, progresses into property damage in the second stage, and then to moderate to serious delinquency as the third stage. The third group follows an "overt pathway" that begins with minor aggression, segues into physical fighting in the second stage, and then progresses to more serious violence in the third stage.

In contrast to these developmental perspectives that posit multiple pathways to delinquency, some life-course theories of offending advance a general explanation that applies for all offenders. The one specific theory that has received the most attention is Sampson and Laub's (1993; Laub and Sampson 2003) age-graded theory of informal social control. Their theory argues that continuity and (especially) change in offending is a function of the strength of an individual's social bonds (to parents and peers early in the life course and then to marriage and employment later in the life course), as well as an individual's purposeful choice, or human agency. According to this perspective, continuity and change in offending reflects changes in the accumulation of social bonds, and especially the strength and attachment of such bonds. Within-individual changes in social bonds, especially in adulthood—i.e., getting married and being invested in a good marriage—are believed to be implicated in desistance from crime. Importantly, the general process underlying continuity and change is similar for most offenders such that offender typologies are unwarranted and unnecessary in their framework. For Sampson and Laub, all offenders desist by middle adulthood regardless of their level of offending or the individual differences or childhood/adolescence variables that relate to their initial and continued offending patterns.

Our review of these developmental/life-course criminological theories shows that there is both overlap and disagreement about the variation within offenders. Some theories strictly adhere to group-based expectations (Patterson, Crosby, and Vuchinich 1992; Moffitt 1993). Other more complicated theories advance both a group-based hypothesis as well as a developmental progression of antisocial behavior from childhood to adolescence and then onto adulthood (Loeber and Hay 1994), while other theories argue against offender typologies but adhere to the importance of a life-course-oriented perspective that allows both continuity and especially change in offending patterns (Sampson and Laub 1993). These theories make vastly different predictions about the nature and patterning of criminal offenders and criminal offending, and several empirical tests have started to examine the veracity and validity of these models. In the next section, we highlight some of the more important studies in this area that have carefully assessed key hypotheses.

V. Ensuing Research Testing

Research on developmental and life-course theories of offending has usually focused on three key hypotheses. The first hypothesis is whether these dynamic theories offer more complete accounts of antisocial behavior over the life course and are superior to static theories in explaining offending throughout the life span. The second hypothesis pertains to whether different causal processes lead to a different progression and pattern of offending for different subgroups of offenders, as suggested by developmental theories, or whether the same causal process operates for all offenders. In addition to this question, researchers have sought to determine how many groups and patterns exist (D'Unger et al. 1998). The third hypothesis focuses on whether and, if so how, changes in local life circumstances in adulthood alter trajectories of offending. For instance, do changes in living situations affect all offenders in a similar manner, or do some offenders react differently to such changes?

The debate over whether the offending population is composed of distinct subgroups of offenders, whose offending is caused by different causes and causal processes, or whether the same general cause and process operates for all offenders has long existed in criminology. The emergence of typological theories, such as those of Moffitt (1993) and Patterson and colleagues (1992), as well as methodological advances, such as the advent of semi-parametric modeling (Nagin and Land 1993), has brought this issue to the fore in recent years. Two studies in particular sought to determine whether developmental theories of offending are superior to general explanations.

Paternoster and Brame (1997) used self-report data from the National Youth Survey (NYS), a large sample of adolescents followed into early adulthood, to determine whether the effects of dynamic factors, such as delinquent peer exposure and prior offending, operate differently in groups of individuals who differ in their offending propensity as predicted by typological theories. Their results suggest that such factors have the same effect on both participation in delinquency and the frequency of offending regardless of offending propensity. They also find strong, positive effects of these dynamic factors on whether and how often individuals offend, even after observed and unobserved individual differences are taken into account.

Bartusch and colleagues (1997) also find greater support for dynamic theories of offending (such as Moffitt's developmental taxonomy) than static explanations in the Dunedin Multidisciplinary Health and Development Study, a birth cohort of over one thousand males and females in Dunedin, New Zealand. In particular, childhood antisocial behavior was related more strongly than adolescent antisocial behavior to low verbal ability, hyperactivity, and negative/impulsive personality, whereas adolescent antisocial behavior was related more strongly to peer delinquency. In addition, childhood antisocial behavior was more strongly associated with convictions for violence, while adolescent antisocial behavior was more strongly related to convictions for nonviolent offenses.

While these studies provide support for dynamic theories of offending, they offer different accounts regarding whether there is a single path to delinquency or whether there are multiple paths. Researchers interested in this question have usually turned to methods, such as trajectory analysis, to identify patterns of continuity and change in offending. Nagin and Land (1993) introduced this methodology to the study of delinquency and crime, seeking to determine whether individual offending trajectories matched the aggregate age–crime curve. Using conviction records for 411 South London males participating in the Cambridge Study in Delinquent Development, they identified four distinct offending trajectories: the never-convicted, adolescence-limited, high-level chronics, and low-level chronics. This four-group finding has been replicated in other samples of serious young offenders (Laub, Nagin, and Sampson 1998; Piquero et al. 2002), although some studies using a more general sample of youth have found as many as five trajectories (Chung et al. 2002; Moffitt 2006).

While trajectory studies have differed in the number of offending patterns, they share some findings in common. For instance, most studies identify a small group of offenders who begin early in life and persist well into adulthood. This group exhibits the features of early onset and persistence throughout life that are predicted by Moffitt's (1993) and Patterson et al.'s (1992) developmental theories. Most trajectory studies also identify the adolescent-peaked pattern predicted by both of these theories (see Piquero 2008). Regardless of the number of groups identified, however, each of these studies demonstrates considerable heterogeneity in the offending population where the vast majority of offenders desist by early (Piquero 2008) or middle (Laub and Sampson 2003) adulthood.

The third area of research that has received considerable attention has been the manner in which changes in life circumstances influence offender trajectories. In an early important study, Horney and colleagues (1995) examined short-term variations in offending and life circumstances in a group of 658 incarcerated male offenders. They found that changes in living arrangements, such as living with their wives, school attendance, and cessation of substance use, reduces the probability of offending at those particular times regardless of an individual's overall level of offending. Further, these circumstances produced the greatest effects in the most serious offenders.

Laub, Nagin, and Sampson (1998) used data from the five hundred Boston-area delinquents included in Glueck's study of criminal careers to study the effect of marriage on offending trajectories to age 32. They found that early marriages characterized by social cohesiveness promoted desistance from offending, and that the effect on offending of these "good" marriages, which were characterized by strong spousal attachment, became stronger over time.

Piquero and colleagues (2002) examined the relationship between local life circumstances and offending in emerging adulthood among a group of 524 serious offenders from the California Youth Authority whom they followed for seven years post-parole. They found four offending trajectories that exhibited different patterns of persistence and desistance from crime. Another significant finding from this study was that although those who ranked low on violent arrests also ranked low on nonviolent arrests, this association did not hold for all groups. For instance, the mean number of nonviolent arrests for one group declined with age at the same time that the average number of arrests for violent offenses increased. Inconsistent findings were obtained for the effects of local life circumstances on offending patterns. For example, a measure of stakes in conformity that included the presence of a marriage had a significant, negative effect on violent arrests in one group and a negative effect on nonviolent arrests for another group. In addition, heroin dependence had a significant and positive effect on nonviolent arrests for some groups, but not for others. A number of other studies have examined similar issues and have yielded similar findings (Paternoster et al. 1997; Chung et al. 2002).

The above research highlights several summary statements. First, although less parsimonious explanations of crime, dynamic theories of offending appear to provide more useful explanations of continuity and change about the nature of offending over the life course when compared to more static theories. At the same time, there still remains mixed evidence with respect to the nature of the pro-dynamic conclusion, as the dynamic/general theory of Sampson and Laub provides a very good portrayal of crime over the life course without the added complexity of offender groups which are characteristic of dynamic/developmental theories. Second, studies that have used the trajectory method to study offending over the life course suggest there is greater heterogeneity in the offending population than current developmental theories would predict. While all of these studies identify a small group of early-onset offenders who persist throughout life, and a larger group of adolescent-onset offenders who desist in early adulthood, other patterns of offending are observed that remain to be explained. Further, the evidence on whether these different trajectories represent different etiologies and causal process at work or whether they reflect differences in the level of severity of the same risk factors is inconsistent. It may be that methodological differences between studies may be partially responsible for these conflicting results. These include, but are not limited to, differences in sample size and the population from which the sample is drawn: whether official records, self-reports, or multi-agent reports are used; the types of crime under study; the length of the study period; and the life stage(s) that the study focuses on (e.g., childhood, adolescence, adulthood). Nonetheless, these differences in offending trajectories suggest there may be multiple pathways to offending. Finally, changes in life circumstances beyond adolescence can alter offending trajectories regardless of offending propensity, although not all offenders may be affected in the same manner.

VI. FUTURE RESEARCH DIRECTIONS

This chapter was designed to provide a very brief overview concerning the heterogeneity that is evident in delinquent and criminal careers. Beginning with the criminal career framework and after reviewing some of the findings associated with research on the various criminal career dimensions, we turned to a brief overview of some of the theories that emerged as a result of the articulation of the criminal career paradigm and its focus on the longitudinal patterning of criminal activity. This was then followed by a short summary of some of the main research studies designed to assess the merits of dynamic and static theories of crime, as well as the differences within dynamic theories, some of which attribute importance to distinct offender typologies. Clearly, a detailed review of the theories and research studies is beyond the scope of this chapter, but fortunately, detailed treatments of this literature already exist (Moffitt et al. 2001; Piquero, Farrington, and Blumstein 2003, 2007; Farrington 2005; Loeber et al. 2008). Thus, while much has been recently learned about offenders and offending over the life course—especially as longitudinal studies continue to gather such information, there remains much more to uncover about the nature and progression of offenders and their offending. We close out this chapter with an identification of some of the most pressing and emerging areas of research that will help fill some of the important gaps in both theory and research on the longitudinal patterning of criminal activity and the heterogeneity that is evidence in delinquent and criminal careers.

First, due to a constellation of historical factors, much of the empirical data and subsequent research findings have been based on samples mainly comprising white males. This has had the unfortunate consequence of limiting our knowledge about offenders and offending over the life course with respect to race/ethnic (Piquero and Brame 2008; Maldonado-Molina et al. 2009) and gender differences (Moffitt et al. 2001; D'Unger, Land, and McCall 2002; Piquero, Brame, and Moffitt 2005). Whether findings based on white male samples replicate to other demographic groups is not only an empirical question, but also highly relevant for existing theories and the extent to which current explanations are applicable across individual characteristics.

Second, many of the older longitudinal studies were based on official data and thus only contain information on offending that emerges from police contact, arrest, and/or conviction files. Only recently have studies begun the expansive and expensive task of collecting self-report records (Loeber et al. 1999; Mulvey et al. 2004). The collection and analysis of offenders and their offending that compares official and self-report records is an important issue in the effort to examine how study conclusions vary according to instruments of data collection (Nagin, Farrington, and Moffitt 1995; Brame et al. 2004; Farrington et al. 2007).

Third, although significant findings have emerged with respect to the relationship of local life circumstances to persistence and desistance from crime, data constraints have limited attention to events like marriage and employment. Other life events, particularly incarceration experiences and neighborhood changes, appear to be important life circumstances worthy of examination (Bhati and Piquero 2008; Nieuwbeerta, Nagin, and Blokland 2009).

Fourth, it has been the case that much of the information concerning offenders and their offending has emerged via quantitative examinations—and recently through the use of sophisticated methodological techniques that permit investigation and identification of distinct typologies. Yet there is much to be gained from qualitative investigations of crime over the life course. As a case in point, Laub and Sampson's (2003) recent life history narratives identified and highlighted important factors and decision-making styles among very active offenders with respect to how various life circumstances influenced their offending behavior, many of which would not have been uncovered with traditional empirical methods. Clearly, integrating both quantitative and qualitative data for the same subjects will permit investigation of important crime over the life-course questions.

Fifth, and in a related manner, the advent of methodological and statistical techniques has permitted researchers to examine the heterogeneity among offenders and their offending patterns. Yet there is a pressing need for methodological investigations into the assumptions and limitations underlying these methods and the implications these issues have for conclusions drawn about offenders and their offending over the life course (Nagin 2005).

Sixth, for the most part, there has not been much recent theoretical development in this area since the introduction of the theories articulated by Moffitt, Patterson, Loeber, and Sampson and Laub. Of course, there may be no reason that "new" theories need to be developed, however, there is a need for unpacking the sequence and meaning of how life circumstances relate to persistence and desistance from crime. For example, why is it that an incarceration stint serves as a deterrent to some offenders but backfires for other offenders, leading to continued criminal activity (Laub and Sampson 2003)? Further, there exists opportunity for fleshing out the notion of human agency in Sampson and Laub as well as the cognitive transformations associated with desistance identified by Giordano, Cernkovich, and Rudolph (2002) and others. An additional point with respect to theory concerns the role and influence of biological factors in the genesis of criminal activity (Peskin et al, Chapter 4 in this volume). Only recently has the knowledge base on biological and biosocial characteristics made headway into criminology, and this information has generated important insight into some of the origins of particular types of offending styles. The integration of these explanations into criminal career research may prove beneficial as criminologists continue to understand the heterogeneity in delinquency and crime over the life course.

Lastly, all of the directions outlined above and the research that will hopefully ensue as a result should be considered in light of current developmental/life-course theories, and any challenges to existing theories should be carefully considered and lead to modifications of the theories as results are replicated. Moffitt (2006) in particular has revised her developmental taxonomy in light of extant research findings identifying other typologies (i.e., low-level chronic) that were not originally anticipated in the original exposition of the theory.

VII. POLICY IMPLICATIONS

Theoretical and empirical knowledge about delinquent and criminal careers suggests that there is important heterogeneity in the nature and patterning of criminal offending over the life course. That is, some offenders offend sparingly and for only a brief period of time, while others are much more persistent as their offending continues across multiple phases of the life course. Further, the characteristics associated with different offenders and their offending patterns appear to evince some similarities but also reveal important differences. In short, a one-size-fits-all prevention and intervention policy aimed at delinquent and criminal offending may not yield significant benefits likely because programmatic efforts may not be addressing the key risk factors for offending onset and offending continuation.

Research that pays attention to the heterogeneity between offenders and follows along the paths suggested above will also be relevant for public policy and programmatic efforts designed to prevent initial criminal activity and intervene in the midst of existing criminal careers so as to deflect offenders away from persistent involvement in crime and related negative outcomes over the life course. In this regard, some programs have attained modest success at addressing risk factors early in the life course, and these efforts have paid dividends across several life-course domains (Greenwood 2006). One particular strategy revolves around early family and parent training efforts, including nurse home visitation programs. A recent meta-analysis of these programs showed that participation in such programs early in the life course evinced significant reductions in delinquency and crime in adolescence and positive gains in other, noncrime life-course domains (Piquero et al. 2009). Given the cost associated with serious and lengthy criminal careers (Cohen and Piquero 2009), it remains important to continue basic research on offenders and their offending over the life course, as the information generated will serve as the backbone to the development and implementation of successful programs designed to turn offenders away from their initial and continued involvement in criminal activity. Further, policy makers must recognize that addressing the correlates of delinquent and criminal activity as early as possible in the life course will pay more dividends than dealing with delinquents well after they have accumulated a healthy stock of offending experience. The classic Quaker State "you can pay me now, or you can pay me later" adage holds true not only for motor oil, but for juvenile delinquency and adult crime as well.

REFERENCES

Bartusch, Dawn R. Jeglum, Donald R. Lynam, Terrie E. Moffitt, and Phil A. Silva. 1997. "Is Age Important? Testing a General versus a Developmental Theory of Antisocial Behavior." *Criminology* 35 (1): 13–48.

Bhati, Avinash Singh, and Alex R. Piquero. 2008. "Estimating the Impact of Incarceration on Subsequent Offending Trajectories: Deterrent, Criminogenic, or Null Effect?" *Journal of Criminal Law & Criminology* 98 (1, Fall): 207–53.

Blumstein, Alfred, Jacqueline Cohen, Somnath Das, and Soumyo D. Moitra. 1988. "Specialization and Seriousness during Adult Criminal Careers." *Journal of Quantitative Criminology* 4: 303–45.

Blumstein, Alfred, Jacqueline Cohen, and Paul Hsieh. 1982. *The Duration of Adult Criminal Careers*. Final report to the U.S. Department of Justice. School of Urban and Public Affairs, Carnegie-Mellon University, Pittsburgh.

Blumstein, Alfred, Jacqueline Cohen, Jeffrey A. Roth, and Christy A. Visher, eds. 1986. *Criminal Careers and "Career Criminals,"* vol. 1. Washington, DC: National Academy Press.

Brame, Robert, Jeffrey Fagan, Alex R. Piquero, Carol Schubert, and Laurence Steinberg. 2004. "Criminal Careers of Serious Delinquents in Two Cities." *Youth Violence & Juvenile Justice* 2: 256–72.

Bushway, Shawn D., Alex R. Piquero, Lisa M. Broidy, Elizabeth Cauffman, and Paul Mazerolle. 2001. "An Empirical Framework for Studying Desistance as a Process." *Criminology* 39: 491–515.

Canela-Cacho, José A., Alfred Blumstein, and Jacqueline Cohen. 1997. "Relationship Between the Offending Frequency of Imprisoned and Free Offenders." *Criminology* 35: 133–76.

Chung, Ick-Joong, Karl G. Hill, J. David Hawkins, Lewayne D. Gilchrist, and Daniel S. Nagin. 2002. "Childhood Predictors of Offense Trajectories." *Journal of Research in Crime and Delinquency* 39: 60–92.

Cohen, Jacqueline. 1986. "Research on Criminal Careers: Individual Frequency Rates and Offense Seriousness." In *Criminal Careers and "Career Criminals,"* vol. 1, edited by Alfred Blumstein, Jacqueline Cohen, Jeffrey A. Roth, and Christy A. Visher. Washington, DC: National Academy Press.

Cohen, Mark A., and Alex R. Piquero. 2009. "New Evidence on the Monetary Value of Saving a High Risk Youth." *Journal of Quantitative Criminology* 25: 25–49.

D'Unger, Amy V., Kenneth C. Land, and Patricia L. McCall. 2002. "Sex Differences in Age Patterns of Delinquent/Criminal Careers: Results from Poisson Latent Class Analyses of the Philadelphia Cohort Study." *Journal of Quantitative Criminology* 18: 349–75.

D'Unger, Amy V., Kenneth C. Land, Patricia L. McCall, and Daniel S. Nagin. 1998. "How Many Latent Classes of Delinquent/Criminal Careers? Results from Mixed Poisson Regression Analyses." *American Journal of Sociology* 103: 1593–630.

Elliott, Delbert S. 1994. "1993 Presidential Address: Serious Violent Offenders: Onset, Developmental Course, and Termination." *Criminology* 32: 1–22.

Farrington, David P. 2003. "Developmental and Life-Course Criminology: Key Theoretical and Empirical Issues—The 2002 Sutherland Award Address." *Criminology* 41: 221–55.

Farrington, David P., ed. 2005. *Integrated Developmental and Life-Course Theories of Offending. Advances in Criminological Theory*, vol. 14. New Brunswick, NJ: Transaction.

Farrington, David P., Darrick Jolliffe, Rolf Loeber, and D.L. Homish. 2007. "How Many Offenses are Really Committed per Juvenile Court Offender." *Victims and Offenders* 2: 227–49.

Giordano, Peggy C., Stephen A. Cernkovich, and Jennifer L. Rudolph. 2002. "Gender, Crime, and Desistance: Toward a Theory of Cognitive Transformation." *American Journal of Sociology* 107: 990–1064.

Gottfredson, Michael R., and Travis Hirschi. 1990. *A General Theory of Crime*. Stanford, CA: Stanford University Press.

Greenwood, Peter W. 2006. *Changing Lives: Delinquency Prevention as Crime Control Policy*. Chicago: University of Chicago Press.

Horney, Julie, D. Wayne Osgood, and Ineke Haen Marshall. 1995. "Criminal Careers in the Short Term: Intra-Individual Variability in Crime and Its Relation to Local Life Circumstances." *American Sociological Review* 60: 655–73.

Kazemian, Lila, and David P. Farrington. 2006. "Exploring Residual Career Length and Residual Number of Offenses for Two Generations of Repeat Offenders." *Journal of Research in Crime and Delinquency* 43: 89–113.

Laub, John H., Daniel S. Nagin, and Robert J. Sampson. 1998. "Good Marriages and Trajectories of Change in Criminal Offending." *American Sociological Review* 63: 225–38.

Laub, John H., and Robert J. Sampson. 2003. *Shared Beginnings, Divergent Lives: Delinquent Boys to Age 70*. Cambridge, MA: Harvard University Press.

Loeber, Rolf, David P. Farrington, Magda Stouthamer-Loeber, and Helene Raskin White. 2008. *Violence and Serious Theft: Development and Prediction from Childhood to Adulthood*. New York: Routledge.

Loeber, Rolf, and Dale F. Hay. 1994. "Developmental Approaches to Aggression and Conduct Problems." In *Development Through Life: A Handbook for Clinicians*, edited by Michael Rutter and Dale F. Hay. Oxford: Blackwell Scientific Publications.

Loeber, Rolf, and Marc Le Blanc. 1990. "Toward a Developmental Criminology." In *Crime and Justice: A Review of Research*, vol. 12, edited by Michael Tonry and Norval Morris. Chicago: University of Chicago Press.

Loeber, Rolf, Evelyn Wei, Magda Stouthamer-Loeber, David Huizinga, and Terence P. Thornberry. 1999. "Behavioral Antecedents to Serious and Violent Offending: Joint Analyses from the Denver Youth Survey, Pittsburgh Youth Study, and the Rochester Youth Development Study." *Studies on Crime and Crime Prevention* 8 (2): 245–63.

Maldonada-Molina, Mildred M., Alex R. Piquero, Wesley G. Jennings, Hector Bird, and Glorissa Canino. 2009. "Trajectories of Delinquency among Puerto Rican Children and Adolescents at Two Sites." *Journal of Research in Crime & Delinquency* 46: 144–81.

Moffitt, Terrie E. 1993. "Life-Course-Persistent and Adolescent-Limited Antisocial Behavior: A Developmental Taxonomy." *Psychological Review* 100: 674–701.

Moffitt, Terrie E. 2006. "Life-Course Persistent versus Adolescence-Limited Antisocial Behavior." In *Developmental Psychopathology*, 2nd ed., edited by Dante Cicchetti and Donald J. Cohen. New York: Wiley.

Moffitt, Terrie E., Avshalom Caspi, Michael Rutter, and Phil A. Silva. 2001. *Sex Differences in Antisocial Behaviour: Conduct Disorder, Delinquency, and Violence in the Dunedin Longitudinal Study*. Cambridge: Cambridge University Press.

Mulvey, Edward P., Laurence Steinberg, Jeffrey Fagan, Elizabeth Cauffman, Alex Piquero, Laurie Chassin, George Knight, Robert Brame, Carol Schubert, Thomas Hecker, and Sandra Losoya. 2004. "Theory and Research on Desistance from Antisocial Activity among Serious Juvenile Offenders." *Youth Violence & Juvenile Justice* 2: 213–36.

Nagin, Daniel S. 2005. *Group-Based Modeling of Development*. Cambridge, MA: Harvard University Press.

Nagin, Daniel S., David P. Farrington, and Terrie E. Moffitt. 1995. "Life-Course Trajectories of Different Types of Offenders." *Criminology* 33: 111–40.

Nagin, Daniel S., and Kenneth C. Land. 1993. "Age, Criminal Careers, and Population Heterogeneity: Specification and Estimation of a Nonparametric, Mixed, Poisson Model." *Criminology* 31: 327–62.

Nieuwbeerta, Paul, Daniel S. Nagin, and Arjan A. J. Blokland. 2009. "Assessing the Impact of First-Time Imprisonment on Offenders' Subsequent Criminal Career Development: A Matched Samples Comparison." *Journal of Quantitative Criminology* 25: 227–57.

Osgood, D. Wayne. 2005. "Making Sense of Crime and the Life Course." *The Annals of the American Academy of Political and Social Science: Developmental Criminology and its Discontents: Trajectories of Crime from Childhood to Old Age* 602: 196–211.

Patterson, G. R., L. Crosby, and S. Vuchinich. 1992. "Predicting Risk for Early Police Arrest." *Journal of Quantitative Criminology* 8 (4): 335–55.

Paternoster, Raymond, and Robert Brame. 1997. "Multiple Routes to Delinquency? A Test of Developmental and General Theories of Crime." *Criminology* 35 (1): 49–84.

Paternoster, Raymond, Charles W. Dean, Alex Piquero, Paul Mazerolle, and Robert Brame. 1997. "Generality, Continuity, and Change in Offending." *Journal of Quantitative Criminology* 13: 231–66.

Piquero, Alex R. 2008. "Taking Stock of Developmental Trajectories of Criminal Activity over the Life Course." In *The Long View of Crime: A Synthesis of Longitudinal Research*, edited by Akiva Liberman. New York: Springer.

Piquero, Alex R., and Robert W. Brame. 2008. "Assessing the Race-Crime and Ethnicity-Crime Relationship in a Sample of Serious Adolescent Delinquents." *Crime & Delinquency* 54: 390–422.

Piquero, Alex R., Robert Brame, Paul Mazerolle, and Rudy Haapanen. 2002. "Crime in Emerging Adulthood." *Criminology* 40: 137–69.

Piquero, Alex R., Robert Brame, and Terrie E. Moffitt. 2005. "Extending the Study of Continuity and Change: Gender Differences in Adolescent and Adulthood Offending." *Journal of Quantitative Criminology* 21: 219–43.

Piquero, Alex R., David P. Farrington, and Alfred Blumstein. 2003. "The Criminal Career Paradigm." In *Crime and Justice: A Review of Research*, vol. 30, edited by Michael Tonry. Chicago: University of Chicago Press.

Piquero, Alex R., David P. Farrington, and Alfred Blumstein. 2007. *Key Issues in Criminal Career Research: New Analyses from the Cambridge Study in Delinquent Development*. Cambridge: Cambridge University Press.

Piquero, Alex R., David P. Farrington, Brandon C. Welsh, Richard Tremblay, and Wesley Jennings. 2009. "Effects of Early Family/Parent Training Programs on Antisocial Behavior and Delinquency." *Journal of Experimental Criminology* 5 (2): 83–120.

Quetelet, Adolphe. 1831. *Research on the Propensity for Crime at Different Ages*. 1984 ed. Cincinnati: Anderson Publishing Company.

Sampson, Robert J., and John H. Laub. 1993. *Crime in the Making: Pathways and Turning Points Through Life*. Cambridge: Harvard University Press.

Shaw, Clifford R. 1931. *The Natural History of a Delinquency Career*. Chicago: University of Chicago Press.

Spelman, William. 1994. *Criminal Incapacitation*. New York: Plenum.

Tarling, Roger. 1993. *Analyzing Offending: Data, Models, and Interpretations*. London: Her Majesty's Stationery Office.

Tracy, Paul E., and Kimberly Kempf-Leonard. 1996. *Continuity and Discontinuity in Criminal Careers*. New York: Plenum.

Tracy, Paul E., Marvin E. Wolfgang, and Robert M. Figlio. 1990. *Delinquency in Two Birth Cohorts*. New York: Plenum.

Visher, Christy A. 2000. "Career Criminals and Crime Control." In *Criminology: A Contemporary Handbook*, edited by Joseph F. Sheley. 3rd ed. Belmont, CA: Wadsworth.

Wolfgang, Marvin E., Robert M. Figlio, and Thorsten Sellin. 1972. *Delinquency in a Birth Cohort*. Chicago: University of Chicago Press.

Zimring, Franklin E., Wesley Jennings, and Alex R. Piquero. 2007. "Juvenile and Adult Sexual Offending in Racine, Wisconsin: Does Early Sex Offending Predict Later Sex Offending in Youth and Young Adulthood?" *Criminology & Public Policy* 6: 507–34.

CHAPTER 3

THE VICTIM-OFFENDER OVERLAP AND ITS IMPLICATIONS FOR JUVENILE JUSTICE

CHRISTOPHER J. SCHRECK AND ERIC A. STEWART

BOTH victimization and offending are problems linked to youth. Thomas Bernard (1992) characterized the pattern where the young commit a disproportionate share of crime as a fact that has remained true for the past two hundred years. This pattern of offending still holds twenty years later (Snyder and Sickmund 2006). Data also consistently show that juveniles have a higher risk of falling victim to crime than other age groups (Hindelang 1976). Recent studies report that one out of every four crime victims are youths (Snyder and Sickmund 2006). The similarities across victims and offenders do not end there: they share the same demographic profiles, with both groups being overrepresented by those who are young, male, and African American (Hindelang, Gottfredson, and Garofalo 1978). The fact that offenders and victims bear strong resemblance to one another may be important not only for academic criminology, but also with respect to the practice of juvenile justice.

This chapter is about the victim-offender overlap, that is to say, a phenomenon where a person's offending activity and victimization experiences are positively correlated. As we shall see, the victim-offender overlap is a well-documented empirical fact, albeit one that we are only now beginning to understand better. Less clear, however, is what juvenile justice ought to do about it. This chapter will focus a great deal of attention on what insights some of the leading criminological theories might offer, particularly cultural deviance, strain, control, and life-course perspectives. Each of these groups of theories proposes distinct policies for how juvenile justice might address the overlap and in so doing reduces not only offending but also the misery that attends victimization. Juvenile justice, for its part, had traditionally operated under its own understanding of the victim-offender overlap—an idea, in fact, that exists in surprising (although not complete) harmony with some of the leading contemporary theories of crime.

We begin with some background on the victim-offender overlap, which should highlight why science can offer relatively little information on this topic. Given how often politics and advocacy intrude into the study of crime victims (e.g., Karmen 2008; Ryan 1971), it is perhaps natural to see victims and offenders as sharing little in common with respect to their deeds and backgrounds. Indeed to suggest that victimization and offending emerge for the same reasons, or are related in some way, is to risk inviting such odious labels as "victim-blamer." In this context, one could be pardoned for believing that victims differ in crucial respects from offenders.

But criminological research discredits the idea that offenders and victims are distinct entities, finding in fact that they are often the same people. Some of the early fathers of victimology made prescient guesses about the offender-victim overlap on the basis of weak or nonexistent data (e.g., Von Hentig 1948). Marvin Wolfgang's (1958) famous study of homicide in Philadelphia was the first to muster credible scientific data showing that victims and offenders in a murder often shared remarkable similarities, particularly in terms of having a background of arrest. Luckenbill (1977) found that homicide victims and offenders behaved similarly during the events leading up to the murder itself, with both parties actively contributing to the escalating situation. Considerable research, most of it of relatively recent vintage, offers further proof (Broidy et al. 2006; Hindelang 1976; Jacobs and Wright 2006; Jensen and Brownfield 1986; Lauritsen, Sampson, and Laub 1991; Mustaine and Tewksbury 2000; Ousey, Wilcox, and Fisher 2010; Peterson, Taylor, and Esbensen 2004; Piquero et al. 2005; Schreck 1999; Schreck, Stewart, and Fisher 2006; Stewart, Schreck, and Simons 2006; Wilkinson 2003). We now know that the correlation between victimization and offending persists across many different data sources, samples, and data-collection techniques. The offender-victim overlap is thus a fact whose existence is beyond dispute.

What scholars can dispute is whether the victim-offender overlap has any scientific meaning and what consequences it might have for the practice of juvenile justice. As persistent as the victim-offender correlation is, few criminological theories say much about it. If academic criminology today is of limited help, it was of almost no help many decades ago. At the time evidence of the victim-offender overlap emerged during the 1940s and 1950s, criminological theory was in a period of remarkable growth. Yet all of the influential theories of this period ignored it.[1] This state of affairs began to change in the late 1970s, with the advent of theories organized to explain the overlap (e.g., Hindelang, Gottfredson, and Garofalo 1978). Only in the last decade have criminologists really begun to wrestle with the substantive implications of the victim-offender overlap (e.g., Agnew 2002; Lauritsen and Laub 2007; Schreck 1999; Stewart, Schreck, and Simons 2006). As theory struggled to catch up with the research, discussion of policy implications has had to wait.

Juvenile justice was more than a century ahead of criminology in recognizing a possible theoretical connection between victimization and offending. The Houses of Refuge during the nineteenth century could admit beaten and neglected children to prevent them from becoming offenders (Mennel 1973). The philosophy of the juvenile court at the turn of the twentieth century was informed by the same idea, an idea supported by the burgeoning social sciences, which took the view that human behavior was determined by antecedent factors (Bernard 1992; Feld 1999). Consequently, the juvenile court would have formal jurisdiction not only over children who broke the law, but also who were dependent, neglected, and abused. Whether children committed crime was not, from the perspective of the juvenile court, the most significant issue for consideration. Instead, the court was to examine the conditions the child lived in. All this of course does not mean that leading scientific theories of that time speculated much about the effects of victimization, but the basic assumption of the juvenile court was that children at high risk of becoming adult offenders had backgrounds characterized by pathology, which included victimization (Pfohl 1984). The juvenile court would then, ideally, direct the youth to programs designed to correct the childhood blighted by victimization. In its own way, juvenile justice historically not only expected a victim-offender overlap, but also operated under an implicit theory that victimization was a factor in shaping youthful and later adult offending.

One can infer additional meanings about the victim-offender overlap from the very organization of the adult and juvenile systems. The use of separate court arrangements on the basis of age tells us that the importance of victimization depends on what stage in the life course it occurs. The experience of victimization was something that the justice system took into account when it came to understanding misconduct out to approximately age 18, which justified the goal of the court intervening to protect the boy or girl from a life of future crime. Finkelhor and Ormrod (2001, p.1) well typify this perspective: "The impact of…crimes on young victims can be devastating and the violent or sexual victimization of children can often lead to an intergenerational cycle of violence and abuse." Victimization was assumed to have a very different meaning for adult offenders. The criminal court's default philosophy was that defendants appearing before it were responsible for their actions. Juveniles might be assaulted in childhood by parents or other adults, or be tormented by peers, and perhaps receive services from the juvenile court to alleviate the effects of these events. But it was assumed that adults have enough maturity to look past earlier (or present) victimization, to be able to restrain impulses to offend that victimization might prompt, and to understand that their current actions may have negative legal consequences. Times changed. Today, while the adult court still assumes that defendants have sufficient mental capacity to choose between criminal and noncriminal conduct, the juvenile system—increasingly interested in forcing accountability on youthful offenders—is less particular about the background of victimization that juveniles often bring into intake. Neither are those who draft the laws governing the affairs of the juvenile system overly concerned with the victim-offender overlap, if the expanded use of automatic or legislative waiver and blended sentences is any indication. So even as academic criminology finally began to come to grips with the idea that among those people where one finds victimization one also finds offending, what actually took place in the juvenile courts was a de-emphasis of this idea as the system abandoned the philosophy of the child-saving movement.

This change in philosophy is remarkable given the near unanimity of the research literature about the effects of childhood victimization. While criminological theory flourished for a time without thought to whether victimization was of causal importance, a huge child abuse research literature developed a very different picture and reported findings that were supportive of the traditional mission of the juvenile court. Glueck and Glueck (1950), in their pioneering study of five hundred juvenile delinquents, reported that the children of parents who were "overstrict" in their use of physical punishment were more likely to become delinquent (see also Sampson and Laub 1993). Today, under some definitions, such adults would be described as child abusers (Karmen 2008). Contemporary research reports similar findings. Women appearing before the criminal courts often were exposed to violence during early childhood (Acoca 2000; Acoca and Dedel 1998). Apart from apparently heightened criminality, female victims of abuse are more likely to mistreat their own children as well as engage in substance use and commit suicide (Baerger et al. 2001; Hoyt and Scherer 1998). Widom (1989) linked the experiencing or witnessing of abuse in the family with an increased probability of violence toward others, including romantic partners. English and her colleagues (2002) reported that abused and neglected children were substantially more likely to have records of adult criminality and violent behavior. Widom and Maxfield (1996) described similar findings with respect to arrests, based upon longitudinal data from several groups of people (some with substantiated histories of child abuse and others who did not have a record).

With few exceptions—such as Menard's (2002) review of the long-term effects of adolescent victimization or MacMillan's (2009) recent commentary on child abuse research—there appears to be little uncertainty about how victimization and offending interrelate. Although the literature sometimes acknowledges that not all or even most abuse or victimization results in greater levels of offending (e.g., Anthony 1974; McGloin and Widom 2001; Widom 1989), where it does, the consistent interpretation is that violence is learned from the experience of victimization.

This literature leaves many questions unanswered. Does the meaning of victimization differ for juveniles and adults, thus requiring separate systems? The child abuse literature certainly coincides with the original philosophy of the juvenile court, thus affirming that the court should return to its former purpose. For our part, we believe that a scientific understanding of the victim-offender overlap, and its implications for juvenile justice, can benefit from an awareness of other theoretical perspectives. We interpret victim-offender overlap from the vantage point of some of the major criminological theories: cultural deviance, strain, and control. We also examine the implications of a life-course approach to the study of the victim-offender overlap.

I. Theoretical Perspectives of the Victim-Offender Overlap

While there is a lot of research showing that victims and offenders are often the same people, this bare fact does not tell us what the connection means or in what way policy should account for it. It is certainly plausible to say that victimized children, through some process, are more likely to offend. But perhaps the correlation is deceptive insofar as it masks other processes that predispose people to become both victims as well as offenders. Obviously, the policy implications of these two interpretations of the victim-offender overlap would be very different than those traditionally followed by the juvenile justice system. As we will see, some well-regarded theoretical approaches would take these positions.

In a paper that has not received the attention it deserved, Janet Lauritsen and her colleagues (1992) used self-report data from the National Youth Survey to compare the substantive correlates of victimization with the correlates of criminal behavior. Their measures tapped such key concepts in theories of delinquency as the elements of the social bond and deviant peer association (Akers and Sellers 2003). It turned out that the correlates of offending and victimization were the same. Whatever the problems of theories of crime and delinquency, they become with this finding an obvious starting point for explaining victimization as well.

This was in one sense good news. As myopic in some respects as criminological theory was, victimization theory was virtually nonexistent. Starting in the late 1990s, researchers who were aware of the victim-offender overlap could begin to take advantage of criminological theory as a starting point to explain victimization. David Forde and Leslie Kennedy (1997) and Christopher Schreck (1999) linked Gottfredson and Hirschi's (1990) self-control theory with victimization risk. (We will outline how this happens later in this chapter.) Other studies examining how low self-control facilitates victimization soon followed (e.g., Holtfreter, Reisig, and Pratt 2008; Piquero et al. 2005; Schreck, Stewart, and Fisher 2006; Stewart, Elifson, and Sterk 2004). Around the same time, Robert Agnew (2002) began to incorporate victimization into his general strain theory, arguing that victimization was a trigger for strain that could manifest as criminal activity. Subculture of violence theories, too, began to take greater interest in the role of victimization (e.g., Stewart, Schreck, and Simons 2006; Stewart, Schreck, and Brunson 2008). Attempts by theorists to account for the victim-offender overlap are perhaps one of the more novel developments in criminological theory in recent years. It should therefore be profitable to see how the three major sociological explanations of crime—cultural deviance, strain, and control—deal with a fact they were once able to ignore.

A. Cultural Deviance Theories

We use the label "cultural deviance theory" because it comprises a coherent set of core assumptions about the nature of crime and its potential connection with victimization (Kornhauser 1978). The cultural deviance perspective is a major force in criminological theory and encompasses a number of leading theories: differential association (Sutherland 1947), subculture of violence (e.g., Anderson 1999; Fagan, Piper, and Cheng 1987), and social learning theory (Burgess and Akers 1968). Cultural deviance theories, in their pure form (e.g., Sutherland 1947), deny the existence of any cause of crime that is not a product of social interaction. People naturally conform to the values and behaviors of those around them. Those who primarily interact with offenders will grow to resemble them. The transmission of criminality occurs through observation; physical attack by role models is but one mode, distinguished from other forms of observation (e.g., witnessing offending against others) only by the fact that the observer-learner can become injured.

Sutherland, of course, never spoke about the implications of his theory for victimization. But implicit in Sutherland's theory is the idea that actions that would result in habitual vulnerability to crime victimization must also be learned. Several ideas seem to follow from this. Given the specificity of learning, there should be no inherent requirement that learning to be vulnerable to crime would teach crime as well (otherwise, we would have to allow that such learning also enhances our language and mathematical abilities). Nor would learning crime require someone to be vulnerable to later crime. In this respect, a child who is beaten may learn to beat other children under specific conditions, but the theory would not assume that physical attack teaches the skills needed to be vulnerable. Cultural deviance theories, at least so far as Sutherland developed that approach, therefore do not predict a victim-offender overlap (Schreck, Stewart, and Osgood, 2008). The victim-offender overlap could still occur, but would require the appropriate combination of cultural influences. Victimization otherwise is happenstance, and the theory cannot—on its own—account for long-term persistence in the victimization-offending overlap, where a victim in the future not only commits crime but also continues to be a victim. In some cultures, as the logic of the theory would go, offending need not necessarily be a trigger for future victimization. For cultural deviance theories to be able to explain the overlap, the theorist must develop the cultural elements that foster a correlation between offending and victimization.

The picture is rather different in subculture of violence theories, where one finds considerable interest in the interrelation between victimization and offending. Simon Singer (1981) proposed that some subcultures that promote violent behavior include norms of retaliation, which results in a pattern where individuals alternate between offender and victim roles. Ethnographic work has identified similar patterns. Elijah Anderson (1999) described how young African American males in socially disorganized areas of Philadelphia adopted a tough, violent persona in order to garner respect and deter victimization. So here is the paradox. The research examining Anderson's conceptual scheme showed that street code values translated into additional violent behaviors (Kubrin and Weitzer 2003; Stewart and Simons 2006; Jacobs and Wright 2006). While the literature generally shows that offending and victimization are positively correlated, Anderson's work indicates a special condition where the offender-victim overlap might not apply. Or at least this is the belief of the African American youth living in disintegrating urban neighborhoods. Yet Stewart, Schreck, and Simons (2006) observed that adolescents who lived in violent neighborhoods and embraced street code values were at heightened—not lessened—risk of victimization. Specifically, they found that adoption of individual-level street code values increased the risk of violent victimization and that this risk was amplified for those adolescents who resided in high-crime settings. The basic causal pattern indicated in this literature is thus a feedback loop between crime and victimization. Youth attack others in response to victimization or to preempt it, which in turn requires victims (former offenders) to get even in order to protect or enhance their personal standing.

Eric Stewart and his colleagues (2008) addressed the general policy implications of the victim-offender overlap. The street-code youth live in conditions that are not favorable for peaceful methods of dispute resolution. They do not have access to the courts. The police are perceived as ineffective, arbitrary, and insensitive to the dignity of local residents. Other authorities, such as teachers and political leaders, are likewise treated with suspicion. Policies emphasizing the juvenile court's role are thus likely to be ineffective. The juvenile court in fact faces a crisis of legitimacy from scholars, political leaders, and jurists (e.g., Feld 1999); one can only imagine the contempt directed toward the juvenile system from within the African American population. The nature of the disorganized community, with its high residential mobility, undermines efforts at informal dispute resolution. The tendency of neighbors to move from place to place—called "residential mobility" in the social disorganization literature—means that they are not trapped in relationships with other residents and have few incentives (and many disincentives) to negotiate with those they injure. With few viable means of peacefully resolving differences, residents are obliged to settle their own problems violently. This, then, is the difficult context in which policy toward juvenile offenders and victims must operate. Some crime control policies, although not explicitly targeted at juveniles, illustrate how governments have attempted to enhance their own standing, and that of other local institutions, with residents (e.g., Braga et al. 2001; Kennedy 1998).

B. Strain Theories

The basic tenet of strain theory is that people naturally would like to obey the law, but external events or circumstances—often, but not always, having to do with the failure to achieve economic success—force them into breaking it. Traditional versions of strain (or anomie) theory, such as Robert Merton's (1938), did not recognize victimization as a form of strain, and there is no evidence to believe that this theory could make sense of a victim-offender overlap (see Schreck, Stewart, and Osgood 2008). Nor do recent variants of this theory give any attention to the overlap (e.g., Messner and Rosenfeld 1994). If one were to speculate what anomie theory might say about whether victimization affects offending, victimization would only matter insofar as it influenced one's position within the social structure. Ross MacMillan's (2000) work, although not executed with strain theory in mind, does show that victimization adversely influences economic success over the long term in a sample of Americans and Canadians. Whether this in turn leads to anomie and more crime is a question no one has examined.

More recently, however, Robert Agnew's General Strain Theory (GST) has explicitly considered the meaning of victimization, arguing that victimization is a type of strain that ultimately would result in a greater level of offending (see Agnew 2002). Robert Agnew (2002, p. 607) wrote: "physical victimization is not only a key type of strain, it is a fairly common type of strain in certain groups." According to the theory, the victimization itself need not be directly experienced in order to have an effect on criminality. Agnew referred to these alternatives as "vicarious strain" and "anticipated strain." Vicarious strain would occur when a person witnesses the victimization of another person. Anticipated strain refers to contexts in which a person feels unsafe and thus expects to become a victim. In all cases, anger is the result and increases the probability that a person will cope in a manner that breaks the law.

Researchers have begun to test these claims. Timothy Brezina (1998) used two waves of the Youth in Transition survey to consider factors that might mediate the relationship between childhood maltreatment and delinquency. Brezina's work offers some evidence that anger and distress can account for the relationship between the experiencing of child abuse and offending. Carter Hay and Michelle Evans (2006) analyzed National Survey of Children data, with a nationally representative sample of over 1,400 individuals, to explore whether victimization functioned as Agnew predicted. They found that the correlation between earlier victimization and later offending held, even after controlling for involvement in previous delinquency. The authors also reported that this correlation diminished somewhat after controlling for anger.

Agnew's (2002) theoretical narrative considers some rival explanations for the connection between victimization and offending—primarily the competing mediating factors (e.g., victimization desensitizes people, reduces school performance). One theory that Agnew did not review was that of Richard Felson (1992), whose social interactionist theory proposes a very different causal pattern. This theory links negative affective states with a greater risk of victimization, primarily because people experiencing difficult emotions tend to be perceived as offensive. For instance, they are more likely to be uncivil toward others, and they tend to perform their tasks at an unsatisfactory level. As a result, people nearby develop grievances with the person and demand satisfaction. If the distressed person fails to respond adequately, the others might then attack. Thus, the social interactionist perspective presents the reverse causal pattern from that of Agnew's general strain theory; negative affect (strain?) does not lead a person to attack others, at least not at first. Instead, victimization occurs and then retaliation. Felson's theory has not been widely tested, but Felson's own test was supportive. Schreck and his colleagues (2007) examined the connection between negative affect and victimization using data from a nationally representative sample of adolescents. They found that depressive symptoms exacerbated the risk of victimization and could even account for the effects of early puberty on the likelihood of victimization (see Haynie and Piquero 2005).

Agnew's strain theory offers some general policy implications. General strain theory indicates that protecting individuals from victimization would reduce strain and thereby reduce offending. At its core, Agnew's theory indicates that those who have the skills or abilities to manage anger are less apt to commit crime. Indeed, many juvenile delinquency prevention programs adopt this basic idea (e.g., Kurtines et al. 2008; Sevin Goldstein et al. 2007). With this skill in place, victimization might occur, but the target will be better able to cope without resorting to crime. Felson's theory, in contrast, indicates that while angry people can attack others, they would prefer to attack the source of their grievance. When this cannot happen, they are more likely to be targets because anger makes them disagreeable. In this case, anger management would include instruction on the broader effects of an angry demeanor, particularly on the behavior of people nearby.

C. Control Theories

Control theories begin with the assumption that humans, thanks to their inherent nature as rational and pleasure-seeking beings, are born capable of understanding when crime is advantageous and then acting accordingly. In this perspective, crime requires no positive causes beyond the fact that breaking the law is often an easy way of getting what one wants. No special motives or training are needed, and crime is not a result of impaired judgment. Unlike cultural deviance or strain theories, the control perspective would not predict that abuse or any form of victimization would teach violence, and neither are victims of crime required by some external force (e.g., a subculture or strain) to lash out at others.

In fact, the theory assumes that society recognizes the danger of allowing people to pursue violence or fraud for private reasons, such as for retaliation, and thus opposes it with a web of legal, physical, and social sanctioning systems (Gottfredson and Hirschi 1990). Control theories therefore focus on identifying and elaborating the systems that exist to deter crime and then explaining why some forms of restraint are more important than others. Social control theories tend to find that crime arises from the breakdown of the bond between an individual and society (e.g., Hirschi 1969; Sampson and Laub 1993). People are aware that crime endangers their relationships and investments and so avoid crime to the degree they value them. Self-control theory views crime as a possible outcome of lack of concern for the long-term negative consequences (whatever they might be) that crime might bring (Gottfredson and Hirschi 1990). Both of these control theories agree that victimization, to the degree it matters at all in connection with crime, functions only to strip away the barriers that humans have created in order to restrain their inherently amoral nature.

1. *Social Control Theory*

The control theorist's next question would be how control is accomplished. We begin with Hirschi's social control theory. There is an extensive literature linking social bonds with offending; however, scholars have also speculated that social bonds enhance the ability of potential protectors to monitor the actions of those they care about (e.g., Felson 1986). For example, the theory would hold that children with weakened bonds to school and parents would naturally prefer to avoid being in proximity to them, thus removing guardians for more extended periods of time and in turn elevating their risk of engaging in crime and falling victim to crime (e.g., Esbensen, Huizinga, and Menard 1999; Schreck and Fisher 2004; Schreck, Wright, and Miller 2002). In this way, elements of the social bond have relevance to offending and victimization.

But how do offending and victimization interrelate? If the factors freeing a person to commit crime are found in fluctuations in the strength of the social bond, it follows that criminal victimization is relevant to offending to the degree it leads to disaffection from others. If a social relationship exposes a person to victimization, such as would occur in intimate partner violence or child abuse, we would expect that the relationship would weaken. Indeed, some research indicates that victims attempt to withdraw from or break off relationships with attackers (e.g., Lammers, Ritchie, and Robertson 2005; Patterson 1982). Victimization is a disincentive for further investment in a relationship. This does not mean that a victim will completely cut off ties with an abusive partner or that a child will leave a school where he or she is bullied or run away from a violent home: the circumstances of some relationships make outright escape too difficult. But the relationship will figure less and less as a deterrent to crime. In short, victimization is inconsistent with the natural conditions that facilitate the development of social bonds. While social control theories are mostly silent about what factors make social bonds stronger, it seems unlikely that criminal injury is among them.

With respect to policy, social control theory offers little specific guidance to juvenile justice about how to address the victim-offender overlap. Social control theorists, however, would question whether a criminal justice response is even required (e.g., Schreck and Hirschi 2009), pointing out that if the theory is correct, all that is necessary to reduce the likelihood that a person will commit crime and be inadequately protected against victimization are social policies calculated to preserve the conditions that foster relationships with others. In such conditions, juvenile justice—assuming it can ever competently administer social welfare (see Feld 1999)—becomes unnecessary or redundant.

Social control theory has rarely been invoked in the research literature as an account for the link between child victimization and contemporaneous or later offending. One of the very few exceptions is the work of Cesar Rebellon and Karen Van Gundy (2005), who analyzed National Youth Survey data to see if measures of social bonding attenuated the effect of earlier physical abuse on later offending behavior. Their findings showed that these measures only modestly reduced the correlation between parental physical attack and offending. These results do not necessarily mean that abuse teaches later violence, but they do indicate that prior experience with abuse is a very strong predictor of later delinquency and that traditional methods of measuring the social bond are not sufficient to account for them. This is unfortunately the extent of the literature; several studies have cited Rebellon and Gundy's work, but none have attempted to confirm their results.

2. *Life Course Theory*

Victimization research has lately begun to use life course arguments to understand victimization (e.g., Daigle, Beaver, and Hartman 2008; Chen 2009; Lauritsen and Davis-Quinet 1995; Wittbrood and Nieuwbierta 2000). It turns out that the academic debate over the life course pertains not only to the victim-offender overlap but also to the very justification of the juvenile justice system (Hirschi and Gottfredson 1993). In their review of the victim-offender correlation, Lauritsen and Laub (2007) in fact organize theories of the overlap using the language of life-course criminology (see also Lauritsen and Davis-Quinet 1995). They distinguished between "individual heterogeneity" and "state-dependent" explanations of the victim-offender overlap. Theories of individual heterogeneity focus on personal or environmental traits connected with both crime and victimization that for the most part remain stable over long periods of time. Such traits, for example, could include levels of self-control (e.g., Gottfredson and Hirschi 1990). State-dependent theories, in contrast, focus on locating those factors that might change a person's risk of future offending or victimization. Life-course theories of crime (e.g., Sampson and Laub 1993) thus assume some degree of state-dependency and identify change in marital status and workforce participation as reasons that levels of offending change.

Some of the life-course literature (e.g., Daigle, Beaver, and Hartman 2008) compares the effects of life-course events on trajectories of offending with their effects on trajectories of victimization. The theoretical linkage, based on what we have described with respect to social control theory, is pretty clear. Victimization represents a potential turning point with implications for future offending. If victimization frees someone from the chains of a relationship, the theory might say, it frees them also to commit crime; but in committing crime, the individual earns disapproval and distrust. The ultimate result of victimization is that the overall quality of social bonds is degraded, and a long-term pattern of increased criminal activity would appear more likely to emerge. Gerald Patterson's (1982) classic observational study of coercive families reports this pattern. The children of explosive parents have a difficult time establishing durable ties with same-age peers; this experience of rejection, in turn, undermines further academic and interpersonal achievements. In the end, the victimization can instigate a long-term process of removing social barriers to crime.

In addition to such straightforward applications of life-course theory to victimization, Lauritsen and Laub (2007) were interested in the interrelationship of desistance from crime and victimization over the life course. Although no one has developed the theoretical linkage, it seems plausible that in some conditions, victimization might act as a turning point that *intensifies* relationships with others, such as perhaps an attack by a stranger pushing someone closer to family members. In this case, desistance might ultimately be the outcome. The literature on the topic is sparse. Lauritsen and Laub are able to cite only the work of Stephen Farrall and Adam Calverley (2006). These researchers expected the decline of offending and victimization to occur simultaneously in a sample of a few hundred probationers. That was not quite what they found: those probationers whose offending decreased and those whose offending did not decrease reported similar levels of victimization. If the results are accurate, this is in fact a meaningful null finding. Note the dissimilarity in outcomes between these ex-offenders and children who are victimized: For many children, victimization is connected with greater criminal involvement; however, if victimization did not improve offending among adult probationers, neither did it make it worse. More recently, Jacques and Wright (2008), using interview data collected from two middle class drug dealers in their 20s, reported that victimization that occurred as a result of criminal involvement did in fact result in desistance from offending. If other research supports Jacques and Wright's findings, then it would appear that victimization in fact is relevant for both adults and juveniles—except that victimization results in diametric outcomes, depending on where one is situated in the life course. For children, victimization enhances the likelihood that offending will occur; for adults, under certain conditions, it can aid in desistance.

A consideration of juvenile justice's traditional assumptions allows us to expand potential research questions offered by a life-course approach still further. Although the reformers who crafted the philosophy of the traditional juvenile court were not informed by life-course theory, the underlying assumptions of both the juvenile system and the life-course approach are practically indistinguishable (Hirschi and Gottfredson 1993). The juvenile court, as we noted earlier, has long assumed that victimized children needed the protection of the state not only for their physical safety, but also to prevent the victimization from cutting off opportunities for the child to grow into a productive and law-abiding adult. Implicit in the separation of adult and juvenile systems, however, is the idea that not only is victimization a "turning point" for offending, the age of 18 represents a transition where victimization switches from a positive cause of crime into something either neutral with respect to the commission of crime or, better still, a justification for desistance from it. Currently, however, there is not enough literature for anyone to claim with certainty that this is the case. Research must establish that the effects of victimization lessen with age, particularly where offending behavior is concerned. If anything, related literature on the general effects of victimization is not encouraging; adults who experience interpersonal violence are more likely to report suffering from a multitude of negative health consequences over the life course, including substance use (e.g., Carbone-Lopez, Kruttschnitt, and MacMillan 2006). Indeed, DeMaris and Kaukinen (2005), examining victimization's effects among a sample of 7,700 people at various ages, in fact found that the health effects of assault victimization did not vary by age. Neither did the results justify making distinctions between childhood and later victimization, so far as health effects were concerned. Juveniles who experience victimization also appear less able to advance themselves educationally or economically, even in adulthood (MacMillan 2001; MacMillan and Hagan 2004).

3. *Self-Control Theory*

Self-control theory offers a different account of the victim-offender overlap, and one that would question the value of a life-course approach as well as the present structuring of the criminal justice system into separate juvenile and adult systems. Self-control is the name that Michael Gottfredson and Travis Hirschi gave to the tendency for a person to act as if long-term negative consequences mattered. Given that crime carried with it negative consequences that were both long-term and uncertain, but at the same time offered quick and certain short-term advantages, it follows that the person who was unimpressed by these risks, that is to say a person who lacked self-control, would be more apt to engage in crime.

As with many other major criminological theories, the presentation of self-control theory was mainly concerned with describing the relation of self-control to crime rather than the victim-offender overlap, but Gottfredson and Hirschi were clear that low self-control resulted in more than just breaking the law. The life of someone with low self-control would tend to have more than its fair share of drug use, accidents, disease, and broken relationships (e.g., Evans et al. 1997; Junger 1994; Sorenson 1994).

In order for a person to avoid a life marked with all the wreckage of low self-control, parents must educate their children in early childhood to respect the consequences of their actions. Building from Patterson's (1982) work, Gottfredson and Hirschi (1990) specified that self-control emerges when a child's family: (1) monitors the child, (2) recognizes deviance for what it is, and (3) punishes the deviance. The combination of these three components teaches the child to respect and fear the long-term consequences of breaking rules and violating expectations. A necessary precondition for all of these is parental attachment for the child; where parents do not love their children, they are less likely to feel obligated to exert themselves with respect to supervision and correction. By late childhood, individual differences in the ability to *habitually* consider long-term consequences become resistant to change.

Schreck (1999) theorized the link between low self-control and victimization. Just as crimes offer the possibility of short-term pleasure, so too do the behaviors that increase vulnerability to victimization. If a person knew for certain that an action would result in victimization, which we might reasonably assume is involuntary and unpleasant, it seems fair to think that he or she would not take the action or at least would take precautions. Among those with low self-control, this sort of clarity of thought would be lacking. Drinking and excessive drug use can bring pleasant sensations and other rewards, but it also makes one much more ineffective at opposing an offender as well as more likely to provoke feelings of disgust and hostility in bystanders (Felson and Burchfield 2004). Belligerence might make one feel good in a confrontation, but it does so at the risk of precipitating an attack. Flashing signs of wealth might amaze those nearby, but may also make an impression on would-be robbers. Those with low self-control will also prefer to spend more time with like-minded peers and less time in the company of protectors whose expectations for behavior are likely to be chafing (Schreck, Fisher, and Miller 2004; Schreck, Wright, and Miller 2002). In sum, low self-control makes victimization easy and gratifying for whoever is inclined to seize advantage of the situation. Those with high self-control are more apt to anticipate risk and take steps to protect their long-term well-being even when doing so entails effort and inconvenience and the foregoing of self-gratification. Inconvenience and effort, in contrast, are perfectly sufficient deterrents toward implementing protective measures among those who naturally prefer the quick and easy. Thus, low self-control is the basis for victimization risk as well as offending. Self-control theory would predict the victim-offender overlap and associate both outcomes with the same basic cause.

The self-control literature, however, does not directly speak to whether victimization influences crime or vice versa. Travis Hirschi (1995) provides perhaps the earliest comments from the perspective of self-control theory on the importance of victimization as a cause of offending. His review of the literature made him skeptical that childhood victimization was an important cause of offending. Cathy Spatz Widom (1989), one of the foremost experts on child maltreatment, collected juvenile and adult criminal data from a sample of nearly 1,600 people. This sample used matching to compare the criminal destinies of neglected and abused children as well as those who never experienced neglect or abuse. What is remarkable in these findings is the huge disproportion of neglect cases relative to abuse cases among those persons with juvenile and adult arrest records. Among the individuals who experienced documented neglect or abuse, the effect of either on later offending appeared to be virtually the same. Hirschi concluded from this that the idea that violence begets violence is considerably less supported than the idea that neglect begets violence. Widom's work also shows that most children who are abused never acquire criminal records as either juveniles or adults (Widom and Maxfield 1996).

But Widom's data and the data of others show that abuse still figures as a cause of crime. Or do they? Complicating this picture is the fact that parents who abuse their children are likely to be "poor parents" along multiple dimensions (Gottfredson and Hirschi 1990). Such parents are more likely to drink, to commit crime, and, most importantly for the future criminality of their offspring, they are less likely to exert themselves to prevent their children from engaging in crime. Put differently, childhood victimization usually coexists with other conditions that would produce a child with low self-control. From the perspective of control theory, it is easy to see why neglect is treated as so pernicious with respect to human behavior. Owing to their basic natures, offenders are not socialized into crime, but rather they are *under*socialized into conformity in the same way an undertrained house pet naturally will snatch food from a table or commit outrages on one's carpet or furniture. Childhood abuse or victimization may matter, but only insofar as it undermines efforts to instill self-control. All of this does not lessen the concern that society should have for abused and victimized children, but it does ask us to question the meaning of abuse and what problems we can hope to solve using policies specifically designed to remedy abuse.

Hirschi and Gottfredson (2005) indirectly address the matter again in another article on the effects of physical punishment by parents. Self-control theory is agnostic about what parents elect to do to punish children, viewing the question about what types of punishment are most effective at instilling self-control as being an empirical question. While there is an extensive literature linking physical punishment with offending, this linkage is also complex and dependent on many factors including the age of the child (Simons 2009). Hirschi and Gottfredson stated that much of this correlation masks the fact that parents who feel obliged to frequently resort to physical punishment have failed at monitoring the behavior of their children and are less likely to feel attachment toward them. In support of this, Hirschi and Gottfredson cite the work of Larzelere and Patterson (1990). These researchers found that multi-method measures of parental monitoring and discipline were so highly correlated that when either one was controlled, the other had no significant effect on delinquency. More important, they found that no single measure of monitoring or discipline was significantly related to delinquency independent of the effects of a "parental management factor" produced by combining the monitoring and discipline measures. Hirschi and Gottfredson concluded from this that what is important is not the specific forms of punishment that parents employ, which can include physical punishment, but the general nature of parent-child relations. Where these relations lack care and affection, no punishment, however mild or severe, will be effective or consistently administered. Hirschi and Gottfredson did point out that physical punishment, for its part, is more challenging to administer because it carries additional risks. The use of hitting can easily be carried too far and destroy attachment, and in turn weaken the parent's ability to supervise and exert discipline in the future.

In sum, self-control theory would explain the correlation between physical abuse and offending as indicating the failure of the relationship between the parent and the child. Abuse does not result in a child learning to be an offender, but is rather a marker of a parent who is struggling with monitoring and ultimately in socializing the child into having self-control. Removing the child from the abusive situation might thus protect the physical safety of the child, but absent a warm relationship with parents or caregivers, the delinquency will continue whether abuse is present or not.

Available writings on self-control theory have not addressed the life-course implications of the victim-offender overlap, at least not directly. However, the internal logic of the theory is skeptical of the life-course approach and thus would question the division of adult and juvenile systems (Hirschi and Gottfredson 1993). Based on our understanding of the theory, we would expect that the effects of victimization on offending behavior—at least after late childhood, which is when the juvenile system most often takes an interest in a juvenile's misconduct—are essentially constant (and nil). Victimization will be positively correlated with offending throughout the entire life course, but both arise from low self-control, and therefore the introduction of one of these cannot exacerbate or worsen the tendency for the other to occur. And the presence of one outcome will not lead to desistance from the other. Both will decline over time, principally due to aging. Action by the juvenile justice system will not accelerate the decline for either crime or victimization.

But what of the findings showing that retaliation is sometimes normative? Subculture of violence theories have alleged that victimization worsens offending, and there is evidence for this. Self-control theory, in our view, does not argue that participants in crime do not look upon their own victimization as a pretext for retaliation. But a person can be a victim and yet seek redress in a manner that is legal. Most people in fact do so, even in disadvantaged communities. One can report crime to the police. One can informally negotiate with the offender. One can turn to the courts or restorative justice centers. Or a victim can take no action at all. The choice the victim makes speaks to his or her self-control, rather than the consequences of victimization itself. Thus, in our view, the superficial perceptions of the actors with regard to their motives, where there is a belief that offending requires getting even, are likely to be misleading.

II. Conclusion

We began with the claim that juvenile justice has operated under its own theory about criminal behavior, one that assumed a victim-offender overlap and, more specifically, that victimization was a cause of crime. This development occurred independently of the leading ideas in contemporary criminology, which tended to locate causes of crime in the peer group, placement in the social structure, or the durability of the elements of the social bond. This did not mean that it was impossible for some of these theories to accommodate a victim-offender relationship, but that theorists did not attach much importance to such a link and so did not speculate or research the topic. All this began to change in a big way in the last several decades.

At this late date, it is not possible to dismiss the finding that victims and offenders are often the same people. But there is room to debate what this finding means. If one uncritically follows the preponderance of the literature, one can only conclude that victimization causes a person's criminality to increase. In this chapter, we described two sets of theories that would reconcile with this idea: cultural deviance and strain. In both cases, a person who is either a natural conformist or who has no natural inclination toward crime suddenly finds, upon victimization, that there is now criminality where there was none before. Control theories, in contrast, assume that conformity when the opportunity and temptation of crime is present is what must be explained. Victimization cannot make criminality worse, but it might peel away those restraints that control our natural amoral tendencies. Although control theories are well known in the criminological community, they have hardly ever been used to make sense of the victim-offender link. This omission has two important consequences. First, accounting for the victim-offender relationship represents a potentially important new direction for control theories of every stripe. This chapter speculates about some possible reasons. Second, their inclusion in the debate about the importance of childhood victimization casts doubt on meaning of such taken-for-granted phrases as "violence begets violence" and "the cycle of violence."

With respect to juvenile justice, two of the three theories—cultural deviance and strain—(with some qualification) support the original mission of juvenile justice. Removing a child from a setting where victimization occurs either eliminates a vector for learning crime or a context that pushes an otherwise good kid into offending. Note that subculture of violence theories introduce a complicating factor: Whatever institutions the state invents to implement assistance toward victimized children must first earn legitimacy among those it seeks to help. Control perspectives do not argue against removing children from violent homes or intervening as a matter of safety when a child is being victimized, but they caution us that hoping such intervention will produce a law-abiding child or adult is likely to end in disappointment. Other factors matter for producing a well socialized child—in particular the nature of parent-child interaction. And juvenile justice, in the view of the control perspective, is poorly situated to effectively attend to these factors. Rather, these theories encourage policies that create the conditions for strengthened family bonds, particularly during early childhood. No theory reviewed here would recommend the current practice of juvenile justice, which increasingly bears a resemblance to a junior adult court.

We should note that the life-course approach is simply a perspective for accounting for change in behaviors over a period of time. The separation of juvenile and adult courts is something consistent with the life-course approach, but the approach would not necessarily endorse it anymore than it would some other division or arrangement. Nevertheless, one can derive from this approach several ideas. First, offending and victimization might co-vary as a result of the same event or else as a function of a transition into a new life stage. Another is that the relationship between offending and victimization itself might change because of specific turning points and transitions. Our criminal justice system identifies this transition at age 18; scientists may speculate other transitions and turning points (e.g., Jacques and Wright 2006).

In sum, our review indicates that the victim-offender nexus is not well understood, notwithstanding the vast literature connecting childhood victimization and mistreatment to offending. Criminology is making a start about what the nexus means; however, there is a scantiness of literature that would address the key theoretical claims of the three major sociological approaches presented here or those of the life-course perspective. Does victimization *cause* offending? Or are both byproducts of something else? Does the nature of the victim-offender relationship change under certain conditions or at some point in the life course? These questions deserve answers, because they speak to not only to the validity of our theories of delinquency, but also the very organization of our adult and juvenile systems and our expectations about what juvenile justice can usefully accomplish.

NOTES

We are very grateful to Donna Bishop and Barry Feld for inviting us to prepare this chapter and for their suggestions. We owe a special debt of gratitude as well to Travis Hirschi and Jean McGloin for so carefully reading and commenting on the manuscript. Direct correspondence to: Christopher J. Schreck, Department of Criminal Justice, Rochester Institute of Technology, 1 Lomb Memorial Drive, Rochester, NY 14623 (email: cjsgcj@rit.edu).

1. Lauritsen and Laub (2007, pp. 65–66), speculated on some of the reasons: (1) the relatively low standing that victimization research has had in criminology, (2) the unwillingness of criminological theorists to consider the linkages between different forms of problem behaviors, (3) lack of data, (4) the belief that linking offending and victimization blames the victim, and (5) the widespread belief that acknowledging an overlap is equivalent to overly sympathizing with offenders. Hirschi (1999), a theorist whose work first gained prominence during this period, further mentioned that the offender-victim relationship was not widely known at this time.

REFERENCES

Acoca, Leslie. 2000. *Educate Don't Incarcerate: Girls in Florida and Duval County Juvenile Justice Systems*. San Francisco: National Council on Crime and Delinquency.

Acoca, Leslie, and Kelly Dedel. 1998. *No Place to Hide: Understanding and Meeting the Needs of Girls in the California Juvenile Justice System*. San Francisco: National Council on Crime and Delinquency.

Agnew, Robert. 2002. "Experienced, Vicarious, and Anticipated Strain: An Exploratory Study on Physical Victimization and Delinquency." *Justice Quarterly* 19: 603–32.

Akers, Ronald L., and Christine Sellers. 2003. *Criminological Theories: Introduction, Evaluation, and Application*. Thousand Oaks, CA: Roxbury.

Anderson, Elijah. 1999. *Code of the Street: Decency, Violence, and the Moral Life of the Inner City*. New York: W. W. Norton and Company.

Anthony, E. James. 1974. "Introduction: The Syndrome of the Psychologically Vulnerable Child." In *The Child in His Family: Children at Psychiatric Risk*, edited by E. J. Anthony and C. Koupernik. New York: Wiley.

Baerger, D. R., J. S. Lyons, P. Quigley, and E. Griffin. 2001. "Mental Health Service Needs of Male and Female Juvenile Detainees." *Journal of the Center for Families, Children & the Courts* 3: 21–29.

Bernard, Thomas J. 1992. *The Cycle of Juvenile Justice*. New York: Oxford University Press.

Braga, Anthony A., David M. Kennedy, Elin J. Waring, and Anne M. Piehl. 2001. "Problem-Oriented Policing, Deterrence, and Youth Violence: An Evaluation of Boston's Operation Ceasefire." *Journal of Research in Crime and Delinquency* 38: 195–225.

Brezina, Timothy. 1998. "Adolescent Maltreatment and Delinquency: The Question of Intervening Processes." *Journal of Research in Crime and Delinquency* 35: 71–99.

Broidy, Lisa M., Jerry K. Daday, Cameron S. Crandall, David P. Sklar, and Peter F. Jost. 2006. "Exploring Demographic, Structural, and Behavioral Overlap among Homicide Offenders and Victims." *Homicide Studies* 10: 155–80.

Burgess, Robert L., and Ronald L. Akers. 1966. "A Differential Association Reinforcement Theory of Criminal Behavior." *Social Problems* 14: 128–47.

Carbone-Lopez, Kristin, Ross MacMillan, and Candace Kruttschnitt. 2006. "Patterns of Intimate Partner Violence and their Associations with Physical Health, Psychological Distress, and Substance Use over the Life Span." *Public Health Reports* 121: 382–92.

Chen, Xiaojin. 2009. "The Linkage between Deviant Lifestyles and Violent Victimization: An Examination from a Life Course Perspective." Journal of Interpersonal Violence 24: 10831–110.

Daigle, Leah E., Kevin M. Beaver, and Jennifer L. Hartman. 2008. "A Life-Course Approach to the Study of Victimization and Offending Behaviors." *Violence and Victims* 3: 365–90.

DeMaris, Alfred, and Catherine Kaukinen. 2005. "Violent Victimization and Women's Mental and Physical Health." *Journal of Research in Crime and Delinquency* 42: 384–411.

English, Diana J., Cathy Spatz Widom, and Carol Brandford. 2002. *Childhood Victimization and Delinquency, Adult Criminality, and Violent Criminal Behavior: A Replication and Extension*. Washington, DC: National Institute of Justice.

Esbensen, Finn-Aage, David Huizinga, and Scott Menard. 1999. "Family Context and Criminal Victimization in Adolescence." *Youth & Society* 31: 168–98.

Evans, T. David, Francis T. Cullen, Velmer S. Burton Jr., R. Gregory Dunaway, and Michael L. Benson. 1997. "The Social Consequences of Self-Control: Testing the General Theory of Crime." *Criminology* 35: 475–504.

Fagan, Jeffrey, E. Piper, and Y. Cheng. 1987. "Contributions of Victimization to Delinquency in Inner Cities." *Journal of Criminal Law and Criminology* 78: 586–613.

Farrall, Stephen, and Adam Calverley. 2006. *Understanding Desistance from Crime: Theoretical Directions in Resettlement and Rehabilitation*. Berkshire, England: Open University Press.

Feld, Barry. 1999. *Bad Kids: Race and the Transformation of the Juvenile Court*. New York: Oxford University Press.

Felson, Marcus. 1986. "Linking Criminal Choices, Routine Activities, Informal Control, and Criminal Outcomes." In *The Reasoning Criminal: Rational Choice Perspectives on Offending*, edited by D. B. Cornish and R. V. Clarke. New York: Springer-Verlag.

Felson, Richard B. 1992. "Kick 'Em When They're Down: Explanations of the Relationship between Stress and Interpersonal Aggression and Violence." *The Sociological Quarterly* 33: 1–16.

Felson, Richard B., and Keri B. Burchfield. 2004. "Alcohol and the Risk of Physical and Sexual Assault Victimization." *Criminology* 42: 837–59.

Finkelhor, David, and Richard Ormrod. 2001. *Offenders Incarcerated for Crimes against Juveniles*. Washington, DC: Office of Juvenile Justice and Delinquency Prevention.

Forde, David R., and Leslie W. Kennedy. 1997. "Risky Lifestyles, Routine Activities, and the General Theory of Crime." *Justice Quarterly* 14: 264–94.

Glueck, Sheldon, and Eleanor Glueck. 1950. *Unraveling Juvenile Delinquency*. New York: Commonwealth Fund.

Gottfredson, Michael R., and Travis Hirschi. 1990. *A General Theory of Crime*. Stanford, CA: Stanford University Press.

Hay, Carter, and Michelle M. Evans. 2006. "Violent Victimization and Involvement in Delinquency: Examining Predictions from General Strain Theory." *Journal of Criminal Justice* 34: 261–74.

Haynie, Dana L., and Alex Piquero. 2005. "Pubertal Development and Physical Victimization in Adolescence." *Journal of Research in Crime and Delinquency* 43: 3–35.

Hindelang, Michael J. 1976. *Criminal Victimization in Eight American Cities: A Descriptive Analysis of Common Theft and Assault*. Cambridge, MA: Ballinger.

Hindelang, Michael J., Michael R. Gottfredson, and James Garofalo. 1978. *Victims of Personal Crime: An Empirical Foundation for a Theory of Personal Victimization*. Cambridge, MA: Ballinger.

Hirschi, Travis. 1969. *Causes of Delinquency*. Berkeley, CA: University of California Press.

Hirschi, Travis. 1995. "The Family." In *Crime*, edited by J. Q. Wilson and J. Petersilia. San Francisco: Institute for Contemporary Studies.

Hirschi, Travis. 1999. "The connection between family decline and family influence." Presented as the keynote address at the 13th International Congress on Juvenile Criminology. Liege, Belgium, May.

Hirschi, Travis, and Michael Gottfredson. 1993. "Rethinking the Juvenile Justice System." *Crime and Delinquency* 39: 262–71.

Hirschi, Travis, and Michael Gottfredson. 2005. "Punishment of Children from the Perspective of Control Theory." In *Corporal Punishment of Children in Theoretical Perspective*, edited by M. Donnelly and M. A. Straus. New Haven, CT: Yale University Press.

Holtfreter, Kristy, Michael D. Reisig, and Travis C. Pratt. 2008. "Routine activities, low self-control, and fraud victimization." *Criminology* 46: 189–220.

Hoyt, Stephanie, and David G. Scherer, 1998. "Female Juvenile Delinquency: Misunderstood by the Juvenile Justice System, Neglected by Social Science." *Law and Human Behavior* 22: 81–107.

Jacobs, Bruce A., and Richard Wright. 2006. *Street Justice: Retaliation in the Criminal Underworld*. New York: Cambridge.

Jacques, Scott, and Richard Wright. 2008. "The Victimization-Termination Link." *Criminology* 46: 1009–38.

Jensen, Gary F., and David Brownfield. 1986. "Gender, Lifestyles, and Victimization: Beyond Routine Activity Theory." *Violence and Victims* 1: 85–99.

Junger, Marianne. 1994. "Accidents." In *The Generality of Deviance*, edited by T. Hirschi and M. Gottfredson. New Brunswick, NJ: Transaction.

Karmen, Andrew. 2008. *Crime Victims: An Introduction to Victimology*. Belmont, CA: Wadsworth.

Kennedy, David M. 1998. "Pulling Levers: Getting Deterrence Right." *National Institute of Justice Journal* 236: 2–8.

Kornhauser, Ruth R. 1978. *Social Sources of Delinquency*. Chicago: University of Chicago Press.

Kubrin, Charis E., and Ronald Weitzer. 2003. "Homicide: Concentrated disadvantage and neighborhood culture." *Social Problems* 50: 157–80.

Kurtines, William M., Laura Ferrer-Wreder, Steven L. Berman, Carolyn Cass Lorente, Earvin Briones, Marilyn J. Montgomery. 2008. "Promoting Positive Youth Development: The Miami Youth Development Project." *Journal of Adolescent Research* 23: 256–67.

Lammers, Marianne, Jane Ritchie, and Neville Robertson. 2005. "Women's Experience of Emotional Abuse in Intimate Relationships: A Qualitative Study." *Journal of Emotional Abuse* 5: 29–64.

Larzelere, Robert E., and Gerald Patterson. 1990. "Parental Management: Mediator of the Effect of Socioeconomic Status on Early Delinquency." *Criminology* 28: 301–24.

Lauritsen, Janet L., and Kenna Davis-Quinet, 1995. "Patterns of Repeat Victimization among Adolescents and Young Adults." *Journal of Quantitative Criminology* 11: 143–66.

Lauritsen, Janet L., and John H. Laub. 2007. "Understanding the Link Between Victimization and Offending: New Reflections on an Old Idea." *Crime Prevention Studies* 22: 55–75.

Lauritsen, Janet L., John H. Laub, and Robert J. Sampson. 1992. "Conventional and delinquent activities: Implications for the prevention of violent victimization among adolescents." *Violence and Victims* 7: 91–108.

Lauritsen, Janet L., Robert J. Sampson, and John H. Laub. 1991. "The Link between Offending and Victimization among Adolescents." *Criminology* 29: 265–91.

Luckenbill, David F. 1977. "Criminal Homicide as a Situated Transaction." *Social Problems* 25: 176–86.

MacMillan, Ross. 2000. "Adolescent Victimization and Income Deficits in Early Adulthood: Rethinking the Costs of Criminal Violence from a Life Course Perspective." *Criminology* 31: 553–87.

MacMillan, Ross. 2001. "Violence and the Life Course: The Consequences of Victimization for Personal and Social Development." *Annual Review of Sociology* 27: 1–22.

MacMillan, Ross. 2009. "The Life Course Consequences of Abuse, Neglect, and Victimization: Challenges for Theory, Data Collection, and Methodology." *Child Abuse & Neglect* 33: 661–65.

MacMillan, Ross, and John Hagan. 2004. "Violence in the Transition to Adulthood: The Socio-Economic Consequences of Adolescent Victimization." *Journal of Research on Adolescence* 14: 127–58.

McGloin, Jean Marie, and Cathy Spatz Widom, 2001. "Resilience among Abused and Neglected Children Grown Up." *Development and Psychopathology* 13: 1021–38.

Menard, Scott. 2002. "Short- and Long-Term Consequences of Adolescent Victimization." *Youth Violence Research Bulletin*. Washington, DC: Office of Juvenile Justice and Delinquency Prevention.

Mennel, Robert M. 1973. *Thorns and Thistles: Juvenile Delinquents in the United States, 1825–1940*. Hanover, NH: University Press of New England.

Merton, Robert K. 1938. "Social Structure and Anomie." *American Sociological Review* 3: 672–82.

Messner, Steven F., and Richard Rosenfeld. 1994. *Crime and the American Dream*. Belmont, CA: Wadsworth.

Mustaine, Elizabeth E., and Richard Tewksbury. 2000. "Comparing the Lifestyles of Victims, Offenders, and Victim-Offenders: A Routine Activity Assessment of Similarities and Differences for Criminal Incident Participants." *Sociological Focus* 33: 339–62.

Ousey, Graham C., Pamela Wilcox, and Bonnie S. Fisher. 2010. "Something Old, Something New: Revisiting Competing Hypotheses of the Victim-Offender Relationship among Adolescents." Unpublished manuscript. Williamsburg, VA: College of William and Mary.

Patterson, Gerald. 1982. *Coercive Family Process*. Eugene, OR: Castalia.

Peterson, Dana, Terrance J. Taylor, and Finn-Aage Esbensen. 2004. "Gang Membership and Violent Victimization." *Justice Quarterly* 21: 793–815.

Pfohl, Stephen J. 1984. "The Discovery of Child Abuse." In *Deviant Behavior*, edited by D. Kelly. New York: St. Martin's Press.

Piquero, Alex R., John MacDonald, Adam Dobrin, Leah Daigle, and Francis T. Cullen. 2005. "Studying the Relationship between Violent Death and Violent Rearrest." *Journal of Quantitative Criminology* 21: 55–71.

Rebellon, Cesar, and Karen Van Gundy. 2005. "Can Control Theory Explain the Link Between Parental Physical Abuse and Delinquency? A Longitudinal Analysis." *Journal of Research in Crime and Delinquency* 42: 247–74.

Ryan, William. 1971. *Blaming the Victim*. New York: Vintage Books.

Sampson, Robert J., and John H. Laub. 1993. *Crime in the Making: Pathways and Turning Points Through Life*. Cambridge, MA: Harvard University Press.

Schreck, Christopher J. 1999. "Criminal Victimization and Low Self-Control: An Extension and Test of a General Theory of Crime." *Justice Quarterly* 16: 633–54.

Schreck, Christopher J., Melissa W. Burek, Eric A. Stewart, and J. Mitchell Miller. 2007. "Distress and Violent Victimization among Young Adolescents: Early Puberty and the Social Interactionist Explanation." *Journal of Research in Crime and Delinquency* 44: 3814–05.

Schreck, Christopher J., and Bonnie S. Fisher. 2004. "Specifying the Influence of Family and Peers on Violent Victimization: Extending Routine Activities and Lifestyles Theories." *Journal of Interpersonal Violence* 19: 1021–41.

Schreck, Christopher J., Bonnie S. Fisher, and J. Mitchell Miller. 2004. "The Social Context of Violent Victimization: A Study of the Delinquent Peer Effect." *Justice Quarterly* 21: 234–8.

Schreck, Christopher J., and Travis Hirschi. 2009. "Social Control Theories." In *21st Century Criminology: A Reference Handbook*, edited by J. Mitchell Miller. New York: Sage.

Schreck, Christopher J., Eric A. Stewart, and Bonnie S. Fisher. 2006. "Self-Control, Victimization, and their Influence on Risky Activities and Delinquent Friends: A Longitudinal Analysis Using Panel Data." *Journal of Quantitative Criminology* 22: 319–40.

Schreck, Christopher J., Eric A. Stewart, and D. Wayne Osgood. 2008. "A Reappraisal of the Overlap of Violent Offenders and Victims." *Criminology* 46: 871–906.

Schreck, Christopher J., Richard A. Wright, and J. Mitchell Miller. 2002. "A Study of Individual and Situational Antecedents of Violent Victimization." *Justice Quarterly* 19: 159–80.

Sevin Goldstein, Naomi E., Amanda Dovidio, Rachel Kalbeitzer, Jennifer Weil, and Martha Strachan. 2007. "Anger Management for Female Juvenile Offenders: Results of a Pilot Study." *Journal of Forensic Psychology Practice* 7: 1–28.

Simons, Leslie Gordon. 2009. "Families and Crime," In *21st Century Criminology: A Reference Handbook*, edited by J. M. Miller. New York: Sage.

Singer, Simon. 1981. "Homogeneous Victim-Offender Populations: A Review and Some Research Implications." *Journal of Criminal Law and Criminology* 72: 779–88.

Snyder and Sickmund 2006. *Juvenile Offenders and Victims: 2006 National Report.* Washington, DC: Office of Juvenile Justice and Delinquency Prevention.

Sorenson, David W. M. 1994. "Motor Vehicle Accidents." In *The Generality of Deviance,* edited by T. Hirschi and M. Gottfredson. New Brunswick, NJ: Transaction.

Stewart, Eric A., Kirk W. Elifson, and Claire E. Sterk. 2004. "Integrating the General Theory of Crime into an Explanation of Violent Victimization among Female Offenders." *Justice Quarterly* 21: 159–82.

Stewart, Eric A., Christopher J. Schreck, and Rod K. Brunson. 2008. "Lessons of the Street Code: Policy Implications for Reducing Violent Victimization among Disadvantaged Citizens." *Journal of Contemporary Criminal Justice* 24: 137–47.

Stewart, Eric A., Christopher J. Schreck, and Ronald L. Simons. 2006. " 'I Ain't Gonna Let No One Disrespect Me': Does the Code of the Street Reduce or Increase Violent Victimization Among African American Adolescents?" *Journal of Research in Crime and Delinquency* 43: 427–58.

Stewart, Eric A., and Ronald L. Simons. 2006. "Structure and Culture in African-American Adolescent Violence: A Partial Test of the Code of the Street Thesis." *Justice Quarterly* 23: 1–33.

Sutherland, Edwin H. 1947. *Criminology,* 4th ed. Philadelphia: Lippencott.

Von Hentig, Hans. 1948. *The Criminal and His Victim.* New Haven, CT: Yale University Press.

Widom, Cathy Spatz. 1989. "The Cycle of Violence." *Science* 244: 160–66.

Widom, Cathy Spatz, and Michael G. Maxfield. 1996. "A Prospective Examination of Risk for Violence among Abused and Neglected Children." In *Understanding Aggressive Behavior in Children,* edited by C. Ferris and T. Grisso. Annals of the New York Academy of Sciences, vol. 794. New York: New York Academy of Sciences Press.

Wilkinson, Deanna. 2003. *Guns, Violence, and Identity among African-American and Latino Youth.* New York: LFB Publishing.

Wittbrood, Karin, and Paul Nieuwbierta. 2000. "Criminal Victimization During One's Life Course: The Effects of Previous Victimization and Patterns of Routine Activities." *Journal of Research in Crime and Delinquency* 37: 91–122.

Wolfgang, Marvin. 1958. *Patterns in Criminal Homicide.* New York: John Wiley & Sons.

PART II

INDIVIDUAL LEVEL VARIABLES

CHAPTER 4

PERSONAL CHARACTERISTICS OF DELINQUENTS
NEUROBIOLOGY, GENETIC PREDISPOSITIONS, INDIVIDUAL PSYCHOSOCIAL ATTRIBUTES

MELISSA PESKIN,
ANDREA L. GLENN,
YU GAO, JIANGHONG LIU,
ROBERT A. SCHUG, YALING YANG,
AND ADRIAN RAINE

I. INTRODUCTION

OVER the past twenty years, researchers have made considerable progress in uncovering various social, psychological, and biological risk factors for juvenile crime and violence. Investigations into the personal characteristics of delinquents have increasingly focused on neurobiological risk factors, as a large body of research has now convincingly demonstrated that several neurobiological risk factors significantly increase risk for antisocial and criminal behavior. Accumulated findings suggest that neurobiological factors are particularly involved in shaping and influencing behavior at a young age, that is, in children and adolescents. Genetic studies have revealed considerable heritability estimates for juvenile delinquency, and genetic research has increasingly focused on identifying candidate genes for antisocial behavior and gene-environment interactions. Functional and structural neuroimaging studies have reported deficits in frontal, temporal, and subcortical brain regions in antisocial youth, which largely parallel the deficits found in older offenders. These studies have been supported by neurological research showing that traumatic brain injuries (TBIs) may result in functional impairments that increase risk for delinquency. Neuropsychological research has also contributed to our understanding of juvenile delinquency, revealing that delinquents have deficits in verbal, spatial, and executive abilities, and that these early childhood risk factors may predict later antisocial behavior. Psychophysiological research has also uncovered predictors of later criminality in autonomic under-arousal and hyporesponsivity, while endocrinological studies have suggested that an imbalance between hormones involved in the fear/stress response and hormones involved in reward-seeking/dominant behavior may contribute to the phenotypic traits of antisocial youth. Empirical support for the importance of neurobiological influences also comes from studies on early health risk factors, including prenatal nicotine and alcohol exposure, birth complications, minor physical anomalies (MPAs), and malnutrition, which demonstrate that these risk factors significantly increase the likelihood of antisocial and criminal behavior throughout life.

In addition to examining the role of neurobiological risk factors in isolation, research has also explored how neurobiological and social risk factors interact to predispose to crime. Juvenile delinquency is thought to be rooted in both biological and social factors, and neurobiological studies have contributed significantly to the formulation of a key biosocial developmental theory of criminality. Moffitt's (1993) proposed taxon of developmental antisocial trajectories includes *life course-persistent* (LCP) offenders—characterized by stable, lifelong antisocial behavior beginning in early childhood—and *adolescence-limited* (AL) offenders, who are typified by late-onset antisociality with recovery by early adulthood. The latter is thought to be driven by social factors and peer influences, while the former represents an interaction of biological vulnerabilities with maladaptive early home environments. This chapter will review research on the personal characteristics of youth that predispose to crime, focusing on the biosocial origins of antisocial behavior. A significant empirical base suggests that certain biological characteristics interact with environmental risk factors to produce higher rates of delinquency. This theme will be explored in reviewing research within the domains of genetics, neuroimaging, neurology, neuropsychology, psychophysiology, endocrinology, and early health risks.

II. Genetics

Research using a wide array of methods has provided persuasive evidence for genetic influences on juvenile delinquency (Popma and Raine 2006; Beaver et al. 2009). Twin studies, adoptive studies, studies in twins reared apart, and molecular genetic studies have been used to ascertain the relative importance of genetic contributions to delinquency. However, heritability estimates, or the magnitude of genetic influences on juvenile delinquency and antisocial behavior, vary widely among studies, ranging from 7% to 85%, with the majority of studies reporting estimates in the 40% to 60% range. (Rowe 1986; Lyons et al. 1995; Miles and Carey 1997; Slutske et al. 1997; Rhee and Waldman 2002; Arsenault et al. 2003; Jaffee et al. 2004; Jaffee et al. 2005; Moffitt 2005; Beaver et al. 2009). Variation in heritability estimates is likely due to methodological differences across studies, including how delinquency is operationalized, sample age, age of delinquency onset, and gender. For instance, studies have operationalized delinquency in terms of behavior (e.g., the violation of legal or social norms), the presence of a psychiatric diagnosis (e.g., conduct disorder), and the severity of aggression, which relates to the broader construct of youth antisocial behavior. Sample age appears to be an important moderator of the magnitude of genetic and environmental influences on delinquency. Studies have shown that the relative importance of genes and environment in the etiology of delinquency changes across the life span (Goldman and Ducci 2007). Most studies have found lower heritability estimates and higher shared environmental influences on delinquency and conduct problems in childhood compared to adolescence (Lyons et al. 1995; Miles and Carey 1997; Jacobson, Prescott, and Kendler 2002). Indeed, genetic influences on delinquency tend to rise with age while shared environmental effects tend to diminish (Goldman and Ducci, 2007). Researchers have also found that delinquent behavior that begins early in life and persists throughout life is more heritable than delinquent behavior that is limited to childhood. In addition, although some genes have been shown to affect delinquent behavior across the life span, others only have an effect during adolescence or adulthood (Goldman and Ducci, 2007).

Differentiating between aggressive and nonaggressive offending in juveniles also appears important, because studies have demonstrated that aggressive offending, which includes physical acts of aggression, such as fighting, is more heritable than nonaggressive offending, which includes acts such as rule-breaking and theft (Eley, Lichtenstein, and Moffitt 2003). In contrast, nonaggressive offending appears to be more influenced by shared environmental factors, such as family criminality, family poverty, and poor parenting, although genetic influences have also been found to affect some of these factors (Moffitt 2005).

Although several candidate genes have been implicated in the development of juvenile delinquency and antisocial behavior, none of these genes have been found to account for a large proportion of the phenotypic variance in juvenile offending

(Goldman and Ducci 2007). This implies not only that multiple genes are involved in creating susceptibility for antisocial behavior, but also that the interaction between genes and environment is likely involved in the etiology of youth delinquency. A recent and influential study by Caspi and colleagues (2002) provides an illustrative example of a gene-environment interaction. Caspi et al. (2002) examined a functional polymorphism in the gene encoding monoamine oxidase A (MAOA, a neurotransmitter-metabolizing enzyme) in a large sample of male children in New Zealand. Maltreated children who had a genotype that conferred high levels of MAOA expression were less likely to develop conduct disorder in adolescence or commit violent crime in adulthood than maltreated children who had a genotype that conferred low levels of MAOA expression. This study was one of the first to demonstrate that specific genotypes can moderate children's susceptibility to negative environmental experiences. Moreover, these findings may shed light on why some children who undergo maltreatment do not themselves become violent or abusive in later life, and are resilient to the effects of environmental adversity, whereas others grow up to perpetuate the cycle of violence. Thus, studies using a diverse array of methodologies have clearly demonstrated that there are genetic influences on juvenile delinquency and conduct problems.

III. Neuroimaging

The growth of neuroimaging research over the past decade has provided considerable evidence for a relationship between brain impairments and antisocial behavior in youth. Brain imaging studies of delinquent children have reported brain abnormalities similar to those found in antisocial personality disordered or aggressive adults. Regions consistently implicated are the amygdala, temporal lobe, orbitofrontal/ventromedial and medial prefrontal cortex, and the anterior and posterior cingulate. Interestingly, these regions have also been implicated in studies of moral decision-making in children and adults. Some researchers have suggested that antisocial behavior may result from impairments in these regions that are important to moral decision-making.

Several functional MRI (fMRI) studies have demonstrated that antisocial youth display reduced amygdala activity. The amygdala is necessary for the formation of stimulus-reinforcement associations, which are necessary for individuals to learn to associate their harmful actions with the pain and distress of others, thus facilitating empathy for victims and discouraging antisocial behavior (Blair 2006a; 2006b). Sterzer et al. (2005) found reduced activation in the amygdala in aggressive children with conduct disorder while viewing negative emotional pictures. Jones et al. (2009) found that boys with conduct problems and callous-unemotional traits demonstrated reduced activity in the amygdala when viewing fearful faces compared to control participants. Similarly, Marsh et al. (2008) found that children with callous-unemotional traits demonstrate reduced amygdala activity to fearful facial expressions, but not to neutral or angry expressions. Furthermore, these children demonstrated reduced connectivity between the amygdala and ventromedial prefrontal cortex, a region important in affective theory of mind (Shamay-Tsoory et al. 2005); processing reward and punishment information (Rolls 2000); inhibiting responses (Aron, Robbins, and Poldrack 2004; Vollm et al. 2006); and regulating emotions (Ochsner et al. 2005). Moreover, the severity of symptoms in the callous-unemotional traits groups was negatively correlated with the degree of connectivity between these brain regions. The amygdala is critical in fear conditioning and emotion reception and generation, while the ventromedial prefrontal cortex is involved in inhibiting behavior and regulating emotional impulses generated by the amygdala and other subcortical structures. Researchers have suggested that connectivity between these regions is important because it allows for emotional input from the amygdala to guide behavioral selection processes in the ventromedial prefrontal cortex.

fMRI studies have also found that youth with conduct disorder (CD) demonstrate reduced functioning in the orbitofrontal cortex, insula, hippocampus, and anterior cingulate during a rewarded continuous performance task (Rubia et al. 2009), and the posterior cingulate and temporal-parietal regions during an inhibition task (Rubia et al. 2008). Reduced activity in the medial and orbitofrontal prefrontal cortex and temporo-parietal junction has been observed in adolescents with conduct disorder when viewing scenes of pain being intentionally inflicted on another individual (Decety et al. 2009). Adolescents with CD also exhibited less amygdala/prefrontal coupling when perceiving others in pain, which may reflect impairment in the ability to regulate emotions. However, some discrepancies remain. Herpertz et al. (2008) found *increased* left-sided amygdala activity in boys with conduct disorder when viewing negative pictures, and no evidence of reduced functioning in orbitofrontal, anterior cingulate, or insular cortices. Similarly, Decety et al. (2009) found greater activity in the amygdala and temporal pole in adolescents with aggressive conduct disorder compared to healthy adolescents when perceiving other individuals in pain. It is hypothesized that this activation may reflect an aroused state of enjoyment or excitement at viewing others in pain. However, the majority of findings from functional neuroimaging studies in antisocial youth tend to parallel those of adult antisocial individuals, demonstrating reduced activity in regions important in moral decision-making. This suggests that brain abnormalities likely exist early in life and affect socialization and moral development in childhood.

Several structural imaging studies have also linked fronto-temporal gray matter volume reductions to antisocial behavior in children and adolescents. This research has found brain abnormalities in children and adolescents with conduct disorder that resemble the brain abnormalities found in adults with antisocial personality disorder. For instance, Sterzer and colleagues (2007) observed reduced gray matter volumes in the amygdala and insula in adolescents with conduct disorder compared to healthy controls. Consistent with these findings, in a recent report, Huebner et al.

(2008) showed reduced gray matter volumes in the orbitofrontal and temporal regions (including the amygdala and hippocampus) in children with conduct disorders compared with healthy controls. Given the importance of the amygdala in fear conditioning and the hippocampus in emotional memory, temporal lobe abnormalities, particularly of the amygdala and hippocampus, may predispose to a lack of fear for punishment and result in the disruption of normal moral development. In another study, Kruesi et al. (2004) detected significant temporal lobe and nonsignificant prefrontal lobe volume reductions in early-onset conduct-disordered children and a trend toward corpus callosum but not prefrontal white matter volume/ratio reductions in youth liars (compared to antisocial controls and healthy volunteers (Kruesi and Casanova 2006)). These findings suggest that reduced brain gray matter volumes in the fronto-temporal regions may predispose to delinquent behavior in children and adolescents and contribute to the continuation of antisocial, criminal behavior into adulthood.

Diffusion Tensor Imaging (DTI) represents a relatively new imaging technique that has provided information on white matter development in the brain and the mapping of neuronal connectivity. This technique has been used in examining the microstructural integrity of white matter in various populations. However, very few studies have applied it to delinquent or antisocial samples. One of the very few studies was conducted by Li et al. (2005) their study showed reduced fractional anisotropy (FA, a measure of the directional diffusivity of water within fiber tracts) in the fronto-temporal regions in adolescents with disruptive behavior disorder compared to normal controls. These findings are consistent with a recent report by Graig et al. (2009) revealing reduced FA in the uncinate fasciculus (a major fiber tract connecting the amygdala and the orbitofrontal cortex) in adult psychopaths with criminal convictions compared to healthy controls. These studies provide initial evidence suggesting that disturbed structural integrity in the morphometry and connectivity of the fronto-temporal regions plays a crucial role in the development of disruptive behavior and emotional deficiency that, especially in the presence of environmental and/or social risk factors, escalate into delinquency and ultimately a lifetime of persistent criminal, violent offending.

In children and adolescents, evidence linking brain damage to antisocial behavior has come largely from studies of youth with traumatic brain injuries (TBIs). These studies reveal that TBIs may result in functional impairments that increase the risk for delinquency. For example, Hux et al. (1998) reported that half of the delinquents studied had experienced a TBI (defined as having ever received a "blow to the head"), while one-third of delinquents with TBIs were thought (by their parents) to have suffered adverse, long-term behavioral problems, including diminished attentional capacity, impaired interpersonal skills, and poor school performance. Another study conducted by Carswell et al. (2004) found 27.7% of the delinquents to have TBIs (defined as a "significant head injury involving loss of consciousness/amnesia with ongoing cognitive or social impairment"). Several longitudinal studies using large samples have also consistently showed an increased incidence of delinquency among children and adolescents who had experienced brain trauma (Butler et al. 1997; Rimel et al. 1981; Asarnow et al. 1991; McAllister 1992; Rantakallio, Koiranen, and Mottonen 1992; Rivara et al. 1994; Bloom et al. 2001). Although the definition of TBIs varied between these studies, findings provide strong evidence that brain lesions may have a causal effect on delinquent behavior. Neuroimaging and neurological research thus suggests that impairment to frontal, temporal, and subcortical brain regions may lead to difficulties with moral socialization, behavioral inhibition, emotion regulation/generation, and fear conditioning. These difficulties may translate into reduced empathy for victims, difficulty regulating anger and inhibiting violent impulses, and failure to learn from punishment.

IV. Neuropsychology

Juvenile delinquency research has also received significant contributions from another key branch of the neurosciences—neuropsychology—that examines the behavioral expression of brain dysfunction. Current understanding of the personal characteristics of juvenile offenders has been advanced by neurobiological investigations of delinquent youth populations (i.e., as defined by judicial status), as well as those examining children and adolescents characterized by criminogenic psychopathology (conduct disorder, psychopathic, or callous/unemotional traits) and other violent, criminal, and aggressive behaviors. These investigations have generally focused upon different domains of cognitive functioning, with an emphasis upon areas such as verbal and spatial intelligence, executive functioning, attention, and emotional processing.

A. Intelligence: Verbal and Spatial

Similar to antisocial adults, lowered Verbal IQ appears largely characteristic of antisocial children and adolescents (Raine 1993; Déry et al. 1999; Teichner and Golden 2000; Vermeiren et al. 2002; Brennan et al. 2003). Moffitt, Lynam, and Silva (1994) found verbal deficits at age 13 predicted delinquency at age 18 for persistent, high-level offending beginning before adolescence; and other longitudinal data suggest Verbal IQ in males to be related negatively to physical violence but *positively* to theft during adolescence and early adulthood (Barker et al. 2007). Verbal deficits may lead to socialization failure (Eriksson et al. 2005) by affecting the development of self-control (Luria 1980). These juvenile offenders may experience reading problems, speech delays, and poor verbal memory; though positive prognosis is associated with environmental modifications and therapy designed to train in the identification of alternative responses (Teichner and Golden 2000). Spatial impairments, however, have also been identified in juvenile delinquent populations. For example, Raine and colleagues (2005) reported both spatial and verbal impairments in a community sample of 325 adolescent schoolboys (childhood-limited offenders were characterized by spatial intelligence deficits; while life-course persistent, childhood-limited and adolescent-limited offenders were characterized by spatial memory deficits). These authors proposed that early visuospatial deficits potentially interfere with mother-infant bonding and may reflect right hemisphere dysfunction that disrupts the processing and regulation of emotions, contributing in turn to life-course antisociality. In aggregate, verbal and spatial intelligence deficits—both associated with childhood and adolescent antisocial behavior—may contribute differentially to the development of juvenile offending.

B. Executive Functioning

Executive functioning (EF) refers to the cognitive processes that allow for goal-oriented, contextually appropriate behavior and effective self-serving conduct (Luria 1966; Spreen and Strauss 1998; Morgan and Lilienfeld 2000; Lezak et al. 2004). Executive dysfunction—thought to represent frontal lobe impairment—is indicated by poor strategy formation, cognitive flexibility, or impulse control on neuropsychological measures of these abilities. One prominent quantitative review of 39 adult and youth neuropsychological studies (Morgan and Lilienfeld 2000) found overall EF deficits in antisocials compared to controls; and though delinquent youth performed .78 standard deviations worse than nondelinquents on EF measures in this meta-analysis (a significant, medium-large effect size, across fifteen studies), other findings have been mixed, with EF deficits characterizing some antisocial youths (White et al. 1994; Nigg et al. 2004; Raine et al. 2005) and not others (Moffitt, Lynam, and Silva 1994; Déry et al. 1999; Nigg et al. 2004). Barker et al. (2007) also found EF to be negatively related to physical violence and positively related to theft in adolescence and early adulthood, though Veneziano and colleagues (2004) did not find differential EF performance among adolescent sex and non-sex offenders. Heterogeneity in EF of antisocial children and adolescents may reflect sample characteristics (Teichner and Golden 2000), methodological weaknesses, inconsistent definitions/operationalizations of EF (Moffitt and Henry 1989), co-occurring EF development and myelination of the frontal cortex into and beyond adolescence (Raine 2002b; Nigg et al. 2004), the influences of comorbid hyperactivity and aggression (Raine 2002b; Séguin et al. 2004), or the functional assessment of differing brain subvolumes. For example, psychopathic-like juvenile delinquents have demonstrated deficits on orbitofrontal tasks indexing response inhibition (i.e., Go/No-Go and stopping tasks) but not dorsolateral prefrontal/diffuse frontal tasks in comparison to nonpsychopathic-like delinquents (Roussy and Toupin 2000). Furthermore, adolescents with psychopathic-like traits and low anxiety have shown less interference than controls on picture-word Stroop tasks (Vitale et al. 2005)—which speaks to the potential influences of comorbid anxiety upon EF. Ultimately, while the relationship between EF deficits and juvenile offending appears intuitively reasonable, the complexities of this relationship require further empirical clarification. However, EF deficits, which are believed to reflect frontal impairment, may affect impulse control, planning activity, and risk assessment, and may contribute to offenders' difficulties with these functions.

C. Attention and Emotional Processing

Neuropsychological abnormalities in selective attention and emotional processing have also been found in children and adolescents who display callous-unemotional traits similar to adult psychopaths. For example, juveniles with psychopathic-like traits have demonstrated reduced asymmetry on a verbal dichotic listening task (Raine et al. 1990), replicating findings in adult psychopaths (Hare and Jutai 1988). Additionally, juveniles with these traits—like adult psychopaths (Newman and Kosson 1986)—have been characterized by passive-avoidance learning task deficits and hyper-responsivity to reward (Scerbo et al. 1990—though these authors found no passive-avoidance learning deficits in their sample). Furthermore, adolescents with callous-unemotional traits have been associated with slower reaction times to negative emotional words, while those characterized by impulsivity demonstrated faster reaction times to negative words in a lexical decision task paradigm (Loney et al. 2003). Reduced lateralization of linguistic processes has been hypothesized to reflect a reduced role for language in mediating and regulating behavior in psychopathic-like juveniles (Hare and Jutai 1988; Raine et al. 1990). Passive avoidance-learning deficits may contribute to failure to modulate responses in the face of physical or social punishment (Blair 2006a), while hyperresponsivity to reward may increase the salience of rewards (e.g., financial gain) for these individuals. Slow response times to negative emotional words may reflect difficulty recognizing fear and sadness in others and/or responding to distress cues. In short, neuropsychological deficits in attention and the processing of emotion appear related to juvenile psychopathic-like traits, and may speak to other etiological mechanisms underlying offending in this population.

D. Biological and Social Influences in Juvenile Offending

Deficits in verbal and spatial intelligence and EF appear to represent biological vulnerabilities particularly characteristic of the life course-persistent offender, that, in interaction with social risk factors, lead to higher rates of delinquency. Earlier prospective neuropsychological studies have found biosocial interactions to significantly increase levels of later violence, aggression, crime, and antisocial behavior over each factor individually (Raine 2002a), and recent longitudinal evidence supports these findings (Aguilar et al. 2000). Brennan et al. (2003) found the interaction of biological risk factors (low age 5 vocabulary ability, poor age 15 VIQ and EF, prenatal/birth complications, maternal illness during pregnancy, and infant temperament) and social risk factors predicted LCP aggression in boys and girls, and LCP versus adolescence-limited aggression in boys. Raine (2002b) proposed that antisocial behavior may result from an overload of the late developing prefrontal cortex by the social and EF demands of late adolescence (e.g., regulation of increasing sexual impulses and emphasis upon career organization/planning)—which leads to prefrontal dysfunction, behavioral inhibition failure, and significantly increased antisocial behavior. Such a proposal illustrates how neuropsychological deficits— indices of biological vulnerability—may interface with social factors to produce juvenile delinquency and underscores the importance of considering biosocial interactions in understanding the etiology of, and potentially preventing, juvenile offending.

V. Psychophysiology

Psychophysiological research has also contributed to a significant empirical understanding of the biological mechanisms underlying delinquent and aggressive behavior in youth. These studies have mostly focused upon the cardiovascular (i.e., heart rate), skin conductance (i.e., electrodermal), and electrocortical (i.e., EEG and ERP; see below for details) concomitants of delinquent behavior.

Heart rate reflects both sympathetic and parasympathetic nervous system activity. Low resting heart rate is the best-replicated biological correlate of antisocial behavior in noninstitutionalized children and adolescents (Ortiz and Raine 2004), and greater heart rate reactivity during behavioral challenge or stress tasks appears characteristic of conduct-disordered children (Kibler, Prosser, and Ma 2004; Lorber 2004). Low heart rate is diagnostically specific of conduct disorder and has demonstrated predictive validity as a childhood predictor of adolescent aggression (Raine 1996; Raine, Venables, and Mednick 1997) and life-course persistent offending (Moffitt and Caspi 2001).

Skin conductance is controlled exclusively by the sympathetic nervous system and reflects both arousal (e.g., skin conductance response frequency, level, and fluctuations at rest) and responsivity (e.g., skin conductance orienting responses to novel stimuli and task responses to emotionally valenced stimuli). Low skin conductance arousal has been associated with conduct problems (Lorber 2004), and reduced skin conductance fluctuations and fear conditioning have been reported in conduct-disordered boys (Herpertz et al. 2005; Fairchild et al. 2008). Longitudinally, reduced skin conductance arousal at age 15 years has been associated with criminal offending at age 24 years (Raine, Venables, and Williams 1990a), and low skin conductance levels measured at age 11 years predict institutionalization at age 13 years in a sample of behavior-disordered children (Kruesi et al. 1992). Orienting deficits have also been reported in conduct-disordered boys (Herpertz et al. 2003), and childhood conduct problems have overall been associated with reduced skin conductance responsivity for nonnegative stimuli (Lorber 2004). Finally, impaired skin conductance fear conditioning at age 3, suggesting retarded maturation of the amygdala, has been found to be associated with aggressive behavior at age 8 as well as criminal behavior 20 years later at age 23 (Gao et al. 2009, 2010). Together, these findings suggest that reduced skin conductance activity in children may be a risk factor for later antisocial behavior and criminality (Raine 2002a), although a recent study has suggested different autonomic correlates of externalizing behavior for girls compared with boys (Beauchaine, Hong, and Marsh 2008).

Diminished autonomic reactivity has also been found in psychopathy-prone adolescents (Fung et al. 2005) and conduct-disordered children with callous-unemotional traits (Loney et al. 2003; Kimonis et al. 2006; Anastassiou-Hadjicharalambous and Warden 2008). Prospective studies have indicated that abnormal skin conductance responses (i.e., longer half-recovery time) to aversive stimuli as early as age 3 predispose to psychopathic personality in adulthood (Glenn et al. 2007). Overall, there is evidence for an early psychophysiological predisposition to the development of aggressive and psychopathic behavior.

Autonomic underarousal and hyporesponsivity have been interpreted in different ways. Fearlessness theory argues that lack of fear, represented by low heart rate or skin conductance arousal, leads in childhood to poor socialization as low fear of punishment reduces the effectiveness of conditioning. Stimulation-seeking theory argues that underarousal represents an aversive state that is compensated for by stimulation/thrill-seeking and risk-taking behavior. In this context, 3-year-old children who show temperamentally high stimulation-seeking and reduced fearlessness have been found to show increased aggression at age 11 (Raine et al. 1998). While both fearlessness and stimulation-seeking theories may be complementary in nature (Raine 2002a), they could also represent independent risk factors, as childhood fearlessness and stimulation-seeking have been found to be independent predictors of later aggression (Raine et al. 1998). Finally, prefrontal dysfunction theory argues that reduced skin conductance orienting is a marker for abnormalities in the prefrontal-cortical-subcortical circuitry involved in arousal regulation and stress responsivity—abnormalities associated with attentional and executive deficiencies (Herpertz 2007).

The electroencephalogram (EEG) is used to detect brain electrical activity. Abnormal EEG activity has been implicated in delinquent and antisocial adolescents (Raine 1993). Developmentally, alpha wave slowing among children and adolescents has been associated with later delinquency, particularly with thefts (Mednick et al. 1981; Petersen et al. 1982). In addition, a prospective longitudinal study of 101 male schoolchildren found that increased age-15 slow-wave EEG activity predicted age-24 criminality (Raine, Venables, and Williams 1990a). EEG abnormalities may reflect cortical immaturity—a developmental lag in those prone to recidivistic crime (Volavka 1987). Additionally, abnormal frontal EEG asymmetry has been found to be associated with antisocial/externalizing behavior problems in children, indicating emotion regulation deficits in these individuals (Ishikawa and Raine 2002; Santesso et al. 2006). Several authors have hypothesized that children with these patterns of abnormal frontal EEG asymmetry might have poor language and analytic-based strategies, rendering emotion regulation harder and their attempts at it less successful. Thus, these children may be more likely to respond to stressful experiences with maladaptive behaviors (Fox 1991, 1994; Santesso et al. 2006).

The Event-Related Potential (ERP) refers to averaged changes in the electrical activity of the brain in response to specific stimuli. Several ERP components appear to be biological markers for antisociality, including P300, a positive-going waveform occurring approximately 300 milliseconds after a stimulus. Reduced P300 amplitude and longer P300 latency have been found to be associated with forms of antisocial behavior in both adolescents and adults (Gao and Raine 2009), indicating somewhat inefficient deployment of neural resources to task-relevant information in these individuals. For example, Bauer and Hesselbrock (1999) found reduced P300 amplitudes in conduct-disordered adolescents younger than 16.5 years old. In one prospective study, increased N1 amplitudes and faster P300 latencies to warning stimuli at age 15 predicted criminality at age 24 (Raine, Venables, and Williams 1990b). Iacono et al. (2002) similarly observed that reduced P300 amplitude at age 17 predicted the development of substance use disorders at age 20. Specifically, it has been reported that there is a trend for younger antisocials to have twice as large a deficit in P300 amplitudes compared to older antisocials (Gao and Raine 2009), suggesting that the sensitivity of the P300 as a putative marker for antisociality may vary with age. These studies suggest that reduced P300 amplitude and longer P300 latency may be a trait marker for antisocial behavior.

The relationship between autonomic factors and antisocial behavior may be moderated by social influences (Farrington 1997; Raine 2002a). Specifically, studies have found that psychophysiological factors, particularly measures of skin conductance and heart rate, show stronger relationships to antisocial behavior in those from *benign* social backgrounds that lack the classic psychosocial risk factors for crime (Raine 2002a). For example, reduced skin conductance orienting and low resting heart rate were shown to be related to age 11 aggression in high but not low social class individuals (Raine et al. 1997). Similarly, poor skin conductance conditioning has been shown to be a characteristic for undersocialized schoolboys from relatively good social backgrounds (Raine and Venables 1981). These findings, explained by the "social push" hypothesis, suggest that psychophysiological risk factors may assume greater importance when social predispositions to crime are minimized. In contrast, social causes may be more important explanations of antisocial behavior in those exposed to adverse early home conditions (Raine 2002a).

Some studies have focused on psychophysiological correlates as protective factors against antisocial and criminal behavior. For example, in a prospective longitudinal study, 15-year-old antisocial adolescents who did not become criminals by age 29 showed higher resting heart rate levels, higher skin conductance arousal, and better skin conductance conditioning when compared to their antisocial counterparts who became adult criminals (Raine, Venables, and Williams 1995, 1996). In another study on adolescents who had criminal fathers and thus were at higher risk for antisocial outcomes, those who desisted from crime had higher skin conductance and heart rate orienting reactivity in comparison with those who eventually became criminals (Brennan et al. 1997). Therefore, enhanced autonomic nervous system functioning, as indexed by higher levels of arousal, better conditioning, and higher orienting responses, may serve as biological protective factors that reduce the likelihood that an individual will become an adolescent or adult criminal.

VI. ENDOCRINOLOGY

Numerous studies have examined the role of hormones in juvenile delinquency. There are two overarching hormone systems that have been implicated. These systems act to maintain an appropriate balance between withdrawing in the presence of fearful or threatening stimuli and approaching in the presence of rewarding stimuli. Juvenile delinquency is hypothesized to be associated with reduced levels of hormones involved in the fear or stress response (e.g., cortisol) and increased levels of hormones involved in reward-seeking and dominant behavior (e.g., testosterone). Such an imbalance results in the combination of traits observed in delinquent children—fearlessness and insensitivity to punishment or threat, combined with dominant, reward-seeking, aggressive behavior.

The primary hormones that have been associated with the fearful or stressful stimuli are cortisol, a hormone released by the hypothalamic-pituitary-adrenal (HPA) axis, and alpha-amylase, a salivary enzyme released by the sympathetic nervous system. Several studies have observed reduced cortisol levels in antisocial children and adolescents. In children, low cortisol levels have been associated with aggression (McBurnett et al. 2000), externalizing behavior and low anxiety (van Goozen et al. 1998b), and symptoms of conduct disorder (Oosterlaan et al. 2005). Low cortisol has been observed in adolescents with conduct disorder (Pajer et al. 2001), callous-unemotional traits (Loney et al. 2006), and conduct problems (McBurnett et al. 2000). In a five-year longitudinal study, Shoal et al. (2003) found that low cortisol in preadolescent boys (ages 10 to 12 years) was associated with low harm-avoidance, low self-control, and more aggressive behavior during adolescence (ages 15 to 17 years). Lower levels of cortisol may indicate that individuals are less responsive to stressors and may be less fearful of negative consequences such as potential punishment. However, some studies have found no such relationship (Schulz et al. 1997; van Goozen et al. 2000; Azar et al. 2004) or even a positive relationship (van Bokhoven et al. 2005). Measures of the cortisol response to a stressor have indicated reduced cortisol *reactivity* in boys with externalizing behaviors (van Goozen et al. 1998a), adolescent males with conduct problems (McBurnett et al. 2005), and children with ODD (van Goozen et al. 2000b). The assessment of cortisol reactivity (in addition to baseline cortisol levels) is important in gaining information about the system's response to threat, which may be especially key in understanding the functioning of the system. As with decreased baseline cortisol levels, decreased cortisol reactivity may suggest that these juveniles are less reactive to stressors and less apprehensive about the possibility of punishment and other aversive outcomes.

Thus far, only one study has examined the salivary enzyme alpha-amylase in relation to aggressive behavior in youth. Gordis, and colleagues (2006) found that alpha-amylase reactivity affected the relationship between cortisol reactivity and aggression. At high levels of alpha-amylase, cortisol was not related to aggression, yet at low levels of alpha-amylase, low cortisol was associated with increased aggression. This may suggest that if sympathetic nervous system functioning is sufficiently high, it may act as a buffer against the development of aggressive behavior, even in individuals with low cortisol.

The hormones that are involved in reward-seeking and dominant behavior are androgens such as testosterone and DHEA. Androgen levels have been associated with approach-related behaviors including reward-seeking (Daitzman and Zuckerman 1980), dominance (Archer 2006), and aggression (Dabbs, Jurkovic, and Frady 1991). In contrast to the stress response system, which increases the probability of *withdrawal* behavior by inducing fear and increasing sensitivity to punishment, androgens increase the probability of *approach* behavior by increasing sensitivity to reward, reducing sensitivity to punishment, and reducing fear (van Honk and Schutter 2006). Testosterone is a gonadal androgen that increases greatly in males during puberty. DHEA is an adrenal androgen that is a precursor to testosterone that starts increasing around the age of 6, in a period called the *adrenarche* (Parker 1999). Some evidence suggests that testosterone may play less of a role in aggression in prepubertal children than DHEA; it is possible that a testosterone–aggression relationship may not emerge until during or after puberty. Although the precise mechanisms by which DHEA is related to aggression are unknown, it has been hypothesized that because DHEA is a precursor to testosterone, it may contribute to a larger pool of endogenous testosterone (Brown et al. 2008).

In general, testosterone tends to be positively related to antisocial behavior in adolescents, but not in prepubertal children. Higher testosterone levels were found in 15- to 17-year-old girls with CD (Pajer et al. 2006), 14-year-old boys with externalizing behaviors (Maras et al. 2003), and late adolescent male offenders (Dabbs, Jurkovic, and Frady 1991). However, no effects were found in aggressive children ages 4 to 10 (Constantino et al. 1993), 8- to 12-year-old boys with ODD (van Goozen et al. 1998a), or 13-year-old males with disruptive behavior (Granger et al. 2003).

There have been fewer studies of DHEA in antisocial youth. Two studies have found increased DHEA levels in children and adolescents with CD (van Goozen et al. 1998a; Dmitrieva et al. 2001), while one study of aggressive children found no relationship (Constantino et al. 1993). One study (Buydens-Branchey and Branchey 2004) in adult cocaine addicts found that DHEA levels were increased in adult males with a retrospective diagnosis of CD in childhood.

Studies have also found interactions between different hormones in predicting juvenile delinquency. For example, an interaction between cortisol and testosterone was found in a recent study of delinquent boys (Popma et al. 2007). At low levels of cortisol, a positive association was found between testosterone and overt aggression, but at high levels of cortisol, no relationship was observed. This may suggest that sufficiently high cortisol levels may buffer against the effects of low testosterone.

Alternatively, it may suggest that the combination of low cortisol and high testosterone predisposes for antisocial behavior. An interaction has also been observed between cortisol and DHEA, both of which are adrenal hormones. Pajer et al. (2006) found that girls with aggressive CD had lower cortisol to DHEA ratios (a result of lower cortisol and higher DHEA). This may suggest that the combined effect of different hormone levels may have more of an effect on aggressive behavior in youth than individual hormone levels. Thus, an imbalance between hormones involved in the fear or stress response, such as cortisol, and hormones involved in reward-seeking and dominant behavior, such as testosterone and DHEA, may be reflected in delinquents' decreased fear and sensitivity to punishment/threat and increased dominant, reward-seeking, aggressive behavior. This implies not only that these juveniles may be less likely to experience fear in threatening or risky situations, but also that potential punishment may not serve as the same deterrent for them as it does for others. Moreover, it suggests that they may be more likely to display aggression and pursue rewards despite possible costs.

Although the interaction between hormones and social factors has rarely been studied, results from a few studies indicate that hormones may interact with social risk factors in predicting juvenile delinquency. Dabbs and Morris (1990) found that high testosterone was associated with higher levels of childhood and adult delinquency in low socioeconomic status (SES) subjects, but not high SES subjects. Mazur (1995) found that a combined biosocial model involving the hormones cortisol, testosterone, and thyroxin, in combination with social factors including age, education, and income, was a better predictor of delinquent behavior than a biological or social model alone.

VII. Early Health Risks

A substantial body of evidence has now convincingly demonstrated that several early health risk factors, including prenatal nicotine and alcohol exposure, birth complications, minor physical anomalies (MPAs), and malnutrition, significantly increase risk for antisocial and criminal behavior across the life span. These early health risk factors can be categorized into those that occur during pregnancy (prenatal), those that occur during the birth of the child (perinatal), and those that occur after the birth (postnatal).

A. Smoking During Pregnancy

Extensive evidence has now strongly established that children who are exposed to maternal smoking during pregnancy are at increased risk for later antisocial behavior that extends over the life course (see Wakschlag et al. 2002 for a review). Maternal prenatal smoking has been shown to predict externalizing behavior in childhood and conduct disorder, delinquency, and offending in adolescence (Rantakallio et al. 1992; Fergusson, Horwood, and Lynskey 1993; Orlebeke, Knol, and Verhulst 1997; Wakschlag et al. 1997; Fergusson, Woodward, and Horwood 1998). Several studies have also reported a dose-response relationship between the extent of maternal smoking during pregnancy and the extent of later antisocial behavior in offspring (Brennan, Grekin, and Mednick 1999; Maughan et al. 2001; Maughan et al. 2004).

The exact mechanism through which maternal tobacco exposure predisposes to behavioral problems in offspring is not clear. In animal studies, the carbon monoxide and nicotine products of cigarette smoking are thought to damage the functioning of the brain by disturbing the noradrenergic system and also the regulation of dopamine (Muneoka et al. 1997), and by reducing brain glucose content (Eckstein et al. 1997). Furthermore, it is thought to impair the basal ganglia, cerebral cortex, and cerebellar cortex (Olds 1997; Raine 2002b), and may contribute to the brain structural and functional deficits found in violent offenders.

In addition to nicotine exposure, it has long been established that fetal alcohol exposure significantly increases risk for antisocial behavior in children and adolescents (Streissguth et al. 1996; Olson et al. 1997; Fast, Conry, and Loock 1999). Heavy alcohol consumption while pregnant can result in Fetal Alcohol Syndrome (FAS), which is characterized by a host of cognitive, behavioral, social, and physical deficits. However, deficits are observed even in those who have been prenatally exposed to alcohol who do not meet diagnostic criteria for FAS (Schonfeld, Mattson, and Riley 2005). For instance, research has found high rates of delinquency in children and adolescents with heavy fetal alcohol exposure, even if they do not have FAS (Roebuck, Mattson, and Riley 1999; Mattson and Riley 2000). In addition, studies have shown that adolescents who were prenatally exposed to alcohol are overrepresented in the juvenile justice system (Fast, Conry, and Loock 1999). One study found that 3% of adolescents in a juvenile inpatient forensic psychiatry unit were diagnosed with FAS, and 22% were diagnosed with fetal alcohol effects (Fast, Conry, and Loock 1999). Another study reported that 61% of adolescents and 14% of children between the ages of 6 to 11 with fetal alcohol exposure had a history of trouble with the law (Streissguth et al. 1996).

B. Birth Complications

In addition to prenatal nicotine and alcohol exposure, research has also focused on obstetric complications, such as premature birth, low birth weight, placement in a neonatal intensive care unit, forceps delivery, Cesarean section, anoxia, resuscitation needed after delivery, preeclampsia in the mother, and low Apgar score. Such complications are believed to directly and indirectly alter brain function in the newborn's CNS (Liu 2004; Liu and Wuerker 2005). A number of well-designed studies have demonstrated that obstetric complications interact with psychosocial risk factors in predicting conduct disorder, delinquency, and impulsive crime and violence in adolescence and adulthood. For example, Raine, Brennan, and Mednick (1994) evaluated whether the early experience of extreme maternal rejection (e.g., unwanted pregnancy, attempts to abort the fetus, and institutional care of the infant during the first year of life) interacted with birth complications in predisposing to violent crime in a sample of 4,269 males born in Copenhagen, Denmark, between 1959 to 1961. The authors found that birth complications significantly interacted with maternal rejection in predisposing to violent crime in late adolescence. The importance of this finding is highlighted by the fact that while only 4% of the sample experienced both birth complications and maternal rejection, this group was responsible for 18% of the violent offenses perpetrated by the whole sample. In a Canadian sample of 849 boys, Arsenault and colleagues (2002) found an interaction between increased serious obstetric complications and family adversity raises the likelihood of violent offending at age 17 years. These findings have been replicated in adult samples in three other countries in the context of a variety of psychosocial risk factors.

A critical question concerns how birth complications predispose to antisocial behavior. In this context, Liu and colleagues recently reported that babies with birth complications were more likely to develop externalizing behavior problems at age 11(Liu et al. 2009). Low IQ was also associated with both birth complications and externalizing behavior, and was found to mediate the birth complications—externalizing behavior relationship. Birth complications such as anoxia (lack of oxygen), forceps delivery, and preeclampsia (hypertension leading to anoxia) are thought to contribute to brain dysfunction, and such brain dysfunction is indirectly reflected in lower IQ. It is known, for example, that hypoxia selectively damages the hippocampus, one component of the limbic system that brain-imaging research indicates is involved in aggression regulation (Raine 2002b; Liu and Wuerker 2005).

C. Minor Physical Anomalies (MPAs)

It has been argued that minor physical anomalies are a biomarker for fetal neural maldevelopment during the first and the second trimester of pregnancy when the fetal brain is undergoing massive growth. Examples of these subtle physical abnormalities include a curved fifth finger, furrowed tongue, single palmer crease, and low-seated ears (Pine et al. 1997). While MPAs may have a genetic basis, they may also be caused by environmental factors affecting fetal growth and development, such as anoxia, bleeding, and infection (Guy et al. 1983). Although multiple studies have found an association between MPAs in children and delinquency and violent behavior in adulthood, fewer studies have investigated MPAs in juvenile populations. Nevertheless, those that have report a similar link. For example, Arseneault et al. (2000) showed that MPAs measured at age 14 in 170 males predicted violent delinquency at age 17, an association that was independent of childhood aggression and family adversity.

Studies have also reported that MPAs interact with social factors in predisposing to violent and antisocial behavior, although, here too, the majority of studies have investigated offending in adult populations. One exception to this is a study by Pine and colleagues (1997) that investigated the interaction of MPAs and environmental risk factors, such as low SES, spousal conflict, and marital disruption in predicting conduct problems in adolescence. The authors found a significant interaction between MPAs and environmental risk, such that individuals with both increased MPAs and environmental risk, assessed at age 7, were at greater risk for disruptive behavior in general and conduct disorder in particular at age 17.

D. Malnutrition

Nutrition factors play an active and critical role in brain development during pregnancy and early childhood. Human studies suggest that a deficiency in macronutrients (e.g., protein), micronutrients (e.g., the trace elements zinc and iron), and a component of omega-3 (docosahexaenoic acid or DHA—a long-chain essential fatty acid) can disturb brain functioning and thus further predispose to antisocial behavior in children and adolescents (Werbach 1992; Rosen et al. 1985; Breakey 1997; Fishbein 2001; Lister et al. 2005; Liu and Raine 2006). For instance, several longitudinal studies have shown that increased aggressive and attention deficit behavior in childhood is related to malnutrition during infancy (Galler et al. 1983a, 1983b; Galler and Ramsey 1989). Studies have also found nutritional deficits in those with a history of delinquent behavior. For example, Rosen et al. (1985) reported that one-third of incarcerated juvenile delinquents suffered from iron-deficient anemia. Research has also examined whether increased consumption of fish rich in omega-3 essential fatty acids is related to lower levels of violent and aggressive behavior. In a large sample of 14,541 pregnant women, mothers who ate more fish during pregnancy had offspring who showed significantly higher levels of prosocial behavior at age 7 years (Hallahan et al. 2007). These findings have been replicated in adult samples.

While the links described above are intriguing, they do not provide conclusive evidence of a relationship between malnutrition and antisocial behavior. More compelling evidence that malnutrition leads to antisocial behavior comes from a number of longitudinal studies in both children and adolescents. A recent longitudinal prospective study by Liu and colleagues (2004) provides a particularly powerful illustration of how early malnutrition may predispose to conduct problems and delinquency in childhood and adolescence. In this study, Liu et al. demonstrated that children with iron, zinc, or protein deficiencies at age 3 had greater antisocial behavior at ages 8, 11, and 17. In comparison to control subjects, malnourished children at age 3 were more aggressive or hyperactive at age 8, had more antisocial behavior at age 11, and greater conduct disorder and excessive motor activity at age 17. Behavior problems were measured with three different instruments at each age, suggesting that findings were largely invariant to the nature of measurement. Findings were also independent of psychosocial adversity and not moderated by gender. Moreover, Liu et al. found a dose-response relationship between the extent of malnutrition at age 3 and the extent of behavior problems at ages 8 and 17, suggesting that malnutrition was an important factor in predisposing to antisocial behavior.

Although the exact nature of how early health risk factors contribute to antisocial behavior is not fully known, researchers have proposed that early health risk factors negatively alter brain structures and functions critical to learning, memory, attention, reward systems, and emotion regulation and thus may both directly and indirectly predispose to aggression.

VIII. Prevention and Intervention

Efforts have been made to integrate biosocial findings into prevention and intervention programs. Interventions have been targeted toward both pre- and postnatal risk factors. For instance, various interventions have been designed to help reduce rates of adverse prenatal behaviors, such as smoking and alcohol use. While interventions aimed at reducing prenatal alcohol use have been somewhat successful (Chang et al. 1999; Chang et al. 2000; Hankin 2002; Chang et al. 2005), interventions targeting prenatal smoking have shown limited effectiveness, rarely producing prenatal quit rates above 20%, despite employing a wide range of approaches (Goldenberg et al. 2000; Wakschlag et al. 2003; Ershoff, Ashford, and Goldenberg 2004; Kodl Middlecamp and Wakschlag 2004). In addition, persistent pregnancy smokers tend to smoke more heavily than pregnancy quitters, have a greater number of problematic health behaviors, poorer adaptive functioning, and an increased history of conduct disorder (Wakschlag et al. 2003; Kodl Middlecamp and Wakschlag 2004). Thus greater attempts to reach this population may be warranted in future interventions.

Intervention research has also focused on the role of malnutrition in antisocial behavior. Studies in children have shown that daily vitamin and mineral supplementation can reduce juvenile delinquency. For instance, in a randomized, double-blind, placebo-controlled trial of 486 unselected, public-school children, Schoenthaler and Bier (2000) found that children given a daily vitamin and mineral supplement showed a reduction of 47% in antisocial behavior after four months compared with children given the placebo. Although results have not always been consistent (e.g., Hirayama, Hamazaki, and Terasawa 2004), several studies have also found that supplementation with omega-3 essential fatty acids may reduce antisocial behavior. For example, in a four-month randomized, double-blind, placebo-controlled trial of fatty acid supplementation in fifty children, Stevens et al. (2003) reported that those in the supplementation condition showed a significant 42.7% reduction in conduct disorder problems compared to those in the control condition.

Effects of early nutritional interventions on later behavior have also been found. Although not specific to nutritional enrichment, one highly successful early intervention for criminal and antisocial behavior consisted of home visits by nurses to mothers in which nutritional guidance was a major component (Olds et al. 1998). A randomized controlled trial by Raine and colleagues (2003) also demonstrated that an enrichment program consisting of nutrition, education, and physical exercise for children from ages 3 to 5 significantly reduced antisocial behavior at age 17 and criminal behavior at age 23. Moreover, the authors found that the beneficial effects of the intervention were greater for children who exhibited signs of malnutrition at age 3, suggesting that the nutritional components of the intervention were the active elements in the enrichment program.

Although only a few studies have examined whether nutritional interventions can reduce antisocial behavior in incarcerated populations, results thus far have been highly promising. In a randomized, controlled, double-blind trial, Schoenthaler et al. (1997) found that vitamin and mineral supplementation significantly reduced violent and nonviolent antisocial behavior by 28% among juvenile delinquents confined to a correctional facility. Particularly striking is the fact that the number of violent acts by the sixteen out of twenty-six subjects who corrected their low blood vitamin and mineral concentrations during the intervention dropped from 131 acts during baseline to 11 during the intervention. Indeed, the success of this intervention led the California legislature to produce a new section in the Health and Welfare Code to determine if the study could be replicated with adult male prisoners. Although the precise way in which nutrition deficits contribute to juvenile delinquency is not well understood, there is speculation that proteins or minerals play a role in either regulating neurotransmitters or hormones, or else exacerbate neurotoxins, and in doing so predispose to brain dysfunction, aggression, and conduct problems (Ferris and Grisso 1996; Coccaro, Kavoussi, and Hauger 1997; Liu and Raine 2006).

Another line of intervention research concerns directly altering one's psychophysiological functioning. For example, in one longitudinal study, better nutrition, more physical exercise, and cognitive stimulation from ages 3 to 5 years was shown to produce long-term psychophysiological changes six years later at age 11 years, including increased skin conductance level, more orienting, and a more aroused EEG profile (Raine et al. 2001; Raine et al. 2003), changes which may serve to protect against the development of criminal offending (Raine, Venables, and Williams 1995; Raine et al. 1996; Brennan et al. 1997).

Future prevention and intervention programs may also be improved by differentiating between subgroups of children based on their psychophysiological characteristics. For example, one study found that a cognitive-behavioral intervention program for children with disruptive behavior problems (aggression, delinquency, and attention problems) was of greater benefit to children with high heart rate levels compared to those with low heart rate levels (Stadler et al. 2008). Similarly, in a pilot study on adolescents at high risk for drug abuse, individuals who were unresponsive to the intervention demonstrated fewer skin conductance responses to two boring and tedious tasks (continuous performance test and delay of gratification) and higher skin conductance responses to the risky choices in a more stimulating task, relative to those who had better responses to the intervention program (Fishbein et al. 2004). Therefore, prevention and intervention programs aimed at reducing antisocial behavior may benefit from targeting their efforts toward individuals based on psychophysiological characteristics or by attempting to directly improve psychophysiological functioning.

IX. CONCLUSIONS

Research from a number of neurobiological domains has yielded greater insight into the etiology of juvenile delinquency and antisocial behavior. Genetic studies reveal considerable heritability estimates of antisocial behavior, and several candidate genes have been implicated in the development of juvenile offending. Research suggests both that multiple genes are involved in creating susceptibility for antisocial behavior, and that the interaction between genes and environment is likely involved in the etiology of youth delinquency. Neuroimaging studies have also made important contributions, revealing structural and functional deficits in frontal, temporal, and subcortical brain regions in antisocial youth that largely resemble those found in adult antisocial populations. Neuropsychological research has found verbal, spatial, and executive functioning deficits in delinquent juveniles and suggests that these early childhood risk factors may predict later offending. Research focused upon psychophysiological factors has also demonstrated that autonomic underarousal, such as low resting heart rate and reduced skin conductance activity, are characteristic of antisocial youth and are important predictors of later criminality, as are EEG and ERP abnormalities. Studies examining the role of hormones in juvenile delinquency have largely found reduced cortisol in antisocial children and adolescents, although other factors, such as sympathetic nervous system activity, may moderate this relationship. In addition, endocrinological research has found a positive association between testosterone and antisocial behavior in adolescents, but not prepubertal children. Numerous studies have demonstrated that several early health risk factors, including prenatal nicotine and alcohol exposure, birth complications, minor physical anomalies (MPAs), and malnutrition significantly increase risk for antisocial behavior throughout life. Thus, the accumulation of evidence through key areas of neurobiological research suggests not only that neurobiological risk factors begin early in life, but also that they represent an important predisposition to later aggression and offending.

Equally, however, attempts to understand the personal characteristics of juvenile delinquents have utilized a biosocial approach, as evidence increasingly suggests that criminal behavior results from a complex interaction of neurobiological and psychosocial risk factors. Although the juvenile justice system may not be in a position to alter biological risk factors, family courts that hear cases of child abuse and neglect may be able to mitigate such psychosocial risk factors by mandating therapies for youth and parenting classes for caretakers. An adverse environment may serve to "trigger" underlying biological vulnerabilities and result in antisocial behavior. Alternatively, the "social push" hypothesis (Mednick 1977; Raine and Venables 1981) suggests that there may be a weaker link between antisocial behavior and biological risk factors in delinquents from adverse backgrounds, relative to delinquents from benign social backgrounds, because the social causes of crime camouflage the biological contribution (Raine 2002a). These perspectives reveal the importance of incorporating both neurobiological and social risks into a framework for understanding the origins of juvenile crime and aggression. Indeed, the adoption of a biosocial approach to understanding juvenile delinquency and violence has turned into a new and perhaps inevitable endeavor for the scientist and educator. Intervention and prevention efforts that utilize this approach represent promising avenues for the future treatment and prevention of criminal and delinquent behavior.

REFERENCES

Aguilar, Benjamin, L. Allen Sroufe, Byron Egeland, and Elizabeth Carlson. 2000. "Distinguishing the early-onset/persistent and adolescent-onset antisocial behavior types: From birth to 16 years." *Development and Psychopathology* 12 (2): 109–32.

Anastassiou-Hadjicharalambous, Xenia, and David Warden. 2008. "Physiologically-indexed and self-perceived affective empathy in conduct-disordered children high and low on callous-unemotional traits." *Child Psychiatry and Human Development* 39: 503–17.

Archer, John. 2006. "Testosterone and human aggression: an evaluation of the challenge hypothesis." *Neuroscience and Biobehavioral Reviews* 30: 319–45.

Aron, Adam R., Trevor W. Robbins, and Russel A. Poldrack. 2004. "Inhibition and the right inferior frontal cortex." *Trends in Cognitive Science* 8 (4): 170–77.

Arseneault, Louise, Terrie E. Moffitt, Avshalom Caspi, Alan Taylor, Fruhlilng V. Rijsdijk, Sara R. Jaffee, Jennifer C. Ablow, and Jeffrey R. Measelle. 2003. "Strong genetic effects on cross-situational antisocial behaviour among 5-year-old children according to mothers, teachers, examiner-observers, and twins' self-reports." *Journal of Child Psychology and Psychiatry* 44: 832–48.

Arsenault, Louise, Richard E. Tremblay, Bernard Boulerice, and Jean-Francois Saucier. 2002. "Obstetrical complications and violent delinquency: Testing two developmental pathways." *Child Development* 73: 496–508.

Arsenault, Louise, Richard E. Tremblay, Bernard Boulerice, Jean R. Seguin, and Jean-Francois Saucier. 2000. "Minor physical anomalies and family adversity as risk factors for violent delinquency in adolescence." *American Journal of Psychiatry* 157: 917–23.

Asarnow, Robert F., Paul Satz, Roger Light, Richard Lewis, and Elizabeth Neumann. 1991. "Behavior problems and adaptive functioning in children with mild and severe closed head injury." *Journal of Pediatric Psychology* 16 (5): 543–55.

Azar, Rima, Mark Zoccolillo, Daniel Paquette, Elsa Quiros, Franziska Baltzer, and Richard E. Tremblay. 2004. "Cortisol levels and conduct disorder in adolescent mothers." *Journal of the American Academy of Child and Adolescent Psychiatry* 43: 461–68.

Barker, Edward D., Jean R. Séguin, Helene R. White, Marsha E. Bates, Eric Lacourse, René Carbonneau, and Richard E. Tremblay. 2007. "Developmental Trajectories of Male Physical Violence and Theft: Relations to Neurocognitive Performance." *Archives of General Psychiatry* 64: 592–99.

Bauer, Lance O., and Victor M. Hesselbrock. 1999. "P300 decrements in teenagers with conduct problems: Implications for substance abuse risk and brain development." *Biological Psychiatry* 46: 263–72.

Beauchaine, Theodore P., James Hong, and Penny Marsh. 2008. "Sex differences in autonomic correlates of conduct problems and aggression." *Journal of American Academy of Child and Adolescent Psychiatry* 47: 788–96.

Beaver, Kevin M., Matt DeLisi, John Paul Wright, and Michael G. Vaughn. 2009. "Gene environment interplay and delinquent involvement: Evidence of direct and indirect, and interactive effects." *Journal of Adolescent Research* 24: 147–68.

Blair, R. J. R. 2006a. "The emergence of psychopathy: Implications for the neuropsychological approach to developmental disorders." *Cognition* 101: 414–42.

Blair, R. J. R. 2006b. "Subcortical brain systems in psychopathy." In *Handbook of Psychopathy*, edited by Christopher J. Patrick. New York: Guilford.

Bloom, Douglas, Harvey S. Levin, Linda Ewing-Cobbs, Ann E. Saunders, James Song, Jack M. Fletcher, and Robert A. Kowatch R. 2001. "Lifetime and novel psychiatric disorders after pediatric traumatic brain injury." *Journal of the American Academy of Child & Adolescent Psychiatry* 40 (5): 572–79.

Breakey, Joan. 1997. "The role of diet and behavior in childhood." *Journal of Pediatric Child Health* 33: 190–94.

Brennan, Patricia A., Emily R. Grekin, and Sarnoff A. Mednick. 1999. "Maternal smoking during pregnancy and adult male criminal outcomes." *Archives of General Psychiatry* 56 (3): 215–19.

Brennan, Patricia A., Jason Hall, William Bor, Jake M. Najman, and Gail Williams. 2003. "Integrating biological and social processes in relation to early-onset persistent aggression in boys and girls." *Developmental Psychology* 39 (2): 309–23.

Brennan, Patricia A., Adrian Raine, Fini Schulsinger, Lis Kirkegaard-Sorensen, Joachim Knop, Barry Hutchings, Raben Rosenberg, and Sarnoff A. Mednick. 1997. "Psychophysiological protective factors for male subjects at high risk for criminal behavior." *American Journal of Psychiatry* 154: 853–55.

Brown, Gerald L., Elizabeth L. McGarvey, Elizabeth A. Shirtcliff, Adrienne Keller, Douglas A. Granger, and Kara Flavin. 2008. "Salivary cortisol, dehydroepiandrosterone, and testosterone interrelationships in healthy young males: A pilot study with implications for studies of aggressive behavior." *Psychiatry Research* 159: 67–76.

Butler, Katy, Byron P. Rourke, Darren R. Fuerst, and John L. Fisk. 1997. "A typology of psychosocial functioning in pediatric closed-head injury." *Child Neuropsychology* 3 (2): 98–133.

Buydens-Branchey, Laure, and Marc Branchey. 2004. "Cocaine addicts with conduct disorder are typified by decreased cortisol responsivity and high plasma levels of DHEA-S." *Neuropsychobiology* 50: 161–66.

Carswell, Kenneth, Barbara Maughan, Hilton Davis, Franscesca Davenport, and Nick Goddard. 2004. "The psychosocial needs of young offenders and adolescents from an inner city area." *Journal of Adolescence* 27: 415–28.

Caspi, Avshalom, Joseph McClay, Terrie E. Moffitt, Jonathan Mill, Judy Martin, Ian W. Craig, Alan Taylor, and Richie Poulton. 2002. "Role of genotype in the cycle of violence in maltreated children." *Science* 297: 851–54.

Chang, Grace, M. A. Goetz, Louise Wilkins-Haug, and Susan Berman. 2000. "A brief intervention for prenatal alcohol use: An in-depth look." *Journal of Substance Abuse Treatment* 18: 365–69.

Chang, Grace, Tay K. McNamara, E. John Orav, Danielle Koby, Alyson Lavigne, Barbara Ludman, Nori Ann Vincitorio, and Louise Wilkins-Haug. 2005. "Brief intervention for prenatal alcohol use: A randomized trial." *Obstetrics and Gynecology* 105: 991–98.

Chang, Grace, Louise Wilkins-Haug, Susan Berman, and M. A. Goetz. 1999. "Brief intervention for alcohol use in pregnancy: A randomized trial." *Addiction* 94: 1499–508.

Coccaro, Emil F., Richard J. Kavoussi, and Richard L. Hauger. 1997. "Serotonin function and antiaggressive response to fluoxetine: A pilot study." *Biological Psychiatry* 42: 546–52.

Constantino, John N., Daniel Grosz, Paul Saenger, Donald W. Chandler, Reena Nandi, and Felton J. Earls. 1993. "Testosterone and aggression in children." *Journal of the American Academy of Child and Adolescent Psychiatry* 32: 1217–22.

Dabbs, James M., Gregory J. Jurkovic, and Robert L. Frady. 1991. "Salivary testosterone and cortisol among late adolescent male offenders." *Journal of Abnormal Child Psychology* 19 (4): 469–78.

Dabbs, James M., and Robin Morris. 1990. "Testosterone, social class, and antisocial behavior in a sample of 4,462 men." *Psychological Science* 1: 2091–1.

Daitzman, Reid, and Marvin Zuckerman. 1980. "Disinhibitory sensation seeking, personality and gonadal hormones." *Personality & Individual Differences* 1: 103–10.

Decety, Jean, Kalina J. Michalska, Yuko Akitsuki, and Benjamin B. Lahey. 2009. "Atypical empathic responses in adolescents with aggressive conduct disorder: a functional MRI investigation." *Biological Psychology* 80: 203–11.

Déry, Michele, Jean Toupin, Robert Pauzé, Henri Mercier, and Laurier Fortin. 1999. "Neuropsychological characteristics of adolescents with conduct disorder: Association with attention-deficit-hyperactivity and aggression." *Journal of Abnormal Child Psychology*: 27 (3): 225–36.

Dmitrieva, Tatyana N., Robert D. Oades, Berthold P. Hauffa, and Christian Eggers. 2001. "Dehydroepiandrosterone sulphate and corticotropin levels are high in young male patients with conduct disorder: Comparisons for growth factors, thyroid and gonadal hormones." *Neuropsychobiology* 43: 134–40.

Eckstein, L. Will, Ivan A. Shibley Jr., J. Sue Pennington, F. Melinda Carver, and Sam N. Pennington. 1997. "Changes in brain glucose levels and glucose transporter protein isoforms in alcohol- or nicotine-treated chick embryos." *Brain Research Developmental Brain Research* 103: 59–65.

Eley, Thalia C., Paul Lichtenstein, and Terrie E. Moffitt. 2003. "A longitudinal behavioral genetic analysis of the etiology of aggressive and nonaggressive antisocial behavior." *Development and Psychopathology* 15: 383–402.

Eriksson, Åsa, Sheilagh Hodgins, and Anders Tengström. 2005. "Verbal intelligence and criminal offending among men with schizophrenia." *International Journal of Forensic Mental Health* 4: 191–200.

Ershoff, Daniel H., Trinita Hall Ashford, and Robert L. Goldenberg. 2004. "Helping pregnant women quit smoking: An overview." *Tobacco Research* 6 (Supp. II): S101–S105.

Fairchild, Graeme, Stephanie H. Van Goozen, Sarah J. Strollery, and Ian M. Goodyer. 2008. "Fear conditioning and affective modulation of the startle reflex in male adolescents with early-onset or adolescence-onset conduct disorder and healthy control subjects." *Biological Psychiatry* 63: 279–85.

Farrington, David P. 1997. "The relationship between low resting heart rate and violence." In *Biosocial bases of violence*, edited by Adrian Raine, Patricia A. Brennan, David P. Farrington, and Sarnoff A. Mednick. New York: Prenum Press.

Fast, Diane K., Julianne Conry, and Christine A. Loock. 1999. "Identifying Fetal Alcohol Syndrome among youth in the criminal justice system." *Journal of Developmental and Behavioral Pediatrics* 20: 370–72.

Fergusson, David M., John L. Horwood, and Michael T. Lynskey. 1993. "Maternal smoking before and after pregnancy." *Pediatrics* 92: 815–22.

Fergusson, David M., Lianne J. Woodward, and John Horwood. 1998. "Maternal smoking during pregnancy and psychiatric adjustment in late adolescence." *Archives of General Psychiatry* 55: 721–27.

Ferris, Craig F. E., and Thomas Grisso. 1996. *Understanding aggressive behavior in children.* New York: New York Academy of Sciences.

Fishbein, Diana. 2001. *Biobehavioral Perspectives in Criminology*. Belmont, CA: Wadsworth/Thomson Learning.

Fishbein, Diana, Christopher Hyde, Brian Coe, and Mallie J. Paschall. 2004. "Neurocognitive and physiological prerequisites for prevention of adolescent drug abuse." *Journal of Primary Prevention* 24: 471–95.

Fox, Nathan A. 1991. "If it's not left, it's right: Electroencephalogram asymmetry and the development of emotion." *American Psychologist* 46: 8637–2.

Fox, Nathan A. 1994. "Dynamic cerebral processes underlying emotion regulation." In *The development of emotion regulation: Behavioral and biological considerations*, edited by Nathan A. Fox. *Monographs of the Society for Research in Child Development* 59 (23–Serial No. 240): 1526–6.

Fung, Michelle T., Adrian Raine, Rolf Loeber, Donald R. Lynam, Stuart R. Steinhauer, Peter H. Venables, and Magda Stouthamer-Loeber. 2005. "Reduced electrodermal activity in psychopathy-prone adolescents." *Journal of Abnormal Psychology* 114: 187–96.

Galler, Janina R., and Frank Ramsey. 1989. "A follow-up study of the influence of early malnutrition on development." *Journal of the American Academy of Child and Adolescent Psychiatry* 26: 23–27.

Galler, Janina R., Frank Ramsey, G. Solimano, and Walter Lowell. 1983a. "The influence of early malnutrition on subsequent behavioral development. II. Classroom behavior." *Journal of the American Academy of Child and Adolescent Psychiatry* 22: 16–22.

Galler, Janina R., Frank Ramsey, G. Solimano, Walter Lowell, and Edward Mason. 1983b. "The influence of early malnutrition on subsequent behavioural development. I. Degree of impairment of intellectual performance." *Journal of the American Academy of Child and Adolescent Psychiatry* 22: 8–15.

Gao, Yu, and Adrian Raine. 2009. "P3 event-related potential impairments in antisocial and psychopathic individuals: A meta-analysis." *Biological Psychology* 82: 199–210.

Gao, Yu, Adrian Raine, Peter H. Venables, Michael E. Dawson, and Sarnoff A. Mednick. 2010. "Association of poor childhood fear conditioning and adult crime." *American Journal of Psychiatry* 167: 56–60.

Gao, Yu, Adrian Raine, Peter H. Venables, Michael E. Dawson, and Sarnoff A. Mednick. 2009. "Reduced electrodermal fear conditioning from ages 3 to 8 years is associated with aggressive behavior at age 8 years." *Journal of Child Psychology and Psychiatry*, 51: 550–58.

Glenn, Andrea L., Adrian Raine, Peter H. Venables, and Sarnoff A. Mednick. 2007. "Early temperamental and psychophysiological precursors of adult psychopathic personality." *Journal of Abnormal Psychology* 116: 508–18.

Goldenberg, Robert L., Lorraine V. Klerman, Richard A. Windsor, and H. Pennington
    Whiteside, Jr. 2000. "Smoking in pregnancy: Final thoughts." *Tobacco Control* 9 (Supp.
    III): iii85–iii86.
Goldman, David, and Francesca Ducci. 2007. "The genetics of psychopathic disorders." In
    International handbook on psychopathic disorders and the law, vol. 1, edited by Alan R.
    Felthous and Henning Sass. West Sussex, England: John Wiley and Sons Ltd.
Gordis, Elana B., Douglas A. Granger, Elizabeth J. Susman, and Penelope K. Trickett. 2006.
    "Asymmetry between salivary cortisol and alpha-amylase reactivity to stress: Relation
    to aggressive behavior in adolescents." *Psychoneuroendocrinology* 31: 976–87.
Graig, Michael C., Marco Catani, Quinton Deeley, Latham Robert, Eileen Daly, Richard A.
    A. Kanaan, Marco Picchioni, Phillip K. McGuire, Tom Fahy, and Declan G. M.
    Murphy. 2009. "Altered connections on the road to psychopathy." *Molecular Psychiatry*
    14 (10): 946–53.
Granger, Douglas A., Elizabeth A. Shirtcliff, Carolyn Zahn-Waxler, Barbara Usher, Bonnie
    Klimes-Dougan, and Paul Hastings. 2003. "Salivary testosterone diurnal variation and
    psychopathology in adolescent males and females: Individual differences and
    developmental effects." *Development and Psychopathology* 15: 431–49.
Guy, James D., Lawrence V. Majorski, Charles J. Wallace, and Margaret P. Guy. 1983. "The
    incidence of minor physical anomalies in adult male schizophrenics." *Schizophrenia
    Bulletin* 9: 571–82.
Hallahan, Brian, Joseph R. Hibbeln, John M. Davis, and Malcolm R. Garland. 2007.
    "Omega-3 fatty acid supplementation in patients with recurrent self-harm—Single-
    centre double-blind randomised controlled trial." *British Journal of Psychiatry* 190:
    118–22.
Hankin, Janet R. 2002. "Fetal alcohol syndrome prevention research." *Alcohol Research and
    Health* 26: 58–65.
Hare, Robert D., and Jeffrey W. Jutai. 1988. "Psychopathy and cerebral asymmetry in
    semantic processing." *Personality and Individual Differences* 9: 329–37.
Herpertz, Sabine C. 2007. Electrophysiology. In *International handbook on psychopathic
    disorders and the law*, vol. 1, edited by Alan R. Felthous and Henning Sass. West Sussex,
    England: John Wiley and Sons Ltd.
Herpertz, Sabine C., Thomas Huebner, Ivo Marx, Timo D. Vloet, Gereon R. Fink, Tony
    Stoecker, N. Jon Shah, Kerstin Konrad, and Beate Herpertz-Dahlmann. 2008.
    "Emotional processing in male adolescents with childhood-onset conduct disorder."
    Journal of Child Psychology and Psychiatry 49 (7): 7819–1.
Herpertz, Sabine C., Bodo Mueller, Mutaz Qunaibi, Christiane Lichterfeld, Kerstin Konrad,
    and Beate Herpertz-Dahlmann. 2005. "Responses to emotional stimuli in boys with
    conduct disorder." *American Journal of Psychiatry* 162: 1100–107.
Herpertz, Sabine C., Bodo Mueller, Britta Wenning, Mutaz Qunaibi, Christiane Lichterfeld,
    and Beate Herpertz-Dahlmann. 2003. "Autonomic responses in boys with externalizing
    disorders." *Journal of Neural Transmission* 110: 1181–95.
Hirayama, Satoshi, Tomohito Hamazaki, and Katsutoshi Terasawa. 2004. "Effect of
    docosahexaenoic acid-containing food administration on symptoms of attention-
    deficit/hyperactivity disorder—a placebo-controlled double-blind study." *European
    Journal of Clinical Nutrition* 58: 467–73.
Huebner, Thomas, Timo D. Vloet, Ivo Marx, Kerstin Konrad, Gereon R. Fink, Sabine C.
    Herpertz, and Herpertz-Dahlmann Beate. 2008. "Morphometric brain abnormalities
    in boys with conduct disorder." *Journal of the American Academy of Child and
    Adolescent Psychiatry* 47 (5): 540–47.

Hux, Karen, Valerie Bond, Suzanne Skinner, Don Belau, and Dixie Sanger. 1998. "Parental report of occurrences and consequences of traumatic brain injury among delinquent and non-delinquent youth." *Brain Injury* 12 (8): 667–81.

Iacono, William G., Scott R. Carlson, Stephen M. Malone, and Matthew McGue. 2002. "P3 event-related potential amplitude and the risk for disinhibitory disorders in adolescent boys." *Archives of General Psychiatry* 59: 750–57.

Ishikawa, Sharon S., and Adrian Raine. 2002. "Psychophysiological correlates of antisocial behavior: A central control hypothesis." In *The neurobiology of criminal behavior*, edited by Joseph Glicksohn. Norwell: Kluwer Academic Publishers.

Jacobson, Kristen C., Carol A. Prescott, and Kenneth S. Kendler. 2002. "Sex differences in the genetic and environmental influences on the development of antisocial behavior." *Development and Psychopathology* 14: 395–416.

Jaffee, Sara R., Avshalom Caspi, Terrie E. Moffitt, Kenneth A. Dodge, Michael Rutter, Alan Taylor, and Lucy A. Tully. 2005. "Nature × nurture: Genetic vulnerabilities interact with physical maltreatment to promote conduct problems." *Development and Psychopathology* 17: 67–84.

Jaffee, Sara R., Avshalom Caspi, Terrie E. Moffitt, and Alan Taylor. 2004. "Physical maltreatment victim to antisocial child: Evidence of an environmentally-mediated process." *Journal of Abnormal Psychology* 113: 44–55.

Jones, Alice P., Kristin R. Laurens, Catherine M. Herba, Gareth J. Barker, and Essi Viding. 2009. "Amygdala hypoactivity to fearful faces in boys with conduct problems and callous-unemotional traits." *American Journal of Psychiatry* 166: 95–102.

Kibler, Jeffrey L., Vicki L. Prosser, and Mindy Ma. 2004. "Cardiovascular correlates of misconduct in children and adolescents." *Journal of Psychophysiology* 18: 184–89.

Kimonis, Eva R., Paul J. Frick, Holly Fazekas, and Bryan R. Loney. 2006. "Psychopathy, aggression, and the processing of emotional stimuli in non-referred girls and boys." *Behavioral Sciences and the Law* 24: 21–37.

Kodl Middlecamp, Molly, and Lauren S. Wakschlag. 2004. "Does a childhood history of externalizing problems predict smoking during pregnancy?" *Addictive Behaviors* 29: 273–79.

Kruesi, Markus J. P., Manuel F. Casanova, Glenn Mannheim, and Adrienne Johnson-Bilder. 2004. "Reduced temporal lobe volume in early onset conduct disorder." *Psychiatry Research Neuroimaging* 132 (1): 1–11.

Kruesi, Markus J. P., and Manuel F. Casanova. 2006. "White matter in liars." *British Journal of Psychiatry* 188: 293–94.

Kruesi, Markus J., Euthymia D. Hibbs, Theodore P. Zahn, Cynthia S. Keysor, Susan D. Hamburger, John J. Bartko, and Judith L. Rapoport. 1992. "A 2-year prospective follow-up study of children and adolescents with disruptive behavior disorders." *Archives of General Psychiatry* 49: 429–35.

Lezak, Muriel D., Diane B. Howieson, David W. Loring, H. J. Hannay, and Jill S. Fischer. 2004. *Neuropsychological Assessment*, 4th ed. New York: Oxford University Press.

Li, Tie-Qiang, Vincent P. Mathews, Yang Wang, David Dunn, and William Kronenberger. 2005. "Adolescents with disruptive behavior disorder investigated using an optimized MR diffusion tensor imaging protocol." *Annals of the New York Academy of Sciences* 1064: 184–92.

Lister, James P., Gene J. Blatt, William A. DeBassio, Thomas L. Kemper, John Tonkiss, Janina R. Galler, and Douglas L. Rosene. 2005. "Effect of prenatal protein malnutrition on numbers of neurons in the principal cell layers of the adult rat hippocampal formation." *Hippocampus* 15: 393–403.

Liu, Jianghong. 2004. "Childhood externalizing behavior: Theory and implications." *Journal of Child and Adolescent Psychiatric Nursing* 17: 93–703.

Liu, Jianghong, and Adriane Raine. 2006. "The effect of childhood malnutrition on externalizing behavior." *Current Opinion in Pediatrics* 18 (5): 565–70.

Liu, Jianghong, Adriane Raine, D. Phil, Peter H. Venables, and Sarnoff A. Mednick. 2004. "Malnutrition at age 3 years predisposes to externalizing behavior problems at ages 8, 11 and 17 years." *American Journal of Psychiatry* 161: 2005–13.

Liu, Jianghong, Adriane Raine, Anne Wuerker, Peter H. Venables, and Sarnoff Mednick. 2009. "The association of birth complications and externalizing behavior in early adolescents." *Journal of Research on Adolescence* 19 (1): 93–111.

Liu, Jianghong and Anne Wuerker. 2005. "Biosocial bases of aggressive and violent behavior—implications for nursing studies." *International Journal of Nursing Studies* 42 (2): 229–41.

Loney, Brian R., Paul J. Frick, Carl B. Clements, Mesha L. Ellis, and Kimberly Kerlin. 2003. "Callous-unemotional traits, impulsivity and emotional processing in adolescents with antisocial behavior problems." *Journal of Clinical Child and Adolescent Psychology* 32: 66–80.

Loney, Brian R., Melanie A. Butler, Elizabeth N. Lima, Carla A. Counts, and Lisa A. Eckel. 2006. "The relation between salivary cortisol, callous-unemotional traits and conduct problems in an adolescent non-referred sample." *Journal of Child Psychology and Psychiatry* 47: 306–.

Lorber, Michael F. 2004. "Psychophysiology of aggression, psychopathy, and conduct problems: A meta-analysis." *Psychological Bulletin* 130: 531–52.

Luria, Alexandr R. 1966. *Higher Cortical Functions in Man.* New York: Basic Books.

Lyons, Michael J., William R. True, Seth A. Eisen, Jack Goldberg, Joanne M. Meyer, Stephen V. Faraone, Lindon J. Eaves, and Ming T. Tsuang. 1995. "Differential heritability of adult and juvenile traits." *Archives of General Psychiatry* 52: 906–15.

Maras, Athanasios, Manfred Laucht, Dirk Gerdes, Cindy Wilhelm, Sabina Lewicka, Doris Haack, Lucie Malisova, and Martin H. Schmidt. 2003. "Association of testosterone and dihydrotestosterone with externalizing behavior in adolescent boys and girls." *Psychoneuroendocrinology* 28 (7): 932–40.

Marsh, Abigail A., Elizabeth C. Finger, Derek G. V. Mitchell, Marguerite E. Reid, Courtney Sims, David S. Kosson, Kenneth E. Towbin, Ellen Leibenluft, Daniel S. Pine, and R. J. R. Blair. 2008. "Reduced amygdala response to fearful expressions in children and adolescents with callous-unemotional traits and disruptive behavior disorders." *American Journal of Psychiatry* 165: 712–20.

Mattson, Sarah N., and Edward P. Riley. 2000. "Parent ratings of behavior in children with heavy prenatal alcohol exposure and IQ-matched controls." *Alcoholism: Clinical and Experimental Research* 24: 226–31.

Maughan, Barbara, Colin Taylor, Alan Taylor, Neville Butler, and John Bynner. 2001. "Pregnancy smoking and childhood conduct Problems: A causal association?" *Journal of Child Psychology and Psychiatry* 42: 1021–28.

Maughan, Barbara, Alan Taylor, Avshalom Caspi, and Terrie E. Moffitt. 2004. "Prenatal smoking and early childhood conduct problems." *Archives of General Psychiatry* 61: 836–43.

Mazur, Allan. 1995. "Biosocial models of deviant behavior among male army veterans." *Biological Psychology* 41: 2719–3.

McAllister, Thomas W. 1992. "Neuropsychiatric sequelae of head injuries." *The Psychiatric Clinic of North America* 15 (2): 661–65.

McBurnett, Keith, Benjamin B. Lahey, Paul J. Rathouz, and Rolf Loeber. 2000. "Low salivary cortisol and persistent aggression in boys referred for disruptive behavior." *Archives of General Psychiatry* 57: 38–43.

McBurnett, Keith, Adrian Raine, Magda Stouthamer-Loeber, Rolf Loeber, Adarsh M. Kumar, Mahendra Kumar, and Benjamin B. Lahey. 2005. "Mood and Hormone Responses to Psychological Challenge in Adolescent Males with Conduct Problems." *Biological Psychiatry* 57: 1109–16.

Mednick, Sarnoff A. 1977. "A bio-social theory of the learning of law-abiding behavior." In *Biosocial bases of criminal behavior*, edited by Sarnoff A. Mednick and K. O. Christiansen. New York: Gardner Press.

Mednick, Sarnoff A., Jan Volavka, William F. Gabrielli, Jr., and Turan M. Itil. 1981. "EEG as a predictor of antisocial behavior." *Criminology* 19: 219–29.

Miles, Donna R., and Gregory Carey. 1997. "Genetic and environmental architecture of human aggression." *Journal of Personality and Social Psychology* 72: 207–17.

Moffitt, Terrie E. 1993. "Adolescence-limited and life-course-persistent antisocial behavior: A developmental taxonomy." *Psychological Review* 100 (2): 674–701.

Moffitt, Terrie E. 2005. "The new look of behavioral genetics in developmental psychopathology: Gene-environment interplay in antisocial behavior." *Psychological Bulletin* 131: 533–54.

Moffitt, Terrie E., and Avshalom Caspi. 2001. "Childhood predictors differentiate life-course persistent and adolescence-limited antisocial pathways among males and females." *Development and Psychopathology* 13: 355–75.

Moffitt, Terrie E., and Bill Henry. 1989. "Neuropsychological assessment of executive functions in self-reported delinquents." *Development and Psychopathology* 1: 105–18.

Moffitt, Terrie E., Donald R. Lynam, and Phil A. Silva. 1994. "Neuropsychological tests predicting persistent male delinquency." *Criminology* 32 (2): 277–300.

Morgan, Alex B., and Scott O. Lilienfeld. 2000. "A meta-analytic review of the relationship between antisocial behavior and neuropsychological measures of executive function." *Clinical Psychology Review* 20 (1): 113–36.

Muneoka, Katsumasa, Tetsuo Ogawa, Kenji Kamei, Shin-ichiro Muraoka, Rika Tomiyosh, Yuichi Mimura, Hitomi Kato, Minoru R. Suzuki, and Morikuni Takigawa. 1997. "Prenatal nicotine exposure affects the development of the central serotonergic system as well as the dopaminergic system in rat offspring: Involvement of route of drug administrations." *Brain Research Developmental Brain Research* 102: 117–26.

Newman, Joseph P., and David S. Kosson. 1986. "Passive avoidance learning in psychopathic and nonpsychopathic offenders." *Journal of Abnormal Psychology* 95: 252–56.

Nigg, Joel T., Jennifer M. Glass, Maria M. Wong, Edwin Poon, Jennifer M. Jester, Hiram E. Fitzgerald, Leon I. Puttler, Kenneth M. Adams, and Robert A. Zucker. 2004. "Neuropsychological executive functioning in children at elevated risk for alcoholism: Findings in early adolescence." *Journal of Abnormal Psychology* 113 (2): 302–14.

Ochsner, Kevin N., Jennifer S. Beer, Elaine R. Robertson, Jeffrey C. Cooper, John D. E. Gabrieli, John F. Kihsltrom, Mark D'Esposito. 2005. "The neural correlates of direct and reflected self-knowledge." *NeuroImage* 28: 797–814.

Olds, David. 1997. "Tobacco exposure and impaired development: A review of the evidence." *Mental Retardation and Developmental Disabilities Research Reviews* 3: 257–69.

Olds, David, Charles R. Henderson, Robert Cole, John Eckenrode, Harriet Kitzman, Dennis Luckey, Lisa Pettitt, Kimberly Sidora, Pamela Morris, and Jane Powers. 1998. "Long-term effects of nurse home visitation on children's criminal and antisocial behavior: 15-year follow-up of a randomized controlled trial." *Journal of the American Medical Association* 280: 1238–44.

Olson, Heather C., Ann P. Streissguth, Paul D. Sampson, Helen M. Barr, Fred L. Bookstein, and Keith W. Thiede. 1997. "Association of prenatal alcohol exposure with behavioral and learning problems in early adolescence." *Journal of the American Academy of Child and Adolescent Psychiatry* 36: 1187–94.

Oosterlaan, Jaap, Hilde M. Geurts, Knol Dirk, and Joseph A. Sergeant. 2005. "Low basal salivary cortisol is associated with teacher-reported symptoms of conduct disorder." *Psychiatry Research* 134: 1–10.

Orlebeke, Jacob F., Dirk L. Knol, and Frank C. Verhulst. 1997. "Increase in child behavior problems resulting from maternal smoking during pregnancy." *Archives of Environmental Health* 52: 317–21.

Ortiz, James, and Adrian Raine. 2004. "Heart rate level and antisocial behavior in children and adolescents: A meta-analysis." *Journal of American Academy of Child and Adolescent Psychiatry* 43: 154–62.

Pajer, Kathleen, William Gardner, Robert T. Rubin, James Perel, and Stephen Neal. 2001. "Decreased cortisol levels in adolescent girls with conduct disorder." *Archives of General Psychiatry* 58: 297–302.

Pajer, Kathleen, Rhonda Tabbah, William Gardner, Robert T. Rubin, R. Kenneth Czambel, and Yun Wang. 2006. "Adrenal androgen and gonadal hormone levels in adolescent girls with conduct disorder." *Psychoneuroendocrinology* 31 (10): 1245–56.

Parker, C. Richard Jr. 1999. "Dehydroepiandrosterone and dehydroepiandrosterone sulfate production in the human adrenal during development and aging." *Steroids* 64: 640–47.

Petersen, Ingemar, Milos Matousek, Sarnoff A. Mednick, Jan Volavka, and Vicki E. Pollock. 1982. "EEG antecedents of thievery." *Acta Psychiatrica Scandinavica* 65: 331–38.

Pine, Daniel S., David Shaffer, Irvin Sam Schonfeld, and Mark Davies. 1997. "Minor physical anomalies: Modifiers of environmental risks for psychiatric impairment?" *Journal of the American Academy of Child and Adolescent Psychiatry* 36: 395–403.

Popma, Arne, and Adrian Raine. 2006. "Will future forensic assessment be neurobiologic?" *Child and Adolescent Psychiatric Clinics of North America* 15: 429–44.

Popma, Arne, Robert Vermeiren, Charlotte A. M. L. Geluk, Thomas Rinne, Wim van den Brink, Dirk L. Knol, Lucres M.C. Jansen, Herman van Engeland, and Theo A. H. Doreleijers. 2007. "Cortisol moderates the relationship between testosterone and aggression in delinquent male adolescents." *Biological Psychiatry* 61 (3): 405–11.

Raine, Adrian. 1993. *The psychopathology of crime: Criminal behavior as a clinical disorder.* San Diego, CA: Academic Press.

Raine, Adrian. 1996. "Autonomic nervous system activity and violence." In *Aggression and violence: Genetic, neurobiological, and biosocial perspective*, edited by David M. Stoff and Robert B. Cairns. Mahwah, NJ: Lawrence Erlbaum Associates.

Raine, Adrian. 2002a. "Biosocial studies of antisocial and violent behavior in children and adults: A review." *Journal of Abnormal Child Psychology* 30: 311–26.

Raine, Adrian. 2002b. "Annotation: the role of prefrontal deficits, low autonomic arousal and early health factors in the development of antisocial and aggressive behavior in children." *Journal of Child Psychology and Psychiatry and Allied Disciplines* 43: 417–34.

Raine, Adrian, Patricia Brennan, and Sarnoff A. Mednick. 1994. "Birth complications combined with early maternal rejection at age 1 year predispose to violent crime at age 18 years." *Archives of General Psychiatry* 51 (12): 984–88.

Raine, Adrian, Kjetil Mellingen, Jianghong Liu, Peter H. Venables, and Sarnoff A. Mednick. 2003. "Effects of environmental enrichment at ages 3–5 years on schizotypal personality and antisocial behavior at ages 17 and 23 years." *American Journal of Psychiatry* 160: 1627–35.

Raine, Adrian, Terrie E. Moffitt, Avshalom Caspi, Rolf Loeber, Magda Stouthamer-Loeber, and Don Lynam. 2005. "Neurocognitive impairments in boys on the life-course persistent antisocial path." *Journal of Abnormal Psychology* 114 (1): 38–49.

Raine, Adrian, Mary O'Brien, Norine Smiley, Angela Scerbo, and Cheryl-Jean Chan. 1990. "Reduced lateralization in verbal dichotic listening in adolescent psychopaths." *Journal of Abnormal Psychology* 99: 272–77.

Raine, Adrian, Chandra Reynolds, Peter H. Venables, and Sarnoff A. Mednick. 1997. "Biosocial bases of aggressive behavior in childhood." In *Biosocial bases of violence*, edited by Adrian Raine, Patricia A. Brennan, David P. Farrington and Sarnoff A. Mednick. New York: Plenum.

Raine, A., Chandra Reynolds, Peter H. Venables, Sarnoff A. Mednick, and David P. Farrington. 1998. "Fearlessness, stimulation-seeking, and large body size at age 3 years as early predispositions to childhood aggression at age 11 years." *Archives of General Psychiatry* 55: 745–51.

Raine, Adrian, and Peter H. Venables. 1981. "Classical conditioning and socialization—A biosocial interaction." *Personality and Individual differences* 2: 273–83.

Raine, Adrian, Peter H. Venables, Cyril Dalais, Kjetil Mellingen, Chandra Reynolds, and Sarnoff A. Mednick. 2001. "Early educational and health enrichment at age 3–5 years is associated with increased autonomic and central nervous system arousal and orienting at age 11 years: Evidence from the Mauritius Child Health Project." *Psychophysiology* 38: 254–66.

Raine, Adrian, Peter H. Venables, and Sarnoff A. Mednick. 1997. "Low resting heart rate age 3 years predisposes to aggression at age 11 years: Evidence from the Mauritius Child Health Project." *Journal of American Academy of Child and Adolescent Psychiatry* 36: 1457–64.

Raine, Adrian, Peter H. Venables, and Mark Williams. 1990a. "Relationships between central and autonomic measures of arousal at age 15 years and criminality at age 24 years." *Archives of General Psychiatry* 47: 1003–1007.

Raine, Adrian, Peter H. Venables, and Mark Williams. 1990b. "Relationships between N1, P300, and contingent negative variation recorded at age 15 and criminal behavior at age 24." *Psychophysiology* 27: 567–74.

Raine, Adrian, Peter H. Venables, and Mark Williams. 1995. "High autonomic arousal and electrodermal orienting at age 15 years as protective factors against criminal behavior at age 29 years." *American Journal of Psychiatry* 152: 1595–600.

Raine, Adrian, Peter H. Venables, and Mark Williams. 1996. "Better autonomic conditioning and faster electrodermal half-recovery time at age 15 years as possible protective factors against crime at age 29 years." *Developmental Psychology* 32: 6243–0.

Rantakallio, Paula, Markku Koiranen, and Jyrka Mottonen. 1992. "Association of prenatal events, epilepsy, and central nervous system trauma with juvenile delinquency." *Archives of Disease in Childhood* 67: 1459–61.

Rantakallio, Paula, Esa Laara, Matti Isohanni, and Kristiina Moilanen. 1992. "Maternal smoking during pregnancy and delinquency of the offspring: An association without causation?" *International Journal of Epidemiology* 21: 1106–13.

Rhee, Soo Hyun, and Irving D. Waldman. 2002. "Genetic and environmental influences on antisocial behavior: A meta-analysis of twin and adoption studies." *Psychological Bulletin* 128: 490–529.

Rimel, Rebecca W., Bruno Giordani, Jeffrey Barth, Thomas Boll, and John Jane. 1981. "Disability caused by minor head injury." *Neurosurgery* 9 (3): 1459–61.

Rivera, May B., Kenneth M. Jaffe, Nayak L. Polissar, Gayle C. Fay, Martin Karen, Hillary A. Shurtleff, and Shiquan Liao. 1994. "Family functioning and children's academic performance and behavior problems in the year following traumatic brain injury." *Archives of Physical Medicine and Rehabilitation* 75 (4): 369–79.

Roebuck, Tresa M., Sarah N. Mattson, and Edward P. Riley. 1999. "Behavioral and psychosocial profiles of alcohol-exposed children." *Alcoholism: Clinical and Experimental Research* 23: 1070–76.

Rolls, Edmund T. 2000. "The orbitofrontal cortex and reward." *Cerebral Cortex* 10: 284–94.

Rosen, Gerald M., Amos S. Deinard, Samuel Schwartz, Clark Smith, Betty Stephenson, and Brenda Grabenstein. 1985. "Iron deficiency among incarcerated juvenile delinquents." *Journal of Adolescent Health Care* 6: 419–23.

Roussy, Sylvain, and Jean Toupin. 2000. "Behavioral inhibition deficits in juvenile psychopaths." *Aggressive Behavior* 26: 413–24.

Rowe, David C. 1986. "Genetic and environmental components of antisocial behavior: A study of 265 twin pairs." *Criminology* 24: 513–32.

Rubia, Katya, Rozmin Halari, Anna B. Smith, Majeed Mohammad, Steven Scott, Vincent Giampietro, Eric Taylor, and Michael J. Brammer. 2008. "Dissociated functional brain abnormalities of inhibition in boys with pure conduct disorder and in boys with pure attention deficit hyperactivity disorder." *American Journal of Psychiatry* 165: 889–97.

Rubia, Katya, Anna B. Smith, Rozmin Halari, Fumie Matsukura, Majeed Mohammad, Eric Taylor, and Michael J. Brammer. 2009. "Disorder-specific dissociation of orbitofrontal dysfunction in boys with pure conduct disorder during reward and ventrolateral prefrontal dysfunction in boys with pure ADHD during sustained attention." *American Journal of Psychiatry* 166: 83–94.

Santesso, Diane L., Dana L. Reker, Louis A. Schmidt, and Sidney J. Segalowitz. 2006. "Frontal electroencephalogram activation asymmetry, emotional intelligence, and externalizing behaviors in 10-year-old children." *Child Psychiatry and Human Development* 36: 311–28.

Scerbo, Angela, Adrian Raine, Mary O'Brien, Cheryl-Jean Chan, Cathy Rhee, and Norine Smiley. 1990. "Reward Dominance and Passive Avoidance Learning in Adolescent Psychopaths." *Journal of Abnormal Child Psychology* 18: 451–63.

Schoenthaler, Stephen J., Stephen Amos, Walter Doraz, Mary-Ann Kelly, George Muedeking, and James Wakefield. 1997. "The effect of randomised vitamin-mineral supplementation on violent and non-violent antisocial behavior among incarcerated juveniles." *Journal of Nutritional and Environmental Medicine* 7: 343–52.

Schoenthaler, Stephen J., and Ian D. Bier. 2000. "The effect of vitamin-mineral supplementation on juvenile delinquency among American schoolchildren: a randomized, doubleblind placebo-controlled trial." *The Journal of Alternative and Complementary Medicine* 6: 19–29.

Schonfeld, Amy M., Sarah N. Mattson, and Edward P. Riley. 2005. "Moral Maturity and Delinquency after Prenatal Alcohol Exposure." *Journal of Studies on Alcohol* 66: 545–54.

Schulz, Kurt P., Jeffrey M. Halperin, Jeffrey H. Newcorn, Vanshdeep Sharma, and S. Gabriel. 1997. "Plasma cortisol and aggression in boys with ADHD." *Journal of the American Academy of Child and Adolescent Psychiatry* 36: 605–609.

Séguin, Jean R., Daniel Nagin, Jean-Marc Assad, and Richard E. Tremblay. 2004. "Cognitive-neuropsychological function in chronic physical aggression and hyperactivity." *Journal of Abnormal Psychology* 113 (4): 603–13.

Shamay-Tsoory, Simone G., Rachel Tomer, B. D. Berger, Dorit Goldsher, and Judith Aharon-Peretz. 2005. "Impaired "affective theory of mind" is associated with right ventromedial prefrontal damage." *Cognitive Behavioral Neurology* 18 (1): 55–67.

Shoal, Gavin D., Peter R. Giancola, and Galina P. Kilrillova. 2003. "Salivary cortisol, personality, and aggressive behavior in adolescent boys: a 5-year longitudinal study." *Child and Adolescent Psychiatry and Mental Health* 42: 1101–107.

Slutske, Wendy S., Andrew C. Heath, Stephen H. Dinwiddie, Pamela A. F. Madden, Kathleen K. Bucholz, Michael P. Dunne, Dixie J. Statham, and Nicholas G. Martin. 1997. "Modeling genetic and environmental influences in the etiology of conduct disorder: A study of 2,682 adult twin pairs." *Journal of Abnormal Psychology* 106: 266–79.

Spreen, Otfried, and Elisabeth Strauss. 1998. *A Compendium of Neuropsychological Tests*, 2nd ed. New York: Oxford University Press.

Stadler, Christina, Dorte Grasmann, Jorg M. Fegert, Martin Holtmann, Fritz Poustka, and Klaus Schmeck. 2008. "Heart rate and treatment effect in children with disruptive behavior disorders." *Child Psychiatry and Human Development* 39: 299–309.

Sterzer, Phillip, Christina Stadler, Annette Krebs, Andreas Kleinschmidt, and Fritz Poustka. 2005. "Abnormal neural responses to emotional visual stimuli in adolescents with conduct disorder." *Biological Psychiatry* 57: 7–15.

Sterzer, Philipp, Christina Stadler, Fritz Poustka, and Andreas Kleinschmidt. 2007. "A structural neural deficit in adolescents with conduct disorder and its association with lack of empathy." *Neuroimage* 37 (1): 335–42.

Stevens, Laura, Wen Zhang, Louise Peck, Thomas Kuczek, Nels Grevstad, Anne Mahon, Sydney S. Zentall, L. Eugene Arnold, and John R. Burgess. 2003. "EFA supplementation in children with inattention, hyperactivity, and other disruptive behaviors." *Lipids* 38: 1007–21.

Streissguth, Ann P., Helen M. Barr, Julia Kogan, & Fred L. Bookstein. 1996. Understanding the occurrence of secondary disabilities in clients with fetal alcohol syndrome (FAS) and fetal alcohol effects (FAE). Washington, DC: Centers for Disease Control and Prevention.

Teichner, Gordon, and Charles J. Golden. 2000. "The relationship of neuropsychological impairment to conduct Disorder in adolescence: A conceptual review." *Aggression and Violent Behavior* 5 (6): 509–28.

van Bokhoven, Irene, Stephanie H.M. van Goozen, Herman van Engeland, Benoist Scaal, Louise Arseneault, Jean R. Seguin, Daniel S. Nagin, Frank Vitaro, and Richard E. Tremblay. 2005. "Salivary cortisol and aggression in a population-based longitudinal study of adolescent males." *Journal of Neural Transmission* 112:10831–896.

van Goozen, Stephanie H.M., Walter Matthys, Peggy T. Cohen-Kettenis, Jan K. Buielaar, and Herman van Engeland. 2000. "Hypothalamic-pituitary-adrenal axis and auonomic nervous system activity in disruptive children and matched controls." *Journal of the American Academy of Child and Adolescent Psychiatry* 39:14384–5.

van Goozen, Stephanie H. M., Walter Matthys, Peggy T. Cohen-Kettenis, Jos H. H. Thijssen, and Herman van Engeland. 1998a. "Adrenal androgens and aggression in conduct disorder prepubertal boys and normal controls." *Biological Psychiatry* 43: 156–58.

van Goozen, Stephanie H. M., Walter Matthys, Peggy T. Cohen-Kettenis, Christien Gispen-de Wied, Victor M. Wiegant, and Herman van Engeland. 1998b. "Salivary cortisol and cardiovascular activity during stress in oppositional defiant disorder boys and normal controls." *Biological Psychiatry* 43: 531–39.

van Honk, Jack, and Dennis J. L. G. Schutter. 2006. "Unmasking feigned sanity: A neurobiological model of emotion processing in primary psychopathy." *Cognitive Neuropsychiatry* 11 (3): 285–306.

Veneziano, Carol, Louis Veneziano, Scott LeGrand, and Linda Richards. 2004. "Neuropsychological executive functions of adolescent sex offenders and nonsex offenders." *Perceptual and Motor Skills* 98: 661–74.

Vermeiren, Robert, Antoine De Clippele, Mary Schwab-Stone, Vladislav Ruchkin, and Dirk Deboutte. 2002. "Neuropsychological characteristics of three subgroups of Flemish delinquent adolescents." *Neuropsychology* 16 (1): 49–55.

Vitale, Jennifer E., Joseph P. Newman, John E. Bates, Jackson Goodnight, Kenneth A. Dodge, and Gregory S. Pettit. 2005. "Deficient behavioral inhibition and anomalous selective attention in a community sample of adolescents with psychopathic traits and low-anxiety traits." *Journal of Abnormal Child Psychology* 33: 461–70.

Volavka, Jan. 1987. "Electroencephalogram among criminals." In *The causes of crime: New biological approaches*, edited by Sarnoff A. Mednick, Terrie E. Moffitt, and Susan A. Stack. Cambridge: Cambridge University Press.

Völlm, Birgit, P. Richardson, S. McKie, R. Elliott, J. F. W. Deakin, and I. M. Anderson. (2006). Serotonergic modulation of neuronal responses to behavioural inhibition and reinforcing stimuli: an fMRI study in healthy volunteers. *European Journal of Neuroscience*, 23, 552–60.

Wakschlag, Lauren S., Benjamin B. Lahey, Rolf Loeber, Stephanie M. Green, Rachel A. Gordon, and Bennett L. Leventhal. 1997. "Maternal smoking during pregnancy and the risk of conduct disorder in boys." *Archives of General Psychiatry* 54: 670–76.

Wakschlag, Lauren S., Kate E. Pickett, Edwin C. Cook, Neal L. Benowitz, and Bennett L. Leventhal. 2002. "Maternal smoking during pregnancy and severe antisocial behavior in offspring: A review." *American Journal of Public Health* 92: 966–74.

Wakschlag, Lauren S., Kate E. Pickett, Molly K. Middlecamp, Laura L. Walton, Penny Tenzer, & Bennett L. Leventhal. 2003. "Pregnant smokers who quit, pregnant smokers who don't: Does history of problem behavior make a difference?" *Social Science and Medicine* 56: 2449–60.

Werbach, Melvyn R. 1992. "Nutritional influences on aggressive behavior." *Journal of Orthomolecular Medicine* 7: 455–1.

White, Jennifer L., Terrie E. Moffitt, Avshalom Caspi, Dawn J. Bartusch, Douglas J. Needles, and Magda Stouthamer-Loeber. 1994. "Measuring impulsivity and examining its relationship to delinquency." *Journal of Abnormal Psychology* 103 (2): 192–205.

CHAPTER 5

ADOLESCENT DEVELOPMENT, DELINQUENCY, AND JUVENILE JUSTICE

JENNIFER L. WOOLARD

SOME form of delinquency is a normative part of adolescence for a majority of teens, yet the consequences of risky behavior and juvenile justice involvement can be severe. Explanations of delinquent behavior that focus on individual development must reconcile its apparent normative nature, at least for some types of offenses, with the fact that most adolescents desist from delinquent behavior as they mature into adulthood. Over the past several decades, an interdisciplinary body of research integrating developmental, clinical, and social psychological studies and neurobiological perspectives has emerged to shed light on the decisional capacities of adolescents to engage in delinquent and criminal behavior, and operate as defendants in the juvenile and criminal justice systems.

Present in cognitive, developmental, and social psychological research, dual process explanations of decision-making incorporate both conscious controlled influences and automatic unconscious influences on decision-making processes and behavior. They have recently been applied to adolescent decision-making, including that of risky behavior generally and delinquent behavior specifically (Byrnes 2005; Klaczynski 2001; Kuhn 2009; Reyna and Farley 2006; Steinberg 2008). Although the details vary across different dual process explanations, commonly one component represents an analytic, deliberate, reasoned set of capacities. The other system is alternatively described as impulsive, spontaneous, intuitive, emotional, and experiential. The two processes may operate simultaneously, but not necessarily equally. Based on behavioral, self-report, and neurobiological data, adolescence appears to be the developmental period in which the analytical cognitive system reaches maturity by the mid-teens, but the experiential or socio-emotional system continues to develop in some aspects well into young adulthood. Thus, the basic cognitive capacities of adolescents aged 16 and older as a class are not easily differentiated from those of the class of young adults. There remains significant heterogeneity within both groups' cognitive capacities, but the differences between groups are more likely due to individual characteristics than they are to normative development per se. By contrast, adolescent socio-emotional capacities include both potentially enduring individual differences and the developmental immaturity that will change once normative development is complete. Because the socio-emotional system is not yet fully mature for adolescents as a group, it is difficult to determine whether an individual adolescent who is socio-emotionally immature will grow out of that immaturity or remain immature throughout adulthood. As a result, the relevant developmental challenges distinguishing the adolescent period from adulthood concern the maturation of the psychosocial and affective, or emotional, factors of the socio-emotional system and its integration with the cognitive system.

Keating (2004) describes three categories of biological changes that are key to understanding cognitive development and relevant to decision-making in adolescence. First, the physical changes of puberty include changes in brain structure and function as well as endocrine and neuro-endocrine changes. Second, changes in the brain itself, specifically in terms of prefrontal cortex maturation and increased connectivity between cortical regions, improve executive functioning and processing speed and efficiency, respectively. Finally, he notes that developmental experience can shape a number of changes in the brain. Biological embedding of experience through neural sculpting is one way in which the physical patterns and neuronal connections in the brain can change depending on sensory input during critical periods of development, for example (Keating and Hertzman 1999).

Self-regulation as a concept comes closest to capturing the nature of this integration between cognitive and socio-emotional systems. Executive function represents the active or "doing" aspect of the self. Baumeister and colleagues (2007) argue that executive function consists of self-regulation and choice, both of which are relevant to adolescent delinquency. Perhaps most simply, they define self-regulation as "the self altering its own responses or inner states" (Baumeister, Schmeichel, and Vohs 2007, p. 517). They describe three basic elements of self-regulation. A commitment to standards represents the ideals and aspirations of what the self should be and the motivation to comply and conform to those standards. Monitoring is the capacity to identify behavior in order to change it. Finally, the capacity to make changes allows individuals to act on those desired changes.

Steinberg (2008) emphasizes three specific aspects of self-regulation relevant to understanding age differences in delinquent behavior: (1) interrupting a trajectory in motion ("getting off a runaway train"); (2) thinking before acting ("not jumping the gun"); and (3) choosing between alternatives ("doing the right thing"). Each requires awareness of behavior and possible choices, the recognition of some standard or "right" choice, and the capacity to make that choice. Byrnes (2005) describes self-regulation in terms of accurate meta-knowledge and appropriate responses to decision outcomes. He also incorporates "the tendency to use strategies to overcome the obstacles and distractions imposed by limited resources, lack of knowledge, certain personality traits, and strong emotion" (Byrnes 2005, p. 14).

Although the terms executive function and self-regulation are used somewhat broadly and sometimes interchangeably in the developmental literature, in this chapter we focus on aspects most relevant to adolescent delinquency and justice processing. In the first section, we examine the cognitive factors developing during adolescence, finding that adolescents appear to perform comparably to adults by about age 16. In the second section, we examine psychosocial factors of susceptibility to peer influence and future orientation and their continued development in the adolescent period. The third section reviews the developing challenge of regulating emotions and affective responses that continues well into young adulthood. For each of these three parts, we briefly describe the biological and brain changes thought to correspond with the behavioral and self-report data reviewed. Finally, in the fourth section, we place adolescents in their ecological context, describing how unique relationships between adolescents, parents, and the state present challenges for adolescents that no other age group faces in the legal system. As defendants, adolescents have constitutional rights and must make their own decisions about confessions and plea agreements; no one can waive their constitutional rights against their will. As developing youths, adolescents do not yet command the full panoply of cognitive and socio-emotional capacities available to adults. As legally dependent children, adolescents are subject to the control and authority of their parents. These characteristics uniquely position adolescents in the justice system.

I. THE COGNITIVE CONTROL SYSTEM

Traditional cognitive computational models presume that actors rationally calculate the risks and benefits of a decision using rules that compute some outcome such as subjective expected utility. Poor decision-making might be a result of incomplete or inaccurate information about the extent of risk generally and for an individual specifically. However, recent reviews suggest that adolescents perceive and estimate risk likelihood in ways comparable to adults (Boyer 2006; Steinberg 2008). In their review, Reyna and Farley (2006) conclude that adolescents do demonstrate optimistic bias—or the tendency to overestimate the potential benefits of important risks—but underestimate harmful consequences. However, they are no more biased in this regard than adults. Even the long-held notion that adolescents perceive themselves as invulnerable compared to adults has been undercut by data suggesting that adolescents have an acute sense of their risk in various situations

(Steinberg 2004). While recognizing benefits and risks to potential decisions, adolescents tend to emphasize the benefits accruing from risky decisions compared to losses (Reyna and Farley 2006).

The cognitive abilities of adolescents have played a significant role in research on adolescents' capacities as defendants in the justice system. The extant literature has taken on two broad challenges: identifying the capacities and capabilities relevant to legal standards such as competence to stand trial or waive *Miranda* rights, and identifying the influences on juveniles' performance under a variety of conditions and contexts (Woolard and Reppucci 2000). Competence to stand trial sets the minimum standard for defendants' capacities that are required for their cases to go forward, although whether an individual will be found to meet the legal standard depends on evidence regarding the person's abilities as well as judicial interpretation of that evidence.

Studies examining youths' knowledge and their capacity to learn required information indicate that adolescents aged 15 and older demonstrate comparable cognitive performance to adults. Grisso and colleagues (2003) assessed adjudicative competence capacities in 1,393 adolescents and adults from the community or incarcerated pending trial. When tested with the MacArthur Competence Assessment Tool for Criminal Adjudication (MacCAT-CA), which measures capacities for understanding relevant legal knowledge, reasoning logically about that information and appreciating the relevance to one's own individual circumstances, juveniles aged 15 and younger were significantly more likely than older adolescents and adults to demonstrate significant impairments on at least one component of the MacCAT-CA that are comparable to those demonstrated by mentally ill adults likely to be found incompetent to stand trial. These age-based differences did not vary by demographic factors such as gender, race, ethnicity, or socioeconomic status. Low IQ interacted with age to disadvantage youth to a greater extent than adults with similar IQ deficits.

To examine whether youth were capable of learning the information that they lacked, Viljoen and colleagues (2007) analyzed a subcomponent of the MacCAT-CA data in which participants with suboptimal scores on six of the eight Understanding subscale items are "taught" the correct information and then assessed again. Adolescents aged 13 and younger, as well as those with low IQ, were less likely to benefit from teaching than older adolescents and adults. Although the causes and longevity of the improvements are not well understood, the findings suggest that the youngest adolescents may have significant capacity issues that the provision of information may not remediate.

Youth under age 15 are also significantly more impaired than older youths and adults in their understanding and appreciation of the *Miranda* warnings, including the right to remain silent, protection against self-incrimination, the right to an attorney before and after questioning, and the right to a court-appointed attorney if indigent (Woolard, Cleary, Harvell, and Chen 2008). In a study of police knowledge among 170 parent-youth pairs, only about half of the 11- to 13-year-olds understood that an individual does not have to answer a police officer's questions and may stop answering questions at any time, compared to approximately two-thirds of 14- to 15-year-olds and more than 80% of 16- to 17-year-olds. Moreover, only 30% of 11- to 13-year-olds correctly understood that the police can lie to them during questioning, compared to 50% of 14- to 15-year-olds and 68% of the 16- to 17-year-olds.

Although performance may vary across individuals, contexts, and tasks, a consensus is emerging in the literature that basic cognitive factors relevant to decision-making likely mature during adolescence, probably somewhere around age 15 or 16 (Kuhn 2009). Boyer (2006) highlights the contradiction that this body of work presents—adolescence is a time of maturing cognitive capacities to understand risk, which would presumably reduce risk-taking behavior; however, adolescence is a time of heightened risk-taking activity. Steinberg (2008) criticizes the extant literature on risky decisions for three reasons: (1) it studies adolescents individually but real-life risk-taking often occurs in groups; (2) it uses hypothetical dilemmas with limited ecological validity; and (3) emotional arousal is usually controlled in research but often important to real-life decision-making contexts.

As one explanation, dual systems theories and related fuzzy trace theories[A] posit that cognitive influences on decision-making derive from both a conscious, rational system and an automatic experiential system (Boyer 2006; Klaczynski 2001; Kuhn 2009; Reyna and Farley 2006). While becoming more sophisticated and efficient during adolescence, the experiential system allows decision-making shortcuts, or heuristics, to play an increasing role in decision-making. With greater development and experience come the capacity to recognize situations, or relate new decisions to similar decisions in the past, and develop shortcuts to more optimal solutions rather than relying on trial and error or more deliberate decision processes. While ultimately perhaps more efficient, these heuristics, or biases, can contradict or bypass the conscious, rational system and result in risky decisions, particularly if they result in ignoring important information (Boyer 2006). Thus, depending on decision context or circumstances, individuals can appear both rational and irrational in their decision-making processes and choices.

II. The Socio-emotional System: Psychosocial Factors

The irrational or risky component of adolescent decision-making derives in part from psychosocial factors and immature self-regulatory processes. In particular, research on delinquency and development emphasizes several psychosocial factors that are particularly relevant to the legal processing of adolescents—especially susceptibility to peer influence and future orientation (Steinberg et al. 2009).

Adolescents are subject to, and sensitive to, peer influence in ways that adults simply are not. Brown and colleagues (2008) conceptualize peer influence in terms of an event-influence-response sequence in which an act occurs, peer influence is activated, a youth responds to that influence (e.g., accepting, rejecting, countering), and the outcome of that attempted influence results. The path between activation of influences and a youth's response can be moderated by individual factors (e.g., age, gender) and contextual factors (e.g., cultural background). Moreover, a youth's openness to influence, salience of influences, relationship dynamics, and the ability/ opportunity to perform a behavior also ultimately affect behavior. For example, Brown and colleagues note that individual peers vary in their importance; pressure brought to bear by a close friend means something different than a casual acquaintance or stranger. Adolescents spend significant time with peers, and crime data confirm that the majority of adolescent delinquency and crime occurs in groups (Zimring 1998). Developmental data confirm that peer relationships become more salient and complex in adolescence (Brown and Larson 2009); salience may be the dimension that makes peer influence more meaningful to adolescents than adults (Scott, Reppucci, and Woolard 1995; Steinberg and Cauffman 1996). Combined, these two statements suggest that decision-making may be influenced by peers in ways that, for most adolescents, will change as they mature into adulthood. Given the social structure of adolescence, though, it is possible that adolescents simply have more opportunities to be influenced by their peers than adults do.

In their study of capacities relevant to adjudicative competence, Grisso and colleagues (2003) examined resistance to peer pressure among adolescents and adults in pretrial detention and the community in response to vignettes about three decision points in the legal process—police interrogation, attorney consultation, and plea agreement consideration. Younger adolescents were more likely to comply with authority (e.g., confess, talk to the attorney, accept a plea agreement) than older adolescents and adults. When presented with information that a peer recommended the opposite choice, interesting age-by-choice interactions emerged for the interrogation scenario. Among all participants who initially chose to confess, willingness to comply with peers increased with age; that is, adults were more likely to change their minds and decide to remain silent, whereas younger adolescents were more likely to stand firm in their decision to confess. The opposite trend occurred among participants who initially chose to remain silent; more of the young adolescents were persuaded by friends' advice to confess than older adolescents and adults.

Gardner and Steinberg (2005) experimentally tested the age-based nature of peer influence in a simulated driving task. Adolescent, college-aged, and adult participants completed a computer task in which the goal was to get a moving car as close to the wall as possible without crashing. A yellow light would signal the proximity of the wall, but each trial varied in the lapsed time between the yellow light and the appearance of the red light and a brick wall. Participants were randomly assigned to complete the task by themselves or in the presence of two same-aged peers they either brought to the laboratory or were acquainted with from the recruiting site (e.g., camp, classroom). All participants took more risks, and emphasized benefits over risks in the risky decision questionnaire, when in the group condition compared to the alone condition. This effect of peer presence on these measures was stronger for the adolescents compared to the adults. Age did not influence measures of risk preference, however. The authors conclude that age-based differences in responses to peer pressure should not be attributed to exposure time, but rather the sensitivity to, and capacity to resist, peer influence changes during the course of adolescence into young adulthood. As Brown and Larson (2009) note, Gardner and Steinberg's findings emphasize that future research on peer influence might usefully distinguish the overt, direct influence of peer pressure with the more subtle aspects of peer encouragement, which may also influence adolescent behavior.

Finally, adolescents have a different future orientation. The broad category of future orientation encompasses a variety of concepts that include cognitive, attitudinal, and motivational components (Steinberg et al. 2009). A recent study of executive function among more than 900 persons aged 11 to 35 examined both self-report dimensions (time perspective, anticipation of future consequences, planning ahead, impulsivity) and behavioral assessments of future orientation using the delay discounting task, which identifies the point at which the value of a larger delayed reward and a smaller immediate reward become equivalent—the "tipping point" (Steinberg et al. 2009). Consistent with prior work, orientation toward the future increased across behavioral and self-report measures from early adolescence into adulthood; findings did not vary by gender or ethnicity. In the delay discounting task, preference for the larger delayed reward grew stronger across adolescence into adulthood. These age differences in discounting were mediated by future orientation but not by impulsivity.

These age-based differences have also been found in studies more directly related to legal constructs such as competence and culpability. In the MacArthur study of adjudicative competence and decision-making (Grisso et al. 2003), the youngest participants, aged 11 to 13, identified fewer long-term consequences of their recommended decisions across interrogation, attorney consultation, and plea agreement vignettes than older adolescents and adults, who did not differ from each other. An innovative video study that asked fifty-six adolescents aged 13 to 18 to identify potential consequences of an unfolding robbery-turned-homicide found that mid-adolescents (aged 14 to 15) had lower future orientation than the younger and older adolescents (Fried and Reppucci 2001).

Self-regulation can affect the perception of time. Greater regulatory attention and effort correlate with longer estimates of time duration; expending resources to control oneself makes time feel slower, perhaps in part because of the increased attention to time and self-monitoring (Vohs and Schmeichel 2003). Moreover, periods of intense self-regulation are often followed by periods of depleted or less effective self-regulation. Thus, it is possible that adolescents expend more effort regulating themselves, may view time as moving more slowly, and may thus react differently to crime and court-processing circumstances than adults with more developed regulatory capacities.

III. The Psychosocial System: Affective and Emotional Factors

The second category of influences in the socio-emotional system are affective and emotional factors (Boyer 2006). Affective influences include how people react to emotion-provoking experiences and how those reactions influence decision-making processes, including encoding information, retrieving information, and making a decision (Dahl 2004). Rivers and colleagues (2008) distinguish several aspects of emotional responses that may affect decision-making: valence (whether something is good or bad); feelings or mood states and their centrality to the decision; arousal (level of physiological activation); and discrete emotional states (e.g., fear, anger, sadness). More generally, the concepts of hot cognition and cold cognition, referring to decision-making under conditions of high and low arousal, respectively, have gained traction in explanations of adolescent delinquency.

Two of the main factors discussed in terms of delinquency and decision-making are impulsivity and sensation-seeking. Although sometimes used interchangeably, impulsivity refers to a lack of inhibitory control over responses, whereas sensation-seeking describes the desire for novel, stimulating experiences (Reyna and Farley 2006; Steinberg et al. 2008). Both sensation-seeking and impulsivity relate to arousal. Emotionally arousing stimuli are attended to and processed preferentially, compared to neutral stimuli (Rivers, Reyna, and Mills 2008). Among adolescents, arousal is associated with greater response to rewards (Rivers, Reyna, and Mills 2008).

The study of executive function by Steinberg and colleagues (Steinberg et al. 2009) examined age-based differences in impulsivity with several scales of the Barratt self-report inventory, including motor impulsivity, inability to delay gratification, and lack of perseverance, as well as behavioral measures. Participants aged 10 through 13 reported significantly higher impulsivity scores than those aged 26 to 30; no other groups were distinguishable. These age differences were consistent with a behavioral index of impulsivity from the Tower of London assessment. The Tower of London task presents three pegs of different sizes with three colored balls. By moving one ball at a time, participants must go from the starting position to a pictured end position in the least number of moves possible. Unbeknownst to participants, the trials increased in complexity from solutions requiring a minimum of three moves to trials requiring a sequence of seven moves. Impulsivity was measured in the latency to first move—how much time participants took between viewing the pegs (start position and end position) and moving the first ball to solve the puzzle.

Older participants took longer than younger participants overall, but a significant age-by-problem complexity interaction demonstrated that young adults (aged 18 to 25 and 26 to 30) took longer to begin solving the most complex puzzles than older teens (aged 16 to 17), who in turn took longer than the youngest participants (aged 10 to 15). This study cannot distinguish whether impulsivity itself decreases across age or whether the capacity to control impulses increases, but either explanation is consistent with increasing executive control well into young adulthood. In that same study, the authors used a subset of items from the Zuckerman Sensation Seeking scale and a behavioral task to assess age differences in sensation seeking. Both behavioral and self-report measures showed higher sensation seeking between ages 12 and 15 than in later adolescence and adulthood.

Hypothesized age differences in the impact of affective and cognitive process are also supported by physiological developments of puberty and changes in brain development during adolescence. Steinberg (2004, 2008) argues that the risky behavior so common in adolescence is not a function of failed or deficient cognitions about risk but rather is in part a function of increased sensitivity to reward of stimulation and novelty. Adolescents may have adult-like capacities to understand risks but simply prefer to engage in more risky activities than adults. This risk preference, or sensation-seeking, is thought to have some biological bases in pubertal changes in the limbic system, which is connected with arousal and emotion (Dahl 2008). Several studies demonstrate adolescents' increased or hypersensitivity to rewards and incentives in subcortical regions (e.g., amygdala and ventral striatum) compared to adults (Somerville, Jones, and Casey 2010).

Brain structures associated with the capacity to self-regulate, or executive control, develop more slowly than the brain areas associated with cognitive control mechanisms. Pubertal development is linked with early changes in the affective system and greater decision-making, but Dahl (2008) reminds us that the relationship is more complex than a simple one-to-one correspondence. Functional MRI studies of adolescent decision-making, compared to adults, see less engagement of prefrontal areas associated with self-regulation. This may allow the affective system to exert more control over adolescents than mature adults (Dahl 2008). It is not only the later development of the affective system but also the emerging integration of the cognitive and affective systems in adolescence and young adulthood that supports increasing self-regulation and executive control (Dahl 2004; Keating 2004). Steinberg and colleagues (2008) argue that the adolescent's interest in sensation-seeking and rewards (compared to losses) develops earlier in adolescence than the capacities for self-regulation, which check or tamp down those proclivities in late adolescence and early adulthood.

The salience of affective influences also derives empirical support from Figner and colleagues' (2009) test of the role of affective and deliberative processes among younger adolescents, older adolescents, and adults. Their series of experiments investigated risk-taking level and complexity of information use in the Columbia Card Task under "hot" and "cold" conditions. Participants could turn over cards so long as each showed a gain. Once a loss card was uncovered, the turning stopped and the loss amount was deducted from the face-up cards. For each trial, participants knew the number of hidden loss cards, gain amount per card, and loss amount. In the hot condition, participants turned one card at a time, receiving immediate feedback on the gain or loss; in the cold condition, participants simply decided how many cards to turn over but did not specify the order; all of them were turned over simultaneously.

As predicted, the two younger groups took more risks and used less complex information strategies than adults in the affectively laden hot condition, focusing on the probability of a loss, failing to take loss amount into account, and considering gain amount less consistently than adults, whose decision involved all three factors. Sensation-seeking predicted risk-taking in the hot condition, whereas measure of executive function did not.

In contrast, adolescents took comparable risks to adults in the cold condition, but their information use complexity was either comparable to or less than adults; in one experiment, adolescents used both probability and loss information (but not gain), whereas adults used all three types of information. The authors interpret the lack of correlation between risk-taking and information use complexity in the cold condition to support the hypothesis that affective arousal influences age differences in risk-taking, rather than cognitive deficits.

IV. Capacities and Competencies in Ecological Context

Keating (2004, p. 63) notes that "the development in adolescence of effective real-world decision-making is interdependent with a wide range of other factors, including non-cognitive aspects of development, the content of the decision, and the context in which decisions are made." Capacities are subject to developmental, clinical, or contextual limits (Woolard and Reppucci 2000). One such context is the family—the role of parents in adolescent development and decision-making. Although a thorough examination of parental influence on adolescent development and decision-making is beyond the scope of this chapter, we highlight a few studies that specifically examine legal assumptions about parents' capacities to assist their children in negotiating the justice system.

Parents can serve a variety of functions once their child is involved with the juvenile justice system, including information-gathering, information provision, advocacy, and support (Osher and Hunt 2002). These functions can assist the adolescent or the system, two parties that may not share the same interests. For example, the court may enlist parents in reporting juveniles' probation violations, actions that have both costs and consequences. Parental reporting might reduce recidivism and enhance compliance with the court, but may also subject youth to negative effects of incarceration and erode the parental relationship in the long term.

A large-scaled survey by the ABA found that a majority of juvenile court judges and probation officers reported that parents attend hearings 80–100% of the time (Davies and Davidson 2001), but there is very little information regarding other ways that parents participate.

A survey of over one thousand law enforcement officers from departments across the nation report than even when parents are present during questioning, the parents never talk (20% of officers) or talk less than half of the time (50% of officers) (Meyer, Reppucci, and Owen 2006). In one of the very few studies of its kind, Grisso (1981) observed parental actions during police interrogation of juveniles. The results documented a consistent pattern of inaction and lack of involvement by parents. Of 390 police interrogations of juveniles, 66% involved no communication between parent and child. Less that 10% of the juveniles asked their parents for advice on how to handle the questioning. In a small, qualitative study, Tobey, Grisso, and Schwartz (2000) found that generally, positive parental participation helped children understand the court process and interact with their attorneys and that a lack of parental involvement was associated with children having a more difficult time navigating the process.

Parents' potential to serve as barriers to or facilitators of confession is explicitly acknowledged in interrogation training. One widely used manual (Inbau et al. 2001) recommends that officers should talk with parents prior to interrogation to enhance parental support for obtaining the truth. This manual counsels investigators to take a positive approach with parents, explaining that the official's primary interest is in ascertaining truth, which could establish innocence as much as responsibility. If parents act in an "overprotective" manner, according to the manual, the investigators should emphasize that no one blames parents, that all children do things that disappoint parents, and that everyone (the investigator and parent included) has done bad things in their youth. Psychological research with adults (e.g., Kassin, Goldstein, and Savitsky, 2003; Kassin and Norwick, 2004) and several high-profile juvenile false confession cases (Deardorff 1999; Hanna 1998; McFadden and Saulny 2002; Possley 1998) raise fundamental questions about the demands that interrogation places on suspects.

In the previously mentioned study of legal knowledge and beliefs among 180 parent-adolescent pairs (Woolard et al. 2008), a majority of parents adequately understood the *Miranda* components and understood that police must notify parents if a youth is taken to the station for questioning (88–96%). However, almost half of parents did not believe the police can lie. Two-thirds incorrectly believed that the police must wait for the parents before questioning a youth, and almost 90% incorrectly believed that police must notify parents if their child is a suspect. Approximately 35% of parents recommended that the youth in the interrogation vignette should confess to police. Thus, parents knew more than younger adolescents about *Miranda* and its behavioral implications but did not necessarily know more about police strategy or the parameters of parental protection. These results question legal assumptions about parents' capacity for protecting youths' interests without intervention.

Moreover, even if youth did receive accurate advice from parents, it is not clear whether they would or should follow that advice. Grisso's (1981) observational study of police interrogation found that less than 10% of the juveniles asked their parents for advice on how to handle the questioning. Koegl (1997) examined the motivational and contextual factors affecting whether Canadian juvenile offenders asserted various rights. Although Canadian law expressly gives juveniles the right to have a parent present during interrogation, only one juvenile in the sample requested it. The main reasons that juveniles failed to ask for their parents were lack of knowledge concerning the right (33%) and police practices or instructions discouraging it (29%). Interestingly, one-fifth of the participants felt that notifying their parents would have negative effects (e.g., anger, worry) or that there was no benefit (25%).

In a study of approximately 150 juveniles and adults awaiting trial, Woolard (1999) asked what a defendant should do in hypothetical scenarios—specifically about confessing to police, consulting with an attorney, and/or considering a plea agreement. After they made a recommendation in each situation and explained their reasons, they were asked what the hypothetical defendant's parents' would have wanted. For certain groups, their view of parents' recommendations differed significantly from their own. For example, virtually all those who thought confessing was a good choice thought that parents would agree. However, conflicts with parental views varied significantly by age for the remainder of the sample who did not recommend confession. Seventy percent of the youngest adolescents thought parents would want them to confess (a choice clearly contrary to a defense attorney's likely recommendation, for example), contrasted with 61.2% of older adolescents and 44% of adults. When subsequently told that the defendant's parents wanted him to confess, 19% of the young juveniles, 32% of the older juveniles, and 12% of adults said that the defendant should not remain silent, but instead should follow his parent's wishes and confess.

Although parents may be perceived as protectors by the legal system, perhaps a more appropriate metaphor is that of scaffolding (Dahl 2004), or of the guided supervision presumably provided while teens drive with a learner's permit (see Zimring 1982). Both invoke a developmental context that allows for experimentation, anticipates mistakes, and expects growth and learning to result. Both scaffolding and guided supervision also protect against the harshest consequences possible for those who do not require or are not accorded such support. This balance occurs during a time when the brain is making important connections between the cognitive control and socioemotional systems (Dahl 2004) and self-regulation is continuing to mature. Once self-regulation is fully developed, effective and appropriate decision-making can usually, but not necessarily, follow, even when an individual is not closely supervised by someone who has a vested interest in that individual's well being (Byrnes 2005).

V. Conclusion

The justice system processes presume that adults have fully developed self-regulatory capacities. Any choice that they might commit crime, therefore, is a deliberate, rational choice on their part based on their own reasoning and proclivities. Decisions made during court processing, such as whether to take a plea agreement, are presumed to reflect the individual's own priorities and values, however different they may be from an observer's. The price and privilege of such autonomy is individual accountability for the results of those decisions. However, when we turn to a developmental explanation, we are suggesting that there are aspects of adolescents' cognition, psychosocial maturity, or other developmental characteristics that are not finished maturing. That is, they will predictably change as the youth grows older, meaning that decisions that she engages in today are likely to be different from decisions that she engages in several years from now. These differences are not solely due to individual characteristics, but are due in part to the fact that their capacities are still developing. This means that adolescents as a class can be considered not fully developed in these capacities as compared to adults.

Developmental differences between adolescents and adults can have implications for all stages of the justice process, both in terms of constitutional rights and system practices. Policy interrogation and *Miranda* procedures differ by state in the degree to which they acknowledge and respond to age-based capacity issues. Some jurisdictions require parents or another adult to be present for custodial interrogation and/or waiver, while others have adopted a per se rule that youth under a certain age are incapable of providing a valid *Miranda* waiver (Szymanski 2004; Woolard et al. 2008). Similarly, legal presumptions about capacities relevant to competence to stand trial vary across states, and the debate about whether juvenile courts can or should have a lesser standard for competence than adult courts continues (Grisso et al. 2003; Steinberg and Scott 2003).

The policy implications of developmental differences implicates foundational legal concepts of culpability and mitigation (e.g., Scott and Steinberg, 2008; Feld 1997). Even among scholars who agree on the existence of developmental differences, the appropriate policy responses can vary from abolishing the juvenile court and creating a youth "discount" in criminal court (e.g., Feld 1997) to reducing the prosecution of youth in criminal court (e.g., Scott and Steinberg, 2008). Competing views of immaturity have received national attention in several recent Supreme Court opinions where the majority and dissenting views disagreed sharply (*Roper v. Simmons*, 543 U.S. 551 [2005]; *Graham v. Florida*, No. 08–7412 [2010]). Differentiating, or at least acknowledging, the contributions of normative development, individual difference, and experience to the choices and consequences of adolescents remains the challenge for research, policy, and practice.

NOTES

1. While both dual systems and fuzzy trace theories posit two systems of influence, fuzzy trace theories hypothesize that decisions about risk are gist-like, that is, based on simpler mental representations of the meaning of information, rather than a verbatim

storage of information itself (Reyna and Rivers 2008). Thus, decision-making improves with the use of gist-based reasoning. In other more traditional theories, reasoning improves with greater computation (Boyer 2006).

REFERENCES

Baumeister, R. F., B. J. Schmeichel, and K. D. Vohs. 2007. "Self-regulation and the executive function: The self as controlling agent." In *Social psychology: Handbook of basic principles*, 2nd ed., edited by A. W. Kruglanski and E. T. Higgin, 516–39. New York: Guilford.

Boyer, T. W. 2006. "The development of risk-taking: A multi-perspective review." *Developmental Review.* 26: 291–345.

Brown, B. B., J. P. Bakken, S. W. Ameringer, and S. D. Mahon. 2008. "A comprehensive conceptualization of the peer influence process in adolescence." In *Understanding Peer Influence in Children and Adolescents*, edited by M. J. Prinstein and K. A. Dodge, 17–44. New York: Guilford.

Brown, B. B., and J. Larson. 2009. "Peer relationships in adolescence." In *Contextual Influences on Adolescent Development Vol. 2*, 3rd ed., edited by R. M. Lerner and L. Steinberg, 74–103. Hoboken, NJ: Wiley.

Byrnes, J. P. 2005. "The development of self-regulated decision making." In *The Development of Judgment and Decision Making in Children and Adolescents*, edited by J. E. Jacobs and P. A. Klaczynski, 5–38. Mahway, NJ: Lawrence Erlbaum.

Dahl, R. 2004. "Adolescent brain development: A period of vulnerabilities and opportunities." *Annals of the New York Academy of Sciences* 1021: 1–22.

Dahl, Robert E. 2008. "Biological, developmental, and neurobehavioral factors relevant to adolescent driving risks." *American Journal of Preventive Medicine* 35(3S): 278–84.

Davies, H. J., and H. A. Davidson. 2001. "Parental involvement practices of juvenile courts: Report to the Office of Juvenile Justice and Delinquency Prevention." Washington, DC: American Bar Association.

Deardorff, J. 1999. "Child's statement on killing disputed: 10-year-old boy allegedly confessed." *Chicago Tribune* (April 7), p. 1.

Feld, B. 1997. *Bad Kids: Race and the Transformation of Juvenile Justice*. Boston: Oxford University Press.

Figner, B., R. Mackinlay, F. Wilkening, and E. Weber. 2009. "Affective and deliberative processes in risky choice: age differences in risk taking in the Columbia card task." *Journal of Experimental Psychology: Learning, Memory, and Cognition* 35: 709–30.

Fried, C., and N. D. Reppucci. 2001. "Criminal decision making: The development of adolescent judgment, criminal responsibility, and culpability." *Law and Human Behavior* 25: 45–61.

Gardner, Margo, and Laurence Steinberg. 2005. "Peer influence on risk taking, risk preference, and risky decision making in adolescence and adulthood: An experimental study." *Developmental Psychology* 41: 625–35.

Grisso, T. 1981. *Juveniles' Waiver of Rights: Legal and Psychological Competence*. New York: Plenum.

Grisso, T., L. Steinberg, J. L. Woolard, E. Cauffman, E. Scott, S. Graham, F. Lexcen, N. Reppucci, and R. Schwartz. 2003. "Juveniles' competence to stand trial: A comparison of adolescents' and adults' capacities as trial defendants." *Law and Human Behavior* 27: 333–63.

Hanna, J. 1998. "Kids' 'competence' a tender issue for courts." *Chicago Tribune* (August 30), p. 1.

Inbau, F. E., J. E. Reid, J. P. Buckley, and B. C. Jayne. 2001. *Criminal Interrogation and Confessions*, 4th ed. Gaithersburg, MD: Aspen.

Kassin, S. M., C. C. Goldstein, and K. Savitsky. 2003. "Behavioral confirmation in the interrogation room: On the dangers of presuming guilt." *Law and Human Behavior* 27: 187–203.

Kassin, S. M., and R. J. Norwick. 2004. "Why people waive their Miranda rights: The power of innocence." *Law and Human Behavior* 27: 187–203.

Keating, D. P. 2004. "Cognitive and brain development." In *Handbook of adolescent psychology*, 2nd ed., edited by R. M. Lerner, and L. Steinberg, 45–84. Hoboken, NJ: John Wiley & Sons.

Keating, D.P. and Hertzman, C. 1999. "Modernity's paradox." In *Developmental health and the wealth of nations*, edited by D.P. Keating and C. Hertzman, 1–18, New York, NY: Guilford Press.

Klaczynski, P. 2001. "Framing effects on adolescent task representations, analytic and heuristic processing, and decision making: Implications for the normative/descriptive gap." *Journal of Applied Developmental Psychology*, 22(3): 289–309.

Koegl, C. J. (1997). "Contextual and motivational factors affecting young offenders' use of legal rights." Unpublished master's thesis, University of Toronto.

Kuhn, D. 2009. "Adolescent thinking." In *Handbook of adolescent psychology (3rd ed.) Vol. 1: Individual bases of adolescent development*, edited by R. M. Lerner and L. Steinberg, 152–86. Hoboken, NJ: Wiley.

McFadden, R., and S. Saulny. 2002. "DNA in Central Park Jogger Case Spurs Call for New Review." *The New York Times* (September 6). http://www.nytimes.com/2002/09/06/nyregion/dna-in-central-park-jogger-case-spurs-call-for-new-review.html

Meyer, J., N. D. Reppucci, and J. Owen. 2006. "Criminal interrogation with young suspects: perspectives and practices of law enforcement." In *Police interrogation of juvenile suspects*. Paper presented at the annual conference of the American Psychology-Law Society (March), J. L. Woolard (chair). St. Petersburg, FL.

Osher, T., and P. Hunt. December 2002. "Involving families of youth who are in contact with the juvenile justice system." Research and program brief. Delmar, NY: National Center for Mental Health and Juvenile Justice.

Possley, M. 1998. "How cops got boys to talk." *Chicago Tribune* (August 30), p. 1.

Reyna, V., and F. Farley. 2006. "Risk and rationality in adolescent decision making: Implications for theory, practice, and public policy." *Psychological Science in the Public Interest.* 7: 1–44.

Reyna, V., and S. Rivers, 2008, "Current theories of risk and rational decision making." *Developmental Review, 28:* 1–11.

Rivers, S., V. Reyna, and B. Mills. 2008. "Risk taking under the influence: A fuzzy-trace theory of emotion in adolescence." *Developmental Review* 28: 107–44.

Scott, E. S., N. D. Reppucci, and J. L. Woolard. 1995. "Adolescent judgment in legal contexts." *Law and Human Behavior* 19: 221–44.

Scott, E. S., and L. Steinberg. 2008. *Rethinking Juvenile Justice*. Boston: Harvard University Press.

Somerville, L.H., R. M. Jones, and B. J. Casey. 2010. "A time of change: Behavioral and neural correlates of adolescent sensitivity to appetitive and aversive environmental cues." *Brain and Cognition* 72: 124–33.

Steinberg, L. 2004. "Risk taking in adolescence: what changes, and why?" *Annals of the New York Academy of Sciences.* 1021: 51–58.

Steinberg, L. 2008. "A social neuroscience perspective on adolescent risk-taking." *Developmental Review*. 28: 78–106.

Steinberg, L., D. Albert, E. Cauffman, M. Banich, S. Graham, and J. L. Woolard. 2008. "Age differences in sensation seeking and impulsivity as indexed by behavior and self-report: Evidence for a dual systems model." *Developmental Psychology* 44: 1764–78.

Steinberg, L., and E. Cauffman. 1996. "Maturity of judgment in adolescence: Psychosocial factors in adolescent decisionmaking." *Law and Human Behavior* 20: 249–72.

Steinberg, L., E. Cauffman, J. Woolard, S. Graham, and M. Banich. 2009. "Are adolescents less mature than adults? Minors' access to abortion, the juvenile death penalty, and the alleged APA 'Flip-flop.'" *American Psychologist* 64: 583–94.

Steinberg, L., and E. S. Scott. 2003. "Less guilty by reason of adolescence: Developmental immaturity, diminished responsibility, and the juvenile death penalty." *American Psychologist* 58: 1009–18.

Szymanski, L. 2004, "Juvenile waiver of *Miranda* rights: Per se age test (2004 update)." *NCJJ Snapshot*, 9(6). Pittsburgh, PA: National Center for Juvenile Justice.

Steinberg, L., S. Graham, L. O'Brien, J. Woolard, E. Cauffman, and M. Banich. 2009. "Age differences in future orientation and delay discounting." *Child Development* 80: 28–44.

Tobey, A., T. Grisso, and R. Schwartz. 2000. "Youths' trial participation as seen by youths and their attorneys: An exploration of competence-based issues." In *Youth on Trial*, edited by T. Grisso and R. G. Schwartz, 225–42. Chicago: University of Chicago Press.

Viljoen, J., C. Odgers, T. Grisso, and C. Tillbrook. 2007. "Teaching adolescents and adults about adjudicative competence proceedings: A comparison of pre- and post-teaching scores on the MacCAT-CA." *Law and Human Behavior* 31: 419–32.

Vohs, K., and B. Schmeichel. 2003. "Self-regulation and the extended now: Controlling the self alters the subjective experience of time." *Journal of Personality and Social Psychology*, 85: 217–30.

Woolard, J. L. 1999. "Competence and effective participation of juvenile defendants: Developmental aspects of the attorney-client relationship." In *Current issues in juvenile research*. Symposium conducted at the Psychology and Law International Conference (July), N. D. Reppucci (chair), Dublin, Ireland.

Woolard, J., H. Cleary, S. Harvell, and R. Chen. 2008. "Examining adolescents' and their parents' conceptual and practical knowledge of police interrogation: A family dyad approach." *Journal of Youth and Adolescence* 37: 685–98.

Woolard, J. L., and N. D. Reppucci. 2000. "Researching juveniles' capacities as defendants." In *Youth on Trial*, edited by T. Grisso and B. Schwartz, 173–91. Chicago: University of Chicago Press.

Zimring, F. 1982. *The Changing Legal World of Adolescence*. New York: The Free Press.

Zimring, F. 1998. *American Youth Violence*. New York: Oxford University Press.

CHAPTER 6

DELINQUENCY AND COMORBID CONDITIONS

TAMARA M. HAEGERICH
AND PATRICK H. TOLAN

YOUTH who engage in delinquent acts are often more troubled than even their most antisocial behavior suggests. It has been estimated that 20% of crime for girls and 15% of crime for boys can be attributed to a child psychiatric disorder, with psychiatric disorder contributing more to crime risk than body mass index (BMI) contributes to heart attack risk (Copeland et al. 2007). Although rates of disorder among delinquent populations vary depending on whether the rates are derived from general population, high risk, or incarcerated samples (community samples of delinquent youth show lower rates of disorder and co-occurring disorder than incarcerated samples), it is clear that mental disorders are often seen in delinquent youth. For example, in an incarcerated sample of youth, Hussey, Drinkard, and Flannery (2007) found that 66% of youth had at least one mental disorder, with 40% having more than one disorder, as defined by the Diagnostic and Statistical Manual of Mental Disorders (DSM-IV; APA 1994). The most common disorders that delinquent youth suffer from include Conduct Disorder (CD), Oppositional Defiant Disorder (ODD), Substance Abuse and Substance Dependence, Depression, Post-Traumatic Stress Disorder (PTSD), and Attention Deficit Hyperactivity Disorder (ADHD) (see Loeber and Keenan 1994; Vermeiren 2003 for reviews).

Delinquent behavior and the co-occurrence of one or more disorders ("comorbidity") may exist for a variety of reasons (Rutter 1997): comorbid disorders may be

The findings and conclusions in this report are those of the author(s) and do not necessarily represent the official position of the Centers for Disease Control and Prevention.

different manifestations of the same disorder (i.e., delinquency and mental disorder may be different expressions of the same underlying disorder at one point in time); may be different stages of the same underlying disorder (i.e., mental disorder may be exhibited in childhood, with delinquency exhibited in adolescence, yet representing the same underlying condition at different points in time); may arise from the same or correlated risk factors (i.e., poor attachment to family and school may underlie both delinquency and other mental disorders); may become meaningfully different with different clinical implications (i.e., one mental disorder is made worse or may morph into a different disorder by engagement in delinquency); or, one disorder may pose a risk for the development of another (i.e., mental disorder may predispose youth to engage in delinquent behavior, or vice versa). Methodological difficulties in assessing the comorbidity of delinquency and other disorders are challenging our understanding of the issue; however, most agree that comorbidity is a true phenomenon and cannot be explained purely by methodological artifacts of the research, such as referral bias or overlap of symptoms across multiple disorders (Angold, Costello, and Erkanli 1999).

In addition to these discriminative validity issues (clarity of whether there are truly different disorders occurring at the same time or in succession), there are other factors that limit our scientific understanding of comorbidity based on the extant research. These include reliance on clinical, single-site, and nonrepresentative samples (e.g., youth in detention facilities); a lack of consideration of how rates discovered within studies could be affected by demographic and historical variables; the use of cross-sectional rather than longitudinal data as a basis for estimating rates; the use of different assessment and classification schemes for disorders across studies (e.g., paper reviews, interviews, surveys, DSM-IV diagnoses); a focus on comorbidity between a given disorder and other disorders rather than the overall patterns across disorders; and differences in symptoms and perhaps comorbidity across developmental stages (e.g., childhood, adolescence, and early adulthood) (Rutter 1997). Specific to delinquency, additional complications include the overlap of delinquent behavior with many of the symptoms of the most prevalent disorders (e.g., disruptive behavior disorders, substance abuse), and underdeveloped theories of (a) the relation between comorbidity and delinquency and (b) how comorbidity relates to different subtypes of offending youth (e.g., adolescence-limited versus life course-persistent; minor versus severe and violent offenders; boys versus girls) (Angold, Costello, and Erkanli 1999; Edens and Ott 1997; Vermeiren 2003). Despite these factors, patterns of comorbidity and the degree to which one disorder predisposes a youth for suffering from another are receiving greater illumination because of a greater focus on studies of individual change, rather than group differences (delinquent versus nondelinquent).

Next, we review the extant evidence of comorbidity of delinquency with CD/ODD and the most common other disorders delinquent youth suffer from, including Substance Abuse and Substance Dependence, Depression, PTSD, and ADHD, discussing prevalence and concurrent and successive comorbidity. We highlight the methodological concerns that have challenged our understanding of comorbidity, including the use of clinical samples and the overlap of symptoms across disorders. When available, we point to longitudinal research studies that are in the best position to inform the knowledge base. We then highlight the complexities in discerning comorbidity given that there are different patterns of co-occurring disorders, that developmental trajectories in offending can lead to different patterns of comorbidity, and that boys and girls can differ in their patterns of comorbidity. We then discuss implications and new directions for research, including the need for developmental psychopathology studies that include representative samples, longitudinal data collection, and careful assessment protocols. We review prevention and treatment approaches to CD, ODD, Substance Abuse and Dependence, Depression, PTSD, and ADHD, with a focus on a greater investment in primary prevention. We conclude with implications for juvenile justice policy, noting the responsibility of the justice system for identifying and treating delinquent youth with comorbid disorders. We focus on enhanced integration of community-based service systems in recognition that youth are still developing emotionally and psychologically and require prevention and treatment strategies that allow them to reach their fullest potential.

I. Comorbidity of Conduct Disorder (CD)/ Oppositional Defiant Disorder (ODD) and Delinquency

The measurement of delinquency, mental disorders, and the two most common child and adolescent disorders—CD and ODD, which overlap considerably—is presenting a challenge for interpreting overall comorbidity rates. Although providing complete diagnostic criteria is beyond the scope of this volume, DSM-IV criteria for CD includes persistent violation of norms and rules in the past year that interferes with social, academic, or occupational functioning, including aggression to people and animals (e.g., bullying, fighting, weapon use, sexual coercion), destruction of property, deceitfulness or theft, and serious violation of rules (e.g., running away, curfew violations, truancy). CD may be diagnosed as childhood-onset type (onset of at least one criterion behavior before the age of 10). Often co-occurring with CD is ODD, a pattern of defiant behavior lasting at least six months that interferes with social, academic, or occupational functioning, including losing one's temper, arguing with adults, refusing to comply with adults' requests, deliberately annoying people, blaming others, or being easily annoyed, angry or resentful, or spiteful or vindictive (APA 1994).

When CD and ODD have been measured independent of delinquency within studies (e.g., through DSM criteria versus self-report of specific delinquent behavior), prevalence of CD/ODD is higher in detained youth populations than in the general youth population. Most delinquent youth will likely obtain a diagnosis of CD (Vermeiren 2003), with only 6.1% receiving a diagnosis of CD/ODD in the general population (NRC/IOM 2009); yet, some have concluded that CD/ODD is independent enough of delinquency to be classified as its own disorder (Loeber et al. 2000). As one can see from the definitions of CD and ODD however, the symptoms used to define those disorders are represented mostly in behaviors considered to be delinquent, begging the question as to whether the co-occurrence of CD and ODD among delinquents is comorbidity or merely counting the same feature twice. This overlap makes it difficult to assess the meaning of high rates of CD and ODD among delinquent youth. Even among those youth who are too young to have their behavior labeled as delinquent, the symptoms that signify these two disorders are ones that if they occurred at a later age, they would be considered delinquent.

Due to the overlap in markers of CD, ODD, and delinquency, our understanding of the comorbidity of these three conditions perhaps has been informed more by the investigation of the co-occurrence of CD and ODD with other mental disorders than by the investigation of "delinquency" per se (e.g., as measured through the use of arrest records); in other words, by research that has treated CD/ODD as essentially equivalent to delinquency. CD and ODD, like delinquency, co-occur with other disorders, mostly with substance use/dependence, depression, and ADHD. The focus on CD/ODD has also informed the prediction of delinquency. For example, Broidy and her colleagues (2003) illustrated the robustness of the association between CD/ODD and delinquency in a study utilizing longitudinal data from multiple studies in six sites and three countries. They reported that conduct problems and oppositional behavior in childhood were consistently predictive of delinquency in adolescence. This and other studies have highlighted mental disorders in childhood as predictors of the onset and severity of delinquency in later adolescence. Accordingly, these studies have helped guide prevention efforts, including the selection of youth for preventive strategies, and the essential measurement of effects over time. A more detailed discussion of the development of conduct disorder and juvenile delinquency, the contributions of the research, and the difficulties associated with identifying causes, correlates, and comorbidity, may be found in Lahey, Moffitt, and Caspi (2003).

II. COMORBIDITY OF SUBSTANCE ABUSE/ DEPENDENCE AND DELINQUENCY

Youth who use substances, including alcohol, marijuana, and illicit drugs, who fail to meet important responsibilities because of their use, who find themselves in dangerous situations when using substances, or who experience legal problems because of use but continue to use over a year's time meet the DSM-IV criteria for substance abuse. More chronic use and impact on functioning denotes a substance dependence disorder (APA 1994). Like CD/ODD, substance use disorders can overlap with delinquency in defining characteristics. Many delinquent arrests are for substance use or substance use-related behavior. Not surprisingly, rates of substance use and disorder are high in delinquents. Examining an incarcerated sample of youths screened for substance abuse or dependence, Hussey and colleagues (2007) reported that 14% of the youths illustrated risk for abuse or dependence, and 9% consented to further assessment. Of these youths, 77% reported using drugs or alcohol weekly during the previous year, and 43% reported drug or alcohol problems (e.g., problems with the law, withdrawal, and physical/mental health). All youths were diagnosed with at least one DSM-IV disorder: 36% were diagnosed with alcohol abuse, 19% were alcohol dependent, 22% were diagnosed with marijuana abuse, and 72% were marijuana dependent. These percentages are higher than the prevalence of substance use disorders among youths in the general population, which is estimated to be around 10% (NRC/IOM 2009).

Understanding what is comorbidity of substance abuse/dependence and delinquency and what is "double counting" is difficult. Also, the relation between substance use/dependence and delinquency may vary among delinquents. For example, possession of substances itself is classified as a delinquent behavior, youth may be involved in the sale of illegal substances, or youth may engage in theft to be able to purchase substances (Loeber, Stouthamer-Loeber, and White 1999). Substance use may also serve as an immediate precipitating factor in delinquency, reducing youths' inhibitory control. Delinquent youth may use substances as a coping strategy (i.e., for self-medication), particularly when delinquency is comorbid with depression (Esposito-Smythers et al. 2008; Turner et al. 2005).

Longitudinal studies may shed light on the relation between substance abuse/dependence and delinquency. Loeber and his colleagues (1999) found that persistent substance use in late adolescence is predicted by persistent delinquency in early adolescence: That is, engaging in delinquent behavior over time leads to persistent use of substances over time. In contrast, Copeland et al. (2007) found that substance use disorder in adolescence predicted arrests for minor offenses in young adulthood. Thus, substance use and delinquency may have a dynamic relationship, such that engagement in early delinquency starts youth on a trajectory for greater substance use which, in turn, promotes criminal behavior in early adulthood. It may also be that substance use and delinquency represent a single syndrome due to shared environmental risk factors and genetic determinants (e.g., Waldman and Slutske 2000). Yet, there is some evidence of differentiating factors of each disorder. For example, exposure to discrimination and early home-leaving predicts criminal violence and alcoholism in adulthood, yet aggression and lack of school attendance in childhood only predict criminal violence, and not alcoholism (McCord and Ensminger 1997).

III. Comorbidity of Depression and Delinquency

Delinquent youth not only suffer from externalizing problems, such as substance use, but internalizing problems as well, such as depression. These disorders have few features that correspond with delinquent behavior. Thus, rates of comorbidity are more easily understood. A major depressive episode is generally characterized by the DSM-IV by depressed mood most of the day nearly every day or diminished interest in activities, and significant weight loss, insomnia or hypersomnia, psycho-motor agitation or retardation, fatigue, feelings of worthlessness, or thoughts of death or suicidal ideation, with five or more of these symptoms occurring during a two-week period, and resulting in distress or impairment in occupational or other areas of functioning (APA 1994).

In an urban detained sample, Teplin and her colleagues (2002) found that approximately 22% of girls and 13% of boys experienced a major depressive episode in the previous six months. Incidence of depression is much higher in detained samples than the general population, with an estimated 5% of all youth suffering from depression (NRC/IOM 2009). Hussey and his colleagues (2007) found in an incarcerated sample that 13% of youths had suicidal thoughts, and of those, 38% attempted suicide, with girls more likely to struggle with suicidal thoughts than boys. Prevalence of suicidal ideation may be more similar among detained youth and youth in the general population, with estimates of suicidal ideation being around 15% for all high school youth (derived from the Youth Risk Behavior Surveillance System, YRBSS; CDC 2008). It is less clear, however, how rates of depression and suicide among delinquent youth in the community (i.e., those not involved in the justice system) differ from rates among nondelinquent youth in the general population, or among a small and distinct minority proportion of detained delinquents from an urban community (like the youth assessed by Teplin et al. 2002). Further, rates of depression in detained and incarcerated samples are difficult to interpret because depression may be an effect of detainment and incarceration itself, rather than delinquency.

Again, longitudinal studies of community samples of youth may provide a clue as to whether engagement in delinquent activity leads to depression and suicide, or vice versa. A longitudinal study of at-risk boys during adolescence by Beyers and Loeber (2003) suggests that depression increases risk for delinquency more than delinquency increases risk for depression. Trajectories of delinquency variety (i.e., number of different delinquent activities) and mood were examined concurrently, and over time. Looking at a specific point in time, higher levels of depressed mood predicted higher levels of delinquency variety. In turn, higher levels of delinquency variety predicted higher levels of depressed mood. These associations could not be attributable to social or contextual factors that influence both disorders. Ultimately, higher depressed mood across adolescence was found to predict a slower decline in delinquency variety over time. That is, over the adolescent period, the developmental trend is for delinquency to decrease; yet for depressed youth, delinquency did not decrease at the same rate. There was no effect of delinquency variety on the rate of change in depressed mood. Thus, depressed mood predicts delinquency trajectories more than delinquency predicts mood trajectories. Depression may result in a failure of youth to desist delinquent activities, leading to continued criminal behavior in adulthood (Beyers and Loeber 2003).

In contrast, when it comes to suicide, studies suggest that delinquency may lead to suicidal ideation. In a longitudinal study of adolescence using a nationally representative sample (Add Health), Thompson, Ho, and Kingree (2007) found that delinquent youth were more likely to seriously consider suicide one to seven years after engaging in delinquent activities. This effect was particularly strong for females, and held even when controlling for other disorders that predict suicidal ideation and delinquency, including alcohol problems, depression, self-esteem, impulsivity, and religiosity.

IV. Comorbidity of Post-Traumatic Stress Disorder (PTSD) and Delinquency

PTSD occurs when a person experiences or witnesses a traumatic event that involves actual or threatened death or serious injury, followed by feelings of fear, helplessness or horror. As described in the DSM-IV, the traumatic event is then re-experienced, such as through recurrent and intrusive thoughts or dreams, feeling that the event is reoccurring, or feeling stress when exposed to cues for the event. Acts of avoidance are also present, such as avoiding thoughts about the event; avoiding people or activities surrounding the event; not remembering aspects of the trauma; not being interested in significant activities; feeling detached from others; having a restricted range of affect; or having a sense of a foreshortened future. People with PTSD also have difficulties falling or staying asleep, feel irritable or angry, have difficulty concentrating, are hypervigilant, and may have an exaggerated startle response. For a diagnosis to be made, the disturbance should last more than one month and cause significant distress or impairment in social, occupational, or other areas of functioning. PTSD can be acute, chronic, or have a delayed onset (APA 1994).

Rates of PTSD have been found to be higher among incarcerated and temporarily detained youth than in the general population of youth. A study by Steiner, Garcia, and Matthews (1997) found rates of PTSD significantly higher among incarcerated youth (31.7%) than a convenience sample of youth (9.3%). Abram et al. (2004) found that 11% of youth met criteria for PTSD. Rates of PTSD in the general youth population have been estimated at .6% of youth (NRC/IOM 2009). Youths who meet the criteria for PTSD have a much higher rate of comorbidity with other mental disorders than youths without a PTSD diagnosis (Abram et al. 2007). Witnessing or experiencing violence in the family or in the community is most often the precipitating factor in delinquent samples (Abram et al. 2004; Steiner, Garcia, and Matthews 1997). PTSD may be a particularly serious diagnosis among delinquents because incarcerated youth with PTSD have been found to have lower levels of self-control than those without PTSD, which is thought to increase recidivism risk (Cauffman et al. 1998).

It remains unclear why PTSD among offending youth is so high. PTSD may be a result of traumatic experiences encountered in the justice system, such as detention and confinement, or exposure to traumatic experiences as part of delinquent behavior (e.g., serious violence threats). Yet delinquent youth are more likely to experience personal violent victimization than nonoffending youth not only as a part of their delinquent behavior, but also through child maltreatment and exposure to community violence (Nofziger and Kurtz 2005; Smith and Thornberry 1995). These represent exposure levels that may be severe enough to induce PTSD symptoms. In addition, engaging in violent behavior may carry traumatizing effects for the young perpetrator. What is clear is that violence exposure, including prior abuse, is a likely major source of PTSD rates among delinquents. Treatment that can affect trauma may be an important part of reducing delinquency.

V. Comorbidity of Attention Deficit Hyperactivity Disorder (ADHD) and Delinquency

ADHD is one of the most commonly diagnosed mental disorders in childhood. DSM-IV criteria for ADHD include symptoms of inattention and/or symptoms of hyperactivity-impulsivity that are present before 7 years of age, with the youth illustrating impairment in two or more settings for at least six months, and in social, academic, or occupational functioning. Symptoms of inattention include failure to pay attention to details, difficulty sustaining attention in activities, not listening when spoken to, not following through on instructions or chores, having difficulty organizing tasks, and avoiding tasks that require sustained attention. Symptoms of hyperactivity include fidgeting, leaving a seat in situations in which remaining seated is expected, running about, having difficulty playing quietly, constantly being on the go, and talking excessively. Symptoms of impulsivity include blurting out answers before questions have been completed, having difficulty awaiting turn, and interrupting others. Types of ADHD include combined type, predominantly inattentive type, predominantly hyperactive type, impulsive type, or not otherwise specified (APA 1994). Rates of ADHD vary substantially between adjudicated, incarcerated, and self-reported delinquents (Vermeiren 2003), but it is clear that ADHD generally occurs at a much higher rate in each of these populations compared to the general population of youth (4.5%, NRC/IOM 2009).

Because a diagnosis of ADHD can be made before the age of 7 and can continue into adolescence, research has primarily investigated the degree to which ADHD predicts delinquency (rather than investigating whether delinquency predicts ADHD). ADHD has been found to predict self-reported delinquency and arrests, convictions, and incarcerations, including early onset, persistence, and severity of delinquency (Loeber and Keenan 1994; Mannuzza, Klein, and Moulton 2007; Moffitt 1990), and uniquely contributes to the development of antisocial behavior in adolescence, above and beyond other variables (Moffitt 1990). Delinquent youth with ADHD fare worse in terms of intelligence, achievement, verbal ability, memory, SES, aggression, and family adversity compared to nondelinquent youth with ADHD and delinquent youth without ADHD (Moffitt 1990). Youth are at particular risk when ADHD is comorbid with CD/ODD and aggression, experiencing greater peer, family, and school problems (Abikoff and Klein, 1992; Angold, Costello, and Erkanli 1999; Loeber and Keenan 1994). Note, however, that some studies have not found that ADHD is independently predictive of delinquency and may only be predictive when ADHD is comorbid with delinquency and other disorders (Broidy et al. 2003; Copeland et al. 2007). Given the documented relation between ADHD, particularly self-control and delinquency, presence of ADHD among delinquents likely represents a key consideration for treatment and prevention.

VI. Comorbidity Among Multiple Disorders and Delinquency

Not only does delinquency co-occur with CD/ODD, Substance Abuse/Dependence, Depression, PTSD, and ADHD independently, but often delinquent youth suffer from multiple concurrent disorders. Compared to nondelinquent youth, delinquent youth are more likely to meet criteria for multiple comorbid disorders, as found in both community and detained/incarcerated samples of youth. The picture of comorbidity among disorders is blurred by different patterns of comorbidity found with different samples; however, it is clear that youth with CD and other mental disorders have more severe symptoms than youth diagnosed with one disorder alone (Stahl and Clarizio 1999).

In a meta-analysis of the associations between the most common mental disorders in community-based samples of youth, Angold, Costello, and Erkanli (1999) concluded that youth with CD are ten times more likely to also have ADHD, and six times more likely to suffer from depression. Using the Add Health study data, Wade (2001) found significant comorbidity among delinquency, depression, and substance use, with increased odds of suffering from one disorder given a second disorder. In comparing incarcerated delinquents to community youth, Ulzen and Hamilton (1998) found that 63.3% of delinquents suffered from two or more disorders, while only 12.2% of community youth exhibited comorbidity. Delinquent youth with ODD also had higher rates of alcohol dependence, depression, ADHD, and CD. Abram, Teplin, McClelland, and Dulcan (2009) investigated the prevalence of comorbidity among detained juvenile delinquents in a cross-sectional study and found that one-third of youths had substance use disorders and ADHD or other behavioral disorders, and half of these youths also suffered from affective disorders and/or anxiety. Approximately 11% of males and 14% of females were diagnosed with both a major mental disorder (psychosis, mania, major depression) and substance use disorder concurrently. The odds of comorbidity in these youth were larger than what one could expect from chance, and the rates were substantially higher than what is usually seen in community samples.

Comorbidity of multiple disorders results in particularly detrimental outcomes for youth. For example, when youths have substance use problems, CD, and ADHD, compared to just ADHD, they have an earlier age of onset of drinking alcohol, more substance use dependence, earlier onset of regular drinking alcohol, and more comorbid psychiatric diagnoses, such as depression, anxiety, and mania (Thompson et al. 1996).

VII. THE COMPLEXITY OF COMORBIDITY IN DELINQUENT YOUTH

The complexity of comorbidity can be understandable through a developmental psychopathology lens. Patterns of psychopathology across development can inform as much about the meaning of comorbidity, risk for comorbidity, and intervention needs in comorbidity, as whether one given disorder is present or not. As highlighted by Loeber and Keenan (1994), it is important to consider the developmental timing of the onset of different disorders when considering concurrent and successive comorbidity. Typically, the onset of ADHD occurs in preschool and elementary school. CD and ODD emerges in middle childhood and is most prevalent during adolescence. The highest risk for comorbidity of ADHD and CD is in the preadolescent period. Substance use and depression often are first noted in adolescence and early adulthood. Mannuzza, Klein, and Moulton (2007) investigated the sequence of comorbidity of delinquency, ADHD, CD, and substance abuse/dependence in a longitudinal study and found that ADHD in childhood is succeeded by CD and/or substance abuse/dependence in adolescence, which is succeeded by delinquency and arrest in late adolescence and early adulthood, generally following the patterns of onset of the disorders as identified by Loeber and Keenan (1994). Similar patterns have been found by Cerdá et al. (2008) in a longitudinal sample of adolescents, which illustrated the pattern of antisocial behavior being succeeded by the comorbidity of antisocial behavior and substance use, succeeded by the comorbidity of substance use and problems with the police.

The heterogeneity of the delinquent population in terms of age of onset, offense trajectories, and offense severity poses another challenge for the understanding of the comorbidity between delinquency and mental disorders. Compared to late-starters, youth with early onset of delinquency have been found to have a greater risk for comorbid depression (Beyers and Loeber 2003) and ADHD/ODD (Taylor, Iacono, and McGue 2000), and greater acceleration of substance use and dependence (Taylor et al. 2002).

Youths following different offense pathways and trajectories have been found to have different patterns of comorbidity. For example, Loeber, and his colleagues (1993) identified three different pathways to delinquency that emerge developmentally: overt, covert, and authority conflict. The overt pathway is characterized by the initiation of aggression, then fighting, followed by serious violence. The covert pathway is characterized by the initiation of minor covert behavior (e.g., lying, shoplifting), followed by property damage (fire-setting, vandalism), followed by moderate to serious delinquency. The authority conflict pathway is characterized by stubborn behavior, followed by defiance, and then authority avoidance. Results indicated that youths with ADHD are over-represented in the overt and authority avoidance pathways, while youths with substance use problems are over-represented in the covert pathway of delinquency. Moffitt (1993) identified two primary types of delinquency trajectories: adolescent limited and life course persistent. Youth following the life course persistent pathway exhibit more comorbidity and psychopathology in adolescence than other offenders (Vermeiren 2003); these patterns remain into adulthood, with life course persistent offenders more likely to suffer from substance abuse and depression (Moffitt et al. 2002).

Offenders have also been classified according to length of involvement in crime (e.g., chronic, escalation, desistance) combined with seriousness of offense (e.g., severe/violent, minor); such classification schemes also reveal differences in comorbidity patterns across subgroups. Sheidow, Strachan, Minden, Henry, Tolan, and Gorman-Smith (2008) examined internalizing problems (withdrawn, somatic complaints, and anxious/depressed syndromes) of high-risk youth falling into four trajectory patterns: nonoffenders, chronic minor offenders, escalating offenders, and serious chronic and violent offenders. Early in adolescence, serious/chronic/violent and minor chronic offenders had higher internalizing symptoms than nonoffenders. Further, internalizing symptoms for nonoffenders decreased over time, while escalators exhibited the same symptoms over time. By late adolescence, all delinquent groups experienced greater symptoms than nonoffenders, with serious/chronic/violent offenders experiencing worse symptoms than minor chronics. Other studies have shown similar findings, with chronic and serious offenders experiencing greater substance abuse and depressive symptoms over time, and greater comorbidity among multiple disorders (Copeland et al. 2007; Doherty,

Green, and Ensminger 2008; Wiesner and Windle 2004; Wiesner and Windle 2006).

Finally, comorbidity among delinquency and mental disorders has been found to vary by gender. Overall, delinquent girls are more likely to suffer from mental health problems than are delinquent boys. Timmons-Mitchell, Brown, Schulz, Webster, Underwood, and Semple (1997) studied a random sample of incarcerated youth and found that 84% of girls and 27% of boys had significant mental health problems. Girls are also more likely to suffer from multiple comorbid disorders compared to boys (Abram et al. 2009). Girls and boys differ in the types of disorders that co-occur. Delinquent girls tend to show comorbidity between CD, substance abuse, depression, suicidal ideation, PTSD, and sexual activity, while delinquent boys tend to show comorbidity between CD and ADHD (Cauffman et al. 1998; Hussey, Drinkard, and Flannery 2007; Stahl and Clarizo 1999; Ulzen and Hamilton 1998).

VIII. Summary

Are youth who suffer from mental disorders more likely to become delinquent? Or are youth who are delinquent more likely to develop mental disorders? Delinquency and comorbidity is a complex issue given the overlap of symptoms from mental disorders (e.g., Conduct Disorder/Oppositional Defiant Disorder, substance use) and delinquency, and the potential contribution of detention and confinement to mental disorders (e.g., depression) resulting in elevated rates. The picture is further obscured by the investigation of the prevalence of mental disorders in detained and incarcerated youth who are not representative of the full population of delinquent youth. Investigations with these biased delinquent samples can lead to distortion in rates of true mental disorder because youths who are involved in serious delinquency and reach the point of detainment and incarceration are more likely to have fewer resources to release them from detention, and more likely to face racial and ethnic discrimination and life adversity—factors that may contribute to mental health problems (similar to Berkson's Bias in clinical samples; Overbeek et al. 2001; Tolan and Titus 2009).

Even so, several themes can be highlighted from the research conducted over the past twenty years—particularly research that has investigated comorbidity longitudinally over the course of development, and research using community samples of youth. Delinquent youth do suffer from Conduct Disorder, Oppositional Defiant Disorder, Substance Abuse and Substance Dependence, Depression, Post-Traumatic Stress Disorder, and Attention Deficit Hyperactivity Disorder to a greater extent than do the general population of youth. The elevated rates are higher than what would be expected from the general population, yet not all delinquent youth suffer from comorbid disorders, and a large proportion of delinquent youth are not diagnosed with mental disorder. Disorders unfold developmentally as children progress from early childhood to young adulthood. Compared to non-delinquent youth, delinquent youth are at greater risk for suffering from each disorder and multiple disorders both concurrently and sequentially. When youths suffer from multiple comorbid disorders, they are more symptomatic, and have greater troubles with peers, family, and school. Detained and incarcerated youths, youths who begin their paths to delinquency early, and youths with chronic and serious delinquent trajectories are at the greatest risk. Male and female delinquents suffer from unique constellations of disorders and thus may require unique prevention and intervention approaches.

A. Implications for Research, Prevention, and Treatment

Given the effect of measurement, sampling, and methodological limitations of existing data on addressing questions about delinquency and comorbidity, there is much need for adequate research. Most essential are those studies that define the delinquent population well and make appropriate comparisons with the general population. Preferably, these samples will be demographically broad or stratified adequately to permit confidence in comparative results. Studies that examine meaningful delinquent subgroups are also needed. Research that measures change in individuals over development, rather than comparing delinquent and nondelinquent youth at one point in time is also advantageous. Epidemiologic studies with repeated measurement over development can help better map out the temporal sequence and relative dependency of disorder occurrence and delinquency. Longitudinal prevention studies would help discover whether treatment of mental disorder can prevent delinquency, or whether early interventions based on risk and protective factors for delinquency can prevent mental disorder later in young adulthood. Finally, it is critical that studies devote attention to the careful measurement of delinquency and diagnostic assessment of mental disorder.

New areas of interest include not only determining which patterns of comorbidity are present at the individual youth level, but also how neighborhood and community conditions may affect these patterns. For example, neighborhood conditions (e.g., concentrated disadvantage) or response to delinquency (e.g., harsh policing, lack of youth and family systems coordination) may contribute to patterns of delinquent behaviors and comorbid disorders (Cerdá et al. 2008).

Youth at risk for or who experience mental disorders in the justice system warrant treatment to stem or ameliorate the impact of the disorder. This may well reduce risk for delinquency by improving overall functioning and may be important even if the effect on delinquency is not direct or immediate. Similarly, linking those identified as having a disorder and the potential for later delinquency with early treatment or prevention efforts may stem delinquency and decrease the prevalence of mental disorder at the population level. However, while there is considerable evidence that both implications will hold and should be important considerations in criminal justice, public health, and mental health policy and practices, it is plausible that the impact may be less substantial and more circuitous or inconsistent than is expected. Thus, research and clinical documentation are needed that can better and more specifically and discriminatively illustrate patterns of comoribidity and the relation of comorbidity patterns to heightened probability of delinquency, seriousness and chronicity of involvement, and response to psychotherapeutic and criminal justice approaches (Tolan and Titus 2009).

A key area of further research is the closer examination of the relation between symptom development and natural change and delinquency to help illuminate how comorbidity should be considered distinct from the presence of a disorder of any sort. It is also important to provide better normative and population-based understanding of comorbidity among disorders of youth. Perhaps one of the most important contributions of such work would be to document how disorders and comorbidity unfold developmentally and how that might differ for those who become delinquent from those who do not. This knowledge can provide key insights about prevention efforts related to early identification of risk for emerging CD, ODD, ADHD, Substance Abuse/Dependence, Depression, and PTSD, and to mount more directed or precise and therefore more effective prevention and early treatment. While reaching that utility rests on considerable additional research effort, the impact should be to substantially decrease delinquency.

A second implication of the comorbidity findings is the need for understanding how interventions affect comorbidity and those with comorbid conditions. There is almost no research in developmental psychopathology or clinical studies of child and adolescent psychopathology that examines how comorbidity patterns change in the process of and as the result of interventions, treatment, or prevention (Tolan and Gorman-Smith 2002). In part, there is need for theory and related intervention methodology that would permit valid understanding. Nevertheless, there is need for studies that can track whether the number and severity of symptoms are decreased during treatment, whether functioning is improved, and whether delinquent behavior is impacted.

A third implication from the comorbidity literature and from the absence of intervention consideration of comorbidity patterns is the need to identify interventions that affect common comorbidity patterns and the process of such impact. The most likely intervention candidates are those with some benefits for a targeted disorder or that lessen delinquency rates. Thus, we suggest value in efforts for secondary analysis as well as primary research designed to examine the impact of existing empirically proven interventions on comorbidity rates, levels, and process of effects.

Identification of the promising efforts should occur across the intervention spectrum from promotion of healthy development, to prevention, to treatment, and to management. Certainly, having identification and treatment occur after substantial involvement in delinquency and the juvenile justice system is useful but may be the least effective, at least in terms of impact on rates of delinquency or of mental health problems among delinquent populations. Even if there was allocation of adequate resources and expertise, if based in the juvenile justice system, it will minimize timely access, effective treatment, and suitable opportunity for building on the benefits of reduced symptoms. Thus, greater investment should be made in primary prevention (stopping serious delinquent behavior before it starts) and secondary prevention (intervening soon after delinquent behavior begins). For those youths who are at risk for CD or ODD, there are several evidence-based, primary prevention, family, school, and community strategies. The most promising strategies for CD and ODD in childhood include parent management training, parent-child interaction training (PCIT), and child cognitive problem-solving skills training (Burke, Loeber, and Birmaher 2004; Kadzin 2007). The Incredible Years Training Series is an example of a parent and child skills training strategy that combines child, parent, and teacher programs to prevent and treat conduct problems in early and middle childhood (Webster-Stratton 2001). The program teaches interactive play, reinforcement skills, nonviolent discipline techniques, problem-solving strategies, self-control, and communication strategies to parents; it teaches behavior management and social and problem-solving skills, and builds positive relationships between students and teachers; and it includes a curriculum for students that is designed to promote social competencies, teach conflict management strategies, and reduce conduct problems in the classroom. The program has been shown to be effective in promoting social competence and reducing children's conduct problems (Brotman et al. 2005; Webster-Stratton 2005). How would this reduce delinquency and affect comorbidity? While there is evidence of reducing later delinquency for this program, there has not been linkage to impact on comorbidity. The linkage to reducing later delinquency is through reducing the level of symptoms marking ODD and CD among those participating. It seems important to track how reduction in these symptoms affects later rates of comorbidity and how that might potentiate effects on delinquency.

Secondary evidence-based prevention strategies for CD and ODD during middle childhood and adolescence include Functional Family Therapy, Multisystemic Therapy, and Multidimensional Treatment Foster Care (Burke, Loeber, and Birmaher 2004; Kadzin 2007). These approaches have also been found to be efficacious in treating substance abuse in adolescents (Waldron and Turner 2008). Multidimensional Treatment Foster Care is an approach that provides youths with close supervision and supports that reinforce prosocial behavior and bonding with peers, enhance work habits and academic skills, improve parenting skills and decrease family conflict, and set clear expectations and limits for behavior (MTFC; Fisher and Chamberlain 2000). In this model, youths are placed with trained foster parents who work closely with program staff, other foster parents, and a treatment team consisting of behavior support specialists, youth specialists, family therapists, consulting psychiatrists, daily report callers, and case managers to implement individualized behavior management plans in the home and provide support services (e.g., individual youth or family therapy). The strategy and its adaptation have been found to be effective in reducing conduct problems and delinquency (Chamberlain, Leve, and DeGarmo 2007; Chamberlain et al. 2008; Chamberlain and Reid 1998; Eddy, Whaley, and Chamberlain 2004). As with the Incredible Years and other valuable prevention efforts, however, there is almost no direct or indirect analysis of impact on comorbidity or on those with comorbid disorders.

Evidence-based prevention approaches for substance use are also important, not only for reducing substance use as a comorbid disorder of delinquency, but for reducing delinquency as well. Family and school-based programs that support children's and adolesents' core competencies, such as behavioral self-regulation, parental involvement, school bonding, and social competence, are the most promising for preventing multiple problem behaviors, including substance use (Haegerich and Tolan 2008). For example, the SAFEChildren program (Gorman-Smith et al. 2007) is a family-focused intervention for elementary-age children and their families that aims to promote family relationships and children's self-control and social competence in childhood that may, in turn, reduce both substance use and delinquency later in adolescence. Initial effects suggest that improvements will result in lower levels of substance use as the children progress into adolescence.

There are also evidence-based strategies for the treatment of ADHD in children, including both behavioral (parent training, school-based contingency management, intensive summer peer interventions) and pharmacological (stimulant therapy) treatments. These treatments are particularly effective when used in combination (see Chronis, Jones, and Raggi 2006; Pelham and Fabiano 2008 for reviews).

Although prevention and intervention strategies in childhood and early adolescence are the best long-term investment in reducing juvenile delinquency and comorbid disorders, youth already engaged in a delinquent trajectory and involved in the justice system require tertiary interventions for the mental health disorders that they suffer from, including treatment for depression, PTSD, and substance abuse/dependence. Evidence-based approaches for depression include cognitive behavior therapy in childhood and adolescence and interpersonal therapy in adolescence (David-Ferdon and Kaslow 2008). Cognitive behavior therapy has also been found to be efficacious in treating children and adolescents with PTSD and substance abuse problems (Silverman et al. 2008; Waldron and Turner 2008).

Youth with comorbid disorders may need to be seen as a sub-population of delinquent youth that perhaps should be considered separately in overall delinquency prevention, treatment, and legal processing. However, it may be the effects for this group are not distinct from those without mental disorders or early signs of such disorders. Prevention and intervention programs that promote social competencies and redirect all youth from a life of delinquency may work differently than those focused on symptom reduction and removal. The impact "difference" between competency-oriented or social functioning-oriented efforts and symptom- or disorder-oriented efforts may be an important consideration in research on intervention effects and the utility for those working to reduce and manage delinquency.

Last, there is a critical need for a developmental understanding of disorders, comorbidity, and delinquency. All juvenile justice approaches need to incorporate psychological knowledge of child development. Psychological research on child development prescribes that children should be treated differently than adults given their lack of adult capacity for judgment, intent, and responsibility, and that the justice system has a therapeutic responsibility for all youth. Therapeutic jurisprudence approaches include interventions aimed at family and other key developmental influences, particularly community-based interventions that allow for continuity of services and greater connections between home and school compared to residential setting interventions (Tolan and Titus 2009).

B. Implications for Policy

The number of youth who experience comorbid disorders brings forth several juvenile justice policy issues. As there is growing acknowledgement of the legitimacy of diminished capacity due to young age, those with disorders seem appropriate for even further protection from strict legal processing. In his book *Double Jeopardy*, Grisso (2004) argues that the justice system holds several obligations for involved youth who suffer from mental health disorders. The first obligation includes providing treatment for crisis conditions, for stabilization of functioning so that rehabilitation efforts can be successful, and for maintenance of treatment even after release, such as through coordination of services in the community. The second obligation is an assurance of due process—that is, assessment of competency for *Miranda* rights waiver, competency to stand trial, and youth understanding of responsibility for illegal activity (i.e., determining whether a mental disorder impairs functioning to a degree that it should be considered a mitigating or perhaps exculpatory factor in their adjudication). The final obligation includes fulfilling the commitment to public safety by providing youths the placement and treatment they need to be free from risk of harming others while in custody and after community release. Each of these issues requires better policy planning around assessment, treatment, and prevention (Grisso 2004).

In 2002, an expert panel of researchers and practitioners convened to develop policy recommendations for identifying and responding to the mental health needs of youth in the justice system (Wasserman et al. 2003). These recommendations include providing a mental health screen within the first twenty-four hours of a youth's arrival at a facility, providing mental health screening and/or assessment for all youths as early as possible to determine the need for mental health services and at the time youths are preparing to leave a facility and return to the community, conducting comprehensive mental health assessments based on a review of information from multiple sources that measure a range of mental health concerns, reassessment on a regular basis, and credentialing and training of staff involved in screening and assessment procedures. Readers are referred to this set of recommendations for focus, organization, and specific procedures to adequately identify and organize treatment for mental health problems in youths in the justice system.

Delinquent youth interface with many service systems, including school, child welfare, juvenile justice, and health. As with other youth with mental disorders, coordination and communication across systems is important for treatment. Systems often operate disjunctively, even though the same children and families are served by each of these systems. Although systems integration has been called upon for years, the time has come for more integrated responses in identifying high-risk youth and providing evidence-based prevention and treatment (Treuting, Haegerich, and Tolan 2002). In 2000, the Surgeon General's Conference on Children's Mental Health called for improvements in the assessment and recognition of mental health needs, encouraging early identification of mental disorders in school, health, social service, and juvenile justice systems, and an increased recognition by policy makers of the role that mental health problems play in placing youths at risk for entering the justice system. The conference also highlighted the need for greater resources to handle psychiatric treatment in juvenile justice settings, and greater follow-up after release to engage clinical and family resources (U. S. Public Health Service 2000).

Most recently, in September 2009, the American Psychological Association (APA) called on Congress to focus on provision of community-based mental health services for youths in the justice system. This call was based on developmental psychology and neuroscience research that illustrates the significant mental health needs of youths and the importance of treatment, the expense of incarceration, and the questioned effectiveness of incarceration in meeting rehabilitation goals. The APA highlighted the importance of a developmentally appropriate response to juvenile crime that considers immaturity and vulnerability, factors that could mitigate the culpability of youths for their actions in certain circumstances. Thus, APA has called for community-based service provision to be integrated into the reauthorization of the Juvenile Justice and Delinquency Prevention Act (APA 2009).

In addition to improving assessment and treatment in the juvenile justice system as it functions today, a major advance for improving attention to mental health would be to base intervention, including sanctions, within community settings as much as possible. There is ample evidence that for criminal behavior and mental health issues, community-based treatment is more effective for youths. Moreover, reparation to the community and reintegration represent opportunities to redirect delinquent youth while minimizing extraction from family and community support. Similarly, drug and mental health courts that integrate the criminal justice and child welfare/mental health concerns can be quite useful. Although these diversion alternatives have not been rigorously evaluated enough to develop a strong science base, specialized drug and mental health courts, restorative justice approaches (e.g., victim-offender mediation, family group conferencing), and teen courts show some promise in providing developmentally appropriate services, improving youth outcomes, and saving costs (Tolan and Titus 2009). Moreover, it is likely that they would improve consideration of comorbidity and its effects on delinquency.

IX. Conclusion

Comorbidity of delinquency and mental disorder is prevalent, even withstanding the sampling and measurement challenges faced in research studies and the overlap of symptoms across disorders. Better integration of mental health prevention and treatment into juvenile justice processing is needed—in particular, community-based service systems. A stronger focus on the promotion of healthy development among high-risk youth and the implementation of empirically based preventive interventions prior to delinquent involvement is desired. Within the juvenile justice system, there needs to be a return to the recognition that youth are still developing emotionally and psychologically, as well as physically, and that our strongest focus is on promoting and, when needed, recovering their socially valuable potential.

REFERENCES

Abikoff, Howard, and Rachel G. Klein. 1992. "Attention-Deficit Hyperactivity and Conduct Disorder: Comorbidity and Implications for Treatment." *Journal of Consulting and Clinical Psychology* 60: 881–92.

Abram, Karen M., Linda A. Teplin, Devon R. Charles, Sandra L. Longworth, Gary M. McClelland, and Mina K. Dulcan. 2004. "Posttraumatic Stress Disorder and Trauma in Youth in Juvenile Detention." *Archives of General Psychiatry* 61: 403–10.

Abram, Karen M., Linda A. Teplin, Gary M. McClelland, and Mina K. Dulcan. 2009. "Comorbid Psychiatric Disorders in Youth in Juvenile Detention." *Archives of General Psychiatry* 60: 1097–108.

Abram, Karen M., Jason J. Washburn, Linda A. Teplin, Kristin M. Emanuel, Erin G. Romero, and Gary M. McClelland. 2007. "Posttraumatic Stress Disorder and Psychiatric Comorbidity Among Detained Youths." *Psychiatric Services* 58: 1311–16.

American Psychiatric Association. 1994. *Diagnostic and Statistical Manual of Mental Disorders (DSM-IV)*, 4th ed. Washington, DC: American Psychiatric Association.

American Psychological Association. "APA Supports Reauthorization of Juvenile Justice Act on Law's 35th Anniversary," press release, Sept. 9, 2009, http://www.apa.org/news/press/releases/2009/09/juvenile-justice.aspx.

Angold, Adrian, Jane Costello, and Alaattin Erkanli. 1999. "Comorbidity." *Journal of Child Psychology, Psychiatry, and Allied Disciplines* 40: 57–87.

Beyers, Jennifer M., and Rolf Loeber. 2003. "Untangling Developmental Relations Between Depressed Mood and Delinquency in Male Adolescents." *Journal of Abnormal Child Psychology* 31: 247–66.

Broidy, Lisa M., Daniel S. Nagin, Richard E. Tremblay, John E. Bates, Bobby Brame, Kenneth A. Dodge, Davide Feergusson, John L. Horwood, Rolf Loeber, Robert Laird, Donald R. Lynam, Terrie E. Moffitt, Gregory S. Pettit, and Frank Vitaro. 2003. "Developmental Trajectories of Childhood Disruptive Behaviors and Adolescent Delinquency: A Six-Site, Cross-National Study." *Developmental Psychology* 39: 222–45.

Brotman, Laurie Miller, Kathleen K. Gouley, Daniel Chesir-Teran, Tracy Dennis, Rachel G. Klein, and Patrick Shrout. 2005. "Prevention for Preschoolers at High Risk for Conduct Problems: Immediate Outcomes on Parenting Practices and Child Social Competence." *Journal of Child Clinical and Adolescent Psychology* 34: 724–34.

Burke, Jeffrey D., Rolf Loeber, and Boris Birmaher. 2004. "Oppositional Defiant Disorder and Conduct Disorder: A Review of the Past 10 years: Part II." *Focus: The Journal of Lifelong Learning in Psychiatry* 2: 558–76.

Cauffman, Elizabeth, S. Shirley Feldman, Jaime Waterman, and Hans Steiner. 1998. "Posttraumatic Stress Disorder Among Female Juvenile Offenders." *Journal of the American Academy of Child and Adolescent Psychiatry* 37: 1209–16.

Centers for Disease Control and Prevention. 2008. "Youth Risk Behavior Surveillance—
    United States, 2007." *Morbidity and Mortality Weekly Report* 57 (SS4): 1–131.
Cerdá, Magdalena, Brisa N. Sánchez, Sandro Galea, Melissa Tracy, and Stephen L. Buka.
    2008. "Estimating Co-occurring Behavioral Trajectories Within a Neighborhood
    Context: A Case Study of Multivariate Transition Models for Clustered Data."
    American Journal of Epidemiology 168: 1190–203.
Chamberlain, Patricia, Leslie D. Leve, and David S. DeGarmo. 2007. "Multidimensional
    Treatment Foster Care for Girls in the Juvenile Justice System: 2-year Follow-up of a
    Randomized Clinical Trial." *Journal of Consulting and Clinical Psychology* 75: 187–93.
Chamberlain, Patricia, Joe Price, Leslie D. Leve, Heidemarie Laurent, John A. Landsverk,
    and John B. Reid. 2008. "Prevention of Problem Behaviors for Children in Foster Care:
    Outcomes and Mediation Effects." *Prevention Science* 9: 17–27.
Chamberlain, Patricia, and John B. Reid. 1998. "Comparison of Two Community
    Alternatives to Incarceration for Chronic Juvenile Offenders. *Journal of Consulting and
    Clinical Psychology* 6: 624–33.
Chronis, Andrea M., Heather A. Jones, and Veronica L. Raggi. 2006. "Evidence-Based
    Psychosocial Treatments for Children and Adolescents with Attention-Deficit/
    Hyperactivity Disorder." *Clinical Psychology Review* 26: 486–502.
Copeland, William E., Shari Miller-Johnson, Gordon Keeler, Adrian Angold, and E. Jane
    Costello. 2007. "Childhood Psychiatric Disorders and Young Adult Crime: A
    Prospective, Population-Based Study." *American Journal of Psychiatry* 164: 1668–75.
David-Ferdon, Corinne, and Nadine J. Kaslow. 2008. "Evidence-Based Psychosocial
    Treatments for Child and Adolescent Depression." *Journal of Clinical Child and
    Adolescent Psychology* 37: 62–104.
Doherty, Elaine E., Kerry M. Green, and Margaret E. Ensminger. 2008. "Investigating the
    Long-Term Influence of Adolescent Delinquency on Drug Use Initiation." *Drug and
    Alcohol Dependence* 93: 72–84.
Eddy, J. Mark, Rachel B. Whaley, and Patricia Chamberlain. 2004. "The Prevention of
    Violent Behavior by Chronic and Serious Male Juvenile Offenders: A 2-Year
    Follow-up of a Randomized Clinical Trial." *Journal of Emotional and Behavioral
    Disorders* 12: 2–8.
Edens, John F., and Randy K. Otto. 1997. "Prevalence of Mental Disorders Among Youth in
    the Juvenile Justice System." *Focal Point* 11: 1–9.
Esposito-Smythers, Christianne, Joseph V. Penn, L. A. R. Stein, Molly Lacher-Katz, and
    Anthony Spirito. 2008. "A Test of Problem Behavior and Self-Medication Theories in
    Incarcerated Adolescent Males." *Journal of Child and Adolescent Substance Abuse* 17:
    41–56.
Fisher, Philip A., and Patricia Chamberlain. 2000. "Multidimensional Treatment Foster
    Care: A Program for Intensive Parenting, Family Support, and Skill Building." *Journal
    of Emotional and Behavioral Disorders* 8: 155–64.
Gorman-Smith, Deborah, Patrick Tolan, David B. Henry, Elana Quintana, Kelly Lutovsky,
    and Amy Leventhal. 2007. "Schools and Families Educating Children: A Preventive
    Intervention for Early Elementary School Children." In *Preventing Youth Substance
    Abuse*, edited by Patrick H. Tolan, J. José Szapocznik, and Soledad Sambrano.
    Washington, DC: American Psychological Association.
Grisso, Thomas. 2004. *Double Jeapordy: Adolescent Offenders with Mental Disorders.*
    Chicago, IL: University of Chicago Press.
Haegerich, Tamara M., and Patrick H. Tolan. 2008. "Core Competencies and the Prevention
    of Adolescent Substance Abuse." In *Core Competencies to Prevent Problem Behaviors*

and Promote Positive Youth Development, edited by Nancy G. Guerra and Catherine P. Bradshaw. New Directions for Child and Adolescent Development 122: 47–60.

Hussey, David L., Allyson M. Drinkard, and Daniel J. Flannery. (2007). "Comorbid Substance Use and Mental Disorders Among Offending Youth." Journal of Social Work Practice in the Addictions 7: 117–38.

Kazdin, Alan E. 2007. "Psychosocial Treatments for Conduct Disorder in Children and Adolescents." In A Guide to Treatments That Work, 3rd ed., edited by Peter E. Nathan and Jack M. Gorman. Oxford University Press: Oxford.

Lahey, Benjamin B., Terrie E. Moffitt, and Avshalom Caspi. 2003. Causes of Conduct Disorder and Juvenile Delinquency. New York: Guilford.

Loeber, Rolf, Jeffrey D. Burke, Benjamin B. Lahey, Alaina Winters, and Marcie Zera. 2000. "Oppositional Defiant and Conduct Disorder: A Review of the Past 10 Years, Part I." Journal of the American Academy of Child and Adolescent Psychiatry 39: 1468–84.

Loeber, Rolf, and Kate Keenan. 1994. "Interaction Between Conduct Disorder and Its Comorbid Conditions: Effects of Age and Gender." Clinical Psychology Review 14: 497–523.

Loeber, Rolf, Magda Stouthamer-Loeber, and Helene R. White. 1999. "Developmental Aspects of Delinquency and Internalizing Problems and Their Association with Persistent Juvenile Substance Use Between Ages 7 and 18." Journal of Clinical Child and Adolescent Psychology 28: 322–32.

Loeber, Rolf, Phen Wung, Kate Keenan, Bruce Giroux, Magda Stouthamer-Loeber, Welmoet Van Kammen, and Barbara Maughan. 1993. "Developmental Pathways in Disruptive Child Behavior." Development and Psychopathology 5: 103–33.

Mannuzza, Salvatore, Rachel Klein, and John L. Moulton III. 2007. "Lifetime Criminality Among Boys with Attention Deficit Hyperactivity Disorder: A Prospective Follow-up Study into Adulthood Using Official Arrest Records." Psychiatry Research 160: 237–46.

McCord, Joan, and Margaret E. Ensminger. 1997. "Multiple Risks and Comorbidity in an African-American Population." Criminal Behaviour and Mental Health 7: 339–52.

Moffitt, Terrie. 1990. "Juvenile Delinquency and Attention Deficit Disorder: Boys' Developmental Trajectories From Age 3 to Age 15." Child Development 61: 893–910.

Moffitt, Terrie. 1993. "Adolescence-Limited and Life-Course-Persistent Antisocial Behavior: A Developmental Taxonomy." Psychological Bulletin 100: 674–701.

Moffitt, Terrie E., Avshalom Caspi, Honalee Harrington, and Barry J. Milne. 2002. "Males on the Life-Course Persistent and Adolescence-Limited Antisocial Pathways: Follow-up at Age 26 Years." Development and Psychopathology 14: 179–207.

National Research Council and Institute of Medicine. 2009. Preventing Mental, Emotional, and Behavioral Disorders Among Young People: Progress and Possibilities, edited by Mary Ellen O'Connell, Thomas Boat, and Kenneth E. Warner. Committee on the Prevention of Mental Disorders and Substance Abuse Among Children, Youth, and Young Adults: Research Advances and Promising Interventions. Board on Children, Youth, and Families, Division of Behavioral and Social Sciences and Education. Washington, DC: The National Academies Press.

Nofziger, Stacey, and Don Kurtz. 2005. "Violent Lives: A Lifestyle Model Linking Exposure to Violence to Juvenile Violent Offending." Journal of Research in Crime and Delinquency 42: 3–26.

Overbeek, Geertjan, Wilma Vollebergh, Wim Meeus, Rutger Engels, and Eric Luijpers. 2001. "Course, Co-occurrence, and Longitudinal Associations of Emotional Disturbance and Delinquency from Adolescence to Young Adulthood: A Six-Year Three-Wave Study." Journal of Youth and Adolescence 30: 401–26.

Pelham, William E. Jr., and Gregory A. Fabiano. 2008. "Evidence-Based Psychosocial Treatments for Attention-Deficit/Hyperactivity Disorder." *Journal of Clinical Child and Adolescent Psychology* 37: 184–214.

Rutter, Michael. 1997. "Comorbidity: Concepts, Claims, and Choices." *Criminal Behaviour and Mental Health* 7: 265–85.

Sheidow, Ashli J., Martha K. Strachan, Joel A. Minden, David B. Henry, Patrick H. Tolan, and Deborah Gorman-Smith. 2008. "The Relation of Antisocial Behavior Patterns and Changes in Internalizing Symptoms for a Sample of Inner-City Youth: Comorbidity Within a Developmental Framework." *Journal of Youth and Adolescence* 37: 821–29.

Silverman, Wendy K., Claudio Ortiz, Chockalingham Viswesvaran, Barbara J. Burns, Kavid J. Kolko, Frank W. Putnam, and Lisa Amaya-Jackson. 2008. "Evidence-Based Psychosocial Treatments for Children and Adolescents Exposed to Traumatic Events." *Journal of Clinical Child and Adolescent Psychology* 37: 156–83.

Smith, Carolyn, and Terence Thornberry. 1995. "The Relationship Between Child Maltreatment and Adolescent Involvement in Delinquency." *Criminology* 33: 451–81.

Stahl, Nicole D., and Harvey F. Clarizio. 1999. "Conduct Disorder and Comorbidity." *Psychology in the Schools* 36: 41–50.

Steiner, Hans, Ivan G. Garcia, and Zakee Matthews. 1997. "Posttraumatic Stress Disorder in Incarcerated Juvenile Delinquents." *Journal of the American Academy of Child and Adolescent Psychiatry* 36: 357–65.

Taylor, Jeanette, William G. Iacono, and Matt McGue. 2000. "Evidence for a Genetic Etiology of Early-Onset Delinquency." *Journal of Abnormal Psychology* 109: 634–43.

Taylor, Jeanett, Steve Malone, William G. Iacono, and Matt McGue. 2002. "Development of Substance Dependence in Two Delinquency Subgroups and Nondelinquents from a Male Twin Sample." *Journal of the American Academy of Child and Adolescent Psychiatry* 41: 1–8.

Teplin, Linda A., Karen M. Abram, Gary M. McClelland, Mina K. Dulcan, and Amy A. Mericle. 2002. "Psychiatric Disorders in Youth in Juvenile Detention." *Archives of General Psychiatry* 59: 1133–43.

Thompson, Laetitia, Paula D. Riggs, Susan K. Mikulich, and Thomas J. Crowley. 1996. "Contribution of ADHD Symptoms to Substance Use Problems and Delinquency in Conduct-Disordered Adolescents." *Journal of Abnormal Child Psychology* 24: 325–47.

Thompson, Martie P., Ching-hua Ho, and J. B. Kingree. 2007. "Prospective Associations Between Delinquency and Suicidal Behaviors in a Nationally Representative Sample." *Journal of Adolescent Health* 40: 232–37.

Timmons-Mitchell, Jane, Christie Brown, Charles Schulz, Susan E. Webster, Lee A. Underwood, and William E. Semple. 1997. "Comparing the Mental Health Needs of Female and Male Incarcerated Juvenile Delinquents." *Behavioral Sciences and the Law* 15: 195–202.

Tolan, Patrick H., and Deborah Gorman-Smith. 2002. "What Violence Prevention Research Can Tell Us About Developmental Psychopathology." *Development and Psychopathology* 14: 713–29.

Tolan, Patrick H., and Jennifer A. Titus. 2009. "Therapeutic Jurisprudence in Juvenile Justice." In *Children as Victims, Witnesses, and Offenders: Psychological Science and the Law* edited by Bette L. Bottoms, Cynthia J. Najdowski, and Gail S. Goodman. New York: Guilford.

Treuting, Jennifer J., Tamara M. Haegerich, and Patrick H. Tolan. 2002. "Preventing Delinquency and Antisocial Behavior." In *Innovative Approaches to the Prevention of*

Delinquency and Antisocial Behavior, edited by David Glenwick and Leonard Jason. New York: Springer.

Turner, Aaron P., Mary E. Larimer, Irwin G. Sarason, and Eric W. Trupin. 2005. "Identifying a Negative Mood Subtype in Incarcerated Adolescents: Relationship to Substance Use." *Addictive Behaviors* 30: 1442–48.

Ulzen, Thaddeus P. M., and Hayley Hamilton. 1998. "The Nature and Characteristics of Psychiatric Comorbidity in Incarcerated Adolescents." *Canadian Journal of Psychiatry* 43: 57–63.

U.S. Public Health Service. 2000. *Report of the Surgeon General's Conference on Children's Mental Health: A National Action Agenda*. Washington, DC: U.S. Department of Health and Human Services.

Vermeiren, Robert. 2003. "Psychopathology and Delinquency in Adolescents: A Descriptive and Developmental Perspective." *Clinical Psychology Review* 23: 277–318.

Wade, Terrance J. 2001. "Delinquency and Health Among Adolescents: Multiple Outcomes of a Similar Social and Structural Process." *International Journal of Law and Psychiatry* 24: 447–67.

Waldman, Irwin D., and Wendy S. Slutske. 2000. "Antisocial Behavior and Alcoholism: A Behavioral Genetic Perspective on Comorbidity." *Clinical Psychology Review* 20: 255–87.

Waldron, Holly B., and Charles W. Turner. 2008. "Evidence-Based Psychosocial Treatments for Adolescent Substance Abuse." *Journal of Clinical Child and Adolescent Psychology* 37: 238–61.

Wasserman, Gail A., Peter S. Jensen, Susan J. Ko, Joseph Cocozza, Eric Trupin, Adrian Angold, Elizabeth Cauffman, and Thomas Grisso. 2003. "Mental Health Assessments in Juvenile Justice: Report on the Consensus Conference." *Journal of the American Academy of Child and Adolescent Psychiatry* 42: 752–61.

Webster-Stratton, Carolyn. 2001. "The Incredible Years: Parents, Teachers, and Children Training Series." *Residential Treatment for Children and Youth* 18: 31–45.

Webster-Stratton, Carolyn. 2005. "The Incredible Years: A Training Series for the Prevention and Treatment of Conduct Problems in Young Children." In *Psychosocial Treatments for Child and Adolescent Disorders: Empirically-Based Strategies for Clinical Practice*, 2nd ed., edited by Euthymia D. Hibbs and Peter S. Jensen. Washington, DC: American Psychological Association.

Wiesner, Margit, and Michael Windle. 2004. "Assessing Covariates of Adolescent Delinquency Trajectories: A Latent Growth Mixture Modeling Approach." *Journal of Youth and Adolescence* 33: 431–42.

Wiesner, Margit, and Michael Windle. 2006. "Young Adult Substance Use and Depression as a Consequence of Delinquency Trajectories During Middle Adolescence." *Journal of Research on Adolescence* 16: 239–64.

CHAPTER 7

....

PREDICTORS OF VIOLENT YOUNG OFFENDERS

....

DAVID P. FARRINGTON

THE main aim of this chapter is to review what is known about childhood predictors of youthful (under age 21) violent offending. As will be explained later, violent offenders tend to be frequent offenders, so the predictors of violent offenders are generally similar to the predictors of persistent offenders. Also, violent offenders disproportionally commit serious nonviolent crimes, but most research on serious offenders concerns violent offenders.

The most basic definition of violence is behavior that is intended to cause, and that actually does cause, physical or psychological injury. The main focus here is on the most important violent crimes that are defined by the criminal law: namely homicide, assault, robbery, and forcible rape. The main emphasis is on results obtained in the United States, Great Britain, and similar Western countries, and on stranger or street violence, not domestic or within-family violence (see, e.g., Desmarais, Gibas, and Nicholls 2010) or sex offenses (see, e.g., Van Wijk et al. 2007). Most research focuses on male offenders and on the offenses of assault and homicide.

This chapter focuses on knowledge gained in studies of individual offenders. It first reviews the development of violent offending, including prevalence at different ages, continuity, and specialization or versatility in offending. It then reviews knowledge about major individual, family, and socioeconomic risk factors. Information about peer, school, and community risk factors is provided in other chapters in this handbook. It also investigates how accurately violent offenders can be predicted in childhood.

I. Risk and Protective Factors

Within one short chapter, it is impossible to review everything that is known about the prediction of violent young offenders. This chapter will focus especially on knowledge gained in major prospective longitudinal studies of offending, in which community samples of at least several hundred people are followed up from childhood into adolescence and adulthood, with repeated personal interviews as well as the collection of record data. More extensive information about violence can be found in Delisi and Conis (2008), Ferguson (2010), Flannery, Vaszonyi, and Waldman (2007), Riedel and Welsh (2008), and Zahn, Brownstein, and Jackson (2004).

During the 1990s, there was a revolution in criminology, as the risk factor prevention paradigm became influential (see Farrington 2000b). The basic idea of this paradigm is very simple: identify the key risk factors for offending and implement prevention methods designed to counteract them. This paradigm was imported to criminology from public health, where it had been used successfully for many years to tackle illnesses such as cancer and heart disease, by pioneers such as Hawkins and Catalano (1992). The risk factor prevention paradigm links explanation and prevention, fundamental and applied research, and scholars, policy makers, and practitioners. Loeber and Farrington (1998) presented a detailed exposition of this paradigm as applied to serious and violent juvenile offenders.

A risk factor for violence is defined as a variable that predicts a high probability of violence. Typically, risk factors are dichotomized so that they are either present or absent. This chapter focuses on changeable risk factors (e.g., excluding gender and race/ethnicity). In order to determine whether a risk factor is a predictor or possible cause of violence, the risk factor must be measured before the violence. Therefore, prospective longitudinal surveys are needed to investigate risk factors for violence.

The paradigm typically also emphasizes protective factors, suggesting that intervention methods to enhance them should also be implemented. However, in the past, the term "protective factor" has been used ambiguously. Some researchers have suggested that a protective factor is merely the opposite end of the scale to a risk factor (e.g., White, Moffitt, and Silva 1989). For example, if poor parental supervision is a risk factor, good parental supervision might be a protective factor. However, this seems to be using two terms for the same variable. Other researchers have suggested that a protective factor interacts with a risk factor to minimize or buffer its effects (e.g., Rutter 1985). Typically, the impact of a protective factor is then studied in the presence of a risk factor. Loeber, Farrington, Stouthamer-Loeber, and White (2008) suggested a consistent terminology. Following Sameroff, Bartko, Baldwin, Baldwin, and Seifer (1998), they defined promotive factors as variables that predict a low probability of violence, and protective factors as variables that predict a low probability of violence among persons exposed to risk factors.

II. Prospective Longitudinal Surveys

This chapter will focus especially on results obtained in two prospective longitudinal surveys: the Cambridge Study in Delinquent Development and the Pittsburgh Youth Study. The Cambridge Study is a prospective longitudinal survey of over four hundred London males from age 8 to age 48 (see Farrington et al. 2006; Piquero, Farrington, and Blumstein 2007). These males were originally assessed in 1961–62, when they were attending six state primary schools in London and were aged 8 to 9. Therefore, the most common year of birth of the males is 1953. All boys of that age in those schools were included in the Study. The Study males have been interviewed and assessed nine times between ages 8 and 48. Attrition has been very low; for example, 95% of those still alive were interviewed at age 18, 94% at age 32, and 93% at age 48.

The assessments in schools measured such factors as intelligence, personality, and impulsiveness, while information was collected in the interviews about such topics as living circumstances, employment histories, relationships with females, leisure activities such as drinking, drug use, and fighting, and of course violence and offending behavior. The boys' parents were also interviewed about once a year from when the boys were aged 8 until when they were aged 15. The parents provided details about such matters as family income, family composition, their employment histories, their child-rearing practices (including discipline and supervision), and the boys' temporary or permanent separations from them. Also, the boys' teachers completed questionnaires when the boys were aged about 8, 10, 12, and 14. These furnished information about such topics as their restlessness or poor concentration, truancy, school attainment, and disruptive behavior in class. Searches of the criminal records of the males, of their biological relatives (fathers, mothers, brothers, and sisters), and of their wives and female partners, were also carried out.

Up to age 40, 16% of the Cambridge Study males were convicted for a violent offense (serious assault, robbery, or weapons); 9% were convicted for violence between ages 10 and 20, and 10% between ages 21 and 40. One-fifth of the males (20% of 389 known) were identified as self-reported violent offenders at ages 15 to 18, because they were highest on number of fights, starting fights, carrying a weapon, and using a weapon in a fight (Farrington 2000a). Between ages 27 and 32, 16% (of 377 males known) were identified as self-reported violent offenders, because they had either (a) been involved in four or more physical fights in which blows were struck, or (b) hit their wife or female partner without her hitting them (Farrington 2001a).

In this chapter, childhood risk factors for youthful violence convictions at ages 10 to 20, and for self-reported violence at ages 15 to 18, will be reported to indicate the predictability of youth violence in a typical longitudinal study. There was a significant overlap between self-reported and official violence in the Cambridge Study. A quarter of young self-reported violent offenders were convicted for violence by age 20, compared with 5% of self-reported nonviolent youth (odds ratio or OR = 6.2, 95% confidence interval or CI = 3.0 to 12.7; the OR is used here as the main measure of predictive efficiency).

In the Pittsburgh Youth Study, over 1,500 boys from Pittsburgh public schools were followed up (see Loeber, Farrington, Stouthamer-Loeber, and van Kammen 1998; Loeber et al. 2008). Initially, five hundred were in first grade (aged about 7), five hundred were in fourth grade (aged about 10), and five hundred were in seventh grade (aged about 13) of public schools in the city of Pittsburgh. Out of about one thousand boys in each grade chosen at random, about 850 were given a screening instrument measuring their antisocial behavior. Based on this instrument, 250 high-risk boys and 250 boys chosen at random from the remainder were followed up in each grade. These boys were mostly born between 1974 and 1980. The youngest and oldest cohorts were assessed at least once a year for 12 years, from age 7 to age 19 (youngest) and from age 13 to age 25 (oldest). The middle cohort was assessed every six months until age 13, and then finally at age 22. Information about risk factors and violence was collected from the boys, their mothers, and their teachers.

By age 19, 26% of the boys in the youngest cohort had been arrested for serious violence (homicide, attacking to injure, robbery, or forcible rape). By age 25, 35% of the boys in the oldest cohort had been arrested for serious violence. Special analyses were carried out to investigate the boys who became convicted homicide offenders (see Farrington, Loeber, Stallings, and Homish, 2008; Loeber et al. 2005). This chapter presents results obtained by comparing childhood risk factors with official and reported violence in the middle cohort of boys (based on Farrington 1998). This cohort was chosen for comparability with the Cambridge Study because childhood risk factors were measured at age 10. About 12% of the boys were petitioned to the juvenile court for Index (serious) violence between ages 10 and 17, while 30% of the boys were reported to have committed violence (attack to hurt, robbery, or rape) between ages 10 and 13. As expected, the official and reported violent boys overlapped significantly. A quarter of reported violent boys were petitioned to court, compared with 7% of the remainder (OR = 4.6, CI 2.6 to 8.1).

Results from the Cambridge and Pittsburgh studies are presented to show illustrative findings and the strength of relationships between childhood risk factors and youthful violent offending. These results are fairly typical, as is shown by more extensive reviews and meta-analyses published by Hawkins et al. (1998), Lipsey and Derzon (1998), and Derzon (2010), based on prospective longitudinal studies. Results obtained in many different longitudinal surveys are presented here; for more information about all of these studies, see Farrington and Welsh (2007, pp. 29–36).

III. Violence Over the Life Course

A. Measurement and Prevalence

The most common ways of identifying violent offenders are by using police or court records or self-reports of offending. For example, in the Seattle Social Development

Project, which is a follow-up of over eight hundred children from age 10 to age 33, 8.6% of youth self-reported a robbery and 3.3% had a court referral for robbery as juveniles (Farrington et al. 2003). The discrepancy was greater for assault, where 61.3% self-reported but only 12.7% were referred to court. The comparison between self-reports and official records gives some indication of the probability of a young violent offender being caught and officially processed. Self-reported violence had predictive validity in the Seattle study: 14% of those who admitted assault had a later court referral for assault, compared with 4% of the remainder (Jolliffe et al. 2003).

Violent offending tends to peak in the teenage years in many different countries. In the United States in 2008, the peak age of arrest for robbery and forcible rape was 18, and for murder and aggravated assault it was 19 (Bureau of Justice Statistics. Sourcebook of Criminal Justice Statistics 2009, Table 4.7). Similar results have been obtained in self-report surveys. For example, in the 2003 English national self-report survey, the percentage admitting violence in the previous year peaked at 23% of males at ages 16 to 17 and 12% of females at ages 14 to 15 (Budd, Sharp, and Mayhew 2005).

Many theories have been proposed to explain why offending (especially by males) peaks in the teenage years. There may be changes with age in physical capabilities and opportunities for crime linked to changes in "routine activities" (Cohen and Felson 1979), such as going out in the evenings with other males. The most popular explanation emphasizes the importance of contextual influences (Farrington 1986). From birth, children are under the influence of their parents, who generally discourage offending. However, during their teenage years, juveniles gradually break away from the control of their parents and become influenced by their peers, who may encourage offending in many cases. After age 20, offending declines again as peer influences give way to a new set of family influences hostile to offending, originating in spouses and female partners.

B. Continuity

In general, there is continuity from childhood aggression to youth violence. In the Orebro (Sweden) longitudinal study of over one thousand children from age 10 to age 45, two-thirds of boys who were officially recorded for violence up to age 26 had high aggressiveness scores at ages 10 and 13 (rated by teachers), compared with 30% of all boys (Stattin and Magnusson 1989). In the Woodlawn (Chicago) follow-up study of over 1,200 African American children, teacher ratings of aggressiveness at age 6 predicted arrests for violent crimes up to age 32 (McCord and Ensminger 1997). Similarly, in the Jyvaskyla (Finland) follow-up of 369 children from age 8 to age 42, peer ratings of aggression at ages 8 and 14 significantly predicted officially recorded violence up to age 20 (Pulkkinen 1987).

There is also continuity from juvenile to adult violence. In Columbus, Ohio, 59% of violent juveniles were arrested as adults in the next five to nine years, and 42% of these adult offenders were charged with at least one Index violent offense (Hamparian et al. 1985). More of those arrested for Index violence as juveniles were rearrested as adults than of those arrested for minor violence (simple assault or molesting) as juveniles.

In the Cambridge Study, 34% of the boys convicted for youthful violence were reconvicted for adult violence, compared with only 8% of those not convicted for youthful violence (OR = 6.1, CI = 2.8 to 13.5). There was also continuity in self-reported violence; 29% of youthful violent offenders were also adult violent offenders, compared with 12% of nonviolent youth (OR = 3.0, CI = 1.7 to 5.4). While it is possible that part of the continuity in officially recorded violence may be attributable to continuity in police targeting, the continuity in self-reported violence indicates that there is real continuity in violent behavior.

Generally, an early age of onset of violence predicts a relatively long career of violence, as found in the Pittsburgh Youth Study (Loeber et al. 2008). Moffitt (1993) suggested that the "life course-persistent" offenders who started early (around age 10) and had long criminal careers were fundamentally different from the "adolescence-limited" offenders who started later (around age 14) and had short criminal careers. Trajectory analyses for violence in the Pittsburgh Youth Study identified an early onset-chronic trajectory and an early desistance trajectory, in agreement to some extent with Moffitt's typology (Loeber, Lacourse, and Homish 2005).

One likely explanation of the continuity in aggression and violence over time is that there are persisting individual differences in an underlying potential to commit aggressive or violent behavior. In any cohort, the people who are relatively more aggressive at one age also tend to be relatively more aggressive at later ages, even though absolute levels of aggressive behavior and behavioral manifestations of violence are different at different ages.

C. Specialization or Versatility

In most research, violent offenders appear to be versatile rather than specialized. They tend to commit many different types of crimes and also show other problems such as heavy drinking, drug use, an unstable job record, and sexual promiscuity (West and Farrington 1977, p.149). There is also versatility in types of violence. For example, males who assault their female partners are significantly likely to have convictions for other types of violent offenses (Farrington 1994), and soccer hooligans are very similar to other types of violent offenders (Farrington 2006a).

As an indication of their versatility, violent people typically commit more nonviolent offenses than violent offenses. In the Oregon Youth Study, which is a follow-up study of 206 boys between ages 10 and 30, the boys arrested for violence had an average of 6.6 arrests of all kinds, compared with the average 3.4 arrests of boys arrested only for nonviolent offenses (Capaldi and Patterson 1996). In the Cambridge Study, the likelihood of committing a violent offense increased steadily with the total number of offenses committed, and violent offenders were very similar to nonviolent frequent offenders (Farrington 1991). Chronic offenders committed more serious crimes than nonchronic offenders (Farrington and West 1993). Piquero (2000) and Piquero and Buka (2002) also found that violent offenders were versatile rather than specialized in the Philadelphia and Providence perinatal cohorts, respectively.

In the Cambridge Study, the strongest childhood (age 8 to 10) predictor of youthful convictions for violence was the rating of troublesomeness in class by teachers and peers; 21% of 90 troublesome boys were convicted, compared with 5% of the remaining 319 nontroublesome boys (OR = 4.8, CI 2.4 to 9.6; see Table 7.1). Troublesomeness also significantly predicted youthful self-reported violence. Childhood dishonesty (rated by peers) significantly predicted convictions but not self-reported violence, and the best measure of childhood aggression (difficult to discipline, rated by teachers: see Farrington 1978) significantly predicted both convictions and youthful self-reported violence. In the Pittsburgh Youth Study, a high risk score (based on reported antisocial behavior in the screening interview), conduct disorder, physical aggression, and covert behavior (concealing, manipulative, untrustworthy) all predicted official and reported youth violence (Table 7.2). In Tables 7.1 and 7.2, all risk factors were dichotomized into the "worst" quarter versus the remainder. These results support generally the idea that continuity in violence from childhood to adulthood largely reflects continuity in general antisocial behavior.

IV. Childhood Risk Factors

A. Impulsiveness

Among the most important personality dimensions that predict violence are hyperactivity, impulsiveness, poor behavioral control, and attention problems, as the systematic review by Jolliffe and Farrington (2009) shows. Conversely, nervousness and anxiety tend to be negatively related to violence. In the Dunedin, New Zealand, follow-up of over one thousand children from age 3 to age 32, ratings of poor behavioral control (e.g., impulsiveness, lack of persistence) at ages 3 to 5 significantly predicted boys convicted of violence up to age 18, compared to those with no convictions or with nonviolent convictions (Henry et al. 1996). In the same study, the personality dimensions of low constraint (e.g., low cautiousness, seeking excitement) and high negative emotionality (e.g., nervousness, alienation) at age 18 were significantly correlated with convictions for violence (Caspi et al. 1994). Impulsiveness is one of the key dimensions of psychopathy, along with an arrogant, deceitful interpersonal style and deficient affective experience (e.g., low empathy, low guilt); all these dimensions are correlated with violence (Cooke et al. 2004).

Table 7.1. Childhood Predictors of Youthful Violence (Cambridge Study)

Age 8 to 10 Predictors	% Convicted Violence (9)			% Self-Reported Violence (20)		
	No	Yes	OR	No	Yes	OR
Behavioral						
Troublesome	5	21	4.8*	15	38	3.3*
Dishonest	7	15	2.4*	19	24	1.4
Difficult to discipline	5	17	3.1*	17	33	2.5*
Individual						
High daring	5	18	4.4*	13	37	3.9*
Low concentration	7	17	2.9*	19	27	1.6
Nervous	9	6	0.7	22	15	0.6
Few friends	9	4	0.5	22	9	0.3*
Unpopular	7	12	1.8	18	26	1.7*
Low nonverbal IQ	6	17	3.0*	18	26	1.6
Low verbal IQ	8	11	1.4	19	24	1.4
Low attainment	7	14	2.1*	19	27	1.6
Family						
Convicted parent	6	17	3.1*	17	31	2.2*
Delinquent sibling	7	20	3.0*	20	26	1.4
Harsh discipline	5	17	3.4*	17	29	1.9*
Poor supervision	6	19	3.6*	18	33	2.3*
Disrupted family	6	19	3.7*	18	29	1.9*
Parental conflict	6	16	2.8*	19	25	1.4
Large family size	7	15	2.5*	16	33	2.6*
Young mother	8	11	1.4	18	30	1.9*
Socioeconomic						
Low SES	8	12	1.5	19	26	1.5
Low family income	7	16	2.7*	16	34	2.6*
Poor housing	7	13	2.1*	16	28	2.1*

Note: OR = Odds Ratio (* $p < .05$)
Based on reanalysis of Farrington (2007b, Table 2.1)

Table 7.2. Childhood Predictors of Youthful Violence (Pittsburgh Study)

Age 10 Predictors	% Court Violence (12)			% Reported Violence (30)		
	No	Yes	OR	No	Yes	OR
Behavioral						
High risk score	9	20	2.6*	23	50	3.3*
Conduct disorder	10	19	2.2*	26	43	2.1*
Physical aggression	10	17	1.9*	21	52	4.0*
Covert behavior	8	23	3.4*	23	52	3.6*
Individual						
Hyperactive	12	12	1.0	26	48	2.6*
Attention deficit	12	12	1.1	26	43	2.1*
High anxiety	14	7	0.4*	30	31	1.0
Depressed	12	11	0.8	27	42	1.9*
Low attainment (P)	10	18	1.9*	26	42	2.0*
Low attainment (CAT)	9	21	2.7*	24	50	3.2*
Family						
Father behavior problems	11	15	1.3	26	44	2.2*
Parent substance use	12	13	1.1	25	43	2.2*
Low reinforcement	10	17	1.8*	30	31	1.1
Harsh discipline	12	13	1.1	27	36	1.6*
Poor supervision	11	14	1.3	30	31	1.1
Disrupted family	5	16	3.4*	17	39	3.1*
Single mother	9	17	2.0*	24	42	2.3*
Parental conflict	6	11	1.8	19	31	2.0*
Large family size	9	20	2.4*	28	35	1.4
Young mother	8	18	2.7*	25	40	2.0*

Socioeconomic

Low SES	10	18	2.0*	26	44	2.2*
Family on welfare	6	19	3.7*	24	39	2.0*
Poor housing	12	13	1.1	30	34	1.2
Unemployed father	8	8	1.0	19	30	1.8*
Unemployed mother	9	18	2.1*	29	32	1.2

Note: OR = Odds Ratio (* p< .05)
Based on reanalysis of Farrington (1998, Table 2)
(P) = Parent
(CAT) = California Achievement Test

Many other studies show linkages between impulsiveness and violence. In the Copenhagen perinatal project of over 4,100 males, hyperactivity (restlessness and poor concentration) at ages 11 to 13 significantly predicted arrests for violence up to age 22, especially among boys experiencing delivery complications (Brennan, Mednick, and Mednick 1993). More than half of those with both hyperactivity and high delivery complications were arrested for violence, compared to less than 10% of the remainder. Similarly, in the Orebro longitudinal study in Sweden, hyperactivity at age 13 predicted police-recorded violence up to age 26. The highest rate of violence was among males with both motor restlessness and concentration difficulties (15%), compared to 3% of the remainder (Klinteberg et al. 1993).

Similar results were obtained in the Cambridge and Pittsburgh studies. High daring or risk-taking at ages 8 to 10 predicted youthful convictions for violence and youthful self-reported violence in the Cambridge Study (Table 7.1). Poor concentration, hyperactivity, and attention difficulties predicted youthful convictions for violence in the Cambridge Study and reported violence in Pittsburgh (Table 7.2). High anxiety/nervousness was negatively related to youthful violence in both studies, although depression positively predicted reported violence in the Pittsburgh study. In the Cambridge Study, social isolation (having few friends) was negatively related to violence. Farrington and colleagues (1988) suggested that shyness and social isolation might act as protective factors against offending for boys from high-risk backgrounds.

There is no doubt that highly aggressive children trend to be rejected by most of their peers (Coie, Dodge, and Kupersmidt 1990). In the Oregon Youth Study, peer rejection at ages 9 to 10 significantly predicted adult antisocial behavior at ages 23 to 24 (Nelson and Dishion 2004). However, low popularity at ages 8 to 10 was only a marginal predictor of youthful violence in the Cambridge Study (Table 7.1).

B. Low School Attainment

The other main group of individual factors that predict violence comprise low intelligence (IQ) and low school attainment. In the Philadelphia perinatal cohort of nearly one thousand African American children (Denno 1990), low verbal and performance IQ at ages 4 and 7, and low scores on the California Achievement Test at ages 13 to 14 (vocabulary, comprehension, math, language, spelling) all predicted arrests for violence up to age 22. In the Woodlawn study in Chicago, low IQ at age 6 predicted arrests for violent crimes up to age 32 (McCord and Ensminger 1997). In Project Metropolitan in Copenhagen, which is a follow-up of over 11,500 boys from age 12 to age 24, low IQ at age 12 significantly predicted police-recorded violence between ages 15 and 22. The link between low IQ and violence was strongest among lower class boys (Hogh and Wolf 1983).

Similar results were obtained in the Cambridge and Pittsburgh studies (Tables 7.1 and 7.2). Low nonverbal IQ at ages 8 to 10 predicted youthful official violence in the Cambridge Study, and low school achievement at age 10 predicted official violence in both studies and reported violence in Pittsburgh. The extensive meta-analysis by Lipsey and Derzon (1998) also showed that low IQ, low school attainment, and psychological factors such as hyperactivity, attention deficit, impulsivity, and risk-taking were important predictors of later serious and violent offending.

Impulsiveness, attention problems, low intelligence, and low attainment could all be linked to deficits in the executive functions of the brain, located in the frontal lobes. These executive functions include sustaining attention and concentration, abstract reasoning and concept formation, goal formulation, anticipation and planning, programming and initiation of purposive sequences of motor behavior, effective self-monitoring and self-awareness of behavior, and inhibition of inappropriate or impulsive behaviors (Moffitt and Henry 1991; Morgan and Lilienfeld 2000). Interestingly, in the Montreal longitudinal-experimental study, a measure of executive functions based on cognitive-neuropsychological tests at age 14 was the strongest neuropsychological discriminator between violent and nonviolent boys (Seguin et al. 1995). This relationship held independently of a measure of family adversity (based on parental age at first birth, parental education level, broken family, and low socioeconomic status).

C. Antisocial Parents

Numerous family factors predict violence. In the Seattle Social Development Project, parental criminality and parental violence predicted a child's violence (Herrenkohl et al. 2000). Also, in the Columbia County (NY) follow-up of over 850 children from age 8 to age 30, parental delinquency predicted children's arrests for violence (Huesmann, Eron, and Dubow 2002). Many other researchers have found that antisocial parents tend to have aggressive children (e.g., Johnson et al. 2004). The meta-analysis by Derzon (2010) also confirms that parental antisocial behavior is a significant predictor of a child's violence. However, it is not clear that there is any specialized intergenerational transmission from violent parents to violent children, as opposed to general transmission from criminal parents to delinquent children (McCord 1977).

In the Cambridge Study, the strongest childhood predictor of adult convictions for violence was having a convicted parent by the tenth birthday (Farrington 2007b). Table 7.1 shows that a convicted parent and a delinquent sibling predicted youth violence in the Cambridge Study, while Table 7.2 shows that the father's behavior problems predicted reported violence in the Pittsburgh study.

Substance use by parents also predicts violence by children, and smoking by the mother during pregnancy is a particularly important risk factor. A large-scale criminal record follow-up of a general population cohort of over 5,600 males in Finland showed that maternal smoking during pregnancy doubled the risk of violent offending by male offspring, after controlling for other biopsychosocial risk factors (Rasanen et al. 1999). Similar results were obtained in the Copenhagen perinatal project (Brennan, Grekin, and Mednick 1999), and in the Philadelphia perinatal project (McGloin, Pratt, and Piquero 2006). Table 7.2 shows that parental substance use predicted reported violence in Pittsburgh.

Farrington and colleagues (2001) reviewed six possible explanations (including contextual and other factors) of why antisocial behavior was concentrated in families and transmitted from one generation to the next. First, there may be intergenerational continuities in exposure to multiple risk factors such as poverty, disrupted families, and living in deprived neighborhoods. Second, assortative mating (the tendency of antisocial females to choose antisocial males as partners) facilitates the intergenerational transmission of antisocial behavior. Third, family members may influence each other (e.g., older siblings may encourage younger ones to be antisocial). Fourth, the effect of an antisocial parent on a child's antisocial behavior may be mediated by environmental mechanisms such as poor parental supervision and inconsistent discipline. Fifth, intergenerational transmission may be mediated by genetic mechanisms. Sixth, there may be labeling and police bias against known criminal families.

D. Child-Rearing Factors

In her classic follow-up of 250 Boston boys in the Cambridge-Somerville Youth Study, McCord (1979) found that the strongest predictors at age 10 of later convictions for violence (up to age 45) were poor parental supervision, parental aggression (including harsh, punitive discipline), and parental conflict. In her later analyses, McCord (1996) showed that violent offenders were less likely than nonviolent offenders to have experienced parental affection and good discipline and supervision. In the Cambridge Study, harsh discipline and poor parental supervision predicted official and self-reported violence (Table 7.1). In Pittsburgh, harsh discipline (physical punishment) predicted reported violence, and low parental reinforcement (not praising) predicted official violence, but poor parental supervision did not predict either measure of violence (Table 7.2).

Similar results have been obtained in other surveys. In the Seattle Social Development Project, poor family management (poor supervision, inconsistent rules, and harsh discipline) predicted self-reported violence (Herrenkohl et al. 2000). In the Columbia County longitudinal study, parental approval of physical punishment predicted children's arrests for violence up to age 30 (Huesmann, Eron, and Dubow 2002). The meta-analysis by Derzon (2010) confirmed that parental supervision, involvement, and discipline were significantly related to a child's violent behavior.

In the Pittsburgh Youth Study, harsh physical punishment predicted violence for Caucasians but not for African Americans (Farrington, Loeber, and Stouthamer-Loeber 2003). It has been suggested (e.g., by Deater-Deckard et al. 1996; Kelley, Power, and Wimbush 1992) that this is because physical discipline is associated with neglect and coldness in Caucasian families but with concern and warmth in African American families. In the Cambridge-Somerville Youth Study, McCord

(1997) found that physical punishment predicted convictions for violence, especially when it was combined with low parental warmth and affection. According to Straus (2001), parental physical punishment predicts children's violence because children learn from their parents that violence is an acceptable method of solving problems.

E. Child Abuse

In a longitudinal study of over nine hundred abused children and nearly seven hundred controls, Widom (1989) discovered that recorded child physical abuse and neglect predicted later arrests for violence, independently of other predictors such as gender, ethnicity, and age. Predictability was greater for females than for males (Widom and White 1997). Child sexual abuse also predicted adult arrests for sex crimes (Widom and Ames 1994). Similarly, child abuse predicted later violence in the Pittsburgh Youth Study (Loeber et al. 2005) and in a Swedish longitudinal survey of nearly three hundred delinquents and controls followed up in criminal records to their 40s (Lang, Klinteberg, and Alm 2002).

Possible environmental causal mechanisms linking childhood victimization and later violence were reviewed by Widom (1994). First, childhood victimization may have immediate but long-lasting consequences (e.g., shaking may cause brain injury; see also Heide and Solomon 2006). Second, childhood victimization may cause bodily changes (e.g., desensitization to pain) that encourage later violence. Third, child abuse may lead to impulsive or dissociative coping styles that in turn lead to poor problem-solving skills or poor school performance. Fourth, victimization may cause changes in self-esteem or in social information-processing patterns that encourage later violence. Fifth, child abuse may lead to changed family environments (e.g., being placed in foster care) that have deleterious effects. Sixth, juvenile justice practices may label victims, isolate them from prosocial peers, and encourage them to associate with delinquent peers.

F. Broken Families and Exposure to Violence

Parental conflict and coming from a broken family predicted violence in both the Cambridge and Pittsburgh studies, and living in a single-parent, female-headed household predicted violence in Pittsburgh (Tables 7.1 and 7.2). A broken family was the strongest explanatory predictor of homicide offending in the Pittsburgh Youth Study (Farrington et al. 2008). Parental conflict also predicted youth violence in the Seattle Social Development Project (Herrenkohl et al. 2000). The meta-analysis by Derzon (2010) found that family discord and parental separation were significantly related to violent behavior, but that coming from a broken home was not.

If a child is exposed to violence between his parents, this predicts the child's later antisocial behavior (Chan and Yeung 2009). In the Christchurch (New Zealand) longitudinal study of over 1,300 children from birth to age 25, Fergusson and Horwood (1998) found that children who witnessed violence between their parents were more likely to commit both violent and property offenses according to their self-reports. The importance of witnessing violence in relation to property crime (but not violent crime) held up after controlling for other risk factors such as parental criminality, parental substance use, parental physical punishment, a young mother, and low family income. Nofziger and Kurtz (2005) discussed various explanations of the link between witnessing and committing violence, and concluded that both were aspects of a continuing violent family lifestyle. Witnessing violence was related to peer violence and violent victimization. They concluded that contextual information about where and with whom exposure to violence occurred, and about the role of routine activities, was important.

G. Large Family Size

Large family size (number of children) predicted youth violence in both the Cambridge and Pittsburgh studies (Tables 7.1 and 7.2). In the Oregon Youth Study, large family size at age 10 predicted self-reported violence at ages 13 to 17 (Capaldi and Patterson 1996). In the Columbia County Longitudinal Study, large family size at age 8 predicted children's arrests for violence up to age 30 (Huesmann, Eron, and Dubow 2002).

There are many possible reasons that a large number of siblings might increase the risk of a child's delinquency (Brownfield and Sorenson 1994). Generally, as the number of children in a family increases, the amount of parental attention that can be given to each child decreases. Also, as the number of children increases, the household tends to become more overcrowded, possibly leading to increases in frustration, irritation, and conflict. In the Cambridge Study, large family size did not predict delinquency for boys living in the least crowded conditions, with two or more rooms than there were children (West and Farrington 1973 p. 33). This suggests that household overcrowding might be an important factor mediating the association between large family size and offending.

H. Young Mothers

Young mothers (mothers who had their first child at an early age, typically as a teenager) tended to have violent sons in the Pittsburgh Youth Study (Table 7.2). A young mother also predicted sons' homicide offending (Farrington et al. 2008). Later analyses in which risk and promotive factors were carefully distinguished demonstrated that the most important effect was that the sons of older mothers had low rates of violence, rather than the sons of younger mothers having high rates (Loeber et al. 2008, p. 200). A teenage mother predicted self-reported violence in the Cambridge Study (Table 7.1). Interestingly, the relationship between a young mother and a convicted son in this study disappeared after controlling for other variables, notably large family size, a convicted parent, and a broken family (Nagin, Pogarsky, and Farrington 1997). A young mother also predicted self-reported violence in the Rochester Youth Development Study of one thousand children between ages 13 and 32 (Pogarsky, Lizotte, and Thornberry 2003). In the Dunedin study in New Zealand, Jaffee and colleagues (2001) concluded that the link between teenage mothers and violent children was mediated by maternal characteristics (e.g., intelligence, criminality) and family factors (e.g., harsh discipline, family size, disrupted families).

I. Socioeconomic Status

In general, coming from a low socioeconomic status (SES) family predicts violence, as shown for Pittsburgh in Table 7.2. For example, in the U.S. National Youth Survey of over 1,700 children followed up between ages 14 and 40, the prevalences of self-reported felony assault and robbery were about twice as high for lower class youth as for middle class ones (Elliott, Huizinga, and Menard 1989). The strongest childhood predictor of official violence in the Pittsburgh Youth Study was family dependence on welfare benefits (Table 7.2), and this also predicted homicide offenders (Farrington et al. 2008). In the Cambridge Study, coming from a low SES family (having a father with an unskilled manual job) did not significantly predict the boy's youthful violence but did predict his adult violence (Farrington 2007b). Low family income and poor housing predicted official and self-reported violence (Table 7.1). In the Columbia County Longitudinal Study, poor family housing at age 8 predicted children's arrests for violence up to age 30 (Huesmann, Eron, and Dubow 2002). In Pittsburgh, an unemployed father and an unemployed mother predicted youth violence (Table 7.2).

The meta-analysis by Derzon (2010) concluded that low SES was a significant, although weak, predictor of violence. Several researchers have suggested that the link between a low SES family and antisocial behavior is mediated by family socialization practices. For example, Larzelere and Patterson (1990) in the Oregon Youth Study concluded that the effect of SES on delinquency was entirely mediated by parental management skills. Fergusson, Swain-Campbell, and Horwood (2004) in the Christchurch Health and Development Study in New Zealand found that the effect of SES on delinquency disappeared after controlling for family factors, conduct problems, truancy, and deviant peers, suggesting that these may have been mediating factors.

J. Accuracy of Prediction

Odds ratios are typically between 2 and 4 in Tables 7.1 and 7.2, suggesting that childhood risk factors double, triple, or quadruple the risk of youth violence. These results are typical. However, depending on the prevalence of youth violence, false positive rates can be high. For example, only 9% of boys in the Cambridge Study were convicted for violence. The best predictor was troublesomeness, and 21% of troublesome boys were convicted, compared with 5% of the remainder (Table 7.1). This means, of course, that 79% of troublesome boys were not convicted, at least up to age 20. False positive rates were lower with self-reported violence, where 20% of boys were identified, and 38% of troublesome boys became violent.

There is always a dose-response relationship between the number of risk factors that a person possesses and the probability of youth violence. This is illustrated in Figure 7.1 for the Pittsburgh Youth Study. This Figure shows the percentage of boys in the middle sample who were violent versus the screening risk score, which was a count of the number of types of antisocial acts that the boy had committed by age 10 (out of 21; see Loeber et al. 1998, p. 50). The percentage of boys who were convicted increased from 3% of those scoring zero to 47% of those scoring 9 to 12. Similarly, the percentage of boys who were reported increased from 5% of those scoring zero to over 50% of those scoring 6 or above.

It is clear that childhood risk factors can identify children with very different risks of becoming violent later. However, of course, it is never possible to predict with 100% accuracy, and there are always a number of high-risk children who do not become violent. This fact should encourage the search for protective factors against youth violence that might suggest methods of early intervention.

V. Conclusions

A. Research Implications

Among the most important childhood risk factors for violent young offenders are impulsiveness, low intelligence and attainment, poor parental supervision, harsh parental discipline, child physical abuse, a violent parent, large family size, a young mother, a broken family, and low socioeconomic status of the family. Other risk factors are important but could not be reviewed in this chapter because of space limitations, especially peer, school, and neighborhood influences. These results should be useful in developing risk assessment instruments.

More research is needed specifically searching for protective factors against violence, for example by investigating why aggressive children do not become violent adults. More research is also needed on protective factors that encourage desistance. Some protective factors may have similar effects on onset and persistence, but others (e.g., life events such as getting married and getting a satisfying job) may have more specific effects on desistance.

In order to investigate development and risk factors for violence and the effects of life events, longitudinal studies are needed. Such studies should include multiple cohorts in order to draw conclusions about different age groups from birth at least to the mid-20s (Farrington, Ohlin, and Wilson 1986). They should include both males and females and the major racial/ethnic groups, so that results can be compared for different subgroups. Longitudinal studies should measure a wide range of risk and especially protective factors, and seek to discover interaction effects. They should be based on large, high-risk samples, especially in inner-city areas, incorporating screening methods to maximize the yield of violent offenders while simultaneously making it possible to draw conclusions about the total population. They should include frequent assessments and a variety of data from different sources (e.g., interviews with participants and parents, official record data). They should include long-term follow-ups to permit conclusions about developmental pathways. They should make a special effort to study careers of violence and to link developmental and situational data.

B. Policy Implications

Violence reduction programs should be based on knowledge about risk and protective factors (Farrington 2001b, 2007a). More systematic reviews and meta-analyses of these factors are needed, and more randomized experiments should be mounted to evaluate the effectiveness of risk-focused prevention. High quality evaluation research shows that many types of programs are effective and that in many cases

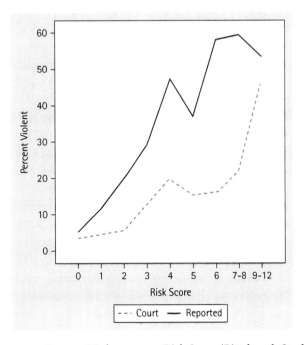

Figure 7.1. Percent Violent versus Risk Score (Pittsburgh Study)

their financial benefits outweigh their financial costs (Farrington and Welsh 2007). However, there have been relatively few attempts to study effects on violence specifically or to follow up experimental and control youth in repeated interviews (see Farrington 2006b).

The major policy implications are as follows: Impulsiveness should be targeted by skills training (Lösel and Beelmann 2006), and low school achievement should be targeted by preschool intellectual enrichment programs (Schweinhart et al. 2005). Smoking, drinking, and drug use in pregnancy, and also early child abuse, should be targeted by home visiting programs in which nurses give advice to mothers about prenatal and postnatal care of the child, about infant development, and about the importance of proper nutrition and avoiding substance use in pregnancy (Olds, Sadler, and Kitzman 2007). Poor parental supervision and inconsistent discipline should be targeted by behavioral parent-management training (Webster-Stratton 1998). Negative peer influence should be targeted by community-based mentoring programs (Jolliffe and Farrington 2008) and by treatment foster care (Chamberlain and Reid 1998).

It is also desirable to implement programs in schools to encourage prosocial development. For example, anti-bullying programs are effective (Farrington and Ttofi 2009), and programs to encourage stable relationships and discourage early pregnancy could be mounted (Theobald and Farrington 2010). Community programs that encourage cohesiveness, collective efficacy, and intervention to prevent crimes can also be recommended.

Communities that Care (CTC) is one of the most promising community-based prevention programs (Hawkins and Catalano 1992). It is modeled on large-scale, community-wide public health programs, and it is a multiple-component program including interventions that have been proved to be effective in high quality research. The choice of intervention strategies depends on empirical evidence about what are the most important risk and protective factors in a particular community. The interventions aim to reduce the identified risk factors and enhance the identified protective factors. CTC has been shown to be effective in reducing substance use and delinquency in a large randomized experiment involving twenty-four communities (Hawkins et al. 2009).

It is also important to target immediate situational influences on violence such as alcohol, guns, gangs, and drugs. For example, the gang prevention program GREAT (Gang Resistance Education and Training) reduced victimization, instilled more negative views about gangs among youth, improved attitudes toward police, and increased the number of prosocial peers (Howell 2009, p. 161). However, it did not prevent youths from joining gangs. As another example, Macintyre and Homel (1997) in Australia found that violence in nightclubs was caused by crowding as well as drunkenness. They made recommendations about how nightclubs could be redesigned to reduce crowding, by changing pedestrian flow patterns (e.g., to and from restrooms).

The time is ripe to adopt a public health approach and embark on risk-focused prevention on a large scale, perhaps based on Communities that Care, in order to reduce youth violence. It is crucial to interrupt the intergenerational transmission of crime and violence, and the financial benefits of risk-focused prevention seem very likely to exceed the financial costs. This approach would have many additional benefits, including improving mental and physical health and life success in areas such as education, employment, relationships, housing, and child-rearing. Early prevention is surely preferable to and more effective than later treatment in the juvenile and criminal justice system.

REFERENCES

Brennan, P. A., E. R. Grekin, and S. A. Mednick. 1999. "Maternal smoking during pregnancy and adult male criminal outcomes." *Archives of General Psychiatry* 56: 215–19.

Brennan, P. A., B. R. Mednick, and S. A. Mednick. 1993. "Parental psychopathology, congenital factors, and violence." In *Mental Disorder and Crime*, edited by S. Hodgins, 244–61. Newbury Park, CA: Sage.

Brownfield, D., and A. M. Sorenson. 1994. "Sibship size and sibling delinquency." *Deviant Behavior* 15: 45–61.

Budd, T., C. Sharp, and P. Mayhew. 2005. *Offending in England and Wales: First Results from the 2003 Crime and Justice Survey*. London: Home Office (Research Study No. 275).

Bureau of Justice Statistics. *Sourcebook of Criminal Justice Statistics*. 2009. www.albany.edu/sourcebook/.

Capaldi, D. M., and G. R. Patterson. 1996. "Can violent offenders be distinguished from frequent offenders? Prediction from childhood to adolescence." *Journal of Research in Crime and Delinquency* 33: 206–31.

Caspi, A., T. E. Moffitt, P. A. Silva, M. Stouthamer-Loeber, R. F. Krueger, and P. S. Schmutte. 1994. "Are some people crime-prone? Replications of the personality-crime relationship across countries, genders, races, and methods." *Criminology* 32: 163–95.

Chamberlain, P., and J. B. Reid. 1998. "Comparison of two community alternatives to incarceration for chronic juvenile offenders." *Journal of Consulting and Clinical Psychology* 66: 624–33.

Chan, Y-C., and J. W-K. Yeung. 2009. "Children living with violence within the family and its sequel: A meta-analysis from 1995–2006." *Aggression and Violent Behavior* 14: 313–22.

Cohen, L. E., and M. Felson. 1979. "Social change and crime rate trends: A routine activity approach." *American Sociological Review* 44: 588–608.

Coie, J. D., K. A. Dodge, and J. Kupersmidt. 1990. "Peer group behavior and social status." In *Peer Rejection in Childhood*, edited by S. R. Asher and J. D. Coie, 17–59. Cambridge, UK: Cambridge University Press.

Cooke, D. J., C. Michie, S. D. Hart, and D. A. Clark. 2004. "Reconstructing psychopathy: Clarifying the significance of antisocial and socially deviant behavior in the diagnosis of psychopathic personality disorder." *Journal of Personality Disorders* 18: 337–57.

Deater-Deckard, K., K. A. Dodge, J. E. Bates, and G. S. Pettit. 1996. "Physical discipline among African American and European American mothers: Links to children's externalizing behaviors." *Developmental Psychology* 32: 1065–72.

Delisi, M. and P. J. Conis, eds. 2008. *Violent Offenders: Theory, Research, Public Policy, and Practice.* Sudbury, MA: Jones and Bartlett.

Denno, D. W. 1990. *Biology and Violence: From Birth to Adulthood.* Cambridge, UK: Cambridge University Press.

Derzon, James H. 2010. "The correspondence of family features with problem, aggressive, criminal, and violent behavior: A meta-analysis." *Journal of Experimental Criminology* 6: 263–92.

Desmarais, S. L., A. Gibas, A., and T. L. Nicholls. 2010. "Beyond violence against women: Gender inclusiveness in domestic violence research, policy, and practice." In *Violent Crime: Clinical and Social Implications*, edited by C. J. Ferguson, 184–206. Thousand Oaks, CA: Sage.

Elliott, D. S., D. Huizinga, and S. Menard. 1989. *Multiple Problem Youth: Delinquency, Substance Use, and Mental Health Problems.* New York: Springer-Verlag.

Farrington, D. P. 1978. "The family backgrounds of aggressive youths." In *Aggression and Antisocial Behavior in Childhood and Adolescence*, edited by L. Hersov, M. Berger, and D. Shaffer. Oxford, UK: Pergamon.

Farrington, D. P. 1986. "Age and crime." In *Crime and* Justice, vol. 7, 189–250, edited by M. Tonry and N. Morris. Chicago: University of Chicago Press.

Farrington, D. P. 1991. "Childhood aggression and adult violence: Early precursors and later life outcomes." In *The Development and Treatment of Childhood Aggression*, edited by D. J. Pepler and K. H. Rubin, 5–29. Hillsdale, NJ: Lawrence Erlbaum.

Farrington, D. P. 1994. "Childhood, adolescent and adult features of violent males." In *Aggressive Behavior: Current Perspectives*, edited by L. R. Huesmann, 215–40. New York: Plenum.

Farrington, D. P. 1998. "Predictors, causes, and correlates of youth violence." In *Youth Violence*, edited by M. Tonry and M. H. Moore, 421–75. Chicago: University of Chicago Press.

Farrington, D. P. 2000a. "Adolescent violence: Findings and implications from the Cambridge Study." In *Violent Children and Adolescents: Asking the Question Why*, edited by G. Boswell, 19–35. London: Whurr.

Farrington, D. P. 2000b. "Explaining and preventing crime: The globalization of knowledge—The American Society of Criminology 1999 Presidential Address." *Criminology*, 38: 1–24.

Farrington, D. P. 2001a. "Predicting adult official and self-reported violence." In *Clinical Assessment of Dangerousness: Empirical Contributions*, edited by G.F. Pinard and L. Pagani, 66–88. Cambridge, UK: Cambridge University Press.

Farrington, D. P. 2001b. "The causes and prevention of violence." In *Violence in Health Care*, edited by J. Shepherd, 2nd ed., 1–27. Oxford, UK: Oxford University Press.

Farrington, D. P. 2006a. "Comparing football hooligans and violent offenders: Childhood, adolescent, teenage and adult features." *Monatsschrift fur Kriminologie und Strafrechtsreform (Journal of Criminology and Penal Reform)* 89: 193–205.

Farrington, D. P. 2006b. "Key longitudinal-experimental studies in criminology." *Journal of Experimental Criminology* 2: 121–41.

Farrington, D. P. 2007a. "Childhood risk factors and risk-focussed prevention." In *The Oxford Handbook of Criminology*, edited by M. Maguire, R. Morgan, and R. Reiner, 4th ed., 602–40. Oxford, UK: Oxford University Press.

Farrington, D. P. 2007b. "Origins of violent behavior over the life span." In *The Cambridge Handbook of Violent Behavior and Aggression*, edited by D. J. Flannery, A. J. Vaszonyi, and I. D. Waldman, 19–48. Cambridge, UK: Cambridge University Press.

Farrington, D. P., J. W. Coid, L. Harnett, D. Jolliffe, N. Soteriou, R. Turner, and D. J. West. 2006. *Criminal Careers Up To Age 50 and Life Success Up To Age 48: New findings from the Cambridge Study in Delinquent Development*. London: Home Office (Research Study No. 299).

Farrington, D. P., B. Gallagher, L. Morley, R. J. St. Ledger, and D. J. West. 1988. "Are there any successful men from criminogenic backgrounds?" *Psychiatry* 51: 116–30.

Farrington, D. P., D. Jolliffe, J. D. Hawkins, R. F. Catalano, K. G. Hill, and R. Kosterman. 2003. "Comparing delinquency careers in court records and self-reports." *Criminology* 41: 933–58.

Farrington, D. P., D. Jolliffe, R. Loeber, M. Stouthamer-Loeber, and L. M. Kalb. 2001. "The concentration of offenders in families, and family criminality in the prediction of boys' delinquency." *Journal of Adolescence* 24: 579–96.

Farrington, D. P., R. Loeber, R. Stallings, and D. L. Homish. 2008. "Early risk factors for homicide offenders and victims." In *Violent Offenders: Theory, Research, Public Policy, and Practice*, edited by M. J. Delisi and P. J. Conis, 79–96. Sudbury, MA: Jones and Bartlett.

Farrington, D. P., R. Loeber, and M. Stouthamer-Loeber. 2003. "How can the relationship between race and violence be explained?": In *Violent Crime: Assessing Race and Ethnic Differences*, edited by D. F. Hawkins, 213–37. Cambridge, UK: Cambridge University Press.

Farrington, D. P., L. E. Ohlin, and J. Q. Wilson. 1986. *Understanding and Controlling Crime: Toward a New Research Strategy*. New York: Springer-Verlag.

Farrington, D. P., and M. M. Ttofi. 2009. "Reducing school bullying: Evidence-based implications for policy." In *Crime and Justice*, vol. 38, 281–345, edited by M. Tonry. Chicago: University of Chicago Press.

Farrington, D. P., and B. C. Welsh. 2007. *Saving Children from a Life of Crime: Early Risk Factors and Effective Interventions*. Oxford, UK: Oxford University Press.

Farrington, D.P., and D. J. West. 1993. "Criminal, penal, and life histories of chronic offenders: Risk and protective factors and early identification." *Criminal Behavior and Mental Health* 3: 492–523.

Ferguson, C. J., ed. 2010. *Violent Crime: Clinical and Social Implications*. Thousand Oaks, CA: Sage.

Fergusson, D. M., and L. J. Horwood. 1998. "Exposure to interparental violence in childhood and psychosocial adjustment in young adulthood." *Child Abuse and Neglect* 22: 339–57.

Fergusson, D., N. Swain-Campbell, and J. Horwood. 2004. "How does childhood economic disadvantage lead to crime?" *Journal of Child Psychology and Psychiatry* 45: 956–66.

Flannery, D. J., A. T. Vaszonyi, and I. D. Waldman, eds. 2007. *The Cambridge Handbook of Violent Behavior and Aggression*. Cambridge, UK: Cambridge University Press.

Hamparian, D. M., J. M. Davis, J. M. Jacobson, and R. E. McGraw. 1985. *The Young Criminal Years of the Violent Few*. Washington, DC: Office of Juvenile Justice and Delinquency Prevention.

Hawkins, J. D., and R. F. Catalano. 1992. *Communities That Care*. San Francisco: Jossey-Bass.

Hawkins, J. D., T. Herrenkohl, D. P. Farrington, D. Brewer, R. F. Catalano, and T. W. Harachi. 1998. "A review of predictors of youth violence." In *Serious and Violent Juvenile Offenders: Risk Factors and Successful Interventions*, edited by R. Loeber and D. P. Farrington, 106–46. Thousand Oaks, CA: Sage.

Hawkins, J. D., S. Oesterle, E. C. Brown, M. W. Arthur, R. D. Abbott, A. A. Fagan, and R. F. Catalano. 2009. "Results of a type 2 translational research trial to prevent adolescent drug use and delinquency: A test of Communities that Care." *Archives of Pediatrics and Adolescent Medicine* 163: 789–98.

Henry, B., A. Caspi, T. E. Moffitt, and P. A. Silva. 1996. "Temperamental and familial predictors of violent and nonviolent criminal convictions: Age 3 to age 18." *Developmental Psychology* 32: 614–23.

Heide, K. M., and E. P. Solomon. 2006. "Biology, childhood trauma, and murder: Rethinking justice." *International Journal of Law and Psychiatry* 29: 220–33.

Herrenkohl, T. I., E. Maguin, K. G. Hill, J. D. Hawkins, R. D. Abbott, and R. F. Catalano. 2000. "Developmental risk factors for youth violence." *Journal of Adolescent Health* 26: 176–86.

Hogh, E., and P. Wolf. 1983. "Violent crime in a birth cohort: Copenhagen 1953–1977." In *Prospective Studies of Crime and Delinquency*, edited by K. T. Van Dusen and S. A. Mednick, 249–67. Boston: Kluwer-Nijhoff.

Howell, J. C. 2009. *Preventing and Reducing Juvenile Delinquency*. Thousand Oaks, CA: Sage.

Huesmann, L. R., L. D. Eron, and E. F. Dubow. 2002. "Childhood predictors of adult criminality: Are all risk factors reflected in childhood aggressiveness?" *Criminal Behavior and Mental Health* 12: 185–208.

Jaffee, S., A. Caspi, T. E. Moffitt, J. Belsky, and P. A. Silva. 2001. "Why are children born to teen mothers at risk for adverse outcomes in young adulthood? Results from a 20-year longitudinal study." *Development and Psychopathology* 13: 377–97.

Johnson, J. G., E. Smailes, P. Cohen, S. Kasen, and J. S. Brook. 2004. "Antisocial parental behavior, problematic parenting, and aggressive offspring behavior during adulthood." *British Journal of Criminology* 44: 915–30.

Jolliffe, D., and D. P. Farrington. 2008. *The Influence of Mentoring on Reoffending*. Stockholm, Sweden: National Council for Crime Prevention.

Jolliffe, D., and D. P. Farrington. 2009. "A systematic review of the relationship between childhood impulsiveness and later violence." In *Personality, Personality Disorder, and Violence*, edited by M. McMurran and R. Howard, 41–61. Chichester, UK: Wiley.

Jolliffe, D., D. P. Farrington, J. D. Hawkins, R. F. Catalano, K. G. Hill, and R. Kosterman. 2003. "Predictive, concurrent, prospective and retrospective validity of self-reported delinquency." *Criminal Behavior and Mental Health* 13: 179–97.

Kelley, M. L., T. G. Power, and D. D. Wimbush. 1992. "Determinants of disciplinary practices in low-income black mothers." *Child Development* 63: 573–82.

Klinteberg, B. A., T. Andersson, D. Magnusson, and H. Stattin. 1993. "Hyperactive behavior in childhood as related to subsequent alcohol problems and violent offending: A longitudinal study of male subjects." *Personality and Individual Differences* 15: 381–88.

Lang, S., B. A. Klinteberg, and P-O. Alm. 2002. "Adult psychopathy and violent behavior in males with early neglect and abuse." *Acta Psychiatrica Scandinavica* 106: 93–100.

Larzelere, R. E., and G. R. Patterson. 1990. "Parental management: Mediator of the effect of socioeconomic status on early delinquency." *Criminology* 28: 301–24.

Lipsey, M. W., and J. H. Derzon. 1998. "Predictors of violent or serious delinquency in adolescence and early adulthood: A synthesis of longitudinal research." In *Serious and Violent Juvenile Offenders: Risk Factors and Successful Interventions*, edited by R. Loeber and D. P. Farrington, 86–105. Thousand Oaks, CA: Sage.

Loeber, R. and D. P. Farrington, eds. 1998. *Serious and Violent Juvenile Offenders: Risk Factors and Successful Interventions*. Thousand Oaks, CA: Sage.

Loeber, R., D. P. Farrington, M. Stouthamer-Loeber, and W. B. Van Kammen. 1998. *Antisocial Behavior and Mental Health Problems: Explanatory Factors in Childhood and Adolescence.* Mahwah, NJ: Lawrence Erlbaum.

Loeber, R., D. P. Farrington, M. Stouthamer-Loeber, and H. R. White. 2008. *Violence and Serious Theft: Development and Prediction from Childhood to Adulthood.* New York: Routledge.

Loeber, R., E. Lacourse, and D. L. Homish. 2005. "Homicide, violence, and developmental trajectories." In *Developmental Origins of Aggression*, edited by R. E. Tremblay, W. W. Hartup, and J. Archer, 202–19. New York: Guilford.

Loeber, R., D. Pardini, D. L. Homish, E. H. Wei, A. M. Crawford, D. P. Farrington, M. Stouthamer-Loeber, J. Creemers, S. A. Koehler, and R. Rosenfeld. 2005. "The prediction of violence and homicide in young men." *Journal of Consulting and Clinical Psychology* 73: 1074–88.

Lösel, F., and A. Beelmann. 2006. "Child social skills training." In *Preventing Crime: What Works for Children, Offenders, Victims, and Places*, edited by B. C. Welsh and D. P. Farrington, 33–54. Dordrecht, Netherlands: Springer.

Macintyre, S., and R. Homel. 1997. "Danger on the dance floor: A study of interior design, crowding and aggression in nightclubs." In *Policing for Prevention: Reducing Crime, Public Intoxication, and Injury*, edited by R. Homel, 91–113. Monsey, NY: Criminal Justice Press.

McCord, J. 1977. "A comparative study of two generations of native Americans." In *Theory in Criminology*, edited by R. F. Meier, 83–92. Beverly Hills, CA: Sage.

McCord, J. 1979. "Some child-rearing antecedents of criminal behavior in adult men." *Journal of Personality and Social Psychology* 37: 1477–86.

McCord, J. 1996. "Family as crucible for violence: Comment on Gorman-Smith et al. (1996)." *Journal of Family Psychology* 10: 147–52.

McCord, J. 1997. "On discipline." *Psychological Inquiry* 8: 215–17.

McCord, J., and M. E. Ensminger. 1997. "Multiple risks and comorbidity in an African-American population." *Criminal Behavior and Mental Health* 7: 339–52.

McGloin, J. M., T. C. Pratt, and A. R. Piquero. 2006. "A life-course analysis of the criminogenic effects of maternal cigarette smoking during pregnancy: A research note on the mediating impact of neuropsychological deficit." *Journal of Research in Crime and Delinquency* 43: 412–26.

Moffitt, T. E. 1993. "Adolescence-limited and life-course-persistent antisocial behavior: A developmental taxonomy." *Psychological Review* 100: 674–701.

Moffitt, T. E., and B. Henry. 1991. "Neuropsychological studies of juvenile delinquency and juvenile violence." In *Neuropsychology of Aggression*, edited by J. S. Milner, 131–46. Boston: Kluwer.

Morgan, A. B., and S. O. Lilienfeld. 2000. "A meta-analytic review of the relation between antisocial behavior and neuropsychological measures of executive function." *Clinical Psychology Review* 20: 113–36.

Nagin, D. S., G. Pogarsky, and D. P. Farrington. 1997. "Adolescent mothers and the criminal behavior of their children." *Law and Society Review* 31: 137–62.

Nelson, S. E., and T. J. Dishion. 2004. "From boys to men: Predicting adult adaptation from middle childhood sociometric status." *Development and Psychopathology* 16: 441–59.

Nofziger, S., and D. Kurtz. 2005. "Violent lives: A lifestyle model linking exposure to violence to juvenile violent offending." *Journal of Research in Crime and Delinquency* 42: 3–26.

Olds, D. L., L. Sadler, and H. Kitzman. 2007. "Programs for parents of infants and toddlers: Recent evidence from randomized trials." *Journal of Child Psychology and Psychiatry* 48: 355–91.

Piquero, A. 2000. "Frequency, specialization, and violence in offending careers." *Journal of Research in Crime and Delinquency* 37: 392–418.

Piquero, A. R., and S. L. Buka. 2002. "Linking juvenile and adult patterns of criminal activity in the Providence cohort of the National Collaborative Perinatal Project." *Journal of Criminal Justice* 30: 259–72.

Piquero, A. R., D. P. Farrington, and A. Blumstein. 2007. *Key Issues in Criminal Career Research: New Analyses of the Cambridge Study in Delinquent Development.* Cambridge, UK: Cambridge University Press.

Pogarsky, G., A. J. Lizotte, and T. P. Thornberry. 2003. "The delinquency of children born to young mothers: Results from the Rochester Youth Development Study." *Criminology* 41: 1249–86.

Pulkkinen, L. 1987. "Offensive and defensive aggression in humans: A longitudinal perspective." *Aggressive Behavior* 13: 197–212.

Rasanen, P., H. Hakko, M. Isohanni, S. Hodgins, M. Jarvelin, and J. Tiihonen. 1999. "Maternal smoking during pregnancy and risk of criminal behavior among adult male offspring in the Northern Finland 1966 birth cohort." *American Journal of Psychiatry* 156: 857–62.

Riedel, M., and W. Welsh. 2008. *Criminal Violence: Patterns, Causes, and Prevention*, 2nd ed. Oxford, UK: Oxford University Press.

Rutter, M. 1985. "Resilience in the face of adversity: Protective factors and resistance to psychiatric disorder." *British Journal of Psychiatry*, 147: 598–611.

Sameroff, A. J., W. T. Bartko, A. Baldwin, C. Baldwin, and R. Seifer. 1998. "Family and social influences on the development of child competence." In *Families, Risk and Competence*, edited by M. Lewis and C. Feiring, 161–85. Mahwah, NJ: Lawrence Erlbaum.

Schweinhart, L. J., J. Montie, X. Zongping, W. S. Barnett, C. R. Belfield, and M. Nores. 2005. *Lifetime Effects: The High/Scope Perry Preschool Study through Age 40.* Ypsilanti, MI: High/Scope Press.

Seguin, J., R. O. Pihl, P. W. Harden, R. F. Tremblay, and B. Boulerice. 1995. "Cognitive and neuropsychological characteristics of physically aggressive boys." *Journal of Abnormal Psychology* 104: 614–24.

Stattin, H., and D. Magnusson. 1989. "The role of early aggressive behavior in the frequency, seriousness, and types of later crime." *Journal of Consulting and Clinical Psychology* 57: 710–18.

Straus, Murray A. 2001. *Beating the Devil Out of Them: Corporal Punishment in American Families and Its Effects on Children.* New Brunswick, NJ: Transaction.

Theobald, D., and D. P. Farrington. 2010. "Should policy implications be drawn from research on the effects of getting married on offending?" *European Journal of Criminology* 7: 239–47.

Van Wijk, A. P., A. A. J. Blokland, N. Duits, R. Vermeiren, and J. Harkink. 2007. "Relating psychiatric disorders, offender and offense characteristics in a sample of adolescent sex offenders and nonsex offenders." *Criminal Behavior and Mental Health* 17: 15–30.

Webster-Stratton, C. 1998. "Preventing conduct problems in Head Start children: Strengthening parenting competencies." *Journal of Consulting and Clinical Psychology* 66: 715–30.

West, D. J., and D. P. Farrington. 1973. *Who Becomes Delinquent?* London: Heinemann.

West, D. J., and D. P. Farrington. 1977. *The Delinquent Way of Life.* London: Heinemann.

White, J. L., T. E. Moffitt, and P. A. Silva. 1989. "A prospective replication of the protective effects of low IQ in subjects at high risk for juvenile delinquency." *Journal of Consulting and Clinical Psychology* 57: 719–24.

Widom, C. S. 1989. "The cycle of violence." *Science* 244: 160–66.

Widom, C. S. 1994. "Childhood victimization and adolescent problem behaviors." In *Adolescent Problem Behaviors,* edited by R. D. Ketterlinus and M. E. Lamb, 127–64. Hillsdale, NJ: Lawrence Erlbaum.

Widom, C. S., and M. A. Ames. 1994. "Criminal consequences of childhood sexual victimization." *Child Abuse and Neglect* 18: 303–18.

Widom, C. S., and H. R. White. 1997. "Problem behaviors in abused and neglected children grown up: Prevalence and co-occurrence of substance use, crime and violence." *Criminal Behavior and Mental Health* 7: 287–310.

Zahn, M. A., H. H. Brownstein, and S. L. Jackson. 2004. *Violence: From Theory to Research.* Lexis Nexis-Anderson.

PART III

SOCIAL CONTEXTS AND DELINQUENCY

CHAPTER 8

LINKING FAMILY PROCESSES AND ADOLESCENT DELINQUENCY

ISSUES, THEORIES, AND RESEARCH FINDINGS

RONALD L. SIMONS,
LESLIE GORDON SIMONS,
AND DONNA HANCOCK

AMERICANS view crime as a major social problem (Tonry 2004), and if asked what they believe to be the major cause of crime, the majority would probably cite lax and ineffective parenting of children (Wilson and Herrnstein 1985). Consistent with this idea, there is compelling evidence that childhood conduct problems are a strong predictor of subsequent involvement in antisocial behavior. Results from a variety of longitudinal studies show that children who are aggressive and noncompliant during elementary school are at risk for adolescent delinquency and adult crime (Caspi and Moffitt 1995; Reid, Patterson, and Snyder 2002; Sampson and Laub 1993; Shaw and Gross 2008; Tremblay et al. 1999). This continuity of deviant behavior has been found in several countries, including Canada, England, Finland, New Zealand, Sweden, and the United States (Caspi and Moffitt 1995). Indeed, support for this continuity is so robust that the Diagnostic and Statistical Manual of Mental Disorders (American Psychiatric Association 1994), the handbook that psychiatrists use as a guide in making psychiatric diagnoses, asserts that oppositional/defiant disorder during childhood is a developmental antecedent to conduct disorder during adolescence, and a diagnosis of adult antisocial personality requires that the person displayed conduct problems during adolescence. As Robins (1978, p. 611) has noted, "adult antisocial behavior virtually requires childhood antisocial behavior." It is extremely rare for a person who was a model child and adolescent to suddenly begin to engage in criminal behavior as an adult.

Thus the roots of an adult antisocial lifestyle appear to be planted during the formative years. Since parents are generally seen as the primary agents of socialization in the early years of a child's life, it follows that parental behavior may somehow contribute to the development of delinquent and criminal behavior. Building upon this idea, several of the more prominent criminological theories identify parenting practices as a major factor in the etiology of youth involvement in antisocial behavior. This chapter explores recent findings, issues, and controversies regarding the role of parenting in the development of youth and adolescent behavior problems.

The chapter is organized around what we believe to be the big questions surrounding this field of inquiry. First, we focus upon two related issues—the dimensions of parenting that foster antisocial behavior and the mechanisms whereby these practices produce this effect. Some theories, for example, emphasize monitoring and discipline, whereas others stress the consequences of hostility and rejection (see Loeber and Stouthamer-Loeber 1986; Simons, Simons, and Wallace 2004). Further, presumably these parenting practices increase risk for adolescent and adult antisocial behavior because of the cognitive and emotional changes that they foster in the child, but the various theories differ regarding the nature of the psychological factors that mediate the effect of parenting on later involvement in delinquency and crime (R. Simons et al. 2007). Thus we will begin by examining the extent to which studies support the contentions of five of the more popular theories regarding the parental behaviors that lead to delinquency and the mediating psychological changes in the child that account for this effect.

Our second big question concerns the link between family structure and delinquency. Recent research has moved beyond a simple comparison of single- and two-parent families to a more nuanced consideration of various types of stepfamilies, cohabiting couples, and divorced individuals. We will examine the impact of each of these family structures on child antisocial behavior. Further, we will consider the extent to which the parenting practices identified by the various theories can account for these family structure effects.

Finally, our third big question involves genetics. In recent years there has been a flurry of studies investigating the role of genetics in the etiology of delinquency and crime. We will examine behavioral genetics research showing that the association between parenting and child antisocial behavior is not simply a spurious consequence of either a passive or evocative gene-environment correlation. We will also

review molecular genetics studies suggesting that children's genetic makeup interacts with the quality of parenting that they receive.

We address these questions in order. First, we discuss five widely accepted theoretical perspectives that emphasize the role of parenting practices in the etiology of
antisocial behavior. In each case, we note the dimensions of parenting and mediating mechanisms specified by the theory and then assess its degree of empirical support. Second, we consider the impact of family structure on child and adolescent
delinquency. Our discussion examines the risk of delinquency posed by various
types of families (e.g., two biological parents, divorced or single parents, stepfamilies, cohabitating partners), as well as the avenues whereby these family structures
influence the probability of involvement in deviant behavior. Finally, we provide a
brief review of behavioral and molecular genetics studies relating to the issue of
parenting and delinquency. This research is examined in order to determine the
degree to which at least a portion of the association between parental behavior and
child or adolescent delinquency might be explained by genetic influences.

I. Dimensions of Parenting and Their Mechanisms of Influence

We begin by discussing two perspectives that emphasize the role of parental control
in the etiology of child antisocial behavior: social learning theory and the general
theory of crime. We then turn to three perspectives that emphasize the parent's
relationship with the child: attachment theory, biased attribution perspective, and
general strain theory. We review recent research relating to the predictions of each
of these approaches.

A. Social Learning Theory

The social learning perspective on adolescent conduct problems grew out of the
work of Bandura and Walters (1963) and Bandura (1969), who took the position
that children learn to be deviant or prosocial during the process of interacting with
family members and peers. Their early writings emphasized both modeling and
operant learning as the determinants of change in social behavior. With time, this
perspective developed into two stems. Bandura (1977, 1986) developed a cognitive
stem that increasingly emphasized vicarious learning (modeling) and the acquisition of rules or expectancies about the consequences of various actions. Aker's (1985,
1998) social learning explanation for criminology is in this vein. In large measure,
research corroborating his perspective has focused on the way that interaction with
deviant peers fosters norms and beliefs supporting the perpetration of deviant
behavior. Since this chapter is concerned with parenting, our focus will be on the

second stem in social learning theory which has continued to investigate the consequences of the contingencies of reinforcement provided by parents. This approach
is best represented by the Coercion Model developed by Gerald Patterson and his
colleagues (e.g., John Reid, Thomas Dishion, Debra Capaldi, and James Snyder).

This research team has been distinctive in its rigorous approach to measurement. Data from family members, teachers, peers, trained observers, and criminal
justice system records are used to develop measures of constructs (see Patterson,
Reid, and Dishion 1992; Reid, Patterson, and Snyder 2002). Their early work indicated that, contrary to popular view, instructing parents of a conduct-disordered
child to focus on reinforcement of competing prosocial behaviors fails to diminish
the child's aggressive behavior (Patterson, Reid and Eddy 2002). The problem, they
discovered, was the parents' inept attempts to control and discipline their child.
These parents often use intimidation and threats to coerce their child into changing
his behavior. This fosters an angry, defiant response from the child with the result
being an escalating spiral of aversive exchanges. Frequently, the parents gave in to
the child, thereby negatively reinforcing the child's aggressive, antisocial behavior
(Patterson 1982). Thus, coercion theory hypothesizes that antisocial behaviors are
performed to the extent that they are functional in escaping or avoiding aversive
conditions in the natural environment (Snyder and Stoolmiller 2002).

This does not mean, however, that aggressive behavior is simply explained by its
having a higher payoff in the families of antisocial compared to conforming youth.
Rather, coercion theory argues that aggression, like any behavior, develops according to the principles of the matching law. The matching law (Hernstein 1974;
Williams and Wixted 1986; Conger and Simons 1997) states that the frequency of
reinforcement that an individual receives for a specific behavior relative to the frequency of reinforcement received by that person for alternative responses determines how frequently she will perform the specific behavior (Snyder and Stoolmiller
2002). Generally, there is a rough match between the functional value of each of a
range of actions and the relative rate at which each of these actions is performed.
Thus in response to parental confrontation, the child might display constructive
behaviors such as complying, apologizing, or compromising, or he might engage in
antisocial acts such as swearing, yelling, threatening, and throwing things. Studies
by Patterson and his colleagues indicate that the relative payoff for child coercive
(versus constructive) acts in terminating family conflict is strongly correlated with
the relative rates of occurrence of coercive (versus constructive) behavior in these
episodes (Snyder and Patterson 1995). Further, the child tends to generalize this
antisocial behavior to interaction outside the home so that rates of coercive interaction with parents predict subsequent commission of delinquent acts (Snyder and
Patterson 1995). When frequency of family conflict bouts (i.e., frequency of training) was also taken into account, over 60% of the variance in delinquency was
explained (Snyder and Stoolmiller 2002).

The coercion model emphasizes the reciprocal relationship that exists between
parents and child. Thus, just as parents' inept discipline serves to inadvertently
intensify the child's coercive behavior, so increases in the child's coercive behavior

decrease parental attempts to control the child (Patterson 2002; Patterson, Bank, and Stoolmiller 1990). Applying the matching law to the parents, their attempts to monitor and discipline are met with coercive behavior, whereas the child's aversive behavior tends to terminate when they give in and withdraw. Since parents' behavior will tend to match the contingencies of reinforcement that they encounter, the result will be a decrease in their involvement with the child. Over time, this results in *premature autonomy* (Dishion, Nelson, and Bullock 2004; Dishion, Poulin, and Skaggs 2000). Just as their child enters adolescence and, like all adolescents, naturally resists and pulls away from parental involvement, the parents of antisocial youth tend to disengage from attempts to exercise control over their child.

This pattern is unfortunate, as research shows that parental monitoring and control is crucial during this developmental period, especially for youth with a history of antisocial behavior (Dishion, Poulin, and Skaggs 2000). As children move into adolescence, the challenges of parenting change, as do the dimensions of parenting that predict antisocial behavior. Delinquency is associated with a lack of parental monitoring of the adolescent's whereabouts, time allocation, and behavior (Dodge, Greenberg, and Malone 2008). In the absence of effective monitoring, these adolescents tend to drift into association with deviant peers who reinforce deviant talk and delinquent behavior (Granic and Dishion 2003; Snyder 2002).

From the beginning, researchers investigating the coercion model have been informed by the dictum: "If you want to understand something, try to change it" (Patterson, Reid, and Eddy 2002). Thus, over the years, they have developed and tested a number of intervention strategies based upon their basic research findings (Reid and Eddy 2002). In various ways, all of these interventions involve assisting parents to become more effective at monitoring and controlling their child's or adolescent's behavior. In large measure, these interventions have shown impressive results (Bullock and Forgatch 2005; Connell et al. 2007, 2008; Dishion and Kavanagh 2003).

In conclusion, both basic and intervention research provide strong support for the coercion model. However, while the approach has identified crucial elements of the process whereby parental behavior fosters delinquency, the approach also omits important elements identified by other theories. For example, coercion theory explicitly discounts the importance of cognitive processes associated with the acquisition of a coercive interactional style, taking the position that such behavior occurs reflexively with little conscious deliberation (Patterson, Reid, and Dishion 1992; Patterson, Reid, and Eddy 2002; Snyder and Stoolmiller 2002). While this may be the case for younger children, cognitive processes become more salient during adolescence and adulthood. Indeed, the coercion model seems to acknowledge the importance of cognition among adults as it includes beliefs and attitudes among the determinants of parental behavior (Patterson 2002). Research generated by the other theories to be discussed in this chapter indicates that, whether deliberately or inadvertently, parents foster attitudes, beliefs, and emotions that influence their offspring's actions while away from home. These cognitions and feelings mediate the effect of parental behavior upon a child's risk of subsequent involvement in antisocial behavior. There is strong evidence, for example, that quality of parenting during childhood and adolescence predicts adult criminal behavior (Johnson et al. 2004; McCord 2001; Sampson and Laub 1993). Thus, while the coercion model is to be commended for its meticulous investigation of the contingencies of reinforcement operating within families, the theory might be enhanced by including the beliefs and patterns of thinking that develop concomitantly with a coercive style of inter-action (MacKinnon et al. 2001). Indeed, research associated with theories to be dis-cussed later in the chapter indicates that cognitive schemas mediate at least a portion of the association between coercive parenting practices and child and adolescent conduct problems.

B. General Theory of Crime

The General Theory of Crime (GTC), developed by Michael Gottfredson and Travis Hirschi (1990), is one of the most popular frameworks in criminology. Like coer-cion theory, GTC views inept parental control as the primary cause of delinquent behavior. Gottfredson and Hirschi (1990) note that we all enter the world low in self-control. Infants and toddlers, for example, are impulsive, self-centered, and want immediate gratification. With time, however, most individuals learn to delay gratification. Rather than giving in to their desire for immediate reward, they exer-cise self-control and act in a manner that takes into account the consequences of their actions for themselves and others.

How do individuals develop self-control? Gottdredson and Hirschi (1990) assert that the answer involves parenting. The child's primary caregiver must set behavior standards, monitor the child's behavior, and be willing to discipline the child when the standards are not met. When caretakers do this in a consistent fashion, the child learns self-control. On the other hand, children fail to develop self-control if they are raised by caretakers who are lax in nurturance, monitoring, and discipline. Thus the theory places quality of parenting center stage and suggests that it is the level of self-control that links parenting to antisocial behavior.

Gottfredson and Hirschi (1990) contend that there is a critical period, a window of opportunity, during which self-control must be taught. Based upon their reading of developmental psychology, they suggested that this window closes around 10 years of age. By age 10, children either have or have not learned self-control. Those who have will go on to live conventional lives, whereas those who have not are expected to manifest a life course trajectory involving adolescent delinquency and adult crime

Consistent with the contentions of GTC, a profusion of studies have reported that low self-control predicts crime and delinquency. A meta-analysis of twenty-one studies found an effect size of .27 with self-control explaining approximately 10–15% of the variance in antisocial behavior (Pratt and Cullen 2000). More recently, a study of young adults in thirty-two Western and non-Western countries found low self-control predicted violence and property crime (Rebellon, Straus, and

Medeiros 2008). The only negative finding is from a study of Chinese adolescents, which found no association between self-control and delinquency once various social factors were controlled (Cheung and Cheung 2008). Thus overall, studies suggest that low self-control is an important predictor of crime.

Several studies have also investigated GTC's prediction that the relationship between exposure to inept parenting during childhood and later antisocial behavior is mediated by low self-control (Burt, Simons, and Simons 2006; Cochran et al. 1998; Gibbs, Giever, and Martin 1998; Hay 2001; Polakowski 1994; Jones, Cauffman, and Piquero 2007). Overall, the evidence from these studies suggests that self-control explains at most one-quarter of the relationship between parental control and anti-social behavior. Thus, while the evidence suggests that low self-control is an impor-tant predictor of delinquency, it appears that parental monitoring and discipline influence a child's risk for deviance in more ways than simply through its impact on self-control.

Finally, research has generally failed to corroborate GTC's contentions regard-ing the stability of self-control after age 10. Studies show that many individuals demonstrate dramatic changes in self-control during late adolescence, sometimes moving from the lowest to the highest quartiles or vice versa (Burt, Simons, and Simons 2006; Hay and Forrest 2006; Mitchell and MacKenzie 2006; Turner and Piquero 2002). Further, these changes are predicted, at least in part, by fluctuations in quality of parenting (Burt, Simons, and Simons 2006; Hay and Forrest 2006). Thus, it appears that the effect of parenting on self-control continues to operate well after the critical period identified by Gottfredson and Hirschi.

C. Attachment Theory

Over the past forty years, attachment theory has become one of the most influential theories in developmental psychology. Its power as an explanation for delinquency, however, did not become evident until the 1990s, and many criminologists remain unfamiliar with the perspective. John Bowlby developed attachment theory during the late 1950s in the midst of a cultural zeitgeist that encouraged stern parental dis-cipline and warned of the dangers of too much warmth and intimacy (see Blum 2002). The dominant psychologies of the day supported this approach. Freud thought that parental love was narcissistic and childish, and John Watson, the father of behaviorism, wrote a best-selling book that urged parents to avoid unconditional love (i.e., holding or cuddling children for no particular reason) as it would make children lazy, spoiled, and weak.

World War II created an unprecedented number of orphans, and in 1950, the World Health Organization commission John Bowlby, an English developmental psychologist and psychoanalyst, to do a study of the adjustment of these children. Bowlby wrote a lengthy report in which he documented the devastating conse-quences for children of being separated from their parents. Through out the 1950s, he continued to develop his ideas regarding the effect of the parent-child relationship upon child development. In the late 1950s, he met Harry Harlow, a psychologist and primatologist at the University of Wisconsin. In a series of studies, Harlow (1958; Harlow and Zimmerman 1959) had demonstrated that rhesus monkeys deprived of contact with parents grow up to be fearful and aggressive when united with their peers. Subsequent studies showed the same sociopathic consequence for other social species such as elephants. These findings had a profound impact upon Bowlby and helped him to formalize his attachment theory of child development.

Bowlby argued that children develop an attachment style based on the nature of the relationship with their primary caregivers. Attachment styles represent internal working models of relationships or relational schemas regarding the nature of people and relationships (e.g., whether others are trustworthy, have good intentions, and can be counted on when needed). These cognitive models are induced from the behavior of caregivers and generalized to interaction with others (Bowlby 1969, 1980). Based upon his work with neglected and orphaned children, he identified three styles of attachment. A loving, supportive caretaker was seen as promoting secure attachment and a trusting, optimistic view of people and relationships. Inconsistent, hit-and-miss parenting was linked to an anxious attachment and fearful, clingy involvement with others. Finally, the most destructive style of parenting, persistent neglect or rejection, was viewed as fostering avoidant attachment expressed as a distrusting, cynical view of people and an emotionally distant approach to relationships.

Scores of studies have corroborated the predicted link between parenting and attachment styles (Ainsworth et al. 1978; van IJzendoorn 1995), and this association holds regardless of race/ethnicity or social class (Bakersmans-Kranenburg, van IJzendoorn, and Kroonenberg 2004). Further, research has shown that attachment styles are relatively stable from childhood into early adulthood (van IJzendoorn 1995), and that they influence peer and romantic partner relationships in expected ways (Bretherton and Munholland 1999; Crowell, Fraley, and Shaver 1999).

Important for our purposes, Bowlby argued that individuals with an avoidant attachment style (i.e., a cynical, distrusting view of relationships) are likely to display aggressive and antisocial behavior. Some studies reported have found this to be the case (Greenberg et al. 1991; Keller, Spieker, and Gilchrist 2005; Renken et al. 1989; van IJzendoorn 1997), whereas others have not (Fagot and Kavanagh 1990; Lewis et al. 1984). Attachment theory became a more powerful explanation for delinquency, however, in the 1990s when researchers began to investigate the consequences of a fourth attachment style. From the beginning, studies had reported that about 15% of children displayed such an inconsistent and bizarre set of behaviors that they could not be classified using Bowlby's three categories. These individuals seemed to lack the goals associated with any of the three standard attachment styles, and Main and Solomon (1990) suggested that they be treated as a fourth group labeled *disorganized* attachment. A meta-analysis of attachment studies including all four types of attachment shows a base rate of 55% secure, 23% avoidant, 8% anxious, and 15% disorganized (van IJzendoorn 1995). In clinical, high-risk samples with a history of parental maltreatment, however, up to 80% are classified as disorganized (Carlson et al. 1989).

In general, studies have reported that children classified as disorganized tend to have been subjected to much more negative parental behavior (tirades, threats, intrusions, depression, withdrawal) than secure, anxious, or avoidant children (Lyons-Ruth 1996; Lyons-Ruth and Jacobvitz 1999; True, Pisani, and Oumar 2001). Indeed, their disorganized behavior appears to be in response to a situation where the attachment figure is both a source of fright and the only possible safe haven (Carlson 1998; Lyons-Ruth 1996). These aversive parental behaviors are presumed to give rise to development by the child of an angry, distrusting view of people and relationships. As these children begin school, many of them begin to display a kind of role reversal where they began to control the caregiver (Lyons-Ruth 1996). The child uses harsh commands, verbal threats, and occasional physical aggression to coerce the parent into submission. These behaviors are functional in that the child gains control over a scary, unpredictable family environment (Jacobvitz and Hazan 1999; Crittenden 1999).

Further, it appears that this aggressive style of interaction is generalized to the classroom and relationships with peers. Several studies have reported a relationship between disorganized attachment based upon observational assessments at approximately 2 years of age and subsequent aggression and conduct problems in the preschool and elementary school years (see reviews by Lyons-Ruth 1996; Lyons-Ruth and Jacobvitz, 1999; Green and Goldwyn 2002). This evidence is impressive as these studies are prospective and use multiple indicators of constructs. A meta-analysis by van IJzendoorn and colleagues (1999) found that effect sizes ranged from .54 to .17, with an average of .29.

While the attachment perspective on delinquency has strong support, it also suffers limitations. First, attachment studies rarely follow children into late adolescence and adulthood. Thus we know little about how childhood attachment styles predict delinquency and crime later in life. Second, there is the issue of the extent to which attachment style mediates the effect of parenting on child conduct problems. Whereas GTC posited that self-control explains the association between parenting and delinquency, attachment theory contends that it is the child's attachment style that mediates this relationship. The few studies that have examined this issue found that attachment style mediates only a modest portion of the impact of harsh parenting on child antisocial behavior (Lyons-Ruth et al. 1990, 1991). This indicates that the mechanism whereby parental behavior increases the probability of delinquency involves more than just the child's attachment style.

Finally, although attachment theory assumes that attachment style influences an individual's relationships with others because it represents a working model of relationships, attachment theorists concerned with childhood aggression do not actually assess these models. Rather, they use behavioral ratings of parent-child interaction to code attachment style. While this approach makes sense when the child is small, the theory would be more compelling if the cognitions assumed to be associated with a disorganized attachment style were assessed during adolescence and shown to predict delinquency and crime. This is the approach utilized by the next theory to be discussed.

D. Hostile Attribution Bias

As noted in the introduction to this chapter, longitudinal studies have shown that some youngsters display high rates of aggression at an early age and that this anti-social behavior escalates into delinquent behavior during adolescence. Since the early 1980s, a number of psychologists, but most notably Ken Dodge and his colleagues, have been investigating the way that these antisocial youth process information when interacting with others. This research indicates that aggressive children and adolescents tend to demonstrate a hostile attribution bias. Persons with this cognitive bias believe that they must be wary and on guard as other individuals have hostile intentions.

When persons committed to this view experience an unpleasant action (e.g., being bumped, being stared at), they assume that the antagonist has a hostile intention. Generally speaking, individuals with this bias do not believe in accidents. All negative actions are perceived as having a hostile intent. This perspective leads them to attribute malevolent motives to others and to assume that an intimidating, confrontational style of interaction is necessary to avoid exploitation. Research has shown that this view of relationships is strongly held by aggressive children and institutionalized delinquents (Burks et al. 1999; Dodge, Bates, and Pettit 1990, 2002; Dodge et al. 2003; Dodge and Newman 1981; Slaby and Guerra 1988; Zelli et al. 1999). A meta-analysis of such studies reported a robust association between hostile attributions and youth aggression, with the relationship being strongest in studies that focused upon extreme forms of aggression (Orbio de Castro et al. 2002). Further, there is evidence that aggressive adults (Bailey and Ostrov 2007), including criminal offenders (Vitale et al. 2005), demonstrate a hostile attribution bias.

Having established a link between a hostile attribution bias and antisocial behavior, researchers began to investigate the hypothesis that children and adolescents learn this cognitive style in interaction with their parents. A profusion of studies have provided support for this idea. This research indicates that youth are at greatest risk for developing a hostile attribution bias when their parents are harsh and rejecting (Camras, Sachs-Alter, and Ribordy 1996; Dodge 1991; Dodge et al. 1995; Dodge, Bates, and Pettit 1990; MacKinnon-Lewis et al. 2001; Palmer and Hollin 2000). There is also evidence that highly authoritarian parenting fosters this cognitive bias in children (Gomez et al. 2001; Runions and Keating 2007). Most of these studies also show that hostile attribution bias only mediates a portion of the association between harsh parenting and child and adolescent antisocial behavior. Thus, like self-control and disorganized attachment, hostile attribution bias appears to be only one mechanism among several whereby inept parenting causes a child to develop conduct problems. Still, there is evidence suggesting that a child's hostile attribution bias may be an effective avenue for preventing delinquent behavior.

At least five intervention experiments have shown that hostile views of people and relationships can be altered and that these changes result in more conventional behavior (see Dodge 2006).

E. General Strain Theory

Robert Agnew (1992, 2006) has formulated a general strain theory of crime which posits that exposure to strain, especially on a persistent basis, increases a child's risk for delinquency (see Agnew, Chapter 14). A strain, according to the theory, is an aversive event involving unfair treatment by others, the inability to achieve a desired outcome, or loss of something of value. For children and adolescents, poor parenting is among the most disruptive of strains (Agnew 2001, 2005). This includes parental rejection and punishments that are erratic, excessive, and harsh (Agnew 2006).

The theory argues that strains lead to delinquency because they foster negative emotions that increase the probability of adopting deviant behavior as a method of coping. The negative emotion that is viewed as most likely to produce this effect is anger. Anger, and its related emotions such as frustration, envy and jealousy, is seen as increasing the probability of delinquency because it fosters irritability and explosiveness, creates pressure for corrective actions such as revenge, and reduces inhibitions and concern with long-term consequences (Agnew 2006). Thus harsh or erratic parenting causes a child to feel angry and frustrated, and these feelings in turn increase the chances of delinquent behavior. The child may vent his negative emotions by fighting, vandalism, and the like, or attempt to assuage these negative feelings through the use of drugs or alcohol.

Consistent with the theory, several studies have demonstrated that feelings of anger increase the probability that an individual will engage in delinquent behavior (Agnew 1985; Berkowitz 1990; Mazerolle and Piquero 1997, 1998; R. Simons et al. 2003, 2006). And, in our earlier discussions of both attachment theory and attribution bias, we noted that a number of studies have demonstrated a link between harsh parenting and delinquency. However, the remaining critical question for general strain theory is the extent to which anger mediates the effect the harsh parenting has on delinquency. Only a few studies have investigated this issue. Broidy (2001) found that anger mediated much of the association between these two variables, whereas evidence from other studies suggests that it mediates only a small portion of this relationship (Brezina 1998; Piquero and Sealock 2000). Thus it appears that feelings of anger and frustration are only part of the explanation for the link between rejecting, harsh, or erratic parenting and adolescent antisocial behavior.

F. Conclusion: Inept Parenting and Mechanisms of Influence

We began our review of theories with two questions: which parenting practices lead to delinquency, and what are the psychological mechanisms whereby they produce this effect? Regarding the first issue, we have seen that studies supporting social learning theory and the general theory of crime suggest that it is the absence of parental control (i.e., lax monitoring and consistent discipline) that fosters child antisocial behavior. On the other hand, research generated by attachment, biased attribution, and general strain theory indicates that it is lack of parental support and nurturance (i.e., hostility, neglect) that promotes antisocial behavior. Which is correct? Research that includes both sets of parenting practices indicates that they are equally important (Loeber and Stouthamer-Loeber 1986; Sampson and Laub 1993; Simons, Simons, Wallace 2004; Wright and Cullen 2001). Children are least likely to engage in antisocial behavior when their caregivers couple warmth and responsiveness with firm control and maturity demands (see Simons, Simons, Wallace 2004; Steinberg 2001). This approach to parenting is usually referred to as "authoritative parenting." Children do best when then have two authoritative parents. However, there is evidence that one authoritative parent can largely buffer the deleterious effects of a second parent who is harsh or uninvolved (Simons and Conger 2007).

Of course, there needs to be a change in the way warmth and control are exercised as the child makes the transitions to adolescence. Studies show that parental monitoring is crucial during this developmental period, especially for youths with a history of antisocial behavior (Dishion, Poulin, and Skaggs 2000). This research indicates that adolescent delinquency is associated with a lack of parental monitoring of the adolescent's whereabouts, time allocation, and peer associations (see Dodge, Greenberg, and Malone 2008). Monitoring is usually measured through assessments of parents' knowledge of their adolescent's everyday life. Parental knowledge has been shown to predict an adolescent's subsequent involvement in delinquent behavior, controlling for past delinquency (see Lahey et al. 2008). However, recently it has become evident that most of the information that parents possess is based upon self-disclosures by the child rather than being derived from parental surveillance (Kerr and Stattin 2000; Soenens et al. 2006; Lahey et al. 2008). This indicates that effective monitoring requires that caregivers establish a warm, involved relationship with their child that includes frequent and open communication. Stated differently, effective control during the adolescent years becomes very difficult in the absence of parental warmth and involvement.

Turning to the question of mechanisms, we saw that each of the various theoretical explanations emphasizes a particular cognitive or affective factor as the avenue whereby parental behavior causes delinquency. Although past research studies have established a strong link between each of these factors and delinquency, none of them completely explain the relationship between parental behavior and delinquency. One might speculate that each of the theories possesses an element of truth and that it is the combination of these psychological factors that explains the effect of parenting on delinquency. This suggests that the various theories may represent complementary, rather than competitive, explanations for conduct problems as each identifies an important element in the mix of factors that leads some youths to often perceive that delinquent behavior is an appropriate line of action. Consistent with this idea, a recent longitudinal study by R. Simons et al. (2007) found that self-control, a hostile model of relationships, and anger each had an independent effect upon delinquency and that together these variables mediated all of the impact of harsh parenting and ineffective discipline.

II. The Effect of Family Structure

Over the past several decades, scores of studies have investigated the association between family structure and delinquency. This research has become even more salient in recent years as less than half of all children grow up in a household consisting of their married biological parents (Simons, Simons, and Wallace 2004; Lugalia and Overturf 2004; Seltzer 2000). The majority of children live with a single parent, a stepfamily, cohabiting biological parents, a foster family, a parent and grandparent, or a parent who is cohabiting with a romantic partner. Studies have consistently found that that youths living with married, biological parents are less likely to display behavior problems than those residing in other types of households (Simons, Simons, and Wallace 2004; Wells and Rankin 1991; Apel and Kaukinen 2008). Evidence suggests that there is roughly a 15% difference in delinquency between the two groups (Apel and Kaukinen 2008; Wells and Rankin 1991). However, recent research suggests that the nature of the risk varies by type of nontraditional family structure, with blended and cohabiting families showing the most negative effects (Apel and Kaukinen 2008; L. Simons et al. 2006). In the previous section we saw that children are at low risk for conduct problems when they are the beneficiaries of authoritative parenting (support and control) from two parents. The evidence suggests that a family structure increases the chances of delinquency to the extent that it is unable to meet this condition.

Numerous studies have shown, for example, that children living with a divorced or never-married single parent (usually a mother) is at higher risk for antisocial behavior than those living with both biological parents (Amato and Keith 1991; Demuth and Brown 2004; Manning and Lamb 2003; McLanahan and Sandefur 1994; Rebellon 2002; Simons 1996). In part, this difference is explained by the fact that single parents are more apt to be poor, to live in disadvantaged areas, and to experience stressful life events like moving and changing jobs than married parents (McLanahan and Sandefur 1994; Apel and Kaukinen 2008). Research shows that these stressors, along with the challenge of managing a household by oneself, have a disruptive effect on the quality of parenting provided by single parents. Hence support and control is often lower in single parent households (Simons and Johnson 1996; White and Rogers 2000).

A second reason for the increased risk for delinquency in single parent households involves the number of parents. In general, children show the strongest developmental outcomes when they receive support and control from two adults

(Dornbusch et al. 1985), whereas only one caregiver is available to nurture, monitor, and discipline in a single parent family. This would suggest that children in single parent households would be less likely to display conduct problems when the non-residential parent, usually the father, is involved in authoritative co-parenting. Several studies show that this is indeed the case (Amato and Gilbreth 1999; Demuth and Brown 2004; Simons 1996). However, one would expect the parenting of a non-residential father to be somewhat less effective than that of fathers who reside in the home with the child, and that is what the evidence suggests (Coley and Medeiros 2007). Finally, if the number of adults engaging in parenting has an impact on child outcomes, children in single parent households should be at lower risk for delinquency when a grandmother or other relative helps the single mother with the task of parenting. There is some evidence indicating that this is the case (Dornbusch et al. 1985; L. Simons et al. 2006).

Several studies indicate that children in stepfamilies are at even greater risk for antisocial behavior than those in single parent households (Apel and Kaukinen 2008; Coleman, Ganong, and Fine 2000; L. Simons et al. 2006). At first glance, this effect might appear puzzling as stepfamilies have the advantage of two adults to parent the children. Studies have found, however, that stepfathers tend to show less warmth, monitoring, and discipline than nondivorced, biological fathers (Hetherington 1993; Kurdek and Fine 1994; L. Simons et al. 2006). Further, research indicates that the birth of new joint biological children in blended families diminishes parental involvement with the stepchildren (Gennetian 2005; Stewart 2005). This reduced support and control in stepfamilies partially explains why stepchildren are at increased risk for antisocial behavior (Apel and Kaukinen 2008; Love and Murdock 2004; L. Simons et al. 2006).

The other factor that seems to account for this elevated risk is that stepparents often lack parental legitimacy in the eyes of their stepchildren (L. Simons et al. 2006). This explains why delinquency is higher in father-stepmother families than mother-stepfather families. Mothers usually provide more parenting than fathers, yet stepchildren are likely to resist a stepmother's attempt to be an involved parent. This same explanation probably accounts for the finding that rates of antisocial behavior are especially high in cohabiting blended families and in foster families (Apel and Kaukinen 2008). Children in cohabiting blended households are likely to perceive their parent's live-in boyfriend or girlfriend as having no legitimacy to play the role of parent. Similarly, foster children often challenge the authority of foster parents.

Finally, there is some evidence that children are at increased risk for delinquency when their biological parents are cohabiting rather than married. Apel and Kaukinen (2008), for example, find that children living with cohabiting biological parents have a risk for delinquency that is approximately the same as that for those residing in single parent families. It is not clear why this might be the case. Perhaps parents who eschew marriage have a less conventional view of parenting and convey less commitment to traditional values to their children. Consistent with this idea, Apel and Kaukinen (2008) found that a significant portion of the difference in delinquency between households with married versus cohabitating biological parents was explained by the tendency of cohabitating parents to engage in less supportive parenting and for their children to be less committed to school.

III. Are Family Effects Simply Genetic Effects?

We have reviewed a rather vast literature showing a link between parental behavior and the chances that a youth will become delinquent. Many of these studies were longitudinal investigations showing that delinquency tends to follow exposure to inept parenting. It is generally assumed that this body of evidence demonstrates that parenting practices promote child and adolescent antisocial behavior, and we reviewed a variety of theoretical explanations regarding the nature of this influence. However, there is another possibility. It may be genes rather than social influence that link quality of parenting to child behavior problems (see Rowe 1994). Behavioral geneticists have posited two avenues whereby these genetic effects might occur.

First, it may be that a child's experience of harsh or uninvolved parenting and subsequent antisocial behavior are likely because the genetic factors transmitted from parents to children foster antisocial behavior in both generations. These genetic factors cause the parents to engage in rejecting or neglecting parenting practices (and perhaps other types of antisocial behavior) and the child to be aggressive and defiant. Stated differently, genetic factors transmitted to children may increase the likelihood that the parents will be ineffectual and that the child will be antisocial. Such a phenomenon is referred to as a *passive gene-environment correlation* (Plomin, DeFries, and Loehlin 1977). Recently, several behavioral genetic studies have reported that parenting continues to influence child antisocial behavior after controlling for this potential genetic effect.

The most straightforward approach to addressing this issue is to use samples of monozygotic twins and their families. This approach relates twin-pair differences in family environment to twin-pair differences in behavior. Since monozygotic twins do not differ genetically, any associations found cannot be attributable to genetics. Using this approach, Asbury, Dunn, Pike, and Plomin (2003) reported that the twin in each pair who received more maternal negativity and harsh discipline tended to display the greater amount of antisocial behavior. The association was particularly strong when the adverse parenting was extreme. Using the same design, Caspi et al. (2004) also found that the twin with more exposure to maternal negativity showed more behavior problems.

In addition to these studies which investigate the effect of parenting, a recent study (Burt et al. 2008) examined the extent to which the association between parental divorce and delinquency might be spurious due to genetic transmission. As noted above, several studies have shown that parental divorce is linked to an increased risk for child antisocial behavior. It could be, however, that a passive gene/environment correlation explains this association. Perhaps divorced parents possess a genetic risk for anger and conflict and they pass this risk to their children with the result being antisocial behavior (Rhee and Waldman 2002). While this is a plausible hypothesis, Burt et al. (2008) found that the experience of parental divorce, and not common genes, accounts for the association between divorce and adolescent delinquency.

Such studies suggest that parental behavior continues to be associated with child behavior problems after removing the effect of any genetically transmitted risk for antisocial behavior. However, this research does not establish the causal priority behind these correlations (Asbury et al. 2003) and therefore does not rule out the possibility of the second avenue, whereby genes may explain the association between parenting and child behavior problems. A child's genotype may increase the likelihood that he or she will engage in disruptive behavior that elicits a punitive response from the caregiver who does not share that genotype. This phenomenon is labeled *evocative or active gene-environment correlation* (Scarr and McCartney 1983). In such cases, the child's noxious actions evoke harsh parenting, rather than harsh parenting causing the child's difficult behavior. This issue has been investigated by researchers using longitudinal data collected from samples of monozygotic twins.

In a study of the effects of physical maltreatment, for example, Jaffee, Caspi, Moffitt, and Taylor (2004) found that the effect of abusive parenting on increases in child conduct problems remained strong after controlling for any genetic transmission of antisocial behavior. They did find, however, that genetic factors accounted for a significant portion of the relationship between maltreatment and children's conduct problems. Similarly, a recent study of over six thousand pairs of twins (Larsson et al. 2008) reported that parents' negativity toward their children continued to predict child antisocial behavior after controlling for genetic influences. Albeit, they also found evidence that genetically influenced antisocial behavior evokes parental negativity toward the child.

Thus, consistent with the contentions of coercion theory as discussed above (Patterson, Reid, Dishion 1992; Reid, Patterson, and Snyder 2002), the relationship between adverse parenting and child antisocial behavior appears to be bidirectional. A wide variety of factors has been shown to increase the probability of harsh or uninvolved parenting. These include economic hardship, marital conflict, quality of parenting in the parent's family of origin, and community context (Conger et al. 1992; Conger et al., 2002; McLoyd et al. 2000; R. Simons et al. 1993; R. Simons et al. 2005). In addition, the behavioral genetics studies just reviewed indicate that children sometimes possess genetically driven tendencies (e.g., difficult temperament) that contribute to their parents' adverse parenting. However, when parents engage in harsh or uninvolved parenting, whether it is a function of past learning, economic stress, or their child's conduct, the consequence is likely to be an amplification of the child's antisocial behavior.

In addition to the studies that focus upon the effect of parental behavior on delinquency, some investigators have examined the extent to which genetics might explain the association between parental behavior and the cognitive mediators identified by some of the theories discussed earlier. For example, several studies have established that the association between quality of parenting and attachment style is not explained by genetic influences (Fearon et al. 2006; Roisman and Fraley 2008). And, Beaver (2008) recently reported that both genetic factors and variations in parenting account for the association between parental behavior and their adolescents' level of self-control.

Thus there is compelling evidence that parental behavior continues to have an effect upon children's cognitive schemas and antisocial behavior after controlling for genetics, especially when adverse parenting practices are extreme. Thus the association between parental behavior and delinquency is far from unity. Although harsh or uninvolved parenting increases the chances of delinquency, many youths exposed to such parenting do not become antisocial. This suggests that some children may be more vulnerable to such parenting practices than others, and recent molecular genetics research indicates that this is indeed the case. Unlike the behavioral genetic approach described above, these studies are concerned with *gene-environment (GxE) interaction*. They focus upon the extent to which variation in a particular gene (i.e., specific genetic polymorphisms) interacts with adverse environments, such as harsh parenting, to produce problem behavior. Several studies have reported positive results (see Moffitt, Caspi, and Rutter 2006; Rutter, Moffitt, and Caspi 2006).

The strongest and most consistent findings involve the monoamine oxidase A (MAOA) gene, which has been shown to interact with harsh or abusive parenting. Results show that exposure to harsh parenting is much more likely to foster adolescent or adult antisocial behavior in individuals with the short rather than long version (allele) of this gene (see meta analysis by Kim-Cohen et al. 2006). Importantly, these analyses show the short allele does not increase the chances of antisocial behavior for individuals who receive conventional forms of parenting. It is only in the presence of adverse parenting that the genetic vulnerability shows its effect. The MAOA gene is sometimes called the warrior gene, as it is associated with anger and aggression in response to provocation (Alia-Klein et al. 2008; McDermott et al. 2009). Thus, this genetic polymorphism may enhance the amount of irritation and hostility experienced in response to unfair treatment such as harsh parenting. If this is the case, we might expect to find that, among individuals exposed to harsh parenting, those with the short MAOA allele are more likely than those with the long allele to develop cognitive schemas that criminological theories have related to delinquency such as a hostile attribution bias or low self-control. Such studies have yet to be completed.

Research has been completed, however, regarding another cognitive mediator—disorganized attachment. Gervai et al. (2007) recently completed a study in which they found a robust association between adverse maternal parenting and the probability of a child developing a disorganized attachment style. However, this association only held for the majority of children who carried the short form of the DRD4 dopamine receptor gene. This gene-by-parenting interaction held after controlling for maternal D4 genotype.

Molecular genetics research is still relatively new. Many more gene-by-parenting interactions are likely to be discovered in the coming years. Thus far, this research has served to underscore the power of parenting. In most studies, adverse parenting shows a main effect on child conduct problems in addition to the impact of its interaction with a particular genetic polymorphism (Moffitt, Caspi, and Rutter 2006; Rutter, Moffitt, and Caspi 2006). This suggests that negative parenting increases the risk of antisocial behavior for all children, but the risk is especially high for those with particular genetic vulnerabilities. On the other hand, genetic vulnerability usually does not show a main effect on child behavior (see Moffitt, Caspi, and Rutter 2006; Rutter, Moffitt, and Caspi 2006). Its influence is limited to its interaction with parenting; it increases the odds of conduct problems when parenting is adverse but exerts no effect upon the chances of antisocial behavior when parenting is more optimal.

This line of research is providing us with a better understanding of the genotypes that make children most vulnerable to negative parental behavior. However, there is a need for studies that go beyond simply analyzing the way that genes and parenting practices interact to influence risk for conduct problems. A real understanding of the manner in which genes and parenting combine to influence child behavior requires information regarding the mechanisms whereby genotypes affect a child's response to parental behavior. Our guess is that polymorphisms associated with genes such as MAOA or DRD4 exert their influence by increasing either the anger or fear that a child experiences in response to adverse parenting.

IV. Conclusion

Parental behavior has been shown to have an impact on child and adolescent antisocial behavior. The evidence suggests that harsh or uninvolved parenting is most detrimental. Child behavior problems are more common in family structures that are at increased risk for these adverse parenting practices (viz., single parent, cohabitating, and stepfamilies). In large measure, harsh or uninvolved parenting elevates the chances of conduct problems by fostering cognitive schemas and traits such as a hostile attribution bias, a negative model of relationships, low self-control, and chronic anger. These characteristics cause situations to be construed in a fashion conducive to aggressive and delinquent behavior.

There is a heritable component to antisocial behavior, but parental behavior exerts an influence beyond any genetic risk transmitted to the child. However, the correlation between adverse parenting and child conduct problems is modest. Although harsh or uninvolved parenting increases the chances of antisocial behavior, many children are resilient in the face of such a family environment. Recent studies involving molecular genetics show promise for providing a better understanding of this fact. This research indicates that some children have a greater genetic vulnerability than others to negative parenting practices. Such studies are providing a more nuanced understanding of when untoward parental behavior is most harmful to a child.

REFERENCES

Agnew, Robert. 1985. "A Revised Strain Theory of Delinquency." *Social Forces* 64: 151–67.

Agnew, Robert. 1992. "Foundation for a General Strain Theory of Crime and Delinquency." *Criminology* 30: 47–87.

Agnew, Robert. 2001. "Building on the Foundation of General Strain Theory: Specifying the Types of Strain Most Likely to Lead to Crime and Delinquency." *Journal of Research in Crime and Delinquency* 38: 319–61.

Agnew, Robert. 2005. *Why Do Criminals Offend?* Los Angeles, CA: Roxbury.

Agnew, Robert. 2006. *Pressured into Crime. An Introduction to General Strain Theory*. Los Angeles, CA: Roxbury.

Ainsworth, Mary D. S., M. D. Blehar, E. Waters, and S. Wall. 1978. *Patterns of Attachment: A Psychological Study of the Strange Situation*. Hillsdale, NJ: Erlbaum.

Akers, R. L. 1985. *Deviant Behavior: A Social Learning Approach*. Belmont, CA: Wadsworth.

Akers, R. L. 1998. *Social Learning and Social Structure: A General Theory of Crime and Deviance*. Boston, MA: Northeastern University Press.

Alia-Klein, Nelly, Aarti Kriplani, Kith Pradhan, Jim Yeming Ma, Jean Logan, Benjamin Williams, Ian W. Craig, Frank Telang, Dardo Tomasi, Rita Z. Goldstein, Gene-Jack Wang, Nora D. Volkow, and Joanna S. Fowler. 2008. "The MAO-A Genotype Does Not Modulate Resting Brain Metabolism in Adults." *Psychiatry Research Neuroimaging* 164: 73–76.

Amato, Paul R., and J. G. Gilbreth. 1999. "Nonresident Fathers and Children's Well-Being: A Meta-Analysis." *Journal of Marriage and the Family* 61: 557–73.

Amato, Paul R., and B. Keith. 1991. "Parental Divorce and the Well-Being of Children: A Meta-Analysis." *Psychological Bulletin* 110: 26–46.

American Psychiatric Association. 1994. *Diagnostic and Statistical Manual of Mental Disorders*, 4th ed. Washington, DC: American Psychiatric Association.

Anderson, E. 1999. *Code of the Street: Decency, Violence, and the Moral Life of the Inner City*. New York: W.W. Norton.

Apel, Robert, and Catherine Kaukinen. 2008. "On the Relationship Between Family Structure and Antisocial Behavior: Parental Cohabitation and Blended Households." *Criminology* 46: 35–70.

Asbury, K., J. Dunn, A. Pike, and R. Plomin. 2003. "Nonshared Environmental Influences on Individual Differences in Early Behavioral Development: An MZ Differences Study." *Child Development* 74: 933–43.

Bailey, Christopher A., and Jamie M. Ostrov. 2007. "Differentiating Forms and Functions of Aggression in Emerging Adults: Associations with Hostile Attribution Biases and Normative Beliefs." *Journal of Youth and Adolescence* 37: 713–22.

Bakermans-Kranenburg, Marinus van IJzendoorn, and Pieter M. Kroonenberg. 2004. "Differences in Attachment Security between African-American and White Children: Ethnicity or Socio-economic Status?" *Infant Behavior and Development* 27: 417–33.

Bandura, A. 1969. *Principles of Behavior Modification*. New York: Holt, Rinehart and Winston.

Bandura, A. 1977. *Social Learning Theory*. Englewood Cliffs, NJ: Prentice-Hall.

Bandura, A. 1986. *Social Foundations of Thought and Action: A Social Cognitive Theory*. Englewood Cliffs, NJ: Prentice-Hall.

Bandura, A., and R. Walters. 1963. *Social Learning and Personality Development*. New York: Holt, Rinehart and Winston.

Beaver, Kevin. 2008. "Nonshared Environmental Influences on Adolescent Delinquent Involvement and Adult Criminal Behavior." *Criminology* 46: 341–69.

Berkowitz, Leonard. 1990. "On the Formation and Regulation of Anger and Aggression: A Cognitive-Associationistic Analysis." *American Psychologist* 45: 494–503.

Blum, Deborah. 2002. *Love at Goon Park: Harry Harlow and the Science of Affection*. Cambridge, MA: Perseus.

Bowlby, J. 1969. *Attachment and Loss*. Vol. 1 of *Attachment*. New York: Basic Books.

Bowlby, J. 1980. *Attachment and Loss*. Vol. 3 of *Loss: Sadness and Depression*. London: Hogarth Press.

Bretherton, Inge, and Kristine A. Munholland. 1999. "Internal Working Models in Attachment Relationships: A Construct Revisited." In *Handbook of Attachment, Theory, Research, and Clinical Applications*, edited by J. Cassidy and P. Shaver, 89–111. New York, NY: Guilford Press.

Brezina, Timothy. 1998. "Adolescent Maltreatment and Delinquency: The Question of Intervening Processes." *Journal of Research in Crime and Delinquency* 35(1): 71–99.

Broidy, Lisa. 2001. "A Test of General Strain Theory." *Criminology* 39: 9–33.

Bullock, Bernadette M., and Marion S. Forgatch. 2005. "Mother in Transition: Model-Based Strategies for Effective Parenting." In *Family Psychology: The Art of the Science*, edited by W. M. Pinsof and Jay Lebow, 349–71. New York: Oxford Univeristy Press.

Burks, Virginia Salzer, Robert D. Laird, Kenneth A. Dodge, Gregory S. Pettit, and John E. Bates. 1999. "Knowledge Structures, Social Information Processing, and Children's Aggressive Behavior." *Social Development* 8: 220–36.

Burt, A., A. Barnes, M. McGue, W. Iacono. 2008. "Parental Divorce and Adolescent Delinquency: Ruling out the Impact of Common Genes." *Developmental Psychology* 44:6, 1668–1677.

Burt, Callie H., Ronald L. Simons, and Leslie Gordon Simons. 2006. "A Longitudinal Test of the Effects of Parenting and the Stability of Self-control: Negative Evidence for the General Theory of Crime." *Criminology* 44: 2353–96.

Camras, Linda A., Ellen Sachs-Alter, and Sheila C. Ribordy. 1996. "Emotion Understanding in Maltreated Children: Recognition of Facial Expressions and Integration with other Emotion Cues." In *Emotional Development in Atypical Children*, edited by Michael Lewis and Margaret Sullivan, 203–25. Hillsdale, NJ, England: Lawrence Erlbaum Associates.

Carlson, E. A. 1998. "A Prospective Longitudinal Study of Attachment Disorganization/ Disorientation." *Child Development* 69: 1107–28.

Carlson, V., D. Cicchetti, D. Barnett, and K. Braunwald. 1989. "Disorganized/Disoriented Attachment Relationships in Maltreated Infants." *Developmental Psychology* 25: 525–31.

Caspi, Avshalom, and T. E. Moffitt. 1995. "The Continuity of Maladaptive Behavior: From Description to Understanding in the Study of Antisocial Behavior." In *Developmental Psychopathology*, edited by D. Cicchetti and J. T. Manly, 472–511. New York: Wiley.

Caspi, Avshalom, Terrie E. Moffitt, Julia Morgan, Michael Rutter, Alan Taylor, Louise Arseneault, Lucy Tully Catherine Jacobs, Julia Kim-Cohen, and Monica Polo-Tomas. 2004. "Maternal Expressed Emotion Predicts Children's Antisocial Behavior Problems: Using Monozygotic-Twin Differences to Identify Environmental Effects on Behavioral Development." *Developmental Psychology* 40: 149–61.

Cheung, Nicole W. T., and Yuet W. Cheung. 2008. "Self-control, Social Factors, and Delinquency: A Test of the General Theory of Crime among Adolescents in Hong Kong." *Journal of Youth and Adolescence* 37: 412–30.

Cochran, J. K., P. B. Wood, C. S. Sellers, W. Wilderson, and M. B. Chamlin. 1998. "Academic Dishonesty and Low Self-control: An Empirical Test of a General Theory of Crime." *Deviant Behavior* 19: 227–55.

Coleman, Marilyn, Larry Ganong, and Mark Fine. 2000. "Reinvestigating Rremarriage: Another Decade of Progress." In *Understanding Families in the New Millinium: A Decade in Review*, edited by Robert M. Milardo, 507–26. Lawrence, KS: National Conference on Family Relations.

Coley, Rebekah Levine, and Bethany L. Medeiros. 2007. "Reciprocal Longitudinal Relations Between Nonresident Father Involvement and Adolescent Delinquency." *Child Development* 78: 132–47.

Conger, R. D., K. J. Conger, G. H. Elder, F. O. Lorenz, Ronald Simons, and L. B. Whitbeck. 1992. "A Family Process Model of Economic Hardship and Influences on Adjustment of Early Adolescent Boys." *Child Development* 63: 526–41.

Conger, R. D., and Ronald L. Simons. 1997. "Life Course Contingencies in the Development of Adolescent Antisocial Behavior: A Matching Law Approach." In *Developmental Theories of Crime and Delinquency*, Edited by T. Thornberry. New Brunswick, NJ: Transaction.

Conger, R. D., L. E. Wallace, Y. Sun, R. L. Simons, V. C. McLoyd, and G. H. Brody. 2002. "Economic Pressure in African-American Families: A Replication and Extension of the Family Stress Model." *Developmental Psychology* 38(2): 179–93.

Connell, Arin, Bernadette M. Bullock, Thomas J. Dishion, Melvin Wilson, Fances Gardner, and Daniel Shaw. 2008. "Family Intervention Effects on Co-occurring Early Childhood Behavioral and Emotional Problems: A Latent Transition Approach." *Journal of Abnormal Child Psychology* 36: 1211–25.

Connell, Arin, Thomas J. Dishion, Miwa Yasui, and Kathryn Kavangh. 2007. "An Adaptive Approach to Family Intervention: Liking Engagement in Family-Centered Intervention to Reductions in Adolescent Problem Behavior." *Journal of Consulting and Clinical Psychology* 75: 568–79.

Crittenden, P. M. 1999. "Danger and Development: The Organization of Self-Protective Strategies." *Monographs of the Society for Research in Child Development* 64: 145–71.

Crowell, J. A., R. C. Fraley, and P. R. Shaver. 1999. "Measurement of Individuals Differences in Adolescent and Adult Attachment." In *Handbook of Attachment, Theory, Research, and Clinical Applications*, edited by J. Cassidy and P. Shaver, 434–465. New York, NY: Guilford Press.

Demuth, S., and S. Brown. 2004. "Family Structure, Family Processes, and Adolescent Delinquency: The Significance of Parental Absence Verses Parental Gender." *Journal of Research in Crime and Delinquency* 41: 58–81.

Dishion, T. J., and K. Kavanagh. 2003. *Intervening in Adolescent Problem Behavior: A Family-Centered Approach*. New York: Guilford Press.

Dishion, T. J., Sarah E. Nelson, and B. Bullock. 2004. "Premature Adolescent Autonomy: Parent Disengagement and Deviant Peer Process in the Amplification of Problem Behavior." *Journal of Adolescence* 27: 515–30.

Dishion, T. J., F. Poulin, and Medici Skaggs. 2000. "The Ecology of Premature Adolescent Autonomy: Biological and Social Influences." In *Explaining Associations between Family and Peer Relationships*, edited by K. A. Kerns, J. Contreras, and A. M. Neal Barrett, 27–45. Westport, CT: Prager.

Dodge, Kenneth A. 1991. "The Structure and Function of Reactive and Proactive Aggression." In *The Development and Treatment of Childhood Aggression*, edited by Debra J. Pepler and Kenneth H. Rubin, 201–18. Hillsdale, NJ: Lawrence Erlbaum Associates.

Dodge, Kenneth A. 2006. "Translational science in action: Hostile attribution style and the development of aggressive behavior problems." *Development and Psychopathology* 18: 791–814.

Dodge, Kenneth A., John E. Bates, and Gregory S. Pettit. 1990. "Mechanisms in the Cycle of Violence." *Science* 250: 1678–83.

Dodge, Kenneth A., Mark T. Greenberg, and Patrick S. Malone. 2008. "Testing an Idealized Dynamic Cascade Model of the Development of Serious Violence in Adolescence." *Child Development* 79: 1907–77.

Dodge, Kenneth A., Robert Laird, John E. Lochman, and Arnoldo Zelli. 2002. "Multidimensional Latent-Construct Analysis of Children's Social Information Processing Patterns: Correlations with Aggressive Behavior Problems." *Psychological Assessment* 14: 60–73.

Dodge, Kenneth A., and Joseph P. Newman. 1981. "Biased Decision-Making Processes in Aggressive Boys." *Journal of Abnormal Psychology* 90: 375–97.

Dodge, Kenneth A., Gregory S. Pettit, John E. Bates, and E. Valente. 1995. "Social Information-Processing Patterns Partially Mediate the Effect of Early Physical Abusive on Later Conduct Problems." *Journal of Abnormal Psychology* 51: 632–43.

Dornbusch, S., J. M. Carlsmith, S. J. Bushwall, P. L. Ritter, H. Leiderman, A. H. Hastorf, and R. T. Gross. 1985. "Single Parents, Extended Households, and the Control of Adolescents." *Child Development* 56: 326–41.

Fagot, B. I., and K. Kavanagh. 1990. "The Prediction of Antisocial Behavior from Avoidant Attachment Classifications." *Child Development* 61: 864–73.

Fearon, R. M. P., M. H. van IJsendoorn, P. Fonagy, M. J. Bakermans-Kranenburg, C. Schuengal, and C. L. Bokhorst. 2006. "In Search of Shared and Nonshared Environmental Factors in Security of Attachment: A Behavior-Genetic Study of the Association between Sensitivity and Attachment Security." *Developmental Psychology* 42: 1026–40.

Gennetian, Lisa. 2005. "One or Two Parents? Half or Step Siblings? The Effect of Family Structure on Young Children's Achievement." *Journal of Population Economics* 18: 415–36.

Gervai, Judit, Alexa Novak, Krisztina Lakatos, Ildiko Toth, Ildiko Danis, Zsolt Ronai, Zsofia Nemoda, Maria Sasvari-Szekely, Jean-Francois Bureau, Elisa Bronfman, and Karlen Lyons-Ruth. 2007. "Infant Genotype May Moderate Sensitivity to Maternal Affective Communications: Attachment Disorganization, Quality of Care, and the DRD4 Polymorphism." *Social Neuroscience* 2: 307–19.

Gibbs, J. J., D. Giever, and J. S. Martin. 1998. "Parental Management and Self-Control: An Empirical Test of Gottfredson and Hirschi's General Theory." *Journal of Research in Crime and Delinquency* 35:40–71.

Gomez, R., A. Gomez, L. DeMello, and T. Tallent. 2001. "Perceived Maternal Control and Support: Effects on Hostile Biased Information Processing and Aggression among Clinic-Referred Children with High Aggression." *Journal of Child Psychology, Psychiatry and Allied Disciplines* 42: 513–22.

Gottfredson, M. R., and T. Hirschi. 1990. *A General Theory of Crime*. Stanford, CA: Stanford University Press.

Granic, Isabela, and Thomas J. Dishion. 2003. "Deviant Talk in Adolescent Friendships: A Step Toward Measuring a Pathogenic Attractor Process." *Social Development* 12: 314–34.

Green, Jonathan, and Ruth Goldwyn. 2002. "Attachment Disorganization and Psychopathology: New Findings in Attachment Research and Their Potential Implications for Developmental Psychopathology in Childhood." *Journal of Child Psychology and Psychiatry* 43: 835–46.

Greenburg, M. T., M. L. Speltz, M. DeKlyen, and M.C. Endriga. 1991. "Attachment Security in Preschoolers with and without Externalizing Problems: A Replication." *Development and Psychopathology* 3: 413–30.

Harlow, Harry F. 1958. "The Nature of Love." *American Psychologist* 13: 573–685.

Harlow, Harry F., and Robert Zimmerman. 1959. "Affectional Responses in the Infant Monkey." *Science*, 130: 421–32.

Hay, Carter. 2001. "Parenting, Self-Control, and Delinquency: A Test of Self-Control Theory." *Criminology* 39: 707–36.

Hay, Carter, and Walter Forrest. 2006. "The Development of Self-Control: Examining Self-control Theory's Stability Thesis." *Criminology* 44: 739–74.

Hernstein, R. J. 1974. "Formal Properties of the Matching Law." *Journal of the Experimental Analysis of Behavior* 21: 159–64.

Hetherington, E. M. 1993. "An Overview of the Virginia Longitudinal Study of Divorce and Remarriage with a Focus on Early Adolescence." *Journal of Family Psychology* 7: 39–56.

Jacobvitz, D., and N. Hazan. 1999. "Developmental pathways from infant disorganization to childhood peer relationships." In *Attachment Disorganization*, edited by J. Solomon and C. George. New York: Guilford Press.

Jaffee, Sara R., Avshalom Caspi, Terrie E. Moffitt, and Alan Taylor. 2004. "Physical Maltreatment Victim Antisocial Child: Evidence of an Environmentally Mediated Process." *Journal of Abnormal Psychology* 113: 44–55.

Johnson, Jeffrey G., Elizabeth Smailes, Patricia Cohen, Stephanie Kasen, and Judith S. Brook. 2004. "Antisocial Parental Behavior, Problematic Parenting and Aggressive Offspring Behavior During Adulthood." *British Journal of Criminology* 44: 915–30.

Jones, Shayne, Elizabeth Cauffman, and Alex Piquero. 2007. "The Influence of Parental Support among Incarcerated Adolescent Offenders: The Moderating Effects of Self-Control." *Criminal Justice and Behavior* 34: 229–45.

Keller, Thomas E., Susan J. Spieker, and Lewayne Gilchrist. 2005. "Patterns of Risk and Trajectories of Preschool Problem Behaviors: A Person-Oriented Analysis of Attachment in Context." *Development and Psychopathology* 17: 349–84.

Kerr, Margaret, and Hakan Stattin. 2000. "What Parents Know, How They Know It, and Several Forms of Adolescent Adjustment: Further Support for a Reinterpretation of Monitoring." *Developmental Psychology* 36: 366–80.

Kim-Cohen, J., A. Caspi, A. Taylor, B. Williams, R. Newcombe, I. W. Craig, and T. Moffitt. 2006. "MAOA, Maltreatment, and Gene-Environment Interaction Predicting Children's Mental Health: New Evidence and a Meta-Analysis." *Mol Psychiatry* 11: 903–13.

Kurdek, Lawrence A., and Mark A. Fine. 1994. "Family Acceptance and Family Control as Predictors of Adjustment in Young Adolescents: Linear, Curvilinear, or Interactive Effects?" *Child Development* 4: 1137–46.

Lahey, Benjamin, Carol Can Hulle, Brian D'Onofrio, Joseph Rodgers, and Irwin Waldman. 2008. "Parental Knowledge of Their Adolescent Offspring's Whereabouts and Peer Associations Spuriously Associated with Offspring Delinquency?" *Journal of Abnormal Child Psychology* 36: 807–23.

Larsson, Henrick, Essi Viding, Fruhling V. Rijsdijk, and Robert Plomin. 2008. "Relationships Between Parental Negativity and Childhood Antisocial Behavior over

Time: A Bidirectional Effects Model in a Longitudinal Genetically Informative Design." *Journal of Abnormal Child Psychology* 36: 633–45.

Lewis, M., C. Feiring, C. McGuffog, and J. Jaskir. 1984. "Predicting Psychopathology in Six-Year-Olds from Early Social Relations." *Child Development* 55: 123–36.

Loeber, R., and Magda Stouthamer-Loeber. 1986. "Family Factors as Correlates and Predictors of Juvenile Conduct Problems and Delinquency." *Crime and Justice*, edited by M. Tonry and N. Morris. Chicago: University of Chicago Press.

Love, K., and M. Murdock. 2004. "Attachment to Parents and Psychological Wellbeing of Young Adult College Students in Intact Families and Stepfamilies." *Journal of Family Psychology* 4: 600–08.

Lugalia, Terry, and Julia Overturf. 2004. *Children and the Households They Live In: Census 2000 Special Report (CENSR-14)*. Washington, DC: U.S. Census Bureau, U.S. Department of Commerce.

Lyons-Ruth, Karlen. 1996. "Attachment Relationships among Children with Aggressive Behavior Problems: The Role of Disorganized Early Attachment Patterns." *Journal of Consulting and Clinical Psychology* 64: 64–73.

Lyons-Ruth, Karlen, David B. Connell, Henry U. Grunebaum, and Sheila Botein. 1990. "Infants at Social Risk: Maternal Depression and Family Support Services as Mediators of Infant Development and Security of Attachment." *Child Development* 61: 85–98.

Lyons-Ruth, K., and D. Jacobvitz. 1999. "Attachment Disorganization: Unresolved Loss, Relationship Violence, and Lapses in Behavioral and Attentional Strategies." In *Handbook of Attachment: Theory, Research, and Clinical Application*, edited by J. Cassidy and P. R. Shaver, 520–54. New York: Guilford Press.

Lyons-Ruth, Karlen, Betty Repachyoli, Sara McLeod, and Eugenia Silva. 1991. "Disorganized Attachment Behavior in Infancy: Short-Term Stability, Maternal and Infant Correlates and Risk-Related Sub-Types." *Development and Psychopathology* 3: 377–96.

MacKinnon-Lewis, Carol, Michael E. Lamb, John Hattie, and Laila P. Baradaran. 2001. "A Longitudinal Examination of the Associations between Mothers' and Sons' Attributions and Their Aggression." *Development and Psychopathology* 13: 69–81.

Main, Mary, and Judith Solomon. 1990. "Procedures for identifying infants as disorganized/disoriented during the Ainsworth Strange Situation." In *Attachment in the preschool years: Theory, research and Intervention*, edited by Mark Greenberg, Dante Cicchetti, and E. Mark Cummings, 121–60. Chicago: University of Chicago Press.

Manning, W. D., and K. Lamb. 2003. "Adolescent Wellbeing in Cohabiting, Married, and Single-Parent Families." *Journal of Marriage and Family* 65: 876–93.

Mazerolle, Paul, and Alex Piquero. 1997. "Violent Responses to Strain: An Examination of Conditioning Influences." *Violence and Victims* 12: 323–43.

Mazerolle, Paul, and Alex Piquero. 1998. "Linking Exposure to Strain with Anger: An Investigation of Deviant Adaptations." *Journal of Criminal Justice* 26: 195–211.

McCord, Joan. 2001. "Forging Criminals in the Family." In *Handbook of Youth and Justice*, edited by S.O. White, 223–35. New York: Plenum.

McDermott, Rose, Dustin Tingley, Jonathan Cowden, Giovanni Frazzetto, and Dominic D. P. Johnson. 2009. "Monoamine Oxidase A Gene (MAOA) Predicts Behavioral Aggression Following Provocation." In *Proceedings of the National Academy of Sciences of the United States of America* 106(7): 2118

McKinnon-Lewis, C., M. Lamb, J. Hattie, and L. Baradaran. 2001. "A Longitudinal Examination of the Associations between Mothers' and Sons' Attributions and their Aggression." *Development and Psychopathology*, 13:1, 69–81.

McLanahan, Sara, and Gary Sandefur. 1994. *Growing Up with a Single Parent*. Cambridge, MA: Harvard University Press.

McLoyd, Vonnie C., Ana Mari Cauce, David Takeuchi, and Leon Wilson. 2000. "Marital Processes and Parental Socialization in Families of Color: A Decade Review of Research." *Journal of Marriage and the Family* 62: 1070–93.

Mitchell, Ojmarrh, and Doris Layton MacKenzie. 2006. "The Stability and Resiliency of Self-Control in a Sample of Incarcerated Offenders." *Crime and Delinquency* 52: 432–49.

Moffitt, T. E., A. Caspi, and M. Rutter. 2006. "Measured Gene-Environment Interactions in Psychopathology: Concepts, Research Strategies, and Implications for Research, Intervention, and Public Understanding of Genetics." *Perspectives on Psychological Science* 1: 5–27.

Orobio de Castro, Bram, Jan W. Veerman, Willem Koops, Joop D. Bosch, and Heidi J. Monshouwer. 2002. "Hostile Attribution of Intent and Aggressive Behavior: A Meta Analysis." *Child Development* 73: 916–34.

Palmer, E. J., and C. R. Hollin. 2000. "The Interrelationships of Socio-Moral Reasoning, Perceptions of Own Parenting and Attributions of Intent with Self-Reported Delinquency." *Legal and Criminological Psychology* 5: 201–18.

Patterson, Gerald R. 1982. *A Social Learning Approach*, Vol. 3 of *Coercive Family Process*. Eugene, OR: Castalia.

Patterson, Gerald R. 2002. "The Early Development of Coercive Family Process." In *Antisocial Behavior in Children and Adolescents*, edited by John Reid, Gerald R. Patterson, and James Snyder, 25–44. Washington, DC: American Psychological Association.

Patterson, Gerald R., L. Bank, and M. Stoolmiller. 1990. *From Childhood to Adolescence: A Transitional Period?* Thousand Oaks, CA: Sage.

Patterson, Gerald R., J. B. Reid, and T. J. Dishion. 1992. *Antisocial Boys*. Eugene, OR: Castalia Publishing Co.

Patterson, Gerald R., John B. Reid, and Mark J. Eddy. 2002. *Antisocial Behavior in Children and Adolescents: A Developmental Analysis and Model for Intervention*. A Brief History of the Oregon Model. Washington, DC: American Psychological Association.

Piquero, Nicole L., and Miriam D. Sealock. 2000. "Generalizing General Strain Theory: An Examination of an Offending Population." *Justice Quarterly* 17: 449–84.

Plomin, Robert, J. C. DeFries, and John C. Loehlin. 1977. "Genotype-Environment Interaction and Correlation in Analysis of Human Behavior." *Psychological Bulletin* 84: 309–22.

Polakowski, M. 1994. "Linking Self- and Social Control with Deviance: Illuminating the Structure Underlying a General Theory of Crime and its Relation to Deviant Activity." *Journal of Quantitative Criminology* 10: 41–78.

Pratt, Travis C., and Francis T. Cullen. 2000. "The Empirical Status of Gottfredson and Hirschi's General Theory of Crime. A Meta Analysis." *Criminology* 38: 931–64.

Rebellon, Cesar. 2002. "Reconsidering the Broken Homes/Delinquency Relationship and Exploring its Mediating Mechanisms." *Criminology* 40: 103–35.

Rebellon, Cesar J., Murray A. Straus and Rose Medeiros. 2008. "Self-Control in Global Perspective: An Empirical Assessment of Gottfredson and Hirschi's General Theory Within and Across 32 National Settings." *European Journal of Criminology* 5: 331–62.

Reid, John B., and M. Eddy. 2002. "Preventive Efforts During the Elementary School Years: The Linking of the Interest of Families and Teachers (LIFT) Project." In *Antisocial Behavior in Children and Adolescents: A Developmental Analysis and Model for*

Intervention, Edited by J. Reid, G. Patterson, and J. Snyder, 219–33. Washington, DC: American Psychological Association.

Reid, John B., Gerald R. Patterson, and James Snyder. 2002. *Antisocial Behavior in Children and Adolescents*. Washington, DC: American Psychological Association.

Renken, Bruce, Bryon Egeland, Denise Marvinney, Sarah Mangelsdorf, and L. Alan Sroufe. 1989. "Early Childhood Antecedents of Aggression and Passive-Withdrawal in Early Elementary School." *Journal of Personality* 57: 257–81.

Rhee, Soo Hyun, and Irwin D. Waldman. 2002. "Genetic and Environmental Influences on Antisocial Behavior: A Meta-Analysis of Twin and Adoption Studies." *Psychological Bulletin* 128: 490–52.

Robins, L. N. 1978. "Sturdy Predictors of Adult Antisocial Behavior, Replications from Longitudinal Studies." *Psychological Medicine* 8: 611–22.

Roisman, Glenn I., and R. Chris Fraley. 2006. "The Limits of Genetic Influence: A Behavior-Genetic Analysis of Infant-Caregiver Relationship Quality and Temperament." *Child Development* 77: 1656–67.

Rowe, David C. 1994. *The Limits of Family Influence: Genes, Experience, and Behavior*. New York: Guilford.

Runions, Kevin C., and Daniel P. Keating. 2007. "Young Children's Social Information Processing: Family Antecedents and Behavioral Correlates." *Developmental Psychology* 43: 838–49.

Rutter, Michael, Terrie E. Moffitt, and Avshalom Caspi. 2006. "Gene-Environment Interplay and Psychopathology: Multiple Varieties but Real Effects." *Journal of Child Psychology and Psychiatry* 47: 226–61.

Sampson, Robert J., and John Laub. 1993. *Crime in the Making*. Cambridge, MA: Harvard University Press.

Scarr, S., and K. McCartney. 1983. "How People Make Their Own Environments: A Theory of Genotype-Environment Effects." *Child Development* 54: 424–35.

Seltzer, J. A. 2000. "Families Formed Outside of Marriage." *Journal of Marriage and the Family* 62: 1247–68.

Shaw, Daniel S., and Heather E. Gross. 2008. "What We Have Learned about Early Childhood and the Development of Delinquency." In *The Long View of Crime: A Synthesis of Longitudinal Research*, edited by Akiva M. Liberman, 23–28. New York: Springer.

Simons, Leslie, Yi-Fu Chen, Ronald L. Simons, Gene Brody, Carolyn Cutrona. 2006. "Parenting Practices and Child Adjustment in Different Types of Households: A Study of African American Families." *Journal of Family Issues* 27: 803–25.

Simons, Leslie Gordon, and Rand Conger. 2007. "Linking Mother-Father Differences in Parenting to a Typology of Family Parenting Styles and Adolescent Outcomes." *Journal of Family Issues* 28: 212–41.

Simons, Ronald L. 1996. *Understanding Differences between Divorced and Two-Biological-Parent Families: Stress, Interaction, and Child Outcome*. Thousand Oaks, CA: Sage Publications.

Simons, Ronald L. and Christine Johnson. 1996. Social Network and Marital Support as Mediators and Moderators of the Impact of Economic Pressure on Parental Behavior. In *The Handbook of Social Support and the Family*. edited by Gregory Pierce, Barbara Sarason, and Irwin Sarason. New York: Plenum, pp. 269–289.

Simons, Ronald L., Jay Beaman, Rand D. Conger, and Wei Chao. 1993. "Childhood Experience, Conceptions of Parenting, and Attitudes of Spouse as Determinants of Parental Behavior." *Journal of Marriage and the Family* 55: 91–106.

Simons, Ronald L., Yi-Fu Chen, Eric A. Stewart, and Gene H. Brody. 2003. "Incidents of Discrimination and Risk for Delinquency: A Longitudinal Test of Strain Theory with an African American Sample." *Justice Quarterly* 20: 827–54.

Simons, Ronald L., Leslie G. Simons, Callie H. Burt, Gene H. Brody, and Carolyn Cutrona. 2005. "Collective Efficacy, Authoritative Parenting, and Delinquency: A Longitudinal Test of a Model Integrating Community- and Family-Level Processes." *Criminology* 43: 989–1029.

Simons, Ronald L., Leslie G. Simons, Callie H. Burt, Hollie Drummund, Eric Stewart, Gene H. Brody, Frederick Gibbons, and Carolyn Cutrona. 2006. "Supportive Parenting Moderates the Effect of Discrimination Upon Anger, Hostile View of Relationships, and Violence among African American Boys." *Journal of Health and Social Behavior* 47: 373–89.

Simons, Ronald L., Leslie G. Simons, Yi-Fu Chen, Gene H. Brody, and Kuie-Hsui Lin. 2007. "Identifying the Psychological Factors that Mediate the Association between Parenting Practices and Delinquency." *Criminology* 45: 451–518.

Simons, Ronald L., Leslie G. Simons, and Lora E. Wallace. 2004. *Families, Delinquency, and Crime: Linking Society's Most Basic Institution to Antisocial Behavior.* Los Angeles: Roxbury.

Slaby, Ronald G., and Nancy G. Guerra. 1988. "Cognitive Mediators of Aggression in Adolescent Offenders: I. Assessment." *Developmental Psychology* 24(4): 580–88.

Snyder, J. 2002. "Reinforcement and Coercion Mechanisms in the Development of Antisocial Behavior: Peer Relationships." In *Antisocial Behavior in Children and Adolescents: A Developmental Analysis and Model for Intervention*, edited by John Reid, Gerald Patterson, and James Snyder, 101–22. Washington, DC: American Psychological Association.

Snyder, J., and G. R. Patterson. 1995. "Individual Differences in Social Aggression: A Test of a Reinforcement Model of Socialization in the Natural Environment." *Behavior Therapy* 26: 371–91.

Snyder, J., and M. Stoolmiller. 2002. "Reinforcement and Coercion Mechanisms in the Development of Antisocial Behavior." In *The Oregon Model of Antisocial Behavior*, edited by J. B. Reid, G. R. Patterson, and J. Snyder, 65–100. Washington, DC: American Psychological Association.

Soenens, Bart, Maarten Vansteenkiste, Koen Luyckx, Luc Goossens. 2006. "Parenting and Adolescent Problem Behavior: An Integrated Model with Adolescent Self-Disclosure and Perceived Parental Knowledge as Intervening Variables." *Developmental Psychology* 42: 305–18.

Steinberg, Laurence. 2001. "We Know Some Things: Parent-Adolescent Relationships in Retrospect and Prospect." *Journal of Research on Adolescence* 11: 1–9.

Stewart, S. D. 2005. "How the Birth of a Child Affects Involvement with Stepchildren." *Journal of Marriage and Family* 67: 461–73.

Tonry, Michael. 2004. *Thinking about Crime: Sense of Sensibility in American Penal Culture.* New York, NY: Oxford University Press.

Tremblay, R.E., Chrita Japel, Daniel Perusse, Pierre McDuff, Michel Boivin, Mark Zoccolillo, and Jacques Montplaisir. 1999. "The Search for the Age of 'Onset' of Physical Aggression: Rousseau and Bandura Revisited." *Criminal Behaviour and Mental Health* 9: 8–3.

True, Mary, Lelia Pisani, and Fadimata Oumar. 2001. "Infant Mother Attachment among the Dogon of Mali." *Child Development* 72: 1451–66.

Turner, Michael G., and Alex R. Piquero. 2002. "The Stability of Self-Control." *Journal of Criminal Justice* 30: 457–71.

van IJzendoorn, Marinus H. 1995. "Adult Attachment Representations, Parental Responsiveness, and Infant Attachment: A Meta-Analysis on the Predictive Validity of the Adult Attachment Interview." *Psychological Bulletin* 117: 387–403.

van IJzendoorn, Marinus. 1997. "Attachment, Emergent Morality, and Aggression: Toward a Developmental Socio Emotional Model of Antisocial Behavior." *International Journal Behavioral Development* 21: 703–27.

van IJsendoorn, Marinus, C. Schuengel, and M. J. Bakermans-Kranenburg. 1999. "Disorganized Attachment in Early Childhood: Meta-analysis of Precursors, Concomitants, and Sequelae." *Development and Psychopathology* 11: 225–49.

Vitale, J. E., Joseph Newman, J. E. Bates, J. A. Goodnight, K. A. Dodge, and G. S. Pettit. 2005. "Deficient Behavioral Inhibition and Anomalous Selective Attention in a Community Sample of Adolescents with Psychopathic and Low-Anxiety Traits." *Journal of Abnormal Child Psychology* 33(4): 461–71.

Wells, E. L., and J. H. Rankin. 1991. "Families and Delinquency: A Meta-Analysis of the Impact of Broken Homes." *Social Problems* 38: 71–93.

White, L. K., and S. J. Rogers. 2000. "Economic Circumstances and Family Outcomes: A Review of the 1990's." *Journal of Marriage and the Family* 62: 1035–51.

Williams, B. A., and J. T. Wixted. 1986. "An Equation for Behavioral Contrast." *Journal of Experimental Analysis of Behavior* 45: 47–62.

Wilson, J. Q., and R. J. Herrnstein. 1985. *Crime and Human Nature*. New York, NY: Simon and Schuster.

Wright, J. P., and F. Cullen. 2001. "Parental Efficacy and Delinquent Behavior: Do Control and Support Matter?" *Criminology* 39: 677–706.

Zelli, Arnoldo, Kenneth A. Dodge, John E. Lochman, and Robert D. Laird. 1999. "The Distinction between Beliefs Legitimizing Aggression and Deviant Processing of Social Cues: Testing Measurement Validity and the Hypothesis that Biased Processing Mediates the Effects of Beliefs on Aggression." *Journal of Personality and Social Psychology* 77: 150–66.

CHAPTER 9

....

SCHOOLS AND DELINQUENCY

....

GARY D. GOTTFREDSON

ONE understanding of delinquency is that it is youth behavior that would be illegal if committed by an adult. According to this view, youth crime can be distinguished from status offenses for which the offender's youthful age is part of the definition, such as school truancy and underage drinking. But as a practical matter, a variety of *problem behaviors*—including behaviors that range from tardiness or absence from school, to damage to property, theft, fighting, drug use, risky driving, unplanned pregnancy, robbery, cheating, rape and other serious assault, and gang crime—seem to share a common set of personal and social-environmental risk factors (Jessor, Donovan, and Costa 1991). A variety of personally risky, socially disapproved, or illegal behaviors tend to be displayed disproportionately by the same individuals and to share common antecedents. This cluster of behaviors includes delinquency even if some of the behaviors are not always officially delinquent. The cluster of behaviors is also interpreted by some (Weissberg, Caplan, and Harwood 1991) as a mental health problem. Although most young people do not become "officially" delinquent by becoming ensnared in the juvenile or criminal justice system, and although most are not "officially" labeled with a diagnosable mental disorder, it has long been clear that most young people engage in some delinquent behavior (Williams and Gold 1972) and that high-risk social and health behavior such as delinquency, school failure, drug use, and pregnancy are common among youths (Dryfoos 1990). Because it is the nature of schools to promote the educational and social development of young people, and because a good portion of young people's problem behavior manifests itself in schools, schooling and delinquency are intertwined.

This chapter examines the nature of delinquent and related problem behavior in schools. It suggests that the changing demography of the United States has increased the difficulty of the task now faced by schools and made that task particularly difficult in some places. It suggests that public perceptions that the quality of many urban schools is low has the effect of exacerbating the concentration of populations of young people at elevated risk of both delinquent behavior and poor educational outcomes in some communities.

Other important topics related to schools and delinquency have been the subject of recent reviews, and so are not treated here. Among these other recent reviews are a chapter on school violence by G. Gottfredson and Gottfredson (2007) and a chapter on school crime, the role of schools in increasing or decreasing crime, and the evidence about school-related delinquency prevention programs by Cook, Gottfredson, and Na (2010). Accordingly, readers interested in reviews of those topics are referred to these other accounts.

I. Crime and Youth

It has long been known that criminal behavior shows a strong association with age (Quetelet [1833] 1984). Interpersonal aggression occurs among very young children at an astoundingly high rate (Holmberg 1980) and declines from age 2 to adolescence (Tremblay et al. 1999), and individuals tend to retain their rank order on aggression from childhood to adulthood (Loeber 1982; Loeber and Dishion 1983; Huesmann et al. 1984; Broidy et al. 2003; Huesmann, Dubow, and Boxer 2009). But aggression that is responded to by authorities as delinquent behavior resulting in arrests increases with age throughout adolescence and declines in early adulthood, in a manner similar to the age curve discovered by Quetelet (M. Gottfredson and Hirschi 1990). Evidently reflecting the interaction of individuals with their social environments at different ages, the peak ages and trajectories for different problem behaviors differ—with "predatory" offenses peaking in the adolescent ages (Sampson and Laub 2005, fig. 2) when youths are generally in high school. What seems to be happening here is that (a) young children are highly aggressive, (b) most children learn to restrain themselves from aggression beginning at an early age, but (c) there are individual differences in aggressiveness so that some children are more aggressive than others and individuals tend to retain their rank order as they age, and (d) the destructive capability of the youths increases and the judged inappropriateness of aggression becomes more salient as children age, so that official responses to aggression increase in adolescence (Tremblay 2006), and then fall off with age as individuals increasingly desist from crime. Children of middle school age are large enough and capable enough of harming other children that—although their rates of aggression may be declining—the aggression is seen as more problematic to those who operate schools. But adolescents learn to restrain themselves further over the course of adolescence (and some of the most delinquent youths leave school), so that educators perceive more problem behavior in middle schools than in elementary schools or high schools (G. Gottfredson and Gottfredson 1985; G. Gottfredson et al. 2000).

II. Delinquency and Related Problem Behaviors in Schools

Delinquency is related to other problem behavior seen in schools. Very early school problem behavior reflected in such things as ratings of aggressiveness by 1st grade teachers predict adolescent delinquency and aggression in adulthood (Ensminger, Kellam, and Rubin 1983; Loeber and Dishion 1983; McCord and Ensminger 1997; Harachi et al. 2006). As children's educational careers continue, delinquency is consistently found to be associated with poor school performance, poor attendance, lack of attachment to school, and limited educational aspirations (G. Gottfredson 1981; Loeber et al. 1998; Hawkins et al. 1998). It is well established that delinquent behavior is inversely related to persistence in education. Those who drop out of school display more delinquent behavior while in school (indexed by self-report, official delinquency, or serious official delinquency) than those who graduate from high school or continue in postsecondary education (Bachman, Green, and Wirtanen 1971; Wolfgang, Figlio, and Sellin 1972; Elliott and Voss 1974; Bachman, O'Malley, and Johnston 1978).

Having been retained in grade has long been known to be a potent predictor of school dropout (Ayers 1909), and grade retention in the 1st grade or later remains a powerful forecast of eventual dropout (Janosz et al. 1997; Alexander, Entwisle, and Kabbani 2001; Jimerson, Anderson, and Whipple 2002). Alexander, Entwisle, and Kabbani (2001) summarized a behavioral disengagement in school that characterizes dropouts—including poor work habit ratings in report cards and teacher ratings of fighting, teasing, and fidgeting—as comportment that does not align "with the values and expectations of the school" (p. 792). Taken together, a great deal of evidence implies that the portrait of school dropouts is not very different from the portrait of delinquents in general. Delinquents and dropouts are engaged in a variety of problem behaviors, and they are low achieving, poorly motivated, and uncommitted to school.

III. Do Similar Individual Characteristics Predispose Young People to Problem Behavior and Poor School Achievement?

Individuals' mental ability and personality are related to delinquency and aggression in ways that are also implicated with difficulty in school. First, there is a modest negative correlation between general mental ability and a variety of indicators of aggression or delinquency (Hirschi and Hindelang 1977; G. Gottfredson 1981; Maguin and Loeber 1996). For example, low intelligence measured at ages 4 and 7 predicted the accumulation of a court record by age 18 (Lipsitt, Buka, and Lipsitt 1990); IQ measured at age 8 showed modest negative correlations with criminal convictions, traffic violations, driving-under-the-influence convictions, and seriousness of offenses at age 30 for men (Huesmann et al. 1984), and both low IQ and poor school attendance in the 1st grade predicted violence in McCord and Ensminger's (1997) study of Chicago 1st graders later interviewed at age 32 for both males and females. Interestingly, aggression at age 8 was a substantial predictor of measured spelling, reading, and arithmetic achievement at age 30 (correlations as high as -.43 for the sample of 211 women) in the Huesmann et al. research. The negative correlation between verbal ability and aggression can be observed at an early age: Dionne et al. (2003) reported a correlation of -.20 in a large sample of 19-month-old twins between expressive vocabulary and physical aggression.

Based on meta-analytic examination of the correlations among school achievement, mental ability, conduct problems, and delinquency, Maguin and Loeber (1996) showed that academic performance is clearly moderately negatively related to delinquency. They also suggested that because both attention problems and intelligence are correlated with both school achievement and delinquency, the achievement-delinquency correlation may be accounted for by their both being influenced by these two shared causes, and they produced evidence based on their meta-analytic estimates of correlations that this may be so. They did not find evidence that socioeconomic status or prior conduct problems may be a common cause accounting for the school performance-delinquency correlation.

Problem behavior is also associated with impulsiveness. M. Gottfredson and Hirschi (1990) have made impulsiveness a centerpiece of their general theory of crime. Abundant empirical evidence implies that more delinquent youths tend to be impulsive and not to defer gratification. For instance, Jessor and colleagues (1968) showed that more delinquent youths would utilize a reinforcement coupon sooner than less delinquent youths when the value of the coupon increased with delay. Kreuger, Caspi, Moffitt, White, and Stouthamer-Loeber (1996) also found that externalizing (aggressive and delinquent) boys less often deferred gratification in laboratory tasks.

Psychologists often describe childhood behaviors involving impulsiveness, aggression, hyperactivity, and disruptive or defiant behavior as *externalizing* or *undercontrolled* behavior. In a review of externalizing behavior and academic underachievement, Hinshaw (1992) distinguished two subtypes of externalizing behavior in children: (a) inattention and hyperactivity and (b) aggression-conduct problems. The first of these subtypes tends to be more associated with developmental immaturity, language delays, poisoning and bone fractures and the second with low family income and dysfunctional families. Hinshaw's review implies that in early and middle childhood, school underachievement is related more to hyperactivity and attention problems than to aggression-conduct problems. By adolescence, delinquent behavior comes to be related more generally to school underachievement and verbal deficits. An additional information-processing or cognitive mechanism that appears involved in aggression is the tendency for aggressive children to perceive approaches by others as hostile (Dodge 1993). Hostile attribution bias is the tendency to perceive hostile intent on the part of others, when no such intent may exist. For example, some children tend to react to approaches by other children as if the other child intended harm or to take something when other children would see the approach as benign. One implication of these findings for school interventions is that the identification of children who show inattention, hyperactivity, and hostile attribution bias would be helpful if interventions to ameliorate the influence of these cognitive individual characteristics are available. Management of attention deficit with hyperactivity by use of stimulant medication is effective (Jadad et al. 1999; King et al. 2006), as are behavioral parent training and behavioral classroom management (Pelham and Fabiano 2008; Fabiano et al. 2009). It seems clear, however, that attention and hyperactivity problems are chronic conditions and may be expected to require continuing behavioral or pharmacological management.

Naturally it is difficult or impossible to disentangle whether attentional or school performance problems lead to aggression and other problem behavior, whether problem behavior leads to school problems, whether causation is reciprocal, or whether both are due to other common causes. However that may be, those who have probed the developmental pathways for these problems (Maguin and Loeber 1996; Trzesniewski et al. 2006) have noted that both educational difficulties and conduct problems are independently important in education and society and that interventions that ameliorate one of these kinds of difficulties may also ameliorate the other and the sequelae of each.

The foregoing discussion pertains to individual differences in delinquency and other problem behavior. About 5% of the variance in individual delinquency lies between schools, and about 14% of the variance in the victimization of teachers lies between schools (Payne, Gottfredson, and Gottfredson 2003), and rates of both (particularly teacher victimization) are substantially associated with community characteristics (G. Gottfredson and Gottfredson 1985). We now shift our attention away from individual differences to differences in community demographics and their influences on schools and delinquency.

IV. The Burden on Schools in Historical Demographic Context

It is easier to educate some young people than it is to educate others, and the task of education is more difficult in some locations than in others. This section spells out the implications of historical demographic phenomena and the current demographic ecology of delinquency and schools. Some demographic influences on schools are self-evident. For example, it is less difficult for schools to achieve high levels of proficiency in reading in the English language for students who have always spoken the language than for those who are English language learners (ELL) or who do not speak English in their homes. Data from the National Assessment of Educational Progress (NAEP; Lee, Grigg, and Donahue 2007) bear out this expectation. In 2007, only 50% of Hispanic 4th graders were at or above the "basic" level of reading achievement compared to 78% of White 4th graders; among Hispanic pupils, only 27% of "English language learners" were at or above basic, but among Hispanics who were not English language learners, 62% were basic or above (tabulations made for this chapter from NAEP data). In 1992, only 7% of 4th graders in the national assessment were Hispanic, but by 2007 the percentage had grown to 19%. The early-grade educational disadvantage is seen in high school completion rates for different groups. In 2005, 7% of native born White persons aged 16 to 24 years were high school dropouts, compared to 14% of native born Mexican Americans and 42% of immigrant Mexican Americans (Ramani et al. 2007). As we have seen, achievement difficulties in schools are robustly associated with delinquency, so it is not surprising to see that estimates of delinquent behavior—particularly violence-related forms—are generally higher for Hispanic (and African American) youths than for the White population (Eaton et al. 2008, tables 7–15).

Of course, the United States has always been a nation of immigrants (Ovando 2003), but such high proportions of immigrants have not always been involved in the schools. One of the demographic trends that contribute to the educational burden of U.S. schools today is the more inclusive participation in education, a second is the shift in the age composition of schools, and a third is a shift of population from rural areas to the cities. Figure 9.1 shows enrollment in grades 9–12 as a percentage of persons aged 14 to 17 years in the United States over the course of the twentieth century. In 1900, 10.6% of persons 14 to 17 years of age were enrolled in high school (grades 9 to 12), and by 2000 94% of this age group was enrolled in high school. A great many of these students do not graduate—essentially failing high school. In 2000, 86% of persons aged 18 to 24 had completed high school (92% of non-Hispanic Whites, 84% of non-Hispanic Blacks, and 64% of Hispanics) (Kaufman, Alt, and Chapman 2001, p. 20). An implication of the dramatic increase in secondary school participation rates over the last century is not only that the social class and ethnic composition of the schools has shifted markedly, but also that the age structure of school enrollment has changed. Estimated age distributions of school enrollment around 1909 and in 2000 are shown in Figure 9.2. Early in the twentieth century, compulsory attendance laws were not as encompassing as they are today, and schools were (from today's perspective) remarkably negligent in ensuring that school-aged youth attended schools—particularly immigrant and minority youth (Ayers 1909; Rury 1988). Ayers showed that in the early 1900s, many pupils did not enter school until they were older than is typical today; many entered school over-age for grade or, because of poor attendance, became over-age for grade over time. Large percentages of these youths left school in the elementary grades. Decennial census data summarized in Figure 9.3 show that in 1900 less than 4% of the K to 12 enrollment in the United States was enrolled in grades 9 through 12. But

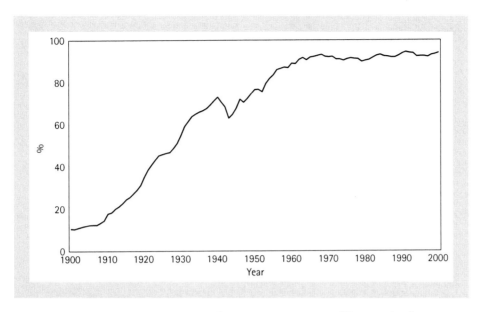

Figure 9.1. Grade 9 Through 12 Enrollment as a Percentage of Persons Aged 14 to 17, United States 1900 to 2000.

Source: U.S. Census Bureau. 2010, Table HS-20. Education Summary–Enrollment 1900 to 2000.

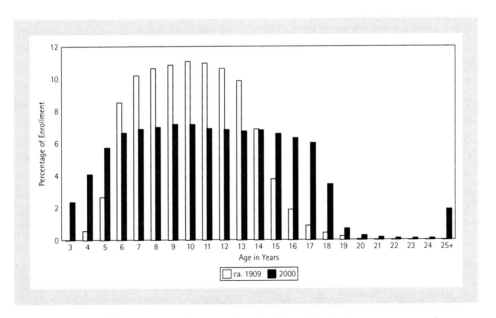

Figure 9.2. Age Distribution of Students Enrolled Pre-K to Grade 12, ca. 1909 and 2000.

Sources: Ayers 1909, p. 11. U.S. Census Bureau. 2006, Table 5S01. Data for 2000 are census enumerations, data for 1909 are estimates based on data 386 cities.

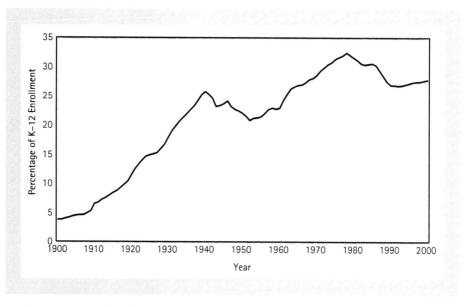

Figure 9.3. Grade 9 Through 12 Enrollment as a Percentage of K to 12 Enrollment,
United States.
Calculated from data presented by U.S. Census Bureau. 2010, Table HS-20. Education
Summary–Enrollment 1900 to 2000.

at the end of the twentieth century, grades 9 through 12 accounted for 28% of elementary and secondary enrollment.

As these shifts in the inclusiveness and age composition of the school population were occurring over the last century, a massive shift in population toward urban
concentration occurred. Figure 9.4 shows that the percentage of the U.S. population
that was urban grew rapidly over the course of the twentieth century. The migration
of Black population from the agrarian south to cities in the industrial north had
two dramatic surges over the course of the century. A first migration occurred
between 1910 and 1930 when, as a result of labor shortages due to World War I, Black
men were employed in industrial work in, for example, manufacturing, steel, and
meat packing in northern cities (Cassidy 1997). Between 1910 and 1930, the Black
population of Chicago grew from 44,000 to 234,000 (from 2% to 7% of population), Newark from 6,700 to 38,900 (from 3% to 9% of population), and Cleveland
from 8,500 to 72,000 (1.5% to 8% of population) (Gibson and Jung 2005). A second,
larger migration occurred between 1940 and 1970, during which time more educated Blacks moved to urban areas in northern and western cities—employed in
industrial, shipyard and other defense-related work (stimulated by World War II) to
which there was less access in the south. For example, between 1940 and 1970, the
Black population of Chicago grew from 278,000 to 1,103,000 (from 8% to 33% of
population), Newark from 46,000 to 207,000 (from 11% to 54% of population), and
Cleveland from 84,500 to 288,000 (from 10% to 38% of population) (Gibson and
Jung 2005).

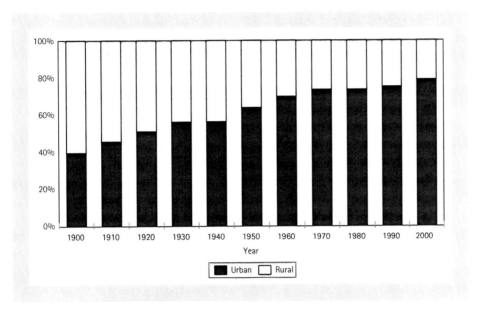

Figure 9.4. Increasing Urbanicity of the U.S. Population, 1900 to 2000.
Source: U.S. Bureau of the Census 2003, Table HS-2.

Wilson (1987) has described circumstances that produced a concentration of truly disadvantaged Black people in many urban centers. The decline in rural agrarian jobs that had employed many young Black workers led to the displacement of populations to the cities, particularly in the industrial north where opportunities were more abundant. But manufacturing jobs in urban centers had been declining when Wilson wrote. By the mid 1950s, manufacturing as a share of total employment had begun to decline—a decline that has continued to the present (Brauer 2004). The numbers of Americans employed in manufacturing was roughly level with periodic intervals of growth and recession from the mid 1960s until about 2000, followed by a sharp decline after 2000. Wilson wrote of a declining "marriageable male index" such that there were few employed Black men per one hundred Black women of a comparable age group, leading to growth in female-headed families. On top of this, the population bulge of baby boomers, including women, in the labor market meant that employers could be picky in their hiring, disadvantaging poorly educated Black men—many now in cities.

Following the 1954 decision of the U.S. Supreme Court in *Brown v. Board of Education of Topeka* (347 U.S. 483), many urban school districts pursued the voluntary desegregation of their schools, and other districts pursued court-ordered desegregation plans. Paradoxically, this eventually led to *increased* segregation in urban centers (Orfield 2001). The 1973 Supreme Court decision in *Millikan v. Bradley* (418 U.S. 717) meant that (a) although *Brown v. Board of Education* had implied that segregated education was not equal and therefore not permissible and (b) an urban school district such as Detroit was so segregated that its schools were mostly Black, a desegregation plan that involved more than one school district could not be required. Associate Justice Marshall noted in his dissent that a Detroit-only decree would fail to integrate the segregated Detroit schools, and it has come to pass over the decades since that metropolitan areas have come to have predominantly Black schools in the center and predominantly White schools in the suburbs.

The history of segregation, integration, resegregation and the concentration of the disadvantaged in Baltimore provides an instructive example. In 1890, Black persons were about 15% of the city's population (Gibson and Jung 2005, table 21). Baltimore's schools were segregated (and remained segregated). In 1910, the city made the first attempt in the United States to use an ordinance to segregate neighborhoods (Silver 1997). Although the ordinance was soon overturned by state (*State v. Gurry*, Maryland Court of Appeals, 88 A. 546 [1913]) and federal courts (*Buchanan v. Warley*, 245 U.S. 60 [1917]), the intention of local political leaders to maintain segregation was clear. By 1930, growth in Baltimore's White population decelerated somewhat, but growth in the Black population continued, accelerating further in the 1940s. Then in 1952, the Baltimore school board (before the decision in *Brown v. Board of Education*) decided to admit a small number of Black youths to the city's all-white Polytechnic High School to save the expense of separate education. Quickly following the decision in *Brown v. Board of Education*, the school board voluntarily integrated the schools. That opened the floodgates for White flight to suburban and private schools. White population in Baltimore fell by 113,000 between 1950 and 1960, and it continued to fall at about this rate in subsequent decades (Gibson and Jung 2005). By the late 1960s, the city's population and its schools' students were mostly Black. Walker, Stinchcombe, and McDill (1967) reported that school integration had proceeded by introducing Black students into previously White schools, and that when the number of Black students reached a "tipping point," the school soon became predominantly Black. School segregation recurred across county lines and school auspices, with county schools and private schools remaining almost all White, while most city schools became almost all Black. Mobility of White residents out of the city led to a concentration of relatively poor Black citizens in the city, and to predominantly Black city schools.

In considering the riots that occurred in Baltimore and elsewhere in the late 1960s, the *Report of the National Advisory Commission on Civil Disorders* in 1968 (often known as the Kerner Commission report) concluded that "Our nation is moving toward two societies, one black, one white—separate and unequal" (p. 1), and that segregation and poverty had created destructive environments in the racial ghettos. The Commission listed twelve grievances that led to the disorders—high among them unemployment, inadequate housing, and inadequate education. Black urban in-migration and White exodus had developed concentrations of impoverished persons.

Public policies creating enclaves of poverty continued after the Kerner Commission issued its report. Baltimore already had ghetto-like enclaves by the 1930s and continued to locate public housing projects in areas of Black population concentration through the 1960s—increasing the density of housing in response to criticisms that federal housing programs were destroying more housing than they created (Samuels 2008). Families displaced by urban renewal projects had to find housing in a city where, as Samuels showed, Baltimore area newspaper housing listings still appeared in 1963 under headings "White" and "Colored." The housing segregation problem did not improve over the decades, with more than 90% of public housing located in Baltimore City in 1990 (Samuels 2008). By 1990 White persons had fallen to 39% of Baltimore's population; by 2008, Whites were 33% of the population. Baltimore's total population had fallen from about 950,000 in 1950 to 637,000 in 2008—a drop of 33%.

Meanwhile, suburban counties surrounding Baltimore City–where schools were perceived to be more attractive—grew in population. Howard County and Baltimore County are two of those suburban counties. Baltimore County surrounds the city except for a portion to the south and extends north to the Pennsylvania border. Howard County is to the west, and is inhabited by many persons who commute to locations in Baltimore, the District of Columbia, and Virginia. Baltimore County and Howard County grew as Baltimore City shrank. Table 9.1 displays demographic characteristics and school outcome data for four high schools—one in Baltimore City (School D), two in Baltimore County (Schools B and C), and the other in Howard County (School A). These schools are all a few miles apart. A Baltimore County school like School C receives students of families who are moving away from Baltimore City. Median income in the area is about double the income in the area around inner city School D, and the portion of families in poverty is lower in the area around School C. But it is a struggle for families to remain in the more affluent area, so there is a great deal of mobility back and forth across the city-county line. In contrast, Schools A and B are beyond the reach of families with children in School D and most of those in School C. The median family income for the mostly married-couple families around School A is 4.5 times the median income of the mostly female-headed families around School D. School A serves children in a community of concentrated affluence and social organization, and School D serves children in a community of concentrated disadvantage. County schools diligently investigate residency to defend against the enrollment of children who do not reside in the counties (e.g., Baltimore County Public Schools 2009).

Much public attention has focused on the problem of student dropout, which we have seen is strongly linked with delinquency: Delinquency predicts dropout and vice versa. We see in Table 9.1 that the four illustrated schools differ greatly in dropout, with 55% *of 12th graders* graduating in the city school (44% of 12th grade males). But this underestimates the magnitude of school failure not only because many students may have left school before reaching grade 12, but also because of the poor quality of the schooling completed. The state of Maryland assesses the rigor of students' educational programs using six indicators.[1] In School A, 93% of graduates completed a rigorous program; in city school D, less than 1% *of graduates* completed a rigorous program. In short, despite being graduates, those who complete high school in School D are not educated at the level usually thought of as representing high school graduation. A few (2.5%) of county School C's *graduates* achieve a

Table 9.1. Four High Schools in the Baltimore Area, 2009

Characteristic	A	B	C	D
Owner occupied housing (%)	89	92	61	30
Families below poverty level (%)	1.3	1.2	8.0	31.3
Family households with children headed by female (%)	7.6	5.8	46.2	70.3
Median 1999 household income ($)	93,400	75,000	41,400	20,600
African American (% students)	8.2	3.1	90.1	98.8
Hispanic (% students)	2.7	2.0	3.9	0.2
Attendance rate (%)	96	96	87	75
Mobility rate (%)	4.0	6.1	49.3	46.5
Teachers with advanced professional certificate (%)	65	72	31	58
Classes not taught by a highly qualified teacher (%)	7.9	5.2	27.1	24.5
Special education (% of students)	4.4	4.5	13.5	19.9
Free or reduced meal participation (%)	4.8	5.0	48.3	65.6
Limited English proficiency (%)	2.3	0.0	3.3	0.0
10th graders meeting state high school requirements (%)*	94	99	36	2
Graduation rate (% of 12th graders)	96	94	73	55
Rigorous high school program (% of graduates)†	92.9	37.1	2.5	0.6
Not proficient in algebra (%)	2	3	37	58

Note. A = Centennial High School in Howard County, B = Hereford High School in Baltimore County, C = Woodlawn High School in Baltimore County, D = Frederick Douglass High School in Baltimore City. First four rows are 2000 census data for zip code tabulation data; remainder are extracted from data published by the Maryland State Department of Education [http://msp.msde.state.md.us/].

* Percentage of 10th graders who attempted and passed the four subject matter tests required prior to high school graduation.

† Percentage of individuals who graduated, who, in the course of their studies, met four of six performance standards related to subjects taken and achievement level (see text).

rigorous program, but the vast majority even of graduates have not completed what is usually thought of as a high school education.

These poor outcomes do not occur only because many students fail to attend school (although a quarter of School D's students are absent on an average day), but also because many subjects are simply not taught. In Maryland, students complete tests in four areas—Algebra, Biology, Government, and English at the end of the courses in these subjects. These tests are completed in middle school for students who take the courses in middle school, and these are not demanding tests.[2] In county Schools A and B, 94% and 99% of 10th graders have already taken the courses and passed all four of these tests. In county School C, 36% of 10th graders have passed the four tests. But in city School D, only 2% of 10th grade students have passed the tests. More specifically, 2.1% took the tests and passed, 3.7% took the end-of-course tests and failed (a 64% failure rate), and 94.2% have not taken the courses or the tests. The city students have mostly not received instruction; of the few who have, most failed the end-of-course tests.

The principal of city School D was removed during the 2005–2006 school year, three of the four assistant principals were replaced before the 2006–2007 school year, and a third of the staff retired or were transferred (Center for Character Education 2009). The mix of teachers working in city School D has recently changed. In 2009, 58% of teachers had "advanced professional certificates," 14% had "conditional certificates," and 7% had "resident teacher certificates"; whereas as recently as 2005, 14% had "resident teacher," and 38% had "conditional" certificates.[3] So in 2005, 52% of the teachers were inexperienced, but in 2009, 21% of teachers were inexperienced. Despite the personnel changes, attendance remained poor: Before the personnel changes, the attendance rate was 85% in 2004 and 83% in 2005; in 2009 it was 75%. A state department of education plan to award an outside management contract for the school failed in 2006 in the midst of an election in which the Baltimore mayor who was running for governor was butting heads with the state superintendent of schools.

County School C also restructured to avoid a state takeover in 2006. All staff had to reapply for their jobs, and Saturday preparation sessions to complete the state tests were instituted (Gencer 2009). Teachers with conditional or resident teacher certification in School C dropped from 25 to 20% between 2006 and 2009, but the attendance rate only went from 88% to 87%, and the 12th grade graduation rate dropped from 83% to 73% (Maryland State Department of Education 2010).

V. Implications of School Demography for Delinquency and Educational Outcomes

Measures of concentrated poverty and disorganization of the community served by schools are correlated with school-level rates of problem behavior, particularly when measured via teacher reports of personal victimization. G. Gottfredson and Gottfredson (1985) found a composite of community poverty and disorganization (including student racial composition and educational disadvantage) correlated .64 with teacher victimization level in a large sample of junior high schools and .37 in a large sample of high schools. In a separate large national sample of secondary schools G. Gottfredson et al. (2005) found a measure of community-concentrated poverty correlated .39 with school teacher victimization. Correlations with school-level student self-reports of delinquent behavior or of student victimization are usually in the same direction but smaller in size. G. Gottfredson, Gottfredson, Gottfredson, and Jones (2002), using data from the same sample of schools, showed that measures of concentrated disadvantage also had correlations of similar size with principals' reports of how easy it was to recruit good teachers: community adult high school noncompletion, -.35; female-headed families, -.24; families below median income, -.26. The data imply that (a) schools serving communities of concentrated disadvantage have difficulty recruiting and retaining teachers, (b) schools in areas of concentrated disadvantage have higher levels of disorder, and (c) schools with difficulty recruiting and retaining staff have more disorder.

It is difficult—perhaps impossible—to disentangle causal processes involving teacher recruitment and retention and delinquency from nonexperimental data. Nevertheless, additional information about the recruitment and retention of teachers suggests that school disorder and delinquency coexist with other educational problems that make it difficult to staff some schools, and that school staffing influences both delinquency and achievement. First, schools differ greatly in the apparent quality of their teachers. This was illustrated in Table 9.1, contrasting four schools in the Baltimore area serving different communities. It was also demonstrated by the examination of teacher sorting among New York state schools by Lankford, Loeb, and Wykoff (2002). Using personnel data for teachers in the state, they showed that urban schools have less qualified teachers, and that low achieving non-White students tend to get less skilled teachers. Furthermore, they showed that teachers with more desirable qualifications tend to leave urban positions for better paid suburban positions.

Ingersoll (2001) has shown that teacher shortages appear to be largely due to teachers leaving teaching for other jobs—with retirement and growth in demand being less important sources of shortage. He also summarized evidence that one of the principal reasons for teacher turnover is job dissatisfaction. Ingersoll argued that negative organizational conditions lead to excess turnover and problems in staffing schools, which in turn lead to poor school academic performance. He showed that lack of administrative support and student conflict are associated with greater odds of teacher turnover. It seems reasonable to conclude that a cycle of reciprocal causation may be operating in which demographic stressors (particularly concentrated disadvantage but possibly also concentrated populations of immigrant language minorities) lead both to delinquent behavior manifested in schools as well as difficulties recruiting and retaining good teachers. Public perceptions that schools serve large numbers of disadvantaged or minority students decrease the attractiveness of the schools, exacerbating the degree to which the communities these schools serve are characterized by concentrated disadvantage. This kind of cycle in which community characteristics, delinquency, achievement, and school attractiveness influence each other is suggested by Figure 9.5. This is not the place for a thorough account of the reasons for believing that this kind of interdependence occurs, but the historical account of demographic influences leading to the current status of urban schools such as those in Baltimore seems consistent with such a cycle. This process can be seen in the contemporary websites (e.g., http://www.schooldigger.com) that rate or provide data on schools for people in the market for real estate. Research implies that housing prices are sensitive to the schools attended by children in the area (Kane, Riegg, and Staiger 2006) and to information about school quality (Crone 1998; Fiva and Kirkeboen 2008) in ways that would be

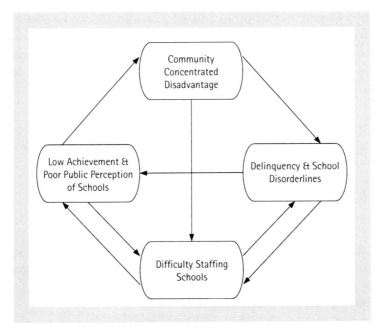

Figure 9.5. Mutual and Cyclical Influences of Community, Delinquency, and School Staffing and Outcomes.

expected to stratify school areas in terms of family economic status. And evidence described earlier implies that community-concentrated poverty or disadvantage is associated both with delinquency and difficulty staffing schools.

Difficulties in staffing are certainly not the only ways in which schools serving disadvantaged populations differ from others. Urban schools serving populations of concentrated poverty typically have older buildings and may have facilities lacking up-to-date labs and computer equipment, for example. These differences are in part a result of the historical demographic phenomena described earlier, where the size of the public school population has sometimes been declining for years. For instance, in Baltimore, enrollment dropped 58% between 1969 and 2007 (Baltimore City Public Schools 2008). As a result, Baltimore, Washington, DC, and other urban school districts with declining enrollments have many older buildings which are often too large for the current populations, may be in deteriorated condition, and require repair. Per capita property values differ greatly across school districts in the United States, making it more difficult for some districts to raise money for education than others. Differences in the quality of educational resources available in different locations have been described by Kozol (1991). Per capita expenditures vary widely across states and local school districts, leading to efforts to diminish inequities in expenditures in many states. These large inequities no doubt feed continuing segregation of schools and contribute to staffing difficulties. A review by Hanushek (1997) implies that it may not be resource inequities per se that lead to differences in student performance, particularly when differences in family inputs are considered—and that simply equalizing resources alone is unlikely to equalize outcomes. Equalizing resources alone seems unlikely to eliminate the link between concentrated educational problems and concentrated community disadvantage, although it will likely also be required.

VI. Should Schools Be Concerned with Prevention of Delinquency?

In recent years, in part because of the 2001 reauthorization of the Elementary and Secondary Education Act (Pub. L. 107–110, 115 Stat. 1425), called the No Child Left Behind (NCLB) Act, schools have increasingly focused on student academic achievement to the exclusion of other potential aims. NCLB required schools to set educational "proficiency" goals linked to specific subject matter tests and to report on progress toward those achievement goals for subgroups of students (e.g., those with disabilities or low family incomes), with the aim of eliminating the discrepancies between goals and performance for each of these subgroups. Schools face sanctions if they fail to make "adequate yearly progress" for all of these groups. NCLB has certainly directed attention toward the academic progress of ethnic and disability subgroups who have in the past often not shown great progress. It has also shifted instruction into the areas tested (particularly reading and mathematics) and away from other curricula (McMurrer 2008).

Prevention programs can take time away from instruction, and it is natural that when accountability mechanisms focus attention on specific achievement indicators, both educators and the general public will also tend to focus on those outcomes to the exclusion of others. Although NCLB required that "persistently dangerous schools" be identified,[4] in practice, education agencies rarely identify such schools, so there is no meaningful public accountability mechanism. Unlike achievement indicators, where great care is taken to secure tests and foster the credibility of assessment data, reporting of delinquent behavior in schools does not take place in such a way that the quantity of crime occurring in specific schools is really measured. But there are several reasons that, as a matter of public policy, we should measure the delinquency outcomes of education and take steps to prevent problem behavior in schools. First, schools are the major social institution with the mission of educating and socializing young people, and participation in elementary and secondary education is now regarded as obligatory for all young people. Second, the vast majority of public money spent on youths is spent on education (Holmes, Gottfredson, and Miller 1992). And third, there is evidence that some forms of preventive intervention in schools may be efficacious (Cook, Gottfredson, and Na, 2010).

But the most important reason to prevent delinquency and improve schools is that schools themselves are weakened by problem behavior. Because of the concentration of the disadvantaged in certain social areas; because schools are now expected to (and should) provide essentially universal education; and because social, economic, and demographic forces concentrate large numbers of difficult-to-educate young people in certain schools, the situation is rigged for the failure of some schools. These forces implicate schools in continuing to disadvantage some communities. Demoralized schools may be unable to implement prevention programs effectively (D. Gottfredson, Gottfredson, and Skroban 1998; G. Gottfredson, Jones, and Gore 2002; Payne, Gottfredson, and Gottfredson 2006),[5] and they are likely to have difficulty recruiting and retaining good teachers and administrators. Accordingly, it is likely that improving schools and their achievement outcomes will both require and result in less concentration of disadvantaged families in certain communities. At present, it is difficult to identify serious public policy initiatives that are directed at the demographic stresses now experienced by some schools. Such initiatives would have to distribute the burden of educating the disadvantaged more equally across schools, or concentrate a great deal more resources and excellent personnel in the overburdened schools. There are occasional proposals for pay increases in some urban schools to help attract and retain good teachers (Prince 2003), but incentives that are large enough to overcome the unattractiveness of working in difficult schools have not been attempted. And initiatives would have to play out over time. A demographic situation that took decades to develop and which persists across generations (Sampson, Sharkey, and Raudenbush 2008; Sharkey 2009) may take decades to unravel, even if practical political and economic tools to do so can be developed.

NOTES

I am grateful for the counsel of Jill Berger and Denise Gottfredson on an earlier version of this chapter.

1. The six indicators are (a) two or more credits of a foreign language with a grade of at least B, (b) one or more credits in a mathematics course beyond Algebra II and Geometry with a grade of at least B, (c) four credits of science with a grade of at least B, (d) two or more credits of technology education with a grade of at least B, (e) a score of at least 1,000 on the SAT or 20 on the ACT, and (f) a grade point average of 3.0. If a student meets four of these criteria he or she is said to have completed a rigorous program.

2. In practice, students need not pass these High School Assessments to graduate, as the state has developed a "Bridge Plan" that allows students to complete instructional projects if they fail the exams.

3. Resident teacher certificates are issued to teachers in special programs for teachers entering the profession through a nontraditional route. A conditional certificate is issued to teachers who do not meet certification requirements.

4. The legislation left it to the states to define persistently dangerous schools (PDS). States adopted varying definitions, most of which in practice were framed such that few if any schools would be identified. For example, Maryland defined a PDS as a school that for

three consecutive years had a number of student expulsions or suspensions for more than ten days equal to 2.5% or more of the number of students enrolled. Five Baltimore schools were designated PDS (Maryland State Department of Education 2007).

5. A useful distinction is the distinction between prevention programs that target students (their skills, attitudes, peer relations, and so on) and those that target school climate, organization, or management. On this distinction see G. Gottfredson and Gottfredson (2007) or Cook, Gottfredson and Na (2010). School-based interventions directed at individual students are reviewed in those two documents. Often these interventions involve curriculum or instruction in social skills, mentoring, or behavior management (G. Gottfredson and Gottfredson 2001). Prevention programs directed at individuals are generally difficult to implement in disorganized, poorly functioning schools (G. Gottfredson, Jones, and Gore 2002; D. Gottfredson, Gottfredson, and Skroban 1998). Accordingly, intervention that improves schools and their capacity to manage student behavior should be given more attention than has been typical in delinquency prevention and intervention.

REFERENCES

Alexander, Karl L., Doris R. Entwisle, and Nader S. Kabbani. 2001. "The Dropout Process in Life Course Perspective: Early Risk Factors at Home and School." *Teachers College Record* 103: 760–822.

Ayres, Leonard P. 1909. *Laggards in the Schools: A Study of Retardation and Elimination in City School Systems*. NY: Charities Publication Committee, Russell Sage Foundation.

Bachman, Jerald G., S. Green, and I. D. Wirtanen. 1971. *Youth in Transition, Vol. 3: Dropping Out–Problem or Symptom?* Ann Arbor, MI: University of Michigan Institute for Social Research.

Bachman, Jerald G., Patrick M. O'Malley, and J. Johnston. 1978. *Adolescence to Adulthood: Change and Stability in the Lives of Young Men*. Ann Arbor, MI: University of Michigan Institute for Social Research.

Baltimore City Public Schools. 2008. "Enrollment Rises: Baltimore City Public Schools Ends Four Decades of Decline," press release, December 28. Baltimore, MD: Baltimore Public Schools. *openaccess.baltimorecityschools.org/News/PDF/Enrollmentupnov82008. pdf*.

Baltimore County Public Schools. 2009. "Rule 5150–Students: Enrollment and Attendance." Towson, MD: Baltimore County Public Schools. http://www.bcps.org/system/ policies_rules/rules/5000Series/RULE5150.pdf.

Brauer, David. 2004. "What Accounts for the Decline in Manufacturing Employment?" *Almanac of Policy Issues* (updated February 19, 2004). Washington, DC: U.S. Congressional Budget Office, Macroeconomic Analysis Division. http://www. policyalmanac.org/economic/archive/manufacturing_employment.shtml.

Broidy, Lisa M., Daniel S. Nagin, Richard E. Tremblay, John E. Bates, Bobby Brahme, Kenneth A. Dodge, David Fergusson, John L. Horwood, Rolf Loeber, Robert Laird, Donald Lynam, Terrie E. Moffitt, Gregory S. Pettit, and Frank Vitaro. 2003. "Developmental Trajectories of Childhood Disruptive Behaviors and Adolescent Delinquency: A Six-Site, Cross-National Study." *Developmental Psychology* 39: 2222–45.

Cassidy, J. G. 1997. "African Americans and the American Labor Movement." *Prologue Magazine* 29(2). http://www.archives.gov/publications/prologue/1997/summer/index.html.

Center for Character Education. 2009. *May: Best Character Education Practices*. Baltimore, MD: Center for Character Education. http://www.mdctrcharacter.org/Best%20Practices%202009/Best%20Practices-May%20%2709-%20Frederick%20Douglass%20High.shtml

Cook, Phillip J., Denise C. Gottfredson, and C. Na. 2010. "School Crime Control and Prevention." In *Crime and Justice: A Review of Research*, vol 39, edited by Michael Tonry.

Crone, Theodore M. 1998. "House Prices and the Quality Of Public Schools: What Are We Buying?" *Business Review* (Federal Reserve Bank of Philadelphia) (September/October): 3–14.

Dionne, Ginette, Richard Tremblay, Michel Boivin, David Laplante, and Daniel Pérusse. 2003. "Physical Aggression and Expressive Vocabulary in 19-month-old Twins." *Developmental Psychology* 39: 261–73.

Dodge, Kenneth A. 1993. "Social-Cognitive Mechanisms in the Development of Conduct Disorder and Depression." *Annual Review of Psychology* 44: 559–84.

Dryfoos, J. G. (1990). *Adolescents at Risk: Prevalence and Prevention*. New York: Oxford University Press.

Eaton, Danice K., Laura Kann, Steve Kinchen, Shari Shanklin, James Ross, Joseph Hawkins, William A. Harris, Richard Lowry, Tim McManus, David Chyen, Connie Lim, Nancy D. Brener, and Howell Wechsler. 2008. Youth Risk Behavior Surveillance—United States, 2007. *Morbidity and Mortality Weekly Report* 57 (No. SS-4). Washington, DC: Government Printing Office. http://www.cdc.gov/mmwr/preview/mmwrhtml/ss5704a1.htm.

Elliott, Delbert S., & Harwin L. Voss. 1974. *Delinquency and Dropout*. Lexington, MA: Lexington Books.

Ensminger, Margaret E., Sheppart G. Kellam, and Barnett R. Rubin. 1983. "School and Family Origins of Delinquency: Comparisons by Sex." in *Prospective Studies of Crime and Delinquency*, edited by Katherine T. Van Dusen and Sarnoff A. Mednick. Boston: Kluwer-Nijhoff.

Fabiano, Gregory A., William E. Pelham, Jr., Erika K. Coles, Andrea Chronis-Tuscano, Briannon C. O'Connor, and Elizabeth M. Gnagy. 2009. "A meta-analysis of behavioral treatments for attention-deficit/hyperactivity disorder." *Clinical Psychology Review* 29, 129–40.

Fiva, J. H., and Lars J. Kirkeboen. 2008. "Does the Hoursing Market React to New information on School Quality?" CESIfo Working Paper No. 2299. http://www.cesifo-group.de/portal/page/portal/ifoHome/b-publ/b3publwp/CESifoWP.

Gencer, Arin. 2009. "2 Schools Show They Can Do It." *Baltimore Sun* (July 23). http://articles.baltimoresun.com/20090-72-3/news/0907220109_1_woodlawn-middle-arbutus-middle-baltimore-county.

Gibson, Campbell, and Kay Jung. 2005. *Historical Census Statistics On Population Totals By Race, 1790 to 1990, and By Hispanic Origin, 1970 to 1990, For Large Cities And Other Urban Places In The United States*. Population Division Working Paper No. 76. Washington, DC: U.S. Bureau of the Census. http://www.census.gov/population/www/documentation/twps0076/twps0076.html.

Gottfredson, Denise C., Gary D. Gottfredson, and Stacy Skroban. 1998. "Can Prevention Work Where it Is Needed Most?" *Evaluation Review* 22: 315–40.

Gottfredson, Gary D. 1981. Schooling and delinquency. In *New Directions in the Rehabilitation of Criminal Offenders*, edited by Susan E. Martin, Lee B. Sechrest, and Robin Redner. Washington, DC: National Academy Press.

Gottfredson, Gary D., and Denise C. Gottfredson. 1985. *Victimization in Schools*. New York: Plenum.

Gottfredson, Gary D., and Gottfredson, Denise C. 2001. "What Schools Do to Prevent Problem Behavior and Promote Safe Environments." *Journal of Educational and Psychological Consultation* 12: 313–44.

Gottfredson, Gary D., and Denise C. Gottfredson. 2007. "School violence." In *Cambridge Handbook of Violent Behavior and Aggression*, edited by D. Flannery, A. Vazonsyi, and I. Waldman. New York: Cambridge University Press.

Gottfredson, Gary D., Denise C. Gottfredson, Ellen R. Czeh, David Cantor, Scott Crosse, and Irene Hantman. 2000. *National Study of Delinquency Prevention in Schools*. Ellicott City, MD: Gottfredson Associates. (NCJ 194129).

Gottfredson, Gary D., Denise C. Gottfredson, Nisha C. Gottfredson, and Elizabeth M. Jones. 2002. "Community Characteristics, Staffing Difficulty, and School Disorder in a National Sample of Secondary Schools." Paper presented at the annual meeting of the American Society of Criminology, Chicago, IL: November.

Gottfredson, Gary D., Denise C. Gottfredson, Allison A. Payne, and Nisha Gottfredson. 2005. "School Climate Predictors of School Disorder: Results from a National Study of Delinquency Prevention in Schools." *Journal of Research in Crime and Delinquency* 42: 412–44.

Gottfredson, Gary D., Elizabeth M. Jones, and Thomas W. Gore. 2002. "Implementation and Evaluation of a Cognitive-behavioral Intervention to Prevent Problem Behavior in a Disorganized School." *Prevention Science* 3: 43–56.

Gottfredson, Michael R., and Travis Hirschi. 1990. *A General Theory of Crime*. Stanford, CA: Stanford University Press.

Hanushek, Eric A. 1997. "Assessing the Effects of School Resources on Student Performance: An Update." *Educational Evaluation and Policy Analysis* 19(2): 141–64.

Harachi, Tracy W., Charles B. Fleming, Helene R. White, Margaret E. Ensminger, Robert D. Abbott, Richard F. Catalano, and Kevin P. Haggerty. 2006. "Aggressive Behavior Among Girls and Boys During Middle Childhood: Predictors and Sequelae of Trajectory Group Membership." *Aggressive Behavior* 32: 279–93.

Hawkins, J. David, T. Herrenkohl, D. P. Farrington, D. Brewer, R. F. Catalano, and T. W. Harachi. 1998. "A Review of Predictors of Youth Violence." In *Serious and Violent Juvenile Offenders: Risk Factors and Successful Interventions*, edited by Rolf Loeber and David P. Farrington. Thousand Oaks, CA: Sage.

Hinshaw, Stephen P. 1992. "Externalizing Behavior Problems and Academic Underachievement in Childhood and Adolescence: Causal Relationships and Underlying Mechanisms." *Psychological Bulletin* 111: 127–55.

Hirschi, Travis, and Michael J. Hindelang. 1977. "Intelligence and Delinquency: A Revisionist Review." *American Sociological Review* 42: 571–87.

Holmberg, Margaret C. 1980. "The Development of Social Interchange Patterns from 12 to 42 Months." *Child Development* 51: 448–56.

Holmes, A. Baron, III, Gary D. Gottfredson, and J. Y. Miller. 1992. "Resources and strategies for funding." In *Communities That Care: Action for Drug Abuse Prevention*, edited by J. David Hawkins and Richard F. Catalano. San Francisco: Jossey-Bass.

Huesmann, L. Rowell, Eric F. Dubow, and Paul Boxer. 2009. "Continuity of Aggression from Childhood to Early Adulthood as a Predictor of Life Outcomes: Implications for the Adolescent-Limited and Life-Course-Persistent Models." *Aggressive Behavior* 35: 136–49.

Huesmann, L. Rowell, Leonard D. Eron, Monroe M. Lefkowitz, and Leopold O. Walder. 1984. "Stability of Aggression Over Time and Generations." *Developmental Psychology* 20: 1120–34.

Ingersoll, Richard M. 2001. "Teacher Turnover and Teacher Shortages: An Organizational Analysis." *American Educational Research Journal* 38: 499–534.

Jadad, Alejandro R., Michael Boyle, Charles Cunningham, Marie Kim, and Russell Schachar. 1999. *Treatment of Attention Deficit/Hyperactivity Disorder*. Evidence Report/Technology Assessment No. 11, AHRQ Publication No. 00-E005. Rockville, MD: Agency for Healthcare Research and Quality, U.S. Department of Health and Human Services.

Janosz, Michel, Marc LeBlanc, Bernard Boulerice, and Richard E. Tremblay. 1997. "Disentangling the Weight of School Dropout Predictors: a Test on Two Longitudinal Samples." *Journal of Youth and Adolescence* 26: 733–62.

Jessor, Richard, J. E. Donovan, and F. M. Costa. 1991. *Beyond Adolescence: Problem Behavior and Young Adult Development*. New York: Cambridge University Press.

Jessor, Richard, T. D. Graves, R. C. Hanson, and S. L. Jessor. 1968. *Society, Personality, and Deviant Behavior: a Study of a Tri-ethnic Community*. New York: Holt, Rinehart and Winston.

Jimerson, Shane R., Gabrielle E. Anderson, and Angela D. Whipple. 2002. "Winning the Battle and Losing the War: Examining the Relation Between Grade Retention and Dropping out of High School." *Psychology in the Schools* 39: 441–57.

Kane, Thomas J., Stephanie K. Riegg, and Douglas O. Staiger. 2006. "School Quality, Neighborhoods, and Housing Prices." *American Law and Economics Review* 8: 183–212.

Kaufman, Phillip, Martha Naomii Alt, and Christopher Chapman. 2001. *Dropout Rates in the United States: 2000* (NCES 2002144). Washington, DC: National Center for Education Statistics.

King, S., S. Griffin, Z. Hodges, H. Weatherly, C. Asseburg, G. Richardson, S. Golder, E. Taylor, M. Drummond, and R. Riemsma. 2006. "A Systematic Review and Economic Model of the Effectiveness and Cost-effectiveness of Methylphenidate, Dexamfetamine and Atomoxetine for the Treatment of Attention Deficit Hyperactivity Disorder in Children and Adolescents." *Health Technology Assessment* 10(23): 1–146.

Kozol, Jonathan. 1991. *Savage Inequalities*. NY: Harper Collins.

Kreuger, Robert F., Avshalom Caspi, Terrie E. Moffitt, Jennifer, White, and Magda Strouthamer-Loeber. 1996. "Delay of Gratification, Psychopathology, and Personality: Is Low Self-Control Specific to Externalizing Problems?" *Journal of Personality* 64: 1071–29.

Lankford, Hamilton, Susanna Loeb, and James Wyckoff. 2002. "Teacher Sorting and the Plight of Urban Schools: A Descriptive Analysis." *Educational Evaluation and Policy Analysis* 24: 37–62.

Lee, J. W. Grigg, and P. Donahue. 2007. *The Nation's Report Card: Reading 2007* (NCES 20071–96). Washington, DC: National Center for Education Statistics.

Lipsitt, P. D., Stephen L. Buka, and Lewis P. Lipsitt. 1990. "Early Intelligence Scores and Subsequent Delinquency: a Prospective Study." *American Journal of Family Therapy* 18: 197–208.

Loeber, Rolf. 1982. "The stability of antisocial and delinquent child behavior: A review." *Child Development* 53: 1431–46.

Loeber, Rolf, and Thomas Dishion. 1983. "Early predictors of male delinquency: A review." *Psychological Bulletin* 94: 68–99.

Loeber, Rolf, David P. Farrington, M. Strouthamer-Loeber, and W. B. Van Kammen. 1998. *Antisocial Behavior and Mental Health problems: Explanatory Factors in Childhood and Adolescence.* Mahwah, NJ: Erlbaum.

Maguin, Eugene, and Rolf Loeber. 1996. "Academic Performance and Delinquency." In *Crime and Justice: A Review of Research*, vol. 20, edited by Michael Tonry. Chicago: University of Chicago Press.

Maryland State Department of Education. (2007). "Five Baltimore City Schools Cited for Dangerous Conditions." *MSDE Bulletin* 18(7): 2. http://www.marylandpublicschools. org/NR/exeres/B18D09544–94C-46DF-9728-E740EB1251FC,frameless.htm?Year=2007& Month=7%%3E.

Maryland State Department of Education. 2010. "Maryland Report Card." Baltimore, MD: Maryland State Department of Education. Data downloads available at http://www. mdreportcard.org/.

McCord, Joan, and Margaret E. Ensminger. 1997. "Multiple Risks and Comorbidity in an African-American Population." *Criminal Behaviour and Mental Health* 7: 339–52.

McMurrer, Jennifer. 2008. *Instructional Time in Elementary Schools: A Closer Look at Changes for Specific Subjects.* Washington, DC: Center on Education Policy.

National Advisory Commission on Civil Disorders. 1969. *Report of the National Advisory Commission on Civil Disorders.* New York: Bantam.

Orfield, Gary. 2001. *Schools More Separate: Consequences of a Decade of Resegregation.* Cambridge, MA: Harvard University, Civil Rights Project. http://www. civilrightsproject.ucla.edu/research/deseg/Schools_More_Separate.pdf

Ovando, C. J. 2003. "Bilingual Education in the United States: Historical Development and Current Issues." *Bilingual Research Journal* 27: 1–24.

Payne, Allison A., Denise C. Gottfredson, and Gary D. Gottfredson. 2003. "Schools as Communities: The Relation Among School Communal Organization, Student Bonding, and School Disorder." *Criminology* 41: 749–77.

Payne, Allison A., Denise C. Gottfredson, and Gary D. Gottfredson. 2006. "School Predictors of the Intensity of Implementation of School-Based Prevention Programs: Results from a National Study." *Prevention Science* 7: 225–37.

Pelham, William E., Jr., and Gregory A. Fabiano. 2008. "Evidence-based Psychosocial Treatments for Attention-deficit/hyperactivity Disorder." *Journal of Clinical Child and Adolescent Psychology* 37: 184–214.

Prince, Cynthia D. 2003. *Higher Pay in Hard-to-Staff Schools: The Case for Financial Incentives.* Oxford, UK: Scarecrow Press.

Quetelet, Adolphe. (1833) 1984. *Research on the Propensity for Crime at Different Ages,* translated by Sawyer F. Sylvester. Cincinnati, OH: Anderson. Originally published as *Recherches sur le penchant au Crime aux Différens Âges.* Brussels: Hayez.

Ramani, Angelina Kewal, Lauren Gilbertson, Mary Ann Fox, and Stephen Provasnik. 2007. *Status and Trends in the Education of Racial and Ethnic Minorities* (NCES 2007039). Washington, DC: National Center for Education Statistics.

Rury, John L. 1988. "Urban School Enrollment at the Turn of the Century: Gender as an Intervening Variable." *Urban Education* 23: 68–88.

Sampson, Robert J., and John H. Laub. 2005. "Developmental Criminology and Its Discontents: Trajectories of Crime from Childhood to Old Age." *Annals of the American Academy of Political and Social Science* 602 (Nov.): 12–45.

Sampson, Robert J., Patrick Sharkey, and Steven W. Raudenbush. 2008. "Durable Effects of Concentrated Disadvantage on Verbal Ability among African-American Children." *Proceedings of the National Academy of Sciences of the United States of America* 105 (3): 845–52.

Samuels, Barbara. 2008. "The 1968 Riots and the History of Public Housing Segregation in Baltimore." Baltimore, MD: American Civil Liberties Union. http://www.aclu-md.org/top-issues/Fair%20ohousing/1968.html.

Sharkey, Patrick. 2009. "The Intergenerational Transmission of Context." *American Journal of Sociology* 114(4): 931–69.

Silver, Christopher. 1997. "The Racial Origins of Zoning in American Cities." In *Urban Planning and the African American Community: In the Shadows*, edited by J. M. Thomas and M. Ritzdorf. Thousand Oaks, CA: Sage.

Tremblay, Richard E. 2006. "Prevention of Youth Violence: Why Not Start at the Beginning?" *Journal of Abnormal Child Psychology* 34: 481–87.

Tremblay, Richard E., Christa Japel, Daniel Pérusse, Pierre McDuff, Michel Boivin, Mark Zoccolillo, and Jacques Montplaisir. 1999. "The Search for the Age of 'Onset' of Physical Aggression: Rousseau and Bandura Revisited." *Criminal Behaviour and Mental Health* 9(1): 8–23.

Trzesniewski, Kali H., Terrie E. Moffitt, Avshalom Caspi, Alan Taylor, and Barbara Maughan. 2006. "Revisiting the Association Between Reading Achievement and Antisocial Behavior: New Evidence of an Environmental Explanation From a Twin Study." *Child Development* 77: 72–88.

U.S. Census Bureau. 2003. *Statistical Abstract of the United States: 2003.* Washington, DC: Author. *www.census.gov/statab/hist/HS-02.pdf*

U.S. Census Bureau. 2006. *United States–School Enrollment of the Population 3 Years and Over by Age, Nativity, and Type of School: 2000.* http://www.census.gov/population/www/cen2000/briefs/phc-t39/tables/tab5S-01.xls

U.S. Census Bureau. 2010. *Statistical Abstract of the United States: 2010.* Washington, DC: Author. http://www.census.gov/compendia/statab/hist_stats.html.

Walker, Dollie, Arthur L. Stinchcombe, and Mary S. McDill. 1967. *School Desegregation in Baltimore* (ERIC No. 03168). Baltimore, MD: Johns Hopkins University, Center for Social Organization of Schools.

Weissberg, Roger P., Marlene Caplan, and Robin L. Harwood. 1991. "Promoting Competent Young People in Competence-enhancing Environments: a Systems-based Perspective on Primary Prevention." *Journal of Consulting and Clinical Psychology* 59: 830–41.

Williams, Jay R., and Martin Gold. 1972. "From Delinquent Behavior to Official Delinquency." *Social Problems* 20: 209–29.

Wilson, William Julius. 1987. *The Truly Disadvantaged: The Inner City, the Underclass, and Public Policy.* Chicago: University of Chicago Press.

Wolfgang, Marvin E., Robert M. Figlio, & Thorsten Sellin. 1972. *Delinquency in a Birth Cohort.* Chicago: University of Chicago Press.

CHAPTER 10

THE SOCIAL SIDE OF DELINQUENT BEHAVIOR

MARK WARR

Let it be remembered that most men live in a world of their own, and that in that limited circle alone are they ambitious for distinction and applause. Sir Mulberry's world was peopled with profligates, and he acted accordingly.

—Charles Dickens, Nicholas Nickleby

IMAGINE the following scenario:

> Jim is 18 years old and lives with his parents. Jim dropped out of school when he was 17 despite pleas from his parents, whom he dislikes and avoids. One Friday evening, Jim "borrows" his parents' car without their knowledge or consent and drives to his old school, where he steals two laptop computers and some sports equipment. Later that evening, he drinks to intoxication after shoplifting some beer from a convenience store, and smashes a streetlight with a rock.

This scenario is largely consistent with what we know about criminal behavior. The offender is a male in the crime-prone ages (about 16 to 24) who is estranged from his parents and school and who has no long-term commitment to a job or career. He often acts impulsively, with little apparent concern for the long-term consequences of his behavior.

As plausible as this example may seem, it is in fact a strikingly *inaccurate* depiction of delinquency in one key respect. That is, Jim acted *alone* during this incident. In reality, when young people break the law, they usually do so in the company of others their age. The Hollywood image of the juvenile delinquent as an isolated loner holds little truth, at least when it comes to illegal behavior.

Is this fact important? Does it tell us something essential about criminal behavior? Or is it merely an incidental feature of criminal events? Thoughtful criminologists can be found on both sides of the argument, and it remains one of the oldest unresolved issues in the field. This chapter explores these questions and sets forth evidence for readers to evaluate.

I. Crime as Group Behavior

Human beings, like other primates, are highly social animals. They crave the company of their own kind, and protracted isolation from other humans (in prisons, for example) can lead to insanity and suicide.

As social animals, what we do at any particular moment depends in part on who we are with and what is considered to be acceptable behavior within that immediate social universe. We behave differently in the presence of a teacher, girlfriend or boyfriend, pastor, coworker, doctor, schoolmate, bar mate, or police officer. This occurs not because we are deceitful or feckless creatures, but because we have acquired role expectations from our culture that define how we are to behave around others (and they with us). We expect those we call "friends," for example, to be loyal, honest, and intimate, and we are hurt or angry when they fall short. In the same way, we do not expect sexual advances from our minister nor loan requests from our mailman. As social beings, we sometimes do things when others are present that we would never contemplate doing alone—things that may be dangerous, illegal, or morally reprehensible. Afterwards, we may look back at our own behavior with amazement and regret. The influence of others is not limited to those who happen to be physically present at any given moment; faraway or former associates can sometimes affect us even in their absence.

During the last century and a half, some scholars have looked to the social nature of human beings in their efforts to explain the origins of criminal conduct. Perhaps humans engage in violence because they want to be respected, admired, or simply accepted by others. Perhaps youths form gangs in order to feel part of a larger, albeit dangerous, community. Edwin Sutherland, among the most sociological of all criminological theorists, insisted that humans learn to commit crimes *from other people* in exactly the same way that they learn to ride a bicycle, order food at a restaurant, or play poker. Crime is learned in the same way that virtually *all* human behavior is learned, he insisted.

The case for a social explanation of crime is buttressed by two persistent characteristics of criminal behavior: (1) Criminal behavior is primarily committed by young people, and, as noted earlier, young people rarely commit crimes without companions; and (2) Among the strongest predictors of delinquent behavior known to criminologists is the number of delinquent friends an individual has. Both of these observations are supported by decades of empirical research. What remains a matter of dispute today is not their veracity, but rather their meaning, as we shall see shortly. First, however, it is instructive to review some evidence on the social nature of crime and delinquency.

II. Companions and Crime

Among the first criminologists to take serious notice of the social nature of delinquency were Shaw and McKay (1931), who discovered that more than 80% of juveniles appearing before the Chicago Juvenile Court had accomplices. Similar findings drawn from official data were routinely reported by scholars from the 1920s through the 1960s (see Klein 1969; Erickson 1971; Reiss 1986). As self-report methods came into common use in the 1960s and 1970s, evidence for the group nature of delinquency accumulated. Gold (1970), for example, reported that 75% of the 2,490 chargeable delinquent offenses reported by his sample of Flint youth were committed in the company of others, and less than 20% of respondents in Shannon's (1991, p. 23) survey of Racine youth said that they had acted alone. Erickson (1971), Erickson and Jensen (1977), and Warr (1996) uncovered consistently high "group violation rates" (the proportion of offenses committed in groups) in self-report data from juveniles. Only one of the eighteen offenses examined by Erickson had a group violation rate below 50%, and the same was true of only four of eighteen offenses in Erickson and Jensen's (1977) study, and only two of twelve in Warr's (1996). Some of the exceptions to the rule were acts that had some inherently solitary element to them (e.g., defying parents, running away; see Erickson and Jensen 1977).

Evidence for the group nature of delinquency also comes from countries outside the United States (Sarnecki 1986; Reiss and Farrington 1991), including England, Sweden, and India. This suggests that the group nature of delinquency is not confined to the United States and perhaps is true wherever delinquency is to be found.

Although delinquent behavior is predominantly group behavior, some offenses are more likely to be committed in groups than others. There is consistent evidence that alcohol and marijuana are used by adolescents almost exclusively in group settings. Likewise, certain property and public order offenses (vandalism, burglary, trespassing) have rates of group offending nearly as high as those for drug offenses, with other property crimes (e.g., auto theft) not far behind. On the other side of the continuum, shoplifting and assault appear to be among the less "groupy" offenses (see Gold 1970; Erickson 1971; Erickson and Jensen 1977; Reiss and Farrington 1991; Warr 1996). In general, the offenses that young people commit most often are also the ones most likely to be committed with others (Gold 1970).

III. Characteristics of Delinquent Groups

If delinquency is primarily a group phenomenon, what are the common features of delinquent groups? How long do they last? Who, if anyone, is "in charge"? How many different groups do adolescents ordinarily belong to?

Before proceeding, it is worthwhile to pause for a moment and distinguish "groups" from "gangs." The point at which a group becomes a gang has been debated for decades in the gang literature, with little prospect of closure. Still, there is general agreement, supported by empirical evidence, that gangs constitute only a small fraction of delinquent groups, and that a gang-like organization (e.g., vertical authority structure, recognized territory, insignia like "tats" or colors) is not a prerequisite for delinquent behavior (see especially Morash 1983; Stafford 1984). By all indications, what is true of delinquent groups—unclear and shifting role assignments and role definitions, predominantly same-sex composition, constantly changing membership—is ordinarily true of gangs as well. Even the size of gangs, which seems clearly to differentiate them from most delinquent groups, is misleading, because gangs are often loose aggregations of smaller, age-segregated cliques (see Klein and Crawford 1967; Sarnecki 1986, 2001).

A focus on group as opposed to gang delinquency is therefore eminently defensible, although gangs, as a logical subset of delinquent groups, surely merit recognition. Gangs are perhaps best understood as *institutionalized* groups, which is to say that they persist through time as identifiable social units, even as their membership changes constantly over the months and years.

A. Examining Delinquent Groups

One established characteristic of delinquent groups is their size; nearly all studies show typical group sizes in the range of two to four members (Shaw and McKay 1931; Gold 1970; Hood and Sparks 1970; Reiss 1986; Sarnecki 1986; Warr 1996). It appears, furthermore, that group size diminishes with age; groups of four or more are typical in late childhood and early adolescence but gradually give way to triads and dyads in middle and late adolescence (Hood and Sparks 1970; Reiss 1986). Lone offending is more typical of adult offenders than juveniles (Reiss and Farrington 1991). Apart from their size, it is also well established that delinquent groups are predominantly unisexual, and they appear to be age homogeneous as well (Miller 1974; Stafford 1984; Sarnecki 1986; Reiss and Farrington 1991; Warr 1996).

As noted earlier, it appears that the small groups that commit most delinquent acts are often subsets of a larger group or clique (Short and Strodtbeck 1965; Klein and Crawford 1967; Reiss 1986; Sarnecki 1986), implying that delinquents commonly have a larger network of co-offenders than might be expected from the small size of offending groups.

Delinquent groups do not appear to be highly stable, nor are they highly organized. Evidently, offenders do not ordinarily stay with the same accomplices over long periods of time, and they often belong to multiple offending groups or cliques at the same time (Reiss 1986; Sarnecki 1986; Warr 1996). Within delinquent groups, role definitions and role assignments appear to be unclear and unstable (Yablonsky 1959; Klein and Crawford 1967; Stafford 1984), and shifting membership due to incarceration, residential mobility, and employment makes such groups intrinsically unstable (Reiss 1986). The result is that "the membership of any group is volatile," and affiliations are "transitory" (Reiss 1986, p. 130). Although there is a tendency toward specialization, most offenders are not exclusively lone offenders or group offenders; rather, they have a history that includes instances of both solo and group offending (Reiss 1986; Reiss and Farrington 1991; Warr 1996).

In an extensive study of group delinquency, Warr (1996) reported that offenders usually belong to multiple delinquent groups over their careers and that they change accomplices frequently; only rarely do delinquents commit more than a few offenses with the same accomplice. Most delinquent groups contain an identifiable instigator, a person who is apt to be older (if only slightly), more experienced, and close to other members. Males almost always follow a male instigator, and although females are also likely to follow an instigator of the same sex, they are far more likely to follow males than vice versa. Most offenders have a history as both instigator and joiner, switching from one role to the other as they shift from one group to another. When Tom is with Randy and Mike, he is the oldest and most experienced of the three. In his other two male peer groups, he is the youngest. When Tom hangs out with his sister's friends, he is the only male. And so on.

One the principal findings of Warr's study was the short life span of delinquent groups. According to his data, delinquent groups are short-lived groups, so short-lived that it may make little sense to even speak of group organization. The extreme instability of most delinquent groups means that offenders will normally have few opportunities to repeat their role in the same group and thereby develop a stable role structure. And the short life span of delinquent groups is scarcely conducive to the establishment of group norms or a sense of group identity (as would be expected in gangs).

If one were to briefly describe delinquent groups using this and other research, one might say that delinquent groups are small, shifting, short-lived, unorganized groups of young males. And according to Gold (1970) and others (Briar and Piliavin 1965; Sarnecki 1986; Erez 1987; Cairns and Cairns 1994), the delinquent behavior that takes place in such groups ordinarily shows little evidence of planning or forethought. This suggests that the motivation to engage in delinquency ordinarily arises *after* a group assembles and as a consequence of group interaction.

IV. A Little Help from My Friends

The case for a social explanation of crime, as noted earlier, rests not only on the group nature of delinquency, but also on the connection between delinquent behavior and delinquent friends. Most offenders have friends who also engage in delinquency (and who may or may not be present during any particular delinquent event), and the number of delinquent friends an adolescent has is one of the strongest known predictors of delinquent behavior.

Like most delinquent youth, delinquent friends tend to have only weak attachments to school and to parents. Adolescents often conceal their delinquent friends from their parents, leading Warr (2007) to describe such friends as "secret friends." Delinquent friends also tend to be "sticky" friends, meaning that, once acquired, they are not quickly lost (Warr 1996). There is strong evidence that adolescents are most strongly influenced by their *current* friends, and that the impact of earlier friends diminishes very quickly with time (Warr 1996). Research also indicates that adolescents are more strongly influenced by the behavior of their friends than the attitudes of their friends (Warr and Stafford 1991). Furthermore, "peers' delinquency has a stronger association with an adolescent's delinquency when the adolescents are located in a central position within their friendship network, when their friendship network is very dense, and when they are nominated as friends by many others" (Haynie 2001, p. 1048). It is also wise to bear in mind that friends tend to be *mutually* influential; a relatively law-abiding youth may exert as much influence on his highly deviant friend as vice versa. McGloin (2009, p. 465) has in fact uncovered evidence that "adolescents seek congruent [i.e., matching] levels of deviance with their close friends."

V. The Implications of Sociality

Few criminologists today dispute the social nature of delinquency. The evidence supporting it is simply too strong to be dismissed. What some *do* dispute is the importance or significance of this fact. To some criminologists, the social nature of delinquency is essential to understanding its etiology. The causal importance of peers, however, has been questioned by other scholars on several grounds. Some argue that the companionship so evident in delinquency is true of most adolescent activities (see especially Kornhauser 1978). Adolescents, they argue, are notoriously gregarious people; they do everything in groups, including breaking the law. Because the group character of delinquency does not distinguish delinquency from other, legal forms of adolescent behavior, it is argued, it remains unclear whether the group nature of delinquency has any causal significance at all.

The validity of this argument, however, is debatable. Even if most adolescent behavior—legal or otherwise—takes place in groups, it is not clear how that is a damning criticism of peer explanations of delinquency. Young people may be influenced by their peers in all categories of behavior—music, speech, dress, sports, and *delinquency*. Indeed, recall that some major theories of delinquent peer influence (Sutherland 1947; Akers 1998) expressly argue that criminal behavior is learned from others in the same way that *all* human behavior is learned.

Causal questions about peer influence arise in another way, however. Recall that proponents of peer influence commonly point to the strong, consistent correlation between delinquent friends and delinquent behavior. Those who doubt the importance of peer influence, however, do not question this correlation, but instead offer an alternative explanation for it. Drawing on the venerable sociological principle of homophily (people make friends with people who are similar to themselves), they argue that the causal direction between delinquency and friends runs in the opposite direction from that implied by peer influence. People do not become delinquent because they acquire delinquent friends, in other words; they acquire delinquent friends after they themselves have become delinquent. The most acclaimed proponents of this position were the Gluecks (1950), who aptly and famously described their point of view with the aphorism "birds of a feather flock together."

Today, however, a number of longitudinal studies support the causal direction favoring peer influence. For example, in a simple but telling investigation, Elliott and Menard (1996) examined the temporal priority between delinquent behavior and exposure to delinquent peers within cohorts of National Youth Survey respondents. They discovered that the acquisition of delinquent peers commonly precedes the onset of delinquency, supporting the notion of peer influence as a causal factor in delinquency.

Even if the acquisition of delinquent friends is necessary for the onset of delinquency, however, many criminologists reasonably maintain that the relation between delinquent behavior and delinquent peers *over time* is likely to be bidirectional or sequential. In other words, acquiring delinquent friends leads to delinquency, which increases the subsequent probability of acquiring still more delinquent friends. Thornberry (1987) posited such reciprocal effects in what he called his "interactional" theory of delinquency. In a test of that theory, he and his associates (Thornberry et al. 1994, p. 74) concluded that "associating with delinquent peers leads to increases in delinquency via the reinforcing environment provided by the peer network. In turn, engaging in delinquency leads to increases in association with delinquent peers."

Similar evidence is provided by Matsueda and Anderson (1998); Meier, Burkett, and Hickman 1984; Burkett and Warren 1987; Paternoster 1988; Agnew 1991; Simons et al. 1994; Aseltine 1995; Fergusson and Horwood 1996; Kandel 1978; Krohn et al. 1996; and Reed and Rountree 1997.

Some of the most compelling evidence on this matter comes from research by Cairns and Cairns (1994). In their longitudinal study of children in grades 4 through 12, these researchers examined socialization and selection effects with respect to a wide variety of characteristics. Summarizing their findings (1994, p. 117), they report that

> There is strong support for the idea that selection and socialization cooperate over time, as far as our own observations are concerned. There is clearly a selection process, where children and adolescents affiliate on the basis of sex, race, and socioeconomic class. There is also a contagion effect, such that once the groups are formed, the "selected" behaviors are escalated for good or ill. The

constraints on escalation typically operate from without, in the case of younger children and adolescents. Equally interesting, however, is the creation of novel behaviors within groups, and their transmission across members. This is a particular problem in the case of deviant groups.

The Cairnses characterize the social scientific literature on socialization and selection effects in this manner:

> A systematic account of social clusters and friendships must take into account the powerful effects of reciprocal influence demonstrated in experimental studies and observational analyses. The message from these investigations is that reciprocal interactions lead to high levels of behavioral and attitudinal similarity, regardless of the initial status of the people involved. The evidence on adolescent group dynamics strongly points to the operation of both differential selection factors and reciprocal influences.... Within the clusters of adolescence, strong reciprocal forces operate on all members toward conformity....Once in a group, there is conformity with respect to a broad spectrum of behaviors and attitudes, including shared linguistic and communication patterns, areas of worry and concern, and "lifestyle" characteristics. For many youth, the problem is to escape from synchrony with deviant or escalating values (1994, pp. 128–29).

In a controversy similar to that over causal direction, some criminologists have asserted that the correlation between delinquent behavior and delinquent peers is simply a consequence of measurement errors or artifacts arising from self-report data. When asked to describe the delinquency of friends, they argue, individuals may impute their own behavior to their friends, for example, or impute friendship to people like themselves (see Gottfredson and Hirschi 1990). Warr (1993a) has raised a number of objections to these claims, however, and Matsueda and Anderson (1998) have shown that the correlation persists even after accounting for measurement error. What many investigators also seem to overlook is that early studies demonstrating a correlation between delinquent behavior and delinquent peers relied on means other than imputational data (i.e., official records or self-reports obtained independently from respondents and friends (see Reiss and Rhodes 1964; Erickson and Empey 1965; Hepburn 1977), as did a more recent study by Aseltine (1995). Consequently, it is difficult to ascribe the correlation to any alleged idiosyncrasies of self-report data. Whatever it may mean, the correlation between delinquency and delinquent friends seems robust with respect to method.

The persistence of causal questions about peer influence may reflect a larger issue in social science generally. Most social science is based on observational data rather than experimental evidence, making causal inference difficult. Ethical concerns, however, preclude many experimental studies of peer influence. For example, one cannot simply place a group of college students in a maximum security prison and observe changes in those students, any more than one can place fifty state felons in a college dormitory and measure the outcome.

Several recent investigations, however, provide relatively unambiguous experimental evidence of peer influence. In one study (Gardner and Steinberg 2005), adolescents and young adults participated in a video game on a laptop computer. In the game, subjects drove a car horizontally across the screen and had the option to either stop or proceed when they encountered a yellow light. Those who "ran" the yellow light risked losing their "life" and all of their accumulated game points. The investigators found that subjects were significantly more likely to run the yellow light when peers were present than when they were alone. This peer effect was stronger among adolescents (those aged 13 to 16) and youth (18 to 22) than among adults (22 and older). Coincidentally, these findings may explain why the probability of a fatal accident in an automobile increases in direct proportion to the number of adolescents in the car (Chen et al. 2000).

In another study (Cohen and Prinstein 2006), white male adolescent subjects were seated at a computer and were instructed to log on to an electronic computer chat room where they could interact with three other students from their high school. In reality, the three other peers were not logged on to the chat room; their presence was simulated by the experimenter. The investigators found that subjects were significantly more likely to endorse aggressive and risky behaviors when they were also endorsed by high-status peers (i.e., popular and accepted students) than by low-status peers. In fact, subjects attempted to distance their attitudes and behaviors from those of low-status peers in their school.

In yet another experimental study, economists Michael Kremer and Daniel Levy (2008) found that college students who were randomly assigned a dorm roommate who drank alcohol had significantly lower grades at the end of the semester than did other students.

Some remarkable new evidence on peer influence comes from physician and sociologist Nicholas Christakis at Harvard University (e.g., Fowler and Christakis 2008). By carefully mapping the social networks of thousands of people over time, he found that the attitudes and behaviors of individuals (e.g., happiness, obesity, smoking) are influenced not only by their friends, but also by the friends of their friends, even when the individual does not directly know those persons. Owing to social contagion, it seems, people often influence others whom they will never meet.

These studies provide compelling evidence of peer influence using experimental methods in relatively naturalistic situations. They leave little room for doubt that peer influence is real, and that it can be very strong.

VI. Peers and the Origins of Delinquency

If peer influence is in fact real, exactly how does it operate? For example, can adolescents be affected by peers they have never actually met (e.g., movie stars, pop figures, television actors)? How long do peer effects last? Weeks? Months? Years? Can parents shut down or counteract peer influence?

To many modern criminologists, the very idea of peer influence is synonymous with Edwin Sutherland and his famous theory of *Differential Association*. The first explicit statement of Sutherland's theory appeared in 1939 in the third edition of his textbook *Principles of Criminology*, a popular textbook of the time. A revised and final version appeared in the fourth edition in 1947, three years before Sutherland's death. The latter statement of the theory took the form of nine propositions, each followed by brief elaborations or clarifications. In essence, Sutherland maintained that criminal behavior is learned in interaction with other persons within intimate groups. The learning includes techniques of committing the crime along with "the specific direction of motives, drives, rationalizations, and attitudes. A person becomes delinquent because of an excess of definitions favorable to violation of law over definitions unfavorable to violation of law." The process of differential association may vary in frequency, duration, priority, and intensity.

Sutherland's theory was, in its time, a radical theory of criminal behavior. It rejected popular biological theories of crime, for example, and by situating the origins of crime in the everyday interactions of ordinary people, it favored a strongly sociological and naturalistic explanation of crime. Perhaps its most radical feature was that it treated criminal behavior like any other form of human behavior (sexual behavior, language, food customs), i.e., as behavior *learned* from others. To Sutherland, the question "Are human beings inherently violent?" is essentially meaningless. Humans can be ruthlessly violent or angelically peaceful, depending on their history of interaction and the cultural context that frames that interaction.

Research on Differential Association has been generally supportive, although some specific precepts of the theory have been called into question. For example, Warr (1993a) examined the effects of priority and duration on self-reported delinquency at age 17 using data from the National Youth Survey. His analysis indicated that these two dimensions of friendship are not entirely independent. Why? Because adolescents who acquire delinquent friends tend to retain them (remember the "sticky friends" phenomenon?), and thus those who acquire such friends at younger ages (greater priority) tend to have longer histories of delinquent friendships (greater duration). Hence the two elements cannot be regarded as entirely independent components of Differential Association. Further analysis by Warr indicated that duration has a substantial and statistically significant effect on delinquency. The effect of priority was also significant for three of the four offenses he examined, but in all four cases, the effect was *negative*, with *recent* rather than early exposure having the greatest effect on delinquency. That is, one's *current* friends appear to be more influential than one's friends at earlier ages. This is exactly the opposite of Sutherland's prediction, although it is quite consistent with social learning theory (see below).

There is another aspect of Sutherland's theory that has consistently failed to receive support from research. Recall that Sutherland argued that individuals become delinquent because they acquire "definitions" (or attitudes) favorable to the violation of law through differential association. In essence, Sutherland was arguing that delinquency is the result of attitude transference, whereby the attitudes of one individual are adopted or absorbed by another. A number of studies over the last three decades, however, have consistently indicated that attitude transference is *not* the process by which differential association operates. For example, after noting that behavior and attitudes are not always consistent, Warr and Stafford reported that the effect of friends' attitudes on adolescents is small in comparison to that of friends' *behavior*, and the effect of friends' behavior is largely direct, meaning that it does not operate through changing attitudes. Consequently, it seems that adolescents are much more sensitive to the behavior of their friends than their attitudes.

A. Social Learning Theory

In 1966, Robert Burgess and Ronald Akers published an important paper in which they restated Sutherland's theory of differential association in the terminology of operant conditioning, a rapidly developing branch of behavioral psychology associated with B. F. Skinner that emphasized the relation between behavior and reinforcement (see Akers and Sellers' Chapter 14 in this volume). In the intervening years, Akers has devoted his career to developing and testing a social learning approach to the explanation of crime, an approach that, like operant conditioning, emphasizes the role of reinforcement (both positive and negative) in criminal behavior:

> Whether individuals will refrain from or initiate, continue committing, or desist from criminal and deviant acts depends on the relative frequency, amount, and probability of past, present, and anticipated rewards and punishments perceived to be attached to the behavior. (Akers 1998, p. 66)

Social learning theory benefits from and builds upon the enormous theoretical and empirical development that took place in behavioral psychology during the second half of the twentieth century. As its name implies, what most distinguishes social learning theory from other learning theories is its sensitivity to the *social* sources of reinforcement in everyday life. Capitalizing on the work of Albert Bandura, Akers, and others, social learning theory emphasizes interpersonal mechanisms of learning, such as imitation (modeling or mimicking the behavior of others) and vicarious reinforcement (observing how other people's behavior is rewarded), as well as direct reinforcement, in the acquisition of behaviors. Thus, an adolescent may adopt the delinquent behavior of his friends (e.g., smoking, theft, drug sales) through imitation, because he observes the adult status it confers on them in the eyes of others his age (vicarious reinforcement), because it brings rewards like sexual attractiveness and money (direct reinforcement), and because participating in those activities gains him the admiration and respect of his friends (direct reinforcement). This example is a bit of an oversimplification, because social learning theory focuses on the precise schedules, quantities, and probabilities of both reward and punishment, which can act in complex ways. But it suffices to illustrate the theory.

The empirical evidence supporting social learning theory is extensive and impressive. However, it is disproportionately concentrated on tobacco, alcohol, and other drug use, and on relatively minor forms of deviance (e.g., cheating). The evidence for the theory, consequently, can best be described as positive and promising, but as yet somewhat limited in scope.

B. Companions in Crime

In a book entitled *Companions in Crime* (2002), Mark Warr identified a number of possible mechanisms of peer influence. What follows is a brief description of some of those mechanisms.

1. *Fear of Ridicule*

Ridicule is an expression of contempt or derision for the actions, beliefs, or features of another. Although it is often expressed verbally, ridicule may be conveyed through facial expressions, gestures, laughter, or through writing (including twittering, texting, and the like). Often, to ridicule another is to call into question his or her fitness for membership in a group (a family, a club, a gang, a clique of friends).

Fear of ridicule can lead adolescents (and sometimes adults) to join others in behavior that they would never engage in if they were alone, behavior they might find morally repugnant and even dangerous. Beyth-Marom and colleagues (1993), for example, asked adult and adolescent subjects to list possible consequences of either accepting or declining to engage in risky behaviors (e.g., smoking marijuana, drinking and driving). The reaction of peers was the most frequently cited consequence (mentioned by 80 to 100% of respondents across situations) of *rejecting* a risky behavior (e.g., "They'll laugh at me"), but was much less salient as a reason for *performing* the behavior ("They'll like me"). Avoiding ridicule, it seems, is a stronger motivation for deviance than a desire to ingratiate.

For adolescents, the sting of ridicule is heightened by the fear of rejection that plagues so many youth and the enormous importance that adolescents place on peer acceptance. It is through peers that young persons first establish an identity independent of their family of origin, an identity whose very existence ultimately rests in the hands of *other* people. By risking ridicule, adolescents are in effect risking their very identity, a prospect that few would wish to entertain. If maintaining that identity entails an occasional foray onto the other side of the law to avoid peer rejection, it may seem a small price to pay to maintain such a valuable possession.

In the modern world, ridicule is often communicated by adolescents via text messaging, e-mail, cell phones, and other electronic media, and these communications sometime have the added feature of being anonymous, hiding not only the source of the message(s) but the number of people behind them. Such messages can be especially disturbing to recipients because they imply organized and widespread disapproval by others. The expansion of modern peer relations onto the Internet and other electronic media, and the capacity for instantaneous and spatially unrestricted communication, are part of what Warr has dubbed the advent of the "virtual peer group."

2. *Loyalty*

Loyalty is a virtue and an element of friendship that is readily appreciated by most people. To remain steadfast to a friend when there are strong pressures to defect is a cultural motif as old as the Last Supper. When asked to define friendship, adolescents typically cite loyalty—along with intimacy—as the principal features of genuine friendship. Adolescent friendships, after all, are *formative* friendships, the first tentative efforts to define an identity outside the family, an identity that may be of enormous importance to a young person emerging into a new phase of life and a new social world, and an identity whose very newness makes it precious and fragile.

When it comes to delinquency, loyalty means more than simply not "ratting" on one's friends, although that is certainly important (see Matza 1964). It often means engaging in risky or illegal behavior in which one would not otherwise participate in order to preserve a friendship or a reputation. Loyalty can be a potent means of demonstrating friendship, and sharing risky behavior provides an excellent opportunity to prove one's loyalty and seal a friendship. In a study using national survey data from young people, Warr (1993a) found that adolescents were more likely than other age groups to say that they would lie to the police to protect their friends.

Loyalty also provides a form of *moral cover* for illegal conduct. It invokes a moral imperative that supersedes or nullifies the moral gravity of the criminal offense. Yes, I took part in the robbery, but I did so out of loyalty to Sonny, who would have done the same for me. As a universally recognized virtue, loyalty imparts legitimacy to otherwise illegitimate acts and confers honor on the dishonorable.

3. *Status*

The term "status" denotes prestige or respect within a group. Like other primates, human beings generally seek and enjoy status. Savin-Williams (1980), for example, found that young males randomly assigned to a summer camp cabin formed a stable dominance hierarchy within hours after meeting, and that contests over status declined rapidly once that hierarchy was established. Other research corroborates the claim that status hierarchies form rapidly in human groups, and it appears that one of the primary objectives of people when participating in groups is to avoid status loss.

In one of the earliest and most influential efforts to understand gang delinquency, Short and Strodtbeck (1965) provided numerous accounts of how gang members in Chicago sought to acquire status in the gang or fend off threats to their existing status. For example, a gang leader who had been away in detention for some time reestablished his status upon returning to the gang by intentionally provoking a fight with members of a rival gang. In another instance, an influential gang member, after losing a prestigious pool tournament to another clique of the gang, robbed and assaulted a stranger along with some of his team members. The offense seemed to defy any economic or other explanation at the time, but because robbery was a source of status within the gang, Short and Strodtbeck concluded that the action was an attempt to reassert status in the gang.

The importance of status in explaining delinquency can only be appreciated by realizing how precious and fragile a commodity status is among adolescents. Industrial societies deny adult status and its perquisites to adolescents until long after physical maturation has occurred, creating what Moffitt (1993) has called a "maturity gap" that persists for years. For many adolescents, the only potential source of status in their lives lies in the world of their age-peers, and the use of violence or other forms of delinquency to attain or maintain that status may appear well worth the potential costs.

If adolescence carries with it a general problem of status deficiency, imagine what it means to be an adolescent *and* a member of a minority group *and* to live in an economically depressed area. That is the social world described so eloquently and chillingly by Elijah Anderson in his book *Code Of the Street* (1999), an account of the social rules of the ghetto. In the inner city world he describes, where status is virtually the only possession that many young persons can claim, there is no greater affront than "dissing" (disrespecting) another, especially in front of others, and the penalty for doing so is often immediate injury, sometimes death. Even the most subtle signs of disrespect (e.g., staring) can produce savage results. This helps to explain why homicides and assaults are so often provoked by seemingly trivial matters (e.g., an argument over a small amount of money, or cutting into a line).

4. *Other Mechanisms of Peer Influence*

In addition to the foregoing, Warr identified several other mechanisms of peer influence. These include the relief from *boredom* that peers often supply for adolescents, the role of *drugs* in encouraging youth to hang together and engage in deviance, a reliance on peers for *protection* in environments that are dangerous (e.g., schools or neighborhoods where violence is ubiquitous), the sense of *anonymity* that groups afford, and the *moral codes* that groups often establish.

Some of Warr's mechanisms, it should be noted, can be logically subsumed under social learning theory. For example, status is a nearly universal reinforcer for humans, just as ridicule is a negative reinforcer (or punishment). Viewed this way, much of Warr's work can be seen as adding greater specificity or detail to the general principles of social learning theory.

VII. Peer Influence and Other Etiological Theories

Even if one concedes that peer influence is important for explaining criminal conduct, it does not mean that peers answer all questions about crime, or that other etiological theories can simply be disregarded. In fact, peer influence can be usefully integrated with a number of major theories of crime and delinquency. For example, Hirschi's (1969) famous control theory of delinquency emphasizes the damaged bond between delinquent youth and their parents. As it happens, youth with weak parental attachment are exactly those most like to acquire delinquent friends, leading Elliott, Huizinga, and Ageton (1985) and many others to integrate control theory with peer-oriented explanations of crime. Similarly, recent evidence indicates that adolescents with low self-control attract delinquent friends, and self-control is the heart of Gottfredson and Hirschi's *General Theory of Crime* (1990). Peers are also important to modern deterrence theory (e.g., Warr and Stafford 1991) because they provide information to potential offenders on the legal and extralegal risks associated with criminal behavior. In Robert Agnew's Revised Strain Theory (Agnew and White 1992), peers are themselves a potential *source* of strain—harassment, cruelty, disloyalty, and so on. Peers, then, figure in important ways in many theories of delinquency.

VIII. Peers and Juvenile Justice

Some approaches to juvenile justice policy attempt to capitalize on the collective nature of delinquency. Modern "peer courts," for example, are designed to expose delinquent youth to peers who do *not* condone delinquent behavior in an attempt to counteract more supportive or tolerant peers. Taking a different tack, some judges try to isolate law-breaking adolescents from their network of friends through no-contact orders or, more traditionally, by sentencing youth to military service. In a study notable for its prescience, Empey and Erickson (1972) found that youth who received counseling in a peer-group context were less likely to recidivate than those who received individual counseling.

Many preventive programs or policies also acknowledge the peer group context of delinquency. For example, after-school and summertime recreational programs for adolescents often are designed to provide an alternative to hanging out with the "wrong crowd." Likewise, parents frequently encourage their children to participate in sports, scouting, or church activities on the grounds that their children will make friends with "good kids." Parents themselves are often urged to supervise their children closely and to pay special attention to those with whom they spend their time.

Do such programs or policies work? Not necessarily, though for reasons that are not always obvious. For example, parents of high school students sometimes encourage their children to get jobs in order to fill their time and keep them away from the wrong kinds of kids. However, employment is *positively* correlated with delinquency among adolescents, and one of the reasons seems to be that adolescents often work in settings where they associate with many of their age-peers and have little or no adult supervision (Ploeger 1997).

Still, there are reasons to believe that regulating exposure to peers can be an effective strategy for delinquency prevention. Warr (1993b) found that adolescents who reported spending much of their time each week with the family had low rates of delinquency *even when they had delinquent friends*. This finding strongly suggests that the family is ultimately capable of counteracting or overcoming peer influence. This may be true merely because spending time with the family limits opportunities to engage in delinquency, but the effect remains the same. In addition, research consistently indicates (see Warr 1993b) that adolescents who are close to their parents are less likely to report having any delinquent friends in the first place. This may occur because their parents monitor their friendships or because such children do not want to displease their parents; but in either case, the point is that parents can reduce the chances that their children will have delinquent friends by remaining emotionally close to their children. Where this proves difficult or impossible to achieve, prohibiting or minimizing contact with delinquent friends ought to be an effective means of delinquency control. At the same time, however, parents who are *overly* restrictive can push their children toward delinquent peers and exacerbate the very problem they seek to avoid (Fuligni and Eccles 1993).

The fundamental dilemma facing parents and legal officials, of course, is that although peer associations carry the risk of delinquency, acquiring friends and achieving intimacy with age-mates is an essential and healthy part of adolescence, and depriving youths of time with their friends may have serious long-term consequences. Moreover, spotting "bad" kids among a child's friends is not always an easy task, and even hanging out with "good" kids can on occasion lead to inappropriate conduct.

IX. Conclusion

Delinquent behavior is predominantly social behavior. Most youthful offenders have accomplices when they violate the law, and most also have delinquent friends who may or may not be accomplices during any given delinquent event. The social character of delinquency, as we have seen, is the foundation for several etiological theories of delinquency, and a component of others.

To critics, however, this evidence remains unpersuasive. Yes, they argue, delinquent youth have accomplices in delinquency, but they have "accomplices" in almost everything they do—dating, sports, driving, or just hanging out. Yes, delinquent youth have delinquent friends, but this is merely homophily, not evidence of peer influence. Some critics even doubt the companionate nature of delinquency itself, arguing that it is merely an artifact of the way criminologists measure crime.

All of these arguments have been countered with empirical evidence by proponents of peer influence, but the search for answers about the social aspects of delinquency remains one of the most vital areas of research in contemporary criminology and one of the most important intellectual challenges for the discipline. If the criminal careers of offenders are indeed interdependent, then studying offenders in isolation, abstracted from their social networks, makes about as much sense as studying only one partner in a marriage, one member of a crowd, or one party to a contract. It can be done, but it surely misses the point.

REFERENCES

Agnew, Robert. 1991. "A Longitudinal Test of Social Control Theory and Delinquency." *Journal of Research in Crime and Delinquency* 28: 126–56.

Agnew, Robert, and Helene Raskin White. 1992. "An Empirical Test of a General Strain Theory." *Criminology* 30: 475–99.

Akers, Ronald L. 1998. *Social Learning and Social Structure: A General Theory of Crime and Deviance*. Boston: Northeastern University Press.

Anderson, Elijah. 1999. Code of the Street: Decency, Violence, and the Moral Life of the Inner City. New York: Norton.

———. 1999. *Code of the Street: Decency, Violence, and the Moral Life of the Inner City*. New York: Norton.

Aseltine, Robert H., Jr. 1995. "A Reconsideration of Parental and Peer Influences on Adolescent Deviance." *Journal of Health and Social Behavior* 36: 103–21.

Beyth-Marom, Ruth, Laurel Austin, Baruch Fischhoff, Claire Palmgren, and Marilyn Jacobs-Quadrel. 1993. "Perceived Consequences of Risky Behaviors: Adults and Adolescents." *Developmental Psychology* 29: 549–63.

Briar, Scott, and Irving Piliavin. 1965. "Delinquency, Situational Inducements, and Commitment to Conformity." *Social Problems* 13: 35–45.

Burgess, Robert L. and Ronald L. Akers. 1966. "A Differential Association–Reinforcement Theory of Criminal Behavior." *Social Problems* 14: 128–47.

Burkett, Steven R., and Bruce O. Warren. 1987. "Religiosity, Peer Influence, and Adolescent Marijuana Use: A Panel Study of Underlying Causal Structures." *Criminology* 25: 109–31.

Cairns, Robert B., and Beverly D. Cairns. 1994. *Lifelines and Risks: Pathways of Youth in Our Time*. Cambridge: Cambridge University Press.

Chen, Li-Hui, Susan P. Baker, Elisa R. Braver, and Guohua Li. 2000. "Carrying Passengers as a Risk Factor for Crashes Fatal to 16- and 17-Year-Old Drivers." *Journal of the American Medical Association* 283: 1578–82.

Cohen, Geoffrey L., and Mitchell J. Prinstein. 2006. "Peer Contagion of Aggression and Health Risk Behavior among Adolescent Males: An Experimental Investigation of Effects on Public Conduct and Private Attitudes." *Child Development* 77: 967–83.

Elliott, Delbert S., David Huizinga, and Suzanne S. Ageton. 1985. *Explaining Delinquency and Drug Use*. Newbury Park, CA: Sage.

Elliott, Delbert S., and Scott Menard. 1996. "Delinquent Friends and Delinquent Behavior: Temporal and Developmental Patterns." In *Delinquency and Crime: Current Theories*, edited by J. David Hawkins. Cambridge: Cambridge University Press.

Empey, Lamar T., and Maynard L. Erickson. 1972. *The Provo Experiment: Evaluating Community Control of Delinquency*. Lexington, MA.: Lexington.

Erez, Edna. 1987. "Situational or Planned Crime and the Criminal Career." In *From Boy to Man, from Delinquency to Crime*, edited by Marvin F. Wolfgang, Terence P. Thornberry, and Robert M. Figlio. Chicago: University of Chicago Press.

Erickson, Maynard L. 1971. "The Group Context of Delinquent Behavior." *Social Problems* 19: 114–29.

Erickson, Maynard L., and Lamar T. Empey. 1965. "Class Position, Peers, and Delinquency." *Sociology and Social Research* 49: 268–82.

Erickson, Maynard L., and Gary F. Jensen. 1977. "Delinquency Is Still Group Behavior!: Toward Revitalizing the Group Premise in the Sociology of Deviance." *Journal of Criminal Law and Criminology* 68: 262–73.

Fergusson, David M., and L. John Horwood. 1996. "The Role of Adolescent Peer Affiliations in the Continuity between Childhood Behavioral Adjustment and Juvenile Offending." *Journal of Abnormal Child Psychology* 24: 205–21.

Fowler, J. H., and N. A. Christakis. 2008. "Dynamic Spread of Happiness in a Large Social Network: Longitudinal Analysis of the Framingham Heart Study Social Network." *British Medical Journal* 337: 2338–47.

Fuligni, Andrew J., and Jacquelynne S. Eccles. 1993. "Perceived Parent-Child Relationships and Early Adolescents' Orientation toward Peers." *Developmental Psychology* 29: 622–32.

Gardner, Margo, and Laurence Steinberg. 2005. "Peer Influence on Risk Taking, Risk Preference, and Risky Decision Making in Adolescence and Adulthood: An Experimental Study." *Developmental Psychology* 41: 625–35.

Glueck, Sheldon, and Eleanor Glueck. 1950. *Unraveling Juvenile Delinquency*. Cambridge, MA: Harvard University Press.

Gold, Martin. 1970. *Delinquent Behavior in an American City*. Belmont, CA.: Brooks/Cole.

Gottfredson, Michael R., and Travis Hirschi. 1990. *A General Theory of Crime*. Stanford, CA: Stanford University Press.

Haynie, Dana L. 2001. "Delinquent Peers Revisited: Does Network Structure Matter?" *American Journal of Sociology* 106: 1013–57.

Hepburn, John R. 1977. "Testing Alternative Models of Delinquency Causation." *Journal of Criminal Law and Criminology* 67: 450–60.

Hirschi, Travis. 1969. *Causes of Delinquency*. Berkeley: University of California Press.

Hood, Roger, and Richard Sparks. 1970. *Key Issues in Criminology*. New York: McGraw-Hill.

Kandel, Denise B. 1978. "Homophily, Selection, and Socialization in Adolescent Friendships." *American Journal of Sociology* 84: 427–36.

Klein, Malcolm W. 1969. "On the Group Context of Delinquency." *Sociology and Social Research* 54: 63–71.

Klein, Malcolm W., and Lois Y. Crawford. 1967. "Groups, Gangs, and Cohesiveness." *Journal of Research in Crime and Delinquency* 4: 63–75.

Kornhauser, Ruth R. 1978. *Social Sources of Delinquency: An Appraisal of Analytic Models*. Chicago: University of Chicago Press.

Kremer, Michael, and Dan Levy. 2008. "Peer Effects and Alcohol Use among College Students." *Journal of Economic Perspectives* 22: 189–206.

Krohn, Marvin D., Alan J. Lizotte, Terence P. Thornberry, Carolyn Smith, and David McDowall. 1996. "Reciprocal Causal Relationships among Drug Use, Peers, and Beliefs: A Five-Wave Panel Model." *Journal of Drug Issues* 26: 405–28.

Matsueda, Ross L., and Kathleen Anderson. 1998. "The Dynamics of Delinquent Peers and Delinquent Behavior." *Criminology* 36: 269–308.

Matza, David. 1964. *Delinquency and Drift*. New York: Wiley.

McGloin, Jean. 2009. "Delinquency Balance: Revisiting Peer Influence." *Criminology* 47: 439–78.

Meier, Robert F., Steven R. Burkett, and Carol A. Hickman. 1984. "Sanctions, Peers, and Deviance: Preliminary Models of a Social Control Process." *Sociological Quarterly* 25: 67–82.

Miller, Walter B. 1974. "American Youth Gangs: Past and Present." In *Current Perspectives on Criminal Behavior*, edited by Abraham S. Blumberg. New York: Knopf.

Moffitt, Terrie. 1993. "Adolescence-Limited and Life-Course-Persistent Behavior: A Developmental Taxonomy." *Psychological Review* 100: 674–701.

Morash, Merry. 1983. "Gangs, Groups, and Delinquency." *British Journal of Criminology* 23: 309–31.

Paternoster, Raymond. 1988. "Examining Three-Wave Deterrence Models: A Question of Temporal Order and Specification." *Journal of Criminal Law and Criminology* 79: 135–79.

Ploeger, Matthew. 1997. "Youth Employment and Delinquency: Reconsidering a Problematic Relationship." *Criminology* 35: 659–75.

Reed, Mark D., and Pamela Wilcox Rountree. 1997. "Peer Pressure and Adolescent Substance Use." *Journal of Quantitative Criminology* 13: 143–80.

Reiss, Albert J., Jr. 1986. "Co-Offender Influences on Criminal Careers." In *Criminal Careers and "Career Criminals,"* edited by Alfred Blumstein, Jacqueline Cohen, Jeffrey Roth, and Christy Visher. Washington, DC: National Academy Press.

Reiss, Albert J., Jr., and David P. Farrington. 1991. "Advancing Knowledge about Co-Offending: Results from a Prospective Longitudinal Survey of London Males." *Journal of Criminal Law and Criminology* 82: 360–95.

Reiss, Albert J., Jr., and A. Lewis Rhodes. 1964. "An Empirical Test of Differential Association Theory." *Journal of Research in Crime and Delinquency* 1: 5–18.

Sarnecki, Jerzy. 1986. *Delinquent Networks*. Stockholm: National Council for Crime Prevention.

———. 2001. *Delinquent Networks: Youth Co-Offending in Stockholm*. Cambridge: Cambridge University Press.

Savin-Williams, Richard C. 1980. "An Ethological Study of Dominance Formation and Maintenance in a Group of Human Adolescents." In *Adolescent Behavior and Society: A Book of Readings*, edited by Rolf E. Muuss, 3rd ed. New York: Random House.

Shannon, Lyle W. 1991. *Changing Patterns of Delinquency and Crime: A Longitudinal Study in Racine*. Boulder: Westview Press.

Shaw, Clifford T., and Henry D. McKay. 1931. *Report on the Causes of Crime*. Vol. II. Washington, DC: U.S. Government Printing Office.

Short, James F., and Fred L. Strodtbeck. 1965. *Group Process and Gang Delinquency*. Chicago: University of Chicago Press.

Simons, Ronald L., Chyi-In Wu, Rand D. Conger, and Frederick O. Lorenz. 1994. "Two Routes to Delinquency: Differences between Early and Late Starters in the Impact of Parenting and Deviant Peers." *Criminology* 32: 247–75.

Stafford, Mark C. 1984. "Gang Delinquency." In *Major Forms of Crime*, edited by Robert F. Meier. Beverly Hills: Sage.

———. 1939. *Principles of Criminology*, 3rd ed. Chicago: J. B. Lippincott.

———. 1947. *Principles of Criminology*, 4th ed. Chicago: J. B. Lippincott.

Thornberry, Terence P. 1987. "Toward an Interactional Theory of Delinquency." *Criminology* 25: 863–91.

Thornberry, Terence P., Alan J. Lizotte, Marvin D. Krohn, Margaret Farnworth, and Sung Joon Jang. 1994. "Delinquent Peers, Beliefs, and Delinquent Behavior: A Longitudinal Test of Interactional Theory." *Criminology* 32: 47–84.

Warr, Mark. 1993a. "Age, Peers, and Delinquency." *Criminology* 31: 17–40.

———. 1993b. "Parents, Peers, and Delinquency." *Social Forces* 72: 247–64.

———. 1996. "Organization and Instigation in Delinquent Groups." *Criminology* 34: 11–37.

———. 2002. *Companions in Crime: The Social Aspects of Criminal Conduct*. Cambridge, England: Cambridge University Press.

———. 2007. "The Tangled Web: Delinquency, Deception, and Parental Attachment." *Journal of Youth and Adolescence* 36: 607–22.

Warr, Mark, and Mark C. Stafford, 1991. "The Influence of Delinquent Peers: What They Think or What They Do?" *Criminology* 29: 851–66.

Yablonsky, Lewis. 1959. "The Delinquent Gang as a Near-Group." *Social Problems* 7: 108–17.

CHAPTER 11

....

GANG DELINQUENCY

....

CHERYL L. MAXSON AND
KRISTY N. MATSUDA

A long line of research confirms that having delinquent peers is a strong negative influence on youth and that co-offending is a hallmark of juvenile offending patterns (see Warr, *supra* Chapter 10). Streets gangs certainly are a form of delinquent peer group. Are street gangs simply an extreme form of a deviant peer group, or are the structure and process of these groups fundamentally different? The effects of gang membership appear to supersede the impact of delinquent friends on a youth's offending profile. Youth who participate in street gangs commit a lot of crime—far more crime than other young people who reside in the same neighborhoods and attend the same schools. Moreover, gang members are more likely to be crime victims than other youth. The experience of gang involvement—and the attendant effects on offending and victimization—is more than just an extreme case of delinquent youth groups.

Gangs are *qualitatively* different than other youth groups, and the group processes and dynamics that make them so have long engaged gang scholars. While gangs are typically less well organized and structured than often presented, they are somewhat more structured than other delinquent groups. Certainly, the dynamics of status, and to some degree loyalty, that Mark Warr presents as mechanisms of peer influence play an important role in gang interactions. However, a strong group identity or orientation toward crime and violence seems to particularly distinguish gangs from other law-violating groups. This orientation involves much talk among gang members about criminal exploits, past and future. Malcolm Klein (1995, p. 30) emphasizes the significance of this criminal orientation:

> It is important, therefore, to emphasize the notion of orientation to crime....At some point, the gang-to-be starts to think of itself as a gang, a group set apart from others. My contention is that this self-recognition is based principally, although not solely, on the group's collective criminal or delinquent

orientation. Very often, part of the process is an acceptance of intergroup, now intergang, rivalries and hostilities.

Klein argues that the evolution of this criminal orientation becomes the "tipping point" that distinguishes a gang from other law-violating groups. Scott Decker (1996; and Decker and Van Winkle 1996) places even stronger emphasis on gang identity revolving around aspects of violence. The role of violence in the attribution of status within the gang, the fostering of gang rivalries, and the defense of territory and identity is critical in understanding the nature of gang social interactions and identity. In fact, this group identity as one, wherein it is acceptable, even admirable, to engage in crime and violence, is an element of a formal definition of gangs recently adopted by an international network of gang researchers, as we will describe shortly.

In the next section, we will continue the discussion of different approaches to defining gangs, including the conceptual and methodological difficulties of measuring gang membership and gang crime and delinquency. We then provide a brief history of gangs that sets the stage for the following section on gang prevalence, joining, and group processes. Later sections focus on trends in gang crime, the individual offending patterns of gang members, and what is known about differential crime patterns in various types of gangs. Thus the unit of analysis is sometimes the individual with gang experience, and other times, the gang group is the focus. We conclude the chapter with a discussion of current approaches to gang prevention, intervention, and control.

For these descriptions, we'll draw from both law enforcement and research studies, relying primarily on information produced in the past two decades. The scope of this chapter reflects the emphasis of existing research in several ways. We focus more on offending than on victimization, but report the latter trends when they are available. Most data on gang offending derives from the United States, but recent interest by European scholars has produced new accounts of gang activity in Europe, particularly in the United Kingdom and the Netherlands. While this volume concentrates on juveniles and responses to delinquency, many gang studies incorporate young adult members as well. Finally, we limit the scope of our inquiry to *street* gangs. While we argue that gangs are a qualitatively different form of delinquent groups, we also note that street gangs are one form among a variety of criminally oriented groups composed primarily of adults. Adult-organized crime groups like La Cosa Nostra, motorcycle gangs like the Hell's Angels, drug cartels, and terrorist groups may offer interesting contrasts to street gangs, but such a discussion is beyond the scope of this chapter.

I. Issues in Definitions of Gangs, Gang Members, and Gang Crime

Gang research has historically suffered from the lack of consensus on definitions of gang, gang membership, and gang crime (Klein 1995; Klein et al. 2001). This has, in turn, limited the generalizability and comparability of research findings. The term "gang" has been used to describe organized crime, motorcycle groups, subversive prison groups, tagging crews, drug distributers, and hate groups. Each of these groups is, in many ways, fundamentally different than the street gang that is the focus of this chapter. The challenge for street gang scholars has been to define gangs with enough detail to be able to distinguish gangs from other social groups (prosocial and criminal), yet still capture a range of organizational structures and behavior. Researchers have been reluctant to agree on the qualities that are necessary and sufficient to define gangs.

Numerous definitions have been proffered during the past eight decades of gang research (e.g., Thrasher 1927; Klein 1971; Miller 1980; National Gang Center 1998; Klein et al. 2001). Most definitions of gangs include group involvement in illegal activity, which distinguishes gangs from prosocial groups. Gang members' involvement in crime makes them of primary concern for citizens and law enforcement, and yet some researchers argue that crime should not be a defining element of gangs (Short 2006). Most previous definitions of street gangs also include an acknowledgement of primarily youth involvement. By and large, street gangs are not adult-run enterprises. This quality distinguishes street gangs from most organized crime, motorcycle groups, drug distribution groups, and hate groups. Definitions have differed in their inclusion of other characteristics, such as the presence of leadership, territoriality, organization, continuity/durability, signs/symbols, and a group name.

To complicate matters, there is even more variation when taking an international perspective. There is a global street gang presence. However, the qualities and characteristics of stereotypical American gangs are rarely recognized in other countries, likely due to misperceptions of "typical" American street gangs (Klein et al. 2001). Cross-national comparisons could not be made without a unifying definition. Could a gang definition be created that would be specific enough to describe a street gang, yet broad enough to encompass gangs across the United States and abroad? Over one hundred American and European researchers and gang policy makers worked for almost a decade to reach consensus on a gang definition (Eurogang Project 2010). Their effort, the Eurogang definition, has resulted in a gang description that can be applied globally: *A street gang is any durable, street-oriented youth group whose involvement in illegal activity is part of its group identity.* Additional information like ethnicity or gender composition, group markers (e.g., name, tattoos, hand signs, colors), and/or organization structure are considered potential "descriptors," but not "definers" of the group.

Researchers often define gang membership by self-report, that is, by responses to a simple question such as "Are you currently [or have you ever been] a member of a street gang?" Sometimes follow-up questions about group delinquency, names, or other characteristics are used to narrow down group membership. Because the "gang" terminology is less recognized outside the United States and can trigger inaccurate stereotypes of organized, violent gangsters (Klein et al. 2001), Eurogang researchers have developed a series of questions that capture the elements of the Eurogang definition (i.e., group duration, age, street orientation, territoriality, and crime orientation within the group) as a supplemental approach to asking the direct question.

Law enforcement personnel approach defining gangs and gang members in a different way. In recent years, many states have included sentencing enhancements to individuals designated to be gang members. Since these designations increasingly have to withstand court challenge, law enforcement has had to establish and train officers on the criteria required to enter an individual into gang databases used to store evidence of gang membership. These criteria often include self-identification, but also identification by informants, associating with known gang members, and gang indicators such as tattoos and costume. In their recent review of statutory codes about gangs, Barrows and Huff (2009) note that states rarely include definitions of gang members in statutes, and just two states, Arizona and New Jersey, employ the same definition. Forty-one states and the District of Columbia define a gang, and these codes vary as to how many people must constitute the group, whether a common name or symbols are required, and whether there must be identifiable leadership, although all include criminal activity as an element.

In summary, even law enforcement and legislators have failed to reach a consensus about what constitutes a gang and who should be designated a gang member. Similarly, there is ongoing debate among researchers regarding best practices for making these determinations. As we shall show below, this lack of uniformity about definitions makes describing the scope of gangs and gang members quite difficult. Moreover, our understanding of the volume and nature of gang crime is complicated by the diversity in both law enforcement and research definitions of gangs and gang members. Even if we could achieve perfect agreement on gang and membership criteria, accurate depictions of the volume of gang crime would still be obscured by different definitional approaches. Gang crime is variously understood as crimes committed by gang members and as crimes committed to further the ends of the gang. The definitional issues clearly challenge a broad depiction of gangs and gang delinquency, but in the sections to follow, we summarize what is known based on these variegated definitional approaches.

II. The History of the Criminal Street Gang

Street gangs have been present in the United States since at least the late 1800s (Curry and Decker 2003). The function of a gang is, generally, to provide a sense of belonging and affiliation to its members. Most people find this kind of support from other groups like family or community. It is not surprising then that individuals from economically and socially marginalized categories are disproportionately involved in gangs and that gangs appear to emerge at times of great social instability (Spergel 1990). The first wave of gangs in the United States appeared in major eastern cities (e.g., New York, Boston, Chicago). The street gangs of the late 1800s and early 1900s were generally composed of recent immigrants to the country (e.g., Italian and Irish), and were most often disorganized groups that committed crimes and protected their "turf." Gangs of this era eventually dissolved likely due to law enforcement response or intervention by social service agencies (Curry and Decker 2003).

Gangs that emerged in the 1960s were more heavily populated with African American and Hispanic minorities, but similarly marginalized youth. Weapon use evolved from fists, bats, and knives to firearms. Gang members became more mobile, and motor vehicles permitted easy incursion into rival territories. Some scholars believe that the expansion of incarceration contributed to the growth of violent gangs, as prisons became an effective training ground for gang recruitment and transmission of gang culture (Curry and Decker 2003). Cities like Los Angeles and Chicago were particularly affected by the prison boom, which may have influenced the gang proliferation in those cities.

In the late 1980s and early 1990s, violent gang crime (like violent juvenile crime in general) garnered national attention. Much of this attention was—and continues to be—focused on the gang problem in California. California has the most cities with a gang presence as compared to all other states (Illinois is second) (W. Miller 2001). In particular, Los Angeles has been considered an epicenter for street gang activity. As we describe below, most gangs are not highly structured, organized, or even durable, however, Los Angeles and Chicago may be more likely to be an exception to this rule (Maxson and Klein 2002). These cities have a longer history of gangs, and therefore may be more likely to have gangs that endure across generations and evidence higher levels of organization than groups in other places (Spergel 1990). To frame the impact of the Los Angeles and Chicago gang problem, in 2001 50% of all of the gang homicides reported by cities with over 100,000 residents or more came from these two cities (Egley, Howell, and Major 2006, p. v).

In previous decades, it may have been accurate to say that street gangs were an urban or big-city problem. This is no longer the case as we will discuss in the following section. Gangs are found in every state in the United States. They are found in big cities and rural towns. They are in the United States and abroad. Perhaps most important, once a city has a gang presence, very rarely does the problem go away (Klein 1995).

III. Prevalence of Gangs and Gang Members

It is a challenge to gain insight into the national (or global) perspective on gangs. There are strong research studies that focus on a small number of gangs in a restricted number of cities. There are far fewer investigations that provide a national estimate of gang prevalence or characteristics. The National Youth Gang Center was created in 1995 and tasked with conducting a systematic survey of law enforcement agencies across the United States regarding the nature and extent of the American gang problem.[1] Each year the agency distributes a survey, the National Youth Gang Survey (NYGS), to all police departments that serve larger cities and all suburban county police and sheriff's departments. They also survey a randomly selected sample of police departments in smaller cities and rural counties. Though the definition is rather broad and subjective,[2] the NYGS data are a rare opportunity to get a national picture of gangs. In the 2007 NYGS, 34.8% of all jurisdictions reported a gang problem. The NYGS estimates the presence of 27,000 gangs and 788,000 gang members across the nation (Egley and O'Donnell 2009, p. 1). Gangs have a stronger presence in large cities. Ninety-nine percent of all agencies serving a population of 100,000 or more report gangs as do 86% of agencies with more than 50,000 residents. In addition, big cities have a greater number of individual gangs (i.e., the modal response is 30 or more), gang members (i.e., 1,000 or more), and a stable presence over time. Gangs are less often present in suburban counties (50%), smaller cities (35%) and rural counties (15%). Smaller jurisdictions that report gangs indicate a small number of gangs (typically, three or fewer) and gang members (i.e., 50 or fewer). The presence of gangs also fluctuates more from year to year in less populated areas (Egley and O'Donnell 2009, pp. 1–2).

How have these numbers changed over time? Since the 1996 survey, the proportion of jurisdictions reporting a gang presence decreased by almost half by 2001 (due largely to small cities and rural counties) and then increased gradually to the 35% figure in 2007, which is slightly less than the 40% figure in the first survey (Egley and O'Donnell 2009, pp. 1–2). Not surprisingly, the national estimates of gangs and gang members have also increased since 2002 (by 25.5% and 7.7%, respectively), following several years of decline. There are no comparable survey efforts on gang presence in other countries, so international estimates or trend analyses are not possible. However, studies of representative youth samples in some cities in Europe suggest that the rate of gang participation may be comparable to some places in the United States, as we describe below.

Prevalence of individual gang membership has been captured using self-report measures, most frequently in individual cities. Data from one nationally representative, longitudinal survey of youth found that by the age of 17, 8% of youths said they had been a member of a gang at some point (Snyder and Sickmund 2006, p. 70). Males were more likely to report gang membership than females (11% versus 6%). Members of racial/ethnic minorities were also more likely to have been affiliated with a gang (Black 12%, Hispanic 12%, and White 7%). Other prevalence estimates are most often provided in sample or site specific research studies. Klein and Maxson (2006, pp. 23–30) review nineteen studies from the last twenty years of gang research that offer prevalence estimates for various locations in the United States and Europe. They find that estimates of current membership in general populations are about 6–8%, while between 13 and 18% of high-risk (by area, sex, or ethnicity) youth are current gang members. Lifetime membership in high-risk populations can vary between 6% and 30%. The definitions and samples used seemed to account for more variation than location; two studies that employed comparable methods found similar gang prevalence rates in U.S. cities and the Netherlands (Esbensen and Weerman 2005) and between Denver and Breman, Germany (Huizinga and Schumann 2001).

The U.S. sample-specific studies reveal comparable demographic patterns of gang joiners to the national study: generally, males join gangs at a higher rate than females, and Black and Hispanic youth report being in gangs more often than White youth. European and Canadian samples also find that ethnic minority youth more often join gangs. While the age of the study samples sometimes are limited, Klein and Maxson (2006) conclude from their overview that the peak age of gang membership is 13 to 15 years old and then declines. Strikingly, these demographic patterns of who joins gangs contrast sharply with the depiction derived from law enforcement data. The NYGS periodically collects these data, most recently in 2007 for sex and in 2006 for age and race/ethnicity. According to law enforcement, only one-third of gang members are juveniles, just 10% are females, and 9% are white (National Gang Center 2009). David Curry (2000) has suggested that there may well be two different types of gang problems: older, male, and ethnic minority gang members most often captured in police data and younger, more diverse gender and race/ethnicity gang distributions that derive from research studies of youth.

IV. JOINING GANGS AND THE DYNAMICS OF GANG LIFE

The picture of gang life is far more complicated than is portrayed in the media (i.e., movies, television, music, news). While there are numerous rich, anecdotal accounts of specific gangs and gang members, these stories often draw attention because of their exceptional quality rather than their generalizability. A general answer about gang life is complicated because gangs vary in structure and composition, and gang members vary in their centrality to the group and their embeddedness in the group ideology.

There can be both environmental and individual factors associated with joining a gang. Our previous discussion highlighted the widespread presence of gangs across cities of different sizes, but within those cities, all areas are not created equal. Gangs are more prevalent in higher crime, disorganized neighborhoods (Short and Strodtbeck 1965; Vigil 1988). However, the research on the effect of residence in these neighborhoods and the likelihood of gang joining has been inconclusive (Klein and Maxson 2006). Even in neighborhoods with a strong gang presence, most youth— perhaps seven or eight out of every ten—do *not* join gangs. Klein and Maxson (2006) review the research on risk factors for gang joining, and they find that the previous twenty years of gang research has not generated many consistently supported risk factors of gang membership. Across numerous dimensions of inquiry (e.g., family, psychological, school, community), only a handful of factors consistently predicted gang membership: experiencing negative life events, engaging in nondelinquent problem behaviors (i.e., antisocial behavior, risk-taking, and impulsiveness), weak parental monitoring, having delinquent friends, and negative peer influences.

Some studies specifically ask gang members about the reasons they joined the gang. The modal response varies by study, but generally, family and/or friends in the gang, protection, neighborhood pride, and desire to engage in illegal activity are commonly offered reasons (e.g., Maxson, Whitlock, and Klein 1997; Decker and Curry 2000; Maxson and Whitlock 2002; Thornberry et al. 2003). In a qualitative study of gang girls, Jody Miller (2001) found that while many girls in the studied neighborhoods experienced neighborhood exposure to gangs, gang-involved family members, or problems within the family, gang-involved girls were more likely to experience most or all of these factors.

Street gangs vary tremendously in size, structure, and member characteristics. Perhaps the most salient feature of gang structure is the proclivity of groups to be segregated along racial/ethnic lines. Bloods and Crips, for example, are most often composed of Black youth. Latin Kings and Queens, in contrast, are generally Hispanic. There are exceptions to this rule, but generally, racial/ethnic homogeneity has been a hallmark of American street gangs.

There are all (or mostly) male, all (or mostly) female, and integrated male and females gangs (Miller 1975). Research suggests that the experience for females will vary significantly depending on the composition of the gang. Females in majority female gangs will experience leadership and planning roles. Females in largely male gangs may never be allowed a central role in the group (Klein 1995; J. Miller 2001).

There have been a variety of attempts to create typologies of gang forms or structures. Maxson and Klein (1995) found that gangs could be arrayed along six structural dimensions: duration, size, age range of members, subgroup or cliquing structures, territoriality and crime versatility. They described five gang types: Traditional, Neo-traditional, Compressed, Collective, and Specialty. Their surveys of police in several hundred gang cities suggested that most street gangs in the United States reflected one of these structural types and the typology worked with European gangs as well (Klein and Maxson 2006).

Two of the gang structures are highly visible in the popular media. As described by Klein and Maxson (2006, pp. 176–77):

> Traditional gangs have generally been in existence for twenty or more years—they keep regenerating themselves. They contain fairly clear subgroups, usually separated by age. O.G.s or Veteranos, Seniors, Juniors, Midgets and various other names are applied to these different age-based cliques. Sometimes the cliques are separated by neighborhoods rather than age. More than other gangs, Traditional gangs tend to have a wide age range, sometimes as wide as from nine or ten years of age into the thirties. These are usually very large gangs, numbering one hundred or even several hundred members. Almost always, they are territorial in the sense that they identify strongly with their turf, 'hood, or barrio,

and claim it as theirs alone. In sum, this is a large, enduring, territorial gang with a wide range and several internal cliques based on age or area.

Juxtapose the Traditional Gang with the Specialty Gang:

> Unlike these other gangs that engage in a wide variety of criminal offenses, crime in this type of group is narrowly focused on a few offenses; the group comes to be characterized by the specialty. The Specialty gang tends to be small—usually fifty or fewer members—without any subgroups in most cases (there are exceptions). It probably has a history of less than ten years, but has developed a well-defined territory. Its territory may be either residential or based on the opportunities for the particular form of crime in which it specialized. The age range of most Specialty gangs is narrow, but in others is broad. In sum, the Specialty gang is crime-focused in a narrow way. Its principal purpose is more criminal than social, and its smaller size and form of territoriality may be a reflection of this focused crime pattern (Klein and Maxson 2006, p. 178)

The Specialty and Traditional gang structures are near opposites of one another. Interestingly, they appear to be far less common than two other types (Klein and Maxson 2006, p. 177):

> The Neotraditional gang resembles the Traditional form, but has not been in existence as long—probably no more than ten years, and often less. It may be medium size—say fifty to one hundred members—or also into the hundreds. It probably has developed subgroups or cliques based on age or area, but sometimes may not. The age range is usually smaller than in the classical Traditional gangs. The Neotraditional gang is also very territorial, claiming turf and defending it. In sum, the Neotraditional gang is a newer territorial gang that looks on its way to becoming Traditional in time. Thus at this point it is subgrouping, but may or may not have achieved territoriality, and size suggests that it is evolving into the Traditional form.
>
>   The Compressed gang is small—usually in the size range of up to fifty members—and has not formed subgroups. The age range is probably narrow—ten or fewer years between the younger and older members. The small size, absence of subgroups, and narrow age range may reflect the newness of the group, in existence less than ten years and maybe for only a few years. Some of these Compressed gangs have become territorial, but many have not. In sum, Compressed gangs have a relatively short history, short enough that by size, duration, subgrouping and territoriality, it is unclear whether they will grow and solidify into the more traditional forms, or simply remain as less complex groups.

The least common and probably least stable structure is the Collective gang (Klein and Maxson 2006, p. 177):

> The Collective gang looks like the Compressed form, but bigger and with a wider age range—maybe ten or more years between younger and older members. Size can be under a hundred, but is probably larger. Surprisingly, given these numbers, it has not developed subgroups, and may or may not be a territorial gang. It probably has a ten to fifteen-year existence. In sum, the Collective gang resembles a kind of shapeless mass of adolescent and young adult members that has not developed the distinguishing characteristics of other gangs.

Notice that these structures are not defined by leadership styles, level of cohesion between members, or indicators of organization such as a gang name, regular meetings, rules of conduct that are enforced, and so on. These are characteristics that vary widely among different types of gangs and require more investigation before we fully understand gang organization.

A hallmark of gang activity, and one very important reason for the study of the groups, is criminal offending. It is an important dimension of the gang life and thus will be the subject of the next few segments of this chapter. We address overall trends in gang crime before turning to the individual offending profiles of gang members and the question of whether crime varies by the type of gang.

V. Gang Crime Trends

While it is appropriate to be cautious about the reliability and validity of police gang record-keeping practices, the NYGS indicates that more than half of law enforcement agencies that report gang problems have implemented procedures for regularly recording criminal offenses as "gang-related" (National Gang Center 2009). Recent reports from law enforcement officials suggest a national pattern of decreasing gang crime and violence. Less than half of agencies that had gang problems in 2007 indicated an increase in gang-related crime over 2006. Moreover, proportionally fewer agencies reported an annual increase in any of six specific crime types compared with 2006 (National Gang Center 2009).

Policy makers and scholars often look at the volume of gang homicides as an indicator of trends in violence, although these most serious incidents are relatively rare events. The NYGS reported the highest annual gang homicide number for survey respondents between 2002 and 2007. During this six-year period, agencies experiencing gang homicides most frequently reported an annual maximum of one or two incidents in their jurisdiction (National Gang Center 2009). Not surprisingly, larger cities (i.e., populations of 50,000 or more) have more homicides, but even among this group, less than 35% reported more than two gang homicides in any year between 2002 and 2007. Just one in five larger cities indicated that 2007 gang homicide levels were greater than in 2006 (Egley and O'Donnell 2009, p. 2).

Researchers have cautioned against extrapolating national trend data from annual homicide counts because a few gang centers such as the Los Angeles area and Chicago can overwhelm the estimates (Maxson, Curry, and Howell 2002, p. 125). For example, Los Angeles county law enforcement designated between seven hundred and eight hundred murders as gang-involved in each year of the first half of the 1990s, but annual figures plummeted to a modern-era low of about 350 homicides in 1999. Such a dramatic decrease would mask any increasing trend in other parts of the country if just annual national total homicides as reported to the NYGS were examined.

Tita and Abrahamse (2004, p. 5) provide a detailed analysis of the patterns of Los Angeles county gang homicide between 1981 and 2001 and compare these trends to gang homicide in the remainder of California. They note that during this period, the proportion of all homicides in Los Angeles that were thought to be gang-involved increased from 10% to nearly half of all homicides, but the proportions in the remainder of California were 4% in 1981 and 14% in 2001. In this study, the researchers took the law enforcement designation of "gang crime" at face value.

Maxson and colleagues (Maxson, Klein, and Sternheimer 2000, p. 29) applied the definitional elements (i.e., any gang member victim or suspect without regard to motive) in a systematic review of the entire contents of police homicide investigation files for several hundred homicides that occurred in various jurisdictions in Los Angeles county. They found that 81% of homicides that involved at least one adolescent (aged 12 to 17 years) as either a victim or a suspect included an identified gang member, as compared to just 28% of other homicides (see Table 11.1). This proportion of gang homicides far exceeded the agencies' official gang designations. When asked about this discrepancy, gang homicide detectives suggested that a more systematic application of the criteria along with a thorough review of case material by researchers likely produced the higher figures.

The Los Angeles figures would undoubtedly be reduced dramatically if local law enforcement adopted a more narrow definition of gang crime. Los Angeles considers crimes that are committed by gang members or against gang members to be gang crimes, regardless of the motive for the incident. In contrast, many other jurisdictions require evidence that a crime was committed to further gang ends or to support gang functions. Maxson and Klein (1990, 1996) investigated the implications of these diverse definitional approaches on the volume and nature of gang homicides in two separate studies. They concluded that Los Angeles gang homicide statistics would be reduced by about half under the narrower, gang-motivated definition. They also found that our basic understanding about the characteristics of these incidents does not vary substantially under the two definitions. Indeed, comparisons of gang and non-gang homicides in Los Angeles and elsewhere suggest that there are relatively stable differences between the two types that transcend loca-

Table 11.1. Gang member participation in adolescent and other homicides in Los Angeles county*

	Adolescent Homicides	Other Homicides
Gang member on suspect side only	30%	10%
Gang member on victim side only	8%	5%
Gang members on both sides	44%	13%
No gang members involved	19%	72%

Reprinted from Maxson, Klein, and Sternheimer (2000, p. 29).
* Weighted percentages provided in table. $p<.001$. Weighted sample Ns are 105 adolescent and 442 other homicides.

tion or definitional approach. Klein and Maxson (2006, p. 81) summarize findings from a series of studies comparing gang and non-gang homicides in Los Angeles and note the similar patterns in other cities as well as one difference:

> Gang homicides are more likely to take place on the street, to involve firearms, and to have more participants of younger ages, who are more often male. Victims and offenders less often have a clear prior personal relationship in gang cases. Motor vehicles are more often present in gang homicides, and the homicides tend to occur in the late afternoon and evening rather than late at night. The presence of more participants in gang incidents leads to other differences: more injuries and additional violent charges. In general, these differences have also emerged in analyses of the two types of homicides in Chicago (Spergel 1995) and in St. Louis (Decker and Curry 2002; Rosenfeld, Bray, and Egley 1999). However, gang homicides without gang motives looked more like nongang homicides than gang-motivated incidents in St. Louis, while the two types of gang homicides were similar in Los Angeles (Maxson and Klein 1996; Rosenfeld, Bray, and Egley 1999).

Scholars and law enforcement express different views on the factors that underlie gang violence. Studies of gang violence in Chicago, St. Louis, and Los Angeles (Block and Block 1995; Maxson and Klein 1996; Decker and Curry 2002) reveal that the catalyst for violent gang encounters most often reflects conflict from ongoing gang rivalries, affiliation challenges, or gang turf. The group identity and sense of belonging that gangs may promise marginalized youth becomes a powerful instigator of gang conflicts. "Where are you from?" is a common affiliation challenge in Los Angeles, and many of the gang homicides studied by Maxson and Klein (1996) began with this query. Ongoing gang rivalries reinforce group identity and solidify the bonds that individual gang members feel to the larger group. The crossing out or defacing of a gang's graffiti represents disrespect or a territorial challenge that necessitates a response from the insulted group. Researchers have observed that violent conflicts less often arise from power struggles over drug business or disputes over deals gone wrong. In contrast, law enforcement tends to perceive a close connection between drug sales and gang violence. In the 2006 NYGS, 73.5% of agencies with gang problems stated that drug-related factors significantly influenced gang-related violence in their jurisdictions; 60.5% of agencies cited conflict between gangs as a major influence (National Gang Center 2009).

Readers might note that we have based our depictions of national gang crime trends and local crime patterns on surveys of the law enforcement, such as those conducted annually by the National Gang Center and on crime reports maintained by law enforcement. There are no comparable research databases that approach the nationally representative samples offered by the NYGS or the individual crime case detail provided by police homicide investigation files. On the other hand, research studies from representative samples of youth in several locations in the United States, Canada, and Europe have proved to be a goldmine for examining patterns of gang participation and individual patterns of offending, the topic addressed in the following section.

VI. CRIME COMMITTED BY GANG MEMBERS

One of the strongest established facts to emerge from gang research over the past five decades is that gang members commit a lot of crime—and substantially more than similarly aged peers from the same communities. Assessments of youth samples in various locations in the United States, Canada, and Europe support this finding, as do tests with officially recorded and self-reported offending. This level of criminal offending by gang members has outraged public officials, engendered fear of victimization within impacted communities, and precipitated public policies that emphasize muscular police and prosecutorial responses and long periods of incarceration. Gang scholars have mined long-term studies of representative samples of youth to uncover the patterns of offending by gang members.

It is important to recognize that gang members vary in their rates of offending—not all gang members commit a lot of crime, and those that do, do not commit crime all the time. Most of the time, gang members are engaged in quite mundane activities like eating and sleeping, hanging out or socializing with friends, or even going to school, working, or doing household chores. While crime often is the spark that engages the interest of scholars in gangs, to say nothing of enormous media and public attention to them, committing crime consumes a relatively small—yet sometimes quite important—portion of gang members' lives. Furthermore, although the violence committed by gang members engages much attention from law enforcement, public officials, community members, researchers, and even other gang members, violent acts are usually just a small portion of any given gang member's diverse offending profile. Think of a gang member offending pattern as a cafeteria line or buffet, a veritable cornucopia of crime choices. The contents on a gang member's tray are very diverse forms of crime. Sometimes there will be a lot on the tray and sometimes very little. In short, gang members, like youth offenders more generally (see Warr, *supra* Chapter 10), rarely specialize in individual forms of crime. They tend not to be muggers, truants, car stealers, drug dealers/users, petty thieves, fighters, burglars, and vandals, but engage in several or all of these activities. Also, far less often, they might commit drive-by shootings, rape, and murder, along with a host of less serious crimes.

The pattern of elevated offending profiles among gang members is reflected in different measures of crime and gang involvement. Gang members commit more violent and serious offenses than non-gang members. Researchers have determined that gang youth commit more crime than non-gang youth that have delinquent peers and prior offending (Battin et al. 1998). The impact of gangs may reach even further than just to its members. Researchers have found that non-gang youth with gang associations (e.g., have gang member friends, wear gang colors) have higher offending and victimization profiles than youth without any gang involvement (Curry, Decker, and Egley 2002). The authors found a similar pattern for both self-reported and official measures of delinquency.

The facilitation of gang membership on delinquency holds across gender as well. Female gang members report committing substantially more crime than non-gang girls (and non-gang boys, for that matter) (Esbensen and Winfree 1998). Gang girls report more serious and frequent delinquency than non-gang girls from the same neighborhood (J. Miller 2001). However, girls in gangs still report markedly fewer offenses than boy gang members (Esbensen and Winfree 1998). While the volume of girl gang offending is less, the pattern of offending is quite similar: versatile offending, including serious and violent crimes, at much higher rates than their non-gang counterparts. This picture of versatile offending and higher volume offending among gang members also holds up in ethnic/race comparisons (Freng and Winfree 2004). White, Hispanic and African American gang members do not appear to display different offending profiles from one another.

One way of describing gang crime patterns is to assess the proportion of all criminal offenses committed by youth in a particular study sample that are accounted for by youth involved with gangs. The scope of gang membership would be expected to vary according to the age and risk level of the sample and/or the nature of the questions posed about gang membership (e.g., Are you a current gang member? Have you ever been involved with gangs? Do you consider your group of friends to be a gang?). But within any given study, we can ask: how much crime do youth that report gang membership commit as compared with those who don't join gangs? Terry Thornberry (1998, p. 225) pursued this question with data from three studies that captured youth reports of gang membership and crime offending throughout adolescence in Rochester, Seattle, and Denver. The figures are startling: in Rochester, 30% of boys and girls in the study reported being a gang member prior to the end of high school. These youths committed about two-thirds of all the delinquent acts reported by all of the study youth, including 68% of all violent incidents and a whopping 86% of all serious crimes. The gang membership prevalence rates were lower in Seattle (15%) and Denver (14%), but the pattern of disproportionate offending is quite evident in these cities also. In Seattle, gang-involved youth committed 58% of all offenses and higher proportions of serious, violent crimes; for example, 85% of robberies were committed by gang members. In Denver, those that reported gang membership at some point through the end of high school were responsible for 79% of all acts of serious violence acknowledged by the entire sample throughout adolescence. There is growing evidence that these patterns occur in the United States, in Canada (Gatti et al. 2005), and in Europe (Esbensen and Weerman 2005; Gatti and Haymoz 2009).

Scholars have investigated factors that might explain these elevated offending patterns. It might be that highly delinquent youth are predisposed to join gangs or are highly attractive targets for gang recruitment. In contrast to this notion that "birds of a feather flock together" is the idea that the catalyst to the high-volume offending occurs upon exposure to the group dynamics within gangs. A strong orientation toward violent resolution of conflict, a street-focused life style, and rivalries and turf challenges between gangs are all aspects of gang membership and normative values that could substantially increase violent activity. These two contrasting views of the relationship between gang membership and crime reflect different theoretical orientations that range from a "kind of person" explanation (such as low self-control from early childhood) to a reliance on group interactional dynamics (such as crime as behavior learned from peers). These are two of three potential gang/crime models proposed by Thornberry and colleagues (Thornberry et al. 1993). The *selection* pattern posits that highly delinquent youth join gangs and continue their high levels of offending throughout adolescence both during gang membership and after they leave. The *facilitation* pattern suggests that gang members offend at levels roughly comparable to other youths before joining. Crime increases substantially during active gang involvement, then decreases to resemble other youth after leaving the gang. The *enhancement* model combines the selection and facilitation explanations, generating the expectation that gang youth display elevated patterns of offending prior to joining gangs, but that crime accelerates during the membership period before falling off after gang exit. This framework has guided complex analyses of gang membership and offending with data from Pittsburgh (Gordon et al. 2004), Rochester (Thornberry et al. 1993; Thornberry et al. 2003), and Montreal (Lacourse et al. 2003; Gatti et al. 2005). These analyses have produced mixed evidence for either facilitation or enhancement, depending on the crime type investigated, length of gang membership, and location. No studies have found evidence of a pure selection effect, i.e., that gangs recruit for high offenders and do not have an impact on individual members' offending. On the contrary, gangs clearly "matter": they have a significant impact on the offending patterns of their members, over and above the crime propensities that members bring to their gang experiences. Other studies suggest that the influence of delinquent peers on gang members' subsequent offending also follows an enhancement pattern (Battin et al. 1998; Lahey et al. 1999). Finally, victimization experienced by gang-involved youth also seems to reflect the enhancement model rather than just selection or group facilitation (Peterson, Taylor, and Esbensen 2004).

This stream of research tells us there is something distinct about the experience of participation in street gangs that spurs higher rates of offending, even if incipient gang members bring more extensive crime histories to the gang environment. These studies have revealed much useful information on the individual offending patterns of gang and non-gang youth, but they are less helpful in signaling what it is about gangs that engenders elevated offending, particularly violence.

VII. Do Crime Patterns Vary By Type of Gang?

About five decades ago, researchers attempted to categorize gangs by the types of crimes they commit. Cloward and Ohlin (1960) advanced a typology that included criminal, retreatist, and conflict groups, while Yablonsky (1963) distinguished violent, delinquent, and social gangs. Twenty years later, Walter Miller (1980) identified turf, gain-oriented, and fighting gangs. Later on, Huff (1989) described hedonistic, instrumental, and predatory gangs, and Fagan (1989) offered a four-fold typology of social, party, conflict, and delinquent gangs. While these typologies have many common elements, it is striking that none have been replicated by other researchers. Perhaps these observations of the crime profiles of gangs are specific to the locations in which the research was conducted, but it is more likely that the effort to produce crime-based typologies is stymied by the pervasive pattern of crime versatility displayed by most gang members (see also Decker, Bynum, and Weisel 1998 on this point). The exception may be—almost by definition—the specialty gang type identified by Klein and Maxson (2006; Maxson and Klein 1995). One of five gang structures emerging from a national study of police gang experts, these crime-specializing groups likely represent less than 20% of gangs in the United States. They most commonly focus on drugs, graffiti vandalism, or fighting (Klein and Maxson 2006, p. 181).

Other typologies have been proposed based on gang structural or organizational characteristics, and researchers have found that these might be useful in understanding variations in the volume of crime in different gangs. For example, the proportion of males and females in gangs appears to produce different levels of delinquency (Peterson, Miller, and Esbensen 2001). Youth in groups with balanced sex ratios or with a majority of male members report more delinquent offending than youths in all male or all or majority female gangs.

A different line of research investigates whether varying levels of organization within gangs is associated with patterns of criminal offending. With the exception of some Chicago-based groups (Decker, Bynum, and Weisel 1998)[3], gang members do not usually describe their gangs as well-organized criminal groups. Even in Chicago, researchers note that there is no evidence that street gang members "graduate" to join traditional organized crime groups.

There are undoubtedly some gangs that produce higher volumes of crime and violence, but the distinguishing structural elements of these groups and interactional mechanisms that provoke these elevated crime levels have thus far eluded gang scholars. As stated earlier, it seems that joining a gang leads many youths to commit more delinquent acts than they committed prior to joining and that disengaging from gang membership reduces criminal involvement. Even after leaving the gang, many youths maintain some of the social and emotional ties with fellow gang members (Decker and Lauritsen 2002). These ties might continue to produce opportunities for offending as well as vulnerabilities to crime victimization, even as former gang members navigate the path of gang desistance (Pyrooz, Decker, and Webb 2009).

VIII. Leaving a Gang

The criminological research on the trajectory of offending reveals that most people age out of crime as they develop into adults. Despite the unique quality of gang membership, most gang members are only active gang members for a short period of time. Among youth members, the average time spent in a gang is less than two years (Thornberry et al 1993; Battin et al 1998). Despite the common conception that once a gang member is in a gang, he or she is in for life, empirical studies show that gang members can and do leave with few problems. In a study of former and current gang members in St. Louis, Decker and Lauritsen (2002) found that the most common reason for gang members to leave is experience with or exposure to violence. Like delinquency in general, many "age out" of offending or find legitimate social commitments (i.e., marriage, employment) (Klein 1971; Horowitz 1990; Vigil 1988; Sanchez-Jankowski 1991). Youth may drop gang affiliation due to incarceration (Vigil 1988; Sanchez-Jankowski 1991) or death (Decker and Lauritsen 2002). And some gangs just fade away, and their members fade out too (Sanchez-Jankowski 1991).

The method by which gang members leave their gang affiliations varies. Some gang members report simply stating their intention to leave or ceasing their affiliation (Decker and Lauritsen 2002). Some members report fighting other gang members for the right to leave. In a study of desistence from gang activity, Decker and Lauritsen (2002) found that a small proportion of gang members and/or their families were threatened after they reported their intention to leave, but none reported retribution to have actually occurred.

IX. Policy Implications and Responses to Gangs

The evidence from many decades of research on gang membership and delinquency in the United States and elsewhere is clear that the volume and seriousness of juvenile delinquency could be decreased substantially if levels of gang association, gang joining, and the length of active gang participation could be reduced. Unfortunately, there is not strong evidence for effective strategies, programs, or policies that could help to accomplish these goals. Klein and Maxson (2006) reviewed documents from nearly sixty gang programs; none met the established effectiveness criteria that have been applied to identify model programs for delinquency, drug use, or youth violence reduction (Elliott and Mihalic 2004). While these model programs might soon be adapted and tested in gang settings (Thornberry 2008), we currently have available only a diverse grab bag of "promising" (but unproven) gang strategies. These are deemed promising because sound evaluations have found them effective in some settings, but not others. Some programs have not been widely tested, or only preliminary information is available. Keeping in mind that the evidence in support of these programs is relatively weak, we offer a description of an array of programs and practices.

While it is becoming increasingly common to recognize the value of comprehensive programs that span the range of prevention, intervention, and suppression goals, many locations confronting gang violence rely primarily upon justice system responses (Greene and Pranis 2007). The toolbox for gang enforcement has grown considerably over the past three decades. Most states have enacted legislation that defines gangs (Barrows and Huff 2009), and about half have codes that aid in the prosecution or enhance the sentence of gang members (National Gang Center 2008). Law enforcement agencies have reorganized to centralize gang expertise in police gang units (Katz 2001), intensive probation and parole caseloads, and in specialized gang prosecution programs like Los Angeles's Operation Hardcore (Dahmann 1982). There is scant evidence that these programs are effective in achieving reductions in gang membership or gang crime. Deterrence-oriented strategies do not take into account the group processes within gangs that might undermine the message of cost over benefit to gang members. These group processes often work to idealize the status of gang "crackdowns" or prioritize a rapid response to perceived insults over the cool calculation of considering the certainty and severity of legal sanctions (Klein 1995; Maxson, Matsuda, and Hennigan 2011).

Civil gang injunctions (CGI) represent a novel gang enforcement approach that has been framed in both deterrence and community policing/prosecution terms (Maxson, Hennigan, and Sloane 2003). Introduced in California but increasingly used elsewhere, CGIs bring civil suits against members of specific gangs under state civil codes against public nuisance. A court order is issued prohibiting a range of behaviors, often including associating with other gang members in the injunction zone. Research has suggested that CGIs may produce a modest decrease in violent crime in the targeted neighborhoods (Grogger 2002). Residents in injunction zones report somewhat less gang visibility and intimidation, although the implementation of CGIs in less active gang areas may backfire (Maxson, Hennigan, and Sloane 2005). More research is needed on CGIs as they continue to be quite popular. In particular, the mechanism through which the strategy appears to achieve a reduction in gang crime is not well understood. Are gang members deterred by the relatively weak punishment for violating a court order? Are the bonds between gang members or social identification to the gang weakened by the injunction prohibitions? Do CGIs provide an excuse, or a viable exit ramp, for gang members that have tired of the gang life? It is important for research to extend beyond the "what works" question to better understand how interventions might be generating the desired outcome.

Another strategy that singles out individual gangs and broadcasts the message of strong law enforcement attention is the Boston Gun Project/Operation Ceasefire program (Braga et al. 2001). Researchers and law enforcement personnel worked together to identify the source of Boston's burgeoning youth gun homicide rate in the late 1980s and early 1990s. They fashioned an intervention and delivered the message to gang members that gun violence would be met with diverse, widespread, and serious penalties. This "pulling levers" or targeted deterrence strategy was credited with a precipitous drop in youth homicides, but has not proven as successful in other gang replications.

Police often are key components of comprehensive gang programs. The Office of Juvenile Justice and Delinquency Prevention (OJJDP) sponsored the development and testing of the Comprehensive Gang Prevention, Intervention and Suppression Model (OJJDP 2008), which is also known as the "Spergel Model" because Irving Spergel pioneered the strategy in the Little Village Project in Chicago (Spergel 2007). He also directed the evaluation of a five-site demonstration of the program. This strategy is quite complex, engaging police, probation, community groups, schools, and youth service agencies in delivering a wide array of services under the broad categories of social intervention, opportunities provision, community mobilization, suppression, and organizational change. The first tests of the model suggested it was difficult to implement, and outcomes were mixed with some sites showing promising results, and others, no differences between the treatment and comparison youth (Klein and Maxson 2006). A similar comprehensive gang intervention, also supported by OJJDP, was the Gang Reduction Program fielded in four sites. The multiyear program evaluation found that only the Los Angeles program generated significant reductions in crime levels, including gang-related crime and serious gang violence, serious violence more generally, and calls of shots fired (Cahill et al. 2008).

Chicago's Ceasefire program (not to be confused with the Boston program described earlier) attempts to achieve reductions in gang violence by employing "violence interrupters" to prevent retaliation for gang conflicts. It also utilizes outreach workers and community agencies to provide job and educational services. There is also community mobilization and a public awareness campaign to try to change community-level norms favorable to violent conflict resolution. The evaluators report positive outcomes on a range of relevant crime indicators, but these were realized in just half or fewer of the neighborhoods in which Ceasefire was implemented (Skogan et al. 2008). As with other multifaceted programs described above, it is clear that faithful implementation of program models is a major challenge but is critical to achieving positive outcomes.

An example of a program that is widespread and has been consistently well implemented is the Gang Resistance Education and Training (G.R.E.A.T.) program. This is a school-based, universal prevention program provided by uniformed law enforcement officers. An established curriculum is delivered to students in middle school classrooms. While some positive results were revealed in a four-year followup of the students, no effect on levels of gang participation was detected (Esbensen et al. 2001). Interestingly, the program developers embarked on an evidence-based curriculum review and revised G.R.E.A.T.'s content and mode of delivery to be more interactive. Preliminary results from the evaluation of the new program are promising (Esbensen 2008).

In addition to this sampling of recent programs, there is a vast array of community-based strategies to prevent gang membership and to steer gang members along more prosocial pathways, most of which have not been adequately evaluated. The evaluation results offer some promise and much discouraging news. Future evaluations may help to clarify what strategies work best in different types of gang settings. The research on gangs and gang programming described here suggests the following for the development of successful programs:

1) Prevention efforts should start early, before the peak ages of gang joining at 13 to 15 years, and should fully incorporate girls and all racial/ethnic groups.

2) Intervention efforts need to be wary of undermining the widespread, natural desistance processes that are suggested by the brief participation patterns of most gang youth.

3) Secondary prevention and intervention efforts need to select clients based on the empirical research on *gang* risk factors described in this chapter. The causes and correlates of juvenile offending are not the same as for gang participation: not all delinquents are gang members, in fact, most are not.

4) Intervention efforts should be informed by knowledge about group process within gangs. Some programs have backfired because they inadvertently increased bonds between gang members or raised the status of gang membership (Klein 1995).

5) Successful efforts will have clearly articulated and carefully implemented program content.

The data on gang prevalence and proliferation suggest that gangs and gang crime continue to be a serious issue in the United States and elsewhere. Thus, there is no lack of available clients for gang prevention and intervention efforts and much to be gained in crime reduction, increased opportunities for youth, and improved quality of communities if effective gang programs and policies were to be broadly and faithfully implemented.

X. Conclusion

Research has provided significant insight into gangs despite a multitude of hurdles. Access to any criminal organization is challenging, but the fluidity of gang membership, definitional issues, and variation in size and structure of gangs add an extra layer of complication. Scholars have not been deterred by the difficulty. While there is always more to do, we do know a lot about gangs, their members, and processes. However, the knowledge base surrounding gangs, perhaps more than other areas of research, competes for legitimacy and salience against contrasting media and pop culture depictions. Research confirms that gang members engage in quite high levels of crime and violence, much more so than non-gang youth. Gang members do not, however, spend a majority of their time committing violent acts. Some traditionally structured gangs (see Klein and Maxson 2006) include adult gang members or "O.G.s" (aka. Original Gangsters), but gangs, for the most part, are a juvenile endeavor that do not require a lifetime commitment. Consistent with their versatility in delinquent offending, gangs engage in drug use and sales, but most gangs do not specialize in drug trafficking. And most gangs are not organized criminal enterprises with hierarchies, detailed operations, or constitutions. Some gangs have ritualistic processes like being "jumped in" or sent on "missions," but this is likely not the norm. While some youths are "jumped out" of gangs with a violent beating, many more just drift away from gang activity, particularly as responsibilities such as legitimate jobs, intimate relationships, and children become more salient. While some gangs continue for decades and reflect multigenerational membership, more typically, groups just appear and disintegrate over time.

Malcolm Klein coined the expression "The Eurogang Paradox," which describes the dismissal of the prospect of European gangs because groups resembling stereotypical American gangs were not uncovered. The "paradox" is in the notion that most American street gangs do not resemble the stereotype either. In this is the ultimate challenge of gang research. The body of work continues to produce information that illuminates the convergence and divergence of commonly accepted stereotypes of the gang as a group and of its individual members. In addition, differences in results taken from self-report and official data have spurred debates and clarification from the field. Much progress has been made from the time of basic descriptions of individual gangs to more generalizable knowledge of the variety and qualities of different gang structures. There is, however, much to be discovered, particularly regarding precisely *how* the gang influences the offending patterns of its members.

NOTES

1. The National Youth Gang Center was merged with the National Gang Center in October 2009 and is now recognized as the National Gang Center.
2. The NYGS defines a gang as "a group of youths or young adults in your jurisdiction that you or other responsible persons in your agency or community are willing to identify as a 'gang.'" Excluded are motorcycle gangs, hate groups, prison gangs, or "exclusively adult gangs."
3. Another exception to this general pattern of low levels of organization may be youth gangs in Kazan, Russia (Salagaev 2001).

REFERENCES

Barrows, Julie, and C. Ronald Huff. 2009. "Gangs and public policy: Constructing and deconstructing gang databases." *Criminology and Public Policy* 8: 675–703.
Battin, Sara R., Karl G. Hill, Robert D. Abbot, Richard F. Catalano, and J. David Hawkins. 1998. "The contribution of gang membership to delinquency beyond delinquent friends." *Criminology* 36: 93–115.
Block, Carolyn Rebecca, and Richard Block. 1995. "Street gang crime in Chicago." In *The Modern Gang Reader*, edited by Malcolm W. Klein, Cheryl L. Maxson, and Jody Miller. Los Angeles, CA: Roxbury.

Braga, Anthony A., David M. Kennedy, Ellin J. Waring, and Anne M. Piehl. 2001. "Problem-oriented policing, deterrence, and youth violence: An evaluation of Boston's Operation-Ceasefire." *Journal of Research in Crime and Delinquency* 38: 195–225.

Cahill, Meagan, Mark Coggeshall, David Hayeslip, Ashley Wolff, Erica Lagerson, Michelle L. Scott, Elizabeth Davies, Kevin Nolan, and Scott Decker. 2008. *Community collaboratives addressing youth gangs: Interim findings from the Gang Reduction Program.* Washington, DC: Justice Policy Center, Urban Institute.

Cloward, Richard A., and Lloyd E. Ohlin. 1960. *Delinquency and Opportunity: A Theory of Delinquent Gangs.* New York, NY: Free Press.

Curry, G. David. 2000. "Self-reported gang involvement and officially recorded delinquency." *Criminology* 38: 1253–74.

Curry, G. David, and Scott H. Decker. 2003. *Confronting Gangs: Crime and Community.* Los Angeles, CA: Roxbury.

Curry, G. David, Scott H. Decker, and Arlen Egley, Jr. 2002. "Gang involvement and delinquency in a middle school population." *Justice Quarterly* 19: 275–92.

Dahmann, Judith. 1982. *An Evaluation of Operation Hardcore: A Prosecutorial Response to Violent Gang Criminality.* McLean, VA: Mitre Corporation.

Decker, Scott H. 1996. "Collective and normative features of gang violence." *Justice Quarterly* 13: 243–64.

Decker, Scott H., Tim Bynum, and Deborah Weisel. 1998. "A tale of two cities: Gangs as organized crime groups." *Justice Quarterly* 15: 395–425.

Decker, Scott H., and G. David Curry. 2000. "Addressing key features of gang membership: Measuring the involvement of young members." *Journal of Criminal Justice* 28: 473–82.

Decker, Scott H., and G. David Curry. 2002. "Gangs, gang homicides, and gang loyalty: Organized crimes of disorganized criminals?" *Journal of Criminal Justice* 30: 1–10.

Decker, Scott H., and Janet L. Lauritsen. 2002. "Leaving the Gang." In *Gangs in America*, 2nd ed., edited by C. Ronald Huff. Thousand Oaks, CA: Sage.

Decker, Scott H., and Barrik Van Winkle. 1996. *Life in the Gang: Family, Friends, and Violence.* Cambridge: Cambridge University Press.

Egley, Arlen, Jr., Jane C. Howell, and Alinek Major. 2006. *National Youth Gang Survey, 1999–2001.* Washington D.C.: Office of Juvenile Justice Delinquency and Prevention.

Egley, Arlen, Jr., and Christina O'Donnell, E. 2009. *Highlights of the 2007 National Youth Gang Survey.* Washington DC: Office of Juvenile Justice Delinquency and Prevention.

Elliott, Delbert S., and Sharon Mihalic. 2004. "Blueprints for violence prevention." Boulder, CO: University of Colorado, Institute of Behavioral Science, Center for the Study and Prevention of Violence.

Esbensen, Finn-Aage. 2008. "Preliminary short-term results from the evaluation of the G.R.E.A.T. program." http://www.iir.com/nygc/publications/2008–12-esbensen.pdf.

Esbensen, Finn-Aage., D. Wayne Osgood, Terrance J. Taylor, Dana Peterson, and Adrienne Freng. 2001. "How great is G.R.E.A.T.? Results from the longitudinal quasi-experimental design." *Criminology and Public Policy* 1: 87–118.

Esbensen, Finn-Aage., and Frank M. Weerman. 2005. "Youth gangs and troublesome youth groups in the United States and the Netherlands: A cross-national comparison." *European Journal of Criminology* 2: 5–37.

Esbensen, Finn-Aage, and L. Thomas Winfree, Jr. 1998. "Race and gender differences between gang and non-gang youth: Results from a multisite survey." *Justice Quarterly* 15: 505–26.

Eurogang Project. 2010. Eurogang. http://www.umsl.edu/~ccj/eurogang/euroganghome. htm.

Fagan, Jeffrey. 1989. "The social organization of drug use and dealing among urban gangs." *Criminology* 27: 633–70.

Freng, Adrienne, and L. Thomas Winfree, Jr. 2004. "Exploring race and ethnic differences in a sample of middle school gang members." In *American Youth Gangs at the Millennium*, edited by Finn-Aage Esbensen, Stephen G. Tibbetts, and Larry Gaines. Long Grove, IL: Waveland Press.

Gatti, Umberto, and Sandrine Haymoz. 2009. "Risk behaviors and victimization among gang members: Gender differences." Paper presented to the annual meeting of the European Society of Criminology. Slovenia, September.

Gatti, Umberto, Richard E. Tremblay, Frank Vitaro, and Pierre McDuff. 2005. "Youth gangs, delinquency and drug use: A test of the selection, facilitation, and enhancement hypotheses." *Journal of Child Psychology and Psychiatry* 46: 1178–90.

Gordon, Rachel A., Benjamin B. Lahey, Eriko Kawai, Rolf Loeber, Magda Stouthamer-Loeber, and David P. Farrington. 2004. "Antisocial behavior and youth gang membership: Selection and socialization." *Criminology* 42: 55–87.

Greene, Judith, and Kevin Pranis. (2007). *Gang Wars: The Failure of Enforcement Tactics and the Need for Effective Public Safety Strategies*. Washington, DC: Justice Policy Institute.

Grogger, Jeffrey. 2002. "The effects of civil gang injunctions on reported violent crime: Evidence from Los Angeles County." *Journal of Law and Economics* 45 (April): 69–90.

Horowitz, Ruth. 1990. "Sociological perspectives on gangs: Conflicting definitions and concepts." In *Gangs in America*, edited by C. Ronald Huff. Thousand Oaks, CA: Sage.

Huff, C. Ronald. 1989. "Youth gangs and public policy." *Crime and Delinquency* 35: 524–37.

Huizinga, David, and Karl F. Schumann. 2001. "Gang membership in Bremen and Denver: Comparative longitudinal data." In *The Eurogang Paradox: Street Gangs and Youth Groups in the U.S. and Europe*, edited by Malcolm W. Klein, Hans-Juergen Kerner, Cheryl L. Maxson, and Elmar G. M. Weitekamp. Dordrect: Kluwer Academic Publishers.

Katz, Charles. 2001. "The establishment of a police gang unit: An examination of organizational and environmental factors." *Criminology*. 39: 37–73.

Klein, Malcolm W. 1971. *Street Gangs and Street Workers*. Englewood Cliffs, NJ: Prentice-Hall.

Klein, Malcolm W. 1995. *The American Street Gang: Its Nature, Prevalence, and Control*. New York, NY: Oxford University Press.

Klein, Malcolm W., Hans-Juergen Kerner, Cheryl L. Maxson, and Elmar G. M. Weitekamp, eds. 2001. *The Eurogang Paradox: Street Gangs and Youth Groups in the U.S. and Europe*. Dordrecht: Kluwer Academic Publishers.

Klein, Malcolm W., and Cheryl L. Maxson. 2006. *Street Gang Patterns and Policies*. New York, NY: Oxford University Press.

Lacourse, Eric, Daniel Nagin, Richard E. Tremblay, Frank Vitaro, and Michel Claes. 2003. "Developmental trajectories of boys' delinquent group membership and facilitation of violent behaviors during adolescence." *Development and Psychopathology* 15: 183–97.

Lahey, Benjamin B., Rachel A. Gordon, Rolf Loeber, Magda Stouthamer-Loeber, and David P. Farrington. 1999. "Boys who join gangs: A prospective study of predictors of first gang entry." *Journal of Abnormal Child Psychology* 27: 261–76.

Maxson, Cheryl L., G. David Curry, and James C. Howell. 2002. "Youth gang homicides in the United States in the 1990s." In *Responding to gangs: Evaluation and research*, edited by Winifred L. Reed and Scott H. Decker. Washington, DC: U.S. Department of Justice.

Maxson, Cheryl L., Karen Hennigan, and David C. Sloane. 2003. "For the sake of the neighborhood?: Civil gang injunctions as a gang intervention tool in Southern California." In *Policing Gangs and Youth Violence*, edited by Scott H. Decker. Belmont, CA: Wadsworth.

Maxson, Cheryl L., Karen Hennigan, and David C. Sloane. 2005. "It's getting crazy out there: Can a civil gang injunction change a community?" *Criminology and Public Policy* 4(3): 501–30.

Maxson, Cheryl L., and Malcolm W. Klein. 1990. "Street gang violence: Twice as great, or half as great?" In *Gangs in America*, edited by C. Ronald Huff. Thousand Oaks, CA: Sage Publishing, Inc.

Maxson, Cheryl L., and Malcolm W. Klein. 1995. "Investigation gang structures." *Journal of Gang Research* 3: 33–40.

Maxson, Cheryl L., and Malcolm W. Klein. 1996. "Defining gang homicide: An updated look at member and motive approaches." In *Gangs in America*, edited by C. Ronald Huff. Thousand Oaks, CA: Sage Publishing, Inc.

Maxson, Cheryl L., and Malcolm W. Klein. 2002. "'Play groups' no longer: Urban street gangs in the Los Angeles region." In *From Chicago to L.A.: Making Sense of Urban Theory*, edited by Michael Dear. Thousand Oaks, CA: Sage.

Maxson, Cheryl L., Malcolm W. Klein, and Karen Sternheimer. 2000. *Homicide in Los Angeles: An analysis of the differential character of adolescent and other homicides*. Report to the National Institute of Justice. Washington, DC: U.S. Department of Justice. http://www.ncjrs.gov/pdffiles1/nij/grants/193812.pdf.

Maxson, Cheryl L., Kristy N. Matsuda, and Karen Hennigan. 2011. "'Deterrability' among gang and nongang juvenile offenders: Are gang members more (or less) deterrable than other juvenile offenders?" *Crime and Delinquency* 57: 516–543.

Maxson, Cheryl L., and Monica L. Whitlock. 2002. "Joining the gang: Gender differences in risk factors for gang membership." In *Gangs in America*, 3rd ed., edited C. Ronald Huff. Thousand Oaks, CA: Sage Publications.

Maxson, Cheryl L., Monica L. Whitlock, and Malcolm W. Klein. 1997. "Gang joining and resistance: Who can 'just say no' to gangs?" Final report submitted to Administration for Children and Families, U.S. Department of Health and Human Services. Los Angeles, CA: University of Southern California.

Miller, Jody. 2001. *One of the Guys: Girls, Gangs, and Gender*. New York, NY: Oxford University Press.

Miller, Walter B. 1975. *Violence by Youth Gangs and Youth Groups as a Crime Problem in Major American Cities*. Washington, DC: U.S. Department of Justice, Office of Juvenile Justice and Delinquency Prevention.

Miller, Walter B. 1980. "Gangs, groups, and serious youth crime." In *Critical Issues in Juvenile Delinquency*, edited by David Schichor and Delos H. Kelly. Lexington, VA: DC Health.

Miller, Walter B. 2001. "The growth of youth gang problems in the United States: 1970–98." Washington, DC: U.S. Department of Justice, Office of Juvenile Justice and Delinquency Prevention.

National Gang Center. 1998. *1996 National Youth Gang Survey Program Summary*. Washington, DC: U.S. Department of Justice, Office of Juvenile Justice and Delinquency Prevention.

National Gang Center. 2008. "Highlights of gang-related legislation Spring 2008." http://www.nationalgangcenter.gov/Legislation/Highlights.

National Gang Center. 2009. "National Youth Gang Survey analysis." http://www.nationalgangcenter.gov/Survey-Analysis.

Office of Juvenile Justice and Delinquency Prevention. 2008. *Best Practices to Address Community Gang Problems: OJJDP's Comprehensive Gang Model.* Washington, DC: U.S. Department of Justice, Office of Juvenile Justice and Delinquency Prevention.

Peterson, Dana, Jody Miller, and Finn-Aage Esbensen. 2001. "The impact of sex compositions in gang and gang member delinquency." *Criminology* 39: 411–39.

Peterson, Dana, Terrence J. Taylor, and Finn-Aage Esbensen. 2004. "Gang membership and violent victimization." *Justice Quarterly* 21: 793–815.

Pyrooz, David, Scott H. Decker, and Vincent Webb. 2009. "The ties that bind: Desistance from gangs." Glendale, AZ: Arizona State University, School of Criminology and Criminal Justice.

Rosenfeld, Richard, Timothy M. Bray, and Arlen Egley, Jr. 1999. "Facilitating violence: A comparison of gang-motivated, gang affiliated and nongang youth homicides." *Journal of Quantitative Criminology* 15: 495–516.

Salagaev, Alexander. 2001. Evolution of delinquent gangs in Russia. In *The Eurogang Paradox: Street Gangs and Youth Groups in the U.S. and Europe*, edited by Malcolm W. Klein, Hans-Juergen Kerner, Cheryl L. Maxson, and Elmar G.M. Weitekamp. Dordrecht: Kluwer Academic Publishers.

Sanchez-Jankowski, Martin. 1991. *Islands in the Street: Gangs and American Urban Society.* Berkeley, CA: University of California Press.

Short, James F., Jr. 2006. "Why study gangs? An intellectual journal." In *Studying Youth Gangs*, edited by James F. Short, Jr. and Lorine A. Hughes. Lanham, MD: Altamira Press.

Short, James F. Jr., and Fred L. Strodtbeck. 1965. *Group Process and Gang Delinquency.* Chicago, IL: University of Chicago Press.

Skogan, Wesley G., Susan M. Harnett, Natalie Bump, and Jill Dubois. 2008. "Evaluation of CeaseFire-Chicago." www.northwestern.edu/ipr/publications/ceasefire.html.

Snyder, Howard N., and Melissa Sickmund. 2006. *Juvenile Offenders and Victims: 2006 National Report*, edited by National Center for Juvenile Justice. Washington, DC: U.S. Department of Justice, Office of Justice Programs, Office of Juvenile Justice and Delinquency Prevention.

Spergel, Irving A. 1990. "Youth gangs: Continuity and change." *Crime and Justice* 12: 171–275.

Spergel, Irving A. 1995. *The Youth Gang Problem: A Community Approach.* New York, NY: Oxford University Press.

Spergel, Irving A. 2007. *Reducing Youth Gang Violence.* Lantham, MD: AltaMira Press.

Thornberry, Terence. 1998. "Membership in youth gangs and involvement in serious and violent offending." In *Serious and Violent Offenders: Risk Factors and Successful Interventions*, edited by Rolf Loeber and David P. Farrington. Newbury Park, CA: Sage Publications.

Thornberry, Terence. 2008 "Blueprints for gang prevention: A concept paper." Boulder, CO: Institute of Behavioral Science, University of Colorado.

Thornberry, Terence, Marvin D. Krohn, Alan J. Lizotte, and Deborah Chard-Wierschem. 1993. "The role of juvenile gangs in facilitating delinquent behavior." *Journal of Research in Crime and Delinquency* 30: 55–87.

Thornberry, Terence, Marvin D. Krohn, Alan J. Lizotte, Carolyn A. Smith, and Kimberly Tobin. 2003. *Gangs and Delinquency in a Developmental Perspective.* Cambridge: Cambridge University Press.

Thrasher, Fredric M. 1927. *The Gang: A Study of 1313 Gangs in Chicago.* Chicago, IL: University of Chicago Press.

Tita, George, and Allan Abrahamse. 2004. "Gang homicides in LA, 1981–2001." Sacramento, CA: California Attorney General's Office.

Vigil, James D. 1998. *Barrio Gangs: Street Life and Identity in Southern California.* Austin, TX: University of Texas Press.

Yablonsky, Lewis. 1963. *The Violent Gang.* New York, NY: Macmillan.

CHAPTER 12

···

COMMUNITIES AND DELINQUENCY

···

CHARIS E. KUBRIN

MUCH of the research on juvenile delinquency focuses on individual dispositional characteristics of youth like impulsivity and feelings of guilt. In these studies, social context often takes a back seat or is ignored altogether. When context is considered, the community context is seldom the focus. The most traditionally examined contexts with respect to juvenile offending include family, school, peers, youth gangs, and even the workplace. Rightly so, these are important contexts with far-reaching consequences for youth, as the other chapters in this section convincingly demonstrate.

Yet the community or neighborhood in which a juvenile lives also constitutes an important context. Neighborhoods vary along multiple dimensions including socioeconomic status, racial composition, access to resources—to name just a few. Given their features, some communities represent high-risk environments for youths (i.e., they generate temptations, provocations, and have low levels of social control), while others are more protective (i.e., they generate low levels of temptation, provocation, and have high levels of social control) (Wikstrom and Loeber 2000, p. 1114).

Apart from serving as a socially meaningful context for youth, communities and their characteristics are important to account for in delinquency studies because to the extent that individual-level studies identify a relationship between, for example, a familial social characteristic (economic status or parental composition) and delinquency, the link remains most often uninterpretable. That is, "no attempt is made to clarify the extent to which the relationship is inherently on the individual-familial level or is moderated by the contexts in which families live (for example, lower- versus middle-class neighborhoods; predominantly two- versus one-parent family neighborhoods)" (Simcha-Fagan and Schwartz 1986:669; see also Hay et al. 2007:594).

The goal of this chapter is to describe the role of communities in the production of delinquency. In the first part of this chapter, I identify community characteristics of importance and describe why these have been most frequently examined by researchers. In the second part, I discuss the various theoretical mechanisms proposed to account for the link between community characteristics and rates of delinquency. In part three, I present two critical weaknesses in the communities and delinquency literature, and explain how they have been addressed to some degree in contextual studies of delinquency. In part four, I review the main findings from the contextual effects literature. And in part five, I conclude by identifying more general issues that warrant attention in communities and delinquency studies and by charting some promising new directions for research.

I. Ecological Conditions of Importance

The idea that communities differ with consequences for delinquency is not a new one. Shaw and McKay (1942) were among the first researchers to document that rates of delinquency varied across communities in Chicago. Their groundbreaking study led to a host of what are often referred to as "delinquency area studies." Early delinquency area studies (e.g., Bordua (1958); Chilton (1964); Gordon (1967); Lander (1954); Polk (1957)) attempted to correlate a collective property of neighborhoods with juvenile delinquency rates for neighborhoods, also a collective property. Many presented evidence that local delinquency rates were associated with underlying community dimensions of socioeconomic status, racial and ethnic composition, and/or anomie. Delinquency area studies continue today, and collectively this literature has identified numerous ecological conditions of importance.

The most common ecological characteristic investigated, dating back to the early Chicago School researchers, is neighborhood socioeconomic status (SES), which has proven a robust predictor of delinquency rates. According to Bursik (2001, p. 395), "It would appear that ... multicity evidence strongly supports the existence of a fundamental socioeconomic status factor that may be called a general component of the community context of delinquency." Most often SES is reflected in the neighborhood's poverty level, but more recent studies have broadened this concept to consider the combined effects of social and economic indicators of disadvantage. In many inner-city communities, as a result of macro-economic changes that have disproportionately affected the urban poor, scholars claim it is the combination of poverty, unemployment, and family disruption that defines the socioeconomic context for residents (Sampson and Wilson 1995; Wilson 1987). They posit that "concentration effects" contribute to social disorganization, which in turn leads to delinquency. They additionally assert that residents living in areas of concentrated disadvantage are geographically and socially isolated, which gives rise to ghetto-specific cultural beliefs that undermine conventional values (e.g., crime is the way to resolve personal disputes). Such cultural beliefs readily develop in the gap created by joblessness, the exodus of middle-class residents, disruptions in the family, and the lack of government support for inner-city institutions. Beyond these claims, "A multidimensional focus on neighborhood disadvantage is…important because it allows for the possibility that not all high-poverty neighborhoods are characterized by high mobility, broken families, chronic unemployment, or excessive cultural heterogeneity; and that these conditions of disadvantage may interact with poverty to produce certain deleterious effects on adolescent development" (Elliott et al. 1996, p. 393).

Consistent with these arguments, researchers typically measure the multiple disadvantages that characterize areas by incorporating several measures (e.g., poverty, unemployment, single-parent families with children) into an overarching index of concentrated disadvantage. Researchers consistently find that neighborhood SES generally, and concentrated disadvantage in particular, are positively associated with rates of juvenile delinquency (Elliott et al. 1996; Haynie et al. 2006; Kupersmidt et al. 1995; Simons et al. 2005; Wikstrom and Loeber 2000). But the effects of concentrated disadvantage are not limited to delinquency. Sampson and colleagues (2002, p. 446) claim, "The range of child and adolescent outcomes associated with concentrated disadvantage is quite wide and includes infant mortality, low birthweight, teenage childbearing, dropping out of high school, child maltreatment, and adolescent delinquency."

Another ecological characteristic often examined in delinquency area studies is neighborhood racial composition. Frequently the focus is on racial heterogeneity or diversity within neighborhoods. Racial heterogeneity has been hypothesized to affect the strength and salience of informal social control. Theorists have posited that in communities with diverse racial groups living in close proximity, interaction between members will be low, or at least lower than in racially homogeneous neighborhoods (Gans 1968). Heterogeneity can also undermine ties between neighbors, limiting their ability to agree on a common set of values or to solve "commonly experienced problems" (Bursik 1988, p. 521; Kornhauser 1978) due to cultural differences between racial groups, language incompatibility, and the fact that individuals prefer members of their own race to members of different races (Blau and Schwartz 1984, p. 14; Gans 1968). As a result, residents will be less likely to look out for one another and will not, to the same extent as in racially homogeneous communities, take an interest in their neighbors' activities. Informal social interactions will be limited, and crime and delinquency rates in such neighborhoods can be expected to be higher. As Kornhauser (1978, p. 78) notes, "Heterogeneity impedes communication and thus obstructs the quest to solve common problems and reach common goals.." Studies of racial heterogeneity and changes in racial heterogeneity find that, in fact, both are associated with increased delinquency rates in communities (Heitgard and Bursik 1987; Kapsis 1978).

The "religious ecology of communities" (Regnerus 2003; Stark, Kent, and Doyle 1982) constitutes a third local dimension of neighborhoods thought to affect delinquency. Religion is theorized to impact the beliefs, attitudes, and behaviors of youths through several mechanisms, including social control, social support, and values/identity. Some examples include religious norms that promote marriage, legitimate sexual relationships, and childbearing, and norms that restrict alcohol sales, access to abortion, or curb Sunday athletic events (Regnerus 2003, p. 527). A key assumption is that religion is a living, salient feature of the larger group. In using the term "moral communities," Stark and colleagues (1982) argue that religion ought to be understood sociologically as a group property more than an individual one. Along these lines, religion is not said to make youth afraid to sin but to bind its adherents to a "moral community" (e.g., a community integrated by shared religious beliefs), compared to a secularized social climate.

It is often argued that religion only serves to bind youth to the moral order if religious influences permeate the culture and social interactions of individuals within communities. In social groups where a religious sanctioning system is the mode and is expressed in daily life, the propensity to deviate from norms will be influenced substantially by the degree of one's commitment to the religious sanctioning system. Where the religious sanctioning system is not pervasive, it is argued, the effects of the youth's religious commitment will be curtailed. In delinquency studies that examine the religious ecology of communities, religion is thought to directly affect the behavior of the group's members as well as indirectly moderate how individuals' religious traits shape their behavior (Regnerus 2003, p. 524; Stark, Kent, and Doyle 1982).

To a lesser degree, the social-ecological literature has considered additional aspects of neighborhood differentiation including life-cycle status, residential stability, home ownership, and density. Whatever neighborhood characteristic under investigation, the argument advanced in this literature is that ecological characteristics either enhance or disrupt the social organizational processes in the community, with implications for juvenile delinquency rates.

II. Intervening Theoretical Mechanisms

The ecological characteristics of communities such as those just discussed are expected to both directly and indirectly affect juvenile delinquency. Indirectly, socioeconomic status, racial composition, and the religious ecology of communities, among other characteristics, are theorized to influence the attitudes, relationships, and behavior of residents through various intervening theoretical mechanisms.

According to the systemic model, closely related to social disorganization theory, community characteristics affect delinquency because they deter neighborhood residents from establishing relationships with one another and thus diminish a neighborhood's capacity for informal social control (Bursik 1988; Bursik and Grasmick 1993). This model is predicated on the notion that neighborhoods are complex systems of friendship and kinship networks and associational ties rooted in families and ongoing social processes (Bursik and Grasmick 1993). Residents living in neighborhoods with large and active social networks are better able to generate social trust and enforce shared community values, including the desire to live in a crime- and delinquency-free neighborhood. As a result, residents have an easier time supervising youths within the neighborhood, socializing them toward conventional values, and preventing them from becoming involved with delinquent peers. When associational ties and local social controls are weak, youths have greater opportunities to engage in delinquency and to become involved with delinquent peers in whose presence delinquency is experienced as highly rewarding (Haynie et al. 2006).

More recently, researchers have discussed the concept of collective efficacy, which combines concepts of social ties, social integration, and social control. Sampson et al. (1997) claim that although social ties are important, the willingness of residents to intervene on behalf of children may depend in large part on conditions of mutual trust and shared expectations among residents. One is unlikely to intervene in a neighborhood context where the rules are unclear and people mistrust or fear one another. It is thus the linkage of mutual trust and the shared willingness to intervene for the public good that captures the neighborhood context of collective efficacy.

Social ties, informal control, and collective efficacy are directly affected by ecological characteristics of neighborhoods, such as those identified in delinquency area studies. Kornhauser (1978, p. 81) notes, "Institutions that cannot supply the means to valued goals fail in all types of control. The attachments and commitments that enmesh the child in interlocking controls cannot be formed. Need satisfaction and goal achievement are conditions for the establishment of indirect control. When they are absent, affective and instrumental bonds to persons and institutions are likewise weak or absent." The result, according to Kornhauser, is heightened delinquency within communities.

Expanding on the systemic model, Elliott et al. (1996, p. 396) identify two additional theoretically relevant organizational and cultural characteristics that link ecological conditions and delinquency rates in neighborhoods. Beyond weak neighborhood organization (e.g., low social integration, weak informal networks, weak informal controls), they cite attenuated neighborhood culture (e.g., low consensus on values, low consensus on norms, normlessness) and illegitimate opportunities (e.g., delinquent gangs, deviant role models, illegitimate job networks) as critical.

Concerning neighborhood culture, Shaw and McKay (1942) long ago discussed the extent to which communities tolerate or sustain social disorder and deviant subcultures. Socially disorganized neighborhoods, in particular, have a diversity (rather than consensus) of norms. Ecological characteristics such as poverty, racial heterogeneity, and residential mobility foster a diverse citizenry so that individuals with all types of values, beliefs, and behaviors are clustered together; that is, "socially disorganized neighborhoods provide 'room' for both conventional and unconventional groups" (Cattarello 2000, p. 36). Youths living in disorganized neighborhoods are thus exposed both to conventional and unconventional groups and norms regarding standards of behavior. In essence, deviant subcultures affect adolescents' normative values as well as the probability of association with delinquent peers which, in turn, results in delinquency. Community deviant subculture, therefore, can affect delinquent behavior via its effect on youth normative values and via the probability of association with delinquent peers. Deviant subcultures can also provide illegitimate opportunities for youth, as suggested by Cloward and Ohlin (1960). For example, delinquent gangs and organized crime provide jobs, food and clothing, role models, and self-affirmation for youths; "they satisfy basic individual and social needs in the same way that stable families, prosocial peers, and legitimate employment satisfy these needs and reinforce conventional behavior" (Elliott et al. 1996, p. 394). In sum then, there are several intervening theoretical mechanisms that help explain why ecological characteristics of communities are found to be associated with juvenile delinquency rates in delinquency area studies.

III. Weaknesses in the Literature

One major problem in the communities and delinquency literature, at least with respect to delinquency area studies, is that studies often assume these mediating processes exist without actually measuring them. Sampson et al. (2002. p. 447) claim: "Although concern with neighborhood mechanisms goes back at least to the early Chicago School of sociology, only recently have we witnessed a concerted attempt to theorize and empirically measure the social-interactional and institutional dimensions that might explain how neighborhood effects are transmitted." Thus, many studies document associations between poverty, racial heterogeneity, and so forth, and rates of juvenile delinquency yet are only able to *theorize* they occur due to intervening processes related to social ties, social control, collective efficacy, attenuated neighborhood culture, and illegitimate opportunities.

One implication of this is that we actually know very little about how neighborhood effects are transmitted to youth—that is, how neighborhoods impact juveniles and encourage or discourage delinquency. The key question remains: What are the relationships among ecological characteristics, family and peer processes, and rates of juvenile delinquency in neighborhoods? Some have suggested that family processes mediate much of the effect of community context on youths (Simons et al. 2005). Others have suggested that involvement in peer networks is the primary mediating factor (Haynie et al. 2006). And still others have claimed that community and family and peer processes interact in ways that amplify delinquency in some communities. Hay et al. (2007, p. 594), for example, argue that community poverty amplifies the effects of family poverty on delinquency, such that these effects become greater when community poverty is also high.

The latter example of an interaction effect suggests complex relationships among the mechanisms at play. An example is illustrative. With respect to community characteristics and their effects on family processes, Simons et al. (2005) describe the potential combined effects of collective efficacy and authoritative parenting on delinquency. Recall that a community is high on collective efficacy to the extent that residents share values, mutual trust, and a disposition to intervene for the public good (i.e., to reduce crime and delinquency). Authoritative parents combine warmth and support with firm monitoring and control. Both authoritative parenting and collective efficacy, according to Simons et al. (2005), function as supportive control, albeit at different levels of analysis (the family and the community), which has a theorized effect on a youth's risk of affiliating with deviant peers and thus engaging in delinquent behavior. Stated another way, just as parental control is an expression of parental affection and concern for the child, so community control appears to be an expression of the residents' concerns and commitment to the community (p. 994). According to these researchers, adults living in communities marked by high levels of collective efficacy exert subtle, as well as not so subtle, pressures upon parents of delinquent youth to become more responsible caretakers. When they witness a child misbehaving, they tend to contact the child's parents or authorities (e.g., school or police). Therefore, parents living in communities with high collective efficacy are apt to be approached by neighbors, school authorities, other parents, or the police when their child misbehaves. Parents might be expected to respond to these complaints by increasing the quality of their parenting in an effort to minimize further difficulties. Uninvolved or permissive parents may be prodded into adopting a more authoritative parenting style in response to the collective efficacy displayed by adult residents in their community (p. 1018). In this way, family- and community-level processes are often correlated and work together to influence juvenile delinquency. Unfortunately, without empirically measuring intervening theoretical mechanisms, our ability to fully and accurately specify how communities and delinquency are related remains limited.

A second problem is apparent in the communities and delinquency literature. Decades ago, Kornhauser (1978, p. 114) asked: "How do we know that area differences in delinquency rates result from aggregative characteristics of communities rather than characteristics of individuals selectively aggregated into communities?" Here Kornhauser raises the possibility that "what appears as a neighborhood effect in the...study could actually be an artifact of not having adequately controlled for neighborhood differences in the background characteristics of local residents" (Kapsis 1978, p. 470). This latter point, often referred to as a selective migration interpretation of the finding (Kapsis 1978, p. 470), implies that residential mobility decisions can artificially create "generative neighborhood effects" when in fact differences across neighborhoods are due, instead, to individual selection effects. Elliott et al. (1996, p. 397) explain: "People are not randomly assigned to neighborhoods but make personal choices that are related to their education, income, race/

ethnicity, and perceived characteristics of the neighborhood.... This selection process produces a compositional effect that is independent of the emerging organizational and cultural effects...."

Researchers are thus left asking: Are neighborhood effects artifactual, reflecting either individual-level compositional effects or self-selection by parents into particular neighborhoods (Haynie et al. 2006)? Some argue yes, and others no, prompting a contextual versus compositional debate. A contextual explanation involves the proposition that the social organization of an area influences the individuals who inhabit it, above and beyond the individuals who reside there. A compositional explanation involves the proposition that variation in delinquency rates across areas is primarily a result of the aggregate characteristics of the individuals who inhabit the areas (e.g., certain kinds of neighborhoods attract persons predisposed to criminality). A challenge for ecological researchers, then, is to demonstrate that neighborhood structure affects adolescent behavior net of compositional and selection factors, and to show that such effects operate through measurable mediating processes.

This has been achieved, to some degree, in neighborhood or contextual effects studies of delinquency, which have proliferated over the last couple of decades (Cattarello 2000; Elliott et al. 1996; Haynie et al. 2006; Gottfredson et al. 1991; Regnerus 2003; Simcha-Fagan and Schwartz 1986; Simons et al. 2005). As Sampson et al. (2002, p. 445) noted in a review of this literature, "the study of neighborhood effects has generated a multidisciplinary research agenda with a strong focus on child and adolescent development." Contextual effects studies address the contextual versus compositional debate because they control for the relevant individual-level traits of residents (e.g., single-parent family, social class, etc.) in order to ensure that a neighborhood-level effect (e.g., disadvantage) is not due to compositional differences among the individuals within neighborhoods. If neighborhood effects on adolescent delinquency are observed net of the individual characteristics on which the neighborhood measure is based, it is argued, we can be more confident that a neighborhood-level effect has indeed been observed (Haynie et al. 2006). Thus, researchers incorporate controls for background demographic characteristics, parental resources, and parenting practices in most neighborhood effects studies.

As noted earlier, parents may choose to reside in a particular neighborhood in part because of the level of crime or delinquency occurring in the area, reflecting selection bias. Selection bias may also produce spurious neighborhood effects because more conscientious parents (an unmeasured trait) may be more likely to select neighborhoods with less crime. If not accounted for, observed neighborhood effects would simply reflect the decision-making of conscientious parents, rather than a true neighborhood effect. In this literature, to help reduce the possibility of selection effects operating in analyses, researchers attempt to incorporate variables indicating parents' reasons for moving into their current neighborhood (Haynie et al. 2006), although this is often difficult to accomplish given data constraints.

IV. Neighborhood Effects Studies and Their Findings

Challenges aside, the neighborhood effects literature has produced many significant findings with respect to communities and delinquency. One set of findings reveals that neighborhood ecological characteristics *directly affect* rates of juvenile delinquency, even after controlling for a variety of individual-level characteristics of residents—findings that speak directly to the contextual versus compositional debate. For example, Kapsis (1978) tests Shaw and McKay's ideas regarding neighborhood racial change and delinquency using 1960–1966 data on a sample of 721 black adolescent males from adjacent low-income neighborhoods that had undergone varying rates of black population change. He finds that delinquency is positively correlated with the rate of racial change of neighborhoods, in line with Shaw and McKay. But perhaps more important, he finds this neighborhood effect remains after controlling for individual attributes of the residents. Similarly, Simcha-Fagan and Schwartz (1986), using survey data from neighborhoods in New York City, find that two neighborhood-level factors—organizational participation and extent of disorder and criminal subculture—significantly affect delinquency, even after controlling for individual-level correlates. Finally, in a contextual study of delinquency using data on 3,729 adolescents who are clustered within diverse social areas in Baltimore, Gottfredson et al. (1991) find that social areas have an independent effect on individual delinquent behavior, although the size of this effect is rather small.

A second set of findings from this literature reveals that neighborhood ecological characteristics *indirectly affect* rates of juvenile delinquency through various intervening processes, such as those identified earlier. That is, according to these studies, community levels of social ties, informal social control, collective efficacy, attenuated neighborhood subculture, and illegitimate opportunities mediate much of the effect of ecological characteristics on juvenile delinquency. Elliott et al. (1996), for example, find that a variety of organizational and cultural features of neighborhoods mediate the effects of concentrated disadvantage on adolescent development and behavior in their study of Chicago and Denver neighborhoods. Likewise, using data on a national sample of youth, Haynie et al. (2006) not only find that neighborhood disadvantage is associated with adolescent violence net of compositional and selection effects, but also that disadvantage is associated with adolescents' exposure to violent and prosocial peers and that peer exposure mediates, in part, the neighborhood disadvantage-adolescent violence association.

A third set of findings documents an *interaction effect* between individual- and community-level characteristics and processes. Neighborhood effects studies of interactions demonstrate that characteristics at both levels matter in unison for understanding and predicting juvenile delinquency. Along these lines, Regnerus (2003, p. 523) notes that "a proper understanding of…delinquency included the joint consideration of individual traits *and* the social contexts in which those traits have meaning." Likewise, a central premise in Furstenberg (1993) and Furstenberg et al. (1999, p. 6) is that "[adolescent] development results from an ongoing process of social change between individuals and their immediate milieus." The work of Furstenberg and his colleagues focuses, in particular, on the interface between the family and the community, and how this interaction affects the course of adolescent development, particularly for disadvantaged youth. Collectively, interaction studies consider a range of social milieus, and as is evident in the Simons et al. (2005) and Hay et al. (2007) research discussed earlier, interaction studies produce perhaps the most complex statements regarding the relationship between communities and delinquency.

As another example, Stark and colleagues (1982) demonstrate how the "religious ecology" of communities affects the individual-level correlation between religiosity and delinquency. Using a national sample of 16-year-old boys from eighty-seven high schools, they find there is a substantial negative relationship between religious commitment and delinquency, but that the relationship vanishes in the most highly secularized West Coast schools. Based on this, they argue that in communities where religious commitment is the norm, the more religious an individual, the less likely he or she will be delinquent. The larger point is that religious effects on delinquency vary according to ecological conditions, namely, the religious climate of the community; religion inhibits a youth from norm violations to the degree that he or she is embedded in a moral community (p. 15).

In a similar study on "religious ecology" and delinquency, Regnerus (2003) tests whether religion, when understood as a group property, is significantly linked to lower delinquency among youths in schools and counties where select religious characteristics are high. He asks: (1) Are adolescents who live or attend school in devoutly religious environments less delinquent, regardless of their own religious practice or affiliation?; (2) Do adolescents who live in religiously homogeneous places (e.g., densely conservative Protestant ones) display less delinquency?; and (3) Does it matter whether they are themselves conservative Protestant as well? Regnerus (2003, p. 546) finds that conservative Protestant homogeneity in both schools and counties constitutes an effective and robust social control against delinquency and, more important, that homogeneity serves to strengthen the inverse relationship between theft and students' self-identification as born-again Christians.

In a third study testing for interaction effects, Wikstrom and Loeber (2000) ask: Is the onset and prevalence of juvenile serious offending invariant by neighborhood SES context when controlling for individual sets of risk and protective characteristics? They report two key findings: first, for those boys scoring high on risk factors, there was no difference in serious offending by neighborhood SES context. That is, there was no evidence of a direct impact of the neighborhood on male juvenile serious offending for those with high risk scores. And second, for those boys having a balanced mix of risk and protective factors, or scoring high on protective factors, the neighborhood SES context influenced serious offending—but only for late onsets (during adolescence). That is, there is a significant direct effect of neighborhood disadvantage on well-adjusted children influencing them to become involved in serious offending as they reach adolescence.

Collectively, the neighborhood and contextual effects literature provides a more comprehensive approach to understanding the relationships among ecological characteristics, neighborhood processes, individual attributes, and juvenile delinquency. This literature begins to answer critical questions, such as those related to how youth living in high-risk environments overcome adversity. On this point Elliott et al. (1996, p. 391) argue: "Our primary interest in neighborhood effects is to understand how youths growing up in disadvantaged neighborhoods manage to complete a successful course of adolescent development in spite of the social and economic adversity that characterizes these social contexts. Our interest in the neighborhood is thus to identify those specific conditions and social processes that interfere with a successful course of youth development, as well as those that buffer or mitigate the potential negative ecological influences and physical dangers found in these environments."

Just as with delinquency area studies, there are some unresolved issues in the neighborhood effects literature. Unanswered is the question: Are community and individual risk factors primarily additive or interactive? That is, do community characteristics matter *in addition to* or *in conjunction with* individual risk factors? A related issue involves identifying the relative importance of neighborhood and individual risk factors for delinquency. One of the most common findings in the literature is that the proportion of variance in juvenile offending explained by community factors is rather low (Cattarello 2000, p. 49; Gottfredson et al. 1991; Simcha-Fagan and Schwartz 1986). Thus, social areas appear to have a small effect on individual delinquent behavior. Why might this be the case? Another finding is that many of the effects of community characteristics on individual offending are mediated by measures of individual characteristics (Cattarello 2000. p. 53; Haynie, Silver, and Teasdale 2006; Simons et al. 2005). Such findings raise the question: What are the implications for neighborhood studies of juvenile delinquency?

V. FUTURE DIRECTIONS IN COMMUNITIES AND DELINQUENCY RESEARCH

Research on communities and delinquency is alive and well. Still, there are several directions scholars can navigate in future studies to advance what is already known. To start, it is important to remember that neighborhoods are not remote and isolated entities. In thinking about neighborhood effects, one must consider, therefore, the presence of external, symbiotic relationships on local rates of delinquency (see, for example, Heitgard and Bursik 1987 who studied the effect of racial change occurring in nearby communities). Along these lines, neighborhoods are influenced by extra-community politics and public policies. Sampson and Wilson (1995, p. 54) emphasize the importance of analyzing crime at the neighborhood level and the policy context in which crime occurs when they contend: "On the basis of our theoretical framework, we conclude that community-level factors...are fruitful areas of future inquiry, especially as they are affected by macrolevel public policies regarding housing, municipal services, and employment." It is also important to remember that neighborhood contexts are not constant. They undergo change in response to broader political, economic, and cultural changes in the larger society, and in response to changes in the characteristics and composition of individual residents (Elliott et al. 1996, p. 392).

An important question for scholars who study communities and delinquency remains: Are patterns in delinquency across communities stable or variable? Unfortunately, most research in this area is cross-sectional, not longitudinal, and thus we know very little about how changes in ecological characteristics, changes in neighborhood social and organizational processes, and changes in rates of delinquency are associated over longer (or even shorter) periods of time. Yet it is argued that "the general omission of temporal considerations from this research tradition is a serious impediment to the community-level study of delinquency, for it forces the analyst to assume that the underlying dimensions associated with delinquency rates during a single time period are in fact real and persistent, regardless of historical changes in urban dynamics that may be taking place" (Bursik 2001, p. 394). In short, community processes related to delinquency should be placed within larger urban dynamics and given a full meaning through longitudinal data (Bursik 2001, p. 395).

Another key issue for future research has to do with determining at which point in the life course it may be most appropriate to measure or study juvenile delinquency. For example, should the focus be on variations in age of onset of delinquency, in terms of early or late onset? Should the focus be on the development of serious offending? What about recidivism rates among juveniles? As Wikstrom and Loeber (2000, p. 1117) point out, "Few studies have addressed the question of influences of community of residence on aspects of criminal careers, such as variations in the age of onset and individuals' development of serious offending," and "The question of whether community context influences the development of individuals' dispositions and social situation relevant to (future) offending has hardly been studied at all" (p. 1134). There is some evidence that neighborhood effects vary by the age of youths; more specifically, "they are minimal on very young children and stronger on older youths, who become increasingly embedded in neighborhood social networks and activities and have longer periods of exposure to the risks in disorganized neighborhoods" (Elliott et al. 1996, p. 417). As such, one could argue researchers should also compare different age groups of juvenile offenders.

Finally, in the conclusion of their review of neighborhood effects studies, Sampson and his colleagues (2002, pp. 470–73) focus on four additional directions for designing research on the neighborhood context of child and adolescent well-being: (1) redefining neighborhood boundaries in ways that are more consonant with social interactions and children's experiences; (2) collecting data on the physical and social properties of neighborhood environments through systematic social observations; (3) taking account of spatial interdependence among neighborhoods; and (4) collecting benchmark data on neighborhood social processes. I think each of these is critically important if the communities and delinquency literature is to make major strides in the future.

Apart from these future directions, criminologists must continue to recognize that adolescent delinquency and violence are a function of multiple social contexts including family, peer group, school, and, as this chapter hopefully has conveyed, the neighborhood. Perhaps of even greater importance, policy makers must begin to direct more attention toward focusing on neighborhoods in their attempts to develop programs and policies to curb juvenile delinquency. Unfortunately, approaches to reducing delinquency that do not involve additional investments within the juvenile justice system have received little attention in the public sphere. In the long list of recommendations for reducing delinquency (e.g., stiffer penalties, job training, boot camp, drug treatment), one arena of change is typically left out of the equation—changing communities. Yet by disregarding community context, we are critically ignoring key influences and pressures that directly and indirectly influence youth behavior. In sum, local areas must be considered when we think about juveniles and juvenile delinquency because they provide the environments that contextualize the lives of youth offenders and nonoffenders alike. As this chapter demonstrates, local areas afford opportunities and constraints for both normative and nonnormative behavior.

REFERENCES

Blau, Peter M., and J.E. Schwartz. 1984. *Crosscutting Social Circles*. Orlando, FL: Academic.

Bordua, David J. 1958. "Juvenile Delinquency and 'Anomie': An Attempt at Replication." *Social Problems* 6: 230–38.

Bursik, Robert J. 1988. "Social Disorganization and Theories of Crime and Delinquency: Problems and Prospects." *Criminology* 26: 519–51.

Bursik, Robert J. 2001. "Urban Dynamics and Ecological Studies of Delinquency." *Social Forces* 63: 393–413.

Bursik, Robert J., and Harold G. Grasmick. 1993. *Neighborhoods and Crime: The Dimensions of Effective Community Control*. New York: Lexington.

Cattarello, Anne M. 2000. "Community-Level Influences on Individuals' Social Bonds, Peer Associations, and Delinquency: A Multilevel Analysis." *Justice Quarterly* 17: 33–60.

Chilton, Roland J. 1964. "Continuity in Delinquency Area Research: A Comparison of Studies for Baltimore, Detroit, and Indianapolis." *American Sociological Review* 29: 71–83.

Cloward, Richard A., and Lloyd E. Ohlin. 1960. *Delinquency and Opportunity: A Theory of Delinquent Gangs*. New York: Free Press.

Elliott, Delbert S., William Julius Wilson, David Huizinga, Robert J. Sampson, Amanda Elliott, and Bruce Rankin. 1996. "The Effects of Neighborhood Disadvantage on Adolescent Development." *Journal of Research in Crime and Delinquency* 33: 389–426.

Furstenberg, Frank F., Jr. 1993. "How Families Manage Risk and Opportunity in Dangerous Neighborhoods." In *Sociology and the Public Agenda*, edited by William Julius Wilson, 231–58. Newbury Park, CA: Sage Publications.

Furstenberg, Frank F., Jr., Thomas D. Cook, Jacquelynne Eccles, Glen H. Elder, and Arnold Sameroff. 1999. *Managing to Make It: Urban Families and Adolescent Success*. Chicago: University of Chicago Press.

Gans, Herbert. 1968. "The Balanced Community: Homogeneity or Heterogeneity in Residential Areas?" In *People and Plans: Essays on Urban Problems and Solutions*, 161–81. New York: Basic Books.

Gordon, R.A. 1967. "Issues in the Ecological Study of Delinquency." *American Sociological Review* 32: 127-144.

Gottfredson, Denise C., Richard J. McNeil III, and Gary D. Gottfredson. 1991. "Social Area Influences on Delinquency: A Multilevel Analysis." *Journal of Research in Crime and Delinquency* 28: 197–226.

Hay, Carter, Edward N. Fortson, Dusten R. Hollist, Irshad Altheimer, and Lonnie M. Schaible. 2007. "Compounded Risk: The Implications for Delinquency of Coming from a Poor Family that Lives in a Poor Community." *Journal of Youth Adolescence* 36: 593–605.

Haynie, Dana L., Eric Silver, and Brent Teasdale. 2006. "Neighborhood Characteristics, Peer Networks, and Adolescent Violence." *Journal of Quantitative Criminology* 22: 147–69.

Heitgard, Janet L., and Robert J. Bursik. 1987. "Extracommunity Dynamics and the Ecology of Delinquency." *American Journal of Sociology* 92: 775–87.

Kapsis, Robert E. 1978. "Residential Succession and Delinquency." *Criminology* 15: 459–86.

Kornhauser, Ruth. 1978. *Social Sources of Delinquency*. Chicago: University of Chicago Press.

Kupersmidt, Janis B., Pamela C. Griesler, Melissa E. DeRosier, Charlotte J. Patterson, Paul W. Davis. 1995. "Childhood Aggression and Peer Relations in the Context of Family and Neighborhood Factors." *Child Development* 66: 360–75.

Lander, B. 1954. *Toward an Understanding of Juvenile Delinquency*. New York: Columbia University Press.

Polk, Kenneth. 1957. "Juvenile Delinquency and Social Areas." *Social Problems* 5(3): 214–17.

Regnerus, Mark D. 2003. "Moral Communities and Adolescent Delinquency: Religious Contexts and Community Social Control." *Sociological Quarterly* 44: 523–54.

Sampson, Robert J., Jeffrey D. Morenoff, and Thomas Gannon-Rowley. 2002. "Assessing 'Neighborhood Effects': Social Processes and New Directions in Research." *Annual Review of Sociology* 28: 443–78.

Sampson, Robert J., Stephen W. Raudenbush, and Felton Earls. 1997. "Neighborhoods and Violent Crime: A Multilevel Study of Collective Efficacy." *Science* 277: 918–24.

Sampson, Robert J., and William Julius Wilson. 1995. "Toward a Theory of Race, Crime and Urban Inequality." In *Crime and Inequality*, edited by John Hagan and Ruth D. Peterson, 37–54. Stanford, CA: Stanford University Press.

Shaw, Clifford R., and Henry D. McKay. 1942. *Juvenile Delinquency and Urban Areas*. Chicago: University of Chicago Press.

Simcha-Fagan, Ora, and Joseph E. Schwartz. 1986. "Neighborhood and Delinquency: An Assessment of Contextual Effects." *Criminology* 24: 667–703.

Simons, Ronald L., Leslie Gordon Simons, Callie Harbin Burt, Gene H. Brody, and Carolyn Cutrona. 2005. "Collective Efficacy, Authoritative Parenting, and Delinquency: A Longitudinal Test of Model Integrating Community- and Family-Level Processes." *Criminology* 43: 989–1030.

Stark, Rodney, Lori Kent, and Daniel P. Doyle. 1982. "Religion and Delinquency: The Ecology of a 'Lost' Relationship." *Journal of Research in Crime and Delinquency* 19: 4–24.

Wikstrom, Per-Olof H., and Rolf Loeber. 2000. "Do Disadvantaged Neighborhoods Cause Well-Adjusted Children to Become Adolescent Delinquents? A Study of Male Juvenile Serious Offending, Individual Risk and Protective Factors, and Neighborhood Context." *Criminology* 38: 1109–41.

Wilson, William Julius. 1987. *The Truly Disadvantaged: The Inner City, the Underclass, and Public Policy*. Chicago: University of Chicago Press.

PART IV

SOCIAL PROCESS AND DELINQUENCY

CHAPTER 13

STRAIN AND DELINQUENCY

ROBERT AGNEW

STRAIN theories state that certain strains or stressors increase the likelihood of delinquency. These strains include such things as harsh parental discipline, negative relations with teachers, peer abuse, criminal victimization, and a desperate need for money. Juveniles who experience these strains experience negative emotions, such as anger and frustration, which create much pressure for corrective action. Delinquency is one possible response. Delinquency may be a way to reduce or escape from strain. For example, juveniles may engage in theft to get the money they need or they may run away from home to escape abusive parents. Delinquency may be a way to seek revenge on those who cause strain or related targets. For example, juveniles may attack the peers who harass them. And delinquency may be a way to alleviate negative emotions. Juveniles, for example, may use illicit drugs to make themselves feel better. Most strained juveniles, however, do not turn to delinquency. Strain theories therefore also discuss those factors that increase the likelihood of delinquent coping. Such factors include poor coping skills, low social support, and association with delinquent peers.

The first section of this chapter provides a brief history of strain theories of delinquency, beginning with Merton (1938) and ending with Agnew's (1992, 2006a, 2006b) general strain theory, which dominates the current literature. The second section describes those strains that are most likely to cause delinquency. The third discusses the reasons *why* these strains increase delinquency. The fourth examines those factors that increase the likelihood that juveniles will cope with strains through delinquency. The fifth draws on strain theory to explain group differences in delinquency, such as the higher rates of offending among males. The sixth section concludes with a discussion of the implications of strain theory for controlling delinquency.

I. A Brief History of Strain
Theories of Delinquency

Merton (1938) presented the first modern version of strain theory in his classic article on "Social Structure and Anomie." This article is in two parts. First, Merton attempts to explain why some societies have higher rates of crime than others. Here he argues that certain societies place much emphasis on monetary success, but little emphasis on the legitimate means for achieving this goal, such as obtaining a good education and then a well-paying job. That is, the focus is not on "how you play the game, but on whether you win or lose." Such societies are said to be high in "anomie" or normlessness. Crime is higher in these societies because people are more likely to pursue monetary success using those means that are most effective, including crime. This part of Merton's theory did not receive much attention for several decades, although it was recently revived and extended by Messner and Rosenfeld (2006) in their "institutional-anomie" theory (also see Baumer and Gustafson 2007; Messner, Thorne, and Rosenfeld 2008). This theory also focuses on explaining societal differences in crime rates; it does not focus specifically on delinquency and so is not considered in this chapter.

The second part of Merton's theory attempts to explain why some groups within a society have higher crime rates than other groups. Merton argues that certain groups are less able to achieve monetary success through legal channels. In particular, lower-class individuals more often lack the training and support necessary to do well in school and secure good jobs. As a result, they experience much frustration and may turn to crime, particularly income-generating crimes such as theft, prostitution, and drug selling. This part of Merton's theory formed the basis for subsequent strain theories in criminology. Cohen (1955) and Cloward and Ohlin (1960), in particular, applied Merton's strain theory to the explanation of delinquency.

Cohen (1955) argued that the dominant goal in the United States is middle-class status, which includes not only monetary success but also the respect associated with a middle-class lifestyle. Lower-class boys were said to be less able to achieve middle-class status through legal channels. In particular, they often fare poorly in the school system since their parents are less able to equip them with the skills and attitudes necessary for success. Cohen argued that such boys are unlikely to turn to delinquency on their own, but if they regularly interact with one another, they might form delinquent gangs. Such gangs are a way to cope with their status frustration. The gangs reject the emphasis on middle-class status and instead focus on goals that the boys can achieve. These lower-class boys, drawing on their hostility toward the middle-class teachers and students who frustrate them, come to define success in terms of being a good criminal (e.g., being a good fighter and thief). (Note: Like most early criminologists, Cohen focused on the explanation of *male* delinquency.)

Cloward and Ohlin (1960), like Merton, argued that the dominant goal in the United States is monetary success. They also stated that lower-class juveniles are less able to achieve this goal through legal channels. Like Cohen, however, they claimed that these juveniles are unlikely to turn to crime unless they first form or join delinquent gangs. Crime is strongly condemned, and juveniles are unlikely to engage in it unless they have some group support. Cloward and Ohlin discussed the factors that influence whether strained juveniles form or join gangs. They stated, among other things, that the type of neighborhood one lives in is especially important, with some neighborhoods proving more opportunities for gang membership. Gangs encourage delinquent coping in several ways; most notably, they provide beliefs that justify or excuse delinquency as a response to strain. The work of Cohen and Cloward and Ohlin played a critical role in the development of strain theory, both because it applied strain theory to delinquency and it shed important light on those factors that influence whether juveniles respond to their strain with delinquency.

Merton, Cohen, and Cloward and Ohlin all argued that the dominant goal in the United States is monetary success or, somewhat more broadly, middle-class status. And the major strain or stressor for them is the inability to achieve this goal through legal channels. Several criminologists, however, later suggested that juveniles pursue a variety of goals, including positive relations with parents, success at school, popularity with peers, autonomy from adults, and masculine status (e.g., Elliott, Huizinga, and Ageton 1979; Greenberg 1977). It was said that the inability to achieve these additional goals might also result in delinquency. Juveniles, for example, might steal money to finance their social activities with peers, or they might drink and engage in sexual behavior as a way of asserting autonomy from adults. Most recently, Agnew (1992, 2006a, 2006b) drew on the stress research in psychology and sociology to point to still other sources of strain, as well as to additional factors that influence whether individuals cope with strains through delinquency. Agnew's general strain theory (GST) is the most comprehensive of the strain theories. The following sections, which describe the major arguments of contemporary strain theory, draw heavily on GST.

II. THE TYPES OF STRAIN MOST CONDUCIVE
TO DELINQUENCY

Strains refer to events or conditions that are disliked by individuals. As stated above, strains may involve the inability to achieve one's goals, including monetary, status, autonomy, and other goals. Strains, however, are not limited to goal blockage. They may also involve the presentation of negative stimuli, such as the experience of verbal and physical abuse. In addition, strains may involve the loss of positive stimuli, such as the loss of material possessions and valued relationships (see Agnew 1992, 2001, 2006a, 2006b).

Further, a distinction can be made between experienced, anticipated, and vicarious strains (Agnew 2002). Strains that are personally experienced should be most conducive to delinquency. However, anticipated and vicarious strains may also lead to delinquency. Anticipated strains refer to individuals' expectations that their current strains will continue into the future or that new strains will be experienced. For example, individuals may anticipate that they will be assaulted if they attend school or encounter certain people in their neighborhood. Like experienced strains, anticipated strains may upset individuals and lead to delinquent coping. For example, individuals may engage in delinquency to prevent anticipated strains from occurring—perhaps skipping school to avoid being assaulted or attacking those they view as a threat. Vicarious strains refer to strains experienced by close others, such as family members and friends. Such strains may also lead to delinquency; for example, an individual may assault members of a rival gang to avenge an attack on a friend.

Finally, it is important to distinguish between "objective strains" and the subjective evaluation of those strains. Objective strains refer to events and conditions that are disliked by most individuals in a given group. Receiving a failing grade at school, for example, is likely an objective strain among juveniles. Individuals, however, sometimes differ in their subjective evaluation of the same objective strain. For example, some juveniles may view a failing grade as a catastrophic event, while others may view it with indifference (see Wheaton 1990). While the experience of objective strains should increase the likelihood of delinquency, we would expect strains to be most likely to increase delinquency when they are also subjectively evaluated as bad or undesirable (see Froggio and Agnew 2007).

There are literally thousands of specific strains, as reflected in scales of stressful life events, stressful conditions, and "daily life hassles" (see Agnew 2006a). Not all of these strains are conducive to delinquency, however. Strains are most likely to result in delinquency when they have four characteristics (Agnew 2001, 2006a, 2006b). First, they are *high in magnitude*. The magnitude of a strain refers to the extent to which it is disliked. Strains are more likely to be disliked if they are high in degree (e.g., a serious versus minor assault, a large versus small loss of money); if they are continuous or frequent (e.g., a juvenile is regularly bullied); if they are of long duration; if they have been recently experienced; and if they are expected to continue into the future. Also important is the extent to which the strain threatens the core goals, needs, values, activities, and/or identities of the individual. For example, a strain is more likely to lead to delinquency if it threatens a core identity, perhaps one's masculine identity, rather than a secondary identity, perhaps one's identity as a good chess player.

Second, the strains are seen as *unjust*. Unjust strains involve the voluntary and intentional violation of a relevant justice norm. Among other things, unjust strains involve deliberate acts (e.g., a deliberate shove rather than an accidental bump). Also, unjust strains are seen as undeserved and not in the service of some greater good (e.g., parents punish a juvenile who did not do anything wrong). Further, the process used to decide whether to inflict the strain may be unjust; that is, juveniles have little opportunity to tell their side of the story, they are treated in a disrespectful manner, and no rationale is provided for the infliction of the strain. In addition, unjust strains frequently involve treatment that differs from the treatment of others in similar circumstances (e.g., a teacher punishes an African American student but ignores a white student who engaged in a similar act).

Third, strains are more likely to lead to delinquency when they are associated with low social control (see Agnew 2009a). There are several types of social control. *Direct control* refers to the extent to which others set clears rules, monitor behavior, and consistently punish rule violations in an appropriate manner. *Stake in conformity* refers to the individual's ties to conventional others, such as parents and teachers, and ties to conventional institutions, such as school. For example, do juveniles have close bonds to their parents, enjoy school, and get good grades. If so, they have much to lose through delinquency. And *beliefs* refer to the extent to which juveniles believe that delinquency is wrong. Certain strains are associated with low levels of social control. This is the case, for example, with parental rejection. Juveniles who are rejected by their parents probably have weak bonds to them and are subject to little direct control by them. Other strains, however, are associated with high social control. Juveniles who are closely supervised by their parents, for example, may dislike such supervision a great deal, but they are nevertheless subject to much direct control. As a consequence, this strain is less likely to result in delinquency.

Fourth, the strains are easily resolved through crime and/or involve exposure to others who promote crime. For example, the type of strain involving a desperate need for money is easily resolved through crime, including theft, selling drugs, and prostitution. The type involving the inability to achieve educational success, however, is not so easily resolved through crime. Also, some strains involve exposure to others who model crime, reinforce crime, or teach beliefs favorable to crime. For example, individuals who are abused by their parents or bullied by peers are exposed to others who model aggression.

Drawing on the above characteristics, it is possible to list those strains that are most conducive to delinquency. Such strains include the following:

- Parental rejection, which involves parents not expressing love or affection for their children, showing little interest in them, and providing little support to them.
- Harsh and erratic parental discipline, which includes the inconsistent use of disciplinary techniques such as physical punishment, screaming, threats, and humiliation and insults.
- Child abuse and neglect, including physical, sexual, and emotional abuse, as well as the failure to provide adequate food, shelter, medical care, and affection and attention.
- Negative school experiences, including low grades, negative relations with teachers (e.g., teachers treat the juvenile unfairly, humiliate the juvenile), and the experience of school as boring and a waste of time.

- Abusive peer relations, including insults, ridicule, gossip, threats, and physical assaults.
- Criminal victimization.
- Residence in economically deprived communities with high rates of violence and other problems.
- Homelessness, which is associated with a range of strains, including a desperate need for money, a need for food and shelter, conflicts with others, and criminal victimization.
- Discrimination based on characteristics such as race/ethnicity, sex, and religion.
- The failure to achieve selected goals, including thrills/excitement, high levels of autonomy, masculine status, and the desire for much money in a short period of time.

Research suggests that most of the above strains have a strong causal effect on delinquency (for overviews, see Agnew 2001, 2006a, 2006b; Kubrin et al. 2009). There has been less research on the effect of certain other of these strains, including peer abuse, criminal victimization, and discrimination. A few recent studies, however, suggest that these strains may also have relatively large effects on delinquency (Agnew 2006a; Baron 2004; Eitle 2002; Hay and Evans 2006; Katz 2000; Simons et al. 2002; Wallace, Patchin, and May 2005). It is important to note, however, that strain theory not only points to the factors which cause delinquency, but also explains *why* those factors cause delinquency.

III. Why Strains Increase the Likelihood of Delinquency

The primary reason that strains increase the likelihood of delinquency is that they lead to a range of negative emotional *states*, such as anger, frustration, and humiliation. These emotions create pressure for corrective action: individuals feel bad and want to do something about it. As indicated, delinquency is one possible response. Delinquency may be a way to reduce or escape from strain, seek revenge, and alleviate negative emotions. Further, certain of these emotions energize the individual for action, reduce inhibitions, create a desire for revenge, and reduce the ability to legally cope (e.g., to calmly and rationally communicate with others). Anger is notable in this regard, and it occupies a special place in strain theory. The continued experience of strains may also lead to negative emotional *traits*. Emotional traits are distinct from emotional states, in that traits refer to the tendency to experience particular emotions. Someone who is high in trait anger, for example, is quick to experience anger and tends to become angrier than others. Several studies have examined whether strains lead to negative emotional states and traits, with a focus on anger, and whether these states and traits in turn lead to delinquency. The results generally support strain theory, especially when it comes to explaining violent crime (for overviews and selected studies, see Agnew 2006a, 2006b; Aseltine, Gore, and Gordon 2000; Boa, Haas, and Pi 2004; Brezina 1998; Broidy 2001; DeCoster and Kort-Bultler 2006; Jang and Johnson 2003; Mazerolle, Piquero, and Capowich 2003; Sigfusdottir et al. 2008). More research is needed in this area, however, including research that looks at emotions besides anger, and that examines whether different strains lead to different emotions and whether different emotions lead to different types of crime (e.g., anger may be most relevant to violence, and depression to drug use).

Strains may also increase the likelihood of delinquency for additional reasons. Strains and the negative emotions associated with them may reduce social control. Many strains involve negative treatment by conventional others, such as parents and teachers. Such treatment may reduce the juvenile's bond to such people and commitment to conventional institutions, such as school. Strains may also reduce direct control and the belief that crime is wrong, since they weaken juveniles' ties to those who exercise direct control and teach such beliefs. Further, strains may foster the social learning of delinquency. As Cohen (1955) and Cloward and Ohlin (1960) point out, strained individuals may form or join delinquent groups in an effort to deal with their strain. These groups, for example, may provide status to juveniles, help juveniles obtain money through illicit activities, and provide some degree of protection from others. Finally, strained individuals may sometimes develop beliefs justifying delinquency. In particular, those who believe they are being unjustly treated by others may justify or excuse delinquent acts. An individual being bullied by others, for example, may come to believe that violence is justified if one is sufficiently provoked. Once more, certain studies provide support for these arguments, suggesting that strains sometimes reduce social control, increase association with delinquent peers, and lead to beliefs favorable to delinquency (see Agnew 2006a; Hoffman and Miller 1998; Hoffman and Su 1997; Paternoster and Mazerolle 1994).

IV. Factors that Increase
the Likelihood of Delinquent Coping

While the strains described above increase the likelihood of delinquency, most juveniles do *not* cope with these strains through delinquency. Delinquency is condemned by most people, it may result in sanction, and juveniles might lose much of what they value if caught. For these reasons, juveniles typically cope with strains in a legal manner. They may avoid or try to negotiate with the people who treat them negatively. They may turn to others, such as parents and teachers, for assistance. This assistance may take several forms, such as advice, emotional support, financial assistance, and advocacy on behalf of the juvenile (e.g., a parent negotiates with the juvenile's teacher). Juveniles may also do such things as listen to music and exercise in order to make themselves feel better. Finally, juveniles may simply endure their strain, suffering in silence.

Some juveniles, however, are more likely than others to cope with strains through delinquency. Strain theory describes the factors that should increase the likelihood of delinquent coping. These factors affect the interpretation of and emotional reaction to strains, the ability to engage in legal and illegal coping, the costs of delinquency, and the juvenile's disposition for delinquency. They include:

- Poor coping skills and resources. Some juveniles are less able than others to cope in a legal manner. These juveniles may have poor problem-solving skills; in particular, they have trouble thinking of different ways to respond to their strain, recognizing the advantages and disadvantages of each response, and enacting the best response. Related to this, they may have poor social skills, which reduce their ability to establish positive ties to others and effectively negotiate with them. Also important are the coping *resources* possessed by juveniles, with power and money being especially important. Juveniles, however, frequently lack these resources. As a consequence, their options for coping with strain are more limited. Imagine, for example, an adult who is having marital problems. This adult may have the resources to hire a marriage counselor, to move out of the house and seek a divorce if the counseling fails, and to hire an attorney to handle negotiations. A juvenile having family problems, however, lacks the money and power to employ these sorts of coping techniques. Juveniles, in particular, are usually compelled to live with their families and endure whatever problems that might exist. The same is often true if juveniles are having problems at school and with peers. This fact may help explain why juveniles have higher rates of offending than adults (more below).
- Delinquent coping skills and resources. It is important to consider not only the ability of juveniles to engage in legal coping, but also their ability to engage in delinquent coping. A range of factors may be relevant here, including physical size and strength, fighting ability, access to weapons, and the belief that one can successfully engage in crime (see Agnew 2006a).
- Low social support. Some juveniles do not have conventional others, such as parents and teachers, that they can turn to for assistance in coping. Their parent(s) may not be willing or able to provide support, and the juveniles may lack ties to other adults who can provide support. Juveniles can turn to their friends for assistance, but other juveniles sometimes have trouble providing effective support. In fact, other juveniles may sometimes suggest that the juvenile cope through delinquency (more below).
- Low social control. Some juveniles have little to lose if they cope through delinquency. The chances that their delinquency will be detected are low because they are poorly supervised by parents, teachers, and neighbors. If they are caught, they have little of value that might be jeopardized. They do

not care about their parents or other conventional adults, they are doing poorly in school, they have bad reputations, and their educational and occupational goals are limited. Finally, they do not believe that delinquency is wrong, so engaging in delinquency does not make them feel guilty.

- Low constraint and negative emotionality (see Agnew et al. 2002). These are personality traits and are a function of both biological factors and the social environment. Juveniles who possess the trait of low constraint are impulsive, giving little thought to the consequences of their behavior; they like to take risks and often find delinquency exciting; and they have little concern for the feelings and rights of others. Juveniles high in negative emotionality are easily upset and quick to anger, they tend to blame their problems on others, and they have an aggressive or antagonistic interactional style. Juveniles with these traits are more likely to interpret events and conditions in a negative manner, experience intense emotional reactions, give little thought to the costs of delinquency, and have a disposition for delinquent coping.
- Association with delinquent peers and beliefs favorable to delinquency. Juveniles who associate with delinquent peers are more likely to engage in delinquent coping because they are more often exposed to delinquent models, reinforced for delinquency, and taught beliefs favorable to delinquency. In particular, they are taught that certain strains are severe and require delinquent coping. Anderson (1999) provides an example of this in his discussion of the "code of the street." The code of the street is said to be common in many poor, inner-city communities, and it essentially states that being treated in a disrespectful manner, especially by others the same age, is perceived to be a serious affront and may require a violent response. Violence is a means of maintaining and enhancing one's status, as well as discouraging disrespectful treatment by others.
- Exposure to situations where the costs of delinquency are low and the benefits are high (see Agnew 2009a). This refers to situations where "attractive targets for crime" are present and "capable guardians" who might intervene are absent (Agnew 2009a). For example, a juvenile with a desperate need for money may encounter an inebriated businessperson carrying a large sum of money on a deserted street.

Researchers have tried to determine whether certain of the above factors increase the likelihood of delinquent coping. The results here have been mixed (for overviews and selected studies, see Agnew 2006a, 2006b; Agnew et al. 2002; Aseltine, Gore, and Gordon 2000; Baron 2004; Eitle and Turner 2003; Jang and Johnson 2003; Kubrin, Stucky, and Krohn 2009; Paternoster and Mazerolle 1994; Tittle, Brody, and Gertz 2008). For example, some studies find that strained juveniles are more likely to engage in delinquency if they have delinquent friends, while other studies do not find this. The reason(s) for these mixed results are unclear. Agnew (2006a) has noted that it is difficult to detect these "interaction" effects for technical reasons. Also, Agnew (2006a) has argued that researchers need to consider the juvenile's standing on all or most of the above factors, something that is rarely done (although see Mazerolle and Maahs 2000). Most researchers look at the above factors in isolation from one another, instead of considering them all together and developing a measure of the individual's overall propensity for delinquent coping.

V. Using Strain Theory to Explain Group Differences in Delinquency

Strain theory has been used primarily to explain why some juveniles are more likely to engage in delinquency than others. The theory, however, has also been applied to the explanation of group differences in delinquency. This section describes how the theory explains gender and age differences in delinquency— gender and age being the strongest socio-demographic correlates of delinquency (Agnew 2009a). It also briefly describes how strain theory has been used to explain race/ethnic and community differences in delinquency. In all cases, it is argued that certain groups have higher rates of delinquency because group members are more likely to experience those strains conducive to delinquency and to cope with them through delinquency.

A. Gender Differences

Males are more likely than females to engage in delinquency, especially serious violent and property crime (Agnew 2009a; Broidy and Agnew 1997). The higher rate of male delinquency is not due to the fact that males experience more strains than females. In fact, some data suggest that females experience more strains (Broidy and Agnew 1997). However, it has been argued that males are more likely to experience many of those strains conducive to delinquency, such as criminal victimization, negative school experiences, and trouble achieving masculinity goals. Many of the strains more often experienced by females, such as close parental supervision and the burdens associated with caring for others, are not conducive to delinquency (or at least other-directed delinquency). Females, however, are more likely to experience certain strains conducive to delinquency, such as sexual abuse and gender discrimination.

Also, the emotional reaction of males to strain is said to differ from that of females. Both males and females are equally likely to experience anger in response to strain, but the anger of females is more often accompanied by emotions such as depression, fear, and anxiety (partly reflecting the fact that anger is viewed as inappropriate for females). These additional emotions are said to reduce the likelihood of other-directed delinquency by females. Finally, males are said to be more likely to cope with strains through delinquency because they more often possess those factors conducive to delinquent coping. In particular, it is said that males are lower in social support, higher in criminal skills and resources, lower in social control, lower in constraint, higher in negative emotionality, more likely to associate with delinquent peers, and more likely to hold beliefs favorable to delinquency.

There has been a moderate amount of research in these areas, but no study has been able to examine the full range of strains and conditioning factors necessary to properly test the above ideas. Nevertheless, there is some evidence that males more often experience many strains conducive to crime, such as criminal victimization. Also, females experience and express anger differently than males. Further, males are more likely to cope with strains through crime, although not all studies find this. In this area, males and females differ on many of those variables that condition the effect of strains on crime. For example, girls are subject to higher levels of control and supervision than boys (which in turn limits opportunities for association with delinquent peers). For overviews and selected studies, see Agnew 2006a, 2009b; Broidy 2001; Broidy and Agnew 1997; Eitle and Turner 2002; Hay 2003; Hoffman and Su 1997; Jang 2007; Mazerolle 1998; Piquero and Sealock 2000; Wallace, Patchin, and May 2005.

B. Age Differences

Adolescents generally have higher rates of offending than children and adults. Strain theory partly explains this by arguing that adolescents are more likely to experience strains conducive to delinquency. Children tend to live in a sheltered world. They stay close to home and school, have a small circle of friends, and are closely supervised by parents and teachers. As a consequence, they are protected from many strains conducive to delinquency. Adolescents, however, enter a larger, more diverse, and more demanding world. They spend more time away from home and school, often unsupervised. They attend larger, more diverse schools, changing classes several times a day. As a result, they interact with many more people, including people they do not know well and people involved in delinquency. They get involved in romantic relationships. Further, school is more demanding; they are subject to more rules, given more work, and graded in a more rigorous manner. And, being physically mature and told to "act like adults," adolescents come to desire many of the privileges of adulthood, such as money, status, and autonomy.

As a result of these changes, adolescents are more likely than children to be treated in a negative manner by others. Further, adolescents more often have trouble meeting the new demands that are placed on them and achieving their new goals. When adolescents become adults, their social world once again narrows and they gain more control over this world. In particular, their circle of friends becomes smaller, they usually settle with a single romantic partner, and the number of people they interact with at their job is typically smaller than the number at school. Also, adults have more control over whom they associate with; and they can more readily change jobs, neighborhoods, and even spouses if they experience negative treatment. Further, adults are better able to achieve goals such as money, autonomy, and status. Adults then experience a decrease in strain. Some limited data support these arguments, suggesting adolescents are more subject to strains conducive to crime than children and adults (see Agnew 1997, 2003, 2006a).

Further, adolescents are less able to legally cope with the strains they experience than are children and adults. Parents and teachers typically cope on behalf of children. They closely monitor the lives of children and intervene when problems arise. This becomes much less true as children become adolescents, partly because adults believe that adolescents should cope on their own and partly because adolescents are much less closely monitored than children. Adolescents, however, lack the coping skills and resources of adults. Among other things, they have poorer problem-solving and social skills; they lack money and power; they are lower in self- and social control; and they are more likely to associate with delinquent peers. Research supports many of these arguments and, at a more general level, suggests that adolescents are more likely than adults to cope in "immature" or maladaptive ways, including delinquency (see Agnew, 1997, 2003, 2006a).

C. Explaining Other Differences in Delinquency

Strain theory has also been used to explain race/ethnic differences in delinquency, particularly the higher level of serious delinquency committed by African Americans relative to whites (Agnew 2009a; Kaufman et al. 2008). While most African Americans are not poor, African Americans are more likely than whites to be poor and to live in high-poverty communities. This contributes to race differences in several types of strain conducive to delinquency, including harsh/erratic discipline, negative school experiences, and, especially, criminal victimization. Also, African Americans at all class levels are more likely to experience discrimination than whites, and this too contributes to race differences in serious offending. Further, African Americans are said to be more likely to cope with strains through crime, given race-related differences in certain of the factors that promote delinquent coping—such as economic resources and social support. Data provide some support for these arguments (Agnew 2006a; Eitle and Turner 2003; Kaufman 2005; Kaufman et al. 2008; Perez, Jennings, and Gover 2008; Simons et al. 2002).

Strain theory has also been used to explain the higher rates of crime in very poor communities (Agnew 1999; Brezina, Piquero, and Mazerolle 2001; Warner and Fowler 2003). The residents of such communities are said to more often experience a range of strains conducive to crime, including discrimination, various family problems, conflicts with others in the community, and trouble achieving economic and status goals. Further, community residents are less able to legally cope with these strains. Among other things, they have fewer coping skills and resources, are lower in conventional social support, are lower in social control, associate more often with criminal others, and hold beliefs conducive to crime.

Finally, strain theory has been used to explain not only differences in offending between individuals and groups, but also changes in the level of offending over the course of an individual's life (Agnew 1997, 2006a; Hoffman and Cerbone 2000; Slocum, Simpson, and Smith 2005). In particular, the theory has been used to explain why most individuals increase their levels of offending as they become adolescents and reduce their offending as they become adults (see above). Also, the theory has been used to explain why some individuals offend at high rates over much of their lives. Such individuals are said to have traits that increase the likelihood that they will evoke negative reactions from others, sort themselves into environments where the likelihood of negative treatment is high, and cope with such treatment through delinquency. Such traits include low constraint and negative emotionality. Individuals with these traits, for example, often evoke negative reactions from their parents, alienate conventional peers and so end up in delinquent peer groups (where juveniles more often mistreat one another), and respond to negative treatment with delinquency. Also, individuals who offend at high rates over the life course are more likely to be very poor and reside in high-poverty communities; these characteristics also increase the likelihood of negative treatment and make it difficult to escape from such treatment. Further, individuals who experience certain strains early in life, such as school failure, are more likely to experience additional strains later in life, such as bad jobs. And this too helps explain offending over the life course.

VI. Recommendations for Reducing Delinquency

Strain theory makes several recommendations for reducing delinquency (see Agnew 2006a, 2010). The first and most obvious is that we eliminate or reduce those strains conducive to delinquency. And, in fact, several successful prevention and rehabilitation programs have shown some success at doing just that (see Agnew 2009a; Farrington and Welsh 2007). For example, certain home visitation and parent-training programs have reduced parental rejection, child abuse and neglect, and harsh/erratic discipline. Among other things, these programs attempt to reduce the stress that parents are under, teach parents how to properly supervise and discipline their children, and teach techniques for better resolving family conflicts. Certain school-based programs have shown success in reducing a range of negative school experiences, including low grades, the experience of school as boring and a waste of time, and negative relations with teachers. These programs provide tutoring and other support to juveniles, train teachers in more effective methods of instruction and discipline, and alter the overall school environment so as to increase student success and satisfaction. Still other programs have shown much success in reducing peer abuse, with some anti-bullying programs reducing the extent of bullying by 50% or more.

It is not always possible, however, to eliminate strains. For example, it is likely that parents will continue to limit the autonomy of their children and teachers will continue to give out low grades. It is possible, however, to alter these strains so as to make them less conducive to crime. Parents and teachers, for example, can better explain the rationale for their actions and take care to treat juveniles with respect. This will reduce the perceived injustice of strains. Also, those students receiving low grades might be assigned tutors and mentors. This will reduce the low control associated with poor grades.

Likewise, officials in the juvenile justice system can take steps to reduce the likelihood that the sanctions they administer will increase offending (see Agnew 2009a). With respect to perceived injustice, such steps include treating suspected offenders in a respectful manner, allowing them to tell their version of events, explaining the rationale behind decisions, reducing discrimination, and avoiding the use of overly harsh sanctions. Several of the chapters in this Handbook discuss these issues in more detail and make specific recommendations for reforming the juvenile justice system. These include the chapters by Tom Tyler, Donna Bishop, Kimberly Kempf-Leonard, Barry Feld, Gordon Bazemore, and Donna Bishop and Barry Feld. The restorative justice approach, in particular, seems to hold much promise for reducing the perceived injustice associated with sanctions (see the chapter by Bazemore).

In still other cases, it may not be possible to eliminate, reduce, or alter strains. The solution here may involve removing juveniles from strains. This includes removing juveniles from abusive families, perhaps placing them in foster care or in group homes. It includes removing juveniles from classes and schools where peer abuse is a problem. And it includes moving families to communities with less crime and violence. Efforts in this area should be used with caution. Sometimes the new environment may be more stressful than the one left behind, as evidenced by tales of abuse in foster care. Also, removing some individuals from a school or community may make conditions worse for those who are left behind.

In addition to the above strategies, we might equip juveniles with the traits and skills to avoid strains conducive to crime. Individuals sometimes provoke negative reactions from others or sort themselves into environments where negative treatment is likely (e.g., delinquent peer groups). This is especially true of individuals who are low in constraint and high in negative emotionality. Certain programs attempt to alter these traits; for example, anger management and social-skills training programs teach juveniles how to interact with others in ways that do not provoke negative reactions. Programs of this type are among the most successful treatment and prevention programs and are being increasingly adopted by juvenile justice agencies (see Agnew 2009a, 2010). Other programs, such as vocational skills training, try to equip juveniles with the skills necessary to achieve their goals through legal channels.

Finally, we can reduce the likelihood that individuals will cope with strains through delinquency. Several programs, in fact, have shown some success in addressing those factors said to increase the likelihood of delinquent coping.

Certain programs try to improve the coping skills and resources of individuals. For example, some programs teach juveniles effective problem-solving skills. Other programs try to increase the conventional social support available to juveniles. For example, they provide juveniles with mentors. Still other programs increase social control, including ties to parents and school; reduce the likelihood that juveniles will join delinquent peer groups; and/or alter those beliefs favorable to delinquent coping.

It is important to emphasize that most of the above programs were *not* explicitly developed to reduce strain or improve coping, but they often have this effect, and it may be one reason for their success.

VII. Summary

Strain theory states that:

1) Certain strains increase the likelihood of delinquency, particularly strains that are high in magnitude, seen as unjust, associated with low social control, easily resolved through crime, and associated with exposure to others who promote crime. Several such strains were described.

2) These strains increase delinquency for several reasons. Most notably, they lead to negative emotions such as anger; these emotions create pressure for corrective action; and delinquency is one possible response.

3) Several factors increase the likelihood that individuals will cope with these strains through delinquency, with these factors affecting the interpretation of and emotional reaction to strains, the ability to engage in legal and delinquent coping, the costs of delinquency, and the disposition for delinquency.

There is a fair degree of support for the first two propositions, and, as a consequence, strain theory stands as one of the major explanations of delinquency. Researchers, however, continue to examine factors that affect the likelihood of delinquent coping. Further, strain theory appears to hold much potential for the reduction of delinquency.

REFERENCES

Agnew, Robert. 1992. "Foundation for a general strain theory of crime and delinquency." *Criminology* 30: 47–87.

Agnew, Robert. 1997. "Stability and change over the life course: A strain theory explanation." In *Developmental Theories in Crime and Delinquency*, edited by Terrence P. Thornberry, 101–32. New Brunswick, NJ: Transaction.

Agnew, Robert. 1999. "A general strain theory of community differences in crime rates." *Journal of Research in Crime and Delinquency* 36: 123–55.

Agnew, Robert. 2001. "Building on the foundation of general strain theory: Specifying the types of strain most likely to lead to crime and delinquency." *Journal of Research in Crime and Delinquency* 38: 319–61.

Agnew, Robert. 2002. "Experienced, vicarious, and anticipated strain." *Justice Quarterly* 19: 603–32.

Agnew, Robert. 2003. "An integrated theory of the adolescent peak in offending." *Youth and Society* 34: 263–99.

Agnew, Robert. 2006a. *Pressured Into Crime: An Overview of General Strain Theory.* New York: Oxford University Press.

Agnew, Robert. 2006b. "General strain theory: Current status and directions for further research." In *Taking Stock: The Status of Criminological Theory*, edited by Francis T. Cullen, John Paul Wright, and Kristie R. Blevins, 101–23. New Brunswick, NJ: Transaction.

Agnew, Robert. 2009a. *Juvenile Delinquency: Causes and Control.* New York: Oxford University Press.

Agnew, Robert. 2009b. "The Contribution of 'Mainstream' Theories to the Explanation of Female Delinquency." In *The Delinquent Girl*, edited by Margaret A. Zahn, 7–29. Philadelphia: Temple University Press.

Agnew, Robert. 2010. "Controlling crime: Recommendations from general strain theory." In *Criminology and Public Policy: Putting Theory to Work*, edited by Hugh Barlow and Scott Decker. Philadelphia: Temple University Press.

Agnew, Robert, Timothy Brezina, John Paul Wright, and Francis T. Cullen. 2002. "Strain, personality traits, and delinquency: Extending general strain theory." *Criminology* 40: 43–72.

Anderson, Elijah. 1999. *Code of the Street.* New York: W. W. Norton.

Aseltine, Robert H., Jr., Susan Gore, and Jennifer Gordon. 2000. "Life stress, anger and anxiety, and delinquency: An empirical test of general strain theory." *Journal of Health and Social Behavior* 41: 256–75.

Bao, Wan-Ning, Ain Haas, and Yijun Pi. 2004. "Life strain, negative emotions, and delinquency: An Empirical test of general strain theory in the People's Republic of China." *International Journal of Offender Therapy and Comparative Criminology* 48: 281–97.

Baron, Stephen W. 2004. "General strain, street youth and crime: A test of Agnew's revised theory." *Criminology*, 42: 457–83.

Baumer, Eric P., and Regan Gustafson. 2007. "Social organization and instrumental crime: Assessing the empirical validity of classic and contemporary anomie theories." *Criminology* 45: 617–64.

Brezina, Timothy. 1998. "Adolescent maltreatment and delinquency: The question of intervening processes." *Journal of Research in Crime and Delinquency* 35: 71–99.

Brezina, Timothy, Alex R. Piquero, and Paul Mazerolle. 2001. "Student anger and aggressive behavior in school: An initial test of Agnew's macro-level strain theory." *Journal of Research in Crime and Delinquency* 38: 362–86.

Broidy, Lisa M. 2001. "A test of general strain theory." *Criminology* 39: 9–33.

Broidy, Lisa M., and Robert Agnew. 1997. "Gender and crime: A general strain theory perspective." *Journal of Research in Crime and Delinquency* 34: 275–306.

Cloward, Richard, and Lloyd Ohlin. 1960. *Delinquency and Opportunity.* Glencoe, IL: Free Press.

Cohen, Albert. 1955. *Delinquent Boys*. Glencoe, IL: Free Press.

DeCoster, Stacy, and Lisa Kort-Butler. 2006. "How General Is General Strain Theory?" *Journal of Research in Crime and Delinquency* 43: 297–325.

Eitle, David J. 2002. "Exploring a source of deviance-producing strain for females: perceived discrimination and general strain theory." *Journal of Criminal Justice* 30: 429–42.

Eitle, David J., and R. Jay Turner. 2002. "Exposure to community violence and young adult crime." *Journal of Research in Crime and Delinquency* 39: 214–37.

Eitle, David J., and R. Jay Turner. 2003. "Stress exposure, race, and young adult crime." *Sociological Quarterly*, 44: 243–69.

Elliott, Delbert, David Huizinga, and Suzanne Ageton. 1979. "An integrated perspective on delinquent behavior." *Journal of Research in Crime and Delinquency* 16: 3–27.

Farrington, David P., and Brandon C. Welsh. 2007. *Saving Children from a Life of Crime*. New York: Oxford University Press.

Froggio, Giacinto, and Robert Agnew. 2007 "The relationship between crime and 'objective' versus 'subjective' strains." *Journal of Criminal Justice* 35: 81–87.

Greenberg, David. 1977. "Delinquency and the age structure of society." *Contemporary Crises*. 1: 189–223.

Hay, Carter. 2003. "Family strain, gender, and delinquency." *Sociological Perspectives* 46: 107–36.

Hay, Carter, and Michael M. Evans. 2006. "Violent victimization and involvement in delinquency: Examining predictions from general strain theory." *Journal of Criminal Justice* 34: 261–74.

Hoffmann, John P., and Felicia Gray Cerbone. 1999. "Stressful life events and delinquency escalation in early adolescence." *Criminology* 37: 343–73.

Hoffmann, John P., and Alan S. Miller. 1998. "A latent variable analysis of general strain theory." *Journal of Quantitative Criminology* 14: 83–110.

Hoffmann, John P., and S. Susan Su. 1997. "The conditional effects of stress on delinquency and drug use: A strain theory assessment of sex differences." *Journal of Research in Crime and Delinquency* 34: 46–78.

Jang, Sung Joon. 2007. "Gender differences in strain, negative emotions, and coping behaviors: A general strain theory approach." *Justice Quarterly* 24: 523–53.

Jang, Sung Joon, and Byron R. Johnson. 2003. "Strain, negative emotions, and deviant coping among African Americans: A Test of general strain theory." *Journal of Quantitative Criminology* 19: 79–105.

Katz, Rebecca. 2000. "Explaining girls' and women's crime and desistance in the context of their victimization experiences." *Violence Against Women* 6: 633–60.

Kaufman, Joanne M. 2005. "Explaining the race/ethnicity-violence relationship: Neighborhood context and social psychological processes." *Justice Quarterly* 22: 224–51.

Kaufman, Joanne M., Cesar J. Rebellon, Sherod Thaxton, and Robert Agnew. 2008. "A general strain theory of racial differences in offending." *The Australian and New Zealand Journal of Criminology* 41: 421–37.

Kubrin, Charis E., Thomas D. Stucky, and Marvin D. Krohn. 2009. *Researching Theories of Crime and Deviance*. New York: Oxford.

Mazerolle, Paul. 1998. "Gender, strain, and delinquency: An empirical examination." *Justice Quarterly* 15: 65–90.

Mazerolle, Paul, and Jeff Maahs. 2000. "General strain theory and delinquency: An alternative examination of conditioning influences." *Justice Quarterly*, 17: 323–43.

Mazerolle, Paul, Alex R. Piquero, and George E. Capowich. 2003. "Examining the links between strain, situational and dispositional anger, and crime." *Youth and Society* 35: 131–57.

Merton, Robert K. 1938. "Social structure and anomie." *American Sociological Review* 3: 672–82.

Messner, Steven F., and Richard Rosenfeld. 2006. *Crime and the American Dream.* Belmont, CA: Wadsworth.

Messner, Steven F., Helmut Thorne, and Richard Rosenfeld. 2008. "Institutions, anomie, and violent crime: Clarifying and elaborating institutional-anomie theory." *International Journal of Conflict and Violence* 2: 163–81.

Paternoster, Raymond, and Paul Mazerolle. 1994. "General strain theory and delinquency: A replication and extension." *Journal of research in crime and delinquency,* 31: 235–63.

Perez, Deanna M., Wesley G. Jennings, and Angela R. Gover. 2008. "Specifying general strain theory: An ethnically relevant approach." *Deviant Behavior* 29: 544–78.

Piquero, Nicole Leeper, and Miriam D. Sealock. 2000. "Generalizing general strain theory: An examination of an offending population." *Justice Quarterly* 17: 449–84.

Sigfusdottir, Inga, Bryndis Asgeirsdottir, Gisli Gudjonsson, and Jon Sigurdsson. 2008. "A model of sexual abuse's effects on suicidal behavior and delinquency: The role of emotions as mediating factors." *Journal of Youth and Adolescence* 37: 699–712.

Simons, Ronald L., Yi-Fu Chen, Eric A. Stewart, and Gene H. Brody, Jr. 2003. "Incidents of discrimination and risk for delinquency: A longitudinal test study of African American adolescents." *Justice Quarterly* 20: 827–54.

Slocum, Lee Ann, Sally S. Simpson, and David A. Smith. 2005. "Strained Lives and Crime: Examining Intra-Individual Variation in Strain and Offending in a Sample of Incarcerated Women." *Criminology* 43: 827–54.

Tittle, Charles, Lisa Brody, and Marc Gertz. 2008. "Strain, crime, and contingencies." *Justice Quarterly* 25: 283–312.

Wallace, Lisa Hutchinson, Justin W. Patchin, and Jeff D. May. 2005. "Reactions of victimized youths: Strain as an explanation of school delinquency." *Western Criminology Review* 6: 104–16.

Warner, Barbara D., and Shannon K. Fowler. 2003. "Strain and violence: Testing a general strain model of community violence." *Journal of Criminal Justice* 31: 511–21.

Wheaton, Blair. 1990. "Life transitions, role histories, and mental health." *American Sociological Review* 55: 209–24.

CHAPTER 14

SOCIAL LEARNING THEORY

RONALD L. AKERS AND
CHRISTINE S. SELLERS

I. DEVELOPMENT OF SOCIAL LEARNING THEORY

THE designation of "social learning theory" has been used to refer to virtually any social behavioristic approach in social science that has a cognitive/behavioral focus (Bandura 1977; Patterson 1975, 1995; Andrews and Bonta 2003). In criminology and criminal justice, social learning theory has been developed and applied primarily in the work of Ronald L. Akers and associates. Social learning theory in criminology was originally proposed in collaboration with Robert L. Burgess (Burgess and Akers 1966b) as a behavioristic reformulation of Edwin H. Sutherland's classic differential association theory of crime.[1] It is a general theory of crime and deviance and is one of the most frequently tested and endorsed theories among academic criminologists (Ellis and Walsh 1999); and also may be considered one of the core theoretical perspectives in the field (Cullen, Wright, and Blevins 2006).

Sutherland's differential association theory (1947) proposed that criminal behavior is learned in a process of symbolic interaction with others in "intimate, face-to-face" groups, and that a person commits criminal acts because he or she has learned "definitions" (rationalizations and attitudes) favorable to violation of law in "excess" of the definitions unfavorable to violation of law. Differential association with criminal or noncriminal patterns varies according to what are called the "modalities" of

This chapter is a revised version of a chapter on social learning theory in Akers and Sellers (2009).

association. Sutherland asserted that all the mechanisms of learning are involved in criminal behavior. However, beyond a brief comment that more is involved than direct imitation, he did not explain what the mechanisms of learning are. These learning mechanisms were specified by Burgess and Akers (1966b) in their "differential association-reinforcement" theory of criminal behavior. Burgess and Akers produced a full reformulation that retained the principles of differential association, combining them with and restating them in terms of the learning principles of operant and respondent conditioning that had been developed by behavioral psychologists.[2] Akers followed up his early work with Burgess to develop social learning theory, applying it to criminal, delinquent, and deviant behavior in general. He has modified the theory, provided a fully explicated presentation of its concepts, examined it in light of the critiques and research by others, and carried out his own research to test its central propositions (Akers 1973, 1977, 1985, 1998; Akers and Sellers 2009).

Social learning theory is not competitive with differential association theory. Instead, it is a broader theory that retains all of the differential association processes in Sutherland's theory (albeit clarified and somewhat modified) and integrates it with differential reinforcement and other principles of behavioral acquisition, continuation, and cessation. But social learning theory explains criminal and delinquent behavior more thoroughly than does the original differential association theory (see, e.g., Akers et al. 1979; Warr and Stafford 1991). The concepts of differential association and definitions from Sutherland's theory are retained, but are conceptualized in both cognitive and behavioral terms. Concepts integrated into the theory from cognitive and behavioral psychology include principally differential reinforcement, whereby "operant" behavior (the voluntary actions of the individual) is conditioned or shaped by the balance of rewards and punishments but also includes "respondent" (involuntary, reflex) actions that can be made to respond to different stimuli through "classical" conditioning. Additional concepts include discriminative stimuli (the environmental and internal stimuli that provide cues or signals for behavior); schedules of reinforcement (the rate and ratio in which rewards and punishments follow behavioral responses); and other principles of behavior modification and the social behavioral mechanism of imitation. Social learning theory retains a strong element of the symbolic interactionism found in the concepts of differential association and definitions from Sutherland's theory (Akers 1985, pp. 39–70). Symbolic interactionism is the theory that social interaction is mainly the exchange of meaning and symbols; individuals have the cognitive capacity to imagine themselves in the roles of others and incorporate this into their conceptions of themselves (Sandstrom, Martin, and Fine 2003). This, and the explicit inclusion of such concepts as imitation, anticipated reinforcement, and self-reinforcement, makes social learning "soft behaviorism" (Akers 1985, p. 65). It assumes human agency, that is, people are capable of making judgments and decisions, and soft determinism, that is, human behavior is predictable on a probability basis, not strictly determined by influences over which individuals have no control and to which they respond automatically.

This chapter presents a detailed discussion of the concepts and propositions of the original social learning model as well as its later expansion, which includes the social structural context within which social learning occurs. A review of the empirical research on social learning theory underscores its validity as an explanation of crime and delinquency. We also analyze several criticisms of social learning theory and conclude with a description of a variety of programs based on principles of social learning theory and an assessment of research testing the effectiveness of these programs in the prevention and treatment of adolescent misbehavior.

II. THE CENTRAL CONCEPTS, PROPOSITIONS, AND PROCESS OF SOCIAL LEARNING THEORY

The word "learning" should not be taken to mean that the theory is only about how behavior is acquired for the first time. Rather it refers to a general process and set of variables in acquiring, maintaining, and changing behavior (Andrews and Bonta 2003; Horney 2006). Social learning theory offers an explanation of crime and deviance that embraces variables that operate both to motivate and inhibit criminal/deviant behavior and both to promote and undermine conformity. The probability of criminal or conforming behavior occurring is a function of the balance of these influences on behavior operative in one's learning history, at a given time, or in a given situation.

> The basic assumption in social learning theory is that the same learning process in a context of social structure, interaction, and situation, produces both conforming and deviant behavior. The difference lies in the direction ... [of] the balance of influences on behavior.... The probability that persons will engage in criminal and deviant behavior is increased and the probability of their conforming to the norm is decreased when they differentially associate with others who commit criminal behavior and espouse definitions favorable to it, are relatively more exposed in-person or symbolically to salient criminal/deviant models, define it as desirable or justified in a situation discriminative for the behavior, and have received in the past and anticipate in the current or future situation relatively greater reward than punishment for the behavior. (Akers 1998, p. 50)

While referring to all social, cognitive, and behavioral dimensions of this process, Akers' development of the theory has relied principally on four major concepts: *differential association, definitions, differential reinforcement, and imitation* (Akers et al. 1979; Akers 1985; 1998).

A. Differential Association

Differential association has both behavioral-interactional and normative dimensions. The interactional dimension is the direct association and interaction with others who engage in certain kinds of behavior, as well as the indirect association and identification with more distant reference groups. The normative dimension is the different patterns of norms and values to which an individual is exposed through this association (see Clark 1972). The groups with which one is in differential association provide the major proximal social contexts in which all the mechanisms of social learning operate. They not only expose one to definitions, but they also present one with models to imitate and with differential reinforcement (source, schedule, value, and amount) for criminal or conforming behavior. The most important of these groups are the primary ones of family and friends, but also may be neighbors, school teachers, physicians, pastors, and other individuals and groups in the community (as well as mass media and other more remote sources of attitudes and models). With the large and growing social interaction taking place over cell phones, the Internet, and other voice, picture, and video technologies these also include what Warr (2002) refers to as "virtual peer groups" that both overlap with and exist apart from groups with which one is in face-to-face interaction. The term "social media" that is so often applied to this phenomenon captures very well the facilitation of interaction that makes not only for virtual peer groups but other groups and even entire "communities." In social learning terms, these would be different variations on "virtual differential association." Those associations that occur earlier (priority), last longer and occupy more of one's time (duration), take place most often (frequency), and involve others with whom one has the more important, significant, or closer relationship (intensity) will have the greater effect on behavior.

B. Definitions

Definitions are one's own attitudes or meanings attached to given behavior. That is, they are orientations, rationalizations, definitions of the situation, and other evaluative and moral attitudes that define the commission of an act as right or wrong, good or bad, desirable or undesirable, justified or unjustified.

In social learning theory, these definitions are both general and specific. General beliefs include religious, moral, and other conventional values and norms that are favorable to conforming behavior and unfavorable to committing any of a whole range of deviant or criminal acts. Specific definitions orient the person to particular acts or series of acts. Thus, one may believe that it is morally wrong to steal and that laws against theft should be obeyed, but at the same time see little wrong with smoking marijuana and rationalize that it is all right to violate laws against drug possession.

The greater the extent to which one holds attitudes that disapprove of certain acts either because they are not in line with one's general values or specific attitudes, the less one is likely to engage in them. Positive definitions favorable to committing criminal acts are beliefs or attitudes that make the behavior morally desirable or wholly permissible ("you gotta be tough and get a rep"). Neutralizing definitions do not view the act as something that is desirable to do, but rather view it as something that is nonetheless all right, justified, excusable, necessary, or not really bad to do under given circumstances. Neutralizing attitudes include such beliefs as "the idiot was in my face and deserved the beating I gave him," "Everybody has a racket," "I can't help myself, I was born this way," "Yes, I did it, but it wasn't my fault," "I was drunk and didn't know what I was doing," "It is OK to steal the batteries because the store can afford it and won't even miss them," and other excuses and justifications for committing law-violating acts and victimizing others. Cognitively, these learned definitions provide a mind-set that makes one more willing to commit the act when the opportunity (itself subject to the person's definition of the situation) occurs. Behaviorally, they affect the commission of deviant or criminal behavior by acting as internal discriminative stimuli that operate as behavioral cues or signals to the individual as to what responses are appropriate or expected in a given situation. For the most part, definitions favorable to crime do not "require" the behavior to be committed. Rather, they are conventional beliefs so weakly held that they provide no restraint or are positive or neutralizing attitudes that facilitate law violation in the right set of circumstances.

C. Differential Reinforcement

Differential reinforcement refers to the balance of anticipated or actual rewards and punishments that follow or are consequences of behavior. Whether individuals will refrain from or commit a crime at any given time (and whether they will continue or desist from doing so in the future) depends on the past, present, and anticipated future rewards and punishments for their actions. The probability that an act will be committed or repeated is increased by rewarding outcomes or reactions to it, e.g., obtaining approval, money, food, or pleasant feelings—positive reinforcement. The likelihood that an action will be taken is also enhanced when it allows the person to avoid or escape aversive or unpleasant events—negative reinforcement. Punishment may also be direct (positive), in which painful or unpleasant consequences are attached to a behavior, or indirect (negative), in which a reward or pleasant consequence is removed. The greater the value or amount of reinforcement for the person's behavior, the more frequently it is reinforced, and the higher the probability that it will be reinforced (as balanced against alternative behavior), the greater the likelihood that it will occur and be repeated. Reinforcers and punishers can be nonsocial; for example, the direct physical effects of drugs and alcohol. Also, there may be a physiological basis for the tendency of some individuals (such as those prone to sensation-seeking) more than others to find certain forms of deviant behavior intrinsically rewarding (Wood et al. 1995; Brezina and Piquero 2003). However, whether or not these effects are experienced positively or negatively is very much affected by previously learned expectations. The peer or other social context in which the actions take place, one's learned moral attitudes, and other social variables affect how much one experiences the intrinsic effects of substance use or committing certain acts as pleasurable and enjoyable or as frightening and unpleasant. "Individual differences in the propensity to derive intrinsic pleasure and reward from substance use appear to be related to social learning factors in ways predicted by the theory" (Brezina and Piquero 2003, p. 284). The prediction is that most of the learning in criminal and deviant behavior is the result of social exchange in which the words, responses, presence, and behavior of other persons directly reinforce behavior, provide the setting for reinforcement (discriminative stimuli), or serve as the conduit through which other social rewards and punishers are delivered or made available.

Individuals can learn behavior without contact, directly or indirectly, with social reinforcers and punishers. The concept of social reinforcement (and punishment) goes beyond the direct reactions of others present while an act is committed. It also includes the whole range of actual and anticipated, tangible and intangible rewards valued in society or subgroups. Social rewards can be highly symbolic. Their reinforcing effects can come from their fulfilling ideological, religious, political, or other goals. Even those rewards which we consider to be very tangible, such as money and material possessions, gain their reinforcing value from the prestige and approval value they have in society. Nonsocial reinforcement, therefore, is more narrowly confined to unconditioned physiological and physical stimuli. In self-reinforcement, the individual exercises self-control, reinforcing, or punishing one's own behavior by taking the role of others, even when alone.

D. Imitation

Imitation refers to the engagement in behavior after the observation of similar behavior in others. Whether the behavior modeled by others will be imitated is affected by the characteristics of the models, the behavior observed, and the observed consequences of the behavior (Bandura 1977). The observation of salient models in primary groups and in the media affects both pro-social and deviant behavior (Donnerstein and Linz 1995). It is more important in the initial acquisition and performance of novel behavior than in the maintenance or cessation of behavioral patterns once established, but it continues to have some effect in maintaining behavior.

E. Process

These social learning variables are all part of an underlying process that is operative in each individual's learning history and in the immediate situation in which an opportunity for a crime occurs. Akers stresses that social learning is a complex process with reciprocal and feedback effects. The reciprocal effects are not seen as equal, however. Akers hypothesizes a typical temporal sequence or process by which persons come to the point of violating the law or engaging in other deviant acts (Akers 1998).

This process is one in which the balance of learned definitions, imitation of criminal or deviant models, and the anticipated balance of reinforcement produces the initial delinquent or deviant act. The facilitative effects of these variables continue in the repetition of acts, although imitation becomes less important than it was in the first commission of the act. After initiation, the actual social and nonsocial reinforcers and punishers affect whether the acts will be repeated and at what level of frequency. Not only the behavior itself, but also the definitions are affected by the consequences of the initial act. Whether a deviant act will be committed in a situation that presents the opportunity depends on the learning history of the individual and the set of reinforcement contingencies in that situation.

> The actual social sanctions and other effects of engaging in the behavior may be perceived differently, but to the extent that they are more rewarding than alternative behavior, then the deviant behavior will be repeated under similar circumstances. Progression into more frequent or sustained patterns of deviant behavior is promoted [to the extent] that reinforcement, exposure to deviant models, and definitions are not offset by negative formal and informal sanctions and definitions. (Akers 1985, p. 60)

The theory does not hypothesize that definitions favorable to law violation only precede and are unaffected by the initiation of criminal acts. Acts in violation of the law can occur in the absence of any thought given to right and wrong. Furthermore, definitions may be applied by the individual retroactively to excuse or justify an act already committed. To the extent that such excuses successfully mitigate others' negative sanctions or one's self-punishment, however, they become cues for the repetition of deviant acts. At that point they precede the future commission of the acts.

Differential association with conforming and nonconforming others typically precedes the individual's commission of the acts. Families are included in the differential association process, and it is obvious that association, reinforcement of conforming or deviant behavior, deviant or conforming modeling, and exposure to definitions favorable or unfavorable to deviance occur within the family prior to the onset of delinquency. On the other hand, it can never be true that the onset of delinquency causes selection into or precedes any interaction whatsoever in the family (except in the unlikely case of the late-stage adoption of a child who is already delinquent who is drawn to and chosen by deviant parents). Parents supervise and control their children's selection of friends (Warr 2005). However, behavioral similarity, including prior deviant behavior or tendencies, can play a role in the youth's friendship selection and initiation of interaction in peer groups. Even so, associations with peers and others are most often formed initially around attractions, friendships, and circumstances, such as neighborhood proximity, that have little to do directly with co-involvement in some deviant behavior. In either case, after the associations have been established and the reinforcing or punishing consequences of the interaction and the deviant or conforming behavior are experienced, both the continuation of old and the seeking of new peer associations (over which one has any choice) will themselves be affected "in proportion to the relative rate of positive reinforcement generated during interaction with each of those peers" (Snyder 2002, p. 109).

> Deviant peers reinforce each other for deviancy. Peers who maximize the child's immediate payoffs get selected as friends.... The selection of deviant peers insures the maintenance of deviant behaviors as well as the development of new forms of deviancy.... The findings show that antisocial boys are mutually reinforcing for rule-breaking talk, and that this talk predicts both later delinquency and later substance use. (Patterson 2002, pp. 12–13)

One may choose further interaction with others based in part on whether they too are involved in similar deviant or criminal behavior, assuming the relationships are mutually reinforcing. But the theory proposes that the sequence of events, in which deviant associations precede the onset of delinquent behavior, will occur more frequently than the sequence of events in which the onset of delinquency precedes the beginning of deviant associations.

This recognition of sequence and reciprocal effects through social interaction is another clear indication that social learning is *not*, as some critics (Gottfredson and Hirschi 1990) claim that it is, simply a "cultural deviance" theory, which assumes that violation of the rules of the larger society occurs only because individuals are conforming to the norms of deviant groups into which they have become completely socialized (see Akers 1996; Sellers and Akers 2006). One may learn deviant attitudes and behavior through exposure to street codes and deviant subcultures (Anderson 1999; Benoit et al. 2003) or immersion in criminal and illegitimate activities as a career criminal (Steffensmeier and Ulmer 2005). Many offenders have come into association with somewhat older criminal "mentors" who go beyond being co-offenders to providing direct tutelage in criminal attitudes and behavior and helping the younger offenders develop and enhance criminal careers (Morselli, Tremblay, and McCarthy 2006). Benoit et al. (2003) have identified the balance of social learning variables, including what they refer to as "inverse imitation" as the main mechanism by which the inner city social structure, neighborhood, and family affect young men's involvement in, and switching between, conforming and deviant norms and behavior such as drug use, trafficking, and violence (Benoit et al. 2003). However, the theory is not confined to delinquent, criminal, or deviant behavior acquired only through differential exposure to such deviant subcultures, environments, and individuals. It does not ignore, as Osgood and Anderson (2004, p. 525) contend it does, "contextual and situational influences" and does not rest solely on "positing a causal role for peer culture that values delinquency." Their finding that delinquency is related to unstructured or unsupervised adolescent peer interaction fits precisely into the notion of differential peer association. The theory proposes that conforming and delinquent, criminal, or deviant behavior is learned through differential exposure to conforming and deviant patterns. This includes incomplete or failed socialization in conventional norms and values as well as countervailing processes of reinforcement, imitation, and exposure to deviant definitions or attitudes. (See Akers and Jensen 2006 and Sellers and Akers 2006 for a review of this and other common misinterpretations of social learning theory.)

III. Social Structure and Social Learning

Akers has proposed a social structure and social learning (SSSL) model in which social structural factors are hypothesized to have an effect on the individual's conduct through their effect on the social learning process and the variables of differential association, differential reinforcement, definitions, and imitation in the individual's life. The social learning variables then have a direct impact on the individual's behavior. That is, the social learning variables are proposed as the main mediating variables in the process by which various aspects of the social structure influence individual behavior.

> The social structural variables are indicators of the primary distal macro-level and meso-level causes of crime, while the social learning variables reflect the primary proximate causes of criminal behavior that mediate the relationship between social structure and crime rates. Some structural variables are not related to crime and do not explain the crime rate because they do not have a crime-relevant effect on the social learning variables. (Akers 1998, p. 322)

In the SSSL model, Akers (1998) identifies four dimensions of social structure that provide the contexts within which the social learning process and variables operate: *Differential Social Organization* refers to the structural correlates of crime in the community or society that affect the rates of crime and delinquency, including age composition, population density, and other attributes that slant societies, communities, and other social systems "toward relatively high or relatively low crime rates" (Akers 1998, p. 332). *Differential Location* in the social structure refers to the sociodemographic characteristics of individuals and social groups that indicate their niches within the larger social structure. Class, gender, race and ethnicity, marital status, and age locate the positions and standing of persons and their roles, groups, or social categories in the overall social structure. *Theoretically Defined Structural Variables* refer to anomie, class oppression, social disorganization, group conflict, patriarchy, and other concepts that have been identified in one or more theories as criminogenic conditions of societies, communities, or groups. *Differential Social Location* refers to individuals' membership in and relationship to primary, secondary, and reference groups such as the family, friendship/peer groups, leisure groups, colleagues, and work groups.

The differential social organization of society and community, as well as the differential location of persons in the social class, race, gender, religion, and other structures in society, provides the general learning contexts for individuals that increase or decrease the likelihood of their committing crime. The differential location in family, peer, school, church, and other groups provides the more immediate contexts that promote or discourage the criminal behavior of the individual. Differences in the societal or group rates of criminal behavior are a function of the extent to which their cultural traditions, norms, and social control systems provide socialization, learning environments, and immediate situations conducive to conformity or deviance. The structural conditions identified in macro-level theories

can affect one's exposure to criminal associations, models, definitions, and reinforcement to induce or retard criminal actions in individuals.

IV. RESEARCH ON RELATIONSHIP OF CRIMINAL AND DELINQUENT BEHAVIOR TO SOCIAL LEARNING VARIABLES

The great preponderance of research conducted on social learning theory has found
strong relationships in the theoretically expected direction between social learning
variables and criminal, delinquent, and deviant behavior. Many studies using direct
measures of one or more of the social learning variables of differential association,
imitation, definitions, and differential reinforcement find that the theory's hypotheses are upheld (Winfree, Sellers, and Clason 1993; Winfree, Vigil-Backstrom, and
Mays 1994; Winfree, Mays, and Vigil-Backstrom 1994; Mihalic and Elliott 1997;
Skinner and Fream 1997; Esbensen and Deschenes 1998; Batton and Ogle 2003;
Sellers, Cochran, and Winfree 2003; Brezina and Piquero 2003; Chappell and Piquero
2004; McGloin, Pratt, and Maahs 2004; Osgood and Anderson 2004; Triplett and
Payne 2004; Matsueda, Kreager, and Huizinga 2006).[3] The relationships between the
social learning variables and delinquent, criminal, and deviant behavior found in
the research are typically strong to moderate, and there has been very little negative
evidence reported in the literature. Most of the research has been done in the United
States, but social learning theory is well supported by research in other societies as
well (Kandel and Adler 1982; Lopez, Redondo, and Martin 1989; Junger-Tas 1992;
Bruinsma 1992; Zhang and Messner 1995; Hwang and Akers 2003, 2006; Wang and
Jensen 2003). Pratt et al.'s (2010) meta-analysis covering the findings of over one
hundred social learning studies found substantial support for the impact of two
social learning variables (differential association and definitions) on offending, and
although the effects of those variables were not stronger than measures of self-control
(Pratt and Cullen 2000), their effect sizes were greater than those for rational choice/
deterrence variables (Pratt et al. 2006) and tended to hold regardless of methodological approach in various empirical tests of the theory. Moreover, when social
learning theory is tested against other theories using the same data collected from
the same samples, it is usually found to have greater support than the theories with
which it is being compared (for instance, see McGee 1992; Benda 1994; Burton et al.
1994; Hwang and Akers 2003, 2006; Rebellon 2002; Preston 2006; Neff and Waite
2007). When social learning variables are included in integrated or combined models that incorporate variables from different theories, it is the measures of social
learning concepts that have the strongest main and net effects (Elliott, Huizinga,
and Ageton 1985; Kaplan, Johnson, and Barley 1987; Thornberry, Moore, and
Christenson 1994; Kaplan 1996; Catalano et al. 1996; Huang et al. 2001; Jang 2002).

Much of this research confirms the effect on criminal and deviant behavior of differential association in primary groups, especially family and peers (Triplett and Payne 2004; Simons, Simons, and Wallace 2004). (For the most recent review of research on the family and delinquency and its implications for social learning and other theories, see Chapter 8 by Simons, Simons, and Hancock in this volume.) The role of the family is usually as a conventional socializer against delinquency and crime. It provides anticriminal definitions, conforming models, and the reinforcement of conformity through parental discipline; it promotes the development of self-control. Patterson and his colleagues at the Oregon Social Learning Center have shown that the operation of social learning mechanisms in parent-child interaction is a strong predictor of conforming/deviant behavior (Patterson 1975; 1995; 2002; Snyder and Patterson 1995; Reid, Patterson, and Snyder 2002; Weisner, Capaldi, and Patterson 2003). Ineffective disciplinary strategies by parents increase the chances that a child will learn behavior in the early years that is a precursor to his or her later delinquency. As Simons, Simons, and Hancock in this volume note in some detail, childhood and adolescent delinquent behavior is related to inconsistent, overly punitive, or too permissive child-rearing and in particular to the development of the kind of parent-child interaction that Patterson and his colleagues refer to as "coercive" (Patterson 1995). Children learn conforming responses when parents consistently make use of positive rewards for proper behavior and impose moderately negative consequences for misbehavior (Capaldi, Chamberlain, and Patterson 1997; see also Ardelt and Day 2002). Having parents and siblings who have engaged in deviant and criminal behavior is a predictor of one's later delinquent and criminal behavior, reflecting both imitative and direct training effects in the family (Adler and Adler 1978; McCord 1991; Rowe and Gulley 1992; Lauritsen 1993; Rowe and Farrington 1997; Ardelt and Day 2002). "[S]ocial learning theory garnered the strongest, most consistent empirical support. Social learning theory directs attention to the behavioral consequences of interaction patterns in families, emphasizing that children tend to adopt behaviors they learn from their parents.... We find that witnessing arguments between parents and being involved in verbal conflicts with parents and siblings is related to higher levels of sibling violence" (Hoffman, Kiecolt, and Edwards 2005, p. 1124).

Among the range of actions and choices directly affected by families are the adolescent's choices of friends and peer associations. Sibling effects in part are peer effects, and delinquent tendencies learned in the family may be exacerbated, while prosocial influences of the family may be counteracted, by differential peer association (Lauritsen 1993; Simons et al. 1994; Simons, Simons, and Wallace 2004). As one moves from childhood to adolescence, family influences diminish and peer groups play an increasingly prominent role in learning conforming and deviant behavior. Other than one's own prior deviant behavior, the best single predictor of the onset, continuance, or desistance of crime and delinquency is differential association with conforming or law-violating peers (Loeber and Dishion 1987; Loeber and Stouthamer-Loeber 1986; Liu 2003; Warr 2002). More frequent, longer-term, and closer association with peers who do not support deviant behavior is strongly correlated with conformity, while greater association with peers who commit and approve of delinquency is predictive of one's own delinquent behavior. It is in peer groups that the first availability and opportunity for delinquent acts are typically provided. Virtually every study that includes a peer association variable finds it to be significantly and usually most strongly related to delinquency, alcohol and drug use and abuse, adult crime, and other forms of deviant behavior (Warr 2002). There is a sizable body of research literature that shows the importance of differential associations and definitions in explaining crime and delinquency.[4] Although some contend that association with delinquent peers has no causal significance in the commission of delinquency or crime (Gottfredson and Hirschi 1990), Mark Warr (2002, p. 40) argues that there is no factor in criminal and delinquent behavior as powerful as peer associations.

> No characteristic of individuals known to criminologists is a better predictor of criminal behavior than the number of delinquent friends an individual has. The strong correlation between delinquent behavior and delinquent friends has been documented in scores of studies from the 1950s up to the present day … using alternative kinds of criminological data (self-reports, official records, perceptual data) on subjects and friends, alternative research designs, and data on a wide variety of criminal offenses. Few, if any, empirical regularities in criminology have been documented as often or over as long a period as the association between delinquency and delinquent friends.

Warr documents these statements by reviewing the large body of research on the group character of, and the role of peers in, crime and delinquency in the United States and societies around the world. In so doing, he reviews some specific ways by which peer influence operates (consistent with social learning theory) in the development of delinquent behavior (see Warr's Chapter 10 in this volume and Warr 2002). Peer influence is most noticeable and strongest in adolescence but is not restricted to the adolescent years. Haynie (2002) found strong support for the social learning principle of differential association, the balance or ratio of association with delinquent and nondelinquent friends, as a predictor of delinquent behavior. The higher the proportion of one's friends who were delinquent, the greater the likelihood that one would become delinquent, even taking into account prior delinquency, time spent with peers, and attachment to peers. Research continues to find the strong influence of gang membership on serious delinquency. Curry, Decker, and Egley (2002) found that gang membership greatly increases involvement in both self-reported and official delinquency; even nonmembers who have only marginal association with gangs are more delinquent than youth who have no involvement at all with gang activities. Battin et al. (1998) found that, controlling for prior delinquency, adolescents with delinquent friends are more likely to engage in delinquent conduct and come before the juvenile court on delinquency charges, even if they are not part of a gang. But they are even more likely to do so if they and their friends are members of an identified delinquent gang. Whatever the frequency and seriousness of one's previous delinquency, joining a gang promotes an even higher level of his or her delinquent involvement, in large part because "group processes and norms favorable to violence and other delinquency within gangs subsequently encourage and reinforce participation in violent and delinquent behavior" (Battin et al. 1998, p. 108). Winfree, Vigil-Backstrom, and Mays (1994; see also Winfree, Mays, and Vigil-Backstrom 1994) found that both gang membership itself and delinquency (gang-related as well as non-gang delinquency) are explained by social learning variables (attitudes, social reinforcers/punishers, and differential association). The processes specified in social learning theory are "nearly identical to those provided by qualitative gang research. Gang members reward certain behavior in their peers and punish others, employing goals and processes that are indistinguishable from those described by Akers" (Winfree, Vigil-Backstrom, and Mays 1994, p. 149). In addition to the consistently positive findings by other researchers, support for the theory comes from cross-sectional, longitudinal, and cross-cultural research conducted by Akers and his associates on a range of behavior from minor deviance to serious criminal conduct in which all of the key social learning variables are measured (Akers 1998; Akers et al. 1979; Krohn et al. 1985; Akers et al. 1989; Boeringer, Shehan, and Akers 1991; Hwang and Akers 2006).

Research has also provided some evidence on the hypothesized relationship between social structure and social learning. This research has found that the relationships of substance use, delinquency, violence, binge drinking, and other forms of crime and deviance to age, sex, race, class, community, family structure, and other aspects of social structure are substantially reduced when the social learning variables are taken into account (See Akers and Jensen 2003, 2006). There are good reasons to believe that the social learning principles provide a solid basis for the macro-level explanation of differences in crime rates across societies as well as structural variations and changes in crime rates within the same society. However, at this time there has not been enough research to confirm that social learning is the principal process mediating the relationship of social structure and crime as expected by the theory. And some research findings suggest the SSSL model may have to be modified to take into account not only "mediating," but also "moderating" effects in the relationship of social structural to social learning variables (Verrill 2008).

V. Critiques of Social Learning Theory

Despite the strong empirical support for social learning theory, the testability of the basic behavioral learning principles incorporated in social learning theory has been challenged. The way in which the principle of reinforcement is often stated by behavioral psychologists makes the proposition true by definition. They define reinforcement by stating that it occurs when behavior has been strengthened; that is, its rate of commission has been increased. If reinforcement is defined this way, then the statement "If behavior is reinforced, it will be strengthened" is tautological.

If reinforcement means that behavior has been strengthened, then the hypothesis states simply, "If behavior is reinforced, it is reinforced." If the behavior is not strengthened, then by definition it has not been reinforced; therefore, no instance of behavior that is not being strengthened can be used to falsify the hypothesis. However, Burgess and Akers (1966a) very early identified and resolved the tautology problem in the reinforcement principle. They separated the definitions of reinforcement and other behavioral concepts from nontautological, testable propositions in social learning theory and proposed criteria for falsifying those propositions. Moreover, social learning theory, as first formulated and as developed to the present time, does not contain any tautological propositions about the relationship between behavior and reinforcement. In research on the theory, variables measured by reward and punishment and the balance of these in the process of reinforcement are always measured separately (and hence nontautologically) from measures of crime and deviance. No attempt is made to use the very behavior hypothesized to result from differential reinforcement as the measure of differential reinforcement itself. No claim is made that the best empirical measures of differential reinforcement (or any aspect of the social learning process) are the very behavior that the process is supposed to explain.

Another criticism of social learning has to do with the temporal and causal sequence of differential peer association and delinquency. Some have argued that the theory proposes that differential association with delinquent peers always precedes, and has only a one-way effect on, delinquent behavior; therefore, the theory does not recognize that one's own delinquent behavior and attitudes can affect peer association. That is, youths become delinquent first, and then seek out other delinquent youths. Rather than delinquent associations causing delinquency, delinquency causes delinquent associations. In fact, some critics argue that differential association with delinquent friends is almost always preceded by and is a consequence of, rather than a cause of, one's delinquent behavior so that no deviance-relevant learning of any kind takes place in peer groups. Contrary to what is proposed by social learning theory, these critics say that association with delinquent friends has an effect on neither the onset nor acceleration, the continuation nor cessation, of delinquent behavior (Hirschi 1969; Gottfredson and Hirschi 1990; Sampson and Laub 1993).

In his chapter in this volume, Warr reviews this criticism of the nature of peer influence in a careful and precise fashion, and concludes that it cannot be sustained. The reciprocal relationship between one's own conduct and association with friends has always been clearly recognized in social learning theory. "A peer 'socialization' process [association preceding deviant behavior] and a peer 'selection' process [behavior preceding association] in deviant behavior are not mutually exclusive, but are simply the social learning process at different times. Arguments that...any evidence of selective mechanisms in deviant interaction runs counter to social learning theory...are wrong" (Akers 1998, p. 56).

The findings from most studies favor the process proposed by social learning theory, which proposes that a youngster associates differentially with peers who are deviant or tolerant of deviance, learns definitions favorable to delinquent behavior, is exposed to deviant models that reinforce delinquency, and then initiates or increases involvement in that behavior, which then is expected to influence further associations and definitions, which then is expected to have further effects on delinquent behavior (Krohn et al. 1985; Sellers and Winfree 1990; Kandel and Davies 1991; Warr 1993; Menard and Elliott 1994; Winfree, Vigil-Backstrom, and Mays 1994; Akers and Lee 1996; Esbensen and Deschenes 1998; Battin et al. 1998; Gordon et al. 2004). Kandel and Davies (1991, p. 442) note that "although assortive pairing plays a role in similarity among friends observed at a single point in time, longitudinal research that we and others have carried out clearly documents the etiological importance of peers in the initiation and persistence of substance use." The considerable amount of research evidence showing that peer associations precede the development of deviant patterns (or increase the frequency and seriousness of deviant behavior once it has begun) more often than involvement in deviant behavior precedes associations with deviant peers is reviewed by Warr in Chapter 8 of this volume (see also Warr 1993).

Some research finds stronger effects of peer associations running in the other direction, and some shows the relationship to be about equal, depending on the measures and methods employed (Kandel 1996; Krohn et al. 1996; Matsueda and Anderson 1998; Gordon et al. 2004). However, experimental research supports the causal ordering of peer influence on behavior (see in particular Warr's discussion in this volume of the research by Gardner and Steinberg 2005 and others). Whatever level of delinquent involvement already exists is increased through differential association with delinquent peers, and "[a]lthough many investigations offer evidence of reciprocal effects, no study yet has failed to show a significant effect of peers on current and/or subsequent delinquency" (Warr 2002, p. 42).

Another criticism of the theory, which Warr earlier (1993) and in this volume considers and concludes is inaccurate, is that asking respondents to report on their friends' behavior as a measure of differential peer association and to relate that measure to the respondents' self-report of their own behavior is simply measuring the same thing twice. But research shows that the two are not the same and that the respondent's reports of friends' behavior is not simply a reflection of, or another way of reporting, one's own delinquent behavior (Menard and Elliott 1990; Agnew 1991b; Thornberry, Moore, and Christenson 1994; Elliott and Menard 1996; Bartusch et al. 1997). The major impact of differential peer association on the adolescent's own behavior, though not as strong, continues to be found in research that measures the proportion of delinquent friends by reports of delinquent behavior of the friends themselves, rather than relying on the adolescent's report or perception of what friends are doing (Haynie 2002; Weerman and Smeenk 2005). Moreover, while both are reasonable indicators of peer influence, the latter, perceptual measure is more relevant and accurate for testing the theory because, "[e]ven if peer behavior is misperceived as more (or less) delinquent than it actually is, the peer influence will still come through that perception" (Akers 1998, p. 119).

VI. Applications of Social Learning Theory in Prevention and Treatment of Crime and Delinquency

If criminal and delinquent behavior is acquired and sustained through the cognitive and behavioral processes in social learning in naturally occurring environments, then it should be possible to modify that behavior to the extent that one is able to manipulate those same processes or the environmental contingencies that impinge on them. This is the underlying assumption of prevention and treatment programs that have relied on the application of social learning principles. Reliance on one or more of the explanatory variables in social learning theory forms the implicit or explicit theoretical basis (often in combination with guidelines from other theories) for many types of group therapies and self-help programs; positive peer counseling programs; gang interventions; family and school programs; teenage drug, alcohol, and delinquency prevention/education programs; and other private and public programs. Behavior modification programs based on cognitive/behavioral learning principles, including both group and individually focused techniques for juveniles and adults, are operating in correctional, treatment, and community facilities and programs and in private practice. (See Morris and Braukmann 1987; Ellis and Sowers 2001; Pearson et al. 2002; Andrews and Bonta 2003; Hersen and Rosqvist 2005). Some historical and more recent examples illustrate how social learning principles have been put into practice and the extent to which they have been effective.

A. Highfields and Pinehills Delinquency Treatment Programs

These are two of the early programs applying principles of differential association to the treatment of adjudicated delinquents in residential and semi-residential facilities for delinquent boys. Both programs were based on the concept of differential peer group influence as a main source of learning delinquent behavior, and therefore peer groups could be formed under adult guidance in the facility to foster learning of sustainable patterns of prosocial attitudes and behavior to counter delinquent peer influences and patterns. Both programs had some success in achieving these goals, and the recidivism of the boys who completed the programs was somewhat lower than the recidivism of delinquent boys who had been committed to state training schools (Weeks 1958; Empey and Erickson 1972; Lundman 1993).

B. The Teaching Family Model

Later community-based residential programs, exemplified by the Teaching Family Model (TFM), moved beyond the almost exclusive reliance on the peer group of the Highfields and Pinehills projects to create more of a family environment. They also explicitly applied the principle of differential reinforcement in order to modify

behavior. The Teaching Family Model is a group home that involves a married couple ("teaching parents") and six to eight delinquent or "at-risk" youth living together
as a family. A "token economy" is in effect in which the youth can earn reward
points by proper behavior or have points taken away for improper behavior in the
home or at school. The parents are responsible for teaching social, academic, and
pre-vocational skills and maintaining mutually reinforcing relationships with the
adolescents. But the youths in the home also operate a peer-oriented self-government
system. Thus, in addition to the shaping of behavior by the teaching parents, the
Teaching Family Model promotes conforming behavior through exposure to a
prosocial peer group. Evaluation research has shown that the model works quite
well to maintain good behavior and retard misconduct and delinquent behavior in
the school and community while living with the teaching family, but that the anti-
delinquency effects are not sustained very well after release from the program
(Braukmann and Wolf 1987; but see Kingsley 2006 for a critique of the methods
used in the evaluations of the TFM).

C. Oregon Social Learning Center (OSLC) Programs

Gerald R. Patterson and his colleagues at the Oregon Social Learning Center
(Patterson 1975; Patterson, Debaryshe, and Ramsey 1989; Patterson, Capaldi, and
Bank 1991; Dishion, Patterson, and Kavanaugh 1992; Patterson and Chamberlain
1994; Snyder and Patterson 1995; Dishion, McCord, and Poulin 1999; Reid, Patterson,
and Snyder 2002) have long been conducting research on social learning theory and
applying it in programs with families and peer groups.

Among these is the OSLC Adolescent Transition Program (ATP), which aims to
prevent delinquency among at-risk youth with parent-focused and parent/teen
groups, teen-focused groups, and individualized sessions. In the parent groups, several sessions are held with a therapist to help parents develop monitoring, discipline, problem-solving, and other effective socialization and disciplinary skills
through instructions, discussion, and role playing. The teen-focused group and
individual sessions are run to help youth develop and improve communication
skills, self-control, prosocial attitudes, and prosocial peer associations. Evaluation
research has shown improvements in parenting skills and reductions in antisocial
behavior among the youths in the program (Dishion, Patterson, and Kavanaugh
1992).

While the ATP is a prevention program, the Multidimensional Treatment Foster
Care (MTFC) program is a treatment program designed for youths who have been
involved in chronic, high-frequency, and serious delinquencies adjudicated by the
juvenile court (Chamberlain, Fisher, and Moore 2002; Eddy and Chamberlain
2000). Competent foster parents were recruited and trained to use "behavior management methods...and to notice and reinforce youngsters" for proper behavior in
a positive way (Eddy and Chamberlain 2000, p. 858). In addition, each youth takes
part in weekly sessions with behavioral therapists "focused on skill building in such
areas as problem solving, social perspective taking, and nonaggressive methods of

self-expression" (Chamberlain, Fisher, and Moore 2002, pp. 205–06). Outcome evaluation has shown that the delinquents in the MTFC treatment group had lower rates of both official and self-reported delinquency than comparable youths placed in other community treatment programs (Chamberlain, Fisher, and Moore 2002). Another example of an OSLC delinquency-prevention project is the Linking the Interests of Families and Teachers (LIFT) program, designed to affect troublesome childhood behavior that is often a precursor to delinquent and violent behavior in adolescence (Reid and Eddy 2002). LIFT provides services to all first and fifth graders (as the transitional grades into elementary and middle schools respectively), their parents, and teachers in areas of the community at high risk for delinquency. LIFT is focused on modifying the interaction of the children with their social environment at home, with peers, and in school. With the cooperation of the schools and voluntary involvement of the children and families, "the three major components of the LIFT are (a) classroom-based child social and problem skills training, (b) playground-based behavior modification, and (c) group-delivered parent training," (Eddy, Reid, and Fetrow 2000, p. 165). By the time the fifth graders were in middle school and the first years of high school, the LIFT participants had experienced significantly fewer police arrests, lower levels of self-reported drug use, and fewer associations with deviant peers (as observed by the teachers) than did the youth in the control group.

D. Seattle Social Development Research Group Programs

The Social Development Model (SDM) is an early intervention, long-term project that has demonstrated some success in preventing adolescent delinquency and misconduct. The SDM is explicitly predicated on principles of social learning (Akers et al. 1979) and social bonding (Hirschi 1969) theories. This model has been developed and implemented in a series of delinquency and substance use prevention programs by J. David Hawkins, Richard F. Catalano, and their associates in the Social Development Research Group (SDRG) at the University of Washington in Seattle (Weis and Hawkins 1981; Hawkins, Von Cleave, and Catalano 1991; Hawkins et al. 1992; Hawkins et al. 1999; Brown et al. 2005). The SDM combines strengthening social attachment and commitment (social bonding theory) with positive reinforcement, modeling, and learning prosocial attitudes and skills and avoiding learning delinquent patterns (social learning theory) in interventions with the family, school, and peer groups.

The Seattle Social Development Project is directed toward children in the first and fifth grade classrooms in Seattle schools. The program was designed to enhance opportunities, develop social skills, and provide rewards for good behavior in the classrooms and families. The teachers in the intervention classrooms were trained to use "proactive classroom management" (e.g., reward desirable student behavior and control classroom disruptions), "interactive teaching" (e.g., state explicit learning objectives and model skills to be learned), "cooperative learning" (teams of students), and other innovative techniques to strengthen bonds to school and teach the students academic and social skills for interacting properly with others. At the same time, parenting skills training was offered on a voluntary basis to students' parents to help them to better monitor their children's behavior, to teach normative expectations to the children (prosocial and anti-delinquent definitions), and to provide consistent discipline in applying positive rewards for desired behavior and negative consequences for undesirable behavior (differential reinforcement). Parents were also encouraged to increase shared family activities, involve their kids in family activities and times together, provide a positive home environment, and cooperate with teachers to develop the children's reading and math skills (differential association and social bonding). The program was evaluated by comparing the intervention and control groups when they were in the fifth grade (Hawkins et al. 1992), and then again when they reached the age of 18 (Hawkins et al. 1999). The findings showed some successful outcomes in the fifth grade and by the time the students were age 18, with significant differences between intervention and control groups in self-reported delinquency, heavy alcohol use, and risky sexual behavior.

Another application of the SDM is found in the SDRG's Raising Healthy Children (RHC) project (Brown et al. 2005) involving youth in the middle and high school years.

> As a theory-based intervention, RHC is guided by the social development model (SDM) which *integrates empirically supported aspects of social control, social learning, and differential association theories into a framework for strengthening prosocial bonds and beliefs*.... [F]our distinct points of intervention were targeted by RHC: (a) opportunities for involvement with prosocial others (e.g., family, teachers, and peers who did not use substances); (b) students' academic, cognitive, and social skills; (c) positive reinforcements and rewards for prosocial involvement; and (d) healthy beliefs and clear standards regarding substance use avoidance (Brown et al. 2005, p. 700, emphasis added).

The goals of the project were (1) to increase the probability of abstinence and reduce the probability of the onset of use of alcohol, marijuana, and tobacco and (2) to reduce frequency or prevent escalation of use once it has been initiated among the students during the years they are passing through grades six to ten. To accomplish these goals, principles of social learning and social bonding were applied in interventions with teachers and their classroom management, with individual students, and with parents of the students.

Longitudinal outcome data on prevalence and frequency of use of alcohol, marijuana, and tobacco were collected through self-reported questionnaires with youth at school and telephone interviews with those youth not in school. The RHC intervention seemed not to affect the youth's decision to remain abstinent or to use any of the substances. However, among the students in the intervention schools, there was significantly lower frequency of use of alcohol and marijuana (but not tobacco) than among those in the nonintervention schools during the middle school to high school years.

VII. Summary

Akers' social learning theory combines Sutherland's differential association theory of criminal behavior with general behavioral learning principles. The theory proposes that criminal and delinquent behavior is acquired, repeated, and changed by the same process as conforming behavior. While referring to all parts of the learning process, social learning theory has focused on the four major explanatory concepts of differential association, definitions, differential reinforcement, and imitation. That process will more likely produce behavior that violates social and legal norms than conforming behavior when persons differentially associate with those who expose them to deviant patterns, when the deviant behavior is differentially reinforced over conforming behavior, when individuals are more exposed to deviant than conforming models, and when their own definitions and attitudes favorably dispose them to commit deviant acts.

Research conducted over many years, including that by Akers and associates, has consistently found that social learning is empirically supported as an explanation of individual differences in delinquent and criminal behavior. The SSSL model hypothesis that social learning processes mediate the effects of structural, sociodemographic, and community variables on behavior has been infrequently studied, but the evidence so far suggests that it will also be upheld. The behavioral, cognitive, and social interactional principles of social learning theory have been applied in a range of prevention and treatment programs for adolescent populations. While the outcomes of these programs are sometimes disappointing, there is also some evidence of success, and generally such programs are more effective than alternative approaches.

NOTES

1. For detailed accounts of Sutherland's career and the way in which he developed this theory, see Cohen, Lindesmith, and Schuessler (1956), Gaylord and Galliher (1988), and Sutherland (1973). For a further study of the development and revisions of differential association theory, see Akers (1998).

2. For classic statements of behavioristic "operant conditioning" principles of learning, see Skinner (1953, 1959). See also the full statement of behavioral learning theory in Burgess and Akers (1966a).

3. See also Conger (1976); Marcos, Bahr, and Johnson (1986); Matsueda and Heimer (1987); Burkett and Warren (1987); White, Pandina, and LaGrange (1987); Winfree, Griffiths, and Sellers (1989); Loeber et al. (1991); Agnew (1991a); Warr and Stafford (1991); Inciardi, Horowitz, and Pottieger (1993); Elliott (1994); Conger and Simons (1995); Simons et al. (1994); and Wood et al. (1995). Research on expanded deterrence models showing the strong effects of moral evaluations and actual or anticipated informal social sanctions on an individual's commission of crime or delinquency also provides support for social learning theory (Anderson, Chiricos, and Waldo 1977; Meier and Johnson 1977; Jensen,

Erickson, and Gibbs 1978; Tittle 1980; Grasmick and Green 1980; Paternoster et al. 1983; Paternoster 1989; Lanza-Kaduce 1988; Stafford and Warr 1993).

4. There is a long list of supportive research on these variables both as part of the original differential association theory and the reformulated social learning theory that covers five decades going back to the pioneering studies by Short (1957, 1958, 1960) and continuing to the present time. For a review of this research see Akers and Jensen (2006).

REFERENCES

Adler, Patricia, and Peter Adler. 1978. "Tinydopers: A Case Study of Deviant Socialization." *Symbolic Interaction* 1: 90–105.

Agnew, Robert. 1991a. "The Interactive Effect of Peer Variables on Delinquency." *Criminology* 29: 47–72.

———. 1991b. "A Longitudinal Test of Social Control Theory and Delinquency." *Journal of Research of Crime and Delinquency* 28: 126–56.

Akers, Ronald L. 1973. *Deviant Behavior: A Social Learning Approach*. Belmont, CA: Wadsworth.

———. 1977 *Deviant Behavior: A Social Learning Approach*, 2nd ed. Belmont, CA: Wadsworth.

———. 1985. *Deviant Behavior: A Social Learning Approach*, 3rd ed. Belmont, CA: Wadsworth. Reprinted 1992. Fairfax, VA: Techbooks.

———. 1996. "Is Differential Association/Social Learning Cultural Deviance Theory?" *Criminology* 34: 229–48.

———. 1998. *Social Learning and Social Structure: A General Theory of Crime and Deviance*. Boston: Northeastern University Press.

Akers, Ronald L., and Gary F. Jensen, eds. 2003. *Social Learning Theory and the Explanation of Crime: A Guide for the New Century*. Vol. 11 of *Advances in Criminological Theory*. New Brunswick, NJ: Transaction.

——— 2006. "The Empirical Status of Social Learning Theory of Crime and Deviance: The Past, Present, and Future." In *Taking Stock: The Status of Criminology Theory*, edited by Francis T. Cullen, John Paul Wright, and Kristie R. Blevins. Vol. 15 of *Advances in Criminological Theory*. New Brunswick, NJ: Transaction.

Akers, Ronald L., Marvin D. Krohn, Lonn Lanza-Kaduce, and Marcia Radosevich. 1979. "Social Learning and Deviant Behavior: A Specific Test of a General Theory." *American Sociological Review* 44: 635–55.

Akers, Ronald L., Anthony J. La Greca, John K. Cochran, and Christine S. Sellers. 1989. "Social Learning Theory and Alcohol Behavior Among the Elderly." *Sociological Quarterly* 30: 625–38.

Akers, Ronald L., and Gang Lee. 1996. "A Longitudinal Test of Social Learning Theory: Adolescent Smoking." *Journal of Drug Issues* 26: 317–43.

Akers, Ronald L., and Christine S. Sellers. 2009. *Criminological Theories: Introduction, Evaluation, and Application*. Fifth Edition. New York: Oxford University Press.

Anderson, Elijah. 1999. *Code of the Street: Decency, Violence, and the Moral Life of the Inner City*. New York: Norton.

Anderson, Linda S., Theodore G. Chiricos, and Gordon P. Waldo. 1977. "Formal and Informal Sanctions: A Comparison of Deterrent Effects." *Social Problems* 25: 103–12.

Andrews, D. A., and James Bonta. 2003. *The Psychology of Criminal Conduct*, 3rd ed. Cincinnati, OH: Anderson.

Ardelt, Monika, and Laurie Day. 2002. "Parents, Siblings, and Peers: Close Social Relationships and Adolescent Deviance." *Journal of Early Adolescence* 22: 310–49.

Bandura, Albert. 1977. *Social Learning Theory*. Englewood Cliffs, NJ: Prentice Hall.

Bartusch, Dawn Jeglum, Donald R. Lynam, Terrie A. Moffitt, and Phil A. Silva. 1997. "Is Age Important?: Testing a General Versus a Developmental Theory of Antisocial Behavior." *Criminology* 35: 375–406.

Battin, Sara R., Karl G. Hill, Robert D. Abbott, Richard F. Catalano, and J. David Hawkins. 1998. "The Contribution of Gang Membership to Delinquency: Beyond Delinquent Friends." *Criminology* 36: 93–115.

Batton, Candice, and Robbin S. Ogle. 2003. "'Who's It Gonna Be—You or Me?': The Potential of Social Learning for Integrated Homicide-Suicide Theory." In *Social Learning Theory and the Explanation of Crime: A Guide for the New Century*, edited by Ronald L. Akers and Gary F. Jensen. Vol. 11 of *Advances in Criminological Theory*. New Brunswick, NJ: Transaction.

Benda, Brent B. 1994. "Testing Competing Theoretical Concepts: Adolescent Alcohol Consumption." *Deviant Behavior* 15: 375–96.

Benoit, Ellen, Doris Randolph, Eloise Dunlap, and Bruce Johnson. 2003. "Code Switching and Inverse Imitation Among Marijuana-Using Crack Sellers." *British Journal of Criminology* 43: 506–25.

Boeringer, Scot, Constance L. Shehan, and Ronald L. Akers. 1991. "Social Contexts and Social Learning in Sexual Coercion and Aggression: Assessing the Contribution of Fraternity Membership." *Family Relations* 40: 558–64.

Braukmann, Curtis J., and Montrose M. Wolf. 1987. "Behaviorally Based Group Homes for Juvenile Offenders." In *Behavioral Approaches to Crime and Delinquency: A Handbook of Application, Research, and Concepts*, edited by Edward K. Morris and Curtis J. Braukmann. New York: Plenum.

Brezina, Timothy, and Alex R. Piquero. 2003. "Exploring the Relationship Between Social and Non-Social Reinforcement in the Context of Social Learning Theory." In *Social Learning Theory and the Explanation of Crime: A Guide for the New Century*, edited by Ronald L. Akers and Gary F. Jensen. Vol. 11 of *Advances in Criminological Theory*. New Brunswick, NJ: Transaction.

Brown, Eric C., Richard F. Catalano, Charles B. Fleming, Kevin P. Haggerty, and Robert D. Abbott. 2005. "Adolescent Substance Use Outcomes in the Raising Healthy Children Project: A Two-Part Latent Growth Curve Analysis." *Journal of Consulting and Clinical Psychology* 73: 699–710.

Bruinsma, Gerben J. N. 1992. "Differential Association Theory Reconsidered: An Extension and Its Empirical Test." *Journal of Quantitative Criminology* 8: 29–49.

Burgess, Robert L., and Ronald L. Akers. 1966a. "Are Operant Principles Tautological?" *Psychological Record* 16: 305–12.

———. 1966b. "A Differential Association Reinforcement Theory of Criminal Behavior." *Social Problems* 14: 128–47.

Burkett, Steven, and Bruce O. Warren. 1987. "Religiosity, Peer Associations, and Adolescent Marijuana Use: A Panel Study of Underlying Causal Structures." *Criminology* 25: 109–32.

Burton, Velmer, Francis Cullen, David Evans, and R. Gregory Dunaway. 1994. "Reconsidering Strain Theory: Operationalization, Rival Theories, and Adult Criminality." *Journal of Quantitative Criminology* 10: 213–39.

Capaldi, Deborah M., Patricia Chamberlain, and Gerald R. Patterson. 1997. "Ineffective Discipline and Conduct Problems in Males: Association, Late Adolescent Outcomes, and Prevention." *Aggression and Violent Behavior* 2: 343–53.

Catalano, Richard F., Rick Kosterman, J. David Hawkins, Robert D. Abbott, and Michael D. Newcomb. 1996. "Modeling the Etiology of Adolescent Substance Use: A Test of the Social Development Model." *Journal of Drug Issues* 26: 429–56.

Chamberlain, Patricia, Philip A. Fisher, and Kevin Moore. 2002. "Multidimensional Treatment Foster Care: Applications of the OSLC Intervention Model to High Risk Youth and Their Families." In *Antisocial Behavior in Children and Adolescents: A Developmental Analysis and Model for Intervention*, edited by John B. Reid, Gerald R. Patterson, and James Snyder. Washington, DC: American Psychological Association.

Chappell, Allison T., and Alex R. Piquero. 2004. "Applying Social Learning Theory to Police Misconduct." *Deviant Behavior* 25: 89–108.

Clark, Robert. 1972. *Reference Group Theory and Delinquency*. New York: Behavioral Publications.

Cohen, Albert K., Alfred R. Lindesmith, and Karl F. Schuessler, eds. 1956. *The Sutherland Papers*. Bloomington: Indiana University Press.

Conger, Rand. 1976. "Social Control and Social Learning Models of Delinquency: A Synthesis." *Criminology* 14: 17–40.

Conger, Rand D., and Ronald L. Simons. 1995. "Life Course Contingencies in the Development of Adolescent Antisocial Behavior: A Matching Law Approach." In *Developmental Theories of Crime and Delinquency*, edited by Terence P. Thornberry. Vol. 7 of *Advances in Criminological Theory*. New Brunswick, NJ: Transaction.

Cullen, Francis T., John Paul Wright, and Kristie R. Blevins, eds. 2006. *Taking Stock: The Status of Criminology Theory*. Vol. 15 of *Advances in Criminological Theory*. New Brunswick, NJ: Transaction.

Curry, G. David, Scott H. Decker, and Arlen Egley, Jr. 2002. "Gang Involvement and Delinquency in a Middle School Population." *Justice Quarterly* 19: 275–92.

Dishion, Thomas J., Joan McCord, and Francia Poulin. 1999. "When Interventions Harm: Peer Groups and Problem Behavior." *American Psychologist* 54: 755–64.

Dishion, Thomas J., Gerald R. Patterson, and Kathryn A. Kavanagh. 1992. "An Experimental Test of the Coercion Model: Linking Theory, Measurement, and Intervention." In *Preventing Antisocial Behavior: Interventions From Birth Through Adolescence*, edited by Joan McCord and Richard E. Tremblay. New York: Guilford.

Donnerstein, Edward, and Daniel Linz. 1995. "The Media." In *Crime*, edited by James Q. Wilson and Joan Petersilia. San Francisco: ICS Press.

Eddy, J. Mark, and Patricia Chamberlain. 2000. "Family Management and Deviant Peer Association as Mediators of the Impact of Treatment Condition on Youth Antisocial Behavior." *Journal of Consulting and Clinical Psychology* 68: 857–63.

Eddy, J. Mark, John B. Reid, and R. A. Fetrow. 2000. "An Elementary School-Based Prevention Program Targeting Modifiable Antecedents of Youth Delinquency and Violence: Linking the Interests of Families and Teachers (LIFT)." *Journal of Emotional and Behavioral Disorders* 8: 165–76.

Elliott, Delbert S. 1994. "Serious Violent Offenders: Onset, Developmental Course, and Termination." *Criminology* 32: 1–22.

Elliott, Delbert S., David Huizinga, and Suzanne S. Ageton. 1985. *Explaining Delinquency and Drug Use*. Beverly Hills: Sage.

Elliott, Delbert S., and Scott Menard. 1996. "Delinquent Friends and Delinquent Behavior: Temporal and Developmental Patterns." In *Delinquency and Crime: Current Theories*, edited by J. David Hawkins. New York: Cambridge University Press.

Ellis, Lee, and Anthony Walsh. 1999. "Criminologists' Opinions About Causes and Theories of Crime and Delinquency." *The Criminologist* 24(4): 1, 4–6.

Ellis, Rodney, and Karen Sowers. 2001. *Juvenile Justice Practice: A Cross-Disciplinary Approach to Intervention.* Belmont, CA: Wadsworth/Brooks Cole.

Empey, LaMar T., and Maynard L. Erickson. 1972. *The Provo Experiment: Evaluating Community Control of Delinquency.* Lexington, MA: Lexington.

Esbensen, Finn-Aage, and Elizabeth Piper Deschenes. 1998. "A Multisite Examination of Youth Gang Membership: Does Gender Matter?" *Criminology* 36: 799–827.

Gardner, Margo, and Laurence Steinberg. 2005. "Peer Influence on Risk Taking, Risk Preference, and Risky Decision Making in Adolescence and Adulthood: An Experimental Study." *Developmental Psychology* 41: 625–35.

Gaylord, Mark S., and John F. Galliher. 1988. *The Criminology of Edwin Sutherland.* New Brunswick: Transaction.

Gordon, Rachel A., Benjamin B. Lahey, Eriko Kawai, Rolf Loeber, Magda Stouthamer-Loeber, and David P. Farrington. 2004. "Anti-social Behavior and Youth Gang Membership: Selection and Socialization." *Criminology* 42: 55–87.

Gottfredson, Michael, and Travis Hirschi. 1990. *A General Theory of Crime.* Palo Alto, CA: Stanford University Press.

Grasmick, Harold G., and Donald E. Green. 1980. "Legal Punishment, Social Disapproval, and Internalization as Inhibitors of Illegal Behavior." *Journal of Criminal Law and Criminology* 71: 325–35.

Hawkins, J. David, Richard F. Catalano, Rick Kosterman, Robert Abbott, and Karl G. Hill. 1999. "Preventing Adolescent Health–Risk Behaviors by Strengthening Protection During Childhood." *Archives of Pediatric and Adolescent Medicine* 153: 226–34.

Hawkins, J. David, Richard F. Catalano, Daine M. Morrison, Julie O'Donnell, Robert D. Abbott, and L. Edward Day. 1992. "The Seattle Social Development Project: Effects of the First Four Years on Protective Factors and Problem Behaviors." In *Preventing Antisocial Behavior: Interventions From Birth Through Adolescence,* edited by Joan McCord and Richard E. Tremblay. New York: Guilford.

Hawkins, J. David, Elizabeth Von Cleve, and Richard F. Catalano, Jr. 1991. "Reducing Early Childhood Aggression: Results of a Primary Prevention Program." *Journal of the Academy of Child and Adolescent Psychiatry* 30: 208–17.

Haynie, Dana L. 2002. "Friendship Networks and Delinquency: The Relative Nature of Peer Delinquency." *Journal of Quantitative Criminology* 18: 99–134.

Hersen, Michel, and Johan Rosqvist, eds. 2005. *Encyclopedia of Behavior Modification and Cognitive Behavior Therapy.* Vol. 1 *Adult Clinical Applications.* Vol. 2 *Child Clinical Applications.* Thousand Oaks, CA: Sage.

Hirschi, Travis. 1969. *Causes of Delinquency.* Berkeley, CA: University of California Press.

Hoffman, Kristi L., K. Jill Kiecolt, and John N. Edwards. 2005. "Physical Violence Between Siblings." *Journal of Family Issues* 26: 1103–30.

Horney, Julie. 2006. "An Alternative Psychology of Criminal Behavior: The American Society of Criminology Presidential Address." *Criminology* 44: 1–16.

Huang, Bu, Rick Kosterman, Richard F. Catalano, J. David Hawkins, and Robert D. Abbott. 2001. "Modeling Mediation in the Etiology of Violent Behavior in Adolescence: A Test of the Social Development Model." *Criminology* 39: 75–108.

Hwang, Sunghyun, and Ronald L. Akers. 2003. "Substance Use by Korean Adolescents: A Cross-Cultural Test of Social Learning, Social Bonding, and Self-Control Theories." In *Social Learning Theory and the Explanation of Crime: A Guide for the New Century,* edited by Ronald L. Akers and Gary F. Jensen. Vol. 11 of *Advances in Criminological Theory.* New Brunswick, NJ: Transaction.

———. 2006. "Parental and Peer Influences on Adolescent Drug Use in Korea." *Asian Journal of Criminology* 1: 59–69.

Inciardi, James A., Ruth Horowitz, and Anne E. Pottieger. 1993. *Street Kids, Street Drugs, Street Crime: An Examination of Drug Use and Serious Delinquency in Miami*. Belmont, CA: Wadsworth.

Jang, Sung Joon. 2002. "The Effects of Family, School, Peers, and Attitudes on Adolescents' Drug Use: Do They Vary With Age?" *Justice Quarterly* 19: 97–126.

Jensen, Gary F., Maynard L. Erickson, and Jack P. Gibbs. 1978. "Perceived Risk of Punishment and Self Reported Delinquency." *Social Forces* 57: 57–78.

Junger-Tas, Josine. 1992. "An Empirical Test of Social Control Theory." *Journal of Quantitative Criminology* 8: 9–28.

Kandel, Denise B. 1996. "The Parental and Peer Contexts of Adolescent Deviance: An Algebra of Interpersonal Influences." *Journal of Drug Issues* 26: 289–316.

Kandel, Denise, and Israel Adler. 1982. "Socialization into Marijuana Use Among French Adolescents: A Cross Cultural Comparison with the United States." *Journal of Health and Social Behavior* 23: 295–309.

Kandel, Denise, and Mark Davies. 1991. "Friendship Networks, Intimacy, and Illicit Drug Use in Young Adulthood: A Comparison of Two Competing Theories." *Criminology* 29: 441–69.

Kaplan, Howard B. 1996. "Empirical Validation of the Applicability of an Integrative Theory of Deviant Behavior to the Study of Drug Use." *Journal of Drug Issues* 26: 345–77.

Kaplan, Howard B., Richard J. Johnson, and C. A. Barley. 1987. "Deviant Peers and Deviant Behavior: Further Elaboration of a Model." *Social Psychology Quarterly* 50: 277–84.

Kingsley, David E. 2006. "The Teaching-Family Model and Post-Treatment Recidivism: A Critical Review of the Conventional Wisdom." *International Journal of Behavioral and Consultation Therapy* 2: 481–96.

Krohn, Marvin D., Alan J. Lizotte, Terence P. Thornberry, Carolyn Smith, and David McDowall. 1996. "Reciprocal Causal Relationships Among Drug Use, Peers, and Beliefs: A Five Wave Panel Model." *Journal of Drug Issues* 26: 405–28.

Krohn, Marvin D., William F. Skinner, James L. Massey, and Ronald L. Akers. 1985. "Social Learning Theory and Adolescent Cigarette Smoking: A Longitudinal Study." *Social Problems* 32: 455–73.

Lanza-Kaduce, Lonn. 1988. "Perceptual Deterrence and Drinking and Driving Among College Students." *Criminology* 26: 321–41.

Lauritsen, Janet L. 1993. "Sibling Resemblance in Juvenile Delinquency: Findings from the National Youth Survey." *Criminology* 31: 387–410.

Liu, Ruth Xiaoru. 2003. "The Moderating Effects of Internal and Perceived External Sanction Threats on the Relationship Between Deviant Peer Associations and Criminal Offending." *Western Criminology Review* 4: 191–202.

Loeber, Rolf, and Thomas J. Dishion. 1987. "Antisocial and Delinquent Youths: Methods for Their Early Identification." In *Prevention of Delinquent Behavior*, edited by J. D. Burchard and Sara Burchard. Newbury Park, CA: Sage.

Loeber, Rolf, and Magda Stouthamer-Loeber. 1986. "Family Factors as Correlates and Predictors of Juvenile Conduct Problems and Delinquency." Vol. 7 of *Crime and Justice: An Annual Review of Research*, edited by Michael Tonry and Norval Morris. Chicago: University of Chicago Press.

Loeber, Rolf, Magda Stouthamer-Loeber, Welmoet Van Kammen, and David P. Farrington. 1991. "Initiation, Escalation, and Desistance in Juvenile Offending and Their Correlates." *Journal of Criminal Law and Criminology* 82: 36–82.

Lopez, Jose Manuel Otero, Lourdes Miron Redondo, and Angeles Luengo Martin. 1989. "Influence of Family and Peer Group on the Use of Drugs by Adolescents." *International Journal of the Addictions* 24: 1065–82.

Lundman, Richard J. 1993. *Prevention and Control of Juvenile Delinquency.* Second Edition. New York: Oxford University Press.

Marcos, Anastasios C., Stephen J. Bahr, and Richard E. Johnson. 1986. "Testing of a Bonding/Association Theory of Adolescent Drug Use." *Social Forces* 65: 135–61.

Matsueda, Ross L., and Kathleen Anderson. 1998. "The Dynamics of Delinquent Peers and Delinquent Behavior." *Criminology* 36: 269–308.

Matsueda, Ross L., and Karen Heimer. 1987. "Race, Family Structure, and Delinquency: A Test of Differential Association and Social Control Theories." *American Sociological Review* 52: 826–40.

Matsueda, Ross L., Derek A. Kreager, and David Huizinga. 2006. "Deterring Delinquents: A Rational Choice Model of Theft and Violence." *American Sociological Review* 71: 95–122.

McCord, Joan. 1991. "Family Relationships, Juvenile Delinquency, and Adult Criminality." *Criminology* 29: 397–418.

McGee, Zina T. 1992. "Social Class Differences in Parental and Peer Influence on Adolescent Drug Use." *Deviant Behavior* 13: 349–72.

McGloin, Jean Marie, Travis C. Pratt, and Jeff Maahs. 2004. "Rethinking the IQ–Delinquency Relationship: A Longitudinal Analysis of Multiple Theoretical Models." *Justice Quarterly* 21: 603–31.

Meier, Robert F., and Weldon T. Johnson. 1977. "Deterrence as Social Control: The Legal and Extralegal Production of Conformity." *American Sociological Review* 42: 292–304.

Menard, Scott, and Delbert S. Elliott. 1990. "Longitudinal and Cross Sectional Data Collection and Analysis in the Study of Crime and Delinquency." *Justice Quarterly* 7: 11–55.

———. 1994. "Delinquent Bonding, Moral Beliefs, and Illegal Behavior: A Three Wave Panel Model." *Justice Quarterly* 11: 173–88.

Mihalic, Sharon Wofford, and Delbert Elliott. 1997. "A Social Learning Theory Model of Marital Violence." *Journal of Family Violence* 12: 21–36.

Morris, Edward K., and Curtis J. Braukmann, eds. 1987. *Behavioral Approaches to Crime and Delinquency: A Handbook of Application, Research, and Concepts.* New York: Plenum.

Morselli, Carlo, Pierre Tremblay, and Bill McCarthy. 2006. "Mentors and Criminal Achievement." *Criminology* 44: 17–43.

Neff, Joan L., and Dennis E. Waite. 2007. "Male Versus Female Substance Abuse Patterns Among Incarcerated Juvenile Offenders: Comparing Strain and Social Learning Variables." *Justice Quarterly* 24: 106–32.

Osgood, Wayne D., and Amy L. Anderson. 2004. "Unstructured Socializing and Rates of Delinquency." *Criminology* 42: 519–49.

Paternoster, Raymond. 1989. "Decisions to Participate in and Desist from Four Types of Common Delinquency: Deterrence and the Rational Choice Perspective." *Law and Society Review* 23: 7–40.

Paternoster, Raymond, Linda E. Saltzman, Gordon P. Waldo, and Theodore G. Chiricos. 1983. "Perceived Risk and Social Control: Do Sanctions Really Deter?" *Law and Society Review* 17: 457–80.

Patterson, Gerald R. 1975. *Families: Applications of Social Learning to Family Life.* Champaign, IL: Research Press.

———. 1995. "Coercion as a Basis for Early Age of Onset for Arrest." In *Coercion and Punishment in Long-term Perspectives*, edited by Joan McCord. Cambridge, England: Cambridge University Press.

———. 2002. "A Brief History of the Oregon Model." In *Antisocial Behavior in Children and Adolescents: A Developmental Analysis and Model for Intervention*, edited by John

B. Reid, Gerald R. Patterson, and James Snyder. Washington, DC: American Psychological Association.

Patterson, Gerald R., D. Capaldi, and L. Bank. 1991. "The Development and Treatment of Childhood Aggression." In *The Development and Treatment of Childhood Aggression*, edited by D. Pepler and R. K. Rubin. Hillsdale, IL: Lawrence Erlbaum Associates, Inc.

Patterson, Gerald R., and Patricia Chamberlain. 1994. "A Functional Analysis of Resistance During Parent Training Therapy." *Clinical Psychology: Science and Practice* 1: 53–70.

Patterson, Gerald R., B. D. Debaryshe, and E. Ramsey. 1989. "A Developmental Perspective on Antisocial Behavior." *American Psychologist* 44: 329–35.

Pearson, Frank S., Douglas S. Lipton, Charles M. Cleland, and Dorline S. Yee. 2002. "The Effects of Behavioral/Cognitive-Behavioral Programs on Recidivism." *Crime and Delinquency* 48: 476–96.

Pratt, Travis C., and Francis T. Cullen. 2000. "The Empirical Status of Gottfredson and Hirschi's General Theory of Crime: A Meta-Analysis." *Criminology* 38: 931–64.

Pratt, Travis C., Francis T. Cullen, Kristie R. Blevins, Leah E. Daigle, and Tamara D. Madensen. 2006. "The Empirical Status of Deterrence Theory: A Meta-Analysis." In *Taking Stock: The Status of Criminology Theory*, edited by Francis T. Cullen, John Paul Wright, and Kristie R. Blevins. Vol. 15 of *Advances in Criminological Theory*. New Brunswick, NJ: Transaction.

Pratt, Travis C., Francis T. Cullen, Christine S. Sellers, L. Thomas Winfree, Jr., Tamara D. Madensen, Leah E. Daigle, Noelle E. Fearn, and Jacinta M. Gau. 2010. "The Empirical Status of Social Learning Theory: A Meta-Analysis." *Justice Quarterly* 27: 765–802.

Preston, Pamela. 2006. "Marijuana Use as a Coping Response to Psychological Strain: Racial, Ethnic, and Gender Differences Among Young Adults." *Deviant Behavior* 27: 397–422.

Rebellon, Cesar J. 2002. "Reconsidering the Broken Homes/Delinquency Relationship and Exploring its Mediating Mechanism(s)." *Criminology* 40: 103–36.

Reid, John B., and J. Mark Eddy. 2002. "Preventive Efforts During the Elementary School Years: The Linking of the Interests of Families and Teachers (LIFT) Project." In *Antisocial Behavior in Children and Adolescents: A Developmental Analysis and Model for Intervention*, edited by John B. Reid, Gerald R. Patterson, and James Snyder. Washington, DC: American Psychological Association.

Reid, John B., Gerald R. Patterson, and James Snyder, eds. 2002. *Antisocial Behavior in Children and Adolescents: A Developmental Analysis and Model for Intervention*. Washington, DC: American Psychological Association.

Rowe, David, and David P. Farrington. 1997. "The Familial Transmission of Criminal Convictions." *Criminology* 35: 177–201.

Rowe, David C., and Bill L. Gulley. 1992. "Sibling Effects on Substance Use and Delinquency." *Criminology* 30: 217–34.

Sampson, Robert J., and John H. Laub. 1993. *Crime in the Making: Pathways and Turning Points Through Life*. Cambridge, MA: Harvard University Press.

Sandstrom, Kent L., Daniel D. Martin, and Gary Alan Fine. 2003. *Symbols, Selves, and Social Reality: A Symbolic Interactionist Approach to Social Psychology and Sociology*. Los Angeles: Roxbury.

Sellers, Christine S., and Ronald L. Akers. 2006. "Social Learning Theory: Correcting Misconceptions." In *The Essential Criminology Reader*, edited by Stuart Henry and Mark M. Lanier. Boulder, CO: Westview.

Sellers, Christine S., John K. Cochran, and L. Thomas Winfree, Jr. 2003. "Social Learning Theory and Courtship Violence: An Empirical Test." In *Social Learning Theory and the*

Explanation of Crime: A Guide for the New Century, edited by Ronald L. Akers and Gary F. Jensen. Vol. 11 of *Advances in Criminological Theory*. New Brunswick, NJ: Transaction.

Sellers, Christine S., and Thomas L. Winfree. 1990. "Differential Associations and Definitions: A Panel Study of Youthful Drinking Behavior." *International Journal of the Addictions* 25: 755–71.

Short, James F., Jr. 1957. "Differential Association and Delinquency." *Social Problems* 4: 233–39.

———. 1958. "Differential Association with Delinquent Friends." *Pacific Sociological Review* 1: 20–25.

———. 1960. "Differential Association as a Hypothesis: Problems of Empirical Testing." *Social Problems* 8: 14–25.

Simons, Ronald L., Leslie Gordon Simons, and Lora Ebert Wallace. 2004. *Families, Delinquency, and Crime: Linking Society's Most Basic Institution to Antisocial Behavior.* Los Angeles: Roxbury.

Simons, Ronald L., C. Wu, Rand D. Conger, and F. O. Lorenz. 1994. "Two Routes to Delinquency: Differences Between Early and Late Starters in the Impact of Parenting and Deviant Peers." *Criminology* 32: 247–76.

Skinner, B. F. 1953. *Science and Human Behavior.* New York: Macmillan.

———. 1959. *Cumulative Record.* New York: Appleton-Century-Crofts.

Skinner, William F., and A. M. Fream. 1997. "A Social Learning Theory Analysis of Computer Crime Among College Students." *Journal of Research in Crime and Delinquency* 34: 495–518.

Snyder, James. 2002. "Reinforcement and Coercion Mechanisms in the Development of Antisocial Behavior: Peer Relationships." In *Antisocial Behavior in Children and Adolescents: A Developmental Analysis and Model for Intervention*, edited by John B. Reid, Gerald R. Patterson, and James Snyder. Washington, DC: American Psychological Association.

Snyder, James J., and Gerald R. Patterson. 1995. "Individual Differences in Social Aggression: A Test of a Reinforcement Model of Socialization in the Natural Environment." *Behavior Therapy* 26: 371–91.

Stafford, Mark, and Mark Warr. 1993. "A Reconceptualization of General and Specific Deterrence." *Journal of Research in Crime and Delinquency* 30: 123–35.

Steffensmeier, Darrell, and Jeffery T. Ulmer. 2005. *Confessions of a Dying Thief: Understanding Criminal Careers and Criminal Enterprise.* New Brunswick, NJ: Transaction Aldine.

Sutherland, Edwin H. 1947. *Principles of Criminology*, 4th ed. Philadelphia: Lippincott.

———. 1973. *On Analyzing Crime*, edited with an Introduction by Karl Schuessler. Chicago: University of Chicago Press.

Thornberry, Terence P., Melanie Moore, and R. L. Christenson. 1994. "Delinquent Peers, Beliefs, and Delinquent Behavior: A Longitudinal Test of Interactional Theory." *Criminology* 32: 47–84.

Tittle, Charles R. 1980. *Sanctions and Social Deviance.* New York: Praeger.

Triplett, Ruth, and Brian Payne. 2004. "Problem Solving as Reinforcement in Adolescent Drug Use: Implications for Theory and Policy." *Journal of Criminal Justice* 32: 617–30.

Verrill, Steven W. 2008. *Social Structure-Social Learning and Delinquency: Mediation or Moderation?* El Paso, TX: LFB Scholarly Publishing.

Wang, Shu-Neu, and Gary F. Jensen. 2003. "Explaining Delinquency in Taiwan: A Test of Social Learning Theory." In *Social Learning Theory and the Explanation of Crime: A*

Guide for the New Century, edited by Ronald L. Akers and Gary F. Jensen. Vol. 11 of
Advances in Criminological Theory. New Brunswick, NJ: Transaction.

Warr, Mark. 1993. "Age, Peers, and Delinquency." *Criminology* 31: 17–40.

———. 2002. *Companions in Crime: The Social Aspects of Criminal Conduct*. Cambridge,
England: Cambridge University Press.

———. 2005. "Making Delinquent Friends: Adult Supervision and Children's Affiliations."
Criminology 43: 77–106.

Warr, Mark, and Mark Stafford. 1991. "The Influence of Delinquent Peers: What They
Think or What They Do?" *Criminology* 4: 851–66.

Weeks, H. Ashley. 1958. *Youthful Offenders at Highfields*. Ann Arbor: University of Michigan
Press.

Weerman, Frank M., and Wilma H. Smeenk. 2005. "Peer Similarity in Delinquency for
Different Types of Friends: A Comparison Using Two Measurement Methods."
Criminology 43: 499–523.

Weis, Joseph G., and J. David Hawkins. 1981. "Preventing Delinquency: The Social
Development Model." *Preventing Delinquency*. Washington, DC: U.S. Government
Printing Office.

Weisner, Margit, Deborah M. Capaldi, and Gerald Patterson. 2003. "Development of
Antisocial Behavior and Crime Across the Life-Span from a Social Interactional
Perspective: The Coercion Model." In *Social Learning Theory and the Explanation of
Crime: A Guide for the New Century*, edited by Ronald L. Akers and Gary F. Jensen.
Vol. 11 of *Advances in Criminological Theory*. New Brunswick, NJ: Transaction.

White, Helene Raskin, Robert J. Pandina, and Randy L. LaGrange. 1987. "Longitudinal
Predictors of Serious Substance Use and Delinquency." *Criminology* 25: 715–40.

Winfree, L. Thomas, Jr., Curt T. Griffiths, and Christine S. Sellers. 1989. "Social Learning
Theory, Drug Use, and American Indian Youths: A Cross Cultural Test." *Justice
Quarterly* 6: 395–417.

Winfree, L. Thomas, Jr., G. Larry Mays, and Teresa Vigil-Backstrom. 1994 "Youth Gangs and
Incarcerated Delinquents: Exploring the Ties Between Gang Membership,
Delinquency, and Social Learning Theory." *Justice Quarterly* 11: 229–56.

Winfree, L. Thomas, Christine Sellers, and Dennis L. Clason. 1993. "Social Learning and
Adolescent Deviance Abstention: Toward Understanding Reasons for Initiating,
Quitting, and Avoiding Drugs." *Journal of Quantitative Criminology* 9: 101–25.

Winfree, L. Thomas, Jr., Teresa Vigil-Backstrom, and G. Larry Mays. 1994. "Social Learning
Theory, Self Reported Delinquency, and Youth Gangs: A New Twist on a General
Theory of Crime and Delinquency." *Youth and Society* 26: 147–77.

Wood, Peter B., John K. Cochran, Betty Pfefferbaum, and Bruce J. Arneklev. 1995.
"Sensation Seeking and Delinquent Substance Use: An Extension of Learning Theory."
Journal of Drug Issues 25: 173–93.

Zhang, Lening, and Steven F. Messner. 1995. "Family Deviance and Delinquency in China."
Criminology 33: 359–88.

CHAPTER 15

AN EMERGENT SITUATIONAL AND TRANSACTIONAL THEORY OF URBAN YOUTH VIOLENCE

DEANNA L. WILKINSON

YOUTH violence is a serious public health problem that compromises the healthy development of youth and communities. Urban youth in high-violence neighborhoods are particularly at heightened risk for violence-related outcomes (Bingenheimer, Brennan, and Earls 2005). Criminologists have examined links between victimization, violent offending, and other outcomes from several interrelated perspectives, including lifestyle/routine activity theory, general strain theory, subcultural theory, and differential association theory. For example, some research argues that exposure to community violence (victimization and vicarious victimization) is a major source of strain or stress on individuals, which is linked to future involvement in violent behavior (Agnew 2002; Eitle and Turner 2003; Kaufman 2005). While criminologists have focused on disentangling the temporal order issues, in terms of the relationship between victimization and violent behavior, they have focused less on the mechanisms involved in both types of experiences; less attention has also been placed on the potential cumulative and reciprocal effects of victimization and offending on other outcomes, such as compromised mental health.

Violence researchers have studied the factors that produce conflict and those that inhibit it, with attention paid to the *occurrence* of violence rather than on individual propensity to aggression. Studies that examine that nuances of violent behavior repeatedly demonstrate that violence is a goal-oriented behavior that can be thought of as purposeful and functional. Both Katz (1988) and Felson (1993) identified three primary goals of violent actions: (1) to compel and deter others, (2) to achieve favorable social identities, and (3) to obtain justice. Given these goals, there are three factors that explain how violence occurs: through the escalation of disputes over goods or status, through competition for status and social identities, and the role of third parties. Felson (1993) described the dynamics of violent incidents much like Luckenbill and Doyle (1989), calling the sequence of events a "social control process" (see also Black 1993; Philips 2003).

In terms of the role of culture in explaining violence, Elijah Anderson's code of the street and Donald Black's theory of crime as self-help have offered explanations for the disproportionate involvement of Black males compared to any other marginalized group. Anderson's study of inner city Philadelphia is perhaps the most widely cited description of violence and inner city life (Anderson 1999). Anderson suggested that the alienation, social isolation, and despair about the future that many inner-city residents experience may have created an alternative system of positive identities and building self-esteem, which is reflected in what Anderson called the "code of the streets." According to the street code, individuals who gain the most status are the most violent and frequently dominate others. Anderson described how the street code has a strong influence over the behaviors of young children, adolescents, and young adults. Children (from both decent and street families) growing up in this environment learn the street code by navigating their way through interpersonal situations that oftentimes involve violent encounters. Social identity and respect are the most important features of the street code. Within this context, there are clear-cut rules for using violence to gain respect. The public nature of a person's image or status identity often requires open displays of "nerve," including attacks on others, getting revenge for previous situations with an opponent, protecting members of one's social group, and having the right to "props." According to Anderson's findings, there is only a limited amount of respect available, and the process of acquiring respect is highly competitive. Projecting the right image is all-important in this context, and backing up the projection with violent behavior is expected. According to Anderson (1999), the street code provides rules for how individuals are to communicate with one another, how respect is to be earned, how and when respect is to be granted to another, and what should happen when someone disrespects you. Violence is used as a tool in promoting one's self-image. Developmentally, as children begin to approach adolescence, there is a stronger need for social approval and status. Ecological theories would predict that these needs would be even stronger in an inner city context where fewer opportunities for receiving positive status (according to middle class values) are available to young adolescents. Though Anderson's work provides a cohesive framework for understanding aspects of inner-city life and violence, this framework is limited in that it was primarily derived from a single research tool (ethnographic study), derived from a restricted setting (Philadelphia neighborhoods), focused on an adult-oriented perspective, and, most important, did not examine how violent offenders made sense of the unfolding of conflict events.

Another cultural view focuses on the social structure of crime. In every society, there are cultural norms for behavior that determine social deviance and the laws that govern social conduct. Cultural norms are produced by the dominant society, and within this framework, the needs, norms, protection, and grievances of marginalized groups are commonly ignored. Within this context, sociologist Donald Black argued that individuals in marginalized groups are forced to take the law "into their own hands" (Black 1983 1993). Black (1983, p. 40) explained that most violent conduct from those who are in subordinate social positions is "intended as a punishment or other expression of disapproval, whether applied reflectively or impulsively with coolness or in the heat of passion." Thus, as an attempt to gain reparation for a violation, a violent act or property damage may ensue instantly or long after the initial violation. What appears to be unimportant to the police may be perceived as a major violation for young minority males—a violation that is accepted as worthy enough to kill for or be killed over (Black 1983, p. 40). In fact, Black reported that an act of self-help is often more unforgiving and harsh than actions that would be taken by the law (1983, p. 41). Since the publication of Black's 1983 original exposition of crime as social control, there have been numerous empirical studies aimed toward applying self-theory to intimate partner homicide (Peterson 2002), vengeance (Philips 2003), retaliation (Jacobs 2004), robberies of drug dealers (Topalli, Wright, and Fornango 2002), bar fights (Oliver 1994), delinquent youth in Sweden (de Haan and Nijboer 2005), and gun violence among youthful offenders (Wilkinson and Carr 2008).

Fagan and Wilkinson (1998b) analyzed the functional aspects of violence for urban adolescents and described five goals important to adolescents that may result in violent acts: achieving and maintaining social status, acquisition of material goods, harnessing power, street justice and self-help, and defiance of authority. They concluded that "violence has become an important part of the discourse of social interactions, with both functional (status and identity), material, and symbolic meaning (power and control), as well as strategic importance in navigating everyday social dangers" (p. 88). Further, Wilkinson (2001) described the adaptive role of violence in building a tough identity in order to avoid stigma and future victimization. She described social hierarchy of violent identities that operate in dangerous neighborhoods and listed three ideal types of social identities that relate to violent performance: the crazy killer/wild identity, the holding your own identity, and the punk or herb identity. She also demonstrated that early victimization experiences shape youths' decisions to develop fighting skills, participate in violent encounters, align with tough (violent) peers, and acquire guns for self-protection (Wilkinson 2001).

One way to examine the adaptive or transactional nature of violence is to utilize an event perspective that examines how violence happens and what processual factors serve as distal (exposure to violence, moral disengagement/neutralization) and proximate (insults, retaliation, group dynamics) causes. Studying violence from an event perspective combines the examination of offenders, victims, and social context to yield a more complete picture of its etiology (Meier, Kennedy, and Sacco 2001; Miethe and Meier 1994). The event perspective considers the co-production of conflict by examining the roles of victim(s), offender(s), and others in a violent experience. It emphasizes event precursors, the event as it unfolds, and the aftermaths (including reporting, harm/injury, gossip, and redress). Most important, the event perspective integrates aspects of the physical and social setting in which violence unfolds. The social geometry of violent conflict provides clues to understanding what distinguishes one conflict situation from another, or, more precisely, what distinguishes a nonviolent conflict from a violent conflict.

Recognizing the need for studies geared toward understanding the situational factors of youth violence, Wilkinson and Fagan conducted a qualitative study of violent events reported by 416 young males recruited from two high-poverty, high-violence New York City neighborhoods in the mid 1990s (see Fagan and Wilkinson 1998a, 1998b; Wilkinson and Fagan 1996, 2001; Wilkinson 2003). The New York City Youth Violence Study (NYCYVS) examined violent events as interactions involving the confluence of motivations, perceptions, technology (in this case, weapons), the social control attributes of the immediate setting, and the ascribed meaning and status attached to the violent act. An event framework is ideal for understanding the schemas or scripts that youths bring into, and modify within, violent contexts. Drawing from the work of several scholars (Abelson 1981; Cornish 1994; Nelson 1986, 2007; Schank and Abelson 1977; Tedeschi and Felson 1994), we use the term *schema* to mean an organizing structure for procedural knowledge stored in memory that shapes behavioral repertoires when activated. Here, we focus on a particular type of schema—namely a script, which is a cognitive framework that organizes a person's understanding of typical situations; when activated, a script provides expectations about the unfolding and potential results of a set of events (Abelson 1981). Prior research on youth violence has not focused on discovering the scripts through which actors integrate information about the characteristic features (e.g., scenes, contextual cues, frames, actors, and slots/roles) and sequencing of events (Nelson 1986). According to Abelson (1981), a script is a cognitive structure or framework stored in memory that, when activated, organizes a person's understanding of typical situations, allowing the person to have expectations and to make conclusions about the potential result of a set of events. Scripts allow the actor to integrate information about the sequencing of events as well as the scenes, contextual cues or script headers, frames, actors, and slots/roles (Nelson 1986). Strong scripts include expectations of how events should unfold, while weak scripts do not provide specific expectations on sequential processes.

This chapter utilizes data from the New York City Youth Violence Study to develop a theoretical model of the situational and transactional features of urban youth violence. In Part I, I describe the research methodology for the study. Part II includes a heuristic presentation of the compositional aspects of the youth violence events focusing on the most central situational characteristics. Then I describe how those characteristics converge in the early stages of a conflict interaction. In understanding the interconnections between the event composition and the sequential patterns, I place particular emphasis on opening interactions, interpretations of social cues, relational distance between actors, and respondents' perceptions of the hostile intent of others. By breaking down event narratives into a sequence of social transactions, I am able to shed light on the micro-decisions actors make during the course of disputes. The analyses focus on the micro-actions by youths in different types of events, thus allowing for a thorough sorting of interactions across domains. Because prior research suggests that the interplay between the principal disputants and others in the immediate setting is important for understanding conflict escalation to violence (see Felson 1982; Felson and Steadman 1983; Hughes and Short 2005; Wilkinson and Fagan 1996), I attempt to identify the causal influence of the temporal antecedents in each of the events described. In Part III, I further specify an emergent transactional model by focusing on the sequential stages of the event and the roles that actors play as the event "moves" through time. Finally, I end the chapter by situating the emergent transactional theory for urban youth violence within the broader violence literature and make suggestions for its relevance to juvenile justice policy.

I. Methods

The NYCYVS consisted of ethnographic life history interviews with a targeted sample of 416 active violent offenders from two New York City neighborhoods, focusing on the social and symbolic construction of violent events (Cornish 1993, 1994; Oliver 1994). The sampling design targeted males between the ages of 16 and 24 from three pools of subjects: individuals convicted of illegal handgun possession or a violent offense (the criminal justice sample, n = 150 or 36%), individuals injured in a violent transaction (the hospital sample, n = 62 or 15%), and individuals identified by screening as having been actively involved in violence in the previous six months (the neighborhood samples, n = 204 or 49%). East New York in Brooklyn and Mott Haven in the South Bronx were selected for this study because at the time of data collection, they were among the most disadvantaged neighborhoods in New York City in terms of poverty and violent crime. The interviews were quite detailed, and in addition to the violent events of primary interest, they covered a wide range of topics, including offenders' neighborhood characteristics, family experiences, school, employment, friendships, youth and street culture, attitudes toward violence, criminal activity, perceptions of the criminal justice system, guns, drug use, and future goals. Respondents were asked to reconstruct three to four violent events that they had engaged in within the previous two-year period: one where guns were present and used; one where guns were present and not used; and one where guns were not present. Data were collected on at least one violent event per person, with an average of 2.27 events per individual. Their narratives offer an opportunity to explore the scripts that youths bring to conflict situations. Events included both completed and non-completed (near) violent situations; the latter group included events where violence was avoided in a variety of situational and social contexts. "Peer" interviewers were used to increase interviewer-respondent rapport and enhance data collection efforts. Interviewers and interviewees were matched by proximate age, race/ethnicity, and gender to facilitate the development of rapport and encourage the recounting of events. The NYCYVS data are a great resource for gaining a deeper understanding of the social worlds of youths whose lives are enmeshed in violence.

The study consisted of qualitative data analysis using an abductive (moving back and forth from inductive to deductive logic) analytical strategy (Adler and Adler 2008; Gilgun 2005) and a modified event structure analysis (Heise 1979, 1991). The rich data set was used to identify typologies of the structure, process, and contingent forms of violent situations focusing on understanding the variations across event domains. The overarching youth violence model that emerged from the qualitative analyses reflects the heterogeneity of violence among male adolescents and young adults. It also captures the varieties of event dynamics by identifying which of many situational factors are likely contingencies in the escalation of conflict to violence. We describe the situational features of the 780 near-violent and violent events coded on a variety of domains. The challenge in creating a typology of youth violence from event narratives is that there are numerous situational factors that are relevant to understanding the heterogeneity of youth violence. Most of the event descriptions were sufficiently detailed to permit us to move beyond the types of past analyses with incidents reported by a younger sample of violent men. The stages of data analysis included open coding (Strauss 1987), sifting and sorting (Wolcott 1994), categorizing, coding in teams and checking for consistency, and examining interactions between and across categories and cases. Coders read the event narratives, identified excerpts, and assigned one or multiple topic codes to each excerpt. In addition, particular domain characteristics, such as weapon type, for example, were assigned to each event case file. The researcher relied on the expertise of the peer interviewers in developing the initial event coding schema, identifying patterns, suggesting interpretations, and validating the investigator's initial interpretations. These efforts facilitated the coding and analysis of the data and permitted checks for consistency in classification among members of the research team. Each code was explicitly defined, and multiple codes were applied as appropriate. The data analysis was managed in QSR N-VIVO software (Version 8.0, Melbourne). To facilitate basic quantitative analysis, the coded data were exported into a statistical analysis program (SPSS 17.0, Chicago).

II. RECURRENT THEMES AND PATTERNS

From the event narratives, I was able to identify some characteristics of violence scripts across a broad range of youth violence incidents. These characteristics illustrate the qualitative differences between violent situations and how actors respond to them. The scenes of youth violence can be divided along two major dimensions:

(1) private versus public and (2) controlled versus uncontrolled spaces. The types of activities that define a physical space and the kinds of people who frequent the location are also important. Violent event action frames include (1) opening moves (threats, attacks, accusations, insults), (2) counter moves (accounts, resistance, denial, attack, threat escalation, warnings), (3) escalation/intensification, (4) closing moves (resolution, disruption, stalling tactics, fleeing the scene, additional threats, injury, injury treatment, arrest), (5) assessments of performance and demands, and (6) aftermaths (fear, avoidance behaviors, acute stress response, enhanced self-protection, gossip, reputational status shifts, revenge planning, self-medications or celebration with drugs/alcohol).

The link between violence scripts and action hinges primarily on how actors read contextual cues related to the harmfulness of the opponent's actions, and/or the opponent's blameworthiness for the action. The most powerful transactional script for violence relates to how youths respond to insults, identity attacks, or issues of disrespect. Youths have internalized a set of beliefs that violence is necessary when someone attacks your identity without either apologizing in a way that restores status or offering a reasonable excuse for his actions. What seems to matter most is what youths think others will think of them if they do not respond aggressively to an identity challenge or a sign of disrespect. Alternative conflict management strategies can be applied, but typically only when the opponent is an associate or friend.

Through careful analysis, I was able to identify characteristics of violence as social interactions that fit nicely into symbolic interactionist language (Anderson 1999; Goffman 1963, 1967, 1974; Heise 1979). Particularly, we can identify how actors move through settings and scenes, read contextual cues, develop action frames, evaluate other actors' potential for violence, and play roles across a broad range of youth violence incidents. The configurations across these event structures provide insights into the qualitative differences between violent situations of varying levels of seriousness and the response of actors to them. The types of activities that define a physical space and the configurations of the people who frequent the location are also important. For example, a majority of these events occur in social venues where other illegal activity is common. These venues attract crowds, facilitate other types of illegal activities such as underage drinking or illegal drug use/sale, are generally ambiguous in terms of territorial rights, and are difficult to monitor, regulate, and control. The actors in youth violence events include the antagonist, the protagonist, the co-offending antagonists, the co-offending protagonists, the allied audience, the neutral audience, the vicarious audience, and the agent of social control. There are several facilitating "props" that are important in understanding how conflict unfolds: the music genre, the presence of desired females, the reputation of the spot, use of controlled substances, the presence of male and female audience members, available weapons, and other objects in the space.

Contextual or situational cues may be verbal or nonverbal. They include threat of physical harm (including concrete facts such as size differentials, being outnumbered, being off, being out-armed), the lethality of the threat (gun versus non-gun, knife versus no weapon), threat of reputational damage, threat of relationship status damage (fear of rejection by peer group, losing the girl), victim vulnerability and relative weakness, and victim blameworthiness. Across the event outcome severity types, there are some general patterns with regard to how events with varying outcomes unfold.

III. The Emergent Transactional and Situational Model

The model that best fits the data across a range of characteristics and levels of event severity includes compositional event features as well as dynamic features. The theoretical model, presented visually in Figures 15.1 and 15.2, is geared toward conveying the most important situational factors as the event emerges and moves through time. Because violence is a form of exchange between two or more parties, the model presented in Figure 15.1 starts with critical characteristics of the identity and status of the major actors. Actors are labeled in terms of sides. The person telling the story is referred to as the respondent and the person(s) he is in conflict with as the opponent, regardless of whether the narrator is the antagonist or protagonist. Across the sample of 780 violent or near-violent events, I identified key factors about the focal participants, specifically: *reputation* (with regard to violence); *group membership, presence, and involvement at* the scene of conflict; *capability* in terms of being armed with a weapon, weapon type, being experienced in violence, age, and physical size and strength; and *arousal* (intoxication, premeditation, and emotional state). Five categories of event injury severity fit the data: near violent; violent–no injury; violent–minor injury; violent–serious injury; and violent–death. As depicted in Figure 15.1, youths on both sides of the conflict make assessments of the situation based on their own and the opposing side's characteristics. When group members or associates are present at the scene of conflicts, their violence potential or capability is factored into the youths' determinations about how the event will turn out.

The opposing sides come together in physical space and in relational space. The social relationships between actors or *social ties* are important for determining how conflict unfolds. Dimensions of social ties in this study include the type of *relationships* between youths involved in conflict, knowledge or information about others; insider versus outsider status; and any *prior history of conflict* between the specific sides. Social ties to third parties or bystanders who may witness the event also play a role in how the event unfolds. Most important among third party characteristics is *partisanship*, *stakes* in the conflict, *capability* (for violence), and *risk of harm* to self. The principal actors in the conflict size up each other as well as the bystanders. This "sizing up" is done rapidly as youths read social cues in the situation to

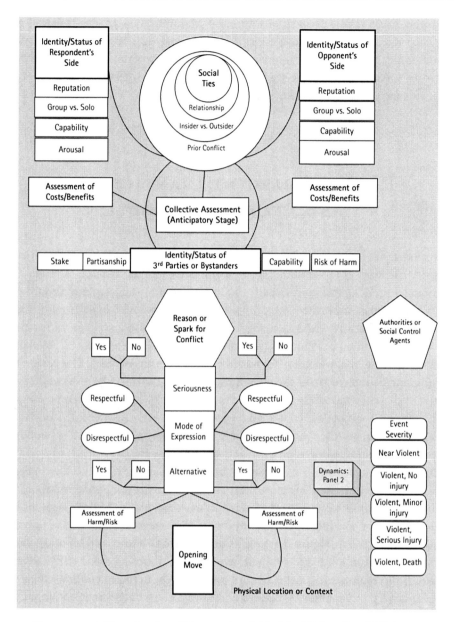

Figure 15.1. A Situational and Transactional Model of Urban Youth Violence

determine what others are likely to do. Youths' perceptions of "the other(s)" and youths' perceptions of how their own behavior and status will be perceived by people in the scene are significant in shaping context-specific action.

The conflict itself can be viewed as a form of communication and coercion. Actors project a certain image from the onset of conflict that includes rejecting stigma, disrespect, and other types of degrading action that may happen in the course of social interaction. Youths make an assessment of the costs/benefits/risk/ harm from the social cues that they read about actors at the scene. Youths will attempt to create ways to avoid violence at a particular time and place if they find themselves at a capability disadvantage or are otherwise uninterested in pursuing violence. Alternatively, youths will capitalize on situations in which their side is clearly advantaged by moving the conflict forward toward violence. Social ties between the sides influence the perceived opportunity for violence. Close ties increase the costs of using serious violence and generally result in low levels of violence.

Youths move through neighborhood spaces with varying degrees of territorial claim and perceived safety. Physical location or context is most likely to spawn violence when the routine activities of physical spaces promote the mixing of youths from different geographic areas, social networks, and greater social distance. Some type of social exchange is typically necessary for violence to erupt, although in some cases one side can dominate the event while the other remains relatively unengaged. In the majority of events, youths point to a spark or reason for the conflict. Spark type is important particularly as it relates to the perceived *seriousness* of the potential conflict. Seriousness relates to the amount of harm or damage the grievance represents to the actors. The issue that sparks a conflict can impact reputation/identity, group memberships, access to resources, health and safety for self and others, and territorial rights. As youths assessed events, the emergent pattern indicated that the greater the likelihood of harm across these categories, the greater the need to use violence. Perhaps even more important than the seriousness is the *mode of expression;* it is the way in which youths confront each other with a grievance. Although simplistic, mode of expression is classified as respectful, disrespectful, or neutral.

In defining and interpreting the spark or reason for conflict, youths are also influenced by potential *alternative* explanations, redirection, and exits. Youths on both sides of the conflict process information about the spark characteristics combined with the information about the identity/status of the actors involved in the conflict. Often the assessment of harm/risk is conducted in the split second after the spark occurs. Youths are particularly concerned about their reputation and status among peers, seeking justice, and the risks to their personal safety. From the youths' perspectives, there are not only safety risks associated with being violent and with others using violence against them, but there are also status risks associated with backing down from a provocation.

To a lesser extent, youths were concerned about whether there would be other negative consequences, such as arrest, incarceration, school expulsion, or prohibitions on access to certain locations such as clubs, homes, or recreational spaces. The likelihood that law enforcement would become aware of violent events played a role in where and how it unfolds. For example, if a young man and his friends were partying in an abandoned apartment building that was surrounded by other empty buildings and they were attacked by a group of armed youths, a shootout could happen without anyone really noticing. Youths assess place in terms of when, how, and what type of violence would be appropriate. This is not to say that all aspects of violent events are calculated or that youths are fully informed of the costs/benefits/ harm/risks when conflicts escalate to violence. They are not. Youths are continuously integrating information about place, people, alliances, obligations, violence potential, harm potential, strategic movement to gain advantage, options for exit, and emotional arousal.

The second model describes the contingencies and decision points as a process. Readers should note that not all events have every component identified, and not all events go through every stage described in Figure 15.2. Most often, the opening move of conflict is an action or inaction that sparks the two sides toward engagement in social interaction. "Moves" were coded as the action/reaction described in the event narrative for each actor as explained by the respondent recounting the incident. The issue or spark may be minor or extremely serious. Participants may agree on the definition of the spark's seriousness or they may disagree completely. Conflict can escalate to violence in either circumstance depending on many contingencies, including how actors express their grievances, who is present, and who might join the conflict if one of the main combatants starts to lose.

As shown in Figure 15.2, violent events unfold across a variety of stages and periods including *anticipatory stage* (reading cues, interpreting action/nonaction as problematic); *opening moves* (threats, attacks, accusations, insults, degrading behavior, inconsiderate behavior); *counter moves* (accounts, resistance, denial, attack, threat escalation, issuing warnings); *escalation/intensification stage; brewing period; casting stage (a sort of who's who and what can they do); persistence stage; early violence stage* (actual violence); *stewing period* (if a pause in action); *intensified violence stage; closing moves* (resolution, disruption, stalling tactics, fleeing the scene, additional threats); *outcomes* (injury, injury treatment, or arrest); *assessment stage* (harm done—physical, emotional, status, and material); *aftermaths* (fear, avoidance behaviors, acute stress response, enhanced self-protection, gossip, reputational status shifts, self-medications with drugs/alcohol, and celebration with drugs/alcohol); *retaliatory planning stage* (additional act of violence linked to a previous event); and *anticipatory stage.*

This "full" sequential model represents how the most complex violent events unfold (over one hundred events fit this complex type). There are ten common sequential configurations in the NYCYVS event data set. Some events are on the other end of the continuum—the opening move is a violent attack without any proximate interaction preceding the attack. In most cases, some prior conflict and typically an earlier violent event between the combatants was part of the backdrop of the violence. Other events move through an average of three to five of the stages. Although narratives provide an opportunity to examine sequential unfolding of events, some respondents were more detailed in their accounts than others. What we captured here suggests that the violence process can vary along a continuum of complexity.

An emergent factor that seems to have a direct influence on violent situations is the group nature of these events, which can take several forms. First and most common is when peers co-participate or co-offend. The decision to co-participate

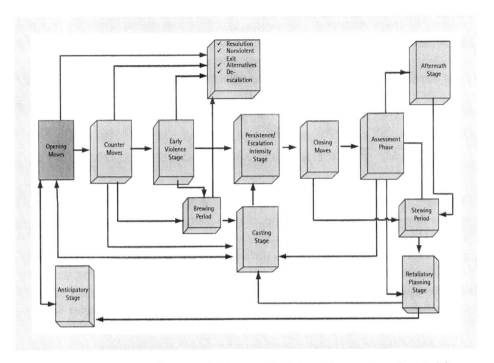

Figure 15.2. Sequential Stages of Urban Youth Violence Events: Complex Model

happens at any stage as violent conflicts unfold. Peer network members become actively involved in conflicts that lead to violence when (1) their involvement in the violent event is strategic and anticipated from the outset, (2) they come to aid an associate who is losing in the confrontation, (3) they are threatened/offended/disrespected at some point during the course of a dispute, (4) they use violence either in the moment or after the fact to get justice or right some wrong that was perpetrated against a group member, or (5) they are influenced by gossip about the performance and reputation of event participants and they take action to restore the reputation of other group members. Peer network members who are present during disputes that escalate into violence play different roles depending on the relationship between the combatants, weapon type, and injury outcomes.

Luckenbill's (1977) early work on the disputatiousness of the victim, as well as many other studies of victim behavior, suggests that violent outcomes will be more likely in conflicts in which the opponents are provocative or disrespectful. The more aggressive the opponent, the greater the likelihood that actors will perceive the situation as serious and feel that violence is necessary.

To summarize, the data on violent events show that there are several sparks that set off violent encounters, which range from preplanned retaliations to violent acts that are committed in self-defense. Some types of violence such as those associated with the drug trade can be seen as symptomatic of moral disengagement, while other violence is predominantly reactive and emergent in nature, thus not adhering to the linear progression of the adaptive model. For instance, in situations where the presence of peers elevates a dispute into a violent gun event, it matters less that the offender has been exposed to violence and has morally disengaged than that the offender is egged on or joined in violence by others. The converse, where others tamp down the potential for violent events, also exists.

IV. DISCUSSION AND CONCLUSIONS

The stages of youth violence events appear to be more complex than Luckenbill's famous four-stage (naming, blaming, claiming, aggressing) explanation. The volleying of blame and responsibility across actors involved in conflict requires a more refined examination of how events unfold. Naming, blaming, and claiming happened frequently, but conflict interactions would not necessarily move to serious violence without stewing, brewing, casting, assessment, aftermaths, and planning for retaliation. The stages of youth violence are perhaps more complex than the stages of violence among older adults (Felson 1993; Luckenbill 1977; Oliver 1998). Alternatively, the more complex sequential typology we have described may reflect differences in the level of detail provided in the accounts available for analysis and/ or our analytical strategy. The main situational factor that differs is the high prevalence of events that include multiple parties in group-on-group interaction. The combination of emergent masculinity, heightened concerns about impression management, immature decision-making, peer support for violence, and being marginalized men who are at extreme structural disadvantage may explain, in part, why youth violence is so complex.

This study reaffirms the importance of the situational perspective for understanding violent behavior as a phenomenon. It suggests that Messerschmidt's *crime as structured action theory* and notions about crime as *doing gender* are not only relevant but also could provide further understanding of disaggregate crime if we pay close attention to the ways that structural constraints relate to various proximal causes. This study has further specified how violent behavior may be scripted, which suggests the need for a dynamic situational or event perspective (Meier, Kennedy, and Sacco 2001). By examining the compositional and sequential features of 780 violent and near-violent events, we were able to develop a refined transactional theory specific to urban male youth violence that fits the data best. Our thinking is influenced by concepts from symbolic interactionism (Blumer 1969; Goffman 1963), Rich Felson's situational interactionism, Miethe and Meier's event perspective, Clarke and Cornish's rational choice theory and situational crime prevention, Marcus Felson and Cohen's routine activity theory, and Paul and Patricia Brantingham's crime pattern theory Brantingham and Brantingham, 1993; Clarke and Cornish, 1985; Felson, 1982; Cohen and Felson, 1979; Miethe and Meier, 1994). As a crime process and situational framework, the ideas presented here highlight the importance of examining how actors make sense of events as they unfold at the transactional level.

This study has implications for policy, practice, and prevention that start with a paradigm shift away from thinking about "violent youth" and propensities toward violence to instead focus on situational, developmental, and structural processes that enable violence to become a resource for youths. Disaggregating youth violence into subtypes and paying careful attention to the nuances in how particular types of violence unfold is critical as a first step toward changing youths' reading of social cues, developing alternative conflict resolution strategies and emotional control, and enhancing youths' ability to think about consequences in moments of angry arousal. The violent event scenarios gleaned from the interviews may be useful in developing materials for violence prevention programs like those developed by Daniel Webster at Johns Hopkins based on some of our findings (Webster 2009). Justice professionals who encounter youths who are perpetrators or victims of violent events could play a vital role in rejecting the use of violence to achieve hegemonic masculinity or other goals. The event narratives reveal many important aspects about how youths are reading social cues and interpreting the behavior of their opponents, associates, and third parties present at events. The narratives also reveal that violent behavior occurs away from positive adult influences that could play a role in guiding youths to consider peaceful alternatives. For example, in many reported violent events that resulted in less serious injuries, there was ample evidence to suggest that the participants were very likely subsequently to threaten, attack, shoot at, or otherwise harm the other side should the opportunity present itself. Following many violent events, youths continue to dwell on their anger toward their opponents. They typically discuss their anger with male peers who often reinforce the storyteller's feelings of mistreatment, injustice, and desire to seek revenge. In terms of scripts that are supportive of violence, the group process plays an incredibly important role before, during, and after particular violent incidents. Intervening following minor and moderately serious events may prevent violence from escalating and spawning new violence.

The examination of the situational characteristics and scripts of youth violence also provide insights into how investigators might incorporate knowledge about third parties and co-offending processes into their crime-solving work. It is important for our crime data systems to systematically capture information that would enable researchers to estimate how prevalent these types of violent events are and whether the elevated rates are adolescent-specific or concentrated among low-income men. Most of the sample reported multiple types of involvement in gun-related behaviors *and* the young men were deeply enmeshed in networks of peers, who, from the respondents' perspectives, were also deeply involved in gun-related behaviors and other crimes. Co-offending in violent events appears to be situational as particular features of the situation are more likely to result in the escalation of conflict when peers co-participate in violent events.

Juvenile justice system responses to urban youth violence should pay close attention to the co-offending issue, particularly when the perceived legitimacy of the system is shaped by observation and personal experience. Juvenile justice interventions for violent offenders should focus on cognitive restructuring, challenging perceived notions of hostile intentionality, positive identity development, analyzing the degree to which group behaviors match individual outcomes, and addressing trauma-related violence scripts. Youths in the juvenile justice system are very likely to have achieved status by violent means. Within juvenile corrections, violence is likely to be a resource for achieving status, but the controlled setting may also provide an opportunity to teach youths alternative scripts for resolving conflict. Youths may respond to opportunities to analyze their own decision-making in prior conflict situations if doing so enables them to come to some type of understanding of how they might avoid similar events in the future.

REFERENCES

Abelson, R. 1981. "Psychological status of the script concept." *American Psychologist* 36: 715–29.

Adler, P., and P. Adler. 2008. "Of rhetoric and representation: The four faces of ethnography." *Sociological Quarterly* 49: 1–30.

Agnew, R. 2002. "Experienced, vicarious, and anticipated strain: An exploratory study on physical victimization and delinquency." *Justice Quarterly* 19(4): 603–32.

Anderson, E. 1999. *The Code of the Street: Decency, Violence and the Moral Life of the Inner City*. New York: Norton.

Bingenheimer, J. B., R. T. Brennan, and F. J. Earls. 2005. "Firearm violence exposure and serious violent behavior." *Science* 308: 1323–26.

Black, D. 1983. "Crime as Social Control." *American Sociological Review* 48(1): 34–45.

Black, D. 1993. *The Social Structure of Right and Wrong*. New York: Cambridge University Press.

Blumer, H. 1969. *Symbolic Interactionism: Perspective and Method*. Englewood Cliffs, NJ: Prentice-Hall.

Brantingham, Patricia and Paul. 1993. "Environment, Routine, and Situation: Toward a Pattern Theory of Crime." *Routine Activity and Rational Choice*, Advances in Criminological Theory, volume 5, edited by Ronald Clarke and Marcus Felson. New Brunswick, NJ: Transaction Publishers.

Clarke, R. V. and Cornish, D.B. 1985. Modeling Offenders' Decisions: A Framework for Research and Policy. In: *Crime and Justice*. Vol. 6,147–178, edited by M. Tonry and N. Morris. Chicago: University of Chicago Press.

Cohen, L.E. and M. Felson, 1979. Social Change and Crime Rate Trends: A Routine Activity Approach. *American Sociological Review*. Vol. 44, 588–608.

Cornish, D. 1993. *Crimes as Scripts*. Paper presented at the Second Annual Seminar on Environmental Criminology and Crime Analysis, University of Miami, Coral Gables, FL.

Cornish, D. 1994. "The Procedural Analysis of Offending and Its Relevance for Situational Prevention." In *Crime Prevention Studies*, 151–96, edited by R. V. Clarke. New York: Criminal Justice Press.

deHaan, W., and J. Nijboer. 2005. "Youth Violence and Self-Help." *European Journal of Crime, Criminal Law and Criminal Justice* 13: 75–88.

Eitle, D., and R. J. Turner. 2003. "Stress exposure, race, and young adult male crime." *Sociological Quarterly*. 44(2): 243–69.

Fagan, J., and D. L. Wilkinson. 1998a. "Guns, youth violence, and social identity in inner cities." In *Crime and Justice: Annual Review of Research*, vol. 24, 105–87, edited by M. Tonry and M. Moore. Chicago: University of Chicago Press.

Fagan, J., and D. L. Wilkinson. 1998b. "The social contexts and functions of adolescent violence." In *Violence in American Schools*, 55–93, edited by D. S. Elliott, B. A. Hamburg, and K. Williams. Cambridge, UK: Cambridge University Press.

Felson, R. B. 1982. "Impression management and the escalation of aggression and violence." *Social Psychology Quarterly* 45(4): 245–54.

Felson, R. B. 1993. "Predatory and dispute-related violence: A social interactionist approach." In *Routine Activity and Rational Choice, Advances in Criminological Theory*, vol. 5, 103–26, edited by R. V. Clarke and M. Felson. New Brunswick, NJ: Transaction Press.

Felson, R. B., and H. J. Steadman. 1983. "Situational factors in disputes leading to criminal violence." *Criminology* 21(1): 59–74.

Gilgun, J. F. 2005. "Qualitative Research and Family Psychology." *Journal of Family Psychology* 19(1): 40–50.

Goffman, E. 1963. *Behavior in Public Places: Notes on The Social Organization of Gatherings*. New York: The Free Press.

Goffman, E. 1967. *Interaction Ritual: Essays on Face-to Face Behavior*. New York: Pantheon Books.

Goffman, E. 1974. *Frame Analysis: An essay on the organization of experience*. Cambridge, MA: Harvard University Press.

Heise, D. 1979. *Understanding Events: Affect and the Construction of Social Action*. New York: Cambridge University Press.

Heise, D. 1991. "Event Structure Analysis: A qualitative model of quantitative research." In *Using Computers in Qualitative Research*, edited by N. Fielding and R. Lee, 136–63. Newbury Park, CA: Sage.

Hughes, L., and J. Short. 2005. "Disputes involving youth street gang members: Micro social contexts." *Criminology* 43(1): 43–76.

Jacobs, B. A. 2004. "A typology of street criminal retaliation." *Journal of Research in Crime and Delinquency* 41(3): 295–323.

Katz, J. 1988. *Seductions of Crime: Moral and Sensual Attractions in Doing Evil*. New York: Basic Books.

Kaufman, J. 2005. "Explaining the race/ethnicity-violence relationship: Neighborhood context and social psychological processes." *Justice Quarterly* 22(2): 224–51.

Luckenbill, D. F. (1977). "Homicide as a situated transaction." *Social Problems* 25: 176–86.

Luckenbill, D. F., and D. P. Doyle. 1989. "Structural position and violence: Developing a cultural Explanation." *Criminology* 27(3): 419–36.

Meier, R. F., L. Kennedy, and V. F. Sacco, eds. 2001. *Advances in Criminological Theory (vol. 9): The Process and Structure of Crime: Criminal Events and Crime Analysis*. New Brunswick, NJ: Transaction.

Miethe, T. D., and R. F. Meier. 1994. *Crime and Its Social Context: Toward an Integrated Theory of Offenders, Victims, and Situations*. Albany, NY: State University of New York Press.

Nelson, K. 1986. "Event knowledge and cognitive development." In *Event Knowledge: Structure and Function in Development*, edited by K. Nelson. Mahwah, NJ: Erlbaum.

Nelson, K. 2007. *Young Minds in Social Worlds: Experience, Meaning, and Memory*. Cambridge, MA: Harvard University Press.

Oliver, W. 1994. *The Violent Social World of Black Men*. New York: Lexington Books.

Oliver, W. 1998. *The Violent Social World of Black Men.* San Francisco, CA: Jossey-Bass.

Peterson, Elicka S.L. 2002. "Varieties of self-help in intimate partner homicide." Unpublished Ph.D. dissertation, University of Missouri at St. Louis, Department of Criminology and Criminal Justice.

Philips, S. 2003. "The social structure of vengeance: A test of Black's model." *Criminology* 41(3): 673–708.

Schank, Roger, and Robert Abelson. 1977. *Scripts, Plans, Goals, and Understanding.* Hillsdale, NJ: Erlbaum.

Strauss, A. L. 1987. *Qualitative Analysis for Social Scientists.* New York: Cambridge University Press.

Tedeschi, J. T., and R. Felson. 1994. *Violence, Aggression, and Coercive Actions.* Washington, DC: American Psychological Association.

Topalli, V., R. Wright, and R. Fornango. 2002. "Drug Dealers, Robbery and Retaliation. Vulnerability, Deterrence and the Contagion of Violence." *British Journal of Criminology,* 42: 337–51.

Webster, Daniel S. 2009. "Public Health Approaches to Reducing Gun Violence." Presentation, Promoting Community Safety and Preventing Violence: Integrating Lessons from Research and Practice, Columbus, Ohio, June 26.

Wilkinson, D. L. 2001. "Violent Events and Social Identity: Specifying the Relationship between Respect and Masculinity in Inner City Youth Violence." In *Sociological Studies of Children and Youth,* edited by N. Mandell and D. A. Kinney, vol. 8, 231–65. Stanford, CT: Elsevier Science.

Wilkinson, D. L. 2003. *Guns, Violence and Identity Among African-American and Latino Youth.* New York: LFB Scholarly Publishing LLC.

Wilkinson, D. L., and P. J. Carr. 2008. "Violent Youths' Responses to High Levels of Exposure to Community Violence: What Violent Events Reveal about Youth Violence." *Journal of Community Psychology* 36: 1026–51.

Wilkinson, D. L., and J. A. Fagan. 1996. "The Role of Firearms in Violence 'Scripts': The Dynamics of Gun Events Among Adolescent Males." *Law and Contemporary Problems* 59(1): 55–90.

Wilkinson, D. L., and J. A. Fagan. 2001. "What we Know About Gun Use Among Adolescents." *Clinical Child and Family Psychology Review* 4(2): 109–32.

Wolcott, H. F. 1994. *Transforming Qualitative Data: Description, Analysis, and Interpretation.* Thousand Oaks, CA: Sage Publications, Inc.

CHAPTER 16

LEGAL SOCIALIZATION AND DELINQUENCY

TOM R. TYLER AND
LINDSAY E. RANKIN

THERE is probably no more dramatic example of the problems in the U.S. criminal justice system than the size of the American prison population (Haney & Zimbardo, 1998). As noted in Part I of this book, the incarceration rates and the costs of the current penal model are staggering. The United States is among the world leaders in the proportion of citizens it holds in prison. In 2000, there were over 2 million Americans in jail or prison (Pew Center for the States, 2008; United States Department of Justice, 2001), far surpassing incarceration rates in Europe and elsewhere (Garland, 2001).

These high rates of punishment reflect a trend in recent decades in the United States in which the exercise of legal authority has become primarily associated with the use of threat and punishment aimed at deterring people from engaging in criminal behavior (Nagin, 1998). In this instrumental approach, the focus is (and should be) on the power of legal authorities and institutions to shape behavior by threatening to deliver negative sanctions for rule breaking. For this model to be credible those who break rules have to receive punishment for their crimes, leading to a need for widespread incarceration. Of course, the model is not only about punishment: it also involves the need for a substantial police force to detect wrongdoing when it occurs. Within legal circles, this way of viewing the instrumental relationship of legal authorities with citizens is referred to as the "deterrence" or "social control" model, and it is this model of human behavior that—for better or worse—currently dominates law and public policy.

We will argue that the current focus is too strongly and too exclusively on such an instrumental approach given its cost and benefit tradeoffs and how it compares to the alternative models that exist. And, we will argue, this overly instrumental orientation is true both in the practices of the legal system and in the opinions of the public. But first, we point out that the attitudes of the public regarding how to prevent and deal with crime is not *solely* instrumental and not *solely* focused on punishment.

We want to first consider how society ended up with such an instrumental system. We will argue that public views can be generally characterized in several ways. First, when the issue is how to prevent crime, members of the public are primarily interested in building people's character or instilling appropriate morals and values. Values are internalized feelings about obligation or right and wrong. They see such values as lacking in those who commit criminal behavior. Second, when considering how to deal with those who have already committed crimes, members of the public have a very pessimistic view of the possibility of rehabilitating these wrongdoers. We characterize this public view as reflecting the belief that there are people beyond the capability of having or being open to influence by morals and values. Such people will commit crimes unless there is a severe threat of punishment to deter them. For this group a value-based approach is not possible and members of the public support an instrumental approach in the form of using punishment to respond to past crime and to deter future crime. The public does not view this punishment approach as effective, but instead sees it as the only possibility for those they regard as beyond the influence of morals and values. This view of criminals as "outsiders" who are not subject to the same motivations and values as the average citizen has dominated the criminal justice system.

In this chapter we will discuss such public attitudes and will consider how these views have led American society to an ambivalent embrace of an instrumental approach to motivating lawful behavior. We note that this strategy is costly and results in negative side effects, and we explore what alternatives are possible. We also discuss the nature of the public opinion that policy makers must confront when seeking to make policy changes.

Public Views on Preventing Crime

How does the public think individuals can be encouraged to behave in accordance with the law? To examine public perceptions about how to motivate such behavior, we can look at research by Tyler and Boeckmann (1997), who interviewed California residents in the wake of the passage of the three-strikes initiative. They asked people about the effectiveness of several different approaches to controlling crime, and the results indicate that people generally believe that shaming and moral education are the most effective ways to control the problem. For example, 70% of those interviewed indicated that shaming people by printing their names in the paper would lower crime, while 85% said that using schools to encourage the development of values such as respect and responsibility to follow rules in children would be effective. These approaches are based on values, specifically social and moral values, and indicate public support for a long-term view of preventing crime by effective socialization in childhood and by the activation of values via responses to wrongdoing like shaming that call upon the values that properly socialized people would hold.

Public support for these approaches that encourage following the law is consistent with research findings that similarly suggest that childhood value creation is a viable approach to encouraging rule following among adults. Specifically, psychologists have studied how to encourage the internalization of social values, that is, the taking values on as one's own and feeling responsible for behaving in accord with them (e.g., Hoffman, 1977). For example, researchers study the factors that shape children's willingness to break rules under conditions in which they believe they are not being observed. Their findings indicate that how children are raised by their parents shapes the degree to which they do or do not break rules under these circumstances. These findings speak to considerations of developing moral values in an effort to prevent later undesirable behavior.

Classic development psychological research points to the effectiveness of two types of child-rearing strategies for building values. One approach involves building social ties with caring others, leading to "identification," that is, the adoption of parental values (Hoffman, 2000; Tangney & Dearing, 2002). The other approach involves the development of reasoning skills through dialogue and discussion with children, so that their moral values become advanced and engaged in guiding their behavior (Blasi, 1980). Both of these strategies are based on the idea of values, rather than an instrumental approach based upon punishment or reward, in an effort to encourage desired behavior. They speak to efforts to prevent or correct misbehavior because research on developmental strategies has also been linked to law-abiding behavior among adults. Specifically, research suggests that strategies of socialization that encourage the development of social ties and cognitive reasoning skills are linked to law-abiding behavior among both adolescents and adults (Jurkovic, 1980; Turiel, 1987).

However, parents do not solely pursue values approaches and in dealing with misbehavior physical discipline is also common. In a recent national sample of American parents of 1–2 year olds, 63% reported using physical discipline, while by fifth grade 80% of children had been physically punished (Gershoff & Bitansky, 2007, p. 232). This supports our argument, expanded upon later, that there is a general culture of punitiveness in the United States. While debate continues about the usefulness of physical discipline, many if not most, researchers argue that it is of very little benefit and carries a substantial risk of harm. For example, Gershoff and Bitansky (2007) conclude that "if parents' goals are to increase children's moral internalization and to decrease their aggressive and antisocial behavior, there is little evidence that corporal punishment is effective in achieving these goals" (p. 235). And physical discipline is linked directly to aggression and violence toward others both in childhood and adolescence (Fine, Trentacosta, Izard, Matow, & Campbell, 2004). So physical punishment is likely ineffective in leading to long-term compliance; does not promote internalization of values; and can lead to aggression. Later, we will argue that similar findings apply to the excessive use of punitive policies in our criminal justice system, but first we turn to public attitudes regarding offenders and prospects of preventing them from engaging in future criminal behavior.

Public Views on Offenders

People do not just want to punish criminals for punitive or retributive reasons. They are also concerned with moral issues. There is a long-standing finding in psychological research on responses to wrongdoing that people punish to restore a moral balance (Vidmar & Miller, 1980). It has recently been affirmed in a compelling series of studies in which appropriate sentencing decisions in criminal cases are driven by moral judgments about deservingness rather than by instrumental judgments concerning how to deter future criminal conduct (Carlsmith, 2006). In making decisions within experimental contexts about whom to punish and/or how severely to punish, people focus primarily upon the issue of moral wrong.

If it were up to the members of the public, in other words, they accept punishment when it accords with their moral sense of what is appropriate given the level and type of wrong committed, but just as important they would prefer to have sincere apologies and other signs that wrongdoers recognized and acknowledge their moral wrongs and were likely to follow their moral values in the future and be law abiding.

But if people view crime as a moral issue, how can they be described as instrumental in their approach to criminals? How does this moral view of punishment contrast with the high rates of incarceration and punitive nature of the criminal justice system? To understand this seeming paradox, we again turn to the study of Californians conducted in the wake of the passage of the three-strikes initiative (Tyler & Boeckmann, 1997). The results on the perceived viability of several different approaches to punishment in response to rule breaking indicated that people had generally pessimistic views about the effectiveness of punishment as a response to wrongdoing. Only 55% said that putting criminals in prison for life would lower the crime rate and only 44% felt that using the death penalty more often would lower the crime rate. Hence, the public generally felt that deterrence in the form of severe punishment was not an especially effective response to crime. But this sample of Californians expressed even higher levels of skepticism regarding rehabilitation, with only 24% indicating that it was possible to rehabilitate burglars and only 5% saying it was possible to rehabilitate violent offenders.

Tyler and Boeckmann (1997) argue that people hold a pessimistic view of rehabilitation both because they believe that there are no common core values that wrongdoers share with others in the community and because they doubt the ability of government to effectively manage the rehabilitation process (Zimring & Johnson, 2006). For whatever reason people see the reconnection of offenders with common moral values as unlikely to occur. Similarly, in that survey of California residents the public supported severe punishment when they felt that children did not learn moral values (Tyler & Boeckmann, 1997). Those respondents who endorsed these views supported the three-strikes initiative and generally punitive policies for law breakers. Again, it seems that people see wrongdoers as lacking the communities' moral values, and therefore appeals to these values will not prevent unlawful behavior. Hence, effective deterrence will necessitate the threat and use of punishment.

In other words, of the alternatives, people expressed reluctant support for deterrence. And, of course, since punishment is not viewed as leading to rehabilitation, it is necessary to impose longer sentences on offenders, who upon their release from jail or prison will pose a danger similar to that which led them to break rules in the first place. As noted, believing that offenders lack moral values is linked to supporting longer sentences (and in the case of the three-strikes law lifetime sentences). The result is the public support for America's currently highly and "unapologetically" punitive policies for dealing with crime and criminals (Roberts & Stalans, 2004).

While the public's ambivalent views of human motivation are supportive of the current instrumental approaches, we will argue that both the public and many policies fail to fully recognize the shortcoming and the problems associated with trying to deter wrongdoing by the threat and use of punishment. Those problems include the material and social costs of deterrence and punishment, as well as the unintended consequence that instrumental approaches contribute to the problem of preventing rule breaking by undermining other human motivations, such as people's values, that could also play a role in keeping people from engaging in criminal behavior. Hence, we will suggest that people ought to be more skeptical of deterrence as a way of preventing crime and punishment as a way of preventing repeat offending, and that greater use of values approaches should be incorporated into public policy. And, as noted, we suggest that such a values-based approach finds resonance within the public, at least if it focuses upon value creation in society, especially among the young, rather than efforts to rehabilitate adult offenders.

Instrumental Approaches in the Legal System

A person looking at American society in the 1960s might have projected a future of declining punishment and increasing efforts at rehabilitation and reintegration for offenders (Garland, 2001). That is, in fact, the direction taken by much of Europe. However, the United States has not moved in that direction. Instead, it has remained a punitive society in which harsh punishment is central to reactions to rule breaking (Garland, 2001). Central to this punitive society are beliefs under which the primary way of motivating compliance with the law is via the application of sanctions.

This instrumental approach of a punishment-based deterrence policy that has come to dominate the legal system has two aspects. First is the suggestion that people's law-related behavior is shaped by their expectations about the punishment that will result from rule breaking. People could potentially be influenced by their estimates of the likelihood of being caught and punished, by their expectation of the severity of punishment, or both. Second, if they are caught and punished for wrongdoing, deterrence models suggest that the severity of the punishment that people receive shapes the likelihood of postpunishment wrongdoing. It is the role of severe punishment in preventing recidivism that is particularly relevant to issues of punitiveness.

The influence of the threat of punishment is ubiquitous in the law. Judges, for example, attempt to influence people's acceptance of their decisions by threatening fines or jail time for failure to comply. Similarly, police officers carry guns and clubs, and they are empowered to threaten citizens with physical injury and incapacitation, among other penalties. The goal is to establish legal authority and, as Reiss (1971) points out, "The uniform, badge, truncheon, and arms all may play a role in asserting authority" in the effort to "gain control of the situation" (p. 46). The police thereby seek to gain control over the individual's behavior "by manipulating an individual's calculus regarding whether 'crime pays' in any particular instance" (Meares 2000, p. 396). All of these authorities seek to bring behavior into line with the law by threatening people with punishment.

More generally, the legal system is charged with producing compliant behavior and based on an instrumental approach it attempts to shape environmental contingencies in such a way that citizens will be faced with the prospect of heavy losses (e.g., incarceration) that are intended to outweigh the anticipated gains of engaging in criminal behavior. This deterrence model dictates that the responsibility of lawmakers is to decide which acts should be prevented, and then to specify sufficiently strict penalties—generally fines or prison terms—so that the prohibited behavior is rarely enacted. The notion that people's behavior with respect to the law is shaped by calculations of expected gains and losses is a core premise of rational choice theory, which is derived from neoclassical economics (Nagin, 1998).

According to the assumptions of rational choice theory, most people will calculate expected utilities by multiplying the probability of an outcome (e.g., getting caught for armed robbery or drunk driving) by its valence (very, very bad). If the laws are well calibrated, people will arrive at the desired conclusion that they should follow the law. Thus, rational self-interest is the motivational engine of the deterrence/social control model. To regulate behavior, this model suggests that decision makers should adjust criminal sanctions to the needed level so that the expected losses associated with law breaking will minimize the likelihood that people will break the law.

Instrumental Views in General Public Attitudes

The general tenor of recent times in the United States is captured by the case of support for the death penalty. During the 1960s, a majority of adult Americans favored ending the death penalty, while public opinion polls during the 1980s and 1990s typically found that 80% or more of those interviewed favored the death penalty (Ellsworth & Gross, 1994). The focus of public discussion has been, both on the issue of the death penalty and punishment more generally, on the view that the legal system is too lenient and that there need to be harsher ways to punish those who commit crimes.

The punitive nature of public views is a theme in most recent writing about the American public. But given some of the support for value building that we discussed earlier, why does the public support ever harsher punishments? We see punitiveness as an expression of frustration in a public who perceives moral values to be in decline and the set of shared values that define a common community transforming into a set of subcommunities of "outsiders" and "strangers" who either lack values or have different values. In this changing social landscape, people view punishment as a mechanism that still works to maintain social order. However, as we are about to argue, its actual effectiveness in preventing law breaking is limited, and over time the appeal of ever more severe sanctions is, in our view, irresistible, since the deterrence model is not preventing crimes and the use of strategies based upon this model has undermined the role of other values in securing compliance. Once rules are broken the general deterrence model can be enhanced by the costly route of building more prisons, as has occurred to a considerable extent in America. Severe punishments hold the promise of keeping dangerous people off the street and, to the degree they can be afforded, seem the only effective route to take. In other words, incapacitation becomes the most seemingly viable option in the wake of failed deterrence strategies. If people cannot be deterred ever more severe punishments can be used to keep criminals under control because they can at least keep them off the streets for lengthy periods of time. In the case of the death penalty the threat posed by someone is completely eliminated by their execution.

Shortcomings of Instrumental Views

Despite such institutional and public support, we argue that the deterrence model is both too costly and at best a minimally effective system of social control. The high costs come in the form of material costs of implementing such a system, the social costs of the negative effects that these methods of surveillance and punishment have on communities and their relationship with the law and law enforcement, and the self-defeating effect that this approach has in undermining individuals' internal motivations for law abiding behavior.

Material Cost of Instrumental Approach

The high material cost of the system stems from the need to create and maintain a credible threat of punishment. According to an instrumental view, people will only change their behavior when they feel that there is a reasonable risk of being caught and punished for wrongdoing. Of course people will try to hide their illegal behavior, so a system of surveillance will be needed to identify wrongdoing.

The problems of surveillance are central to deterrence models, because research suggests that it is the probability of punishment, more than punishment severity, that shapes rule-related behavior (Tyler, 2006a, 2006b). In other words, if a person is considering rule breaking, he or she is more influenced by the likelihood that he or she will be caught and punished at all than by considerations of how severe that punishment will be. As a consequence, a system for detecting wrongdoing must be created and maintained. For this reason, as Meares (2000) notes, the effectiveness of "instrumental means of producing compliance always depend[s] on resource limits" (p. 401). It is not realistic to substitute draconian punishments for a more costly system that creates credible risks of being detected while engaging in wrongdoing because it will not be effective in motivating behavior. The relevant questions are how much in terms of financial and other benefits and burdens authorities are willing to expend in order to control crime, and how much power to intrude into citizens' lives people are willing to allow the authorities to have?

Deterrence works reasonably well in at least some cases, such as murder, because society has devoted considerable resources to making the risk of being caught high and to enforcing penalties for it by punishing those who commit murder with lengthy incarceration. The objective risk of being caught and punished for murder is relatively high: approximately 45% (Robinson & Darley, 1997). The likelihood of being caught for committing a murder is high enough for deterrence to be effective in lowering the murder rate. Even in this case, however, criminals are not as sensitive to the magnitude of the penalty as they are to the estimated probability of being apprehended. As a result, capital punishment does not serve to deter murder more effectively than does life imprisonment (Ellsworth & Mauro, 1998).

For offences less severe than murder, using surveillance to shape law-related behavior becomes even more problematic. For example, in examining the problem of drunk driving, Ross (1982) suggests that raising risk estimates to a level that is high enough to lower the rate of law-breaking behavior, while not necessarily impossible, involves prohibitively high costs in terms of police manpower and people's willingness to accept state intrusions into their personal lives. Ross further points out that even the intensive efforts of Scandinavian authorities to create high estimates of risk using random road blocks and other similarly expensive and intrusive law enforcement measures are insufficient to create and maintain subjective risk estimates that are high enough to deter drunk driving over the long term.

In addition to deterring a potential offender, the instrumental approach would argue that punishing an individual after he or she does something wrong discourages the individual from future law breaking, which provides an additional reason for incarceration. This is referred to as specific deterrence, the belief that punishing a person for wrongdoing leads that person to be less likely to commit rule-breaking behavior in the future. The high material costs of this extension of the instrumental strategy are incurred through the administration of the actual punishment such as incarceration time, as discussed in Part I of this book.

However, just as we have argued that the threats of severe punishment fail to motivate behavior, the delivery of punishments is also a strategy of uncertain effectiveness. This is true of the practice of widespread punishment for minor crimes. One example is the use of what is called the broken windows approach to policing. That approach argues that the police should punish minor crimes to discourage more serious crimes. However, evaluations suggest that the use of this approach does not lower the rate of serious crime (Harcourt & Ludwig, 2006). More broadly, variations in the severity of punishment are not found to be related to the rate of reoffending among offenders (Lipsey & Cullen, 2007; Lynch & Sabol, 1997), while among juveniles incarceration increases the risk of recidivism (McCord, Widom, & Crowell, 2001; Mendel, 2002).

As already noted, it would be wrong to argue that estimates of risk and punishment have no effect on behavior. Research does support the argument that variations in the perceived certainty of punishment do affect people's compliance with the law, at least to some degree in some cases. People's behavior is often, though not always, shaped by their estimate of the likelihood that, if they disobey the law, they will be caught and punished (Nagin, 1998). But perceptions of the likelihood of being caught and punished generally have a relatively minor influence on people's behavior. Consequently, social control strategies based exclusively on a deterrence model of human behavior have at best limited success (Tyler, 2009).

Further demonstrating the minor effect of deterrence by examining both the certainty and severity of punishment, MacCoun (1993) found that these considerations account for approximately 5% of the variance in drug use behavior, a finding consistent with the suggestion of Paternoster (1987) that "perceived certainty [of punishment] plays virtually no role in explaining deviant/criminal conduct" (p. 191). A recent review similarly concluded that the relationship between crime/deviance and variables specified by deterrence theory is "modest to negligible" (Pratt, Cullen, Blevins, Daigle, & Madensen, 2008, p. 383). And after decades of research the voluminous literature on the deterrence effects of the death penalty suggests that "the relationship between executions and murders still lacks clear proof" (Weisberg, 2005, p. 163). Hence, deterrence is a very high cost strategy that yields, at best, identifiable but weak results.

Social Costs of Instrumental Approaches

Deterrence involves material investments of resources and would require high costs to be effective. Further, the implementation of deterrence strategies also results in social costs. Many material costs are concrete and visible on state and federal budgets. In contrast, social costs, by which we mean the negative effects on the relationships of people within a community and between communities and law enforcement, may be more invisible but no less important to consider. The heavy costs of the large-scale imprisonment to individuals and communities have had a strong impact, especially on urban communities and especially among members of racial and ethnic minority groups, which are overrepresented in the prison system (Patillo, Weiman, & Western, 2004).

For example, surveillance systems have deleterious effects on the social climate of groups because their use implies distrust, which decreases people's ability to feel positively about themselves, their groups, and the system itself (Kramer & Tyler, 1996). Furthermore, people may experience intrusions into their lives as procedurally unfair, leading to anger and other negative emotions often associated with perceptions of injustice (e.g., Gurr, 1970). Whether surveillance works or not, then, it is often demotivating and introduces new costs in terms of distrust and perhaps even paranoia in subsequent social interaction. Such costs are borne by groups, organizations, and societies to which people belong, as they lose the gains that occur when people are willing to cooperate with each other.

Research suggests that the increasing use of deterrence strategies and social control has exerted precisely this type of negative influence on the American social climate. It has created an adversarial relationship between legal authorities and members of the communities they serve, especially with respect to racial and ethnic minority group members (Tyler & Huo, 2002), leading the public to grow less compliant with the law and less willing to help the police to fight crime (Sunshine & Tyler, 2003).

Undermining of Motivation Through Instrumental Approach

Furthermore, general principles of human motivation suggest that if people comply with the law only in response to coercive power, they will be less likely to obey the law in the future because acting in response to external pressures diminishes internal motivations to engage in a behavior. This follows from the well-known distinction in social psychology between intrinsic and extrinsic motivation. Research shows that when people are motivated solely by the prospect of obtaining external rewards and punishments they become less likely to perform the desired behavior in the absence of such environmental reinforcements (e.g., Deci, 1975). On the other hand, if people are motivated by intrinsic reasons for behaving in a certain way, then their compliance becomes much more reliable and less context dependent. And external contingencies that are too strong can even dampen the motivation for behaviors they were previously intrinsically motivated, even for formerly enjoyable activities.

The undermining effects of deterrence do not only occur among the people being regulated. When authorities manage people by surveillance, they do not build up any basis for trusting them. For example, employees who have been given the opportunity to follow rules for internal reasons demonstrate to workplace authorities when they do so that they can be trusted. Subsequently, authorities are more comfortable allowing those individuals to work without supervision. However, when authorities are constantly present, they have no basis for trust and can suspect that the moment they leave people will stop following the rules (Strickland, 1958). Hence, the very behavior of surveillance creates the conditions requiring future surveillance. And, as noted earlier, their suspicions are at least partially justified, since their surveillance has probably had the effect of undermining people's value-based motivations for obeying the law.

Thus, overall the deterrence or instrumental model has, at best, only minor influence on people's behavior. In the social sciences even small effects can be meaningful, but as we have outlined, these small effects come at high costs in terms of resources for enforcement and punishment and in terms of negative social impact. Therefore, these small effects, we argue, are not worth these high costs, and furthermore the side effects over time can be cumulative because it can create a self-fulfilling prophecy, a perpetuating cycle of lessening intrinsic motivation and trust in authorities which lead to less voluntary cooperation and rule following and greater reliance and enforcement of deterrence models by both law enforcement and in the minds of the public. Despite these disadvantages, our society is currently committed to a deterrence approach to bringing behavior into line with rules. This commitment is strong in spite of empirical evidence that suggests that this approach is not very effective and that value-based regulation is more effective. As we have noted, the public is focused upon moral issues when dealing with the law, so the deterrence approach is a poor fit to "true" public concerns. However, the public has a generally skeptical view about both the possibility of who can be motivated to adhere to rules based upon values and of preventing recurrences of wrongdoing based upon rehabilitation. As a consequence, the public focuses reluctantly upon deterrence and incapacitation (Tonry, 1999). Our argument is that in reality empirical findings support the value of the approach that the public actually favors, a focus upon preventing rule-breaking behavior through the development and maintenance of the values that support rule following.

Alternative Value-Based Approaches Rather Than Instrumental

We noted that the public generally falls back on instrumental approaches for motivating rule following, despite recognizing the limits of punishment. They see punishment as more effective or at least the only option for dealing with individuals who have committed crimes because they view rehabilitation as not viable. However, while the public has a generally negative view about the possibility of rehabilitation, the public is more positive toward efforts to prevent criminal behavior, not by deterrence, but by the development of values. This strong public support for values is important because, we will suggest, there is considerable evidence that values are a viable and effective approach to motivating rule adherence. Hence, it may be more politically reasonable to focus upon changing approaches to preventing wrongdoing, and it may require more convincing of the public that similar efforts can be directed at rehabilitating those who have committed crimes.

Our argument is that there is an alternative model to deterrence that can inform criminal justice policies, a self-regulatory model in which individuals' behavior is internally motivated by their values. In this chapter, we use the term *values* to refer to internalized feelings that people have about their obligations to obey authorities and follow moral principles; that is, we focus on the values of legitimacy and moral beliefs (see Tyler, 2009). Because these values are held by people as their own, they are motivated to follow them irrespective of whether there are punishments or rewards associated with such actions. Hence, their behavior in following rules is voluntary and occurs without surveillance. We argue that people are more likely to obey a law if they think it is legitimate and/or consistent with their moral values. We will argue are that these values are actually better at preventing criminal behavior than instrumental approaches, that such values can be developed and encouraged, and that people who have committed crimes are still sensitive to these values despite public skepticism about such motivations within people who have committed crimes in the past.

Legitimacy

Legitimacy is the feeling of responsibility and obligation to follow the law; to accept the decisions of legal authorities; and to cooperate with and help legal authorities to do their jobs. Legitimacy is defined as "a property that a rule or an authority has when others feel obligated to voluntarily defer to that rule or authority. In other words, a legitimate authority is one that is regarded by people as entitled to have its decisions and rules accepted and followed by others" (Skogan & Frydl, 2004, p. 297). Legitimacy, therefore, is a quality that people perceive an authority, a law, or an institution to possess that leads others to feel obligated to obey its decisions and directives. Successful leaders and institutions use more than brute force to execute their will. They strive to gain the consent of the governed so that their commands will be voluntarily accepted.

One way to think about legitimacy is people's belief that it is a property of an institution. Studies of the legitimacy of legal authorities typically ask people to evaluate their general feelings of responsibility and obligation to obey the law and legal authorities (see Tyler, 2006a). This focus on the importance of legitimacy reflects concern with the circumstances under which people follow the directives of social rules and social authorities. Legitimacy is important to the success of such authorities because they are enabled to gain public deference to a range of decisions by virtue of their social role (Tyler, 2006a, 2006b). Widespread voluntary cooperation with the law and legal authorities allows those authorities to concentrate their resources most effectively on pursuing the long-term goals of society. The authorities do not need to provide incentives or sanctions to all citizens to get them to support every rule or policy they enact, and the resources needed for order maintenance can be deployed in other ways.

Legitimacy can also be perceived as the property of a person. In early policing, for example, the beat officer patrolled a particular area, an area in which he or she often lived. They developed personal relationships with the public—that is, people knew them. So they had legitimacy as individuals, and they built or undermined that legitimacy by the manner in which they exercised their authority. In modern police forces, which are rooted in police cars, the officer who steps out of a car to respond to a particular situation is generally someone that the people involved do not know. That officer has institutional legitimacy, marked by a uniform, a cap, a badge. Their authority comes from the authority of their office, not from anything about them as particular people.

Legitimacy can be created by the actions of the institution or individuals. One of the primary ways examined in research that legitimacy is created in the minds of people is through authorities' use of fair procedures. This means by making decisions via neutral procedures and by treating people fairly and with respect, ideas referred to in the psychological literature as procedural justice (Tyler, 2009). The centrality of procedural justice to legitimacy suggests that policy makers can effectively create and maintain legitimacy and can, therefore, enact strategies based upon legitimacy (Tyler, 2009).

Moral Values

The second social value we are discussing is personal morality—the motivation to behave in accord with one's sense of what is appropriate and right to do in a given situation. The influence of moral values is based on the internalization of feelings of responsibility to follow principles of personal morality (see Robinson & Darley, 1995). A core element of moral values is that people feel a personal responsibility to follow those values and feel guilty when they fail to do so. Hence, moral values, once they exist, are self-regulatory in character, and those who have such values are personally motivated to bring their conduct into line with their moral standards. And, like the social value of legitimacy, morality is internal and shapes actions distinct from consideration of being caught and punished for wrongdoing. What unites the study of legitimacy and morality? In both cases, the key is that people accept as their own feelings of responsibility and obligation for their actions in society.

These feelings about the morality of particular behaviors also shape people's rule-following behavior. People are less likely to obey laws not consistent with their moral values (Tyler, 2006b). Further, discrepancies can generalize beyond a particular law and shape adherence to a broader range of laws. This can pose problems for the legal system, but looked at from the other direction people are more willing to comply with the law to the extent that they view it as consistent with their moral values; their internalized sense of morality acts as a force for law abidingness (e.g., Robinson & Darley, 1995; Tyler, 2006a).

Robinson and Darley (1995) and Finkel (1995) show gaps between law and public morality. To the extent that such gaps are widely known, they would undermine public compliance with the law. The law can enlist people's moral values as a motivational force supporting deference to the law by pursuing ends that people view as moral. They argue that the law is less likely to be able to call upon people's moral motivations to support the legal system when its values are viewed as discrepant from those of the public. Hence, the law can engage moral values when and if the law is consistent with the moral values held by the public.

Building upon moral values requires first that people have moral values and that they are widely shared within the community. It is precisely this issue that forms the focus of public concern, with the lack of common moral values seen as a problem, and the building of moral values seen as the best long-term solution to issues of crime. Here, we suggest, public views and our arguments converge. We join the public in arguing that creating moral values is the best approach to exercising social control. How do you build such values? One focus should be upon childhood socialization because, as we have indicated, psychological research supports the importance of socializing values in children. And that developmental literature is directed at moral values. Second, studies of adults suggest that procedural justice, which as we have noted increases legitimacy, also increases moral value congruence. If legal authorities enforce the law using fair procedures, people also infer that they share their moral values (Tyler & Blader, 2005).

Values Advantages Over Instrumental Approaches

In empirical studies of the general population, legitimacy and morality are found to be as or more important in shaping compliance than instrumental approaches. Tyler (2006a, 2006b, 2009), for example, compared the risk of deterrence to that of legitimacy and moral value congruence and found that both values were stronger predictors of compliance than was estimated risk. In other words, when these alternative value-based models are compared to deterrence, the alternative models are found to be stronger. Further, studies find that results "consistent with a large body of research that shows that when other inhibitions are strong (such as those provided by one's moral beliefs), the deterrent effect of sanction threats are irrelevant [to whether adolescents and young adults engage in criminal behavior]" (Wright, Caspi, Moffit, & Paternoster, 2004, p. 206).

In other words, when people have values, such as their morality or belief in an institution's legitimacy, risk calculations may become less relevant or even irrelevant to their behavioral calculations. Tyler (2005) similarly found that values and risk perceptions interacted in shaping peoples' everyday law-related behavior, with risk calculations assuming a smaller role in behavioral choices when values were important. Further, values are more important than sanctions in shaping both the voluntary acceptance of rules and willing cooperation with legal authorities. Because voluntary acceptance and cooperation are gains to the legal system, self-regulation is a superior strategy.

Given the positive effects of values on influencing behavior, we think policy should include promotion of legitimacy and moral values as approaches to preventing and dealing with crime. There have been institutions that have beneficially moved from instrumental approaches toward self-regulation based upon values, as demonstrated in the research on business (Tyler & Blader, 2005). Employee behavior was traditionally thought of as being shaped by command and control models in which authorities shaped actions by providing rewards and/or threatening punishments, but it has been recognized within the regulatory community that more self-regulatory models are important and that businesses need to tap into the values that exist within their workplaces, drawing upon employees own motivations to follow rules and policies in their workplace. Such self-regulatory approaches have the advantage we have noted—they minimize surveillance costs and maximize behavior based upon employee values (see Tyler, Dienhart, & Thomas, 2007). Hence, efforts to deal with recent corporate crises should focus on building value-based cultures in work organizations.

The average employee might, understandably, be seen by the public as quite different from the average person in contact with the criminal justice system. We would not argue that a self-regulation model will prevent all crime, just as the deterrence model cannot prevent murders even when its detection and punishment rates are high. And we would not argue that punishment and instrumental methods should never be used; for one thing, people have reactions to extreme injustice, and deterrence is not the only reason for the use of punishment. But once a crime has been committed, if just putting people in jail or prison does not lower the rate of reoffending, what can be done? Many strategies of rehabilitation focus on reconnecting people with their values and their ties to society and its rules and authorities (Braithwaite, 2002; Tyler, 2006c) and by building social ties and encouraging the development and engagement of values (Gendreau, 1996).

Developing Values

A large psychological literature speaks to the idea of value socialization in childhood (see Chapter 3). That literature makes clear that it is possible to socialize values and that doing so shapes both adolescent and adult law-related behavior. Further, specific approaches to value development have been identified and proven to be effective. Hence, it is possible enact the public's agenda with considerable confidence of success.

The more challenging issue—in the public's mind, at least—is to get adults who have committed crimes to develop and act on their values. Is this possible to do once a person is beyond childhood? Public opinion seems to be skeptical, but research suggests that many approaches to rehabilitation are successful. While Part III of this book will address in greater detail specific strategies to reduce recidivism, for the purposes of arguing that values can be engaged in such a population we will point out a few methods and findings in this area of research relevant to our arguments about the contexts that succeed and fail at steering people away from crime.

One specific approach of a successful program is restorative justice. Restorative justice involves conferences that include the offender, the offender's family, the victim, and members of the community. At the conference all of those involved discuss the offender's behavior, the offender acknowledges responsibility for wrongdoing, and the group crafts an approach to restoring justice. The focus is on a "bad behavior, good person" approach in which those present seek to reconnect the offender to his or her values, with the goal of motivating the offender to want to follow the rules in the future. The restorative justice approach seeks ways to heighten the offender's future motivations to engage psychologically and behaviorally in society. This engagement includes developing or becoming more committed to social values that promote self-regulation, and consequently adhering more closely to laws and social regulations in the future, that is, to lower levels of rearrest. In other words, one important goal is being able to create better community members. Research results support the facilitative role of restorative justice conferences (Roberts & Stalans, 2004; Sherman, 1999). Studies suggest that, at least with regard to some types of crime such as those committed by juveniles who have social ties, participating in a restorative justice conference leads to greater cooperation with the law in the future (Bradshaw, Roseborough, & Umbriet, 2006; Latimer, Dowden, & Muise, 2005; Nugent, Williams, & Umbreit, 2003; Poulson, 2003). Such conferences, it seems, do increase the motivation to accept the law and the decisions of legal authorities and to be a law-abiding citizen.

Latimer, Dowden, and Muise (2005) directly examined evidence concerning the impact of restorative justice on recidivism in adults. They concluded that in approximately two-thirds of the programs studied, restorative justice programs "yielded reductions in recidivism compared to nonrestorative approaches to criminal behavior" (p. 137), a difference which they found statistically significant. While these authors do not examine the psychological mechanisms by which these effects occur, we argue that they are using approaches consistent with our argument for an increased focus on values and a less singular focus on instrumental approaches.

Of course, we do not want to overstate our case. Studies suggest that rehabilitation is most successful among adolescents. It can be effective among adults, but results are weaker. We know it is most difficult to change "hardened" criminals such as violent or career offenders. Is it possible to do so at all? Research reviewed elsewhere in this volume suggests that the answer is yes.

We noted at the beginning that it is almost as if the public sees criminals as different and not subject to motivations related to values. Evidence addressing some aspects of this view contradicts these beliefs and shows that this group is sensitive to issues of values. For example, Casper, Tyler, and Fisher (1988) analyzed the results of a panel study of defendants arrested for felonies, defendants who were generally young, minority, and male, demographic characteristics that are common among much of the population in contact with criminal justice in the United States. They found that the evaluations of the procedural justice of the case disposition process made by these defendants had a strong influence upon both their satisfaction with their experiences and was the primary factor shaping their generalization from their personal experience to their overall views about the legitimacy of the law and the legal system. And elsewhere we have argued that legitimacy corresponds with rule-following behavior. Other studies similarly suggest that procedural justice plays an important role in shaping the attitudes and behaviors of "criminals" (see Tyler, 2009).

Summary

The general message of this chapter is that law enforcement and the public have ambivalently embraced an instrumental approach, that is, the threat of or actual punishment as a mechanism through which to shape the behavior of both wrongdoers and people in general. This is not to say that others approaches do not exist, or that people do not disagree; however, the dominant model clearly follows instrumental approaches. We have argued that not only does empirical research show that this approach is not particularly effective in determining behavior, but it also is very costly in terms of both resources and negative side effects. Hence, there is a widespread disconnect between policy and empiricism. It has led to a dramatic growth in the American prison population and has soured the relationship between the law, legal authorities, and the members of society. It has had a particularly negative impact on the minority community.

Given these problems it is important to emphasize that there are alternatives to a solely instrumental approach. In particular, we point to a series of findings that suggest the importance of focusing on values, an approach which has the goal of enhancing self-regulation. But the main purpose of considering these issues is to ask whether alternatives to instrumental approaches that do receive empirical support can actually be implemented with public support or at least without widespread resistance. That is, one problem lies in public punitiveness—the support of the public for harsh punishment. These public views are linked to public conceptions of human nature. In particular, the issue is whether people believe that people can develop and act on values.

The public seems to generally favor and see the potential of approaches that build values and mutual respect among members of the public. The findings of Tyler and Boeckmann (1997) suggest that people support efforts to build values and rely on self-regulation methods to prevent crime. Thus, policy makers would do well to focus on building on these existing beliefs of people in order to shift from dependency on a purely surveillance deterrence model to a model that encourages the development and activation of moral values and beliefs in the legitimacy of the legal system (Tyler, 2009).

The core to the effectiveness of a value-based strategy is value socialization. Studies show it works, but they clearly suggest that it works most effectively among children and adolescents. The socialization of adults is harder and the socialization of rule breakers may be especially difficult. While rehabilitation can work, it is not an optimum place to start.

Further, policy changes related to rehabilitation face more resistance from the public. Of course, additional research is clearly needed to establish the nature of punitive attitudes, but the findings of Tyler and Boeckmann (1997) suggest that the public does not see rehabilitation as feasible, especially for violent adult offenders. Thus, in the case of the rehabilitation of adults who are already criminals, policy makers would not be able to rely solely on emphasizing certain aspects of the existing attitudes of the public and instead would have to focus more on communicating to people that there are methods that *are* effective or that the preventative measures the public abstractly support *can* also be applied to reducing recidivism. And, of course, that would be more difficult because the research evidence is less strikingly positive for programs aimed at adult offenders.

Is value creation a panacea that can increase law abidingness among everyone? No, it is not. Public skepticism is justified to a degree. But we suggest that it is clearly a superior strategy in general, particularly when societies begin with a focus on value creation during childhood and adolescence and do not wait until people have already offended to attempt to create or reactivate values. While restoration can occur, it is not as effective as is a strategy focused on value creation prior to offending. And the public reveals considerable awareness of these distinctions. As a result, the public supports the superior strategy of childhood value creation when it feels that effectively implementing such a strategy is feasible.

REFERENCES

Blasi, A. (1980). Bridging moral cognition and moral action. *Psychological Bulletin, 88*, 1–45.

Bradshaw, W., Roseborough, D., & Umbriet, M. S. (2006). The effects of victim offender mediation on juvenile offender recidivism. *Journal of Conflict Resolution, 24*, 87–98.

Braithwaite, J. (2002). *Restorative justice and responsive regulation.* Oxford, England: Oxford University Press.

Carlsmith, K. M. (2006). The roles of retribution and utility in determining punishment. *Journal of Experimental Social Psychology, 42*, 437–451.

Casper, J. D., Tyler, T., & Fisher, B. (1988). Procedural justice in felony cases. *Law and Society Review, 22*(3), 483–507.

Deci, E. L. (1975). *Intrinsic motivation.* New York: Plenum Press.

Ellsworth, P. C., & Gross, S. R. (1994). Hardening of the attitudes: Americans' views on the death penalty. *Journal of Social Issues, 50*, 19–52.

Ellsworth, P. C., & Mauro, R. (1998). Psychology and law. In D. T. Gilbert, S. T. Fiske, & G. Lindzey (Eds.), *Handbook of social psychology* (pp. 684–732). New York: McGraw Hill.

Fine, S. E., Trentacosta, C. J., Izard, C. E., Mastow, A. J., & Campbell, J. L. (2004). Anger perception, caregivers' use of physical discipline, and aggression in children at risk. *Social Development, 13*, 213–228.

Finkel, N. J. (1995). *Commonsense justice: Juror's notions of the law.* Cambridge, MA: Harvard University Press.

Garland, D. (2001). *The culture of control.* Chicago: University of Chicago Press.

Gendreau, P. (1996). The principles of effective intervention with offenders. In A. T. Harland (Ed.), *Choosing correctional interventions that work: Defining the demand and evaluating the supply* (pp. 117–130). Newbury Park, CA: Sage.

Gershoff, E. T., & Bitensky, S. H. (2007). The case against corporal punishment of children. *Psychology, Public Policy, and Law, 13*, 231–272.

Gurr, T. R. (1970). *Why men rebel.* Princeton, NJ: Princeton University Press.

Haney, C., & Zimbardo, P. (1998). The past and future of U.S. prison policy: Twenty-five years after the Stanford prison experiment. *American Psychologist, 53*, 709–727.

Harcourt, B. E., & Ludwig, J. (2006). Broken windows: New evidence for NYC and a five-city social experiment. *University of Chicago Law Review, 73*, 271–320.

Hoffman, L. W. (1977). Changes in family roles, socialization and sex differences. *American Psychologist, 32*, 644–657.

Hoffman, M. L. (2000). *Empathy and moral development: Implications for caring and justice.* Cambridge, England: Cambridge University Press.

Jurkovic, G. J. (1980). The juvenile delinquent as a moral philosopher: A structural- developmental perspective. *Psychological Bulletin, 88*, 709–727.

Kramer, R. M., & Tyler, T. R. (Eds.). (1996). *Trust in organizations.* Thousand Oaks, CA: Sage.

Latimer, J., Dowden, C., & Muise, D. (2005). The effectiveness of restorative justice practices. *The Prison Journal, 85*, 127–144.

Lipsey, M. W., & Cullen, F. T. (2007). The effectiveness of correctional rehabilitation: A review of systematic reviews. *Annual Review of Law and Social Science, 3*, 297–320.

Lynch, J. P., & Sabol, W. J. (1997). *Did getting tough on crime pay?* Crime Policy Report. Washington, DC: American University, The Urban Institute.

MacCoun, R. J. (1993). Drugs and the law: A psychological analysis of drug prohibition. *Psychological Bulletin, 113*, 497–512.

McCord, J., Widom, C. S., & Crowell, N. A. (2001). *Juvenile justice*. Committee on Law and Justice, National Research Council, Juvenile Justice. Washington, D.C.

Meares, T. L. (2000). Norms, legitimacy, and law enforcement. *Oregon Law Review, 79*, 391–415.

Mendel, R. A. (2002). *Less hype, more help: Reducing juvenile crime: What works and what doesn't*. Washington, DC: National Urban League, American Youth Policy Forum.

Nagin, D. S. (1998). Criminal deterrence at the onset of the 21st century. *Crime and Justice, 23*, 1–42.

Nugent, W., Williams, M., & Umbreit, M. S. (2003). Participation in victim-offender mediation and the prevalence and severity of subsequent delinquent behavior. *Utah Law Review, 2003*, 137–166.

Paternoster, R. (1987). The deterrent effect of the perceived certainty and severity of punishment: A review of the evidence and issues. *Justice Quarterly, 4*(2), 173–217.

Patillo, M., Weiman, D., & Western, B. (Eds.). (2004). Imprisoning America: The social effects of mass incarceration. New York: Russell-Sage.

Pew Center for the States. (2008). One in 100: Behind bars in America. *Pew's Public Safety Performance Project*. Pew Center on the States. "www.pewcenteronthestates.org"

Poulson, B. (2003). A third voice: A review of empirical research on the psychological outcomes of restorative justice. *Utah Law Review, 2003*, 167–203.

Pratt, T. C., Cullen, F. T., Blevins, K. R., Daigle, L. E., & Madensen, T. D. (2008). The empirical status of deterrence theory: A meta-analysis. In F. T. Cullen, J. P. Wright, & K. R. Blevins (Eds.), *Taking stock: The status of criminological theory* (pp. 367–396). New Brunswick, NJ: Transaction.

Reiss, A. J. (1971). *The police and the public*. New Haven, CT: Yale University Press.

Roberts, J. V., & Stalans, L. J. (2004). Restorative sentencing: Exploring the views of the public. *Social Justice Research, 17*, 315–334.

Robinson, P. H., & Darley, J. (1995). *Justice, liability, and blame*. Boulder, CO: Westview.

Robinson, P. H., & Darley, J. (1997). The utility of desert. *Northwestern University Law Review, 91*, 453–499.

Ross, H. L. (1982). *Deterring the drinking driver: Legal policy and social control*. Lexington, MA: Lexington Books.

Sherman, L. (1999, January). *Consent of the governed*: Police, democracy and diversity Presentation at the Law School of Hebrew University. Jerusalem.

Skogan, W. G., & Frydl, K. (Eds.). (2004). *Fairness and effectiveness in policing: The evidence*. Washington, DC: The National Academies Press.

Strickland, L. H. (1958). Surveillance and trust. *Journal of Personality, 26*, 200–215.

Sunshine, J., & Tyler, T. R. (2003). The role of procedural justice and legitimacy in shaping public support for policing. *Law and Society Review, 37*(3), 555–589.

Tangney, J. P., & Dearing, R. L. (2002). *Shame and guilt*. Oxford, England: Oxford University Press.

Tonry, M. (1999). Why are US incarceration rates so high? *Crime and Delinquency, 45*, 419–437.

Turiel, E. (1987). Potential relations between the development of social reasoning and childhood aggression. In D. H. Crowell, I. M. Evans, & C. R. O'Connell (Eds.), *Childhood aggression and violence* (pp. 95–114). New York: Plenum.

Tyler, T. R. (2005). Managing conflicts of interest within organizations: Does activating social values change the impact of self-interest on behavior. In D. Moore, D. Cain, G. Loewenstein, & M. Bazerman (Eds.), *Conflicts of interest* (pp. 13–35). Cambridge, England: Cambridge University Press.

Tyler, T. R. (2006a). Legitimacy and legitimation. *Annual Review of Psychology, 57*, 375–400.

Tyler, T. R. (2006b). *Why people obey the law.* Princeton, NJ: Princeton University Press.

Tyler, T. R. (2006c). Restorative justice and procedural justice: Dealing with rule breaking. *Journal of Social Issues, 62*, 307–326.

Tyler, T. R. (2009). *Legitimacy and criminal justice: The benefits of self-regulation.* Reckless/Dinize Memorial Lecture. Retrieved from http://moritzlaw.osu.edu/osjcl/Articles/Volume7_1/Tyler-FinalPDf.pdf

Tyler, T. R., & Blader, S. L. (2005). Can businesses effectively regulate employee conduct?: The antecedents of rule following in work settings. *Academy of Management Journal, 48*, 1143–1158.

Tyler, T. R., & Boeckmann, R. J. (1997). Three strikes and you are out, but why? The psychology of public support for punishing rule breakers. *Law and Society Review, 31*, 237–265.

Tyler, T. R., Dienhart, J., & Thomas, T. (2007). The ethical commitment to compliance. *California Management Review, 50*, 31–51.

Tyler, T. R., & Huo, Y. (2002). *Trust in the law.* New York: Russell-Sage.

United States Department of Justice, Bureau of Justice Statistics. (2001). *Prisoners in 2000.* Washington, DC: US Department of Justice

Vidmar, N., & Miller, D. T. (1980). The social psychology of punishment. *Law and Society Review, 14*, 565–602.

Weisberg, R. (2005). The death penalty meets social science. *Annual Review of Law and Social Science, 1*, 151–170.

Wright, B. R. E., Caspi, A., Moffitt, T. E., & Paternoster, R. (2004). Does the perceived risk of punishment deter criminally prone individuals? *Journal of Research in Crime and Delinquency, 41*, 180–213.

Zimring, F. E., & Johnson, D. T. (2006). Public opinion and the governance of punishment in democratic political systems. *The Annals of the American Academy of Political and Social Science, 605*, 265–280.

CHAPTER 17

....

UNDERSTANDING DESISTANCE FROM JUVENILE OFFENDING

CHALLENGES AND OPPORTUNITIES

....

JOHN H. LAUB AND
SARAH L. BOONSTOPPEL

I. INTRODUCTION

....

ADOLESCENT involvement in crime is nearly ubiquitous, and it is seen by some as a normative aspect of growing up (see, e.g., Moffitt 1993; Laub, Eggleston, and Sampson 2007; Scott and Steinberg 2008).[1] As common as adolescent delinquency is, desistance—"maturational reform" or aging out of delinquency—is also considered a normative part of the transition from adolescence to adulthood. However, although many adolescents age out of crime at this critical life stage, some do continue offending into adulthood (Moffitt 1993). Early exit from involvement in crime has clear benefits. If fewer adolescents continue offending into adulthood there

We thank Shelly Schaefer and Chris Uggen for graciously sharing their forthcoming chapter, "Juvenile Delinquency and Desistance," with us while we were working on this paper. We also thank Donna Bishop and Barry Feld for comments on an earlier version of this paper.

would be less crime, smaller prison populations, and improved public safety. Those who desist from crime also enjoy additional benefits, including long-term employment, fulfilling relationships, and better health outcomes (see, e.g., Laub and Sampson 2003).

In spite of the evidence indicating that the prevalence of offending declines during late adolescence (Steffensmeier et al. 1989), much of the research on desistance from crime neglects this critical time period, focusing instead on early adulthood or later. As a result, we know very little about the factors associated with the processes and mechanisms of desistance during the period when desistance begins for most offenders. Several reasons may account for this gap in the literature, but how we conceptualize and operationalize desistance may play an important role here as well. In particular, permanent abstinence from delinquency is nearly impossible to identify during adolescence, and the heterogeneity in criminal offending over the life span makes it difficult to make accurate predictions about the course a particular delinquent trajectory might take (Kazemian, Farrington, and Le Blanc 2009). Factors related to differences in offending during adolescence are poor predictors of persistence and desistance in offending later in life, perhaps in part because delinquent trajectories are rarely unidirectional, and many offenders "drift" in and out of crime over time (Matza 1964; Laub and Sampson 2003; Kazemian, Farrington, and LeBlanc 2009).

In this chapter, we will review the current state of knowledge and perspectives on desistance from juvenile offending. We start by locating juvenile delinquency and desistance within the context of adolescent development. Then we describe both the conceptual and methodological challenges of studying desistance from juvenile offending. There is no agreed-upon definition of desistance or method to assess whether or not desistance has in fact occurred. Next, we review what we have learned so far in spite of those challenges. Much of what is known is from studies of young adults; however, there is a small but growing body of research focusing on desistance during adolescence. We conclude by highlighting some of the gaps in both theory and research on desistance during adolescence, and we offer suggestions for how juvenile justice policy might benefit from desistance research.

II. Juvenile Delinquency and Adolescent Development

Adolescence has been described repeatedly as the most difficult period in a person's life as it marks a time when many changes are occurring. Not only do adolescents progress to physical maturity, but they must meet social, emotional, and cognitive milestones as well. Moreover, the events and experiences of adolescence place youths on pathways into adulthood that may have lasting influence. Education, employment, relationships, and other activities, including delinquency and other problem behaviors, all shape individuals' worldview and set the stage for future successes and failures (see Lerner and Galambos 1998). Finally, involvement in delinquency and crime is perhaps at its most dynamic during adolescence, as it marks a period in which there is a dramatic increase in the participation in delinquency. In this section, we explain *why* adolescence is such an important period in understanding delinquency and desistance from crime.

One aspect of adolescent development that is important to understanding juvenile delinquency and desistance from crime is the development of decision-making skills and judgment. Recent advances in neuroscience inform the perspective on adolescent decision-making that contends that behavioral choices result from both logical reasoning and psychosocial factors (Steinberg 2004). Adolescent brain development, especially development in executive functioning, contributes to improvements in cognitive functioning (for reviews, see Rutter 2007; Steinberg 2007). Cognitive development progresses quickly during adolescence, thereby improving understanding and reasoning skills and expanding the capacity for abstract, planned, and hypothetical thought and contributes to one's ability to perceive risks and estimate one's own vulnerability to risk (Steinberg 2007). Indeed, studies of decision-making generally find no differences in risk-processing between older adolescents and adults when they are presented with hypothetical scenarios under controlled conditions (see Steinberg 2007, p. 57).

Whereas cognitive development occurs relatively quickly during adolescence, psychosocial maturity occurs at a much slower pace and continues well into young adulthood (for an excellent overview, see Scott and Steinberg 2008). Psychosocial development affects impulse control, emotional regulation, future orientation to the consequences of one's actions, and resistance to peer influence—key factors in decision-making processes. Further, the impact of psychosocial immaturity on decision-making interacts with social context. For example, Gardner and Steinberg (2005) found that people made riskier decisions in the presence of their peers than they did when they were alone, but the impact of peers was magnified for adolescents and young adults relative to older adults.

Personal identity formation is also a key developmental task during adolescence. As youths work to expand their independence from their parents and prepare for adult roles, risky behaviors such as delinquency challenge parental authority and orient youth toward their peers. Adolescents also "try on" different behaviors, attitudes, and beliefs during this period as part of the search for self-definition, and experimentation with delinquency and other risky behavior may contribute to this process (Scott and Steinberg 2008). As Silbereisen and Noack (1988) conclude, when considered in the context of normal adolescent development, problem behaviors may have positive instrumental value.

The ecological context in which psychosocial development and identity formation occurs also has significance for the understanding delinquency. Drawing on Bronfenbrenner (1979), individuals are viewed as embedded in a broader social developmental and structural context, and individual development is regarded as the product of reciprocal interaction between the individual and social contexts (e.g., families, schools, peer groups, neighborhoods, and culture). Social contexts can have a negative impact on development and delinquency, including neglectful, abusive, or absent parents; membership in delinquent peer groups; and low commitment to school (Sampson and Laub 1993). On the other hand, social contexts can also facilitate positive development. For example, Scott and Steinberg (2008, pp. 55–60) highlight three contextual conditions that facilitate positive development, including the presence of an involved and invested adult, membership in prosocial peer groups, and involvement in activities that encourage independent decision-making and critical thinking.

In short, adolescent development and the nature of juvenile offending (e.g., less serious crime, more property crime, and more offending in groups) suggest that juvenile offenders are generally different from adult offenders.[2] As we stated above, in spite of improvements in cognitive ability, adolescents are still developing. Of course, as they approach adulthood, many of these differences become less distinct, and many adolescents involved in delinquency begin to desist. Adolescent development and psychosocial maturity may be central to understanding why involvement in delinquency starts to decline as youth approach adulthood. For example, Mulvey and Aber (1988) found that compared to youths who continued involvement in offending, desisting delinquents were better able to identify appropriate responses to situations and to see themselves as able to accomplish that response. They suggest that desisting youths were better able to recognize and take advantage of prosocial opportunities and relationships, to consider the long-term outcomes of their decisions, and to estimate the potential success of changes they make. These developing skills serve to facilitate the transition to adult social roles, but they also facilitate desistance from delinquency.

In the next section, we review the challenges of studying desistance from delinquency and crime, highlighting key conceptual and methodological issues that are especially relevant for studying desistance in adolescence.

III. The Challenges of Studying Desistance in Adolescence

The conceptual and methodological issues in the study of desistance from crime are many, and have recently been reviewed at length elsewhere (for example, see Laub and Sampson 2001; Kazemian 2007). In this section, we focus on those issues that are most salient for the study of desistance during adolescence. These issues loom large in desistance research generally, but they gain considerable import when turning the spotlight to desistance from offending during adolescence.

A. Conceptual Issues

First, there is no agreed-upon definition of desistance from offending (see Bushway et al. 2001), though desistance is generally defined as ceasing to do something. Desistance from crime is commonly acknowledged in the research literature, yet there is relatively little theoretical conceptualization about crime cessation. In practice, most definitions describe it as an event or state of nonoffending. Increasingly, criminologists are turning to more dynamic definitions that emphasize the processes by which criminality declines (see, e.g., Laub and Sampson 2001; Bushway et al. 2001). As Maruna (2001, p. 17) noted: "Desistance from crime is an unusual dependent variable for criminologists because it is not an event that happens, but rather it is the sustained *absence* of a certain type of event (in this case, crime)." Compounding this lack of conceptualization is the confounding of desistance with aging. It is well known that crime declines with age in the aggregate population (Gottfredson and Hirschi 1990), but as Loeber and LeBlanc suggest, desistance does not occur "merely as a function of individuals' chronological age" (1990, p. 452). In fact, desistance can take place at any time during the life span.

In addition to identifying a straightforward definition of desistance, several conceptual questions remain unanswered. Many of these questions address the ambiguities faced when determining the boundaries of desistance. For example, how much delinquency must ensue before one is defined as a "delinquent"? Given the ubiquity of offending during adolescence, these questions are especially important for conceptualizing desistance *during* adolescence. Can desistance occur after one act of crime? If so, are the processes of desistance from a single act of crime different from desistance after several acts of crime? Moreover, are the processes of desistance from more common forms of delinquency, such as vandalism or shoplifting, different from desistance from serious theft or violence? Can desistance occur spontaneously, without any external intervention?

A second boundary issue concerns the time period that must be observed in order to identify desistance. That is, how long must a delinquent be crime-free before we can say that he or she has desisted? How can "intermittency in offending" be distinguished from "true desistance"? Given the age range encapsulated by adolescence, is desistance during adolescence even possible to identify? Can periods of nonoffending in an intermittent or zigzag career (Laub and Sampson 2003) tell us something about the process of desistance that we might miss if we narrowly focus on true or permanent desistance?

A third boundary issue concerns whether de-escalation to less serious delinquency is an indication of desistance. For example, if serious delinquency ceases, but problem behavior remains or increases, what does that say about desistance? Some offenders, even though they desist from predatory criminal activity, such as serious theft or violence, might continue to engage in a variety of acts that are more income-oriented, such as drug dealing, or acts that are considered "deviant" or the functional equivalents of crime. For instance, de-escalation of delinquency and increase of substance use is a common pattern in late adolescence (see, e.g., Massoglia

2006). Can such "offenders" accurately be called desisters? Perhaps from the narrow confines of the criminal justice system they are, but from a theoretical vantage point, they display traits that imply little change in their antisocial trajectory.

B. Measurement Issues

Many of the conceptual problems in the study of desistance have direct implications for the measurement of desistance and, ultimately, for what we think we know about desistance. One challenge to the study of desistance is the difficulty distinguishing between a "pause" in a long-term pattern of crime and actual deceleration and termination of involvement in delinquency. To identify such patterns, desistance research requires longitudinal data. Although the number of longitudinal studies of criminal behavior has increased in the last few decades (see, e.g., Liberman 2008), such studies are not without their weaknesses.

One primary concern is the source of the data used to measure desistance. Measures of desistance typically are derived from official records of crime, such as arrests or convictions, or from self-reported offending measures. By using official measures of crime, one risks underestimating the prevalence and incidence of crime and overestimating desistance from crime (Massoglia and Uggen 2007). Thus, it seems that official records of offending lack the variability in offending over time that self-reported measures offer. As a result, studies utilizing official records to measure desistance may miss important changes in offending, particularly during adolescence. An alternative is to use self-reported offending measures based on surveys, which have the benefit of getting at the "dark figure of crime," as they are less vulnerable to criminal justice biases. An important paper by Nagin, Farrington, and Moffitt (1995) bears on this issue. Based on official records of conviction from the Cambridge Study of Delinquent Development, they found that a group of offenders desisted from crime (starting at age 20) even though self-reported data from these same subjects revealed continued involvement in drugs, alcohol, and violence outside of the home at age 32. LeBlanc and Frechette (1989) also found varying rates of desistance depending on the source of information. Using official records as the criterion, 62% of the official male delinquents desisted from crime. However, using self-report data, only 11% of the delinquents desisted by age 30. The main limitation of self-reports, however, is that studies differ by what "self-reported offending" actually measures along several dimensions of offending, including seriousness, frequency, and variety.

How desistance is measured also has implications for the conclusions we draw about the causes and correlates of desistance (Kazemian 2007). Kazemian, Farrington, and LeBlanc (2009) found that the factors associated with desistance differed according to whether official or self-report measures were used. For example, improvements in employment were associated with less crime as indicated by official records but were not correlated with self-report measures of desistance. In a sample of young adults followed from high school to age 30, Massoglia and Uggen (2007) examined desistance as marked by four different measures: self-reported offending, arrests, subjective desistance (subjects were asked about their current level of involvement in delinquent behavior relative to their involvement five years prior), and relative desistance (subjects were asked to compare their level of involvement in crime to those of their same-age peers). They found that though each of the measures indicated a general desisting trend, differences in the prevalence of desistance were highest when measured by official desistance (85%) and lowest for reference group desistance (60%). Moreover, the influence of variables that are most associated with desistance (gender, race, prior involvement in crime, work quality, relationship quality, children, and friends) differed by the measure of desistance.

Whether desistance is measured as a static event or a dynamic process also has serious implications for research findings. Like Laub and Sampson (2001), Bushway and colleagues (2001) argue that desistance should be studied as a process in which criminality (propensity) changes over time rather than as a state of nonoffending. As such, desistance can be operationalized as a change in the rate of offending (a measure of propensity) "from a non-zero level to a stable rate empirically indistinguishable from zero" (Bushway et al. 2001, p. 500). Using data from the Rochester Youth Development study, Bushway, Thornberry and Krohn (2003) found that the two modes of measuring desistance (event and process) identified different people as desisters. Brame, Bushway, and Paternoster (2003) go a step further to argue that in addition to strict behavioral desistance (desistance as an event) and approximate desistance (desistance as a process), statistical models of desistance should also account for underlying propensity to commit crime. They found that models that do not control for propensity overestimate the prevalence of desistance.

Finally, few studies of desistance take seriously the issue of displacement of offending. Studies that fail to account for these kinds of behaviors, some argue, may overestimate the prevalence of desistance from crime. For example, using data from the National Youth Survey, Massoglia (2006) found that nearly 25% of the sample were less involved in predatory crimes, including violence, during adulthood than they were during adolescence, but there was little change in hard drug use, marijuana use, and general deviance over the same time period.

C. Ground Rules

The topic of desistance elicits conceptual, definitional, and measurement concerns. In order to increase clarity and provide guidance for the remainder of this review, we believe two issues stand out. First, we must identify the population for which the desistance from delinquency is a meaningful concern. Because low-rate offending is regarded as normative during adolescence, we argue that researchers should not spend much time on studying termination and desistance for low-rate offenders (defined as involvement in a single event or a series of relatively isolated events over a long period of time). Furthermore, termination and desistance should be studied among those who reach some reasonable threshold of frequent or serious criminal offending. The precise details of measurement depend on the data set and the research question under investigation.

Second, once an operational definition of the offender pool has been constructed and defended, we believe it is important to distinguish termination of offending from the concept of desistance. Following Laub and Sampson (2001), we argue that termination is the time at which criminal activity stops. Desistance, by contrast, is the causal process that supports the termination of offending. While it is difficult to ascertain when the process of desistance begins, it is apparent that it continues after the termination of offending and maintains the continued state of nonoffending. Thus, both termination and the process of desistance need to be considered in understanding cessation from offending. By using different terms for these distinct phenomena, we separate termination (the outcome) from the dynamics underlying the process of desistance (the cause).

IV. What do we know about Desistance from Juvenile Offending?

Much of what we know about the correlates of desistance from crime as well as explanations of desistance derives from research focusing on the transition to young adulthood (for reviews, see Laub and Sampson 2001; Siennick and Osgood 2008). In this section, we briefly discuss several theoretical frameworks that may be applicable to explaining desistance from juvenile offending. Then, we briefly review what we have learned about the correlates of desistance during adulthood, emphasizing both social events and subjective changes. We then turn our focus on the small group of studies that have directly examined desistance from crime during adolescence.

A. Frameworks for Understanding the Desistance Process

A variety of theoretical accounts have been offered to explain desistance from crime. Laub and Sampson (2001) group these accounts into five categories: maturational reform and spontaneous remission, developmental accounts, rational choice accounts, social learning accounts, and life course accounts. Each of these frameworks presents compelling accounts of desistance as a general phenomenon, but they vary in the extent to which they are applicable to understanding desistance across the life span, and during adolescence in particular.

With respect to adolescent offending, the frameworks that are most commonly invoked are Moffitt's dual taxonomy theory and Sampson and Laub's life course theory (see Scott and Steinberg 2008; Schaefer and Uggen 2009). Moffitt's (1993) dual taxonomy theory focuses on two types of adolescent offenders: life course-persistent offenders and adolescence-limited offenders. Life course-persistent offenders suffer from numerous problems and challenges, including neurological difficulties, cognitive impairment, poor impulse control, and discordant parent-child interactions. Moffitt argues that the age at desistance is a function of the age of onset of offending, the mastery of prosocial skills, and the number and severity of events that may ensnare the offender. From this perspective, life course-persistent offenders are more likely to engage in antisocial behavior very early in life, fail to develop prosocial skills, and become ensnared by the outcomes of their antisocial behavior. In contrast, adolescent-limited offending is limited to this developmental stage of the life span and is sporadic in nature. The key point is that most adolescent-limited offenders will naturally desist with age.

Sampson and Laub's age-graded theory of social control contends that crime occurs when the social bond to society is weak or broken. They emphasize that social ties and bonds to society at all ages across the life course are important to understanding involvement in crime, and changes in informal social control explain changes in criminal behavior. In particular, their theory focuses on social role transitions such as marriage, employment, and the like, and subsequent change in behavior. In a recent elaboration of their theory, Laub and Sampson argue that social bonds facilitate desistance through "the confluence of social controls, structured routine activities, and purposeful human agency" (2003, p. 37). Social institutions such as marriage, military, and employment contribute to the initiation and maintenance of desistance through a knifing off from the past, supervision and monitoring, as well as opportunities for social support and growth, change and structure to routine activities, and an opportunity for identity transformation (Laub and Sampson 2003, p. 148–49). Though their emphasis is on adult social institutions, these mechanisms might also be found in family, school, and peer contexts.

These theoretical accounts are not necessarily mutually exclusive. To illustrate, Scott and Steinberg (2008, pp. 53–54) state: "Most teenagers desist from criminal behavior during the period when risky experimentation generally diminishes as individuals develop a stable sense of identity, a stake in the future, and mature judgment. The assumption of adult roles that Sampson and Laub associate with desistance from crime may facilitate this process; at the same time, it seems likely that psychological maturation makes it possible for individuals effectively to assume those roles."

B. Social and Subjective Factors

The correlates of desistance might be organized along the lines of social change and subjective shifts. The relationships between these two factors are complicated and often reciprocal. Social factors include changes in social institutions, life events, and markers of the transition to adulthood. Much of the research indicates that desistance during adulthood is correlated with social factors, including *marriage* (Sampson, Laub, and Wimer 2006), *employment* (Uggen 2000), *military service* (Laub and Sampson 2003), and *parenthood* (Edin, Nelson, and Paranal 2004; Giordano, Cernkovich, and Rudolph 2002).

An emerging body of research emphasizes the importance of dynamic subjective factors in the process of desistance. LeBel and colleagues define subjective factors as those that "refer to changes in the way individuals experience, understand, interpret, and make sense of the world around them" (2008, p. 133). Changes in *identity* or *self-concept* (Maruna 2001), *cognitive transformations* (Giordano, Cernkovich, and Rudolph 2002), *agency* (Laub and Sampson 2003), and *emotions* (Giordano, Schroeder, and Cernkovich 2007) have all been implicated in the desistance process.

C. Desistance During Adolescence

While our understanding of the processes of desistance certainly benefits from this body of research, it is unclear whether these findings apply to desistance during adolescence, particularly as much of the research on adults focuses on adult institutions and age-graded life events such as marriage. Adolescents simply have fewer opportunities to experience these kinds of events. Unfortunately, few studies focus on desistance from juvenile delinquency during adolescence, and those exceptions suggest some divergence from research utilizing adult samples with respect to the impact of salient life events and social institutions. For example, Stouthamer-Loeber and colleagues (2008) found that life circumstances measured at ages 17 to 19, including marriage, cohabitation, high job skills, and military service, were not related to desistance from serious theft and violence during this early adulthood. By contrast, among the participants of the same age in Mulvey and Aber's (1988) qualitative study, high-rate offenders reported less employment and less work experience than those reporting a decline in offending, and high-rate offenders were more likely to report "hustling" to get money when they needed it.

There is a growing body of research on early work experiences and adolescent crime (for a review, see Uggen and Wakefield 2008). This research has implications for desistance during the adolescent period. Of course, a key challenge in this research is adequately taking into account self-selection (see Apel et al. 2007). Staff and Uggen (2003) found that the type of employment experience mattered with respect to adolescent criminal outcomes. More specifically, jobs that had greater autonomy, conflicted with school, paid higher wages, and increased contact with deviant peers did not reduce offending. However, jobs that did not conflict with school and offered opportunities for learning new skills reduced offending.

As with the adult literature, there is some evidence that different kinds of relationships facilitate desistance during adolescence. In their recent analysis of data from the National Longitudinal Study of Adolescent Health (Add Health), McCarthy and Casey (2008) found that romantic love might encourage desistance among adolescents, although engaging in sexual activity outside of a committed relationship was associated with an increase in crime. Similarly, in their qualitative study of ten young men (ages 15 to 20), Mulvey and LaRosa (1986) found that desistance was associated with support from a significant person, such as a girlfriend or a sibling.

Family structure and process factors are also related to desistance during adolescence. Stouthamer-Loeber and colleagues (2008) found that low socioeconomic status and being from a family on welfare were associated with a lower likelihood of desistance during adolescence, while low parental stress and good housing quality increased the probability of desistance. Mulvey and LaRosa (1986) reported that a change in home situations and relationships with family members was also related to desistance.

In a number of qualitative studies, family formation, especially fatherhood, has been linked to desistance during adolescence (Hughes 1998; Nurse 2004). This is intriguing because there is a high correlation between juvenile delinquency and adolescent fatherhood (Stouthamer-Loeber and Wei 1998). Using repeated interviews with a very small sample, Shannon and Abrams (2007) revealed that becoming a father and establishing a relationship with a child could motivate an offender to desist from crime. However, a number of structural obstacles were identified that make achieving that goal difficult at best.

Maintaining relationships with delinquent peers decreases the likelihood of desistance during adolescence (Stouthamer-Loeber et al. 2008), whereas adolescents on a desisting pathway tend to put more space between themselves and their delinquent peers (see also Warr 2002). The adolescent boys interviewed by Mulvey and LaRosa (1986) reported changing their social networks either through "trimming" friends or moving from the community, which in turn reduced drug use. In a qualitative study of youths recruited from detention centers, drug treatment centers, youth centers, and high schools in Quebec, Brunelle, Cousineau, and Brochu (2005) found that cessation of drug use and delinquency was associated with entering or reuniting with a conformist circle of friends. How kids spend time with peers may also affect the desistance process. Mulvey and Aber's (1988) qualitative work revealed that boys who continued involvement in delinquency reported regular contact with a large number of people with whom they spent time on the streets and in other public areas. In contrast, boys on a desisting pathway reported being more selective about their friends, spent little time with them, and were more likely to spend time at home.

Some evidence suggests that involvement in different antisocial behaviors reduces the likelihood of desistance. For example, adolescents in the Pittsburgh Youth Study who reported high involvement in drug dealing were less likely to desist from serious theft and violence Stouthamer-Loeber et al. 2008). Further, substance use, including alcohol use, reduces the likelihood of desistance (Stouthamer-Loeber et al. 2008), and reductions in drug use (but perhaps not abstinence) might be related to desistance from delinquency (Mulvey and LaRosa 1986). Of course, drug selling, drug use, and alcohol use are all illegal activities for adolescents, but these behaviors stand out as factors that may make it difficult to desist from violent or property crimes.

Findings regarding the role of perceptions about the risk of being caught and punished diverge somewhat. For example, Stouthamer-Loeber and colleagues (2008) found that adolescents reporting a low perceived likelihood of being caught were less likely to desist from serious theft and violence. By contrast, Mulvey and

Aber (1988) found that boys who continued to report a high rate of involvement in delinquency perceived that doing time in the adult system was inevitable, and they seemed to accept imprisonment as a part of their lives.

The role of sanctions—perceived and actual—and adolescent decision-making warrants more serious attention by the research community. Glassner and colleagues (1983) found that youths stopped committing crimes because they feared being apprehended, convicted, and jailed as adults. They contended that this change in a behavior was "a conscious decision" based on the perceptions of available sanctions for juvenile offenders compared to adult offenders (Glassner et al. 1983, p. 219). However, Scott and Steinberg (2008, p. 197) point out that "because of their psychosocial immaturity, youths may be less responsive to the impact of criminal penalties than adults." Moreover, the existing research evidence suggests that sanctioning juvenile offenders as adults does not reduce offending (see Scott and Steinberg 2008, pp. 195–203).

Subjective factors may also be related to desistance during adolescence, including appraisals of one's life circumstances and involvement in crime. For example, participants desisting from crime in Mulvey and LaRosa's (1986) study identified a time period in which things began to change for the better, and the participants tied that change to boredom, a sense of lack of direction, and events that served to reinforce one's resolve to change. Brunelle, Cousineau, and Brochu (2005) found that those on a desisting trajectory reported reaching a cognitive limit (a feeling as if there was too much to lose or nothing to gain from continuing involvement) and a morality limit (a feeling of too much to lose based on a personal value system).

Though the research on desistance during adolescence is limited, we have identified some emerging themes that differ somewhat from the literature on adult desistance; nonetheless, the two bodies of literature resonate. Though involvement in institutions such as work and marriage is not common among adolescents, some literature suggests that bonds to others, including romantic partners, family, and prosocial peers, may facilitate desistance from offending, while involvement in substance use and drug markets may inhibit desistance from other antisocial behaviors. The literature reviewed here also suggests that subjective factors, including assessments of the risk of being caught and imprisoned, as well assessments of one's life circumstances, might also contribute to the desistance process.

D. Demographic Factors

In spite of the growing research, we still know little about the role of demographic correlates in the desistance process, including race and ethnicity, social class and neighborhood disadvantage, and gender. In spite of this research shortage, some research on structural factors and demographic correlates is starting to emerge. For example, Smith (2006) found that though family structure factors (family deprivation, intact family, and social class) had no impact on desistance from self-reported delinquency, neighborhood context was an important predictor of desistance among youths participating in the Edinburgh Study on Youth Transitions and

Crime. Specifically, desistance was more common in advantaged neighborhoods than in deprived neighborhoods, and it was less likely in neighborhoods where residents were dissatisfied with their neighborhood and perceived their neighborhood to be disorderly.

Few studies have explored the role of race in desistance from delinquency and crime, and what we know is derived from studies focused on desistance during early adulthood rather than during adolescence. Elliott (1994) found race differences in patterns of prevalence of self-reported serious violent offending over time in the National Youth Survey. African Americans' involvement in serious violent offending started earlier and ended later than did whites', and nearly twice as many African American males (34%) as white males (18%) continued violent offending from adolescence to adulthood. Piquero, MacDonald, and Parker (2002) found a similar pattern with regard to violent offending among California Youth Authority parolees. Race was unrelated to the accumulation of total arrests or nonviolent arrests, whereas nonwhites were more likely to accumulate violent arrests.

In comparing whites to nonwhites (typically African Americans) on other correlates of desistance, there are similarities in broad domains such as marriage and employment, but differences in the details within those domains. For example, Elliott (1994) found that although there were no significant differences in continuity rates for African Americans and whites who were living with a spouse or partner or who were employed between ages 18 and 20, differences did exist for those who were not partnered or who were unemployed. That is, marriage and employment benefited the desistance process regardless of race, but African Americans were less likely to desist than whites were if they were not married or unemployed. Elliott speculated that contextual differences—where one was living or working—might explain these differences. Similarly, Piquero and colleagues (2002) found that among parolees released from the California Youth Authority, traditional marriage was associated with a reduction in nonviolent arrests for whites and nonwhites, but had no impact on violent arrests for either group. Only nonwhites, however, experienced an *increase* in arrest when in a common-law marriage.

There is even less research on race and ethnic variation in subjective factors associated with desistance. In one of the few qualitative studies to examine desistance among African American and Latino American inner-city young men, Hughes (1998) found four significant factors influencing the move away from antisocial behavior. These factors included respect and concern for their children; fear of physical harm, incarceration, or both; time away from one's immediate environment which provided an opportunity for self reflection and contemplation about their past and future life course; and support and modeling from a dedicated person (e.g., a counselor or mentor). Although derived from a small convenience sample, these findings are generally consistent with the findings from qualitative studies focusing on white men.

Gender is yet another under-explored area in the desistance research due in part to the low rate of delinquency among women and girls relative to men and boys. Evidence from quantitative and qualitative studies suggests that though that the age-crime curves for males and females are similar in shape, females tend to offend at a much lower rate than males, the prevalence of female offending peaks earlier than it does for males, and females are more likely to desist than males (Elliott 1994; Uggen and Kruttschnitt 1998). Among those studies that compare males and females, evidence suggests both similarities and differences in the impact of the correlates of desistance. Education measures (Graham and Bowling 1995), having prosocial peers (Uggen and Kruttschnitt 1998), limited opportunities for illegal earnings (Uggen and Kruttschnitt 1998), avoiding delinquent peers and family members (McIvor, Murray, and Jamieson 2004), and subjective or emotional changes (Giordano, Cernkovich, and Rudolph 2002; Giordano, Schroeder, and Cernkovich 2007) tend to influence desistance for both men and women, though there is little agreement across studies. Starting a family and having children (Giordano, Cernkovich, and Rudolph 2002), leaving home (Graham and Bowling 1995), avoiding romantic relationships (Leverentz 2006), and religion (Giordano, Cernkovich, and Rudolph 2002) tend to be important for the desistance process among women. Living at home (Graham and Bowling 1995), legal work (Uggen and Kruttschnitt 1998), having a family in general (rather than having children) (Giordano, Cernkovich, and Rudolph 2002), and prison and treatment experiences (Giordano, Cernkovich, and Rudolph 2002) tend to be important for men.

V. The Next Steps in Furthering our Understanding of Desistance

A number of research and theoretical questions about desistance have been reviewed elsewhere (see, for example, Laub and Sampson 2001). Here we focus on those questions that are of particular concern with respect to furthering our understanding of desistance from juvenile offending.

A. Data Gaps

A major issue in the study of desistance concerns the availability of data. Much of what we know about desistance is drawn from official data and, increasingly, self-report measures. We need to look beyond even self-reported behavioral measures. Subjective assessments of desistance—whether one sees oneself as doing more or less crime than before—may reflect movement away from crime, thereby lending insight into the process of desistance and how adolescents view their participation in delinquency (see Massoglia and Uggen 2007). Further, qualitative life history narratives may offer crucial details regarding the underlying processes associated with desistance during adolescence that might be missed in quantitative studies.

Research has not yet reached a consensus on the relationship between adolescent desistance and the factors typically associated with adult desistance (e.g., serious long-term relationships and full-time employment). One reason for this is that many adolescents have not yet had the opportunity to experience salient life events such as marriage (see Stouthamer-Loeber et al. 2008). Given what we know about adolescent development and psychosocial maturity, it might also be that adolescents are more influenced by immediate contexts (such as spending time unsupervised with peers) and short-term circumstances. Thus, we need to understand how peer influence, future orientation, and risk assessment are related to serious juvenile offending over short periods of time. Often research on desistance compares a few time points, thereby missing potential variability in delinquent involvement over time. Further, it risks overlooking circumstances and contexts that change quickly or over a brief period of time. One useful tool to gain insight into these issues is space-time budget methodology. Wikström and colleagues (2009) have successfully employed this method to capture exposure to particular settings and detailed activity patterns among adolescents.

B. Research Gaps

Aside from the overall dearth of research on desistance during adolescence, several specific gaps require attention. One important question is whether the mechanisms of desistance differ by race/ethnicity, gender, and social class. More research is needed to determine how the predictors and processes of desistance differ across various subgroups in the population, particularly for adolescents. Additionally, we know neighborhood contexts vary, and it is expected that these neighborhood differences will interact with individual differences to increase the probability of crime and violence (Moffitt 1997); exactly how these interactions between person and context affect the desistance process is a key research question.

Sampson and Laub's research examining the lives of disadvantaged men who experienced the transition from adolescence to young adulthood in the 1950s and 1960s showed that desistance from crime during adulthood was related to job stability, marital attachment, and successful military experiences. However, the extent to which these mechanisms explain desistance from crime today is not known, although the evidence suggests that they do (see Siennick and Osgood 2008). The link between macro-historical shifts and individual-level transitions is a central theme of life-course research and an important consideration in the study of desistance. For example, national-level changes in presidential administrations, natural disasters, and shifting economic prospects can have important implications for individual lives. Moreover, local events that catalyze structural or institutional change, including changes in neighborhood policing tactics or in district-wide school policies, may also change the context within which individuals desist from delinquency. Focusing on local events such as these may provide natural experiments for desistance researchers, especially for those conducting ongoing longitudinal studies, and can contribute to our understanding of how macro-level shifts affect desistance.

It is also unclear how substance use affects desistance from juvenile offending. Focusing on adults, Horney, Osgood and Marshall (1995) found that recently released offenders were more involved in crime when using drugs. Similarly, Schroeder, Giordano, and Cernkovich (2007) found that alcohol and drug use reduced the likelihood of desistance among a sample of delinquent youth during adulthood. Along the same lines, Stouthamer-Loeber and colleagues (2008) found that high alcohol use reduced the likelihood of desistance during later adolescence, but it was not related to desistance during early adolescence or young adulthood. By contrast, Massoglia (2006) found that though youths moved away from violent crime during late adolescence, they initiated or continued substance use into young adulthood. Thus, we have reason to believe substance use and desistance are negatively correlated, but its role in adolescent desistance is an empirical question that has not yet been adequately addressed.

C. Theoretical Questions

Theoretical accounts of desistance should focus on what explains the variation in offending trajectories *within* individuals in addition to focusing on between individual differences. As there is no way to know whether adolescent desistance is "true" desistance or merely a suspension in delinquent activity, to our mind, the most fruitful desistance theory will focus on the causes of variability in within-individual offending patterns rather than on heuristic persister/desister dichotomies. Examining desistance during adolescence demands a theoretical appreciation of the concept of the zigzag or intermittent path of offending. As Daniel Glaser pointed out forty years ago, "Criminals go from noncrime to crime and to noncrime again. Sometimes this sequence is repeated many times, but sometimes criminals clearly go to crime only once; sometimes these shifts are for long durations or even permanent, and sometimes they are short-lived" (1969, p. 58). This may be particularly true when studying desistance during adolescence.

Research in the life-course and developmental traditions has made great strides in identifying and explaining factors associated with continuity and change during adulthood, but as yet, there has been little in the way of explaining desisting patterns of delinquency during adolescence. Clearly, we need to know more about the underlying mechanisms of desistance during adolescence. Future research should test Laub and Sampson's (2003) age-graded theory to determine whether the mechanisms they identified as facilitating the process of desistance—separating the past from the present, providing opportunities for social support as well as supervision and monitoring, changing routine activities, and offering options to develop new identities—can be activated by those social institutions that are most salient to adolescents involved in serious, chronic delinquency, including family, school, and peer networks.

VI. Implications for Juvenile Justice Policy

Our review of the literature on adolescent development and delinquency has led us to conclude that rather than pathological or abnormal behavior, delinquency is a normative aspect of adolescent development (Silbereisen and Noack 1988; Laub, Eggleston and Sampson 2007) and a part of the process of individuation and identity formation (Scott and Steinberg 2008). This raises the important question: Do juvenile justice sanctions facilitate or inhibit desistance? The irony is that if delinquency and drug use are viewed as a normative stage in adolescent development, societal reaction to delinquency can result in weakened bonds and continued delinquency though the dynamic process of "cumulative disadvantage" (Sampson and Laub 1997). In support of this idea, Sampson and Laub (1997) found that incarceration as a juvenile and as an adult had negative effects on later job stability, which in turn was related negatively to continued involvement in crime over the life course. These indirect "criminogenic effects" are substantively important, as arrest and incarceration may spark school failure, unemployment, and weak community bonds, in turn increasing adult crime. This finding is consistent with Western's (2006) study of a contemporary sample showing that the negative effects of youth incarceration on adult employment time exceed the large negative effects for dropping out of high school and living in an area with high unemployment. These effects are further compounded for youths facing structural disadvantages such as class and race (Hagan 1991; Pager 2007). The precise impact of sanctions for adolescent desistance, however, is unknown; more research is required in this area.

From a policy standpoint, the message is that change is possible, and therefore it is critical that juvenile offenders are not snared by their contact with the criminal and juvenile justice systems. Instead, juvenile offenders should be provided with opportunities to retain or establish connections to institutions that might provide the social support and monitoring they need, including family, school, and prosocial peers. Further, rather than focusing solely on sanctions which may in fact retard psychosocial development (Chung, Little, and Steinberg 2005), interventions should emphasize positive youth development, whereby each adolescent might be equipped with the basic personal and social assets needed for healthy development and a productive adulthood. These assets include physical, intellectual, psychological, and social dimensions (Eccles and Gootman 2002), areas in which serious, chronic juvenile delinquents are particularly deficient (Sampson and Laub 1993). Indeed, the interventions aimed at adjudicated delinquents that are deemed most effective or promising for reducing delinquency are multidimensional and centered, in part, on enhancing family attachments and family functioning while youths remain in the community (for reviews, see Greenwood 2006; MacKenzie 2006). When such programs are successful, they can provide the structure, social support, and opportunities serious adolescent delinquents need to desist from criminal offending. In addition, Chung, Little, and Steinberg (2005, p. 86) argue that "in order to make a successful transition into adult roles and responsibilities, individuals need to enter adulthood with sufficient psychosocial maturity to make autonomous decisions, establish satisfying interpersonal relationships, maintain gainful employment, and exercise self-governance" (see also Scott and Steinberg 2008).

VII. CONCLUSION

Perhaps an under-appreciated assumption in thinking about and studying desistance, particularly desistance during adolescence, is the belief in amenability to change. As a society, we have long assumed that children and adolescents are far more adaptable and redeemable than are adults; indeed, our juvenile justice system was once based on this conviction (see Scott and Steinberg 2008). Though the juvenile and criminal justices systems might have abandoned this belief, we maintain a theoretical commitment to the idea of social malleability across the life course and the constancy of change. There are multiple pathways through delinquency and desistance, and as Silbereisen and Noack (1988) suggest, some delinquency may be a developmental asset that youths need to experience in order to be "fully prepared" for adulthood. Yet desistance from delinquency is plainly valuable to healthy development across the life course. A focused research program on the underlying mechanisms of desistance during adolescence is needed to advance our understanding of this topic. Moreover, with the notion of malleability and change in mind, we need to step back and think seriously about ways to restructure our response to juvenile delinquency, especially by the formal system of justice, in order to allow for the possibility of desistance from crime and other behavioral change to take effect.

NOTES

1. Wikström and Butterworth (2006) make an important observation. They write: "While adolescent offending may not be regarded as a statistically highly deviant phenomenon, this is not the same as to say that there are no differentiating factors between those who have and those who have not offended" (2006, p. 239). Indeed, Wikström and Butterworth's study of adolescent crime reveals that there are important individual and lifestyle differences between offenders and nonoffenders.

2. This is not to say that all juvenile offenders are similar. In fact, there is good reason to believe that there is important heterogeneity in offending patterns among adolescent offenders (see Wikström and Butterworth 2006).

REFERENCES

Apel, Robert, Shawn D. Bushway, Robert Brame, Amelia Haviland, Daniel Nagin, and Raymond Paternoster. 2007. "Unpacking the Relationship between Adolescent Employment and Antisocial Behavior: A Matched Samples Comparison." *Criminology* 45: 67–97.

Brame, Robert, Shawn D. Bushway, and Raymond Paternoster. 2003. "Examining the Prevalence of Criminal Desistance." *Criminology* 41: 423–48.

Bronfenbrenner, Urie. 1979. *The Ecology of Human Development*. Cambridge, MA: Harvard University Press.

Brunelle, Natacha, Marie-Mathe Cousineau, and Serge Brochu. 2005. "Juvenile Drug Use and Delinquency: Youths' Accounts of Their Trajectories." *Substance Use and Issues* 40: 721–34.

Bushway, Shawn D., Alex Piquero, Lisa Broidy, Elizabeth Cauffman, and Paul Mazerolle. 2001. "An Empirical Framework for Studying Desistance as a Process." *Criminology* 39: 491–516.

Bushway, Shawn D., Terence P. Thornberry, and Marvin D. Krohn. 2003. "Desistance as a Developmental Process: A Comparison of Static and Dynamic Approaches." *Journal of Quantitative Criminology* 19: 123–53.

Chung, He Len, Michelle Little, and Laurence Steinberg. 2005. "The Transition to Adulthood for Adolescents in the Juvenile Justice System: A Developmental Perspective." In *On Your Own without a Net: The Transition to Adulthood for Vulnerable Populations*, edited by D. Wayne Osgood, E. Michael Foster, Constance Flanagan, and Gretchen R. Ruth. Chicago: University of Chicago Press.

Eccles, Jacquelynne S., and Jennifer Appleton Gootman, eds. 2002. *Community Programs to Promote Youth Development*. Washington, DC: National Academy Press.

Edin, Kathryn, Timothy J. Nelson, and Rechelle Paranal. 2004. "Fatherhood and Incarceration as Potential Turning Points in the Criminal Careers of Unskilled Men." In *Imprisoning America: The Social Effects of Mass Incarceration*, edited by Mary Patillo, David Weiman, and Bruce Western. New York: Russell Sage Foundation.

Elliott, Delbert. 1994. "Serious Violent Offenders: Onset, Developmental Course, and Termination." *Criminology* 32: 1–22.

Gardner, Margo, and Laurence Steinberg. 2005. "Peer Influence on Risk-Taking, Risk Preference, and Risky Decision-Making in Adolescence and Adulthood: An Experimental Study." *Developmental Psychology* 41: 625–35.

Giordano, Peggy C., Stephen A. Cernkovich, and Jennifer L. Rudolph. 2002. "Gender, Crime, and Desistance: Toward a Theory of Cognitive Transformation." *American Journal of Sociology* 107: 990–1064.

Giordano, Peggy C., Ryan D. Schroeder, and Stephen A. Cernkovich. 2007. "Emotions and Crime over the Life Course: A Neo-Median Perspective on Criminal Continuity and Change." *American Journal of Sociology* 112: 1603–61.

Glaser, Daniel. 1969. *The Effectiveness of a Prison and Parole System*. Abridged ed. Indianapolis: Bobbs-Merrill.

Glassner, Barry, Margret Ksander, Bruce Berg, and Bruce D. Johnson. 1983. "A Note on the Deterrent Effect of Juvenile vs. Adult Jurisdiction." *Social Problems* 31: 219–21.

Gottfredson, Michael, and Travis Hirschi. 1990. *A General Theory of Crime*. Stanford, CA: Stanford University Press.

Graham, John, and Benjamin Bowling. 1995. *Young People and Crime*. Research Study 145. London: Home Office.

Greenwood, Peter W. 2006. *Changing Lives: Delinquency Prevention as Crime Control Policy*. Chicago: University of Chicago Press.

Hagan, John. 1991. "Destiny and Drift: Subcultural Preferences, Status Attainments, and the Risks and Rewards of Youth." *American Sociological Review* 56: 21–36.

Horney, Julie, D. Wayne Osgood, and Ineke Haen Marshall. 1995. "Criminal Careers in the Short-Term: Intra-individual Variability in Crime and Its Relation to Local Life Circumstances." *American Sociological Review* 60: 655–73.

Hughes, Margaret. 1998. "Turning Points in the Lives of Young Inner-City Men Forgoing Destructive Criminal Behaviors: A Qualitative Study." *Social Work Research* 22: 143–51.

Kazemian, Lila. 2007. "Desistance from Crime: Theoretical, Empirical, Methodological, and Policy Considerations." *Journal of Contemporary Criminal Justice* 23: 5–27.

Kazemian, Lila, David P. Farrington, and Marc LeBlanc. 2009. "Can We Make Accurate Long-Term Predictions About Patterns of De-Escalation in Offending Behavior?" *Journal of Youth and Adolescence* 38: 384–400.

Laub, John H., Elaine Eggleston Doherty, and Robert J. Sampson. 2007. "Social Control and Adolescent Development: A View from Life-Course Criminology." In *Approaches to Positive Youth Development*, edited by Rainer K. Silbereisen and Richard M. Lerner. Thousand Oaks, CA: Sage Publications.

Laub, John H., and Robert J. Sampson. 2001. "Understanding Desistance from Crime." In *Crime and Justice: A Review of Research*, vol. 28, edited by Michael Tonry. Chicago: University of Chicago Press.

Laub, John H., and Robert J. Sampson. 2003. *Shared Beginnings, Divergent Lives: Delinquent Boys to Age 70*. Cambridge, MA: Harvard University Press.

LeBel, Thomas P., Ros Burnett, Shadd Maruna, and Shawn Bushway. 2008. "The 'Chicken and the Egg' of Subjective and Social Factors in Desistance from Crime." *European Journal of Criminology* 5: 131–59.

LeBlanc, Marc, and Marcel Frechette. 1989. *Male Criminal Activity from Childhood through Youth: Multilevel and Developmental Perspectives*. New York: Springer.

Lerner, Richard M., and Nancy L. Galambos. 1998. "Adolescent Development: Challenges and Opportunities for Research, Programs, and Policies." *Annual Review of Psychology* 49: 413–46.

Leverentz, Andrea M. 2006. "The Love of a Good Man? Romantic Relationships as a Source of Support or Hindrance for Female Ex-offenders." *Journal of Research in Crime and Delinquency* 43: 459–88.

Liberman, Akiva M., ed. 2008. *The Long View of Crime: A Synthesis of Longitudinal Research*. New York: Springer.

Loeber, Rolf and Marc LeBlanc. 1990. "Toward a Developmental Criminology." In *Crime and Justice: A Review of the Research*, vol. 12, edited by Michael Tonry and Norval Morris. Chicago: University of Chicago Press.

MacKenzie, Doris Layton. 2006. *What Works in Corrections: Reducing the Criminal Activity of Offenders and Delinquents*. New York: Cambridge University Press.

Maruna, Shadd. 2001. *Making Good: How Ex-Convicts Reform and Rebuild Their Lives*. Washington, DC: American Psychological Association Books.

Massoglia, Michael. 2006. "Desistance or Displacement? The Changing Patterns of Offending from Adolescence to Young Adulthood." *Journal of Quantitative Criminology* 22: 215–39.

Massoglia, Michael, and Christopher Uggen. 2007. "Subjective Desistance and the Transition to Adulthood." *Journal of Contemporary Criminal Justice* 23: 90–103.

Matza, David. 1964. *Delinquency and Drift*. New York: Wiley.

McCarthy, Bill, and Teresa Casey. 2008. "Love, Sex, and Crime: Adolescent Romantic Relationships and Offending." *American Sociological Review* 73:944–69.

McIvor, Gil, Cathy Murray, and Janet Jamieson. 2004. "Desistance from Crime: Is it Different for Women and Girls?" In *After Crime and Punishment: Pathways to Offender Reintegration*, edited by Shadd Maruna and Russ Immarigeon. United Kingdom: Willan Publishing.

Moffitt, Terrie E. 1993. "Adolescence-Limited and Life-Course Persistent Antisocial Behavior: A Developmental Taxonomy." *Psychological Review* 100: 674–701.

Moffitt, Terrie E. 1997. "Neuropsychology, Antisocial Behavior, and Neighborhood Context." In *Violence and Childhood in the Inner City*, edited by Joan McCord. Cambridge, UK: Cambridge University Press.

Mulvey, Edward P., and Mark Aber. 1988. "Growing Out of Delinquency: Development and Desistance." In *The Abandonment of Delinquent Behavior*, edited by Richard L. Jenkins and Waln K. Brown. New York: Praeger Publishers.

Mulvey, Edward P., and John F. LaRosa. 1986. "Delinquency Cessation and Adolescent Development: Preliminary Data." *American Journal of Orthopsychiatry* 56: 212–24.

Nagin, Daniel, David P. Farrington, and Terrie E. Moffitt. 1995. "Life-Course Trajectories of Different Types of Offenders." *Criminology* 33: 111–39.

Nurse, Anne M. 2004. *Fatherhood Arrested*. Nashville, TN: Vanderbilt University Press.

Pager, Devah. 2007. *Marked: Race, Crime, and Finding Work in an Era of Mass Incarceration*. Chicago: University of Chicago Press.

Piquero, Alex R., John M. MacDonald, and Karen F. Parker. 2002. "Race, Local Life Circumstances, and Criminal Activity." *Social Science Quarterly* 83: 654–70.

Rutter, Michael. 2007. "Psychopathological Development Across Adolescence." *Journal of Youth and Adolescence* 36: 101–10.

Sampson, Robert J., and John H. Laub. 1993. *Crime in the Making: Pathways and Turning Points through Life*. Cambridge, MA: Harvard University Press.

Sampson, Robert J., and John H. Laub. 1997. "A Life-Course Theory of Cumulative Disadvantage and the Stability of Delinquency." In *Developmental Theories of Crime and Delinquency*, edited by Terence P. Thornberry. New Brunswick, NJ: Transaction.

Sampson, Robert J., John H. Laub, and Christopher Wimer. 2006. "Does Marriage Reduce Crime? A Counterfactual Approach to Within-individual Causal Effects." *Criminology* 44: 465–508.

Schaefer, Shelly, and Christopher Uggen. 2009. "Juvenile Delinquency and Desistance." In *Handbook of Youth and Young Adulthood*, edited by Andy Furlong. Abingdon, Oxfordshire: Routledge.

Schroeder, Ryan D., Peggy C. Giordano, and Stephen A. Cernkovich. 2007. "Drug Use and Desistance Processes." *Criminology* 45: 191–222.

Scott, Elizabeth S., and Laurence Steinberg. 2008. *Rethinking Juvenile Justice*. Cambridge, MA: Harvard University Press.

Shannon, Sarah K. S., and Laura S. Abrams. 2007. "Juvenile Offenders as Fathers: Perceptions of Fatherhood, Crime, and Becoming an Adult." *Families in Society: The Journal of Contemporary Social Services* 88: 183–91.

Siennick, Sonja E., and D. Wayne Osgood. 2008. "A Review of Research on the Impact on Crime of Transitions to Adult Roles." In *The Long View of Crime: A Synthesis of Longitudinal Research*, edited by Akiva M. Liberman. New York: Springer.

Silbereisen, Rainer K., and Peter Noack. 1988. "On the Constructive Role of Problem Behavior in Adolescence." In *Persons in Context: Developmental Process*, edited by Niall Bolger, Avshalom Caspi, Geraldine Downey, and Martha Moorehouse. Cambridge, UK: Cambridge University Press.

Smith, David J. 2006. *Social Inclusion and Early Desistance from Crime*. Edinburgh Study of Youth Transitions and Crime, Number 12. Edinburgh, Scotland: Center for Law and Society, University of Edinburgh.

Staff, Jeremy, and Christopher Uggen. 2003. "The Fruits of Good Work: Early Work Experiences and Adolescent Deviance." *Journal of Research in Crime and Delinquency* 40: 263–90.

Steffensmeier, Darrell J., Emile Andersen Allan, Miles D. Harer, and Cathy Streifel. 1989. "Age and the Distribution of Crime." *American Journal of Sociology* 94: 803–31.

Steinberg, Laurence. 2004. "Risk-Taking in Adolescence: What Changes and Why?" *Annals of the New York Academy of Sciences* 1021: 51–58.

Steinberg, Laurence. 2007. "Risk-Taking in Adolescence: New Perspectives from Brain and Behavior Science." *Current Directions in Psychological Science* 16: 55–59.

Stouthamer-Loeber, Magda, Rolf Loeber, Rebecca Stallings, and Eric LaCourse. 2008. "Desistance from and Persistence in Offending." In *Violence and Serious Theft: Development and Prediction from Childhood to Adulthood*, edited by Rolf Loeber, David P. Farrington, Magda Stouthamer-Loeber, and Helene Raskin White. New York: Routledge.

Stouthamer-Loeber, Magda, and Evelyn Wei. 1998. "The Precursors of Young Fatherhood and its Effect on the Delinquency Career of Teenage Males." *Journal of Adolescent Health* 22: 56–65.

Uggen, Christopher. 2000. "Work as a Turning Point in the Life Course of Criminals: A Duration Model of Age, Employment, and Recidivism." *American Sociological Review* 65: 529–46.

Uggen, Christopher, and Candace Kruttschnitt. 1998. "Crime in the Breaking: Gender Differences in Desistance." *Law and Society Review* 32: 339–66.

Uggen, Christopher, and Sara Wakefield. 2008. "What Have We Learned from Longitudinal Studies of Adolescent Employment and Crime?" In *The Long View of Crime: A Synthesis of Longitudinal Research*, edited by Akiva Liberman. New York: Springer.

Warr, Mark. 2002. *Companions in Crime: The Social Aspects of Criminal Conduct*. Cambridge, UK: Cambridge University Press.

Western, Bruce. 2006. *Punishment and Inequality in America*. New York: Russell Sage Foundation.

Wikström, Per-Olof H., and David A. Butterworth. 2006. *Adolescent Crime: Individual Differences and Lifestyles*. United Kingdom: Willan Publishing.

Wikström, Per-Olof H., Vania Ceccato, Beth Hardie, and Kyle Treiber. 2009. "Activity Fields and the Dynamics of Crime: Advancing Knowledge about the Role of the Environment in Crime Causation." Unpublished Manuscript. Cambridge, United Kingdom: University of Cambridge.

CHAPTER 18

....

DELINQUENCY
PREVENTION

....

BRANDON C. WELSH

DELINQUENCY prevention involves intervening in the lives of children and youths before they engage in delinquency in the first place—that is, before the first delinquent act. In this respect, it includes interventions applied to the whole community to prevent the onset of delinquency, and interventions targeted at children and youths who are at risk for becoming offenders because of the presence of one or more risk factors. Delinquency prevention involves measures that are largely of a developmental or social nature—preventing the development of criminal potential in individuals and improving the social conditions and institutions (e.g., families, peers, social norms) that influence offending. A social structure perspective is often a key focus in the design of prevention programs.

By contrast, delinquency control or repression responds to individuals after the fact—once a delinquent act has been committed. This marks the initiation of the juvenile justice process. In large measure, delinquency prevention takes place outside of the juvenile justice system. But delinquency prevention programs are not designed with the intention of excluding justice personnel. Some types of prevention programs, especially those that address the needs of older juveniles, involve justice personnel like the police. In these cases, justice personnel work in close collaboration with those in such fields as education, public health, recreation, and family and social services.

The history of the prevention of delinquency in the United States is closely tied to the history of juvenile justice in this country. From the founding of the House of Refuge in New York City in 1825 to more contemporary events, such as amendments to the federal Juvenile Justice and Delinquency Prevention Act of 1974, child-saving organizations and law makers have had an interest in both the prevention and control of delinquency. However, many scholars have noted that efforts to prevent juveniles from engaging in delinquency in the first place were secondary to and often overlooked in favor of juvenile justice responses to youths who had come in conflict with the law (Krisberg and Austin 1978; Lundman 2001; Weis and Hawkins 1981).

While this imbalance between delinquency prevention and control continues to this day (and remains a cause for concern), there are signs that prevention, especially targeted at the early years of the life course, is enjoying an unusually higher profile of late. This has come about in large measure because of a number of research developments. One of these developments concerns the substantial knowledge base on the "root causes" of offending. After decades of rigorous research in the United States and across the Western world—using prospective longitudinal studies—a great deal is known about early risk factors for delinquency and later criminal offending (Farrington and Welsh 2007). By definition, a risk factor is a variable that predicts an increased probability of offending (Kazdin et al. 1997). For example, children who experience poor parental supervision have an increased risk of committing delinquent acts later on. Early risk factors that are strongly associated with delinquency and later criminal offending can be found at the individual, family, and environmental levels. Disappointingly, less is known about protective and promotive factors, but recent research provides some important insights (see Loeber et al. 2008; Lösel and Bender 2003).

Another development concerns the growing body of high quality scientific evidence on the effectiveness of prevention programs designed to tackle these risk factors and from which evidence-based conclusions can be drawn. At the heart of this is the concept of risk-focused prevention. The basic idea of this approach is straightforward: identify key risk factors for offending and implement prevention methods designed to counteract them. Risk-focused prevention links explanation and prevention, fundamental and applied research, and scholars, policy makers, and practitioners. Many early prevention trials have followed children long enough to measure delinquency. Model programs and systematic reviews and meta-analyses of early prevention programs provide scientific evidence that a wide range of programs in different domains can be effective and others promising in preventing delinquency and later offending (Farrington and Welsh 2007; Greenwood 2006; Mihalic et al. 2004).

An increasing number of cost-benefit and cost-effectiveness analyses show that many prevention programs provide value for money and can be a worthwhile investment of government resources compared with prison and other juvenile justice responses (Aos et al. 2004; Karoly, Kilburn, and Cannon 2005). Research has also documented the widespread public support that exists in the United States and in other countries for prevention programs compared with more punitive measures (Cullen et al. 2007; Nagin et al. 2006; Roberts and Hastings 2007).

Moreover, findings of neuroscience, behavioral research, and economics show a "striking convergence on a set of common principles that account for the potent effects of early environment on the capacity of human skill development," which affirms the need for greater investments in disadvantaged children in the early years of the life course (Knudsen et al. 2006, p. 10155; see also Heckman 2006). Recent U.S. national scientific commissions on early childhood development and juvenile offending that have examined much of this evidence have also identified the many benefits of early prevention programs and called for concrete action to make early prevention a top government priority (McCord, Widom, and Crowell 2001; Shonkoff and Phillips 2000; U.S. Department of Health and Human Services 2001).

This chapter sets out to review the research on and key issues facing the prevention of delinquency. The next three sections review the scientific evidence on what works to prevent delinquency (as well as later criminal offending) through individual, family, and environmental (peer, school, and community) interventions that are delivered in the early years of the life course. Only the highest quality research studies (i.e., experiments and quasi-experiments) and the most rigorous literature reviews (i.e., systematic and meta-analytic reviews) that include only high quality projects are included. This approach ensures that conclusions are based on the best available evidence. The chapter concludes with a discussion of the implications of this research for juvenile justice policy and practice.

I. INDIVIDUAL PREVENTION

Individual-based prevention programs target risk factors for delinquency and later offending that are found within the individual. Among the most important of these risk factors include low intelligence and attainment, low empathy, impulsivity, and hyperactivity. These programs are targeted on the child. As noted by Duncan and Magnuson (2004, p. 94), "Individual interventions focus directly on the person whose development is targeted, and can occur very early in life, as with intensive preschool education." This is distinguished from family-based interventions, which are directed at both the child and parent or caregiver (see below).

Early childhood programs help society's most vulnerable members. They have as explicit aims the betterment of children's immediate learning and social and emotional competencies, as well as the improvement of children's success over the life course. In addition, they are implemented at a time when children are most impressionable and hence receptive to intervention (Duncan and Magnuson 2004). With a primary emphasis on improving school readiness, providing families in need with various other services, and reaching about half of all impoverished children (Currie 2001), Head Start is considered the nation's most important early childhood program (Ripple and Zigler 2003).

Two main types of individual-based programs have been found to be effective in preventing delinquency and later criminal offending: preschool intellectual enrichment and child skills training.

A. Preschool Intellectual Enrichment

Preschool intellectual enrichment programs are generally targeted on the risk factors of low intelligence and attainment. As noted by Duncan and Magnuson (2004, p. 105), "Child-focused early-education intervention programs are designed to provide economically disadvantaged children with cognitively stimulating and enriching experiences that their parents are unlikely to provide at home." Improved cognitive skills, school readiness, and social and emotional development are the main goals of these programs (Currie 2001). Some of the key features of these programs include the provision of developmentally appropriate learning curricula, a wide array of cognitive-based enriching activities, and activities for parents, usually of a less intensive nature, so that they may be able to support the school experience at home (Duncan and Magnuson 2004, pp. 105–06).

On the basis of four evaluations of preschool programs (three evaluated with randomized experimental designs), a meta-analysis found that this type of early developmental prevention produced a significant 12% reduction in delinquency and offending (e.g., from 50% in a control group to 38% in an experimental group) (Farrington and Welsh 2007).

The most famous of the programs included in this meta-analysis was the Perry Preschool project carried out in Ypsilanti, Michigan, by Lawrence Schweinhart and David Weikart (1980). This was essentially a Head Start program targeted at disadvantaged African American children. A sample of 123 children was allocated (approximately at random) to experimental and control groups. The experimental children attended a daily preschool program, backed up by weekly home visits, usually lasting two years (covering ages 3 to 4). The aim of the "plan-do-review" program was to provide intellectual stimulation, to increase thinking and reasoning abilities, and to increase later school achievement.

This program had long-term benefits. Berrueta-Clement and his colleagues (1984) showed that at age 19, the experimental group was more likely to be employed, more likely to have graduated from high school, more likely to have received college or vocational training, and less likely to have been arrested. By age 27, the experimental group had accumulated only half as many arrests as the controls—an average of 2.3 compared to 4.6 arrests (Schweinhart, Barnes, and Weikart 1993). In addition, they were more likely to have graduated from high school, had significantly higher earnings, and were more likely to be home owners.

The most recent follow-up of Perry, at age 40, which included 91% of the original sample (112 out of 123), found that the program continued to make an important difference in the lives of the participants (Schweinhart et al. 2005). Compared to the control group, program group members had significantly fewer lifetime arrests for violent crimes (32% versus 48%), property crimes (36% versus 58%), and drug crimes (14% versus 34%), and were significantly less likely to be arrested five or more times (36% versus 55%). Improvements were also recorded in many other important life-course outcomes. For example, significantly higher levels of schooling (77% versus 60% graduating from high school), better records of employment (76% versus 62%), and higher annual incomes were reported by the program group compared to the controls. A cost-benefit analysis at age 40 found that Perry produced just over seventeen dollars of benefit per dollar of cost, with 76% of this being returned to the general public—in the form of savings in crime, education, and welfare, and increased tax revenue—and 24% benefiting each program participant.

Duncan and Magnuson's (2004) review of preschool education programs distinguished between "intensive efficacy interventions" (or research and demonstration projects) and "more policy-relevant, less intensive interventions" (or routine practice). Their coverage of the former group of preschool intellectual enrichment programs is similar to those in the foregoing meta-analysis, and they, too, found that these programs have long-term beneficial effects on children's criminal behavior (as well as on other outcomes). On the matter of less intensive preschool education interventions like Head Start, the authors found that the evidence was less clear about the ability of these programs to produce results similar to the intensive efficacy ones. However, they concluded that "the weight of the evidence to date indicates that these programs may also improve children's life courses" (p. 105).

The economist Janet Currie (2001) reviewed early childhood education programs, defined more broadly than preschool programs. She too distinguished between "small-scale model programs" (or research and demonstration projects) and "large-scale public programs" (or routine practice), with the former "typically funded at higher levels and run by more highly trained staff" (p. 217). The findings of the routine practice programs, specifically Head Start, are relevant here. As in Duncan and Magnuson's (2004) review, Currie (2001) found that the evidence in support of favorable long-term effects (e.g., on offending) of Head Start was less than conclusive. She attributed this result mostly to a paucity of well-designed studies that have measured long-term effects.

B. Child Skills Training

Interpersonal skills training or social competence programs for children are generally targeted on the risk factors of impulsivity, low empathy, and self-centeredness. As noted by Carolyn Webster-Stratton and Ted Taylor (2001, p. 178), this type of individual-based program is designed to "directly teach children social, emotional, and cognitive competence by addressing appropriate social skills, effective problem-solving, anger management, and emotion language." A typical program includes one or more of these elements and is highly structured with a limited number of sessions, thus lasting for a relatively short period of time (Lösel and Beelmann 2003).

The criminologists Friedrich Lösel and Andreas Beelmann (2006; see also Lösel and Beelmann 2003) carried out a systematic review and meta-analysis of the effects of child skills training on antisocial behavior (including delinquency). The review included fifty-five randomized controlled experiments with eighty-nine separate experimental-control group comparisons. A meta-analysis found that almost half of the comparisons produced desirable results favoring the children who received the treatment compared to those who did not, while less than one out of ten revealed undesirable results (i.e., the control group fared better than the treatment group). Control participants typically received non-intensive, basic services.

Four evaluations (all randomized controlled experiments) measured delinquency. Effects of the intervention on delinquency were consistent at two different follow-up periods. At immediate outcome or post-intervention (defined as within two months after treatment) the meta-analysis yielded a significant 9% reduction in delinquency in an experimental group compared to a control group. At later follow-up (defined as three months or more after treatment), the average effect was slightly higher—a 10% reduction in delinquency (also a significant effect). The meta-analysis also found that the most effective skills training programs used a cognitive-behavioral approach and were implemented with older children (aged 13 years and over) and higher risk groups who were already exhibiting some behavioral problems.

II. Family Prevention

Family-based prevention programs target risk factors for delinquency and later offending that are associated with the family, such as poor child rearing, poor supervision, and inconsistent or harsh discipline. Broadly speaking, family-based prevention programs have developed along the lines of two major fields of study: psychology and public health. When delivered by psychologists, these programs are often classified into parent management training, functional family therapy, or family preservation (Wasserman and Miller 1998). Typically, they attempt to change the social contingencies in the family environment so that children are rewarded in some way for appropriate or prosocial behaviors and punished in some way for inappropriate or antisocial behaviors.

Family-based programs delivered by health professionals such as nurses are typically less behavioral, mainly providing advice and guidance to parents or general parent education. Home visiting with new parents, especially mothers, is perhaps the most popular form of this type of family intervention. In the early 1990s, Hawaii became the first state to offer free home visits for all new mothers. A small number of other states, with Colorado at the forefront, have more recently implemented more intensive but targeted versions of home visiting programs with the aim of eventually providing universal coverage (Calonge 2005).

Two main types of family-based programs have been found to be effective in preventing delinquency and later criminal offending: general parent education (in the context of home visiting and parent education plus day care services) and parent management training.

A. Parent Education

Home visiting with new parents, especially mothers, is a popular, although far from universal, method of delivering the family-based intervention known as general parent education. The main goals of home visiting programs center around educating parents to improve the life chances of children from a very young age, often beginning at birth and sometimes as early as the final trimester of pregnancy. Some of the main goals include the prevention of preterm or low weight births, the promotion of healthy child development and school readiness, and the prevention of child abuse and neglect (Gomby, Culross, and Behrman 1999, p. 4). Home visits very often also serve to improve parental well-being, linking parents to community resources to help with employment, education, or addiction recovery. Home visitors are usually nurses or other health professionals with a diverse array of skills in working with families.

In a meta-analysis that included four home visitation programs (all randomized controlled experiments), it was found that this form of early intervention was effective in preventing antisocial behavior and delinquency, corresponding to a significant 12% reduction (e.g., from 50% in a control group to 38% in an experimental group) (Farrington and Welsh 2007).

Oleg Bilukha and his colleagues (2005) carried out a systematic review of the effectiveness of early childhood home visitation in preventing violence. Four studies were included that reported the effects of home visitation programs on violence by the visited children. Mixed results were found for effects on criminal violence (in adolescence) and child externalizing behavior across the four programs: two reported desirable but nonsignificant effects; one reported a significant desirable effect; and one reported mixed results. On the basis of these results, the authors concluded that the "evidence is insufficient to determine the effectiveness of home visitation interventions in preventing child violence" (p. 17).

Using these and many other studies, the systematic review by Bilukha and colleagues also assessed the effectiveness of early childhood home visitation on parental violence, intimate partner violence, and child maltreatment. For the first two outcomes, there was also insufficient evidence to make a determination of effectiveness. Strong evidence of effectiveness was found, however, for home visiting programs in preventing child abuse and neglect.

The best known home visiting program (and the only one with a direct measure of delinquency) is the Nurse-Family Partnership (NFP) carried out in the semi-rural community of Elmira, New York, by David Olds and his colleagues (1998). The program enrolled four hundred women prior to their thirtieth week of pregnancy. Women were recruited if they had no previous live births and had at least one of the following high-risk characteristics prone to health and developmental problems in infancy: under 19 years of age, unmarried, or poor. The women were randomly assigned to receive home visits from nurses during pregnancy, or to receive visits both during pregnancy and during the first two years of life, or to a control group who received no visits. Each visit lasted about one and one-quarter hours, and the mothers were visited on average every two weeks. The home visitors gave advice about prenatal and postnatal care of the child, about infant development, and about the importance of proper nutrition and avoiding smoking and drinking during pregnancy.

The results of this experiment showed that the postnatal home visits caused a significant decrease in recorded child physical abuse and neglect during the first two years of life, especially by poor, unmarried, teenage mothers (Olds et al. 1986), and in a fifteen-year follow-up, significantly fewer experimental compared to control group mothers were identified as perpetrators of child abuse and neglect (Olds et al. 1997). At the age of 15, children of the higher risk mothers who received prenatal or postnatal home visits or both had incurred significantly fewer arrests than their control counterparts (twenty as opposed to forty-five per one hundred children; Olds et al. 1998). Several cost-benefit analyses show that the benefits of this program outweighed its costs for the higher risk mothers (see Aos et al. 2004; Karoly et al. 1998).

A small number of parent education programs that include day care services for the children of the participating parents have also measured delinquency. Day care programs are distinguished from preschool programs in that the former are not necessarily focused on the child's intellectual enrichment or on readying the child for kindergarten and elementary school, but serve largely as an organized form of child care to allow parents (especially mothers) to return to work. Day care also provides children with a number of important benefits, including social interaction with other children and stimulation of their cognitive, sensory, and motor control skills.

In a meta-analysis of three day care programs, it was found that this form of parent education resulted in a small but nonsignificant 7% reduction in antisocial behavior and delinquency (e.g., from 50% in a control group to 43% in an experimental group) (Farrington and Welsh 2007).

B. Parent Management Training

Many different types of parent training have been used to prevent and treat child externalizing behavior problems and delinquency (Wasserman and Miller 1998). Parent management training refers to "treatment procedures in which parents are trained to alter their child's behavior at home" (Kazdin 1997, p. 1349). Gerald Patterson (1982) developed behavioral parent management training. His careful observations of parent-child interaction showed that parents of antisocial children were deficient in their methods of child rearing. These parents failed to tell their children how they were expected to behave, failed to monitor their behavior to ensure that it was desirable, and failed to enforce rules promptly and unambiguously with appropriate rewards and penalties. The parents of antisocial children used more punishment (such as scolding, shouting, or threatening), but failed to make it contingent on the child's behavior.

Patterson attempted to train these parents in effective child-rearing methods, namely, noticing what a child is doing, monitoring behavior over long periods, clearly stating house rules, making rewards and punishments contingent on behavior, and negotiating disagreements so that conflicts and crises did not escalate. His treatment was shown to be effective in reducing child stealing and antisocial behavior over short periods in small-scale studies (Patterson, Chamberlain, and Reid 1982; Patterson, Reid, and Dishion 1992).

On the basis of ten high quality evaluations of parent management training programs, a meta-analysis found that this type of early intervention produced a significant 20% reduction in antisocial behavior and delinquency (e.g., from 50% in a control group to 30% in an experimental group) (Farrington and Welsh 2007). Each of the ten parent management training programs included in this meta-analysis aimed to teach parents to use rewards and punishments consistently and contingently in child rearing. The programs were usually delivered in guided group meetings of parents, including role-playing and modeling exercises, and three of the programs were delivered by videotape. Just one of the ten programs combined parent management training with another intervention (child skills training).

Alex Mason and his colleagues (2003) evaluated the effectiveness of an early family-based program that included, as a main component, parent management training. Known as Preparing for the Drug Free Years (PDFY), this universal program to "enhance family protection and reduce children's risk for early substance initiation" was designed to aid parents on many fronts: "teaching parents about the risk and protective factors for substance abuse and helping them to develop skills for establishing and communicating clear behavioral expectations, monitoring their children's behavior and enforcing norms, managing family conflict, promoting child involvement, and strengthening family bonds" (p. 206).

In their evaluation, the first to assess the program's impact on delinquency, thirty-three rural schools in nineteen contiguous counties in the state of Iowa were randomly allocated—using a randomized block design that blocked on "enrollment and on the proportion of lower income students"—to one of three conditions. These conditions included the PDFY program, a minimal contact group (the control group), and another treatment condition known as the Iowa Strengthening Families Program (which the authors did not evaluate as part of this study) (Mason et al. 2003, p. 205). Altogether, the study included 429 6th grade students (average age 11.3 years) and their families. The PDFY program was carried out in a group format and was fairly short in duration, involving five weekly parenting sessions, each lasting about two hours. Children were involved in one of the sessions.

At the latest follow-up (three and a half years post-intervention), it was found that the experimental group had experienced a significantly slower rate of increase in delinquency and substance use compared to the control group. The authors speculated that other comprehensive family-focused drug prevention programs should be able to produce "effects that generalize to nondrug-related delinquency" (Mason et al. 2003, p. 210).

The psychologists Wendy Serketich and Jean Dumas (1996) carried out a meta-analysis of twenty-six controlled studies of behavioral parent training (also called parent management training) with young children up to age 10. Most were based on small numbers (average total sample size was twenty-nine), and most were randomized experiments. They concluded that parent management training was effective in reducing child antisocial behavior, especially for (relatively) older children.

Alex Piquero and his colleagues (2009) carried out a much broader systematic review and meta-analysis of parent training and found it to be effective in reducing child behavior problems, including antisocial behavior and delinquency. The review, which included fifty-five randomized controlled experiments, investigated the full range of early/family parent training programs for children up to age 5 years, including home visiting, parent education plus day care, and parent management training. Significant differences were not detected across program type (traditional parent training versus home visiting) or outcome source (parent, teacher, or direct observer reports).

III. Peer, School, and Community Prevention

Peer, school, and community prevention programs target environmental-level risk factors for delinquency and later offending. The most important of these risk factors includes associating with delinquent friends; attending high-delinquency rate schools, which have high levels of distrust between teachers and students, low commitment to the school by students, and unclear and inconsistently enforced rules; and growing up in a poor, disorganized neighborhood.

School-based prevention programs have become increasingly popular in recent years. This is due in part to increased attention to school crime that has come about from high-profile school shootings and other violent incidents. Most of the programs that have been set up in the wake of these tragic events focus on the safety of students within schools, with fewer focused on the prevention of delinquency in the wider community. Less can be said about early intervention programs targeted at peer risk factors to prevent delinquency. However, peer-based programs have been used extensively to help children resist peer influences to initiate drug use. Community-based prevention covers a wide array of programs, including after-school, mentoring, and youth and resident groups. These programs hold wide appeal among the public and political leaders alike, but are often among the first programs to lose funding in times of federal or state budget cuts (Butterfield 2003). This state of affairs has hampered the knowledge base on the effectiveness of this type of early intervention. An examination of this group of preventive interventions together stems in large part from their shared focus on environmental factors.

A. Peer-Based Programs

Peer-based programs to prevent delinquency and offending are ostensibly designed with two related aims: to reduce the influence of delinquent friends and increase the influence of prosocial friends. Teaching children to resist antisocial peer pressures that encourage delinquent activities can take many forms, including modeling and guided practice. Peers must be older, preferably in their later teens, and influential; such peers are sometimes known as high-status peer leaders.

Unfortunately, no systematic review or meta-analysis has been carried out to assess the effects of peer-based programs on delinquency or later offending. The reviews that have been completed to date have focused on substance use. For example, a large-scale meta-analysis of 143 substance use prevention programs by Nancy Tobler (1986) concluded that programs using peer leaders were the most effective in reducing smoking, drinking, and drug use.

The National Research Council and Institute of Medicine's Panel on Juvenile Crime (McCord, Widom, and Crowell 2001) reviewed four randomized experiments of peer-based interventions, two with delinquency measures. The Panel did not attempt to synthesize program effects on delinquency or other outcomes, but rather cautioned against the practice of grouping deviant or high-risk peers together during early adolescence (p. 138). This was largely because of the research of Joan McCord (the Panel's Co-Chair) on harmful effects of delinquency prevention programs (see Dishion, McCord, and Poulin 1999; McCord 2002, 2003), which began with her long-term follow-up of the famous Cambridge-Somerville Youth Study (McCord 1978).

In addition, there are no outstanding examples of effective intervention programs for delinquency or later offending based on peer risk factors. The most hopeful programs involve using high-status conventional peers to teach children ways of resisting peer pressure; this has been shown to be effective in reducing drug use (Tobler et al. 1999). In addition, in a randomized experiment in St. Louis, Ronald Feldman, John Wodarski, and Timothy Caplinger (1983) showed that placing antisocial adolescents in activity groups dominated by prosocial adolescents led to a reduction in their antisocial behavior (compared with antisocial adolescents placed in antisocial groups). Over four hundred boys around the age of 11 were included in the study, and the focus was on group-level behavior modification. The findings of this study suggest that the influence of prosocial peers can be harnessed to reduce offending.

B. School-Based Programs

Schools are a critical social context for crime prevention efforts, from the early to later grades (Elliott, Hamburg, and Williams 1998). All schools work to produce vibrant and productive members of society. According to Denise Gottfredson and her colleagues (2002, p. 149), "Students who are impulsive, are weakly attached to their schools, have little commitment to achieving educational goals, and whose moral beliefs in the validity of conventional rules for behavior are weak are more likely to engage in crime than those who do not possess these characteristics." The school's role in influencing these risk factors and preventing delinquency in both school and the wider community (the focus here) differs from situational and administrative measures taken to make the school a safer place (e.g., through metal detectors, police in school, or closed-circuit television surveillance cameras).

There have been a number of comprehensive, evidence-based reviews on the effectiveness of early school-based programs to prevent delinquency and offending.

David Wilson, Denise Gottfredson, and Stacy Najaka (2001; see also Gottfredson et al. 2002; Gottfredson, Wilson, and Najaka 2006) conducted a meta-analysis that included 165 randomized and quasi-experimental studies with 216 experimental-control group comparisons. Their meta-analysis identified four types of school-based programs as effective in preventing delinquency: school and discipline management, classroom or instructional management, reorganization of grades or classes, and fostering self-control or social competency using cognitive behavioral or behavioral instructional methods. Reorganization of grades or classes had the largest mean effect size ($d = .34$), corresponding to a significant 17% reduction in delinquency. Three of these four effective types of school-based programs (other than school and discipline management) were also effective in preventing alcohol and drug use, and fostering self-control or social competency with cognitive behavioral or behavioral instructional methods was effective in preventing other problem behaviors.

Two other meta-analyses, one by Sandra Wilson and Mark Lipsey (2007) and the other by Julie Mytton and her colleagues (2002), provide further support for the effectiveness of school-based prevention programs in general, especially those targeted on the highest risk children.

One of the most important early school-based prevention experiments was carried out in Seattle by David Hawkins and his colleagues (1991). They implemented a multicomponent program (known as the Seattle Social Development Project) combining parent training, teacher training, and skills training. About five hundred 1st grade children (aged 6) in twenty-one classes were randomly assigned to be in experimental or control classes. The children in the experimental classes received special treatment at home and school, which was designed to increase their attachment to their parents and their bonding to the school, based on the assumption that delinquency was inhibited by the strength of social bonds. In addition, the treated children were trained in interpersonal cognitive problem solving. Their parents were trained to notice and reinforce socially desirable behavior in a program called "Catch Them Being Good." Their teachers were trained in classroom management, for example, to provide clear instructions and expectations to children, to reward children for participation in desired behavior, and to teach children prosocial (socially desirable) methods of solving problems.

In an evaluation of this program eighteen months later, when the children were in different classes, Hawkins and his colleagues (1991) found that the boys who were in the experimental program were significantly less aggressive than the control boys, according to teacher ratings. This difference was particularly marked for Caucasian boys compared to African American boys. The experimental girls were not significantly less aggressive, but they were less self-destructive, anxious, and depressed. Julie O'Donnell and her colleagues (1995) focused on children in low-income families and reported that, in the 6th grade (age 12), experimental boys were less likely to have initiated delinquency, while experimental girls were less likely to have initiated drug use. In the latest follow-up of offending outcomes, at age 18, Hawkins and his colleagues (1999) found that the full intervention group (those receiving the intervention from grades 1 through 6) admitted less violence, less alcohol abuse, and fewer sexual partners than the late intervention group (grades 5 and 6 only) or the controls. A cost-benefit analysis of the program by Steve Aos and his colleagues (2004) found that for every dollar spent on the program, more than three dollars was saved to government and crime victims.

Noticeably absent from this discussion of effective school-based delinquency prevention programs is the widely popular DARE (Drug Abuse Resistance Education) program, which brings uniformed law enforcement officers into elementary schools to educate children about the dangers of drug use and the skills needed to resist peer pressure to use drugs. The reason for its absence here is that large-scale evaluations (many of which employed randomized experimental designs) and independent reviews have consistently found that the program has a trivial effect on substance use and delinquency (see Gottfredson et al. 2006; U.S. General Accountability Office 2003). Key reasons for its ineffectiveness include the fact that it targets children who are too young to appreciate its message and it does not employ a cognitive-behavioral focus. These results have led to hundreds of school districts to discontinue its use, as well as its removal from the "List of Exemplary and Promising Prevention Programs" administered by the U.S. Department of Education's Safe and Drug-Free Schools program (Weiss et al. 2008). An evaluation of a new DARE curriculum designed for older students, known as "Take Charge of Your Life," found that it had no effect on the onset or initiation of drug use (Sloboda et al. 2009)

C. Community-Based Programs

More often than not, community-based efforts to prevent delinquency and later offending are some combination of developmental prevention, with its focus on reducing the development or influence of early risk factors—or root causes—for delinquency and later offending (Tremblay and Craig 1995), and situational prevention, with its focus on reducing opportunities for crime (Clarke 1995). Unlike these two general crime prevention strategies, there is little agreement in the academic literature on the definition of community prevention and the types of programs that fall within it (Bennett 1996). Hope's (1995) definition that it involves actions designed to change the social conditions and institutions that influence offending in residential communities is perhaps the most informative.

The latest research on the effectiveness of community-based crime prevention finds that after-school programs are promising and mentoring programs are effective in preventing juvenile crime.

1. After-School Programs

This type of program is premised on the belief that providing prosocial opportunities for young people in the after-school hours can reduce their involvement in delinquent behavior in the community. After-school programs target a range of crime risk factors, including alienation and association with delinquent peers. There are many different types of these programs, including recreation-based programs, drop-in clubs, and tutoring services.

Welsh and Hoshi (2006) identified three high quality after-school programs with an evaluated impact on delinquency. Each program produced desirable effects on delinquency, and one program also reported lower rates of drug activity for participants compared to controls. Welsh and Hoshi concluded that community-based after-school programs represent a promising approach to preventing juvenile offending, but this conclusion only applies to areas immediately around recreation centers.

Denise Gottfredson and her colleagues (2004), as part of a larger study to investigate the effects of after-school programs on delinquency in Maryland, reported on a brief review of the effectiveness of these programs. They concluded that there is insufficient evidence at present to support claims that after-school programs are effective in preventing delinquency or other problem behaviors. However, they noted that, among a small number of experimental and quasi-experimental studies (which included two of the three programs in Welsh and Hoshi's review), after-school programs that "involve a heavy dose of social competency skill development...may reduce problem behavior" (p. 256). In the Maryland study, which used randomized experimental and quasi-experimental methods with statistical matching designs to evaluate the effects of fourteen after-school programs, it was found that participation in the programs reduced delinquent behavior among children in middle school but not elementary school. Increasing intentions not to use drugs and positive peer associations were identified as the mechanisms for the middle school programs' favorable effects on delinquency, while decreasing time spent unsupervised or increasing involvement in constructive activities played no significant role (pp. 263–64).

2. *Mentoring*

This type of program usually involves nonprofessional adult volunteers spending time with young people at risk for delinquency, dropping out of school, school failure, and other social problems. Mentors behave in a "supportive, nonjudgmental manner while acting as role models" (Howell 1995, p. 90). In many cases, mentors work one-on-one with young people, often forming strong bonds. Care is taken in matching the mentor and the young person.

Darrick Jolliffe and David Farrington's (2008) systematic review and meta-analysis of eighteen mentoring programs found this to be an effective approach to preventing delinquency. The average effect across the studies corresponded to a significant 10% reduction in offending. The authors found that mentoring was more effective in reducing offending when the average duration of each contact between mentor and mentee was greater, in smaller scale studies, and when mentoring was combined with other interventions.

IV. CONCLUSIONS AND POLICY IMPLICATIONS

This chapter opened by drawing attention to two important yet seemingly divergent issues that confront the present state and future of delinquency prevention in the United States. On the one hand, there is the research, which has never before been so robust and wide-ranging in its support for the prevention of delinquency. Importantly, this research shows that delinquency prevention programs can be effective and worthwhile in their own right, as well as compared to prison and other delinquency control measures. On the other hand, there is the reality of the policy and practice of delinquency prevention, which shows that it holds a small place in the nation's response to juvenile crime. Delinquency control strategies operated by the juvenile justice system dominate.

Efforts to address this imbalance have received some attention. Perhaps the most promising initiative is the Comprehensive Strategy for Serious, Violent, and Chronic Juvenile Offenders developed by John Wilson and James Howell (1993). Programs are based on a continuum of care that begins in early childhood and progresses through late adolescence. There are six components to the strategy: (1) prevention in early childhood; (2) intervention with pre-delinquents and child delinquents; (3) immediate intervention for first-time delinquent offenders; (4) intermediate sanctions for first-time serious or violent juvenile offenders; (5) secure placement for the most serious of these offenders; and (6) aftercare or reentry (Howell 2009, p. 222).

This strategy recognizes that effective prevention programs will go some way toward reducing the number of young people who come in contact with the juvenile justice system. How much the case flow of delinquents through the justice system could be reduced by expanded use of effective prevention programs is not known. What is known is that the current evidence base on effective delinquency prevention programs (as reviewed above) satisfies the key elements of the strategy to help achieve this objective. First, effective programs are targeted on the most important early risk factors for delinquency and later offending. Second, effective programs can be found in different domains and are targeted at different age groups. At the individual level, effective programs include preschool intellectual enrichment and child skills training. At the family level, effective programs include general parent education in the context of home visiting and day care as well as parent management training. At the environmental level, effective programs include a number of school-based programs and mentoring, and after-school programs are promising.

In the interest of achieving maximum effectiveness, this strategy also recognizes the need for a comprehensive, locally driven program that includes several of these effective prevention programs. Communities That Care (CTC) has many attractions to serve as the model for delivering these delinquency prevention programs. It is both risk-focused and evidence-based, and it is widely used across the United States, at the last count in several hundred communities (Harachi et al. 2003). In the first randomized controlled trial of CTC, David Hawkins and his colleagues (2008) report promising findings in reducing targeted risk factors and initiation of delinquent behavior.

Another important consideration for a strategy that values prevention is the determination about the authority that will be responsible for administering it. Peter Greenwood (2006) excellently reviews the pros and cons of different government departments that could have primary responsibility for delinquency prevention programs in general (Justice, Education, and Health and Human Services, or HHS). Ultimately, he argues that HHS should be the lead department for early prevention programs, while Justice is the more appropriate department for serving the needs of high-risk and adjudicated youths. Greenwood summarizes his arguments in favor of HHS with the following principle: "*Primary responsibility for developing and operating delinquency-prevention programs should be assigned to an appropriate agency in HHS unless immediate public protection is an overriding concern*" (p. 179, emphasis in original). One argument in favor of HHS is that the benefits of prevention are not restricted to delinquency, but include many other aspects of a successful or healthy lifestyle (including education, employment, substance use, relationships, and mental health).

Striking a greater balance between prevention and control offers to go a long way toward addressing the multiple needs of at-risk children and their families and reducing juvenile crime. Getting there will require a number of important steps and will not necessarily be easy. Making sure that the research evidence is at center stage in this process will ensure it is on the right track. And that will be a good start.

REFERENCES

Aos, Steve, Roxanne Lieb, Jim Mayfield, Marna Miller, and Annie Pennucci. 2004. *Benefits and Costs of Prevention and Early Intervention Programs for Youth*. Olympia: Washington State Institute for Public Policy.

Bennett, Trevor H. 1996. "Community Crime Prevention in Britain." In *Kommunale Kriminalprävention: Paradigmenwechsel und Wiederentdeckung alter Weisheiten*, edited by Thomas Trenczek and Hartmut Pfeiffer. Bonn, Germany: Forum Verlag Godesberg.

Berrueta-Clement, John R., Lawrence J. Schweinhart, W. Steven Barnett, Ann S. Epstein, and David P. Weikart. 1984. *Changed Lives: The Effects of the Perry Preschool Program on Youths Through Age 19*. Ypsilanti, MI.: High/Scope Press.

Bilukha, Oleg, Robert A. Hahn, Alex Crosby, Mindy T. Fullilove, Akiva Liberman, Eve Moscicki, Susan Snyder, Farris Tuma, Phaedra Corso, Amanda Schofield, and Peter A. Briss. 2005. "The Effectiveness of Early Childhood Home Visitation in Preventing Violence: A Systematic Review." *American Journal of Preventive Medicine* 28(2S1): 11–39.

Butterfield, Fox. 2003. "Proposed White House Budget Cuts Imperil a Lifeline for Troubled Oregon Teenagers." *New York Times* (June 7), p. A20; available at: www.nytimes.com.

Calonge, Ned. 2005. "Community Interventions to Prevent Violence: Translation into Public Health Practice." *American Journal of Preventive Medicine* 28(2S1): 4–5.

Clarke, Ronald V. 1995. "Situational Crime Prevention." In *Building a Safer Society: Strategic Approaches to Crime Prevention. Crime and Justice: A Review of Research*, vol. 19, edited by Michael Tonry and David P. Farrington. Chicago: University of Chicago Press.

Cullen, Francis T., Brenda A. Vose, Cheryl N. L. Jonson, and James D. Unnever. 2007. "Public Support for Early Intervention: Is Child Saving a 'Habit of the Heart'?" *Victims and Offenders* 2: 108–24.

Currie, Janet. 2001. "Early Childhood Education Programs." *Journal of Economic Perspectives* 15: 213–38.

Dishion, Thomas J., Joan McCord, and François Poulin. 1999. "When Interventions Harm: Peer Groups and Problem Behavior." *American Psychologist* 54: 755–64.

Duncan, Greg J., and Katherine Magnuson. 2004. "Individual and Parent-Based Intervention Strategies for Promoting Human Capital and Positive Behavior." In *Human Development Across Lives and Generations: The Potential for Change*, edited by P. Lindsay Chase-Lansdale, Kathleen Kiernan, and Ruth J. Friedman. New York: Cambridge University Press.

Elliott, Delbert S., Beatrix A. Hamburg, and Kirk R. Williams. 1998. "Violence in American Schools: An Overview." In *Violence in American Schools: A New Perspective*, edited by Delbert S. Elliott, Beatrix A. Hamburg, and Kirk R. Williams. New York: Cambridge University Press.

Farrington, David P., and Brandon C. Welsh. 2007. *Saving Children from a Life of Crime: Early Risk Factors and Effective Interventions*. New York: Oxford University Press.

Feldman, Ronald A., John S. Wodarski, and Timothy E. Caplinger. 1983. *St. Louis Conundrum: The Effective Treatment of Antisocial Youth*. Englewood Cliffs, NJ: Prentice-Hall.

Gomby, Deanna S., Patti L. Culross, and Richard E. Behrman. 1999. "Home Visiting: Recent Program Evaluations—Analysis and Recommendations." *The Future of Children* 9(1): 4–26.

Gottfredson, Denise C., Stephanie A. Gerstenblith, David A. Soulé, Shannon C. Womer, and Shaoli Lu. 2004. "Do After School Programs Reduce Delinquency?" *Prevention Science* 5: 253–66.

Gottfredson, Denise C., David B. Wilson, and Stacey S. Najaka. 2002. "The Schools." In *Crime: Public Policies for Crime Control*, 2nd ed., edited by James Q. Wilson and Joan Petersilia. Oakland, CA: Institute for Contemporary Studies Press.

Gottfredson, Denise C., David B. Wilson, and Stacey S. Najaka. 2006. "School-Based Crime Prevention." In *Evidence-Based Crime Prevention*, rev. ed., edited by Lawrence W. Sherman, David P. Farrington, Brandon C. Welsh, and Doris L. MacKenzie. New York: Routledge.

Greenwood, Peter W. 2006. *Changing Lives: Delinquency Prevention as Crime-Control Policy*. Chicago: University of Chicago Press.

Harachi, Tracy W., J. David Hawkins, Richard F. Catalano, Andrea M. Lafazia, Brian H. Smith, and Michael W. Arthur. 2003. "Evidence-Based Community Decision Making for Prevention: Two Case Studies of Communities That Care." *Japanese Journal of Sociological Criminology* 28: 26–38.

Hawkins, J. David, Eric C. Brown, Sabrina Oesterle, Michael W. Arthur, Robert D. Abbott, and Richard F. Catalano. 2008. "Early Effects of Communities That Care on Targeted Risks and Initiation of Delinquent Behavior and Substance Abuse." *Journal of Adolescent Health* 43: 15–22.

Hawkins, J. David, Richard F. Catalano, Rick Kosterman, Robert Abbott, and Karl G. Hill. 1999. "Preventing Adolescent Health Risk Behaviors by Strengthening Protection During Childhood." *Archives of Pediatric and Adolescent Medicine* 153: 226–34.

Hawkins, J. David, Elizabeth von Cleve, and Richard F. Catalano. 1991. "Reducing Early
  Childhood Aggression: Results of a Primary Prevention Program." *Journal of the
  American Academy of Child and Adolescent Psychiatry* 30: 208–17.

Heckman, James J. 2006. "Skill Formation and the Economics of Investing in
  Disadvantaged Children." *Science* 312: 1900–02.

Hope, Tim. 1995. "Community Crime Prevention." In *Building a Safer Society: Strategic
  Approaches to Crime Prevention. Crime and Justice: A Review of Research*, vol. 19, edited
  by Michael Tonry and David P. Farrington. Chicago: University of Chicago Press.

Howell, James C., ed. 1995. *Guide for Implementing the Comprehensive Strategy for Serious,
  Violent, and Chronic Juvenile Offenders*. Washington, DC: U.S. Department of Justice,
  Office of Juvenile Justice and Delinquency Prevention.

Howell, James C. 2009. *Preventing and Reducing Juvenile Delinquency: A Comprehensive
  Framework*, 2nd ed. Thousand Oaks, Calif.: Sage.

Jolliffe, Darrick, and David P. Farrington. 2008. *The Influence of Mentoring on Reoffending*.
  Stockholm, Sweden: National Council for Crime Prevention.

Karoly, Lynn A., Peter W. Greenwood, Susan S. Everingham, Jill Houbé, M. Rebecca
  Kilburn, C. Peter Rydell, Matthew Sanders, and James Chiesa. 1998. *Investing in Our
  Children: What We Know and Don't Know About the Costs and Benefits of Early
  Childhood Interventions*. Santa Monica, CA: RAND.

Karoly, Lynn A., M. Rebecca Kilburn, and Jill S. Cannon. 2005. *Early Childhood
  Interventions: Proven Results, Future Promise*. Santa Monica, CA: RAND.

Kazdin, Alan E. 1997. "Parent Management Training: Evidence, Outcomes, and Issues."
  Journal of the American Academy of Child and Adolescent Psychiatry 36: 1349–56.

Kazdin, Alan E., Helena C. Kraemer, Ronald C. Kessler, David J. Kupfer, and David R.
  Offord. 1997. "Contributions of Risk-Factor Research to Developmental
  Psychopathology." *Clinical Psychology Review* 17: 375–406.

Knudsen, Eric I., James J. Heckman, Judy L. Cameron, and Jack P. Shonkoff. 2006.
  "Economic, Neurobiological, and Behavior Perspectives on Building America's Future
  Workforce." *Proceedings of the National Academy of Sciences* 103: 10155–62.

Krisberg, Barry, and James Austin. 1978. *The Children of Ishmael: Critical Perspectives on
  Juvenile Justice*. Palo Alto, CA: Mayfield.

Loeber, Rolf, David P. Farrington, Magda Stouthamer-Loeber, and Helene Raskin White.
  2008. *Violence and Serious Theft: Development and Prediction from Childhood to
  Adulthood*. New York: Routledge.

Lösel, Friedrich, and Andreas Beelmann. 2003. "Effects of Child Skills Training in
  Preventing Antisocial Behavior: A Systematic Review." *Annals of the American Academy
  of Political and Social Science* 587: 84–109.

Lösel, Friedrich, and Andreas Beelmann. 2006. "Child Social Skills Training." In *Preventing
  Crime: What Works for Children, Offenders, Victims, and Places*, edited by Brandon C.
  Welsh and David P. Farrington. New York: Springer.

Lösel, Friedrich, and Doris Bender. 2003. "Protective Factors and Resilience." In *Early
  Prevention of Adult Antisocial Behaviour*, edited by David P. Farrington and Jeremy
  W. Coid. New York: Cambridge University Press.

Lundman, Richard J. 2001. *Prevention and Control of Juvenile Delinquency*, 3rd ed. New York:
  Oxford University Press.

Mason, W. Alex, Rick Kosterman, J. David Hawkins, Kevin P. Haggerty, and Richard L. Spoth.
  2003. "Reducing Adolescents' Growth in Substance Use and Delinquency: Randomized
  Trial Effects of a Parent-Training Prevention Intervention." *Prevention Science* 4: 203–12.

McCord, Joan. 1978. "A Thirty-Year Follow-Up of Treatment Effects." *American Psychologist* 33: 284–89.

McCord, Joan. 2002. "Counterproductive Juvenile Justice." *Australian and New Zealand Journal of Criminology* 35: 230–37.

McCord, Joan. 2003. "Cures that Harm: Unanticipated Outcomes of Crime Prevention Programs." *Annals of the American Academy of Political and Social Science* 587: 16–30.

McCord, Joan, Cathy Spatz Widom, and Nancy A. Crowell, eds. 2001. *Juvenile Crime, Juvenile Justice*. Washington, DC: National Academy Press.

Mihalic, Sharon F., Abigail Fagan, Katherine Irwin, Diane Ballard, and Delbert S. Elliott. 2004. *Blueprints for Violence Prevention*. Washington, DC: Office of Juvenile Justice and Delinquency Prevention, U.S. Department of Justice.

Mytton, Julie A., Carolyn DiGuiseppi, David A. Gough, Rod S. Taylor, and Stuart Logan. 2002. "School-Based Violence Prevention Programs: Systematic Review of Secondary Prevention Trials." *Archives of Pediatric and Adolescent Medicine* 156: 752–62.

Nagin, Daniel S., Alex R. Piquero, Elizabeth S. Scott, and Laurence Steinberg. 2006. "Public Preferences for Rehabilitation Versus Incarceration of Juvenile Offenders: Evidence from a Contingent Valuation Survey." *Criminology and Public Policy* 5: 627–52.

O'Donnell, Julie, J. David Hawkins, Richard F. Catalano, Robert D. Abbott, and L. Edward Day. 1995. "Preventing School Failure, Drug Use, and Delinquency Among Low-Income Children: Long-Term Intervention in Elementary Schools." *American Journal of Orthopsychiatry* 65: 87–100.

Olds, David L., John Eckenrode, Charles R. Henderson, Harriet Kitzman, Jane Powers, Robert Cole, Kimberly Sidora, Pamela Morris, Lisa M. Pettitt, and Dennis W. Luckey. 1997. "Long-Term Effects of Home Visitation on Maternal Life Course and Child Abuse and Neglect: Fifteen-Year Follow-Up of a Randomized Trial." *Journal of the American Medical Association* 278: 637–43.

Olds, David L., Charles R. Henderson, Robert Chamberlin, and Robert Tatelbaum. 1986. "Preventing Child Abuse and Neglect: A Randomized Trial of Nurse Home Visitation." *Pediatrics* 78: 65–78.

Olds, David L., Charles R. Henderson, Robert Cole, John Eckenrode, Harriet Kitzman, Dennis W. Luckey, Lisa M. Pettitt, Kimberly Sidora, Pamela Morris, and Jane Powers. 1998. "Long-Term Effects of Nurse Home Visitation on Children's Criminal and Antisocial Behavior: 15-Year Follow-Up of a Randomized Controlled Trial." *Journal of the American Medical Association* 280: 1238–44.

Patterson, Gerald. 1982. *Coercive Family Process*. Eugene, OR: Castalia.

Patterson, Gerald, Patricia Chamberlain, and John B. Reid. 1982. "A Comparative Evaluation of a Parent Training Program." *Behavior Therapy* 13: 638–50.

Patterson, Gerald, John B. Reid, and Thomas J. Dishion. 1992. *Antisocial Boys*. Eugene, OR: Castalia.

Piquero, Alex R., David P. Farrington, Brandon C. Welsh, Richard E. Tremblay, and Wesley G. Jennings. 2009. "Effects of Early/Family Parent Training Programs on Antisocial Behavior and Delinquency." *Journal of Experimental Criminology* 5: 83–120.

Ripple, Carol H., and Edward Zigler. 2003. "Research, Policy, and the Federal Role in Prevention Initiatives for Children." *American Psychologist* 58: 482–90.

Roberts, Julian V., and Ross Hastings. 2007. "Public Opinion and Crime Prevention: A Review of International Findings." In *Learning from the Past—Planning for the Future*, edited by Ross Hastings and Melanie Bania. Ottawa, Canada: Institute for the Prevention of Crime, University of Ottawa.

Schweinhart, Lawrence J., Helen V. Barnes and David P. Weikart. 1993. *Significant Benefits: The High/Scope Perry Preschool Study through Age 27.* Ypsilanti, MI: High/Scope Press.

Schweinhart, Lawrence J., Jeanne Montie, Xiang Zongping, W. Steven Barnett, Clive R. Belfield, and Milagros Nores. 2005. *Lifetime Effects: The High/Scope Perry Preschool Study Through Age 40.* Ypsilanti, MI: High/Scope Press.

Schweinhart, Lawrence J., and David P. Weikart. 1980. *Young Children Grow Up: The Effects of the Perry Preschool Program on Youths Through Age 15.* Ypsilanti, MI: High/Scope Press.

Serketich, Wendy J., and Jean E. Dumas. 1996. "The Effectiveness of Behavioral Parent Training to Modify Antisocial Behavior in Children: A Meta-Analysis." *Behavior Therapy* 27: 171–86.

Shonkoff, Jack P. and Deborah A. Phillips, eds. 2000. *From Neurons to Neighborhoods: The Science of Early Childhood Development.* Washington, DC: National Academy Press.

Sloboda, Zili, Richard C. Stephens, Peggy C. Stephens, Scott F. Grey, Brent Teasdale, Richard D. Hawthorne, Joseph Williams, and Jesse F. Marquette. 2009. "The Adolescent Substance Abuse Prevention Study: A Randomized Field Trial of a Universal Substance Abuse Prevention Program." *Drug and Alcohol Dependence* 102: 1–10.

Tobler, Nancy S. 1986. "Meta-Analysis of 143 Drug Treatment Programs: Quantitative Outcome Results of Program Participants Compared to a Control or Comparison Group." *Journal of Drug Issues* 16: 537–67.

Tobler, Nancy S., Terri Lessard, Diana Marshall, Peter Ochshorn, and Michael Roona. 1999. "Effectiveness of School-Based Drug Prevention Programs for Marijuana Use." *School Psychology International* 20: 105–37.

Tremblay, Richard E., and Wendy M. Craig. 1995. "Developmental Crime Prevention." In *Building a Safer Society: Strategic Approaches to Crime Prevention. Crime and Justice: A Review of Research*, vol. 19, edited by Michael Tonry and David P. Farrington. Chicago: University of Chicago Press.

U.S. Department of Health and Human Services. 2001. *Youth Violence: A Report of the Surgeon General.* Rockville, MD: U.S. Department of Health and Human Services.

U.S. General Accountability Office. 2003. *Youth Illicit Drug Use Prevention: DARE Long- Term Evaluations and Federal Efforts to Identify Effective Programs.* Report GAO-03–172R. Washington, DC: U.S. General Accountability Office.

Wasserman, Gail A., and Laurie S. Miller. 1998. "The Prevention of Serious and Violent Juvenile Offending." In *Serious & Violent Juvenile Offenders: Risk Factors and Successful Interventions*, edited by Rolf Loeber and David P. Farrington. Thousand Oaks, CA: Sage.

Webster-Stratton, Carolyn, and Ted Taylor. 2001. "Nipping Early Risk Factors in the Bud: Preventing Substance Abuse, Delinquency, and Violence in Adolescence Through Interventions Targeted at Young Children (0–8 Years)." *Prevention Science* 2: 165–92.

Weis, Joseph G., and J. David Hawkins. 1981. *Preventing Delinquency.* Washington, DC: Office of Juvenile Justice and Delinquency Prevention, U.S. Department of Justice.

Weiss, Carol H., Erin Murphy-Graham, Anthony Petrosino, and Allison G. Gandhi. 2008. "The Fairy Godmother—and Her Warts: Making the Dream of Evidence-Based Policy Come True." *American Journal of Evaluation* 29: 29–47.

Welsh, Brandon C., and Akemi Hoshi. 2006. "Communities and Crime Prevention." In *Evidence-Based Crime Prevention*, rev. ed., edited by Lawrence W. Sherman, David P. Farrington, Brandon C. Welsh, Doris L. MacKenzie. New York: Routledge.

Wilson, David B., Denise C. Gottfredson, and Stacy S. Najaka. 2001. "School-Based Prevention of Problem Behaviors: A Meta-Analysis." *Journal of Quantitative Criminology* 17: 247–72.

Wilson, John J., and James C. Howell. 1993. *A Comprehensive Strategy for Serious, Violent, and Chronic Juvenile Offenders*. Washington, DC: U.S. Department of Justice, Office of Juvenile Justice and Delinquency Prevention.

Wilson, Sandra Jo, and Mark W. Lipsey. 2007. "School-Based Interventions for Aggressive and Disruptive Behavior: Update of a Meta-Analysis." *American Journal of Preventive Medicine* 33(2S): 130–43.

PART V

JUVENILE COURT: HISTORY AND CONTEXT

CHAPTER 19

......

THE ELUSIVE JUVENILE COURT
ITS ORIGINS, PRACTICES, AND RE-INVENTIONS

......

DAVID S. TANENHAUS

[T]he highest motives and most enlightened impulses led to
a peculiar system for juveniles, unknown to our law in any
comparable context. The constitutional and theoretical
basis for this peculiar system is—to say the least—
debatable. And in practice...the results have not been
entirely satisfactory.

—Justice Abe Fortas, United States Supreme Court,
In re Gault, 387 U.S. 1, 17–18 (1967)

ALTHOUGH there are legal casebooks on juvenile justice, there is neither a comprehensive history of a single juvenile court in the United States from its inception to the present nor a standard text on the history of American juvenile justice (Marcus and Rosenberg 2007; Feld 2009).[1] Instead, the scholarship by criminologists, historians, lawyers, and sociologists is a patchwork of generalizations about past and present trends in the history of juvenile justice,[2] intellectual histories, jurisprudential accounts (Ryerson 1978; Zimring 2005), close historical examinations of particular courts during their formative eras,[3] exposés of modern juvenile courts at work,[4] nuanced studies of gender and sexuality,[5] and recently, several insightful examinations of race and juvenile justice (Hawkins and Kempf-Leonard 2005; Chavez-Garcia 2007; Chavez-Garcia 2009; Ward 2009, Ward forthcoming; Bush 2010).[6] To assess this disparate body of literature, this essay proceeds chronologically from the Anglo-American revolution against authority in the seventeenth and eighteenth centuries to the present, pausing within specific historical eras to assess significant thematic issues.

The essay makes three interrelated arguments. First, even though the nation's first juvenile court did not open its doors until 1899, the ideological origins of the juvenile court predate the American Revolution and are embedded in democratic theory. The long history of the idea that children are different from adults and are less culpable for their actions helps to explain the resiliency of the juvenile court ideal in the United States (i.e., that the law should treat children differently from adults). Second, the juvenile court is an elusive institution. The diversity of juvenile court practices within and among states has made it nearly impossible to study *the* juvenile court.[7] Third, the protean character of the juvenile court also helps to explain its popularity in the United States and abroad. Communities across the globe have been able to use the idea of a separate court to hear children's cases to implement their own conceptions of juvenile justice.

Part I of this chapter traces the ideological origins and legal foundations of the juvenile court. Part II examines juvenile courts at work in the early twentieth century, their guiding principles, and the later development of federal juvenile justice in the 1930s. Part III assesses the U.S. Supreme Court's due process revolution that introduced more procedural requirements as well as lawyers into juvenile court during the 1960s, but simultaneously undercut one of the rationales (i.e., "the rehabilitative ideal") for having a separate justice system for juveniles. Part IV focuses on the "get tough" era of the 1980s and 1990s, a time when most states made it easier to prosecute adolescents in the criminal justice system. A brief conclusion focuses on the future of the juvenile court.

I. The Ideological Origins and Legal Foundation of Juvenile Court

The ideological and legal justifications for treating children accused of committing crimes differently from adults were forged in the seventeenth and eighteenth centuries. As historian Holly Brewer has shown, by emphasizing that people had a right to consent in religion and politics, English and American reformers launched a democratic revolution that fundamentally changed the nature of Anglo-American society. The architects of modern democratic theory, including the influential political and educational theorist John Locke, also argued that children lacked reason and thus should not be allowed to participate in self-government, have a voice in legal proceedings, or make binding contracts. Instead, it was the responsibility of their parents and/or the state to educate them so that they could later exercise the rights and obligations of citizenship. In theory and practice, children had a right to custody, not liberty (Brewer 2005).

This paternalistic understanding of children as a class in need of protection marked the beginning of a new chapter in the history of childhood. Previously, it was a parent's duty to rush his or her children toward adult status. As historian Steven Mintz has noted, "The middle of the eighteenth century saw the emergence of a new set of attitudes, which came to define modern childhood. A growing number of parents began to regard children as innocent, malleable, and fragile creatures who needed to be sheltered from contamination. Childhood was increasingly viewed as a separate stage of life that required special care and institutions to protect it" (Mintz 2004, p. 3). In the nineteenth century, middle-class families promoted this ideal of protected childhood by extending both how long children remained in their parents' home and at school. Over time, middle-class parents also became more conscious of the stages of child development, including the invention of the concept of adolescence in the early twentieth century (Mintz 2004).

By asserting that children lacked reason and required protection, the architects of democratic theory argued that children were less culpable for criminal offenses. The compilers of the common law, including the treatise writers Matthew Hale and William Blackstone, incorporated these assumptions about reasoning and responsibility into the criminal law and helped codify a tripartite schema for handling the cases of minors. Children under age 7 were immune from prosecution because they were considered incapable of having felonious discretion. "By the mid-nineteenth century," Brewer points out, "Hale's and Blackstone's dictum that those under age fourteen generally should not be held responsible for their crimes had become the standard guideline, repeated in the superior courts of most states"(Brewer 2005, pp 225–26). The state could rebut this presumption that a child between ages 7 and 14 was not responsible for his or her actions. Once children reached 14 years of age, they were tried and sentenced as adults.

The same legislators in the United States who were working out the implications of democratic theory, including a ban on children participating in self government, also redefined how citizens should be punished. The revolutionary generation, as Brewer reminds us, "initiated a sudden transformation away from such bodily punishments as branding, whipping, cutting off ears, castrating, and hanging toward imprisonment in its varied forms as the punishment for all crimes" (Brewer 2005, p. 228). By the 1830s, all of the states except two had established penitentiaries to rehabilitative offenders. They also built the first houses of refuge to separate juveniles from adult offenders.[8]

The opening in the 1820s and 1830s of Houses of Refuge laid the legal foundations for the juvenile court (Fox 1970; Cogan 1970; Curtis 1976; Grossberg 1996; Feld 1999; Schlossman 2005). The case of *Ex Parte Crouse*, 4 Wharton 9 (Pa. 1838), decided by the Pennsylvania Supreme Court, became the leading antebellum decision on the authority of the state to use indeterminate sentences to incarcerate children whose parents could not or would not care for them properly. The case involved Mary Ann Crouse. Her mother had filed a complaint against her, and an alderman serving as a justice of the peace had Mary Ann committed to the Philadelphia House of Refuge. Although her father filed a writ of habeas corpus asking for Mary Ann's release, the Pennsylvania Supreme Court did not free her. Instead, the court applied the concept of *parens patriae* (the state as parent) to justify the community acting as her guardian. In a per curium opinion, the court asked rhetorically:

> May not the natural parents, when unequal to the task of education, or unworthy
> of it, be superseded by the *parens patriae*, or common guardian of the
> community? It is to be remembered that the public has a paramount interest in
> the virtue and knowledge of its members, and that, of strict right, the business of
> education belongs to it. That parents are ordinarily entrusted with it, is because it
> can seldom be put into better hands; but where they are incompetent and
> corrupt, what is there to prevent the public from withdrawing their faculties, held
> as they obviously are, at its sufferance?

This decision was emblematic of what the legal historian William Novak has characterized as "the common law vision of a well-regulated society" that emphasized the social nature of human beings, including their place in local communities (Novak 1996). This vision of a well-regulated society granted discretionary power to local officials to police individual behavior for the sake of the welfare of the community.

In addition to its invocation of *parens patriae, Crouse* also analogized the reformatory to a school, not a prison. By characterizing the Philadelphia House of Refuge as a school, the Pennsylvania high court began a legal tradition of differentiating juvenile correctional institutions from adult prisons, even though houses of refuge and reform schools often became brutal mini-prisons for children (Schlossman 1993). Finally, by focusing on all children as dependent, *Crouse* downplayed potential differences between how the state should handle cases of child neglect and juvenile delinquency.

At the end of the nineteenth century, progressive child savers embedded the principle of undifferentiated handling of children's cases into the foundation of the juvenile court. They also made *Crouse*-like arguments to contend that juvenile courts, like house of refuges, did not punish children, but instead saved them. Accordingly, since juvenile courts were not adversarial settings like a criminal court, they should not have to follow formal criminal procedure and instead should be considered civil or chancery courts (Mack 1909, 1925). In her remembrance of the opening of the Chicago Juvenile Court in 1899, Jane Addams explained:

> There was almost a change in *mores* when the Juvenile Court was established. The
> child was brought before the judge with no one to prosecute him and with no one
> to defend him—the judge and all concerned were merely trying to find out what

could be done on his behalf. The element of conflict was absolutely eliminated and with it, all notion of punishment as such with its curiously belated connotation (Addams 1935, p. 137).

From this perspective, the needs of children mattered more than due process.

Although the common law vision of a well-regulated society gradually gave way to the rise of a more individually based conception of constitutional law after the Civil War, state courts continued to use *Crouse* as a precedent (Tanenhaus 2005). In 1905, for example, the Pennsylvania Supreme Court decided *Commonwealth v. Fisher*, 213 Pa. 48 (1905). Like *Crouse* more than a half century earlier, *Fisher* became the leading case of its time. Once again, the Pennsylvania Supreme Court used the theory of *parens patriae* to justify state intervention in the lives of children and their families. The court also brushed aside the argument that the juvenile court deprived children of the due process that they would have received if they had been prosecuted in criminal court. As the court explained,

> The objection that "the act offends against a constitutional provision in creating, by its terms, different punishments for the same offense by a classification of individuals," overlooks the fact, hereafter to be noticed, that it is not for the punishment of offenders, but for the salvation of children, and points out the way by which the state undertakes to save, not particular children of a special class, but all children under a certain age, whose salvation may become the duty of the state in the absence of proper parental care or disregard of it by wayward children. *No child under the age of sixteen is excluded from its beneficent protection* (213 Pa. at 53, emphasis added).

The intertwined ideas that children as a class were entitled only to custody and that the state should and could act as a caring parent protected the juvenile court until the 1960s from critics who questioned its constitutionality in more than forty jurisdictions (Paulsen 1996; Manfredi 1998; Feld 1999).

II. Progressive Juvenile Justice

The literature on the juvenile court in the early twentieth century has focused on urban courts to address two overarching questions. First, did the creation of the juvenile court, as the sociologist Anthony Platt famously argued, represent a radical break with the past (Platt 1969)? Second, did the early juvenile court function as the benevolent social welfare institution that Jane Addams described, or, as Platt argued, did middle-class child savers use it to expand state control over the lives of poor children and their families? (Addams 1935; Platt 1969) Or was it a combination of the two? To answer these questions about the workings of the first juvenile courts, historians have used primary sources, including case files, newspaper articles, and academic and government publications, to investigate these courts in Boston, Chicago, Detroit, Los Angeles, Memphis, and Milwaukee.

As these studies have shown, the political process ensured that the juvenile court had an inchoate beginning (Eliot 1914; Tanenhaus 2002).[9] Although the creators of the Chicago Juvenile Court, such as Addams, imagined that its hearings would be closed to the public and the press, a child's record would remain confidential, and no lawyers or juries would be present, the Illinois General Assembly instead passed a watered-down version of their bill. Thus the court initially had open hearings and public records, used juries in dependency cases, and lacked funding to pay probation officers or to maintain a detention home for children. A private association initially paid the salaries of the court's probation officers and ran the detention home. Protestant reformers and Catholic leaders also clashed repeatedly over the extent of the court's authority to police children and their families. The progressive juvenile court was a work in progress (Tanenhaus 2002, Tanenhaus 2004).

Although the structure and procedures of the juvenile court were developed over time, its clientele remained similar. The children of juvenile court came from predominantly poor and marginalized ethnic communities. In the early twentieth century, Poles and Italians were disproportionately represented in juvenile court, and later the same was true of African Americans and Latinos. The concentration of children from poor families explains why scholars have used class as the primary analytical category with which to analyze the rise of the juvenile court, including emphasizing the status differences between the court's creators and wards. The focus on northern and midwestern cities that had small African American populations also helps to explain why scholars focused less attention on race than they did on class (Schlossman and Tanenhaus 2009).

Now that scholars are studying the South, the Southwest, and the West, race is receiving more attention in the historical literature, including exploring how juvenile courts handled the cases of African American and Latino children. Writing about the disproportionate imprisonment of black youth in South in the early twentieth century, William S. Bush observes, "The roots of such disparities ran back to slavery and shaped the thinking of child savers who created juvenile justice and corrections. Put simply, white reformers did not include black children in the emerging idea of modern childhood, and unequal treatment largely persisted despite the strenuous efforts of African American reformers" (Bush 2010, p. 20). In the West and Southwest, Mexican American youth were treated much the same way that children from ethnically marginalized communities were in the Midwest and Northeast (Chavez-Garcia 2006).

Since the 1970s, scholars have used feminist theories to explain why juvenile courts treated boys' and girls' antisocial behavior differently. Although the original juvenile court law granted the Chicago Juvenile Court jurisdiction only over violations of ordinances and laws, reformers across the nation quickly amended juvenile court laws to include status offenses (i.e., behaviors such as incorrigibility or truancy that are only illegal because of the status of the person who commits them). This expanded jurisdiction allowed juvenile courts to charge girls with the "crime of precocious sexuality," or any behavior that challenged middle-class notions of gender and sexuality (Schlossman and Wallach 1978; "The Crime of Precocious

Sexuality" 2009). Girls, who constituted fewer than 20% of the cases in juvenile court, were incarcerated at substantially higher rates than boys for much of the twentieth century. Policing girls for status offenses became an entrenched practice in juvenile courts across North America (Sprott and Doob 2010).

As Mary Odem's work on Los Angeles in the early twentieth century has revealed, single mothers often used the juvenile court as a means to reassert parental control over their adolescent daughters. These girls, who embraced modern youth culture, were seeking more autonomy over their lives, including their wages or sexuality. The role of parents in initiating complaints challenged Platt's characterization of the juvenile court as an unwelcome intruder in the lives of working-class families (Odem 1995; Schlossman 2005), but also demonstrated how gendered juvenile justice has been since its inception.

Another prominent theme in the scholarship has been the central role that probation officers played in the administration of juvenile justice. As Schlossman revealed in his pioneering study of the Milwaukee Juvenile Court, the use of probation demonstrated a commitment on the part of the child savers to keep families together, including poor, immigrant ones (Schlossman 2005). He explained: "The main object of the child savers was not to invent new rationales, laws, and means to incarcerate lower-class children in long-term custodial institutions. Instead, without eliminating the option of commitment, indeed, using it quite consciously as a threat to motivate better behavior—the child savers sought primarily to develop effective oversight of delinquents in their own homes and under the watch of their own parents or guardians" (Schlossman 2005, xx). Although we still know very little about the lives of the men and women who staffed probation departments in the United States, they did much of the court's heavy lifting.[10] This included investigating a child's life and home, making recommendations to the judge, representing children during a hearing, and supervising them during probation.

The historical literature also reveals that the opening of a juvenile court did result in more children being arrested, but there were also simultaneous efforts to limit the number of children appearing before a juvenile court judge. For example, David Wolcott's work on the police and delinquency shows that the opening of a juvenile court in Detroit increased the number of arrests (Wolcott 2005). Yet judges also sought to limit the number of cases they heard. In Chicago, during his first three years as a juvenile court judge, Julian Mack heard more than 14,000 cases (Tanenhaus 2004, p. 47). The courtroom experience in early juvenile courts (as well as later ones) could be disorienting for children, their families, and even lawyers (Van Waters 1925; Molloy 1962; Buss 2009). Under the Illinois Juvenile Court Act, the court had to hear all cases in which a petition had been filed. Mack instituted an important change of procedure that became known as the complaint system. Instead of filing petitions against children, the court asked that concerned individuals file an informal complaint with the court's probation department. This allowed the probation department to investigate cases to determine whether they merited judicial attention. The complaint system, which became a defining feature of progressive juvenile justice by the 1920s, provided probation officers the necessary discretion to handle many cases informally (Tanenhaus 2002; see also Daniel Mears' Chapter 24 in this volume on intake and diversion in this volume).

Probation officers were also vital to the court's mission of transforming delinquent youth into law-abiding, productive citizens. According to Francis Allen's famous formulation, this rehabilitative ideal assumed that "human behavior is the product of antecedent causes" (Allen 1964, p. 26). Like a medical condition, delinquency could be diagnosed, treated, and cured. Moreover, the rehabilitative ideal assumed that the interests of the child and the state were identical, so that therapeutic measures could "be designed to effect changes in the behavior of the convicted person in the interest of his own happiness, health, and satisfaction and in the interest of social defense" (Allen 1964, p. 26). This interventionist vision of juvenile justice was based on the related beliefs that human beings are malleable and that there was a societal consensus about how people should be taught to live their lives properly (Allen 1981).

The rehabilitative ideal was not limited to children and youth (Polsky 1991). The rise of positivist criminology that emphasized environmental factors over individual free will and faith in a therapeutic state also reshaped the administration of criminal justice, including promoting the use of indeterminate sentencing, probation, and parole for adult offenders (Rothman 1980; Willrich 2003). The later erosion of a social consensus about moral values in the 1960s and 1970s, including the breakdown of "dominant norms about the family, gender roles, age, and even reproduction as they were subjected to radical change and revision," ultimately undermined the rehabilitative ideal (Allen 1981; Mintz 2004, p. 4).

The rehabilitative ideal was only the most prominent rationale for juvenile justice. Sparing children "from the savagery of the criminal courts and prison," as Franklin E. Zimring has shown, was also a guiding principle of the juvenile court (Zimring 2000, p. 2480). This diversionary rationale made increasing sense in a society in which the modern ideal of a sheltered childhood became nearly universal by the 1950s (Mintz 2004). By the late twentieth century, the social revolution in values that had already shattered the rehabilitative ideal also threatened to undermine the modern ideal of childhood as well as the diversionary rationale.

From the creation of the juvenile court, judges had to address difficult cases involving adolescents who had committed serious and violent offenses and/or appeared to be mentally ill. Although judges did transfer a small percentage of adolescents to the criminal court in the early twentieth century, progressive child savers and the courts did not compile detailed reports on these cases. Moreover, once a child was transferred out of juvenile court, he or she ceased to be considered a child who would be counted in the official tabulation of "children in the courts" (Tanenhaus 2002, p. 25).

The problem of what to do with recidivists, especially older adolescents, threatened the legitimacy of the juvenile court from the beginning. The problem of recidivists, in fact, led to the first intensive medical and psychological study of juvenile delinquents in the twentieth century. Beginning with the 1909 opening in Chicago of the Juvenile Psychopathic Institute, the neurologist William Healy studied the children of juvenile court. In 1915, Healy published his findings in *The Individual Delinquent* (Healy 1915). Considered by modern criminologists to be a classic in the field of multiple-factor approach to understanding juvenile offending, many of Healy's findings, including calling for early intervention, mirror many of the recommendations by current experts on serious and violent juvenile offenders (Laub 2002). Although few juvenile courts opened clinics, psychological and psychiatric approaches to the prevention of juvenile delinquency became increasingly popular in the child guidance movement of the 1920s and 1930s. As Kathleen W. Jones has shown (Jones 1991), this psychological approach also informed parental guidance manuals, including Dr. Benjamin Spock's bestseller *Common Sense Book of Baby and Child Care* (Spock 1957).

By 1920, however, the juvenile court movement was in crisis. Although forty-six states had passed juvenile court laws, a comprehensive study by the U.S. Children's Bureau revealed that many jurisdictions still detained children in jails, fewer than half of the nation's juvenile courts had probation departments, and only 7% provided psychiatric services (U.S. Children's Bureau 1920). These findings prompted the Children's Bureau and the National Probation Association to work together to develop national standards for the administration of juvenile court.

Completed in 1923, *Juvenile-Court Standards*, which the Children's Bureau published without any changes until 1954, served as the programmatic capstone of progressive juvenile justice (U.S. Children's Bureau 1923). In her foreword to the standards, chief of the Children's Bureau Grace Abbott highlighted the report's four overarching principles:

(1) That the court dealing with children should be clothed with broad jurisdiction, embracing all classes of cases in which a child is in need of the protection of the State, whether the legal action is in the name of the child or an adult who fails in his obligations toward the child.

(2) that the court should have a scientific understanding of each child;

(3) that treatment should be adapted to individual needs;

(4) that there should be a presumption in favor of keeping the child in his own home and his own community, except when adequate investigation shows this not be in the best interests of the child.

As the need for the standards themselves demonstrated, these principles about individualized justice were aspirations and did not reflect general practice across the nation.

By 1930, the efforts of progressive child savers, including the National Probation Association and the United States Children's Bureau, did prompt the majority of states to raise the maximum age of jurisdiction for children's courts to 18; and Arkansas, California, Colorado, Iowa and Wyoming set theirs at 21. Simultaneously, state legislatures also began to exclude serious and violent offenses, including murder and other crimes punishable by death or life imprisonment, from the jurisdiction of juvenile court. The combination of higher jurisdictional age limits and legislatively excluded offenses remained fairly constant in most states, with few exceptions, until the 1970s (Tanenhaus 2000).

The juvenile court movement, however, remained a state phenomenon in the early twentieth century. For example, in her 1922 Children's Bureau study, "The Federal Courts and the Delinquent Child," Ruth Bloodgood reported: "No separate provisions exist under Federal law for jurisdiction over juvenile cases; and so the children who violate such acts as the postal, interstate-commerce, internal-revenue, and drug laws, or those who are arrested for larceny of United States property, trespassing on United States property, forgery, and embezzlement of Government property, are under the jurisdiction of the United States district courts" (Bloodgood 1922, p. 3). And, as Grace Abbott noted in her letter of transmittal to the Secretary of Labor, "It will doubtless surprise many who have been interested in the development of the juvenile-court system to find that our Federal laws, like the old common criminal law, makes no distinction between adults and children. In consequence little children are still proceeded against in the United States courts by the ordinary method of arrest, detention in jail with adults pending arraignment for bail, indictment by the grand jury, and final discharge or sentence of fine or imprisonment" (Abbott 1922, p. v).

There were three outcomes in these federal cases. First, juries convicted children, "sometimes in spite of doubt in the minds of the authorities as to whether such disposition is in accord with real justice." The second outcome was "the dismissing or nol-prossing of the case or refusal to indict." Third, and most important was "the use of various expedients not specifically provided by law, which it is hoped will more nearly achieve justice, the correction and training of the offender, and the protection of the community" (Bloodgood 1922, p. 66). These "expedients" included "immediate reference of the case to the juvenile courts by post-office inspectors and United States attorneys"; "the use of informal probation by the Federal authorities themselves, prior to the hearing or pending continuance on condition of good behavior" (this informal practice predated the passage of a federal probation law in 1924); "short-term jail sentences"; and "sentences to one day in the custody of the United States marshal" (Bloodgood 1922, p. 67). As Bloodgood noted: "Except the reference to juvenile courts, none of these methods of handling children's cases is satisfactory, because the authorities have no facilities for ascertaining the necessary facts about the child and his environment, nor the means for the intensive supervision and reconstructive work essential to treatment of delinquents in the community" (p. 67). Thus, federal officials were implementing quasi-legal responses to juvenile crime.

In 1932 and 1938, Congress passed the first two federal juvenile justice laws, including the Act to Provide for the Care and Treatment of Juvenile Delinquents.[11] This law allowing federal district courts to operate like juvenile courts when they heard delinquency cases was significant for two reasons. First, it demonstrated the continued attractiveness of the juvenile court ideal. Second, federal cases later played an important role in the U.S. Supreme Court developing its juvenile court jurisprudence (Manfredi 1998).

In conclusion, the historical scholarship on progressive juvenile justice has focused almost exclusively on urban courts in the early twentieth century. The literature demonstrates that the child savers' vision for the juvenile court often proved elusive in practice. The juvenile court movement did succeed, however, in institutionalizing the idea that all children and adolescents, with few exceptions, should have their cases heard in a separate court system. Yet more work on the juvenile court in the middle decades of the twentieth century remains to be done, including studies of the administration of juvenile justice in the nation's rural jurisdictions and also by federal district courts.

III. The Transformation of the Juvenile Court

From 1961 to 1972, the Supreme Court issued eleven decisions, collectively known as the "due process revolution," that sought to nationalize due process in the nation's courts. (Manfredi 1998). The constitutional revolution, which initially focused on criminal courts, ultimately affected juvenile justice. Scholars argue that the court's 1967 decision *In re Gault*, 387 U.S. 1 (1967), written by Justice Abe Fortas, by stripping the juvenile court of its traditional rationale, transformed it (Manfredi 1998; Feld 1999). Drawing on Nicholas de B. Katzenbach's *The Challenge of Crime in a Free Society* (1967) and studies of juvenile courts by leading lawyers and social scientists, including many funded by grants from the U.S. Department of Health, Education, and Welfare, Justice Fortas demonstrated how much the reality of juvenile justice in the 1960s contradicted the benevolent rhetoric that had long justified its informal proceedings. In *Gault*, the court extended limited due process protections to minors in juvenile court adjudicatory hearings, including the right to notice, counsel, confrontation and cross-examination of witnesses, and the privilege against self-incrimination. *Gault* also left many constitutional questions unanswered, including the standards that juvenile court should use to determine guilt, whether bail, appellate review and juries were required, and if double jeopardy applied (Dorsen and Reznick 1967).[12]

Barry Feld contends that this landmark decision had deleterious consequences because "the Court's insistence on greater procedural safeguards transformed the juvenile court from a social welfare agency into a wholly owned subsidiary of the criminal justice system" (Feld 1999, p. 81).[13] Moreover, he adds, "*Gault*'s insistence on procedural safeguards legitimated the imposition of punitive sentences that now fall disproportionately heavily on minority offenders" (Feld 1999, p. 81). According to Feld, a combination of structural changes in American society, including the baby boom, a rising crime rate, the great migration of African Americans from the South to the North, the civil rights movement, and a general loss of faith in coercive governmental programs to change people's behavior, all helped to set the stage for the Supreme Court to critically examine the juvenile court in the 1960s (Feld 1999).

In addition, a number of states, including New York, California, and Illinois, had revised their laws to provide more procedural protections for children in juvenile court. Finally, the American Civil Liberties Union was also becoming interested in children's rights cases at this time and ultimately played a leading role in convincing the Supreme Court to hear *Gault* (Tanenhaus 2011)

The year before its *Gault* decision, the U.S. Supreme Court decided *Kent v. United States*, 383 U.S. 541 (1966), a District of Columbia case that involved the transfer from juvenile court to adult court of 16-year-old Morris Kent Jr., whose fingerprints were found in the apartment of a woman who had been raped and robbed. Although the Court decided *Kent* on statutory rather than constitutional grounds, Fortas's opinion for the Court established the intellectual framework for *Gault*. For instance, Fortas explained that studies of the juvenile court had revealed "grounds for concern that the child receives the worst of both worlds: that he gets neither the protections accorded to adults nor the solicitous care and regenerative treatment postulated for children" (383 U.S. at 556). In his assessment of the significance of *Kent*, Christopher Manfredi explains: "Without any opposition within the Court on the merits, the majority opinion acknowledged procedural and substantive deficiencies in juvenile proceedings, agreed that certain aspects of juvenile proceedings should be subject to constitutional review on due process grounds, and suggested a standard to apply in that review—the 'essentials of due process and treatment'"(Manfredi 1998, p. 78.).

The next year, the Supreme Court used the case of 15-year-old Gerald Gault to extend the logic of *Kent* to hold that children during adjudicatory hearings in juvenile court were constitutionally entitled to procedural due process protections. Gault, who had been accused of making a lewd phone call to a neighbor, was serving an indeterminate sentence in the Arizona State Industrial School. Thus, he could possibly spend six years in prison. In Arizona, an adult charged with the same offense could be sentenced to only sixty days in jail and fined $50. It appeared that the juvenile court had provided Gerald Gault with the worst of both worlds (Cortner and Lytle 1971; Manfredi 1998; Tanenhaus 2011).[14]

Like the U.S. Supreme Court's landmark decision in *Brown v. Board of Education*, 347 U.S. 483 (1954), that declared segregated schools unconstitutional, *Gault* proved difficult to implement.[15] For example, Norman Lefstein, Vaughan Stapleton, and Lee Teitelbaum studied three urban courts before and after *Gault*. They found that judges in one of the court systems did not inform juveniles of their right to counsel. The second court system informed only 3% of the juveniles of this constitutional right, and the third system informed them in 56% of the cases. Judges in these courts also rarely informed juveniles of their rights to confrontation and the privilege against self-incrimination (Lefstein, Stapleton, and Teitelbaum 1969). Studies of rural courts also revealed that judges rarely followed the court's *Gault* opinion (Canon and Kolsen 1971). The lack of procedural due process protections in many of the nation's juvenile courts, including notifying juveniles of their right to counsel, continues to the present (Feld 1999; see also Feld's Chapter 27 on juvenile procedural rights in this volume).

As the U.S. Supreme Court's due process revolution came to an end in the early 1970s, in *McKeiver v. Pennsylvania*, 403 U.S. 528 (1971), writing for a divided Burger Court, Justice Harry Blackmun stopped short of requiring juvenile courts to provide jury trials. As he explained, they would "remake the juvenile proceeding into a fully adversary process and put an effective end to what has been the idealistic prospect of an intimate, informal protective proceeding" (403 U.S. at 545). Thus, the U.S. Supreme Court did not require juvenile courts to provide juveniles with all the due process protections required in criminal court, including a right to a jury trial and also a right to appellate review.

Significantly, in an argument similar to Feld's, Christopher Manfredi contends that the U.S. Supreme Court's trilogy of juvenile justice decisions (*Kent, Gault,* and *Winship*) collectively "articulated a new conception of childhood that embodied a broader understanding of children's capacity for independent judgment and action. This new perspective encouraged both reform advocates and state legislatures to shift the focus on juvenile court proceedings from identifying and eliminating the behavioral causes of delinquency to holding juveniles more directly accountable for the harm caused by their offenses" (Manfredi 1998, p. 159). Increasingly, the philosophy of "just deserts" became the rallying cry of crime control advocates who argued that state legislatures should pass mandatory transfer laws that transformed children and adolescents who committed serious and violent crimes into automatic adults whose cases should be prosecuted in criminal court.[16]

Following the pattern that had begun in the Progressive Era, national experts continued to strive to make the juvenile court experience more uniform within and between states. Unlike earlier periods, they could no longer rely on *parens patriae* ideology to justify the existence of a separate justice system for juveniles. Instead, they turned to core common law concepts that undergirded criminal law. For example, the Institute of Judicial Administration and the American Bar Association joined forces to draft new standards for juvenile justice and in 1977 published twenty-three volumes of juvenile justice standards and commentary. Collectively, they called for replacing juvenile courts with family courts that had broad jurisdiction, including divorce and adoption. They focused attention on the dismal state of juvenile corrections, argued that courts should make objective dispositional decisions based on "theories of fairness, justifiable intervention, proportionality, [and] determinacy," and advocated mandatory appointment of counsel (Manfredi 1998, p. 160.)

The following year, the Twentieth Century Fund's Juvenile Justice Task Force produced an influential report on the sentencing of young offenders in both juvenile and criminal court (Zimring 1978). This report also called for integrating traditional legal norms, including culpability and proportionality, into sentencing. Significantly, the Task Force rejected the conception of rehabilitation and instead called for providing "room to reform" for adolescents, which meant providing them "with the opportunity to pass through this crime-prone stage of development with their life chances intact" (Zimring 1978, p. 163). This innovative approach laid the groundwork for later attempts by the MacArthur Foundation, beginning in the 1990s, to use research on adolescent development to refocus juvenile justice policy.[17]

The federal government also now played a more prominent role in developing and implementing national standards. The enactment of the Juvenile Justice and Delinquency Prevention Act in 1974 created the Office of Juvenile Justice and Delinquency Prevention, provided block grants to states, created advisory groups to assist state governors in the allocation of federal funds, and established the National Advisory Committee for Juvenile Justice and Delinquency Prevention to develop national standards for the administration of juvenile justice. The federal law required states participating in the program to remove within two years all status offenders from secure detention and correctional facilities and to ensure that all juvenile prisoners were separated from adult offenders in prisons. As a result, by the end of the twentieth century, the cases of status offenders dropped to approximately 15% of the juvenile court's caseload. Status offenders were also institutionalized much less frequently than they had been earlier in the twentieth century (Teitelbaum 2002). The overall drop in the number of status offender cases, however, masks how girls' cases were handled, including the use of valid court order violations and private facilities to incarcerate them (Sprott and Doob 2010; Kempf-Leonard's Chapter 21 in this volume on girls).

In 1980, the National Advisory Committee published its own standards that sought to "provide for greater equity, consistency and fairness in proceeding affecting juveniles, a more efficient and respected court, and a stronger, more effective system of justice for juveniles, their families, and the public" (Department of Justice 1980, p. ix). Building on important work done by the Institute of Judicial Administration, the American Bar Association, and the Twentieth Century's Juvenile Justice Task Force, the standards, according to Manfredi, emphasized "the reorganization of jurisdiction over juveniles and the gradual narrowing of its delinquency component; the need for formal adjudication procedures and the expansion of due process in juvenile courts; a somewhat greater emphasis on offenses than on offenders; and the need to limit dispositional discretion" (Manfredi 1998, p. 169.)

The Committee sought to combine the traditional ideal of the juvenile court as a protective institution committed to rehabilitation with the due process protections, including limiting the discretion of judges in their dispositional decisions. As the Committee stressed, juveniles deserved the best of both worlds, including the due process protections "accorded to adults" in criminal court, coupled with the "solicitous care and regenerative treatment postulated for children" in the ideal juvenile court (Department of Justice 1980, p. 13.)

Yet these proposals never had a chance to take root. Instead, as Elizabeth Scott and Laurence Steinberg have pointed out, "violent juvenile crimes rates started to climb in the late 1980s, triggering a new wave of reforms under which young criminals increasingly were either classified as adults or punished severely within the juvenile system. Thus, the youth advocates who sought to change the traditional juvenile system ultimately lost control of the reform process. The justice system that has emerged is a far cry from the ideal that the reformers in the 1970s envisioned" (Scott and Steinberg 2008, p. 91).[18]

In retrospect, the 1980 standards represented the end of an era that sought to reconcile the ideology of *parens patriae* with procedural due process protections to produce a juvenile court that would provide children with the best of both worlds. The "get tough" approach developed first at the state level, and later endorsed by the National Advisory Committee during the Reagan Administration, shifted the focus of juvenile justice from child protection to emphasizing public safety (Manfredi 1998). Thus, the constitutional domestication of the juvenile court ultimately transformed the juvenile court, undercut its rehabilitative rationale, and contributed to recriminalizing juvenile justice in the 1980s and 1990s.

IV. The Get Tough Era

In response to a soaring rate of juvenile arrests for serious and violent juvenile crime in the late 1980s and early 1990s, including the doubling of the murder rate, and concerns that a new breed of "superpredators" had emerged, most states passed laws making it easier to prosecute children's cases in the criminal court system (Fox 1995, 1997; Bennett, DiIulio, and Walters 1996; Fagan and Zimring 2000; Feld's Chapter 32 in this volume on waiver; Snyder's Chapter 1 on juvenile crime trends in this volume).[19] By 1995, for instance, twenty-seven states allowed for the prosecution of a 10-year-old, charged with murder, as an adult (Department of Justice 1995, pp. 86–87). The trend to punish adolescents more severely in both juvenile and criminal courts was part of the dramatic increase in the use of imprisonment in the United States during the late twentieth century. "From 1929 to 1967," as the criminologist Mona Lynch notes, "the U.S. state and prison incarceration rate hovered around 100 prisoners per 100,000 population," and then in the early 1970s began "a slow but consistent decline, which seemed to signify a new horizon in penology that moved corrections away from isolated total institutions and back into less restrictive community settings." Yet "[b]y the late 1970s, the U.S. prison population began a rather sharp ascent, and this acceleration, it turned out, has continued (although it has slowed since the late 1990s) into the twenty-first century. Consequently, a mere 25 years after what looked like the demise, or at least the diminution of incarceration, the national imprisonment rate had nearly quintupled to 410 prisoners per 100,000 population. By the end of 2006, more than 1.5 million people were in state and federal prisons in the United States—about 1.1 million more than were incarcerated just 25 years earlier" (Lynch 2010, p. 2). The historian Heather Ann Thompson has argued that the rise of mass incarceration ultimately shaped the lives of all Americans in fundamental ways by the early twenty-first century (Thompson 2010).

Initially, the juvenile justice system spared many children and adolescents from the "get tough" approach. As Zimring has shown, during the 1970s and 1980s "the diversionary objective of the juvenile justice insulated delinquents from the brunt of a high magnitude expansion in incarceration in the criminal justice system" (Zimring

2000, p. 2493). The success of diverting youths from the criminal justice system helps to explain why in the 1990s the juvenile court became a target for "get tough" proponents. The punitive turn in American juvenile law, including transferring younger adolescents to criminal court, raised troubling questions about differential handling of cases based on race and ethnicity (Hawkins and Kempf-Leonard 2005; Tonry 2008; Bishop and Leiber's chapter in this volume on racial and ethnic differences); the competency of younger adolescents to stand trial, (Grisso and Schwartz 2000; Viljoen, Penner, and Roesch's chapter on competence and criminal responsibility in this volume); the related issue of the culpability of adolescent offenders for their offenses; and the economic costs and effectiveness of prosecuting juveniles as adult offenders (Zimring 1998; Feld 1999; Scott and Steinberg 2008; Mulvey and Schubert's chapter 33 on youth in prison in this volume).

The "get tough" era for adults and children, as Michael Tonry has noted, meant that Americans supported punishing their fellow citizens in ways that were "unimaginable in most other Western countries," including allowing "capital punishment, sentences for life without the possibility of parole, mandatory minimum sentences measured in decades, and prosecution of children as if they were adults" (Tonry 2008, p. 3). These harsh practices led scholars to mine American history and culture for explanations of the widening divide between American and European approaches to criminal punishment (Whitman 2003; Tonry 2008).

Significantly, by the time that many "tough on crime" laws were being adopted in the mid 1990s, the nation's rate of youth violence had already begun to decline rapidly. This drop in crime opened up the possibility of refocusing juvenile justice policies. The John T. and Catherine D. MacArthur Foundation, for example, spent $150 million to support research on adolescent psychological development to develop sound public policies that addressed the related issues of competency and culpability. The MacArthur Foundation also launched model programs in Pennsylvania, Illinois, Louisiana, and Washington. Proponents of using a developmental framework, such as Elizabeth Scott and Laurence Steinberg, contend that using science to develop rational policy "is the key to creating a stable regime that is fair to juvenile offenders and promotes social welfare" (Scott and Steinberg 2008, p. 27; Bishop and Feld's Chapter 35 in this volume on current trends).

V. Conclusion: The Resilient Juvenile Court

In hindsight, the deep roots of the idea that the law should treat children differently from adults in American law and democratic theory made the invention of the juvenile court seem inevitable. They also make its abolition appear unlikely, especially since scientists and the courts continue to reaffirm the longstanding idea that children and adolescents are immature, vulnerable, and malleable (*Roper v. Simmons*, 543 U.S. 551 [2005]).[20] American democracy, however, is a messy process. That social fact has ensured that the borders of juvenile justice have always been (and will always be) contested. They have changed over the course of a more than a century, with the get tough reforms of the 1980s and 1990s standing out. Despite jurisdictional changes, procedural reforms, and the erosion of the rehabilitative ideal, the juvenile court remains a flawed but resilient fixture in modern American governance.

NOTES

For their valuable comments on drafts of this chapter, I would like to thank the editors, Donna Bishop and Barry Feld, and my fellow historians, William S. Bush, Joseph "Andy" Fry, Marcia Gallo, Michael S. Green, Colin Loader, Mary Wammack, Paul Werth, Tom Wright, and David Wrobel. I also would also like to thank Dina Titus for inviting me to present this chapter at the interdisciplinary research roundtable "On Top of Black Mountain" and to express my appreciation to Carol Harter, Executive Director of the Black Mountain Institute, and Associate Director Richard Wiley.

1. Rosenheim, et al. (2002) provide historical perspectives on juvenile justice practices and policy, but it is not a comprehensive history of the American juvenile court.

2. For an overview of the evolution of the historical literature on juvenile court, see Chavez-Garcia (2009) and Schlossman and Tanenhaus (2009). Excellent accounts of more recent trends include Feld (1999); Fagan and Zimring (2000); and Scott and Steinberg (2008).

3. Case studies include two books on Boston (Schneider 1992; Holloran 1994); several on Chicago (Gittens 1994; Getis 2000; Knupfer 2001; Tanenhaus 2004; Platt 2009); two on Los Angeles (Odem 1995; Wolcott 2005); and ones on Milwaukee (Schlossman 2005) and Memphis (Trost 2005).

4. This genre also includes works by judges, probation officers, and journalists. Notable studies include Prescott (1981), Bortner (1982), Polier (1989), Butterfield (1995), Humes (1996), and Corriero (2006).

5. Meda Chesney-Lind's pioneering scholarship on female delinquency inspired much of the later historical scholarship on gender and juvenile justice (Chesney-Lind 1973; Chesney-Lind 1974; Alexander 1995; Odem 1995; Knupfer 2001). There is also excellent work on gender and Canadian juvenile justice (Strange 1995; Myers 2006) and an outstanding comparative study of the United States and Canada (Sprott and Doob 2009).

6. Race is also a central theme in Feld (1999); Trost (2005); and Penn, Greene, and Gabbion (2006).

7. On this point, see Rothman (1980, p. 236). The National Center for Juvenile Justice provides profiles of the systems used in all fifty states and the District of Columbia: http://www.ncjj.org/stateprofiles/.

8. The classic accounts of the response to juvenile delinquency in the nineteenth century include Pickett (1969); Hawes (1971); Bremner (1970–1974); Mennel (1973); Brenzel (1983). On the rise of the prison in the United States more generally, see Rothman (1971) and McLennan (2008).

9. On the role of women's organizations in the juvenile court movement, see Clapp (1998).

10. In her study of girl delinquency in Montreal, Myers provides the best biographical descriptions of probation officers in the early twentieth century (Myers 2006).

11. In 1932, the United States enacted the Act to Provide for the Transportation of Certain Juvenile Offenders to States Under the Law of Which They Have Committed Offenses or Are Delinquent, and For Other Purposes.

12. In *In re Winship*, 397 U.S. 358 (1970), the Court held the that the "beyond a reasonable doubt" standard that is required in criminal trials must also be used in juvenile delinquency proceedings; in *Breed v. Jones*, 421 U.S. 519 (1975), the Court declared that the "the double jeopardy" rule (i.e., a person cannot be prosecuted twice for the same crime) required in criminal law must also be applied to juvenile proceedings; and in *Schall v. Martin*, 467 U.S. 253 (1984), the Court allowed for the preventive detention of juveniles who posed a serious risk to commit an offense before trial.

13. Manfredi (1998) makes a similar argument about the unintended consequences of the Supreme Court's juvenile justice decisions. He draws, however, more explicitly on the political science literature that examines the institutional capacity of courts, including the Supreme Court, to enact policy. Important works on this subject include Horowitz (1977) and Rosenberg (1991).

14. The National Juvenile Defender Center hosts a website devoted to the case. http://www.njdc.info/gaultat40/gault_home.htm.

15. For the difficulties in implementing *Brown*, see (Rosenberg 1991). Manfredi (1998) provides a succinct overview of the similar problems with implementing *Gault*.

16. In 1978, for example, New York passed the Juvenile Offender Act that allowed adolescents as young as 13 to be prosecuted for murder and face the same sentences as adults (Butterfield 1995).

17. For an introduction to the MacArthur Foundation Initiative see Grisso and Schwartz (2000).

18. For an overview of the structure of modern juvenile justice, see Rosenheim (2002).

19. For an excellent account of the impact of new legislation on one state, see Singer (1996).

20. Since the early twentieth century, several critics have called for the abolition of the juvenile court. Feld (1999) provides the most compelling case for its abolition.

REFERENCES

Abbott, Grace. 1922. "Letter of Transmittal, Nov. 19, 1921." In *The Federal Courts and the Delinquent Child: A Study of the Methods: A Study of the Methods of Dealing with Children Who Have Violated Federal Laws*. Washington, DC: U.S. Government Printing Office.

Addams, Jane. 1935. *My Friend, Julia Lathrop*. New York: MacMillan.

Alexander, Ruth M. 1995. *The "Girl Problem:" Female Sexual Delinquency in New York, 1900–1930*. Ithaca, NY: Cornell University Press.

Allen, Francis A. 1964. "Legal Values and the Rehabilitative Ideal." In *The Borderland of Criminal Law: Essays in Law and Criminology*. Chicago: University of Chicago Press.

Allen, Francis A. 1981. *The Decline of the Rehabilitative Ideal: Penal Policy and Social Purpose*. New Haven, CT: Yale University Press.

Bennett, William, John DiIulio, Jr., and John Walters. 1996. *Body Count: Moral Poverty and How to Win America's War against Crime and Drugs*. New York: Simon & Schuster.

Bloodgood, Ruth. 1922. *The Federal Courts and the Delinquent Child: A Study of the Methods of Dealing with Children who have violated federal laws*. Washington, DC: U.S. Government Printing Office.

Bortner, M.A. 1982. *Inside a Juvenile Court: The Tarnished Ideal of Individualized Justice*. New York: New York University Press.

Bremner, Robert H. 1970–1974 ed. *Children and Youth in America: A Documentary History*. Cambridge, MA: Harvard University Press.

Brenzel, Barbara M. 1983. *Daughters of the State: A Social Portrait of the First Reform School for Girls in North America, 1856–1905*. Cambridge, MA: MIT Press.

Brewer, Holly. 2005. *By Birth or Consent: Children, Law, & the Anglo-American Revolution in Authority*. Chapel Hill, NC: University of North Carolina Press.

Bush, William S. 2010. *Who Gets a Childhood?: Race and Juvenile Justice in Twentieth-Century Texas*. Athens, GA: University of Georgia Press.

Buss, Emily. 2009. "Rethinking the Connection between Developmental Science and Juvenile Justice." *University of Chicago Law Review* 76: 493–515.

Butterfield, Fox. 1995. *All God's Children: The Bosket Family and the American Tradition of Violence*. New York: Knopf.

Canon, Bradley C., and Kenneth L. Kolson. 1971. "Rural Compliance with *Gault*: Kentucky, a Case Study." *Journal of Family Law* 10: 300–26.

Chavez-Garcia, Miroslava. 2006. "Youth, Evidence, and Agency: Mexican and Mexican American Youth at the Whittier State School, 1890–1920." *Azlan: A Journal of Chicano Studies* 31(Fall): 55–83.

Chavez-Garcia, Miroslava. 2007. "Anthony M. Platt's *The Child Savers: The Invention of Delinquency*." *Reviews in American History* 35: 464–81.

Chavez-Garcia, Miroslava. 2009. "Introduction." In *The Child Savers: The Invention of Delinquency*, 40th anniversary ed. New Brunswick, NJ: Rutgers University Press.

Chesney-Lind, Meda. 1973. "Judicial Enforcement of the Female Sex Role: The Family Court and the Female Delinquent." *Issues in Criminology* 8(Fall): 51–69.

Chesney-Lind, Meda. 1974. "Juvenile Delinquency: The Sexualization of Female Crime." *Psychology Today* 8(July): 43–46.

Clapp, Elizabeth J. 1998. *Mothers of All Children: Women Reformers and the Rise of Juvenile Courts in Progressive Era America*. University Park, PA: Pennsylvania State University Press.

Cogan, Neil H. 1970. "Juvenile Law, Before and After the Entrance of 'Parens Patriae.'" *South Carolina Law Review* 22: 147–81.

Corriero, Michael. 2006. *Judging Children as Children: A Proposal for a Juvenile Justice System*. Philadelphia, PA: Temple University Press.

Cortner, Richard C., and Clifford M. Lytle. 1971. *Constitutional Law and Politics: Three Arizona Cases*. Tucson, AZ: University of Arizona Press.

Curtis, George B. 1976. "The Checkered Career of Parens Patriae: The State as Parent or Tyrant?" *DePaul Law Review* 25: 895–915.

Department of Justice. 1980. National Advisory Committee for Juvenile Justice and Delinquency Prevention. *Standards for the Administration of Juvenile Justice*. Washington, DC: U.S. Government Printing Office.

Department of Justice. 1995. *Juvenile Offenders and Victims: A National Report*. Washington, DC: U.S. Government Printing Office.

Dorsen, Norman, and Daniel Rezneck. 1967. "*In re Gault* and the Future of Juvenile Law." *Family Law Quarterly* 1: 1–46.

Eliot, Thomas D. 1914. *The Juvenile Court and the Community*. New York: MacMillan.

Fagan, Jeffrey, and Franklin E. Zimring, eds. 2000. *The Changing Borders of Juvenile Justice: Transfer of Adolescents to the Criminal Court*. Chicago, IL: University of Chicago Press.

Feld, Barry C. 1999. *Bad Kids: Race and the Transformation of the Juvenile Court*. New York: Oxford University Press.

Feld, Barry C. 2009. *Cases and Materials on Juvenile Justice Administration*, 3rd ed. St. Paul, MN: Thompson/West.

Fox, James A. 1995. "Trends in Juvenile Violence: A Report to the United States Attorney General on Current and Future Rates of Juvenile Offending." *Bureau of Justice Statistics*. Washington, DC: U.S. Government Printing Office.

Fox, James A. 1997. "Trends in Juvenile Violence: An Update." *Bureau of Justice Statistics*. Washington, DC: U.S. Government Printing Office.

Fox, Sanford. 1970. "Juvenile Justice Reform: An Historical Perspective." *Stanford Law Review* 22(June): 1187–239.

Getis, Victoria. 2000. *The Juvenile Court and the Progressives*. Urbana-Champaign, IL: University of Illinois Press.

Gittens, Joan. 1994. *Poor Relations: The Children of the State in Illinois, 1818–1990*. Urbana-Champaign, IL: University of Illinois Press.

Grisso, Thomas, and Robert G. Schwartz, eds. 2000. *Youth on Trial: A Developmental Perspective on Juvenile Justice*. Chicago, IL: University of Chicago Press.

Grossberg, Michael. 1996. *A Judgment for Solomon: The D'Hauteville Case and Legal Experience in Antebellum America*. New York: Cambridge University Press.

Hawes, Joseph. 1971. *Children in Urban Society: Juvenile Delinquency in Nineteenth-Century America*. New York, NY: Oxford University Press.

Hawkins, Darnell F., and Kimberly Kempf-Leonard, eds. 2005, *Our Children, Their Children: Confronting Racial and Ethnic Differences in American Juvenile Justice*. Chicago, IL: University of Chicago Press.

Healy, William. 1915. *The Individual Delinquent: A Text of Diagnosis and Prognosis for All Concerned in Understanding Offenders*. Boston, MA: Little, Brown.

Holloran, Peter C. 1994. *Boston's Wayward Children: Social Services for Homeless Children, 1830–1930*. Boston, MA: Northeastern University Press.

Horowitz, Donald L. 1977. *The Courts and Social Policy*. Washington, DC: The Brookings Institution.

Humes, Edward. 1996. *No Matter How Loud I Shout: A Year in the Life of Juvenile Court*. New York: Simon and Schuster.

Jones, Kathleen W. 1991. *Taming the Troublesome Child: American Families, Child Guidance, and the Limits of Psychiatric Authority*. Cambridge, MA: Harvard University Press.

Katzenbach, Nicholas de B. 1967. *The Challenge of Crime in a Free Society: A Report by the President's Commission on Law Enforcement and the Administration of Justice*. Washington, DC: U.S. Government Printing Office.

Knupfer, Anne Meis. 2001. *Reform and Resistance: Gender, Delinquency and America's First Juvenile Court*. New York: Routledge.

Laub, John H. 2002. "A Century of Delinquency Research and Delinquency Theory." In *A Century of Juvenile Justice* edited by Margaret K. Rosenheim, Franklin E. Zimring, David S. Tanenhaus, and Bernardine Dohrn. Chicago: University of Chicago Press.

Lefstein, Norman, Vaughan Stapleton, and Lee Teitelbaum. 1969. "In Search of Juvenile Justice: *Gault* and Its Application." *Law and Society Review* 3: 491–562.

Lynch, Mona. 2010. *Sunbelt Justice: Arizona and the Transformation of American Punishment*. Palo Alto, CA: Stanford University Press.

Mack, Julian W. 1909. "The Juvenile Court." *Harvard Law Review* 23: 104–22.

Mack, Julian W. 1925. "The Chancery Procedure in the Juvenile Court." In *The Child, the Clinic, and the Court*, edited by Jane Addams. New York: New Republic.

McLennan, Rebecca M. 2008. *The Crisis of Imprisonment: Protest, Politics, and the Making of the American Penal State, 1776–1941*. Cambridge, MA: Harvard University Press.

Manfredi, Christopher P. 1998. *The Supreme Court and Juvenile Justice*. Lawrence, KS: University Press of Kansas.

Marcus, Ellen, and Irene Rosenberg. 2007. *Children and Juvenile Justice*. Durham, NC: Carolina Academic Press.

Mennel, Robert M. 1973. *Thorns & Thistles: Juvenile Delinquents in the United States, 1825–1940*. Hanover, NH: University of New Hampshire Press.

Mintz, Steven. 2004. *Huck's Raft: A History of American Childhood*. Cambridge, MA: The Belknap Press of Harvard University Press.

Molloy, John J. 1962. "Juvenile Court—A Labyrinth of Confusion for the Lawyer." *Arizona Law Review* 4: 1–25.

Myers, Tamara. 2006. *Caught: Montreal's Modern Girls and the Law, 1869–1945*. Toronto: University of Toronto Press.

Novak, William J. 1996. *The People's Welfare: Law and Regulation in Nineteenth-Century America*. Chapel Hill, NC: University of North Carolina Press.

Odem, Mary. 1995. *Delinquent Daughters: Protecting and Policing Adolescent Sexuality in Los Angeles, 1885–1920*. Chapel Hill, NC: University of North Carolina Press.

Paulsen, Monrad G. 1966. "Kent v. United States: The Constitutional Context of Juvenile Cases," *Supreme Court Review* 1966: 167–92.

Penn, Everette B., Helen Taylor Greene, and Shaun L. Gabbion. 2006. *Race and Juvenile Justice* Durham, NC: Carolina Academic Press.

Pickett, Robert. 1969. *Houses of Refuge: Origins of Juvenile Reform in New York States, 1815–1857*. Syracuse, NY: Syracuse University Press.

Platt, Anthony M. 1969. *The Child Savers: The Invention of Delinquency*. Chicago, IL: University of Chicago Press.

Platt, Anthony M. 2009. *The Child Savers: The Invention of Delinquency*, 40th ed. New Brunswick, NJ: Rutgers University Press. (Originally published 1969. Chicago: University of Chicago Press.)

Polier, Justine Wise. 1989. *Juvenile Justice in Double Jeopardy: The Distanced Community and Vengeful Retribution*. Hillsdale, NJ: L. Erlbaum, Associates.

Polsky, Andrew J. 1993. *The Rise of the Therapeutic State*. Princeton, NJ: Princeton University Press.

Prescott, Peter S. 1981. *The Child Savers: Juvenile Justice Observed*. New York: Knopf.

Rosenberg, Gerald N. 1991. *The Hollow Hope: Can Courts Brings About Social Change?* Chicago, IL: University of Chicago Press.

Rosenheim, Margaret K. 2002. "The Modern Juvenile Court." In *A Century of Juvenile Justice*, edited by Margaret K. Rosenheim, Franklin E. Zimring, David S. Tanenhaus, and Bernardine Dorhn. Chicago, IL: University of Chicago Press.

Rosenheim, Margaret K., Franklin E. Zimring, David S. Tanenhaus, and Bernardine Dohrn, eds. 2002. *A Century of Juvenile Justice*. Chicago, IL: University of Chicago Press.

Rothman, David J. 1971. *Discovery of the Asylum: Social Order and Disorder in the New Republic*. Boston, MA: Little, Brown and Co.

Rothman, David J. 1980. *Conscience and Convenience: The Asylum and Its Alternative in Progressive America*. Boston, MA: Little, Brown, and Co.

Ryerson, Ellen. 1978. *The Best-Laid Plans: America's Juvenile Court Experiment*. New York: Hill and Wang.

Schlossman, Steven L. 1993. "Delinquent Children: The Juvenile Reform School." In *Oxford History of the Prison: The Practice of Punishment in Western Society*, edited by Norval Morris and David J. Rothman. New York: Oxford University Press.

Schlossman, Steven L. 2005. *Transforming Juvenile Justice: Reform Ideals and Institutional Realities, 1825–1920*, revised ed. DeKalb, IL: Northern Illinois Press.

Schlossman, Steven L., and David S. Tanenhaus. 2009. "Juvenile Court." In *The Child: An Encyclopedic Companion*, edited by Richard A. Shweder. Chicago: University of Chicago Press.

Schlossman, Steven L., and Stephanie Wallach. 1978. "The Crime of Precocious Sexuality: Female Juvenile Delinquency in the Progressive Era." *Harvard Educational Review* 48(Feb.): 65–94.

Schneider, Eric C. 1992. *In the Web of Class: Delinquents and Reformers in Boston, 1810s–1930s*. New York: NYU Press.

Scott, Elizabeth S., and Laurence Steinberg. 2008. *Rethinking Juvenile Justice*. Cambridge, MA: Harvard University Press.

Singer, Simon I. 1996. *Recriminalizing Juvenile Justice: Violent Juvenile Crime and Juvenile Justice Reform*. New York: Cambridge University Press.

Spock, Benjamin. 1957. *The Common Sense Book of Baby and Child Care*. Revised ed. New York: Duell, Sloane, and Pearce.

Sprott, Jane B., and Anthony N. Doob. 2009. *Justice for Girls? Stability and Change in the Youth Justice Systems of the United States and Canada*. Chicago, IL: University of Chicago Press.

Strange, Carolyn. 1995. *Toronto's Girl Problem: The Perils and Pleasures of the City, 1885–1930*. Toronto: University of Toronto Press.

Tanenhaus, David S. 2000. "The Evolution of Transfer out of the Juvenile Court." In *The Changing Borders of Juvenile Justice: Transfer of Adolescents to the Criminal Court*, edited by Jeffrey Fagan and Franklin E. Zimring. Chicago: The University of Chicago Press.

Tanenhaus, David S. 2002. "The Evolution of Juvenile Courts in the Early Twentieth Century: Beyond the Myth of Immaculate Construction." In *A Century of Juvenile Justice*, edited by Margaret K. Rosenheim, Franklin E. Zimring, David S. Tanenhaus, and Bernardine Dohrn. Chicago, IL: University of Chicago Press.

Tanenhaus, David S. 2004. *Juvenile Justice in the Making*. New York: Oxford University Press.

Tanenhaus, David S. 2005. "Between Dependency and Liberty: The Conundrum of Children's Rights in the Gilded Age." *Law and History Review* 23(Summer): 351–86.

Tanenhaus, David S. 2011. *The Constitutional Rights of Children: In re Gault and Juvenile Justice*. Lawrence, KS: University Press of Kansas.

Teitelbaum, Lee. 2002. "Status Offenses and Status Offenders." In *A Century of Juvenile Justice*, edited by Margaret K. Rosenheim, Franklin E. Zimring, David S. Tanenhaus, and Bernardine Dohrn. Chicago: University of Chicago Press.

"The Crime of Precocious Sexuality: Female Juvenile Delinquency in the Progressive Era." Symposium. Winter 2009. *Journal of Childhood and Youth* 2: 85–126.

Thompson, Heather Ann. 2010. "Why Mass Incarceration Matters: Rethinking Crisis, Decline, and Transformation in Postwar American History." *Journal of American History* 97 (December): 703–734.

Tonry, Michael. 2008. "Crime and Human Rights—How Political Paranoia, Protestant Fundamentalism, and Constitutional Obsolescence Combined to Devastate Black

America: The American Society of Criminology 2007 Presidential Address."
Criminology 46: 1–33.

Trost, Jennifer. 2005. *Gateway to Justice: The Juvenile Court and Progressive Child Welfare in a Southern City*. Athens, GA: University of Georgia Press.

United States Children's Bureau. 1920. *Courts in the United States Hearing Children's Cases: A Summary of the Juvenile-court Legislation in the United States*. Report by Evelina Belden. Publication No. 65. Washington, DC: Government Printing Office.

United States Children's Bureau. 1923. *Juvenile-Court Standards: Report of the Committee Appointed by the Children's Bureau, August, 1921, to Formulate Juvenile-court Standards, Adopted by a Conference Held under the Auspices of the Children's Bureau and the National Probation Association*. Washington, DC: Government Printing Office.

Van Waters, Miriam. 1925. "The Juvenile Court from the Child's Viewpoint: A Glimpse into the Future." In *The Child, the Clinic and the Court*, edited by Jane Addams. New York: New Republic.

Ward, Geoff. Forthcoming. *The Black Child Savers: Racial Democracy and American Juvenile Justice*. Chicago, IL: University of Chicago Press.

Ward, Geoff. 2009. "The 'Other' Child Savers: Racial Politics of the Parental State." In *The Child Savers: The Invention of Delinquency*, 40th anniversary ed. New Brunswick, NJ: Rutgers University Press.

Whitman, James Q. 2003. *Harsh Justice: Criminal Punishment and the Widening Divide between America and Europe*. New York: Oxford University Press.

Willrich, Michael. 2003 *City of Courts: Socializing Justice in Progressive Era Chicago*. New York: Cambridge University Press.

Wolcott, David. 2005. *Cops and Kids: Policing Juvenile Delinquency in Urban America, 1890–1940*. Columbus, OH: Ohio State University Press.

Zimring, Franklin E. 1978. *Confronting Youth Crime: Report of the Twentieth Century Fund Task Force on Sentencing Policy Toward Young Offenders*. New York: Holmes and Meier Publishers.

Zimring, Franklin E. 1998. *American Youth Violence*. New York: Oxford University Press.

Zimring, Franklin E. 2000. "The Common Thread: Diversion in Juvenile Justice." *California Law Review* 88: 2477–95.

Zimring, Franklin E. 2005. *American Juvenile Justice*. New York: Oxford University Press.

PART VI

JUVENILE COURT CLIENTELE

CHAPTER 20

RACIAL AND ETHNIC DIFFERENCES IN DELINQUENCY AND JUSTICE SYSTEM RESPONSES

DONNA M. BISHOP AND
MICHAEL J. LEIBER

I. Introduction

NATIONALLY, police arrest minority youths—especially African Americans and Hispanics—in numbers greatly disproportionate to their representation in the general population (Lauritsen 2005). They are over-represented among young people held in secure detention, petitioned to juvenile court, and adjudicated delinquent. Among those adjudicated delinquent, they are more often committed to the "deep end" of the juvenile system. When confined, they are more often housed in large public institutions rather than smaller private facilities. And, at "the end of the line," prosecutors and judges are more apt to relinquish jurisdiction over them, transferring them to criminal court for prosecution and punishment as adults (Bilchik 1999; Hartney and Vuong 2009). Finally, criminal courts judges confine in prisons larger proportions of minority youths than white youths convicted of similar crimes.

Despite decades of research, there is no clear consensus on why minority youths enter and penetrate the juvenile justice system at such disproportionate rates. Both public and academic discourse have tended to highlight two explanations. The first is that minority over-representation reflects race and ethnic differences in the incidence, seriousness, and persistence of delinquent involvement (the "differential offending" hypothesis). The second is that over-representation is attributable to inequities—intended or unintended—in juvenile justice practice (the "differential treatment" hypothesis). The purpose of this chapter is to review the research literature bearing on these positions and to shed light on the intervening mechanisms by which race and ethnicity influence juvenile justice outcomes.

This chapter is organized into four parts. In the first part, we review national data on the minority presence in the juvenile justice system from arrest to post-dispositional confinement. The second part examines research bearing on the "differential offending" thesis. In the third part, we review the research literature on race bias in justice processing. Our overall assessment is that racial disparities in processing are attributable in part to differences in offending, yet race differences in offending alone are insufficient to account for minority over-representation in the juvenile justice system (see also Pope and Feyerherm 1990a, 1990b, 1993; Pope and Leiber 2005; Huizinga et al. 2007). Moreover, while there is some truth to both the "differential offending" and "differential treatment" arguments, there is also truth that lies beyond and between these positions, in the politico-legal climate responsible for law-making and its enforcement, and in the conditions and circumstances that at once place youths at risk for delinquency and simultaneously provide the rationale for juvenile justice intervention. The issue is no longer simply whether whites and youths of color are treated differently. Instead, the preeminent challenge is to explain how these differences come about. Understanding the intervening mechanisms is essential if we are to replace speculative and often ill-conceived efforts to reduce disproportionate minority contact with strategic choices in policy and practice that hold more promise of success. In the concluding section of the chapter, we explore implications for justice policy in a preliminary way.

II. Disproportionate Minority Representation in the Juvenile Justice System

Table 20.1 presents national data on the racial composition of the delinquency population at successive stages in processing. Rates and relative rates—comparing each minority group to whites—are presented to illustrate racial disparities and guide the discussion.

A. Arrest

In 2005, the Uniform Crime Reports recorded 1.8 million juvenile arrests (Puzzanchera and Adams 2008). White youth, who make up 78% of the at-risk population aged 10 to 17, accounted for 68% of arrests. African Americans were greatly overrepresented: they comprise 17% of the youth population, but accounted for 30% of arrests. At the national level, Native Americans are arrested in numbers proportionate to their numbers in the population. However, within the states where they are most populous, they are over-represented among arrestees (data not shown). Only youths in the "other" category are under-represented among arrestees.

Overall racial disparities are perhaps best expressed in terms of arrest rates. In 2005, the total arrest rate (per 1,000) for African American juveniles was 101; for Native American youth, 52; and for other minority youths, 15—compared to a rate of 49 for whites. African American youth were over two times more likely to be arrested than white youth (relative rate = 2.1). There were also important differences by race in rates of arrest for different offense types. African American youth were arrested for violent index crimes at a rate of 851 per 100,000, more than four times the rate for whites and nearly twelve times the rate for Asian youth (Snyder 2008, data not shown). For property index crimes, the arrest rate for African Americans was nearly double that of whites and five times the rate of Asian youth (Snyder 2008, data not shown).

B. Court Referral

Table 20.1 shows that nearly 1.7 million youths were referred to the juvenile court in 2005 (Puzzanchera and Adams 2008). Nearly every nonwhite youth arrested was referred to court, compared to 90% of whites arrested.

C. Detention

In 2005, 354,000 cases resulted in preadjudicatory detention. The over-representation of minorities was fairly pronounced at this stage: 26% of cases involving African Americans were detained between referral and disposition, compared to 20% for Native Americans, 22% for other races, and 18% for whites. When we compare race-specific detention rates for each of the four offense categories recorded in the Juvenile Court Statistics (See Table 20.2), we find that African Americans and other minority youths were more likely to be detained than whites in nearly every offense comparison. Racial disparities were most striking in the handling of drug offenses, for which African Americans were detained at a rate 2.2 times that for whites. For drug offenses, 14% of whites were detained, compared to 32% of African Americans, 15% of Native Americans, and 17% for other youths.

D. Formal Charging

Racial disparities in rates of formal charging are also apparent (Table 20.1). Sixty-two percent of cases involving African American youth resulted in formal charging,

Table 20.1. The Processing of Juveniles by Race/Ethnicity, 2005

	White	African American	Native American	Other[a]	Total
Population aged 10–17	26,108,000	5,589,300	475,300	1,489,900	33,661,500
Percent	(78)[b]	(17)	(1)	(4)	(100)
Arrested	1,281,000	564,800	24,700	22,600	1,893,400
	(68)	(30)	(1)	(1)	(100)
Arrest Rate per 1,000 persons	49	101	52	15	56
Relative Rate to White =		2.1	1.1	.3	
Referred to Court	1,090,200	559,100	24,600	23,900	1,697,900
	(64)	(33)	(2)	(1)	(100)
Percentage of arrests referred	90	99	100	106	90
Relative Rate to White =		1.2	1.2	1.2	
Detained	197,100	147,000	4,800	5,200	354,000
	(56)	(42)	(1)	(1)	(100)
Percentage of referrals detained	18	26	20	22	21
Relative Rate to White =		1.5	1.1	1.2	
Formally Charged	573,900	347,500	13,900	14,000	949,300
	(60)	(37)	(1)	(1)	(100)
Percentage of referrals charged	53	6	56	58	56
Relative Rate to White =		1.2	1.1	1.1	

Adjudicated Delinquent					
	390,300	214,200	9,700	9,700	623,900
	(63)	(34)	(1)	(1)	(100)
Percentage of charged adjudicated	68	62	70	69	66
Relative Rate to White=		.9	1.0	1.0	
Placed Out of Home	80,600	54,800	2,600	2,100	140,100
	(58)	(39)	(2)	(1)	(100)
Percentage of adjudicated placed	21	26	26	22	23
Relative Rate to White	1.2	1.2	1.9	.6	

Source: Puzzanchera, Charles and Ben Adams. 2008. "National Disproportionate Minority Contact Databook." National Center for Juvenile Justice. Office of Juvenile Justice and Delinquency Prevention. http://ojjdp.ncjrs.gov/ojstatbb/dmcdb/.

a Other includes Asian, Hawaiian, and Pacific Islander.
b Numbers in parentheses are percentages.

Table 20.2. Juvenile Court Processing By Race/Ethnicity and Offense Type, 2005

Offense Type	Detained				Formally Charged				Placed Out of Home			
	W	AA	NA	Other	W	AA	NA	Other	W	AA	NA	Other
Person												
Percent	23	28	24	30	55	64	57	63	23	27	31	28
Relative Rate to W=		1.2	1.0	1.3		1.2	1.0	1.2		1.1	1.4	1.2
Property												
Percent	14	22	13	17	51	60	53	52	20	24	26	20
Relative Rate to W=		1.6	1.0	1.2		1.2	1.0	1.0		1.2	1.3	1.0
Drugs												
Percent	14	32	15	17	52	71	51	58	15	29	19	17
Relative Rate to W=		2.2	1.0	1.2		1.4	1.0	1.1		2.0	1.3	1.2
Public Order												
Percent	22	29	28	24	54	60	64	66	23	25	26	21
Relative Rate to W=		1.3	1.3	1.1		1.1	1.2	1.2		1.1	1.1	.9

Source: Puzzanchera, Charles and Ben Adams. 2008. National Disproportionate Minority Contact Databook. National Center for Juvenile Justice. Office of Juvenile Justice and Delinquency Prevention. http://ojjdp.ncjrs.gov/ojstatbb/dmcdb/.

Note: W = White, AA= African American, NA= American Indian or Alaskan Native, Other= Asian, Hawaiian, or Pacific Islander.

compared to 58% for youths of other races, 56% for Native Americans, and 53% for whites. Table 20.2 shows that, as was true at detention, cases involving African American youth were more likely to be formally charged than cases involving whites in all offense categories. Again, disparities were pronounced for drug referrals. In this offense category, prosecutors petitioned 52% of cases involving whites, but 71% of cases involving African Americans.

E. Adjudication

Of all cases in which formal charges were brought, 66% resulted in adjudications of delinquency. Table 20.1 shows that the patterns of racial disparity observed at previous stages are not evident at adjudication. In fact, the probability of being adjudicated delinquent among those formally charged is lower for African Americans than for other youths. The relative rate comparing African Americans to whites is .9, whereas for the two other race groups it is 1. Nevertheless, due to the cumulative effect of minority overrepresentation at earlier decision points, minority youth remain over-represented.

F. Disposition

Racial disparities at disposition are somewhat smaller than at the front end of the system. The relative rate of out-of-home placement for African Americans is 1.2; for Native Americans, 1.9; and for youths of other races, .6. Although African Americans were only slightly more likely to be placed than whites when adjudicated for person, property, or public order crimes, disparities in the disposition of drug offenses were more pronounced. Table 20.2 shows that 29% of drug cases involving African Americans resulted in out-of-home placement, compared to only 15% of cases involving whites. In the Native American and other race categories, youths were removed from their homes at slightly higher rates than whites.

In sum, racial disparities—especially for African American youth—are quite prominent at the front end of the system. Minority over-representation is not as marked at the back end of the system but still exists, in part, due to the carryover of disparities introduced at earlier stages. It is noteworthy, however, that even at judicial disposition, we find marked differences in the handling of whites and African Americans arrested for drug offenses.

G. Youths in Juvenile Correctional Facilities

Correctional placement is the only point in the system for which we have data on both race and ethnicity. Table 20.3 presents race/ethnic-specific custody rates for juvenile correctional facilities from the 2006 Census of Juveniles in Residential Placement (a one-day count). Here we see that minorities are greatly over-represented: Youths of color comprise 65% of the institutionalized population

Table 20.3. One-Day Count of Juveniles in Correctional Placement by Race and Ethnicity, 2006

	Total	White	African American	Hispanic	Native American	Asian	Other
N	92,854	32,495	37,337	19,027	1,828	1,155	1,012
Percent	100	35	40	20	2	1	1
Rate[a]	295	170	767	326	540	85	—[b]

Source: Sickmund, M., T. J. Sladky, and W. Kang. 2008. "Census of Juveniles in Residential Placement Databook." Washington, DC: National Center for Juvenile Justice, Office of Juvenile Justice and Delinquency Prevention. http://www.ojjdp.gov/ojstatbb/cjrp/

a Rates are calculated per 100,000 youths in the population age 10 to the upper age of juvenile court jurisdiction.
b No rate is shown because there are no data for the comparable reference population.

(Sickmund, Sladky, and Kang 2008), more than twice their proportion in the youth population. The disparities across groups are striking: For every 100,000 whites in the youth population, 170 were in residential placement. The comparable rates for Asian youth are low (85), and those for Hispanics (326), Native Americans (540), and African Americans (767) are strikingly higher. African Americans were more than four times as likely to be incarcerated as whites, while Hispanic and Native American youth were incarcerated at rates two and three times greater than whites, respectively.

III. RACE DIFFERENCES IN OFFENDING

As noted above, African Americans are more likely to be arrested than whites in nearly every offense category. But some have questioned whether arrest data reflect bias in police decision-making. Fortunately, we have other sources of data on youth crime with which to address the issue of race differences in offending. If these other sources reveal race differences in crime that are in basic agreement with arrest data, we can have more confidence that race differences in arrest reflect real differences in offending. If they do not, then the system bias hypothesis becomes more plausible.

Self-reports and victimization surveys are alternative methods of measuring crime independent of the police. Unfortunately, they too are not without shortcomings. Self-reports ask high school and other samples of youths anonymously to report any offenses they have committed, whether or not they were apprehended. But self-reports may not be equally valid for all racial groups. Some researchers have suggested that African Americans tend to under-report serious misconduct (Hindelang, Hirschi, and Weis 1981; Huizinga and Elliott 1987), while others have found no differences in the accuracy of reporting across racial groups (Knight, Little, Losoya and Mulvey 2004). Victimization surveys ask household residents to report personal victimizations, regardless of whether they reported these crimes to the police. But victims can only tell researchers about characteristics of offenders where there has been face-to-face contact. For "victimless" crimes (e.g., drug offenses), property crimes, and homicides, victim descriptions of offenders are unavailable. Furthermore, even in crimes involving face-to-face contact, victims may not always be able accurately to identify the offender's age and race. With these caveats in mind, we look briefly at what these data tell us about race differences in offending.

The National Youth Survey is a self-report administered to a nationally representative sample of teens. Using these data, Elliott (Elliott 1994;) found that African American youth admitted greater involvement in violent behavior than Hispanic youth, who in turn reported greater involvement than whites. These findings are consistent with those from the Denver, Pittsburgh, and Rochester Youth Studies, where white youth reported involvement in violent crimes at lower rates than Hispanic youth, and African American youth reported the highest levels of involvement (Huizinga, Loeber, and Thornberry 1994). Although the self-reported race differences in violent offending across all these studies are substantial, they are not nearly as great as those found in police arrest data.

Another national self-report study examined patterns for lesser offenses (Snyder and Sickmund 2006). Thirty-nine percent of white youth and 33% of African Americans reported that they had vandalized property; 44% of whites and 38% of African Americans reported that they had committed thefts of items worth less than $50; there were no race differences in the proportion of youths who admitted carrying guns. With respect to drug offenses, Monitoring the Future—an annual national survey of high school students begun in 1975—has consistently shown that the highest proportions of drug use of all kinds is found among whites, followed by Hispanics, with African Americans reporting the lowest levels of illicit drug use. These race differences in self-reported crime are not at all consistent with police arrest data, which show substantial over-representation of minorities for vandalism, theft, weapons, and drug offenses.

Victim reports, obtained from the annual National Crime Victimization Survey (NCVS), indicate that minorities are over-represented among offenders who commit serious violent crimes (e.g.,———-delete and insert Rand, 2008, Rand 2008.). For robbery, the proportion of juvenile offenders whom victims identified as African American is only slightly lower than the proportion shown in police data. For sexual and aggravated assaults, African Americans are also over-represented, although not nearly to the extent indicated in arrest data.

Taken together, self-report and victimization data suggest that African American youth are considerably more likely to commit violent crimes than whites, although the disparities are not as great as those reported in official arrest data. For property and drug crimes (for which victimization data are not available), self-reports indicate minimal race differences in offending. The differences that do appear more often suggest greater delinquent involvement among whites. In sum, these comparisons of arrest data with self-report and victimization data seem to support the following general conclusion: Racial disparities in arrest are attributable *both* to differential offending *and* to differences in the way justice officials respond to white and minority juveniles who engage in the same sorts of behaviors.

A. Explaining Race Differences in Offending

In their analysis of race differences in offending, Joan McCord and colleagues and the National Research Council and Institute of Medicine (2001) concluded that minority youths are more often exposed than whites to "contexts of risk," i.e., social structural conditions that contribute to delinquency and crime. This explanation of race differentials in offending calls attention to the economic status of racial and ethnic minorities, the effects of poverty and disorder on the family, and the impact of neighborhood conditions on the development of traditions of crime and delinquency in urban areas (see Walker, Spohn, and DeLone 2000; Wilson 1987; Hawkins et al. 1998; Sampson and Groves 1989; Sampson and Lauritsen 1997; Sampson and Wilson 1995).

The roots of this perspective are found in social disorganization theory. After showing that high-crime areas of cities are characterized by high-population density, poverty, and unemployment, racial and ethnic heterogeneity, and highly transient populations, Shaw and McKay (1969) argued that these structural features produced a condition in which social networks—informal intergenerational ties and friendships, as well as formal neighborhood organizations—are attenuated and unable to provide the supervision and control necessary for the effective socialization of children. When a neighborhood is constantly in flux, when most residents are poor and unemployed, when families are broken and isolated from one another, neighborhood residents mistrust each other and do not forge networks of association that might help them to deal more effectively with local community problems. They lack collective efficacy (Sampson, Raudenbush and Felton 1997), the will to support each other, to look out for each other's children, and to work together to control neighborhood crime. Because crime flourishes in socially disorganized areas, children are routinely exposed to deviant role models. They see persons involved in drugs, gambling, prostitution, theft, and violence, which become behavioral options they might not otherwise have considered. In this way, structural conditions give rise to traditions of crime and delinquency that are transmitted from one generation of young residents to the next.

The social disorganization perspective has recently been applied to an understanding of race differences in offending in contemporary America, especially by Sampson and his colleagues (see, e.g., Sampson and Groves 1989; Sampson and Wilson 1995; Sampson et al., 1997; Sampson, Morenoff, and Earls 1999). They note that the inner city has undergone a social transformation in the past few decades, resulting in the ghettoization of an impoverished black population—consisting especially of female-headed families—who live in relative social isolation in pockets of concentrated poverty. While in the past, poor inner-city residents were able to secure fairly well-paying jobs in manufacturing and other industries (e.g., steel and textile mills) that allowed them eventually to move out of the urban core, this is no longer possible for vast numbers of urban residents. In the 1970s and 1980s, the urban industrial sector of the nation's economy largely shut down, and economic growth relocated to suburban areas. Jobs that remain in the city tend to be either professional-level (requiring higher education) or, far more often, jobs in the retail sales and service sectors (e.g., salesclerk, cashier, waiter, housekeeper) (Sklar 1995, p. 32). Most of these latter jobs pay only a minimum wage. At that rate, a single breadwinner supporting three dependents will live far below the official poverty level (Walker, Spohn, and DeLone 2000, p. 69). Even if two parents work, they will barely rise above the poverty line. In short, the poor are essentially trapped in the inner city.

Further contributing to the development of a largely minority urban underclass are practices of residential segregation that relegate poor minorities to urban ghettoes, where they live in relative isolation from the more affluent majority (Wilson 1987). To be sure, many poor white families live in cities as well, but they are less apt to live in areas where everyone else is poor.

For blacks, poverty and residential segregation have had devastating effects on the family. The strains of poverty, high rates of male unemployment, and welfare-to-work policies for single parents have combined to produce high rates of family disruption. Although the national rate of family disruption and poverty among blacks is two to four times higher than among whites, the number of distinct ecological contexts in which blacks achieve equality to whites is striking. In not one city over 100,000 in the United States do blacks live in ecological equality to whites when it comes to the basic features of economic and family organization. Accordingly, race differences in poverty and family disruption are so strong that the "worst" urban contexts in which whites reside are considerably better off than the average context of black communities (Sampson and Lauritsen 1997, p. 337).

Poverty in the inner city has many additional ramifications. Because the poor cannot afford health insurance, pregnant women often receive no prenatal care, increasing the risk that their children will be born with neurological deficits that impair learning and social development, both of which have been linked to antisocial behavior (see, e.g., Fishbein 2001, pp. 63–70). Inner city neighborhoods tend also to be characterized by "critically low performing" schools—which do little to improve youth's life chances—and by a dearth of recreation programs and other organized activities for adolescents. It is difficult if not impossible for a single parent, especially one who must work to support the family, to provide the instruction needed to compensate for inferior schools, to organize and supervise children's after-school activities, and to provide guidance sufficient to counterbalance the negative influence of deviant role models on the streets. These factors in combination are believed to contribute heavily to minority youth crime.

IV. The Role of the Justice System in the Generation of Racial and Ethnic Disparities

Racial and ethnic disparities in juvenile justice processing derive in part from laws that differentially target the behaviors, statuses, and life conditions associated with youths of color. Enforcement of the law is constrained most obviously by the content of the law itself. At the national level, the "get tough," "law and order" climate of the past twenty-five years has spawned legislation and strategic initiatives that have promoted racial disparities in the juvenile system. In some instances, the law reflects institutionalized racism by supporting policies and practices that, while perhaps not racist in intent, nevertheless have a differential and sometimes profoundly negative impact on minority populations. The "war on drugs" is perhaps the best recent example.

Although self-report studies showed little change in drug use from the mid-1980s into the 1990s, legislatures nonetheless targeted drug offenders with stepped up enforcement and harsher punishments (Beckett and Sasson 2004; Tonry 1995). Arrest rates for drug offenses among white youth were higher than those for African American youth throughout the 1970s. However, after the initiation of the war on drugs, white drug arrest rates declined, while arrests of African American youth skyrocketed. By the early nineties, arrest rates for drug offenses among African American youth were four to five times those for whites (Miller 1996, p. 85).

The National Criminal Justice Commission observed more than ten years ago that racial disparities in drug arrests are attributable largely to enforcement strategies that focus almost exclusively on low-level dealers in minority neighborhoods. "Police found more drugs in minority communities because that is where they looked for them" (Donziger 1996, p. 115). That the war on drugs has been waged differentially against young minority offenders was undoubtedly influenced by the media, which promulgated the view that drug crime is exclusively an urban African American male phenomenon (Walker, Spohn, and DeLone 2000, p. 45). Contributing to differential enforcement was the ease of making arrests in underclass neighborhoods, where drug sales more often take place on the street, dealers more often sell to strangers and, because of high unemployment rates, a steady stream of young people is available to replace those who are arrested (Tonry 1994, pp. 485–87). It should also be noted that in some instances, changes in the law may actually have encouraged the targeting of underclass neighborhoods for drug enforcement activities. For example, the Illinois legislature passed a law in the early 1990s mandating the transfer to criminal court of 15- and 16-year-olds charged with drug violations committed within 1,000 feet of public housing, where minorities are more likely to reside. A study of transfers in Cook County following the law's implementation revealed that all of the juveniles transferred under this provision were African American (Clarke 1996, p. 9).

Another illustration of how the politico-legal climate has exacerbated racial disparities involves the focus on juvenile gangs. Fueled by public fear of youth crime and by the perceived connection between drugs and gangs, legislatures provided monetary incentives for gang suppression activities and enhanced penalties for gang-related crimes. "Sweeps" and "crackdowns" on minority gangs became part of drug enforcement strategies (Eschholz, Mallard, and Flynn 2004; Walker, Spohn, and DeLone 2006; Freng and Esbensen 2007). Since 1995, the Office of Juvenile Justice and Delinquency Prevention (OJJDP) has sponsored the National Youth Gang Survey, gathering information from local law enforcement agencies on the scope of youth gangs and characteristics of gang members. Beginning in 1995 and continuing to the present, police officials have estimated that the vast majority of youth gang members are nonwhite (primarily African American and Hispanic), and that much violence and drug crime is gang-related (National Youth Gang Center 2009). Although these estimates are almost certainly inflated (Esbensen and Osgood 1999; Walker, Spohn, and DeLone 2006), they provide a rationale for differential enforcement of anti-gang initiatives in minority communities.

Numerous additional examples could be cited (e.g., curfew laws in urban communities, transfer laws that target violent offenders regardless of age or prior record). The point is that in order to fully understand racial disparities in the juvenile justice system, it does not suffice merely to examine the operation of police, court, and correctional agencies. It is essential to also consider the politics of race and crime and the ways that minority youths differentially become the objects of social control.

A. Police and Juvenile Processing

There are strong theoretical grounds for believing that the impact of race and ethnicity on police handling of juveniles is potentially quite substantial. Although police officers' actions are constrained by statutes, regulations, directives, and the formal and informal norms of the departments in which they work, rules cannot cover all situations and many situations are legally ambiguous (Lipsky 1980). In cases involving serious and violent crimes, discretion is limited. But the vast majority of police-suspect encounters involve minor offenses, where arrests are made no more than 10% to 15% of the time, leaving a large margin for discretionary decision-making (Black and Reiss 1970; Engel, Sobol, and Worden 2000; Terrill and Paoline 2007). That there is little review of or accountability for many front-end decisions adds to the potential for bias (Black and Reiss 1970; Worden and Myers 1999). If minority youths are more often arrested in situations where similar white youths are released or handled informally, these differentials will be almost impossible to detect. That police decisions must often be made quickly based on very little information adds to the potential for bias. Officers draw on their personal backgrounds and experiences in assessing situations and making on-the-spot decisions (Smith and Visher 1981; see also Irwin 1985; Rubinstein 1973; Wilson 1968). Differentiating between dangerous and nondangerous places, and between suspicious and nonsuspicious persons, is essential to police work (Skolnick 1966) but, in the context of a society suffused in inequality, race- and class-linked stereotypes may become bases of differentiation (Lipsky 1980).

Despite the theoretical grounds for suspecting police bias, we know less about the influence of race on police handling of juveniles than about processing in other contexts. The dearth of information is especially unfortunate because police are the primary gatekeepers of the juvenile court. Selection bias introduced by the police is very likely to affect outcomes at later stages, even if no bias occurs at later stages (Farrell and Swigert 1978). Moreover, bias introduced at the police stage is likely to be amplified at later stages and, more insidiously, to be subsumed under the cover of offense-related considerations whose legitimacy is unlikely to be challenged. If minority youths are systematically overcharged by police,[1] the probability that they will penetrate deeper into the juvenile system is increased. Similarly, if police are more likely to arrest minorities in situations where white youths are released or handled informally, this will translate into race differences in prior record. Seriousness of the offense and prior record are key predictors of outcomes at nearly every stage in court processing, and their validity as proxies for actual behavior is seldom questioned. The dual problems of "bias amplification" (Dannefer and Schutt 1982; Farrell and Swigert 1978; Liska and Tausig 1979) and what might best be termed "offense contamination" are potentially critical consequences of the impact of race on police decision-making.

Observational studies are the primary sources of information on police decision-making in the field. Survey research, studies of police records, and comparisons of self-reported and official delinquency constitute other methodologies. All of these sources suggest that police-juvenile encounters and arrests are influenced not only by offending but also by aspects of the encounter and the context in which it occurs (see Dunham and Alpert 2009). Studies also suggest that, for the most part, racial and ethnic disparities in police decision-making are not manifestations of intentional bias or prejudice. Instead, race effects are largely indirect: they reflect decisions based on considerations that, from the standpoint of the decision-maker, appear to be race-neutral and legitimate.

Racial disparities in police handling of juveniles are linked to at least three features of police administration and organization. One involves routine deployment decisions. In general, patrols are disproportionately distributed to geographic areas with the greatest numbers of calls for service and the highest rates of reported crime (Walker 1999), which tend to be areas characterized by higher concentrations of minorities and the poor (Piliavin and Briar 1964; Conley 1994). While geographic assignment of officers based on need for police protection may be rational and defensible for some purposes, its effect is to increase police surveillance over minority populations (Werthman and Piliavin 1967).

A second aspect of police administrative decision-making that contributes to racial disparities has to do with strategic choices, such as whether to focus on "hot spots," to initiate "sweeps," to conduct "crackdowns" on certain kinds of crime, and the like (Braga 2006). Recently, targeting "hot spots" and creating "drug free zones" have become popular strategies that concentrate law enforcement resources in high-crime neighborhoods where minorities disproportionately reside. A third aspect of police organization/administration that affects racial disparities in arrest has to do with characteristic styles of policing (Wilson 1968). There is some evidence that modern urban police departments tend to be legalistic in orientation: officers make arrests more often for minor offenses that in suburban or rural areas would be handled informally (Bridges et al. 1993). Again, the concentration of minority populations in urban areas places them at a disadvantage relative to whites.

Numerous researchers have found that neighborhood characteristics structure the exercise of officers' discretion in ways that make youth of color more vulnerable to stops and arrests (Smith, Visher, and Davidson 1984; Sampson 1986; Smith 1986). They suggest that typifications of neighborhoods based on considerations of race and class provide a heuristic for identifying "dangerous areas," "suspicious persons," and "unusual activity." Irwin (1985), for example, reports that officers tend to impute to persons who reside in "bad neighborhoods" the moral liability of the area itself, prompting a more aggressive stance in terms of officer-initiated stops and arrests. In an extensive observational study of twenty-four police departments in sixty neighborhoods, Smith (1986) found that irrespective of neighborhood crime rates, in racially mixed and primarily African American neighborhoods, police were more likely to initiate contacts with suspects and also to use or threaten to use force (see also Terrill and Reisig 2003). Neighborhood socioeconomic status (SES) also had a direct effect on the probability of arrest, independent of characteristics of offenders or offenses. Citizens encountered in lower-class (disproportionately minority) neighborhoods were three times as likely to be arrested.

In a Seattle study that combined survey data and police records, Sampson (1986) found that neighborhood SES affected the likelihood of police-juvenile contacts independent of individual race, individual SES, or self-reported delinquent involvement. Delinquent involvement was the strongest predictor of police contact, followed by race (minorities were more likely to be arrested) and individual-level SES. But even when these variables were controlled, neighborhood SES had a significant effect, suggesting, consistent with Smith's research, that officers intensify efforts at social control in economically depressed neighborhoods where minorities more often reside (see also Conley 1994; Huizinga et al. 2007).

Although studies of police-juvenile encounters are few, most suggest that, for minor offenses, race has an indirect effect on arrest that is mediated by a youth's demeanor. In an early study, Piliavin and Briar (1964) observed officers in a single metropolitan department over a period of several months. About 10% of police-juvenile contacts involved serious offenses, which uniformly resulted in arrest and referral to court, irrespective of other factors. Outcomes in the remaining cases were determined in large measure by the nature of the officer-suspect interaction. Juveniles who appeared tough and disrespectful were more often arrested while those who were polite and respectful were more often released. African American youth more often displayed demeanor that prompted officers to view them as "potential troublemakers." In a clear example of racial stereotyping, officers recognized the potential prejudice involved in these attributions but justified their decisions by pointing to departmental crime statistics showing that African Americans committed more crimes than whites. Similar findings regarding the effects of demeanor have been reported by Black and Reiss (1970), Lundman, Sykes, and Clark (1978),Worden and Myers (1999), and others. Bittner (1990, p. 336) reported that officers frequently interpret hostile demeanor as an indicator of criminal propensity as well as a signal that the situation may get out of control. But demeanor can be misleading. Because most juvenile crime involves group offending (Zimring 1981), encounters with juveniles routinely occur in situations where youths are "on stage" before an audience of their peers. In such settings, "copping an attitude" of toughness or hostility may be a face-saving tactic rather than a harbinger of danger. A hostile attitude may also be a response to real or perceived police prejudice, especially if police concentrate surveillance on underclass areas and differentially stop minority youths. Such practices generate antagonism and perpetuate a vicious cycle (Anderson 1990; Winfree and Griffiths 1977; Griffiths and Winfree 1982).

Police responsiveness to the dispositional preferences of complainants also contributes to racial disparities in arrests for minor offenses (Black and Reiss 1970; Lundman, Sykes, and Clark 1978). The vast majority of police encounters with suspects are citizen-initiated (Black and Reiss 1970). Especially if the offense is not serious, the suspect is more likely to be released if the complainant does not support prosecution. Several studies have found that complainants more often urge arrest in cases involving African American suspects (Black and Reiss 1970; Lundman, Sykes, and Clark 1978; Smith and Visher 1981).

In many jurisdictions, police officers are responsible for deciding whether youths who have been taken into custody should be diverted from the system or referred to the court for formal processing. Most of the research indicates that minority youths are more likely to be referred for formal processing than are legally similar whites (Bell and Lang 1985; Fagan, Slaughter, and Hartstone 1987; Wordes and Bynum 1995; Sealock and Simpson 1998). Interactions between race and offense type have also been reported. In serious cases, the offense itself becomes an overriding consideration. In less serious cases, extralegal considerations come into play and redound to the disadvantage of youth of color (e.g., Fagan, Slaughter, and Hartstone 1987). There is some evidence that the link between race and court referral is also mediated by youths' demeanor (Bell and Lang 1985; Kurtz, Giddings, and Sutphen 1993).

Finally, structural factors also may condition the impact of race on police referrals. Dannefer and Schutt (1982), for example, found that in urban counties with high proportions of minorities, police were significantly more likely to refer African American and Hispanic youth to court than their white counterparts. (In urban counties, race was a stronger predictor of referral than even severity of the offense.) By contrast, race had a much weaker effect in suburban counties with small minority populations.

In sum, the literature indicates that, for a number of reasons, minority youths are more likely than whites to be stopped, arrested, and referred to court by police. Because urban underclass neighborhoods have the highest rates of officially recorded crime, they are subject to higher levels of police surveillance. Concentrated surveillance in these areas results in more police-initiated encounters and arrests. The research also suggests that police are more suspicious of persons in low SES neighborhoods with high minority concentrations, which tend to be typified as "bad" and "dangerous" areas. These typifications, which rest on race and class stereotypes, condone and even encourage a more aggressive posture with respect to stops, arrests, and use of coercive authority. At the level of the police-juvenile encounter, the extant research indicates that whites and minorities tend to be treated similarly when they are suspected of serious crimes. However, when the threat is less serious, extralegal factors—especially demeanor—influence police decision-making. Because African American and Hispanic youth tend to be (or are perceived to be) less cooperative, more gang-involved, and more threatening, they are disadvantaged relative to whites. At all stages of police processing, differential treatment of white and minority youths seems to be affected most by behavioral and attitudinal indicators of risk (danger and hostility) and structural factors that are linked to class and race.

B. Processing in Juvenile Courts

Conceived in a social welfare model, the overriding goal of the juvenile court at its inception was to respond to the individual needs of the young people brought before it. Until the 1960s, when a radical reformation of the court took place, notions of equality under the law (i.e., treating legally similar cases alike) had little place in the juvenile court. In theory, at least, offenses were important only insofar as they were symptomatic of some underlying need or problem, which could as easily be signaled by a truancy or a shoplifting as by a robbery or an aggravated assault. The potential for race and class to influence processing decisions was great given the enormous discretionary authority granted to justice officials, the lack of criteria to guide decision-making, the informality and secrecy of court proceedings, the confidentiality of case records, and—laudatory though the goal might have seemed—the sheer arrogance embodied in the presumption that a cadre of predominantly white, middle-class court personnel could diagnose impartially and treat effectively the problems of "other people's children."

Beginning in the 1960s and 1970s and continuing to the present, juvenile court philosophy, policy, and practice have undergone a series of fundamental changes. Although the court has not altogether abandoned its rehabilitative purpose, the additional objectives of punishment and community protection have been conferred upon it in many states. That treatment objectives remain a focus of the juvenile court process provides strong grounds for believing that the potential impact of race on court processing is substantial. Court officials lack substantive criteria to assist them in determining what needs or problems should be considered or what weight they (individually or collectively) should be accorded, and they lack the tools for identifying intervention strategies most conducive to their resolution.

Contributing to the potential for bias is the fact that, especially at the "front end" of the system, decisions to divert or refer for formal processing, and to release from custody or detain, often must be made within a matter of hours based on little information. In these circumstances, officials may rely on typifications—shorthand cues based on race and class stereotypes—in their attempts to differentiate between youths who pose a risk to the community and those who do not, and between those who are likely and unlikely to respond to treatment.

It is somewhat telling that, after controlling for severity of the current offense and prior record, race effects are relatively rare in studies of processing in the criminal courts (Sampson and Lauritsen 1997; Walker, Spohn, and DeLone 2006), yet they are common and often quite pronounced in research on juvenile court processing (e.g., Pope and Feyerherm 1993; Bishop 2005; Bishop, Leiber, and Johnson 2010). Recent studies of the juvenile court process that have examined more than one decision point and employed multivariate models with controls for offense-related variables consistently report significant race effects, usually at multiple processing stages (Bishop and Frazier 1988, 1996; Kempf-Leonard and Sontheimer 1995; Engen, Steen, and Bridges 2002; Guevara, Herz, and Spohn 2006; Leiber and Johnson 2008; Leiber, Brubaker, and Fox 2009). The review that follows traces the sequence of court decision-making, highlighting studies that point to sources of racial disparity independent of race differentials in offending.

C. Intake

This stage is the first point of contact with the juvenile court, where initial decisions are made regarding formal processing and detention. Perhaps because of differences in orientation and function between police organizations and juvenile court intake divisions, referral decisions made by intake personnel hinge to a lesser extent on offense and demeanor (the criteria most often used by police) and more on appraisals of youths' backgrounds and life circumstances.

The consensus of prior research is that legal variables are the strongest predictors: lesser offenses are more often dropped and first offenders more often diverted (e.g., Bishop and Frazier 1988, 1996; Kempf et al. 1990; Smith and Paternoster 1990; DeJong and Jackson 1998). However, most studies also reveal racial and ethnic disparities in outcome that cannot be explained solely by legal factors (e.g., Bishop and Frazier 1988, 1996; Bridges et al. 1993; Leiber and Fox 2005).

Several factors have been identified that help explain why minority youths are less likely than whites to be diverted from the system. One involves simple failure to meet the criteria for diversion. As a matter of policy in many jurisdictions, juveniles are ineligible for diversion and must be automatically detained if their parents cannot be contacted and do not appear for a face-to-face interview. In a Florida study, Bishop and Frazier (1996) reported that minority families were less likely to have phones, access to transportation, access to childcare, and the ability to take leave time from work without loss of pay, all of which made it more difficult for them to comply with official policy. Bond-Maupin, Lujan, and Bortner (1995) documented the devastating effects of a similar policy on Native American adolescents living on reservations.

In many jurisdictions, diversion to informal probation or other community-based sanctions or services also requires an admission of guilt (Snyder and Sickmund 1999). Such admissions tend to be perceived by officials as a sign of receptivity to treatment. Leiber (1994) and Kempf, Decker, and Bing (1990) reported that white youths more often admit guilt than African Americans. Reluctance to admit guilt on the part of minority youths may say far more about their distrust of justice officials than about their amenability to treatment (Leiber 1994; Bishop and Frazier 1996). Nevertheless, officials tend to draw the inference that those who do not admit guilt lack remorse. As we will see below, the image of the "remorseless" minority offender extends well beyond the intake stage.

Disaggregation of data by offense type suggests another reason for racially disparate intake outcomes. Juveniles arrested for drug offenses are especially likely to be referred to court (Bell and Lang 1985; Kempf, Decker, and Bing 1990; Kempf-Leonard and Sontheimer 1995). We have already seen that police more often target minority communities for enforcement of drug laws (Tonry 1994, 1995). That drug cases are disproportionately referred for formal processing at intake amplifies these racial disparities.

Family assessment also plays an important role in contributing to disparate outcomes. Evaluation of the family's ability to provide a wholesome environment for the socialization of children has traditionally been a dominant focus of juvenile court inquiry (Cicourel 1968; Emerson 1969; Feld 1999). While critics view these assessments as means by which elites rationalize extensions of control over minorities and the poor (Platt 1977; Schlossman 1977), defenders point to studies suggesting the centrality of family dysfunction (especially child-parent conflict and inadequacy of parental supervision) in the etiology of delinquency (e.g., Hirschi 1969; Patterson, Reid, and Dishion 1992; Gottfredson and Hirschi 1990).

In their study of juvenile courts in Missouri, Kempf, Decker, and Bing (1990) found that both family structure and judgments about the adequacy of parental supervision were strong predictors of intake referral decisions. Minority youths were less likely than white youths to reside in two-parent homes. In addition, the case records of minority youths more often reported that parents were unwilling to supervise their children and incapable of exercising proper control even when they expressed a willingness to do so. Although the basis for these judgments is unclear, the danger of racial stereotyping is unmistakable.

Kempf et al.'s findings have been replicated in other jurisdictions. Austin (1995), Corley et al. (1996), Frazier and Bishop (1995), Krisberg and Austin (1993), and Smith and Paternoster (1990) also found that intake decisions to handle cases formally were linked to broken homes, perceptions of inadequate parental supervision, and perceptions of parental unwillingness to work with court personnel. On all three dimensions, youths of color fared less well.

Some qualitative research suggests that officials' assessments of family life and parental supervision are affected by racial stereotypes. Frazier and Bishop (1995) interviewed juvenile court officials and found they generally viewed African American families in more negative terms than white families. Even when two African American parents were in the home, they tended to be perceived as less capable of exercising control over their children than the parents of white youth. Negative attributes may be linked to minority families because African Americans in the aggregate have higher rates of broken homes, poverty, and unemployment, and reside more often in neighborhoods where officials believe that crime and drugs are prevalent (see also Leiber 2003).

Racial disparities have also been linked to social class, sometimes in terms of demeanor (Kurtz, Giddings, and Sutphen 1993) but, most often, in terms of differential access to resources. Bishop and Frazier (1996) reported that justice officials in Florida attributed racially disparate intake outcomes to the fact that middle-class families were able to purchase services privately (e.g., counseling, substance abuse treatment), while comparable services for poor youths could only be obtained by court order following an adjudication of delinquency.

School problems (attendance and performance) have also been found to predict intake decisions to refer youths for formal processing, independent of controls for legal and other social factors (Leiber 1995; Kempf-Leonard and Sontheimer 1995.) While difficulties in school are common among youths referred to intake, they are more common among African Americans, Native Americans, and Hispanics (e.g., Jarjoura 1993; McCarter 1997).

D. Detention

Juveniles may be detained if there is reason to believe they will fail to appear at upcoming hearings. They are also eligible for "preventive detention" if they are predicted to commit further crimes. However, the standards that apply to the preventive detention of juveniles are vague and invite subjective decision-making with enormous potential for misapplication (Holman and Ziedenberg 2006).

Detention is one of the most frequently studied decision points in the juvenile system. It is also the point at which race effects unexplained by offense-related variables are most often found (e.g., Frazier and Cochran 1986; Bishop and Frazier 1996; Armstrong and Rodriguez 2005; Leiber and Fox 2005; Leiber forthcoming; Guevara, Herz, and Spohn 2006; Kurtz, Linnemann, and Spohn 2008). Studies that have included Native American and Hispanic youth report significant disadvantages to these groups as well (Wordes, Bynum, and Corley 1994; Corley et al. 1996; Rodriguez 2007).

While some states have tried to regulate the use of detention by adopting risk assessment instruments and admissions screening criteria, drug offenders and gang members are sometimes targeted for presumptive detention (Orlando 1999). As we have already seen, drug enforcement tends to be heaviest in underclass, minority neighborhoods. Minority youths also have higher rates of gang membership than whites and are more often suspected of gang membership, regardless of their involvement (Austin 1995; Miller 1996, p. 109; Esbensen and Winfree 1998).

As was the case at referral, decisions to place youths in detention are apparently linked to judgments regarding the adequacy of parental supervision and control. Assessments of parental supervision play a prominent role in detention decisions (e.g., Fenwick 1982; Bridges et al. 1993; Corley et al. 1996; Kempf, Decker, and Bing 1990; Wu, Cernkovich, and Dunn 1997). Fenwick (1982) found that the strongest predictors of detention were not legal variables, but family structure, parents' expressed interest in the juvenile, and the quality of child-parent interaction. As noted above, there is considerable risk of racial stereotyping in assessments of parental attitudes and family dynamics.

School and work represent other sources of control and supervision. Whether youths are attending and/or performing well in school (Cohen and Kluegel 1979; Wu, Cernkovich, and Dunn 1997) or are employed (Cohen and Kluegel 1979; Rodriguez 2007) has been linked to detention outcomes. As noted above, compared to whites, African American and Hispanic youth are more likely to have problems in school and are less likely to be employed.

E. Formal Charging

Relatively few studies have explored the influence of race or ethnicity on prosecuto-rial decisions to file formal charges, and they have produced mixed results. Bishop and Frazier (1988, 1996) found that race was only weakly related to formal charging once legal variables were controlled. However, race affected charging decisions indi-rectly: juveniles who were detained were more likely to be charged, and minority youths were considerably more likely to be detained than otherwise similar whites. Other researchers report direct race effects at prosecutorial charging that put minor-ity youth at a disadvantage (Kempf-Leonard and Sontheimer 1995; MacDonald and Chesney-Lind 2001).

F. Adjudication

At the adjudicatory stage, judges decide whether to dismiss the case or make a find-ing of delinquency. Contrary to the results at virtually every other decision point, the most common finding is that, after controlling for offense and prior record, whites are considerably more likely than minority youths to be adjudicated delinquent (Secret and Johnson 1997; Wu and Fuentes 1998). A few studies report no race effect (Leiber and Jamieson 1995; Kempf-Leonard and Sontheimer 1995), while findings of minority disadvantage are less common (MacDonald and Chesney-Lind 2001).

G. Judicial Disposition

Judges in most jurisdictions tend to rely heavily on pre-disposition reports pre-pared by probation officers. These reports commonly address issues of harm and culpability (e.g., the youth's statement regarding the offense, probation officer's assessments of moral character, victim's statement); issues of danger and risk (e.g., details of the prior record, the youth's behavior on probation or other previous dispositions); and matters relevant to treatment (e.g., alcohol and substance abuse; family, school, and peer influences that may have contributed to the offense; and offender expressions of guilt or remorse).

   The consensus of the extant research is that offense history is the strongest pre-dictor of dispositional outcomes. Previous dispositions are also highly influential, much more so than current offense (e.g., Henretta, Frazier, and Bishop 1986; Thornberry and Christensen 1984). That offense history and prior disposition are stronger predictors than current offense is consistent with the conclusion that judges are most concerned about community protection (predictions of risk) and treatment (what interventions have already been tried?). Emerson (1969) suggests that judges at disposition are especially interested in assessing moral character. If a youth reappears in court multiple times, he is generally perceived as a hard-core delinquent with criminal values. Multiple previous (and, by definition, unsuccess-ful) dispositions ultimately lead to the conclusion that the youth is not amenable to treatment (Emerson 1969).

Unfortunately, prior record and previous dispositions, although apparently race neutral, are contaminated to unknown degrees. As we have seen, youth of color are more vulnerable to arrest and formal processing than otherwise similar whites. Compared to white youths engaged in the same behaviors, minorities more readily accumulate offense histories and dispositions from which inferences are drawn about character and capacity for reform.

The vast majority of studies indicate that race has a significant direct effect on dispositional outcomes after legal variables are controlled (e.g., McCarthy and Smith 1986; Bishop and Frazier 1988, 1992, 1996; Rodriguez, Smith, and Zatz 2009; Rodriguez 2010). Moreover, researchers who have examined the effects of decisions made at earlier points in processing almost without exception report indirect effects of race operating through detention status. Two of the most consistent findings in the literature are that minority youths are more likely to be detained than otherwise similar whites, and that being detained strongly predicts harsher treatment at disposition (e.g., Bishop and Frazier 1988, 1992, 1996; Leiber and Fox 2005; Leiber, forthcoming; Rodriguez 2010).[2] Research suggests that the effects of race on judicial disposition may also be contingent on offense type. Several recent studies report that minority youths convicted of drug offenses are especially likely to receive more severe dispositions (Horowitz and Pottieger 1991; DeJong and Jackson 1998). Because the drug problem has become so thoroughly linked to minorities in the public view (Miller 1996; Bortner, Zatz, and Hawkins 2000), minority drug offenders are apt to be perceived as more threatening than their white counterparts (Sampson and Laub 1993).

As was the case with respect to referral and detention, family considerations play a role at disposition in ways that work to the disadvantage of minority offenders. Youths from single-parent families and youths experiencing (or perceived to be experiencing) family problems receive more severe dispositions (e.g., Horwitz and Wasserman 1980; Kempf, Decker, and Bing 1990). Other evidence of the importance of the family—and of the intersection of race, class, and family—is provided in research by Sanborn (1996), who interviewed one hundred court officials in three eastern communities regarding factors that influence judicial disposition. Asked what they believed should be considered at disposition, officials identified family most often. Asked whether the juvenile court in fact discriminated against any particular youths, 87% of the respondents answered positively. They most often identified African American males from dysfunctional families in lower class neighborhoods (see also Rodriguez 2007).

Interactions between race and family disadvantage have also been reported by Kempf-Leonard and Sontheimer (1995) and Wu and Fuentes (1998), who found that African American youths from very poor and welfare families were especially likely to be removed from their homes. Wu and Fuentes' interpretation of this result is that judges view minority youths as especially needy when they live in socially disorganized, underclass areas that weaken families and promote crime (see also Frazier and Bishop 1995). In other words, because minority youths are more likely to live in impoverished areas (due in no small part to racial prejudice, racial segregation, and lack of employment), they are more likely to be removed from their homes. The irony is that, however well intended the court might be in taking this action, it is powerless to alter the neighborhood environments from which youths come and to which they will almost certainly return. An alternative explanation is suggested by conflict theory (Blalock 1967; Quinney 1977). From this perspective, minority youths from indigent families, especially if they are part of the urban underclass, are more often removed from their homes not because they are perceived to be particularly needy but because they are viewed as particularly threatening.

That race is an influential factor in perceptions and evaluations of delinquent youths has been demonstrated by Bridges and Steen (1998) (see also Steen, Sara, Engen, and Gainey 2005; Graham and Lowery (2004); Rodriguez, Smith, and Zatz (2009)). They examined predisposition reports prepared by juvenile probation officers in three counties in a western state and found pronounced differences in probation officers' assessments of the causes of offending among white versus minority offenders. Causal attributions were heavily influenced by prior record and current offense. However, race remained a significant predictor of probation officer assessments and recommendations even after these legal factors were controlled. Offending among African American youths was more often attributed to enduring defects of character rather than external features of their environments. In reports to the court, African American youths were more often described as non-amenable to treatment and dangerous to the community. In contrast, reports on white offenders significantly more often focused on the negative effects of family conflict, delinquent peers, poor school performance, and other external factors. By attributing the delinquency of white youths to external factors, probation officers portrayed them as fundamentally good kids who were victims of unfortunate circumstances. Consequently, they were regarded as less threatening and less likely to reoffend. Not surprisingly, then, probation officers recommended significantly more lenient sentences for whites than for African Americans. This study provides some of the most compelling evidence to date of racial stereotyping by juvenile justice officials and of the power of racial stereotypes to influence decision-making (see also Graham and Lowery 2004; Rodriguez, Smith, and Zatz 2009). More broadly, it suggests that racist characterological and behavioral expectancies in the larger culture are reproduced in the juvenile courts.

H. Contextual Effects

The studies of juvenile court processing discussed thus far have focused on the connection between individual-level case characteristics and decision outcomes. While studies of this type constitute the bulk of the extant research, increasingly scholars are adopting a macrosociological perspective, inquiring whether racial and ethnic disparities in processing may be explained by or linked to the larger context in which processing occurs. Juvenile courts do not operate uniformly within the United States, or even within states (Feld 1991; Pope and Feyerherm, 1993). Because courts are organized at the local level, practices vary greatly from one place to another. Local practice reflects structural features of communities, the availability of resources, as well as political, legal, and ideological features of courts and the communities in which they are located (e.g., Sampson and Laub 1993; Bridges et al. 1995; Leiber 2003; Armstrong and Rodriguez 2005; Rodriguez, 2007, 2010). Cross-jurisdictional variations in juvenile justice practice, for example, have been linked to idiosyncrasies of individual judges (e.g., Podkopacz and Feld 1996), to the bureaucratic structure of prosecutors' offices (Barnes and Franz 1989; Bishop and Frazier 1991), to methods of judicial appointment and levels of judicial specialization in juvenile justice matters (Hasenfeld and Cheung 1985; Kempf, Decker, and Bing 1990), and to organizational culture, reflected in the shared beliefs and expectations of juvenile court officials (Aday 1986; Smith and Paternoster 1990).

I. Urban-Rural Variation

Feld (1991, 1995, 1999) suggests that level of urbanization is linked to organizational characteristics of juvenile courts, which in turn have important implications for how cases are processed He argues that because urban counties are more heterogeneous, diverse, and less stable than rural counties, with fewer mechanisms of informal social control, their juvenile courts tend to be more formal, bureaucratic, and due process-oriented. They screen out fewer cases, process more cases formally, and make greater use of commitment. But they also handle cases more equitably than do rural courts: their legalistic orientation results in a focus on offense and prior record, rather than social characteristics of offenders. By contrast, in rural courts, justice administration tends to be more informal. More cases are filtered out of the system at intake. Judges exercise more discretion and youths who have committed similar offenses may be treated very differently. "Equal treatment under the law" gives way to the traditional *parens patriae* mandate to provide individualized treatment based on a youth's personal and social needs.

Consistent with this perspective, Feld (1990), Smith and Paternoster (1990), and Kempf-Leonard and Sontheimer (1995) found that cases referred to courts in urban and suburban areas were more likely to progress beyond the initial referral stage. Processing in urban courts was more offense-driven, social characteristics being less influential at intake than in rural areas (see also DeJong and Jackson 1998; Kempf, Decker, and Bing 1990). Although urban courts were more evenhanded than rural ones in the referral and petitioning of cases, their propensity to move cases deeper into the system ultimately worked to the disadvantage of African Americans, who reside more often in urban areas. Urban areas are also more likely than rural ones to have local detention centers, which tend to be kept filled to capacity regardless of fluctuations in juvenile crime rates (Krisberg, Litsky, and Schwartz 1984; Schwartz and Willis 1994). Simply by virtue of urban residence, then, African Americans are more likely than whites to be detained. Mixed results have been reported with respect to urban-rural differences in sentencing (e.g., compare Feld 1990 to DeJong and Jackson 1998).

J. Minority Composition, Poverty, and Racial Inequality

Racial disparities have been linked to other aspects of social structure. In their analysis of juvenile court disposition across thirty-one Florida counties, Tittle and Curran (1988) found that dispositional severity was predicted by the relative size of the nonwhite and youth populations. Irrespective of crime rates, significant racial disparities occurred only in communities with large percentages of nonwhites and young people, and especially for drug and sex offenses (see also Bridges et al. 1993 and Dannefer and Schutt 1982; but see, contra, Frazier, Bishop, and Henretta 1992). Tittle and Curran interpreted these results by proposing a variant of conflict theory, suggesting that it is not the objective level of threat posed by minority groups that impels efforts to control them but, rather, "symbolic" aspects of threat. When whites perceive that there are concentrated populations of minorities disproportionately engaged in behaviors that provoke fear, anger, and the like, they subject them to intensified social control (Tittle and Curran 1988, p. 52).

In a study of juvenile court processing in 322 counties in twenty-one states, Sampson and Laub (1993) found that counties with greater underclass poverty and racial inequality detained youths and sentenced them to out-of-home placement at higher rates. The effects of structural context were more pronounced for African Americans than for whites. Particularly strong were the effects of concentrations of underclass poverty and levels of racial inequality on rates of African American out-of-home placement, especially for drug offenses. Sampson and Laub also interpret their findings in terms of symbolic threat, proposing that economic elites in counties with high concentrations of the underclass, racial poverty, and inequality use the juvenile justice system to exert greater control over populations viewed as offensive and threatening (Sampson and Laub 1993, p. 293).

Bridges et al. (1995) explored the effects of several features of community social structure on racial disparities in juvenile confinement across counties in Washington State. They found that racial disparities in confinement were very unevenly distributed across counties and were unrelated to race differences in rates of arrest. Instead, low white confinement rates were found in urban communities and those with large minority concentrations, while high minority confinement rates were found in counties with high rates of violent crime.

K. Local Culture

Feld (1991) and Mahoney (1987) propose that cross-jurisdictional variations in juvenile justice processing are also related to the socio-political environments in which justice system agencies operate and upon which they rely for legitimation, resources, and clients. Mahoney conducted a two-year study of a single juvenile court and showed that case processing and outcomes were affected by local issues and events, including resource shifts, political infighting, personality characteristics of key players, and changing political climates. Hers is a revealing account of the ways in which courts are embedded in, dependent on, and interactive with the socio-political environment. Cross-jurisdictional variations in juvenile justice practice have also been linked to idiosyncrasies of individual judges (e.g., Podkopacz and Feld 1996), to the bureaucratic structure of prosecutors' offices (Barnes and Franz 1989; Bishop and Frazier 1991), to methods of judicial appointment and levels of judicial specialization (Hasenfeld and Cheung 1985; Kempf, Decker, and Bing 1990), and to organizational culture, reflected in the shared beliefs and expectations of juvenile court officials (Aday 1986; Stapleton, Aday, and Ito 1982; Smith and Paternoster 1990). Researchers have only begun to explore most of these issues, whose implications for understanding minority over-representation in the justice system are presently unclear.

V. Discussion and Conclusions

While race and ethnic differentials in processing are attributable in part to differential involvement in crime, disparities that cannot be explained by race differences in offending are apparent at nearly every stage in the juvenile justice process. At the police level, decisions to deploy resources differentially to urban underclass neighborhoods put minority offenders at greater risk of detection and arrest. In lower-class and primarily nonwhite neighborhoods, police officers more often make proactive investigative stops, arrests, and use coercive authority, especially toward minority offenders. At the level of the police-juvenile encounter, race influences police decisions indirectly, at least with respect to minor offenses. Because minority youth suspects are more often perceived to be insolent and uncooperative, officers more often arrest them and refer them to court compared to white youth involved in similar offenses.

Most individual-level studies of juvenile court processing have shown a substantial direct effect of race at multiples processing stages even after legal factors are controlled. Race differentials introduced by the police are compounded in the juvenile courts (especially at intake), eventually culminating in marked disparities in minority confinement. Although legal variables have the strongest effects on court processing from intake through final disposition, they are contaminated to an unknown degree. Because minority youths are more likely to be arrested, charged with more serious offenses, and formally processed than their white counterparts, race bias is incorporated into and masked by the offense, prior record, and prior disposition variables that inform processing decisions.

The empirical record on individual-level case decision-making in the juvenile courts provides strong evidence that race has a substantial effect on decisions made at the "front end" of the system. Minority youths are less often diverted, more often referred for formal processing, and more often held in secure detention than white youths who are legally similar. By contrast, evidence of differential treatment at the prosecutorial charging stage is mixed. Contradictory results may reflect cross-jurisdictional differences in the extent to which cases are pre-screened for evidentiary sufficiency. At adjudication, where evidentiary consider-ations presumably take precedence, there is little evidence of minority disadvantage. To the contrary, research suggests that judges may compensate at this stage for disparities introduced at earlier stages in processing. At judicial disposition, evi-dence of race differentials is again more pronounced. Many studies report a direct race effect. Moreover, it is clear that much of the effect of race is indirect and hid-den due to selection effects: minority youths are considerably more likely than legally similar whites to be detained, and detainees receive more intrusive dispositions.

Recent cross-jurisdictional analyses also suggest that the structural context of juvenile courts influences justice system responses. There is evidence that courts in urban areas, areas characterized by racial inequality and underclass poverty, com-munities with high rates of violent crime, and communities with high proportions of minorities and the young process cases more formally, use detention more fre-quently, and impose harsher dispositions, especially for minority youths. Although the findings are far from conclusive, they hint that in impoverished high-crime areas where minorities are highly visible, youth of color are perceived by justice officials—and perhaps by the community at large—as especially needy, especially threatening, or both.

A. Explaining Differential Treatment

There is little evidence of overt bias on the part of police officials. Instead, it appears that race and ethnic differentials in handling are due in part to policies and prac-tices that appear to be race neutral but that are discriminatory in effect. Although it makes sense to deploy more police resources to neighborhoods where crime rates are highest, these neighborhoods are those in which minorities disproportionately reside. Subjecting poor, minority neighborhoods to differential surveillance and police-initiated investigative stops may provoke attitudes of antagonism among minority youths who perceive that they are being harassed, which in turn increases their likelihood of arrest, detention, and court processing.

Differential treatment by police also appears to reflect more subtle forms of bias related to the meanings officers attach to places and people. Because police officers seldom have sufficient information to accurately assess either the level of criminal activity or the dangers associated with the places they patrol and the peo-ple they encounter, they develop "typescripts" of the neighborhoods in which they work based on stereotypes that are linked to class and race: lower-class, racially mixed neighborhoods tend to be perceived as disreputable and dangerous, and so too the people within them. That minorities are more likely to be stopped, arrested, and treated coercively in these neighborhoods may reflect this ecological bias (Smith 1986, p. 335).

Interpretations of differential treatment in the juvenile courts may benefit from consideration of two research findings. First, there is much more evidence of race effects in the juvenile than in the criminal courts (e.g., Sampson and Lauritsen 1997). Second, legal variables typically account for much less of the explained variance in juvenile compared to criminal court outcomes. Taken together, these findings suggest that features of the juvenile court that distinguish it from its criminal counterpart are especially important in explaining racial disparities in processing. From its inception, the juvenile court has tried to balance the dual functions of social welfare and social control. The focus on individualized treatment is a unique feature of the juvenile court, calling for an assessment of youths' needs and life circumstances and identification of responses that will effectively address their problems. Not surprisingly then, studies that include controls for personal and social factors (e.g., family structure, willingness and ability of parents to provide control and supervision, school performance, employment status) report that these variables inform court referral, detention, and disposition decisions. From the perspective of juvenile court officials charged with acting "in the best interests of the child," these are key factors that should inform their decisions. That each of these factors tends also to be correlated with race makes it inevitable that minority youths will enter the juvenile court system more frequently and receive more intrusive dispositions.

Also contributing to racially disparate outcomes are class differences in access to resources. Parents' ability to comply with requirements for diversion are affected by access to phones and transportation, resulting in greater formal processing of youth of color. At least equally important, socioeconomic status is linked to the availability of insurance to defray the costs of private mental health and substance abuse treatment; to financial resources to purchase services such as alternative education, legal assistance, tutoring, recreational programs, and other developmental benefits; and to knowledge about private service options and providers, and how to access them. Economically disadvantaged adolescents are often processed through the system in order to make them eligible for treatment at state expense, while those from more affluent families can be diverted to purchase services on their own. Many justice officials view such practices as not only defensible but enlightened (Frazier and Bishop 1995, p. 32).

Insofar as the problems to which court officials respond are rooted in underlying social and economic conditions (e.g., poverty, racial inequality)—and there is considerable evidence that they are (Sampson and Groves 1986)—the same structural factors responsible for race differentials in offending also contribute to race disparities in justice system responses. In other words, differential offending and disparities in processing influence one another and are mutually affected by underlying structural conditions and the cultural contexts in which they occur (see also McCord, Widom, and Crowell 2001, pp. 228–60; Bortner, Zatz, and Hawkins 2000; Kempf-Leonard 2007; Piquero 2008).

While racial disparities may be due in part to real differences in youths' backgrounds and circumstances and to differential access to resources, research suggests that these disparities also result from racial stereotyping in the filtering and processing of information on which decisions are based. Because justice officials rarely have either the information or assessment tools on which to base reliable and valid assessments of an offender's dangerousness or amenability to treatment, they develop a "perceptual shorthand" (Hawkins 1981, p. 280; Steffensmeier, Ulmer, and Kramer 1998, p. 767) based on stereotypes and attributions that are linked to offender characteristics, including race and ethnicity. Because the unique substantive considerations of the juvenile court—i.e., those related to diagnosing youth problems and developing appropriate treatments—tend to be especially vague and amorphous (e.g., what is a "dysfunctional" family?), the juvenile court would appear to be an especially receptive host to these more subtle forms of discrimination.

In addition to assessing the role that external factors play in contributing to a youth's offending, juvenile court officials (like their criminal court counterparts) are asked to make judgments about youths' culpability and their propensity for future crime. The risk that youth of color will be perceived differently than whites based on factors other than offense and prior record is particularly great: stereotypes of minority offenders as especially threatening and dangerous and are deeply imbedded in popular culture. This interpretation also fits the results of cross-jurisdictional studies showing higher levels of formal social control in counties with high concentrations of impoverished minority populations and in counties with high violent crime rates. In sum, at both the individual and community levels, it seems that the unique social welfare concerns of the juvenile court (based on real and perceived family, school, and other problems) combine with traditional social control concerns (focused on real and perceived culpability and danger to society) to produce greater minority involvement in the juvenile justice system.

B. Policy Implications

The problem of minority over-representation in the juvenile justice system is complex and does not lend itself to easy solutions. It is attributable to race differences in offending; to the reproduction by justice officials of cultural stereotypes of minority offenders, their families, and the neighborhoods in which they live; to law-making and enforcement that differentially disadvantage minority youths; and to racial disparities in processing, especially those introduced by consideration of youths' family and school status. All of these seem to be inextricably intertwined and mutually reinforcing. If they are, and if all are rooted in macrostructural factors, then none are likely to be reduced short of broad-scale social and economic change. Race differentials in both offending and justice system responses have common origins in social and economic features of contemporary American life. Because higher rates of offending among minority youths are attributable in great part to the impoverished conditions in which minority families disproportionately reside—in socially isolated and economically impoverished urban neighborhoods where traditions of crime and deviance are pervasive—minority over-representation in the juvenile justice system cannot be addressed effectively through reforms in the justice system itself. It is essential that we attend to structural conditions—poverty, unemployment, racial segregation, underfunded and poor-quality schools, family disruption, inadequate housing, lack of access to physical and mental health care, neighborhood powerlessness—if we hope to reduce offending and eliminate the "needs" to which juvenile justice officials respond. Tragic is the failure to recognize that "individual-ized needs" are not individual, but social and economic, as is the concomitant expectation that minority over-representation in the juvenile justice system can be addressed effectively by tinkering with juvenile justice operations. To be sure, there are some improvements that can be made within the system, but these are ancillary to the social and economic restructuring that will be required to produce lasting change. Because stereotyping of minority neighborhoods, families, and youths by justice officials increases the probability of arrest, referral, formal charging, and intrusive dispositions, efforts to combat myths and misconceptions—especially those that portray minority offenders as threatening and morally defective, and their families as disinterested or incapable of providing adequate guidance and supervision—can be helpful. Training justice officials in cultural awareness and sensitivity may produce greater consciousness of stereotypical attitudes and beliefs and facilitate more objective assessments of youths and their families.

Steps can also be taken to modify formal and informal agency policies that work to the disadvantage of poor minority youths. The common intake require-ment that there be a face-to-face interview with a parent as a precondition of diver-sion and release is a case in point. Home visits and phone visits could keep many youths out of detention. Moreover, adjudications of delinquency should not be the backdoor through which youths obtain counseling and treatment services which their parents cannot afford. Resources could be allocated to the front end of the system in the form of vouchers for mental health and other services available in the community. These services could then be accessed by financially disadvantaged youths and their families without legal penalty.

The greater need is for state and national attention to the problems faced by impoverished inner city families. The creation of jobs (e.g., by providing industry incentives to relocate to the urban core, including tax breaks and employee subsi-dies) and systems of universal health care are essential. So too are efforts to improve schools—by incorporating skilled trades curricula, updating equipment and educa-tional materials, providing incentives to attract good teachers, replacing out-of-school suspension with in-school behavioral management, and providing after-school tutoring for at-risk youth. Improving schools would reduce dropout, and better prepare youths for higher education and for positions other than dead-end, minimum wage jobs in the service sector. Efforts to organize and empower residents in minority communities are also essential. Numerous strategies might be employed (e.g., beginning with community policing and enlisting the support of local churches) to encourage inner-city residents to come together in civic organi-zations for mutual support in addressing crime and other neighborhood problems. It will take neighborhood organization to bring community problems to the atten-tion of local and state officials and to exert sufficient pressure to institute change (e.g., codes enforcement; rehabilitating abandoned houses that become havens for illicit activity; establishing daycare centers, free clinics, and recreational programs). In the final analysis, reducing minority offending and disparities in the processing of minority offenders will require nothing less than elevating the problems faced by impoverished inner-city families to a national priority. Unless "other people's children" are seen as "our children," and their nurturance becomes a major public health issue, there can be little hope for real and sustained change.

NOTES

1. Although formal charging is a prosecutorial function, the charges that police make a record of at the arrest stage undoubtedly influence prosecutorial decision-making.

2. These findings highlight the importance of analyzing juvenile justice as a series of decision points. When research is restricted to a single, late-stage outcome, race effects can be obscured due to correlations between race and earlier processing decisions that predict these later outcomes. It is noteworthy that most of the studies reporting no race effect at disposition involve single-stage analyses.

REFERENCES

Aday, David P., Jr. 1986. "Court Structure, Defense Attorney Use, and Juvenile Court Decisions." *Sociological Quarterly* 27: 107–19.

Anderson, Elijah. 1990. *Street Wise: Race, Class, and Change in an Urban Community*. Chicago, IL: University of Chicago Press.

Armstrong, Gayle, and Nancy Rodriguez. 2005. "Effects of Individual and Contextual Characteristics on Preadjudication Detention of Juvenile Delinquents." *Justice Quarterly* 22(4): 521–39.

Austin, James. 1995. "The Overrepresentation of Minority Youths in the California Juvenile Justice System: Perceptions and Realities." In *Minorities in Juvenile Justice*, edited by Kimberly Kempf Leonard, Carl E. Pope, and William H. Feyerherm. Thousand Oaks, CA: Sage.

Barnes, Carole W., and Randal S. Franz. 1989. "Questionably Adult: Determinants and Effects of the Juvenile Waiver Decision." *Justice Quarterly* 6(1): 117–35.

Beckett, Katherine, and Ted Sasson. 2004. *The Politics of Injustice: Crime and Punishment in America*, 2nd ed. Thousand Oaks, CA: Sage.

Bell, Duran, Jr., and Kevin Lang. 1985. "The Intake Dispositions of Juvenile Offenders." *Journal of Research in Crime and Delinquency* 22: 309–28.

Bilchik, Shay. 1999. "Minorities in the Juvenile Justice System." In *1999 National Report Series Juvenile Justice Bulletin*. Washington, DC: Office of Juvenile Justice and Delinquency Prevention.

Bishop, Donna M. 2005. "The Role of Race and Ethnicity in Juvenile Justice Processing." In *Our Children, Their Children: Confronting Racial and Ethnic Differences in American Juvenile Justice*, edited by Darnell Hawkins and Kimberly Kempf-Leonard. MacArthur Foundation Research Network on Adolescent Development and Juvenile Justice. The John D. and Catherine T. MacArthur Foundation. Chicago, IL: University of Chicago Press.

Bishop, Donna M., and Charles E. Frazier. 1988. "The Influence of Race in Juvenile Justice Processing." *Journal of Research in Crime and Delinquency* 25: 242–63.

———. 1991. "Transfer of Juveniles to Criminal Court: A Case Study and Analysis of Prosecutorial Waiver." *Notre Dame Journal of Law, Ethics, and Public Policy* 5: 281–302.

———. 1992. "Gender Bias in Juvenile Justice Processing: Implications of the JJDP Act." *Journal of Criminal Law and Criminology* 82: 1162–86.

———. 1996. "Race Effects in Juvenile Justice Decision-Making: Findings of a Statewide Analysis." *Journal of Criminal Law and Criminology* 86: 392–414.

Bishop, Donna M., Michael Leiber, and Joseph Johnson. 2010. "Contexts of Decision Making in the Juvenile Justice System: An Organizational Approach to Understanding Minority Overrepresentation" *Journal of Youth Violence & Juvenile Justice* 22: 213–233.

Bittner, Egon. 1990. "Policing Juveniles: The Social Context of Common Practices." In *Aspects of Police Work*, edited by Egon Bittner. Boston, MA: Northeastern University Press.

Black, Donald J., and Albert J. Reiss. 1970. "Police Control of Juveniles." *American Sociological Review* 35: 63–77.

Blalock, Hubert M. 1967. "Toward a Theory of Minority-Group Relations." New York: Wiley.

Bond-Maupin, Lisa J., Carol Chiago Lujan, and M. A. Bortner. 1995. "Jailing of American-Indian Adolescents: The Legacy of Cultural Domination and Imposed Law." *Crime, Law, and Social Change* 23: 1–16.

Bortner, M. A., Marjorie S. Zatz, and Darnell Hawkins. 2000. "Race and Transfer: Empirical Research and Social Context." In *The Changing Borders or Juvenile Justice: Transfer of Adolescents to the Criminal Court*, edited by Jeffrey Fagan and Franklin E. Zimring. Chicago, IL: University of Chicago Press.

Braga, Anthony. 2006 "Policing Crime Hot Spots." In *Preventing Crime: What Works for Children, Offenders, Victims and Places*, edited by Brandon C. Welsh and David P. Farrington. New York: Springer.

Bridges, George S., Darlene Conley, George Beretta, and Rodney L. Engen. 1993. "Racial Disproportionality in the Juvenile Justice System: Final Report." Olympia, WA: State of Washington, Department of Social and Health Services.

Bridges, George S., Darlene Conley, Rodney L. Engen, and Townsend Price-Spratlen. 1995. "Racial Disparities in the Confinement of Juveniles: Effects of Crime and Community Social Structure on Punishment." In *Minorities in Juvenile Justice*, edited by Kimberly Kempf-Leonard, Carl Pope, and William H. Feyerherm. Thousand Oaks, CA: Sage.

Bridges, George S., and Sara Steen. 1998. "Racial Disparities in Official Assessments of Juvenile Offenders: Attributional Stereotypes as Mediating Mechanisms." *American Sociological Review* 63: 554–70.

Cicourel, Aaron V. 1968. *The Social Organization of Juvenile Justice*. New York: Wiley.

Clarke, Elizabeth E. 1996. "A Case For Reinventing Juvenile Transfer." *Juvenile and Family Court Journal* 47: 3–22.

Cohen, Lawrence E., and James R. Kluegel. 1979. "The Detention Decision: A Study of the Impact of Social Characteristics and Legal Factors in Two Metropolitan Courts." *Social Forces* 58: 146–61.

Conley, Dale J. 1994. "Adding Color to a Black and White Picture: Using Qualitative Data to Explain Racial Disproportionality in the Juvenile Justice System." *Journal of Research in Crime and Delinquency* 31: 135–48.

Corley, Charles J., Timothy S. Bynum, Angel Prewitt, and Pamela Schram. 1996. "The Impact of Race on Juvenile Court Processes: Quantitative Analyses with Qualitative Insights." *Caribbean Journal of Criminology and Social Psychology* 1: 1–23.

Dannefer, Dale, and Russell K. Schutt. 1982. "Race and Juvenile Justice Processing in Court and Police Agencies." *American Journal of Sociology* 87: 1113–32.

DeJong, Christina, and Kenneth C. Jackson. 1998. "Putting Race into Context: Race, Juvenile Justice Processing, and Urbanization." *Justice Quarterly* 15: 487–504.

Donziger, Steven R., ed. 1996. *The Real War on Crime: The Report of The National Criminal Justice Commission*. New York: HarperCollins.

Dunham, Roger, and Geoffrey Alpert. 2009. "Officer and Suspect Demeanor: A Qualitative Analysis of Change." *Police Quarterly* 12(1): 6–21.

Elliott, Delbert S. 1994. "Serious Violent Offenders: Onset, Developmental Course, and Termination—The American Society of Criminology 1993 Presidential Address." *Criminology* 32: 1–21.

Emerson, Robert M. 1969. *Judging Delinquents: Context and Process in the Juvenile Court*. Chicago, IL: Aldine.

Engel, Robin Shepherd, James J. Sobol, and Robert E. Worden. 2000. "Further Exploration of the Demeanor Hypothesis: The Interaction Effects of Suspects' Characteristics and Demeanor on Police Behavior." *Justice Quarterly* 17: 235–58.

Engen, Rodney, Sarah Steen, and George Bridges. 2002. "Racial Disparities in the Punishment of Youth: A Theoretical and Empirical Assessment of the Literature." *Social Problems*. 49(2): 194–220.

Esbensen, Finn-Aage, and D. Wayne Osgood. 1999. "Gang Resistance Education and Training (GREAT): Results From the National Evaluation." *Journal of Research in Crime and Delinquency* 36: 194–225.

Esbensen Finn-Aage, and L. Thomas Winfree. 1998. "Race and Gender Differences Between Gang and Nongang Youths: Results from a Multisite Survey." *Justice Quarterly* 15: 505–26.

Eschholz, Sarah, Matthew Mallard, and Stacy Flynn. 2004. "Image of Prime Time Justice: A Content Analysis of 'NYPD Blue' and 'Law and Order.'" *Journal of Criminal Justice and Popular Culture* 10: 161–80.

Fagan, Jeffrey, Ellen Slaughter, and Eliot Hartstone. 1987. "Blind Justice? The Impact of Race on the Juvenile Justice Process." *Crime and Delinquency* 33: 224–58.

Farrell, Ronald, and Victoria Swigert. 1978. "Prior Offense Record as a Self-Fulfilling Prophecy." *Law and Society Review* 12: 437–53.

Feld, Barry C. 1990. "The Punitive Juvenile Court and the Quality of Procedural Justice: Distinctions Between Rhetoric and Reality." *Crime and Delinquency* 36: 443–66.

———. 1991. "Justice by Geography: Urban, Suburban, and Rural Variations in Juvenile Justice Administration." *Journal of Criminal Law and Criminology* 82: 156–210.

———. 1995. "The Social Context of Juvenile Justice Administration: Racial Disparities in an Urban Juvenile Court." In *Minorities in Juvenile Justice*, edited by Kimberly Kempf-Leonard, Carl E. Pope, and William H. Feyerherm. Thousand Oaks, CA: Sage.

———. 1999. *Bad Kids: Race and the Transformation of the Juvenile Court*. New York: Oxford University Press.

Fenwick, C. R. 1982. "Juvenile Court Intake Decision-Making: The Importance of Family Affiliation." *Journal of Criminal Justice* 10: 443–53.

Fisbein, Diana. 2001. Bio-Social Perspectives in Criminology. Wadsworth.

———. 1995. "Reflections on Race Effects in Juvenile Justice." In *Minorities in Juvenile Justice*, edited by Kimberly Kempf-Leonard, Carl E. Pope, and William H. Feyerherm. Thousand Oaks, CA: Sage.

Frazier, Charles E., Donna M. Bishop, and John C. Henretta. 1992. "The Social Context of Race Differentials in Juvenile Justice Dispositions." *Sociological Quarterly* 33: 447–58.

Frazier, Charles E., and John K. Cochran. 1986. "Detention of Juveniles: Its Effects on Subsequent Juvenile Court Processing Decisions." *Youth and Society* 17: 286–305.

Freng, Adrienne, and Finn-Aage Esbensen. 2007. "A Comparative Analysis of Race and Gang Affiliation: Is Race a Marginalizing Factor?" *Justice Quarterly* 24: 600–28.

Gottfredson, Michael, and Travis Hirschi. 1990. *A General Theory of Crime*. Palo Alto, CA: Stanford University Press.

Graham, Sandra, and Brian Lowery. 2004. "Priming Unconscious Racial Stereotypes About Adolescent Offenders." *Law and Human Behavior* 28(5): 483–504.

Griffiths, Curt T., and L. Thomas Winfree, Jr. 1982. "Attitudes Toward the Police— A Comparison of Canadian and American Adolescents." *International Journal of Comparative and Applied Criminal Justice* 6: 128–41.

Guevara, Lori, Denise Herz, and Cassia Spohn. 2006. "Gender and Juvenile Justice Decision Making: What Role Does Race Play?" *Feminist Criminology* 1: 258–82.

Hartney, Christopher, and Linh Vuong. 2009. *Created Equal: Racial and Ethnic Disparities in the U.S. Criminal Justice System*. Oakland, CA: National Council on Crime and Delinquency.

Hasenfeld, Yeheskel, and Paul P. Cheung. 1985. "The Juvenile Court as a People-Processing Organization: A Political Economy Perspective." *American Journal of Sociology* 90: 801–24.

Hawkins, Darnell. 1981. "Causal Attribution and Punishment for Crime." *Deviant Behavior* 1: 207–30.

Hawkins, J. David, Todd I. Herrenkohl, David P. Farrington, Devon Brewer, Richard F. Catalano, and Tracy W. Harachi. 1998. "A Review of Predictors of Youth Violence." In *Serious and Violent Juvenile Offenders: Risk Factors and Successful Interventions*, edited by Rolf Loeber and David P. Farrington. Thousand Oaks, CA: Sage.

Henretta, John C., Charles E. Frazier, and Donna M. Bishop. 1986. "The Effect of Prior Case Outcomes on Juvenile Justice Decision-Making." *Social Forces* 65: 554–62.

Hindelang, Michael J., Travis Hirschi, and Joseph Weis. 1981. *Measuring Delinquency*. Beverly Hills, CA: Sage.

Hirschi, Travis. 1969. *Causes of Delinquency*. Berkeley, CA: University of California Press.

Holman, Bill, and John Ziedenberg. 2006. *The Dangers of Detention: The Impact of Incarcerating Youth in Detention and Other Secure Facilities*. Washington, DC: Annie E. Casey Foundation, Justice Policy Institute.

Horowitz, Ruth, and Anne E. Pottieger. 1991. "Gender Bias in Juvenile Justice Handling of Seriously Crime-Involved Youths." *Journal of Research in Crime and Delinquency* 28: 75–100.

Horwitz, Allan and Michael Wasserman. 1980. "Some Misleading Conceptions About Sentencing Research in the Juvenile Court." *Criminology* 18: 411–424.

Huizinga, David, and Delbert S. Elliott. 1987. "Juvenile Offenders: Prevalence, Offender Incidence, and Arrest Rates by Race." *Crime and Delinquency* 33: 206–23.

Huizinga, David, Rolf Loeber, and Terence P. Thornberry. 1994. *Urban Delinquency and Substance Abuse: Initial Findings*. Washington, DC: Office of Juvenile Justice and Delinquency Prevention.

Huizinga, David, Terence Thornberry, Kelly Knight, and Peter Lovegrove. 2007. "Disproportionate Minority Contact in the Juvenile Justice System: A Study of Differential Minority Arrest/Referral to Court in Three Cities." Washington, DC: U.S. Department of Justice.

Irwin, John. 1985. *The Jail: Managing the Underclass in American Society*. Berkeley, CA: University of California Press.

Jarjoura, G. Roger. 1993. "Does Dropping Out of School Enhance Delinquent Involvement? Results from a Large-Scale National Probability Sample." *Criminology* 31: 149–71.

Kempf, Kimberly L., Scott H. Decker, and Robert L. Bing. 1990. *An Analysis of Apparent Disparities in the Handling of Black Youth Within Missouri's Juvenile Justice Systems.* St. Louis, MO: Department of Administration of Justice, University of Missouri-St. Louis.

Kempf-Leonard, Kimberly, and Henry Sontheimer. 1995. "The Role of Race in Juvenile Justice in Pennsylvania." In *Minorities in Juvenile Justice*, edited by Kimberly Kempf-Leonard, Carl E. Pope, and William H. Feyerherm. Thousand Oaks, CA: Sage.

Kempf-Leonard, Kimberly. 2007. "Minority Youths and Juvenile Justice: Disproportionate Minority Contact After Nearly 20 Years of Reform Efforts." *Youth Violence and Juvenile Justice* 5(1): 71–87.

Knight, George, Michelle Little, Sandra Losoya and Edward Mulvey. 2004. "The Self-Report of Offending Among Serious Juvenile Offenders: Cross-Gender, Cross-Ethnic/Race Measurement Equivalence." *Youth Violence and Juvenile Justice* 2: 273–295.

Krisberg, Barry, and James F. Austin. 1993. *Reinventing Juvenile Justice.* Newbury Park, CA: Sage.

Krisberg, Barry, Paul Litsky, and Ira M. Schwartz. 1984. "Youth in Confinement: Justice by Geography." *Journal of Research in Crime and Delinquency* 21(2): 153–81.

Kurtz, P. David, Martha M. Giddings, and Richard Sutphen. 1993. "A Prospective Investigation of Racial Disparity in the Juvenile Justice System." *Juvenile and Family Court Journal* 44: 43–59.

Kurtz, Don, Travis Linnemann, and Ryan Spohn. 2008. "Investigating Racial Disparity at the Detention Decision: The Role of Respectability." *Southwest Journal of Criminal Justice* 5(2): 140–57.

Lauritsen, Janet L. 2005. "Social and Scientific Influences on the Measurement of Criminal Victimization." *Journal of Quantitative Criminology* 21: 245–66.

Leiber, Michael J. 1994. "A Comparison of Juvenile Court Outcomes for Native Americans, African Americans, and Whites." *Justice Quarterly* 11: 257–79.

———. 1995. "Toward Clarification of the Concept of 'Minority' Status and Decision-Making in Juvenile Court Proceedings." *Journal of Crime and Justice* 18: 79–108.

———. 2003. *The Contexts of Juvenile Justice Decision Making: When Race Matters.* Albany, NY: State University of New York Press.

———. Forthcoming. "Race, Pre- and Post-Detention, and Juvenile Justice Decision Making." *Crime and Delinquency.*

Leiber, Michael J., Sarah Jane Brubaker, and Kristan Fox. 2009. "A Closer Look at the Individual and Joint Effects of Gender and Race on Juvenile Court Decision Making" *Feminist Criminology* 4(4): 333–58.

Leiber, Michael J., and Kristan Fox. 2005. "Race and the Impact of Detention on Juvenile Justice Decision Making." *Crime and Delinquency* 51(4): 470–97.

Leiber, Michael J., and Katherine M. Jamieson. 1995. "Race and Decisionmaking Within Juvenile Justice: The Importance of Context." *Journal of Quantitative Criminology* 11: 363–88.

Leiber, Michael J., and Joseph Johnson. 2008. "Being Young and Black: What Are Their Effects On Juvenile Justice Decision Making?" *Crime and Delinquency* 54(4): 560–81.

Lipsky, Michael. 1980. *Street-Level Bureaucracy: Dilemmas of the Individual in Public Services.* New York: Russell Sage.

Liska, Allen E., and Mark Tausig. 1979. "Theoretical Interpretations of Social Class and Racial Differentials in Legal Decision-Making for Juveniles." *Sociological Quarterly* 20: 197–207.

Lundman, Richard J., R. E. Sykes, and John P. Clark. 1978. "Police Control of Juveniles:
      A Replication." *Journal of Research in Crime and Delinquency* 15: 74–91.
MacDonald, John M., and Meda Chesney-Lind. 2001. "Gender Bias and Juvenile Justice
      Revisited: A Multiyear Analysis." *Crime and Delinquency* 47: 173–95.
Mahoney, Anne Rankin. 1987. *Juvenile Justice in Context.* Boston, MA: Northeastern
      University Press.
McCarter, Susan. 1997. *Understanding the Overrepresentation of Minorities in Virginia's
      Juvenile Justice System.* Ann Arbor, MI: UMI Dissertation Services.
McCarthy, Belinda R., and Brent L. Smith. 1986. "The Conceptualization of Discrimination
      in the Juvenile Justice Process: The Impact of Administrative Factors and Screening
      Decisions on Juvenile Court Dispositions." *Criminology* 24: 41–64.
McCord, Joan, Cathy Spatz Widom, and Nancy A. Crowell, eds. 2001. *Juvenile Crime,
      Juvenile Justice.* National Research Council and Institute of Medicine. Washington,
      DC: National Academy Press.
Miller, Jerome. 1996. *Search and Destroy.* New York: Cambridge University Press.
National Youth Gang Center. 2009. *National Youth Gang Survey Analysis.* Washington, DC:
      Office of Juvenile Justice and Delinquency Prevention. http://www.nationalgangcenter.
      gov/Survey-Analysis.
Orlando, Frank. 1999. "Controlling the Front Gates: Effective Admissions Policies and
      Practices." Vol. 3 in *Pathways to Juvenile Detention Reform.* Baltimore, MD: Annie
      E. Casey Foundation.
Patterson, Gerald R., John B. Reid, and Thomas J. Dishion. 1992. *Antisocial Boys.* Eugene,
      OR: Castalia.
Piliavin, Irving, and Scott Briar. 1964. "Police Encounters with Juveniles." *American Journal
      of Sociology* 69: 206–14.
Piquero, Alex. 2008. "Disproportionate Minority Contact." *The Future of Children.* 18(2):
      59–79.
Platt, Anthony M. 1977. *The Child Savers.* Chicago, IL: University of Chicago Press.
Podkopacz, Marcy Rasmussen, and Barry C. Feld. 1996. "The End of the Line: An Empirical
      Study of Judicial Waiver." *Journal of Criminal Law and Criminology* 86: 449–92.
Pope, Carl E., and William H. Feyerherm. 1990a. "Minority Status and Juvenile Justice
      Processing: An Assessment of the Research Literature (Part I)." *Criminal Justice
      Abstracts* 22: 327–35.
———. 1990b. "Minority Status and Juvenile Justice Processing: An Assessment of the
      Research Literature (Part II)." *Criminal Justice Abstracts* 22: 527–42.
———. 1993. *Minorities and the Juvenile Justice System.* Washington, DC: National Institute
      of Justice, Office of Juvenile Justice and Delinquency Prevention.
Pope, Carl E., and Michael Leiber. 2005. "Disproportionate Minority Contact (DMC): The
      Federal Initiative." In *Our Children, Their Children: Confronting Racial and Ethnic
      Differences in American Juvenile Justice,* edited by Darnell F. Hawkins and Kimberly
      Kempf-Leonard. Chicago, IL: University of Chicago Press.
Puzzanchera, Charles, and Bill Adams. 2008. National Disproportionate Minority Contact
      Databook. Updated May 17, 2010. Washington, DC: National Center for Juvenile
      Justice, Office of Juvenile Justice and Delinquency Prevention. http://ojjdp.ncjrs.gov/
      ojstatbb/dmcdb/.
Quinney, Richard. 1977. *Class, State and Crime: On the Theory and Practice of Criminal
      Justice.* New York: David McKay.
Rand, Michael. 2008. Criminal Victimization, 2007. Bureau of Justice
      Statistics Bulletin, U.S. Department of Justice, Washington, DC.

Rodriguez, Nancy. 2007. "Juvenile Court Context and Detention Decisions: Reconsidering the Role of Race, Ethnicity, and Community Characteristics in Juvenile Court Processes." *Justice Quarterly* 24: 629–56.

———. 2010. "The Cumulative Effect of Race and Ethnicity in Juvenile Court Outcomes and Why Preadjudication Detention Matters." *Journal of Research in Crime and Delinquency* 47(3): 391–413.

Rodriguez, Nancy, Hillary Smith, and Marjorie Zatz. 2009. "'Youth is Enmeshed in a Highly Dysfunctional Family System': Exploring the Relationship Among Dysfunctional, Parental Incarceration, and Juvenile Court Decision Making." *Criminology* 47(1): 177–207.

Rubinstein, Jonathan. 1973. *City Police*. New York: Farrar, Straus and Giroux.

Sampson, Robert J. 1986. "Effects of Socioeconomic Context on Official Reaction to Juvenile Delinquency." *America Sociological Review* 51: 876–85.

Sampson, Robert J., and W. Byron Groves. 1989. "Community Structure and Crime: Testing Social-Disorganization Theory." *American Journal of Sociology* 94(4): 774–802.

Sampson, Robert J., and John H. Laub. 1993. "Structural Variations in Juvenile Court Processing: Inequality, the Underclass, and Social Control." *Law and Society Review* 27: 285–311.

Sampson, Robert J., and Janet L. Lauritsen. 1997. "Racial and Ethnic Disparities in Crime and Criminal Justice in the United States." In *Ethnicity, Crime, and Integration: Comparative and Cross-National Perspectives*. Vol. 21 of *Crime and Justice: A Review of Research*, edited by Michael Tonry. Chicago, IL: University of Chicago Press.

Sampson, Robert J., Jeffrey D. Morenoff, and Felton Earls. 1999. "Beyond Social Capital: Spatial Dynamics of Collective Efficacy for Children." *American Sociological Review* 64: 633–60.

Sampson, Robert J., Stephen W. Raudenbush, and Felton Earls. 1997. "Neighborhoods and Violent Crime: A Multilevel Study of Collective Efficacy." *Science* 277: 918–24.

Sampson, Robert J., and William J. Wilson. 1995. "Toward a Theory of Race, Crime, and Urban Inequality." In *Crime and Inequality*, edited by J. Hagan and R. D. Peterson. Stanford, CA: Stanford University Press.

Sanborn, Joseph, Jr., 1996. "Factors Perceived to Affect Delinquent Dispositions in Juvenile Court: Putting the Sentencing Decision Into Context." *Crime and Delinquency* 42: 99–113.

Schlossman, Steven. 1977. *Love and the American Delinquent: The Theory and Practice of "Progressive" Juvenile Justice*. Chicago, IL: University of Chicago Press.

Schwartz, Ira M., and Deborah A. Willis. 1994. "National Trends in Juvenile Detention." In *Reforming Juvenile Detention: No More Hidden Closets*, edited by I. M. Schwartz and W. H. Barton. Columbus, OH: Ohio State University Press.

Sealock, Miriam D., and Sally S. Simpson. 1998. "Unraveling Bias in Arrest Decisions: The Role of Juvenile Offender Type-Scripts." *Justice Quarterly* 15: 427–57.

Secret, Philip E., and James B. Johnson. 1997. "The Effect of Race on Juvenile Justice Decision Making in Nebraska: Detention, Adjudication, and Disposition, 1988–1993." *Justice Quarterly* 14: 445–78.

Shaw, Clifford R., and Henry D. McKay. 1969. *Juvenile Delinquency and Urban Areas*. Chicago, IL: University of Chicago Press.

Sickmund, Melissa, T. J. Sladky, and Wei Kang. 2008. "Census of Juveniles in Residential Placement Databook." http://www.ojjdp.gov/ojstatbb/dmcdb/index.html.

Sklar, Holly. 1995. "The Upper Class and Mothers in the Hood." In *Race, Class, and Gender: An Anthology*, edited by M. L. Anderson and P. H. Collins. Belmont, CA: Wadsworth.

Skolnick, Jerome. 1966. *Justice Without Trial: Law Enforcement in a Democratic Society*. New York: Wiley.

Smith, Douglas A. 1986. "The Neighborhood Context of Police Behavior." In *Communities and Crime*. Vol. 8 of *Crime and Justice: A Review of Research*, edited by Albert J. Reiss and Michael Tonry. Chicago, IL: University of Chicago Press.

Smith, Douglas A., and Raymond Paternoster. 1990. "Formal Processing and Future Delinquency: Deviance Amplification as Selection Artifact." *Law and Society Review* 24: 1109–31.

Smith, Douglas A., and Christy A. Visher. 1981. "Street-Level Justice: Situational Determinants of Police Arrest Decisions." *Social Problems* 29: 167–77.

Smith, Douglas A., Christy A. Visher, and Laura A. Davidson. 1984. "Equity and Discretionary Justice: The Influence of Race on Police Arrest Decisions." *Journal of Criminal Law and Criminology* 75: 234–49.

Steen, Sara, Rodney L. Engen, and Randy R. Gainey. 2005. "Images of Danger and Culpability: Racial Stereotyping, Case Processing, and Criminal Sentencing." *Criminology* 43(2): 435–468.

Snyder, Howard J. and Melissa Sickmund. 2006. *Juvenile Offenders and Victims: 2006 National Report*. Washington, DC: U.S. Department of Justice.

Snyder, Howard. 2008. *Juvenile Arrests 2005*. Juvenile Justice Bulletin. Washington, DC: U.S. Department of Justice.

Snyder, Howard J., and Melissa Sickmund. 1999. *Juvenile Offenders and Victims: 1999 National Report*. Washington, DC: Office of Juvenile Justice and Delinquency Prevention.

Stapleton, W. Vaughn, David P. Aday, Jr., and Jeanne A. Ito. 1982. "An Empirical Typology of American Metropolitan Juvenile Courts." *American Sociological Review* 88: 549–61.

Steffensmeier, Darrell, Jeffrey Ulmer, and John Kramer. 1998. "The Interaction of Race, Gender, and Age in Criminal Sentencing: The Punishment Cost of Being Young, Black, and Male." *Criminology* 36: 763–97.

Terrill, William, and Eugene Paoline. 2007. "Nonarrest Decision Making in Police-Citizen Encounters." *Police Quarterly* 10(3): 308–31.

Terrill, William, and Michael D. Reisig. 2003. "Neighborhood Context and Police Use of Force." *Journal of Research in Crime and Delinquency* 40: 291–321.

Thornberry, Terence P., and R. L. Christenson. 1984. "Juvenile Justice Decision-Making as a Longitudinal Process." *Social Forces* 63: 433–44.

Tittle, Charles R., and Debra A. Curran. 1988. "Contingencies for Dispositional Disparities in Juvenile Justice." *Social Forces* 67: 23–58.

Tonry, Michael. 1994. "Racial Politics, Racial Disparities, and the War on Crime." *Crime and Delinquency* 40: 475–94.

Tonry, Michael. 1995. *Malign Neglect: Race, Crime, and Punishment in America*. New York: Oxford University Press.

Walker, Samuel. 1999. *The Police in America*. Boston: McGraw-Hill.

Walker, Samuel, Cassia Spohn, and Miriam DeLone. 2000. *The Color of Justice: Race, Ethnicity, and Crime in America, Second Edition*. Belmont, CA: Wadsworth.

———. 2006. *The Color of Justice: Race, Ethnicity, and Crime in America*, 3rd ed. Belmont, CA: Wadsworth.

Werthman, Carl, and Irving Piliavin. 1967. "Gang Members and The Police." In *The Police: Six Sociological Essays*, edited by David Bordua. New York: Wiley.

Wilson, James Q. 1968. "The Police and the Delinquent in Two Cities." In *Controlling Delinquents*, edited by Stanton Wheeler. New York: Wiley.

Wilson, William Julius. 1987 *The Truly Disadvantaged: The Inner City, the Underclass, and Public Policy.* Chicago, IL: University of Chicago Press.

Winfree, L. Thomas, Jr., and Curt T. Griffiths. 1977. "Adolescents' Attitudes Toward the Police: A Survey of High School Students." In *Juvenile Delinquency: Little Brother Grows Up*, edited by Theodore N. Ferdinand. Beverly Hills, CA: Sage.

Worden, Robert E., and Stephanie M. Myers. 1999. "Police Encounters with Juvenile Subjects." Unpublished paper commissioned by the Panel of Juvenile Crime: Prevention, Treatment, and Control. Washington, DC: National Academy of Sciences.

Wordes, Madeline, and Timothy S. Bynum. 1995. "Policing Juveniles: Is There Bias Against Youths of Color?" In *Minorities in Juvenile Justice*, edited by Kimberly Kempf-Leonard, Carl E. Pope, and William H. Feyerherm. Thousand Oaks, CA: Sage.

Wordes, Madeline, Timothy S. Bynum, and Charles J. Corley. 1994. "Locking Up Youth: The Impact of Race on Detention Decisions." *Journal of Research in Crime and Delinquency* 31: 149–65.

Wu, Bohsiu, Stephen Cernkovich, and Christopher S. Dunn. 1997. "Assessing the Effects of Race and Class on Juvenile Justice Processing in Ohio." *Journal of Criminal Justice* 25: 265–77.

Wu, Bohsiu, and Angel Ilarraza Fuentes. 1998. "Juvenile Justice Processing: The Entangled Effects of Race and Urban Poverty." *Juvenile and Family Court Journal* 49: 41–53.

Zimring, Franklin E. 1981. "Kids, Groups, and Crime: Some Implications of a Well-Known Secret." *Journal of Criminal Law and Criminology* 72: 867–902.

CHAPTER 21

THE CONUNDRUM OF GIRLS AND JUVENILE JUSTICE PROCESSING

KIMBERLY KEMPF-LEONARD

For nearly all types of delinquency and crime, females comprise the minority of offenders. This disproportionate under-representation of females has been observed across time, place, race, ethnic group, data source, and age. Often the over-representation of males is of such magnitude as to nearly eclipse female offenders, for example, about nine to one for violent felony arrests. It is only for less serious crimes, such as minor property offenses and status violations, that the gender imbalance is not so large. Girls constitute a majority only for offenses like running away and incorrigibility—offenses related to "precocious sexuality" and dysfunctional family interactions—both of which generally occur outside of public view. Because of the chronic under-representation of females in the juvenile and criminal justice systems, public officials have paid far less attention to understanding their offending or to developing and assessing effective prevention and intervention strategies for them. However, this "out of sight, out of mind" approach to female offenders is changing. Attention to female offenders is now considered important because their numbers are growing in all spheres of criminal justice, but police, court, and corrections officials are ill-prepared to provide them effectively and equitably with justice. The justice experiences of adolescent girls is particularly difficult to understand given the current status of research, and potentially troubling in juvenile justice systems where informal, private processing and independent discretionary decisions are deeply institutionalized.

This chapter explains what currently is known about girls and their juvenile justice experiences. First, I discuss the difficulty that exists in identifying gender bias because of the nature of juvenile justice processing. Then I describe data sources and information about offending patterns of girls and boys. I examine how gender appears to affect the sequential stages of juvenile justice processing: arrest and referral; intake screening and pre-hearing detention; adjudication and dispositional court decisions—including differences due to type of offending, race, ethnicity, and social class; and out-of-home residential placement. Next, I identify difficulties for girls in access to effective treatment and services, both in community and institutional settings. Recent advances in understanding what constitutes effective interventions are highlighted, including deficiencies in knowledge about female-specific treatment. I look at risks, needs, and protective factors for girls and the contributions etiological explanations have made to understanding female offending. Throughout the chapter I assess the status quo and offer ways to overcome obstacles that have prevented greater advances. I conclude with recommendations for an integrated framework from which I believe we could learn more about the problems girls face and ways to make their experiences with juvenile justice systems more successful.

I. Juvenile Justice and Assessing Gender Bias

Separate systems of justice for juveniles have evolved in the United States for more than a century. They are considered favorable alternatives to adult criminal justice systems and have been adopted by several countries. Like adult systems of criminal justice, we expect juvenile justice systems to be fair and effective in promoting public safety. Perhaps unlike our expectations for adults, however, we also want interventions with youths to be "in the best interests of the child." This goal of helpful benevolence, manifested as the legal doctrine of *parens patriae*, attributes responsibilities to these government systems of justice similar to those expected of parents. Treatment and assistance was the goal established by the Progressive reformers in setting up the original juvenile courts and reformatories (Platt 1977; Rothman 1978; Tanenhaus 2004). Due process and equity concerns were added by the *In re Gault* decision of the Supreme Court in 1967 (Feld 1999).

Today, the three objectives (i.e., fairness, effectiveness, helpfulness) are pursued through juvenile justice procedures that are primarily private, informal, and individualized. Juveniles seldom have legal representation because attorneys are considered superfluous to the court work group's aim to assist youth (Feld 1993; Burruss and Kempf-Leonard 2002; Feld and Schaefer 2010; Kempf-Leonard 2010). For similar reasons, hearings occur out of public view and without a transcribed record to document the proceedings (Bernard 1992). Dispositional decisions also are closed to protect youths and enable them to overcome any negative stigma from public knowledge of their juvenile records.

Officials who try to deliver juvenile justice are tasked with pursuing multiple, potentially conflicting goals, and with very little direction or guidance on procedures or understanding about what constitutes successful case outcomes. This lack of clarity, along with the informality and discretion in decision-making, enables officials to opt for benevolent services in the best interest of the child in some cases and punitive sanctions in other cases. These factors make juvenile justice very difficult to be effective or to understand (Gottfredson and Gottfredson 1980). Criminal justice decisions can be evaluated solely on criteria based on characteristics of the offense, so when "extra-legal" factors based on sex or other individual traits affect case outcomes, suspicions about the process are raised. In contrast, juvenile justice decisions are much more complicated. They require consideration of the offense, but along with individual characteristics and achievements and social and family histories. Often personal traits weigh more heavily than the youths' behavior in decisions on case outcome. There is an institutionalized tension between empowering and infantilizing youths (Schaffner 2008, p. 35). Many experiences and characteristics are shaped by context and perspectives of gender, race, class, age, and location. This is true both for youths and the juvenile justice officials who evaluate them. Thus, juvenile justice is much more difficult than criminal justice to assess in terms of bias and differential treatment, but it is almost unavoidable that gender affects the decision-making process and case flow.

Simple interpretations of chronic under-representation of girls in juvenile justice outcomes might be considered either positively or negatively for girls depending upon the emphasis placed on a particular court objective. The objective of fairness is the easiest to assess because it is the most similar to criminal justice and requires a measure of equity. For justice to be fair, interventions must be commensurate to the behavior and applied uniformly to similarly situated offenders. Assuring that "similarly situated" cases are compared is the key to an interpretation of disparity and bias. When dispositional decisions differ among offenders who are similarly situated on all factors relevant to the offense, but differ only by sex of the offender, we conclude that differential treatment exists and that gender bias is affecting the decisions.

When judging other juvenile justice objectives, however, interpretations of gender disparities differ. For example, less intensive interventions for girls than boys might be viewed negatively in terms of evaluating the "best interests of the child" goal, suggesting that judges accord girls less consideration in meeting their needs. Such different outcomes might be viewed positively in terms of effectiveness, perhaps interpreting that leniency works better to help girls than boys. In terms of fairness, "less severe outcomes" suggests a mixed finding that while justice isn't meted out evenly, girls are the beneficiaries of this gender bias. To adequately understand juvenile court interventions with girls, the interpretation is not nearly as straightforward as that available in criminal justice.

In attempting to achieve multiple, incompatible objectives for youths, juvenile justice systems operate with a level of informality and lack of transparency that do not exist in any other system of law. While some youths might benefit from their experiences, there is reason to suggest that juvenile justice systems include unfair and ineffective processing and reach decisions that are not in accord with the best interests of youths and from which youths often fail to benefit. Nowhere is justice for juveniles as suspect, and yet as complicated to understand, as when applied to girls.

II. Offending, Initial Referrals, and Arrests

Juvenile justice is initiated with a referral or arrest, and gender differences in type of offense are clearly evident at this initial stage. Table 21.1 shows the Uniform Crime Reports (UCR) arrest data for those aged 18 and younger by sex and offense type for 1990, 1998, and 2007. Males predominate over females in all offense types except runaway and prostitution. Overall rates of offending (as measured by arrest and court referral data) of both males and females follow the same trends, increasing during the 1990s, then decreasing more recently. The magnitude of these changes differed considerably, with the increase for females more than double that for males in the early period (53.1% compared to 24.3%), and the decline for females less than that for males (13.5% compared to 23.0%) in the later period. If we consider only violent crime, the increase for female offending during the 1990s is even greater and the gender difference more pronounced (65.1% compared to 6.3%), although the subsequent decline by 2007 is similar (12.7% versus 14.3%). For property crimes, female offending increased 22.2% and then declined 17.7%, whereas male offending declined continually and markedly by 12.6%, then 38.9%. The greater presence of female violence is driven by an observed 84.1% increase in arrests for aggravated assault, along with increases for non-index offense categories (123.9% other assaults, 74.8% weapons, 139.7% disorderly conduct, and 232.3% offenses against family and children). Females also had much larger gains and smaller declines than males in all property crimes, drug and alcohol offenses, and curfew violations.

The "gendered" nature of juvenile cases can occur either because of actual behavioral differences between girls and boys or because the justice system casts a net of formal social control in a way that treats boys and girls differently. To determine which of these two alternatives is more likely true, we can consider self-report surveys of juvenile offending, which are unaffected by actions taken by justice officials. The Centers for Disease Control provides one such source in the National Youth Risk Behavior Survey (YRBS), which monitors risk-taking behavior for a nationally representative sample of students in grades 9 through 12 in public and private schools. Table 21.2 shows these data separately by sex for three years, extending nearly two decades. Boys report higher levels of risky behaviors, with the exception of suicide, which girls consider, plan, and attempt about twice as often as males. Both boys and girls report declining prevalence of carrying a weapon, physical

Table 21.1. Juvenile Arrest Trends by Sex, 1990, 1998, 2007

Offense charged	Boys under age 18					Girls under age 18				
	1990	1998	2007	Percent change 1990–98	Percent change 98–2007	1990	1998	2007	Percent change 1990–98	Percent change 98–2007
TOTAL[1]	897,082	1,114,987	858,746	+24.3	−23.0	269,578	412,694	357,093	+53.1	−13.5
Murder and nonnegligent manslaughter	1,397	898	702	−35.7	−21.8	81	85	51	+4.9	−40.0
Forcible rape	2,814	2,914	2,005	+3.6	−31.2	57	61	29	+7.0	−52.5
Robbery	16,580	16,813	17,654	+1.4	+5.0	1,516	1,626	1,896	+7.3	+16.6
Aggravated assault	29,667	33,029	25,602	+11.3	−22.5	5,068	9,329	7,712	+84.1	−17.3
Burglary	72,290	62,217	42,872	−13.9	−31.1	6,778	7,954	6,031	+17.4	−24.2
Larceny-theft	178,745	169,452	100,042	−5.2	−41.0	71,384	89,088	75,519	+24.8	−15.2
Motor vehicle theft	43,600	24,689	12,701	−43.4	−48.6	5,593	5,193	2,588	−7.2	−50.2
Arson	4,070	4,832	3,880	+18.7	−19.7	406	575	511	+41.6	−11.1
Violent crime[2]	50,458	53,654	45,963	+6.3	−14.3	6,722	11,101	9,688	+65.1	−12.7
Property crime[2]	298,705	261,190	159,495	−12.6	−38.9	84,161	102,810	84,649	+22.2	−17.7
Other assaults	61,770	96,249	91,986	+55.8	−4.4	18,994	42,531	46,809	+123.9	+10.1
Forgery and counterfeiting	2,683	2,754	1,146	+2.6	−58.4	1,401	1,496	553	+6.8	−63.0
Fraud	2,993	3,969	2,849	+32.6	−28.2	1,524	2,097	1,631	+37.6	−22.2

(continued)

Table 21.1. (continued)

Offense charged	Boys under age 18					Girls under age 18				
	1990	1998	2007	Percent change 1990–98	Percent change 98–2007	1990	1998	2007	Percent change 1990–98	Percent change 98–2007
Embezzlement	353	575	618	+62.9	+7.5	210	443	454	+111.0	+2.5
Stolen property; buying, receiving, possessing	22,266	17,289	10,809	−22.4	−37.5	2,413	2,580	2,421	+6.9	−6.2
Vandalism	64,701	66,314	56,177	+2.5	−15.3	5,982	9,104	8,750	+52.2	−3.9
Weapons; carrying, possessing, etc.	20,850	24,048	21,999	+15.3	−8.5	1,343	2,347	2,329	+74.8	−0.8
Prostitution and commercialized vice	427	349	170	−18.3	−51.3	482	394	615	−18.3	+56.1
Sex offenses (except forcible rape and prostitution)	8,367	8,870	7,450	+6.0	−16.0	494	661	656	+33.8	−0.8
Drug abuse violations	38,005	99,691	91,800	+162.3	−7.9	5,208	16,661	17,644	+219.9	+5.9
Gambling	383	479	347	+25.1	−27.6	28	16	13	−42.9	−18.8
Offenses against the family and children	1,287	3,648	1,885	+183.4	−48.3	637	2,117	1,210	+232.3	−42.8
Driving under the influence	9,478	9,849	7,513	+3.9	−23.7	1,553	2,068	2,354	+33.2	+13.8
Liquor laws	58,613	66,251	47,505	+13.0	−28.3	22,021	28,006	27,443	+27.2	−2.0
Drunkenness	12,692	13,056	8,697	+2.9	−33.4	2,252	2,908	2,821	+29.1	−3.0

Disorderly conduct	47,475	72,357	69,051	+52.4	−4.6	12,267	29,410	35,329	+139.7	+20.1
Vagrancy	1,949	1,505	1,917	−22.8	+27.4	367	300	802	−18.3	+167.3
All other offenses (except traffic)	119,742	199,315	153,225	+66.5	−23.1	34,403	66,923	53,999	+94.5	−19.3
Suspicion	2,175	686	189	−68.5	−72.4	515	217	66	−57.9	−69.6
Curfew and loitering law violations	33,890	73,163	51,116	+115.9	−30.1	12,729	31,813	22,101	+149.9	−30.5
Runaways	39,995	40,412	27,028	+1.0	−33.1	54,387	56,908	34,822	+4.6	−38.8

1. Does not include suspicion.
2. Violent crimes are offenses of murder, forcible rape, robbery, and aggravated assault.
3. Property crimes are offenses of burglary, larceny-otor vehicle theft, and arson.
4. Includes arson.

Population estimates:
1990: 128,207,000
1998: 154,013,711
2007: 171,876,948

Adapted from Crime in the U.S., Table 33.

fights, injuries, contemplating suicide, and sexual intercourse. Contrary to the arrest data, these self-report data show a decline during both the 1990s and the current decade that is similar by gender. Exceptions to the pattern of decline occur for some drug use and attempted suicide, which increased during the 1990s. Among boys, these behaviors subsequently declined. Among girls, however, there is no change or perhaps a continuing increase (in use of alcohol, episodic heavy drinking, DUI, and marijuana and cocaine use.)

Although the types of delinquency observed in the two sources of data are not equivalent, they are sufficiently similar to suggest that caution should be taken in interpreting arrest and referral data as accurately representing the behavior of males and females. Data drawn from juvenile justice systems may instead represent actions taken by officials. A recent comparison of data on crime trends by gender, and the subsequent debate between two prominent research teams on how best to interpret these trend results, serves to underscore the difficulty we have in making sense of existing data.

First, Lauritsen, Heimer, and Lynch (2009) computed the gender rate ratio (or the rate of female offending divided by the rate of male offending) based on UCR arrest data and based on victim reports of offenders as found in the National Crime Survey/National Crime Victimization Survey (NCS/NCVS) for 1973 through 2005. For aggravated assault, robbery, and simple assault, they found "remarkable

Table 21.2. Self- Risk Behaviors by Sex, 1991, 1997, 2007

	Percent of Boys, Grades 9–12			Percent of Girls, Grades 9–12		
	1991	1997	2007	1991	1997	2007
Ever driven car while drinking alcohol	22.0	19.8	12.8	9.6	9.7	8.1
Carried a weapon at least 1 day during past 30 days	42.0	30.0	28.5	12.7	9.0	7.5
Ever in a physical fight	51.5	46.1	44.4	35.7	27.9	26.5
Ever injured in a fight	6.6	7.7	n/a	2.8	2.1	n/a
Ever seriously considered attempting suicide	19.6	14.6	10.3	35.5	26.4	18.7
Ever made a plan to commit suicide	11.7	11.7	9.2	23.6	19.8	13.4
Ever attempted suicide	4.0	5.5	4.6	10.9	12.5	9.3
Currently use alcohol (>=1 drink during past 30 days)	53.2	51.1	44.7	45.6	45.2	44.6
Episodic heavy drinking (>=5 drinks w/in a few hours on >=1 day during past 30 days)	36.2	33.5	27.8	22.7	23.3	24.1
Used marijuana at least once	35.6	50.1	41.6	27.4	39.4	34.5
Used cocaine at least once	8.0	10.4	7.8	4.4	6.5	6.5
Ever had sexual intercourse	62.6	57.5	49.8	50.8	50.6	45.9

consistency in upward trends in the gender rate ratios over time" (Lauritsen, Heimer, and Lynch 2009, p. 383). They "conclude that there has been an apparent long-term decline in the gender gap in violent offending, and that this is reflected not only in UCR arrest data, but also in victims' reports of the gender of the perpetrator" (p. 435). The NCVS data show a decline in both male and female rates of offending, and they contend that the gender gap has narrowed "in large part because male rates declined more than female rates" (p. 383). Lauritsen and her colleagues refute the notion of more frequent and heinous female offending over time

In response, Schwartz and her colleagues (2009) disagree that the gap between male and female offending is lessening, and take issue with the methodology used by the Lauritsen team. Schwartz et al. argue that there is measurement error in the observed trend because of instrumentation changes in the NCVS. The survey redesign that was implemented in the early 1990s now includes more household crime and less serious offending, for which females have higher representation (2009, p. 405; see also Steffensmeier and Allan 1996). This may be true, but Lauritsen et al. control for offense type. Schwartz and colleagues also suggest an internal validity threat due to general societal changes in how women are perceived, which likely contributed to an increase among victims in willingness to report female perpetrators. Finally, they extend a general argument that the social construction of crime, particularly violent crime, has greatly expanded the nature of behavior that now gets included within that category. They argue that "assault is driving claims and conceptions of rising female-to-male violence. But even for assault, arguably the most ambiguously defined violent crime, there is contrary evidence depending on data source and method. Evidence from data triangulation strategies show more stability than change in the violence gender gap" (2009, p. 420). Heimer, Lauritsen, and Lynch (2009) contend that Schwartz and her colleagues' triangulation of arrest data with the criminal justice system confound the activities of officials and, as such, the NCVS data are superior.

Despite criticism of the Lauritsen et al. study, Steffensmeier and his colleagues (2005, pp. 378, 393) and Steffensmeier and Schwartz (2009) offer some agreement with their conclusion that there has been a decline in male and female arrests. They also offer as plausible factors in the male decline some male-specific deterrence policies and prevention programs, and social changes that produce "civilizing messages" (Lauritsen and Heimer 2008) that make male criminality seem more unacceptable (Schwartz, Steffensmeier, and Feldmeyer 2009). However, declines in offending by males are not the answer that Schwartz's group accepts for the narrowing gender gap in arrests (Heimer, Lauritsen, and Lynch 2009, p. 435). To explain this, they point to changes in criminal justice processing rather than changes in offending. They suggest that because traditional views have changed, victims and police officers no longer view violence by females as less problematic than that by males (Steffensmeier et al. 2006, p. 9).

In response, Heimer, Lauritsen, and Lynch agree that there have been changes in the ways police view male and female offenders, but they dismiss any potential difficulty with changes in victim reporting. They argue that the NCVS survey item that requests the sex of the offender appears long after a detailed account of the incident, at which point victims already have overcome any embarrassment or reluctance to identify females (2009, p. 388). They consider the "civilizing hypothesis," i.e., whether public domains are safer now because women have a greater presence and thereby females serve as "capable guardians" exerting informal social control over males (Lauritsen and Heimer 2008). For example, perhaps public domains have changed but spheres of private life have not? Although there have been overall declines in domestic violence and intimate partner homicides since the early 1990s, there also now are zero-tolerance policies applied to domestic violence, and females are now more often arrested as a result (Gaarder, Rodriguez, and Zatz 2004). Finally, they speculate that the change reflects economic marginalization: during a recent period of economic growth (Rosenfeld and Fornango 2007), females made fewer gains and suffered some losses due to changes in welfare policies (Lauritsen et al. 2009).

The close of this lively debate between researchers leaves many questions unanswered, including how the gender gap is observed and explained for juvenile delinquency and juvenile justice. Steffensmeier and his colleagues have presented trends for juveniles based on arrest statistics of the UCR, NCVS data in which the victim identifies both the sex and age of the offender, and offending self-reports from both the Monitoring the Future and National Youth Risk Behavior Surveys with similar arguments for youths as they made in this debate on adult data. They argue that juvenile offending patterns have not changed as much as actions of officials and policies that more often formally snare girls (Steffensmeier et al. 2005; Steffensmeier and Schwartz 2009). However, no comparable youth-specific analyses, data comparisons, or discussion exists. Indeed, according to Lauritsen and her colleagues, no such youth-specific exercise should be undertaken because much juvenile crime involves multiple offenders, and for those incidents the NCVS data are not specific enough to assess age by gender rates (2009, p. 398).

The interpretation available to us at this point in our understanding of information sources and analyses is that most available data show fairly stable gender variation with males disproportionately more involved than females for most but not all types of crime and delinquency. There is a gender gap both in criminality and desistance, although that gap appears to have narrowed some. What seems most important is that offending rates of males are dropping more quickly than those for females during the 1990s. It is unknown whether these trends in gender-specific offending will continue into the future, whether the gender gap will change, and whether these patterns will vary across offense type. The principal issues that remain involve offense type, direction, and what the trends portend for the future.

Gender differences in juvenile referrals and arrests may reflect actual gender variations in behavior, although even older studies based on self-reports suggest this is not the case (Canter 1982; Figueira-McDonough 1985; Brener et al. 1999). Alternatively, cases involving girls may reflect the stereotypic belief that girls generally need more protection than boys. Stereotypes such as these may influence how officials respond to juvenile cases. This is likely, according to Schaffner who contends that much about the behavior of today's adolescent girls "contradicts the strict binary mainstream concepts of gender" (2008, p. 34) held by many juvenile justice officials.

Police are the primary source of delinquency referrals. According to some policing scholars, police officers are likely to intervene more restrictively when girls appear at risk of victimization, including being sexually vulnerable. The intervention can take the form of a status offense referral (McCluskey, McCluskey, and Huebner 2003, p. 49). Police charging practices may have changed too, and behavior characterized as assault is one for which there is tremendous police discretion (Blumstein 2000). Because family-violence calls for service require an arrest now, they implicate a growing number of adolescent girls (Gaarder, Rodriguez, and Zatz 2004). As a result of zero tolerance policies adopted in the past decade, schools also more often rely on police for interventions with students. Harsher charging practices by police, particularly for criminal assault, is the principal reason offered by Feld (2009b) for the increase in rates of arrest and referral of girls.

Unfortunately, most scholarly attention to factors that affect police arrest decisions does not attend to gender effects or observe interactions with females. Chesney-Lind (1973) found that police arrested young females, but not males, for sexual activity. She concluded that the range of behavior deemed acceptable for girls was much narrower than for boys, and that even minor infractions committed by girls were considered problematic. A decade later, Visher (1983) found that arrest decisions for females were made "on the basis of a more limited set of individual cues," while decisions for males seemed "more multidimensional" (p. 15). Female-specific decisions by police also differed by race. Visher reported: "chivalrous attitudes that may exist among police officers are apparently directed towards white females and withdrawn from their black sisters" (p. 17). Moreover, "young, black, or hostile women receive no preferential treatment" (p. 23).

Visher's study was important as a methodological advance, too, in showing the necessity of gender-specific analyses. The majority of previous research on policing had either omitted females or assumed gender-neutrality in general analyses. Any female-specific factors are obscured in tests that aggregate data because of the far smaller number of females. Visher's study included 24 police departments, 900 patrol shifts, 5,688 police-citizen counters, and multivariate analyses. It is the most rigorous study to date, yet includes only 142 encounters with females, 22 arrests, and no information specifically about juveniles.

Family members, school administrators, and community residents also may respond to stereotypes in ways that bring girls into the juvenile justice system earlier and for different reasons than boys (Krause and McShane 1994). Parents are a major source of referrals for status offenses, especially incorrigibility and behavior deemed "beyond parental control." Aggression by girls more often involves family members, while boys more often fight with people outside the family (Hoyt and Scherer 1998; Bloom et al. 2002; Franke, Huynh-Hohnbaum, and Chung 2002). In the past decade, new zero-tolerance policies in schools have resulted in juvenile justice referrals of truancy and disruptive behavior that previously were handled informally by school officials. It is clear that some of the offenses for which girls are more represented are those referred by sources other than the police (Office of Juvenile Justice and Delinquency Prevention 2008).

III. Intake Screening and Pre-hearing Detention

Initial screening and classification of juvenile referrals is another likely source of gender bias early in the process. For example, stereotypical views held by intake officers can influence the way in which case files are constructed to reflect gender bias. Rosenbaum and Chesney-Lind (1994) identified handwritten notes made at intake screening on the physical appearance, maturity, and sexuality of girls, but not of boys. Stereotypical expectations of intake officers are also criticized by Johansson and Kempf-Leonard (2007), who suspect that despite an existing policy that required intake officers to adhere to a uniform screening protocol, some questions asked of girls, such as questions regarding abuse and neglect experiences and emotional feelings, were not routinely asked of boys. Acoca (1998, p. 82) also blames the low prevalence of victimization reflected in juvenile court records on the lax method used to prepare case files.

The differential effect of early classification decisions on subsequent stages in the juvenile justice system is identified in an unpublished dissertation. Robinson (1990) compared a very small sample of fifteen Massachusetts girls processed by the child welfare system with fifteen delinquent girls committed to the Department of Youth Services. The girls' problems and backgrounds were virtually identical, leading Robinson to conclude the difference was in the way the police and authorities initiated referrals or charges. Interviews with the girls also suggested a race effect of differential classification.

In 1974, Congress took federal action aimed at limiting the number of youths in pre-hearing detention, which is confinement in either a secure or nonsecure facility and can occur anytime between referral and secure residential placements. The intent of the Juvenile Justice and Delinquency Prevention (JJDP) Act of 1975 (Pub. L. No. 93–415, 88 Stat. 1109 (codified at codified at 42 USC §§ 5601 et seq.) was to preclude states from confining youths referred for status offense and dependency cases in secure facilities and to prohibit any youths from being jailed with adults. The effect was a marked decline in confinement, including a disproportionate benefit for girls (Krisberg et al. 1986; Feld 1999, 2009a). The policy was difficult to implement, however, due to the lack of nonsecure and community-based alternatives, and many judges felt they were without options for processing girls for status offenses. As a result of lobbying efforts on behalf of the National Council of Juvenile and Family Court Judges, the JJDP Act was amended in 1980 to allow secure custody of status offenders who subsequently violate court orders, and to jurisdictions in which good faith efforts at compliance are made (Schwartz 1989). The effects of

JJDP Act revisions and creative adaptations in which offenses are reclassified are not actually known, but there is strong speculation of a detrimental impact, especially on girls (Weithorn 1988; Bishop and Frazier 1992; Chesney-Lind and Shelden 1998; Kempf-Leonard and Sample 2000; Feld 2009a and 2009b, pp. 237–39).

Since implementation of the JJDP Act, many studies have identified that pre-hearing detention is likely to contribute to harsher, more restrictive final case outcomes for youths (Krisberg and Schwartz 1983; Fagan, Forst, and Vivona 1987; Kempf, Decker, and Bing 1990; Feld 1995; Frazier and Bishop 1995; Kempf-Leonard 2001). While females consistently have lower rates of detention, there is some evidence to suggest that they are held in custody for a lower threshold of offending and for longer (Krisberg et al. 1986). A Florida study of the characteristics common to a sample of youths entering detention found that girls were more likely to have abuse histories and contact with the system because of a status offense, while boys had more involvement with delinquency (Dembo, Williams, and Schmeidler 1993). In one effort to understand the detention process, the only gender-specific criteria that increased the likelihood of detention were abuse and neglect for girls and substance abuse for boys. For both girls and boys—and more often for minorities and older youths—risk of detention increased with multiple charges, including serious offenses, prior delinquency, and more often for minorities and older youths (Kempf-Leonard and Sample 2000, p. 107).

Inequitable and unavailable services and treatment while in detention is sometimes more problematic for pre-adjudicated girls than those who proceed deeper within the system (Belknap and Cady 2008, pp .260, 276–77). Conditions of custody, including concerns about unwarranted and humiliating tests for sexually transmitted diseases and pelvic exams for girls, but no similar tests for boys, also have been raised (Chesney-Lind and Shelden 1998, p. 173; Schaffner 2008). The leading cases on strip searching juveniles prior to admission to detention facilities—N.G. and S.G. v. Connecticut, 382 F.3d 225 (2d Cir. 2004), and Smook v. Minnehaha County Detention Center, 457 F.3d 806 (8th Cir. 2006)—both concerned strip searches of girls detained for status offenses for which there was no individualized suspicion. Although there is no evidence available on how extensive such practices are, these recent cases suggest that detention officials may disregard the privacy concerns of young women and what is in their "best interests" instead to investigate adolescent girls invasively and without due cause as potential smugglers of contraband into facilities with strip searches and body cavity searches. The effect of such extreme, and generally unnecessary, investigative measures is likely harmful both to the individual psyche and the youths' perceptions of the justice system. Indeed, focus group research with girls and professionals in Colorado juvenile detention settings reported this overall effect: "The girls report experiencing poor treatment from staff, which makes them feel disrespected and powerless. They detect the contradictory messages they receive about taking charge of their lives and increasing their self-esteem, when at times they are not provided the capacity to influence their circumstances or afforded the positive regard that would help boost their sense of worth" (Belknap and Cady 2008, p. 269).

In addition, "justice by geography" has been a long-standing concern about differential treatment in detention (Krisberg, Litsky, and Schwartz 1984; Krisberg et al. 1987; Schwartz, Harris, and Levi 1988; Feld 1991). For example, large crowded urban detention facilities can mirror the custody problems of adult jails. Solitary confinement, particularly if due to only one female in custody, still occurs in some rural locations. In addition, if rural courts must transport juvenile detainees long distances to access detention facilities, the effect both on youth and their legal cases can be detrimental. When multiple factors are controlled in predictive models of detention, studies also show different findings. In my Missouri study, gender-neutral detention decisions were likely to differ by geographic location because urban courts had large secure facilities and more nonsecure residential options than rural courts (Kempf-Leonard and Sample 2000). Others agree that rural jurisdictions are less likely to detain overall, but argue that rural courts also intervene more restrictively for females for more minor infractions (Frazier and Cochran 1986; Feld 1995).

IV. Adjudication and Dispositional Court Decisions

The role of gender throughout the juvenile court adjudication and disposition process has been examined by various means and with differing results. For example, direct observations of national data for court dispositions suggest either that courts handle cases in the same way regardless of sex (Snyder and Sickmund 1995), or that "at all stages of juvenile court processing, delinquency cases involving girls received less severe outcomes than cases involving boys" (Poe-Yamagata and Butts 1996, p. 10). A recent trend study tracking juvenile court dispositions for more than twenty years found that not only has formal processing and adjudication increased overall, but also that the greatest increases are shown for females across all offense categories (Tracy, Kempf-Leonard, and Abramoske-James 2009).

Juvenile court processing has been examined for gender bias with adequate statistical controls to compare similarly situated girls and boys, but still with mixed results. In assessing the role of gender in the adjudication and disposition processes, some scholars find disparity (Bishop and Frazier 1992; Pope and Feyerherm 1982; Rhodes and Fisher 1993; Kempf-Leonard and Johansson 2007) but others report more gender similarities (Teilmann and Landry 1981; Dannefer and Schutt 1982; Corley, Cernkovich, and Giordano 1989; Horowitz and Pottieger 1991; Leiber 1994; Hoyt and Scherer 1998; Kempf-Leonard and Sample 2000). Some studies suggest that the court provides preferential treatment to girls (Johnson and Scheuble 1991; Kempf-Leonard and Johansson 2007); others observe a double standard with negative effects on girls (Bishop and Frazier 1992). Sometimes the gender effect is observed only conditionally, such as by a specific offense type (Datesmann and Scarpitti 1980; Bishop and Frazier 1992) or race (Sarri 1983).

The complicated nature of gendered relationships in court processing is illustrated in one Missouri study (Kempf-Leonard and Sample 2000). First, the authors distinguished informal handling from formal dispositions by gender with controls for several offense, prior record, and personal characteristics. They found that processing and outcomes for girls were based on virtually the same reasons as for boys. Only one female-specific criteria distinguished the type of interventions; girls with prior abuse or neglect were more likely to be formally adjudicated. Next, a test for the effect of gender on formal disposition type showed that the factors that increased the likelihood of placement were the same for girls and boys, with the exception of two significant differences. Females were more likely to be committed based only on a single charge; number of charges was not important for males, but a prior record increased their risk of placement. The more intensive interventions for girls because of abuse and a single charge suggests an element of differential treatment that can be hidden among the host of other gender-neutral factors affecting juvenile court decisions.

V. Type of Offending and Juvenile Justice Processing

Another way gender bias can be examined among similarly situated cases is by focusing exclusively on a single type of offense. The most obvious target is the status offense of runaway, a common violation and one for which girls are much more represented among the referrals. Surprisingly, studies of runaway using data sources outside of juvenile justice settings have found that girls and boys runaway at similar rates (Teilmann and Landry 1981; Canter 1982; Figueira-McDonough 1985; Finkelhor et al. 1990; Kaufman and Widom 1999; Hammer, Finkelhor, and Sedlack 2002).

The higher level of arrests of girls for running away has been explained both as protective care for their safety and wellbeing (McCord, Widom, and Crowell 2001, p. 56) and as unfair and discriminatory actions because juvenile justice officials have a "unique and intense preoccupation with girls' sexuality and their obedience to parental authority" (Chesney-Lind and Shelden 1998, p. 135). Both explanations are merely speculative, however, because nearly all of the information available on runaways is based on data collected completely outside of juvenile justice processing. Characteristics and experiences of runaways are observed in subjects identified primarily at homeless shelters (Stiffman et al. 1987; Hagan and McCarthy 1997; Whitbeck et al. 2001; Chapple, Johnson, and Whitbeck 2004), but also from inmates who retrospectively report this as an adolescent experience (Silbert and Pines 1981; Chesney-Lind and Rodriguez 1983; Arnold 1990; Gilfus 1992; Snell and Morton 1994).

One specific study of runaway youths in juvenile justice processing found remarkable similarities by gender. The risk factors of runaways were significantly different from those of youths referred to juvenile court for other offenses for both girls and boys (Kempf-Leonard and Johansson 2007). For both girls and boys, informal warnings were the most common juvenile court intervention, but runaway boys received probation and out-of-home placement more often than runaway girls because they had additional referrals. When other referrals were controlled for statistically, juvenile justice interventions differed by race; black youths got more restrictive outcomes—exacerbated by substance abuse, gang involvement, and household situation—but not by sex. Child abuse victimization did not affect responses to runaways from the juvenile justice system.

The latter finding is a particular curiosity because the literature is replete with assertions that juvenile court processing serves to "criminalize girls' strategies to survive abuse," one of which is running away from abusers (Chesney-Lind and Shelden 1998). This is supported by one sample of runaway youths, in which females with sexual abuse victimization were significantly more likely than nonabused girls to commit delinquency (McCormack, Janus, and Burgess 1986, pp. 392–393). Indeed, the prevalence of childhood victimization among adult women in prison runs as high as 92% (Acoca and Austin 1996), and abuse is what many incarcerated girls and women attribute their crime problems to (Silbert and Pines 1981; Chesney-Lind and Rodriguez 1983; Daly 1992; Arnold 1990; Gilfus 1992; Snell and Morton 1994; Richie 1996; Owen 1998). To illustrate the problems of female offenders, researchers often highlight an in-depth interview of a woman whose adolescence included horrific sexual victimization. Such practice helps to reinforce the severity of the impact of abuse on these victims, but also may serve to distort the true prevalence of sexual abuse as well as minimize the harmful effects of neglect and other types of victimization. In addition, no such male-specific research attention has addressed boyhood victimization to allow for gender comparisons.

Not all studies rely on retrospective accounts from convenience samples. That abuse and neglect serve as risk factors in crime is clearly evident in Widom's important longitudinal follow-up of abuse and neglect victims and a matched control group of children who had no record of maltreatment Her research shows that girls who were officially identified as abused or neglected were much more likely than other girls to acquire a criminal record—a relationship that also held for boys (Widom and Ames 1994). Victimization did not increase the risk of reoffending in two studies of released female inmates (Bonta et al. 1995; Blanchette 1996).

VI. Race, Ethnicity, Social Class, and Juvenile Court Processing

Considerable evidence suggests that juvenile court processing may treat youths differently by race and social class. The interaction of gender and race is underscored by several studies on juvenile courts, although regrettably, most of the many inquiries supported by the Office of Juvenile Justice and Delinquency Prevention (OJJDP) Disproportionate Minority Confinement (DMC) initiative following amendments in 1992 and 2002 to the JJDP Act to address minority concerns did not include females or failed to examine them separately. Intake staff noted in case files of minority girls negative comments about their appearance (Rosenbaum and Chesney-Lind 1994) and descriptions that made them appear threatening and culpable, while similarly situated white girls were described as needing protection (Bridges and Steen 1998; Steen et al. 2005). At the disposition stage of court processing, Miller (1994) found that juvenile court officials recommended treatment for white girls but restrictive sanctions for African American and Latina girls. These recommendations were framed with arguments that minority girls made "inappropriate 'lifestyle' choices," while white girls were products of "abandonment," had low self-esteem, and were easily manipulated (Miller 1994, p.20). In another study, informal supervision was more often given to white girls, whereas similarly situated black girls and all boys were more often formally adjudicated (Kempf, Decker, and Bing 1990). In contrast, in one Texas county, the risk of detention was greater for white girls than their Latina and African American counterparts (Tracy 2005). In other Texas counties studied, the number of girls detained was too small to examine with multivariate techniques. Another study found racial bias in the outcomes of juvenile court decisions that sent white girls to private facilities and black girls to public institutions, in addition to gender bias that confined girls with a lower standard than that used to commit boys (Bartollas 1993). Such "racialized gender expectations" (Miller 1994), in which girls from minority groups receive more limited options, harsher interventions, but fewer services, have been observed since the inception of juvenile justice systems (Odem and Schlossman 1991; Knupfer 2001; Tanenhaus 2005, p. 115).

VII. Out-of-Home Residential Placement

Although most youths exit the juvenile justice system without commitment to an out-of-home placement, it is in residential facilities where the most intensive treatment and restrictive supervision occur. Custodial treatment requires more resources than other juvenile justice procedures, and the small number of girls in placement (e.g., 13% of all commitments in 2001, Sickmund, Sladky, and Kang 2004) has minimized the resources allocated specifically to services for them. Between 1975 and 1995, the number of boys in placement increased 57%, whereas girls increased only 2% (Smith 1998). Crowding was an issue during this time, and, "as a result of increasing caseloads and restricted budgets, many correctional facilities have experienced deteriorating conditions of confinement and basic lapses in meeting professional standards" (Krisberg 1995, p. 154).

More recently, between 1997 and 2006, the number of males in placement decreased 16.2% from 66,450 to 55,672, while the number of girls dropped less than

1% from 8,956 to 8,886. Table 21.3 shows the rate of out-of-home placement by categories of offense and sex for 1997, 2001, and 2006. Placement rates for males far exceed those for females for all categories except status offenses. With the exception of technical violations, the rates for males have declined. For females, all rates have remained stable or shown small increases during this decade. The custody rate varies considerably by state, so situations of "justice by geography," including situations related to gender, also are likely to exist (Davis et al. 2008).

Privately run correctional facilities also merit attention because they are growing in popularity and use (Austin et al. 1995; Moone 1993), and because the reasons for placement of youths in private institutions may differ from those that are state-run. A 1990 survey found 90% of juvenile court jurisdictions had at least one contract for intervention and services with a private treatment provider (Levenson and Taylor 1991, p. 248). This may not be new, however, as private facilities have always been a part of juvenile justice systems in the United States. (Bernard 1992). What appears to have changed is that a growing number of private providers now treat delinquents; historically, nonoffenders or youths with dispositions as status offenders were the typical clientele (Smith 1998).

It is important to recognize that the boundaries between public-run state facilities and private residential treatment are somewhat fluid. This fluidity is primarily a result of policy mandates in the 1974 Juvenile Justice and Delinquency Prevention Act that require nonoffenders, namely youths accused of status offenses or referred as child welfare victims, not be held in secure facilities (Feld 2009a and 2009b). As was noted earlier in this chapter, this mandate pertains to both pre-hearing detention and out-of-home placement facilities. There was considerable resistance by judges to the provision for deinstitutionalization of status offenders (DSO), because

Table 21.3. Juvenile Court-Placement Rate by Sex, 1997, 2001, 2006

	Male rate per 100,000			Female rate per 100,000		
	1997	2001	2006	1997	2001	2006
Total	439	417	345	62	65	58
Delinquency	422	403	332	47	55	48
Person	159	147	126	17	20	17
Violent Index	125	106	91	9	9	7
Other Person	33	41	34	8	11	10
Property	147	128	93	15	16	13
Property Index	126	107	77	13	13	10
Other Property	21	21	16	3	3	3
Drug	41	39	31	3	4	5
Public Order	42	44	38	4	4	5
Technical Violation	34	45	44	7	11	9
Status Offense	17	14	13	16	10	10

Source: Sickmund et al. 2008. *Census of Juveniles in Residential Placement Databook.*

few or no alternatives exist in most jurisdictions. The strategies adopted by juvenile court administrators and judges to circumvent the federal mandate, yet remain in general compliance for federal funding, appear to follow three patterns of "net-widening." In one strategy, status offending is reclassified as a minor law violation, thereby elevating the severity of the charge, which has been called variously "boot-strapping" (Federele and Chesney-Lind 1992) or "up-criming" (Acoca 1998). Second, court-ordered requirements that are especially difficult to achieve are issued to juveniles, who are then remanded to custody for technical violations which are classified as violations of law, another form of escalation of severity. As noted previously, the JJDP Act was amended in 1980 to allow secure confinement of youths for violations of court orders to accommodate the recommendations of the National Council of Juvenile and Family Court Judges (Schwartz 1989). Third is a process of "transinstitutionalization" (Federele and Chesney-Lind 1992) in which youths are placed in private custodial settings "voluntarily," following informal negotiations with parents in exchange for no formal record. The use of voluntary commitments to private institutions was affirmed by the U.S. Supreme Court in *Parham v. J.R.* (442 U.S. 609 [1979]).

There is little information regarding the extent to which these methods of circumvention prevail across juvenile justice systems, or whether they are gender-specific. This is some evidence that bootstrapping disproportionately affects girls, placing them at elevated risk of incarceration for lesser offenses than for boys. This has been observed in a few studies (Costello and Worthington 1981–1982; Schwartz, Jackson-Beeck, and Anderson 1984; Weithorn 1988; Frazier and Bishop 1990; Schwartz, Steketee, and Schneider 1990; Kempf-Leonard and Sample 2000). Bishop and Frazier (1992) explicitly tracked how juvenile courts in Florida used contempt of court charges to bootstrap status offenders, with detrimental effects more often for girls. Another study reported that facilities with female-specific beds more often than other, primarily male-only, facilities accepted youths (girls) referred directly from their parents, physicians, and even schools (Kempf-Leonard and Sample 2000, p. 115). Most notably, Weithorn (1988) identified a dramatic increase in the 1980s in private mental health admissions of children and their protracted hospital stays. She also determined that hospitalized juveniles had fewer problems than adults in treatment. Most of Weithorn's case studies involved girls who were merely "acting out."

Weithorn concluded that it was financial profit motives that led private hospital administrators to accommodate requests for residential treatment of youths from public juvenile justice officials (1988, p. 786). Schichor and Bartollas (1990) reported on a policy in one state that provided a financial incentive for juvenile court officials specifically to place youths in private facilities. Schwartz (1999), however, argued that the previously identified social class divide in type of institutionalization subsequently diminished because changes in Medicaid benefits led to more funding for private care providers, while private insurance options declined. The relative quality of care provided by public and private facilities is controversial regardless of health care changes, but there is somewhat dated evidence that at least some private custodial stays have been long, secure, and included medication of youths to facilitate social control (Schwartz, Jackson-Beeck, and Anderson 1984; Castellano 1986). We do know that most private facilities are smaller, newer, and require intensive admission screening and classification (Armstrong 2001). Moreover, those private facilities that are large are more likely to have secure operations, including intimidating structures and razor-wire fencing (Bartollas 1997). Because current monitoring requirements for state compliance with the JJDP Act do not extend to private institutions, the prevalence of these situations or the extent to which they differ by gender is unknown.

Meanwhile, descriptive information about females while they are actually in out-of-home placement also is not easily accessible. In 1990, the American Correctional Association provided a profile of girls in correctional facilities that typifies prior physical abuse victimization, often repeatedly; runaway experiences; substance abuse; prior arrests for minor crime; and elevated rates of attempted suicide. Minorities were over-represented in this profile. One-fifth of the girls were mothers (ACA 1990). Similarly, Acoca and Dedel (1998) describe the characteristics of incarcerated girls in four California counties. The majority (81%) had been either physically or sexually abused. They also identified high-risk behaviors among the girls prior to their confinement—drug use, sex with multiple partners, gang membership, failure in school, health problems, and early pregnancy. One-third of the girls had been forced to leave home (Acoca 1998). More recent information of this type is not available.

VIII. ACCESS TO EFFECTIVE TREATMENT AND SERVICES

Knowledge about institutional experiences and effective correctional treatment for girls also is severely limited, in large part because the smaller numbers of girls than boys is even more acute at this back-end stage of the system, and thus the level of resources they garner is likely proportionately even lower. Some of the issues relate only to facility care, but many equally concern community treatment. A similar problem of access to resources exists for adult women, for whom there is more information.

One way in which adult women inmates receive services more closely comparable to men's services involves gender-mixed, "co-correctional" institutional campus settings, which enable treatment and training programs to be accessible regardless of sex. Belknap (1996) attributes criticism of sex-segregated prisons to recognition in the 1970s that "although segregated facilities had significantly decreased the (especially sexual) abuse of women prisoners, they had also served to promote damaging gender stereotypes and restricted incarcerated women's opportunities" (1996, p. 97). Of course, mere access by females to services developed and traditionally provided only to males certainly is not sufficient to speculate that women are served well (Belknap 1996; Chesney-Lind 1991; Jackson and Stearns 1995).

Most problematic for juveniles is the lack of any parallel discussions about co-corrections and the extension of existing programs and services in boys' juvenile facilities to girls. According to Schaffner (2008, p. 161), sex-segregated juvenile facilities and treatment reflect the overzealous patriarchal view that girls need to be isolated from boys for reasons of sexuality. There appears to be an implicit assumption that girls are boy-crazy, so they are treated as though they indeed are; this Schaffner also criticizes as based on the false assumption of heterosexuality.

In addition, it is easy to extend the criticisms of women's prisons—isolated locations, lack of diverse educational, vocational, and skill-based programs, and the low levels of specialization in classification and treatment (Belknap 1996; Bloom and Chesney-Lind 1999; Gray, Mays, and Stohr 1995; Muraskin 1999; Prendergast, Wellisch, and Falkin 1995)—to custodial facilities for girls. While large, sexually integrated urban detention facilities tend to have a separate corridor for girls and therefore can provide comparable services—although inadequate overall—to boys and girls in short-term pre-hearing custody, public placement institutions for girls are more apt to be located in remote rural settings far from the facilities housing boys or other beneficial service providers.

There are several concerns about the nature of the treatment and services delivered to adjudicated girls. One concern is that interventions to help girls focus disproportionately on their physical and mental health, while boys more often are helped to develop their skills. Restricted access to health care professionals, excessive medication, vaginal searches, and disciplinary policies more harsh than administered to boys also have been observed in juvenile facilities serving girls (Belknap 1996; Kersten 1989; Leonard 1983; McClellan 1994). Recent focus group research on girls in custody and in juvenile corrections concluded that "while girls do not appear to receive the same opportunities as boys for appropriate programs and services, life skills, or vocational training, they do tend to receive more focus as far as treatment and therapy" (Belknap and Cady 2008, p. 210). The health and medical emphasis raises an issue of gender bias in terms of the proper perspective of individualized problems. If the health emphasis for girls also reflects an overzealous attention to female sexuality, then there is need for a better balance that assures the identification of health-related issues that can be addressed but that does not intervene needlessly, nor preclude beneficial life skill and vocational training.

Historically, life skill and vocational programs for girls targeted training consistent with traditional domestic functions and stereotypical feminine behavior (Dobash et al. 1986; Morris 1987; Rafter 1985; Gelsthorpe 1989). Fortunately, correctional experiences seldom prepare girls for unprofitable careers as laundresses and seamstresses anymore, although concerns about gender bias in programming services and training remain fervent. One current difficulty occurs when programs designed for boys are merely delivered to girls without due consideration to the new clients. That is not to say that no gender-neutral services are effective, but merely to underscore that generally it is inaccurate to assess the performance of girls based on standards established only on boys' experiences.

Another problem is that even when consideration is given to implementing services specifically for girls, some characteristics advanced as female-specific often are poorly conceived. For example, in programs to counter aggression, the nature of the problem is sometimes viewed as more likely to be instrumental among boys while relational among girls (Schaffner 2008, p. 161). As Schaffner identifies, this can result in the physically violent assaults for which many girls are adjudicated not being adequately addressed. It also too often reduces relational aggression to manipulative, backstabbing verbal assaults, which serve to reinforce gender biases. Similarly, programs for girls sometimes emphasize their need to process information verbally. In talking things through, girls might develop good communication skills, but sacrifice the opportunity to learn substantive content, which is emphasized in program delivery to boys and needed for everyone to achieve success.

Part of the difficulty with juvenile justice interventions for girls is a lack of appreciation for female-specific services and program delivery. Many treatment service providers and facility staff express a general bias against, or specific resistance to, working with females (Baines and Alder 1996; Rasche 1999; Bond-Maupin, Maupin, and Leisenring 2002; Goodkind 2005; McCorkel 2003; Gaarder, Rodriguez, and Zatz 2004). Some of this hostility appears directed toward special physical and medical needs of sexually active and pregnant females (Belknap 1996, p. 100), the attribution of more emotional and mental health problems to adolescent girls (Chesney-Lind 1997), or perhaps merely that more administrative time is required to access resources to serve girls than boys. Some of the sentiments also likely reflect the large number of inadequately trained career staff intent merely on completing their shift work (Schaffner 2008, p. 158).

Perhaps the biggest obstacle to providing effective interventions for girls is the lack of attention to understanding what does, and what should, actually happen. Ten years ago the dearth of information about experiences of girls in confinement forced Chesney-Lind and Shelden (1998) to rely on two outdated studies (Giallambardo 1974; Propper 1978), one unpublished inquiry, and the ACA profile (1990) to guide their entire discussion of juvenile corrections. At that time, based more on speculation than sufficient data, they suggested: "Institutional practices that are routine in boys' facilities have to be scrutinized for their impact on girls. In particular, there needs to be a sensitivity to the fact that girls' victimization histories make such practices as routine strip searches and isolation extremely risky" (1998, p. 182). They also warned: "With the increasing 'invisibility' of girls in such institutions comes the possibility for extreme correctional neglect and abuse" (p. 184).

In what should have led to better knowledge and services for girls, the reauthorization of the JJDP Act in 1992 added a requirement that states assess the adequacy of their services, particularly for girls, as a condition of receiving federal funds (Section 223[a][8] of the JJDP Act, as modified in 1992). Concomitantly, the Office of Juvenile Justice and Delinquency Prevention initiated a new opportunity for funding improvements specifically for girls as part of its challenge grant program

(Bownes and Albert 1996). The challenge grant program called for reallocation of resources to promote gender equity, a discontinuation of putting girls into "boys' programs," and a concerted effort to establish substantive female-specific services (Bownes and Albert 1996, p. 1; see also Community Research Associates 1997; Girls, Inc. 1996).

The challenge grant program was short-lived, unfortunately, and funding supported more exploratory and descriptive research about girls than program evaluation or development (Community Research Associates 1997; Kempf-Leonard and Sample 2000; Bloom et al. 2002; MacDonald and Chesney-Lind 2001; Kempf-Leonard, Johansson, and Jacobs 2005). The findings of most inquiries echo Ross and Fabiano (1986) that female offenders are "correctional afterthoughts." Schaffner's (2008, p. 163) conclusions that gender-specific policies and programs she observed "promoted the teaching of outdated, static framings of gender, ignored the existence of transgender youth altogether, and encouraged girls to conform to archaic feminine identifies that are not a part of their reality, let alone,... in their best interests" illustrate many of the disappointments. Thus, while concern exists about treatment of boys, the services provided to girls likely are of poorer quality and narrower in scope and availability than those provided to males.

IX. "What Works" for Girls

In recent years, knowledge about what constitutes effective correctional treatment has improved considerably (Andrews, Bonta, and Hoge 1990; Howell et al. 1995; Gendreau 1996; Lipsey 1995; Loeber and Farrington 1998; Andrews and Bonta 2003; Gendreau, French, and Gionet 2004; Ogloff and Davis 2004). Effective interventions are those shown to reduce crime and delinquency. Many scholars agree that "what works" is intervention that meets the following four criteria.

- First, clients and programs must be matched appropriately through valid assessment and classification procedures. Youths should be assessed for risks of reoffending, needs for treatment, and protective factors that can be targeted to strengthen their resilience. Classification schemes help guide decisions about treatment and services, caseload management, and release from supervision.
- Second, treatment plans need to be comprehensive because many juvenile offenders have a collection of personal problems, family situations, and limited opportunities that they need help in overcoming in order to succeed. The focus should include dynamic, criminogenic risk factors (Andrews and Bonta 2003) and strength-based approaches that improve individual capabilities (Sorbello et al. 2002; Van Wormer 2001; Ward and Brown 2004). This holistic approach is facilitated best with case management

administration and oversight that keeps the focus on the individual youth. The focus should be on interventions with dynamic, changeable characteristics.

- Third, service providers must be well trained in the specific treatment protocols they deliver.
- Fourth, services must be delivered in safe, nurturing settings and administered sufficiently long enough to sustain an effect.

A recent evaluation of sixty-two intervention programs for girls' delinquency in the United States found that no programs could be rated as effective—even as effective with some reservations, and that most would be rated as having insufficient evidence. Only four programs were identified has having substantial promise for girls, but none of them are even still in operation (Zahn et al. 2008, p. 6).

The difficulty for girls in juvenile justice systems is that nearly all of the information about effective treatment is based on research findings from male-only or gender-neutral analyses and often only for adults. There has been little effort to determine the validity of assessment and classification instruments specifically for females (Hardyman and Van Voorhis 2004). The best available assessment instruments for females take gender-neutral or male-only derived tools, then add or delete specific elements, reweight other factors, and modify cutoff scores to create different risk categories for females (Van Voorhis and Presser 2001). Among these instruments, classification improves if they include "gender-responsive" variables for relationships, mental health, and child abuse (Hardyman and Van Voorhis 2004). There is some disagreement, however, on whether the improvement for females based on adjusted male-based models is significant (Funk 1999), or only minor (Blanchette 2005).

Using recidivism to assess effectiveness among females is problematic, girls have low levels of recidivism and are a relatively small number in the first place. Therefore, at least some of the dilemma in judging predictive accuracy is a statistical artifact of the low base rate of reoffending among females (Blanchette and Brown 2006, p. 80). "The development of a good actuarial classification tool requires a large representative sample: criteria more easily met within the dominant male correctional population. Whether it is because the overwhelming majority of offenders are male, or whether it is because females are viewed as comparatively lower risk, actuarial classification tools for women are virtually absent" (Blanchette and Brown 2006, p. 51).

This is more than a problem of analytical deficiency. Indeed, there are important policy gains to be made with better substantive information. The potential reach of such gains is underscored by the following comments by Schaffner:

> [A] largely unarticulated benefit that gender-appropriate responses provide is promotion of the perspective that gender is crucial for understanding children's life pathways. After all, every aspect of adolescence is imbued with the implications of gender: youth development, physical and mental health care; understanding sexualities; mentoring; relating to family and neighbors; education; and work—all are experienced through prisms of gender (2008, p. 156).

X. Risks, Needs, and Protective Factors of Girls

In the absence of effective female-specific assessment instruments, robust indicators of female criminality observed in explanatory and predictive research should help to identify reliable risks, needs, and protective factors for girls (Blanchette and Brown 2006, p. 111). Unfortunately, the first body of etiological research to address female criminality targeted only static biological and physiological sex characteristics. Several critiques identify attempts to link female offending with biological deficiencies of girls compared to boys, abnormal female characteristics, or other stereotypes based on sexuality (e.g., Denno 1990). For example, Thomas (1923) attributed a sexual and manipulative nature to female offending because of inherent sex differences (Smart 1976; Heidensohn 1985). Sexuality and emotional difficulties, thought to be typical of females, were offered as the cause of girls' offending in *The Adolescent Girl in Conflict* (Konopka 1966). The "abnormal female" notion was advanced by Thrasher (1927), who argued that the few girls in gangs were "tomboys" who were uncomfortable with their own sex (p. 158). Inherent problems with the individual, both because of female inadequacies and abnormal girls, appear in explanations for delinquency by Cowie, Cowie, and Slater (1968) and Vedder and Sommerville (1970), who also added ethnocentric dimensions (Klein 1980, p. 99). Although all of the ideas offered by these scholars have been generally dismissed because they failed to recognize the gendered social world apart from anatomy and fell far short of modern scientific standards, it is still possible to discern their effect in helping to shape views about girls' delinquency held by some teachers and school administrators, juvenile justice officials, parents, and scholars.

Many of the prominent delinquency theories also have been chastised for the manner in which they addressed the delinquency of girls: disregard and omission. Beginning with Shaw and McKay (1942), but continuing as common practice today, the general term "delinquency" is used to refer only to boys but never only to girls. Both Cohen (1955) and Miller (1958) ignored girls on purpose in their subcultural explanations for delinquency. Cohen's justifications for ignoring girls have been openly criticized as both arrogant and sexist (Chesney-Lind and Paskos 2004, p. 18). Cloward and Ohlin's extension of subcultural theory and integration of strain theory (1960) also ignored girls, which is ironic because girls probably had more "blocked opportunities" than boys. Surprisingly, Hirschi (1969) even ignored the girls for whom he had already collected data, albeit apologetically and promising to return to examine them, although he never did.

Even when girls were not included in observations from which theories developed or in analyses that assessed the viability of these explanations, some criminologists accept their applicability also to girls (e.g., Simons, Miller, and Aigner 1980; Canter 1982; Smith and Paternoster 1987; Rowe, Vazsonyi, and Flannery 1995;

Baskin and Sommers 1997; Steffensmeier and Allan 1996; Moffit et al. 2001; Lanctot and LeBlanc 2002; Jensen 2003; Blanchette and Brown 2006; Agnew 2009). Others are ardent critics of the validity of this "add females and stir" approach (Jagger 2008) to understanding female delinquency (e.g., Leonard 1983; Gilfus 1992; Daly 1992, 1994; Naffine 1996; Chesney-Lind 1995, 1997; Acoca and Dedel 1998; Belknap and Holsinger 1998, 2006). Many of these authors advocate for a female-specific pathway to offending that includes victimization, mental health deficiencies, substance abuse, running away, behavior injurious to self, and poverty. The theoretical linkages between these factors are not yet identified; some of them can coexist or may even covary.

A lot of the evidence used to advance these female-specific traits comes primarily from results of qualitative exploratory studies with incarcerated female offenders. In-depth interviews and observations of a few "established" female offenders enable the subjects to speak freely about their lives, including experiences and their perceptions of causal connections with their offending. Recurrent findings underscore that abuse and victimization, dysfunctional families, and social barriers have impeded these women. The value of this evidence would be stronger, however, if we also knew the prevalence of these factors and their priority in relation to other correlates of offending. Such knowledge cannot be discerned from purposive samples and phenomenological explorations. These observations do serve a purpose in inductive approaches to theory building, such as Howell's (2003) female-specific theory of serious, violent, and chronic offending. There has been only one empirical test of Howell's theory, and only a partial test, but significant factors were equally applicable to girls and boys (Johansson and Kempf-Leonard 2009). No other female-specific theory has fared better. Tests of causal delinquency theories leave the question of explanatory pathways specifically for females unresolved.

Descriptive and predictive studies offer another avenue from which we can observe factors that place females at higher risk or need. Unfortunately, the "persistent invisibility of girls" (Acoca 1998, p. 562) has not been the purview only of theory-building. Researchers aimed at exploration, description, and prediction also have foregone attention to females based on "the tyranny of small numbers." For example, Wolfgang, Figlio, and Sellin (1972) failed to include girls in their prominent longitudinal cohort study because they relied on military registration data, which did not include females, as one method to identify subjects. Their pragmatic argument did not hold for school records, another source they used (1972), and the research team corrected this weakness in the second cohort study (Tracy et al. 1990). When delinquency career trajectories such as early onset of offending, escalating severity, crime specialization, persistent and chronic offending, and desistance were examined, the patterns were similar for females and males, except that the offense levels for females were far lower (Tracy and Kempf-Leonard 1996; Kempf-Leonard, Tracy, and Howell 2001). When the effect of juvenile justice interventions was examined, even the large number of fourteen thousand females experienced only 1,962 encounters with police for delinquency, and too few girls had formal juvenile court dispositions to sustain statistical analyses of informative patterns (Tracy and Kempf-Leonard 1996).

More recently, the major initiative to understand the causes and correlates of delinquency funded by the Office of Juvenile Justice and Delinquency Prevention (OJJDP) in 1986 led to prospective longitudinal data collection efforts in youth surveys and supplemental data administered in Pittsburgh, Denver, and Rochester. In Pittsburgh, the sample included 500 boys in First, fourth, seventh grades; in Rochester, 271 girls and 729 boys who had been oversampled because of their greater likelihood to exhibit serious delinquency; in Denver, 806 boys and 721 girls. Although the sampling designs varied considerably, the initial aim of most findings was a description of serious, chronic, and violent offending, plus comparison across sites. As such, often girls were either not separately identified or excluded from analyses from two sites. Rolf Loeber, chief investigator of the Pittsburgh Youth Survey also directs the Developmental Trends Study, a National Institute of Mental Health initiative following 177 boys and nearing its twentieth year in 2012. In addition, after more than a decade of the OJJDP Causes and Correlates program, Loeber started the Pittsburgh Girls Study to track 2,451 girls ages 5 through 8 until they reach grade 9. These three studies contribute significant information about factors associated with delinquency and ways in which these factors affect developmental pathways, trajectories, or careers involving crime (OJJDP 2011); the area in which they have offered the least expertise is female offending and gendered crime. Our knowledge about how these and other factors relate to girls' offending would be much better now had all of the original study designs included provisions to study and oversample girls.

The only other recent major research initiative to understand female offending and juvenile justice processing has been the OJJDP Girls' Study Group (RTI International 2011 http://girlsstudygroup.rti.org; Zahn 2009). This consortium of scholars examines existing data sets and literature but does not receive support to develop new and better ways to observe female delinquency and crime. Either as part of or complementary to the Girls Study Group, there are several recent meta-analyses of research including gender and risk of offending. Meta-analyses based on female offenders and family process variables identify attachment, affection, and supervision as robust, inverse predictors of recidivism (Dowden and Andrews 1999; Simourd and Andrews 1994). Associates are also important (Simourd and Andrews 1994); having antisocial peers was among the strongest risk factors identified for adolescent girls (Dowden and Andrews 1999). The meta-analysis by Dowden and Brown (2002) found primarily gender-neutral findings for substance abuse and treatment. The exception was a stronger effect on girls than boys for alcohol and drug use by parents.

Of course there are many other independent efforts in which the aim is to describe and advance our understanding of female offending. It is not necessary to review them all here; they would only lend further support to what is already evident. The current body of knowledge is not sufficient to allow us to make informed decisions about accurate and effective responses to female delinquents.

XI. Conclusions and Recommendations

With more than a century of experience in intervention with juvenile offenders, juvenile justice systems in the United States should be highly effective, operate fairly, and prove beneficial to the country's youths—including girls, who comprise half of the adolescent population. By now, the evidence of virtuous juvenile justice processing should be both compelling and widely known, too, because scholars have been studying female delinquency and juvenile justice interactions all along. It is very disappointing, therefore, to report that this is not the case. Instead, the information is equivocal, at best, on whether juvenile justice systems actually achieve these goals for girls, or that our level of understanding is sufficient to direct implementation of reformed and better systems. The fault lies with an immature science and qualities inherent to the original design of juvenile justice systems.

That the collective evidence from an important area of scientific inquiry falls short of where it should be is not unexpected, however, given the haphazard manner in which the research has progressed. Good science builds chronologically, taking the best information from prior work and improving upon it with new insights and methodological advancement. That has not happened in this line of inquiry. Rather than a cumulative process, research on female delinquency and juvenile justice might best be viewed as conflicting ontological views of girls and epistemological expectations about science. For example, it is fairly easy to dismiss as not scientifically rigorous, and no longer having much relevance, most of the work by scholars who attributed female crime only to sexuality, ignoring any role of social and cultural expectations of gender conformity.

The contributions of two other groups of scholars, however, are both important but have not yet benefitted from each other. One sphere includes scholarship based primarily on positivism and the modern view that objective scientific tests of delinquency and juvenile justice can be conducted. Most of this work is social science, although increasingly it is more multidisciplinary. The minimal roles accorded females and "androcentric bias" of this scholarship has been challenged and criticized as systematically ignoring the problems of victimization that affect girls (e.g., Chesney-Lind and Paskos 2004). Although it is true that some of these studies are dismissive of females, and others gender-neutral, a lot of research in this category does treat gender as a variable.

Conducted primarily by critics of the first group, another body of work adheres to feminist standpoint theory and mainly qualitative methods that emphasize phenomenology. Female subjects are chosen purposively to meet criminality criteria, and then potential risks, needs, and protective factors are explored through retrospective personal accounts of their life histories. This body of research values the individualized, contextual views available in the in-depth interviews and observations. Males are seldom observed. The difficulty here is that although these data are rich in details about select subjects, they are of limited utility from which to deduce generalizable results or to draw conclusions about female delinquency and juvenile justice.

An important next step will be to move beyond "androcentric" or "gynocentric" dismissals and pursue good science capable of understanding female delinquency and suggesting effective responses. In recommending the way to advance etiological understanding of girls' delinquency, Miller and Mullins endorse this juncture. They say, "the most promising approach for understanding girls' delinquency is to develop scholarship that draws from the important insights of broader criminological though, but does so while critically examining the gendered life situations of girls and boys and their impact on delinquency" (2009, p. 33). Moreover, an effort to meld achievements from both groups likely is the only way to garner resources sufficiently large to support a study design able to sustain the large number of girls and enough offending to be observed systematically, both of which must be tracked through imaginative methods. Knowledge grows quickly when science achieves this level of maturity. For example, regarding other social science topics Leckenby (2007, p. 48) writes:

> The varied and vibrant contributions of feminist empiricists have created an environment where paradigm shifts are already taking place. These contributions are leading to better and more objective science and are often subsumed into the establishment's notions of good science, frequently leaving their feminist label behind. Feminist empiricists are hardly monolithic in their epistemology, methodology, and use of method.

Blanchette and Brown (2006) conclude their review of research with a proposal that such synergy also is possible for understanding female delinquency and advancing effective treatment:

> The empirical evidence to date clearly indicates that gender-neutral theories have a sizeable role to play in the explanation of female criminal conduct. Moreover, while a number of "female-centered" paradigms have emerged, they are relatively more novel and have not been studied to the same extent as their gender-neutral counterparts. Nonetheless, the extant research suggests that our understanding of female criminal conduct may be enhanced by incorporating elements from "gender-informed" and "female-centered" perspectives. In fact, we observed that a number of seemingly divergent theoretical perspectives were actually complementary. This holds promise for prospective theoretical advancements that adopt conciliatory rather than adversarial approaches (p. 139).

A research consortium of diverse perspectives is likely to advance our knowledge about male delinquency and juvenile justice too, because "incorporating feminist insights about women and the feminine into existing systems of knowledge requires simultaneously reexamining prevailing understanding of men and the masculine" (Jagger 2008, p. viii).

Once epistemological differences are set aside and good scientific investigations commence routinely, the remaining obstacles in understanding female delinquency and intervening justly involve the policy structure of juvenile justice systems. The way to reduce disparity is by building cooperation and competency, and holding the justice system accountable (Hawkins and Kempf-Leonard 2005). A competent justice system requires clear objectives, access to adequate alternatives, and information from which to determine the circumstances in which each option is most effective (Gottfredson and Gottfredson 1980). Particularly for girls, juvenile justice systems lack all three of these elements of competency.

Available evidence suggests that juvenile justice processing initiates at arrest and referral in a somewhat biased, stereotypical manner, proceeds with more fair and balanced adjudication, and then concludes with differential treatment, which may be especially detrimental for girls who are placed out of home. Problems also vary by stage of process and size or location of the system. The experiences are not uniformly distributed across girls either, as females in disadvantaged race, ethnicity, and social class groups often are marginalized even more by juvenile justice. These difficulties exist because juvenile justice decisions typically are individualized, discretionary, and not informed by structured guidelines. Most of these decisions are allowed to occur in private, informal settings in which there is no independent advocate for the youth, and little recourse by which to oppose any decision. Moreover, there is a lack of clear, consistent goals guiding decisions because punitive public safety can be substituted for helpful benevolent treatment at the whim of any official. Most officials receive little or no feedback on the effects of their decisions, so there is no impetus to modify their decision-making strategies. Given such lack of standardization, juvenile justice processing cannot and does not function in a systematic way.

At the front-end, fewer girls than boys become involved with juvenile justice, and generally for behavior that is less serious and more related to family problems and sexuality. The prevalence of arrest of females is growing, however, and for many reasons. Some reasons are beyond the scope of formal juvenile justice policies, but others involve decisions made by police and intake officers who respond to complaints and could be guided more systematically than they are now. Police officers may be public safety experts, but often lack the knowledge of adolescent development required to make decisions in the best interests of youths. With training and structured guidelines, these early-stage decisions could be made both more fair and effective. Most assuredly, informed front-end decisions could reduce the current situation in which the process is initiated for some girls with a lower threshold of fewer, less serious charges and family problems than the factors that formally ensnare boys. A wider array of alternatives to pre-hearing detention and knowledge about how options help troubled girls and boys also would likely achieve gains in public safety, benefit individual youths, and provide cost savings.

Decisions during the adjudication and disposition stages appear to be the most fair, or at least show fewer disparities. This likely occurs because court bureaucracies have adapted routine processing to expedite cases efficiently. The bigger and busier the court, the more likely the decisions are to become habitual, and thereby more equitable and fair. In addition, courts respond but do not initiate interventions with youths, so court officials may be more likely to organize their decisions according to recurrent factors that end up helping them to situate girls similarly to boys. Courts operate within a realm of multiple options, but all involve fixed, short lengths, which also may contribute to the perception of more gender-balanced decisions. Fair, equitable decisions do not equate to effective crime reduction or public safety out-comes. Knowledge about effectiveness requires feedback to decision makers, the mechanisms for which rarely exist in America's juvenile courts.

Girls who are placed out of home may have the most detrimental of juvenile justice experiences. In contrast to boys, these girls often live in more restrictive resi-dential settings, where they receive a more narrow range of services that also are of poorer quality. The first difficulty is lack of access for girls to services readily avail-able to boys. The allocation of resources at the back-end of the system generally is inadequate, but constrained even more when girls are relegated to remote rural locations far away from service providers for the larger number of boys. Second, the adequacy of services and treatment girls receive has not yet been determined. After more than a century of developing juvenile justice interventions in the United States, the time is past due that we devote good scientific inquiry to understanding risks and needs of troubled girls, extending to them through fair and effective pro-cedures comprehensive treatment and services that are delivered by well-trained experts in safe settings.

REFERENCES

Acoca, Leslie. 1998. "Outside/Inside: The Violation of American Girls at Home, on the Streets, and in the Juvenile Justice System." *Crime and Delinquency* 44: 561–89.

Acoca, Leslie, and James Austin. 1996. *The Hidden Crisis: Women in Prison*. San Francisco: National Council on Crime and Delinquency.

Acoca, Leslie, and Kelly Dedel. 1998. *The California Girls' Story*. San Francisco, CA: National Council on Crime and Delinquency.

Agnew, Robert. 2009. "The Contribution of 'Mainstream' Theories to the Explanation of Female Delinquency." In *The Delinquent Girl*, edited by Margaret A. Zahn, 7–29. Philadelphia: Temple University Press.

American Correctional Association (ACA). 1990. *The Female Offender: What Does the Future Hold?* Washington, DC: St. Mary's.

Andrews, D. A., and James Bonta. 2003. *The Psychology of Criminal Conduct*, 3rd ed. Cincinnati, OH: Anderson.

Andrews, D. A., James Bonta, and R. D. Hoge. 1990. "Classification for Effective Rehabilitation: Rediscovering Psychology." *Criminal Justice and Behavior* 17: 19–52.

Armstrong, Gaylene S. 2001. *Private vs. Public Operation of Juvenile Correctional Facilities*. New York: LFB publishing.

Arnold, R. A. 1990. "The Process of Victimization and Criminalization of Black Women." In *The Criminal Justice System and Women*, edited by B. R. Price and N. Sokoloff, 136–46. New York: McGraw-Hill.

Austin, James, Barry Krisberg, Robert DeComo, Sonya Rudenstine, and Dominic Del Rosario. 1995. *Juveniles Taken into Custody: Fiscal Year 1993*. Washington, DC: Office of Juvenile Justice and Delinquency Prevention.

Baines, Margaret, and Christine Alder. 1996. "Are Girls More Difficult to Work With? Youth Workers' Perspectives in Juvenile Justice and Related Areas." *Crime and Delinquency* 42: 467–85.

Bartollas, Clemens. 1993. "Little Girls Grown Up: The Perils of Institutionalization."
In *Female Criminality: The State of the Art*, edited by Concetta C. Culliver, 469–82.
New York: Garland.

Bartollas, Clemens. 1997. *Juvenile Delinquency, fourth edition*. Boston: Allyn & Bacon.

Baskin, Deborah R., and Ira B. Sommers. 1997. *Casualties of Community Disorder: Women's
Careers in Violent Crime*. New York: Westview Press.

Belknap, Joanne. 1996. *The Invisible Woman: Gender, Crime, and Justice*. Belmont, CA:
Wadsworth.

Belknap, Joanne, and Bonnie Cady. 2008. "Pre-Adjudicated and Adjudicated Girls' Reports
on Their Lives Before and During Detention and Incarceration." In *Female Offenders:
Critical Perspectives and Effective Interventions*, edited by Ruth T. Zaplin, 2nd ed.,
251–81. Sudbury, MA: Jones and Bartlett.

Belknap, Joanne, and Kristi Holsinger. 1998. "An Overview of Delinquent Girls: How
Theory and Practice Have Failed and the Need for Innovative Change." In *Female
Offenders: Critical Perspectives and Effective Interventions*, edited by R. T. Zaplin, 31–64.
Gaithersburg, MD: Aspen.

Belknap, Joanne, and Kristi Holsinger. 2006. "The Gendered Nature of Risk Factors for
Delinquency." *Feminist Criminology* 1: 48–70.

Bernard, Thomas J. 1992. *The Cycle of Juvenile Justice*. New York: Oxford University Press.

Bishop, Donna, and Charles Frazier. 1992. "Gender Bias in Juvenile Justice Processing:
Implications of the JJDP Act." *Journal of Criminal Law and Criminology* 82: 1162–86.

Blanchette, Kelley. 1996. *The Relationship Between Criminal History, Mental Disorder, and
Recidivism Among Federally Sentenced Female Offenders*. Unpublished Master's Thesis,
Carleton University, Ottawa, Ontario, Canada.

Blanchette, Kelley. 2005. *Field Test of a Gender-Informed Security Reclassification Scale for
Female Offenders*. PhD. Dissertation, Carleton University, Ottawa, Ontario.

Blanchette, Kelley, and Shelley L. Brown. 2006. *The Assessment and Treatment of Women
Offenders: An Integrative Perspective*. West Sussex, England: John Wiley and Sons.

Bloom, Barbara, and Meda Chesney-Lind. 1999. "Women in Prison: Vengeful Equity." In *It's
a Crime: Women and Justice*, edited by R. Muraskin, 2nd ed., 183–204. Englewood
Cliffs, NJ: Prentice-Hall.

Bloom, Barbara, Barbara Owen, Elizabeth P. Deschenes, and Jill Rosenbaum. 2002.
"Improving Juvenile Justice for Females: A Statewide Assessment in California." *Crime
and Delinquency* 4: 526–52.

Blumstein, Albert. 2000. "Disaggregating the Violence Trends." In *The Crime Drop in
America*, edited by Alfred Blumstein and Joel Wallman, 13–44. New York: Cambridge
University Press.

Bond-Maupin, Lisa, James Maupin, and Amy Leisenring. 2002. "Girls' Delinquency and the
Justice Implications of Intake Workers' Perspectives." *Women and Criminal Justice* 13:
51–77.

Bonta, James, Bessie Pang, and Suzanne Wallace-Capretta. 1995. "Predictors of Recidivism
among Incarcerated Female Offenders." *The Prison* Journal 75: 277–294.

Bownes, Donna, and Rodney L. Albert. 1996. "State Challenge Activities." *OJJDP Juvenile
Justice Bulletin*. September. Washington, DC: U.S. Department of Justice, Office of
Juvenile Justice and Delinquency Prevention.

Brener, Nancy D., Thomas R. Simon, Etienne G. Krug, and Richard Lowry. 1999. "Recent
Trends in Violence-Related Behaviors Among High School Students in the United
States." *Journal of the American Medical Association* 282: 330–446.

Bridges, George S., and Sara Steen. 1998. "Racial Disparities in Official Assessments of Juvenile Offenders: Attributional Stereotypes as Mediating Mechanisms." *American Sociological Review* 63: 554–70.

Burruss, George, and Kimberly Kempf-Leonard. 2002. "The Questionable Advantage of Defense Counsel in Juvenile Court." *Justice Quarterly* 17: 37–68.

Canter, Rachelle J. 1982. "Sex Differences in Self-Reported Delinquency." *Criminology* 20: 373–93.

Castellano, Thomas C. 1986. "The Justice Model in the Juvenile Justice System: Washington State's Experience." *Law and Policy* 8: 397–418.

Chapple, Constance L., K. D. Johnson, and Lee B. Whitbeck. 2004. "Gender and Arrest Among Homeless and Runaway Youth: An Analysis of Background, Family, and Situational Factors." *Youth Violence and Juvenile Justice* 2: 129–47.

Chesney-Lind, Meda. 1973. "Judicial Enforcement of the Female Sex Role." *Issues in Criminology* 8: 51–70.

Chesney-Lind, Meda. 1991. "Patriarchy, Prisons, and Jails: A Critical Look at Trends in Women's Incarceration." *Prison Journal* 71: 51–67.

Chesney-Lind, Meda. 1995. "Girls, Delinquency, and Juvenile Justice: Toward a Feminist Theory of Young Women's Crime." In *The Criminal Justice System and Women: Offenders, Victims, and Workers*, edited by B. R. Price and N. J. Sokoloff, 71–88. New York: McGraw-Hill.

Chesney-Lind, Meda. 1997. *The Female Offender: Girls, Women, and Crime*. Thousand Oaks, CA: Sage.

Chesney-Lind, Meda, and Lisa Pasko. 2004. *The Female Offender; Girls, Women, and Crime*. Thousand Oaks, CA: Sage.

Chesney-Lind, Meda, and Nancy Rodriguez. 1983. "Women Under Lock and Key." *Prison Journal* 63: 47–65.

Chesney-Lind, Meda, and Randall H. Shelden. 1998. *Girls, Delinquency, and Juvenile Justice*, 2nd ed. Pacific Grove, CA: Brooks/Cole.

Cloward, Richard A., and Lloyd E. Ohlin. 1960. *Delinquency and Opportunity*. Glencoe, IL: Free Press.

Cohen, Albert K. 1955. *Delinquent Boys: The Culture of the Gang*. New York: Free Press.

Community Research Associates. 1997. *Status of the States: Female-Specific Services*. Champaign, IL: Community Research Associates.

Corley, Charles J., Steven Cernkovich, and Peggy Giordano. 1989. "Sex and the Likelihood of Sanction." *Journal of Criminal Law and Criminology* 80: 540–56.

Costello, Jan C., and Nancy L. Worthington. 1981–1982. "Incarcerating Status Offenders: Attempts to Circumvent the Juvenile Justice and Delinquency Prevention Act." *Harvard Civil Rights-Civil Liberties Law Review* 16: 41–81.

Cowie, John, Valerie Cowie, and Eliot Slater. 1968. Delinquency in Girls. London: Heinemann.

Daly, Kathleen. 1992. "Women's Pathways to Felony Court: Feminist Theories of Law Breaking and Problems of Representation." *Review of Law and Women's Studies* 2: 11–52.

Daly, Kathleen 1994. *Gender, Crime, and Punishment*. New Haven, CT: Yale University Press.

Dannefer, Dale, and Russell K. Schutt. 1982. "Race and Juvenile Justice Processing in Police and Court Agencies." *American Journal of Sociology* 87: 1113–32.

Datesman, Susan K., and Frank R. Scarpitti. 1980. "Unequal Protection for Males and Females in the Juvenile Court." In *Women, Crime and Justice*, edited by S. K. Datesmann and F. R. Scarpitti, 300–19. New York: Oxford University Press.

Davis, Antoinette, Chris Tsudian, Susan Marchionna, and Barry Krisberg. 2008. *The Declining Number of Youth in Custody in the Juvenile Justice System. Focus.* National Council on Crime and Delinquency.

Dembo, Richard, Linda Williams, and James Schmeidler. (1993. "Gender Differences in Mental Health Service Needs Among Youths Entering a Juvenile Detention Center." *Journal of Prison and Jail Health* 12: 73–1010.

Denno, Deborah. 1990. *Biology and Violence: From Birth to Adulthood.* Cambridge, UK: Cambridge University Press.

Dobash, Russell P., R. Emerson Dobash, and Sue Gutteridge. 1986. *The Imprisonment of Women.* Oxford: Blackwell.

Dowden, Craig, and D. A. Andrews. 1999. "What Works for Female Offenders: A Meta-Analytic Review." *Crime and Delinquency* 45: 438–52.

Dowden, Craig, and Shelley L. Brown. 2002. "The Role of Substance Abuse Factors in Predicting Recidivism: A Meta-Analysis." *International Journal of Crime, Psychology, and Law* 8: 243–64.

Fagan, Jeffrey, Martin Forst, and T. S. Vivona. 1987. "Racial Determinants of the Judicial Transfer Decision: Prosecuting Violent Youth in Criminal Court." *Crime and Delinquency* 33: 259–86.

Federele, Katherine H., and Meda Chesney-Lind. 1992. "Special Issues in Juvenile Justice: Gender, Race, and Ethnicity." In *Juvenile Justice and Public Policy: Toward a National Agenda*, edited by I. Schwartz, 165–95. New York: Lexington Books.

Feld, Barry C. 1991. "Justice by Geography: Urban, Suburban, and Rural Variations in Juvenile Justice Administration." *Journal of Criminal Law and Criminology* 82: 156–210.

Feld, Barry C. 1993. *Justice for Children: The Right to Counsel and the Juvenile Court.* Boston: Northeastern University Press.

Feld, Barry C. 1995. "The Social Context of Juvenile Justice Administration: Racial Disparities in an Urban Juvenile Court." In *Minorities in Juvenile Justice*, edited by K. Kempf-Leonard, C. E. Pope, and W. H. Feyerherm, 66–97. Thousand Oaks, CA: Sage.

Feld, Barry C. 1999. *Bad Kids: Race and the Transformation of the Juvenile Court.* New York: Oxford University Press.

Feld, Barry C. 2009a. "Girls in the Juvenile Justice System." In *The Delinquent Girl*, edited by Margaret A. Zahn, 225–64. Philadelphia: Temple University Press.

Feld, Barry C. 2009b. "Violent Girls or Relabeled Status Offenders? An Alternative Interpretation of the Data." *Crime and Delinquency* 55: 241–65.

Feld, Barry C., and Shelly Schaefer. 2010. "The Right to Counsel in Juvenile Court: Law Reform to Deliver Legal Services and Reduce Justice by Geography." *Criminology and Public Policy* 9: 327–56.

Figueira-McDonough, Josefine. 1985. "Are Girls Different? Gender Discrepancies Between Delinquent Behavior and Control." *Child Welfare* 64: 273–89.

Finkelhor, David, Gerald T. Hotling, I. A. Lewis, and Christine Smith. 1990. "Sexual Abuse in a National Survey of Adult Men and Women: Prevalence, Characteristics, and Risk Factors." *Child Abuse and Neglect* 14: 19–28.

Franke, Todd Michael, Anh-Luu T. Huynh-Hohnbaum, and Yunah Chung. 2002. "Adolescent Violence: with Whom They Fight and Where." *Journal of Ethnic and Cultural Diversity in Social Work* 11: 133–58.

Frazier, Charles E., and Donna Bishop. 1990. "Jailing Juveniles in Florida: The Dynamics of Compliance with a Sluggish Federal Reform Initiative." *Crime and Delinquency* 36: 427–41.

———. 1995. "Reflections on Race Effects in Juvenile Justice." In *Minorities in Juvenile Justice*, edited by K. Kempf-Leonard, C. E. Pope, and W. H. Feyerherm, 16–46. Thousand Oaks, CA: Sage.

Frazier, Charles E., and John K. Cochran. 1986. "Detention of Juveniles: Its Effects on Subsequent Juvenile Court Processing Decisions." *Youth and Society* 17: 286–385.

Funk, Stephanie J. 1999. "Risk Assessment for Juveniles on Probation: A Focus on Gender." *Criminal Justice and Behavior* 26: 44–68.

Gaardner, Emily, Nancy Rodriguez, and Marjorie S. Zatz. 2004. "Criers, Liars, and Manipulators: Probation Officers' Views of Girls." *Justice Quarterly* 21: 547–78.

Gelsthorpe, Lois. 1989. *Sexism and the Female Offender: An Organizational Analysis.* Aldershot, UK: Gower.

Gendreau, Paul, Sheila French, and Angela Gionet. 2004. "What Works (What Doesn't Work): The Principles of Effective Treatment." *Journal of Community Corrections* 13: 4–30.

Gendreau, Paul. 1996. "The Principles of Effective Intervention with Offenders." In *Choosing Correctional Interventions that Work: Defining the Demand and Evaluating the Supply*, edited by A. T. Harland, 117–30. Newbury Park, CA: Sage.

Giallambardo, Rose. 1974. *The Social World of Imprisoned Girls: A Comparative Study of Institutions for Juvenile Delinquents.* New York: John Wiley and Sons.

Gilfus, Mary E. 1992. "From Victims to Survivors to Offenders: Women's Routes of Entry and Immersion into Street Crime." *Women and Criminal Justice* 4: 63–90.

Girls, Inc. 1996. *Prevention and Parity: Girls in Juvenile Justice.* Indianapolis: Girls Incorporated National Resource Center.

Goodkind, Sara. 2005. "Gender-Specific Services in the Juvenile Justice System: A Critical Examination." *Affilia* 20: 52–70.

Gottfredson, Michael R., and Don M. Gottfredson. 1980. *Decision Making in Criminal Justice: Toward the Rational Exercise of Discretion*, 2nd ed. New York: Plenum.

Gray, Tara, G. Larry Mays, and Mark K. Stohr. 1995. "Inmate Needs and Programming in Exclusively Women's Jails." *Prison Journal* 75: 186–202.

Hagan, John, and Belinda McCarthy. 1997. *Mean Streets: Youth Crime and Homelessness.* New York: Cambridge University Press.

Hammer, Heather, David Finkelhor, and Andrea Sedlack. 2002. *Runaway/Thrownaway Children: National Estimates and Characteristics.* National Incidence Studies of Missing, Abducted, Runaway, and Thrownaway Children (NISMART). Washington, DC: U.S. Department of Justice, Office of Justice Programs, Office of Juvenile Justice and Delinquency Prevention.

Hardyman, Patricia L., and Patricia Van Voorhis. 2004. *Developing Gender-Specific Classification Systems for Women Offenders.* Washington, DC: National Institute of Corrections (NIC Accession number 018931).

Hawkins, Darnell F., and Kimberly Kempf-Leonard, eds. 2005. *Our Children, Their Children: Confronting Racial and Ethnic Differences in American Juvenile Justice.* Chicago: University of Chicago Press.

Heidensohn, Francis. 1985. *Women and Crime: The Life of the Female Offender.* New York: New York University Press.

Heimer, Karen, Janet L. Lauritsen, and James P. Lynch. 2009. "The National Crime Victimization Survey and the Gender Gap in Offending: Redux." *Criminology* 47 (2): 427–38.

Hirshi, Travis. 1969. *Causes of Delinquency.* Berkeley: University of California Press.

Horowitz, Ruth, and Anne Pottieger. 1991. "Gender Bias in Juvenile Justice Handling of Serious Crime-Involved Youth." *Journal of Research in Crime and Delinquency* 28: 75–100.

Howell, James C. 1993. *Preventing and Reducing Juvenile Delinquency: A Comprehensive Framework*. Thousand Oaks, CA: Sage.

Howell, James C., Barry Krisberg, J. D. Hawkins, and John J. Wilson, eds. 1995. *A Sourcebook: Serious, Violent, and Chronic Juvenile Offenders*. Thousand Oaks, CA: Sage.

Hoyt, Stephanie, and David G. Scherer. 1998. "Female Juvenile Delinquency: Misunderstood by the Juvenile Justice System, Neglected by Social Science." *Law and Human Behavior* 22: 81–107.

Jackson, Patrick G., and Cindy Stearns. 1995. "Gender Issues in the New Generation Jail." *Prison Journal* 75: 203–21.

Jagger, Alison M. 2008. *Just Methods: an Interdisciplinary Feminist Reader*. New York: Paradigm.

Jensen, Gary F. 2003. "Gender Variation in Delinquency: Self-Image, Beliefs and Peers as Mediating Mechanisms." In *Social Learning Theory and the Explanation of Crime: A Guide for the New Century*, edited by M. D. Krohn and R. I. Akers, vol. 11, 119–36. Beverly Hills, CA: Sage.

Johansson, Pernilla, and Kimberly Kempf-Leonard. 2009. "A Gender-Specific Pathway to Serious, Violent and Chronic Offending? Exploring Howell's Risk Factors for Serious Delinquency" *Crime and Delinquency* 55 (2): 215–40.

Johnson, David R., and Laurie K. Scheubel. 1991. "Gender Bias in the Disposition of Juvenile Court Referrals: The Effects of Time and Location." *Criminology* 29: 677–99.

Kaufman, Jeanne G., and Cathy S. Widom. 1999. "Childhood Victimization, Running Away, and Delinquency." *Journal of Research in Crime and Delinquency* 36: 347–71.

Kempf, Kimberly L., Scott H. Decker, and Robert Bing, II. 1990. *An Analysis of Apparent Disparities in the Handling of Black Youth within Missouri's Juvenile Justice Systems*. Report submitted to the Governor's Advisory Group on Juvenile Justice. St. Louis, MO: University of Missouri-St. Louis.

Kempf-Leonard, Kimberly. 2001. "Race, Gender, and Pre-hearing Detention of Juveniles." In *Juvenile Delinquency, Crime and Society*, vol. 2., edited by J. Weis, R. Crutchfield, and G. Bridges, 538–47. Thousand Oaks, CA: Pine Forge Press.

Kempf-Leonard, Kimberly. 2010. "Does Having an Attorney Provide a Better Outcome? The Right to Counsel Doesn't Mean Attorneys Help Youths." *Criminology and Public Policy* 9(2): 357–63.

Kempf-Leonard, Kimberly, and Pernilla Johansson. 2007. "Gender and Runaways: Risk Factors, Delinquency, and Juvenile Justice Experiences" *Youth Violence and Juvenile Justice* 5(3): 308–27

Kempf-Leonard, Kimberly, Pernilla Johansson, and Bruce Jacobs. 2005. *The Role of Gender in Juvenile Referrals, Case, Processing, and Treatment in Dallas County Juvenile Department*. Report Submitted to the Criminal Justice Division, Office of the Governor, and Federal Office of Juvenile Justice and Delinquency Prevention.

Kempf-Leonard, Kimberly, and Lisa L. Sample. 2000. "Disparity Based on Sex: Is Gender-Specific Treatment Warranted?" *Justice Quarterly* 17: 89–128.

Kempf-Leonard, Kimberly, Paul E. Tracy, and James C. Howell. 2001. "Serious, Violent, and Chronic Juvenile Offenders: The Relationship of Delinquency Career Types to Adult Criminality." *Justice Quarterly* 18: 449–78.

Kersten, Joachim. 1989 "The Institutional Control of Girls and Boys: An Attempt at a Gender-Specific Approach." In *Growing Up Good*, edited by M. Cain, 129–44. London: Sage.

Klein, Dorie. 1980. "The Etiology of Female Crime: A Review of the Literature." In *Women, Crime, and Justice*, edited by S. K. Datesman and F. R. Scarpitti, 70–10. New York: Oxford University Press.

Knupfer, Anne M. 2001. *Reform and Resistance: Gender, Delinquency and America's First Juvenile Court*. New York: Routledge.

Konopka, Gisela. 1966. *The Adolescent Girl in Conflict*. Englewood Cliffs, NJ: Prentice-Hall.

Krause, W., and Marilyn D. McShane. 1994. "A Deinstitutionalization Retrospective: Relabeling the Status Offender." *Journal of Crime and Justice* 17: 45–67.

Krisberg, Barry, Ira M. Schwartz, Gideon Fishman, Zvi Eisikovits, and Edna Guttman. 1986. *The Incarceration of Minority Youth*. Minneapolis: Hubert Humphrey Institute of Public Affairs.

Krisberg, Barry, Ira M. Schwartz, Gideon Fishman, Zvi Eisikovits, Edna Guttman, and Karen Joe. 1987. "The Incarceration of Minority Youth." *Crime and Delinquency* 33: 173–204.

Krisberg, Barry, Paul Litsky, and Ira M. Schwartz. 1984. "Youth in Confinement: Justice by Geography." *Journal of Research in Crime and Delinquency* 21: 153–81.

Krisberg, Barry. 1995. "The Legacy of Juvenile Corrections." *Corrections Today* 57: 122–54.

Krisberg, Barry, and Ira M. Schwartz. 1983. "Re-Thinking Juvenile Justice." *Crime and Delinquency* 29: 381–97.

Lanctot, Nadine, and Marc LeBlanc. 2002. "Explaining Deviance by Adolescent Females." In *Crime and Justice: A Review of Research*, edited by M. Tonry, vol. 29, 113–202. Chicago: University of Chicago Press.

Lauritsen, Janet L., and Karen Heimer. 2008. "The Gender Gap in Violent Victimization, 1983–2004." *Journal of Quantitative Criminology* 24: 125–47.

Lauritsen, Janet L., Karen Heimer, and James P. Lynch. 2009. "Trends in the Gender Gap in Violent Offending: New Evidence from the National Crime Victimization Survey." *Criminology* 47(2): 361–400.

Leckenby, Denise. 2007. "Feminist Empiricism: Challenging Gender Bias and 'Setting the Record Straight.'" In *Feminist Research Practice*, edited by S. N. Hesse-Beber and P. L. Leavy, 27–52. Thousand Oaks, CA: Sage.

Leonard, Eileen. 1983. *Women, Crime, and Society*. New York: Longman.

Levinson, R. B., & Taylor, W. J. 1991. "ACA Studies Privatization in Juvenile Corrections." *Corrections Today*, 53, 242–48.

Lieber, Michael. 1994. "A Comparison of Juvenile Court Outcomes for Native Americans, African Americans, and Whites." *Justice Quarterly* 11: 257–79.

Lipsey, Mark. 1995. "What Do We Learn From 400 Research Studies on the Effectiveness of Treatment with Juvenile Delinquents?" In *What Works? Reducing Reoffending*, edited by J. McGuire, 63–78. New York: Wiley.

Loeber, Rolf, and David P. Farrington, eds. 1998. *Serious and Violent Juvenile Offenders: Risk Factors and Successful Interventions*. Thousand Oaks, CA: Sage.

MacDonald, John M., and Meda Chesney-Lind. 2001. "Gender Bias and Juvenile Justice Revisited: A Multiyear Analysis." *Crime and Delinquency* 47: 173–95.

McClellan, Dorthy S. 1994. "Disparity in the Discipline of Male and Female Inmates in Texas Prisons." *Women and Criminal Justice* 5: 71–97.

McCluskey, John D., Cynthia McCluskey, and Beth Huebner. 2003. "Juvenile Female Arrests: A Holistic Explanation of Organizational Functioning." *Women and Criminal Justice* 14: 35–52.

McCord, Joan, Cathy S. Widom, and Nancy A. Crowell. 2001. *Juvenile Crime, Juvenile Justice*. Washington, DC: National Academy Press.

McCorkel, Jill. 2003. "Embodied Surveillance and the Gendering of Punishment." *Journal of Contemporary Ethnography* 32: 41–76.

McCormack, Arlene, Mark-David Janus, and Ann. W. Burgess. 1986. "Runaway Youths and Sexual Victimization: Gender Differences in Adolescent Runaway Populations." *Child Abuse and Neglect* 10: 387–95.

Miller, Jody. 1994. "An Examination of Disposition Decision-Making for Delinquent Girls." In *The Intersection of Race, Gender and Class Decision-Making in Criminology*, edited by M. D. Schwartz and D. Milovanic, 219–56. New York: Garland.

Miller, Jody, and Christopher W. Mullins. 2009. "Feminist Theories of Girls' Delinquency." In *The Delinquent Girl*, edited by Margaret Zahn, 30–49. Philadelphia: Temple University Press.

Miller, Walter C. 1958. "Lower Class Culture as a Generating Milieu of Gang Delinquency." *Journal of Social Issues* 14: 5–19.

Moffit, Terrie E., Avshalom Rutter Michael, and Phil A. Silva. 2001. *Sex Differences in Antisocial Behavior: Conduct Disorder, Delinquency, and Violence in the Dunedin Longitudinal Study*. London: Cambridge University Press.

Moone, Joseph. 1993. *Children in Custody: Private Facilities*. Washington, DC: Office of Juvenile Justice and Delinquency Prevention.

Morris, A. 1987. *Women, Crime and Criminal Justice*. New York: Blackwell.

Muraskin, Roslyn. 1999. "Disparate Treatment in Correctional Facilities." In *It's a Crime: women and Justice*, edited by R. Muraskin and T. Alleman, 225–52. Englewood Cliffs, NJ: Prentice-Hall.

Naffine, N. 1996. *Female Crime: The Construction of Women in Criminology*. Sydney, Australia: Allen & Unwin.

Odem, Mary, and Steven Schlossman. 1991. "Guardians of Virtue: The Juvenile Court and Female Delinquency in Early 20th Century Los Angeles." *Crime and Delinquency* 37: 186–203.

Office of Juvenile Justice and Delinquency Prevention. 2008. Juvenile Court Statistics, 2005. Washington D.C., U.S. Government Printing Office. http://www.ojjdp.gov/publications/PubResults.asp#2008

Office of Juvenile Justice and Delinquency Prevention (OJJDP) 2011. "Program of Research on the Causes and Correlates of Delinquency." Accessed Feb. 18. http://www.ojjdp.ncjrs.gov/programs/ccd

Ogloff, James R., and Michael R. Davis. 2004. "Advances in Offender Assessment and Rehabilitation: Contributions of the Risk-Needs-Responsivity Approach." *Psychology, Crime and Law* 19: 229–42.

Owen, Barbara. 1998. *In the Mix: Struggle and Survival in a Women's Prison*. New York: State University of New York.

Platt, Anthony M. 1977. *The Child Savers: The Invention of Delinquency*. Chicago: University of Chicago Press.

Poe-Yamagata, Eileen, and Jeffrey A. Butts. 1996. *Female Offenders in the Juvenile Justice System*. Washington, DC: U.S. Department of Justice.

Pope, Carl, and William Feyerherm. 1982. "Gender Bias in Juvenile Court Dispositions." *Social Service Research* 6: 1–17.

Prendergast, Michael L., Jean Wellisch, and Gregory P. Falkin. 1995. "Assessment Of and Services For Substance-Abusing Women Offenders in Community and Correctional Settings." *Prison Journal* 75: 240–56.

Propper, A. 1978. "Lesbianism in Female and Coed Correctional Institutions." *Journal of Homosexuality* 3: 265–74.

Rafter, Nicole H. 1985. *Partial Justice: Women in State Prisons, 1800–1935*. Boston: Northeastern University Press.

Rasche, Christine E. 1999. "The Dislike of Female Offenders Among Correctional Officers: A Need For Specialized Training." In *It's a Crime: Women and Justice*, edited by R. Muraskin, 2nd ed., 237–52. Englewood Cliffs, NJ: Prentice-Hall.

Rhodes, Jean, and Karla Fisher. 1993. "Spanning the Gender Gap: Gender Differences in Delinquency Among Inner City Adolescents." *Adolescence* 28: 880–89.

Richie, Beth. 1996. *Compelled to Crime: The Gender Entrapment of Battered Black Women*. New York: Routledge.

Robinson, Robin A. 1990. "Violations of Girlhood: A Qualitative Study of Female Delinquents and Children in Need of Services in Massachusetts." PhD Dissertation, Brandeis University, Waltham, MA.

Rosenbaum, Jill, and Meda Chesney-Lind. 1994. "Appearance and Delinquency: A Research Note." *Crime and Delinquency* 40: 250–61.

Rosenfeld, Richard, and Robert Fornango. 2007. "The Impact of Economic Conditions on Robbery and Property Crime: The Role of Consumer Sentiment." *Criminology* 45: 745–69.

Ross, Robert R., and Elilzabeth A. Fabiano. 1986. *Female Offenders: Correctional Afterthoughts*. Jefferson, NC: McFarland.

Rothman, David J. 1978. "The State as Parent: Social Policy in the Progressive Era." In *Doing Good: The Limits of Benevolence*, Willard Gaylin, Ira Glasser, Steve Marcus, and David J. Rothman, eds. New York: Pantheon Books.

Rowe, David, Alexander Vazsony, and Daniel Flannery. 1995. "Sex Differences: Do Means and Within-Sex Variation Have Similar Causes?" *Journal of Research in Crime and Delinquency* 32: 84–100.

RTI International. 2011. "Girls Study Group: Understanding and Responding to Girls' Delinquency." Accessed Feb. 18. http://girlsstudygroup.rti.org

Sarri, Rosemary A. 1983. "Gender Issues in Juvenile Justice." *Crime & Delinquency* 29: 381–397.

Schaffner, Laurie. 2008. *Girls in Trouble with the Law*. New Brunswick, NJ: Rutgers University Press.

Schichor, David, and Clemons Bartollas. 1990. "Private and Public Juvenile Placements: Is There a Difference?" *Crime and Delinquency* 36: 286–99.

Schwartz, Ira M. 1989. *[In]justice for Juveniles: Rethinking the Best Interests of the Child*. Lexington, MA: Lexington Books.

Schwartz, Ira M. 1999. *Kids Raised by the Government*. Westport, CT: Praeger.

Schwartz, Ira M., Linda Harris, and Lauri Levi. 1988. "The Jailing of Juveniles in Minnesota: A Case Study." *Crime and Delinquency* 34: 133–49.

Schwartz, Ira M., Marilyn Jackson-Beeck, and Roger Anderson. 1984. "The 'Hidden' System of Juvenile Control." *Crime and Delinquency* 30: 371–85.

Schwartz, Ira M., M. W. Steketee, and Vicki W. Schneider. 1990. "Federal Juvenile Justice Policy and the Incarceration of Girls." *Crime and Delinquency* 36: 503–20.

Schwartz, Jennifer, Darrell J. Steffensmeier, and Ben Feldmeyer. 2009. "Assessing Trends in Women's Violence via Data Triangulation: Arrests, Convictions, Incarcerations, and Victim Reports." *Social Problems* 56: 494–525.

Schwartz, Jennifer, Darrell Steffensmeier, Hua Zhong, and Jeff Ackerman. 2009. "Trends in the Gender Gap in Violence: Reevaluating NCVS and Other Evidence." *Criminology* 47(2): 401–26.

Shaw, Clifford R., and Henry D. McKay. 1942. *Juvenile Delinquency and Urban Areas*. Chicago: University of Chicago Press.

Sickmund, Melissa, T. J. Sladky, and Wei Kang. 2004. *Census of Juveniles in Residential Placement Databook*. Washington, D.C.: U.S. Government Printing Office. http://www. ncjrs.gov/App/publications/abstract.aspx?ID=182521

Silbert, Mimi H. and Ayala M. Pines. 1981. "Sexual Child Abuse as an Antecedent to Prostitution." *Child Abuse and Neglect* 5: 407–411.

Simons, Ronald L., Martin G. Miller, and Stephen M. Aigner. 1980. "Contemporary Theories of Deviance and Female Delinquency: An Empirical Test." *Journal of Research in Crime and Delinquency* 17: 42–57.

Simourd, Linda, and D. A. Andrews. 1994. "Correlates of Delinquency: A Look at Gender Differences." *Forum on Corrections Research* 6: 26–31.

Smart, Carol. 1976. *Women, Crime and Criminology: A Feminist Critique*. London: Routledge & Kegan Paul.

Smith, Bruce. 1998. "Children in Custody: 20-year Trend in Juvenile Detention, Correctional, and Shelter Facilities." *Crime and Delinquency* 44: 526–43.

Smith, Douglas A., and Raymond Paternoster. 1987. "The Gender Gap in Theories of Deviance: Issues and Evidence." *Criminology* 57: 451–81.

Snell, Tracy L., and Danielle C. Morton. 1994. *Women in Prison (Special Report)*. Washington, DC: Bureau of Justice Statistics.

Snyder, Howard, and Melissa Sickmund. 1995. *Juvenile Offenders and Victims: A National Report*. Pittsburgh: National Center for Juvenile Justice.

Sorbello, Laura, Lynne Eccleston, Tony Ward, and Robin Jones. 2002. "Treatment Needs of Female Offenders: A Review." *Australian Psychologist* 37: 196–205.

Steen, Sara, Christine E. W. Bond, George S. Bridges, and Charis E. Kubrin. 2005. "Explaining Assessments of Future Risk: Race and Attributions of Juvenile Offenders in Presentencing Reports." In *Our Children, Their Children: Confronting Racial and Ethnic Differences in American Juvenile Justice*, edited by D. F. Hawkins and K. Kempf-Leonard, 245–69. Chicago: University of Chicago Press.

Steffensmeier, Darrell, and Emilie Allan. 1996. "Gender and Crime: Toward a Gendered Paradigm of Female Offending." *Annual Review of Sociology* 22: 459–87.

Steffensmeier, Darrell, and Jennifer Schwartz. 2009. "Trends in Girls' Delinquency and the Gender Gap: Statistical Assessment of Diverse Sources." In *The Delinquent Girl*, 50–83, edited by Margaret A. Zahn. Philadelphia: Temple University Press.

Steffensmeier, Darrell, Jennifer Schwartz, Hua Zhong, and Jeff Ackerman. 2005. "An Assessment of Recent Trends in Girls' Violence Using Diverse Longitudinal Sources: Is the Gender Gap Closing." *Criminology* 43: 355–405.

Steffensmeier, Darrell, Hua Zhong, Jeff Ackerman, Jennifer Schwartz, and S. Agha. 2006. "Gender Gap Trends for Violent Crimes, 1980–2003." *Feminist Criminology* 1: 72–98.

Stiffman, Arlene R., Felton Earls, Jave Powell, and Lee N. Robins. 1987. "Correlates of Alcohol and Illicit Drug Use in Adolescent Medical Patients." *Contemporary Drug Problems* 14: 295–314.

Tanenhaus, David. 2004. *Juvenile Justice in the Making*. New York: Oxford University Press.

Tanenhaus, David S. 2005. "Degrees of Discretion: The First Juvenile Court and the Problem of Difference in the Early Twentieth Century." In *Our Children, Their Children: Confronting Race and Ethnic Differences in American Juvenile Justice*, edited by D. F. Hawkins and K. Kempf-Leonard, 105–19. Chicago: University of Chicago Press.

Teilmann, Katherine, and Pierre Landry. 1981. "Gender Bias in Juvenile Justice." *Journal of Research in Crime and Delinquency* 18: 47–80.

Thomas, William I. 1923. *The Unadjusted Girl*. New York: Harper.

Thrasher, Frederick. 1927. *The Gang: A Study of 1,313 Gangs in Chicago*. Chicago: University of Chicago Press.

Tracy, Paul E. 2005. "Race, Ethnicity, and Juvenile Justice: Is There Bias in Postarrest Decision Making?" In *Our Children, Their Children: Confronting Race and Ethnic Differences in American Juvenile Justice*, edited by D. F. Hawkins and K. Kempf-Leonard, 300–49. Chicago: University of Chicago Press.

Tracy, Paul E., and Kimberly Kempf-Leonard. 1996. *Continuity and Discontinuity in Criminal Careers: The Transition from Delinquency to Crime*. New York: Plenum Press.

Tracy, Paul E., Kimberly Kempf-Leonard, Stephanie Abramoske-James. 2009. "Gender Differences in Delinquency and Juvenile Justice Processing: Evidence from National Data." *Crime and Delinquency* 55: 171–215.

Tracy, Paul E., Marvin E. Wolfgang, and Robert M. Figlio. 1990. *Delinquency Careers in Two Birth Cohorts*. New York: Plenum.

Van Voorhis, Patricia V., and Lois Presser. 2001. *Classification of Women Offenders: A National Assessment of Current Practices*. Washington, DC: U.S. Department of Justice, National Institute of Corrections.

Van Wormer, Katherine. 2001. *Counseling Female Offenders and Victims: A Strength-Restorative Approach*. New York: Springer.

Vedder, Clyde B., and Dara B. Sommerville. 1970. *The Delinquent Girl*. Springfield, IL: Charles C. Thomas.

Visher, Christy A. 1983. "Gender, Police Arrest Decisions, and Notions of Chivalry." *Criminology* 21: 5–28.

Ward, Tony, and Mark Brown. 2004. "The Good Lives Model and Conceptual Issues in Offender Rehabilitation." *Psychology, Crime and Law* 10: 243–57.

Weithorn, Lois A. 1988. "Mental Hospitalization of Troublesome Youth: An Analysis of Skyrocketing Admission Rates." *Stanford Law Review* 40: 773–838.

Whitbeck, Les B., Dan Hoyt, Kevin Yoder, Ana Cauce, and Matt Paradise. 2001. "Deviant Behavior and Victimization Among Homeless and Runaway Adolescents." *Journal of Interpersonal Violence* 16: 1175–204.

Widom, Cathy Spatz, and M. Ashley Ames. 1994. "Criminal Consequences of Childhood Sexual Victimization." *Child Abuse and Neglect* 18: 303–18.

Wolfgang, Marvin E., Robert Figlio, and Thorsten Sellin. 1972. *Delinquency in a Birth Cohort*. Chicago: University of Chicago Press.

Zahn, Margaret A., ed. 2009. *The Delinquent Girl*. Philadelphia: Temple University Press.

Zahn, Margaret A., Stephanie R. Hawkins, Janet Chiancone, and Ariel Whitworth. 2008. *The Girls Study Group—Charting the Way to Delinquency Prevention for Girls*. Washington DC: U.S. Printing Office.

CHAPTER 22

COMPETENCE AND CRIMINAL RESPONSIBILITY IN ADOLESCENT DEFENDANTS

THE ROLES OF MENTAL ILLNESS AND ADOLESCENT DEVELOPMENT

JODI VILJOEN,

ERIKA PENNER, AND

RONALD ROESCH

SINCE at least the 1700s, the law has required that adult defendants cannot be tried unless they have an ability to adequately understand and participate in legal proceedings against them (Bonnie and Grisso 2000). If a defendant lacks these capacities due to mental illness, then he or she can be deemed *incompetent to stand trial*. This requirement arose as a way of protecting defendants with mental health conditions. Another legal protection for mentally ill defendants is what is commonly referred to as the *insanity defense* or *criminal responsibility* laws (Borum 2003). Under these laws, defendants may be judged to be *not guilty by reason of insanity* (NGRI) if, as a result of mental illness, they were unable to understand and/or control their criminal behavior.

While competence and criminal responsibility laws have a long history within adult criminal court, historically these legal protections were not applied to adolescents tried in juvenile court (Grisso 2005a). Prior to the establishment of the juvenile court system, children younger than 7 were presumed incapable of forming intent and thus could not be charged. There was also a presumption that children aged 7 to 14 could not form the requisite intent, but prosecutors could rebut that presumption by proving that the child appreciated the difference between right and wrong. Those over 14 were automatically presumed to have the capacity to form criminal intent (LaFave and Scott 1986).

When it was established early in the twentieth century, the goal of the juvenile justice system was primarily to rehabilitate youth (Mack 1909), which was a substantial shift from the punishment philosophy that was dominant in the adult criminal justice system at the time. The Illinois Juvenile Justice Court Act (see Fox 1996) initially created a separate division within the adult court to deal with juveniles, and this was expanded just a few years later to become an independent juvenile court. In addition to a shift of focus from punishment to rehabilitation, the Act provided for confidentiality of records, physical separation of youth from adults if incarcerated in the same facility, and a ban on jail detention for those under 12. The juvenile court also incorporated the infancy defense barring the prosecution of children under 7. The reform that began in Illinois quickly caught on in other jurisdictions. By 1910, thirty-two states adopted similar provisions, and by 1925, all but two states had a separate juvenile court.

Given the juvenile justice system's focus, legal protections were deemed irrelevant or unnecessary. Over the past several decades, however, the juvenile justice system has changed considerably, evolving to become much more adult-like in nature (Redding, Goldstein, and Heilbrun 2005). During the 1980s and 1990s, for instance, concerns about youth violence, which were largely reactive in nature and sparked by public fear and misinformation, led to legislative changes excluding some offenses from juvenile court and providing waiver provisions allowing the prosecution of juveniles in adult court (Feld 2000; Benekos and Merlo 2008). In addition, laws in the United States, Canada, and other countries were changed to enable juvenile courts to administer longer and more severe sanctions.

These dramatic changes to the juvenile justice system have since slowed. In fact, there have been some declines in the number of youth transferred to adult court and incarcerated in prisons (Benekos and Merlo 2008). Nevertheless, it is clear that the juvenile justice system today is dramatically different than the juvenile justice system as it was first developed and envisioned in the early 1900s. Given that youths can now receive similar sanctions as adults, it important that they be provided with

similar protections as adults, including the right not to be tried unless competent
and the right to raise an NGRI plea (Mulford et al. 2004; Scott and Grisso 2005).
It has been challenging however for courts to extend competence and criminal
responsibility laws to adolescents in a manner that is attentive to adolescents' developmental status. For instance, while mental illness is a primary factor that may lead
to incompetence to stand trial in adults, in adolescents, incompetence may
sometimes simply stem from young age and the fact that youths are still developing
and maturing (Grisso 2005a). In addition, as we review later in this chapter, recent
research has highlighted the high prevalence of mental illness among juveniles, and
this may serve to compound the deficits associated with youths' developmental
immaturity.

The purpose of this chapter is to examine the application of competence and
criminal responsibility laws to adolescents, with a focus on some of the challenges
that have arisen. We discuss relevant legal standards and the role of mental illness
and developmental immaturity. In addition, we highlight implications for courts,
attorneys, and mental health clinicians.

I. Competence to Stand Trial

A. Legal Standards and Proceedings

Concerns about a defendant's competence (i.e., his or her ability to understand
and participate in legal proceedings) typically arise at the time of the trial. As such,
our focus in this chapter is on competence to stand trial. However, concerns about
competence can arise in other legal contexts and at any stage of the proceedings,
such as waiver of the right to an attorney or the right to an appeal. The term *adjudicative competence* is sometimes used to capture the broad contexts in which the
issue of competence is raised (Bonnie 1992). Comprehension of *Miranda* rights is
another facet or type of competence, which is discussed by Barry Feld's chapter in
this book, Chapter 27, "Procedural Rights in Juvenile Courts: Competence and
Consequences."

In the United States, the legal standard for competence to stand trial was established in *Dusky v. United States* (362 U.S. 402 [1960]). This case held that defendants
must have adequate *factual understanding* (e.g., understanding of the roles of the
defense attorney and judge), *rational understanding* (e.g., appreciation of the possible consequences of a finding of guilt), and an ability to communicate with their
attorney (see also *Drope v. Missouri*, 420 U.S. 162 [1975]). In addition, more recent
cases have been interpreted to mean that defendants must also be able to adequately
reason about decisions that arise during legal proceedings, such as decisions about
how to plead (*Godinez v. Moran*, 509 U.S. 389 [1993]). Canadian legal standards are
similar but set a lower threshold or level of competence (Zapf and Roesch 2001).

If there is evidence that a defendant lacks one of more of these competence-related legal capacities (i.e., understanding, appreciation, communication, and reasoning), the court typically requests a competence evaluation from a mental health professional (Melton et al. 2007). Then, based on this evaluation, the court makes a formal determination as to whether the defendant is competent. If deemed incompetent, the defendant's trial is suspended until competence is restored. During this period of restoration, the defendant may receive various types of treatment, such as psychotropic medication (e.g., medication to treat psychotic disorders), and/or psychoeducational programs, in which defendants are taught didactic information about legal proceedings.

The requirement that defendants must be competent to be tried was typically restricted to adult defendants. However, competence requirements were first applied to adolescents starting in approximately the 1970s and 1980s, following a series of legal cases that extended due process rights to adolescents (*Kent v. United States*, 383 U.S. 541 [1966]; *In re Gault*, 387 U.S. 1 [1967]). During the 1990s, the juvenile court shifted to become more punitive in focus, and it became even more important for juvenile defendants to be competent to stand trial (Grisso 1997). Although it is difficult to obtain exact figures regarding how frequently the issue of juvenile competence is now raised, there is some evidence that requests for juvenile competence evaluations increased substantially during the 1990s and 2000s (Kruh and Grisso 2009). Furthermore, the number of scholarly articles on juvenile competence grew dramatically during this period, reflecting the surge of interest and concern regarding this issue (Viljoen 2011).

B. Factors That May Contribute to Incompetence

While concerns about competence in adults are typically raised in cases in which the defendants have a serious mental illness or mental retardation, youth may be incompetent as a result of mental illness, mental retardation, and/or simply normal age-appropriate developmental immaturity. These potential sources of incompetence are discussed in the following section.

1. Mental Disorders and Intellectual Disabilities

Based on recent research, rates of mental disorders are remarkably high among adolescent offenders (Fazel, Doll, and Långström 2008). Teplin and colleagues (2002), for instance, found that approximately 60% of detained male adolescents and 70% of detained female adolescents met criteria for a current mental disorder; this was true even after Conduct Disorder, a disorder characterized by antisocial behavior, was excluded. Substance use disorders were particularly prevalent, as were depression and Attention-Deficit/Hyperactivity Disorder (ADHD).

Some of the mental disorders that are commonly found in adolescent offenders could conceivably lead to impairments in competence-related legal capacities (Grisso 2005a). For instance, a youth with ADHD may have difficulty communicating effectively with his or her attorney and testifying coherently, and a youth with depression may lack motivation to adequately defend himself or herself (Viljoen and Roesch 2005). Indeed, research has found that adolescents who are found incompetent have a wide range of mental disorders, including ADHD, depression or other mood disorders, and anxiety disorders (Kruh et al. 2006).

The types of disorders found in adolescents deemed incompetent differ from those found in adults deemed incompetent. For instance, psychotic disorders, such as schizophrenia, are a particularly common source of incompetence in adults. However, such disorders are very rare among adolescents, as these disorders typically do not develop until late adolescence or early adulthood (APA 2000). Consistent with this, rates of psychotic disorders are much lower among juveniles found incompetent than adults found incompetent (i.e., 3 to 15% of incompetent juveniles versus approximately 34 to 63% of incompetent adults have psychotic disorders: McKee and Shea 1999; Cooper and Zapf 2003; Kruh et al. 2006; Warren et al. 2006). Nevertheless, adolescents with psychotic disorders are more likely to be found incompetent than adolescents with other types of mental disorders, indicating that while rare, psychotic disorders are an important predictor of findings of incompetence.

In addition to mental disorders such as ADHD, depression, and psychotic disorders, the presence of intellectual disabilities may jeopardize a youth's ability to competently stand trial. In some jurisdictions, a sizable proportion of youths who are found incompetent to stand trial are diagnosed with mental retardation (Kruh et al. 2006). For instance, a Florida study reported that 58% of youths who were found incompetent were mentally retarded (McGaha et al. 2001). This prevalence rate of intellectual disabilities is higher than what is typically seen among adults who are judged incompetent, and adolescents who are deemed incompetent due to mental retardation appear particularly difficult to remediate or restore to competence (McGaha et al. 2001).

Even when an adolescent does not meet criteria for mental retardation, deficits in cognitive abilities (e.g., borderline IQ, verbal ability, attention, memory) may contribute to competence-related legal impairments (Viljoen and Roesch 2005). Not surprisingly, for instance, a number of studies demonstrate that adolescents with low IQ scores have greater difficulty understanding and appreciating legal proceedings and communicating with their attorneys (Grisso et al. 2003; Viljoen and Roesch 2005). Further, poor verbal abilities appear to be a particularly strong predictor of competence-related difficulties (Viljoen and Roesch 2005).

2. Developmental Immaturity

Adolescents differ from adults in a number of important ways. Compared to adults, adolescents are less able to act in an autonomous manner, appreciate the long-term consequences of their decisions, and resist influence by peers or authority figures (Scott, Reppucci, and Woolard 1995; Steinberg and Cauffman 1996). In addition, while it was previously believed that adolescents' cognitive functioning by mid-adolescence was comparable to that of adults, more recent research demonstrates that brain development continues to occur for much longer than previously thought, up until at least an individual's early 20s (Giedd et al. 1999; Coalition for Juvenile Justice 2006).

As a result of their incomplete development and relative immaturity compared to adults, adolescents may be more likely to have difficulties understanding and participating in their legal proceedings *even if they do not have a mental disorder or cognitive impairments* (Scott et al. 1995; Steinberg and Cauffman 1996). For instance, adolescents may have difficulty reasoning about critical legal decisions, such as how to plea, due to their more limited focus on long-term consequences. Also, they may have more difficulty understanding legal processes and concepts (e.g., guilty pleas) as a result of their incomplete cognitive development and limited abstract thinking abilities. In other words, normally developing adolescents may have significant competence-related deficits simply due to their developmental stage. Clinicians are increasingly viewing maturity as a factor that should be considered in competency evaluations, suggesting that it is viewed as a cause of incompetence in much the same way that mental disorder can be a cause of incompetence in adults (Kruh and Grisso 2009).

The relevance of maturity is particularly salient for younger adolescents. Research has shown that many adolescents aged 15 and under have substantial limitations in their ability to understand and adequately participate in legal proceedings (Peterson-Badali and Abramovitch 1992; Grisso et al. 2003; Burnett, Noblin, and Prosser 2004). A leading study in this area, the MacArthur Juvenile Adjudicative Competence study, reported that approximately one-third of adolescents aged 11 to 13 and one-fifth of adolescents aged 14 to 15 had significant impairments in their competence-related abilities (Grisso et al. 2003). Further, younger adolescents with below-average IQ performed even more poorly on measures of trial competency than older juveniles with comparably low IQs. The study also found that adolescents were more likely than adults to be make choices (e.g., plea agreements) that reflected compliance with authority, and that young adolescents were less likely to consider the risks and long-term consequences of their legal decisions.

In addition, research has found that young adolescents who are referred to mental health clinicians for competence evaluations are significantly more likely to be found incompetent by the courts than older adolescents (McKee and Shea 1999; Kruh et al. 2006). This is not to say that all young adolescents are incompetent to stand trial, but rather that they are more likely than adults or older youths to have significant limitations in the legal capacities that are required to be competent defendants.

C. Implications for Courts, Attorneys, and Clinicians

The application of competence standards to adolescents carries important implications for judges and courts, defense attorneys, and mental health clinicians. The central problem is that juvenile courts have yet to reconcile the fact that adult competency laws are not easily applied to youths. The relevance of developmental immaturity as a basis for a finding of incompetence suggests that courts may need to develop laws and policies that are appropriate in light of adolescents' developmental status, and that clinicians may need to tailor assessment and remediation approaches so that they are relevant to adolescents. These implications are discussed below.

1. Clarification of Legal Standards

Legal professionals (including judges and attorneys) report that they consider it important that juveniles adjudicated in juvenile and adult criminal court are able to understand, appreciate, and participate in legal proceedings against them (Viljoen and Wingrove 2007). Furthermore, with the exception of Oklahoma (*G.J.I. v. State*, 778 P.2d 485 [Okla. Crim. App. 1989]), all state courts that have considered this issue have held that juveniles who are adjudicated in court must be competent. However, beyond basic agreement that competence is applicable to juveniles, there is considerable variability, inconsistency, and ambiguity in legal standards that pertain to adolescents' adjudicative competence (Scott and Grisso 2005).

One key issue that courts face is whether to allow youths to be found incompetent to stand trial if they do not have a mental disorder or mental retardation, but rather competence-related deficits that stem from normal developmental immaturity (Scott and Grisso 2005). As described, historically, legal standards for competence focused on mental illness and mental retardation as possible sources of incompetence. Many statutes explicitly state that a defendant must be mentally ill or mentally retarded in order to be found incompetent (e.g., WASH. REV. CODE § 10.77.010). However, given that many youths have impairments in their legal capacities that stem from developmental immaturity, it is critical that courts carefully consider developmental factors so as to preserve the underlying purpose of competence laws, which is to ensure that legal proceedings are reliable and fair (Bonnie 1992).

Thus far, at least two court cases have held that developmental immaturity provides an adequate basis for a finding of incompetence (Louisiana: *In re Causey*, 363 So. 2d 472 [La. 1978]; Washington: *State v. E.C.*, 922 P.2d. 145 [Wash. 1996]; see also Scott and Steinberg 2008 for a discussion of *State v. Tate*, 864 So. 2d 44 [Fla. Dist. Ct. App. 2003], a case in which developmental immaturity was noted as a potential basis for incompetence). Furthermore, in many cases, judges appear to recognize developmental immaturity as a basis for incompetence findings even without an explicit mandate to do so (Grisso 2005a).

A second issue that courts currently face is whether to adopt the same competence standard for juveniles adjudicated in juvenile court as is used in adult criminal court. Applying an adult standard (i.e., understanding, appreciation, communication, and reasoning) might potentially result in a high number of youths who are found incompetent to stand trial (Viljoen, Zapf, and Roesch 2007). As such, some juvenile courts have adopted more relaxed (lower) standards (e.g., *In re Carey*, 615 N.W.2d 742 [Mich. Ct. App. 2000]), such as requiring that a juvenile have only a basic understanding of legal proceedings and an ability to communicate with attorneys. However, applying a lower standard in juvenile court is only justifiable if the consequences of adjudication are less severe in juvenile court than in adult court. In some jurisdictions, it is not clear whether juvenile court sanctions are, in fact, sufficiently less severe as to justify a lower threshold of competence, because many juvenile courts have adopted more punitive sanctions (Scott and Grisso 2005). Therefore, courts must give this issue careful consideration prior to adopting more relaxed standards for juvenile court. Furthermore, even if a lower standard is adopted in juvenile court, the adult standard of competence must presumably still be applied to adolescents tried in adult criminal court.

2. Attorney Representation of Juveniles Who May be Incompetent

Not surprisingly, attorneys report that defending potentially incompetent juveniles is challenging and time-consuming (Viljoen, McLachlan, and Wingrove 2008). Attorneys play an important role in first detecting whether a youth may be incompetent. If an attorney has a "bona fide" doubt regarding his client's competence, he is obligated to inform the courts so that a competence evaluation can be requested; this is called raising the issue of competence (see Melton et al. 2007). To help provide some guidance to attorneys regarding competence evaluations, Grisso (2005b) recently published a manual for attorneys (see also Rosado 2000).

Although attorneys appear to have some knowledge of the factors that may contribute to incompetence in youths (Viljoen et al. 2008), it is likely that they may sometimes inadvertently miss instances of incompetence. Due to high caseloads, for instance, attorneys for juveniles often have very limited time to spend with individual defendants, making it difficult to detect whether a particular youth is having difficulties. Furthermore, attorneys report that they sometimes do not formally raise the issue of competence, even when they suspect their client may be incompetent (Viljoen et al. 2008). They cite various reasons for this, some of which reflect legitimate concerns about competence proceedings. For instance, some attorneys express concerns about whether raising the issue might delay the trial and therefore not be in their clients' best interests.

Instead of formally raising the issue of competence, attorneys sometimes first attempt to enhance youths' legal capacities, such as by attempting to teach them about legal proceedings (Viljoen et al. 2008). While such efforts may improve an adolescent's legal understanding to some degree (Viljoen and Grisso 2007), it is unlikely that youths with serious legal impairments can be made competent through such means; instead, more intensive interventions and services are likely needed. Another strategy that attorneys sometimes take is to further involve the youths' parents or guardians so that parents can provide assistance to their child (Viljoen et al. 2008). However, research indicates that some parents have inadequate legal capacities themselves (Woolard et al. 2008), and that they sometimes advise their child to waive his or her rights (Grisso and Ring 1979). Therefore, again, this strategy cannot necessarily be relied upon to compensate for true instances of incompetence and does not appear to be a sound alternative to raising the issue of competence, when appropriate.

3. Competence Evaluations by Mental Health Clinicians

In addition to posing challenges for attorneys and the courts, the application of the competence requirements to juveniles raises unique challenges for mental health clinicians. As the number of requests for juvenile competence evaluations has grown, mental health clinicians are now increasingly faced with the task of evaluating a youth's competence. Until recently, clinicians have had little guidance as to how to best approach this task. Nevertheless, there is evidence that judges heavily rely on these evaluations in making determinations as to whether a juvenile is competent (Kruh and Grisso 2009), and as such, it is critical that clinicians use sound and appropriate methods.

In conducting competence evaluations, some clinicians rely on what is referred to as "unstructured clinical judgment"; that is, the clinician himself designs the assessment method rather than relying on any structured or standardized approach. Often, the main component of this approach is a clinical interview rather than forensic or psychological testing. However, research has indicated that this approach may result in inconsistencies between evaluators, and that clinicians may neglect to assess key domains (Grisso 2003). For instance, while competence evaluations appear to adequately describe a youth's general psychological functioning, clinicians often provide only limited information about the legal capacities that are relevant to competence (Christy et al. 2004).

Given the potential limitations of unstructured methods, a number of "competence assessment tools" have been developed (Kruh and Grisso 2009). These are tests designed specifically to evaluate competence-related legal capacities. A key advantage of using a competence assessment tool is that it may provide a way of structuring the evaluation and ensuring a comprehensive and systematic assessment of legal capacities. However, while such tools are recommended and seen as valuable (Kruh and Grisso 2009), most tools have been designed for *adults* rather than youths, and it is unclear whether adult tools are appropriate for adolescents (Viljoen and Roesch 2008).

One limitation of using adult competence assessment tools with youths is that adult tools do not explicitly consider developmental factors that are relevant to youths' competence, such as youths' incomplete cognitive development and more limited autonomy (Grisso 2005a; Viljoen and Roesch 2008). As we have discussed, maturity is often a factor in competency evaluations of youths. For instance, Grisso and Quinlan (2005) found that about 20% of a sample of evaluators cited inadequate development as the most common basis for an opinion that a youth was not competent. The role of maturity poses a difficult assessment problem, as the construct of maturity has been difficult to define and measure. Kruh and Grisso (2009) make a distinction between cognitive and emotional maturity, and urge clinicians to make clear the link between the type of immaturity and specific legal abilities. Some researchers have proposed a broader perspective encompassing aspects of psychosocial development (Scott et al. 1995; Steinberg and Cauffman 1996). While some measures of maturity have been incorporated into some adolescent assessment instruments (e.g., Salekin 2004), assessment of maturity is an area in which instrument development is essential. One promising instrument is the Juvenile Adjudicative Competence Interview (JACI; Grisso 2005a). This tool guides evaluators to attend to developmental considerations (e.g., autonomy, perceptions of risk, time perspective, abstract/concrete thinking) and focuses on legal capacities that are relevant to juvenile court proceedings.

4. *Competence Remediation Programs*

When an adolescent is formally deemed incompetent to stand trial by the courts, the trial is typically suspended and efforts are made to enhance the adolescent's legal capacities so that the trial can continue. In cases where it is not possible to restore a defendant to competence, the charges against the defendant may be dropped and/or the defendant may be civilly committed to a psychiatric facility. Given that dismissing charges is an outcome that is unlikely to be satisfactory to courts or the general public, courts are invested in ensuring that adolescents are effectively remediated so that their trials may continue.

At this point, there is a lack of knowledge regarding how to make an incompetent adolescent competent (Viljoen and Grisso 2007). Many times, adult defendants who are found incompetent are treated with psychotropic medications as many of these defendants have psychotic disorders. However, as discussed earlier, the factors that contribute to incompetence in adolescents and adults may be quite different, and, as such, different types of treatments may be required. In addition, while some psychoeducational programs have been developed for adult defendants, in which adults are taught information about legal proceedings, such programs are likely to require adaptation for adolescent populations.

Moreover, while incompetence in adults is thought to be a transient and treatable state that often stems from mental disorders, it is not clear how easy it is to accelerate the acquisition of adult-like legal capacities in youth. There is reason to believe that it may be challenging to remediate adolescents who are found incompetent, particularly when legal deficits stem from developmental immaturity (Viljoen and Grisso 2007). Cooper (1997), for instance, found that adolescents who participated in a brief videotape intervention showed some improvement in their legal capacities after viewing the training videotape. Even so, most did not attain the level of competence required (see also Viljoen et al. 2008). Despite these challenges, research indicates that most adolescents in some jurisdictions are deemed competent after treatment (McGaha et al. 2001), suggesting that treatment may be effective in some cases. However, there may sometimes be pressure to deem a youth competent so that the trial may proceed, even when his or her competence remains questionable.

While research in this area is slow to progress, clinicians have made some notable efforts to develop sound and developmentally appropriate remediation services.

For instance, Virginia offers a comprehensive community-based juvenile compe-tency restoration program that integrates a number of interesting and innovative teaching methods, such as a board game, workbook, a video called "Going to the Court," a coloring book for use with younger children, flash cards with vocabulary items, and an interactive CD Rom (Warren et al. 2009). The initial research on this program has yielded promising results. Subsequent research is needed to evaluate the success of various types of remediation efforts.

II. Criminal Responsibility

While competency standards largely refer to a defendant's mental capacities at the time of adjudication, questions of criminal responsibility relate to the defendant's mental capacities at the moment of the offense (Bonnie and Grisso 2000). To be found guilty of a crime, an individual must have both acted in an unlawful manner (*actus reus*) and have done so with a "guilty mind" (*mens rea*); that is, defendants can only be held responsible for their actions if they had unlawful intent (Borum 2003). If an individual's ability to form an intention is impaired and that impair-ment is beyond their control, the extent to which they can be held responsible for their actions is reduced. A defendant acting under these circumstances may enter a plea of *not guilty by reason of insanity* (NGRI).

A. Legal Standards and Proceedings

The definition of the legal construct of NGRI varies across states. At present, the two predominant insanity defense standards used in the United States are the McNaughtan rule and the American Law Institute's Model Penal Code standard (ALI 1962), with about half of states adhering to one or the other (Giorgi-Guarnieri et al. 2002). The McNaughtan rule is the longest-standing principle, dating back to the nineteenth century, and states that the accused need not have known the nature and consequences of the act, or that it was wrong, to be prosecuted (*McNaughan's Case*, 10 Cl. and F. 200, 8 Eng. Rep. 718 [H.L. 1843]). The ALI's Model Penal Code (1962) is broader in that it also allows for volitional impairments; under this stan-dard, individuals can be found NGRI if they do not understand the wrongfulness of their actions or if they are unable "to conform [their] conduct to the requirements of the law" (Section 4.01). Legal standards in other countries, particularly common-wealth countries like Canada, Australia, and Great Britain, similarly emphasize the understanding of wrongfulness and, in some cases, volitional control.

In the adult criminal system, insanity is rarely raised as a defense (Zapf, Golding, and Roesch 2005; Packer 2009). Even when it is raised, it is unlikely to be successful. This stands in contrast to public perceptions; studies indicate that the general population vastly overestimates the number of defendants who are found NGRI

(Silver, Cirincione, and Steadman 1994). Further, when a defendant is found not criminally responsible for his actions, he is likely to be civilly committed to treatment in a psychiatric hospital (Borum 2003), rather than "let free," as many people believe (Silver et al. 1994).

Some states provide the insanity defense to juveniles, others have chosen not to, and the vast majority have remained silent on the issue (Taylor 2001). States that allow juveniles to enter a plea of NGRI have provided this right either through case law (e.g., *Winburn v. Wisconsin*, 145 N.W.2d 178 [Wis. 1966]) or through legislation (e.g., Arizona: ARIZ. REV. STAT. ANN. §§ 8–291–8.291.03, 2001; Colorado: Colo. Rev. Stat. § 19–2–702 [2001], COLO. REV. STAT. § 16–8–203 [2001]; Massachusetts: Mass. Gen. Laws Ann., ch. 123, §§ 15 (a)–(f) [2002]). In Canada, the right of young offenders to plead *not criminally responsible on account of mental disorders* is written into the legislation (Youth Criminal Justice Act, S.C. 2002, c. 1 [2002]).

When courts have determined that juveniles must be provided with the right to an insanity defense, they have largely reasoned that this defense is a due process right that must be provided to juveniles in accordance with *In re Gault*. For example, in *Winburn v. Wisconsin*, the court stated that "juvenile procedures, to some degree at least, smack of 'crime and punishment'" and that all individuals have "a fundamental right...not to answer criminally for misdeeds committed under the influence of an insane mind" (p. 161) (see *also In re M.G.S.*, 172 Cal. Rptr. 810 [Cal. Ct. App. 1968]; *In re Stapelkempr*, 562 P.2d 815 [Mont. 1977]; *In re Causey*, 363 So. 2d 472 [La. 1978]).

In contrast, several American states have explicitly stated that the insanity defense is not needed within the juvenile justice system. The District of Columbia, Ohio, and Virginia have determined that juveniles do not have the right to enter a plea of insanity (Ohio: *In re Chambers*, 688 N.E.2d 25, 25 [Ohio Ct. App. 1996]); Virginia: *Commonwealth v. Chatman*, 538 S.E.2d 304 [Va. 2000]) and VA. CODE ANN. § 16.1–280 [2001]; District of Columbia: D.C. CODE § 16–2315(d) [2001]). The primary argument for denying juveniles the insanity defense is that this right is contradictory to the rehabilitative focus of the juvenile justice system and that juveniles whose mental condition renders them unable to control or understand the nature of their actions would receive treatment rather than punishment if found guilty (Mulford et al. 2004). In accordance with this line of reasoning, juveniles transferred to adult court would be allowed to enter a plea of NGRI if it was available within the criminal system of that state, as those juveniles would no longer be afforded the protections purportedly inherent in the juvenile system.

B. Factors That May Contribute to Reduced Culpability

1. *Mental Disorders and Intellectual Disabilities*

Given both that very few states allow juveniles to enter a plea of NGRI and that this defense is very rarely used even when it is available, the pool of youths who have asserted the NGRI defense in the United States is likely extremely small (Newman et al. 2007). Researchers have yet to examine the primary grounds upon which youths assert an NGRI defense, the mental and physical health status of these youth, or the proportion of youths who are successfully acquitted on the basis of their NGRI plea. However, the small volume of research on NGRI pleas in the adult criminal system may shed some light on the possible circumstances under which a youth may be acquitted on the basis of insanity.

In general, the majority of adults who are successful in their NGRI defenses have psychotic symptoms. In Canada and the United States, most studies show that just over half of those acquitted on the basis of an NGRI plea have a diagnosis of schizophrenia or a related psychotic disorder (Roesch et al. 1997; Melton et al. 2007). Other major mental illnesses that are commonly associated with successful NGRI pleas include major affective disorders, primarily anxiety and depressive disorders (Warren et al. 1991; Cirincione, Steadman, and McGreevy 1995; Roesch et al. 1997). Personality disorders, such as borderline personality disorder or obsessive compulsive personality disorder, also occasionally lead to an acquittal on the basis of an NGRI plea, as does a finding of mental retardation (Warren et al. 1991).

In contrast, substance use is not typically seen as an adequate basis for an NGRI finding as it is considered to be voluntary (Marlowe, Lambert, and Thompson 1999). Indeed, being under the influence of a substance during the commission of a crime or being charged with a drug crime is inversely related to the success of an NGRI plea (Warren et al. 2004), although there are some circumstances under which a substance use diagnosis may underlie a successful insanity plea. In reality, those acquitted based on a defense of insanity often have multiple diagnoses and have frequently been previously hospitalized for mental health issues (Cirincione et al. 1995).

The types of disorders that are associated with NGRI pleas among adults might also be the basis for findings of NGRI among juveniles. However, developmental differences between juveniles and adults may produce variability in the types of mental impairments that are likely to present or be diagnosed. For instance, given that schizophrenia and other psychotic disorders typically have their onset in late adolescence or early adulthood (APA 2000), a smaller proportion of juveniles than adults may be found NGRI due to psychotic symptoms. Research on the characteristics of adolescents found NGRI would help to clarify which mental impairments may underlie an absolution of criminal responsibility in youth.

2. Developmental Immaturity and Culpability

In the area of competence, arguments have been made that youths may be incompetent due to developmental immaturity alone even if they do not meet criteria for a mental disorder or mental retardation. While it is unlikely that youths would ever be found NGRI on the basis of young age alone (Steinberg and Scott 2003), adolescents' lesser developmental maturity is relevant to considerations of their criminal responsibility. In fact, the recognition that youths may be less culpable than adults was one of the factors that led to the development of a separate justice system for juveniles

(Scott and Woolard 2004). It also impelled juvenile courts to establish minimum age restrictions for criminal responsibility whereby children who have not reached a state's chosen age of criminal responsibility—usually 7 years of age in American states, although substantially higher in commonwealth countries like Canada (Youth Criminal Justice Act 2002)—are absolved of blame for actions that might otherwise have been viewed as criminal (*In re Gladys R.*, 464 P.2d 127 [Cal. 1970]; *State v. Q.D.*, 685 P.2d 557 [Wash.1984]; *In re William A.*, 548 A.2d 130, 133 [Md.1988]).

As American juvenile justice systems become increasingly punitive and adult-like in nature (Reppucci 1999; Scott and Steinberg 2003), some scholars have made a call to further consider the impact of juveniles' developmental immaturity on their criminal responsibility (Scott and Steinberg 2003). Basic principles of proportionality dictate that criminal punishment should be meted out not only based on the nature of the perpetrator's criminal actions, but also by his blameworthiness (Scott and Steinberg 2003). Included among the factors that the courts have traditionally considered when determining the degree to which a person is held responsible or blameworthy for criminal actions are the individual's decision-making capacity, the circumstances under which the crime was committed, and the individual's character (*Roper v. Simmons*, 543 U.S. 551 [2005]; Steinberg and Scott 2003). A volume of research attests to the fact that juveniles may differ from adults in ways relevant to offending behavior in each of these domains (Scott et al. 1995; Modecki 2008, 2009).

First, adolescents' decision-making capacities, including their decisions to engage in antisocial behavior, may be impaired by their immature cognitive development (Scott et al. 1995; Scott 2000). Research confirms that children's and adolescents' ability to reason and think about the world around them is less well-developed than that of adults (Piaget 2008); indeed, the adolescent brain is still in a state of development (e.g., Giedd et al. 1999; Coalition for Juvenile Justice 2006). Second, adolescents' psychosocial immaturity may influence their tendency to engage in antisocial behavior. In particular, adolescents tend to be more vulnerable to peer influence or situational pressures (Scott et al. 1995; Steinberg and Cauffman 1996), to focus on short-term outcomes over long-term consequences (Halpern-Felsher and Cauffman 2001; Steinberg and Scott 2003), and to base their decisions on anticipated rewards while discounting potential risks (Furby and Beyth-Marom 1992; Halpern-Felsher and Cauffman 2001). Finally, adolescence is a time of identity development (Scott and Steinberg 2003). As such, criminal behavior in an adolescent is less likely to reflect a permanent, characterologically-based propensity than it is in adults.

C. Implications for Courts, Clinicians, and Researchers

1. Extension of NGRI to Adolescents

The vast majority of states that have considered the question of whether juveniles should have the right to plead NGRI have concluded in the affirmative (Frost and Shepherd 1996). Indeed, scholars have argued that denying juveniles the insanity defense may not be legally and ethically justifiable (Heilbrun, Hawk, and Tate 1996; Mulford et al. 2004).The insanity defense is considered a fundamental due process right for adults in most American states and over the last two decades, the majority of the fundamental due process rights provided to adults (e.g., the right to notice of criminal charges, the right to counsel, the right against self-incrimination, etc.) have been extended to juveniles (*Kent v. United States*, 383 U.S. 541 [1966]; *In re Gault*, 387 U.S. 1 [1967]; *In re Winship*, 397 U.S. 358 [1970]). The Supreme Court has repeatedly recognized that the potentially adversarial and adult-like nature of juvenile proceedings requires that juveniles have the same protections as adults; indeed, in *Kent*, the Court stated that "the child receives the worst of both worlds... gets neither the protections accorded to adults nor the solicitous care and regenerative treatment postulated for children" (p. 556). As such, a *failure* to extend the insanity defense to juveniles is inconsistent with the general trends in juvenile justice and may, in fact, be contraindicated by the Supreme Court's regular extension of adult due process rights to juveniles.

A variety of explanations have been offered by states that have declined to extend this protection to juveniles, among them that the juvenile justice system is rehabilitative rather than punitive and that juveniles are not consistently provided with the same rights as adults (see, e.g., *Golden v. State*, 21 S.W.3d 801 [Ark. 2000]). While the juvenile court was originally conceived as a venue in which young people were to be treated rather than punished (Mack 1909), the common consensus among scholars and law makers is that the distinctions between adult criminal systems and juvenile justice systems have become increasingly indistinct over the past century (e.g., Redding et al. 2005; Benekos and Merlo 2008).As such, the notion that juveniles do not require the protection of an insanity defense because of the rehabilitative nature of the juvenile justice system is questionable. Courts should carefully consider the relative punitiveness of the juvenile court and the degree to which the Supreme Court has chosen to extend adult rights to juveniles when making determinations about the applicability of NGRI pleas to juveniles.

2. *Clinical Assessments and Treatment of Youth Found NGRI*

When the question of NGRI is raised, most often by the defense, a clinical evaluation is undertaken to determine whether there is merit to the claim (Grisso 2004). Research on adult criminal responsibility assessments have found that this information is weighed heavily by the court (Petrella and Poythress 1983; Borum 2003). As such, it is vital that assessments of criminal responsibility be conducted as reliably and accurately as possible. However, NGRI assessments are extremely challenging to conduct for a number of reasons. They require clinicians to retrospectively evaluate a defendant's mental state at the time of the crime; there are substantial variations in legal standards regarding the definition of insanity and in the amount and type of information the expert is permitted to present to the court (Borum 2003); and there is always a possibility of malingering on the part of the defendant (Melton et al. 2007).

With adolescents, the assessment of criminal responsibility is likely to be even more challenging because there is an absence of guidelines or empirical studies to aid clinicians. Although some specialized tools, like the Rogers Criminal Responsibility Assessment Scales (R-CRAS) (Rogers 1984) and the Mental Health at the Time of the Offense Screening Evaluation (MSE) (Slobogin, Melton, and Showalter 1984) have been developed for adult criminal responsibility evaluations, it is unclear whether such tools would be appropriate for adolescents. For instance, baseline adolescent behavior would be expected to differ from adult behavior (e.g., level of socially responsible behavior in previous week), which would influence ratings, and the relationship between mental impairments and criminal responsibility in adolescents is currently unknown.

As a first step in conducting an NGRI evaluation of a juvenile defendant, clinicians must become familiar with relevant legal standards in their jurisdiction and then tailor their assessment so that it is legally relevant. If adult-like criteria for NGRI are adopted, the primary referral questions would be to determine (1) whether, at the time of the crime, the youth had a mental disorder consistent with legal definitions; (2) whether the defendant had the capacity to understand the nature of his or her actions and/or control his or her actions; and (3) whether deficits in understanding or behavioral control were rooted in the defendant's mental disease or impairment (Roesch, Viljoen, and Hui 2004). To assist clinicians, researchers should work to develop relevant assessment instruments that are appropriate for adolescents, as well as outlining best practice guidelines.

Similarly, further research on the treatment of adolescents found NGRI is needed. Until then, clinicians should focus on assessing and mitigating risk for recidivism in youths deemed NGRI and should ensure that rehabilitative measures continue beyond hospitalization into the community (Woodworth et al. 2004). A focus on community-based relapse prevention is likely extremely important, as research with NGRI adults suggests that rates of recidivism among this population are high and that poor monitoring and support in the community is related to the likelihood of reoffending (McNamara and Andrasik 1982; Vaughan and Stevenson 2002).

3. *Consideration of Developmental Issues and Reduced Culpability*

As described, new research indicates that adolescents may not possess the same decision-making capacities as adults. While youths are unlikely to be found NGRI on the basis of developmental immaturity, scholars have recently argued that adolescents are inherently less culpable than adults and that reduced penalties may be warranted (Scott and Steinberg 2003; Feld 2008). In line with principles of proportionality, courts should be careful to consider the impact of youths' developmental status on their blameworthiness and ensure that punishments take into account the degree to which youths should be held responsible for their actions.

Encouragingly, there is some evidence that some courts have begun to recognize the impact of adolescents' developmental immaturity on their decision-making and criminal culpability. For instance, North Carolina's Sentencing and Policy

Advisory Commission (2007) recommended increasing the upper age limit under which the juvenile court has jurisdiction to 18 years of age, stating that:

> A significant volume of scientific evidence on stages of human development points to immaturity and its effect on reduced criminal culpability in youth up to age 18 and beyond, well into their 20's. At least four areas of developmental immaturity may bear directly on the criminal culpability of youth: impaired risk perception, foreshortened time perspective, greater susceptibility to peer influence, and reduced capacity for behavioral controls. (p. 8)

In addition, recent Supreme Court rulings have prohibited courts from using the two most severe penalties when sentencing juveniles: the death penalty (*Roper v. Simmons*) and life without parole (for juveniles who have committed non-homicide offenses; *Graham v. Florida*, 560 U.S. ___ [2010]). In reaching their decision in *Roper*, the Supreme Court noted that "juveniles are more vulnerable or susceptible [than adults] to negative influences and outside pressures, including peer pressure" and acknowledged juveniles' "underdeveloped sense of responsibility" (at 569); unfortunately, as noted by Feld (2008), "the Court provided minimal social science support for its categorical conclusion" (p. 102). In *Graham*, the Supreme Court reaffirmed these findings and stated that "No recent data provide reason to reconsider the Court's observations in *Roper* about the nature of juveniles" (at 17). Prior to this latter ruling, 37 States and the District of Columbia allowed juveniles who had committed non-homicidal acts to be sentenced to life without parole (*Graham v. Florida*, at 11).

While it appears that some courts are recognizing that adolescents are inherently different from adults, and that responses to youth crime should reflect these differences, the distinction between adult and youth courts remains blurry. Juvenile sentences have become longer and harsher over time, and the notion that an adult crime deserves an adult penalty is common in the public mind (Pollock 2000). In most states, children as young as 7 can be held responsible for criminal actions even if their level of maturity and understanding are believed to render them less blameworthy. As such, it is vital that researchers continue to work to examine differences between adult and youth decision-making, vulnerability to environmental pressures, and general cognitive and biological developmental. At the same time, policy makers must endeavor to convey this research to the courts in the hopes that adolescents will be treated in a manner appropriate to their developmental level.

III. CONCLUSION

Competence and criminal responsibility laws have a long history within adult criminal court and were designed to protect mentally ill adult criminal defendants (Grisso 2003). As discussed in this chapter, these laws have been increasingly applied to adolescents as the juvenile justice system has become more punitive in nature. While mental illness is clearly an important source of findings of incompetence and NGRI in adolescents, adolescents' competence and culpability is also affected by their lesser developmental maturity, and, as such, the extension of these laws to adolescents requires careful thought and consideration.

At the present time, many issues pertaining to potentially incompetent and NGRI adolescents remain undecided. For instance, there is a fair degree of inconsistency and ambiguity in legal standards, and clinicians who assess and treat these youths have very little guidance, with few well-developed assessment and treatment approaches at their disposal. As such, courts, attorneys, and clinicians who work with these adolescents face a challenging task. To assist practitioners and guide the courts, there is a need for further research on the characteristics and needs of these adolescents and appropriate assessment and treatment approaches.

REFERENCES

American Law Institute (ALI). 1962. *Model Penal Code* (proposed official draft). Philadelphia, PA: American Law Institute.

American Psychiatric Association (APA). 2000. *Diagnostic and Statistical Manual of Mental Disorders*, 4th ed., text revision. Washington, DC: American Psychiatric Association.

Benekos, Peter J., and Alita V. Merlo. 2008. "Juvenile Justice: The Legacy of Punitive Policy." *Youth Violence and Juvenile Justice* 6(1): 28–46.

Bonnie, Richard. J. 1992. "The Competence of Criminal Defendants: A Theoretical Reformulation." *Behavioral Sciences and the Law* 10(3): 291–316.

Bonnie, Richard J., and Thomas Grisso. 2000. "Adjudicative Competence and Youthful Offenders." In *Youth on Trial: A Developmental Perspective on Juvenile Justice*, edited by Thomas Grisso and Robert G. Schwartz. Chicago, IL: University of Chicago Press.

Borum, Randy. 2003. "Not Guilty by Reason of Insanity." In *Evaluating Competencies*, 2nd ed., edited by Thomas Grisso. New York: Kluwer/Plenum Press.

Burnett, Darla M. R., Charles D. Noblin, and Vicki Prosser. 2004. "Adjudicative Competency in a Juvenile Population." *Criminal Justice and Behavior* 31(4): 438–62.

Christy, Annette, Kevin S. Douglas, Randy K. Otto, and John Petrila. 2004. "Juveniles Evaluated Incompetent to Proceed: Characteristics and Quality of Mental Health Professionals' Evaluations." *Professional Psychology: Research and Practice* 35(4): 380–88.

Cirincione, Carmen, Henry J. Steadman, and Margaret A. McGreevy. 1995. "Rates of Insanity Acquittals and the Factors Associated with Successful Insanity Pleas." *Bulletin of the American Academy of Psychiatry and Law* 23(3): 399–409.

Coalition for Juvenile Justice. 2006. *What are the Implications of Brain Development for Juvenile Justice? Emerging Concepts Brief*. Washington, DC: Coalition for Juvenile Justice.

Cooper, Deborah K. 1997. "Juveniles' Understanding of Trial-Related Information: Are They Competent Defendants?" *Behavioral Sciences and the Law* 15(2): 167–80.

Cooper, Virginia G., and Patricia Zapf. 2003. "Predictor Variables in Competency to Stand Trial Decisions." *Law and Human Behavior* 27(4): 423–36.

Fazel, Seena, Helen Doll, and Niklas Långström. 2008. "Mental Disorders among Adolescents in Juvenile Detention and Correctional Facilities: A Systematic Review and Metaregression Analysis of 25 Surveys." *Journal of the American Academy of Child and Adolescent Psychiatry* 47(9): 1010–19.

Feld, Barry C. 2000. "Legislative Exclusion of Offenses from Juvenile Court Jurisdiction: A History and Critique." In *The Changing Borders of Juvenile Justice: Transfer of Adolescents to the Criminal Justice System*, edited by Jeffrey Fagan and Franklin E. Zimring. Chicago, IL: University of Chicago Press.

———. 2008. "A Slower Form of Death: Implications of *Roper v. Simmons* for Juveniles Sentenced to Life without Parole." *Notre Dame Journal of Law, Ethics, and Public Policy* 22: 101–58.

Fox, Sanford J. 1996. "The Early History of the Court." *The Juvenile Court* 6(3): 29–39.

Frost, Lynda E., and Robert E. Shepherd. 1996. "Mental Health Issues in Juvenile Delinquency Proceedings." *Criminal Justice* 11(3): 52–59, *available at* http://www.abanet.org/crimjust/juvjus/cjmental.html.

Furby, Lita, and Ruth Beyth-Marom. 1992. "Risk Taking in Adolescence: A Decision-Making Perspective." *Developmental Review* 12(1): 1–44.

Giedd, Jay N., Jonathan Blumenthal, Neal O. Jeffries, F. X. Castellanos, Hong Liu, Alex Zijdenbos, Tomas Paus, Alan C. Evans, and Judith A. Rapoport. 1999. "Brain Development During Childhood and Adolescence: A Longitudinal MRI Study." *Nature Neuroscience* 2: 861–63.

Giorgi-Guarnieri, Deborah, Jeffrey Janofsky, Emily Keram, Sarah Lawsky, Philip Merideth, Douglas Mossman, Donna Schwartz-Watts, Charles Scott, John Thompson, and Howard Zonana. 2002. "Practice Guideline: Forensic Psychiatric Evaluation of Defendants Raising the Insanity Defense." *Journal of the American Academy of Psychiatry and Law* 30 (Supp.): 31–37.

Grisso, Thomas. 1997. "The Competence of Adolescents as Trial Defendants." *Psychology, Public Policy, and Law* 3(1): 3–32.

———. 2003. *Evaluating Competencies: Forensic Assessments and Instruments*, 2nd ed. New York: Kluwer Academic/Plenum Press.

———. 2004. *Double Jeopardy: Adolescent Offenders with Mental Disorders*. Chicago, IL: University of Chicago Press.

———. 2005a. *Evaluating Juveniles' Adjudicative Competence: A Guide for Clinical Practice*. Sarasota, FL: Professional Resource Press.

———. 2005b. *Evaluating Juveniles' Adjudicative Competence: A Guide for Legal Professionals*. Sarasota, FL: Professional Resource Press.

Grisso, Thomas, and Melissa Ring. 1979. "Parents' Attitudes toward Juveniles' Rights in Interrogation." *Criminal Justice and Behavior* 6(3): 211–26.

Grisso, Thomas, and Judith Quinlan. 2005. "Juvenile Court Clinical Services: A National Description." *Juvenile and Family Court Journal* 56(4): 9–20.

Grisso, Thomas, Laurence Steinberg, Jennifer Woolard, Elizabeth Cauffman, Elizabeth Scott, Sandra Graham, Fran Lexcen, N. Dickon Reppucci, and Robert Schwartz. 2003. "Juveniles' Competence to Stand Trial: A Comparison of Adolescents' and Adults' Capacities as Trial Defendants." *Law and Human Behavior* 27(4): 333–63.

Halpern-Felsher, Bonnie L., and Elizabeth Cauffman. 2001. "Costs and Benefits of a Decision: Decision-Making Competence in Adolescents and Adults." *Journal of Applied Developmental Psychology* 22(3): 257–73.

Heilbrun, Kirk, Gary Hawk, and David C. Tate. 1996. "Juvenile Competence to Stand Trial: Research Issues in Practice." *Law and Human Behavior* 20(5): 573–78.

Kruh, Ivan, and Thomas Grisso. 2009. *Evaluation of Juveniles' Competence to Stand Trial.* New York: Oxford University Press.

Kruh, Ivan, Lynne Sullivan, Mesha Ellis, Frances Lexcen, and Jon McClellan. 2006. "Juvenile Competence to Stand Trial: A Historical and Empirical Analysis of a Juvenile Forensic Evaluation Service." *International Journal of Forensic Mental Health* 5(2): 109–23.

LaFave, Wayne R., and Austin W. Scott, Jr. 1986. *Criminal law*, 2nd ed. St. Paul, MN: West.

Mack, Julian. 1909. "The Juvenile Court." *Harvard Law Review* 104(23): 119–20.

Marlowe, Douglas B., Jennifer B. Lambert, and Robert G. Thompson. 1999. "Voluntary Intoxication and Criminal Responsibility." *Behavioral Sciences and the Law* 17(2): 195–217.

McGaha, Annette, Randy K. Otto, Mary D. McClaren, John Petrila. 2001. "Juveniles Adjudicated Incompetent to Proceed: A Descriptive Study of Florida's Competence Restoration Program." *Journal of the American Academy of Psychiatry and Law* 29(4): 427–37.

McKee, Geoffrey R., and Steven J. Shea. 1999. "Competency to Stand Trial in Family Court: Characteristics of Competent and Incompetent Juveniles." *Journal of the American Academy of Psychiatry and the Law* 27(1): 65–73.

McNamara, John R., and Frank Andrasik. 1982. "Recidivism Follow-Up for Residents Released From a Forensic Psychiatry Behavior Change Treatment Program." *Journal of Psychiatric Treatment and Evaluation* 4: 423–26.

Melton, Gary B., John Petrila, Normal G. Poythress, and Christopher Slobogin. 2007. *Psychological Evaluations for the Courts: A Handbook for Mental Health Professionals and Lawyers*, 3rd ed. New York: Guilford.

Modecki, Kathryn. 2008. "Addressing Gaps in the Maturity of Judgment Literature: Age Differences and Delinquency." *Law and Human Behavior* 32(1): 78–91.

———. 2009. "'It's a Rush': Psychosocial Content of Antisocial Decision Making." *Law and Human Behavior* 33(3): 183–93.

Mulford, Carrie F., N. Dickon Reppucci, Edward P. Mulvey, Jennifer L. Woolard, and Sharon L. Portwood. 2004. "Legal Issues Affecting Mentally Disordered and Developmentally Delayed Youth in the Justice System." *International Journal of Forensic Mental Health* 3(1): 3–22.

Newman, Stewart S., Marie C. Buckley, Senia P. Newman, and Joseph D. Bloom. 2007. "Oregon's Juvenile Psychiatric Security Review Board." *Journal of the American Academy of Psychiatry and Law* 35(2): 247–52.

North Carolina Sentencing and Policy Advisory Commission. 2007. *Report on Study of Youthful Offenders Pursuant to Session Law 2006–248, Sections 34.1 and 34.2.* http://www.nccourts.org/Courts/CRS/Councils/spac/Documents/yo_finalreporttolegislature.pdf.

Packer, Ira K. 2009. *Evaluation of Criminal Responsibility.* New York: Oxford University Press.

Peterson-Badali, Michele, and Rona Abramovitch. 1992. "Children's Knowledge of the Legal System: Are They Competent to Instruct Legal Counsel?" *Canadian Journal of Criminology* 34(2): 139–60.

Petrella, Russell C., and Norman G. Poythress. 1983. "The Quality of Forensic Examinations: An Interdisciplinary Study." *Journal of Consulting and Clinical Psychology* 51(1): 76–85.

Piaget, Jean. 2008. "Intellectual Evolution from Adolescence to Adulthood." *Human Development* 51(1): 40–47.

Pollock, Emily S. 2000. "Those Crazy Kids: Providing The Insanity Defense In Juvenile
    Courts." *Minnesota Law Review* 85: 2041–79.
Redding, Richard E., Naomi E. S. Goldstein, and Kirk Heilbrun. 2005. "Juvenile
    Delinquency: Past and Present." In *Juvenile Delinquency: Prevention, Assessment, and
    Intervention*, edited by Kirk Heilbrun, Naomi E. S. Goldstein, and Richard E. Redding.
    New York: Oxford University Press.
Reppucci, N. Dickon. 1999. "Adolescent Development and Juvenile Justice." *American
    Journal of Community Psychology* 27(3): 307–26.
Roesch, Ronald, James R. P. Ogloff, Stephen D. Hart, Rebecca J. Dempster, Patricia A. Zapf,
    and Karen E. Whittemore, K. E. 1997. "The Impact of Canadian Criminal Code
    Changes on Remands and Assessments of Fitness to Stand Trial and Criminal
    Responsibility in British Columbia." *Canadian Journal of Psychiatry* 42(5): 509–14.
Roesch, Ronald, Jodi L. Viljoen, and Irene Hui. 2004. "Assessing Intent And Criminal
    Responsibility." In *Handbook Of Forensic Psychology: Resource For Mental Health And
    Legal Professionals*, edited by William T. O'Donohue and Eric Levensky. New York:
    Academic Press.
Rogers, Richard. 1984. *Rogers Criminal Responsibility Assessment Scales*. Odessa, FL:
    Psychological Assessment Resources.
Rosado, Lourdes M., ed. 2000. *Understanding Adolescents: A Juvenile Court Training
    Curriculum*. Washington, DC: American Bar Association Juvenile Justice Center,
    Juvenile Law Center, and Youth Law Center.
Salekin, Randall T. 2004. *Risk-Sophistication-Treatment-Inventory (RST-i): Professional
    Manual*. Lutz, FL: Psychological Assessment Resources.
Scott, Elizabeth S. 2000. "The Legal Construction of Adolescence." *Hofstra Law Review* 29:
    547–98.
———. (2008). *Rethinking Juvenile Justice*. Cambridge, MA: Harvard University Press.
Scott, Elizabeth S., and Thomas Grisso. 2005. "Developmental Incompetence, Due Process,
    And Juvenile Justice Policy." *North Carolina Law Review* 83: 101–47.
Scott, Elizabeth S., N. Dickon Reppucci, and Jennifer L. Woolard. 1995. "Evaluating
    Adolescent Decision Making in Legal Contexts." *Law and Human Behavior* 19(3):
    221–44.
Scott, Elizabeth S., and Laurence Steinberg. 2003. "Blaming Youth." *Texas Law Review* 81:
    799–840.
Scott, Elizabeth S., and Jennifer L. Woolard. 2004. "The Legal Regulation of Adolescence."
    In *Handbook of Adolescent Psychology*, edited by Richard M. Lerner and Laurence D.
    Steinberg. Hoboken, NJ: Wiley.
Silver, Eric, Carmen Cirincione, and Henry J. Steadman. 1994. "Demythologizing
    Inaccurate Perceptions of the Insanity Defense." *Law and Human Behavior* 18(1):
    63–70.
Slobogin, Christopher, Gary B. Melton, and C. Robert Showalter. 1984. "The Feasibility of a
    Brief Evaluation of Mental State at the Time of the Offense." *Law and Human Behavior*
    8(3–4): 305–20.
Steinberg, Laurence, and Elizabeth Cauffman. 1996. "Maturity of Judgment in Adolescence:
    Psychosocial Factors in Adolescent Decision-Making." *Law and Human Behavior*
    20(3): 249–72.
Steinberg, Laurence, and Elizabeth Scott. 2003. "Less Guilty by Reason of Adolescence:
    Developmental Immaturity, Diminished Responsibility, and the Juvenile Death
    Penalty." *American Psychologist* 58(12): 1009–18.

Taylor, William C. 2001. "Golden v. State: Should the Insanity Defense Exist in Juvenile Court?" *Arkansas Law Review and Bar Association Journal* 54: 703–25.

Teplin, Linda A., Karen M. Abram, Gary M. McClelland, Mina K. Dulcan, and Amy A. Mericle. 2002. "Psychiatric Disorders in Youth in Juvenile Detention." *Archives of General Psychiatry* 59: 1133–43.

Vaughan, Phillip J., and Susan Stevenson. 2002. "An Opinion Survey of Mentally Disordered Offender Service Users." *British Journal of Forensic Practice* 4(3): 11–20.

Viljoen, Jodi L. 2011. "Extending Clinical Forensic Assessment to Adolescent Offenders: Emerging Knowledge on Juvenile Violence Risk and Competence Assessments." Paper presented at the Annual Conference of the American Psychology-Law Society, Miami, FL., March.

Viljoen, Jodi L., and Thomas Grisso. 2007. "Prospects for Remediating Juveniles' Adjudicative Incompetence." *Psychology, Public Policy, and Law* 13(2): 87–114.

Viljoen, Jodi L., Kaitlyn McLachlan, and Twila Wingrove. 2008. *Defense Attorneys' Concerns about the Legal Capacities of Juvenile Defendants.* Paper presented at the Annual Conference of the American Psychology-Law Society, Jacksonville, FL., Mar. 5–8.

Viljoen, Jodi L., and Ronald Roesch. 2005. "Competence to Waive Interrogation Rights and Adjudicative Competence in Adolescent Defendants: Cognitive Development, Attorney Contact, and Psychological Symptoms." *Law and Human Behavior* 29(6): 723–42.

———. 2008. "Assessing Adolescents' Adjudicative Competence." In *Learning Forensic Assessment*, edited by Rebecca Jackson. New York: Routledge/Taylor and Francis.

Viljoen, Jodi L., and Twila Wingrove. 2007. "Adjudicative Competence in Adolescent Defendants: Judges' and Defense Attorneys' Views of Legal Standards for Adolescents in Juvenile and Criminal Court." *Psychology, Public Policy, and Law* 13(3): 204–29.

Viljoen, Jodi L., Patricia A. Zapf, and Ronald Roesch. 2007. "Adjudicative Competence and Comprehension of Miranda Rights in Adolescent Defendants: A Comparison of Legal Standards." *Behavioral Sciences and the Law* 25(1): 1–19.

Warren, Janet I., Jeanette DuVal, Irina Komarovskaya, Preeti Chauhan, Jacqueline Buffington-Vollum, and Eileen Ryan. 2009. "Developing a Forensic Service Delivery System for Juveniles Adjudicated Incompetent to Stand Trial." *The International Journal of Forensic Mental Health* 8(4): 245–262.

Warren, Janet I., Lawrence W. Fitch, Park E. Dietz, and Barry D. Rosenfeld. 1991. "Criminal Offense, Psychiatric Diagnoses, and Psycholegal Opinion: An Analysis of 894 Pretrial Referrals." *Bulletin of the American Academy of Psychiatry and the Law* 19(1): 63–69.

Warren, Janet I., Daniel C. Murrie, Preeti Chauhan, Park E. Dietz, and James Morris. 2004. Opinion Formation in Evaluating Sanity at the Time of the Offense: An Examination of 5175 Pre-Trial Evaluations. *Behavioral Sciences and the Law* 22(2): 171–86.

Warren, Janet I., Daniel C. Murrie, William Stejskal, Lori H. Colwell, James Morris, Preeti Chauhan, and Park E. Dietz. 2006. "Opinion Formation in Evaluating The Adjudicative Competence And Restorability Of Criminal Defendants: A Review Of 8,000 Evaluations." *Behavioral Sciences and the Law* 24(2): 113–32.

Woodworth, Mike, Kristine A. Peace, Cedar O'Donnell, and Steve Porter. 2004. "Forensic Community Programs: Recommendations for the Management of NCRMD Patients in the Community." *Journal of Forensic Psychology Practice* 3(4): 1–22.

Woolard, Jennifer L., Hayley M. D. Cleary, Samantha A. S. Harvell, and Rusan Chen. 2008. "Examining Adolescents' and Their Parents' Conceptual and Practical Knowledge of Police Interrogation: A Family Dyad Approach." *Journal of Youth and Adolescence* 37(6): 685–98.

Zapf, Patricia A., Stephen L. Golding, and Ronald Roesch. 2005. "Criminal Responsibility and the Insanity Defense." In *Handbook of Forensic Psychology*, 3rd ed., edited by Allen K. Hess and Irving B. Weiner. New York: Wiley.

Zapf, Patricia A., and Ronald Roesch. 2001. "A Comparison of Maccat-CA and the FIT for Making Determinations of Competency to Stand Trial." *International Journal of Law and Psychiatry* 24(1): 81–92.

PART VII

JUVENILE COURT CASE PROCESSING: SCREENING, DETENTION, AND TRIAL

CHAPTER 23

POLICING JUVENILES

EDMUND F. MCGARRELL

OVER two million people under the age of 18 are arrested annually by law enforcement agencies in the United States. Juveniles comprised 16% of all arrests for violent crimes and 26% of all property crime arrests in 2007 (Puzzanchera 2009). Given that most police-citizen contacts, including contacts with juveniles, do not result in an arrest, it is clear that interactions with juveniles are a significant component of police work and that many youths are affected every day by decisions made by the police.

In many respects, the historic experience of the police and juveniles parallels that of the emergence and development of the juvenile court and juvenile justice system. Similarly, just as the juvenile court has faced contradictory pressures inherent in the tension between community crime control and the individualized needs of youth, so too have the police. Further, the wide range of behaviors that bring juveniles and the police in contact with each other—ranging from child abuse and neglect issues, to witnesses of violence, to status offense behaviors, to property offenses, to the most serious and violent types of offending—heightens these tensions between individualized treatment, prevention, and crime control. It also blurs the lines between juvenile and criminal jurisdiction. The tensions are magnified by the lack of evidence-based practice that could more clearly inform policing policy and practice and more effectively guide prevention, intervention, and enforcement activities (Mears 2007). Finally, because youth victimization and offending is embedded in family, peer, school, neighborhood, and economic contexts, policing juveniles necessarily brings the police in contact with other governmental agencies, social services, education, community groups, and many other elements of community. How the police navigate these multiple missions, contradictory pressures, and the level and extent of such external collaboration and partnerships is likely to ultimately determine the "fairness and effectiveness" of policing juveniles.

I. A Brief History of Policing Juveniles

Like the forces that ultimately resulted in the creation of the juvenile court (Platt 1969; Mennel 1973), the modern police were the product of urbanization, industrialization, and immigration whereby large urban centers created police forces to exert social control that was previously the responsibility of families, communities, and local institutions. Within the United States, New York City, Philadelphia, and Boston created police forces in the 1830s and 1840s with the major growth occurring in the first part of the twentieth century following World War I and the recommendations of the Wickersham reform commission[1] (President's Commission on Law Enforcement and Administration of Justice 1967). Specialized juvenile police bureaus emerged with the juvenile court in Chicago at the turn of the twentieth century and became more common in the post-World War I period. The early juvenile bureaus tended to adopt the juvenile court's *parens patriae* philosophy and emphasized prevention and intervention. They also reflected the gendered nature of the juvenile justice system as often juvenile bureaus were the units where female officers were assigned.

The 1960s called into question the informal procedures of the juvenile justice system through a series of Supreme Court cases that imposed a number of constitutional safeguards on the police as they processed juveniles charged with status and criminal offenses (Snyder and Sickmund 2006; see also Empey and Stafford 1991, ch. 20). The period from the 1970s through the early 1990s witnessed increases in serious juvenile offending with a corresponding political emphasis on juvenile crime, legislation, and policy to criminalize juvenile offending, increase sanctions, and limit the discretion and treatment orientation of the juvenile justice system (McGarrell 1988; Bernard 1992). These trends seemed to influence the police as indicated by the long-term trend whereby the police refer more juvenile arrests to the juvenile and adult courts as opposed to informally disposing the cases (Empey and Stafford 1991; Snyder and Sickmund 2006).

In order to consider contemporary policing of juveniles, it is helpful to consider what is known about the nature and recent trends of juvenile offending.

II. Trends in Juvenile Crime and Arrests

The limitations of measuring crime are magnified in the context of juvenile crime. The most standardized measurement system, the FBI's Uniform Crime Reporting System, does not have specific categories of juvenile offenses other than arrests of juveniles. Arrest data are problematic in a number of ways. First, they are primarily indicators of police activity as opposed to direct measures of crimes committed by juveniles. Second, although limiting to a common category such as arrests of people under the age of 18 provides a common metric, it does not align with the varying jurisdictional definitions of what constitutes a juvenile as opposed to an adult offense. This picture is further complicated in states with juvenile court jurisdiction ending at ages 15 or 16. In such states, youths under age 18 may be counted as juveniles in arrest statistics but be prosecuted in criminal court. Third, arrests represent the total number of arrests as opposed to arrests of particular individuals. Thus, repeat offending individuals are over-represented in these data. Similarly, the data include situations where multiple arrests are made for a single offense. Indeed, given that youths typically offend in groups, reliance on arrest statistics can overstate the extent of juvenile offending relative to adult offending (Zimring 1981;Snyder and Sickmund 2006). Law enforcement agencies that participate in the National Incident Based Reporting System (NIBRS) can identify incidents involving juveniles as well as incidents in which victims may report that they believed the perpetrator was a juvenile, but these data do not currently provide consistent national trend data. Consequently, juvenile arrests remain the most commonly used, though imperfect, proxy measure of the level of juvenile crime.

The most recent data indicate that over 2.18 million arrests of persons under age 18 were made in 2007. This represented a 20% decline since 1998. Juveniles were more likely to be arrested for property offenses than violent crimes. Indeed, despite the seeming constant outcry about the increasing number and violent nature of juvenile crime, there were some encouraging signs in juvenile arrest trends. For example, after years of an upward trend in juvenile violence, with a peak rate of 14.4 juvenile arrests for murder per 100,000 juveniles in 1993, the juvenile murder arrest rate in 2007 was 4.1 arrests per 100,000 juveniles. This represented a 72% decline in a little over a decade.

Despite these positive trends, the fact that over 1,800 juveniles were murdered in 2007 stood as a sobering reminder of an unacceptable level of lethal violence. Juvenile murder victims were most likely to be male, and most were killed with a firearm (80% of victims were ages 13 to 17). Research also demonstrated that the significant increase in juvenile homicide during the late 1980s and early 1990s was almost entirely accounted for by homicides involving 15–17-year-olds and involving firearms (Snyder and Sickmund 2006). African American youths were particularly at risk for being homicide victims with a victimization rate four times that of white youths (Snyder and Sickmund 2006). Research indicates that the elevated risk for African American and Hispanic youths for violence is partly accounted for by living in disadvantaged neighborhoods and in single-parent households (Lauritsen 2003; Snyder and Sickmund 2006; but see Zimring 1998).

Juvenile arrests for property offenses in 2007 had also declined since 1998 (a 33% decline), and the decline in juvenile arrests for both violent and property index crimes was greater than the decline for adults (Puzzanchera 2009). The arrest data were consistent with trends in reported victimization that indicated that serious and violent victimization of youth declined since the peak rates in 1993 for all juvenile age groups, males and females, and all races. Violent victimizations were more likely to occur at school, and the peak time for such victimization was in the hours after school. The victimization data indicated that the overall reduction in violence against juveniles mirrored declines in victimization in school as well as during travel to and from school. (Snyder and Sickmund 2006.)

Like adults, juvenile males have long been more likely to be arrested and involved in the justice system, but recent years have witnessed more involvement of females. For example, whereas in 1980, 20% of juvenile arrests involved females, this increased to 29% in 2003 (Snyder and Sickmund 2006). This was true for both violent and property offenses.

An additional risk factor suggested by research was the involvement of youths in gangs. Analyses of the National Longitudinal Survey of Youth indicated that gang-involved youth were four times as likely to have committed a serious assault and five times as likely to have carried a gun (Snyder and Sickmund 2006; see also Thornberry et al. 1993). Indeed, gang membership significantly increased the likelihood of youth victimization as well as offending (Hill, Liu, and Hawkins 2001; Thornberry et al. 2003; Melde, Taylor, and Esbensen 2009).

The arrest data also indicated disproportionate minority contact. For example, whereas African American youth comprise 17% of the total juvenile population, they accounted for just over one-half of all arrests for violent index crimes and approximately one-third of property index crime arrests (Puzzanchera 2009). However, there was some indication that this disparity was declining in recent years. For example, while the African American arrest rate for violent offenses was six times the rate for white youth during the late 1980s, it was four times the white rate in 2003 (Snyder and Sickmund 2006). For drug offenses, where African American youth have long been disproportionately arrested (Tonry 1994), the African American rate fell from five times the rate for whites to just less than twice the rate. Despite these indications of a reduced level of disproportionate minority arrest rate, the higher arrest rates for minority youth remain troubling. Indeed, Huizinga et al. (2007) reported findings from longitudinal studies conducted in Denver, Pittsburgh, and Rochester that found that even after controlling for self-reported offending, minority youth had greater contact with the police and higher rates of arrest and referral to juvenile court. The race effect was reduced when considering risk factors such as neighborhood characteristics, family economic status, family structure, age of mother at first birth, and youth educational problems, but it remained a significant factor in police contact and referral to the court. Thus, minority youth who may experience higher levels of risk for delinquency also experience a higher likelihood of formal police intervention. Some of the reasons for this are discussed later in the chapter.

The manner in which law enforcement agencies processed juvenile arrests in 2007 reflected the continued trend toward greater reliance on referral to the juvenile court. Seventy percent of juvenile arrests were referred to the juvenile court, and an additional nine percent were referred to adult criminal court. Just under one-fifth of the cases were handled informally within the police department (Puzzanchera 2009). Law enforcement agencies were also the major source of cases entering the juvenile court system (84% in 2000; see Snyder and Sickmund 2006). For status offenses—those offenses such as running away, violating curfew, illegal possession of alcohol, and being truant, which are only "criminalized" for youths—law enforcement made about one-half of the court referrals with others being made by child welfare agencies, schools, families, probation, and similar sources (Snyder and Sickmund 2006).

Finally, the national juvenile arrest data reflected the wide variation in the like-lihood of juveniles being arrested across the states. For example, nationally the juve-nile arrest rate for violent index crimes was 301 per 100,000 youths ages 10 to 17. This ranged from 42 in West Virginia and 63 in Maine to 591 in Delaware and 913 in Illinois. For property crimes, the national juvenile arrest rate was 1,293 per 100,000 youths but ranged from 368 in West Virginia and 521 in Massachusetts to over 2,000 in Kentucky and Wisconsin. Arrests for drug offenses also witnessed significant variation, with a national average of 590 per 100,000 ranging from 161 (West Virginia) to 2,152 (Illinois). These data, although influenced by a variety of factors, seem to reflect the observation made by Feld (1991) nearly two decades ago of "justice by geography." Although based on county-level variation within the state of Minnesota, Feld noted that the way juvenile offending was handled was to a signifi-cant extent determined by local justice system practices. Similarly, Wilson's (1968) classic study of the styles of policing found that juvenile arrest rates varied dramati-cally across what he referred to as legalistic, service, and watchman styles of policing based on local norms and traditions. These national data suggest that contempo-rary policing of juveniles continues to be influenced by these policing styles and local political norms and traditions.

As will be discussed subsequently, these patterns and trends in juvenile victim-ization, offending, and arrest provide valuable information for policing juveniles. For example, the high rates of victimization associated with schools and with the after-school hours time period suggests opportunities for focused prevention and intervention efforts. Similarly, the high risk for victimization and offending associ-ated with disadvantaged neighborhoods suggests the need for educational, eco-nomic, and community development as well as for focused prevention. In addition to addressing crime and victimization, increasing evidence-based prevention and intervention programs focused on disadvantaged neighborhoods could also carry benefits in terms of reducing the level of disproportionate minority contact with the juvenile justice system. Research demonstrating the high offending and victim-ization rates for periods when youth are gang-involved have driven prevention, intervention, and suppression gang strategies. Similarly, the heavy involvement of firearms in youth homicide also suggests strategies focused on youths' illegally pos-sessing and using firearms.

III. Specialized Police Units

Police departments have a long history of specialized units and programs focused on youth. In the era following the development of the juvenile court at the turn of the twentieth century through the Wickersham Commission in the 1930s, many departments, particularly in larger cities, developed juvenile aid bureaus. These often included specialized police detectives. Although all patrol officers were likely to encounter youths, when an arrest of a youth occurred, it would typically be referred to the youth bureau. Youth bureaus developed a variety of youth prevention activities including programs such as the Police Athletic League.

Since the years following the due process revolution of the 1960s, a period that also witnessed a more formalized response to juvenile offending by the police as indicated by increasing referrals of arrested youth to the courts, specialized youth programs have tended to follow concerns with various forms of crime. For example, concern with illegal drug abuse led to the emergence of the Drug Abuse Resistance Education (DARE) program. Also, the community policing movement, coupled with beliefs about the importance of schools as an institution affecting the socialization of youth, resulted in the emergence of School Resource Officers (SROs) and school-based police liaison officers. SRO programs typically involve officers who are assigned to schools to build relationships with youths, identify potential problems at early stages, and gather intelligence. The emergence of after-school programs could be linked to research indicating that the often unsupervised after-school time period was a high-risk period for delinquency. Concern about the spread of gangs and the criminogenic influence of gangs resulted in the emergence of gang units as well as gang prevention activities such as the Gang Resistance Education and Training Program (GREAT). Increases in serious and violent offending by youths resulted in the Serious and Habitual Violent Offender Program.

Although not all departments have developed or maintained juvenile aid bureaus or implemented all of these specialized programs, some type of bureau or programs are common across police departments. The Bureau of Justice Statistics conducts a periodic survey of the nation's law enforcement agencies known as the Law Enforcement Management and Administrative Statistics (LEMAS) program. It includes questions about specialized units intended to address youth-related problems. In the 2000 LEMAS survey, 70% of local police agencies reported providing drug education in schools, and just over 60% had a juvenile unit. Just less than one-half of the agencies reported gang, child abuse, domestic violence, or missing children units (Snyder and Sickmund 2006).

IV. Promising Practices and the Movement toward Evidence-Based Practice

For decades, specialized police services intended to prevent or reduce juvenile offending have operated on the basis of good intentions and good ideas about what could influence youth behavior in a positive manner. Few of these initiatives operated on the basis of sound empirical research. One such example is the very popular

DARE program, which involves police officers providing educational programs in the schools that are intended to teach youths about the dangers of drug abuse and strengthen their capacity to resist the temptation to use illegal drugs. A number of studies, however, found that the program did not result in significantly reduced levels of drug abuse (Ennett et al. 1994; Dukes, Ullman, and Stein 1996).

Somewhat more promising results emerge from studies of the GREAT program, which also involves police-led instruction in schools. Several studies found more prosocial attitudes and reduced self-reported offending for youths who participated in the GREAT program in contrast to comparison group youths (Esbensen and Osgood 1999; Esbensen et al. 2001; but see Klein and Maxson 2006). The authors, however, call for more rigorous evaluation designs, and there is clearly a need for additional research before GREAT can be considered an example of evidence-based practice.

As noted above, another development in the community policing era has been the emergence of School Resource Officers (SROs) and police-liaison officers in schools. There is some evidence that SRO programs are popular with school administrators and parents and that youths with positive attitudes toward SROs feel safe at school and are more comfortable reporting crimes (Finn and McDevitt 2005; McDevitt and Panniello 2005). An early study of SROs found that school infractions decreased significantly after the introduction of the SRO program (Johnson 1999), but other research found SROs to be unrelated to school disorder or to even relate to increased disorder (Schreck, Miller, and Gibson 2003; Mayer and Leone 1999).[2] Others have raised the concern that the presence of police in schools will criminalize behavior previously handled informally by school officials (Hirschfield 2008). One of the few systematic studies of the "criminalization" hypothesis produced mixed findings. Schools with SROs did have increased arrests compared to schools without SROs, but the differences disappeared when economic disadvantage was controlled (Theriot 2009). Schools with SROs actually had lower levels of arrests for assault and weapons charges; there was no relationship between SROs and arrests for drug and alcohol charges. The presence of an SRO did result in increased arrests for disorderly conduct, a finding likely to reflect discretion on the part of an SRO and that may indicate a response to teachers' and administrators' requests for assistance in dealing with "problem students." Clearly there is a need for additional research on the impact of school-based officers on school climate, infractions and safety, and perceptions of the police as well as on the unintended effects of criminalizing youth and potentially disrupting school careers.

In contrast to the experience with DARE, which has involved decades of significant funding in the absence of evidence of benefit, recent years have witnessed increased attention to moving toward evidence-based practices (Office of Justice Programs 2006). The U.S. Department of Justice's (DOJ) Office of Justice Programs, which includes DOJ's research and funding agencies including the Office of Juvenile Justice and Delinquency Prevention (OJJDP), has sponsored several efforts intended to identify promising and best practices and the movement toward evidence-based practice. Examples of such efforts include a review of evidence on the impact of policing on crime prevention (Sherman 1997), OJJDP's Model Program Guide (Office of Juvenile Justice and Delinquency Prevention 2009), the Blueprints for Violence Prevention at the Center for the Study and Prevention of Violence (Mihalic et al. 2004), the Campbell Collaboration (2009), and the Center for Evidence-Based Crime Policy (2009). These reviews go beyond police-based prevention and intervention programs, and several go beyond juvenile crime, but all promote a commitment to basing practice on evidence.

A review of the Blueprints documents and OJJDP website's reports on promising practices for reducing delinquency and youth crime reveals that many do not directly involve the police. For example, in a 182-page Blueprints document, the police are mentioned only three times (Mihalic et al. 2004). Among the model programs were those focused on changing the home environment, including home visitation, early child education, parent training, and family therapy. A second major category included programs aimed at changing the school environment. These included antibullying programs, school and classroom discipline, and classroom management programs. A third category focused on changing the community, though with fewer model programs identified. One of these, CASASTART, included the police as an important partnering agency for this program that focused on youth in high-risk community, school and family contexts. The final category was focused on individual change for youths and included programs such as life skills training, alternative thinking skills, drug abuse prevention, and mentoring.[3] The OJJDP website of promising practices includes several additional community intervention programs that involve the police, some of which are discussed later in this chapter, yet the main focus is on individual, family, school, and community prevention and intervention programs (Office of Juvenile Justice and Delinquency Prevention 2009).

As evidence accumulates about these promising interventions, the police can play an important role as advocates for evidence-based practice. The National Research Council (2004, pp. 87–88) noted that to deal with "youth trajectories" toward crime and with "criminogenic circumstances" that generate youth offending, the police can play an important role by working with schools, youth service and social work agencies, community groups, and other local resources to develop, implement, and test prevention and intervention programs.

In addition to these non-police-focused programs, several promising practices directly involving the police have emerged over the last several decades to address some of the most vexing problems involving youth offending. Although not intended to be a comprehensive review of promising practices, these emerging practices include restorative and balanced alternatives to juvenile court processing, as well as interventions intended to address gun-, gang-, and drug-related crime and violence.

A. Restorative Justice

Critics of the juvenile court have complained that the typical overcrowded and under-resourced courts fail to adequately respond to youth offending or meet the needs of victims. In traditional juvenile courts, victims are largely excluded from the court, and youths are diverted, counseled, and released, or placed on probation until they have accumulated a significant criminal record, at which time they might be removed from the community with the result of weakened bonds to family and school. The last few decades have witnessed increasing reliance on a variety of restorative justice practices including victim-offender mediation, sentencing circles, community accountability boards, and family group conferences (Bazemore and Umbreit 2001; Van Ness, Morris, and Maxwell 2001; Presser and Voorhis 2002; Crawford and Newburn 2003). All are intended to increase the accountability for offending, to better address victim needs, but to do so in a community of care and without removing the youths from the community.

The so-called Wagga Wagga model of family group conferences (so named because it was developed by the Wagga Wagga, Australia, Police Department) involves trained police officers who serve as facilitators for conferences that involve the offending youth, the victim, and supporters of both offender and victim. The conference offers the opportunity for everyone to hear an account of why the youth committed the offense, for the victim(s) to question the youth and explain how they were harmed, and for supporters of both victim and offender to express their concerns over the incident. The conference typically involves an apology as well as a consensually based reparation plan for how the youth can make amends.

Research on family group conferences has tended to show substantial increases in victim satisfaction in comparison to cases that are handled in court or other court-related processes (McGarrell 2001; Braithwaite 2002). Although many of the studies have involved relatively weak designs, experiments conducted in Canberra, Australia, and Indianapolis, Indiana, have found reductions in reoffending, at least for some offenses (Sherman, Strang, and Woods 2000; McGarrell and Hipple 2007; see also Braithwaite 2002; Rodriguez 2005, 2007). Further, although some restorative justice advocates argue for the exclusion of police and formal criminal justice actors, the one study that provided a comparison found that there were no differences in terms of youth reoffending between police- and civilian-run conferences (Hipple and McGarrell 2008).

B. Directed Police Patrol of Gun Hotspots

During the 1980s and early 1990s, concerns emerged about increasing involvement of youths in gun violence (Zimring 1998; Snyder and Sickmund 2006). Although not specifically aimed at youth gun crime, one of the promising practices for addressing gun violence identified by the National Research Council (2004; see also Koper and Mayo-Wilson 2006) involved directed police patrol of gun hotspots. Studies in Kansas City, Indianapolis, and Pittsburgh found that such patrols, focused on illegal gun carrying in hot spot locations, were associated with significant declines in gun crime (Sherman and Rogan 1995; McGarrell et al. 2001; Cohen and Ludwig 2003).

Citizen surveys associated with these studies found general support for these police efforts (Shaw 1995; Chermak, McGarrell, and Weiss 2001). However, these surveys typically did not include youths, and a concern arises that these directed patrol initiatives may result in excessive stopping of poor and minority youth. Such practices may thus exacerbate tensions between minority youths and the police and perhaps a loss in the perceived sense of justice and police legitimacy among these youths.

C. "Pulling Levers"

Also aimed at violence involving youths and young adults, an intervention emerged in Boston in the mid-1990s that has come to be known as pulling levers. In Boston, a multi-agency criminal justice team involving the police department, U.S. Attorney's Office, local prosecutors, and probation and parole worked with local researchers and community groups to attempt to reduce levels of youth gun violence. Following a problem-solving model, the researchers found that much of the city's youth violence involved a very small number of youths involved in gangs and neighborhood crews. These youths tended to have extensive prior criminal histories and were often under probation or parole supervision or had outstanding warrants. The multi-agency team used this legal status to influence these high-risk youths through face-to-face meetings. The message of the meeting was that the violence stops or the police and prosecutors would use all available levers to remove the youths from the streets. The message included offers of social support through youth service providers, and examples were offered of gang members who were subject to long prison sentences, including federal prosecution, due to their continued involvement in gun violence. The pulling levers program was associated with a very large decline in youth offending (Braga et al. 2001; Kennedy et al. 2001).

The Boston pulling levers model has been implemented in a number of additional cities, and a series of studies have indicated the program's promise in reducing homicide and gun violence. These have included studies in Chicago, Illinois; Indianapolis, Indiana; Los Angeles, California; Lowell, Massachusetts; and Stockton, California (Tita et al. 2003; McGarrell et al. 2006; Papachristos, Meares, and Fagan 2007; Braga et al. 2008; Braga 2008).

D. Drug Market Intervention

A variation on the pulling levers program was developed by police in High Point, North Carolina, to address the problem of open-air drug markets. These drug markets are typically associated with high levels of disorder, crime, and fear of crime by local residents. For youths, these markets often serve as an entrée into drug-selling operations with youths often serving as lookouts and lower-level street dealers. Such involvement also results in high levels of arrest and the accumulation of criminal records for drug selling.

The High Point model includes systematic analysis of the drug markets to identify the nature of the market and the players involved. Traditional undercover operations are implemented with the goal of building cases against all the people involved in the drug market. Offenders with records of violence are then prosecuted. Lower-level dealers, often including youths and young adults, however, are subject to a lever pulling approach. They are confronted with the evidence against them in a public meeting and informed that they could be prosecuted immediately. They also learn about the prosecution of other individuals involved in the market. They are then offered a second chance and the opportunity to access various services, but with the provision that the drug market is closed. During this time, the police work closely with community members to reassert control over the former drug market location. High Point officials report significant declines in crime in the four areas where the program was implemented. Preliminary time series analysis supports these reports of a positive impact on the neighborhoods affected by these drug markets (Hipple et al. 2009; see also Kennedy 2009).

Given the reports from High Point, a number of cities have implemented this program, and the Bureau of Justice Assistance has developed a national training and technical assistance program to assist communities seeking to implement the program (Hipple et al. 2009; Bureau of Justice Assistance 2009). Initial evaluations in Rockford, Illinois, and Nashville, Tennessee, have found reductions in crime and calls for police service following the implementation of the drug market intervention (Corsaro, Brunson, and McGarrell 2009; Corsaro, Brunson, and McGarrell 2010). Although further research is warranted, the drug market intervention appears to hold promise as a more effective response to the problems generated by drug markets and with the promise of keeping young, nonviolent drug offenders out of court and prison.

E. Comprehensive Gang Model

As noted above, gang involvement has been identified as a significant risk factor for youths in terms of their involvement in serious and violent offending. The OJJDP has advocated a comprehensive and balanced approach to gang intervention that places emphasis on gang prevention, intervention, and suppression. It is based on the model developed by Irving Spergel and David Curry (Spergel and Curry 1993; see also Decker 2003; Klein and Maxson 2006). In the Chicago community of Little Village, Spergel (1994) worked with a network of police, youth outreach workers, probation officers, court service workers, and former gang members to reduce violence between conflicting coalitions of street gangs. Evaluation results of this project indicated a reduction in gang-related violence, increased community organization and mobilization, and the transition of gang-involved youths into educational programs and jobs (Spergel, Grossman, and Wa 1998; Spergel and Wa 2000).

One of the ironies of the above mentioned LEMAS survey on specialized youth programs was that the most commonly mentioned program was drug education in schools (see Snyder and Sickmund 2006). Yet the existing evaluations of DARE have not provided supportive evidence of its positive impact. Hopefully, the increased focus on identifying promising and best practice will assist the police and others to focus limited resources on risk-based and empirically supported programs. As the next section emphasizes, it is also important to assess the implementation of such programs to avoid unintended and potentially harmful effects.

V. DISPROPORTIONATE MINORITY CONTACT

One of the central tensions facing the police is the desire to respond to crime problems that are concentrated in particular geographic contexts but where increased police presence and proactive intervention may result in differential impact on people of color and on the poor. The potential for such differential impact is illustrated at both ends of the seriousness of crime spectrum. Research has demonstrated that violent crime is concentrated in disadvantaged neighborhoods, typically measured by factors such as extreme poverty, single-parent households, and minority population (Curry and Spergel 1988; Bursik and Grasmick 1993; Rosenfeld, Bray, and Egley 1999; Sampson and Raudenbush 1999). Thus, proactive police strategies focused on addressing high levels of violence are very likely to increase contact with minority youth. At the other end of the spectrum, truancy and school dropout have been shown to be risk factors for involvement in serious crime and delinquency (Huizinga and Jakob-Chien 1998), and truancy and dropout rates are often highest in urban school systems and for poor and minority youth (Snyder and Sickmund 2006). Policing strategies focused on truancy, likely designed for crime prevention goals, may also have a differential effect on minority and impoverished children.

The concern with these strategies is that the differential contact with the police may result in disproportionate minority involvement in all stages of the juvenile justice system (Leiber 2002). Such involvement can have a long-term negative impact on youths as early involvement can lead to the accumulation of a delinquency record that influences subsequent legal decisions, can disrupt bonds with family and schools, can lead to association with other at-risk youths, and may result in perceptions of unfairness and defiance, all of which may be associated with future offending (Tyler 1990; Sherman 1993). Concern with these issues has led to a national effort to reduce disproportionate minority contact that involves monitoring rates of contact and examination of processes that may inadvertently produce such differential contact (Leiber 2002).

Studies of youth attitudes toward the police suggest that youths tend to have less favorable attitudes when compared to adults (Apple and O'Brien 1983; Brandl et al. 1994) and that there are racial and ethnic differences in views of the police (Browning et al. 1994). Several older studies found that while whites, middle-class youths, and girls were more likely to have positive attitudes toward the police, African Americans and youths having contact with the police had more negative attitudes (Portune 1971; Winfree and Griffiths 1977). A more recent study by Hurst, Frank, and Browning (2000) uncovered an interesting pattern in the perceptions of black and white youths of the police. Black youths were significantly less positive in their overall assessment of police performance, but the race differences disappeared when asked about specific encounters with the police. Hurst and colleagues interpreted this as indicating general cultural beliefs about patterns of mistreatment and unequal enforcement in the black community. Similarly, Leiber, Nalla, and Farnworth (1998) found that minority youths, particularly those expressing delinquent subcultural norms and having contact with the police, had much less favorable attitudes toward the police.

The evidence of racial differences in youths' perceptions of the police seems to reflect findings from a series of studies of police encounters with youths (Piliavan and Briar 1964; Bittner 1976; Black 1980; Terrill and Reisig 2003). They also reflect the finding that a series of organizational, neighborhood, and situational factors conspire to make it more likely that minority youth will find their behavior under police surveillance, will more likely be stopped and questioned by the police, will more likely be arrested, and will more likely be detained and referred to court (Bishop 2005).

Given that many of the encounters between police and youths involve order maintenance and minor offenses, the police have substantial discretion in terms of how they handle the situation. Youths often travel in groups (Bittner 1976), congregate in public places, and are subject to behavior restrictions such as truancy laws and curfew ordinances (Black 1980), all of which increase the likelihood of police intervention.

These characteristics of youth behavior and offending are also influenced by organizational practices and neighborhood characteristics. Contemporary police practices such as the COMPSTAT program[4] that uses crime patterns for the deployment of police personnel (Silverman 1999) and "hot-spot" policing (Weisburd and Braga 2006) result in greater police presence and surveillance in disadvantaged neighborhoods with a disproportionate minority population. Research suggests that the police are likely to use more formal control tactics in minority and disadvantaged neighborhoods (Smith 1986; Terrill and Reisig 2003). Further, these factors appear to converge to increase the likelihood of formal police response to minority youths. For example, although Sampson (1986) found that self-reported delinquency was the strongest predictor of formal police action, the race and socioeconomic status of the youth, as well as the neighborhood socioeconomic status, all related to increased formal social control being exerted by the police.

Given the focus on minority and disadvantaged neighborhoods, situational factors can further magnify disproportionate minority confinement by the police. Conley (1994) found that police patrolling communities of color made more frequent stops, and Wordes and Bynum (1995) found that youths hanging out in the "wrong neighborhood" were more likely to be stopped by the police. Both studies are consistent with what Piliavin and Briar (1964) described as the "neighborhood bias" effect. Given high rates of violence in some such neighborhoods, the police may perceive greater threat when dealing with black youths, and the youths may anticipate disrespect from the police (Anderson 1990). Although in the case of serious offending the discretion of the police is constrained, for minor offenses, the police are likely to respond based on their perception of the youth's demeanor and attitude (Bittner 1976), as well as complainant preferences (Black and Reiss 1970; Lundman, Sykes, and Clark 1978). As Bittner noted, conflictual interactions between the police and minority and economically disadvantaged youth can have long-term effects on the youths' perceptions of the police and the legal system.

The end result of these patterns is a vicious cycle (Bittner 1990; Bishop 2005). Police organizations focus on disadvantaged neighborhoods, thereby increasing surveillance of minority youths. Youths are more likely to be stopped and questioned. Youths feel hostility toward the police, and the police respond to real or perceived hostility with an increased likelihood to detain, arrest, and refer cases to the courts (Zimring 1981; Bishop 2005).

These findings become increasingly important given research on the role of the perceived legitimacy of the law and legal actors, such as the police, and future compliance with the law (Tyler 1990; Fagan and Tyler 2005; Piquero et al. 2005). In brief, loss of respect and legitimacy reduce conformity with the law. This research suggests that efforts on behalf of the police to increase youths' perceptions of fair and respectful policing may have long-term crime prevention potential. Conversely, it suggests that even well-intended police tactics undertaken to address high levels of violent victimization in disadvantaged neighborhoods run the risk of ultimately reducing compliance if such tactics are perceived as illegitimate.

For the police, managing this tension becomes a central issue. On the one hand, the failure to respond to geographically concentrated levels of violence can be a form of benign neglect for neighborhoods suffering from high levels of violence. Similarly, inattention to truancy and dropout may set disadvantaged youth to a life of limited opportunity. On the other hand, absent attention to the potential for differential impact, these crime prevention and control strategies may inadvertently generate police-community conflict as well as negatively affect disadvantaged youth of color. At a minimum, an emphasis on respectful policing, on fostering relationships with the community, and on implementing evidence-based prevention programs in disadvantaged neighborhoods appears critical. Evidence from Chicago suggests that these steps, at least in terms of developing relationships with the community, can have a positive impact on the relationship between the police and citizens in minority neighborhoods (Skogan and Hartnett 1997).

VI. Conclusion

As noted at the outset, policing juveniles reflects the multiple goals and values that the police are expected to pursue and that result in competing tensions for the police to manage. Thus, the contemporary police organization is expected to control crime, and in the COMPSTAT-era is often held accountable for levels of crime. At the same time, the police are expected to respect the civil liberties of citizens and be the guardians of due process. Research informs the police that the effectiveness of their crime control efforts is often a product of the extent to which they focus their efforts on the specific crime problems and the specific contexts driving crime (National Research Council 2004). Yet citizens and neighborhood groups demand responses to a broad range of problems, including traffic enforcement, litter and trash collection, unruly youths and graffiti, as well as serious crime. Further, the focus on specific crime contexts can readily translate to concerns about biased or targeted enforcement. In a constitutional democracy these tensions are inherent to the institution of policing and thus the call for a commitment to policing that is both fair and effective (National Research Council 2004).

These tensions are particularly apparent in thinking about juvenile crime and delinquency. The teenage and young adult years are characterized by the high prevalence of offending and a wide range of behaviors included under the labels of crime and delinquency. Most youths will engage in some type of illegal behavior, most of which will be of a less serious nature, and most of which will be episodic. Some juveniles will begin offending early, will engage in serious and violent behavior, and will persist into adulthood (Loeber and LeBlanc 1990; Nagin and Farrington 1992; Moffitt 1993; Nagin, Farrington, and Moffitt 1995). The juvenile years also carry the heightened risk of victimization (Snyder and Sickmund 2006). Policing juveniles involves responding to this diverse range of juvenile crime and delinquency. Further, much of this response must occur, at least today, in the absence of clear, evidence-based practice. At the prevention end of the spectrum, after-school programs or recreational programs such as, for example, "midnight basketball" might seem to offer an enlightened response to delinquency that emerges from unsupervised time. However, some evidence suggests that absent effective supervision during and after such programs, these programs may actually create opportunities for crime and delinquency. At the other end of the spectrum, research suggests that directed police patrol in gun crime hotspots may reduce levels of gun violence. Yet what are the unintended impacts on law-abiding youths who find themselves regularly stopped by the police in such hot spot locations?

The emphasis on evidence-based practice offers police executives one guiding principle for improving police practice as it relates to juveniles and the juvenile justice system. At a minimum, in an era of shrinking public resources. it becomes critical to eliminate ineffective programs (e.g., DARE), to demand assessment and accountability for unproven programs (e.g., various prevention programs, GREAT, SROs), and to invest in strategies that research suggests have the most promise for addressing particular problems.

Additional research suggests the need for a broader perspective on what is meant by "evidence-based" practice and on the performance metrics used to judge police performance. What if SROs and beat officers were assessed on the extent to which their interactions with youths were perceived as legitimate and fair, in addition to levels of school and neighborhood victimization? What if police departments measured youth perceptions along with adult citizen assessments of the police (and trends in crime)? Improving youths' perceptions of the police, the most visible representatives of the justice system, may be one of the most effective long-term delinquency and crime prevention strategies available to the police. Such an emphasis also has considerable implications for police training so that the fairness dimension moves from being perceived as a constraint on police behavior to a key component of crime prevention and control.

Contemporary policing has been influenced by a number of philosophies including community policing, problem-solving, and evidence-based policing (Goldstein 1990; Skogan and Hartnett 1997; Sherman 1998; Weisburd and Braga 2006; Lum 2009). All of these models appear to hold some promise for improving practice related to policing juveniles. Clearly, the police should not be saddled with full responsibility for addressing the needs of youths who are at risk for involvement in crime and delinquency. Community partnerships with schools, youth service organizations, parents, neighborhood groups, employers, recreational programs, and other local agencies and institutions offer promise for enhancing prevention and intervention efforts. Problem-solving approaches that break down the full range of youth crime and delinquency into specific problems that can be analyzed and assessed hold promise for more tailored and accountable strategies for crime prevention and control. A commitment to evidence-based practice and continued development of the requisite body of knowledge should assist police leaders in deciding where to invest limited resources. Whatever the model of policing, ultimately police executives responsible for policing juveniles must continually ask: is this going to be seen as fair and respectful by the community, including by juveniles, and is it likely to be effective in reducing youth offending and victimization?

NOTES

1. The National Committee on Law Observance and Enforcement, which came to be known as the Wickersham Commission, was appointed by President Herbert Hoover in 1929 (Calder 1993; Law Enforcement Assistance Administration 1976). The Commission conducted a broad review of the criminal justice system with a particular focus on prohibition, organized crime, and police misconduct. The report on police misconduct was considered a significant factor in the emergence of the "professional era" of policing.

2. Both studies used "security guard" to measure law enforcement/security presence and thus are not strictly tests of the impact of SROs.

3. CASASTART is a program developed by the National Center on Addiction and Substance Abuse (CASA) known as Striving Together to Achieve Rewarding Tomorrows (START) (See National Center on Addiction and Substance Abuse 2009).

4. The COMPSTAT program was originally developed by the New York Police Department and has since been adopted by many police departments. It refers to a managerial initiative involving regular meetings of the command staff with the leadership

of all divisions and units to systematically review crime patterns with the goal of responding to such patterns to reduce levels of future offending. The program combines review of crime data with managerial accountability (Silverman 1999).

REFERENCES

Anderson, Elijah. 1990. *Streetwise: Race, Class and Change in an Urban Community.* Chicago: University of Chicago Press.

Apple, Nancy, and David J. O'Brien. 1983. "Neighborhood Racial Composition and Residents' Evaluation of Police Performance." *Journal of Police Science and Administration* 11: 76–84.

Bazemore, Gordon, and Mark Umbreit. 2001. "A Comparison of Four Restorative Conferencing Models." *OJJDP Bulletin.* Washington, DC: U.S. Department of Justice, Office of Juvenile Justice and Delinquency Prevention.

Bernard, Thomas. 1992. *The Cycle of Juvenile Justice.* New York: Oxford University Press.

Bishop, Donna M. 2005. "The Role of Race and Ethnicity in Juvenile Justice Processing." In *Our Children, Their Children: Confronting Racial and Ethnic Differences in American Juvenile Justice,* edited by Darnell F. Hawkins and Kimberly Kempf-Leonard. Chicago: University of Chicago Press.

Bittner, Egon. 1976. "Policing Juveniles." In *Pursuing Justice for the Child,* edited by Margaret Rosenheim. Chicago: University of Chicago Press.

Bittner, Egon. 1990. "Race Effects in Juvenile Justice Decision-Making: Findings from a Statewide Analysis." *Journal of Criminal Law and Criminology* 86: 392–414.

Black, Donald. 1980. *The Manners and Customs of the Police.* London: Academic Press.

Black, Donald, and Albert J. Reiss. 1970. "Police Control of Juveniles." *American Sociological Review* 35: 63–77.

Braga, Anthony. 2008. "Pulling Levers Focused Deterrence Strategies and the Prevention of Gun Homicide." *Journal of Criminal Justice* 36: 332–43.

Braga, Anthony A., David M. Kennedy, Elin J. Waring, and Anne M. Piehl. 2001. "Problem-Oriented Policing, Deterrence, and Youth Violence: An Evaluation of Boston's Operation Ceasefire." *Journal of Research in Crime and Delinquency* 38: 195–226.

Braga, Anthony A., Glenn L. Pierce, Jack McDevitt, B.J. Bond, and Shea Cronin. 2008. "The Strategic Prevention of Gun Violence Among Gang-Involved Offenders." *Justice Quarterly* 25(1): 132–62.

Braithwaite, John. 2002. *Restorative Justice and Responsive Regulation.* New York: Oxford University Press.

Brandl, Steven G., James Frank, Robert E. Worden, and Timothy S. Bynum. 1994. "Global and Specific Attitudes Toward the Police: Disentangling the Relationship." *Justice Quarterly* 11: 119–34.

Browning, Sandra L., Francis T. Cullen, Liqun Cao, Renee Kopache, and Thomas J. Stevenson. 1994. "Race and Getting Hassled by the Police: A Research Note." *Police Studies* 17(1): 482–89.

Bureau of Justice Assistance. 2009. Drug Market Intervention Program. Accessed Feb. 23, 2011. http://www.ojp.usdoj.gov/BJA/topics/DMII.pdf.

Bursik, Robert J., and Harold Grasmick. 1993. *Neighborhoods and Crime: The Dimensions of Effective Community Control.* New York: Lexington Publishing.

Calder, James D. 1993. *The Origins and Development of Federal Crime Control Policy: Herbert Hoover's Initiatives*. Westport, CT: Praeger.

Campbell Collaboration. 2009. Accessed Feb. 23, 2011. http://www.campbellcollaboration.org/.

Center for Evidence-Based Crime Policy. 2009. Accessed Feb. 23, 2009. http://gunston.gmu.edu/cebcp/.

Chermak, Steven, Edmund F. McGarrell, and Alexander Weiss. 2001. "Citizens' Perceptions of Aggressive Traffic Enforcement Strategies." *Justice Quarterly* 18(2): 365–91.

Cohen, Jacqueline, and Jens Ludwig. 2003. "Policing Crime Guns." In *Evaluating Gun Policy: Effects on Crime and Violence*, edited by Jens Ludwig and Philip J. Cook. Washington, DC: Brookings Institution Press.

Conley, Dale J. 1994. "Adding Color to a Black and White Picture: Using Qualitative Data to Explain Racial Disproportionality in the Juvenile Justice System." *Journal of Research in Crime and Delinquency* 31(2): 135–48.

Corsaro, Nicholas, Rod K. Brunson, and Edmund F. McGarrell. 2009. "Problem-Oriented Policing and Open-Air Drug Markets: Examining the Rockford Pulling Levers Deterrence Strategy." *Crime and Delinquency* Published Online First October 14, 2009 doi: 10.1177/001128 709345955.

Corsaro, Nicholas, Rod K. Brunson, and Edmund F. McGarrell. 2010. "The Systematic Disruption of Open-air Drug Markets: A Mixed Methods Examination of Pulling Levers." *Evaluation Review* 34: 513–548.

Crawford, Adam, and Tim Newburn. 2003. *Youth Offending and Restorative Justice: Implementing Reform in Youth Justice*. Portland, OR: Willan Publishing.

Curry, G. David, and Irving A. Spergel. 1988. "Confronting Gangs: Crime and Community." *Criminology* 26: 381–403.

Decker, Scott. 2003. *Policing Gangs and Youth Violence*. Newbury Park, CA: Wadsworth.

Dukes, Richard L., Jodie B. Ullman, and Judith A. Stein. 1996. "Three-Year Follow-Up of Drug Abuse Resistance Education (DARE)." *Evaluation Review* 20(1): 49–66.

Empey, Lamar T., and Mark C. Stafford. 1991. *American Delinquency: Its Meaning and Construction*. Belmont, CA: Wadsworth.

Ennett, Susan T., Nancy S. Tobler, Christopher L. Ringwalt, and Robert L. Flewelling. 1994. "How Effective is Drug Abuse Resistance Education? A Meta-analysis of Project DARE Outcome Evaluations." *American Journal of Public Health* 84(9): 1394–401.

Esbensen, Finn-Aage, and D. Wayne Osgood. 1999. "Gang Resistance Education and Training (GREAT): Results From the National Evaluation." *Journal of Research in Crime and Delinquency* 36(2): 194–225.

Esbensen, Finn-Aage, D. Wayne Osgood, Terrance J. Taylor, Dana Peterson, Adrienne Freng. 2001. "How Great Is G. R. E. A. T.? Results From a Longitudinal Quasi-Experimental Design." *Criminology & Public Policy* 1(1): 87–118.

Fagan, Jeffrey, and Tom R. Tyler. 2005. "Legal Socialization of Children and Adolescents." *Social Justice Research* 18(3): 217–42.

Feld, Barry C. 1991. "Justice by Geography: Urban, Suburban, and Rural Variations in Juvenile Justice Administration." *Journal of Criminal Law and Criminology* 82(1): 156–210.

Finn, Peter, and Jack McDevitt. 2005. "National Assessment of School Resource Officer Programs: Final Project Report." Report to the National Institute of Justice. Washington, DC: U.S. Department of Justice.

Goldstein, Herman. 1990. *Problem-Oriented Policing*. Philadelphia, PA: Temple University Press.

Hill, Karl, Christina Lui, and J. David Hawkins. 2001. "Early Precursors of Gang Membership: A Study of Seattle Youth." *Juvenile Justice Bulletin* (December).

Washington, DC: U.S. Department of Justice, Office of Justice Programs, Office of Juvenile Justice and Delinquency Prevention.

Hipple, Natalie K., and Edmund F. McGarrell. 2008. "Comparing Police- and Civilian-Run Family Group Conferences." *Policing: An International Journal of Police Strategies & Management* 31(4): 553–77.

Hipple, Natalie K., Edmund F. McGarrell, Timothy S. Bynum, Heather A. Perez, Nicholas Corsaro, and Melissa Garmo. 2009. "Drug Market Intervention: Implementation Guide and Lessons Learned." Report to the U.S. Department of Justice, Bureau of Justice Assistance. School of Criminal Justice, Michigan State University, East Lansing, MI.

Hirschfield, Paul J. 2008. "Preparing for Prison? The Criminalization of School Discipline in the USA." *Theoretical Criminology* 12(1): 79–101.

Huizinga, David, and Cynthia Jakob-Chien. 1998. "The Contemporaneous Co-occurrence of Serious and Violent Juvenile Offending and Other Problem Behaviors." In *Serious & Violent Juvenile Offenders*, edited by Rolf Loeber and David P. Farrington. Thousand Oaks, CA: Sage.

Huizinga, David, Terence Thornberry, Kelly Knight, Peter Lovegrove, Rolf Loeber, Karl Hill, and David P. Farrington. 2007. "Disproportionate Minority Contact in the Juvenile Justice System: A Study of Differential Minority Arrest/Referral to Court in Three Cities." Report to the Office of Juvenile Justice and Delinquency Prevention. Washington, DC: U.S. Department of Justice.

Hurst, Yolander, James Frank, and Sandra L. Browning. 2000. "The Attitudes of Juveniles toward the Police: A Comparison of Black and White Youth." *Policing* 23(1): 37–53.

Johnson, Ida M. 1999. "School Violence: the Effectiveness of a School Resource Officer Program in a Southern City." *Journal of Criminal Justice* 27(2): 173–92.

Kennedy, David M. 2009. "Drugs, Race, and Common Ground: Reflections on the High Point Intervention." *NIJ Journal* 262: 12–17.

Kennedy, David M., Anthony A. Braga, Anne M. Piehl, and Elin J. Waring. 2001. *Reducing Gun Violence: The Boston Gun Project's Operation Ceasefire*. Washington, DC: U.S. Department of Justice, National Institute of Justice.

Klein, Malcolm, and Cheryl L. Maxson. 2006. *Street Gang Patterns and Policies*. New York: Oxford University Press.

Koper, Christopher S., and Evan Mayo-Wilson. 2006. "Police Crackdowns on Illegal Gun Carrying: A Systematic Review of Their Impact on Gun Crime." *Journal of Experimental Criminology* 2: 227–61.

Lauritsen, Janet. 2003. "How Families and Communities Influence Youth Victimization." *Juvenile Justice Bulletin* (November). Washington, DC: U.S. Department of Justice, Office of Justice Programs, Office of Juvenile Justice and Delinquency Prevention.

Law Enforcement Assistance Administration. 1976. *Two Hundred Years of American Criminal Justice*. U.S. Department of Justice. Washington, DC: U.S. Government Printing Office.

Leiber, Michael. 2002. "Disproportionate Minority Confinement (DMC) of Youth: An Analysis of State and Federal Efforts to Address the Issue." *Crime and Delinquency* 48(1): 3–45.

Leiber, Michael, Mahesh Nalla, and Margaret Farnworth. 1998. "Explaining Juveniles' Attitudes Toward the Police." *Justice Quarterly* 15(1): 151–74.

Loeber, Rolf, and Marc Le Blanc. 1990. "Toward a Developmental Criminology." *Crime and Justice: A Review of Research* 12: 375–473.

Lum, Cynthia. 2009. *Translating Police Research into Practice*. Ideas in American Policing Series. Washington, DC: Police Foundation.

Lundman, Richard J., Richard E. Sykes, and John P. Clark. 1978. "Police Control of Juveniles: A Replication." *Journal of Research in Crime and Delinquency* 15(1): 74–91.

Mayer, Matthew J., and Peter E. Leone. 1999. "A Structural Analysis of School Violence and Disruption: Implications for Creating Safer Schools." *Education and Treatment of Children* 22(3): 333–56.

McDevitt, Jack, and Jenn Panniello. 2005. "National Assessment of School Resource Officer Programs: Survey of Students in Three Large New SRO Programs." Report to the National Institute of Justice. Washington, DC: U.S. Department of Justice.

McGarrell, Edmund F. 1988. *Juvenile Correctional Reform: Two Decades of Policy and Procedural Change.* Albany, NY: State University of New York Press.

McGarrell, Edmund F. 2001. *Restorative Justice Conferences as an Early Response to Young Offenders.* Washington, DC: U.S. Department of Justice, Office of Juvenile Justice and Delinquency Prevention.

McGarrell, Edmund F., Steven Chermak, Alexander Weiss, and Jeremy Wilson. 2001. "Reducing Firearms Violence through Directed Police Patrol." *Criminology and Public Policy* 1(1): 119–48.

McGarrell, Edmund F., Steven Chermak, Jeremy M. Wilson, and Nicholas Corsaro. 2006. "Reducing Homicide through a 'Lever-Pulling' Strategy." *Justice Quarterly* 23: 214–31.

McGarrell, Edmund F., and Natalie K. Hipple. 2007. "Family Group Conferencing and Re-offending among First-Time Juvenile Offenders: The Indianapolis Experiment." *Justice Quarterly* 24(2): 221–46.

Mears, Daniel P. 2007. "Towards Rational and Evidence-based Crime Policy." *Journal of Criminal Justice* 35: 667–82.

Melde, Christopher, Terrance J. Taylor, Finn Esbensen. 2009. " 'I've Got Your Back': An Examination of the Protective Function of Gang Membership in Adolescence." *Criminology* 47(2): 565–94.

Mennel, Robert. 1973. *Thorns and Thistles: Juvenile Delinquents in the United States 1825–1940.* Hanover, NH: University of New Hampshire Press.

Mihalic, Sharon, Abigail Fagan, Katherine Irwin, Diane Ballard, and Delbert Elliott. 2004. *Blueprints for Violence Prevention.* Washington, DC: U.S. Department of Justice, Office of Justice Programs, Office of Juvenile Justice and Delinquency Prevention.

Moffitt, Terri E. 1993. "Adolescence-Limited and Life-Course Persistent Antisocial Behavior: A Developmental Taxonomy." *Psychological Review*, 100: 674–701.

Nagin, Daniel S., and David P. Farrington. 1992. "The Stability of Criminal Potential from Childhood to Adulthood." *Criminology* 30: 235–60.

Nagin, Daniel S., David P. Farrington, and Terri E. Moffitt. 1995. "Life-Course Trajectories of Different Types of Offenders." *Criminology* 33: 111–39.

National Center on Addiction and Substance Abuse. 2009. CASASTART. Accessed Feb. 23, 2011. http://casastart.org/.

National Research Council. 2004. *Fairness and Effectiveness in Policing: The Evidence.* Washington, DC: National Academies Press.

Office of Justice Programs. 2006. *Office of Justice Programs Strategic Plan: Fiscal years 2007–2012.* Washington, DC: U.S. Department of Justice, Office of Justice Programs.

Office of Juvenile Justice and Delinquency Prevention. 2009. OJJDP Model Programs Guide. Accessed Feb. 23, 2011. http://www2.dsgonline.com/mpg/.

Papachristos, Andrew, Tracey Meares, and Jeffrey Fagan. 2007. "Attention Felons: Evaluating Project Safe Neighborhoods in Chicago." *Journal of Empirical Legal Studies* 4: 223–72.

Piliavin, Irving, and Scott Briar. 1964. "Police Encounters with Juveniles." *American Journal of Sociology* 70(2): 206–14.

Piquero, Alex R., Jeffrey Fagan, Edward P. Mulvey, Laurence Steinberg, and Candace Odgers. 2005. "Developmental Trajectories of Legal Socialization Among Serious Adolescent Offenders." *Journal of Criminal Law and Criminology* 96(1): 267–98.

Platt, Anthony. 1969. *The Child Savers*. Chicago, IL: University of Chicago Press.

Portune, Robert. 1971. *Changing Adolescent Attitudes Toward Police*. Cincinnati, OH: Anderson.

President's Commission of Law Enforcement and Administration of Justice. 1967. *Task Force Report: The Police*. Washington, DC: U.S. Government Printing Office.

Presser, Lois, and Patricia Van Voorhis. 2002. "Values and Evaluation: Assessing Processes and Outcomes of Restorative Justice Programs." *Crime and Delinquency* 48(1): 162–88.

Puzzanchera, Charles. 2009. "Juvenile Arrests 2007." *Juvenile Justice Bulletin* (April). Washington, DC: U.S. Department of Justice, Office of Justice Programs, Office of Juvenile Justice and Delinquency Prevention.

Rodriguez, Nancy. 2005. "Restorative Justice, Communities, and Delinquency: Whom Do We Reintegrate?" *Criminology & Public Policy* 4(1): 103–30.

Rodriguez, Nancy. 2007. "Restorative Justice at Work: Examining the Impact of Restorative Justice Resolutions on Juvenile Recidivism." *Crime & Delinquency* 53(3): 355–79.

Rosenfeld, Richard, Timothy M. Bray, and Arlen Egley. 1999. "Facilitating Violence: A Comparison of Gang-Motivated, Gang-Affiliated, and Nongang Youth Homicides." *Journal of Quantitative Criminology* 15(4): 495–516.

Sampson, Robert J. 1986. "Effects of Socioeconomic Context on Official Reaction to Juvenile Delinquency." *American Sociological Review* 51: 876–85.

Sampson, Robert J., and Steven W. Raudenbush. 1999. "Systematic Social Observation of Public Spaces: A New Look at Disorder in Urban Neighborhoods." *American Journal of Sociology* 105: 603–51.

Schreck, Christopher J., J. Mitchell Miller, and Chris L. Gibson. 2003. "Trouble in the School Yard: A Study of the Risk Factors of Victimization at School." *Crime and Delinquency* 49: 460–84.

Shaw, James W. 1995. "Community Policing against Guns: Public Opinion of the Kansas City Gun Experiment." *Justice Quarterly* 12: 695–710.

Sherman, Lawrence W. 1993. "Defiance, Deterrence, and Irrelevance: A Theory of the Criminal Sanction." *Journal of Research in Crime and Delinquency* 30(4): 445–73.

Sherman, Lawrence W. 1997. "Policing for Crime Prevention." In *Preventing Crime: What Works, What Doesn't, What's Promising?*, edited by Lawrence W. Sherman, Denise Gottfredson, Doris Mackenzie, John Eck, Peter Reuter, and Shawn Bushway. Washington, DC: U.S. Department of Justice, National Institute of Justice.

Sherman, Lawrence W. 1998. *Evidence-Based Policing*. Ideas in American Policing Series. Washington, DC: Police Foundation.

Sherman, Lawrence W., and Dennis P. Rogan. 1995. "Effects of Gun Seizure on Gun Violence: 'Hot Spots' Patrol in Kansas City." *Justice Quarterly* 12(4): 673–93.

Sherman, Lawrence W., Heather Strang, and Daniel Woods. 2000. "Recidivism Patterns in the Canberra Reintegrative Shaming Experiment." Centre for Restorative Justice, RSSS, Canberra, Australia: Australian National University.

Silverman, Eli. 1999. *NYPD Battles Crime: Innovative Strategies in Policing*. Boston: Northeastern University Press.

Skogan, Wesley, and Susan Hartnett. 1997. *Community Policing, Chicago Style*. New York: Oxford University Press.

Smith, Douglas A. 1986. "The Neighborhood Context of Police Behavior." In *Communities and Crime*, edited by Albert J. Reiss and Michael Tonry. Chicago: University of Chicago Press.

Snyder, Howard N., and Melissa Sickmund. 2006. *Juvenile Offenders and Victims: 2006 National Report*. Washington, DC: U.S. Department of Justice, Office of Justice Programs, Office of Juvenile Justice and Delinquency Prevention.

Spergel, Irving. 1994. *Gang Suppression and Intervention: Problem and Response*. Washington, DC: Office of Juvenile Justice and Delinquency Prevention.

Spergel, Irving, and G. David Curry. 1993. "The National Youth Gang Survey: A Research and Development Process." In *Gang Intervention Handbook*, edited by A. P. Goldstein and C. R. Huff. Champaign, IL: Research Press.

Spergel, Irving, Susan F. Grossman, and Kwai M. Wa. 1998. *Evaluation of the Little Village Gang Violence Reduction Project: The First Three Years Executive Summary*. Washington, DC: U.S. Department of Justice, Bureau of Justice Assistance.

Spergel, Irving, and Kwai M. Wa. 2000. "Combating Gang Violence in Chicago's Little Village Neighborhood." *On Good Authority* 4(2): 1–4.

Terrill, William, and Michael D. Reisig. 2003. "Neighborhood Context and Police Use of Force." *Journal of Research in Crime and Delinquency* 40(3): 291–321.

Theriot, Matthew T. 2009. "School Resource Officers and the Criminalization of Student Behavior." *Journal of Criminal Justice* 37: 280–87.

Thornberry, Terence P., Marvin D. Krohn, Alan J. Lizotte, and Deborah Chard-Wierschem. 1993. "The Role of Juvenile Gangs in Facilitating Delinquent Behavior." *Journal of Research in Crime and Delinquency* 30(1): 55–87.

Thornberry, Terence P., Marvin D. Krohn, Alan J. Lizotte, Carolyn A. Smith, and Kimberly Tobin. 2003. *Gangs and Delinquency in Developmental Perspective*. Cambridge, U.K.: Cambridge University Press.

Tita, George, K. Jack Riley, Greg Ridgeway, Clifford Grammich, Allan F. Abrahamse, and Peter W. Greenwood. 2003. *Reducing Gun Violence: Results from an Intervention in East Los Angeles*. Santa Monica, CA: RAND Corporation.

Tonry, Michael. 1994. "Racial Politics, Racial Disparities and the War on Crime." *Crime and Delinquency* 40: 475–91.

Tyler, Tom R. 1990. *Why People Obey the Law*. New Haven, CT: Yale University Press.

Van Ness, Daniel, Allison Morris, and Gabrielle Maxwell. 2001. "Introducing Restorative Justice." In *Restorative Justice for Juveniles: Conferencing, Mediation and Circles*, edited by Allison Morris and Gabrielle Maxwell. Portland, OR: Hart Publishing.

Weisburd, David, and Anthony A. Braga. 2006. "Hot Spots Policing as a Model for Police Innovation." In *Police Innovation: Contrasting Perspectives*, edited by David Weisburd and Anthony A. Braga. New York: Cambridge University Press.

Wilson, James Q. 1968. *Varieties of Police Behavior*. Cambridge, MA: Harvard University Press.

Winfree, L. Thomas and Curt T. Griffiths. 1977. "Adolescents' Attitudes Toward the Police: A Survey of High School Students." In *Juvenile Delinquency: Little Brother Grows Up*, edited by Theodore N. Ferdinand. Beverly Hills, CA: Sage Publishing.

Wordes, Madeline, and Timothy S. Bynum. 1995. "Policing Juveniles: Is There Bias Against Youths of Color?" In *Minorities in Juvenile Justice*, edited by Kimberly Kempf-Leonard, Carl Pope, and William Feyerherm. Thousand Oaks, CA: Sage Publications.

Zimring, Franklin E. 1981. "Kids, Groups, and Crime: Some Implications of a Well-Known Secret." *Journal of Criminal Law and Criminology* 72: 867–902.

Zimring, Franklin E. 1998. *American Youth Violence*. New York: Oxford University Press.

CHAPTER 24

THE FRONT END OF THE JUVENILE COURT

INTAKE AND INFORMAL VERSUS FORMAL PROCESSING

DANIEL P. MEARS

I. INTRODUCTION

THE "front end" of juvenile justice refers to initial court decisions about how to process cases. When law enforcement agents, schools, or parents believe that youths have committed acts that violate the law, they refer them to juvenile court. There, the first contact typically occurs with an intake unit staffed by court personnel. These individuals, usually probation officers but not infrequently prosecutors, make decisions that may profoundly affect what happens to referred youths. Indeed, they have been aptly referred to as the "gatekeepers" of the juvenile court (Lindner 2008, p. 48). Certain decisions have been made, of course, prior to intake. For example, police officers will have decided whether the behavior of a specific youth in a particular context warranted referral to the court (Sanborn and Salerno 2005; Carrington and Schulenberg 2008; Piquero 2008). Frequently—in approximately

I thank Christina Mancini, Adam Friedman, Joshua Cochran, and Joshua Kuch for their assistance in collecting information and literature, and Jeff Butts, Buddy Howell, Melissa Sickmund, Howard Snyder, and especially Barry Feld and Donna Bishop, for their helpful insights and recommendations.

20% of juvenile arrests—police officers will make no referral to juvenile court (Snyder and Sickmund 2006, p. 104; see also Edmund McGarrell's Chapter 23 in this volume, "Policing Juveniles"). However, only when a youth enters an intake unit or its equivalent does the formal authority of the juvenile justice system begin.

Because they provide the first point of official contact with the court system and because of their responsibilities, the individuals—whether intake officers or prosecutors—who initially review a referral wield considerable influence over what happens to referred youths. For example, intake officers conduct assessments, help determine whether youths are detained, and make or influence decisions about whether youths are diverted from the juvenile justice system. More generally, they influence how various court actors view and handle a given case. Intake does not occur in a vacuum, though. It occurs in a context in which multiple court personnel and a tension between promoting punishment and rehabilitation exists. Not least, it occurs in a context in which caseload pressures, local culture, and relationships among courtroom actors may influence front-end processing decisions and, ultimately, the fate of referred youths.

The goal of this chapter is to describe front-end processing in the juvenile court, with a focus on intake, the historical context within which it emerged, and its consequences for youths and society. First, I describe what is meant by the "front end" of juvenile justice. Second, I discuss how the traditional mission of the juvenile court, which emphasizes punishment, treatment and services, and individualized attention, contributes to the goals and structure of front-end decision-making. Third, I describe two critical front-end activities: (a) screening and assessment and (b) informal and formal processing. In so doing, I discuss the roles of intake officers and prosecutors in these activities and how they comport with the juvenile court's traditional mission. I also discuss the fact that there has been a trend toward having prosecutors conduct initial screenings—that is, instead of referrals going first to an intake officer, they go to prosecutors for review. This change enhances prosecutorial control over processing and in turn reflects a toughening of juvenile justice by increasing the power of the executive branch of government and decreasing the power of the judiciary (Rubin 1980; Feld 2009). Fourth, I discuss the stakes involved in front-end decision-making, including the potential impacts on how cases are processed. Fifth, I discuss the implications of front-end processing for policy and practice. The chapter concludes with a call for better monitoring of and research on front-end juvenile court processing and its impacts on recidivism, juvenile crime rates, and other outcomes.

II. An Overview of Front-End Juvenile Court Processing

Juvenile justice is different than criminal justice, or at least in theory it is (see David Tanenhaus's Chapter 19, "The Elusive Juvenile Court: Its Origins, Practices, and Re-Inventions," in this volume; see also Bernard 1992; Feld 1999; Butts and Mears

2001; Scott and Steinberg 2008; Howell 2009). It operates according to a different set of laws, it uses different terminology, and, not least, it is guided by a different mandate. In particular, the juvenile court, as envisioned by its founders, is supposed to serve as the equivalent of a parent who looks out for the "best interests" of his or her children. That means that punishment should occur when rules are violated. But it also means that any necessary services and treatments should be applied to address a child's particular problems or needs. Put differently, the juvenile court operates with both a punishment and a social welfare orientation. Thus, for example, even if an adolescent commits a relatively trivial violation, the mandate of the juvenile court demands that an intervention should be undertaken if evidence of important problems, needs, or a risk of committing future crime exists. Intervention is especially indicated if the court determines that the family lacks the capacity to resolve the youth's problems (Sanborn and Salerno 2005).

This approach contrasts markedly with criminal justice, where the primary focus centers on the offense and on establishing guilt or innocence. The juvenile court, by contrast, focuses primarily on the offender and his or her needs (Feld 1999). That does not mean it achieves that mission. As some accounts suggest, the juvenile court may even operate in ways that run counter to its mission (see Feld and Bishop's Chapter 32, "Transfer of Juveniles to Criminal Court," in this volume). Regardless, the mission still stands as a central guiding feature of juvenile justice. The court is supposed to provide for the best interests of young offenders— "delinquents"—and to do so, where possible, through informal, case-by-case decision-making and with an emphasis on both punishment and rehabilitation.

The question thus arises: how exactly should juvenile justice systems operate to achieve this mission? Many considerations come into play. Ideally, for example, court personnel would work together to determine the sanctions, services, and treatment that provide for the best interests of youth referred to juvenile court. One critical part of an overall approach, however, has to involve front-end decision-making to determine which youth merit closer attention.

It is the nature of the juvenile court, as originally conceived, that each youth referred to it be carefully assessed and that less serious cases be informally handled rather than have a delinquency petition filed with the court. A petition in juvenile court is the legal equivalent to "a prosecutor's filing of a complaint or information, or a grand jury's indictment in the adult criminal process" (Feld 2009, p. 361). The informally processed cases might be diverted or receive a sanction (e.g., restitution or supervision). However, the youths in these instances would not have an official record of a formal adjudication. They also would be less likely to face the more serious sanctions that arise through formal proceedings. At the same time, the court would be freed to focus greater attention on more serious cases.

To achieve these goals, it only makes sense that a unit or division within the court be charged with the responsibility of determining how referred cases should be processed. Historically, parents and police could file delinquency petitions directly. Over time, however, that function fell to probation, in part to reduce the caseload of formally processed referrals (Rubin 1980). Today, it remains the case that probation officers typically conduct intake screenings (Feld 2009, p. 366; see also Snyder and Sickmund 2006).

The philosophy of the juvenile court, with its emphasis on informality and the social welfare of children, underlies the logic of having probation officers conduct intake proceedings. However, with the toughening of the juvenile justice system in recent decades, there has been a corresponding trend toward greater prosecutorial involvement in initial screenings. Petrucci and Rubin (2004, p. 264), for example, have argued that "prosecutors now dominate the intake-processing stage in many jurisdictions" (see also Lindner 2008, p. 51). Put differently, there appears to have been a shift of discretion from the judiciary to the executive (prosecutorial) branch of government in determining how referrals are handled (Feld 2009, pp. 368, 388).

The precise arrangements through which prosecutors may affect intake processing vary. Petrucci and Rubin (2004) have described five arrangements (see also Sanborn and Salerno 2005; Lindner 2008; Feld 2009). The first—and weakest—version involves prosecutorial review of cases for which intake officers have filed petitions. A second and somewhat stronger version delimits the intake officer's discretion and holds that the officer "cannot dismiss or divert a felony charge without prosecutor concurrence" (Feld 2009, p. 264). A third and even stronger version requires that prosecutors review all intake officer recommendations for filing *and* for not filing petitions. A fourth version bypasses intake officers altogether and requires that cases involving more serious charges by sent directly to the prosecutor for review "with the expectation of a formal petition" (Feld 2009, p. 204). In such cases, the prosecutors may, if they deem it appropriate, send a case to intake for informal processing. Finally, the strongest version requires that "all police referrals bypass intake and go directly to a prosecutor...who exclusively determines whether to prepare a petition for the court" (Feld 2009, p. 204).

No national inventory exists to document which arrangement is most common or how intake practices actually work in practice (see, however, Sanborn and Salerno 2005; Griffin and King 2009; see also Willison et al. 2009). For example, few studies have examined whether greater prosecutorial involvement at intake changes how youth are processed. Rubin's (1980) study is one exception—he found that prosecutors almost invariably followed the recommendation of intake officers concerning recommendations to file delinquency petitions. However, in some places, prosecutors agreed less often with the recommendations. To illustrate, in Fort Lauderdale, Florida, prosecutors approved petitions in only 54% of the cases where intake officers recommended that a petition be filed. The study suggests that prosecutors may view cases in much the same way that intake officers do, but also that they may disagree. The precise level of overlap or disagreement likely will vary from place to place, depending on local court cultures and how intake officers adapt their processing to accord with their views of how prosecutors or the courts will act (Needleman 1981; Petrucci and Rubin 2004; Feld 2009).

Figure 24.1—Front-End Processing in the Juvenile Justice System—depicts a simplified diagram of the front-end processing of juvenile referrals. As the figure shows and as the discussion above highlights, initial intake decisions may be

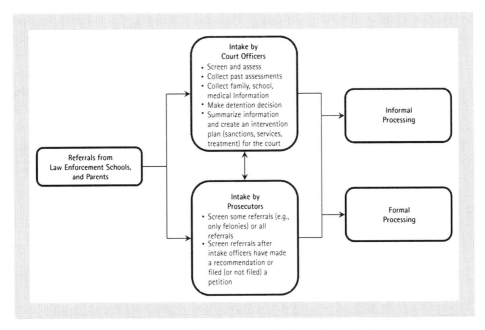

Figure 24.1. Front-End Processing in the Juvenile Justice System.

undertaken by court officers or by prosecutors. Prosecutors, for example, may review all police referrals. In some places, however, they may only review decisions intake officers have made to file petitions, or, in other places, they may review both filed and non-filed referrals. The primary focus for prosecutors consists of determining the legal sufficiency of a case and, in turn, whether to proceed informally or formally.

Intake officers focus, too, on legal sufficiency (Snyder and Sickmund 2006, p. 104). However, their mandate generally is broader than that of prosecutors. For example, they must determine whether a youth is a risk to himself or to others and should be detained, and, if detention occurs, what treatment or services may be needed (Feld 2009, p. 416). In addition, they must make recommendations to the court about how a case should be handled (e.g., formally or informally). In many instances, the officers may have the authority to divert a case or to informally process it themselves (Lindner 2008).

To assist in making these decisions, intake officers collect information through a screening and assessment process that allows them to identify possible areas of concern, such as mental health or physical problems, prior contact with the justice system, family context, behavioral or other problems at school, and the like. This process typically provides intake officers with discretion in how much weight they give to specific dimensions, such as the age or perceived maturity of the youth, the youth's attitude, the possibility that the youth's behavior stemmed from a temporary problem at home, and the like (Linder 2008; Feld 2009). As the discussion below highlights, such discretion can enable them to greatly affect what will happen to youth.

Given an initial determination about the legal sufficiency of a case and whether detention is warranted, the case can go in one of two directions—it can be informally processed or formally processed. Intake officers typically determine or drive this decision (Feld 2009, p. 366), but, again, prosecutors increasingly have become involved in such decisions. If a case is informally processed, a critical decision is whether the case should be dismissed or diverted from the formal purview of the juvenile justice system (Roberts 2004). If a case is formally processed—for example, if the intake officer decides to file a petition with the court—a prosecutor and a juvenile court judge become the central actors in determining how the case will proceed.

III. Front-End Processing and the Juvenile Court's Mission

Front-end processing in the juvenile court is complicated by the tension that derives from the court's dual emphasis on punishment and social welfare when determining the "best interests" of youth (Feld 1999; Scott and Steinberg 2008; Howell 2009). By design, the court should act as the equivalent of a parent who wants not only to punish his or her child when wrongs occur but also to ensure that the child's problems and needs are adequately addressed. Indeed, the doctrine of *parens patriae* ("the state as parent") is frequently used to characterize the philosophical orientation of juvenile justice (Feld and Schaefer 2010). Accordingly, the scope of what the court considers to be relevant is broad—it wants information not only about possible guilt but also about the services that the youth may need to have a better chance at leading a successful, prosocial life. This scope necessitates creating a unit or stage of processing at intake that allows for a crime-focused and a welfare-focused assessment (Pabon 1978; Lindner 2008).

Much has been written about the traditional mission of the juvenile court. Some scholars have argued that it is critically flawed (e.g., Feld 1999). How, for example, can one institution adequately focus both on punishment and the best interests of a child? Moreover, how would we know when an appropriate balance of these two outcomes occurred? Reasonable people will and do disagree about such matters. It thus can be expected that within and across juvenile courts, variation exists in the balance that is achieved, what sometimes has been referred to as "justice by geography" (Feld 1999; Feld and Schaefer 2010). Some juvenile courts may be more "child-friendly" than others and so quicker to divert youth, deemphasize punishment, and provide a range of specialized services and treatments. Others may be tougher and thus quicker to punish and to minimize rehabilitative services (see, e.g., Mears and Field 2000).

This tension pervades juvenile justice and extends to the earliest stages of processing. It is evident, for example, in the administration of front-end processing, with probation officers conducting initial intake proceedings in some places and prosecutors doing it in others. Probation officers are typically charged with not only supervising youth but also helping them to obtain needed assistance. Accordingly, they may have more of a social welfare orientation than prosecutors, who focus primarily on establishing guilt and obtaining punishments. Juvenile court prosecutors do not differ from criminal court prosecutors in this respect, although they may be more likely to embrace the traditional philosophy espoused by the founders of the juvenile court.

The relevance of these observations lies in the fact that the traditional mission of the juvenile court, and the tension inherent to it, provides the context for understanding the structure of front-end processing, the reason intake officers traditionally have been afforded considerable discretion in how cases are handled, and the implications of allowing prosecutors to have more control over front-end decisions. For example, given the goal of providing for the best interests of youths, it makes sense that probation officers, with their social worker emphasis, rather than a prosecutor, might be responsible for initially assessing a youth. It makes sense, too, that probation officers would be allowed to exercise discretion concerning the dismissal, diversion, and informal processing of delinquency referrals—among other things, it affords them the flexibility to consider the totality of a youth's context and to devise a course of action that seems best for a particular youth. That is not to say that this arrangement is best. It may be the case, for example, that probation officers give insufficient weight to legal factors. Prosecutors thus would seem to be logical candidates for conducting intake. However, such an arrangement thereby puts the juvenile court a step closer to becoming a criminal court, which clearly runs counter to the vision that its founders espoused (Rubin 1980; Feld 2009).

The traditional mission of the juvenile court is relevant to a discussion of front-end decision-making for another reason—it highlights that multiple outcomes should be considered when assessing this decision-making. To illustrate, the focus on the "best interests" of youths clearly implies that reduced recidivism is not the only measure of success. Effective front-end decisions ideally should ensure that physical and mental health needs are identified and treated and that youths learn effective ways for negotiating difficult family, school, or community environments. They should ensure that an appropriate balance of punishment and treatment occur (Guarino-Ghezzi and Loughran 2004). And, not least, they should ensure that cases are diverted or dismissed when appropriate. Few juvenile justice policy or program evaluations examine these decisions and outcomes (Mears and Butts 2008). Nonetheless, as will be discussed in the final section of this chapter, they are central to evaluating the effectiveness of front-end processing. Indeed, the importance of diversion, achieving a balance between punishment and treatment, and improving multiple life domains among youths constitute the very reason for having a separate system of justice for young people (Roman and Butts 2005).

IV. Two Critical Features of Front-End Processing

A. Screening and Assessment

1. *Triage, Legal Decisions, and the Mission of the Juvenile Court*

Any type of front-end decision-making typically involves a triage approach, much as one might use in a hospital emergency room. In emergencies, cases receive a rapid assessment to determine if they require attention or can be best managed through discharge or diversion to some other care. Emergency room cases that require intensive attention get prioritized over others.

Similarly, in juvenile court, intake typically involves making a rapid assessment about the kind of attention a case merits. If youths present a danger to themselves or others, they are immediately detained pending further assessment. Regardless of whether youths are detained, decisions must be made about how to proceed. For example, some nondetained cases may merit further assessment, others may be readily dispensed with informally, and still others may warrant transfer to adult court.

Intake begins with an initial screening, which may or may not include use of a screening instrument (Mears and Kelly 1999). When prosecutors receive referrals, they focus primarily on the legal sufficiency of the case. Intake officers are, of course, concerned with assessing the legal sufficiency of a case, but they typically will take a broader approach to collecting information and to assessing the case. For example, the intake officer usually will conduct a preliminary investigation of the incident and available records, including information provided by the referring agent (e.g., police or parents), and hold a conference with the child and his or her parents (Sanborn and Salerno 2005). The officer will attempt to answer a range of questions. Has an offense occurred? What specific risks does the youth pose? What needs may merit attention? What is the family context? Can the family afford certain services?

Answering such questions can be difficult. Consider first the question of whether an offense has occurred. That is fundamentally a legal question. Imagine a situation in which the police say that you assaulted someone at a bar. Your view is that you sidestepped someone who then tripped and fell. The police arrest you for "simple assault" and transfer you to the station. Then a probation officer interviews you and determines that your case merits formal processing by the court, which in turn means that a prosecutor will investigate your case. The probation officer has no legal training and yet is deciding whether your case will be officially processed. Consider a similar situation: you are assaulted by a 15-year-old and you believe it is severe. However, a probation officer determines that really it was a misdemeanor offense and so chooses to dismiss or divert the case rather than file a delinquency petition with the court.

The juvenile court traditionally has proceeded as if this situation—one where officers of the court render a legal assessments or decisions even though they lack legal training—were not a problem. Yet clearly it would be a problem in adult court. Few of us would want an official who is untrained in the law determining whether we committed a crime. Perhaps more important, prosecutors would not stand for it. So why, then, have they allowed it in juvenile court? Historically, prosecutors focused little attention on juvenile offenders. Juvenile cases were viewed as low in prestige relative to more serious offenses committed by adults. In recent decades, however, juvenile crime has garnered greater attention from the public and policy makers. As a result, prosecutors have begun to take greater interest in what happens to juvenile offenders (Petrucci and Rubin 2004; Sanborn and Salerno 2005; Lindner 2008).

That shift has profound implications for front-end decision-making. A prosecutor is better positioned than a probation officer to determine the legal sufficiency of a case (Rubin 1980). However, he or she arguably is ill-equipped, and certainly ill-positioned, to assess a youth's home or school environment, drug or mental health needs, or risk not only for criminal behavior but also for abuse, victimization, drug addiction, or school drop-out. Probation officers, by contrast, are much better equipped and positioned to render such an assessment because the mandate and philosophy of juvenile probation typically centers around supervising and coordinating care for young offenders. Even so, the dilemma remains: legal determinations must be made, but so, too, must social welfare determinations concerning the best interests of referred youths. Regardless, any front-end decision-making involves both legal and social welfare determinations, and these require that intake officers, whether in consultation with prosecutors or not, screen and assess referred youths to determine how to proceed.

2. The Screening and Assessment Process

So how does screening and assessment unfold? It depends. Until recently, it occurred informally. That is, an intake officer would exercise his or her professional judgment as to whether a case merited attention by the court, detention pending a detention hearing or further processing, diversion, or dismissal. (Detention hearings typically must occur within twenty-four to seventy-two hours of a referral. Petrucci and Rubin 2004, p. 262.) "The intake officer," as Krisberg and Austin (1993, p. 96) have observed, "may decide that the allegations are without basis or that the case may be difficult to substantiate, and suggest that the juvenile be informally processed without further court intervention." Certain cases, such as those involving felonies, might make the screening process simple. Aggravated assault? File a petition. Truancy? Perhaps warn the youth that he faces considerable trouble if he continues down an errant path? Repeat offenders would likely be among the easiest calls. Screeners would probably file a petition. Research suggests that, as with criminal justice processing, where a prior record increases the likelihood of receiving a tougher sanction (Wang and Mears 2009), a prior record in juvenile court—more so than other factors—typically leads to formal processing (Henretta, Frazier, and Bishop 1986; Lee 1995; cf. Thornberry and Christenson 1984). Why is this? Intake officers and prosecutors may view youths who have had contact with the juvenile justice system as less-than-ideal candidates for more rehabilitative-focused interventions and sanctioning.

Observe here that "gray area" cases would likely garner a less consistent response within or across jurisdictions, leading in turn to "justice by geography." For example, what one person views as a serious offense might be viewed by another as relatively trivial. In one county, the local court culture may view marijuana use as meriting a formal and serious sanction, while in another county such an offense may be viewed as inconsequential (Mears 1998). The result? The initial decisions made by individual intake officers and by different intake units can vary dramatically. And, of course, the fact that in some places prosecutors are more involved in or actually conduct the initial intake screening creates even more variability in how referrals are handled.

In recent years, considerable attention has been given to formalizing the intake process. Instead of relying solely on professional judgment, intake officers frequently are required to rely on a list of explicitly identified criteria as well on the results of screening and assessment instruments. For example, Sanborn and Salerno (2005, p. 188) list twelve general categories—including the youth's age, maturity, and culpability; the nature and circumstances of the offense; the youth's prior record; the likelihood that the youth will cooperate with or be successful in a diversion program; the youth's problems at school or home; and the attitude of the youth and his or her parents, to name but a few—that intake officers are supposed to consider in some jurisdictions.

The basic idea is that such lists or instruments result in more consistent and appropriate decisions (Mears 2004). Clearly, however, considerable leeway exists in how much weight intake officers, as well as prosecutors, give specific criteria in certain contexts. An explicit set of considerations or instrument-created facts thus may not create more consistency. In addition, although consistency sounds like a good idea, it runs counter to the notion of individualized treatment that the juvenile court's founders advocated and to the view that local culture should influence the handling of cases. At the same time, inconsistency, or "justice by geography," runs counter to notions of fair treatment. Why should a youth's processing depend largely on where he or she lives? It also runs counter to the national trend in juvenile and criminal justice to reduce inconsistency in sentencing (Mears 2002). For these and other reasons, the use of formal risk and needs assessment has emerged as one of the most prominent trends in juvenile justice.

A good screening instrument should help us to flag cases that merit greater attention and to dismiss or divert those that do not. For example, many youths referred to juvenile court may suffer from some type of a mental disorder or a disability of some kind (Mears and Aron 2003). To illustrate, estimates typically indicate that the prevalence of mental disorders and learning disabilities is at least two to three times greater among youths in the juvenile justice system than with youth in the general population (Mears and Aron 2003, p. 28; Grisso 2004, p. 13). Although no national census exists of the screening instruments used in juvenile justice systems, two increasingly used instruments include the Brief Symptom Inventory (BSI) and the Massachusetts Youth Screening Instrument (MAYSI) (Grisso 2004, p. 60).

While a good screening instrument should raise flags about potential problems, a good assessment instrument should provide a more accurate and detailed description of a youth's conditions or problems. For example, a better, more valid mental health assessment would be one that identified whether a youth actually has a mental illness, learning disability, drug, or other problem (Mears 2004). Because assessments take time and thus require resources, an effective screening stage is paramount. Indeed, if screening procedures fail to flag cases that potentially merit greater attention, even the best assessment instruments will be of little use.

When conducting a screening or assessment, intake officers use questionnaires to collect information about a range of dimensions, including a youth's past criminal history, education, home environment, and so on. They include information obtained from the youth and also from schools, juvenile justice system records, parents, and other sources. Ultimately, a screening instrument provides a recommendation about dismissing the case, diverting it, and the need for further assessment; it also may be used to inform decisions about detention and whether to file a delinquency or waiver petition with the court. By contrast, an assessment instrument provides a preliminary diagnosis and information about what type of action, such as crisis intervention, drug or mental health treatment, and/or family counseling, may be appropriate or needed. These questionnaires use items similar to those found in instruments that have been created for determining the level of supervision that youth should receive. The focus differs in that the aim is to inform decisions prior to adjudication (i.e., the juvenile court equivalent of conviction). However, because informal processing constitutes a central feature of juvenile court, screening and assessment instruments generate information that can and does contribute to decisions by intake units about sanctions, treatments, and services that youths should receive.

3. Screening and Assessment: Themes from the Literature

A large literature on risk and needs assessment exists, and so here I will emphasize a few key themes. First, in general, risk and needs instruments provide more consistent and more accurate assessments about the risk of offending, the needs or problems that youth may have, and the types and levels of punishment and treatment that may be most effective with specific types of offenders (Cullen and Gendreau 2000; Loeber and Farrington 2001; Griffin and Torbet 2002; Howell 2009). They also can aid in making determinations relevant to legal proceedings. For example, a mental health assessment might identify that a youth lacked the competency or capacity to appreciate the nature of court proceedings and so should not be allowed to waive his right to legal counsel (Grisso 2004).

Second, the validity of many instruments varies greatly and in many instances is quite limited in predicting the likelihood of general offending or of specific types of offending, in identifying competency or specific drug or mental health problems or disabilities, or in making valid predictions or diagnoses for different groups or populations (e.g., young/old, males/females, whites/blacks) (Grisso 2004, 2008; Sanborn and Salerno 2005; Borum 2006; Olver, Stockdale, and Wormith 2009). Numerous drug assessment instruments exist, for example, and yet many have not been evaluated (Mears 2004). Among those that have been evaluated, the degree of validity can depend on the dimension of concern. For example, some instruments generate many false positives—that is, they indicate that a youth has a drug problem when really he or she does not. Other instruments may generate many false negatives—that is, they classify a youth as not having a drug problem when really the youth does. Few instruments fare well on both of these dimensions or others. Some instruments may have not been normed or validated for different groups (e.g., juveniles versus adults, males versus females, different racial or ethnic groups). Many others require a considerable investment of time and resources. They may require, for example, that a trained professional administer them. As a result, if nonprofessionals administer the instruments, the resulting information may be of questionable validity or usefulness. The validity of an instrument matters because it can have profound ripple effects on decision-making. For example, if an instrument is overly conservative about assessing risk, it can result in overuse of detention. Conversely, if it is too conservative, it can result in under-use of it.

Third, most front-end decision-making in juvenile court still involves professional judgment alone: "The reality is that formal decision-making tools such as risk assessment and need assessment instruments are not widely used in juvenile justice" (Howell 2009, p. 229; see also Towberman 2002). Even when instruments are used, the information they provide may be problematic or used inappropriately (Janku and Yan 2009). For example, instruments may not be administered or scored correctly and staff may misinterpret results (Winters 1999). Also, intake officers may follow the results of instruments alone rather than exercise professional judgment, even though the recommended practice typically is to rely on both (Mears 2004).

Fourth, although considerable attention has been given to developing better screening and assessment instruments, we know little about the actual use of such instruments in day-to-day practice (Towberman 1992; Mears and Kelly 1999; Grisso 2004; Janku and Yan 2009). Many jurisdictions lack the capacity or resources to use some instruments. Others may use instruments but ignore the resulting information. In addition, the information in the instruments may be inaccurate. For example, an intake officer may be required to score a child's family relationships on a scale of 1 (very stable) to 4 (highly unstable) and provide a score based on a hunch or the statement of a referred youth, both of which may be wrong. Still other jurisdictions may misuse the information (Mears and Kelly 1999). Prosecutors, for example, may be allowed to use drug treatment assessments to inform their decisions about whether to pursue formal legal processing. How prevalent these different uses and problems are remains unknown.

Screening and assessment occurs, whether it is structured or formalized through the use of instruments. But the actual practices—the laws, procedures, protocols, and instruments—vary greatly in their details and how they are implemented. Such variation in turn lays the groundwork for considerable differences in how cases are handled by different officers and intake units, and, in turn, how cases are handled within and across jurisdictions (Pabon 1978; Sanborn and Salerno 2005). It also perforce leads to differences in how closely decision-making corresponds to the traditional mission of the juvenile court, including the provision of individualized, case-by-case decision-making that considers a youth's social context and best interests. Consider, for example, that the increased use of screening and assessment instruments fits neatly with an increased use of sentencing guideline approaches to juvenile sanctioning, a strategy that more closely corresponds to the mission of the criminal justice system rather than that of the juvenile justice system (Mears 2002). Of course, the uses to which information from such instruments are put may well accord with the traditional mission of juvenile justice, but it just as easily could be used in other ways. To illustrate, if jurisdictions follow a rote, follow-the-book approach to using screening and assessment instruments, they would seem necessarily to compromise the logic of providing individualized, case-by-case attention to each referred youth.

B. Informal versus Formal Processing

The juvenile court was founded on informality; formal, adversarial proceedings were anathema. Juvenile court actors were to decide, based on discussions rather than a rigid adherence to law or a battle over determining guilt or innocence, what would best advance the well-being of youths. Over time, proceedings became more formalized, with juvenile probation departments conducting intakes and thus making critical decisions about how referred youths were processed. Traditionally, for example, intake officers could file a delinquency petition with the court without consulting a prosecutor. As emphasized above, that approach is widely used today, but prosecutors increasingly play a role in the intake process.

Informal processing—which occurs when a delinquency petition is not filed with the court or when, as occurs in some jurisdictions, a petition is withdrawn (Sanborn and Salerno 2005)—remains a central feature of the juvenile court. It allows cases that may not merit intensive or official attention from the court to be diverted or to receive services, treatment, or sanctions but without a formal record being created. In so doing, it provides a potentially more effective response for juveniles while facilitating a more efficient case flow for the juvenile court.

Formal processing is also central to how delinquency referrals are handled. It constitutes the more legal approach to case processing, one that results in the creation of an official record and that allows for youths to be placed in secure confinement, the equivalent of juvenile prisons. It also allows for a range of other sanctions, including fines, community service, probation, and other sanctions that can occur through informal processing.

Probation officers hold a pivotal role in whether cases proceed informally or formally. Indeed, they frequently determine which route a case will take. Typically, for example, they can (1) file a petition with the court; (2) adjust a case (i.e., resolve it without filing a delinquency petition) and in so doing impose some type of informal disposition (e.g., dismissal, warning, counseling, probation) or divert the case through referral to another agency or community service; or (3) recommend to prosecutors and the court that a petition be filed (Lindner 2008, p. 48; Feld 2009, p. 361). These officers exercise considerable influence over informally processed cases and the services, treatment, and sanctions youth receive who are handled in this manner; they also can influence court decisions about the formal processing of cases. The sum result is that intake officers wield a great influence over decision-making in and for the court.

Consider, for example, the processing of youth referrals. As shown in Figure 24.2, during much of the 1990s, over half of all cases referred to juvenile court were processed informally, meaning that no delinquency petition was filed with the court. Corresponding with a general trend toward more criminal-like processing, the percentage of cases informally processed declined in the 1990s and, since then, has hovered at around 43 to 44%. Despite the decline, a large number of referred youths are informally processed annually. In 2005, for example, almost 750,000 cases were processed this way, as compared to the approximately 950,000 who were formally processed (Puzzanchera and Kang 2008).

Figure 24.2—Informally Processed Juvenile Court Referrals as Percentage of Total Referrals, 1985–2005—highlights that informal processing is not restricted to property crime. Certainly, a greater percentage of property crime referrals than

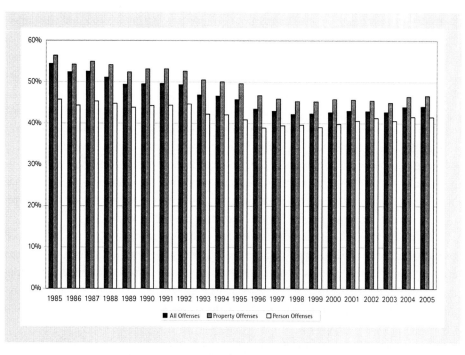

Figure 24.2. Puzzanchera and Kang (2008).

person crime referrals are informally processed. Even so, the difference is small and has become smaller in the last decade. Observe, for example, the 10 percentage point difference in the rates of informal processing of property and person offenses in 1985 (56% and 46%, respectively), compared with the only 5 percentage point difference in 2005 (47% and 42%, respectively).

Informal processing varies greatly by age, sex, and race. For example, youths who are 15 or younger, female, or white are more likely to be informally processed (Puzzanchera and Sickmund 2008, pp. 38–39). Racial differences in processing are especially pronounced for drug offenses. Nationally, 29% of black juveniles referred for drug crimes were informally processed, compared with 52% of white juveniles (p. 39). Put differently, black youth faced a far greater likelihood of being formally processed for such crimes.

Racial disparities bear special mention both because of the widespread concern about such disparities and because of research that suggests that front-end decision-making may contribute greatly to such disparities. Some studies, for example, have found that, even after controlling for crime rates, police may be "more likely to initiate contacts with suspects in racially mixed and primarily African American neighborhoods" (Bishop 2005, p. 40). As Bishop (2005, p. 39) has emphasized, differences in how white and black youth are processed may be "subsumed under the cover of offense-related considerations whose legitimacy is unlikely to be challenged" (p. 39), thereby masking the possibility that the police are biased (cf. Lauritsen 2005, p. 100).

Regardless of whether police bias occurs, racial disparities in arrests exist that then may be amplified during intake. Studies show, for example, that African American and Hispanic youth are less likely to be diverted and more likely to be referred for formal processing as compared with white youth (Bishop 2005, p. 48). Such differences may stem from different causes, such as differences in offending or perceptions that court workers have about minority youth. For example, intake officers may be more likely to hold negative views of minority youth and the ability of the parents of such youth to provide adequate supervision, and they may also believe that minority youth will be more likely to offend in the future (p. 50). It also is possible that court workers perceive formal processing as a means by which to provide needed services and treatment for minority youth, whose parents may be less likely to afford them (p. 50). In short, considerable room exists for front-end decision-making, especially arrest and intake decisions, to contribute to racial disparities in the processing of young people. (See Donna Bishop and Michael Lieber's Chapter 20, "Racial and Ethnic Differences in Delinquency and Justice System Responses," in this volume for a more general discussion of race and sanctioning.)

The relevance of informal processing in juvenile court is not just that it occurs, but also that it has implications for the dispositions youth experience. Turning to Figure 24.3—Disposition of Informally Processed Juvenile Court Referrals, 1985–2005—we can see that half or fewer of all informally processed cases are dismissed. From 1985 to 2005, the percentage declined from 49% to 40%, reflecting a general toughening of the court in its response to juvenile

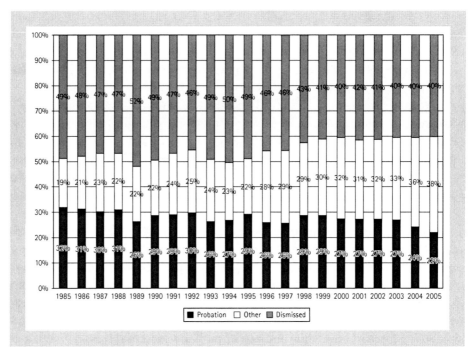

Figure 24.3. Disposition of Informally Processed Juvenile Court Referrals, 1985–2005.
Source: Puzzanchera and Kang (2008)

crime. Even so, the magnitude of the dismissals bears emphasizing—in 2005, over 301,000 informally processed referrals were dismissed. Observe here that a dismissal can be undertaken entirely or largely at the discretion of an intake officer, thus underscoring the considerable influence that intake officers have for how youthful offenders are handled.

Of course, informal processing can result in dispositions other than dismissal. In these cases, "the juvenile *voluntarily agrees* to serve a period of informal probation, to pay victim restitution, to pay a fine, to perform community service, or to submit to some other sanction" (Snyder 1996, p. 57, emphasis in original). Such sanctions carry the weight of the law. The main difference, as compared with a formal sanction, is that successful completion of an informal sanction results in the case being dismissed. If, however, the youth "fails to abide by the agreement, the case can then be reassessed and, in most instances, handled formally" (Snyder 1996, p. 57).

As can be seen in the figure, many informally processed youth receive probation or some other sanction. In 2005, 22% of such youths were placed on probation and 38% were given some other sanction. As can also be seen in the figure, the trend in recent decades has been toward fewer dispositions involving probation and more that involve other sanctions. In 1985, only 19% of informally processed referrals (122,900 cases) received such a sanction. By 2005, that percentage doubled to 38% (283,400), an increase that stemmed from decreases in the percentages of cases dismissed or receiving probation.

Informal processing via intake is not the only way to generate an informal sanction. An alternative route is via formal processing. In these cases, formally processed youths are given the option of receiving an informal sanction. If youths agree to this option, they are not adjudicated delinquent and must successfully complete the conditions of the sanction. Failure to comply with the agreement can result in being adjudicated delinquent, thereby generating an official record of delinquency and creating the possibility of a more severe sanction.

Table 24.1 depicts the processing outcomes for informally and formally processed youths in 2005. It differentiates between formally processed youths who were not adjudicated delinquent and those who were. In addition, it excludes waived cases (there were 6,900 such cases). The table highlights that only formally processed youth who are adjudicated delinquent typically receive placement in secure confinement. It also shows that intake-driven informal processing accounted for 30% of all probation dispositions nationally and 62% of all "other" sanctions (not counting placements). Formally processed, nonadjudicated youths account for a relatively small, but nonetheless nontrivial, percentage of all probation dispositions (3%) and "other" dispositions (13%).

Table 24.1. Dispositions Resulting from Informal versus Formal Processing, 2005

	Number	Percentage
Total Placements		
Informally Processed (Intake)	0	0
Formally Processed, Nonadjudicated	0	0
Formally Processed, Adjudicated	140,100	100
Total Probation Dispositions		
Informally Processed (Intake)	164,000	30
Formally Processed, Nonadjudicated	19,100	3
Formally Processed, Adjudicated	373,400	67
Total "Other" Dispositions		
Informally Processed (Intake)	283,400	62
Formally Processed, Nonadjudicated	60,900	13
Formally Processed, Adjudicated	110,400	24
Total Dismissals		
Informally Processed (Intake)	301,200	56
Formally Processed, Nonadjudicated	0	0
Formally Processed, Adjudicated	238,500	44
Total	1,691,000	

Source: Puzzanchera and Sickmund (2008, p. 58).

Note: Excludes 6,900 cases waived to adult court. Percentages may not add to 100 due to rounding.

V. The Potential Impacts of Front-End Decision-Making

As the preceding discussion highlights, front-end decision-making is central to the processing of delinquency referrals and thus can have profound impacts on court operations and how youths are handled. Following are a brief description of some of these impacts.

First, as the national statistics indicate, informal processing allows for efficient caseload management in the juvenile justice system. Without such processing, much greater involvement of prosecutors and the courts would be required.

Second, the critical role of informal processing places probation officers in a unique position, one in which they essentially serve as prosecutor and judge as well as social worker (Krisberg and Austin 1993, p. 96; see also Needleman 1981). Of course, the severity of certain cases circumscribes this power. Most felonies, for example, will be examined by prosecutors; and in increasingly more jurisdictions, prosecutors have assumed a greater role at intake. Even so, intake officers on the whole have extraordinary discretion in whether to detain or divert youths, proceeding with informal processing and making recommendations to prosecutors and judges about formal processing, including waiver to adult court (Snyder and Sickmund 2006, p. 105).

This discretion and the authority that comes with it should not be underestimated (Sanborn and Salerno 2005). Needleman's (1981) study of intake screening—one of the few in-depth treatments of the topic—found that intake workers viewed intake as "the most important part of the whole system" (p. 251) and that they took special pride in their prominent role in handling all types of cases, even serious ones, and in "saving" children. For example, intake workers she interviewed reported using a variety of tactics to convince parents to proceed with informal rather than formal processing as well as to convince the court to sanction a youth. To illustrate, they might "tailor the contents of the petition so that the court outcome will correspond to what they feel the child needs" (p. 257). The workers might also use coded language in the petition to let judges know that a case probably should be diverted. Intake workers may use these and many other approaches to prompt parents and court actors to take specific actions, including dismissal, diversion, detention, formal processing, and imposition of specific sanctions (see also Curtis and Reese 1994). The result may be better decisions than otherwise might occur. But it may be that inappropriate, unfair, and inconsistent decisions instead result (Linder 2008, p. 49).

In short, intake officers guide, and sometimes dictate, both the informal and formal processing of many youths. Consider, for example, that they sometimes serve as the officers who prepare disposition plans for the court. In these cases, the decisions officers make at intake may drive not only whether a case is informally or formally processed but also, if formally processed, the final disposition. That is because judges frequently must rely heavily on intake officers to efficiently manage their caseloads and so take seriously the officers' recommendations.

Third, informal dispositions are not necessarily or likely trivial. Dismissing cases where youths have substantial problems creates the risk of allowing the youths to engage in more serious offending or of allowing serious emotional problems to go unaddressed. The decision to detain a youth can greatly increase the likelihood that a youth will be adjudicated delinquent and receive a more serious disposition. Referrals to other agencies expose youths to the control and authority of such agencies. Not least, informal sanctions can consist of far more than a "slap on the wrist." Probation, for example, is sometimes viewed by youths and their defense counsel as a more serious disposition than short-term placement in secure confinement (Mears 1998; see also Petersilia 1997). It is true that informal probation may differ from formal probation—for example, it may entail less intense supervision or fewer conditions, but that is not necessarily true. For example, informal probation can involve supervision that "may be just as stringent as the conditions of formal probation" and can range "from a few months to several years" (Krisberg and Austin 1993, p. 98). Ultimately, then, the only difference between many informal and formal sanctions is that completion of the terms of an informal sanction can eliminate any official record of a formal court intervention.

Fourth, although informal dispositions sometimes are characterized as progressive because they offer youths a chance at avoiding an official record, they expose youths to the prospect of more serious sanctioning. Why? If a youth fails to successfully comply with the conditions of probation, they then face a greater likelihood that they will be adjudicated delinquent. One reason is that "the youth must *admit* that he or she committed the [delinquent] act before informal processing is permitted" (Snyder 1996, p. 57, emphasis added). That holds for intake-driven and prosecutor-driven informal sanctions. Thus, if youths then fail, for whatever reason, to complete the terms of the informal sanction, they essentially guarantee that a successful adjudication will follow. By contrast, had they not provided an admission of guilt, prosecutors might have faced a more difficult challenge in adjudicating the youths as delinquent.

This last point bears elaboration. If a prosecutor offers an informal sanction, he or she may do so as part of a plea bargaining negotiation (see Krisberg and Austin 1993, p. 100; see also Sanborn 1992, 1993, 1994; Mears 1998). More than likely, then, there are cases where, at least some of the time, prosecutors would fail to adjudicate a youth as delinquent if the youth challenged the case. Such cases then would be dismissed. By admitting guilt and accepting an informal sanction, youths essentially close off any possibility of a dismissal. In addition, they create a situation where their case may appear worse—because of the admission of guilt and a record of violating the agreed-upon sanction—than if the original petition were challenged. In these cases, youths may face stiffer penalties, including placement in secure confinement. Informal sanctioning thus is not intrinsically a progressive step. Rather, it can be progressive or punitive, depending upon how it is used (Krisberg and Austin 1993, pp. 82, 99).

Fifth, such concerns aside, intake officers provide a mechanism by which the juvenile court can try to achieve its original mission in providing for the best interests of youths. By making these officers the central conduit for managing delinquency referrals, the court institutionalizes an emphasis on both the punishment and the social welfare of children. That emphasis may be undermined by excessive caseloads, prosecutor-like attitudes among probation officers, local court cultures that emphasize one extreme or another, and placing greater discretion about intake decisions with prosecutors. Regardless, it is an emphasis that intake officers more so than the police or prosecutors, by dint of their position and training, appear situated to provide. For example, from the perspective of the court founders and probation officers, it makes sense that one would want to intervene in the lives of referred youths, even in cases where there is insufficient evidence to adjudicate youths as delinquent.

Sixth, as with screening and assessment practices, informal versus formal processing practices vary considerably within and across jurisdictions. The variation stems, as Krisberg and Austin (1993) have observed, from such factors as the severity of the offenses committed (p. 107), "community tolerance, the frequency of referrals, existing alternative resources, and resources available within the juvenile court itself" (p. 98), and the "personal preference of the intake officers" (p. 100). Processing also may vary based on how intake officers take into account the family context from which youth come (Needleman 1981, p. 253). More generally, it may vary depending on police practices—especially relevant since the police account for 80% or more of delinquency referrals nationally (Snyder and Sickmund 2006, p. 104)—and the race and ethnicity of referred youths, their age or sex, their maturity or mental health, and other such factors (Krisberg 2005; Sanborn and Salerno 2005; see also the chapters by William Barton, Donna Bishop and Michael Leiber, Kimberly Kempf-Leonard, Edmund McGarrell, and Jodi Viljoen, Erika Penner, and Ron Roesch in this volume). As but one example, Bridges and Steen (1998) found that probation officers were prone, in their predisposition reports, to characterize black youth as committing crime due to personal flaws and to characterize white youth as committing crime due to environmental conditions. These differences can lead to black youth receiving more punitive dispositions. And, of special relevance here, the differences may result from assessments that probation officers make during their initial contact with youths at intake, especially if the officers who conduct intake are the same ones who create predisposition reports for the court.

Seventh, front-end juvenile court processing entails decision-making that can greatly affect youths, the courts, the juvenile justice system, and society. Consider, again the fact that front-end processing can influence the following decisions about referred youths: how cases are screened; whether and what kind of in-depth assessments occur; whether youths are detained; whether their cases are informally or formally processed; whether youths are diverted from the juvenile justice system; whether they receive or are referred to receive specific services and treatment; and how prosecutors and judges may view and handle specific cases.

Defense counsel can serve as a check against decisions that may not be in a juvenile's best interests. However, the right to counsel does not typically exist until a delinquency petition is filed (Feld 2009, p. 361), although some states (e.g., Arkansas and New Jersey) provide for the right to counsel at intake. As a result, many of the front-end decisions about youths occur without the assistance of counsel; indeed, many youths lack legal representation at later decision-making stages, such as arraignment and pretrial detention hearings (pp. 361, 458), and adjudication (p. 820). In addition, even if youths have legal representation, their attorneys may be unfamiliar with juvenile law, may work under excessive caseloads, or may readily capitulate to court worker recommendations (pp. 822–824; see also Puritz et al. 1995; Mears 1998; Grisso 2004). Moreover, studies suggest that the presence of defense counsel at later stages of processing can contribute to more punitive sanctions (Feld and Schaefer 2010). It thus may be that the presence of attorneys at intake may result in formal processing or tougher sanctions, whether due to incompetence of legal counsel, punishment of youths for exercising their legal rights, or some other factor.

The range of potential impacts of early decision-making means that the risks associated with bad front-end decisions can have profound ripple effects (Mears and Butts 2008; Mears and Bacon 2009). In aggregate, these decisions have the potential to affect case flows, the frequency and manner in which detention is used, the amount of informal and formal sanctioning that occurs, the use of various services and treatments, and differences in how different groups (e.g., males versus females, minorities, the mentally ill) are processed. Ultimately, impacts along these dimensions can influence whether the juvenile court achieves larger goals, such as achieving the best interests of youths, fair processing, decreased recidivism and crime, and increased prosocial outcomes (e.g., a better educated youth population and greater employment).

No body of empirical research has systematically identified how all of these decisions ultimately relate to one another and thus whether juvenile courts in specific jurisdictions achieve their goals. Indeed, it remains unclear exactly what the benchmarks or criteria would be for defining "success" (Roman and Butts 2005). Even so, and as prior work shows, the potential for front-end processing to affect many of these decisions is considerable.

VI. FRONT-END DECISION-MAKING: IMPLICATIONS FOR POLICY AND PRACTICE

Given that front-end decision-making in the juvenile court can have a considerable impact on youths, the fact that many of the decisions continue to occur in what is largely a "black box" raises concerns about the fairness, effectiveness, and efficiency of the juvenile justice system (Sanborn and Salerno 2005; Mears and Butts 2008; Piquero 2008). Consider the analogous situation in law enforcement—arrest has long served as a central feature of law enforcement activity, yet few rigorous studies have assessed the relative deterrent effect associated with being arrested as against being arrested and receiving a sanction (Huizinga and Henry 2008).

Much the same can be said of front-end juvenile processing decisions. Specifically, we know little about the actual decisions made within and across jurisdictions or the actual impacts of these decisions on youths, juvenile justice, or society. That situation presents clear implications for policy and practice. Failure to take action risks allowing a youth to continue or enter a trajectory of offending or to reduce the deterrent effect of the juvenile court (Needleman 1981, p. 252). At the same time, taking action when it is not needed wastes resources and risks creating a labeling effect that leads to more—not less—offending. Against that backdrop, I discuss below several critical implications that front-end processing has for policy and practice.

A. Front-End Decision-Making and Diversion

The term "diversion" became a prominent part of juvenile justice policy discussions in the 1960s and 1970s. For example, the U.S. Juvenile Justice and Delinquency Prevention Act was enacted in 1974 and provided large-scale funding for "diversion programs" (Roberts 2004, p. 187). The programs varied greatly but were similar in their intent on providing an alternative to formal court processing. Diversion thus included an emphasis on providing educational services, vocational and job training, skill development, counseling, advocacy, and social services (Klein 1979, pp. 168–69), with individual, group, or family counseling constituting the primary programming effort (p. 170). The goals of diversion include reduced labeling of youth as "delinquents," reduced use of detention and incarceration, lower recidivism, and fewer costs (p. 191). The argument, for example, is that informal processing can provide a more flexible and efficient approach to sorting and routing cases and to providing youths with access to community resources, treatment, and services (Feld 2009, p. 365).

Despite the seemingly self-evident idea connoted by "diversion," substantial confusion exists about what diversion is. Consider, for example, some of the ways in which it has been conceptualized. First, the juvenile justice system itself can be viewed as existing to divert youths from the criminal justice system. Second, diversion can be viewed simply as a dismissal of a case. Third, diversion can be defined as any effort aimed at ensuring that less serious cases are turned away from the juvenile justice system to receive services or treatment from some other agency or organization. This practice has constituted a central feature of juvenile justice since its inception (Pabon 1978, p. 27; Roberts 2004, p. 185). For example, if youths can be counseled and released, warned to good effect, or sent to a program or social service agency that can help them, these "diversionary" avenues would be preferred over formal adjudication proceedings. Fourth, diversion can be viewed as any effort to provide a less serious juvenile justice intervention or sanction relative to what otherwise would occur, what sometimes is termed "minimization of penetration" (Klein 1979, p. 152). From this perspective, placing a youth on probation rather than incarcerating him or her would constitute diversion.

The last two definitions arguably provide the clearest foothold for describing the range of "diversion" programs that have emerged in recent decades. Even then, however, ambiguity exists. For example, if, per the third definition, we intend diversion to mean the referral of youth to a social service agency for further handling, we conflate two types of cases—those that would have been referred without a diversion program (i.e., usual practice) and those that would not have been referred without the program (i.e., diversionary practice). The latter situation seems more clearly to involve diversion. Put differently, diversion as a term that describes a new policy or practice makes sense only if it describes a situation where the juvenile justice system handles a case in a manner different from how it otherwise would and where it is associated with less oversight or less penetration further into this system (Klein 1979, p. 153).

In reality, no consensus exists about how diversion should be defined. The result, in turn, is that it remains difficult to compare diversion evaluations much less to arrive at a verdict concerning diversion's effectiveness (Klein 1979; McCord, Widom, and Crowell 2001; Sanborn and Salerno 2005; Feld 2009). For example, if we find that one diversion program is effective, that does not mean that other types of diversion "work" anymore than a study of one antibiotic's effectiveness establishes the effectiveness of other antibiotics. Consider a simple example—many states view diversion as an event that occurs prior to and instead of filing a petition, but some view it as occurring after a petition has been filed and when a youth successfully completes a program, at which point the adjudication is voided (Sanborn and Salerno 2005). The effectiveness of "diversion" might well vary depending on when it occurs.

Making a definitive statement about the effectiveness or ineffectiveness of diversion is difficult for another reason. Specifically, the vague conceptual underpinnings of many diversion efforts impedes our ability to draw valid inferences about their effectiveness even when evaluations have been undertaken. For example, informal probation frequently is described as a form of diversion, yet informal sanctions have been central to the juvenile court since its creation (Bernard 1992; Krisberg and Austin 1993; Feld 1999). Consequently, if a jurisdiction expands its use of informal probation and then finds that informal probation reduces recidivism, that does not mean that diversion "works"; rather, it means that a common practice in juvenile justice may be effective. In addition, it would not mean that some other type of diversion was effective.

One way to appreciate the challenges of validly assessing the effectiveness of diversion is to consider how one would establish the need for diversion. Ideally, before implementing a new diversion program, we would identify that a problem exists for which diversion constitutes an obvious solution. That requires defining the problem and then measuring it. Perhaps, for example, intake officers or prosecutors are filing too many delinquency petitions for first-time youth referrals. That sounds like a problem. However, a necessary first step to establishing whether it really is a problem involves empirically measuring how many such referrals exist and identifying a standard for determining "too many." For example, some first-time youth referrals clearly may merit formal processing. One jurisdiction may have many such youths, and another may have few. Without a standard and empirical evidence, it is impossible to determine which jurisdiction formally processes cases that perhaps should be informally processed.

Other problems plague the diversion literature. For example, an additional reason that we know little about the effectiveness of diversion is that most evaluations have lacked sufficient methodological rigor to generate credible results (Klein 1979). Effective diversion programs certainly exist and, under the right conditions and with appropriate populations and quality implementation, may achieve some benefits (Roberts 2004). By and large, however, the combination of conceptual ambiguity underlying many different diversion programs, the poor implementation of them, and the lack of methodological rigorous impact evaluations have made it difficult to arrive at a definitive assessment about the effectiveness of such programs (Klein 1979; Sanborn and Salerno 2005). In short, it remains unclear whether diversion in general reduces labeling, detention, incarceration, recidivism, or court or societal costs.

At the same time, studies suggest that diversion actually creates more harm than good. For example, a goal of diversion is to reduce further system penetration. However, net-widening—whereby social control efforts expand rather than contract—has been documented (Feld 2009, p. 365). To illustrate, a diversion program might result in some youths receiving supervision and services in cases that historically might have been dismissed (Blomberg 1980; Polk 1984; Sanborn and Salerno 2005). Here, then, formal processing remains largely the same, but informal processing greatly expands. The precise extent of net-widening is not known, but sufficient examples exist to suggest that the problem exists. Some reviews, for example, have found that many diversion programs serve a supplemental role rather than as an alternative to traditional court processing (Klein 1979, p. 185).

Against this backdrop, what then is the relevance of intake to diversion? Intake processing is central to any discussion of diversion because of its critical role at the front end of the juvenile justice system. When probation officers conduct intake, that role enables them, in many instances, to divert youths out of the juvenile justice system through dismissal or to some service, treatment, or other agency. Even when intake officers' decisions must be reviewed by prosecutors, the officers may influence whether diversion occurs by how they characterize cases or through the recommendations they make to prosecutors and judges.

More generally, given their philosophical outlook—which emphasizes the social welfare of youths—intake officers can play a central role in greatly expanding the state's authority over youths through diversion programs. Consider, for example, the ways in which intake officers are able to influence case processing even without a new diversion program:

> [Intake workers] know… that the court calendar is so crowded that several
> months may elapse before a child they petition to court will be seen by a judge.
> Therefore, if the case seems to require major intervention, [they] will open it for
> informal adjustment and try either to give direct service or to connect the child

with some community social service—such as a therapist, mental health clinic or youth program—rather than let the problem "sit around getting worse" while waiting for court action. (Needleman 1981, p. 252)

Such discretion is, if anything, amplified in settings where diversion programs proliferate. Of course, the influence of intake officers may be diminished in contexts where prosecutors take a more active role in screening referrals (Rubin 1980). Even then, however, officers may greatly affect which cases prosecutors select for diversion versus dismissal or formal processing.

B. Rehabilitative versus Tougher, More Criminal-Like Decision-Making

The juvenile justice system has been characterized as becoming more criminal-like (see Bishop and Feld's Chapter 35 in this volume, "Trends in Juvenile Justice Policy and Practice"). Evidence of that trend can be seen in the increased number of ways that youths can be transferred to adult court. As discussed earlier, it also can be seen in the increased role and power of prosecutors during intake (Petrucci and Rubin 2004; Feld 2009). Three decades ago, for example, just as juvenile justice systems developed new, more punitive ways to sanction youths, Rubin (1979, pp. 287–288) observed: "If the entry of defense counsel into juvenile court proceedings best symbolized the impact of the *Gault* decision, perhaps the expanded role of the juvenile court prosecutor best exemplifies the 'new' juvenile courts of the late 1970s. Today, the prosecutor is entering the juvenile court processing at its beginning." That shift appears to have continued in the decades since Rubin made that observation (see, e.g., Petrucci and Rubin 2004; Sanborn and Salerno 2005; Feld 2009).

Despite such changes, it remains unclear whether actual case decisions or outcomes have been affected. Here again, the "black box" problem surfaces. To say whether a policy created a change, we need information on baseline decision-making and outcomes. However, few jurisdictions systematically monitor court decisions, especially those involving informal negotiations between intake workers and parents, prosecutors, and judges (Needleman 1981; Sanborn and Salerno 2005; Mears and Butts 2008). Consequently, whether changes in intake decision-making have led to processing that more closely resembles what occurs in the criminal justice system is unknown. We do know that juvenile justice operates as a system and that changes in one part frequently are offset by changes in another (Snyder, Sickmund, and Poe-Yamagata 2000). We also know that even as the juvenile justice system toughened throughout the 1980s and 1990s, many countervailing forces emerged that accorded with the juvenile court's traditional mission (Butts and Mears 2001). However, absent a coherent and credible body of empirical research on front-end decision-making, it is difficult to say whether changes in intake policies or practices have generated tougher, more criminal-like processing or not. What can be said is that the punishment-versus-rehabilitation tension evident at the founding of the juvenile court continues to the present and can be seen in the structure and practice of intake processing.

C. Approaches to Front-End Decision-Making

There is no one system of juvenile justice in the United States, but rather a panoply of systems at the state and local levels. The same observation holds for front-end processing in juvenile courts. Thus, although highly efficient and effective approaches to structuring front-end decision-making may exist, evidence of them has not emerged. However, in 2005, the National Council of Juvenile and Family Court Judges (NCJFCJ) issued guidelines for administering juvenile justice that include many detailed recommendations not only for intake but also for all other aspects of the juvenile justice system. The Council recommended, among other things, that prosecutors review all decisions to file or not to file a delinquency petition with the court (NCJFCJ 2005, p. 66). Separately, the National Center for Juvenile Justice has issued a publication, the *Desktop Guide to Good Juvenile Probation Practice* (Griffin and Torbet 2002), which describes recommended approaches for conducting intake and improving diversion and detention decisions. For example, it advises that "intake interviews with juveniles must strike a balance between the need for information and the rights of the accused" and that policies should be in place that "ensure appropriate confidentiality and prevent misuse of intake information" (p. 44). The concern, as the Guide emphasizes, is that intake officers ask questions of a sensitive nature and do so with juveniles, as well as their families, who know little about juvenile court procedures and who typically have not consulted with a defense attorney (Feld 2009).

One specific promising approach is the use of Juvenile Assessment Centers (JACs), which first emerged in Florida in 1993 (Dembo, Schmeidler, and Walters 2004). The motivation for developing JACs derived in part from a concern that many youth were involved in a vicious cycle, one that resulted from a failure to intervene early and in a manner that addressed the many risks and needs of referred youth. That problem stemmed in part from inadequate screening and assessment of youth. To address these problems, JACs emphasize immediate, and typically comprehensive, assessment of juveniles at a centralized unit. They also rely on management information systems that make it easier to combine multiple sources of information about youth, to identify counseling, treatment, and other services that would be appropriate for specific youth, and to provide integrated case management of youth to ensure that youth participated in or received intended services (Dembo, Schmeidler, and Walters 2004). However, as one could anticipate, considerable variation exists in how specific JACs operate. For example, some JACs may use well-established and validated screening and assessment instruments, while others may use ones that have been developed by local juvenile court personnel (p. 518).

Despite the potential of JACs, it remains unknown whether they produce efficiencies or impacts along a range of dimensions that, admittedly, are difficult to assess. Certainly, it appears likely that JACs perform better at identifying youths who have mental disorders or other problems or needs and that they provide more efficient and integrated services (Rivers and Anwyl 2000; McReynolds et al. 2008). The central role that assessment plays in their operations accords with the recommendations scholars have made to improve efforts to identify youths with mental health and other problems (Grisso 2004, 2008; Mears 2004). Even so, minimal empirical evidence exists to support claims about the impacts of JACs on the fairness or appropriateness of intake officer decisions, informal or formal processing decisions, sanctioning, recidivism, or crime. At the same time, the risk of net-widening exists—and with a greater capacity to assess needs comes the potential for increasingly larger numbers of youths to receive interventions in cases where dismissal would be the better option (Dembo, Schmeidler, and Walters 2004, p. 529).

It may well be that variation in front-end court processing will remain for the indefinite future. That does not mean, however, that such processing cannot be improved. As the NCJFCJ (2005, p. 29) has emphasized, "different [intake] models can work equally well as long as they are consistently followed [and there are] clear guidelines specifying which cases will be handled formally" and as long as well-trained staff are used. Ultimately, however, any assessment of effectiveness requires empirical research.

D. The Need for Improved Monitoring of and Research on Front-End Decision-Making

Front-end juvenile court decision-making has received relatively little attention from researchers. In the 1970s, a number of studies examined the topic, but few studies of intake occurred thereafter, perhaps due to the emergence of many new reforms, such as a plethora of transfer statutes, that garnered more interest or were deemed to be more important. Regardless, the result is the same: there currently is no national, systematic, comprehensive research on the precise nature of informal processing in American juvenile justice, the role of the intake officer in this processing, or the impacts of specific front-end processing policies and practices. (There also is little research on police processing of cases prior to intake—see Feld 2006; see also Edmund McGarrell's chapter in this volume.)

Certainly, many studies have examined individual-level correlates of intake worker decisions (e.g., Thomas and Sieverdes 1975; Cohen and Kluegel 1979). However, the bulk of these studies fail to include measures of a wide range of factors that may affect front-end processing decisions. For example, intake worker decisions may be influenced by their assessment of a youth's family context, how they think prosecutors and the court will proceed with the case, available treatment and service options, and so on (Cicourel 1968; Needleman 1981; Thomas and Fitch 1981). Few studies exist that empirically examine these different possibilities, much less that do so for more than one or two jurisdictions at a select period in time. The problem lies in the fact that existing case studies may not generalize to other jurisdictions or over time. Yet it is because of such studies (e.g., Emerson 1969; Kupchik 2006), as well as research on sentencing in general (Mears 1998), that we know that the above factors, as well as the local court culture, organizational pressures, quality of defense representation, and other such dimensions, may affect front-end processing decisions (McCarthy and Smith 1986; Sanborn 1992; Curtis and Reese 1994; Feld 1999; Grisso 2004; Sanborn and Salerno 2005).

From a policy perspective, research is needed that describes front-end processing and the factors that influence the type and impact of front-end processing decisions that occur in specific jurisdictions. Any such research should include a focus on systems-level factors that affect decision-making (Boyd, Huss, and Myers 2008). For example, in a given jurisdiction, police may be reluctant to refer certain cases to juvenile court if they feel that intake officers or prosecutors will dismiss the cases. Conversely, if they believe the screeners will process certain cases in a manner that they view is appropriate, they may be more likely to refer them. Of course, serious offenses almost invariably will get referred, but many referrals involve acts that could be described as "gray" in that it may not be clear that an offense occurred, that sufficient evidence exists to prosecute it, or that a youth has needs that merit court-related intervention (Needleman 1981). A similar process can unfold between intake officers and prosecutors. For example, in a study I undertook, a chief juvenile probation officer in a large metropolitan county stated that the practice in his office was to avoid formally reporting violations of the conditions of probation because the new District Attorney had a policy of automatically seeking revocation in such cases. A systems-level focus would examine such dynamics and investigate how the actions that law enforcement, intake officers, prosecutors, and judges take may influence front-end processing decisions (Sanborn and Salerno 2005).

Because disjunctures between ideal and actual practice likely constitute the norm rather than the exception in juvenile justice (see, e.g., Feld and Schaefer 2010; Mears et al. 2010), research should focus not only on the laws and policies that govern front-end processing but also the actual implementation of them and whether they lead to intended outcomes. The risk otherwise is that we draw inferences that may be incorrect. To illustrate, many states have enacted laws for transferring youths to adult court. Such efforts unquestionably reflect a punitive trend. Even so, inspection of how frequently the laws actually are used might reveal no substantial difference in the case processing of youth (see, e.g., Snyder, Sickmund, and Poe-Yamagata 2000). Rubin's (1980) analysis of the prosecutorial review of intake officer decisions, which found that the review frequently led to no change in how cases were processed, underscores the possibility that much the same may hold for new approaches to front-end processing.

The focus on a broad range of outcomes is especially important. Front-end processing approaches should be graded along multiple dimensions. Implementation, of course, is important. Are screening protocols followed? Are youth appropriate for detention in fact detained? Are cases appropriate for informal processing so processed? And so on. Ultimately, however, we want to know if the approaches achieve long-term goals. For example, do front-end decisions to informally process some youths in a specific manner result in less recidivism or crime than otherwise would occur? Do these decisions result in improvements in the ability of youths to develop prosocial relationships, obtain an education, or find employment? More generally, do they result in changes to youths that benefit the youths—that are in their best interests—as compared what would happen to the youths if they were processed differently? Not least, do they benefit not only youthful offenders but also victims and communities?

Special research and policy attention should be accorded to detention and diversion decision-making, given the potential for unnecessary costs and potential harms if youths inappropriate for these placements receive them. Some promising work in this area includes the Detention Diversion Advocacy Project (DDAP) and the Juvenile Detention Alternatives Initiative (JDAI), both of which involve system-atic efforts to decrease the use of inappropriate detention and increase investment in more efficient and effective alternatives for reducing delinquent behavior (Holman and Ziedenberg 2006). (See William Barton's Chapter 26, "Detention," in this volume for a more general discussion of these efforts.)

Finally, although risk and needs assessment instruments hold the potential for more accurately identifying at-risk youth, there is, as Grisso (2004, p. 199) has emphasized, a "need for empirically validated measures and strategies for assessing risk of future aggression among youths," with attention given to validating instru-ments for specific populations and areas (see, e.g., Miller and Lin 2007; Onifadea et al. 2008; Schwalbe 2008). More generally, there is a need for identifying not only the risk of delinquent activity, but also the presence of specific illnesses and prob-lems, such as suicidal ideation and competency, that may merit attention from the court (NCJFCJ 2005; Scott and Steinberg 2008).

The focus on strategies is as important as a focus on valid instruments. Otherwise, the risk is that the instruments will be improperly administered and/or that the resulting information will be misused (Mears and Kelly 1999). Indeed, qual-ity screening and assessment ultimately are of little help if they are not coupled with mechanisms to ensure that the information from them will be used appropriately and in a way that leads to better front-end decisions (NCJFCJ 2005). For example, if an instrument identifies a youth as being at risk of violent behavior, the mission of the juvenile court demands that steps be taken to protect the public. But the mission of the court also demands that a youth's needs be addressed. To that end, the court would fail in its mission if an instrument focused only on risk of offending, or if the court focused only on results from risk assessments rather than risk and needs assessments. Sending a youth to secure confinement might satisfy the first mandate but likely would compromise the court's mission to promote the social welfare of children since custodial treatment options may be less effective than those available in the community (Grisso 2004, p. 201). No easy answer to this dilemma exists, but the point is that it cannot be resolved simply through better instruments. Instead, strategies are needed, such as the incorporation of identified "best practices," careful monitoring of actual practices, and a constant effort to define, operationalize, and evaluate the impacts of these practices to hold the juvenile justice system account-able (Mears and Butts 2008).

REFERENCES

Bernard, Thomas J. 1992. *The Cycle of Juvenile Justice*. New York: Oxford University Press.

Bishop, Donna M. 2005. "The Role of Race and Ethnicity in Juvenile Justice Processing." In *Our Children, Their Children: Confronting Racial and Ethnic Differences in American Juvenile Justice*, 23–82, edited by Darnell F. Hawkins and Kimberly Kempf-Leonard. Chicago: University of Chicago Press.

Blomberg, Thomas G. 1980. "Widening the Net: An Anomaly in the Evaluation of Diversion Programs." In *Handbook of Criminal Justice Evaluation*, edited by Malcolm W. Klein and Katherine S. Teilmann, 572–92. Beverly Hills, CA: Sage.

Borum, Randy. 2006. "Assessing Risk for Violence among Juvenile Offenders." In *The Forensic Assessment of Children and Adolescents*, edited by Steven N. Sparta and Gerald P. Koocher, 190–202. New York: Oxford University Press.

Boyd, Rebecca J., Sheila M. Huss, and David L. Myers. 2008. "Antecedents and Consequences of Juvenile Case Processing: Where Are We Now, and Where Do We Go From Here?" *Youth Violence and Juvenile Justice* 6: 195–220.

Bridges, George S., and Sara Steen. 1998. "Racial Disparities in Official Assessments of Juvenile Offenders: Attributional Stereotypes as Mediating Mechanisms." *American Sociological Review* 63: 554–71.

Butts, Jeffrey A., and Daniel P. Mears. 2001. "Reviving Juvenile Justice in a Get-Tough Era." *Youth and Society* 33: 169–98.

Carrington, Peter J., and Jennifer L. Schulenberg. 2008. "Structuring Police Discretion: The Effect on Referrals to Youth Court." *Criminal Justice Policy Review* 19: 349–67.

Cicourel, Aaron V. 1968. *The Social Organization of Juvenile Justice*. New York: Wiley.

Cohen, Lawrence E., and James R. Kluegel. 1979. "Selecting Delinquents for Adjudication: An Analysis of Intake Screening Decisions in Two Metropolitan Juvenile Courts." *Journal of Research in Crime and Delinquency* 16: 143–63.

Cullen, Francis T., and Paul Gendreau. 2000. "Assessing Correctional Rehabilitation: Policy, Practice, and Prospects." In *Policies, Processes, and Decisions of the Criminal Justice System*, edited by J. Horney, 109–75. Washington, DC: National Institute of Justice.

Curtis, Russell L., and William A. Reese II. 1994. "Framed Attributions and Shaped Accounts: A Study of Dispositional Process in Juvenile Justice." *Criminal Justice Review* 19: 244–70.

Dembo, Richard, James Schmeidler, and Wansley Walters. 2004. "Juvenile Assessment Centers." In *Juvenile Justice Sourcebook: Past, Present, and Future*, edited by Albert R. Roberts, 511–36. New York: Oxford University Press.

Emerson, Robert M. 1969. *Judging Delinquents: Context and Process in the Juvenile Courts*. Chicago: Aldine.

Feld, Barry C. 1999. *Bad Kids: Race and the Transformation of the Juvenile Court*. New York: Oxford University Press.

Feld, Barry C. 2006. "Police Interrogation of Juveniles: An Empirical Study of Policy and Practice." *Journal of Criminal Law and Criminology* 97: 219–316.***

Feld, Barry C. 2009. *Cases and Materials on Juvenile Justice Administration*, 3rd ed. St. Paul, MN: West.

Feld, Barry C., and Shelly Schaefer. 2010. "The Right to Counsel in Juvenile Court: The Conundrum of Attorneys as an Aggravating Factor at Disposition." *Justice Quarterly* 27: 713–41.

Griffin, Patrick, and Melanie King. 2009. *State Juvenile Justice Profiles*. Pittsburgh, PA: National Center for Juvenile Justice.

Griffin, Patrick, and Patricia Torbet, eds. 2002. *Desktop Guide to Good Juvenile Probation Practice.* Pittsburgh, PA: National Center for Juvenile Justice.

Grisso, Thomas. 2004. *Double Jeopardy: Adolescent Offenders with Mental Disorders.* Chicago: University of Chicago Press.

Grisso, Thomas. 2008. "Adolescent Offenders with Mental Disorders." *The Future of Children* 18: 143–64.

Guarino-Ghezzi, Susan, and Edward J. Loughran. 2004. *Balancing Juvenile Justice.* New Brunswick, NJ: Transaction Publishers.

Henretta, John C., Charles E. Frazier, and Donna M. Bishop. 1986. "The Effect of Prior Case Outcomes on Juvenile Justice Decision-Making." *Social Forces* 65: 554–62.

Holman, Barry, and Jason Ziedenberg. 2006. *The Dangers of Detention: The Impact of Incarcerating Youth in Detention and Other Secure Facilities.* Washington, DC: The Justice Policy Institute.

Howell, James C. 2009. *Preventing and Reducing Juvenile Delinquency: A Comprehensive Framework.* 2nd ed. Thousand Oaks, CA: Sage.

Huizinga, David, and Kimberly L. Henry. 2008. "The Effect of Arrest and Justice System Sanctions on Subsequent Behavior: Findings from Longitudinal and Other Studies." In *The Long View of Crime: A Synthesis of Longitudinal Research,* edited by Akiva M. Liberman, 220–54. New York: Springer.

Janku, Anne D., and Jiahui Yan. 2009. "Exploring Patterns of Court-Ordered Mental Health Services for Juvenile Offenders: Is There Evidence of Systemic Bias?" *Criminal Justice and Behavior* 36: 402–19.

Klein, Malcolm W. 1979. "Deinstitutionalization and Diversion of Juvenile Offenders: A Litany of Impediments." *Crime and Justice* 1: 145–201.

Krisberg, Barry. 2005. *Juvenile Justice: Redeeming Our Children.* Thousand Oaks, CA: Sage.

Krisberg, Barry, and James Austin. 1993. *Reinventing Juvenile Justice.* Newbury Park, CA: Sage.

Kupchik, Aaron. 2006. *Judging Juveniles: Prosecuting Adolescents in Adult and Juvenile Courts.* New York: New York University Press.

Lauritsen, Janet L. 2005. "Racial and Ethnic Differences in Juvenile Offending." In *Our Children, Their Children: Confronting Racial and Ethnic Differences in American Juvenile Justice,* edited by Darnell F. Hawkins and Kimberly Kempf-Leonard, 83–104. Chicago: University of Chicago Press.

Lee, Leona. 1995. "Factors Influencing Intake Disposition in a Juvenile Court." *Juvenile and Family Court Journal* 46: 43–61.

Lindner, Charles. 2008. "Probation Intake: Gatekeeper to the Family Court." *Federal Probation* 72(1): 48–53.

Loeber, Rolf, and David P. Farrington, eds. 2001. *Child Delinquents: Development, Intervention, and Service Needs.* Thousand Oaks, CA: Sage Publications.

McCarthy, Belinda R., and Brent R. Smith. 1986. "The Conceptualization of Discrimination in the Juvenile Justice Process: The Impact of Administrative Factors and Screening Decisions on Juvenile Court Dispositions." *Criminology* 24: 41–64.

McCord, Joan, Cathy S. Widom, and Nancy A. Crowell, eds. 2001. *Juvenile Crime, Juvenile Justice.* Washington, DC: National Academy Press.

McReynolds, Larkin S., Gail A. Wasserman, Robert E. DeComo, Reni John, Joseph M. Keating, and Scott Nolen. 2008. "Psychiatric Disorder in a Juvenile Assessment Center." *Crime and Delinquency* 54: 313–34.

Mears, Daniel P. 1998. "The Sociology of Sentencing: Reconceptualizing Decisionmaking Processes and Outcomes." *Law and Society Review* 32: 667–724.

Mears, Daniel P. 2002. "Sentencing Guidelines and the Transformation of Juvenile Justice in the Twenty-First Century." *Journal of Contemporary Criminal Justice* 18: 6–19.

Mears, Daniel P. 2004. "Identifying Adolescent Substance Abuse." In *Juvenile Drug Courts and Teen Substance Abuse*, edited by Jeffrey A. Butts and John Roman, 185–220. Washington, DC: Urban Institute Press.

Mears, Daniel P., and Laudan Y. Aron. 2003. *Addressing the Needs of Youth with Disabilities in the Juvenile Justice System: The Current State of Knowledge*. Washington, DC: The Urban Institute.

Mears, Daniel P., and Sarah Bacon. 2009. "Improving Criminal Justice through Better Decisionmaking: Lessons from the Medical System." *Journal of Criminal Justice* 37: 142–54.

Mears, Daniel P., and Jeffrey A. Butts. 2008. "Using Performance Monitoring to Improve the Accountability, Operations, and Effectiveness of Juvenile Justice." *Criminal Justice Policy Review* 19: 264–84.

Mears, Daniel P., and Samuel H. Field. 2000. "Theorizing Sanctioning in a Criminalized Juvenile Court." *Criminology* 38: 983–1020.

Mears, Daniel P., and William R. Kelly. 1999. "Assessments and Intake Processes in Juvenile Justice Processing: Emerging Policy Considerations." *Crime and Delinquency* 45: 508–29.

Mears, Daniel P., Tracey L. Shollenberger, Janeen B. Willison, Colleen E. Owens, and Jeffrey A. Butts. 2010. "Practitioner Views of Priorities, Policies, and Practices in Juvenile Justice." *Crime and Delinquency* 56: 535–63.

Miller, Joel, and Jeffrey Lin. 2007. "Applying a Generic Juvenile Risk Assessment Instrument to a Local Context." *Crime and Delinquency* 53: 552–80.

National Council of Juvenile and Family Court Judges (NCJFCJ). 2005. *Juvenile Delinquency Guidelines: Improving Court Practice in Juvenile Delinquency Cases*. Reno, NV: NCJFCJ.

Needleman, Carolyn. 1981. "Discrepant Assumptions in Empirical Research: The Case of Juvenile Court Screening." *Social Problems* 28: 247–62.

Olver, Mark E., Keira C. Stockdale, and J. Stephen Wormith. 2009. "Risk Assessment with Young Offenders: A Meta-Analysis of Three Assessment Measures." *Criminal Justice and Behavior* 36: 329–53.

Onifadea, Eyitayo, William Davidson, Sarah Livsey, Garrett Turke, Chris Horton, Jill Malinowski, Dan Atkinson, and Dominique Wimberly. 2008. "Risk Assessment: Identifying Patterns of Risk in Young Offenders with the Youth Level of Service/Case Management Inventory." *Journal of Criminal Justice* 36: 165–73.

Pabon, Edward. 1978. "A Re-examination of Family Court Intake." *Federal Probation* 42: 25–32.

Petersilia, Joan. 1997. "Probation in the United States." *Crime and Justice* 22: 149–200.

Petrucci, Carrie J., and H. Ted Rubin. 2004. "Juvenile Court: Bridging the Past and the Future." In *Juvenile Justice Sourcebook: Past, Present, and Future*, edited by Albert R. Roberts, 247–88. New York: Oxford University Press.

Piquero, Alex R. 2008. "Disproportionate Minority Contact." *The Future of Children* 18: 59–79.

Polk, Kenneth. 1984. "Juvenile Diversion: A Look at the Record." *Crime and Delinquency* 30: 648–59.

Puritz, Patricia, Sue Burrell, Robert Schwartz, Mark Soler, and Loren Warboys. 1995. *A Call for Justice: An Assessment of Access to Counsel and Quality of Representation in Delinquency Proceedings*. Washington, DC: American Bar Association.

Puzzanchera, Charles, and William Kang. 2008. *Juvenile Court Statistics Databook*. Pittsburgh, PA: National Center for Juvenile Justice. Accessed Feb. 24, 2011. http://ojjdp.ncjrs.gov/ojstatbb/jcsdb.

Puzzanchera, Charles, and Melissa Sickmund. 2008. *Juvenile Court Statistics 2005.* Pittsburgh, PA: National Center for Juvenile Justice.

Rivers, James E., and Robert S. Anwyl. 2000. "Juvenile Assessment Centers: Strengths, Weaknesses, and Potential." *The Prison Journal* 80: 96–113.

Roberts, Albert R. 2004. "The Emergence and Proliferation of Juvenile Diversion Programs." In *Juvenile Justice Sourcebook: Past, Present, and Future*, edited by Albert R. Roberts, 183–95. New York: Oxford University Press.

Roman, John, and Jeffrey A. Butts. 2005. *The Economics of Juvenile Jurisdiction.* Washington, DC: The Urban Institute.

Rubin, H. Ted. 1979. "Retain the Juvenile Court? Legislative Developments, Reform Directions, and the Call for Abolition." *Crime and Delinquency* 25: 281–98.

Rubin, H. Ted. 1980. "The Emerging Prosecutor Dominance of the Juvenile Court Intake Process." *Crime and Delinquency* 26: 299–318.

Sanborn, Joseph B., Jr. 1992. "Pleading Guilty in Juvenile Court: Minimal Ado about Something Very Important to Young Defendants." *Justice Quarterly* 9: 127–50.

Sanborn, Joseph B., Jr. 1993. "Philosophical, Legal, and Systemic Aspects of Juvenile Court Plea Bargaining." *Crime and Delinquency* 39: 509–27.

Sanborn, Joseph B., Jr. 1994. "The Juvenile, the Court, or the Community: Whose Best Interests Are Currently Being Promoted in Juvenile Court?" *The Justice System Journal* 17: 249–66.

Sanborn, Joseph B., Jr., and Anthony W. Salerno. 2005. *The Juvenile Justice System: Law and Process.* Los Angeles, CA: Roxbury.

Schwalbe, Craig S. 2008. "A Meta-analysis of Juvenile Justice Risk Assessment Instruments Predictive Validity by Gender." *Criminal Justice and Behavior* 35: 1367–81.

Scott, Elizabeth S., and Laurence Steinberg. 2008. *Rethinking Juvenile Justice.* Cambridge, MA: Harvard University Press.

Snyder, Howard N. 1996. "The Juvenile Court and Delinquency Cases." *The Future of Children* 6: 53–63.

Snyder, Howard N., and Melissa Sickmund. 2006. *Juvenile Offenders and Victims: 2006 National Report.* Pittsburgh, PA: National Center for Juvenile Justice.

Snyder, Howard N., Melissa Sickmund, and Eileen Poe-Yamagata. 2000. *Juvenile Transfers to Criminal Court in the 1990's: Lessons Learned from Four Studies.* Washington, DC: Office of Juvenile Justice and Delinquency Prevention.

Thomas, Charles W., and W. Anthony Fitch. 1981. "The Exercise of Discretion in the Juvenile Justice System." *Juvenile and Family Court Journal* 32: 31–50.

Thomas, Charles W., and Christopher M. Sieverdes. 1975. "Juvenile Court Intake: An Analysis of Discretionary Decision-Making." *Criminology* 12: 413–32.

Thornberry, Terence P., and R. L. Christenson. 1984. "Juvenile Justice Decision-Making as a Longitudinal Process." *Social Forces* 63: 433–44.

Towberman, Donna B. 1992. "National Survey of Juvenile Needs Assessment." *Crime and Delinquency* 38: 230–38.

Wang, Xia, and Daniel P. Mears. 2009. "A Multilevel Test of Minority Threat Effects on Sentencing." *Journal of Quantitative Criminology* 26: 191–215.

Willison, Janeen B., Daniel P. Mears, Tracey Shollenberger, Colleen E. Owens, and Jeffrey A. Butts. 2009. *Past, Present, and Future of Juvenile Justice: Assessing the Policy Options.* Washington, DC: The Urban Institute.

Winters, Ken C. 1999. *Screening and Assessing Adolescents for Substance Use Disorders.* Treatment Improvement Protocol (TIP) 31. Rockville, MD: Substance Abuse and Mental Health Services Administration, Center for Substance Abuse Treatment.

CHAPTER 25

VARIETIES OF JUVENILE COURT

NONSPECIALIZED COURTS, TEEN COURTS, DRUG COURTS, AND MENTAL HEALTH COURTS

JEFFREY A. BUTTS, JOHN K. ROMAN, AND JENNIFER LYNN-WHALEY

I. INTRODUCTION

JUVENILE courts in the United States have varying responsibilities and come in a variety of structures. In fact, many types of courts exercise legal jurisdiction over children and youths. Some communities do not have a specialized juvenile court. Other courts handle matters involving juveniles, including probate courts, juvenile divisions of circuit courts, or comprehensive family courts that also respond to cases involving abused and neglected children and family violence. In every community, however, some type of court must respond when a young person still under the legal age of criminal responsibility is accused of violating the law. When a court exercises jurisdiction over juvenile law-breakers, and when it follows the procedures of juvenile or family law, it is conventional to refer to such a court as a juvenile court.

A juvenile court is a type of specialized court or a court docket devoted to one or more specific categories of legal matter. Today, there are many specialized courts. Some even operate within the juvenile justice system. Many of the new specialized courts are also known as problem-solving courts. Drug courts are the most visible type of problem-solving court, but other varieties exist, including courts for mental health cases, domestic violence cases, and offenders charged with gun crimes. Problem-solving courts are increasingly popular but controversial (Hoffman 2000; Orr et al. 2009). Several characteristics distinguish problem-solving courts from traditional courts, but the essential ingredients are enhanced judicial oversight, active case management, longer post-sentencing supervision, and a general philosophy of rehabilitation and restorative justice rather than simply punishment and retributive justice (Berman and Feinblatt 2005). Problem-solving courts begin with the premise that people should be accountable for harmful behavior, but the justice system should do more than simply punish them for that harm; it should attempt to prevent future harm. Problem-solving courts extend the role of the legal system beyond fact-finding and the imposition of sanctions. They use the legal authority of the court system to maintain the social health of communities. Ironically, these are largely the same characteristics once used to describe the "new" juvenile courts of the early 1900s.

This chapter addresses the growing use of specialized, problem-solving courts for delinquent juveniles. After introducing the specialized nature of the juvenile court itself, we describe three of the most popular forms of specialized courts for youths (teen courts, juvenile drug courts, and juvenile/family mental health courts), and we examine several key policy and practice issues related to their operation. Where did the idea for each court originate? How many exist in the United States today? What type of legal matters do they handle? How do they process cases, and what do we know about their effectiveness?

II. NONSPECIALIZED COURTS

States organize their court systems in varying ways. Most trial courts are either courts of general jurisdiction (responsible for all types of criminal and civil matters within a defined geographic area) or limited jurisdiction (authorized to handle only certain types of cases, such as traffic, family, probate, etc.). Juvenile courts are usually established as a court of limited jurisdiction, but some communities in the United States do not have specialized juvenile courts. The court responsible for handling young people accused of law violations may be a division of some other court (Rottman and Strickland 2006). In Connecticut, for example, juvenile matters may be heard in Superior Courts or Probate Courts, which are courts of general and limited jurisdiction, respectively. In other states, lawmakers may have established distinct juvenile courts, but not all areas of the state have adopted the juvenile model. In Georgia, the juvenile court is a separate court of limited juris-diction, but not all counties have juvenile court judges. In some Georgia counties, judges from the Superior Court assume responsibility for delinquency matters. Even in states with true juvenile courts, the structure of the juvenile system may vary. Colorado handles delinquency cases in twenty-two district courts, which are courts of general jurisdiction, but the city of Denver has a separate juvenile court that is also a court of general jurisdiction. Juvenile courts in the state of Utah, on the other hand, belong to a single, statewide structure of twenty limited jurisdic-tion courts.

Juvenile courts across the United States vary in their responsibilities and activ-ities, as defined by state laws and local policies. In most communities, juvenile courts handle delinquent acts, or illegal behaviors for which adults can be prose-cuted in criminal court. This includes everything from relatively minor offenses (e.g., loitering and vandalism) to serious offenses, including weapons violations, drug offenses, arson, property offenses (e.g., theft and burglary), and person offenses (e.g., assault and robbery). Many states give their juvenile courts legal jurisdiction over cases involving not only delinquency, but also child abuse and neglect, and status offense proceedings (acts that would not be illegal for an adult, including truancy and curfew violations). Some juvenile courts have jurisdiction over adoptions, terminations of parental rights, interstate compact matters, eman-cipation, and consent (i.e., to marry, enlist in the armed services, be employed, etc.). Occasionally, juvenile courts have jurisdiction over traffic violations and child support matters.

The age range of juvenile court jurisdiction varies from state to state (Snyder and Sickmund 2006, ch. 4). In the majority of states and the District of Columbia, the upper age of juvenile court jurisdiction is 17. In other words, law violations involving youths begin under the jurisdiction of the juvenile court so long as the young person has not reached age 18 at the time of the offense. Juvenile court juris-diction extends only through age 16 in some states (e.g., Georgia, Illinois, Louisiana, Massachusetts, Michigan, Missouri, New Hampshire, South Carolina, Texas, and Wisconsin). In three states, Connecticut, New York, and North Carolina, juvenile court jurisdiction applies only through age 15. In 2007, however, Connecticut began a process to raise the age of juvenile court jurisdiction, and North Carolina officials have considered similar changes (Action for Children 2007). In every state, of course, there are exceptions in which a youth still within the age of juvenile jurisdiction may fall under the jurisdiction of the criminal (adult) court. This practice, known generically as criminal court transfer, is both popular and controversial (McGowan et al. 2007; see also Feld and Bishop, Chapter 32 this volume).

These wide variations in structure are reflected in the formal goals and pur-poses of juvenile courts across the United States. Especially during the 1980s and 1990s, a number of states modified the missions of their juvenile courts to incorpo-rate a greater emphasis on punishment or accountability (Snyder and Sickmund 2006). In nine states, lawmakers gave their juvenile courts a stronger mandate to hold young offenders accountable for their law violations by exacting proportionate retribution or punishment (Arkansas, Georgia, Hawaii, Illinois, Iowa, Louisiana, Michigan, Missouri, and Rhode Island). Other states emphasized prevention and rehabilitation as the formal goals of their juvenile courts (for example, Kentucky, Massachusetts, North Carolina, Ohio, South Carolina, Vermont, and West Virginia). In most states, the formal mission of the juvenile court continues to be a combination of youth rehabilitation and public safety, but achieving a proper balance between these competing goals leads to conflict and controversy.

As the responsibilities of juvenile courts became more elaborate during the twentieth century, the policies and procedures used to govern their operations became increasingly contentious. Before the 1960s, juvenile court judges were not required to follow detailed procedures or adhere to complex legal rules. With fewer legal formalities, juvenile courts were free to intervene as they pleased with each youth. Even in cases where a juvenile was merely suspected of criminal involvement, a judge was empowered to take jurisdiction over the matter, place the youth on probation, or even order incarceration. Due to a series of rulings by the U.S. Supreme Court and several decades of policy changes enacted at the state level, juvenile courts of today are more tightly regulated (Manfredi 1998). State and federal lawmakers have blended the original philosophy of the juvenile court with the rules and procedures of the criminal court. Many states have reduced the confidentiality of juvenile court proceedings and juvenile court records, increased the legal formalities used in juvenile court, and shifted the focus of the juvenile justice process away from individualized intervention and rehabilitation (Butts and Mitchell 2000). Juvenile courts now focus more on public safety, offender accountability, formal procedures, and due process. In essence, today's juvenile courts are "scaled-down criminal courts" (Feld 1999, p. 11). They are, in other words, less specialized than they once were.

As policy makers focus on the need to build an effective youth justice system, they have become increasingly attracted to the wide variety of new problem-solving court models. Some experts have even advised policy makers to turn to problem-solving courts as a way of avoiding the impasse between the youth advocates who demand stronger juvenile court programs and the law-and-order hardliners who promote adult court trials for younger and younger juveniles (Butts and Harrell 1998). Meaningful reforms in juvenile justice policy are always difficult to achieve. Lawmakers want to defend the traditional juvenile court, but they also find it easy to respond to public fears of crime by sending more youths to the adult court system. The emergence of "new" problem-solving courts presents lawmakers with an opportunity to break the stalemate over the future of juvenile justice. Policymakers are drawing upon these alternative courts in growing number to construct a more diverse youth justice system. Three court models in particular have become very popular in the past decade: teen courts, juvenile drug courts, and juvenile mental health (or treatment) courts. We consider each of these models and the policy issues they present for future decision makers.

III. Teen Courts

Teen courts, sometimes known as youth courts, peer courts, and peer juries, exist in hundreds of cities and nearly every state across the country. In 2006, the National Association of Youth Courts estimated that more than 1,100 courts were in operation nationwide (National Association of Youth Courts 2006). Teen court programs have obvious appeal for the parents and neighbors of troublesome youths. Teen courts ensure that youths face memorable, albeit unofficial, consequences soon after they begin to violate the law, often after the very first offense. Young people arrested the first time for a minor offense such as vandalism or shoplifting receive little attention from the regular juvenile justice system, often nothing more than a warning letter. When young offenders appear in teen court, they not only receive meaningful consequences for their behavior, they see young people their own age acting responsibly and receiving the respect of others. They see that their lawyer is a teenager, as is the prosecutor. They see juries made up of other youths, and the judge (or judges) may be young as well. Youths are responsible for much of what happens in the courtroom.

Young offenders never "get off with a warning" in teen court. Every case ends with some type of sanction or penalty. Defendants (or "participants") may be required to repair the property they vandalized, replace the goods they stole, or work in community service jobs to repay the community in general for their behavior. They may be required to write apology letters to their victims, their parents, or both. Some youths may even have to return to teen court to serve on a jury themselves. The dominant presence of other youths in teen court demonstrates to young offenders that most young people are law abiding, that breaking the law has consequences, and that law breakers are not admired.

A. Origins

The modern idea of teen courts began to take shape in the 1970s, although precursors existed long before then. In the 1940s, for example, teens in Mansfield, Ohio, served as judges and attorneys in a "Hi-Y" bicycle court (Mansfield News Journal 1949). The court convened on Saturday mornings to hear cases of minor traffic violations committed by bike-riding juveniles. Using the facilities of the municipal courthouse, teenagers were arraigned for infractions such as violating the stop sign ordinance or riding at night without reflectors. As punishment, the court often required offenders to write three hundred-word essays about traffic laws.

A dramatic growth in teen courts occurred during the 1990s. According to some estimates, there were only eighty teen courts in the United States as recently as 1993 (Godwin 2000). During the late 1990s and early 2000s, the number of teen courts swelled, in part due to the active, financial support of the Office of Juvenile Justice and Delinquency Prevention (OJJDP) in the U.S. Department of Justice. By 2001, OJJDP had funded the National Youth Court Center, and there were more than eight hundred operating teen courts, with more in the planning stage (Butts, Buck, and Coggeshall 2002). The total number of programs had reached 1,100 by 2006 (National Youth Court Association 2006).

B. Operations

Teen courts are diversion programs that mimic the style and ambience of courts. Their only authority derives from the force of an agreement between prosecutors and police to defer formal charges if a youth agrees to participate in teen court (see Mears, Chapter 24 this volume). Teen courts provide a voluntary diversion alternative for young offenders charged with less serious law violations like shoplifting, vandalism, and disorderly conduct. Proceedings in teen court mirror those of the traditional justice system except that youths, not adults, are in charge of the courtroom. Youth volunteers serve as judges, prosecuting attorneys, defense lawyers, jurors, bailiffs, and clerks. Youths are responsible for much of the key decision-making in each case. They weigh the severity of charges and determine what sanctions to impose. The goal of court hearings in these programs is to review the facts of each case, consider any mitigating or aggravating circumstances that may be involved, and then impose a "sentence." In some programs (about 5% of all teen courts), defendants may also dispute the allegations and the teen court will hold a hearing to consider the evidence (Butts, Buck, and Coggeshall 2002). This does not mean that youths in teen court are actually on trial or that teen courts establish legal culpability. Still, in programs offering the option of "trials," youth defendants who are successful in arguing the facts of a case and creating sufficient doubt about the charges may avoid further court involvement. The teen court can waive "sentencing" and the youth's participation in the diversion program is completed.

The teen court process is similar to that of a traditional juvenile court. In most jurisdictions, teen court proceedings and all program records are confidential. Every youth goes through an intake process that includes an interview with an adult program worker. A parent is often required to be present, and sometimes the intake interview may occur just prior to the teen court hearing. During the interview, the program staff member explains the teen court process to the youth and parent and reiterates that their participation is voluntary. Adults usually administer all teen court activities outside of the courtroom itself. They are responsible for client screening, fund-raising and budgeting, office management, and personnel. Adults typically coordinate the community service placements where offenders work to fulfill the terms of teen court sentences.

The extent of youth responsibility for teen court hearings depends on the courtroom model used by each particular program. In about half of all teen courts, adults perform the role of the judge in teen court hearings while youths serve as attorneys, clerks, bailiffs, and jurors (Butts and Buck 2000). Teen court models are divided into four basic types: (1) adult judge, (2) youth judge, (3) youth tribunal, and (4) peer jury. The youth judge and youth tribunal models maximize youth involvement because youths perform all courtroom roles, including that of judge. Youth tribunals involve a panel of (usually three) judges who hear cases presented by youth attorneys. There is no jury in the tribunal model. Programs using the youth judge model follow a traditional hearing with opposing counsel, juries, and a single judge. Adults may assist with courtroom management in these programs, but the teen court hearings themselves are run by youths. Adult judge programs, representing approximately half of all U.S. teen courts, function much like programs using youth judges, except that the role of the judge is filled by an adult who also manages the dynamics within the courtroom (Butts and Buck 2000). The peer jury model works much like a grand jury. An adult or youth volunteer presents each case to a jury of teens, and the jury questions the defendant directly. The jury members choose the most appropriate disposition, albeit with guidance and oversight of the adult judge.

Teen courts are usually administered by, or housed within, agencies that are part of the traditional juvenile justice system. Law enforcement agencies, juvenile probation, or prosecutor's offices serve as the lead agency for more than half of all teen courts (Butts and Buck 2000). Only a handful of programs are operated by schools, social service agencies, or other private organizations, although the number of school-based programs appears to be growing. Most teen courts are small and handle relatively few cases. In a 2000 survey, more than half (59%) of all teen courts reported handling one hundred or fewer cases annually; just 13% of all programs handled more than three hundred cases per year (Butts and Buck 2000).

C. Clients

Police, courts, and juvenile probation agencies are the primary sources of referrals to teen courts. In some jurisdictions, schools may also refer youth to teen courts, especially truancy cases and school behavior problems. All teen courts, however, handle relatively minor law violations. Shoplifting, disorderly conduct, minor assaults, and alcohol possession are the most common offenses referred to teen courts (Butts and Buck 2000). Very few programs handle more serious crimes, although some programs accept low-level felony offenses, most often property crimes involving first-time offenders.

The dispositions imposed by teen courts include those used by traditional courts, including fines, payments of restitution, and community service. In addition, many teen courts use alternative dispositions, such as requiring young offenders to attend educational workshops or discussion groups focused on decision-making skills or victim awareness. Many teen courts require offenders to write formal apologies to their victims. Others require offenders to serve on teen court juries. If offenders fail to comply with these sanctions the case usually is transferred back to juvenile or family court for formal handling.

D. Theory

Many ideas underlie the development and operation of teen courts. The Urban Institute proposed seven theoretical perspectives that might explain the origins of teen courts and their intended effect on youth recidivism (Butts, Buck, and Coggeshall 2002). Although sometimes known by other names, the seven theoretical schools were: (1) peer justice, (2) procedural justice, (3) deterrence, (4) labeling, (5) restorative justice and repentance, (6) law-related education, and (7) skill building. The Urban Institute considered each category for its relevance to teen court operations. All seven perspectives provided at least some explanation for the high demand for teen court programs across the country, but only the first theoretical perspective—peer justice—was intricately related to teen court operations. The outcomes suggested by the other six theoretical perspectives could be achieved equally well by interventions other than teen court. The concerns of procedural justice, for example, could be addressed by reforming the juvenile court process in a way that encourages youthful defendants to speak more often during court proceedings and to watch the hearings of other youths to confirm the impartiality of the court process. In accordance with deterrence theory, diversion programs in the juvenile justice system could be structured to ensure that sanctions are imposed more swiftly and with greater certainty. Many diversion programs are consistent with the recommendations of labeling theory as they allow juvenile offenders to avoid formal adjudication.

The peer-to-peer justice element of the teen court model was the only unique and viable explanation for the appeal and possible impact of teen courts. Even this perspective, however, leaves court officials with little guidance as to how teen courts should be designed. Until more research is available on the theoretical questions underlying teen court effectiveness, policy makers and practitioners must rely on their own instincts to choose which elements of teen court to emphasize to increase program effectiveness. There are many arguments that have and could be made to support the effectiveness of teen courts, but little sound evidence exists that would allow researchers to judge the validity of each argument.

E. Effectiveness

Despite their popularity, there are still no definitive studies about teen court outcomes. The studies that exist often use weak designs (e.g., no comparison groups), or they involve so few cases that statistical analysis is not highly reliable. The overall impression one gets from the evaluation literature is positive, yet researchers have yet to identify exactly why teen courts are such a promising juvenile justice alternative. Most important, no studies have investigated whether some teen court models are more effective than other models. Some programs place youths in prominent and responsible roles; others do not. Some involve youth judges; others permit only adults to serve as judges. Are these differences important? Do they affect the ability of teen courts to reduce recidivism? Do they shape the experiences of youths, either volunteers or defendants? Researchers have not addressed these important questions.

A few studies have measured recidivism in credible ways, and most have reported very low rates of reoffending among former defendants. Several researchers found rates of post-program recidivism ranging from 3 to 8% within six to twelve months of an appearance in teen court (McNeece et al. 1996; SRA Associates 1995). Others have estimated recidivism to be between 10 and 25% (Harrison, Maupin, and Mays 2001; LoGalbo and Callahan 2001). A few researchers have found higher recidivism rates, but these are often evaluations of teen courts that accept adjudicated rather than diverted juveniles. Minor and his colleagues, for example, found that nearly one third (32%) of teen court alumni reoffended within one year, but the program involved in that study handled youths referred to teen court as a dispositional alternative after juvenile court adjudication (Minor et al. 1999). The offenders it served could have been from a more delinquent population than would be true of the typical teen court caseload.

Some studies have used comparison groups to measure the possible effects of teen courts on recidivism. Hissong (1991) suggested that teen court participants were significantly less likely to reoffend than a comparison group (24% versus 36%). A North Carolina study (North Carolina Administrative Office of the Courts 1995) matched teen court cases and comparison group cases using several factors and failed to find statistically significant differences in the recidivism of the two groups. Seyfrit and her colleagues (1987) tracked recidivism outcomes in a Georgia teen court and also found little difference in the recidivism of teen court youth and comparison youth.

The 2002 study by the Urban Institute is still one of the best teen court studies available (Butts, Buck, and Coggeshall 2002). The project used a quasi-experimental design to study teen courts in four jurisdictions (Alaska, Arizona, Maryland, and Missouri). Researchers compared more than five hundred teen court cases with similar cases handled in the traditional juvenile justice process. In three of the four study sites, recidivism was lower for teen court youth than for the comparison group. In Alaska, for example, recidivism for teen court cases was 6%, compared with 23% of cases handled by the traditional juvenile justice system and matched with the teen court sample on variables such as age, sex, ethnicity, and offense history ($p < .01$). In Missouri, the recidivism rate was 9% in teen court and 27% in the traditional process ($p < .01$).

F. Policy and Practice Issues

Teen courts are considered a "promising" model of intervention, but their procedures and operations vary significantly, as do their effects. Some teen court programs are youth programs in name only. In these teen courts, adults are responsible for nearly everything, including all facets of the public hearing process and any courtroom procedures necessary to complete each case. Youth volunteers may serve as the lawyers, clerks, and bailiffs, but an adult judge calls the cases, instructs the jury, guides the questioning of defendants, and determines an appropriate sentence for each case. Even a casual observer would conclude that youth participation in such a courtroom was largely symbolic.

In other teen courts, young people are very much in charge. From the moment a young defendant and his or her parent enters the courtroom, they see teenagers filling all of the major courtroom roles, including that of judge. Youths as young as 14 or 15 years of age are responsible for maintaining order and moving each case through to completion. In the strongest teen court models, adults are not even allowed to speak in court unless they have been explicitly recognized by the youth judge or judges. Programs using this model are sometimes supported by well-organized "youth bar associations" whose members design and manage their own bar exams and hold periodic training programs, mock trials, and so forth (Butts, Buck, and Coggeshall 2002).

It would seem obvious that these two different styles of teen court could have very different effects on youth volunteers, youth defendants, and their parents. Teen courts run by youths themselves may be more effective in encouraging youth responsibility and community engagement. Yet no studies have investigated the differential impact of the competing models of teen court. Teen courts are proliferating at a rapid pace in the United States, but there is no research information to guide the choices of local officials as they develop new teen courts. Most communities continue to adopt the adult judge model, perhaps because it is the easier model to manage and it is more familiar to local juvenile justice officials, but researchers have yet to answer important questions about its effectiveness.

IV. Juvenile Drug Courts

Rapidly growing numbers of drug arrests during the 1980s and 1990s led law enforcement agencies and criminal courts to devise new approaches for dealing with drug-involved offenders. Many jurisdictions turned to drug courts, a model that first appeared in Florida during late 1980s. The idea behind drug courts in the criminal (or adult) justice system is relatively simple. Drug courts provide defendants with an opportunity to have their charges dismissed or their sentences modified in return for completing a course of drug treatment under court supervision. Those who fail in drug court, however, may serve a sentence as long as—or perhaps longer than—they otherwise would have. Drug court programs employ a variety of techniques to ensure that offenders complete their treatment program. Case managers coordinate a comprehensive service-delivery plan, including drug treatment, mental health services, job training, educational and housing assistance, and any other program as needed. Clients are required to comply with frequent drug tests and to appear in regular review hearings, often held in open or public sessions. During drug court hearings, a judge reviews the progress of each case and discusses recent developments with the program staff, the defendant, and often the defendant's family. Offenders are usually involved in the drug court process until they have established a sustained period of program compliance and a lengthy record of clean drug tests—typically twelve to eighteen months.

A. Origins

The drug court concept is more than twenty years old and still growing in popularity. Less than a decade after the first Florida program opened in 1989, drug courts were operating in hundreds of communities across the United States. By 2010, there were more than two thousand drug courts either in operation or in the planning stages (Office of National Drug Control Strategy 2010). The first drug courts were for adult offenders, and adult programs are still the most common type of drug court. Juvenile drug courts, however, began to appear in the mid-1990s. By 2009, about five hundred juvenile drug courts were operating in the United States.

There are many reasons for the rapid expansion of adult drug courts in the United States. First, drug arrests nearly tripled during the 1980s and 1990s. According to law enforcement data collected annually by the Federal Bureau of Investigation, the total number of drug arrests in the United States grew from 580,900 to 1,702,537 between 1980 and 2008 (Federal Bureau of Investigation 2009). With drug offenders overwhelming court systems, the need for effective diversion programs was clear. Funding was also a powerful impetus. The federal government invested heavily in promoting and implementing drug courts. Federal funding for drug courts was first authorized in Title V of the Violent Crime Control and Law Enforcement Act of 1994 (Public Law No. 103–322). The U.S. Department of Justice then established a Drug Courts Program Office (DCPO) to administer the funds and to provide leadership for program development. By 1997, federal appropriations for drug courts had grown to $30 million annually. During the early years of the twenty-first century, federal investments in drug courts averaged $40 million annually. With federal and state expenditures combined, the total investment in drug courts likely exceeds $2 billion. As many as one million individuals have participated in drug court (Roman and Markman 2010).

B. Operations

The appeal of the drug court model in the adult justice system is compelling and easy to understand. Drug courts allow the criminal justice system to intervene promptly and more aggressively in cases where untreated drug problems will likely result in additional criminal charges and higher court costs. Using the drug court model, the adult justice system is able to increase its oversight of drug-related cases. It can use judicial authority to ensure the delivery of appropriate treatment for drug-involved offenders.

The reasons for introducing drug courts inside the juvenile justice system are more complicated. The traditional juvenile court process is designed to identify the needs of offenders and to monitor their compliance with court-ordered treatment. The creation of juvenile drug courts in the 1990s seemed to be largely the result of funding incentives (Butts and Roman 2004). Many juvenile drug courts began with federal funding, and there were few specific requirements for program operations linked to that funding. At best, the agencies that received funding to start the first juvenile drug courts were merely encouraged to adopt the "10 Key Components" of effective programs, as promulgated by drug court advocacy groups (National Association of Drug Court Professionals 1997). These components represented general guidance rather than a specific framework for program design or a theory of effectiveness based on research or client outcome data. The lack of specifics led to broad experimentation in drug courts, much of it driven by ad hoc policy-making (Butts and Roman 2004). Thus, there is tremendous variation in program operations, including substantial variation in the target population, the type and severity of participant drug use, and the requirements for program completion (referred to as graduation).

In general, however, juvenile drug courts share the following five elements:

1) Individualized and less adversarial courtroom procedures allow judges and other drug court staff to collaborate openly in motivating young offenders to desist from drug use and sustain desistance.
2) Treatment plans are consistent with the goals established for each youth during court hearings.
3) A visible and consistent system of sanctions and rewards (both in and out of the courtroom) encourages prosocial behavior while deterring deviant behavior among juvenile clients.
4) An effective system of case management services matches offenders and services to ensure consistency in the application of rewards and sanctions.
5) Courts, and especially judges, draw upon their community standing and their leadership skills to ensure the availability of high-quality treatment and supervision services and to hold the services system accountable for youths, their families, and the community.

The working environment in juvenile drug courts is different from that of traditional juvenile courts. Instead of the bureaucratic, sometimes impersonal atmosphere of the contemporary juvenile courtroom, juvenile drug courts employ a more personal, team-oriented courtroom where procedures are highly interactive, even theatrical. Practitioners place great value on the dynamic interaction between offenders and judges in drug court proceedings. Juvenile drug court judges motivate participants by maintaining close and frequent communication with each youth and by keeping track of each offender's personal situation from one hearing to the next. A judge may confront a young offender with the results of a failed drug test and apply a sanction in one hearing, and then praise the youth for a clean drug test and provide a reward in the next hearing. During court hearings, the judge plays the role of a concerned authority figure, compassionate when possible but always ready to impose sanctions (including detention) so that offenders understand their actions have consequences. Juvenile drug courts share many of the characteristics of adult drug courts. Both are designed to provide intensive supervision of drug-involved offenders and to use an array of treatment and social services to assist (or coerce) offenders to desist from drug use. In juvenile as well as adult drug courts, shared hearings with fellow participants are a central part of the process. All aspects of the drug court process should convey the message that the only way to avoid sanctions and deeper involvement with the justice system is to follow program rules and to make a sincere effort to change.

The period of participation in juvenile drug courts is somewhat shorter than adult drug courts, usually less than twelve months. There are other important differences between juvenile drug courts and adult drug courts. Juvenile drug courts place a greater emphasis on the role of the family in all facets of court operations, from assessment and treatment, to courtroom procedures, and to the structure of rewards and sanctions. Juvenile drug courts usually include more significant outreach to each offender's home and community. They are more likely to mobilize the efforts of other significant people in each youth's life to create teams of program partners that can teach, supervise, coach, and discipline youthful offenders. Ideally, they also incorporate development-based treatment strategies that take into account the age and cognitive capacity of each client, and they consider each offender's school performance and peer relationships as well as their work and family obligations.

C. Theory

Juvenile drug courts reflect the key features of the juvenile justice process. They are founded on the notion that adolescents are different from adults and that the root causes of adolescent substance use often are found in developmental challenges and family-related risk factors. The juvenile drug court process is similar to that of traditional juvenile courts, but with several important differences: (1) juvenile drug courts involve greater judicial oversight of case progress; (2) there are many more court appearances; and (3) the purposes and goals of substance abuse treatment are closely integrated with the entire court process.

Substantial research literature links substance use and abuse to criminal behaviors, although little of that research specifically looks at the relationship between juvenile substance use and delinquent behavior (Anglin and Perrochet 1998; Ball, Shaffer, and Nurco 1983; Boyum and Kleiman 2002; Brownstein et al. 1992; Condon and Smith 2003; Dawkins 1997; Harrison and Gfroerer 1992; Inciardi et al. 1996; Inciardi 1992; Inciardi and Pottieger 1994; MacCoun and Reuter 2001; Miller and Gold 1994; Mocan and Tekin 2003). The psychopharmacologic effects of substance use may lead drug users to commit crimes when intoxicated, while the economic-compulsive effects of drug use lead users to commit crimes to gain resources to buy drugs (Goldstein 1985). The violence associated with illegal drug trade and the victimization of intoxicated drug users also contribute to drug-related crime (Boyum and Kleiman 2002; Cottler et al. 1992; Goldstein 1985; MacCoun, Kilmer, and Reuter 2003). Drug sellers are often drug users (Reuter, MacCoun, and Murphy 1990), and young drug users and suppliers are more likely than other youths to be violent (Blumstein and Cork 1996; MacCoun, Kilmer, and Reuter 2003). Criminal activity increases as the frequency and intensity of drug use increases (Anglin, Longshore, and Turner 1999; Anglin and Maugh 1992; Chaiken and Chaiken 1990; Stewart et al. 2000; Vito 1989). Conversely, crime decreases as drug use declines, particularly income-generating crimes (Anglin, Longshore, and Turner 1999; Chaiken and Chaiken 1982; Degenhardt et al. 2005; Inciardi 1987; Nurco, Kinlock, and Hanlon 1990; Speckert and Anglin 1986).

Juvenile drug courts build on three theoretical concepts to break the link between drug use and crime: (1) therapeutic jurisprudence, (2) substance abuse treatment, and (3) specific deterrence. Therapeutic jurisprudence is a legal philosophy that defines the courts' approach to justice (Hora, Schma, and Rosenthal 1999; Senjo and Leip 2001). Therapeutic jurisprudence builds upon procedural justice theory, which states that a fair process will result in more positive participant attitudes, which are associated ultimately with better outcomes. A number of studies have found that participation in adult drug court reduces recidivism rates (Finigan 1998; Goldkamp and Weiland 1993; Gottfredson and Exum 2002; Harrell and Roman 2001; Jameson and Peterson 1995; Peters and Murrin 2000; Wilson, Mitchell, and MacKenzie 2006). A critical factor in the effectiveness of courtroom procedures may be their conformance to the concepts of procedural justice (see Tyler 1990 for a review of procedural justice). According to Harrell and Hirst (2000), courts provide effective procedural justice when they ensure that:

- mutual "trust" exists among all court participants;
- all participants have sufficient opportunities to be heard ("voice");
- the fact-finding process operates with demonstrable "accuracy";
- the hearing and sanctioning process is transparent, impartial, and fair ("neutrality"); and
- participants are granted "standing" by being treated with respect.

The theoretical concepts underlying treatment for substance abuse often focus on cognitive behavioral linkages between youth coping strategies and specific developmental goals, including desistance from drug use. There is a substantial literature linking substance abuse treatment to reductions in demand for drugs and associated offending, although again this literature mainly concerns adults. Studies have found that:

- treatment is more cost-effective than incarceration in producing behavior change (Caulkins and Reuter 1997; MacKenzie 2006; Lipsey and Cullen 2007);
- intensive and long-term treatment is more effective than less intensive and shorter treatment (National Institute on Drug Abuse 2009);
- direct interaction with a judge is more effective for serious drug users (Marlowe, Festinger, and Lee 2004); and
- violent offenses cause the greatest economic damage to communities (Cohen and Miller 2003).

Specific deterrence causes improved participant compliance by imposing swift, certain, and increasingly severe punishments in response to client infractions, thus creating strong incentives for compliance. Deterrence is one of the founding principles of the justice system in that people adjust their behavior according to how effectively the law rewards desirable conduct and punishes unwanted conduct (Nagin 1998). The three classic ingredients of punishment are certainty, severity, and celerity (or swiftness). Of these, the most important may be certainty. When individuals perceive that punishments are very likely to follow illegal or unwanted behavior, they are less likely to engage in such behavior. In fact, once certainty is taken into account, the severity and speed of punishment seems to have less effect on behavior (Grogger 1991). In juvenile drug court, deterrence takes two forms. First, successful drug court participants are often diverted from the traditional delinquency process. Thus, the threat of adjudication itself deters new offending. Second, graduated sanctions are imposed for noncompliance with drug court rules, and these sanctions, including brief stays in detention, often become incrementally more severe for each new infraction. Thus, the immediate threat of sanctioning contributes to desistance.

D. Clients

Juvenile drug courts vary substantially in the types of clients they serve. Programs in rural areas are more likely to serve clients for whom alcohol and/or marijuana are the drugs of choice; access to treatment is often limited. Juvenile drug courts in urban areas may have access to sophisticated treatments, including Multisystemic Therapy, and they may serve youths with more serious drug problems. The mix of clients in any juvenile drug court stems in part from the attributes of the drug- and alcohol-using population in the area, and partly from the risk tolerance of the court, the prosecutor, and the community in general. Drug courts have traditionally excluded individuals with current or prior violence in their criminal histories. In addition, drug courts may reject some potential participants because the community lacks resources to treat those individuals and their behavioral challenges. For instance, many communities lack residential treatment facilities for adolescents; few communities have outpatient programs that are appropriate for adolescents; and resources for treating non-English speakers are often scarce. Other criteria leading to disqualification for drug court include co-occurring disorders of substance abuse and mental illness, youths who have failed prior treatment attempts, or those who simply appear to be bad risks to a court or prosecutor.

Hiller and his colleagues (1998) noted more than ten years ago that the research literature on juvenile dug courts was extremely limited, and unfortunately, it remains limited. With respect to the core activity of treating substance abuse, "little is known about drug treatment as it is provided within JDCs, and it is likely that principles for evidence-based practice are not closely followed in some programs" (Hiller et al. 1998, p. 17). Juvenile drug courts may attempt to link juveniles with drug treatment providers in the community, but many are forced to use inappropriate models (such as Alcoholics Anonymous) to supplement that treatment. Because many communities have limited treatment options for youths, the target population of the juvenile drug court can vary according to the availability and accessibility of appropriate treatments. Typically, most participants in juvenile drug courts are 15 to 17 years of age and are using marijuana and alcohol almost exclusively (Butts and Roman 2004; Hiller et al. 1998).

E. Effectiveness

Much of what passes for knowledge about juvenile drug court effectiveness comes from studies of adult courts. From these studies, it is fair to conclude that about half of drug court participants will graduate successfully and that drug court participation appears to yield moderate reductions in new offending. Meta-analyses of fifty prior drug court studies found a 10% to 20% reduction in new offending, and recidivism among drug court graduates is well below the average for drug-involved offenders. Drug courts appear to be cost-effective and have the potential to yield even larger benefits if policies for client eligibility were more controlled. Research on adult drug courts suggests that desistance in drug use may not persist beyond the period of drug court participation, and there is little evidence to evaluate whether other important outcomes related to health, education, and labor market participation are improved by drug court. Drug courts almost certainly cost more than business-as-usual court processing, excluding any associated costs of incarceration. Most studies estimate between $4,000 and $5,000 in new costs for each drug court participant. Courts serving clients with more serious substance problems and thus likely to require more expensive services, such as residential treatment, may experience higher costs, but if effective, could generate higher returns as well.

Research on juvenile drug courts is very limited. Quasi-experimental studies of juvenile drug courts have shown mixed results. Matched comparison studies found no significant reductions in drug use or delinquency (Rodriguez and Webb 2004; Gilmore, Rodriguez, and Webb 2005). Not surprisingly, studies that compared dropouts to program completers found improvements in the incidence of delinquency (Applegate and Santana 2000; Miller, Scocas, and O'Connell 1998; O'Connell, Nestlerode, and Miller 1999; Shaw and Robinson 1998). Recently, a series of studies have tested whether incorporating Multisystemic Therapy into juvenile drug courts yields better participant outcomes. A series of random controlled trials have demonstrated substantial improvements in drug use and delinquency outcomes (Henggeler 2007; Henggeler et al. 2006). However, while Multisystemic Therapy has been shown to be a cost-effective strategy (Aos et al. 2001), it is very expensive to operate and has been employed in few juvenile drug courts. It is not clear from these studies whether juvenile drug courts would be capable of generating similar outcomes with other, less expensive therapeutic approaches.

Despite a growing consensus that substance abuse treatment promotes desistance, few juvenile arrestees receive sufficient treatment through the juvenile justice system to reduce their offending. Strict eligibility rules and scarce resources limit access to treatment, even in jurisdictions operating juvenile drug courts. While there are drug courts operating in most mid- and large-sized counties in the United

States, most are very small and serve fewer than thirty clients annually. Thus, only a small number of drug-involved arrestees are likely to receive intensive and long-term treatment in lieu of detention. As a result, existing linkages between the justice system and the substance abuse treatment system are so constrained that at best, only small reductions in crime are being achieved (Bhati, Roman, and Chalfin 2008).

F. Policy and Practice Issues

Does the availability of a juvenile drug court cause some drug-using youth to penetrate the justice system further than what their criminal charges would suggest? Many juvenile drug courts accept youths with limited criminal histories and no reliable indications of severe drug problems (Butts and Roman 2004). A single arrest for marijuana possession could be enough to qualify a youth for drug court in many jurisdictions. If youths with only minor drug problems end up in a juvenile drug court, what does the community gain? For some of these youths, drug court may help them to avoid future drug abuse and costly legal trouble. For others, drug court could turn out to be just as damaging to their futures as drug use. Formalized legal intervention with adolescents is not risk-free. Young people who are arrested and brought to court may be more likely to grow up to become adult criminals than similar youths who are allowed to discover for themselves how to be law-abiding and drug-free (Bernburg and Krohn 2003). If a drug court program were to accept many clients without serious drug problems or criminal involvement, the program would not only fail to have a significant effect on drug-related crime in the community, it also could turn out to be harmful for some youths. Nearly twenty years after the first juvenile drug courts appeared, these important questions remain unanswered.

V. Juvenile Mental Health Courts

Like drug courts, mental health courts respond to a particular type of case that traditional courts find challenging—offenders with mental health problems. Mental health courts first emerged in the criminal justice system in the late 1990s, beginning in the state of Florida. As the model met with early success and growing optimism, it spread quickly throughout the adult justice system. A few years later, the strategy appeared in the juvenile court system as well. Juvenile mental health courts evolved like other problem-solving courts. They are designed to address unmet needs among a targeted group of people—in this case, chronic low-level juvenile offenders with severe mental illness.

In 2001, Santa Clara County, California, opened the first juvenile mental health court. Court officials hoped the Court for the Individualized Treatment of

Adolescents (CITA) would not only address the needs of juvenile offenders with serious mental illness using a multidisciplinary team approach, but also underscore the critical gap in resources for these youths (Behnken, Arredondo, and Packman 2009). The strategy was to embrace an offender-based rather than offense-based approach that considers an array of factors related to the juvenile, including the youth's mental health, developmental stage, emotional needs, and public safety (Arredondo 2003). Practitioners associated with a juvenile mental health court see crimes through a lens in which behaviors are possible symptoms of mental illness, and their goal is to create a safety net of appropriate treatment options for youthful offenders (National Council on Disabilities 2003).

Juvenile mental health courts share many structural and procedural characteristics with other specialized courts. They emphasize individualized case processing, coupled with a multidisciplinary team approach and regular judicial supervision. They offer a balance of swift and consistent sanctions combined with treatment. Santa Clara County implemented CITA based on the "systems of care" approach, focusing on the family context and working across organizational systems. The court is guided by the notion that early and appropriate intervention allows juveniles with mental health issues to receive services and thereby avoid further legal trouble (Behnken, Arredondo, and Packman 2009). Juvenile mental health courts are beginning to catch on in communities across the United States. As of 2007, the National Center for Mental Health and Juvenile Justice identified eighteen operating juvenile mental health courts, and twenty other jurisdictions had signaled their intention to open juvenile mental health courts (Council of State Governments 2008). To understand the context in which these courts are growing in popularity, it is important to review the reasons for their creation.

A. Origins

The dearth of mental health services for youths in the justice system has long been decried by mental health professionals. They support their arguments by pointing to high rates of mental health disorders among young offenders. One study, for example, found that nearly two-thirds of the juveniles held in Chicago's juvenile detention center had mental health problems, although the figure included many youths with minor disorders and substance use issues (Teplin et al. 2002). The Coalition for Juvenile Justice estimated in its 2000 report to Congress that 50 to 75% of the youthful offenders placed in secure correctional facilities nationwide had diagnosable mental health disorders (Coalition for Juvenile Justice 2000). The data confirmed what advocates had long argued: facilities holding juvenile offenders were becoming a "dumping ground" for youths with various forms of mental illness (Lang 2003; Behnken, Arredondo, and Packman 2009).

The reasons behind these disturbing figures are complex. The proportion of youth with detectable mental health problems appears to increase as juveniles move through the justice process. McReynolds and her colleagues (2008) measured the prevalence of mental health disorders among youths soon after their arrest by law enforcement, regardless whether their arrest resulted in formal legal charges. Among these youths, just 29% had some form of diagnosable mental disorder, and a third of those disorders involved substance use. Wasserman and her colleagues (2005) measured mental health problems among youths referred to a juvenile probation intake department. In other words, they examined youths deeper into the justice system than the youths studied by McReynolds and her colleagues, but not as deeply in the system as youths held in correctional facilities. In the Wasserman sample, 46% of youths had some form of diagnosable disorder, including substance abuse.

The pattern is clear. As one looks deeper into the juvenile justice process—from initial contact, to probation intake, to incarceration—the prevalence of mental health problems among young offenders increases. Whether the pattern reflects a correlation between mental health problems and juvenile offending or it results from the effects of differential handling by justice authorities who are more likely to intervene in cases involving mental health problems, the policy conclusions are the same. Communities need better intervention strategies for youths with mental health disorders to prevent them from moving into the deep end of the justice system (Behnken, Arredondo, and Packman 2009).

Juvenile mental health courts appear to fill a service gap caused by the failure of two systems—mental health and juvenile justice (Grisso 2004; Steadman et al. 1999). This failure stems from a number of problems in the way mentally disordered juveniles are managed by traditional courts, including inadequate screening and assessment, a shortage of mental health treatment, a lack of collaboration among relevant agencies, and poor coordination between youth, families, and service providers. Given the cross-agency nature of these issues, organizational collaboration must play a central role. Juvenile mental health courts, with their emphasis on a multidisciplinary team approach, may provide such a framework (National Council on Disabilities 2003).

B. Clients

Juvenile mental health courts serve a population of offenders with very specific characteristics. Broadly speaking, most courts accept nonviolent youths who have committed a criminal offense and been diagnosed with a severe mental illness. Some courts prohibit youths from participating if they have been charged with serious offenses—for example, murder, arson, and rape—or if they are suspected of gang involvement. Other courts serve only youths with co-occurring diagnoses, or those with both mental health and substance abuse issues. Most juvenile mental health courts screen youths for eligibility based on the severity of their mental illness, excluding those with minor or transient disorders. Nearly all courts, for example, exclude youths diagnosed with only oppositional defiant disorder or conduct disorder (Cocozza and Shufelt 2006).

The National Center for Mental Health and Juvenile Justice identified several key aspects of juvenile mental health courts (Cocozza and Shufelt 2006).

- Courts are most effective when they are just one component of a broader approach to meet the mental health needs of juveniles, including treatment initiatives and alternatives to detention.
- Most courts use a post-adjudication model, while there are a few that operate at the pre-adjudication stage.
- The majority of courts do not restrict access based on type of offense, admitting juveniles who have committed either misdemeanors or felonies, though several exercise discretion regarding whether to accept offenders who have committed very violent felonies.
- There is little consensus among juvenile mental health courts on diagnostic criteria for program admission.

C. Operations

Juvenile mental health courts are similar to adult mental health courts in many ways, and they present many of the same benefits and challenges. Because of their participants' status as minors, however, mental health courts for juveniles involve other issues, including the effect of developmental issues on cognition and behavior, the effectiveness of mental health treatment with adolescents, the critical involvement of parents and guardians, and the role of schools and other service systems (Council of State Governments 2008). Most juvenile mental health courts operate inside the juvenile court system, but some are administered by probation, and others may be operated by a state family services agency (Cocozza and Shufelt 2006). All juvenile mental health courts function as a separate docket, frequently overseen by a single judge, and have as their primary mission connecting participating youths to existing community-based mental health services. Most of these courts identify their clients through mental health screening and assessment, usually after adjudication but prior to disposition. Other courts function at the pre-adjudication stage, while some may serve as an aftercare program for juveniles transitioning out of residential facilities.

Most juvenile mental health courts involve multidisciplinary teams consisting of probation staff, defense attorneys, prosecutors, case managers, and treatment providers. Teams work together to develop individualized treatment plans, to monitor client progress and compliance with treatment, and to make recommendations to the court. The members of such teams often address institutional and structural barriers that can complicate cross-agency collaboration. For example, the team may tackle issues related to jargon, conflicting departmental objectives, and different means of achieving "success" (Behnken, Arredondo, and Packman 2009). Juvenile mental health courts provide a range of treatment to participating youths that includes traditional services, such as individual, group, and family therapy; case management; and medication management services.

The length of a youth's participation in juvenile mental health court varies widely, from a few months to two years or more. An offender's participation may end when the term of probation is over, the youth's mental health issues are stabilized, or after successful program completion. The terms of program compliance commonly include electronic monitoring (e.g., ankle bracelet), home visits, community supervision, and regular judicial review hearings to ensure adherence to the treatment plan. Participation may end prematurely if the juvenile fails to comply with terms of probation, commits a new crime, or the youth and/or parent chooses to withdraw from the program (Arredondo et al. 2001; National Council on Disabilities 2003).

D. Effectiveness

There is very little empirical research on the effectiveness of mental health courts, especially for programs serving youths. In a review of the literature, Cocozza and Shufelt (2006) found that nearly all research on mental health courts focused on adult courts, and most studies are program descriptions (e.g., Goldkamp and Irons-Guynn 2000), policy papers (e.g., Redlich 2006), or process evaluations (e.g., Steadman et al. 2005). To the extent that researchers have examined mental health courts for juveniles, they appear to have incorporated the basic components seen in other specialty courts, such as collaboration among stakeholders and swift and consistent sanctions (Roman and Harrell 2001). Preliminary investigations into the first two mental health courts for juveniles suggested that they focus on strengthening relationships between the juvenile justice and mental health systems—a critical ingredient to the effectiveness and success of any specialty court (Mears 2001)—but the findings of the studies are subject to interpretation (Behnken, Arredondo, and Packman 2009).

Like other specialized courts, the absence of a standardized program model suitable for replication across jurisdictions has inhibited the clarity of evaluation findings for juvenile mental health courts. The heterogeneity of program models makes it impractical to compare any one court to another. There is no consensus regarding what defines a mental health court. Every jurisdiction reinvents the model, which leads to highly varying eligibility criteria, target populations, program lengths, and intensity (Council of State Governments 2008). In addition, every court has access to different community resources and funding streams (Trupin and Richards 2003; Watson et al. 2001). At best, the research suggests that the model has merit, but the realities of program implementation render client results unpredictable.

E. Policy and Practice Issues

As juvenile mental health courts expand across the county, it is clear that communities see them as an attractive alternative to the traditional court system for juvenile offenders with mental health disorders. More research, however, will be necessary to determine how successful they are in reducing recidivism and to explore the impact of the courts on participating service systems. There are several potential benefits associated with juvenile mental health courts, including the ability of the judiciary to leverage youth access to community-based mental health services and the court's ability to mandate youth and family compliance with treatment orders. The monitoring strategies employed by the courts may enhance client adherence to treatment orders, and the presence of the mental health court itself may help to expand dispositional alternatives for youths. Communities may benefit from the introduction of the multidisciplinary team approach favored by mental health courts. Collaboration among systems improves the coordination of services for youths, and each effort to form an interagency partnership raises new awareness of the issues and challenges faced by individual organizations. This increased awareness helps to draw attention to resource limitations and may increase support among community members for adding additional services.

Although there are many benefits associated with the implementation of juvenile mental health courts, there are also risks. The National Mental Health Association (2009) summarized the concerns seen across the professional literature (Tyuse and Linhorst 2005; Powell 2003; Wolff 2002). Many of these issues relate to whether the courts are too coercive and whether they stigmatize and criminalize the mentally ill. The most pressing issue, common to other specialized courts, is whether the existence of the courts contributes to "net-widening" by drawing youths into the juvenile justice system who previously would not have received legal sanctions, merely in order to facilitate service delivery. Some believe that because the courts wield considerable power in breaking down barriers to mental health services, their actions may unintentionally coerce youths into participation. Research indicates that in order for mental health interventions to have lasting effects, client participation must be voluntary (Monahan et al. 2001). Taking into account a youth's mental health status, together with the power asymmetry implicit in a minor's status, critics argue that risks remain even for youths agreeing to participate voluntarily. Some research exploring this dynamic, however, reveals that participants do not report feeling coerced; to the contrary, they report feeling more positive toward the court and toward the legal system due to their extensive interactions with the judge (Poythress et al. 2002).

Aside from the potential misuse of judicial resources and the collateral consequences for youths associated with unnecessary contact with the justice system, there are other concerns related to the potential for juvenile mental health courts to disrupt effective community service systems. Because the mental health resources available to courts are the same hard-to-access resources that exist for other agencies in the community, some critics question whether a court's efforts to secure treatment for its clients may be tantamount to "cutting in line," as court-ordered youths receive priority while others wait longer for service (Cocozza and Shufelt 2006).

Finally, policy makers must confront fundamental questions about whether juvenile mental health courts are even necessary. Even proponents question whether the key elements of mental health court—the multidisciplinary team approach and its orientation toward treatment—could just as well operate in a traditional juvenile court (Cocozza and Shufelt 2006). However, the fact remains that juvenile mental health courts, despite their limitations, fill an apparent gap in services and connect youths with treatment resources that would otherwise remain unavailable to them. The research is very clear that ignoring mental illness among youth offenders can have tragic consequences. Mental health courts are advocated as an effective way for the legal system to support "the evolution of policy toward more contemporary standards of decency" (Behnken, Arredondo, and Packman 2009, p. 25). Despite their benefits, however, a number of substantive issues and implementation challenges remain.

VI. Conclusion

Problem-solving courts first appeared in the adult justice system in the late 1980s and early 1990s. Soon after, the juvenile justice system began to develop them as well. Thousands of teen courts, juvenile drug courts, and juvenile mental health courts now exist in communities across the United States. Ironically, the principles underlying these problem-solving courts are largely the same as those advanced by the American juvenile court movement of the late nineteenth and early twentieth century (Tanenhaus 2004). Lawmakers founded the original juvenile courts because they believed that many young people charged with crimes were still redeemable and that the crimes of children deserved a different kind of legal response. The juvenile court process was to focus on the offender, not the offense. Juvenile court intervention was to correct harmful behavior and not simply to punish it. Instead of merely imposing a sentence that was proportionate to their offenses, the juvenile court was to involve each youth in a program of treatment and rehabilitation and then monitor the youth's participation in treatment.

In other words, juvenile courts were founded on the same ideas that today inspire the "new" movement toward problem-solving courts. Noting this irony, some experts have observed that drug courts—the most popular type of specialized court—are essentially juvenile courts for adults (Butts and Roman 2004). Why then, is it necessary to invent new, problem-solving courts for juveniles within the existing juvenile court system? The growing use of problem-solving courts for juveniles may be tacit acknowledgement that juvenile courts have strayed so far from their historical mission that the legal system needs a new version of the original juvenile court model as an alternative to contemporary juvenile justice.

Of course, one could make a similar argument for the criminal (or adult) justice system. The goals advanced by problem-solving courts—harm reduction, individualized behavior correction, and community well-being—were not new in the 1980s when drug courts first appeared. They were not new even in the late 1800s when the juvenile court movement adopted a similar mission. Ameliorating social problems and reducing harmful behavior has always been a basic purpose of the law. Problem-solving courts may be new in one sense, but their mission is very old. The model of a problem-solving court is simply a reformulation of the foundational goals of justice.

The growing presence of problem-solving courts in the legal system today may be due less to their revolutionary approach than to their effectiveness at correcting a long-standing imperfection in the operations of the justice system. In practice, the justice system may have allowed some elements of its mission—namely, retribution and deterrence—to supplant other, equally important elements—rehabilitation, equity, and social justice. It is easy to see why a new court structure to correct such imbalances would improve the effectiveness of the criminal justice system. That the same strategy may now be necessary in juvenile justice is certainly more intriguing and perhaps more regrettable.

REFERENCES

Action for Children. 2007. "Putting the Juvenile Back in Juvenile Justice." *Juvenile Justice Issue Brief*. Raleigh, NC: Action for Children North Carolina.

Anglin, M. Douglas, Douglas Longshore, and Susan Turner. 1999. "Treatment Alternatives to Street Crime: An Evaluation of Five Programs." *Criminal Justice and Behavior* 26(2): 168–95.

Anglin, M. Douglas, and Thomas H. Maugh, II. 1992. "Ensuring Success in Interventions with Drug Using Offenders." *The ANNALS of the American Academy of Political and Social Science* 521(1): 66–90.

Anglin, M. Douglas, and Brian Perrochet. 1998. "Drug Use and Crime: A Historical Review of Research Conducted by the UCLA Drug Abuse Research Center." *Substance Use & Misuse* 33(9): 1871–914.

Aos, Steve, Polly Phipps, Robert Barnoski, and Roxanne Lieb. 2001. *The Comparative Costs and Benefits of Programs to Reduce Crime Version 4.0*. Olympia: Washington State Institute for Public Policy.

Applegate, Brandon K., and Susan Santana. 2000. "Intervening with Youthful Substance Abusers: A Preliminary Analysis of a Juvenile Drug Court." *The Justice System Journal* 21: 281–300.

Arredondo, David E. 2003. "Child Development, Children's Mental Health and the Juvenile Justice System: Principles for Effective Decision-Making." *Stanford Law & Policy Review* 14(1): 13–28.

Arredondo, David. E., Kurt Kumli, Larry Soto, Enrique Colin, Jill Ornellas, Judge Raymond J. Davilla, Judge Leonard P. Edwards, and Judge Eugene M. Hyman. 2001. "Juvenile Mental Health Court: Rationale and Protocols." *Juvenile and Family Court Journal* 52(4): 1–19.

Ball, John C., John W. Shaffer, and David N. Nurco. 1983. "Day to Day Criminality of Heroin Addicts in Baltimore: A Study in the Continuity of Offense Rates." *Drug and Alcohol Dependence* 12: 119–42.

Behnken, Monic P., David E. Arredondo, and Wendy L. Packman. 2009. "Reduction in Recidivism in a Juvenile Mental Health Court: A Pre- and Post-Treatment Outcome Study." *Juvenile and Family Court Journal* 60(3): 23–44.

Berman, John, and John Feinblatt. 2005. Good Courts—The Case for Problem-Solving Justice. New York: The New Press.

Bernburg, Jón Gunnar, and Marvin D. Krohn. 2003. "Labeling, Life Chances, and Adult Crime: The Direct and Indirect Effects of Official Intervention in Adolescence on Crime in Early Adulthood." *Criminology* 41(4): 1287–318.

Bhati, Avinash S., John K. Roman, and Aaron Chalfin. 2008. *To Treat or Not to Treat: Evidence on the Prospect of Expanding Treatment to Drug-Involved Offenders.* Washington, DC: Urban Institute.

Blumstein, Alfred, and Daniel Cork. 1996. "Linking Gun Availability to Youth Gun Violence." *Law and Contemporary Problems* 59: 5–24.

Boyum, David A., and Mark A. Kleiman. 2002. "Substance-Abuse Policy from a Crime Control Perspective." In *Crime: Public Policies for Crime Control,* edited by James Q. Wilson and Joan Petersilia, 331–82. Oakland, CA: Institute for Contemporary Studies.

Brownstein, Henry H., Hari R. Shiledar Baxi, Paul J. Goldstein, and Patrick J. Ryan. 1992. "The Relationship of Drugs, Drug Trafficking, and Drug Traffickers to Homicide." *Journal of Crime and Justice* 15: 25–44.

Butts, Jeffrey A., and Janeen Buck. 2000. "Teen Courts: A Focus on Research." *Juvenile Justice Bulletin.* Washington, DC: U.S. Department of Justice, Office of Juvenile Justice and Delinquency Prevention.

Butts, Jeffrey A., Janeen Buck, and Mark Coggeshall. 2002. *The Impact of Teen Court on Young Offenders.* Washington, DC: The Urban Institute.

Butts, Jeffrey A., and Adele V. Harrell. 1998. *Delinquents or Criminals? Policy Options for Juvenile Offenders.* Washington, DC: The Urban Institute.

Butts, Jeffrey A., and Ojmarrh Mitchell. 2000. "Brick by Brick: Dismantling the Border Between Juvenile and Adult Justice." In *Boundary Changes in Criminal Justice Organizations,* Vol. 2 of *Criminal Justice 2000,* edited by Charles M. Friel, 167–213. Washington, DC: U.S. Department of Justice, National Institute of Justice.

Butts, Jeffrey A. and John K. Roman, eds. 2004. *Juvenile Drug Courts and Teen Substance Abuse.* Washington, DC: The Urban Institute Press.

Caulkins, Jonathan P., and Peter Reuter. 1997. "Setting Goals for Drug Policy: Harm Reduction or Use Reduction?" *Addiction* 92: 1143–50.

Chaiken, Jan M., and Marcia Chaiken. 1982. "Varieties of Criminal Behavior." *Rand Report R-2814-NIJ.* Santa Monica, CA: Rand Corporation.

Chaiken, Jan M., and Marcia R. Chaiken. 1990. "Drugs and Predatory Crime." *Crime and Justice* 13: 203–39.

Coalition for Juvenile Justice. 2000. "Handle with Care—Serving the Mental Health Needs of Young Offenders." *2000 Annual Report.* Washington, DC: Coalition for Juvenile Justice.

Cocozza, Joseph J., and Jennie L. Shufelt. 2006. "Juvenile Mental Health Courts: An Emerging Strategy." *Research and Program Brief.* Washington, DC: National Center for Mental Health and Juvenile Justice.

Cohen, Mark A., and Ted R. Miller. 2003. "'Willingness to Award' Nonmonetary Damages and the Implied Value of Life from Jury Awards." *International Review of Law and Economics* 23: 165–81.

Condon, Joanne, and Nicola Smith. 2003. *Prevalence of Drug Use: Key Findings from the 2002/2003 British Crime Survey.* London: Home Office.

Cottler, Linda B., Wilson M. Compton, Douglas Mager, Edward L. Spitznagel, and Aleksander Janca. 1992. "Posttraumatic Stress Disorder Among Substance Users from the General Population." *American Journal of Psychiatry* 149: 664–70.

Council of State Governments. 2008. *Mental Health Courts: A Primer for Policymakers and Practitioners.* New York: Council of State Governments Justice Center, Criminal Justice/Mental Health Consensus Project.

Dawkins, Marvin P. 1997. "Drug Use and Violent Crime among Adolescents." *Adolescence* 32: 395–405.

Degenhardt, Louisa, Elizabeth Conroy, Stuart Gilmour, and Linette Collins. 2005. "The Effect of a Reduction in Heroin Supply in Australia upon Drug Distribution and Acquisitive Crime." *The British Journal of Criminology* 45: 2–24.

Feld, Barry C. 1999. *Bad Kids—Race and the Transformation the Juvenile Court*. New York: Oxford University Press.

Finigan, Michael. 1998. *An Outcome Program Evaluation of the Multnomah County S.T.O.P. Drug Diversion Program*. West Linn, OR: Northwest Professional Consortium.

Gilmore, Amna Saddik, Nancy Rodriguez, and Vincent J. Webb. 2005. "Substance Abuse and Drug Courts: The Role of Social Bonds in Juvenile Drug Courts." *Youth Violence and Juvenile Justice* 3: 287–315.

Godwin, Tracy. 2000. *National Youth Court Guidelines*. Washington, DC: U.S. Department of Justice, Office of Juvenile Justice and Delinquency Prevention.

Goldkamp, John S., and Cheryl Irons-Guynn. 2000. *Emerging Judicial Strategies for the Mentally Ill in the Criminal Caseload: Mental health Courts in Fort Lauderdale, Seattle, San Bernardino, and Anchorage*. Washington, DC: U.S. Department of Justice, Office of Justice Programs.

Goldkamp, John S., and Doris Weiland. 1993. *Assessing the Impact of Dade County's Felony Drug Court*. Washington, DC: U.S. Department of Justice, Office of Justice Programs, National Institute of Justice.

Goldstein, Paul. 1985. "The Drug/Violence Nexus: A Tripartite Conceptual Framework." *Journal of Drug Issues* 14: 493–506.

Gottfredson, Denise C., and M. Lyn Exum. 2002. "The Baltimore City Drug Treatment Court: One-year Results from a Randomized Study Effectiveness." *Journal of Research in Crime and Delinquency* 39: 3.

Grisso, Thomas. 2004. *Double Jeopardy: Adolescent Offenders with Mental Disorders*. Chicago, IL: The University of Chicago Press.

Grogger, Jeffrey. 1991. "Certainty vs. Severity of Punishment." *Economic Inquiry* 29(2): 297–309.

Harrell, Adele V., and Alexa Hirst. 2000. "Measuring Perceptions of Procedural Justice among Court-Monitored Offenders." Presented at the American Society of Criminology. Washington, DC: Urban Justice.

Harrell, Adele V., and John K. Roman. 2001. "Reducing Drug Use and Crime among Offenders: The Impact of Graduated Sanctions." *Journal of Drug Issues* 31(1): 207–32.

Harrison, Lana, and Joseph Gfroerer. 1992. "The Intersections of Drug Use and Criminal Behavior: Results from the National Household Survey on Drug Abuse." *Crime and Delinquency* 38: 422–43.

Harrison, Paige, James R. Maupin, and G. Larry Mays. 2001. "Teen Court: An Examination of Processes and Outcomes." *Crime and Delinquency* 47: 243–64.

Henggeler, Scott W. 2007. "Juvenile Drug Court: Emerging Outcomes and Key Research Issues." *Opinions in Psychiatry* 20: 242–46.

Henggeler, Scott W., Colleen A. Halliday-Boykins, Phillippe B. Cunningham, Jeff Randall, Steven B. Shapiro, and Jason E. Chapman. 2006. "Juvenile Drug Court: Enhancing Outcomes by Integrating Evidence-Based Treatments." *Journal of Consulting and Clinical Psychology* 74: 42–54.

Hiller, Matthew L., Kevin Knight, Kirk M. Broome, and D. Wayne Simpson. 1998. "Legal Pressure and Treatment Retention in a National Sample of Long-Term Residential Programs." *Criminal Justice and Behavior* 25(4): 463–81.

Hissong, Rod. 1991. "Teen Court—Is It an Effective Alternative to Traditional Sanctions?" *Journal for Juvenile Justice and Detention Services* 6: 14–23.

Hoffman, Morris B. 2000. "The Drug Court Scandal." *North Carolina Law Review* 78: 1477–2000.

Hora, Peggy Fulton, William G. Schma, and J. Rosenthal. 1999. "Therapeutic Jurisprudence and the Drug Treatment Court Movement: Revolutionizing the Criminal Justice System's Response to Drug Abuse and Crime in America." *Notre Dame Law Review* 74(2): 439–527.

Inciardi, James A. 1987. "Heroin Use and Street Crime." In *Chemical Dependencies: Patterns, Costs, and Consequences*, edited by Carl D. Chambers, David Petersen, James A. Inciardi, Harvey A. Siegel, and O. Z. White. Athens, OH: Ohio University Press.

Inciardi, James A. 1992. *The War on Drugs II: The Continuing Epic of Heroin, Cocaine, Crack, Crime, AIDS, and the Public Policy*. Mountain View, CA: Mayfield Publishing Co.

Inciardi, James A., Steven S. Martin, Clifford A. Butzin, Robert M. Hooper, and Lana D. Harrison. 1996. "An Effective Model of Prison-based Treatment for Drug-Involved Offenders." *Journal of Drug Issues* 27(2): 261–78.

Inciardi, James A., and Anne E. Pottieger. 1994. "Crack Cocaine Use and Street Crime." *Journal of Drug Issues* 24: 273–92.

Jameson, Robert, and N. Andrew Peterson. 1995. *Evaluation of the First Year of Operation of the Jackson County Drug Court*. Kansas City, MO: Ewing Marion Kauffman Foundation.

Lang, Meghan. 2003. "Mental Health Court Partnership Helps Youth with Serious Mental Illness." *Youth Law News*. April–June.

Lipsey, Mark W., and Francis T. Cullen. 2007. "The Effectiveness of Correctional Rehabilitation: A Review of Systematic Reviews." *Annual Review of Law and Social Science* 3: 297–320.

LoGalbo, Anthony P., and Charlene M. Callahan. 2001. "An Evaluation of Teen Court as a Juvenile Crime Diversion Program." *Juvenile and Family Court Journal* 52: 1–11.

MacCoun, Robert J., Beau Kilmer, and Peter Reuter. 2003. "Research on Drug-Crime Linkages: The Next Generation." In *Toward a Drugs and Crime Research Agenda for the 21st Century*. Special Report. Washington, DC: U.S. Department of Justice, National Institute of Justice.

MacCoun, Robert, and Peter Reuter. 2001. *Drug War Heresies: Learning from other Vices, Times, & Places*. Cambridge, UK: Cambridge University Press.

Mackenzie, Doris L. 2006. *What Works in Corrections Reducing the Criminal Activities of Offenders and Delinquents*. New York: Cambridge University Press.

Manfredi, Christopher P. 1998. *The Supreme Court and Juvenile Justice*. Lawrence, KS: University Press of Kansas.

Mansfield News Journal. "Sentences Meted Out." 1949. *Mansfield News Journal* (May 16). Mansfield, Ohio.

Marlowe, Douglas B., David S. Festinger, and Patricia A. Lee. 2004. "The Judge Is a Key Component of Drug Court." *National Drug Court Institute Review* 4(2): 1–34.

McGowan, Angela, Robert Hahn, Akiva Liberman, Alex Crosby, Mindy Fullilove, Robert Johnson, Eve Moscicki, LeShawndra Price, Susan Snyder, Farris Tuma, Jessica Lowy, Peter Briss, Stella Cory, and Glenda Stone. 2007. "Effects on Violence of Laws and Policies Facilitating the Transfer of Juveniles from the Juvenile Justice System to the Adult Justice System: A Systematic Review." *American Journal of Preventive Medicine* 32(4S): S7–28.

McNeece, Aaron, Mary Kay Falconer, Chalandra M. Bryant, and Michael Shader. 1996. *Hernando County Teen Court: Evaluation of 1996 Continuation Grant Activity*.

Tallahassee, FL: Florida State University, Institute for Health and Human Services
    Research.
McReynolds, Larkin S., Gail A. Wasserman, Robert E. DeComo, Reni John, Joseph M.
    Keating, and Scott Nolen. 2008. "Psychiatric Disorder in a Juvenile Assessment Center."
    Crime and Delinquency 54(2): 313–34.
Mears, Daniel P. 2001. "Critical Challenges in Addressing the Mental Health Needs of
    Juvenile Offenders." *Justice Policy Journal* 1: 41–61.
Miller, Marsha L., Evelyn A. Scocas, and John P. O'Connell. 1998. *Evaluation of the Juvenile
    Drug Court Diversion Program*. Dover, DE: Statistical Analysis Center.
Miller, Norman S., and Mark S. Gold. 1994. "Criminal Activity and Crack Addiction." *The
    International Journal of Addictions* 29: 1069–78.
Minor, Kevin I., James B. Wells, Irina R. Soderstrom, Rachel Bingham, and Deborah
    Williamson. 1999. "Sentence Completion and Recidivism among Juveniles Referred to
    Teen Courts." *Crime and Delinquency* 45(4): 467–80.
Mocan, H. Naci, and Erdal Tekin. 2003. "Guns, Drugs and Juvenile Crime: Evidence from a
    Panel of Siblings and Twins." *Working Paper 9824*. Cambridge, MA: National Bureau of
    Economic Research.
Monahan, John, Richard J. Bonnie, Paul S. Applebaum, Pamela S. Hyde, Henry J.
    Steadman, and Marvin S. Swartz. 2001. "Mandated Community Treatment: Beyond
    Outpatient Commitment." *Psychiatric Services* 52: 1198–205.
Nagin, Daniel. 1998. "Criminal Deterrence Research at the Outset of the Twenty-First
    Century." *Crime and Justice*, 23: 1–42.
National Association of Drug Court Professionals. 1997. *Defining Drug Courts: The Key
    Components*. Washington, DC: U.S. Department of Justice, Drug Courts Program
    Office.
National Council on Disability. 2003. *Addressing the Needs of Youth with Disabilities in the
    Juvenile Justice System: The Current Status of Evidence-Based Research*. Washington,
    DC: National Council on Disability.
National Institute on Drug Abuse. 2009. *Principles of Drug Addiction Treatment*, 2nd ed.
    Rockville, MD: National Institute on Drug Abuse.
National Mental Health Association. 2009. *NMHA Position Statement 53: Mental
    Health Courts*. Accessed Feb. 25, 2011. http://www.mentalhealthamerica.net/go/
    position-statements/53.
National Association of Youth Courts. 2006. "Youth Courts Across America." http://www.
    youthcourt.net.
North Carolina Administrative Office of the Courts. 1995. *Report on the Teen Court
    Programs in North Carolina*. Raleigh, NC: North Carolina Administrative Office of the
    Courts.
Nurco, David N., Timothy W. Kinlock, and Thomas E. Hanlon. 1990. "The Drugs Crime
    Connection." In *Handbook of Drug Control in the United States*, edited by James A.
    Inciardi, 71–90. Westport, CT: Greenwood Press.
O'Connell, John P., Evelyn Nestlerode, and Marsha L. Miller. 1999. *Evaluation of the
    Delaware Juvenile Drug Court Diversion Program*. Dover, DE: Statistical Analysis
    Center.
Office of National Drug Control Strategy. 2010. *Drug Courts*. Washington, DC: Office of
    National Drug Control Strategy.
Orr, Cynthia Hujar, John Wesley Hall, Norman L. Reimer, Edward A. Mallett, Kyle O'Dowd,
    Angelyn C. Frazer. 2009. *America's Problem-Solving Courts: The Criminal Costs of*

Treatment and the Case for Reform. Washington, DC: National Association of Criminal Defense Lawyers.

Peters, Roger H., and Mary R. Murrin. 2000. "Effectiveness of Treatment-Based Drug Courts in Reducing Criminal Recidivism." *Criminal Justice and Behavior* 27(1): 72–96.

Powell, Jill. 2003. Letter to the editor. *Issues in Mental Health Nursing* 24: 463.

Poythress, Norman G., John Petrila, Annette McGaha, and Roger Boothroyd. 2002. "Perceived Coercion and Procedural Justice in the Broward Mental Health Court." *International Journal of Law and Psychiatry* 25: 517–33.

Redlich, Allison D. 2006. "Voluntary, but Knowing and Intelligent? Comprehension in Mental Health Courts." *Psychology, Public Policy and the Law* 11(4): 605–19.

Reuter, Peter H., Robert MacCoun, and Patrick Murphy. 1990. *Money from Crime*. Santa Monica, CA: RAND.

Rodriguez, Nancy, and Vincent J. Webb. 2004. "Multiple Measures of Juvenile Drug Court Effectiveness: Results of a Quasi-experimental Design." *Crime and Delinquency* 50: 292–314.

Roman, John K., and Adele V. Harrell. 2001. "Assessing the Costs and Benefits Accruing to the Public from a Graduated Sanctions Program for Drug-Using Defendants." *Law and Policy* 23: 237–68.

Rottman, David B., and Shauna M. Strickland. 2006. *State Court Organization, 2004*. Washington, DC: U.S. Department of Justice, Office of Justice Programs, Bureau of Justice Statistics.

Senjo, Scott R., and Leslie A. Leip. 2001. "Testing and Developing Theory in Drug Court: A Four-part Logit Model to Predict Program Completion." *Criminal Justice Policy Review* 12(1): 66–87.

Seyfrit, Carole L., Philip L. Reichel, and Brian L. Stutts. 1987. "Peer Juries as a Juvenile Justice Diversion Technique." *Youth and Society* 18(3): 302–16.

Shaw, Michelle, and Kenneth Robinson. 1998. "Summary and Analysis of the First Juvenile Drug Court Evaluations." *National Drug Court Institute Review* 1: 73–85.

Snyder, Howard N., and Sickmund, Melissa. 2006. *Juvenile Offenders and Victims: 2006 National Report*. Washington, DC: U.S. Department of Justice, Office of Justice Programs, Office of Juvenile Justice and Delinquency Prevention.

Speckert, George R., and M. Douglas Anglin. 1986. "Narcotics and Crime: A Causal Modeling Approach." *Journal of Quantitative Criminology* 2: 3–28.

SRA Associates. 1995. *Teen Court Evaluation of 1994 Activities and Goals: Characteristics, Backgrounds, and Outcomes of Program Referrals*. Santa Rosa, CA: SRA Associates.

Steadman, Henry J., Allison D. Redlich, Patricia Griffin, John Petrila, and John Monahan. 2005. "From Referral to Disposition: Case Processing in Seven Mental Health Courts." *Behavioral Sciences and the Law* 23: 1–12.

Steadman, Henry J., Martha Williams Deane, Joseph P. Morrissey, Mary L. Westcott, Susan Salasin, and Steven Shapiro. 1999. "A SAMHSA Research Initiative Assessing the Effectiveness of Jail Diversion Programs for Mentally Ill Persons." *Psychiatric Services* 50: 1620–23.

Stewart, Duncan, Michael Gossop, John Marsden, and Alexandra Rolfe. 2000. "Drug Misuse and Acquisitive Crime among Clients Recruited to the National Treatment Outcome Research Study (NTORS)." *Criminal Behaviour and Mental Health* 10(1): 10–20.

Tanenhaus, David S. 2004. *Juvenile Justice in Making*. New York: Oxford University Press.

Teplin, Linda A., Karen M. Abram, Gary M. McClelland, Mina K. Dulcan, and Amy A. Mericle. 2002. "Psychiatric Disorders in Youth in Juvenile Detention." *Archives of General Psychiatry* 59(Dec.): 1133–43.

Trupin, Eric, and Henry Richards. 2003. "Seattle's Mental Health Courts: Early Indicators of Effectiveness." *International Journal of Law and Psychiatry* 26: 33–53.

Tyler, Tom R. 1990. *Why People Obey the Law*. New Haven, CT: Yale University.

Tyuse, Sabrina W., and Donald M. Linhorst. 2005. "Drug Courts and Mental Health Courts: Implications for Social Workers." *Health and Social Work* 30: 233–40.

Vito, Gennaro F. 1989. "The Kentucky Substance Abuse Program: A Private Program to Treat Probationers and Parolees." *Federal Probation* 53: 65–72.

Wasserman, Gail A., Larkin S. McReynolds, Susan J. Ko, Laura M. Katz, and Jennifer R. Carpenter. 2005. "Gender Differences in Psychiatric Disorders at Juvenile Probation Intake." *American Journal of Public Health* 95(1): 131–37.

Watson, Amy, Patricia Hanrahan, Daniel Luchins, and Arthur Lurigio. 2001. "Mental Health Courts and Complex Issue of Mentally Ill Offenders." *Psychiatric Services* 52: 477–81.

Wilson, David B., Ojmarrh Mitchell, and Doris L. MacKenzie. 2006. "A Systematic Review of Drug Court Effects on Recidivism." *Journal of Experimental Criminology* 2(4): 459–87.

Wolff, Nancy. 2002. "Courts as Therapeutic Agents: Thinking Past the Novelty of Mental Health Courts." *Journal of the American Academy of Psychiatry and the Law* 30: 431–37.

CHAPTER 26

....

DETENTION

....

WILLIAM H. BARTON

I. INTRODUCTION

....

THE term "detention" refers to that part of the juvenile justice system that handles youths between the time of their arrest and court hearings. Detention centers are secure facilities intended to hold youths deemed too risky to release during that time period. These are distinct from nonsecure shelters that are used to temporarily house children in the child welfare system who are removed from their families because of alleged abuse or neglect. Shelters at times also house youths temporarily who have been arrested, whose risk may be low, but who have no place to stay. Police typically make an initial recommendation to detain; court intake staff (or sometimes probation officers) screen cases and make an initial determination regarding detention; and a judge reviews these initial determinations at a detention hearing within one to three days. In addition to holding pretrial youths, detention centers also hold some youths after adjudication while they await disposition and placement.

All states' statutes mention some variation on three generic detention criteria: danger to self, danger to others, or risk of flight (Snyder and Sickmund 2006). Statutory language seems to be fairly specific and restrictive, but allows for considerable interpretive flexibility. The wording of the Indiana juvenile code regarding release or detention of a child is representative:

> (a) The juvenile court shall release the child on the child's own recognizance or to the child's parent, guardian, or custodian upon the person's written promise to bring the child before the court at a time specified. However, the court may order the child detained if the court finds probable cause to believe the child is a delinquent and that:

(1) the child is unlikely to appear for subsequent proceedings;

(2) detention is essential to protect the child or the community.

(IND. CODE ANN. § 31–37–6–6 (2005)).

In other circumstances, such as when the parent or guardian cannot be located or is unable or unwilling to take the child, if the court believes that sending the child home would not be in the child's best interests and harmful to the safety or health of the child, or if the child requests that the child not be released, the Indiana law permits holding the child, but not in a secure facility (IND. CODE ANN. § 31–37–7–1 (2005)). However, data regarding who is actually held in secure detention, as will be presented later in this chapter, show that secure detention is used far more frequently than would be suggested by a conservative reading of the law.

This chapter attempts to provide an overview of juvenile detention in the United States and to address a range of questions and issues concerning its use. What is juvenile detention and why does it exist? Does its reality match its intended purpose? How many young people are placed in juvenile detention? How and why do they end up there? What are the consequences of juvenile detention policies and practices for society and for the children who are affected by them? Is there a better way to structure this part of the juvenile justice system?

II. History of Controversy

Juvenile detention practices and policies over the years have generated many concerns and controversies. What purposes is detention intended to serve, who should be detained and for how long, what activities should occur while they are detained, and in what conditions should they be held. These issues take on even more urgency when, as will be argued below, detention serves as the gateway to the rest of the juvenile justice system. It is thus critical to be sure that its use effectively serves the purposes of the broader juvenile justice system and society, and does not exacerbate the problem of juvenile delinquency it is intended to address.

Detention centers emerged with the separation of the juvenile and adult justice systems marked by the establishment of the first juvenile court in Chicago in 1899. Juvenile courts spread gradually throughout the country until the middle of the twentieth century, when they could be found in all states (Mennel 1973). There is a familiar adage that the more things change, the more they remain the same. Almost from the beginning, critics raised concerns about detention policies and practices. More than sixty years ago, Norman (1949) decried the overuse of detention and widespread misunderstanding of its purposes. About a decade later, Milton Rector, then Director of the National Probation and Parole Association, observed that construction of detention facilities produced a "sharp increase in the number of cases in which detention is used, out of a mistaken notion of the purpose of detention" and that resulting detention use "will not be restricted to the more disturbed, serious offenders who need secure custody" (1960, p. iv).

Going back a bit further in time, Warner (1933) commented on the wide variations in detention practices from community to community. More recently, Feld (1991) provided extensive documentation of geographical variations in juvenile justice policy and practices. He argued that more diverse, urban jurisdictions employ more formal procedures than do more stable, homogeneous rural jurisdictions, and that this formality leads to greater use of pretrial detention and harsher sentencing practices. Feld's study examined all juvenile cases formally petitioned in the state of Minnesota in 1986 and found that urban counties detained "proportionally two to three times as many youths as [did] suburban or rural counties" (1991, p. 197). Although juvenile crime rates were higher in urban counties, these counties also used "detention disproportionately for juveniles charged with misdemeanors…and status offenses…." (Feld 1991, p. 197).

In the 1960s and 1970s, advocates grew increasingly concerned about the overuse and poor conditions of detention centers and secure juvenile placement facilities. A Senate Subcommittee to Investigate Juvenile Delinquency found that large numbers of youths held in secure facilities were status offenders (e.g., runaways, truants, and "incorrigible," whose acts would not be considered crimes if committed by adults) or victims of parental neglect (Schwartz 1989). As a result, Congress passed and President Ford signed the Juvenile Justice and Delinquency Prevention Act (JJDPA) in 1974, making it illegal to securely confine status offenders in detention centers or secure placement facilities. However, this push for deinstitutionalization included no accompanying requirement to provide community-based services that status offenders might need. As a result, although the number of status offenders in detention and secure placements fell, the juvenile justice system adjusted its practices to maintain control over these children. Jurisdictions adopted practices that transformed some of what were previously considered status offenses into delinquent offenses eligible for secure detention. For example, "bootstrapping" emerged, whereby courts hold in contempt (misdemeanor) status offenders placed on probation who fail to comply with the terms of their probation (such as staying out past curfew or not attending counseling sessions) or who commit another status offense (such as running away or skipping school) (Bishop and Frazier 1992; Feld 2009). In addition, Feld (2009) analyzed national data to demonstrate that since 1980, the numbers and rates of girls charged with simple assaults increased dramatically, and concluded that officials were charging youths engaged in minor peer altercations and many domestic disputes with simple assault rather than handling the situation informally, as in the past.

As mentioned above, juvenile detention centers were an extension of the idea of separating juvenile from adult offenders. Even after the emergence of the juvenile justice system, however, many children were still held in adult jails rather than juvenile detention centers. Advocates now and in the past have argued for the abolition of the jailing of juveniles (Sarri 1974; Schwartz 1989; Campaign for Youth Justice

2007), claiming that it disrupts adolescent development, places youths at risk for suicide and victimization by prison violence including rape, and exposes them to more dangerous, adult criminals. The 1980 reauthorization of the JJDPA contained an amendment prohibiting the holding of juveniles in adult jails or police lockups without sight and sound separation from adults. While the number of youths in adult jails fell after the passage of that legislation, the practice still continued to some extent (e.g., Schwartz 1989, estimated that one-day counts of juveniles in jail had decreased to from more than 7,000 to 1,692 by 1985).

As stated in the introduction, detention refers to the time between arrest and court hearings. Locking up a child who has not yet been found "guilty" because he or she might commit another offense or might not appear for a court hearing amounts to preventive detention. Although challenged as an unconstitutional deprivation of liberty, the Supreme Court upheld the preventive detention of juveniles in *Schall v. Martin*, 467 U.S. 253 (1984). In that case, the Supreme Court overturned a decision by a New York district court that had ruled that the state's statute authorizing the preventive detention of juveniles violated due process protections and amounted to punishment prior to a determination of guilt. As discussed and analyzed in detail by Feld (1984–1985), the Supreme Court's decision in the *Schall* case rested on the *parens patriae* philosophy that the court can replace parental custody with state custody. The majority opinion, authored by Justice Rehnquist, argued that, although preventive detention may be an inappropriate deprivation of liberty for adults, children are presumed to be unable to care for themselves and thus always under some form of custody (e.g., of their parents). Therefore, if parental control is inadequate, the state may intervene and provide pretrial custody, in the child's best interest and in the state's legitimate interest in protecting public safety. The majority opinion also expressed satisfaction that detention decisions could be based reasonably on a prediction of risk of future offending.

The dissent in *Schall v. Martin*, authored by Justice Marshall, supported the earlier district court ruling, and argued that the prediction literature concluded that it was not possible to predict dangerousness with any degree of accuracy, so that judges' detention decisions based on predictions of risk were arbitrary. The dissent also referred to evidence that the majority of detainees were not charged with serious offenses, countering the majority opinion that detention was justified on public safety grounds, and further that conditions of confinement in detention centers were reprehensible and dangerous, countering the majority view that short-term detention was not punitive but merely mirrored parental care. In addition, the dissent argued that preventive detention limited juveniles' ability to prepare an adequate defense and resulted in stigmatization and negative self-labeling.

As illustrated by the *Schall v. Martin* arguments, controversies about the proper purposes of detention reflect the historical tension between the *parens patriae* philosophy, presumably pursuing the best interests of the child, and a due process approach. Using the lens of *parens patriae*, officials view detention as another opportunity to provide treatment or rehabilitation to the child. An early example here is Norman (1949), who advocated a therapeutic model as opposed to simple confinement, arguing that detention "may be more destructive than helpful unless the "storage only" concept is abandoned in favor of beginning the process of rehabilitation at the point of arrest" (p. 29).

Due process advocates (e.g., Feld 1984–1985; Schwartz 1989; Feld 1999; Arthur 2001) take a narrower view, particularly regarding the use of detention prior to adjudication, and clearly recognize detention as punitive. This view considers "treatment" services at this stage inappropriate, beyond meeting basic safety, health, and education needs, since the child has not yet been adjudicated delinquent.

III. Detention Today

As outlined in the previous section, disagreements about the purpose of juvenile detention, and widely varying policies and practices, are recurring themes in the literature. To this day, many secure detention facilities continue to be chronically overcrowded, exhibit all-too-common abusive conditions and practices, and comingle many kinds of young people whose primary commonality is that the police apprehended them in connection with some offense or that the juvenile justice system is the only one that cannot refuse to deal with them. In most jurisdictions, another commonality among these youths is that disproportionately many are children of color (Snyder and Sickmund 2006; Puzzanchera and Sickmund 2008; Sickmund et al. 2008).

On a given day, if one were to look at the children in a typical juvenile detention center, one would find some who are very young, many who have mental illnesses or developmental disabilities, a few who have committed very violent acts, but many more whose offenses are less serious, many who have been in detention multiple times, some who have been adjudicated delinquent and are awaiting openings at training schools or other placements, some who are serving brief periods of confinement as a sanction for violating the terms of their probation, and some who would have been released except that their parents could not be located or refused to pick them up.

A. Juvenile Crime, Juvenile Court, and Detention Statistics

Given the confusion over the appropriate conceptualization and use of detention, it should not be surprising that a look at recent statistics and trends in its use reveals a somewhat disturbing picture. Despite fluctuations in the volume and rate of juvenile crime over the last three decades, the use of secure detention has steadily increased (Snyder and Sickmund 2006; Puzzanchera and Sickmund 2008; Puzzanchera 2009; Sickmund 2009). Beginning in 1981, the rate of juvenile crime held steady until a sharp increase in the early 1990s, peaking in 1994, then falling off sharply to return to the 1980s level by 2003 (Snyder and Sickmund 2006). There was little change from

2003 through 2007, the most recent year for which such data are available (Puzzanchera 2009). However, the overall arrest trends mask some differences for specific offenses. While the most serious violent and property crimes have followed the pattern described above, the rate of arrest for drug abuse violations, though declining slightly after 1994, has remained at a level well above its 1980s rate, and the arrest rate for simple assault has not declined since 1994 (Puzzanchera 2009).

Despite the fluctuations in juvenile arrest rates noted above, the volume of delinquency cases processed by the nation's juvenile court system increased steadily from 1960 through 1997; it then declined slightly through 2002, thereafter remaining at a level twice that of the mid-1980s (Puzzanchera and Sickmund 2008). In addition, the proportion of cases receiving formal as opposed to informal court processing has increased since the early 1990s, even though the rate of arrests involving the most serious offenses declined (Puzzanchera and Sickmund 2008). Similarly, the number of cases for which a youth was adjudicated delinquent nearly doubled between 1985 and 2005 (Puzzanchera and Sickmund 2008). On the other hand, the number of cases receiving dispositions involving out-of-home placements, while increasing in the 1980s through the mid-1990s, has dropped since 1997 (Puzzanchera and Sickmund 2008).

In 2005, the most recent year with available data, detention was used in 354,100 delinquency cases and 11,900 status offense cases nationally (Puzzanchera and Sickmund 2008). That status offenders continue to be detained at all, albeit comprising less than 5% of detention referrals, is problematic given the JJDPA's prohibition of incarcerating status offenders. In recent years there have been efforts, such as "Becca's Law" in Washington State, to permit the secure detention of certain status offenders deemed to be at high risk of harm. This particular law resulted from the high-profile murder of a runaway girl who had frequently come to the attention of the authorities but had not been detained.

Between 1985 and 2005, the proportion of cases involving detention has remained steady at about 20%, yet the increase in the volume of delinquency cases has led to a 48% increase in the number of cases involving detention (Snyder and Sickmund 2006; Puzzanchera and Sickmund 2008). Even as the volume of juvenile court cases declined after its 1997 peak, the number of cases involving detention continued to rise (Sickmund 2009). During this period, the number of detentions for person, drug, and public order offenses rose sharply, while the number of detentions for property offenses actually declined; since 2002 public order offense cases have made up the largest segment of detained cases (Puzzanchera and Sickmund 2008).

The chart in Figure 26.1 shows national trends in the types of referral offenses leading to detention from 1985 to 2005. The chart documents the overall increase in detention referrals from about 240,000 in 1985 to about 370,000 in 1998, and a relatively steady rate since then. The area for each of four offense types reflects its share of the detention referrals. Property offenders make up the largest group of the detention referrals, although their proportion has dropped from more than half to about a third. The percentage of person offenders increased somewhat from about 20% in the 1980s to between 25% and 30% in more recent years. Public order

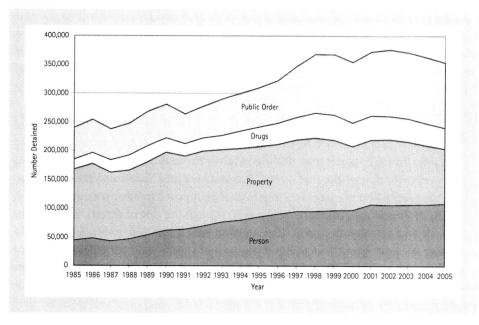

Figure 26.1. Detention Referral Offenses, 1985–2005.
Source: National Centre for Juvenile Justice 2008. "National Juvenile Court Data Archive: Juvenile court case records 1985–2005 [machine-readable data files]." Pittsburgh, PA: National Center for Juvenile Justice [Producer].

offenders make up about the same proportion of detention referrals as person offenders, while the percentage of drug offenders has increased slightly from about 7% to 10%. Although these broad offense categories mask variations in offense seriousness between, for example, aggravated assault and simple assault, these data suggest that the bulk of detention referrals are not for highly serious offenses, a point that will be addressed in more detail below.

When looking at who is in detention at any one time, a slightly different picture emerges. Table 26.1 summarizes data from the 2006 One-Day Census of Youth in Detention (Sickmund et al. 2008). The vast majority of detention centers (about 90%) are public, and most of these are operated by local jurisdictions, usually juvenile courts or probation departments. The majority of detainees reside in relatively large detention centers (about 54% are in facilities with more than fifty residents), and nearly one in five (19%) are in extremely large facilities housing more than two hundred youths. About half are being held between the time of their arrest and court hearing, but many are there following adjudication, either awaiting disposition (20%), an opening at a placement (25%), or for other reasons (4%) such as awaiting transfer to or hearings in the adult criminal justice system. Most are male (82%), and more than two-thirds (69%) are children of color. Fewer than a third (31%) are there for person offenses; one-fourth are there for technical violations of probation or parole; and, despite federal legislation on the books since the 1970s prohibiting their secure confinement, a few status

Table 26.1. National One-Day Census of Youth in Detention, 2006 (Total
              Number Detained: 26,344)

Characteristic	N	Pct.	Characteristic	N	Pct.
Auspice:			Race:		
Public (State)	5,111	19.4	White	8,167	31.0
Public (Local)	18,496	70.2	Black	11,089	42.1
Private	2,631	10.0	Hispanic	5,993	22.7
Tribal	106	0.4	Other	1,095	4.2
Facility Size:			Most Serious Offense:		
1–20 residents	3,389	12.9	Person offenses	8,171	31.0
21–50 residents	6,165	23.4	Property offenses	5,786	22.0
51–150 residents	9,830	37.3	Drug offenses	2,179	8.3
151–200 residents	1,892	7.2	Public order offenses	2,790	10.6
> 200 residents	5,068	19.2	Technical violations	6,582	25.0
Status:			Status offenses	836	3.2
Pre-adjudication	13,280	50.4	Days Since Admission:		
Post-adjud./pre-disposition	5,291	20.1	0–6 days	6,782	25.7
Post-dispos./pre-placement	6,631	25.2	7–13 days	4,770	18.1
Other	1,142	4.3	14–30 days	6,974	26.5
Gender:			31–90 days	5,368	20.4
Male	21,653	82.2	90–365 days	2,226	8.4
Female	4,691	17.8	> 365 days	224	0.9

Source: Sickmund, Melissa, T. J. Sladky, Wei Kang, and Charles Puzzanchera. 2008. "Easy Access to the Census of Juveniles in Residential Placement." National Center for Juvenile Justice, Office of Juvenile Justice and Delinquency Prevention. http://ojjdp.ncjrs.gov/ojstatbb/ezacjrp/.

offenders are still held. Most detention stays are short, between a few days and two or three weeks. However, a one-day snapshot will oversample youths who have been in detention relatively longer than others, so that the One-Day Census finds more than half who had been there for more than two weeks, and some whose stays had been several months.

More detailed offense data are available from the one-day census counts of youths in detention, collected periodically from 1997 to 2006, as shown in Figure 26.2, than from the referral data in Figure 26.1. Since one-day counts oversample those with longer stays, and those with longer stays are more likely to be charged with relatively more serious offenses, these data over-represent serious offenders. In Figure 26.2, the most serious offenses, most likely felonies (e.g., homicide, sexual assault, robbery, aggravated assault, arson, burglary, auto theft, and drug trafficking) appear in the checkered areas at the bottom of the chart. The top two areas reflect status offenses and technical violations, while mostly misdemeanor level

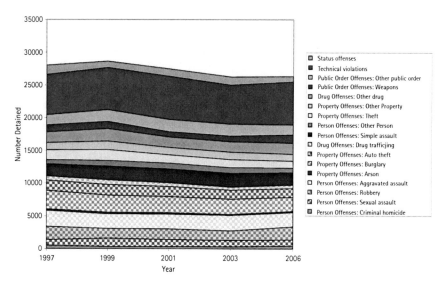

Figure 26.2. Most Serious Offense, One-Day Detension Census, 1997–2006.
Source: Sickmund, Melissa, T.J.Sladky, Wei Kang, and Charles Puzzanchera, 2008. "Easy Access
to the censes of Juveniles in Residential Placement." National Center for Juvenile Justice, Office of
Juvenile Justice and Delinquency Prevention. http://ojjdp.ncjrs.gov/ojstatab/ezacjsp/

offenses (e.g., simple assault, theft, public order offenses, etc.) appear in the middle
areas. Less than 40% of the detainees fall in the serious offense categories. The largest single group (nearly 25%) is comprised of youths who have committed technical
violations of the terms of their probation or parole. Despite over-representing serious offenders, these data clearly show that the majority of those detained are not
serious, violent offenders.

To sum up, the increase in juvenile crime in the 1990s was accompanied by
increases in court cases for all kinds of offenses, increases in the proportion of cases
handled formally, and increases in the use of secure detention. These increases led
to a series of "get tough" juvenile justice policies (three strikes, zero tolerance, more
transfers of youths to adult criminal court jurisdiction, etc.). The presence of these
policies, along with the routinization of practices that accompanied them, meant
that the subsequent declines in the volume and rate of juvenile crime had little
impact on the use of detention. Moreover, detention practices, like so many other
aspects of the juvenile justice system, have put children of color at a particular disadvantage. The next section examines the negative impact of detention on the future
life chances of those detained, rendering the statistics and trends discussed above
particularly troubling.

B. Detention as Gateway to the Juvenile Justice System

In medicine, the term *iatrogenic* refers to a treatment that actually worsens the condition it was intended to cure. Several studies in the United States and Canada demonstrate that aspects of juvenile justice system processing, especially confinement in

secure detention and placement facilities can be iatrogenic, that is, they may foster further delinquency rather than suppress it (Holman and Ziedenberg 2006; Gatti, Tremblay, and Vitaro 2009; Loughran et al. 2009). There are at least two distinct theoretical interpretations of such iatrogenic effects. On the one hand, social learning theory (Akers 1985) would posit that exposure to deviant peers as occurs in detention and other juvenile justice interventions provides a youth with negative role models. Studies and meta-analyses conducted by Dishion and colleagues have found evidence of peer deviancy "training" in a variety of group settings, including juvenile justice interventions, supporting this view (Dishion, Spracklen, and Patterson 1996; Dishion, McCord, and Poulin 1999; Dodge, Dishion, and Lansford 2006; however, see Weiss et al. 2005 for opposing evidence). On the other hand, labeling theory (Lemert 1951; Becker 1963; Goode 1975) suggests that others in and outside of the juvenile justice system develop self-fulfilling expectations that youths handled by the system will continue to commit delinquent acts. Once "labeled" as delinquent, an individual cannot easily overcome these negative expectations, and, furthermore, the label may become part of the individual's self-concept. Johnson, Simons, and Conger (2004) found that formal processing of a youth in juvenile court increased future criminal offending, even after controlling for prior offending, and argued that the results from their longitudinal analyses support labeling theory. In addition, simply being detained poses other procedural, social, and psychological challenges for youths. It limits their ability to mount a defense, because they cannot interview witnesses. They also become "prisonized" in behavior and appearance, (e.g., appearing in detention uniforms and shackles for court hearing), thus making a negative impression on judges.

Regardless of the theoretical mechanism involved, several studies suggest that the use of detention itself leads to a greater likelihood of formal case processing, harsher dispositions, and more restrictive placement outcomes, even after controlling for demographic and offense-related factors (Frazier and Bishop 1985; Frazier and Cochran 1986; Feld 1991). That means that if two youths with identical demographic backgrounds, offense histories, and current offenses appear in court, one of whom has been held in secure detention, that youth is more likely to receive formal and punitive treatment by the juvenile justice system simply as a result of having been detained. What seems to happen in practice is that many youths are arrested repeatedly for relatively minor offenses. At some point they get placed on probation, and many violate the terms of their probation by, for example, missing curfew. As a result of the probation violation, they may be held in secure detention pending a review hearing. At that hearing, noting that they have already been on probation, have violated probation, and have been held in detention, the judge may order a commitment to the state juvenile correctional institution or some other residential placement. At every step, officials feel compelled to toughen the sanction, although the youth may never have committed a particularly serious offense. Then, with deeper penetration into the system comes the increased likelihood of more, rather than less, frequent and serious subsequent offending behavior, as noted previously.

It is clear, then, that detention serves as a gateway to the juvenile justice system, and to the lessening of opportunities for successful life outcomes for youths securely held.

This alone would warrant extreme caution in its use, limited to those youths who truly pose an unacceptable risk to public safety or a flight risk. Yet detention policies and practices are fraught with additional problems, as discussed in the next section.

IV. Salient Issues

Juvenile detention centers in the United States face a plethora of challenges. Many detention centers are overcrowded, elevating the risks to the safety of both youths and staff. The crowding, high volume of juveniles (many of whom are there for very brief periods), and high rates of staff turnover make it difficult for detention centers to offer quality services. Conditions of confinement may be poor, including under-staffing, insufficient supervision, poor design, or deteriorating facilities. Children of color are greatly overrepresented in detention compared with their percentages in the general population. While the majority of detainees are male, as noted earlier, the number of females has increased in recent years, and gender-specific program-ming is often lacking. Many detained youths have substance abuse problems and/or mental health conditions that may never have been diagnosed, let alone treated. Some have developmental disabilities that detention centers are not designed to accommodate. Although detention centers must provide basic education services, their quality may be variable, and special education services may be lacking.

A. Overcrowding and Other Conditions of Confinement

Concern about overcrowding and other conditions of confinement in juvenile detention centers is not new. Warner (1933) reported that few public detention cen-ters in her field study of 141 facilities met even minimal standards recommended by the United States Children's Bureau: sufficient space to avoid overcrowding; layout permitting separation by sex, character, and physical condition; separate bathing and toilet facilities for boys and girls; proper lighting and ventilation; dining rooms, recreation rooms, and schoolrooms; security against escape; adequate fire protec-tion; and outdoor play space. Three decades later, the National Council on Crime and Delinquency (1961) proposed standards and guides for detention that met four objectives: minimizing the damaging effects of confinement; providing construc-tive activities building on youths' strengths; offering individual and group guidance to promote a youth's constructive use of the detention experience; and screening for undetected mental and emotional illness. Sarri (1974) noted a shortage of profes-sional staff trained to handle the kind of youths detained, overall staff-youth ratios that correlated inversely with facility size, and deficiencies in supervision and train-ing of child care staff.

Overcrowded facilities tend to be at elevated risk for a number of other prob-lems. These include injuries to youth and staff, more use of short-term isolation, more suicidal behavior, and higher staff turnover (Parent et al. 1994). Lubow (2005) noted that the proportion of detained youths residing in overcrowded facilities had risen steadily, from 20% in 1985 to 62% in 1995. While there is some evidence that the extent of overcrowding in juvenile detention centers has lessened in recent years, it still remains a problem in many centers, especially the larger, public facilities. On the day of the 2002 Juvenile Residential Facility Census, 18% of all juvenile detention facilities (and 21% of all public detention centers) were above their capacity for number of youths held (Snyder and Sickmund 2006). By 2004, only 12% of all detention centers (14% of public detention centers) were above capacity (Livesy, Sickmund, and Sladky 2009). Unfortunately, these more recent reports do not include data regarding the proportion of detained youths in these overcrowded facilities.

In a comprehensive study of conditions of confinement that included both detention centers and placement facilities, Parent et al. (1994) found low rates of conformity (less than 50% of confined juveniles in conforming facilities) to standards regarding basic needs (living space, health care, food, clothing, hygiene, and living accommodations), order and security, and juvenile rights, and only slightly higher rates of conformity to programming standards. More recently, Gallagher and Dobrin (2007) investigated the extent to which detention centers met standards for health care promulgated by the National Commission on Correctional Health Care. Using national data from juvenile justice residential facilities, they found that few detention centers met even minimal standards of care, with considerable racial and geographic variation in quality and accessibility of care.

The issues highlighted in the Parent et al. (1994) report have provided a backdrop for recent attempts to improve conditions of confinement in detention. As part of the Annie E. Casey Foundation's Juvenile Detention Alternatives Initiative (JDAI), to be discussed in more detail later in this chapter, some jurisdictions have undertaken ongoing, systematic self-assessments of conditions of confinement (Burrell 2000). The instruments for assessing conditions of confinement cover a range of issues including physical and mental health care, access to counsel, programming activities, staff supervision and training, physical conditions of the facility, behavior management practices, and safety issues for both staff and children (Burrell 2000, p. 23). Those conducting the assessment look for written policies or procedures around each of the issues, whether these meet legal standards and whether they are actually followed in practice. Burrell (2000) reports that these assessments have helped participating JDAI sites achieve measurable improvements in conditions.

A continuing history of lawsuits challenging the conditions and practices in detention centers demonstrates that conditions of confinement remain problematic in many sites (Youth Law Center 2009). Although arguing that at the time there had been relatively few lawsuits regarding detention conditions, Dale (1998) makes a strong case for the utility of litigation as a reform advocacy strategy. Yet changes grudgingly made to settle lawsuits may be fleeting and may only result in minimally adequate conditions (Winfield 2008). Barton (1994) suggests that changes are more likely to persist when local stakeholders have developed consensus policies that lead to internalization of the changes and when sites can identify a strong reform champion.

B. Disproportionate Confinement of Minorities

As shown previously in Table 26.1, based on the 2006 one-day count of youths in detention facilities, 42.1% of the detained youth were African American, 31% were White, 22.7% were Hispanic, and 4.2% were classified as other (Sickmund et al. 2008). The percentage of minority youths in detention greatly exceeds their percentage in the general population. Nationwide in 2006, among youths aged 10 to 17 (the years most commonly associated with juvenile justice system jurisdiction), only 16.6% were African American, 18.3% were Hispanic, 59.1% were White, and 5.9% were of other racial/ethnic groups (Puzzanchera, Sladky, and Kang 2008). When considering the rate of detention per youth in the population base, in comparison to Whites, African American youth are detained 5.3 times as often, Latino youth 2.4 times as often, and Native American youth 3.5 times as often (Sickmund, Sladky, and Kang 2008).

This kind of over-representation, known as disproportionate minority contact (DMC), is evident throughout the juvenile justice system. The 1998 amendment to the Juvenile Justice and Delinquency Prevention Act required states seeking federal juvenile justice funding to address disproportionate minority confinement, and since the Act's 2002 amendment, this requirement was broadened to include DMC at any point in the juvenile justice system (Hsia 2006). Although DMC exists at all decision points in the juvenile justice system, from arrest through disposition, the detention stage is especially critical (Armour and Hammond 2009). Therefore, efforts to reduce DMC include careful examination of the factors related to the secure detention decision, the development of objective intake screening, and the provision of appropriate alternatives (Armour and Hammond 2009).

While DMC at the point of detention is clearly demonstrable, its causes are complex and not completely understood. Since it is also true that minorities, especially African Americans and Hispanics, are arrested at higher rates than their White counterparts (Puzzanchera and Adams 2008), it might seem logical that DMC reflects a higher rate of offending among minority youth. Several studies suggest that this is not the case (Frazier and Bishop 1985; Wordes, Bynum, and Corley 1994; Leiber and Fox 2005). As discussed more fully elsewhere in this volume, differences in delinquent behavior, arrests, or the presence of risk factors known to be related to the likelihood of future offending cannot account for DMC completely. The results of Lieber and Fox's (2005) study of juvenile detention decision-making, in particular, support the symbolic threat thesis (Tittle and Curran 1988) and its related differential attribution thesis (Bridges and Steen 1998). The symbolic threat thesis suggests that decision makers employ negative stereotypical perceptions of African American youth (Tittle and Curran 1988), and the differential attribution thesis specifies that these stereotypes reflect a tendency to attribute the delinquency of African American youth to internal causes and the delinquency of White youth to external causes (Bridges and Steen 1998). Decision makers perceive that delinquency attributed to internal causes is more likely to be repeated than is delinquency attributed to external causes; thus they recommend more punitive system responses to African American youth than to White youth.

Since the decision to detain also affects subsequent case outcomes, including raising the probability of placement in training schools and other residential programs, and since such placements increase rather than decrease the odds of future offending, DMC at the point of detention is especially pernicious. Recent detention reform efforts explicitly and appropriately set the reduction of DMC as a goal, and some have achieved promising results (Feyerherm 2000; Hoytt et al. 2005; Armour and Hammond 2009).

C. Gender

As noted previously, the arrest rate for juveniles increased in the late 1980s and early 1990s, followed by a sharp decrease from 1994 through 2003 and little change since then (Puzzanchera 2009). However, "arrests of juvenile females decreased less than male arrests in most offense categories (e.g., aggravated assault, burglary, and larceny-theft); in some categories (e.g., simple assault, drug abuse violations, and DUI), female arrests increased, while male arrests decreased" (Puzzanchera 2009, p. 8). As also mentioned above, despite these trends, juvenile court caseloads and detention populations have consistently increased.

Although the large majority of delinquency cases involves boys, the number and proportion of cases involving girls has increased at a faster rate in recent years. Between 1985 and 2005, the number of cases involving girls more than doubled, whereas the number of cases involving boys increased by about one-third (Sickmund 2009). The proportion of delinquency cases involving girls increased from 19% in 1985 to 27% in 2005, and these proportional increases were found across all types of offenses (Sickmund 2009). Girls also showed a larger increase in petitioned status offenses (33%) than did males (25%) between 1995 and 2005 (Puzzanchera and Sickmund 2008). National data from 2005 show that secure detention continues to be used relatively more often in cases involving boys (22%) than girls (17%), but that the proportion of detained girls whose most serious offense was a person offense increased from 16% in 1985 to 35% in 2005 (Puzzanchera and Sickmund 2008). However, as discussed previously, Feld's (2009) analysis attributes this rise to a relabeling of girls' status offenses in the wake of the JJDPA to enable the system to continue to detain and control them. It is also likely that bootstrapping occurs, whereby girls are more likely than boys to be detained for probation violations, and often their assignment to probation was the result of a status offense. Sherman (2005) provides recent evidence of bootstrapping across several detention sites.

As discussed in detail elsewhere in this volume, researchers and practitioners alike have come to recognize that there are important gender differences in the risk and needs profiles of youths in the juvenile justice system. In comparison to boys, girls are more likely to experience family dysfunction, trauma and sexual abuse, mental health and substance abuse problems, high-risk sexual behaviors, school problems, and affiliation with deviant peers (Hubbard and Pratt 2002; Lederman et al. 2004; Gavazzi, Yarcheck, and Chesney-Lind 2009). Especially given the prevalence of trauma and victimization experienced by girls who come into contact with the juvenile justice system, it is easy to see how being locked in detention centers can exacerbate problems for girls and reinforce feelings of powerlessness. Sherman (2005) reviews a range of gender-responsive programs that have been created to address the needs of girls in the context of detention. These approaches emphasize tailoring responses to individual girls and their circumstances, with an eye toward empowerment. Gender-responsive detention reform includes developing collaborations with gender-responsive community-based agencies; creating detention alternatives that are designed to address the specific needs of girls; cross-system (juvenile justice and child welfare) case conferencing, legal representation, and data sharing; female-focused probation units; and crisis intervention programs to deal with the family tensions found especially often in cases in involving girls (Sherman 2005).

D. Mental Health, Substance Abuse and Developmental Disabilities

Unlike other service systems, the juvenile justice system cannot refuse to deal with youths who enter it. A large proportion of the youths in the system, particularly those in detention and other residential placements, face challenges from mental illnesses, substance abuse, developmental disabilities, or some combination of these conditions. Detention centers are ill-equipped to address such conditions. Several recent studies have documented the high level of psychiatric disorders among youths in juvenile correctional facilities, finding that two-thirds or more of the youths have one or more diagnosable mental illness and/or an indication of substance abuse (Teplin et al. 2002; Grisso 2004; Wasserman, Ko, and McReynolds 2004; Teplin et al. 2006; Fazel, Doll, and Långström 2008). This prevalence greatly exceeds that of adolescents in the general population, estimated at about 16% (Roberts, Attkisson, and Rosenblatt 1998). Moreover, a substantial number of youths in detention centers meet criteria for two or more disorders; Abram and colleagues (2003; 2004) found comorbidity rates of 45.9% for males and 56.5% for females, with rates of comorbidity being higher for non-Hispanic Whites and older adolescents. Finally, there is evidence that large proportions of youths with mental illness in juvenile correctional settings do not receive mental health services (Desai et al. 2006; Pumariega et al. 1999), and that minority youth are less likely than Whites to access mental health services, either in the community or in the juvenile justice system (Rawal et al. 2004). Further evidence of the inadequacy of the mental health system in addressing the needs of adolescents comes from studies that document a high incidence of parents placing children in the juvenile justice system in order to access mental health services otherwise unavailable to them (National Alliance for the Mentally Ill 2001; United States General Accounting Office 2003).

In response to such findings, advocates have called for mental health screening of all youths at detention intake (Skowyra and Cocozza 2007). The National Center for Mental Health and Juvenile Justice (2009) reports that as many as thirty-nine states now use the Massachusetts Youth Screening Instrument Version 2 (MAYSI-2) (Grisso and Barnum 2000) in at least some juvenile correctional settings. Scores exceeding clinical cutoff levels on one or more of the MAYSI-2 scales alert officials to the need for further, more systematic assessment and the provision of mental health services as indicated.

The issue of children with disabilities in detention overlaps with, to some degree, and extends the discussion regarding mental health issues above. Mears, Aron, and Bernstein (2003) note that there is no universally accepted definition of disability, but that disability may be thought of as "the outcome of an interaction between impairments, or functional limitations, and behavioral/performance expectations of socially defined roles" (p. 49). Disabilities commonly discussed within educational or juvenile justice settings include a variety of learning disabilities, emotional disturbance, and mental retardation. The best estimates suggest that youths with disabilities are overrepresented in juvenile justice at a rate of four to five times that in the general population (Rutherford et al. 2002; Quinn et al. 2005).

Mears and colleagues (2003) argue that the over-representation of youths with disabilities in juvenile justice is not the result of their disabilities causing them to commit offenses at an elevated rate, but is more likely caused by differential targeting and processing by schools, police, and the courts. Although little empirical support currently exists, they suggest that adults may misinterpret behaviors commonly seen in youths with disabilities, such as impulsiveness or an inability to follow directions, and react punitively towards them (Osher et al. 2002; Mears, Aron, and Bernstein 2003).

The Individuals with Disabilities Education Act (IDEA), passed in 1975, mandates that "public schools and state-operated programs, such as juvenile correctional facilities, provide each eligible child with a free appropriate public education in the least restrictive environment" (Leone and Meisel 1997, p. 1.). Yet detention centers and juvenile correctional facilities have often failed to provide appropriate special education, or have done so only as a result of litigation (Leone and Meisel 1997).

V. CURRENT DETENTION REFORM EFFORTS

The last few decades have seen several efforts to reform juvenile detention. Lawsuits challenging some of the more outrageous conditions in some jurisdictions prompted some of these. Others were voluntary, as some stakeholders (persons working within and around local juvenile justice systems) envisioned better policies and practices. Some reform efforts have persisted, and model detention sites now exist. Others, however, could not withstand the political pressures to "get tough" that periodically sweep the country. Schwartz and Barton (1994) describe some of the earliest of these reform efforts. The most comprehensive, wide-ranging effort to date has been the Annie E. Casey Foundation's Juvenile Detention Alternatives Initiative (JDAI), described in detail below.

A. JDAI

The Annie E. Casey Foundation's first foray into detention reform occurred in Broward County, Florida (Fort Lauderdale) in the late 1980s when the Foundation provided funds to assist Florida in its response to a federal lawsuit (Barton, Schwartz, and Orlando 1994). This reform effort focused on mobilizing stakeholders to develop a consensus and understanding of the purposes of detention, developing objective intake criteria, expanding the availability of alternatives to secure detention, expediting the cases of youths held in secure detention to reduce lengths of stay, and collecting and using relevant data to guide policy decisions (Barton, Schwartz, and Orlando 1994). As a result, Broward County (capacity: 109 beds) reduced its average daily population in secure detention from a highly overcrowded 161 before the reform effort to 88 three years later, with no increased risk to public safety (Barton, Schwartz, and Orlando 1994).

Buoyed by these results, the Casey Foundation sought to expand the reform effort to the entire state of Florida. This attempt met with less success, as imposing the reforms on jurisdictions without sufficient site preparation proved impossible, especially in the increasingly conservative political climate of the early 1990s (Bishop and Griset 1999). Nevertheless, the Foundation had learned a great deal from the experiences in Broward County and the rest of Florida, and in 1993 formally launched JDAI in five sites: Cook County (Chicago), Sacramento, Multnomah County (Portland, OR), Milwaukee County, and New York City (Stanfield 1999). By 2009, JDAI had expanded to "105 local jurisdictions in 25 states and the District of Columbia," covering "29% of the nation's youth," and continues to grow (Mendel 2009, p. 10).

Although not all sites have seen long-term success, many have, and the quality and sustainability of implementation in some, such as Multnomah County and Bernalillo County (Albuquerque, NM) serve as models. The number of youths securely detained has fallen dramatically in these and many other JDAI sites, by as much as 50% in several, with no concomitant increases in juvenile crime or failures to appear (Feldman, Males, and Schiraldi 2001; Chen 2009; Mendel 2009).

In addition to reducing sites' reliance on secure detention, the JDAI approach can reduce minority over-representation (Feyerherm 2000; Hoytt et al. 2005) and serve as a catalyst for broader juvenile justice system reforms (Mendel 2007). For example, after the first five years of JDAI implementation, Multnomah County reduced its use of secure detention by more than 50% despite an increase in delinquency referrals, and greatly reduced the gap between the proportion of minority and White youths detained (Feyerherm 2000). Several other JDAI sites produced similar results (Lubow 2007). Mendel (2007) describes how JDAI implementation led to many other juvenile justice system improvements in several sites, including reductions in commitments to state juvenile correctional facilities, expansion of community-based programs, increased use of data to guide decisions, and greater collaboration among juvenile justice stakeholders. The key elements of the JDAI approach are outlined below.

1. *Stakeholder Mobilization*

JDAI reform efforts require a broad collaborative with strong leadership from a coordinator trained by Foundation consultants. At a minimum, partners include key juvenile justice system actors (judges, prosecutors, public defenders, probation officers, and police), along with representatives from related community service providers and youth advocates. The Foundation provides technical assistance and materials to stakeholders through consultant site visits, an online "JDAI Help Desk," and annual conferences to which representatives from each JDAI site are invited to share their successes and challenges.

2. *Definitional Consensus*

An early task for the collaborative is to develop a consensus around a definition of detention that views detention as a process rather than a building and that sees secure detention as only appropriate when no less restrictive alternatives can adequately protect public safety or prevent failures to appear at court hearings.

3. *Objective Intake Screening*

JDAI sites develop objective intake screening tools that guide recommendations for placement into secure detention, assignment to nonsecure alternatives, or outright release (Orlando 1999). Although JDAI refers to these as risk assessment instruments (RAIs), they are not actuarial prediction tools but rather are based on stakeholder consensus regarding what kinds of cases are appropriate for detention. Given the difficulties in predicting future offending, and a discomfort with ordering preventive detention on the basis of weak prediction, carefully developed consensus instruments at least make detention screening decisions more consistent and objective. These tools weight the youths' current and prior offense history most heavily. Multnomah County, with more than fifteen years of experience and data-driven refinement, perhaps provides the best example of an RAI (Dedel and Davies 2007).

4. *Alternatives to Secure Detention*

Stakeholders are uncomfortable releasing certain kinds of youths without some level of supervision. Often, community-based supervision is a sufficient alternative to locking up the youths. A broad array of alternatives can help a jurisdiction limit its use of secure detention, and the alternatives typically cost far less than a stay in detention. JDAI recommends and has developed a range of alternatives across its many sites, including:

- home detention, where a youth may only leave home for school, work, or when accompanied by a parent, and probation staff or trackers make frequent unannounced home visits (the frequency of the visits may vary depending upon the level of risk);
- home detention with electronic monitoring, an ankle bracelet that broadcasts a signal indicating the youth's whereabouts;
- afterschool or evening reporting centers can supervise youths and engage them in positive activities during the late afternoon and early evening hours;
- day reporting centers for youths who are not in school during the day;
- nonsecure shelter beds for temporary, supervised housing of youths whose parents cannot or will not take them, or when the victim of the alleged offense is in the youth's home.

(DeMuro 2005).

5. Case Expediting

While limiting admissions through an objective intake instrument helps to reduce detention populations, so does limiting lengths of stay by looking for ways to streamline the court processes. In addition to their influence on detention bed space, lengthy stays increase the likelihood of failures to appear, extend the time until victims receive their day in court, increase the risk of new offenses committed before the case process is completed, and make it more difficult for youths to see the relationship between the offense and the disposition (Henry 1999). JDAI sites have developed several strategies to reduce delays, such as appointing defense counsel prior to preliminary hearings so that the attorney has an opportunity to meet with the child before the hearing, reducing the likelihood of continuances; designating someone as a case expeditor, whose charge is to identify every opportunity to move cases forward and get youths out of detention; and holding weekly case reviews where the case of every child in detention is reviewed to see if there are any unnecessary delays (Henry 1999).

6. Use of Data for Continuous Monitoring and Evaluation

JDAI sites conduct ongoing collection and reporting of relevant data and use these data to inform policy and practice decisions (Busch 1999). As JDAI's efforts in a site begin, current data regarding admissions, average daily population, and length of stay provide compelling evidence that reform is needed. As the JDAI effort progresses, sites track outcome data (e.g., new offenses, failures to appear) on a regular basis. Stakeholders review this information to see if reform strategies are working as intended and to determine whether modifications or additional approaches should be tried.

B. DDAP

In the 1990s, the Center on Juvenile and Criminal Justice (CJCJ) developed the Detention Diversion Advocacy Project (DDAP) to divert high-risk juvenile offenders from the juvenile justice system in San Francisco, which had been long plagued with an overcrowded juvenile detention center (Shelden 1999). DDAP is an intensive case management model providing lay case advocacy, supervision and support, and linkage to other service resources for youths at the point of detention intake who have been identified as high-risk according to an instrument developed by the National Council on Crime and Delinquency. DDAP staff present a comprehensive community service plan at the detention hearing, and, if the plan is accepted, the judge diverts the youth to DDAP rather than ordering detention. Program goals include not only ensuring that the youth attends court hearings and is not rearrested while in the program, but also reducing the secure detention population, reducing disproportionate minority contact, and demonstrating that community-based interventions can be effective even with high-risk youths (Shelden 1999).

An evaluation of DDAP compared 271 program participants with a systematic random sample of 271 detained youths. The DDAP participants scored higher on initial risk than the comparison group (e.g., most were felony offenders), yet showed markedly lower rates of re-arrest, including fewer re-arrests for serious offenses. On most indicators, the comparison group's recidivism was two or three times as high as that of the DDAP youth (Shelden 1999). Moreover, the majority of DDAP youths remained successfully in the community prior to their dispositions, and most were not sent to residential programs at disposition (Shelden 1999). DDAP has expanded to other sites, with the Philadelphia program showing good early results (Feldman and Kubrin 2002).

Unlike JDAI, DDAP is not a comprehensive reform strategy, but, as a promising alternative to secure detention, it merits attention. Both San Francisco (Macallair and Males 2004) and Philadelphia (Griffin 2003) continue to experience problems with detention overall, but DDAP demonstrates that secure detention is not necessary even for high-risk youths, those that most jurisdictions absolutely believe require secure pretrial detention.

VI. Summary

As this chapter has suggested, the apparently simple concept of secure juvenile detention as a last resort to protect public safety and the integrity of the court process has proven anything but simple in practice. Secure detention does not and is not intended to deter crime, reform young offenders, or protect them from themselves. It does, however, populate the rest of the juvenile justice system. It bears little relationship to rates of juvenile crime, and its use varies widely from jurisdiction to jurisdiction. It contains far too many youths whose offenses are minor. Its use tends to lead to harsher dispositional outcomes that, in turn, result in increased subsequent offending. As it over-represents children of color, those with mental illness, and those with developmental disabilities, it amplifies many of society's most noxious inequities.

None of this is news, as observers have recognized problems with the nation's detention system for decades. The recurring calls for reform have produced little dramatic progress, although perhaps, through its continually expanding reach, JDAI's impact is encouraging. Some time ago, Schwartz (1994) argued that the greatest impediment to true detention reform was the politicized nature of the juvenile justice system, and that is probably still the case. No prosecutor, sheriff, or judge gets elected on a platform of *not* locking people up. Then, as now, the road to reform is paved with an awareness of the long-term fiscal impact of greater public safety benefits and better developmental outcomes for youths at lower cost, resulting from a more rational, limited, and better-focused use of secure detention and its alternatives.

It is tempting to call for the abolition of the use of secure pretrial juvenile detention, as did Fagan and Guggenheim (1996), who analyzed a "natural experiment" that resulted from the circumstances surrounding the *Schall v. Martin* (1984) case discussed previously. For three years prior to the resolution of that case, a district court ruling prohibited New York from using preventive detention for juveniles. During that time, judges still issued orders for detention based on their determination of serious risk that the juvenile would commit a crime prior to the court hearing, but released *Schall* cases immediately in accordance with the injunction against preventive detention. In other words, these were cases in which a judge had determined that detention was warranted but had released the youth as a result of the ongoing *Schall* litigation. A control group was constructed of cases not judicially ordered to be detained during that period, but who matched the *Schall* cases on a number of relevant legal and social structural variables. For both the *Schall* and control cases, the researchers compared all re-arrests within ninety days, the maximum period allowable in New York City between initial court appearance and disposition. Although the *Schall* cases did have significantly more re-arrests than the controls, the majority in both groups did not reoffend, and the groups did not significantly differ on re-arrests for violent offenses. In other words, judges' determinations of dangerousness were anything but certain. Fagan and Guggenheim (1996) conclude:

> There are reasonable and constitutional arguments to incapacitate a presumptively innocent individual when we are certain he or she is dangerous. But whenever a significant number of persons are preventively detained, many individuals will be deprived of their liberty even though they would not have endangered the community. In light of the great cost to defendants in terms of case outcomes and sanctions, and the marginal gains to society in crimes averted, preventive detention appears to be unjustified (p. 448).

However, without broader social and economic changes in communities, there will continue to be some youths perceived to pose such a serious threat to public safety that their secure detention will be necessary. At the very least, detention policies and practices can benefit from the research on detention and its effects, such as that reviewed in this chapter. The JDAI principles and strategies offer guidance for policy makers as they continue to grapple with the challenges of detention and the rest of the juvenile justice system. Developing a clear, limited definition of detention, applying objective intake screening, providing a continuum of community-based alternatives, and conducting diligent monitoring of conditions, practices, and outcomes is essential for minimizing abuse. As in medicine, the admonition of "at least do no harm" applies.

REFERENCES

Abram, Karen M., Linda A. Teplin, Devon R. Charles, Sandra L. Longworth, Gary M. McClelland, and Mina K. Dulcan. 2004. "Posttraumatic Stress Disorder and Trauma in Youth in Juvenile Detention." *Archives of General Psychiatry* 61(4): 403–10.

Abram, Karen M., Linda A. Teplin, Gary M. McClelland, and Mina K. Dulcan. 2003. "Comorbid Psychiatric Disorders in Youth in Juvenile Detention." *Archives of General Psychiatry* 60(11): 1097–108.

Akers, Ronald L. 1985. *Deviant Behavior: A Social Learning Approach*, 3rd ed. Belmont, CA: Wadsworth.

Armour, Jeff, and Sarah Hammond. 2009. *Minority Youth in the Juvenile Justice System: Disproportionate Minority Contact*. Denver, CO: National Conference of State Legislatures.

Arthur, Judge Lindsay G. 2001. "Ten Ways to Reduce Juvenile Detention." *Juvenile and Family Court Journal* 52(1): 29–36.

Barton, William H. 1994. "Implementing Detention Policy Changes." In *Reforming Juvenile Detention: No More Hidden Closets*, edited by Ira M. Schwartz and William H. Barton. Columbus: Ohio State University Press.

Barton, William H., Ira M. Schwartz, and Frank A. Orlando. 1994. "Reducing the Use of Secure Detention in Broward County, Florida." In *Reforming Juvenile Detention: No More Hidden Closets*, edited by Ira M. Schwartz and William H. Barton. Columbus: Ohio State University Press.

Becker, Howard S. 1963. *Outsiders: Studies in the Sociology of Deviance*. New York: Free Press.

Bishop, Donna M., and Charles E. Frazier. 1992. "Gender Bias in Juvenile Justice Processing: Implications of the JJDP Act." *Journal of Criminal Law and Criminology* 82(4): 1162–86.

Bishop, Donna M., and Pamela L. Griset. 1999. "Replicating Juvenile Detention Reform: Lessons from the Florida Detention Initiative." Vol. 12 of *Pathways to Juvenile Detention Reform*. Baltimore: Annie E. Casey Foundation.

Bridges, George S., and Sara Steen. 1998. "Racial Disparities in Official Assessments of Juvenile Offenders: Attributional Stereotypes as Mediating Mechanisms." *American Sociological Review* 63(4): 554–70.

Burrell, Sue. 2000. "Improving Conditions of Confinement in Secure Juvenile Detention Centers." Vol. 6 of *Pathways to Juvenile Detention Reform*. Baltimore: Annie E. Casey Foundation.

Busch, Deborah. 1999. "By the Numbers: The Role of Data and Information in Detention Reform." Vol. 7 of *Pathways to Juvenile Detention Reform*. Baltimore: Annie E. Casey Foundation.

Campaign for Youth Justice. 2007. "*Jailing Juveniles: The Dangers of Incarcerating Youth in Adult Jails in America*." Washington, DC: Campaign for Youth Justice. http://www.campaign4youthjustice.org/Downloads/NationalReportsArticles/CFYJ-Jailing_Juveniles_Report_2007-11-15.pdf.

Chen, Ronald K. 2009. "*Reinvesting in New Jersey Youth: Building on Successful Juvenile Detention Reform*." Trenton, NJ: New Jersey Office of the Child Advocate. http://www.state.nj.us/childadvocate/publications/PDFs/Reinvesting%20in%20NJ%20Youth.pdf.

Dale, Michael J. 1998. "Lawsuits and Public Policy: The Role of Litigation in Correcting Conditions in Juvenile Detention Centers." *University of San Francisco Law Review* 32(4): 675–734.

Dedel, Kelly, and Garth Davies. 2007. "Validating Multnomah County's Juvenile Detention Risk Assessment Instrument." Portland, OR: One in 37 Research, Inc., Multnomah County Department of Community Justice. http://www.onein37.com/storage/RAI%20Validation%20REPORT.pdf.

Desai, Rani A., Joseph L. Goulet, Judith Robbins, John F. Chapman, Scott J. Migdole, and Michael A. Hoge. 2006. "Mental Health Care in Juvenile Detention Facilities: A Review." *Journal of the American Academy of Psychiatry and the Law Online* 34(2): 204–14. http://jaapl.org/cgi/reprint/34/2/204.

DeMuro, Paul. 2005. "Consider the Alternatives: Planning and Implementing Detention Alternatives." Vol. 4 of *Pathways to Juvenile Detention Reform*. Baltimore: Annie E. Casey Foundation.

Dishion, Thomas J., Joan McCord, and François Poulin. 1999. "When Interventions Harm: Peer Groups and Problem Behavior." *American Psychologist* 54(9): 755–64.

Dishion, Thomas J., Kathleen M. Spracklen, and Gerald R. Patterson. 1996. "Deviancy Training in Male Adolescent Friendships." *Behavior Therapy* 27(3): 373–90.

Dodge, Kenneth A., Thomas J. Dishion, and Jennifer E. Lansford. 2006. "Deviant Peer Influences in Intervention and Public Policy for Youth." *Social Policy Report* 20(1). http://www.srcd.org/index.php?option=com_content&task=view&id=232&Itemid=550

Fagan, Jeffrey, and Martin Guggenheim. 1996. "Preventive Detention and the Judicial Prediction of Dangerousness for Juveniles: A Natural Experiment." *The Journal of Criminal Law and Criminology* 86(2): 415–48.

Fazel, Seena, Helen Doll, and Niklas Långström. 2008. "Mental Disorders among Adolescents in Juvenile Detention and Correctional Facilities: A Systematic Review and Metaregression Analysis of 25 Surveys." *Journal of the American Academy of Child and Adolescent Psychiatry* 47(9): 1010–19.

Feld, Barry C. 1984–1985. "Criminalizing Juvenile Justice: Rules of Procedure for the Juvenile Court." *Minnesota Law Review* 69(1): 191–276.

Feld, Barry C. 1991. "Justice by Geography: Urban, Suburban, and Rural Variations in Juvenile Justice Administration." *The Journal of Criminal Law and Criminology* 82(1): 156–210.

Feld, Barry C. 1999. *Bad Kids: Race and the Transformation of the Juvenile Court*. New York: Oxford University Press.

Feld, Barry C. 2009. "Violent Girls or Relabeled Status Offenders? An Alternative Interpretation of the Data." *Crime and Delinquency* 55(2): 241–65.

Feldman, Lisa B., and Charis E. Kubrin. 2002. *Evaluation Findings: The Detention Diversion Advocacy Program Philadelphia, Pennsylvania*. Washington, DC: George Washington University Center for Excellence in Municipal Management. http://www.cjcj.org/files/ddap_philly.pdf.

Feldman, Lisa, Michael Males, and Vincent Schiraldi. 2001. *A Tale of Two Jurisdictions: Youth Crime and Detention Rates in Maryland and the District of Columbia*. Washington, DC: Youth Law Center, Building Blocks for Youth.

Feyerherm, William H. 2000. "Detention Reform and Overrepresentation: A Successful Synergy." *Corrections Management Quarterly* 4(1): 44–51.

Frazier, Charles E., and Donna M. Bishop. 1985. "The Pretrial Detention of Juveniles and its Impact on Case Dispositions." *The Journal of Criminal Law and Criminology* 76(4): 1132–52.

Frazier, Charles E., and John C. Cochran. 1986. "Detention of Juveniles: Its Effects on Subsequent Juvenile Court Processing Decisions." *Youth and Society* 17(3): 286–305.

Gallagher, Catherine A., and Adam Dobrin. 2007. "Can Juvenile Justice Detention Facilities Meet the Call of the American Academy of Pediatrics and National Commission on Correctional Health Care? A National Analysis of Current Practices." *Pediatrics* 119(4): 815–16.

Gatti, Uberto, Richard E. Tremblay, and Frank Vitaro. 2009. "Iatrogenic Effect of Juvenile Justice." *Journal of Child Psychology and Psychiatry* 50(8): 991–98.

Gavazzi, Stephen M., Courtney M. Yarcheck, and Meda Chesney-Lind. 2006. "Global Risk Indicators and the Role of Gender in a Juvenile Detention Sample." *Criminal Justice and Behavior* 33(5): 597–612.

Goode, Erich. (1975). "On Behalf of Labeling Theory." *Social Problems* 22(5): 570–83.

Griffin, Patrick. 2003. "Juvenile Detention: The Philadelphia Alternative." *Pennsylvania Progress: Juvenile Justice Achievements in Pennsylvania* 9(4): 1–12. http://www.ncjj-servehttp.org/NCJJWebsite/pdf/july2003.pdf.

Grisso, Thomas. 2004. *Double Jeopardy: Adolescent Offenders with Mental Disorders*. Chicago: University of Chicago Press.

Grisso, Thomas, and Richard Barnum. (2000). "*Massachusetts Youth Screening Instrument-2: User's Manual and Technical Report*." Worcester MA: University of Massachusetts Medical School.

Henry, D. Allen. 1999. "Reducing Unnecessary Delay: Innovations in Case Processing." Vol. 5 of *Pathways to Juvenile Detention Reform*. Baltimore: Annie E. Casey Foundation.

Holman, Barry, and Jason Ziedenberg. 2006. *The Dangers of Detention: The Impact of Incarcerating Youth in Detention and Other Secure Facilities*. Washington, DC: Justice Policy Institute. http://www.justicepolicy.org/images/upload/06–11_REP_DangersOfDetention_JJ.pdf.

Hoytt, Eleanor H., Vincent Schiraldi, Brenda V. Smith, and Jason Ziedenberg. 2005. "Reducing Racial Disparities in Juvenile Detention." Vol. 8 of *Pathways to Juvenile Detention Reform*. Baltimore: Annie E. Casey Foundation.

Hsia, Heidi. 2006. "Introduction." In *Disproportionate Minority Contact: Technical Assistance Manual*, edited by the Office of Juvenile Justice and Delinquency Prevention, 3rd ed. Washington, DC: U.S. Department of Justice, Office of Justice Programs, Office of Juvenile Justice and Delinquency Prevention. http://www.ncjrs.gov/html/ojjdp/dmc_ta_manual/dmcfull.pdf.

Hubbard, Dana Jones, and Travis C. Pratt. 2002. "A Meta-Analysis of the Predictors of Delinquency Among Girls." *Journal of Offender Rehabilitation* 34(3): 1–13.

Johnson, Lee Michael, Ronald L. Simons, and Rand D. Conger. 2004. "Criminal Justice System Involvement and Continuity of Youth Crime." *Youth and Society* 36(1): 3–29.

Lederman, Cindy S., Gayle A. Dakof, Maria A. Larrea, and Hua Li. 2004. "Characteristics of Adolescent Females in Juvenile Detention." *International Journal of Law and Psychiatry* 27(4): 321–37.

Leiber, Michael J., and Kristan C. Fox. 2005. "Race and the Impact of Detention on Juvenile Justice Decision Making." *Crime and Delinquency* 51(4): 470–97.

Lemert, Edwin M. 1951. *Social Pathology*. New York: McGraw-Hill.

Leone, Peter E., and Sheri Meisel. 1997. "Improving Education Services for Students in Detention and Confinement Facilities." *Children's Legal Rights Journal* 17(1): 1–12. http://www.edjj.org/Publications/list/leone_meisel-1997.html.

Livesy, Sarah, Melissa Sickmund, and Anthony Sladky. 2009. "Juvenile Residential Facility Census, 2004: Selected Findings." *Juvenile Offenders and Victims: National Report Series*. Washington, DC: U.S. Department of Justice, Office of Justice Programs, Office of Juvenile Justice and Delinquency Prevention.

Loughran, Thomas A., Edward P. Mulvey, Carol A. Schubert, Jeffrey Fagan, Alex R. Piquero, and Sandra H. Losoya. 2009. "Estimating a Dose-Response Relationship Between Length of Stay and Future Recidivism in Serious Juvenile Offenders." *Criminology* 47(3): 699–740.

Lubow, Bart. 2005. "Safely Reducing Reliance on Juvenile Detention." *Corrections Today* 67(5): 66–68, 70–72.

Lubow, Bart. 2007. "Preface Update." In Richard A. Mendel, "Beyond Detention: System Transformation through Juvenile Detention Reform." Vol. 14 of *Pathways to Juvenile Detention Reform*. Baltimore: Annie E. Casey Foundation.

Macallair, Daniel, and Mike Males. 2004. "A Failure of Good Intentions: An Analysis of Juvenile Justice Reform in San Francisco during the 1990s." *Review of Policy Research* 21(1): 63–78. http://www3.interscience.wiley.com/cgi-bin/fulltext/118818130/PDFSTART.

Mears, Daniel P., Laudan Aron, and Jenny Bernstein. 2003. *Addressing the Needs of Youth with Disabilities in the Juvenile Justice System: The Status of Evidence-Based Research*. Washington, DC: National Council on Disability.

Mendel, Richard A. 2007. "Beyond Detention: System Transformation through Juvenile Detention Reform." Vol. 14 of *Pathways to Juvenile Detention Reform*. Baltimore: Annie E. Casey Foundation.

Mendel, Richard A. 2009. *Two Decades of JDAI: From Demonstration Project to National Standard. A Progress Report*. Baltimore, MD: Annie E. Casey Foundation.

Mennel, Robert M. 1973. *Thorns and Thistles: Juvenile Delinquents in the United States, 1825–1940*. Hanover, NH: University Press of New England.

National Alliance for the Mentally Ill. 2001. *Families on the Brink: The Impact of Ignoring Children with Serious Mental Illness*. Arlington, VA: National Alliance for the Mentally Ill.

National Center for Juvenile Justice. 2008. "National Juvenile Court Data Archive: Juvenile court case records 1985–2005 [machine-readable data files]." Pittsburgh, PA: National Center for Juvenile Justice [producer].

National Center for Mental Health and Juvenile Justice. 2009. *Mental Health Screening within Juvenile Justice: The Next Frontier*. Delmar, NY: National Center for Mental Health and Juvenile Justice. Accessed July 13, 2009. http://www.ncmhjj.com/pdfs/MH_Screening.pdf.

National Council on Crime and Delinquency. 1961. *Standards and Guides for the Detention of Children and Youth*, 2nd ed. New York: National Council on Crime and Delinquency.

Norman, Sherwood. 1949. "New Goals for Juvenile Detention." *Federal Probation* 13: 29–35.

Orlando, Frank. 1999. "Controlling the Front Gates: Effective Admissions Policies and Practices." Vol. 3 of *Pathways to Juvenile Detention Reform*. Baltimore: Annie E. Casey Foundation.

Osher, David, Mary Magee Quinn, Kimberly Kendziora, and Darren Woodruff. 2002. *Addressing Invisible Barriers: Improving Outcomes for Youth with Disabilities in the Juvenile Justice System*. College Park, MD: Center for Effective Collaboration and Practice, American Institutes for Research.

Parent, Dale G., Valerie Leiter, Stephen Kennedy, Lisa Livens, Daniel Wentworth, and Sarah Wilcox. 1994. *Conditions of Confinement: Juvenile Detention and Corrections Facilities. Research Summary*. Washington, DC: U.S. Department of Justice, Office of Justice Programs, Office of Juvenile Justice and Delinquency Prevention.

Pumariega, Andres J., D. Lanette Atkins, Kenneth Rogers, Larry Montgomery, Cheryl Nybro, Robert Caesar, and Donald Millus. 1999. "Mental Health and Incarcerated Youth. II: Service Utilization." *Journal of Child and Family Studies* 8(2): 205–15.

Puzzanchera, Charles. 2009. "Juvenile Arrests 2007." *Juvenile Justice Bulletin*. Washington, DC: U.S. Department of Justice, Office of Justice Programs, Office of Juvenile Justice and Delinquency Prevention.

Puzzanchera, Charles, and Ben Adams. 2008. "National Disproportionate Minority Contact Databook," Updated May 17, 2010. National Center for Juvenile Justice, Office of Juvenile Justice and Delinquency Prevention. http://ojjdp.ncjrs.gov/ojstatbb/dmcdb/.

Puzzanchera, Charles, and Melissa Sickmund. 2008. *Juvenile Court Statistics 2005*. Pittsburgh, PA: National Center for Juvenile Justice.

Puzzanchera, Charles, Anthony Sladky, and Wei Kang. 2008. "Easy Access to Juvenile Populations: 1990–2007." http://www.ojjdp.ncjrs.gov/ojstatbb/ezapop/.

Quinn, Mary Magee, Robert B. Rutherford, Peter E. Leone, David M. Osher, and Jeffrey M. Poirier. 2005. "Youth with Disabilities in Juvenile Corrections: A National Survey." *Exceptional Children* 71(3): 339–45. http://web.ebscohost.com/ehost/pdf?vid=3andhid=101andsid=5788d219-eada-4530-b6a4-af38d7db5858%40sessionmgr110.

Rawal, Purva, Jill Romansky, Michael Jenuwine, and John S. Lyons. 2004. "Racial Differences in the Mental Health Needs and Service Utilization of Youth in the Juvenile Justice System." *Journal of Behavioral Health Services and Research* 31(3): 242–54.

Rector, Milton G. 1960. Preface. In Sherwood Norman, *Detention Practice: Significant Developments in the Detention of Children and Youth*. New York: National Probation and Parole Association.

Roberts, Robert E., C. Clifford Attkisson, and Abram Rosenblatt. 1998. "Prevalence of Psychopathology among Children and Adolescents." *American Journal of Psychiatry* 155(6): 715–25.

Rutherford, Robert B. Jr., Michael Bullis, Cindy W. Anderson, and Heather M. Griller-Clark. 2002. *Youth with Disabilities in the Correctional System: Prevalence Rates and Identification Issues*. College Park, MD: Center for Effective Collaboration and Practice, American Institutes for Research.

Sarri, Rosemary C. 1974. *Under Lock and Key: Juveniles in Jails and Detention.* Ann Arbor: University of Michigan, National Assessment of Juvenile Corrections.

Schwartz, Ira M. 1989. *(In) Justice for Juveniles.* Lexington, MA: Lexington Books.

Schwartz, Ira M. 1994. "What Policymakers Need to Know about Juvenile Detention Reform." In *Reforming Juvenile Detention: No More Hidden Closets,* edited by Ira M. Schwartz and William H. Barton. Columbus: Ohio State University Press.

Schwartz, Ira M., and William H. Barton, eds. 1994. *Reforming Juvenile Detention: No More Hidden Closets.* Columbus: Ohio State University Press.

Shelden, Randall G. 1999. "Detention Diversion Advocacy: An Evaluation." *Juvenile Justice Bulletin.* Washington, DC: U.S. Department of Justice, Office of Justice Programs, Office of Juvenile Justice and Delinquency Prevention. http://www.ncjrs.gov/pdffiles1/ojjdp/171155.pdf

Sherman, Francine T. 2005. "Detention Reform and Girls: Challenges and Solutions." Vol. 13 of *Pathways to Juvenile Detention Reform.* Baltimore: Annie E. Casey Foundation.

Sickmund, Melissa. 2009. "Delinquency Cases in Juvenile Court, 2005." *OJJDP Fact Sheet.* Washington DC: U.S. Department of Justice, Office of Justice Programs, Office of Juvenile Justice and Delinquency Prevention.

Sickmund, Melissa, T. J. Sladky, and Wei Kang. 2008. "Census of Juveniles in Residential Placement Databook." http://www.ojjdp.ncjrs.gov/ojstatbb/cjrp/.

Sickmund, Melissa, T. J. Sladky, Wei Kang, and Charles Puzzanchera. 2008. "Easy Access to the Census of Juveniles in Residential Placement." National Center for Juvenile Justice, Office of Juvenile Justice and Delinquency Prevention. http://ojjdp.ncjrs.gov/ojstatbb/ezacjrp/.

Skowyra, Kathleen, and Joseph J. Cocozza, 2007. *Blueprint for Change: A Comprehensive Model for the Identification and Treatment of Youth with Mental Health Needs in Contact with the Juvenile Justice System.* Delmar, NY: Policy Research Associates, National Center for Mental Health and Juvenile Justice. http://www.ncmhjj.com/Blueprint/pdfs/Blueprint.pdf.

Snyder, Howard N., and Melissa Sickmund. 2006. *Juvenile Offenders and Victims: 2006 National Report.* Washington, DC: U.S. Department of Justice, Office of Justice Programs, Office of Juvenile Justice and Delinquency Prevention.

Stanfield, Rochelle. 1999. "The JDAI Story: Building a Better Juvenile Detention System." *Pathways to Juvenile Detention Reform, Overview.* Baltimore, MD: Annie E. Casey Foundation.

Teplin, Linda A., Karen M. Abram, Gary M. McClelland, Mina K. Dulcan, and Amy A. Mericle. 2002. "Psychiatric Disorders in Youth in Juvenile Detention." *Archives of General Psychiatry* 59(12): 1133–43.

Teplin, Linda A., Karen M. Abram, Gary M. McClelland, Amy A. Mericle, Mina K. Dulcan, and Jason J. Washburn. 2006. "Psychiatric Disorders of Youth in Detention." *Juvenile Justice Bulletin.* Washington, DC: U.S. Department of Justice, Office of Juvenile Justice and Delinquency Prevention.

Tittle, Charles R., and Debra A. Curran. 1988. "Contingencies for Dispositional Disparities in Juvenile Justice." *Social Forces* 67(1): 23–58.

United States General Accounting Office. 2003. *Child Welfare and Juvenile Justice: Federal Agencies Could Play a Stronger Role in Helping States Reduce the Number of Children Placed Solely to Obtain Mental Health Services.* Publication No. GAO-03-397. Washington, DC: United States General Accounting Office.

Warner, Florence W. 1933. *Juvenile Detention in the United States: Report of a Field Survey of the National Probation Association.* Chicago: University of Chicago Press.

Wasserman, Gail A., Susan J. Ko, and Larkin S. McReynolds. 2004. "Assessing the Mental Health Status of Youth in Juvenile Justice Settings." *Juvenile Justice Bulletin.* Washington, DC: U.S. Department of Justice, Office of Juvenile Justice and Delinquency Prevention.

Weiss, Bahr, Annalise Caron, Shelly Ball, Julie Tapp, Margaret Johnson, and John R. Weisz. 2005. "Iatrogenic Effects of Group Treatment for Antisocial Youth." *Journal of Consulting and Clinical Psychology* 73(6): 1036–44.

Winfield, Emily N. 2008. "Judicial Policymaking and Juvenile Detention Reform: A Case Study of Jimmy Doe et al. v. Cook County." *Journal of Gender, Race and Justice* 12(1): 225–55.

Wordes, Madeline, Timothy S. Bynum, and Charles J. Corley. 1994. "Locking up Youth: The Impact of Race on Detention Decisions." *Journal of Research in Crime and Delinquency* 31(2): 149–65.

Youth Law Center. 2009 "Resources." San Francisco, CA: Youth Law Center. Accessed June 23. http://www.ylc.org/resources.php.

CHAPTER 27

....

PROCEDURAL RIGHTS IN JUVENILE COURTS

COMPETENCE AND CONSEQUENCES

....

BARRY C. FELD

I. INTRODUCTION

....

PROGRESSIVE reformers envisioned a juvenile court judge who made dispositions in the child's "best interests." Juvenile courts separated children from adult offenders, treated them rather than punished them, and rejected the procedural safeguards of criminal prosecutions. They maximized judicial discretion to rehabilitate abused, dependent, and delinquent youths. Because delinquency proceedings focused primarily on a child's background and future welfare rather than the crime alleged, juvenile courts dispensed with formal procedures such as lawyers, juries, and rules of evidence (Feld 1999; Tanenhaus 2004).

In 1967, the Supreme Court in *In re Gault* (387 U.S. 1 [1967]) began a "due process revolution" that substantially transformed the juvenile court from a social welfare agency into a more formal, legal institution (Feld 1999; Scott and Steinberg 2008). Among other safeguards, *Gault* granted delinquents a constitutional right to counsel and to the Fifth Amendment privilege against self-incrimination, and initiated a procedural convergence between juvenile and criminal courts. In subsequent decisions, the Court further emphasized the criminal aspects of delinquency proceedings. In *In re Winship* (397 U.S. 358 [1970]), the Court held that the state must prove delinquency "beyond a reasonable doubt" rather than by the lower, civil "preponderance of the evidence" standard of proof. However, in *McKeiver v. Pennsylvania* (403 U.S. 528 [1971]), the Court declined to give delinquents all criminal procedural safeguards and denied them a constitutional right to a jury trial. By contrast, in *Breed v. Jones* (421 U.S. 519 [1975]), the Court posited a functional equivalence between delinquency and criminal trials and held that the Fifth Amendment's double jeopardy clause barred criminal re-prosecution of a youth after a judge had adjudicated him delinquent.

Developmental psychologists have examined adolescents' adjudicative competence, their capacity to exercise or waive *Miranda* rights or the right to counsel, and their ability to participate in legal proceedings. This research questions whether juveniles possess the cognitive ability and judgment necessary to exercise legal rights. It indicates that younger and mid-adolescent youths exhibit substantial deficits in understanding and competence compared with adults.

Despite developmental differences between adolescents and adults, the Court and most states do not provide youths with additional procedural safeguards to protect them from their immaturity and vulnerability. Instead, states use the adult legal standard—"knowing, intelligent, and voluntary under the 'totality of the circumstances'"—to gauge juveniles' waivers of rights. Because developmental differences reduce youths' competency to exercise rights, formal legal equality results in practical inequality. By contrast, when states have the option to provide delinquents with procedural safeguards comparable to those of criminal defendants, such as a jury trial, the vast majority instead use less effective juvenile court procedures that provide an advantage to the state. It is easier to convict a youth in juvenile court without a jury than it would be to convict an adult in criminal court. Many states use those procedurally deficient delinquency convictions to enhance adults' criminal sentences and to impose other collateral consequences.

This chapter examines the "law on the books" and the "law in action" in juvenile courts. The first section examines juveniles' Fifth Amendment privilege against self-incrimination and *Miranda* rights. It then analyzes developmental psychological research on juveniles' competence to exercise rights. Youths' reduced competency increases their vulnerability and renders them less able than adults to effectively exercise rights. The second part examines the impact of juveniles' limited competence to exercise and waive their right to counsel. Juveniles' developmental limitations adversely affect the delivery of legal services in juvenile courts and increase the risks of erroneous adjudications. Youths' diminished competence and the absence of counsel compounds the risks of erroneous convictions because the vast majority of juveniles plead guilty rather than receive a trial. The third part of this chapter examines the Court's rationale to deny juveniles a constitutional right to a jury trial and analyzes why that makes it easier to convict delinquents than criminals and how the subsequent use of delinquency convictions to enhance criminal sentences compounds that procedural disparity. The chapter concludes that more than four decades after *Gault*, "the child receives the worst of both worlds:...he gets neither the protections accorded to adults nor the solicitous care and regenerative treatment postulated for children" (Kent v. United States, 383 U.S. 541, 556 [1966]).

II. COMPETENCE TO EXERCISE PROCEDURAL RIGHTS: FIFTH AMENDMENT AND *MIRANDA*

In re Gault involved the delinquency trial and institutional commitment of a 15-year-old boy who allegedly made an obscene telephone call. The state took him into custody, detained him overnight without notifying his parents, and conducted a hearing the next day. The juvenile court judge did not hear the complaining witness, receive sworn testimony, or prepare a record of the proceedings. At the hearing, the judge neither advised Gault of a right to counsel or to remain silent, nor did he provide an attorney. Instead, he questioned Gault about the telephone call and elicited some incriminating responses. The judge adjudicated Gault a delinquent and committed him to the State Industrial School "for the period of his minority [that is, until age 21], unless sooner discharged by due process of law." If Gault had been an adult, his offense could have resulted in a $50 fine or two months' imprisonment, rather than six years, the duration of his minority.

Gault identified two crucial disjunctions between juvenile justice rhetoric and reality: the theory versus the practice of rehabilitation, and the differences between the procedures available to criminal defendants and to delinquents. The Court reviewed the history of juvenile courts and the traditional justifications to deny procedural rights, such as claims that proceedings were neither adversarial nor criminal. *Gault* noted that the absence of procedures frequently resulted in arbitrary decisions rather than "careful, compassionate, individualized treatment." The Court assessed the rhetoric of juvenile justice against the realities of procedural arbitrariness, paucity of appropriate treatments (reflected in high rates of recidivism), and stigma of delinquency labels.

The Court concluded that the Constitution requires states to provide fundamentally fair delinquency procedures. These protections included notice of charges, a fair and impartial hearing, assistance of counsel, an opportunity to confront and cross-examine witnesses, and the Fifth Amendment privilege against self-incrimination. *Gault* asserted that adversarial procedural safeguards were essential to determine the truth—accurate fact-finding—and to preserve individual freedom by limiting the power of the state—prevent governmental oppression. It did not believe that providing these protections would impair juvenile courts' ability to treat juveniles.

The Court based delinquents' rights to notice, counsel, and to confront and cross-examine witnesses on the Fourteenth Amendment due process clause's standard of fundamental fairness rather than the specific provisions of the Sixth

Amendment. However, it explicitly relied on the Fifth Amendment to provide juveniles with the privilege against self-incrimination. As a result, juvenile courts' proponents no longer could characterize delinquency adjudications as either noncriminal or nonadversarial, because the Fifth Amendment privilege is the bulwark of the adversary system and only available to criminal defendants (Feld 1984). *Gault* precipitated an incomplete procedural convergence with adult criminal procedures. Juvenile courts' increased procedural formality, in turn, unintentionally legitimated punishment, contributed to greater severity in juvenile sentencing policy and practice, and made providing adequate safeguards more critical (Feld 1988a, 2003b).

A. *Miranda* and Interrogating Juveniles—Legal Framework

After *Gault* applied the Fifth Amendment to delinquency proceedings, juveniles also received the right to a *Miranda* warning prior to custodial interrogation. Earlier, the Court in *Haley v. Ohio* (332 U.S. 596 [1948]) and in *Gallegos v. Colorado* (370 U.S. 49 [1962]) cautioned judges to closely scrutinize how youthfulness and inexperience affected the voluntariness of statements, and it excluded the confessions extracted from 14- and 15-year-old youths. *Gault* reiterated the Court's concerns about the impact of youthfulness on juveniles' exercise of legal rights. Thus, the Court long had recognized that children are not the equals of adults during interrogation and that they required additional safeguards, such as assistance of a parent or an attorney, to compensate for their vulnerability (Bishop and Farber 2007).

In *Fare v. Michael C.* (442 U.S. 707 [1979]), a more conservative Court considered the validity of a *Miranda* waiver given by a 16 1/2-year-old who had several prior arrests and who had "served time" in a youth camp. Despite Michael C.'s repeated requests to see his probation officer, the Court ruled that he did not invoke the *Miranda* privilege or request counsel. Instead, *Fare* held that trial judges should use the adult standard—"knowing, intelligent, and voluntary" under the "totality of the circumstances"—to evaluate juveniles' waivers of rights and the admissibility of confessions. *Fare* rejected the view that developmental differences between juveniles and adults required special procedures to protect youths during interrogation and required children to assert legal rights clearly and unambiguously. *Fare* dismissed concerns that trial courts could not accurately use the adult standard to gauge juveniles' exercise or waiver of *Miranda* rights.

In *Yarborough v. Alvarado* (541 U.S. 652 [2004]), a 5–4 majority of the Court again rejected youthfulness and inexperience as special factors when juveniles waive rights. *Miranda* requires police to administer a warning whenever they interrogate a suspect who is in custody. In *Alvarado*, police instructed the parents of a 17-year-old juvenile to bring him to the station for questioning and denied their request to be present. Because the officer did not give Alvarado a *Miranda* warning before she questioned him alone for two hours, the issue was whether he was in custody. The Court concluded that custody is an objective status—whether a reasonable person would feel free to leave—and does not include how a suspect's age or lack of experience with police might affect his feelings of restraint. By contrast, the *Alvarado* dissent argued that youthfulness bears directly on whether a reasonable person would feel she was in custody.

About one dozen states provide additional safeguards beyond the "totality" approach endorsed by *Fare* (Feld 2006a, 2006b). These states require the presence of a parent or other interested adult at a juvenile's interrogation as a prerequisite to a valid waiver of *Miranda* rights. They presume that most juveniles lack competence to exercise *Miranda* rights and require an adult's assistance. Rather than trying to assess after-the-fact the impact of immaturity on waivers of rights, they simply require parents to be present during interrogation. They assume that a parent's presence enhances juveniles' understanding of their rights, mitigates the dangers of unreliable statements, provides an independent witness of what occurs, and reduces police coercion. As juvenile justice has become more punitive, youths need additional procedural safeguards to achieve functional parity with adult defendants (e.g., State v. Presha, 748 A.2d 1108 [N.J. 2000]). Moreover, parents are the practical means by which juveniles can exercise their *Miranda* right to counsel. Most commentators endorse parental presence safeguards, even though empirical research and experience challenge the validity of the assumptions or the utility of the rule (Feld 2006a, 2006b).

The Supreme Court in *Fare* and *Alvarado*, and the vast majority of states treat juveniles as the functional equals of adults during interrogation. Just as they must with an adult, trial judges must decide whether, after examining the totality of the circumstances, a youth has made a "knowing, intelligent, and voluntary" waiver of her rights. The "totality of the circumstances" includes characteristics of the offender—e.g., age, education, IQ, and prior contacts with police—and circumstances surrounding the interrogation, such as the location, methods, and lengths of interrogation (Feld 2006a, 2006b). Youthfulness, inexperience, or parents' presence are relevant factors in judges' "totality" assessment.

While appellate courts identify factors for judges to consider when they assess suspects' *Miranda* waivers, they do not assign controlling weight to any one and remit their weighing to trial judges' discretion (Grisso 1980; Feld 2006a). In practice, judges apply the "totality" standard conservatively, find valid *Miranda* waivers whenever police testify that they advised a juvenile of her rights and she said she understood them, and exclude only the most obviously invalid waivers and confessions (Feld 1984, 2006a). Trial judges find voluntary *Miranda* waivers despite coercive interrogation techniques, young age, or mental deficiencies (Feld 1984, 2006a). Judges have found valid *Miranda* waivers and admitted confessions made by 10-year-old children and by illiterate, mentally retarded youths with IQs in the 60s whom psychologists characterize as incapable of abstract reasoning (see, e.g., People v. Cheatham, 551 N.W.2d 355 [Mich. 1996]; *In re B.M.B.*, 955 P.2d 1302 [Kan. 1998]; Drizin and Leo 2004; Feld 2006a). Although the totality approach theoretically enables trial judges to protect immature youths who are unable to exercise rights or who succumb to coercion, in practice, judges give police considerable leeway to exploit youths' vulnerability.

B. Juveniles' Competence to Exercise *Miranda* Rights and Stand Trial

Developmental and social psychologists question whether juveniles have the cognitive capacity or psychosocial maturity to make "knowing, intelligent, and voluntary" waivers. The foremost research, conducted by Thomas Grisso, reports that most juveniles simply do not understand a *Miranda* warning well enough to invoke or waive rights in a knowing and intelligent manner (Grisso 1980, 1981). Without adequate understanding, juveniles are at a comparative disadvantage with adults. Juveniles most frequently misunderstood that they had the right to consult with an attorney and to have a lawyer present when police questioned them (Grisso 1980, 1981). Children 15 years of age and younger exhibited significantly poorer understanding of *Miranda* rights than did older adolescents (Grisso 1980). Even though juveniles 16 years of age and older exhibited a level of understanding comparable to adults, substantial minorities of both groups failed to grasp at least one element of the standard warning.

Although *Miranda* focuses primarily on suspects' understanding the words of the warning, a valid waiver of rights also requires the ability to appreciate the adverse consequences of waiving and to make rational decisions. Juveniles often fail to appreciate the significance of rights or to understand that they can exercise them without adverse consequences (Grisso 1997a; Grisso et al. 2003).[1] There is an asymmetrical power relationship in which children's lower social status and expectations of obedience to authority make them more vulnerable than adults to interrogation techniques. For example, when females, African Americans, or young people deal with authority figures, they often speak less assertively and use indirect patterns of speech to avoid conflict (Ainsworth 1993). During interrogation, youths respond more passively and acquiesce more easily to police suggestions (Kaban and Tobey 1999). *Fare* requires juveniles to invoke *Miranda* rights clearly, unambiguously, and with adult-like technical precision, even though this expectation conflicts with the normal responses and verbal styles of most youths.

Developmental psychological research on adolescents' adjudicative competence raises further doubts about juveniles' ability to exercise legal rights. To conduct a fundamentally fair trial, constitutional due process requires a defendant to be able to understand the proceedings, to make rational decisions, and to assist counsel (Drope v. Missouri, 420 U.S. 162 [1975]). Legal competence hinges on a defendant's ability to understand proceedings; to provide, receive, and understand information from counsel; and to make reasonable choices (Bonnie and Grisso 2000; Grisso 2000). Judges assess defendants' competency to stand trial when mental illnesses or developmental disabilities substantially impair their ability to understand or participate (Dusky v. United States, 362 U.S. 402 [1960]).

Developmental psychologists contend that adolescents' immaturity produces the same deficits of understanding, impairment of judgment, and inability to assist counsel as does severe mental illness, and renders many juveniles legally incompetent (Grisso 1997b, 2000; Scott and Grisso 2005). Generic developmental limitations rather than mental illness or mental retardation adversely affect adolescents' ability to understand proceedings, to assist counsel, and to make rational decisions (Grisso 1997a; Redding and Frost 2001; Scott and Grisso 2005).

Grisso's research on adolescents' adjudicative competence, like his earlier research on youths' competence to exercise *Miranda* rights, found significant age-related developmental differences in understanding and judgment (Grisso et al. 2003). Most juveniles younger than 13 or 14 years of age exhibited impairments similar to adults with severe mental illnesses and lacked the ability to assist or participate in their defense (Bonnie and Grisso 2000; Grisso et al. 2003). A significant proportion of juveniles younger than age 16 lacked competence to stand trial, to make legal decisions, or to assist counsel, and many older youths exhibited substantial impairments (Grisso et al. 2003). Juveniles of below-average intelligence exhibited greater impairment of competence than did either low-intelligence adults or juveniles of normal intelligence (Grisso et al. 2003). Research on adolescents' psychosocial maturity and quality of judgment identifies several areas—risk perceptions, emotions, temporal orientation, loyalty to peers, susceptibility to the influence of others, and the like—in which youths think differently than adults and that contribute to more immature and impetuous decisions by adolescents (Scott, Reppucci, and Woolard 1995; Steinberg and Cauffman 1996; Scott and Grisso 1997). Even formally competent adolescents made poorer decisions than did young adults because they emphasized short-term over long-term outcomes and sought peer approval (Scott and Grisso 1997; Steinberg and Cauffman 1999; Bonnie and Grisso 2000).

To summarize, developmental psychological research spanning decades and assessing several domains consistently indicates that adolescents as a class are at a significant disadvantage in the interrogation room, at trial, or, more often, at arraignment when entering a guilty plea. For youths 15 years of age and younger, these disabilities are clear and substantial. While juveniles aged 16 and 17 exhibit some degree of impairment, they appear to function comparably to adults. Because of these developmental differences, using the same legal framework to judge juveniles' and adults' waivers of rights puts youths at a considerable disadvantage.

C. Juveniles in the Interrogation Room

Four decades after *Miranda*, we still know remarkably little about what actually happens when police interrogate suspects (Leo 1996; Feld 2006a, 2006b). Studies conducted in the immediate aftermath of *Miranda* attempted to gauge compliance with the warning requirements and to assess the impact of warnings on subsequent rates of confessions and convictions (reviewed in Feld 2006a, 2006b; Leo 2008). Richard Leo (1996) has conducted the only empirical research on police interrogation of adults in the United States in the last three decades, based on his observations of 122 interrogations in an urban California police department and his review of sixty audio and videotapes of interrogations from two other police departments.

Barry Feld (2006a, 2006b) has reported the first empirical data of custodial interrogation of juveniles, based on analyses of recordings of sixty-six interrogations in one county in Minnesota. England's Police and Criminal Evidence Act 1984 (PACE) requires police to record interrogations of suspects arrested for indictable offenses. Gisli Gudjonsson (2003) and colleagues have coded and analyzed tapes and transcripts of British interrogations, assessed the techniques police employ and examined how suspects with different personal or psychological characteristics responded. Saul Kassin (1997, 2005; Kassin and Gudjonsson 2004) has conducted laboratory studies to analyze the psychology of interrogation, to assess how social influences affect susceptible subjects, and to identify the individual characteristics and police practices likely to elicit false confessions. Finally, Drizin and Leo (2004) examined cases of DNA exonerations and proven false confessions to identify the features of the interrogations that produced them.

Empirical studies of interrogations of older juveniles and the characteristics of defendants who gave proven false confessions shed light on police practices and adolescents' vulnerability. Feld (2006a; 2006b) reported that 80% of the 16- and 17-year-old juveniles charged with a felony waived their *Miranda* rights. These rates are virtually identical to the very high waiver rates reported in studies of adults (Grisso 1981; Leo 1996; Gudjonsson 2003). Once officers secured a juvenile's *Miranda* waiver, they used a two-pronged strategy like that employed with adults to overcome suspects' resistance and to enable them more readily to admit responsibility. Maximization techniques intimidate suspects and impress on them the futility of denial, while minimization techniques provide moral justifications or face-saving alternatives to enable them to confess (Leo 1996; Kassin 2005; Feld 2006a, 2006b). Juveniles fully confessed in about one-fifth of the cases, provided some statements of evidentiary value in about half of the cases, and denied involvement or made no incriminating admissions in about one-third of the cases. These outcomes are similar to the results reported in studies of adult interrogations (Wald et al. 1967; Leo 1996). The same proportion of juveniles and adults waived *Miranda* rights, following which police used the same strategies and tactics to question them (Leo 1996; Feld 2006a, 2006b). Juveniles responded to those tactics, cooperated or resisted, and provided incriminating evidence at about the same rate as did adults. As with adults (Leo 1996), police interrogated the vast majority of juveniles for relatively brief periods of time (Feld 2006b). In short, the law treats juveniles just like adults, and police question them just as they do older suspects.

Steven Drizin and Richard Leo (2004) examined 125 cases involving proven false confessions based on DNA-exonerations. Three factors consistently contributed to police-induced false confessions—youthfulness, coercive interrogation techniques, and prolonged questioning. Youths' diminished competence relative to adults increases their susceptibility to interrogation techniques and concomitant risks of false confessions. Their limited understanding of rights or appreciation of legal consequences increases their vulnerability to interrogation tactics (Bonnie and Grisso 2000; Redlich and Goodman 2003; Redlich et al. 2004; Kassin and Gudjonsson 2005; McMullen 2005). Their imperfect ability to think strategically makes them more likely than adults to assume responsibility for their confederates out of a misguided feeling of loyalty to peers (Kaban and Tobey 1999; Grisso et al. 2003; Scott and Steinberg 2008). They have a greater tendency than adults to comply with authority figures and to acquiesce to police officials (Gudjonsson 2003; Tanenhaus and Drizin 2003). A violent or brutal crime may create perceptual bias against young people when police officers question them (Birckhead 2008). Interviewer bias may elicit confirmatory statements consistent with prior beliefs and disregard contradictory information (Birckhead 2008; Leo 2008). Interrogation techniques designed for adults—especially coercive or prolonged questioning—may prove particularly problematic when deployed against young suspects (Magid 2001). Police obtained 35% of all of the proven false confessions from youths younger than 18 years of age and 19% from youths aged 15 or younger, even though younger juveniles comprise a very small proportion of serious offenders (Drizin and Leo 2004). Police obtained the vast majority (84%) of false confessions only after interrogations that lasted six hours or longer, and half of those interrogations continued for twelve hours or longer (Drizin and Leo 2004).

Fare, *Alvarado*, and most states' laws treat juveniles as the functional equals of adults during interrogation. By contrast, over the past quarter-century, developmental psychological research consistently has emphasized adolescents' limited adjudicative competence and reduced ability to understand or exercise *Miranda* rights. While older juveniles perform about as well—or as badly—as adults during routine interrogations (compare, e.g., Leo 1996 with Feld 2006b), research on false confessions underscores the unique vulnerability of youths when police question suspects under the age of 18 (Drizin and Leo 2004).

The Court's rulings in juvenile interrogation cases—*Haley*, *Gallegos*, *Gault*, *Fare*, and *Alvarado*—excluded statements elicited from defendants 15 years of age or younger and admitted those obtained from 16- and 17-year-old youths. This *de facto* line tracks research findings that juveniles 15 years old or younger lack the ability to exercise *Miranda* rights, while older juveniles perform about on par with adults. Courts and legislatures should formally adopt the functional line that the Court drew and that psychologists report between older and younger youths. Policy makers should provide additional protections, such as the mandatory presence of counsel, for more vulnerable children.

Within the past decade, near unanimity has emerged among policy groups and scholars to mandate the recording of all interrogations to reduce coercion, to minimize dangers of false confessions, and to increase the visibility and transparency of the process (e.g., Gudjonsson 2003; Drizin and Reich 2004; Feld 2006b; Leo 2008). Recording creates an objective record with which to resolve credibility disputes between police and youths about *Miranda* warnings, waivers, or statement, and reduces the risks of false confessions (Drizin and Leo 2004). After expressing repeated frustration with police interrogation practices with juveniles, the Wisconsin Supreme Court in *In re Jerrell C.J.* (699 N.W.2d 110 [Wis. 2005]) finally required police to record all custodial interrogations of juveniles. Several states have similar recording requirements for all interrogations (Feld 2006a; Leo 2008).

III. Competence to Exercise Procedural Rights: Right to Counsel and Plead Guilty

Gault likened the seriousness of a delinquency proceeding to a felony prosecution and granted juveniles a constitutional right to counsel. *Gault* relied on the Fourteenth Amendment Due Process Clause rather than the Sixth Amendment, which guarantees criminal defendants the right to counsel (Gideon v. Wainwright, 372 U.S. 335 [1961]), and did not order automatic appointment of counsel. Instead, the Court only required a judge to advise a child and parent of a right to counsel and, if indigent, to have counsel appointed (*Gault*). *Gault* also acknowledged that juveniles could make a knowing, intelligent, and voluntary waiver of counsel. Most states do not use any special measures to protect delinquents from their own immaturity, such as mandatory appointment of counsel (Feld 1984, 2006a). As with *Miranda* waivers, formal equality results in practical inequality, and lawyers represent delinquents at much lower rates than they do adult criminal defendants (Feld 1988b, 1991; Harlow 2000; Burruss and Kempf-Leonard 2002).

Despite statutes, procedural rules, and judicial decisions that apply equally throughout a state, juvenile justice administration varies with urban, suburban, and rural context and produces "justice by geography" (Feld 1991, 1993; Burruss and Kempf-Leonard 2002; Bray, Sample, and Kempf-Leonard 2005; Guevara, Spohn, and Herz 2008; Feld and Schaefer 2010a, 2010b). Lawyers appear more often in urban courts, which tend to be more formal, bureaucratized, and due-process-oriented (Feld 1991, 1993; Burruss and Leonard 2002). In turn, more formal courts place more youths in pre-trial detention and sentence them more severely. Rural courts tend to be procedurally less formal and sentence youths more leniently than their urban counterparts (Feld 1991; Burruss and Kempf-Leonard 2002). Finally, the presence of a lawyer appears to be an aggravating factor when judges sentence delinquents. Regardless of structural context and controlling for legal variables, judges sentence youths who appear with counsel more severely than they do those appear without an attorney (Feld 1988b, 1991; Burruss and Kempf-Leonard 2002; Feld and Schaefer 2010a). Several explanations account for this consistent finding: lawyers who appear in juvenile court are incompetent and prejudice their clients' cases; judges predetermine sentences and appoint counsel when they anticipate out-of-home placements; or judges punish delinquents for exercising procedural rights (Feld 1989, 1993).

A. Presence of Counsel in Juvenile Courts

When the Court decided *Gault*, lawyers seldom appeared in juvenile courts (Note 1966). Although states amended their juvenile codes to comply with *Gault*, the law-in-action lagged behind changes of the law-on-the-books, and most states failed to provide counsel. Evaluations of initial compliance with *Gault* found that most judges did not advise juveniles of their rights, and the vast majority did not appoint counsel (Lefstein, Stapleton, and Teitelbaum 1969; Canon and Kolson 1971; Ferster, Courtless, and Snethen 1971; Stapleton and Teitelbaum 1972). Studies of counties or courts in several jurisdictions in the 1970s and early 1980s reported that juvenile courts failed to appoint counsel for most juveniles (Clarke and Koch 1980; Bortner 1982; Aday 1986). Research in Minnesota in the mid-1980s reported that most youths appeared without counsel (Feld 1988b, 1989, 1993), that rates of representation varied widely between urban, suburban, and rural counties (Feld 1991, 1993), and that nearly one-third of youths whom judges removed from their homes and about one-quarter of those whom they confined in institutions were unrepresented (Feld 1989, 1993). A decade later, about one-quarter of juveniles removed from home were unrepresented despite law reform efforts to eliminate the practice (Feld and Schaefer 2010a; 2010b). A study of delivery of legal services in six states reported that only three of them appointed counsel for a substantial majority of juveniles (Feld 1988b). Studies in the 1990s described juvenile court judges' failure to appoint lawyers for many youths who appeared before them (GAO 1995; Burruss and Kempf-Leonard 2002). In 1995, the General Accounting Office (1995) replicated and confirmed Feld's (1988b) findings that rates of representation varied widely among and within states, and that judges tried and sentenced many unrepresented youths. Burruss and Kempf-Leonard (2002) found urban, suburban, and rural variation in rates of representation in Missouri and reported that an attorney's presence increased a youth's likelihood of receiving out-of-home placements. Guevara reported that race, gender, and type of representation influenced sentencing severity in different court settings (Guevara et al. 2008).

In the mid-1990s the American Bar Association published two reports on juveniles' legal needs. In *America's Children at Risk*, the ABA reported that many children in the juvenile justice system appeared without counsel (ABA 1993). Many lawyers who represented youths lacked adequate training, and they often failed to provide effective assistance (ABA 1993; Bishop and Farber 2007). In *A Call for Justice*, the ABA focused on the quality of defense lawyers, reported that many youths appeared without counsel, and concluded that many attorneys failed to appreciate the complexities of representing young defendants (ABA 1995). Since the late 1990s, the ABA and the National Juvenile Defender Center have conducted about a dozen state-by-state assessments of juveniles' access to and quality of counsel. These studies report that many, if not most, juveniles appear without counsel and that lawyers who represent youths often provide substandard assistance because of structural impediments to effective advocacy (see, e.g., Celeste and Puritz 2001; Puritz and Brooks 2002; Puritz, Scali, and Picou 2002; Brooks and Kamine 2004; Bookser 2004). Moreover, regardless of how poorly lawyers perform, juvenile and appellate courts appear incapable of correcting their errors (Berkheiser 2002). Juvenile defenders rarely, if ever, appeal adverse decisions and often lack a record with which to challenge an invalid waiver of counsel or trial errors (Harris 1994; Crippen 2000; Puritz and Shang 2000; Berkheiser 2002; Bookser 2004).

B. Waivers of Counsel and Guilty Pleas in Juvenile Court

There are several reasons so many youths appear in juvenile courts without counsel. Public defender legal services may be inadequate or nonexistent in nonurban areas (ABA 1995). Judges may give cursory advisories of the right to counsel, imply that a rights colloquy and waiver are just legal technicalities, and readily find waivers to ease courts' administrative burdens (ABA 1995; Cooper, Puritz, and Shang 1998; Berkheiser 2002; Bookser 2004). In other instances, judges may not appoint counsel if they expect to impose a noncustodial sentence (Lefstein, Stapleton, and Teitelbaum 1969; Feld 1984, 1989; Burruss and Kempf-Leonard 2002).

Waiver of counsel is the most common reason that so many juveniles are unrepresented (ABA 1995; Feld 1989; Cooper et al. 1998; Berkheiser 2002). As with *Miranda* waivers, judges in most states use the adult standard—knowing, intelligent, and voluntary—to gauge juveniles' waivers of counsel (Johnson v. Zerbst, 304 U.S. 458 [1938]; Fare v. Michael C., 442 U.S. 707 [1979]; Berkheiser 2002). They consider the same factors—age, education, IQ, prior police contacts, or experience with delinquency trials—to decide whether youths understood and voluntarily waived counsel (Feld 1984, 1989, 2006a). Many juveniles waive their rights without consulting with either a parent or an attorney (Berkheiser 2002). In addition to advising youths of their right to counsel, judges are supposed to determine whether a child possesses sufficient intelligence and ability to represent herself; whether she understands the charges and potential consequences; and whether she appreciates the dangers and disadvantages of self-representation (*In re* Manuel R., 207 A.2d 719 [Conn. 1988]; *In re* Christopher H., 596 S.E.2d 500 [S.C. Ct. App. 2004]). However, a review of appellate cases reveals that judges frequently failed to give delinquents any counsel advisory, often neglected to create a record of a waiver colloquy, and readily accepted waivers from manifestly incompetent children (Berkheiser 2002).

The research on juveniles' adjudicative competence and exercise of *Miranda* rights reviewed earlier applies equally to their ability to make knowing, intelligent, and voluntary waiver of counsel or to plead guilty—a much more frequent outcome. Many juveniles simply do not understand the meaning of a *Miranda* warning, counsel advisory, or a plea colloquy and cannot exercise their rights effectively (Grisso 1980, 1981, 2000). Even youths who understand a *Miranda* warning or a counsel advisory may not appreciate the function or importance of rights as well as do adults (Grisso 1980, 1997a; Grisso et al, 2003; ABA 1995). Juveniles' diminished competence to exercise rights, their inability to understand legal proceedings, and judicial encouragement to waive counsel results in larger proportions of youths than criminal defendants without lawyers (Feld 1988b; Harlow 2000). These disabilities are even more consequential for the vast majority of unrepresented juveniles who then plead guilty without understanding or appreciating the consequences.

As with adult criminal defendants, very few delinquency cases go to trial, and nearly all juveniles plead guilty and proceed to sentencing (Feld 1993). Because most states deny juveniles the right to a jury trial (McKeiver v. Pennsylvania, 403 U.S. 528 [1971]), delinquents have very little plea bargaining leverage (Rosenberg 1993). Juvenile courts eschew "sentencing bargains" because prosecutors and defense counsel cannot restrict judges' discretion (Sanborn 1993). Even though pleading guilty is the most critical decision a delinquent makes, states use adult legal standards to evaluate juveniles' competence and ability to enter a plea (Sanborn 1992, 1993; Singleton 2007). In addition to making a knowing, intelligent, and voluntary waiver of all procedural rights associated with trial, an offender must also admit to or acknowledge the underlying factual basis to establish substantive guilt of an offense. A youth must understand the nature of the charges, the consequences of pleading guilty, and the potential sentence the court may impose (Boykin v. Alabama, 395 U.S. 238 [1969]). Courts must conduct a colloquy with the delinquent on the record to comply with the procedural and substantive requirements for entry of a valid plea (Singleton 2007). Because appellate courts seldom review juveniles' waivers of counsel (Berkheiser 2002), scrutiny of pleas made without counsel receive even less judicial attention (Sanborn 1992, 1993).

C. Justice by Geography in Juvenile Courts

Despite statutes and procedural rules that apply throughout a state, most states administer juvenile courts at the county or judicial district level, and justice administration varies with locale (Feld 1991; GAO 1995; Burruss and Kempf-Leonard 2002; Bray, Sample, and Kempf-Leonard 2005; Feld and Schaefer 2010b). For example, urban juvenile courts typically operate in a milieu that provides fewer mechanisms for informal social control than do rural courts. Urban courts tend to be more formal and due process-oriented, place more youths in pretrial detention, and sentence offenders more severely than do suburban or rural courts (Feld 1991). No reasons exist to believe that rural youths are more competent than urban juveniles to waive legal rights, but rural judges appoint attorneys for delinquents far less often than do their urban counterparts (Feld 1991; Burruss and Kempf-Leonard 2002; Feld and Schaefer 2010b). Attorneys in Minnesota appeared with 63% of urban youths and 55% of suburban juveniles, but only 25% of rural youths (Feld 1991). In Missouri, attorneys appeared with 73% of youths in urban courts as contrasted with only 25% in suburban courts and 18% in rural settings (Burruss and Kempf-Leonard 2002). The GAO reported that rural youths were four times more likely to appear without counsel than their urban counterparts (GAO 1995). Variability in rates of appointment of counsel more likely reflects differences in courts' policies to appoint attorneys than variations in youths' competence to waive rights. While appointment of counsel provides an indicator of juvenile courts' due process orientation, greater procedural formality is also associated with more severe sentencing practices as well. After controlling for legal variables, high-representation urban courts sentenced youths more severely than did suburban or rural courts (Feld 1991; Burruss and Kempf-Leonard 2002).

D. Counsel as an Aggravating Factor in Sentencing

Historically, juvenile court judges discouraged adversarial representation, and organizational pressures to cooperate with other people in the system impeded effective advocacy (Blumberg 1967; Stapleton and Teitelbaum 1972; Clarke and Koch 1980; Bortner 1982; Feld 1984). The presence of lawyers in juvenile courts may put their clients at a disadvantage (Bortner 1982; Feld 1988b; 1989; Burruss and Kempf-Leonard 2002; Feld and Schaefer 2010a). After controlling for legal variables—present offense, prior record, pretrial detention status, and so forth—judges removed from home and incarcerated delinquents who appeared with counsel more frequently than they did unrepresented youths (Duffee and Siegel 1971; Clarke and Koch 1980; Bortner 1982; Feld 1989, 1993; Burruss and Kempf-Leonard 2002; Guevara, Spohn, and Herz 2004; Feld and Schaefer 2010a). Evaluations of law reform efforts to improve delivery of legal services in juvenile courts report the aggravating effect of representation on sentences actually increases (Feld and Schaefer 2010a; 2010b).

Several reasons explain why the presence of counsel is an aggravating factor in juveniles' dispositions. First, lawyers who appear in juvenile courts may be incompetent and prejudice their clients' cases (Lefstein, Stapleton, and Teitelbaum 1969; Stapleton and Teitelbaum 1972; Knitzer and Sobie 1984; Cooper et al. 1998). Even in states in which judges routinely appoint counsel for juveniles, many lawyers provide ineffective representation (Knitzer and Sobie 1984). Public defender offices may assign their least capable lawyers or send their newest attorneys to juvenile court to gain trial experience (Handler 1965; Flicker 1983). Court-appointed lawyers may place a higher priority on maintaining good relations with judges who assign cases to them than vigorously defending their oft-changing clients (Flicker 1983; Feld 1989). More significantly, conditions under which many defense attorneys work constitute a structural impediment to quality representation (ABA 1995; Cooper, Puritz, and Shang 1998; Jones 2004). Observations and qualitative assessments in several jurisdictions consistently report adverse working conditions—crushing caseloads, penurious compensation, lack of support services, inexperienced attorneys, and inadequate supervision—that detract from or even preclude effective representation (Celeste and Puritz 2001; Puritz and Brooks 2002; Puritz, Scali, and Picou 2002; Brooks and Kamine 2004; Jones 2004).

Second, the relationship between attorneys' presence and more severe dispositions may occur because judges appoint lawyers when they expect to impose more severe sentences (Canon and Kolson 1971; Aday 1986). Supreme Court decisions prohibit "incarceration without representation" (Scott v. Illinois, 440 U.S. 367 [1979]), and judicial efforts to comply with that requirement strengthen the relationship between judges' initial decisions to appoint counsel and their subsequent decisions to remove youths from their homes (Feld and Schaefer 2010a). In most states, the same judge presides at a youth's arraignment, detention hearing, adjudication, and disposition; they may appoint counsel when they anticipate imposing a more severe sentence (Feld 1984). However, if judges appoint lawyers at delinquents' arraignments or detention hearings because they expect to incarcerate them later,

have they already prejudged the case? If they only appoint lawyers when they antici-
pate more severe dispositions, then can an attorney still provide an effective defense
(Burruss and Kempf-Leonard 2002; Guevara, Spohn, and Herz 2008; Feld and
Schaefer 2010a)?

Third, judges may sentence represented delinquents more severely than unrepresented ones because a lawyer's presence effectively insulates judges from appellate
reversal (Duffee and Siegel 1971). While judges may not punish juveniles just because
they have a lawyer, they may sentence more leniently youths who "throw themselves
on the mercy of the court" (Burruss and Kempf-Leonard 2002; Guevara, Spohn,
and Herz 2004). The sentencing differential associated with counsels' presence mirrors the harsher sentences adults receive who exercise their right to a jury trial rather
than plead guilty (Engen and Steen 2000). Juvenile court judges may punish youths
whose lawyers invoke formal procedures, disrupt routine procedures, or question
their discretion.

Some may question why to require counsel if many effects of representation are
negative. However, cumulative legal changes since *Gault* have transformed many
aspects of juvenile justice into a scaled-down, second class criminal justice system
(Feld 1988a, 1999, 2003b). Youths require and deserve safeguards that only lawyers
can effectively invoke to protect against erroneous state intervention. The direct consequence of delinquency convictions and sentences makes procedural justice critical
(Feld 1988a). The use of prior delinquency convictions to sentence delinquents more
harshly, to waive juveniles to criminal court, and to enhance adult sentences makes
providing competent counsel all the more imperative (Feld 2003a).

IV. Right to Jury Trial—Accurate
Fact-Finding and Collateral Consequences

In a plurality decision that produced five separate opinions, the Supreme Court in
McKeiver v. Pennsylvania (403 U.S. 528 [1971]) declined to extend all of the procedural safeguards of criminal trials to delinquents. Although *Duncan v. Louisiana*
(391 U.S. 145 [1968]) previously held that the Sixth Amendment right to a jury trial
applied to state criminal proceedings, the Court decided *McKeiver* solely on the
basis of Fourteenth Amendment Due Process and "fundamental fairness." It insisted
that "the juvenile court proceeding has not yet been held to be a 'criminal prosecution,' within the meaning and reach of the Sixth Amendment, and also has not yet
been regarded as devoid of criminal aspects merely because it usually has been given
the civil label" (*McKeiver* at 541). The plurality reasoned that fundamental fairness
in delinquency proceedings emphasized accurate fact-finding, which a judge could
satisfy as well as a jury.

McKeiver's exclusive focus on fact-finding differed from *Gault's* and *Winship's*
analyses that recognized the dual functions of procedural safeguards: to assure

accurate fact-finding and protect against government oppression. *Gault* granted delinquents the Fifth Amendment privilege against self-incrimination to protect against government oppression even though it might impede fact-finding. In contrast, *McKeiver* invoked the imagery of a sympathetic, paternalistic juvenile court judge, disregarded delinquents' need for protection from coercive state intervention, and rejected concerns that juvenile courts' informality could compromise accurate fact-finding (Feld 2003b). The need for protection from the state may be especially critical in low-visibility delinquency proceedings where punitive sentences fall disproportionately heavily on racial minorities (Poe-Yamagata and Jones 2000; McCord and Spatz-Widom 2001).

The dissent in *McKeiver* argued that once a state charged a youth with a crime for which it could incarcerate her, she then enjoyed the right to a jury trial. It argued for procedural parity with criminal defendants based on the Sixth Amendment rather than vague notions of fundamental fairness. The dissent argued, as in *Gault*, that the punitive elements of delinquency adjudications—criminal charges carrying the possibility of confinement—required criminal procedural safeguards. They feared that informal procedures could contaminate judicial fact-finding and rebuffed the plurality's concerns about the administrative burdens of providing a jury trial.

McKeiver feared that jury trials would adversely affect juvenile courts' informality, flexibility, and confidentiality. Although the plurality found faults with juvenile courts, it did not believe that jury trials would correct those deficiencies, but would instead make the process more formal. *McKeiver* recognized that granting jury trials would make juvenile and criminal courts procedurally indistinguishable and could lead to the elimination of juvenile courts. *McKeiver* did not discuss whether any advantages might accrue from increased formality or why it would be incompatible with treatment dispositions.

Most important, *McKeiver* did not analyze the differences between juvenile courts' treatment and criminal courts' punishment that justified dissimilar procedures. The Court did not have before it a record of juvenile courts' dispositional practices, conditions of confinement, or evaluations of treatment effectiveness. *McKeiver* emphasized juvenile courts' "rhetoric" rather than their "reality," and denied delinquents procedural parity with adults without examining whether they also required protection from the state.

Most juveniles, like adult defendants, plead guilty rather than face trial by judge or jury (Feld 1989, 1993). In criminal courts, however, the possibility of a jury trial provides important checks on prosecutors' over-charging and on judges' evidentiary rulings, and helps to uphold the standard of proof beyond a reasonable doubt. The prospect of a jury trial also increases the visibility and accountability of justice administration and enhances the performance of lawyers and judges. Procedural safeguards may be even more critical in low-visibility juvenile courts that deal with vulnerable, dependent youths.

Although a few states give juveniles a right to a jury trial as a matter of state law (e.g. Feld 2003b; *In re L.M.*, 186 P.3d 164 [Kan. 2008]), the vast majority of states uncritically follow *McKeiver*. For four decades, advocates of jury trials have advanced several constitutional theories to avoid the impact of *McKeiver*. Some have argued that juveniles enjoy a constitutional right to a jury as a matter of Equal Protection, rather than Due Process (*In re D.J.*, 817 So. 2d 26 [La. 2002]). Others have urged supreme courts to interpret their state constitutions to find a right to a jury trial (e.g., State v. Hezzie R., 580 N.W.2d 660 [Wis. 1998]). The most fundamental challenges contend that *McKeiver's* basic premise that juvenile courts treat, rather than punish, delinquents is flawed.

Since *McKeiver*, every state has revised its juvenile code, adopted get-tough provisions, fostered a punitive convergence with criminal courts, and eroded the rationale for less effective procedures in delinquency trials (Feld 1988b; Torbet et al. 1996). The increased emphasis on punishment is reflected in legislative amendments of the purposes clauses of juvenile codes, court opinions endorsing punishment, states' enactment of determinate and mandatory minimum sentencing statutes, evaluations of judges' sentencing practices, and harsh conditions of confinement (Feld 1988b, 1999; Ainsworth 1991; Torbet et al. 1996). These get-tough changes cumulatively indicate that juvenile courts punish youths, and therefore the youths require protection from the state.

Despite substantial change in juvenile court jurisprudence and sentencing practices since *McKeiver*, state courts generally reject these constitutional arguments (see, e.g., *In re D.J.*; State v. Hezzie R.; *In re J.F. and G.G.*, 714 A.2d 467 [Pa. Super Ct. 1998]). State courts sometimes use a "glass half-full" rather than "glass half-empty" logic to distinguish between delinquency dispositions and criminal sentences (e.g., *In re D.J.*; State v. Schaff, 743 P.2d 240 [Wash. 1987]). "[N]otwithstanding the changes in the juvenile justice system,…there remains a great disparity in the severity of penalties faced by a juvenile charged with delinquency and an adult defendant charged with the same crime" (*In re D.J.* at 33). Other courts unquestioningly invoke *McKeiver* as continuing authority despite the legislative erosion of its four-decades-old foundation (State v. Hezzie R.). While state courts caution that a juvenile system may become sufficiently punitive as to require a jury trial, they only invalidate sentences when states confine youths in adult prisons after they were convicted in juvenile court without a jury trial (*In re C.B.*, 708 So. 2d 319 [La. 1998]; State v. Hezzie R.).

In contrast with most state courts' uncritical reliance on *McKeiver*, the Kansas Supreme Court in *In re L.M.* held that juveniles have a constitutional right to a jury trial under the Sixth and Fourteenth Amendments *and* the state constitution. The court in *L.M.* reasoned that two decades of legislative changes to the Kansas juvenile code had eroded the benevolent, rehabilitative, and *parens patriae* character of juvenile courts that distinguished them from the criminal justice system. As evidence of that erosion, the court noted changes in the juvenile code purpose clause to emphasize public protection and accountability, replacement of nonpunitive juvenile justice rhetoric with terminology similar to that used in the criminal code, adoption of a sentencing guidelines matrix based on the seriousness of the present offense and prior record that used the same principles as the adult guidelines, and removal of protections such as closed and confidential proceedings.

[B]ecause the juvenile justice system is now patterned after the adult criminal
system, we conclude that the changes have superseded…*McKeiver*['s] … reasoning
and those decisions are no longer binding precedent for us to follow.… [T]he
Kansas juvenile justice system has become more akin to an adult criminal
prosecution, [and] we hold that juveniles have a constitutional right to a jury trial
under the Sixth and Fourteenth Amendments.

In re L.M. at 170. The dissent in *L.M.* acknowledged that the juvenile system had
become more punitive, but objected that the majority overemphasized those punitive changes and failed to recognize the protective and rehabilitative features that
continued to distinguish it from the adult criminal system.

A danger exists in advocating jury trials for delinquents. As noted earlier, a relationship exists between procedural formality and the severity of sentences judges
impose. Providing a right to a jury trial and procedural parity with adults might
encourage some legislators to seek more penal "bang-for-the-buck" and to impose
even longer sentences on delinquents (Feld 1995). Procedural formality creates
additional incentives to plea bargain, which subverts any rights granted. Ultimately,
as *McKeiver* feared, granting delinquents the right to a jury may provide impetus to
abolish juvenile courts. On the other hand, if juvenile courts impose punitive sanctions, then don't delinquents deserve the same constitutional protections as adults?
Moreover, the denial of a jury right raises substantial questions about the quality
and accuracy of delinquency adjudications and use of those convictions to enhance
criminal sentence.

A. Accurate Fact-Finding and Judge versus Jury Reasonable Doubt

McKeiver's premise that states do not need juries to assure accurate fact-finding
contradicts the logic of *Winship* and highlights differences between judge and jury
fact-finding. *Winship* reasoned that the seriousness of the proceedings and the
potential consequences for a defendant—whether juvenile or adult—required proof
beyond a reasonable doubt. The same rigorous standard of proof for both adults
and juveniles assures factual accuracy, protects against government oppression,
maintains public confidence in trial decisions, and fosters similar outcomes in juvenile and criminal proceedings.

McKeiver's rejection of jury trials undermines factual accuracy and increases
the likelihood that outcomes will differ in delinquency and criminal trials. Because
there is no way to know the correct outcome of a factual dispute, most research
compares jurors' decisions with those of judges. Although judges and juries agree in
their judgments of defendants' guilt or innocence in about four-fifths of criminal
cases, when they differ, juries acquit defendants more often than do judges (Kalven
and Zeisel 1966; Greenwood, Abrahamse, and Zimring 1983).

Fact-finding by judges and juries is intrinsically different, because the former
may preside over hundreds of cases annually while the latter may hear only one or

two cases in a lifetime (Kalven and Zeisel 1966; Ainsworth 1991; Saks 1997). Because judges hear many cases, they sometimes become less meticulous when they weigh evidence, more casual when they evaluate facts, and apply less stringently the reasonable doubt standard than do jurors (Guggenheim and Hertz 1998). Appellate courts have noted that cases appealed from juvenile court "have often shown much more extensive and fundamental error than is generally found in adult criminal cases, and [we] wonder whether secrecy is not fostering a judicial attitude of casualness toward the law in children's proceedings" (R.L.R. v. State, 487 P.2d 27 [Alaska 1971]). Although judges' and jurors' backgrounds differ, defendants have greater difficulty to learn how a judge's characteristics might affect her decision (Saks 1997). And although *voir dire* enables litigants to assess how jurors' beliefs and experiences might affect their decisions, they have no similar opportunity to examine judges.

Juries and judges evaluate testimony differently. Judges hear testimony from police and probation officers on a recurring basis and develop settled opinions about their credibility (Feld 1984; Guggenheim and Hertz 1998). Similarly, judges may have an opinion about a youth's credibility, character, or the merits of the case from hearing earlier charges against her or presiding at her detention hearing. Judicial fact-finding also differs from that by a jury because a judge does not have to discuss either the law or evidence before reaching a decision (Saks 1997). By contrast, some group members may remember facts that others forget, and the give-and-take of deliberations and airing of competing points of view promotes more accurate outcomes (Guggenheim and Hertz 1998). Although a judge instructs a jury about the law to apply to the case, in bench trials, judges do not give explicit instructions, which makes it more difficult for an appellate court to know whether the judge understood or applied the law correctly.

A defendant's youthfulness elicits jury sympathy and accounts for some differences between jury and judge trial outcomes (Kalven and Zeisel 1966). Juvenile court judges may be predisposed to find jurisdiction to help an errant youth (Guggenheim and Hertz 1998). It is easier to convict a youth in a juvenile court bench trial than to convict a younger person in a criminal proceeding when the state presents similar evidence to a jury (Greenwood, Abrahamse, and Zimring 1983).

The informality of delinquency proceedings compounds the differences between judge and jury reasonable-doubt and places delinquents at a further disadvantage. When juvenile court judges preside at detention hearings, they receive information about a youth's offense, criminal history, and social circumstances. This non-guilt-related evidence increases the likelihood that a judge will convict and subsequently institutionalize the youth (Feld 1984; Saks 1997). The absence of a jury enables judges to conduct suppression hearings during trial, exposes them to prejudicial information about youths, and further increases the likelihood of erroneous conviction (Feld 1984; Guggenheim and Hertz 1998). Finally, the absence of a jury enables juvenile courts to adjudicate many juveniles without the assistance of an attorney, which further prejudices the accuracy and reliability of fact-finding (Feld 1993; Cooper, Puritz, and Shang 1998).

Criminal guilt does not involve just factual guilt, but entails a complex assessment of culpability and responsibility (Packer 1968). Analysts attribute differences in outcomes between juries and judges to differences in their evaluations of evidence, jury sentiments about the law or jury equity, and jury sympathy for the defendant (Duncan v. Louisiana (391 U.S. 145 [1968]); Kalven and Zeisel 1966). Jurors use a higher evidentiary standard of "proof beyond a reasonable doubt" than do judges (Kalven and Zeisel 1966). Kalven and Zeisel conclude that "[i]f a society wishes to be serious about convicting only when the state has been put to proof beyond a reasonable doubt, it would be well advised to have a jury system" (pp. 89–90). The factual and legal issues in delinquency hearings and criminal trials are exactly the same: has the state proven that the defendant committed a crime beyond a reasonable doubt? Given the importance of juries to answer this question for criminal defendants, *McKeiver* made it easier to convict a youth in juvenile court than it would be to convict an adult before a jury.

B. Use of Delinquency Convictions to Enhance Criminal Sentences

Providing criminal courts with access to records of delinquency convictions poses a policy conflict between the rehabilitative, nonstigmatic goals of juvenile courts and the interests of public safety to incapacitate or punish career offenders more severely (Feld 1999, 2003a). Although juvenile courts historically restricted access to delinquency records to avoid stigmatizing youths, confidentiality may not be reasonable for youths who continue to offend into adulthood. Research on criminal careers provides ample justification to use delinquency convictions to enhance the sentencing of young adult offenders (Blumstein et al. 1986). A strong relationship exists between age and offending—crime rates peak in mid- to late adolescence for most offenses. Most delinquents—"adolescent-limited" offenders—desist after one or two contacts with the justice system, but once a youth becomes a chronic offender— "life-course persistent"—then he likely will persist in criminal activity as an adult (Scott and Steinberg 2008). Chronic offenders comprise a small subset of delinquents but account for a disproportionate amount of serious, violent, and repetitive crime. Historically, juvenile courts' confidential proceedings and expunction of records hindered criminal courts' access to records of delinquency convictions (Blumstein et al. 1986).

Despite policies to restrict access to juvenile records, states' use of delinquency convictions to enhance adult sentences has a long lineage (Feld 2003a). Many state and the federal sentencing guidelines include some delinquency convictions in a defendant's criminal history score (Miller 1995). Under California's "three-strikes" sentencing law, some juvenile felony convictions constitute "strikes" for sentence enhancements (People v. Smith, 1 Cal. Rptr. 3d 901 [Cal. Dist. Ct. App. 2003]; Packel 2002).

States' use of delinquency convictions to enhance criminal sentences raises troubling questions about the quality of justice delinquents receive in juvenile courts. Recall that juvenile courts in many states adjudicate many youths delinquent without the assistance of counsel, including some convicted of felonies. The vast majority of states deny juveniles a right to a jury trial. And the vast majority of delinquents plead guilty—with or without the assistance of counsel—and those pleas constitute convictions for purposes of subsequent sentence enhancement. As a result, many delinquency adjudications occur that would not have resulted in criminal convictions or pleas if defendants received adequate procedural safeguards (Feld 2003a). While *McKeiver* found delinquency convictions sufficiently reliable to support juvenile dispositions, they may not be reliable enough to support punitive enhancements of criminal sentence.

In *Apprendi v. New Jersey* (530 U.S. 466 [2000]), the Court, by a 5–4 vote, held that "[o]ther than the fact of a prior conviction, any fact that increases the penalty for a crime beyond the statutory maximum, must be submitted to a jury and proved beyond a reasonable doubt" (at 490). *Apprendi* reasoned that a jury must find the facts beyond a reasonable doubt that result in an increased sentence, rather than to allow a judge to do so by a preponderance of the evidence at a sentencing hearing. *Apprendi* exempted the "fact of a prior conviction" from its holding because criminal defendants enjoyed the right to a jury trial in the proceeding that led to that "prior conviction." Because *McKeiver* denied and most states do not provide a jury, states' use of delinquency adjudications for sentence enhancements may not satisfy *Apprendi*'s rationale to exempt "the fact of a prior conviction" (Feld 2003a).

Lower courts are divided on whether delinquency convictions fall within *Apprendi*'s "prior conviction" exception. A majority have concluded that even without a jury right, delinquency trials are sufficiently reliable to permit the sentencing judge to use those adjudications for sentence enhancements (e.g., U.S. v. Smalley, 294 F.3d 1030 [8th Cir. 2002]; U.S. v. Jones, 332 F.3d 633 [3d Cir. 2003]; People v. Superior Court, 7 Cal. Rptr. 3d 74 [Cal. Ct. App. 2003]; State v. McFee, 721 N.W.2d 607 [Minn. 2006]). They reason that when a judge adjudicates a juvenile guilty beyond a reasonable doubt in a bench trial or accepts a voluntary guilty plea, then the youth has received all the due process protections required. Convictions that are valid for one purpose, e.g., to impose a therapeutic disposition, are sufficiently reliable for other purposes as well, e.g., punitive criminal sentence enhancement. Unfortunately, none of these cases adequately examine the rationale to provide delinquents fewer procedural safeguards or the differences in purposes for which the state initially obtained those convictions. Rather, they mechanically rely on the idea that a conviction that is valid for one purpose is valid for all purposes. Moreover, none of these courts sufficiently evaluate the reliability of those prior convictions compared with those of adult defendants.

By contrast, a substantial minority of courts deem delinquency procedures inadequate to allow the use of juvenile convictions to enhance criminal sentences (e.g., United States v. Tighe, 266 F.3d 1187 [8th Cir. 2001]; State v. Brown, 879 So .2d 1276 [La. 2004]; State v. Harris, 118 P.3d 236 [Ore. 2005]). *Apprendi* reasoned that proving a defendant's guilt in a jury trial beyond a reasonable doubt guaranteed the reliability of prior criminal convictions. These courts limited *Apprendi*'s "prior conviction" exception to prior convictions that were themselves obtained through proceedings that included the right to a jury trial, a feature most delinquency adjudications lack. These courts reason that *McKeiver* denied all the constitutional procedures granted adult criminals because of the remaining "civil nature" of a delinquency adjudication, the focus on rehabilitation, and the state's role as *parens patriae* (State v. Brown). Others reason that under state law, delinquency adjudications do not constitute convictions of any crime (State v. Harris). These courts conclude that "[i]t seems contradictory and fundamentally unfair to provide youths with fewer procedural safeguards in the name of rehabilitation and then to use adjudications obtained for treatment purposes to punish them more severely as adults" (State v. Brown at 1289).

V. CONCLUSION

The decades since *Gault*, *Winship*, and *McKeiver* have witnessed a substantial procedural and substantive convergence between juvenile and criminal courts. The greater procedural formality and adversarial nature of delinquency proceedings reflect juvenile courts' shift in emphases from rehabilitating offenders to protecting public safety. Despite these changes, most states do not provide delinquents with procedural safeguards that provide formal or functional protections comparable to those of adult criminal defendants. Juveniles waive their *Miranda* rights and right to counsel under a standard—"knowing, intelligent, and voluntary" under the "totality of circumstances"—that is unlikely to discern whether they understand and are competent to exercise the rights they relinquish. The high rates of waiver of counsel constitute an indictment of the entire delinquency process, because assistance of counsel is the essential prerequisite to the exercise of other procedural safeguards. The denial of jury trials calls into question the validity and reliability of delinquency adjudications, both for initial dispositions and for collateral use such as sentence enhancements. In short, states do not provide juveniles with special procedural safeguards to protect them from their own immaturity and vulnerability, nor do they provide them with the full panoply of criminal procedural safeguards to protect them from punitive state intervention. Instead, juvenile courts assure that youths continue to "receive the worst of both worlds"—treating juvenile offenders just like adult criminal defendants when formal equality redounds to their disadvantage and providing less effective juvenile court procedures when they provide an advantage to the state.

NOTES

1. Developmental and social psychologists conduct their research under laboratory conditions that cannot capture the stressful situations and psychological pressures that police exert during an actual interrogation (Abramovitch, Higgins-Biss, and Biss 1993; Redlich and Goodman 2003). In addition, public school youths who participate in many of these studies do not directly compare with delinquents who come from poorer households, have more limited verbal skills, and exhibit greater difficulty understanding legal abstractions (e.g., Viljoen, Klaver, and Roesch 2005; Grisso 1997a).

REFERENCES

Abramovitch, Rona, Karen L. Higgins-Biss, and Stephen R. Biss. 1993. "Young Persons' Comprehension of Waivers in Criminal Proceedings." *Canadian Journal of Criminology* 35: 309–22.

Aday, David P., Jr. 1986. "Court Structure, Defense Attorney Use, and Juvenile Court Decisions." *Sociological Quarterly* 27: 107–19.

Ainsworth, Janet E. 1991. "Re-Imagining Childhood and Reconstructing the Legal Order: The Case for Abolishing the Juvenile Court." *North Carolina Law Review* 69: 1083–133.

Ainsworth, Janet E. 1993. "In a Different Register: The Pragmatics of Powerlessness in Police Interrogation." *Yale Law Journal* 103: 259–322.

American Bar Association. 1993. *America's Children at Risk: A National Agenda for Legal Action.* Washington, DC: American Bar Association Presidential Working Group on the Unmet Needs of Children and their Families.

American Bar Association. 1995. *A Call for Justice: An Assessment of Access to Counsel and Quality of Representation in Delinquency Proceedings.* Washington, DC: American Bar Association Juvenile Justice Center.

Berkheiser, Mary. 2002. "The Fiction of Juvenile Right to Counsel: Waiver in the Juvenile Courts." *Florida Law Review* 54: 577–686.

Birckhead, Tamar R. 2008. "The Age of the Child: Interrogating Juveniles After *Roper v. Simmons.*" *Washington and Lee Law Review* 65: 385–450.

Bishop, Donna M., and Hillary B. Farber. 2007. "Joining the Legal Significance of Adolescent Developmental Capacities with the Legal Rights Provided by *In re Gault.*" *Rutgers Law Review* 60: 125–73.

Blumberg, Abraham S. 1967. "The Practice of Law as a Confidence Game: Organizational Cooptation of a Profession." *Law & Society Review* 1: 15–39.

Blumstein, Alfred, Jacqueline Cohen, Jeffrey A. Roth, and Christy A. Visher, eds. 1986. *Criminal Careers and "Career Criminals."* Washington, DC: National Academy Press.

Bonnie, Richard, and Thomas Grisso. 2000. "Adjudicative Competence and Youthful Offenders." In *Youth on Trial: A Developmental Perspective on Juvenile Courts,* Thomas Grisso and Robert G. Schwartz, eds. Chicago: University of Chicago Press.

Bookser, Susanne M. 2004. "Making *Gault* Meaningful: Access to Counsel and Quality of Representation in Delinquency Proceedings for Indigent Youth," *Whittier Journal of Child & Family Advocacy* 3: 297–328.

Bortner, M. A. 1982. *Inside a Juvenile Court: The Tarnished Ideal of Individualized Justice.* New York: New York University Press.

Bray, Timothy, Lisa L. Sample, and Kimberly Kempf-Leonard. 2005. "Justice by Geography: Racial Disparity and Juvenile Courts." In *Our Children, Their Children: Confronting Racial and Ethnic Differences in American Juvenile Justice*, edited by Darnell Hawkins and Kimberly Kempf-Leonard. Chicago: University of Chicago Press.

Brooks, Kim, and Darlene Kamine. 2003. *Justice Cut Short: An Assessment of Access to Counsel and Quality of Representation in Delinquency Proceedings in Ohio*. Washington, DC: American Bar Association Juvenile Justice Center.

Burruss, George W. Jr., and Kimberly Kempf-Leonard. 2002. "The Questionable Advantage of Defense Counsel in Juvenile Court." *Justice Quarterly* 19: 37–68.

Canon, Bradley C., and Kenneth Kolson. 1971. "Rural Compliance with *Gault*: Kentucky, A Case Study." *Journal of Family Law* 10: 300–26.

Celeste, Gabriella, and Patricia Puritz. 2001. *The Children Left Behind: An Assessment of Access to Counsel and Quality of Legal Presentation in Delinquency Proceedings in Louisiana*. Washington, DC: American Bar Association Juvenile Justice Center.

Clarke, Stevens H., and Gary G. Koch. 1980. "Juvenile Court: Therapy or Crime Control, and Do Lawyers Make a Difference?," *Law & Society Review* 14: 263–308.

Cooper, N. Lee, Patricia Puritz, and Wendy Shang. 1998. "Fulfilling the Promise of *In re Gault*: Advancing the Role of Lawyers for Children," *Wake Forest Law Review* 33: 651–79.

Crippen, Gary L. 2000. "Can the Courts Fairly Account for the Diminished Competence and Culpability of Juveniles? A Judge's Perspective." In *Youth on Trial: A Developmental Perspective on Juvenile Justice*, edited by Thomas Grisso and Robert Schwartz. Chicago: University of Chicago Press.

Drizin, Steven A., and Richard A. Leo. 2004. "The Problem of False Confessions in the Post-DNA World." *North Carolina Law Review* 82: 891–1007.

Drizin, Steven A., and Marissa J. Reich. 2004. "Heeding the Lessons of History: The Need for Mandatory Recording of Police Interrogations to Accurately Assess the Reliability and Voluntariness of Confessions." *Drake Law Review* 52: 619–46.

Duffee, David, and Larry Siegel. 1971. "The Organization Man: Legal Counsel in the Juvenile Court." *Criminal Law Bulletin* 7: 544–53.

Engen, Rodney L., and Sara Steen. 2000. "The Power to Punish: Discretion and Sentencing Reform in the War on Drugs." *American Journal of Sociology* 105: 1357–95.

Feld, Barry C. 1984. "Criminalizing Juvenile Justice: Rules of Procedure for the Juvenile Court." *Minnesota Law Review* 69: 141–276.

Feld, Barry C. 1988a. "The Juvenile Court Meets the Principle of Offense: Punishment, Treatment, and the Difference it Makes." *Boston University Law Rev.* 68: 821–915.

Feld, Barry C. 1988b. "*In re Gault* Revisited: A Cross-State Comparison of the Right to Counsel in Juvenile Court." *Crime & Delinquency* 34: 393–424.

Feld, Barry C. 1989. "The Right to Counsel in Juvenile Court: An Empirical Study of When Lawyers Appear and the Difference They Make." *Journal of Criminal Law & Criminology* 79: 1185–346.

Feld, Barry C. 1991. "Justice by Geography: Urban, Suburban, and Rural Variations in Juvenile Justice Administration." *Journal of Criminal Law & Criminology* 82: 156–210.

Feld, Barry C. 1993. *Justice for Children: The Right to Counsel and the Juvenile Courts*. Boston: Northeastern University Press.

Feld, Barry C. 1995. "Violent Youth and Public Police: A Case Study of Juvenile Justice Law Reform." *Minnesota Law Review* 79: 965–1128.

Feld, Barry C. 1999. *Bad Kids: Race and the Transformation of the Juvenile Court*. New York: Oxford University Press.

Feld, Barry C. 2003a. "The Constitutional Tension Between *Apprendi* and *McKeiver*: Sentence Enhancements Based on Delinquency Convictions and the Quality of Justice in Juvenile Courts." *Wake Forest Law Review* 38: 1111–224.

Feld, Barry C. 2003b. "Race, Politics, and Juvenile Justice: The Warren Court and the Conservative 'Backlash.'" *Minnesota Law Review* 87: 1447–577.

Feld, Barry C. 2006a. "Juveniles' Competence to Exercise Miranda Rights: An Empirical Study of Policy and Practice." *Minnesota Law Review* 91: 26–100.

Feld, Barry C. 2006b. "Police Interrogation of Juveniles: An Empirical Study of Policy and Practice." *Journal of Criminal Law and Criminology* 97: 219–316.

Feld, Barry C., and Shelly Schaefer. 2010a. "The Right to Counsel in Juvenile Court: The Conundrum of Attorneys as an Aggravating Factor at Disposition." *Justice Quarterly* 27: 713–41.

———. 2010b. "The Right to Counsel in Juvenile Court: Law Reform to Deliver Legal Services and Reduce Justice by Geography." *Criminology & Public Policy* 9: 327–56.

Ferster, Elyce Zenoff, Thomas Courtless, and Edith Snethen. 1971. "The Juvenile Justice System: In Search of the Role of Counsel." *Fordham Law Review* 39: 375–412.

Flicker, Barbara. 1983. *Providing Counsel for Accused Juveniles*. New York: Institute of Judicial Administration.

Greenwood, Peter W., Allan Abrahamse, and Franklin E. Zimring. 1983. *Youth Crime and Juvenile Justice in California: A Report to the Legislature*. Santa Monica, CA: Rand Corporation.

Grisso, Thomas. 1980. "Juveniles' Capacities to Waive *Miranda* Rights: An Empirical Analysis." *California Law Review* 68: 1134–66.

Grisso, Thomas. 1981. *Juveniles' Waiver of Rights: Legal and Psychological Competence*. New York: Plenum Press.

Grisso, Thomas. 1997a. "The Competence of Adolescents as Trial Defendants." *Psychology, Public Police & Law* 3: 3–11.

Grisso, Thomas. 1997b. "Juvenile Competency to Stand Trial: Questions in an Era of Punitive Reform." *Criminal Justice* 3: 5–11.

Grisso, Thomas. 2000. "What We Know about Youths' Capacities as Trial Defendants." In *Youth on Trial: A Developmental Perspective on Juvenile Justice*, edited by Thomas Grisso and Robert G. Schwartz. Chicago: University of Chicago Press.

Grisso, Thomas, Laurence Steinberg, Jennifer Woolard, Elizabeth Cauffman, Elizabeth Scott, Sandra Graham, Fran Lexcen, and N. Dickon Reppucci. 2003. "Juveniles' Competence to Stand Trial: A Comparison of Adolescents' and Adults' Capacities as Trial Defendants." *Law & Human Behavior* 27: 333–63.

Gudjonsson, Gisli H. 2003. *The Psychology of Interrogations and Confessions: A Handbook*. New York: John Wiley & Sons.

Guevara, Lori, Cassia Spohn, and Denise Herz. 2004. "Race, Legal Representation and Juvenile Justice: Issues and Concerns." *Crime & Delinquency* 50: 344–71.

———. 2008. "Race, Gender, and Legal Counsel: Differential Outcomes in Two Juvenile Courts." *Youth Violence and Juvenile Justice* 6: 83–104.

Guggenheim, Martin, and Randy Hertz. 1998. "Reflections on Judges, Juries, and Justice: Ensuring the Fairness of Juvenile Delinquency Trials." *Wake Forest Law Review* 33: 553–93.

Handler, Joel F. 1965. "The Juvenile Court and the Adversary System: Problems of Form and Function." *Wisconsin Law Review* 1965: 7–51.

Harlow, Caroline Wolf. 2000. *Defense Counsel in Criminal Cases*. Washington, DC: U.S. Department of Justice, Bureau of Justice Statistics.

Harris, Donald J. 1994. "Due Process vs. Helping Kids in Trouble: Implementing the Right to Appeal from Adjudications of Delinquency in Pennsylvania." *Dickinson Law Review* 98: 209–35.

Jones, Judith B. 2004. *Access to Counsel*. Washington, DC: Office of Juvenile Justice and Delinquency Prevention.

Kaban, Barbara, and Ann E. Tobey. 1999. "When Police Question Children, Are Protections Adequate?" *Juvenile Center for Children & Courts* 151: 150–58.

Kalven, Harry Jr., and Hans Zeisel. 1966. *The American Jury*. Chicago: University of Chicago Press.

Kassin, Saul. 1997. "The Psychology of Confession Evidence." *American Psychologist* 52: 221–38.

Kassin, Saul. 2005. "On the Psychology of Confessions: Does Innocence Put Innocents at Risk?" *American Psychologist* 60: 215–28.

Kassin, Saul, and Gisli H. Gudjonsson. 2004. "The Psychology of Confessions: A Review of the Literature and Issues." *Psychological Sciences in Public Interest* 5: 33–69.

Knitzer, Jane, and Merril Sobie. 1984. *Law Guardians in New York State: A Study of the Legal Representation of Children*. Albany, NY: New York State Bar Association.

Lefstein, Norman, Vaughan Stapleton, and Lee Teitelbaum. 1969. "In Search of Juvenile Justice: *Gault* and Its Implementation," *Law & Society Review* 3: 491–562.

Leo, Richard A. 1996. "Inside the Interrogation Room." *Journal of Criminal Law & Criminology* 86: 266–303.

Leo, Richard A. 2008. *Police Interrogation in America*. Cambridge, MA: Harvard University Press.

Magid, Laurie. 2001. "Deceptive Police Interrogation Practices: How Far is Too Far?" *Michigan Law Review* 99: 1168–210.

McCord, Joan, and Cathy Spatz-Widom. 2001. *Juvenile Crime, Juvenile Justice*. National Research Council, Washington DC: National Academy Press.

McMullen, Patrick M. 2005. "Questioning the Questions: The Impermissibility of Police Deception in Interrogations of Juveniles." *Northwestern University Law Review* 99: 971–1005.

Miller, Neal. 1995. *State Laws on Prosecutors' and Judges Use of Juvenile Records*. Washington. DC: National Institute of Justice.

Note. 1966. "Juvenile Delinquents: The Police, State Courts and Individualized Justice." *Harvard Law Review* 79: 775–810.

Packel, Amanda K. 2002. "Juvenile Justice and the Punishment of Recidivists Under California's Three Strike Law." *California Law Review* 90: 1157–202.

Packer, Herbert. 1968. *The Limits of the Criminal Sanction*. Stanford, CA: Stanford University Press.

Poe-Yamagata, Eileen, and Michael A. Jones. 2000. *And Justice For Some*. Davis, CA: National Council on Crime and Delinquency.

Puritz, Patricia, and Kim Brooks. 2002. *Kentucky: Advancing Justice: An Assessment of Access to Counsel and Quality of Representation in Delinquency Proceedings*. Washington, DC: American Bar Association Juvenile Justice Center.

Puritz, Patricia, Mary Ann Scali, and Ilona Picou. 2002. *Virginia: An Assessment of Access to Counsel and Quality of Representation in Delinquency Proceedings*. Washington, DC: American Bar Association Juvenile Justice Center.

Puritz, Patricia, and Wendy Shang. 2000. "Juvenile Indigent Defense: Crisis and Solutions," *Criminal Justice* 15: 22–28.

Redding, Richard E., and Lynda E. Frost. 2001. "Adjudicative Competence in the Modern Juvenile Court." *Virginia Journal of Social Policy & the Law* 9: 353–409.

Redlich, Allison D., & Gail S. Goodman. 2003. "Taking Responsibility for an Act Not Committed: The Influence of Age and Suggestibility." *Law & Human Behavior* 27: 141–56.

Redlich, Allison D., Melissa Silverman, Julie Chen, and Hans Steiner. 2004. "The Police Interrogation of Children and Adolescents." In *Interrogations, Confessions, and Entrapment*, edited by G. Daniel Lassiter. New York: Springer Science.

Rosenberg, Irene Merker. 1993. "Leaving Bad Enough Alone: A Response to the Juvenile Court Abolitionists." *Wisconsin Law Review* 1993: 163–88.

Saks, Michael J. 1997. "What Do Jury Experiments Tell Us About How Juries (Should) Make Decisions?" *Southern California Interdisciplinary Law Journal* 6: 1–53.

Sanborn, Joseph B. Jr. 1992. "Pleading Guilty in Juvenile Court: Minimal Ado About Something Very Important to Young Defendants." *Justice Quarterly* 9: 127–49.

Sanborn, Joseph B. Jr. 1993. "Philosophical, Legal, and Systemic Aspects of Juvenile Court Plea Bargaining." *Crime & Delinquency* 39: 509–27.

Scott, Elizabeth S., and Thomas Grisso. 1997. "The Evolution of Adolescence: A Developmental Perspective on Juvenile Justice Reform." *Journal of Criminal Law & Criminology* 88: 137–89.

———. 2005. "Developmental Incompetence, Due Process, and Juvenile Justice Policy." *North Carolina Law Rev.* 83: 793–846.

Scott, Elizabeth S., N. Dickon Reppucci, and Jennifer L. Woolard. 1995. "Evaluating Adolescent Decision Making in Legal Contexts." *Law & Human Behavior* 19: 221–44.

Scott, Elizabeth S., and Laurence Steinberg. 2008. *Rethinking Juvenile Justice*. Cambridge, MA: Harvard University Press.

Singleton, Lacey Cole. 2007. "Say 'Pleas': Juveniles' Competence to Enter Plea Agreements." *Journal of Law & Family Studies* 9: 439–55.

Stapleton, Vaughan, and Lee Teitelbaum. 1972. *In Defense of Youth: A Study of the Role of Counsel in American Juvenile Courts*. New York: Russell Sage Foundation.

Steinberg, Laurence, and Elizabeth Cauffman. 1996. "Maturity of Judgment in Adolescence: Psychosocial Factors in Adolescent Decision Making." *Law & Human Behavior* 20: 249–72.

———. 1999. "The Elephant in the Courtroom: A Developmental Perspective on the Adjudication of Youthful Offenders." *Virginia Journal of Social Policy & the Law* 6: 389–417.

Tanenhaus, David S. 2004. *Juvenile Justice in the Making*. New York: Oxford University Press.

Tanenhaus, David S., and Steven A. Drizin. 2003. "Owing to the Extreme Youth of the Accused: The Changing Legal Response to Juvenile Homicide." *Journal of Criminal Law & Criminology* 92: 641–705.

Torbet, Patricia, Richard Gable, Hunter Hurst, IV, Imogene Montgomery, Linda Szymanski, and Douglas Thomas. 1996. *State Responses to Serious and Violent Juvenile Crime: Research Report*. Washington, DC: U.S. Department of Justice, Office of Juvenile Justice and Delinquency Prevention.

U.S. General Accounting Office. 1995. *Juvenile Justice: Representation Rates Varied as Did Counsel's Impact on Court Outcomes*. Washington, DC: Government Printing Office.

Viljoen, Jodi L., Jessica Klaver, and Ronald Roesch. 2005. "Legal Decisions of Preadolescent and Adolescent Defendants: Predictors of Confessions, Pleas, Communication with Attorneys, and Appeals." *Law & Human Behavior* 29: 253–77.

Wald, Michael et al. 1967. "Interrogations in New Haven: The Impact of *Miranda*." *Yale Law Journal* 76: 1519–623.

PART VIII

SANCTIONING DELINQUENTS

RESTORATION, SHAME, AND THE FUTURE OF RESTORATIVE PRACTICE IN U.S. JUVENILE JUSTICE

GORDON BAZEMORE

RESTORATIVE justice and reintegrative shaming theory became prominent on the North American juvenile justice scene in the mid- to late 1990s. Ironically, this occurred as the juvenile court experienced what some consider the most serious attack in its history. This paper considers the impact of Braithwaite's macro theory of reintegrative shaming and also the larger strengths and weaknesses of the restorative justice movement on juvenile justice policy, practice, and research. To move forward in the United States, restorative justice, as an evidence-based practice, must be viewed as a mainstream, "problem-oriented" intervention capable of responding effectively to a range of chronic juvenile justice and community concerns. Currently, widespread implementation of restorative policies and practices in U.S. juvenile justice appears to be limited by: the absence of a legislative mandate or incentives for presumptive referral to restorative programs; the political role of elected prosecutors in justice decision-making; and an almost unshakeable commitment to punishment and maximum use of adversarial and quasi-adversarial dispositional decision-making at the expense of informal decision-making.

I. Introduction

The term "postmodern juvenile justice" (Bazemore and Leip 2007) might be used to describe the aftermath of the historic, comprehensive transformation that occurred in juvenile justice in the early to mid-1990s (Torbet et al. 1996). It may also describe the way juvenile justice leaders and practitioners have responded to changes that created a new set of options for a criminal court alternative that, in theory at least, promised to limit the court's jurisdiction over more serious offenders in many states (Butts and Mitchell 2000). While most offenders, including most of the more serious ones, remain in juvenile court and the juvenile justice system, loss of the presumption that the juvenile court would retain responsibility for addressing youth crime challenges the traditional, exclusive, "best interests" mandate. In doing so, it may add significantly to a loss of grounding and the capacity for "*sensemaking*" (Weik 1995) in a system that still seeks to justify its existence based on the "best interest of the child."[1]

In what is now the third decade of the so-called "new juvenile justice" (Forst 1995), familiar terms like treatment, punishment, probation, diversion, "continuum of services and sanctions," and assessment may no longer mean what they used to (Bazemore and Leip 2007). More significantly, despite relatively limited use of more punitive criminal court options, terms like "direct file," "transfer" to criminal court, and "adult time" no longer seem disturbing in a system that is generally more formal and punitive than it was twenty years ago. The juvenile court can, however, be very informal when it needs to be (Feld 1993a, 1999 and practitioners continue to use the "best interest" rhetoric even in this far more punitive context. Practices such as shackling juveniles for court hearings, extended stays in pre-adjudicatory detention, arrest and detention of 10-year-olds for minor school disciplinary violations, and of course, the possibility in some states of an expedited transfer of 14-year-olds to criminal court, no longer shock us—despite the growing body of empirical data on the harsh consequences associated with these decisions (Bishop 2000, 2005; Stinchcomb, Bazemore, and Riestenberg 2005; Blueprint Commission 2008).

In this postmodern context, a process and theory known as "reintegrative shaming" may not be viewed as an oxymoron. Indeed, such terms may fit nicely into what has become a kind of Alice-in-Wonderland juvenile justice milieu in which (as the Mad Hatter said), "words mean what I want them to mean." To say this in no way disparages the reintegrative shaming (RISE)[2] model, which has become a robust "general theory" of intervention in response to crime and harm, nor its author, John Braithwaite. Rather, the positive emphasis on shame as a natural emotion (Harris 2006), and "shaming" as a process aimed at denouncing and separating the harmful *act* from the character of the offender (Harris, Walgrave, and Braithwaite 2004), offers a significant, if simple, breakthrough. Yet those still not so comfortable with the new juvenile justice may understandably fear that words like "shaming" can be quite dangerous in the United States, where, as one restorative justice practitioner put it, "these kids have already gone through more than enough shaming to last a lifetime." (Kay Pranis, 2004).

In the new juvenile justice era, few may question why, having lost a significant portion of their jurisdiction over more serious offenders, juvenile justice agencies appear to have begun expanding their mandate on the "front end" of the system. For example, in the "pre-systems" of schools, zero tolerance policies have created an increasingly efficient school-to-jail pipeline (Freeman 2009; Stinchcomb, Bazemore, and Riestenberg 2006). Similarly, critics may also raise questions about the proliferation of what appear to be dozens of new "specialty court" models (most aimed at young people), as well as truancy centers, new juvenile Assessment Centers, and other ways of managing the youth population, at least temporarily. While none of this seems to be about informality, "best interest," effective treatment, or for that matter, just punishment or deterrence, it does seem clearly to be about the application of what Feely and Simon (1992) referred to more than a decade ago as "managerial criminology." Indeed, decision-makers in the new juvenile justice era appear to have agreed to again assume responsibility for controlling status offenders such as truants and runaways (see Bazemore et al 2004). In the new courts, centers, and other spaces, they have also done a good job of incapacitation—if not of treatment, deterrence, or due process. Arguably, this youth management function alone may have kept juvenile justice alive in the early years of the new century—even while it has led some observers to express concern about net-widening and iatrogenic effects of much juvenile justice intervention (Dishon, McCord, and Poulin 1999; Brown and Horowitz 1993; Gottfredson 2009), and even new calls for a "radical nonintervention" (Sheldon 2007; Schur 1973).

It was in this confusing and less than hopeful context that the new promising practices of restorative justice and reintegrative shaming theory became visible on the U.S. juvenile justice scene. Juvenile justice professionals most likely learned about reintegrative shaming in the mid-to late 1990s after first hearing about restorative practices, while most academics typically were exposed to reintegrative shaming theory first and then restorative justice later. The new restorative justice models that began to be imported to the States (from Australia for the most part) offered a different version of what had become generally familiar alternative sentencing and conflict resolution practices (i.e., victim-offender mediation) by adding the "family group conference" into the mix. In any case, restorative justice, in several North American and imported forms, was beginning to spread widely by the late 1990s. By 2001, advocacy and support had reached a high point, with some 770 programs identified in U.S. states (Bazemore and Schiff 2004).

The timing of passage of explicitly retributive juvenile justice legislation in a number of U.S. states—coupled with advocacy and support for inclusion of restorative justice in juvenile court purpose clauses and other policy in a number of states (for example, Pennsylvania, Illinois, California, and Oregon) (O'Brien 2000; Whitehead and Lab 2009; Ryan 2007), may have been coincidental.[3] Nonetheless, constituencies concerned about new options for transfer of youth to criminal court and other punitive legislation began to mobilize in support of restorative justice in part to mitigate some of the most punitive impact of these statutes. New policy and legislation in support of restorative justice from Australia, New Zealand, and the

UK also began to give important new credibility to existing restorative programs in the U.S.. Observers also began to grasp the essence of these practices as grounded in an understanding of justice intervention as different from traditional treatment/*parens patriae*, but also distinctly at odds with the retributive model and the goals of expanded punishment (Braithwaite and Mugford 1994; Bazemore 1998).

Whether these trends had any real "softening" impact on the new retributive legislation is doubtful, however, practitioners in states such as Pennsylvania, Idaho, and Colorado, and Illinois by the late 1990s claimed to be promoting restorative justice as a new and different paradigm for juvenile justice reform (Griffin and Thomas 2004; Whitehead and Lab 2009). With or without new punitive statutes, by the late 1990s, some thirty-five states had adopted some form of restorative justice legislation and/or policy (O'Brien 2000; Whitehead and Lab 2009), with supporters suggesting that they did so in part as a means of successfully holding off, or softening, more retributive legislation (Krisberg 2005; Griffin and Thomas 2004). The good news for restorative justice advocates then and now is that objective opinion polls in the past two decades asking citizens about preferences for punishment, rehabilitation, and/or restorative or reparative justice practices have typically concluded that the public is *not* as punitive as policy makers believe them to be (Bazemore 1998; Bishop 2006). Specific citizen support for restorative justice in the 1990s was seen in both national and state polls—which, in several cases, ranked restorative practices at the top of the list of various types of juvenile justice interventions favored by the public (Schwartz, Guo, and Kerbs 1991; Pranis and Umbreit 1992; Moon et al. 2000).

This chapter considers the impact of reintegrative shaming and restorative justice as related but distinct concepts (Braithwaite 2002; Bazemore and Schiff 2004). Although there is much overlap between the emergence and continued advancement of reintegrative shaming theory and restorative justice, the former concept is both more *and less* than restorative justice. Similarly, restorative practice, theory, and research, and restorative movements internationally are much bigger than RISE and take place in multiple system and community contexts—schools, workplaces, and neighborhoods. First, I briefly define restorative justice according to its core principles of intervention and then consider the multitheoretic status of restorative justice research and practice. Second, reintegrative shaming (RISE) is discussed as a "general theory" of intervention in response to crime, which has been especially influential in the international development of restorative theory and practice (Braithwaite 2002). Third, I consider the impressive empirical support for restorative justice that has emerged especially in the past decade and its standing as a robust, evidence-based practice (e.g., Sherman and Strang 2007; Bonta et al. 2002). Fourth, while restorative justice practice in the United States since the late 1990s has been widely embraced by juvenile justice systems in a number of states, I argue that despite excellent and effective U.S programs, use of restorative practice in the United States is limited and sporadic in comparison to use in New Zealand, Europe, the UK, Canada, Australia, and many other countries. In part, this is because use of these practices in the United States is neither mandated nor presumptive, even for specific categories of crimes (e.g., first offenses, mid-level felonies) (Masters 2003). Fifth, I suggest that challenges to expanding current limited use of restorative practices (in a most states) are presented in part by: the political role of elected prosecutors and judges in court decision-making; an almost unshakeable systemic commitment to retributive punishment and adversarial processes that leaves little space for less formal community involvement in decision-making; and an absence of funding streams that could promote such involvement and program development. Finally, advocates, practitioners, and academics must share responsibility for moving U.S. restorative justice beyond its current status as a specialized, "boutique" program. To do so, I argue that advocates and policy makers must adopt a more ambitious New Zealand-style approach to restorative justice grounded in a generic problem solving or "problem-oriented" model (Scott 2000; Felson 1995). With an agenda of intervention beyond individual "cases" and "programs," such a holistic restorative model would address chronic, practical juvenile justice system and community problems (e.g., overcrowding, disproportionate minority confinement) and broader collective levels of impact while displacing expensive and ineffective practices.

II. Literature Review

The history of restorative justice can be traced to the settlement practices of both communal and highly organized early human civilizations (Weitekamp 1999). Modern roots of restorative justice practice in North America date back to the 1970s (Hudson and Galoway 1990). Restorative justice is most accurately described as a model for "*doing* justice" by *repairing the harm of crime* (Van Ness and Strong 1997; Bazemore and Walgrave 1999). Specifically, restorative intervention seeks, to the greatest extent possible, to heal the wounds crime and associated conflict causes to victims, communities, families, and relationships. Restorative justice is not, however, simply a different model of offender treatment or rehabilitation, or a diversionary alternative to punishment. It is also a comprehensive approach to crime and harm, not limited to the juvenile justice context.

Restorative justice and the RISE model have different origins, although both became widely popular at a time when juvenile justice itself was in the process of dramatic change. Looking back, despite many flaws which I will address below, the popularity of restorative justice as a "new justice" movement (Daly 1996; Daly and Immarigeon 1998) can be summarized in a few big ideas that made restorative justice unique. It is also around these ideas that restorative justice and reintegrative shaming come together, and to some degree reinforce each other.

A. Understanding and Misunderstanding Restorative Justice

Restorative justice became popular as a response to youth crime in part because it appeared to offer new insight that seemed capable of filling a troublesome gap in juvenile justice. The historic vulnerability of juvenile justice that came to a head for some average citizens by the end of the 1970s rested not so much with the post-*Gault* issues of due process, the need for more diversion, and the promise of deinstitutionalization. Though these issues remain controversial to some, they must also remain as largely unfulfilled promises (Feld 1987, 1993b). Of more importance historically was the failure of the "best interest" mission to (1) actually be implemented and to (2) articulate any reasonable sense of youth *accountability* for crime.

The failure of the "best interests" mission as the foundation of the juvenile court has been widely and critically discussed (Platt 1969; Polk, 1987; Garland 1990). Historically, had it really been about the best interests of children and youths, juvenile courts might have developed something very different than a rather anemic treatment model. For example, juvenile court judges might have been charged with a clear child advocacy mission, focused, for example, on legal action against abusive landlords who profited from income from families living in squalor; strong advocacy for decent schools; and other issues. While the rhetoric of "best interests" and treatment remains surprisingly strong even today, the recent reality is a much more formal juvenile justice system (though still without many of the protections and rights of the criminal justice system) (Feld 1993b, 1999).

Although punishment has always been a key feature of the juvenile justice system (Krisberg and Austin 1978), by the late 1980s, many of the trappings of just deserts/retributive justice that affirmed the value of punishment began to appear prominently in juvenile justice codes (Feld 1990; Torbet et al. 1996). It was against this backdrop of a fading best interest idea, and new respectability and policy-maker support for punishment (von Hirsch 1993), that restorative justice advocates entered the debate about the future of a new juvenile justice. One important part of this was a nonretributive conceptualization of accountability (Braithwaite 1989; Bazemore and Walgrave 1999; Walgrave and Bazemore, (1999).

1. *Justice, Restorative Accountability, and the Fit with Other Models*

"Accountability" in a restorative justice process must be sharply distinguished from retributive punishment. While most restorative justice advocates continue to strongly oppose retributive punishment (Braithwaite 1999; Braithwaite and Petit 1990), they also emphasize the necessity of appropriate measures of offender accountability for crime (Van Ness and Strong 1997). However, restorative justice encourages a higher and more productive standard of *justice* as "active accountability" (Braithwaite and Roche 2001). From this perspective, the offender is not expected to passively "take the *punishment*," but rather is encouraged to take *responsibility* for repairing harm caused to crime victims and/or the community. Such active accountability—along with emphasis on the sense of an obligation owed to the victim and community rather than the state—is indeed what most distinguishes restorative justice, both from passive retributive punishment by the state, and from the singular focus on "best interest." In general, the amount and quality of "justice" achieved in a given response to crime is gauged in a restorative justice process by attention to the extent to which *harm is repaired*, rather than the degree to which "justice deserts" is delivered (Maloney, et. al, 2000). Although there are many restorative justice practices, restorative responses do not require a *program* or a formal process, and indeed, some of the best examples of restorative justice occur serendipitously both in and outside of criminal/juvenile justice environments (Sullivan and Tifft 2001).

2. *Principles and Practice of Restorative Justice*

Though restorative justice is not limited to a program or set of programs, primary restorative practice includes two broad intervention components:

(1) <u>Restorative decision-making or "conferencing" programs</u>. These nonadversarial decision-making practices allow victims, offenders, their supporters, and other stakeholders a way to provide input into a plan to repair harm caused by a crime or harmful act (e.g., school disciplinary violations). Conferencing processes share a focus on maximizing stakeholder involvement, but may assume many variations within four general structural models: (1) family group conferencing, (2) victim-offender mediation/dialogue, (3) neighborhood accountability boards, and (4) peacemaking circles (Bazemore and Schiff 2004).

(2) <u>Restorative obligations</u>. These obligations may include restitution, community service, apologies, victim service, behavioral agreements, and a wide array of other efforts that allow offenders to make amends for harm caused by their offense. Such actions hold offenders accountable by allowing them to "right the wrong" in a way that provides evidence to the community and victim that the offender has "*earned* redemption" by concrete, behavioral actions.

More important than programs and practices, however, are *core principles* of restorative justice. Grounded in value-based assumptions that provide goals and objectives to be achieved in a justice process, these principles (Van Ness and Strong 1997) provide normative guidelines for gauging the actual strength and integrity of any response to crime and harm. Guidelines can in turn be linked to theories of intervention, which suggest immediate or intermediate outcomes of any restorative process. Such outcomes, or dimensions, as proposed by practitioners in qualitative research on restorative processes (Bazemore and Schiff 2004), help to connect intervention in a restorative decision-making process to impact on victim, offender, and community (See Appendix 1 for a list of theoretical dimensions and italicized material below that define successful outcomes). Core principles and theoretical dimensions are as follows:

> <u>The Principle of Repair:</u> Justice requires that we work to heal victims, offenders, and communities that have been injured by crime. The extent to which harm is repaired is based on the degree to which all parties identify the damage of a crime that needs to be addressed, and develop and carry out a plan to do so. Operative intervention models include: exchange theories that gauge the extent to which offenders *make amends* to victims of crime (Molm and Cook 1995), and social support theories

(Cullen 1994), which suggest that rebuilding *relationships* or *building new ones* between offender, victim, and/or supporters of both is essential to all parties.

The Principle of Stakeholder Involvement: Victims, offenders, and communities should have the opportunity for active involvement in the justice process as early and as fully as possible. The quality of stakeholder involvement is assessed by the degree to which victims, offenders, and their supporters and community members are intentionally and actively engaged in decision-making about how to accomplish this repair. Theories that posit the importance of dimensions of stakeholder participation include: reintegrative shaming, which emphasizes a conference outcome of *respectful disapproval* of the behavior/offense (Bazemore and Schiff 2004); a theory of "healing dialogue" (Umbreit 1999) that gives priority to *open exchange* between victim and offender regardless of the outcome of the conference; and a theory of "common ground" (Stuart 1996) based on a dimension/ outcome of *mutual transformation* between parties wherein small connections between multiple stakeholders (beyond victim and offender)—and/or minute points of agreement—are often a necessary prerequisite for addressing the issue at hand (Bazemore and Schiff 2004).

The Principle Community and Government Role Transformation: The extent to which *the community/government relationship is transformed* in a restorative process is assessed by the degree to which a response to crime is grounded in a rethinking and reshaping of the role of justice systems in the context of an expanded role for community members and groups. Theories related to this principle include: (1) theories of social disorganization, which would suggest that participants in a community decision-making process may need to articulate core values and engage in *norm affirmation* to establish common objectives and facilitate trust; (2) theories of social capital which create a sense of *collective ownership* of common problems leading to crime, and efficacy among stakeholders in processes that build skills and confidence to intervene effectively in neighborhood conflict; and (3) a theory of *collective efficacy* (Sampson et al. 1997) grounded in *shared leadership* and ownership of the problem being addressed.

Appendix I

Table 28.1* Core Principles and Theoretical Dimensions

Repairing Harm	Stakeholder Involvement	Community/Government Role Transformation
Dimensions:	*Dimensions:*	*Dimensions:*
➤Making Amends	➤Victim-offender exchange	➤Norm Affirmation/Values Clarification
	➤Mutual Transformation	➤Collective Ownership
➤Relationship Building	➤Respectful Disapproval	➤Skill Building

*Adapted from Bazemore and Schiff 2004.

B. Understanding Reintegrative Shaming

Reintegrative shaming (RISE) is but one of many theories that can be linked to restorative justice practice (Bazemore and Schiff 2004; Braithwaite 2002). Although it was to a great extent Braithwaite's writing on reintegrative shaming theory (Braithwaite 1989) that brought international attention and academic legitimacy to restorative justice in North America and other countries, RISE theory is both more *and less* than restorative justice. RISE has, for example, been applied quite extensively to international disputes and conflicts, multiple forms of white-collar crime, and "responsive regulation" (Braithwaite and Roche 2001). Because restorative justice is also linked, as suggested above, to a wide range of other normative and causal theories and practices (Bazemore and Schiff 2004), it is also larger than RISE theory.

Reintegrative shaming is first a *general theory* of intervention (Braithwaite 1989, 2002) also linked to a macro theory of the state based on what Braithwaite calls "non-denomination" or "dominion" (Braithwaite and Petit 1990). Braithwaite's "republican theory" of criminal justice is a departure from both offender-centered treatment and justice models, with the latter most problematic in its focus on proportional punishment grounded in liberal individualism. Republican theory, according to Braithwaite, must focus as much attention on victimization as on offending because the purpose of criminal justice should be to protect "liberty as non-domination of victims"(Braithwaite and Parker 1999, p. 107). While the theory is concerned with equality, it "does not value formal equality for its own sake," but rather prioritizes "those forms of equality that will increase freedom as *non-domination*" (emphasis mine). From this perspective, the formal equality of the liberal justice model "unfortunately creates an oppressive punitive complex in which domination is rampant." While the republican model shares with just desserts "an equitable concern with upper limits," it does not value formal equality for its own sake because this liberal model of equal punishment "creates an oppressive punitive complex in which domination is rampant (Braithwaite and Petit, 1990; see Garland 2001)." In practice the liberal model "delivers just deserts to the poor and impunity to the rich…due to the way the dominations of punishment interact with the dominations of unequal wealth and power." (Braithwaite and Parker 1999, p. 108).

Examples of problems that may be invited by restorative and other forms of informal justice in this larger climate include: failure to take violence seriously, lack of procedural accountability, failure to deal with unequal bargaining power or allowing too much unaccountable power over serious criminal problems—while, as Braithwaite and Parker (p. 109) suggest, potentially "empowering the 'victim advocacy' of the lynch mob." They argue, however, that these problems can be addressed by three republican strategies: "1) contestability under the rule of law whereby legal formalism empowers informalism while checking its excesses; 2) de-individualizing restorative justice (to challenge power imbalances) by using community conferences rather than one-on-one mediation; 3) support for a vibrant social movement politics that percolates into the deliberation of conferences, defends minorities against tyrannies of the majority and connects to campaigns for public transformation."

1. *Global Propositions*

In Crime Shame and Reintegration (CSR), Braithwaite develops and builds upon two primary global propositions about crime, and about the difference between low- and high-crime societies or communities. First, consistent with well-known social disorganization theories in the United States (Kornhauser 1978; Bursik and Grasmik 1993; Sampson et. al. 1997), Braithwaite argued at the macro level that low-crime societies around the world are those in which members do *not* "mind their own business."(1989, p.178). This assertion is of course consistent with the research of Sampson and his colleagues on Chicago neighborhoods that reveals that low-income communities, where residents are not afraid to intervene with other peoples' children, are often likely to have lower crime rates than similar, even more affluent, neighborhoods. In the latter, adults may lack relationships of social capital (Putnam 2000) that inspire trust and a sense of belonging, which enables the active response that flows from "collective efficacy" (Sampson et al. 1997).

The second, best-known, and most widely discussed part of Braithwaite's "general theory" of low-crime societies, Reintegrative Shaming, focuses on how community members bring about a successful, reintegrative outcome for those who violate laws or community norms. Here, at a generally more micro level of decision-making, Braithwaite proposes a kind of destigmatizing, "reverse labeling" process, in which extended family members and community participants denounce harmful *acts*, while emphasizing the good qualities of the offender. In the context of accountability for wrongdoing, participants seek to separate clear disapproval of the harmful *behavior* from disapproval of the offender. Viewed as an aberration best interpreted as inconsistent with the offender's "true self," questions and observations such as "what were you thinking," or "that's not like you," characterize the discussion of the offense/act (see Braithwaite and Mugford 1994).

2. *Shaming and Affect Theory*

At a more micro, psychological level, RISE theory also builds on the "affect theories" of Nathanson (1992) and Tomkins (1962), who argue that shame may become a destructive, criminogenic emotion when it leads the offender to "attack others, attack self, avoid, or withdraw" (Harris, Walgrave, and Braithwaite 2004, p. 195). Braithwaite (2002, p. 79) argues that his original theory (Braithwaite 1989) was "just a theory of shaming, with the emotion of shame left un-theorized." While some shame may be a healthy emotive response when one harms others, "chronic shame" that is unrecognized or by-passed is typically "the culprit in the shame-rage spirals that characterize our worst violence domestically and internationally." (Braithwaite 2002, p. 79); Retzinger and Scheff 1996. Shame *not addressed* and "managed" by offenders can therefore provoke further violence (Ahmed and Braithwaite 2005). Recent studies in school crime and discipline, for example, emphasize that restorative dialogue may assist in this management when responders emphasize both harmful and positive characteristics of the rule violator or aggressor (e.g., a bully) (Morrison 2001). On the other hand, "shaming" practices that attempt to humiliate and degrade offenders by requiring them to carry signs declaring that they are "losers" or "predators" (Kahan 1999) work against reintegrative shaming and restorative justice. Such practices and similar informal responses also tend to provoke defiance (Karp 1998; Sherman 1993), because in general, "disrespect begets disrespect" (Zehr 2000). The result of this, as was demonstrated in the follow-up to the domestic violence studies in the 1980s (Sherman and Berk 1984), is that shame-based sanctions become counterdeterrents.

Reintegrative shaming and restorative justice responses, according to Braithwaite, have also been applied at a more global or aggregate level, with important implications for macro issues of accountability of international corporate criminals, responses to hate crimes with global impact, post-apartheid truth and reconciliation, and even post-genocide healing in Rwanda (Braithwaite 2002). It is in such challenging contexts that nonstigmatizing shame may be truly reintegrative and may fit quite naturally within restorative theory and practice. Even in these contexts, however, most restorative justice advocates agree that the emphasis must be much less on shaming than on healing or repairing the harm of crime (Weitekamp et. al. 2006). More parochial, but equally challenging applications of restorative conferencing in family violence cases (Pennell 2006; Burford and Pennell 1995) also illustrate the resiliency of the general restorative model, *and* what I argue is an under-application of restorative practice in low-level cases, with little or no use in addressing serious crime and harm.

C. Applications of RISE, Restorative Justice: New Zealand and Australian Experiences and Impact

Despite broad application as a guide to research in multiple contexts (Harris et al. 2006; McGivern 2009), reintegrative shaming practice has been criticized even by advocates of restorative justice who are sympathetic to the value of the theory itself (Crawford and Clear 2001; Braithwaite and Roche, 2001; Bazemore 2009). Indeed, some do not view RISE as a restorative justice theory at all—because of its primary focus, at least in some places, on the offender rather than victim (Daly 2005), while others view the theory as resilient and robust.

The New Zealand Phenomenon

Despite the global significance of RISE theory, the most important development bringing attention to the term "restorative justice" was a then little-known legislative change in New Zealand's juvenile justice statute. At the turn of the decade in 1989, a truly indigenous justice decision-making model became the primary component of the juvenile justice code in what remains a highly anglicized, former commonwealth country. Adopted directly from the "whanau conference," practiced by Maori Aboriginals for centuries, the statute made the Family Group Conference an essentially mandated process to be applied in virtually all juvenile justice cases. The whanau conference became the "government's default legal process for handling all youth offenses in New Zealand (Van Ness and Strong 2006, p. 61)," and a primary basis for determining the content of court dispositions.

While court adjudication of guilt and responsibility when contested continues to be based on the seriousness of the offense or public safety concerns, the conference itself, in essence, provides the basis for maximum family/community input into a disposition that might also include information from arresting officers, juvenile justice professionals, mental health workers, and other expert practitioners who may sit in an outer circle around the family group to assist, for example, with intervention or placement decisions. The family group is also allowed "caucus time" to develop a plan to present to victims and justice officials for discussion in a process that—depending on the offense and other issues—may be entirely informal, with the outcome viewed essentially as a legal disposition.

Though shaming was never a part of New Zealand or Maori practice (Maxwell 2005), the statute recognized the primary importance of an accused person *standing with* his or her extended family group. While conference participants honor the role of group (extended family) disapproval of deliberate acts of harm and crime, this expression is also to be coupled with maximum support, in a way that does *not* condemn (or shame) the offender (McElrae 1996).

1. *The Wagga Wagga Model*

But while some proponents of an emerging Australian conferencing approach were said to have modeled their approach after New Zealand conferencing, Van Ness and Strong (2001, p. 61) assert that the Maori model was "adapted and significantly changed in Australia" as it was in its introduction to the United States and Canada. Although distinct differences include the use of a conference "script" and other more formal process components, few North Americans became familiar with the more inclusive, free-flowing New Zealand approach until several years after the country's passage of its new juvenile code. Thus, by the early 1990s, an Australian police-based program, developed by officer Terry O'Connell in the New South Wales town of Wagga Wagga, became an emerging international prototype for Family Group Conferencing based on reintegrative shaming.

While O'Connell developed and operated a restorative program consistent with Braithwaite's RISE theory and restorative justice (O'Connell 2008), replication of the Wagga Wagga model at times appeared to give more emphasis to "shaming" rather than reintegrative aspects of the model, therefore raising concerns among juvenile justice practitioners and academics (Alder and Wundersitz 1993). Nonetheless, the Canadian government (via the Royal Canadian Mounted Police) soon began to invest heavily in the Wagga Wagga model by purchasing training from the United States. The "Real Justice" group marketed such training across North America (O'Connnell 2008). Eventually, many U.S. practitioners, including a number of police officers, received training on this reintegrative shaming approach, later referred to by some as the "purist" model of restorative conferencing (McCold 2000).

Canadian and U.S. juvenile and criminal justice professionals also began to receive training on what some viewed as less rigid conferencing options that did not, for example, incorporate shaming as a necessary goal (Bazemore and Griffiths

1997; Pranis et. al. 2006). Though the Wagga Wagga/Real Justice model continues to have strong support, by the late 1990s, a number of Canadians had begun to embrace and utilize their own indigenous aboriginal practice models, including what were originally called "sentencing circles," and later "peacemaking circles," which also were adapted for use in a number of juvenile and criminal justice programs in the United States. (Stuart 1996; Bazemore and Griffiths 1999). Borrowing from other traditions, including victim-offender mediation/dialogue and Neighborhood Accountability Boards (Karp, Bazemore, and Chesire 2004), other preexisting and new models found converts, and some programs added new components, including use of the peacemaking circle dialogue format that encouraged maximum group input by use of a "talking piece" that allowed its holder to speak without being interrupted until the piece was passed to the next participant (Stuart 1996).

Today, reintegrative shaming as applied in these early Australian and U.S. efforts appears to have been rejected by conferencing practitioners in much of Australia, the United States, Canada, and other countries that have since implemented restorative justice—including Northern Ireland and much of the UK (McEvoy and Erickson 2002). Regarding the empirical impact of shaming versus other factors, in Daly's South Australia studies (Daly 2005) and follow-up on New Zealand longitudinal research on hundreds of offenders and victims (Maxwell 2005), the primary explanatory variable for recidivism reduction appears to be remorse and empathy with the victim, rather than reintegrative shaming.

III. The Evidence Base: Empirical Studies of Rise and Restorative Justice

A large body of research spanning thirty years or more has demonstrated the general effectiveness of restorative justice in recidivism reduction, victim satisfaction, and other outcomes (Bonta et al. forthcoming)[2011]. In the past two decades, researchers launched a number of evaluation studies, many employing randomized experiments and meta-analyses. While the great majority of studies in the past decade emphasize conferencing processes and offender outcomes, related research has also focused on several related components: crime victim impact, reparative practices or restorative sanctions, and reintegrative shaming.

A. Victim Impact

Most restorative justice supporters also view themselves as victim advocates. Indeed, many believe that restorative principles require a maximum focus on victim participation and healing (Achilles and Zehr 2001), that may alone justify investment in restorative programs. Consistent with a growing body of research on the impact of restorative justice on crime victims (e.g., Umbreit et al. 2003; Sherman and Strang. 2007) findings in the Canberra research demonstrate significant improvements in victim satisfaction and other outcomes for victims assigned to restorative justice groups compared with those going through the typical court process. Victim *dissatisfaction* with court and other aspects of the adversarial process is indeed one of the most widely replicated findings in victimology and restorative justice research, and recent studies find even stronger negative feelings about court among victims of violent crime (e.g., Daly 2005). Overall, consistently large differences in victim satisfaction with restorative justice compared with traditional court or related processes are now arguably the most consistent finding in restorative justice research (see Daly 2005; Sherman and Strang 2007).[4] Beyond satisfaction, new frontiers for meeting victim needs are illustrated by a recent randomized experiment wherein victims of Post-Traumatic Stress Disorder assigned to restorative conferences had significantly lower PTS than a control group receiving traditional PTS intervention (Angel 2009).

B. Reparative Practices

The important focus on the restorative decision-making process (i.e., conferencing) has often minimized the value of research on vital components of a holistic restorative intervention: completion of agreements to repair harm, improvements in victim well-being, changes in offender behavior, and the successful reintegration of offender and victim. For example, Van Ness and Strong (2006) argue that the restorative victim/offender/community "encounter" (e.g., through a conference) is the critical component of a restorative process. They note, however, that a complete restorative model must also include four additional phases: (1) *making "amends"* as an essential set of actions to repair harm, including *apology* (accompanied by offender behavior change); (2) *"reintegration"* of victims and offenders; and (3) *inclusion*, or the "opportunity for direct and full involvement of each party in the procedures that follow crime," (Van Ness and Strong 2006 p. 126).[5]

From this perspective, studies that demonstrate the positive impact of reparative activity—i.e., restitution and community service on recidivism reduction and victim satisfaction (e.g., Schneider 1986; Butts and Snyder 1991)—are important to the overall consideration of the value and impact of the restorative justice approach.. In a multisite, extensive randomized field experiment involving reparative programs in six cities, for example, Schneider (1990) found significant reductions in recidivism in four of six community trials on the impact of restitution and community service, and similar studies suggest positive victim impact for restitution payment (e.g., Hudson and Galoway 1990) Schneider's research found that *completion* of restitution and service obligations had an independent added impact on recidivism reduction, and findings from one site found that victim-offender mediation improved rates of completion of restitution (Umbreit, 1999). Though not an experiment, in a Utah sample of 18,000 juvenile justice cases referred to either probation or diversion programs, Butts and Snyder (1991) found significant differences in recidivism for youths who participated in community service and those who did not. While statistically significant, 8 and 10 percent reductions in reoffending for probation and diversion respectively—though perhaps not impressive to some—have practical implications when considering cost savings in reoffending based on the simple choice of a reparative intervention (see Uggen and Janikula, 1999). Indeed, a number of studies of community service generally show positive impact on reoffending with or without use of restorative conferencing (see also Wilkinson 1999). Future restorative justice research should examine *both* restorative process and initial outcomes as intervening variables potentially linked to reoffending and other outcomes.[6]

C. Reintegrative Shaming Research

Like the theory itself, reintegrative shaming research is quite expansive (see Braithwaite 2002 for summaries). Studies of impact of RISE on youth and delinquent populations, however, are generally mixed in their outcomes. This may be a result of the fact that researchers rely heavily on survey questionnaire data and hypothetical scenarios that may not provide a true test of either the impact of reintegrative shaming or the restorative experience. In a survey research study on incarcerated populations of juvenile offenders in Florida, for example, Hay (2001) found that reintegrative shaming reduced secondary delinquency, but contrary to the theory, *stigmatization* also reduced offending. Zhang and Zhang (1995) used National Youth Survey data to test reintegrative shaming on a sample of 1,725 adolescents, but also found that support for reintegrative shaming did not reduce reoffending. McGivern (2009), however, using a different statistical method, found significant differences in a study using the same sample. Summarizing this research, McGivern suggests that the lack of consensus on the impact of RISE should not be discouraging due to the difficulty of developing consistent measures of the complex and subtle concept of reintegrative shaming using survey data (McGivern 2009).

The generally successful Canberra RISE experiments also show somewhat mixed results that nonetheless help to determine types of restorative conferences that may be expected to be *unsuccessful*. In 1995, 1,300 offenders were randomly assigned to three different treatment and control conditions to examine four different offense types: juvenile property offenses; drunk driving offenses; juvenile shoplifting; and violent youth offenses. First, offenses decreased for *all* violent offenders—regardless of whether they attended a conference—but rates for those attending a conference decreased by an additional 38 percent. Neither drunk driving offenders nor the shoplifting offenders showed decreases in offending subsequent to the conference, though in hindsight, both were considered to be weak applications of restorative justice (e.g., few victims were present in these trials and implementation of restorative principals was viewed as weak) (Braithwaite 2002). Finally, in later trials on school bullying, reintegrative shaming coupled with forgiveness at home appeared to significantly reduce self-initiated bullying, while *shame displacement* (blaming others) seemed to increase school bullying (Ahmed and Braithwaite 2005).

D. Restorative Conferencing Research

Overall, research in the UK, meta-analyses in Canada, the United States, and elsewhere—including the original Canberra study in Australia and early results from studies in the UK—report significant, if not dramatic, levels of recidivism reduction (Sherman and Strang 2007; Bonta et al. 2002, 2007). As suggested above, some studies also provide clues about what does *not* work—i.e., including conferences with little or no victim participation and the lack of emotional commitment often common in more trivial cases (e.g., shoplifting) versus violent crime (Sherman 2003). For the most part, international studies provide strong support for the impact of restorative justice on reoffending, victim satisfaction, and other outcomes with adult and juvenile offenders and victims. More research is needed in different contexts (e.g., as part of offender reentry, in secure facilities, and in school-based contexts) (Bazemore and Maruna 2009).

Overall, conferencing research is beginning to span a wide range of offense types and seriousness levels. Findings from recent intervention studies, for example, include: Sherman's randomized trials with serious and violent adult offenders showing stronger effects on reoffending than what has been found in trials with medium-range young juvenile offenders (Sherman and Strang 2007); a large juvenile diversion program that randomly assigned youths to conferencing or control group receiving traditional intervention that yielded significant results in a three-year follow-up study (McGarell 2001; and several quasi-experimental studies of restorative programs contrasted with probation alternatives (e.g., Rodriguez 2004) Karp et al. 2004). Together, these provide growing support for the proposition that restorative applications at different points in justice systems, and multiple levels of offense seriousness, reduce reoffending and increase victim satisfaction in a variety of contexts (Bonta et. al. 2002).

E. Why It Works

Although randomized experiments provide the strongest possible test of impact as a function of *assignment to experimental and control* groups,[7] it is sometimes difficult in randomized studies to draw conclusions about the *specific* independent variable or theoretical process producing reductions in reoffending (or other outcomes). While randomization provides the clearest possible answer regarding the impact of a general intervention (conferencing), experimental and control conditions may encompass multiple embedded variables, intervention approaches, and theoretical frameworks (e.g., reintegrative shaming, amends-making, social support). Thus, experiments may not address the relative importance of one or more independent or "intervening variables" or other factors that may vary *within* the experimental group. To improve practice, it is important to understand how and why restorative justice works when it does (see Agnew 1993; Hagan 1989). For example, what is the impact of reintegrative shame versus the effect of "healing dialogue, "making amends," or other initial conference outcomes that may lead to long-term changes in offenders, victims, and other stakeholders. It is not therefore completely clear whether the real *intervening variable* is a *restorative* process, or perhaps simply procedural justice (Tyler 1990), or some other factor. It is therefore possible that restorative practices may be effective *not* for the reasons proposed in this chapter, but because they lead to a more robust form of procedural justice (Braithwaite 2002; Tyler 2006). While all restorative practices focus on the general goals of active accountability, restoration, and reintegration, practitioners appear to vary in their pursuit of immediate conferencing outcomes (i.e., theoretical dimensions such as remorse, sense of fairness, social support, and healing dialogue are expected to be most important to achieving long-term goals) (Weiss 1997; Walgrave 2004).

Finally, despite some claims of "superior" conferencing *models* (McCold 2000), to date, no studies directly compare the impact of any one restorative conferencing model against another. To improve practice and consistency, future studies may therefore find ways to contrast the impact of distinct restorative program *models* (e.g., victim-offender mediation, family group conferencing), or better yet, document the impact of specific theoretical and practical model *components* (e.g., different victim involvement strategies, use of volunteers) in studies that contrast participants randomly assigned to one of several different restorative conferencing models (e.g., peacemaking circles, neighborhood boards, family group conferencing, New Zealand versus other models).[8]

IV. Potential Dangers, Red Herrings, and Real Worries About the Future: Misuse and Underuse of Restorative Justice

The sudden appearance of new restorative practices in the United States in the late 1990s brought early criticism. While some presented legitimate, reality-based concerns about the dangers of unchecked informalism (Feld 1999; Crawford and Clear 2001), others posed anticipatory litanies of critical scrutiny *even prior to* examination of restorative conferencing practice (Levrant et al. 1999). Legal scholars based their concerns on problems with what was forty years ago called "mediation," and attacked restorative justice conferencing as if it were the same practice (e.g., Delgado 2000). Treatment advocates mounted preemptive anticipatory critiques, concluding that the new restorative programs were already, or would immediately begin to: (1) hamper rehabilitation efforts, (2) widen the net of social control while imposing longer and more punitive sanctions on offenders; (3) increase incarceration; and (4) (somehow) worsen already high rates of disproportionate minority confinement (Levrant et. al. 1999), even while African American leaders suggested that these programs might likely have the opposite result (e.g., Landry, 2007).

At a time when the net is indeed being widened by a variety of forces reaching down into schools and communities to manage new youth populations (especially those of color) (Sheldon 2007), these general concerns are valid ones. But they have little to do with restorative justice in most of the United States—largely because restorative practices are simply not used frequently enough to be singled out for blame for negative outcomes, or praised for positive ones. Although increased use could make restorative practice more vulnerable to net-widening, policy makers in countries with far more routine application (Sherman and Strang 2007; Maxwell 2005) have typically placed strict floors on eligibility for admission to programs. In Canada and several Australian states, for example, police and other front-end decision-makers must follow *lower limit* restrictions on eligibility for participation in restorative justice (e.g., several informal police diversions) prior to referral to programs, and some pilot programs have provided legal counsel for youths about options for court (Griffiths and Corrado, 1999; Bargen 1996).

A. America's Got Courts

Realistic worries about U.S. restorative justice have more to do with (1) the absence of mandates or even presumptive requirements for referral and (2) competition with ineffective, or marginally effective, popular early intervention programs of the "Scared Straight" or Jail Tour variety (Finkenhauer and Gavin 1999). Critics concerned with informalism and net-widening should focus also on the growing number of other untested or marginally successful programs that have become popular with some judges and other juvenile justice professionals. In general, the bulk of these "informal" diversion and probation alternatives have the word "court" in their titles, and are differentiated by specialized focus: drug, truancy, smoking, family, gun, alcohol, grade, and—of course—teen/peer courts, to name but a few popular interventions on the juvenile justice scene. While evidence-based restorative programs flourish in many countries, U.S. juvenile justice typically favors "feel good" programs that in some cases clearly do *not* work (e.g., Boot Camps).

The argument against restorative justice as an open door for net-widening, for now at least, should be viewed as a red herring. Indeed, arguments against use of less formal restorative justice processes in predispositional decision-making (Delgado 2000) seem to presume the court is really more formal than it really is. In the real world of juvenile justice, a robust *legal informalism* thrives as attorneys negotiate in hallways to make deals, hopefully related to their clients' needs and wishes, while also seeking to maximize their own interests without meaningful input from family, victim, offender, or other stakeholders. Ultimately, a key obstacle limiting wider and more effective use of restorative justice in the United States is the politicization of the role of prosecutor and judge. With few exceptions, and regardless of political affiliation and ideology, district or state attorneys must express almost absolute support for more punishment to continue to run for office. Thus, while the public is actually not as punitive as policy makers think they are (e.g., Bishop 2005; Shiraldi and Soler 1998), the addiction to punishment survives in criminal and juvenile justice in part because we do not provide effective, nonretributive, inclusive paths to accountability and public safety.[9]

B. Can Restorative Justice Prosper in the United States? Avoiding the "Oprah Curse"

The problem with increasing use of restorative justice practices, however, is not limited to the behavior of prosecutors, judges, or other legal decision makers—many of whom have become strong advocates for restorative justice despite potential political risks. A more serious challenge is the limited perception of restorative justice as an "interesting" model with a few specific applications to mostly minor offenses. Much blame for limited use of these evidence-based practices is therefore due to the failure of advocates, practitioners, and community groups to make the case for use of an intervention, which, as the New Zealand experience reveals, is useful in almost all cases (McElrae 1996).

Instead, what may be called the "Oprah Effect"—for many a surefire approach to effective marketing of products ranging from cupcakes, to automobiles, to bathrobes, to Dr. Phil—has, in the case of restorative justice, become a curse. As an advocate, Oprah has featured live restorative conferences as well as interviews with conference participants on some half-dozen televised broadcasts. While some suggest that televised restorative justice of this variety misrepresents practice (Zehr 2007), the Oprah effect is neither the fault of the famous host nor of television, but rather the perception of restorative justice as a "boutique" program. Like one of Oprah's "favorite things"—restorative justice is often viewed as "perfect for" just the right (unfortunately rare) case.

As reflected in research polls mentioned earlier, and in hundreds of conversations with practitioners, the desire to expand the use of restorative justice is apparent. The problem is that current juvenile justice practitioners (whether in probation, diversion, or residential care) claim to want restorative practices, while in fact marginalizing them. In much of the world, on the other hand, restorative justice is either mandated for many cases, or used in some fashion as a vital non-adversarial, problem-solving, decision-making process ideal for developing diversion, and dispositional and reentry recommendations.

V. Discussion: Making it Work Through Problem Solving And Community Building

While restorative principles demand that interventions first meet the needs of victims, offenders, and communities, successful implementation must focus on use of restorative justice to *solve core problems* facing managers and communities. In New Zealand, for example, problems included (1) overcrowding in the primary youth facility and (2) disproportionate minority confinement among Maori youth (McAlrae 1996). Rather than the usual process of imposing solutions on indigenous populations, the key feature of the plan for addressing these needs was the adoption of the Maori justice decision-making process. Though the United States is not New Zealand, if restorative justice is to expand beyond its status as a boutique practice, supporters must move aggressively toward a pragmatic *problem-oriented* approach (Felson 1995; Scott 2000) also aimed at building community and system capacity for sustained practice. A brief template for a problem-oriented and community-building juvenile justice follows.

A. System Problem Solving and Juvenile Justice: A Checklist

1. <u>Systemic Reform.</u> Following New Zealand, practical restorative problem-solving initiatives include: reducing crowded court dockets; providing police with effective alternatives to arrest; reducing assaults in facilities; creating a more robust reentry process; reducing school referrals through restorative justice alternatives to zero tolerance; providing an alternative to probation violations; and so on.

2. <u>Deemphasize "Programs."</u> Programs are by definition "alternatives" to how most cases will be processed, and, as such, tend to have little impact on dominant practice. Used only as a program, restorative justice is unlikely to survive and will certainly fail to address the needs of more than a few victims and offenders.

3. <u>Find a Restorative *Way.*</u> Rather than *programs*, develop principle- and theory-based restorative *strategies* to address common system problems and to transform basic system functions practically applying appropriate practice to the correct problem and point in the system (e.g., restorative diversion, restorative discipline in facilities and schools, restorative probation, restorative reentry).

4. <u>Displace versus "Add On."</u> While restorative justice can supplement other practices (e.g., an intensive treatment program in serious cases), it should, however, be viewed as capable of becoming a self-sufficient response (rather than an add-on), which fails to save time or resources (e.g., replacing the formal dispositional process).

B. Community Building and Juvenile Justice: A Checklist

1. <u>Build capacity in various community institutions and organizations (neighborhoods, schools).</u> Restorative strategies emphasize the responsibility of civil society, *socializing* institutions (e.g., schools), and community groups for raising, supporting, and disciplining young people. Practice can and should be used intentionally to teach new skills to adults in support of increasing capacity for informal social control and social support.

2. <u>Address and measure collective, community skill-building outcomes.</u> Such outcomes should be primary indicators of the impact of restorative justice on families, schools, neighborhoods, faith community groups, and a range of parochial organizations.

3. <u>Increase the number of shared core decision-making functions.</u> Juvenile justice systems should cede most system functions (other than those that determine guilt and innocence) to community groups (supported, rather than led, by professionals).

NOTES

1. It is important to note that some states (e.g., Connecticut) to some degree actually moved in the direction of shoring up the integrity of the juvenile court by *raising* the minimum age of the court's original jurisdiction from 16 to 18—with related changes in Virginia, Arizona, and Colorado, while twenty-two states adopted reverse waiver legislation. In states like Florida, where transfer decisions are a relatively routine part of the conversation of prosecutors and juvenile justice administrators, the possibilities of very young offenders in criminal court present a frightening reality.

2. In fact, theoretically and empirically, Braithwaite's work spans much of criminology and law beyond juvenile justice. In this chapter, I use the acronym RISE (actually a commonly used abbreviation for the Reintegration Shaming Experiments in Canberra, Australia).

3. Moreover, with the exception of a few jurisdictions that wisely attached programs more or less permanently to probation departments or other more permanent entities, few U.S. states or local jurisdictions currently set aside funding resources to support restorative programs. By comparison, much weaker, marginally related programs, such as teen courts, truancy courts, and drug and alcohol courts have managed to build judicial and court constituencies that find ways to continue funding and even expand use.

4. Sherman and Strang's (2007) studies on impact on crime victims also demonstrate significant positive results for victims assigned to restorative justice compared with those going through the typical court process (Sherman and Strang, 2007). Because this finding is no doubt one of the most widely replicated outcomes in restorative justice research based on thirty years of evidence (see Umbreit et al. 2003), it is clear that further research may no longer justify the expense, and stress, of random assignment of victims to control groups.

5. Forms that this inclusion take, for example, from less to more inclusive, are: receiving information, observing proceedings, making a formal impact presentation in court, and the right of legal standing in the criminal/juvenile justice process to pursue reparation.

6. It is important to acknowledge that reparative interventions *alone*—including court ordered restitution and community service—are typically not viewed as "restorative" in their own right in the absence of a restorative justice process. Some argue, however, that these reparative measures have restorative value when they are proposed as alternatives to retributive punishment, and when crime victims unable to participate in a conference receive restitution—especially when restorative conferences are not an option (Bazemore and Walgrave 1999).

7. The goal of randomized studies is to differentiate and contrast outcomes for experimental and control groups as a whole rather than specific conditions that happen to vary within these groups (e.g., a focus on reintegrative shaming versus healing dialogue). Whether or not shaming may have been a core feature of these programs, randomized studies do not generally report data on the specific impact of reintegrative shaming as a variable, or the nature and strength of focus of restorative justice.

8. Bonta et al. (2002) provide a partial exception to the rule of a general lack of comparison of the impact of program components in calculating effect sizes for various restorative and other interventions as part of experimental and quasi-experimental program comparisons. As an early critic of restorative justice—and its value relative to effective treatment programs—both of Bonta's meta-analyses find stronger effect sizes for restorative practices with an expanded sample (on average, a phi value of .07). In the 2007 study, differences are stronger still (phi = .10) when programs administered by criminal justice officials under court order were eliminated from the sample.

9. This is not to say that prosecutors and judges have not also been leaders in restorative justice. Ronnie Earl of Austin, Texas; Bill Ritter of Denver (currently Governor of Colorado); Fred Gay of Iowa; and Richard Devine of Chicago have been both smart and courageous in aligning themselves and their campaigns with restorative justice. Juvenile Deputies who have led restorative efforts in their respective states include Kathy Ryan, of Chicago and John Delaney, of Philadelphia.

REFERENCES

Achilles, Mary, and Howard Zehr. 2001. "Restorative Justice for Crime Victims: The Promise, the Challenge." In *Restorative Community Justice: Repairing Harm and Transforming Communities*, edited by Gordon Bazemore and Mara Schiff. Cincinnati, OH: Anderson Publishing.

Agnew, Robert. 1993. "Why Do They Do It? An Examination of the Intervening Mechanisms between 'Social Control' Variables and Delinquency." *Journal of Research in Crime and Delinquency* 30: 245–66.

Ahmed, Eliza, and John Braithwaite. 2005. "Forgiveness, Shaming and Bullying." *Australian and New Zealand Journal of Criminology* 38(3): 298–323.

Alder, Christine, and Joy Wundersitz, eds. 1994. *Family Group Conferencing and Juvenile Justice: The Way Forward or Misplaced Optimism?* Canberra, Austl.: Australian Institute of Criminology.

Angel, Carolyn M. 2005. "Crime Victims Meet Their Offenders: Testing the Impact of Restorative Justice Conferences on Victims' Post-Traumatic Stress Symptoms." PhD dissertation, University of Pennsylvania.

Bargen, Jenny. 1996. "Kids, Cops, Courts, Conferencing and Children's Rights—A Note on Perspectives." *Australian Journal of Human Rights* 2(2): 209–28.

Bazemore, Gordon. 1998. "Restorative Justice and Earned Redemption: Communities, Victims & Offender Reintegration." *American Behavioral Scientist* 41(6): 768–813.

Bazemore, Gordon. 2009. "Getting and Keeping It Real: Less than Perfect Restorative Justice Intervention and the Value of Small Connections," *Journal for Peace and Justice Studies* 18(1–2): 54–73.

Bazemore, Gordon and Curt Griffiths. (1997). "Conferences, Circles, Boards, and Mediation: The New Wave in Community Justice Decisionmaking." *Federal Probation*, 59(2): 25–37.

Bazemore, Gordon, and Leslie Leip. 2007. "Making Sense of Community Supervision: Diversion and Probation in Postmodern Juvenile Justice," In *Juvenile Offenders and Victims*, edited by Marilyn D. McShane and Frank. P. Williams III. Vol. 1 of *Youth Violence and Delinquency: Monsters and Myths*. Westport, CT: Praeger Publishers.

Bazemore, Gordon and Shadd Maruna (2009) Restorative justice in the reentry context: Building new theory and expanding the evidence base. Victims & Offenders 2009; 4(4): 375–384.

Bazemore, Gordon and Martha Schiff. 2004. *Juvenile Justice Reform and Restorative Justice: Building Theory and Policy from Practice*. Cullompton, UK: Willan Publishing.

Bazemore, Gordon, and Lode Walgrave. 1999. "Restorative Juvenile Justice: In Search of Fundamentals and an Outline for Systemic Reform." In *Restorative Juvenile Justice: Repairing the Harm of Youth Crime*, edited by Gordon Bazemore and Lode Walgrave. Monsey, NY: Criminal Justice Press.

Bishop, Donna M. 2000. "Juvenile Offenders in the Adult Criminal Justice System" In *Crime and Justice: A Review of Research*, edited by Michael Tonry, vol. 27. Chicago: University of Chicago Press.

Bishop, Donna M. 2005. "The Role of Race and Ethnicity in Juvenile Justice Processing." In *Our Children. Their Children: Confronting Racial and Ethnic Differences in American Juvenile Justice*, edited by D. F. Hawkins and K. Kempf-Leonard. Chicago: University of Chicago Press.

Bishop, Donna M. 2006. "Public Opinion and Juvenile Policy: Myths and Misconceptions—Reaction Essay." *Criminology and Public Policy* 5: 653–64.

Blueprint Commission. 2008. "Getting Smart About Juvenile Justice in Florida." Tallahassee, FL: Blueprint Commission, Florida Department of Juvenile Justice. January.

Bonta, James, Susan Wallace-Capretta, James Rooney, K. Mackanoy. (2002). "An Outcome Evaluation of a Restorative Justice Alternative to Incarceration." *Contemporary Justice Review* 5: 319–38.

Braithwaite, John. 1989. *Crime, Shame, and Reintegration*. Cambridge: Cambridge University Press.

Braithwaite, John. (2002). *Restorative Justice and Responsive Regulation*. New York: Oxford University Press.

Braithwaite, John, and Steven Mugford. 1994. "Conditions of Successful Reintegration Ceremonies: Dealing with Juvenile Offenders." *British Journal of Criminology* 34: 139–71.

Braithwaite, John, and Cristine Parker. 1999. "Restorative Justice is Republican Justice." In *Restorative Juvenile Justice: Repairing the Harm of Youth Crime*, edited by Gordon Bazemore and Lode Walgrave. Monsey, NY: Criminal Justice Press.

Braithwaite, John, and Philip Petit. 1990. *Not Just Deserts: A Republican Theory of Criminal Justice*. Oxford, UK: Oxford University Press.

Braithwaite, John and Declan Roche. 2001. "Responsibility and Restorative Justice." In *Restorative Community Justice: Repairing Harm and Transforming Communities*, edited by G. Bazemore and M. Schiff. Cincinnati: Anderson Publishing.

Brown, Joel H., and Jordon E. Horowitz. 1993. "Why Adolescent Substance Use Prevention Programs Do Not Work." *Evaluation Review* 17: 529–55.

Burford, Gale, and John Pennell. 1995. *Family Group Decisionmaking: New Roles for "Old" Partners in Resolving Family Violence: Implementation Report Summary*. Saint Johns, Newfoundland, Memorial University of Newfoundland.

Bursik, Robert J. Jr., and Harold G. Grasmick. 1993. *Neighborhoods and Crime: The Dimensions of Effective Community Control*. New York: Lexington.

Butts, Jeffery, and Oliver Mitchell. 2000. "Brick by Brick: Dismantling the Border Between Juvenile and Adult Justice" In *Boundary Changes in Criminal Justice Organizations*, ch. 5. Washington, DC: National Institute of Justice.

Butts, Jeffery, and Howard Snyder. (1991). *Restitution and Juvenile Recidivism*. Monograph. Pittsburgh, PA, National Center for Juvenile Justice.

Crawford, Adam, and Tod Clear. 2001. "Community Justice: Transforming Communities through Restorative Justice?" In *Restorative Community Justice: Repairing Harm and Transforming Communities*, edited by Gordon Bazemore and Mara Schiff. Cincinnati, OH: Anderson Publishing.

Cullen, Frank T. 1994. "Social Support as an Organizing Concept for Criminology: Residential Address to the Academy of Criminal Justice Sciences." *Justice Quarterly*. 11: 527–59.

Daly, Kathy (1996). "Diversionary Conferences in Australia: A Reply to the Optimists and Skeptics." Paper presented at the annual meeting of the American Society of Criminology, San Francisco, November.

Daly, Kathy. 2005. "A Tale of Two Studies: Restorative Justice From a Victim's Perspective." In *New Directions in Restorative Justice: Issues, Practice, and Evaluation*, edited by Elizabeth Elliot and Robert M. Gordon. Cullompton, Devon, UK: Willan Publishing.

Daly, Kath, and Russel Immarigeon. 1998. "The Past, Present, and Future of Restorative Justice: Some Critical Reflections." *Contemporary Justice Review* 1: 21–45.

Delgado, Robert. 2000. "Goodbye to Hammerabi: Concerns About Restorative Justice." *Stanford Law Review* 52(4): 751–73.

Dishion, Thomas J., Joan McCord, and François Poulin. 1999. When Interventions Harm: Peer Groups and Problem Behavior. *American Psychologist* 54(9): 755–64.

Feely, Malcom, and Jonathan Simon. 1992. "The New Penology: Notes on the Emerging Strategy of Corrections and Is Implications." *Criminology*, 30(4): 449–74.

Feld, Barry C. 1987. "The Juvenile Court Meets the Principle of the Offense: Punishment, Treatment, and the Difference It Makes." *Journal of Criminal Law and Criminology* 68: 473–99.

Feld, Barry C. 1990. "The Punitive Juvenile Court and the Quality of Procedural Justice: Disjunctions between Rhetoric and Reality." *Crime and Delinquency*, 36(4): 443–66.

Feld, Barry C. 1993a. "The Criminal Court Alternative to Perpetuating Juvenile (In)Justice." In *The Juvenile Court: Dynamic, Dysfunctional, or Dead?* Philadelphia: Center for the Study of Youth Policy, School of Social Work, University of Pennsylvania.

Feld, Barry C. 1993b. "Juvenile (In)Justice and the Criminal Court Alternative." *Crime and Delinquency* 39: 403–24.

Feld, Barry C. (1999). "Rehabilitation, Retribution and Restorative Justice: Alternative Conceptions of Juvenile Justice," pp. 17–44 in *Restorative Juvenile Justice: Repairing the Harm of Youth Crime*, G. Bazemore and L. Walgrave (Eds.) Monsey, New York: Criminal Justice Press.

Felson, Marcus. 1995. "Those Who Discourage Crime." In *Crime and Place: Crime Prevention Studies*, vol. 4, edited by John Eck and David Weisburg. Monsey, NY: Criminal Justice Press.

Finkenhauer, James and Gavin, P. (1999). *Scared Straight: The Panacea Phenomenon Revisited*. Prospect Heights, IL: Waveland Press.

Forst, Martin, ed. 1995. *The New Juvenile Justice*. New York: Nelson Hall.

Freeman, James. 2009. *Turning Words Into Actions: Guidance on Implementing Florida's Zero Tolerance Law*. Florida State Conference of the NAACP Advancement Project.

Garland, David. (1990). Punishment and Modern Society. Oxford: Clarendon Press.

Gottfredson, Denise. 2009. "Developing an Experiment in the Negative Impacts of Treatment." Paper presented at the American Society of Criminology Meetings, Philadelphia, PA, November.

Griffin, Patrick, and Doug Thomas. 2004. "The Good News: Measuring Juvenile Court Outcomes at Case Closing." *Pennsylvania Progress* 10(2). Harrisburg, PA: Pennsylvania Commission on Crime and Delinquency, National Center for Juvenile Justice.

Griffiths, Curt T. and Ray Corrado. (1999). "Restorative Justice: Repairing the Harm of Youth Crime," In *Restorative Justice: Repairing the Harm of Youth Crime*, edited by Gordon Bazemore and Lode Walgrave. Monsey, NY: Willow Tree Press.

Hagan, John. 1989. "Why Is There So Little Criminal Justice Theory? Neglected Macro and Micro Links between Organization and Power." *Journal of Research in Crime and Delinquency* 26: 116–35.

Harris, Nathan. 2006. "Reintegration Shaming, Shame, and Criminal Justice." *Journal of Social Issues* 62: 327–46.

Harris, Nathan, Lode Walgrave, and John Braithwaite. 2004. "Emotional Dynamics in Restorative Conferences." *Theoretical Criminology* 8(2): 191–210.

Hay, Carter. 2001. "An Exploratory Test of Braithwaite's Reintegrative Shaming Theory." *Journal of Research in Crime and Delinquency* 38: 132–53.

Hudson, Joe, and Burt Galaway. 1990. "Introduction: Towards Restorative Justice." In *Criminal Justice, Restitution, and Reconciliation*, edited by Burt Galaway and Joe Hudson, Monsey, NY: Willow Tree Press.

Kahan, D. M. 1999. "Punishment Incommensurability." *Buffalo Criminal Law Review* 1: 691–708.

Karp, David R. 1998. "The Judicial and Judicious Use of Shame Penalties," *Crime and Delinquency* 44: 277–94.

Karp, David R., G. Bazemore, and J. Chesire. 2004. "The Role and Attitudes of Restorative Board Members: A Case Study of Volunteers in Community Justice." *Crime and Delinquency* 50(4): 487–553.

Kornhauser, Ruth R. 1978. *Social Sources of Delinquency*. Chicago: University of Chicago Press.

Krisberg, Barry. 2005 *Juvenile Justice: Redeeming Our Children*. Thousand Oaks, CA: Sage.

Landry, Dale (2009). Florida Department of Juvenile Justice: Restorative Justice Philosophy Training and Implementation Guide. (Available from the Florida Department of Juvenile Justice, Office of Prevention and Victim Services, 2737 Centerview Drive, Tallahassee, FL 32399–3100)

Levrant, Sharon, Frank Cullen, Barbara Fulton, and John Wozniak. 1999. "Reconsidering Restorative Justice: The Corruption of Benevolence Revisited?" *Crime and Delinquency*, 45(1): 3–27.

Maloney, Dennis, Gordon Bazemore, and Joe Hudson. (2000). "The End of Probation and the Beginning of Community Justice," *Perspectives*. 3:Summer, pp.1–14.

Masters, Guy. 2003. "What Happens When Restorative Justice is Encouraged, Enabled and/or Guided by Legislation?" In *Critical Issues in Restorative Justice*, edited by Howard Zehr and Barbara Toews. Cullompton, Devon, UK: Willan Publishing.

Maxwell, Gabrielle. (2005). "Achieving effective outcomes in you justice: implications for new research for principles, policy and practice." In *New Directions in Restorative Justice: Issues, Practice and Evaluation*, edited by Elizabeth Elliott and Robert M. Gordon, Portland, OR: Willan Publishing.

McCold, Paul. 2000. "Toward a Holistic Vision of Restorative Juvenile Justice: A Reply to the Maximalist Model." *Contemporary Justice Review* 3(4): 357–72.

McElrae, Fred W. 1996. "The New Zealand Youth Court: A Model for Use with Adults." In *Restorative Justice: International Perspectives*, edited by B. Galaway and J. Hudson. Monsey, NY: Criminal Justice Press.

McEvoy, Kieran, and Anna Eriksson. 2006. "Restorative Justice in Transition: Ownership, Leadership and 'Bottom Up' Human Rights." In *Handbook of Restorative Justice*, edited by Dennis Sullivan and Larry Tifft. New York: Routledge.

McGarrell, Edward. 2001. "Restorative Justice Conferences as an Early Response to Young Offenders." *OJJDP Juvenile Justice Bulletin*. August. Washington, DC: U.S. Department of Justice, Office of Juvenile Justice and Delinquency Prevention.

Molm, Lawrence, and Kathleen Cook. 1995. "Social Exchange and Exchange Networks." *In Sociological Perspectives on Social Psychology*, edited by K. Cook, G. Fine, and J. House. Boston: Allyn and Bacon.

Moon, Melissa, John Sundt, Francis Cullen, and John Wright. 2000. "Is Child Saving Dead? Public Support for Rehabilitation." *Crime and Delinquency*. 46: 38–60.

Morrison, Brenda. 2001. "The School System: Developing its Capacity in the Regulation of a Civilized Society." In *Restorative Justice and Civil Society*, edited by J. Braithwaite and H. Strang. Cambridge: Cambridge University Press.

O'Brien, Sandra. 2000. *Restorative Juvenile Justice Policy Development and Implementation Assessment: A National Survey of States*. Ft. Lauderdale, FL: Florida Atlantic University, Balanced and Restorative Project.

O'Connell, T. 2008. "The Origins of Restorative Conferencing," *Journal for Peace Studies* 18(2): 87–94.

Pennell, Joan. 2006. "Restorative Practices and Child Welfare: Toward an Inclusive Civil Society." *Journal of Social Issues* 62(2) 2: 259–79.

Platt, A. (1969). *The Child Savers*. Chicago: University of Chicago Press.

Polk, K. (1987). "When Less Means More: An Analysis of Destructuring in Criminal Justice." *Crime and Delinquency*, 33: 358–78.

Pranis, K. (2004). Comment in presentation at Restorative Justice Conference, Florida Atlantic University, Fort Lauderdale, Florida, June.

Pranis, Kay, Barry Stuart, and Mark Wedge. 2006. *Peacemaking Circles: From Crime to Community*, St. Paul: Living Justice Press.

Pranis, Kay, and Mark Umbreit. 1992. *Public Opinion Research Challenges Perception of Wide Spread Public Demand for Harsher Punishment*. Minneapolis MN: Minnesota Citizens Council on Crime and Justice.

Putnam, Robert. 2000. *Bowling Alone: The Collapse and Revival of American Community*. New York: Simon and Shuster.

Rodriguez, N. 2004. "Restorative Justice, Communities and Delinquency: Whom Do We Reintegrate?" *Criminology and Public Policy* 4: 103–30.

Sampson, Robert, Steven Raudenbush, and Felton Earls. (1997). " Neighborhoods and violent crime: A multi-level study of collective efficacy." *Science Magazine*, 77, 918–24.

Schneider, A. 1986. "Restitution and Recidivism Rates of Juvenile Offenders: Results from Four Experimental Studies." *Criminology* 24: 533–52.

Schneider, A. 1990. *Deterrence and Juvenile Crime: Results from a National Policy Experiment.* New York: Springer-Verlag.

Schur, Edwin M. 1973. *Radical Non-intervention: Rethinking the Delinquency Problem.* Berkeley: University of California Press.

Schwartz, Ira, Steven Guo, and John Kerbs. 1991. *Public Attitudes toward Juvenile Crime and Juvenile Justice: Implications for Public Policy.* Ann Arbor, MI: Center for the Study of Youth Policy.

Scott, Michal. (2000). *Problem-Oriented Policing: Reflections on the First 20 years.* Washington, DC: U.S. Department of Justice, Office of Community Oriented Policing Services.

Sheldon, Randal. 2007. "Resurrecting Radical Nonintervention: Stop the War on Kids." In *Youth Violence and Delinquency: Monsters and Myths*, edited by M. McShane and F. P. Williams III. London: Praeger.

Sherman, Lawrence. 1993. "Defiance, Deterrence, and Irrelevance: A Theory of Criminal Sanction." *Journal of Research in Crime and Delinquency* 30: 445–73.

Sherman, Lawence, and Richard Berk. 1984. "The Specific Deterrence Effects of Arrest for Domestic Assault." *American Sociological Review* 49: 261–72.

Sherman, Lawrence W., and Heather Strang. 2007. *Restorative Justice: The Evidence.* London, UK: The Smith Institute.

Sherman, Lawrence. 2003. "Reason for Emotion: Reinventing Justice With Theories, Innovations, and Research: The American Society of Criminology Presidential Address." *Criminology* 41(1): 1–38.

Shiraldi, Vincent, and Mark Soler. 1998. "The Will of the People? The Public's Opinion of the Violent and Repeat Juvenile Offender Act of 1997." *Crime and Delinquency.* 44(4): 490–601.

Stinchcomb, Jeanne, Gordon Bazemore, and Nancy Riestenberg. 2006. "Beyond Zero Tolerance: Restoring Justice in Secondary Schools." *Youth Violence and Juvenile Justice* 4: 123–47.

Stuart, Barry. 1996. "Circle Sentencing: Turning Swords Into Plowshares," in *Restorative Justice: International Perspectives*, edited by B. Galoway and J. Hudson. Monsey, New York: Criminal Justice Press.

Sullivan, Dennis, and Larry Tift. 2001. *Restorative Justice: Healing the Foundation of Our Everyday Lives.* Monsey, New York: Willow Tree Press.

Tomkins, Sylvan S. 1962. *Affect, Imagery, Consciousness: Volume I, The Positive Affects.* New York: Springer.

Torbet, Patricia, Richard Gable, Hunter Hurst, Ian Montgomery, Laurence Szymanski, and Douglas Thomas. 1996. *State Responses to Serious and Violent Juvenile Crime.* Pittsburgh, PA: Office of Juvenile Justice and Delinquency Prevention Research Report, National Center for Juvenile Justice.

Tyler, Thomas R. 1990. *Why People Obey the Law.* New Haven, CT: Yale University Press.

Tyler, Thomas R. 2006. "Restorative Justice and Procedural Justice: Dealing with Rule Breaking." *Journal of Social Issues* 62(2): 307–26.

Uggen, C., and J. Janikula. (1999). "Volunteerism and arrest in the transition to adulthood." *Social Forces*, 78:331–62.

Umbreit, M. 1999. "Avoiding the Marginalization and McDonaldization of Victim Offender Mediation: A Case Study in Moving Toward the Mainstream." In *Restoring Juvenile Justice: Repairing the Harm of Youth Crime*, edited by G. Bazemore and L. Walgrave. Monsey, NY: Criminal Justice Press.

Umbreit, Mark, Betty Voss, Robert Coates, and Kenneth Brown. 2003. *Facing Violence: the Path of Restorative Dialogue*. Monsey, New York: Criminal Justice Press.

Van Ness, D., and K. H. Strong. 1997. *Restoring Justice*. Cincinnati OH: Anderson.

Van Ness, D., and K. H. Strong. (2001). *Restoring Justice* (2nd Edition), Cincinnati OH: Anderson.

Van Ness, D., and K. H. Strong. (2006). *Restoring Justice* (3rd Edition), Cincinnati OH: Anderson.

von Hirsch, A. (1993). *Censure and Sanctions*. Clarendon Press. Oxford.

Walgrave, Lode. (2004). "Restoration in Juvenile Justice," in M. Tonry and A. Doob (eds.), *Youth Crime and Juvenile Justice: Comparative and Cross-National Perspectives*. Crime and Justice: A Review of the Researh, Vol. 31. Chicago: Chicago University Press.

Walgrave, Lode, and Gordon Bazemore, (1999). "Reflections on the Future of Restorative Justice. In G. Bazemore and L. Walgrave (Eds.), *Restorative juvenile justice: Repairing the harm of youth crime* (359–99). Monsey, NY: Criminal Justice Press.

Weick, Kenneth E. 1995. *Sensemaking in Organizations*. Thousand Oaks, CA: Sage.

Weitekamp, Elmar G. 1999. "The History of Restorative Justice." In *Restorative Juvenile Justice: Repairing the Harm of Youth Crime*, edited by G. Bazemore and L. Walgrave. Monsey, NY: Criminal Justice Press.

Weitekamp, Elmar G. M., Steven Parmentier, K. Vanspauwen, M. Valinas, and R. Gerits. 2006. "How to Deal with Mass Victimization and Gross Human Rights Violations: A Restorative Approach." In *Large-Scale Victimization as a Potential Source of Terrorist Activities*, edited by Uwe Ewald and Ksenija Turkovic. Amsterdam: IOS Press.

Whitehead, John, and Steven Lab. 2009. *Juvenile Justice: An Introduction*. New York: LexisNexis.

Wilkinson, Reginald A. (2005). Engaging Communities: An Essential Ingredient to Offender Reentry. *Corrections Today*; *67 (2), 86–89.*

Zehr, Howard. 2000. "Journey to Belonging." Paper presented at the Fourth International Conference on Restorative Justice for Juveniles, Tubingen, Germany, September.

Zhang, L., and S. X. Zhang.(1995) "Reintegrative Shaming and Predatory delinquency." *Journal of Research in Crime and Delinquency* 41(4): 433–53.

CHAPTER 29

....

PROBATION AND OTHER NONINSTITUTIONAL TREATMENT

THE EVIDENCE IS IN

....

PETER W. GREENWOOD
AND SUSAN TURNER

I. Introduction

....

THERE are many reasons society should try to prevent juvenile offenders from reoffending and continuing as adult offenders. The most obvious reason is that delinquency puts a youth at risk for drug use and dependency, school dropout, incarceration, injury, early pregnancy, and adult criminality. Saving youths from further delinquency saves them from wasted lives (Farrington and Welsh 2007). But there are other reasons as well.

Most adult criminals began their so-called "criminal careers" as juveniles. A delinquency record is one of the strongest predictors of adult criminality. Preventing delinquency helps stop the onset of adult criminal careers and thus reduces the burden of crime on its victims and on society. Delinquents and adult offenders take a heavy toll, both financially and emotionally, on victims and on taxpayers, who must share the cost of arresting, prosecuting, incarcerating, and treating offenders. Corrections has been the fastest growing part of most state budgets over the past decade and now runs into the billions of dollars a year. Yet recent analyses have shown that investments in appropriate delinquency intervention programs can save taxpayers seven to ten dollars for every dollar invested, primarily in the form of reduced spending on prisons (Aos, Miller, and Drake 2006).

The prospect of reaping such savings, by preventing further delinquency, is not a new one. Achievement of these savings was one of the original missions of the Juvenile Court, but it is only recently that officials have begun to measure how well this mission is being fulfilled. During the past fifteen years, researchers have begun to clearly identify both the risk factors that promote delinquency and interventions that consistently reduce the likelihood that delinquency will reoccur. Some of the identified risk factors for delinquency are genetic or biological and cannot easily be changed (see Peskin et al., Chapter 4, "Personal Characteristics of Delinquents: Neurobiology, Genetic Predispositions, Individual Psychosocial Attributes," this volume). Others are dynamic—meaning they can be changed—and involve the quality of parenting, school participation, peer group associations, or skill deficits. Studies that monitor the social development of groups of at-risk youth beginning in infancy and early childhood are used to help us refine our understanding of how these risk factors develop and interact with each other over time (Lipsey and Derzon 1998).

Fairly strong evidence now demonstrates the effectiveness of three or four "proven" delinquency-intervention program models and another dozen or so generalized strategies (Elliot 1997). Somewhat weaker evidence supports the effectiveness of another dozen "promising" programs that still need further testing (Greenwood 2008). A number of public and private agencies have been implementing the proven programs for a number of years, some of which have been closely monitored by independent evaluators (Mihalick et al. 2002), and their experiences can benefit others.

In this chapter we focus on community-based programs for youths. We review the concept of evidence-based practice in juvenile justice, its benefits, and the challenges for adoption by agencies. We begin by reviewing traditional juvenile justice programming, or what is referred to in the experimental literature as "treatment as usual." We then review the methods currently accepted as the best way to identify the most effective programs. We follow with a comprehensive overview of community-based programs that work, with some information about programs that are proven failures. We conclude by describing how jurisdictions are implementing the best of these programs and overcoming the challenges they meet.

II. Treatment as Usual

Since the disposition of juvenile cases in most states is supposed to be tailored to the individual needs and circumstances of each juvenile, it should come as no surprise that a wide variety of programs have been developed to meet these needs. For those juveniles whose crimes or records are not very serious, and whose families are sufficiently supportive that the youths can continue to reside at home, there are a variety of programs such as informal or formal probation, electronic monitoring and intensive supervision, tracking and in-home supervision by private agencies, mentoring programs, after-school or all-day programs in which a youth reports to the program site for part of the day and then returns home. For those youths who must be placed out of their homes, but do not represent such a risk that they must be removed from the community, many jurisdictions provide or contract for a wide variety of group homes, foster care, and other treatment or community living situations. Placements in such facilities are typically in the range of six to twenty-four months, depending on the program and seriousness of the youth's offense. For those youths who represent a more serious risk to the community, or who cannot function appropriately in an open setting, most states provide a continuum of increasingly restrictive settings ranging from isolated wilderness camps and ranches to secure fenced and locked facilities, often referred to as "training schools."

The primary criticisms leveled against traditional training schools have been that they offered sterile and unimaginative programs, were inappropriate places in which to run rehabilitative programs, and fostered abuse and mistreatment of their charges. These concerns have led many states to begin shifting more of their youths to privately run, community-based programs; however the vast majority of youth in custody (69%) are still housed in large public facilities. Community programs appear to offer a wide array of settings and methods. Part of the reason may be that community-based programs are more likely to be run by private (usually nonprofit) providers, rather than the county or state. In addition to offering a greater variety of programming, privately run programs offer more treatment services compared to publicly run programs, and are less likely to be overcrowded (Greenwood 2006).

III. Determining What Works: Evolving Standards

For more than a century, efforts to reduce delinquency have been guided more by the prevailing theories about the causes of delinquent behavior than by whether the efforts achieved the desired effects. At various times, the primary causes of delinquency were thought to be the juvenile's home or neighborhood, or lack of socializing experiences, or lack of job opportunities, or the labeling effects of the juvenile justice system (Laub 2002). The intervention strategies promoted by these theories included removal of urban children to more rural settings, enrollment in residential training schools, placement in industrial schools, summer camps, and job programs, and diversion from the juvenile justice system. None turned out to be consistently helpful. A systematic review of rigorous evaluations of these strategies by a special panel of the National Research Council in 1993 concluded that none could be described as effective (Reiss and Roth 1993). These conclusions reaffirmed similar conclusions reached by Robert Martinson and his colleagues two decades previously (Lipton, Martinson, and Wilks 1975).

The "gold standard" for evaluations in the social sciences—experiments that compare the effects on youths who have been assigned randomly to alternative interventions—are seldom used in criminal justice settings (Shadish, Cook, and Campbell 2002). Although such rigorous designs, along with long-term follow-up, are required to assess accurately the lasting effect of an intervention, they are far too expensive for most local agencies or even most state governments to conduct. Such evaluations are thus fairly rare and not always applied to the most promising programs. Instead, researchers typically evaluate delinquency-intervention programs using a quasi-experimental design that compares outcomes for an experimental treatment group with outcomes for a nonrandom comparison group, which is claimed to be similar in characteristics to the experimental group, though it seldom is.

The second problem in identifying successful programs is a lack of consistency in how analysts review the research base, making it hard to compare programs. Some reviews simply summarize the information contained in selected studies of individual programs, grouping evaluations together to arrive at conclusions about particular strategies or approaches that they have defined. Such reviews are highly subjective, with no standard rules for choosing which evaluations to include or how their results are to be interpreted. More rigorous reviews use meta-analysis, a statistical method of combining results across studies, to develop specific estimates of effects for alternative intervention strategies. Finally some "rating or certification systems" use expert panels or some other screening process to assess the integrity of individual evaluations, as well as specific criteria to identify proven, promising, or exemplary programs. These reviews also differ from each other in the outcomes they emphasize (for example, delinquency measures, drug use, mental health, or school-related behaviors), their criteria for selection, and the rigor with which empirical evidence is screened and reviewed. Cost-effectiveness and cost-benefit studies make it possible to compare the efficiency of programs, allowing policy makers to compare the possible crime-reduction effects for a given level of funding.

IV. WHAT WORKS AND WHAT DOESN'T

For anyone in a position to decide which programs should be continued or enhanced, which should be scrapped, and which new programs should be adopted, the ultimate question is "what works" and "how well" does it work? The answers to these questions now come in three distinct categories: generic, brand name, and principles. The "generics" are generalized strategies that have been tried by various investigators in different settings. Counseling, behavior modification, and group therapy all fall into this category. The second category includes the "brand name" programs such as Functional Family Therapy and Multisystemic Therapy. These are programs that were developed by a single investigator or team over a number of years and have been proven through careful replications, often supported by millions of dollars in federal grants. The generic methods are identified by meta-analysis and represent the efforts of independent researchers, each testing particular versions of the method. The brand name programs have met the criteria established by various review groups for identifying proven programs. The third category of "what works" includes a number of principles that have been found to be true across a variety of strategies. Principles are not programs per se, but techniques or approaches that have been proven successful in reducing delinquency. For example, research has shown that focusing on the higher-risk offenders has the most impact on recidivism (Andrews and Bonta 1998, Latessa, Cullen, and Gendreau (2002) and increasing fidelity to exemplary models advances positive outcomes (Landenberger and Lipsey 2005).

A. Developing a Local List of What Works

There are so many lists of "what works" now in circulation that one cannot avoid a decision about which to use The most recent reviews, meta-analyses, certified lists, and cost-benefit analyses provide a variety of perspectives and a wealth of information regarding what does and does not work in reducing youth crime and violence. At the very top of the evidence-based practice pyramid is a small group of rigorously evaluated brand name programs that have consistently demonstrated significant positive effects and contain protocols to help others replicate their programs and achieve similar results. At the bottom are programs and strategies that have been evaluated but have proven to have no effects or adverse effects. In the middle are programs and strategies for which there is some scientific evidence to support effectiveness. There are three reliable sources of information regarding program effectiveness for community-based programs that can be combined to provide us with all the relevant information we need to make intelligent programming choices: (1) Blueprints for Prevention, (2) work published by Mark Lipsey, PhD, and (3) the Washington State Institute for Public Policy. These sources stand out because they employ a rigorous scientific standard of evaluation, are relatively comprehensive, and are periodically updated.

The Blueprints for Prevention, or Blueprints, list has been developed by a research team headed by Professor Delbert Elliott at the Center for the Study and Prevention of Violence at the University of Colorado (Elliot 1997). For Blueprints to certify a brand name program as *proven* ("model"), the program must demonstrate its effects on problem behaviors with a rigorous experimental design, show that its effects persist after youths leave the program, and be successfully replicated at least once. In order for a brand name program to be certified as *promising*, the program must demonstrate effects using a rigorous experimental design. The current Blueprints website (www.colorado.edu/cspv/blueprints/) lists eleven "model" programs and nineteen "promising" programs that were identified from a review of over eight hundred programs. These eleven proven programs include the Midwestern Prevention Project, Big Brothers Big Sisters of America, Functional Family Therapy, Life Skills Training, Multisystemic Therapy, Nurse-Family Partnership, Multidimensional Treatment Foster Care, Olweus Bullying Prevention Program, Promoting Alternative thinking Strategies, The Incredible Tears: Parent, Teacher, and Child Training Series, and Project Towards No Drug Abuse. Many of these programs target school-aged youths, before they are involved in the juvenile justice system.

Mark Lipsey, Director of the Peabody Research Institute at Vanderbilt University, conducted the first meta-analysis that focused specifically on juvenile justice (Lipsey 1992; Lipsey and Wilson 1998). In the most basic terms, a meta-analysis combines the results of independent studies with a shared research focus in order to analyze an overall effect, specifically called an *effect size*. Accordingly, Lipsey's analysis did not identify specific programs but did begin to identify specific strategies and methods that were more likely to be effective than others. Lipsey continued to expand and refine this work to include additional studies and many additional characteristics of each study (Lipsey 2003, 2006, 2009; Lipsey and Cullen 2007).

Based on his research, Lipsey found that effective programs and strategies were those implemented well and on high-risk offenders. He also found strategies with a therapeutic component, such as counseling and skill building, are more effective than those with a control component, such as surveillance and discipline (Lipsey 2009).

The Washington State Institute for Public Policy (WSIPP) uses the meta-analysis methodology to conduct evaluations of programs, but also considers the cost of such programs and strategies to taxpayers and crime victims and weighs these costs against possible benefits. Programs and strategies are not ranked, but effects on recidivism are measured and the number of evaluations is reported. Recidivism, cost to taxpayers and crime victims, and benefits are estimated using data specific to Washington State. In this chapter, all cost and benefit information refers to the analysis conducted by WSIPP for the State of Washington. Accordingly, the information should be considered an estimate for the potential cost and dollar benefits for other states.[1]

B. Rating Evidence-Based Practices

For this chapter, we reviewed the evidence provided by the Blueprints, Lipsey meta-analyses, and WSIPP cost analysis to place programs into one of five categories. Programs or strategies that can be found in these sources but not included in our analyses were omitted either because of outdated evaluations or because a program or strategy was not evaluated for crime or risk factor effects and outcomes. The programs and strategies were sorted by the strength of the evidence supporting their effectiveness and the degree to which the program or strategy has been replicated or could be replicated using the findings and conclusions of the above-referenced sources. The categories are described below:

PROVEN PROGRAMS are brand name programs that have been shown to reduce delinquency and recidivism, substance use, and/or antisocial behavior in at least two trials by using a strong research design.

PROVEN STRATEGIES are generic strategies that have been shown through rigorous meta-analysis to reduce recidivism.

PROVEN PRINCIPLES OF EFFECTIVENESS are generalized principles that appear to increase effectiveness across the spectrum of programs and strategies.

PROMISING PROGRAMS are brand name programs that have been shown to reduce delinquency and recidivism, substance use, and/or antisocial behavior by using a strong research design, but outcomes have not yet been replicated.

PROVEN INEFFECTIVE are those programs and strategies that have been shown not to reduce recidivism or substance use, and those that have an adverse outcome.

Table 29.1 presents the results of our analysis and is organized into the five categories described above: Within each category, programs and/or strategies are divided into three sections when applicable: delinquency and recidivism, substance use, and antisocial behavior. The categories of Promising Strategies and Proven Ineffective are not divided because they share the same outcome measure, namely, effect on recidivism (excluding DARE). For purposes of organization, the Proven Ineffective category is divided into programs and strategies. When effect on recidivism is the only outcome listed, programs and strategies were organized from highest reduction in recidivism to lowest within the respective category. Additionally, for each program or strategy the following is provided:

SOURCE OF RATING: Indicates which list(s) the program or strategy derives from: Blueprints, Washington State Institute for Public Policy (WSIPP), or Mark Lipsey. The program or strategy may be from multiple lists. In those cases, a brief summary of effects and outcomes from each source is listed.

DESCRIPTION: A brief description of the program or strategy is provided for quick reference. Each description includes the following elements: the intervention method, who implements the program or strategy, and where it is implemented.

OUTCOMES: Each program and strategy has at least one outcome listed. Generally, the outcome of interest is the effect (if any) on the rate of recidivism. This number is reported as an average percentage reduction in recidivism after a program or strategy is implemented. When recidivism outcomes were not available, other outcomes, such as effects on substance abuse and antisocial behavior, are listed. Due to limited space, in some cases only a few outcomes are listed. For additional outcomes that may not have been listed, please consult the source of rating as indicated.

COST-BENEFIT ANALYSIS: When calculated and evaluated by WSIPP, cost-benefit analysis is provided for each program or strategy. Benefits are calculated based on costs paid by taxpayers (for law enforcement, courts, juvenile detention services, etc.) and those suffered by crime victims (monetary and quality of life losses). Costs were estimated based on offender participation in a program or strategy versus not participating. For more information regarding WSIPP's cost-benefit analysis, please visit their website at www.wsipp.wa.gov.

Table 29.1. Evidence-Based Crime and Violence Intervention Practices

PROVEN PROGRAMS

| | Source of Rating | | | Description | Cost-Benefit Analysis (if available) | | | |
	Blueprints	Lipsey	WSIPP		Outcomes	Benefits	Costs	Benefit minus Cost
DELINQUENCY & RECIDIVISM								
Functional Family Therapy (FFT)	X		X	Intervention administered by therapist in-home focusing on family motivation, engagement, & problem-solving	18.1% reduction in recidivism	$52,156	$2,380	$49,776.00
Multidimensional Treatment Foster Care (MTFC)	X		X	Intervention administered by specially trained foster parents taking teen into their home; therapy for bio-parents	17.9% reduction in recidivism	$95,879	$6,926	$88,953.00
Aggression Replacement Training (ART)			X	Intervention administered by trained staff to Improve moral reasoning, aggression & anger management	8.3% reduction in recidivism	$23,933	$918	$23,015.00
Multisystemic Therapy (MST)	X		X	Intervention administered by therapist to family & provides assistance with other systems	7.7% reduction in recidivism	$22,058	$4,364	$17,694.00

PROVEN STRATEGIES

	Source of Rating				Cost-Benefit Analysis (if available)			
	Blueprints	Lipsey	WSIPP	Description	Outcomes	Benefits	Costs	Benefit minus Cost
DELINQUENCY & RECIDIVISM								
Cognitive Behavioral Therapy		X	X	Prevention or intervention using structured goal setting, planning, & practice	26% reduction in recidivism (Lipsey) 2.6% reduction in recidivism (WSIPP)			
Behavioral Programs		X	X	Prevention or intervention that awards selected behaviors	22% reduction in recidivism			
Group Counseling		X		Prevention or intervention using group counseling led by a therapist	22% reduction in recidivism			
High School Graduation			X	Prevention or intervention: graduation from high school	21.1% reduction in recidivism			
Mentoring		X		Prevention or intervention: using mentoring by volunteer or paraprofessional	21% reduction in recidivism			
Case Management		X		Prevention or intervention using case manager or case team to develop service plan & arranges services for juvenile	20% reduction in recidivism			
Counseling/Psychotherapy		X	X	Prevention or intervention: individual counseling	16.6% reduction in recidivism (WSIPP) 5% reduction in recidivism (Lipsey)			
Mixed Counseling		X		Prevention or intervention: combination of individual, group, and/or family	16% reduction in recidivism			

(continued)

Table 29.1. (continued)

| | Source of Rating | | | | Cost-Benefit Analysis (if available) | | | |
	Blueprints	Lipsey	WSIPP	Description	Outcomes	Benefits	Costs	Benefit minus Cost
Teen Court			X	Intervention for juvenile offenders in which they are sentenced by their peers	14% reduction in recidivism	$16,908	$937	$15,971.00
Family Counseling		X	X	Prevention or intervention: family counseling	13% reduction in recidivism			
Social Skills Training		X		Prevention or intervention: teaching social skills	13% reduction in recidivism			
Challenge Programs		X		Prevention or intervention: provide opportunities for experimental learning by mastering tasks	12% reduction in recidivism			
Family Crisis Counseling		X		Prevention or intervention: short-term family crisis counseling	12% reduction in recidivism			
Mediation		X		Intervention where offender apologizes to victim & meets under supervision	12% reduction in recidivism			
Multiple Coordinated Services		X		Intervention providing a package of multiple services to juveniles	12% reduction in recidivism			
Skill Building Programs		X		Prevention or intervention aimed at developing skills to control behavior and prosocial functions	12% reduction in recidivism			
Restorative Justice for Low-Risk Offenders		X	X	Intervention using victim-offender conferences & restitution	10% reduction in recidivism (Lipsey) 8% reduction in recidivism (WSIPP)	$9,609	$907	$8,702.00

| | Source of Rating | | | | Cost-Benefit Analysis (if available) | | | Benefit |
	Blueprints	Lipsey	WSIPP	Description	Outcomes	Benefits	Costs	minus Cost
Academic Training		X		Prevention or intervention: tutoring, GED programs, etc.	10% reduction in recidivism			
Service Broker		X		Intervention using referrals for juvenile services with minimal role afterward	10% reduction in recidivism			
Sex Offender Treatment			X	Intervention using a cognitive-behavioral approach specifically for juvenile sex offenders	9.7% reduction in recidivism	$57,504	$33,842	$23,662.00
Restitution		X		Intervention: offender provides financial compensation to victim and/or community service	9% reduction in recidivism			
Mixed Counseling with Referral		X		Intervention: supplementary referrals for other services	8% reduction in recidivism			
Job-Related Interventions		X		Prevention or intervention: vocational counseling, job placement, training	6% reduction in recidivism			
Peer Counseling		X		Prevention or intervention: peer group plays therapeutic role	4% reduction in recidivism			
Diversion with Services			X	Intervention using citizen accountability boards & counseling compared to court supervision	3.1% reduction in recidivism			

(continued)

Table 29.1. (continued)

PROMISING PROGRAMS

| | Source of Rating | | | | | Cost-Benefit Analysis (if available) | | |
	Blueprints	Lipsey	WSIPP	Description	Outcomes	Benefits	Costs	Benefit minus Cost
DELINQUENCY & RECIDIVISM								
Seattle Social Development Project	X			Intervention administered by parents & teachers using social control & social learning	15.7% reduction in recidivism			
Family Integrated Transitions (FIT)			X	Intervention for the reentry of juveniles with mental illness & substance abuse	10.2% reduction in recidivism	$54,045	$9,970	$44,753.00
TeamChild			X	Intervention: attorneys advocate on behalf of juvenile for education, treatment, housing	9.7% reduction in recidivism			
SUBSTANCE USE								
Project Northland	X			Intervention implemented through-out the community to reduce substance abuse	Decreased tendencies to use alcohol; less alcohol, cigarette, and marijuana use			
ANTISOCIAL BEHAVIOR								
Brief Strategic Family Therapy (BSFT)	X			Intervention administered by a therapist improving family interactions	Significant reductions in Conduct Disorder and Socialized Aggression			

PROVEN INEFFECTIVE

	Source of Rating				Cost–Benefit Analysis (if available)			
	Blueprints	Lipsey	WSIPP	Description	Outcomes	Benefits	Costs	Benefit minus Cost
PROGRAMS								
Guided Group Interaction			X	Intervention using a peer group to promote prosocial & restructure peer interaction	No reduction in recidivism			
STRATEGIES								
Boot Camps			X	Intervention emphasizing drill, teamwork, etc.	No reduction in recidivism			
Court Supervision			X	Intervention using court supervision compared to releasing juvenile without services	No reduction in recidivism			
Intensive Probation			X	Intervention using more than usual contact compared to incarceration	No reduction in recidivism			
Intensive Probation Supervision			X	Intervention using more than the usual contacts	No reduction in recidivism	$0	$1,650	−$1,650.00

(continued)

Table 29.1. (continued)

| | Source of Rating | | | | Cost-Benefit Analysis (if available) | | | |
	Blueprints	Lipsey	WSIPP	Description	Outcomes	Benefits	Costs	Benefit minus Cost
Intensive Parole Supervision			X	Intervention using more than the usual contacts	No reduction in recidivism	$0	$6,670	–$6,670.00
Regular Surveillance-Oriented Parole			X	Intervention involving post-release monitoring	No reduction in recidivism	$0	$1,237	–$1,237.00
Deterrence		X		Intervention dramatizing the negative consequences of behavior	2% increase in recidivism			
Scared Straight			X	Intervention using prison inmates to confront first-time offenders about the downside of criminal life	6.1% increase in recidivism	–$17,410	$60	–$17,470.00
Discipline		X		Intervention teaching discipline to succeed & avoid reoffending	8% increase in recidivism			

PRINCIPLES OF IMPLEMENTATION

	Source of Rating				Cost-Benefit Analysis (if available)			
	Blueprints	Lipsey	WSIPP	Description	Outcomes	Benefits	Costs	Benefit minus Cost
FIDELITY: Integrity of Treatment Implementation	X	X	X	Having procedure to ensure staff stick to protocol improves outcomes				
Focus on High-Risk Youth		X		More needs, more room for improvement, higher costs of failure				
Longer Duration of Treatment		X		Dosage matters: too few sessions can be ineffective				
Tracking Outcomes	X	X	X	Track outcomes, particularly when implementing strategies				

Source: Adapted from Peter W. Greenwood. 2010. *Preventing and Reducing Youth Crime and Violence: Using Evidence-Based Practices.* Sacramento, CA: Governor's Office of Gang and Youth Violence Policy.

V. What Works

We begin this review with the most proven programs, followed by proven strategies, then promising programs, then principles of effectiveness, and finally end with programs and strategies that have been shown not to work. Programs/strategies in the table represent a wide range of settings and target youth. Delinquency-intervention programs in community settings can be created for various purposes such as diverting youths out of the juvenile justice system, serving youths placed on informal or formal probation, or serving youths on parole who are returning to the community after a residential placement. Settings can range from individual homes, to schools, to teen centers, to parks, to the special facilities of private providers. They can involve anything from a one-hour monthly meeting to intensive family therapy and services.

The most successful programs are those that emphasize family interactions, probably because they focus on providing skills to the adults who are in the best position to supervise and train the child (Greenwood 2004). For example, for youths on probation, two family-based programs designated as proven by Blueprints and the Surgeon General (U.S. Department of Health and Human Services 2001) are Functional Family Therapy and Multisystemic Therapy. Functional Family Therapy (FFT) targets youths aged 11 to 18 facing problems with delinquency, substance abuse, or violence. The program focuses on altering interactions between family members and seeks to improve the functioning of the family unit by increasing family problem-solving skills, enhancing emotional connections, and strengthening parents' ability to provide appropriate structure, guidance, and limits for their children (Alexander, Pugh, and Parsons 1998). It is a relatively short-term program (twelve to sixteen sessions over three to four months) that is delivered by specially trained therapists, usually in the home setting. Each team of four to eight therapists works under the direct supervision and monitoring of several more experienced therapist and trainers. The program is well documented and readily transportable.

Multisystemic Therapy (MST), also a family-based program, is designed to help parents deal effectively with their youth's behavior problems, including engaging with deviant peers and poor school performance. To accomplish family empowerment, MST also addresses barriers to effective parenting and helps family members build an indigenous social support network. To increase family collaboration and generalize treatment, MST is typically provided in the home, school, and other community locations. Master's level counselors provide fifty hours of face-to-face contact over four months (Henngeler 1998). MST works with an individual family for as long a period as FFT does, but it is more intensive and more expensive. In addition to working with parents, MST will locate and attempt to involve other family members, teachers, school administrators, and other adults in supervising the youths.

For youths who have traditionally been placed in group homes—homes that are usually licensed to care for six or more youths who need to be removed from their home for an extended period, but do not pose a serious risk to themselves or others—the preferred alternative is Multidimensional Treatment Foster Care (MTFC). In MTFC, community families are recruited and trained to take one youth at a time into their homes. MTFC parents are paid a much higher rate than regular foster parents, but have additional responsibilities. One parent, for example, must be at home whenever the child is. Parent training emphasizes behavior management methods to provide youths with a structure and therapeutic living environment. After completing a preservice training, MTFC parents attend a weekly group meeting run by a case manager for ongoing supervision. Supervision and support are also provided to MTFC parents during daily telephone calls. Family therapy is also provided for biological families. Random assignment evaluations find that arrest rates fall more among participants in the MFTC model than among youths in traditional group homes (Chamberlain 1998). Although it costs approximately $7,000 more per youth to support MFTC than a group home, the Washington State Institute for Public Policy estimates that MFTC produces $26,300 in criminal justice system savings and $69,519 in benefits to potential crime victims.

Aggression Replacement Therapy (ART) is a special form of cognitive behavioral therapy that can be offered in classroom or other group settings. There are three components to the program. The first is "anger control," which teaches participants what triggers their anger and how to control their reactions. The second is "behavioral skills," which teach a series of prosocial skills through modeling, role playing, and performance feedback. The third is "moral reasoning," in which participants work through cognitive conflict in dilemma discussion groups (Glick 1996). Several studies have shown ART reduces recidivism. In Washington State, moderate- to high-risk adjudicated youths were randomly assigned to ART of standard juvenile court services. The recidivism rate for ART youths at eighteen months was reduced 16% compared with those who received standard court services (Barnoski 2004).

Effective intervention strategies that can be used in the community include: Cognitive Behavioral Therapy (CBT); behavioral programs; group counseling; assisting with high school graduation; mentoring; case management; individual counseling; mixed counseling; teen court; family counseling; social skills training; challenge programs; family crisis counseling; mediation; multiple coordinated services; skill building programs; restorative justice; academic training; service brokers; sex offender treatment; restitution; mixed counseling; job-related interventions; peer counseling; and diversion with services.

The general principles that appear to apply to all forms of effective intervention include:

- Focusing on the fidelity or integrity with which the program is delivered.
- Focusing resources on higher-risk youth.
- Ensuring an adequate amount of training or services.
- Allowing for a program to mature for one to two years in order to achieve high fidelity.

- Preparing and assisting community leaders in selecting and implementing appropriate programs.

Contrasted with effective programs that have a therapeutic or social-skill-building component, those that rely on surveillance, punishment, or scare tactics generally are not effective. The last category of ineffective programs includes intensive supervision, surveillance, extra services, and early release and deterrence approaches such as Scared Straight.

VI. Implementing Best Practices

With more than ten years of solid evidence now available regarding what does and does not work in reducing recidivism, jurisdictions should be adopting an evidence-based approach to implementing new programs. Taking this approach will prevent wasted lives, save taxpayer dollars, and protect communities from unnecessary crime.

Cost-benefits studies conducted by the Washington State Institute for Public Policy (WSIPP), summarized in the far right-hand column of Table 29.1, indicate that many evidence-based programs can produce savings on the order of five to ten times their cost. When confronted with a projected requirement to build two additional prisons, the Washington State legislature asked WSIPP to estimate how a substantial increase in spending on evidence-based programs would affect projected prison bed requirements. The analysis, published in 2006, showed that doubling current investments in high-quality programs could eliminate the need for additional prison capacity (Aos, Miller, and Drake 2006). In addition to early prevention and adult corrections programs, the WSIPP analysis recommended expansion of FFT, ART, Family Integrated Transition (FIT), and Restorative Justice for juvenile offenders (see Chapter 29 by Bazemore, this volume).

A. Intervention and Impediments to Implementation

Before a jurisdiction can begin to identify successful programs, it should conduct a needs assessment to determine what programs are currently available to serve the various populations with which the Juvenile Court must deal. If there are any high-risk youths not being served by the proven programs or strategies listed in Table 29.1, or if the programs serving such youths are not routinely audited for their fidelity, there is a clear service gap that needs to be filled.

After completing the service needs assessment, a jurisdiction can follow one of two basic paths to identify successful programs. It can follow the Blueprints and WSIPP recommendations and replace existing programs with the models these agencies have identified as proven. Or it can use results of Lipsey's and WSIPP's meta-analyses as a guide to improve existing programs. The steps involved and financing required for these two approaches are quite different, with the Blueprints approach being the costlier and more intense of the two.

If a jurisdiction opts to implement the Blueprints approach to fill service gaps, it should begin by selecting the program model that best fits both the clients to be served and the capabilities of the agency and staff that will provide the service. In addition to carefully reviewing the Blueprints publication describing the model, the jurisdiction may need to speak with the model's developer and other agencies that have adopted it before making a final choice.

The second step in the Blueprints approach is to arrange for training. Most developers of Blueprints model programs have established organizations to provide training, technical assistance, oversight, and certification to sites desiring to adopt their model. Most require applicants to meet a number of qualifying conditions before being considered for implementation. Initial training fees can range from $20,000 to more than $50,000, and annual licensing fees can cost more than $100,000. Some developers offer training on a regular schedule in one or two locations. Others will send their trainers to the applicant's site if a sufficient number of staff needs to be trained. The waiting period for training may be as long as six to nine months.

Once training has been scheduled, the third step is to designate or hire appropriate staff. Many agencies make the mistake of selecting and training staff who are not comfortable with the requirements of the program and do not last long in the job. Some programs require only one type of staff, such as a family therapist, while others require several different types, such as a case manager, skills trainer, and family therapist. The fourth step is to "sell" the program to potential customers and agency personnel. Without a strong champion within the host agency, a demanding new program has little chance of ever getting off the ground. The fifth step is to arrange for ongoing monitoring and feedback, preferably from the developer, by having weekly telephone conferences to discuss cases or by reviewing videotapes of project staff in action. The final step, implementing a quality assurance mechanism, usually involves questionnaires or observational rating sheets to assess the fidelity of the program to the original model.

If a jurisdiction opts for the meta-analytic (or Lipsey) approach to improve the effectiveness of its existing programs, its first step should be to identify the programs most in need of improvement based on the risk level of the youths served and the quality of the current programming. . The second is to identify the key elements of each program and compare them with the "best practice" standards identified by meta-analysis and shown in Table 29.1. If the program does not include any of the proven strategies or follow the principles listed in Table 29.1, then some of those strategies and principles must be added to the program for it to be considered evidence-based.

For instance, a community residential program or group home containing no evidence-based elements can be made more effective by adding cognitive-behavioral therapy or aggression replacement training. Likewise, a community supervision program with no evidence-based elements can be made more effective by adding a family therapy or parent training component. Mark Lipsey and several colleagues have used this approach to improve the effectiveness of locally developed programs in North Carolina and Arizona (Howell and Lipsey 2004).

After selecting an evidence-based program, an agency should adopt and implement a validated risk assessment instrument that can help provide a basis for assigning youths to specific programs—for comparing the effectiveness of alternative programs in treating similar youth, and for measuring the progress of individual youth. These instruments are readily available from a number of vendors, some of which offer training in using the instrument as well as in online data entry and analysis.

The next step in developing an evidence-based practice is to develop a way to assign youths to the most appropriate program, taking into account all of the relative costs and differences in effectiveness of each program. Whenever uncertainty exists about the programs to which particular types of youth should be assigned, an evaluation should be conducted to determine which of the competing alternatives is best.

Finally, once programs have been implemented, they must be monitored to ensure that they follow the program model as intended. Vendors of many proven programs have developed their own fidelity measurement instruments. Locally developed programs will require local development of such instruments.

As an example, let's suppose the Juvenile Probation Department of a medium-sized jurisdiction has decided to undertake a review of its programs. As a first step, it directs its Research Unit to conduct an analysis of the various types of programming provided to all of the youths it serves, broken down into three age groups (12 and under, 13 to 15, and 16 to 17) and three levels of risk, with cut points chosen to identify three risk levels representing approximately one-third of the population. As part of conducting this exercise, they learn, as would many other Probation Departments, that they do not have very good records on program participation and attendance levels. After much discussion, the Department decides that the most underserved youths are the more serious 13- to 15-year-olds, who now are sentenced primarily to monitoring, community service, and restitution. It is obvious that some type of intervention that could improve the capabilities of parents to monitor and discipline these youths would be helpful.

The options from Table 29.1 for filling this service gap would appear to be FFT, MST, or some generic family therapy. It is easiest to learn more about the two Blueprint programs, FFT and MST: they have websites, and a booklet about each program was published by Blueprints in 1998. FFT and MST both require some minimal number of therapists (four to six) and therapist caseloads in order to implement their coaching style of supervision. Other types of family therapy or parent training may work with smaller numbers, but then their integrity is harder to ensure. If staff are available, the best option for this department's current capabilities and budget would seem to be FFT, especially after they learn that they can bill the costs for FFT therapists to their state Medicaid system.

VII. Challenges and Obstacles to Implementing Evidence-Based Practice

Despite more than ten years of research on the nature and benefits of evidence-based programs, such programming is the exception rather than the rule. Only about 5% of youths who should be eligible for evidence-based programs participate in one (Henggeler 1998).

One reason for the slow progress is the general lack of accountability for performance within the juvenile justice system, or even an ability to measure outcomes. Only rarely does a jurisdiction take delinquency intervention seriously enough to measure the outcome of its efforts. Rather, it tends to evaluate agencies on how well they meet standards for protecting the health and safety of their charges and preventing runaways or incidents requiring restraints. Without the availability of such data as re-arrests or high school graduation rates, there is little pressure on agency officials to improve their performance.

A second challenge is a lack of funding. Implementing evidence-based programs, especially the Blueprint models, is expensive. Training a single team of therapists and their supervisor can cost more than $25,000. The agency may have to hire new staff who meet higher credentialing standards before start-up, without any revenue to cover their costs. State and local agencies have a hard time finding that kind of funding even in good economic times. Today it is difficult indeed. Even after youths start being referred to the program, it may still take time for the flow of cases to fully occupy all the staff charged to the program.

To fund start-up activities, some states have set up grant mechanisms for which local communities compete. Some jurisdictions seek grants from state or federal agencies. Even after an evidence-based program is implemented, it may be hard to find funds to continue its operation. Most of the savings from effective programs accrue to the state in the form of lower corrections costs. If some of these anticipated savings are not passed down to the local entities that must fund the programs, they may have trouble competing for scarce local funding against better-established programs. Some sites have solved this problem by working with state licensing officials to ensure adequate funding and reimbursement rates from Medicaid, Mental Health, or other federally subsidized funding streams.

Another big problem is resistance from staff. It is one thing to sell the director of an agency on the value of evidence-based programs. It is quite another to sell the staff who must adopt the new behaviors, because they have spent their whole career developing their own intuitive approaches. When they begin the training, they are reluctant to admit that someone at some distant university has come up with a better approach than they have. As in all cognitive-behavioral therapy, there is a certain amount of cognitive dissonance when they start applying the new methods. It just does not feel right. Some staff never overcome this initial resistance and must be shifted to other programs.

A different question is whether an agency has the competence or capacity to take on a Blueprints program. Some of these programs are very demanding in terms of staff qualifications, supervision, information systems, and quality assurance. Often program developers find that an applicant agency needs a year or two to develop the capacity to even begin the first steps of implementing their model.

VIII. Conclusions

Over the past decade, researchers from a variety of disciplines have identified or developed an array of intervention strategies and specific program models demonstrated to be effective in reducing delinquency and promoting more prosocial development. They have developed a variety of training methods and other technical assistance to help others replicate these successful methods. They have accumulated evidence that many of these programs are cost-effective, returning more than five times their cost in future taxpayer savings. Evidence also confirms that the general public overwhelmingly prefers treatment and rehabilitation over confinement and punishment for juvenile offenders. Still, only about 5% of the youths who could benefit from these improved programs now have the opportunity to do so. Juvenile justice options in many communities remain mired in the same old tired options of custodial care and community supervision.

In the long run, the authority of science may win out and the necessary changes will occur. But the authority of science is undermined on a daily basis by those who refuse to distinguish the difference between fact and opinion. Every year of delay in implementing evidence-based reforms consigns another cohort of juvenile offenders to a recidivism rate that is 50% higher than necessary.

Practitioners who are going to work with juvenile offenders and at-risk youth will have to be trained and monitored to ensure that they are delivering services in the prescribed and most appropriate manner. Achieving the consistency and fidelity that effective programs appear to require will necessitate new ways of supervising and managing those who have direct contact with youths and their families. Shifting from a management focus on preventing abuse or infractions to one that empowers employees to provide effective services to their clients is going to be a major struggle.

Those who wish to develop or promote new methods of intervention will have to learn how to play by the new set of rules and protocols that have made possible by the programming advances of the past decade. Programs can no longer be promoted for wide-scale dissemination until they have been proven effective by a rigorous evaluation.

None of these challenges is impossible. Efforts to expand the use of Blueprints programs in Florida, Pennsylvania, and Washington have been under way for several years now, with considerable success. Both North Carolina and Arizona have undertaken efforts in collaboration with Mark Lipsey to evaluate all their programs (Howell and Lipsey 2004). Hundreds of communities have adopted and implemented proven program models and are reaping the benefits of reduced delinquency and lower system costs. The challenge now is to move beyond these still relatively few early adopters and push these reforms into the mainstream of juvenile justice.

NOTES

1. The data used for this project can be found in the article by Drake, Aos, and Miller (2009) and can be downloaded from their website, www.wsipp.wa.gov.

REFERENCES

Alexander, James, Christie Pugh, and Bruce Parsons. 1998. "Functional Family Therapy." In *Blueprints for Violence Prevention*, edited by Delbert S. Elliott. Boulder, Colorado: Center for the Study and Prevention of Violence, Institute of Behavioral Science, University of Colorado.

Andrews, Don A., and James Bonta. 1998. *The Psychology of Criminal Conduct*, 2nd ed. Cincinnati: Anderson Publishing Co.

Aos, Steve, Marna Miller, and Elizabeth Drake. 2006. *Evidence-Based Public Policy Options to Reduce Future Prison Construction, Criminal Justice Costs, and Crime Rates.* Olympia, WA: Washington State Institute for Public Policy.

Barnoski, Robert. 2004. *Outcome Evaluation of Washington State's Research-Based Programs for Juvenile Offenders.* Olympia, WA: Washington State Institute for Public Policy.

Chamberlain, Patricia. 1998. "Multidimensional Treatment Foster Care." In *Blueprints for Violence Prevention*, edited by Delbert S. Elliott. Boulder, CO: Center for the Study and Prevention of Violence, Institute of Behavioral Science, University of Colorado.

Elliot, Delbert. 1997. *Blueprints for Violence Prevention.* 1997. Boulder, CO: Center for the Study and Prevention of Violence, University of Colorado.

Drake, Elizabeth, Steve Aos, and Marna Miller. (2009). *Evidence-Based Public Policy Options to Reduce Crime and Criminal Justice Costs: Implications in Washington State.* Olympia, WA: Washington State Institute for Public Policy.

Farrington, David P., and Brandon C. Welsh. 2007. *Saving Children from a Life of Crime: Early Risk Factors and Effective Interventions.* New York: Oxford University Press.

Glick, Barry. 1996. "Aggression Replacement Training in Children and Adolescents." *The Hatherleigh Guide to Child and Adolescent Therapy* 5: 191–226.

Greenwood, Peter W. 2004. "Special Issue on Youth Violence: Scientific Approaches on Youth Violence." *Cost-Effective Violence Prevention through Targeted Family Interventions, Annals of the New York Academy of Sciences* 1036(Dec.): 201–14.

Greenwood, Peter W. 2006. *Changing Lives: Delinquency Prevention as Crime Control Policy.* Chicago: University of Chicago Press.

Greenwood, Peter W. 2008. "Prevention and Intervention Programs for Juvenile Offenders: The Benefits of Evidence Based Practice." *Future of Children* 18(2)(Fall): 185–210.

Greenwood, Peter W. 2010. *Preventing and Reducing Youth Crime and Violence: Using Evidence-Based Practices*. Sacramento, CA: Governor's Office of Gang and Youth Violence Policy.

Henggeler, Scott W. 1998. "Multisystemic Therapy." In *Blueprints for Violence Prevention*, edited by Delbert S. Elliott. Boulder, CO: Center for the Study and Prevention of Violence, Institute of Behavioral Science, University of Colorado.

Howell, James C., and Mark W. Lipsey. 2004. "A Practical Approach to Evaluating and Improving Juvenile Justice Programs." *Juvenile and Family Court Journal* 55(1): 35–48.

Landenberger, Nana A., and Mark Lipsey. 2005. "The Positive Effects of Cognitive-Behavioral Programs for Offenders: A Meta-analysis of Factors Associated with Effective Treatment." *Journal of Experimental Criminology* 1: 451–76.

Latessa, Edward J., Frank Cullen, and Paul Gendreau. 2002. "Beyond Correctional Quackery—Professionalism and the Possibility of Effective Treatment." *Federal Probation* 66(2): 43–49.

Laub, John. 2002. "A Century of Delinquency Research and Delinquency Theory." In *A Century of Juvenile Justice*, edited by Margaret K. Rosenbaum, Franklin E. Zimring, and David S. Tanenhaus. Chicago: University of Chicago Press.

Lipsey, Mark W. 1992. "Juvenile Delinquency in Treatment: A Meta-analytic Inquiry into the Variability of Effects." In *Meta-Analysis for Explanation: A Casebook*, edited by Thomas D. Cook, Harris Cooper, David S. Cordray, Heidi Hartmann, Larry V. Hedges, Richard J. Light, Thomas A. Louis, and Frederick Mosteller. New York: Russell Sage Foundation.

Lipsey, Mark W. 2003. "Those Confounded Moderators in Meta-analysis: Good, Bad, and Ugly." *The Annals of the American Academy of Political and Social Science* 587: 69–81.

Lipsey, Mark W. 2006. "The Effects of Community-Based Group Treatment for Delinquency: A Meta-analytic Search for Cross-Study Generalizations," In *Deviant Peer Influences in Programs for Youth: Problems and Solutions*, edited by Kenneth A. Dodge, Thomas J. Dishion, and Jennifer E. Lansford. New York: Guilford Press.

Lipsey, Mark W. 2009. "The Primary Factors That Characterize Effective Interventions with Juvenile Offenders: A Meta-Analytic Overview." *Victims and Offenders* 4(2): 124–47.

Lipsey, Mark W., and Frank Cullen. 2007. "The Effectiveness of Correctional Rehabilitation: A Review of Systematic Reviews." *Annual Review of Law and Social Science* 3: 279–320.

Lipsey, Mark W., and James H. Derzon. 1998. "Predictors of Violent and Serious Delinquency in Adolescence and Early Adulthood." In *Serious and Violent Juvenile Offenders*, edited by Rolf Loeber and David P. Farrington, Thousand Oaks, CA: Sage.

Lipsey, Mark W., and David B. Wilson. 1998. "Effective Intervention for Serious Juvenile Offenders: A Synthesis of Research." In *Serious and Violent Juvenile Offenders: Risk factors and Successful Interventions*, edited by Ralph Loeber and David P. Farrington. Thousand Oaks, CA: Sage.

Lipton, Douglas, Robert Martinson, and Judith Wilks. 1975. *The Effectiveness of Correctional Treatment: A Survey of Treatment valuation Studies*. New York: Praeger Press.

Mihalick, Sharon, Abigail Fagan, Katherine Irwin, Diane Ballard, and Delbert Elliot. 2002. "Factors for Implementation Success." In *Blueprints for Violence Prevention*. Boulder, Colorado: Center for the Study and Prevention of Violence, Institute of Behavioral Science, University of Colorado.

Reiss, Albert J., and Jeffrey A. Roth. 1993. *Understanding and Preventing Violence*. Washington: National Academy Press.

Shadish, William R., Tomas D. Cook, and Donald T. Campbell. 2002. *Experimental and Quasi-Experimental Designs for Generalized Causal Inference*. Boston: Houghton-Mifflin Co.

U.S. Department of Health and Human Services. 2001. *Youth Violence: A Report of the Surgeon General*. Rockville, Maryland: U.S. Department of Health and Human Services.

CHAPTER 30

JUVENILE CORRECTIONS

AN OVERVIEW

BARRY KRISBERG

IN the summer of 2009, the California Division of Juvenile Justice, formerly known as the California Youth Authority (CYA), announced the closure of the Heman G. Stark Youth Correctional Facility (HGSYCF), which held over four hundred young people and was one of the most violence-prone juvenile institutions in America. When it first opened in the 1960s, the HGSYCF was known as the Youth Training School and was celebrated as a new model for treating troubled adolescents. During its years of operation, HGSYCF held as many as one thousand residents. It was regularly plagued with riots, high levels of violence, and documented abusive practices against youths by its staff (Office of Inspector General 2000).

The closure of HGFYC followed decisions by the State of California in 2004 to close five youth correctional facilities. These were some of the largest juvenile correctional facilities in the United States. California also closed a number of Youth Conservation Camps that had previously held juvenile offenders. The state youth corrections system had shrunk dramatically; from 1997 to 2007, the population in state juvenile facilities dropped from almost 10,000 residents to just 1,600. For years, the CYA had been regarded as the "gold standard" in juvenile corrections (Lemert 1972), and now state officials were moving aggressively to shut it down. Indeed, a nonpartisan task force known as the Little Hoover Commission actually proposed the closure of the Division of Juvenile Justice.

California was not alone in the movement to reduce the number of youths in state juvenile correctional facilities. Texas, New York, and Michigan all experienced substantial declines in their incarcerated youth populations. Indeed, data from the federal Office of Juvenile Justice and Delinquency Prevention showed a 14 percent decline in youth in custody nationwide from 1997 to 2006.

This chapter will review the forces that led to the decline in the population of juvenile correctional institutions and will begin with the history of the first specialized corrections facilities for young people. It will consider how this enterprise of juvenile justice started and how well it has met its mission and goals. The evolution of juvenile corrections has been an ongoing struggle between advocates for secure congregate care and the reformers who pushed for more community-based solutions for juvenile offenders. A sampling of major scandals and abusive practices has dominated juvenile corrections throughout its history and has become especially pronounced in recent years. These trends contributed to the closures of many juvenile facilities across the nation.

Also discussed are basic data on contemporary juvenile corrections such as who is confined in these facilities and programs and the effectiveness of juvenile corrections, including "boot camps," in reducing recidivism. The chapter concludes with some observations about policy directions for the future.

I. The History and Evolution of Juvenile Corrections

In the early part of the nineteenth century, a group of religious leaders created the first specialized correctional facility for juveniles—the New York House of Refuge (Pickett 1969; Mennel 1973). This group, the Society for the Prevention of Juvenile Delinquency, expressed alarm about the growing number of young people living on the streets of New York with little or no parental supervision. At that time, arrested youths were held in the same jails or workhouses as adults. The Society for the Prevention of Juvenile Delinquency argued that the exposure of wayward youths to criminal adults would only make the children more criminal. Further, these advocates warned that some juries would acquit serious juvenile offenders rather than see them placed in adult jails.

Members of the Society for the Prevention of Juvenile Delinquency were "conservative reformers" in that they were primarily worried that the spread of urban poverty and the growing wave of immigrants from Europe (especially new arrivals from Ireland) were leading to a breakdown in the social order and perhaps a lower class revolt against established moral and political authority. These reformers cared less about the well-being of poor children than about their own power and privileges (Krisberg 2005). The goal was to create institutions to control the behavior of poor children and their families. In short order, the New York Refuge idea spread to other eastern cities. The early decades of the nineteenth century witnessed a migration of people from rural areas into the cities. There was also a surge of immigration into the United States from countries in Northern Europe, especially England, Ireland, and Italy. The new Americans were escaping severe poverty and starvation in Europe and brought few financial resources with them. Further, the early nine-teenth century witnessed the beginning of factory and industrial production, which exploited the new immigrants from both the rural areas and overseas. Wages for urban workers remained very low, and living conditions among the working poor were horrid. There was a growing sense among better-off Americans that "informal social controls" were weakening, and more formal tools of maintaining social order were needed (Rothman 1971; Friedman 1993).

In most eastern cities, there were Houses of Refuge that operated in a similar fashion to the first one that was established in New York City. The New York House of Refuge would send out agents to pick up children on the streets and bring them to the Refuge. There was no judicial process to govern this practice. Children who were impoverished, neglected, or abused by their guardians, or who had committed a vari-ety of delinquent acts were rounded up. Occasionally, the parents of these children would go to court arguing that they were being unfairly deprived of their property, since children were regarded as similar to chattel slaves. The courts generally sup-ported the Houses of Refuge, arguing that rescuing children from harmful or inatten-tive parents justified a very lax legal process (*Ex Parte* Crouse, 4 Whart. 9 [Pa. 1838]). The court held that parents possessed a natural right but not an inalienable right to control of their children. This jurisprudence was heavily influenced by the antago-nism toward Irish parents who were regarded by more established Americans as cor-rupt and ineffectual. The courts generally held that the traditional conceptions of criminal law did not apply to the Refuge. The overriding values involved protecting the social order from the potential threat posed by a growing army of impoverished youths. The Houses of Refuge were racially segregated, and members of the African American religious community opened their own institutions for wayward youths of color. Young women were thought to be promiscuous and incapable of reformation. There were few options for girls other than the adult facilities.

The Houses of Refuge relied on a regimen of religious indoctrination, forced labor, and unyielding discipline. The Refuge was both a school and a prison (Pickett 1969). The managers of the Refuge believed that unwavering routines and harsh punishment for misconduct were the keys to controlling these dangerous youths. Physical exercise was also part of the Refuge routine, but work was the central activ-ity of the Refuge. The labor of inmates was sold to private contractors to subsidize the budget of the Refuge. There were frequent allegations that the young inmates were abused by the private contractors and that the managers of the Houses of Refuge received bribes to steer business to certain entrepreneurs. Upon release, the Refuge inmates were placed in apprenticeships, most often on the ships of the emerging merchant marine.

Like subsequent juvenile correctional facilities, the Houses of Refuge were beset with many problems. Mennel (1973) estimated that about 40% of the inmates ran away. Refuge residents regularly rioted and set fires. Violence in these facilities was commonplace.

Political opposition to them was also building. The Catholic Church accused the Refuges of coercing their children into converting to Protestantism. Early labor unions and local businesses complained that the system of contracted labor created unfair wage competition. The local press often reported about deplorable working conditions for the youths and corruption on the part of the Refuge managers. The growing concerns expressed about the Houses of Refuge led to the government taking over the operation of these new juvenile correctional facilities from the private charitable and religious organizations that had started them. State oversight bodies developed, which in turn led to the creation of the first statewide juvenile correctional facility in 1847, the Thomas Lyman School in Massachusetts.

The first half of the nineteenth century also witnessed the rise of another set of juvenile corrections reformers that were harshly critical of the new large-scale congregate facilities for troubled youths. In New York City, Charles Loring Brace founded the Children's Aid Society and argued that the Houses of Refuge were harmful to young people and the social order. Brace advocated for a very different approach in which the young urban dispossessed would be placed with farm families in the Midwest (Brace 1872). Brace held a romantic notion of how rural farm families could provide the right rehabilitative environment for the street urchins of New York.

The followers of Brace, who came to be known as the "child savers," were in reality no more sympathetic to the plight of the urban poor than the founders of the Society for the Prevention of Juvenile Delinquency (Platt 1968; Bremner et al. 1970). Both groups primarily feared social revolts and the undermining of American democracy. The difference between these two groups was a debate about the most effective methods to control the "dangerous classes." Like the managers of the Refuge, the agents of the Children's Aid Society would round up youths on the streets without due process of law or the protection of legal rights. Large numbers of urban youths were sent on trains to the Midwest where they were placed in apprenticeships for terms of at least seven years. The child savers made minimal attempts to keep siblings together. There are tragic stories of brothers and sisters who were "placed out" and later spent many years trying to locate family members (Holt 1992; O'Connor 2001).

Proponents of the Refuges and the Children's Aid Society debated each other for several years. The managers of the large-scale congregate institutions for delinquents tried to respond to their critics by relocating the institutions in rural areas, by naming the custody staff as "house parents," and by calling the residential units "cottages." Despite these superficial changes, the basic approach of the House of Refuge continued to be religious study, harsh discipline, basic education, and forced labor as the core program components. At the Elmira Reformatory in the late 1890s, noted corrections expert Zebulon Brockway added military drill and physical exertion to the model.

The pattern of abuse also continued. For example, at the Arthur G. Dozier School for Boys—Florida's oldest training school—youths were housed behind razor wire fences. There were well-documented cases of young people being beaten by guards, hog-tied, or kept in extreme isolation and becoming psychotic as a result of these abuses. Hundreds of former inmates at Dozier in the 1950s and 1960s sued the state for their maltreatment. There are dozens of unmarked graves at Dozier and little information on how these youths died (Montgomery and Moore 2009). As we will see, many of these terrible practices continue today.

The landmark U.S. Supreme Court decision in *In re Gault* exerted a profound impact on the juvenile justice system and on juvenile corrections. Chief Justice Abe Fortas observed that the benign rhetoric of the juvenile court sometimes clashed with its reality. The Court wrote as follows:

> The boy is committed to an institution where he may be restrained of liberty for years.…His world becomes "a building with whitewashed walls, regimented routine and institutional hours." Instead of mother and father and sisters and brothers and friends and classmates, his world is populated by guards, custodians, state employees and "delinquents" confined with him for anything from waywardness to rape and homicide" (387 U.S. 1, 27 [1967]).

The *Gault* case decision established the basic procedural and due process rights that must be accorded to minors in the juvenile justice system. Eventually, the extension of these rights in several jurisdictions raised very serious concerns about the treatment of juveniles in youth correctional systems.

It was not until the 1970s that major lawsuits were filed, addressing the child abuse and neglect taking place in juvenile training schools. Most notably, the federal courts intervened in Texas, North Carolina, Florida, and the District of Columbia. In Massachusetts, an investigation by the Department of Health and Human Services revealed the terrible treatment of delinquent youths.

Some states such as New Jersey and California started limited experimentation with community-based alternatives to the training schools in the 1960s and 1970s (Empey and Lubeck 1971; Empey and Erickson 1972; Lerman 1975). However, the most dramatic change in juvenile corrections occurred in Massachusetts in the early 1970s.

There were a number of ethnographic studies from the 1960s and 1970s that documented the problems of juvenile correctional facilities. One of the classic studies was Howard Polsky's (1962) *Cottage Six*, which described how the staff at a New York residential treatment center were unable to prevent the development of an inmate culture in which some youths exploited and brutalized the more vulnerable youngsters. Polsky showed how the victimization of the weaker youth inmates led to severe mental health issues among these youngsters, and ultimately their placement in mental hospitals. There were other ethnographies by Fisher (1961), Bartollas and Miller (1997), and Street, Vinter, and Perrow (1966) that showed the corrosive and violent nature of juvenile facilities.

Besides these social science studies, there are a range of personal autobiographies and journalist accounts that raised public awareness of the destructive nature of juvenile facilities. Most notable are Brendan Behan's *Borstal Boy* (1958); Alex Haley (1964), *The Autobiography of Malcolm X*; Piri Thomas's *Down These Mean Streets* (1967); and Sonny Carson's (1972) *The Education of Sonny Carson*. An extraordinary piece of journalism by Kenneth Wooden (1976), *Weeping in the Playtime of Others*, galvanized national attention to the need for new federal laws that protected youth in juvenile facilities.

In the wake of well-publicized scandals and abusive practices in its state training schools, Massachusetts recruited Dr. Jerome Miller, a professor of social work at Ohio State University, to run its Department of Youth Services (DYS). Dr. Miller had been a psychotherapist in the U.S. Air Force and was well known for his work on building therapeutic communities. He began with the goal of establishing therapeutic treatment settings in Massachusetts training schools. Feld (1977), in *Neutralizing Inmate Violence*, documented some early progress in creating less toxic institutional environments. But Dr. Miller quickly faced staunch opposition to his ideas from state corrections workers. The DYS custody staff opposed even small reforms, such as permitting youths to wear normal adolescent clothing rather than prison garb, ending the practice of shaving the heads of the young DYS inmates, or any limitations of the practice of solitary confinement. Deciding that even modest changes would be impossible, and seeing little hope of initiating comprehensive therapeutic communities, Dr. Miller concluded that the entire Massachusetts DYS had to be shut down (Miller 1991).

From 1970 to 1972, Massachusetts closed all of its state training schools. The first institution to close was the Thomas Lyman School, the nation's oldest statewide juvenile facility. Under Dr. Miller's direction, almost one thousand inmates were moved to a diverse network of small, secure facilities (most with fewer than fifteen beds) or a broad range of community placements (Bakal 1973). The dramatic and rapid way in which the training schools were closed grabbed worldwide attention. Initial research on the closures by Lloyd Ohlin and his colleagues at Harvard Law School suggested that the radical DYS reforms had worked reasonably well in terms of improving the quality of care without impacting public safety (Coates, Miller, and Ohlin 1978). Later research by the National Council on Crime and Delinquency (NCCD) showed that the new Massachusetts DYS system had better youth outcomes and was considerably less expensive than the older training school system (Krisberg, Austin, and Steele 1991). Political opposition to closing the training schools, and resistance by public employee unions who feared job losses, led to Dr. Miller being replaced as the head of DYS.

Dr. Jerome Miller was later hired by Pennsylvania and Illinois to run the youth corrections systems in those states. Although the results in Pennsylvania and Illinois were not as far-ranging as in Massachusetts, Dr. Miller did close Camp Hill—the worst juvenile prison in the Quaker State—and substantially reduced the number of youths in all state juvenile institutions. In Illinois, there was some progress in diverting delinquent youths into intensive community-based options (Murray and Cox 1979).

The well-publicized Massachusetts reforms of the 1970s and the continuing wave of lawsuits alleging violations of the Eighth and Fourteenth Amendments of the U.S. Constitution led many other jurisdictions to consider following the Massachusetts DYS model. Litigation on the "right to treatment" for juveniles was spawned in cases such as *White v. Reid* (1956), which held that juveniles could not be held in institutions that did not provide for their rehabilitation. *Morales v. Turman* (364 F. Supp. 166, 173 [E.D. Tex. 1973]) and *Nelson v. Heyne* (491 F.2d 353 (7th Cir.

1974) reaffirmed that juveniles had a right to treatment, mental health services, and education, although the courts were guarded in the granting of these rights. Other cases decried the use of solitary confinement, gassing of juvenile inmates, beatings, sexual assaults, and other forms of torture.

The Edna McConnell Clark Foundation supported conferences, training, and technical assistance for states that wanted to end or avoid lawsuits by replicating the Massachusetts approach. Places as diverse as Utah, Vermont, Missouri, Texas, Florida, Maryland, Indiana, Colorado, Oregon, New Jersey, and Arizona closed one or more large-scale juvenile correctional facilities. The federal Office of Juvenile Justice and Delinquency Prevention endorsed the Massachusetts DYS model as part of its Comprehensive Strategy on Serious, Violent, and Chronic Juvenile Offenders (Howell 1995).

Very small facilities for the few dangerous juvenile offenders and greatly expanded community-based programs emerged as the new standard for juvenile corrections across the nation. Many believed that the traditional training school would become extinct. But historical circumstances conspired to keep the traditional youth corrections facilities in business.

Starting in the early 1990s, arrests for juvenile crime spiked up for a few years. The media, ambitious politicians, and some very questionable criminological research by James Q. Wilson, John DiIulio, and Charles Murray raised fears about a growing tidal wave of "juvenile super predators" that would wreak havoc in urban America (DiIulio 1995; Wilson 1995). Further, an increasingly conservative crime policy was dominant through two Bush administrations and the Clinton presidency and in many states. One result of the tougher attitude toward offenders was the passage of the Prison Reform Litigation Act in 1995, which made it much harder for juveniles and adults to challenge the legality of conditions of confinement.

Few jurisdictions built more large juvenile facilities in the late 1990s and the early twenty-first century, but the conditions in existing facilities continued to deteriorate, and the movement to close more training schools stalled. What followed next was a sad return to the abusive and illegal practices that had dominated juvenile corrections since its inception. Lawsuits and investigations by the U.S. Department of Justice under the Civil Rights of Institutionalized Persons Act (CRIPA) were becoming more common in many of the larger states, especially California, Florida, Maryland, Texas, Illinois, and New York.

A comprehensive investigation of state youth facilities requested by California's Attorney Bill Lockyer in 2003 found that youths were held during the day in cage-like structures that were not fit for zoo animals (Krisberg 2003). The cages were used for "high-risk" youths as their school classrooms or recreation areas. Violence and use of chemical agents to quell fights and riots were commonplace. Some facilities used guard dogs to maintain order in the institutions. Racial conflict and gang-related fights occurred daily. Four youths committed suicide in just two years. Youths reported that sexual assaults in the living units were part of their experience. Many youths were held in isolation for twenty-one hours a day for extended periods of time. In addition, this investigation found a wide range of violations of state and federal laws in the areas of education, health care, mental health services, and the rights of the disabled. Faced by the uncontroverted results of the Attorney General's investigation in 2004, California agreed to a substantial and multifaceted consent decree to fix these horrid conditions and the poor treatment of incarcerated young people.

The circumstances for youths in Texas were equally abhorrent. In 2007, stories emerged about the sexual abuse of youths by staff and managers in a West Texas juvenile facility in Pyote. A high-level investigation ordered by state officials uncovered the facts that top managers at Pyote were among the offenders (Swanson 2007a). The Texas Youth Commission, which was responsible for the Pyote facility, denied any knowledge of these alleged problems, even though caseworkers at the facility documented numerous efforts to expose the sexual abuse of incarcerated youths. A former school principal and an assistant superintendent at Pyote were charged with engaging in multiple incidents of inappropriate sexual contact with youths. These top staff at Pyote allegedly offered their victims extra privileges or threatened them with punishment, including added time to their sentences, if they refused sexual advances. It turned out that the horrors were not limited to the Pyote School.

Eventually, over 750 employees of the Texas Youth Commission supported the claims of sexual abuse and misconduct by other staff (Swanson 2007b). Over two thousand offenses by staff in the Texas Youth Commission were confirmed by investigators between 2003 and 2006. The U.S. Department of Justice was unable to take decisive legal action, despite knowledge of the abuse for over four years. As the media reported more about the sexual scandals, the legislature ordered the overhaul of the Texas Youth Commission. The Commission members and top staff were replaced, and the governor appointed a conservator to run the agency.

Florida was another large state that experienced major problems in its juvenile correctional facilities. In 2005 the legislature closed a maximum security facility for girls because of ongoing problems. The abuses continued right up until the closure as a long-term corrections officer was charged with sexually assaulting a 15-year-old female resident of the facility. At another Florida juvenile corrections program for girls—the Sawmill Academy—a staff supervisor was charged with eight felony counts of illegal contact with youths.

Boys' programs in Florida were also caught up in scandal and abuse. The Miami-Dade County juvenile detention facility was the site of the death of Omar Paisley, who died of a ruptured appendix in 2003. Despite the youth's obviously severe symptoms, he received no medical attention from staff. In 2007, 14-year-old Martin Lee Anderson was beaten by seven guards, and he later suffocated when staff attempted to revive him with ammonia capsules. This tragedy occurred at a state-funded boot camp operated by the Bay County Sheriff's Department. Initially, the state medical examiner attempted to say that Anderson died due to complications from sickle cell anemia. A courageous medical director for the Florida Department of Juvenile Justice (DJJ) disputed this finding, and another autopsy ruled that the death was a potential homicide. Later, a Bay County jury acquitted the staff of the murder charges after just ninety minutes of deliberations. Outrage over the death of Martin Lee Anderson led the Florida DJJ to cut off funding for all juvenile boot camps.

Even before these horrible events, it was clear that Florida juvenile justice programs were deeply troubled. During 2000 and 2001, there were 2,285 allegations of abusive practices in Florida juvenile facilities (Hurtibise 2002). Beginning in 2004, Florida closed fifty-six juvenile corrections programs for boys and twenty-five programs for girls. These closures were in response to complaints about staff falsifying log books, giving drugs to young inmates, and failing to provide pregnant teens with even rudimentary prenatal medical care.

In both Florida and Texas, the State had stopped doing criminal background checks on new staff. Juvenile facilities in both states unknowingly hired convicted sex offenders and pedophiles to work in some of their institutions. In Maryland, state employees broke the arms of youths who were confined in a juvenile corrections program. In Marion County, Indiana, a local district attorney indicted nine staff for inappropriate sexual contact with detained girls. These problems led to comprehensive investigations by the U.S. Department of Justice, Civil Rights Division under CRIPA. The Department of Justice also conducted full investigations of Los Angeles County juvenile institutions for excessive use of isolation, poor mental health services, and a pervasive culture of violence in these facilities. Federal investigators found excessive use of physical force and unacceptable mental health care in New York State juvenile facilities.

These scandals prompted lawsuits and legislative hearings in many jurisdictions. Attorney General Janet Reno made the improvement of the conditions in juvenile facilities a priority, but Attorneys General Albert Gonzales and Michael Mukasey seemed much less focused on the crisis in juvenile facilities.

Legal challenges and growing adverse media and political attention to the severe problems in juvenile corrections led to a national trend of sending fewer youths to these facilities. Despite a lack of focus on the deteriorated conditions in juvenile facilities, national data show a trend of sending fewer youths to state and local correctional facilities (Davis et al. 2008). This contrasted sharply to most of the 1990s, during which the population of juvenile facilities increased by 36%. From 1997 to 2006, the number of youths who were incarcerated in juvenile correctional facilities dropped by 14%. In California, the number of confined youths declined by 33% from 1997 to 2006. Louisiana's number of youths in custody went down by 49%, and Georgia saw a drop of 40%. Other states also experienced a decline in confined youths; Washington and Tennessee each had a population decrease of 38% in their juvenile facilities. Although the OJJDP has not yet released its data on juveniles in custody for years later than 2006, anecdotal evidence indicates that the number of incarcerated youngsters has continued to decline. Despite fears fomented by the national "get tough" rhetoric on juvenile offenders, there was no evidence that states were sending more young people to adult prisons and jails (Hartney 2006). From 1999 to 2006, the number of persons under age 18 in adult prisons and jails declined from 13, 652 to 8,494—a decrease of almost 38%.

Several states such as California and Texas enacted new laws designed to divert juvenile offenders from state juvenile facilities. Florida created a Blue Ribbon Task Force that urged that fewer youths be placed in state facilities.

A prominent philanthropy—the Annie E. Casey Foundation—launched a major national campaign to cut down on the number of youths who were held unnecessarily in secure detention facilities. The Juvenile Detention Alternatives Initiative (JDAI) is now being implemented in 110 sites in twenty-seven states. These sites have already witnessed a decline in their detained populations since they began the reform effort.

It is worth noting that as states and counties were reducing their confined juvenile populations, the number of adult inmates continued to climb to historic levels. Further, juvenile arrest rates decreased by 28% as localities continued to reduce the number of young people in secure confinement.

II. THE VARIED WORLD OF JUVENILE CORRECTIONS

The term "juvenile corrections" covers a wide range of facilities and programs. Most juvenile corrections facilities are quite small, perhaps fewer than fifty beds. Although there are some juvenile training schools that hold more than three hundred youths, there are none that rival the size of many adult prisons and jails. The last data compiled by OJJDP reported that almost 93,000 youths were housed in juvenile corrections facilities based on a one-day census in 2006 (Sickmund et al. 2008). About one-third of these confined youths were held in facilities operated by state governments; roughly another third of these youths resided in facilities operated by counties. The last third of the youths were placed in private juvenile correctional institutions. Although there is a growing but still limited trend of privatization in prisons and jails, many juveniles are sent to facilities operated by nonprofit agencies and for-profit corporations. Recall that the origin of juvenile corrections was led by private charitable groups that started the Houses of Refuge.

Juvenile facilities can include institutions of maximum security custody with all of the trappings of adult prisons, such as razor wire perimeters, locked rooms, and uniformed correctional staff who may carry guns. But other juvenile correctional facilities may be environmental conservation camps, boot camps, or other open facilities where doors are unlocked and security is provided solely by staff. Juvenile corrections also include community-based residential facilities and supervised independent living programs for those youths who are about to be released. Some juvenile correctional facilities are virtually identical to group homes run by the child welfare system. There are some juvenile corrections programs in Florida and, previously, in Los Angeles, which were situated on sailing ships. There are several juvenile facilities with a capacity of fewer than fifty beds. Most youths are held in juvenile facilities with fewer than one hundred and fifty beds. Only about one-quarter of confined youths are in institutions that have a capacity of more than two hundred beds.

Most confined youths (about 83%) are housed in locked institutions with physically secure perimeters. The last major building boom in juvenile corrections occurred more than three decades ago, and many of these older facilities are in severe disrepair. States and localities have been much more willing to sell bonds to build new prisons and jails than to update or replace antiquated juvenile institutions.

Most inmates of juvenile corrections facilities are males (85%) and members of racial and ethnic minority groups. In 2006, just 35% of youths in custody were white. Youths in custody are generally age 15 or 16. Five percent of the juvenile inmates were under 13, and 14% were over age 18.

About one-third of confined juveniles were charged with a violent crime. The bulk of youths in juvenile corrections are there for property offenses, drug crimes (mostly possession for use), or technical violations of their conditions of probation. Approximately 5% of juveniles in custody are charged with juvenile status offenses such as truancy, running away, or incorrigibility—behaviors that are not considered criminal for adults.

Youths in juvenile facilities spend less time locked up than adults who are sent to prisons or jails. The 2006 Census found that about 80% of youths had been incarcerated for less than six months. These shorter stays are primarily a function of youths being committed for less serious crimes than adult inmates. Young people who commit very serious and violent crimes are often sentenced to adult facilities. While juvenile facilities are often plagued with fights and other problems, juvenile corrections does not confront the high levels of real or potential lethal violence of adult facilities. Unlike adult corrections, juvenile facilities are mandated by state and federal laws to provide education and special education services to school-age inmates. Few juvenile facilities are in full compliance with these educational requirements; a growing number of legal challenges to juvenile corrections systems cover educational issues, the provision of mental health treatment, and appropriate responses to the needs of disabled youths.

Juvenile facilities usually possess a richer staffing ratio than adult facilities, and, as a consequence, they are much more costly to operate than adult prisons. For example, the average annual per capita cost to confine a prisoner in California in 2008 was $49,000, but the Division of Juvenile Justice was spending over $225,000 a year for each inmate in its state youth facilities. The high cost of operating juvenile institutions that meet even minimal legal standards has been another reason public officials have become more open to less costly community-based programming.

III. Disproportionate Confinement
of Youth of Color

As noted above, youth of color comprise a large percentage of the residents of juvenile corrections facilities. For Detention Centers, African American youth are incarcerated at 5.3 times the rate for Whites, and Latino youth and Native American youth are detained 2.4 and 3.5 times the rate of White youngsters, respectively (Hartney and Vuong 2009). The same disproportion holds for post-adjudication residential programs, where African American youth are confined at 4.5 times the rate for Whites, Latino youth are locked up at 1.9 times the White rate, and Native American youth are 3.2 times more likely to be residential placements than White youth (Hartney and Vuong 2009).

These disparities exist even when one controls for the severity of the offense or the number of prior placements (Hartney and Vuong 2009; NCCD 2007). Youth of color are also more likely to be confined in more secure facilities and in crowded juvenile correctional facilities. This disproportionality is true for both young men and young women.

One might speculate that youth of color are more likely to be assigned to residential placements because of harsher attitudes toward their misconduct and the lack of available alternative treatment options (Krisberg 1975). Juvenile justice reformer Jerome Miller often asks his audiences what they would want to happen if their own children were brought into juvenile court. He makes the distinction between "our children and other peoples' children." Miller would argue that youth of color are incarcerated at much higher levels because the Whites who dominate the juvenile justice system view them as "others"—a phrase made famous by Toni Morrison. The issue of race may also explain the slow pace of reform in juvenile corrections and the willingness to tolerate abusive practices against confined youths.

IV. Juvenile Corrections and Young Women

Although arrests for juveniles declined generally, the drop in male juvenile arrests has been greater than that for girls; since 1997, that decline was 18% for boys compared to 8% for girls. Moreover, there were fourteen states in which the rate of incarceration for girls grew by more than 30% since 1997 (Davis et al. 2008). Young women comprise approximately 15% of the incarcerated juvenile population, but in some states, that figure is almost one third.

The profile of incarcerated young women shows that they are confined for less serious crimes than their male counterparts. As far back as the research of Paul

Tappan (1947), it was observed that girls were often locked up to "protect" them from their nascent sexual behavior and potential exploitation by others. Later research by Chesney-Lind and Shelden (1992) and Bishop and Frazier (1992) has shown that this pattern has continued in the post-*Gault* era. Girls are more likely than boys to be confined for juvenile status offenses such as running away and incorrigibility. Chesney-Lind (1997) described the process by which young women were placed in residential programs through "bootstrapping," in which minor misconduct was treated as probation violations or breaches of court orders. A study in Maryland by Mayer (1994) found that even young women who are incarcerated for assaultive behavior were actually involved in family disputes involving mutual combat.

Because boys dominate the population of juvenile correctional facilities, there has been much less attention paid to the unique needs of young women. It is often observed that programs for young women are just "boys programs painted pink." There are few if any juvenile corrections programs that are designed specifically for the needs of adolescent women. Some have observed that incarcerated girls have less access to vocational or recreational programs than boys. Many girls' programs reinforce traditional societal stereotypes about young women—that "they love tea parties" and that proper selection of a mate is a first priority. Vocational programs channel girls into conventional female employment roles such as cosmetology, dog grooming, or child care. The limited resources for troubled young women often means that girls are sent to out-of-state facilities in jurisdictions in which there are local options for boys but not for girls.

There is much less research on incarcerated girls, but the rigorous studies that do exist point to very high levels of mental illness, serious drug abuse problems, heightened levels of self-harming behavior, and early exposure to trauma (Hoyt and Scherer 1998; Obeidallah and Earls 1999; Acoca 2000; and Freitag and Wordes 2001). These life challenges can lead girls to clinical depression, other forms of severe mental illness, suicidal behavior, and maltreatment of their own children.

The emerging literature on evidence-based practices in juvenile justice is almost exclusively based on research on boys. A recent Girls Study Group convened by the Office of Juvenile Justice and Delinquency Prevention decried the lack of sound research on female programs and the paucity of theory and empirical data about girls in the juvenile justice system.

Beyond the lack of programming, there are several reports about high levels of abusive practices in juvenile corrections for girls. Giallombardo (1974) in *The Social World of Imprisoned Girls* documented physical and sexual victimization among the residents of girl's facilities. Acoca and Dedel (1998) described the horrid and degrading treatment of incarcerated young women in several California counties. Krisberg (2009) has written about the "cycle of abuse" that incarcerated girls experienced in Florida, California state youth facilities, and Indiana. National surveys of incarcerated young people report much higher levels of sexual abuse aimed at girls compared to boys (Beck, Guerino, and Harrison 2010).

As profound as the problems are that boys face in boys' correctional facilities, girls in girls' facilities face equal or greater issues. National attention and litigation has only recently been focused on the plight of incarcerated young women. An agenda of reforms is urgently needed. As a beginning step, the Jessie Ball duPont Fund helped establish the National Center for Girls and Young Women to be a resource for policy makers, practitioners, and concerned citizens who wish to make improvements in this arena.

V. How Successful Is Juvenile Corrections at Reducing Future Crime?

As we passed the centennial of the juvenile court, it is still true that there are very few objective data on how well youth corrections systems function to reduce future crime. Only a handful of states collect any data at all, and there is no agreed-upon standard to measure recidivism; no comprehensive data exist on the topic. Some studies have tracked the outcome of selected cohorts of young people released from various corrections programs. Overall, these data suggest that a majority of institutionalized juveniles are rearrested and incarcerated in future years. At one extreme are failure rates. In a recent follow-up analysis of youths who were paroled from the California Division of Juvenile Justice in 2004–2005, over 81% were arrested for a new felony or were incarcerated for a parole violation within three years of release (CDCR 2009). Other studies suggest that states that use smaller facilities and that have moved away from the more traditional prison-like environments—such as Missouri, Massachusetts, and Pennsylvania—appear to have lower recidivism rates (Krisberg 2005; Howell 1997). However, comparing failure rates across youth corrections systems is difficult because states handle very different youth populations in their facilities. For example, different ages of juvenile court jurisdictions mean that youths in some state systems will be much older or younger than in other jurisdictions. In New York, Connecticut, and North Carolina, offenders over the age of 16 can be sent to adult facilities, but in California, the maximum age in the state youth facilities is 25. Because the odds of committing future crimes goes up for all youths in their late teens and early 20s, this can influence failure rates (Beck et al. 2010). States also differ on the use of probation or community-based sanctions in lieu of incarceration. States with higher rates of juvenile incarceration tend to send offenders to their facilities for lesser crimes and with shorter prior records. These facts can profoundly affect recidivism rates. Policies also differ across jurisdictions on the use of technical parole violations to return youths to custody. Recidivism rates can be influenced by policy decisions, such as law enforcement priorities or resources attached to drug offenses, gang behavior, or other youth-related offenses. Some states such as Florida, Colorado, and Georgia operate all juvenile corrections through a state agency. Other states operate state facilities and county facilities. States also differ on whether juvenile corrections are exclusively staffed by public employees, private agencies, or a combination of the two.

Further complexity is added to the assessment of recidivism rates because different jurisdictions make variable use of mental health or special education facilities, foster care placements, or sending some of their youthful offenders out of state. Judges decide the location of youth confinement and the length of stay in some states, whereas youth corrections agencies or parole boards may decide these issues in others. Laws governing juvenile sentencing are currently in flux (Dedel 1998). States also differ on the nature and extent of aftercare or reentry services and supervision that are available to released youths. Much more sophistical data analyses are needed to make meaningful comparisons of recidivism rates between jurisdictions or within a single jurisdiction over time.

Arguments about the effectiveness of juvenile corrections programs are as old as the nineteenth century work of Charles Loring Brace (1872) and the founders of the juvenile court, such as Julia Lathrop and Jane Addams (Platt 1968). Advocates for youth corrections like Edward Rhine (1996) and Charles Murray (Murray and Cox 1979) have asserted that the institutional experience can have a positive impact on a youth's future criminal behavior, but the evidence to support this viewpoint is very limited or contradictory. Other researchers at the Washington Institute for Public Policy have reported positive effects on recidivism of some community-based programs, but scant data support either the deterrent or rehabilitative impact of juvenile incarceration.

More than the acknowledged difficulties of comparing the outcomes of various juvenile corrections approaches, few states or counties collect any recidivism data on incarcerated youths. By contrast, there exist national-level data on the number of adult prisoners who return to custody during the three years after their release. The Bureau of Justice Statistics collects data on most states through the National Corrections Reporting Program. Because juveniles may reach the age of adulthood after their release from youth corrections, accurate studies must examine rates on reincarceration in both juvenile and adult systems. Further, most states possess statewide registries of felony arrests for adults, but juvenile data are often kept by local juvenile courts and may not be available to researchers; some jurisdictions jealously guard the confidentially of juvenile arrest data.

In the mid-1990s, the National Council on Crime and Delinquency (NCCD) was funded by OJJDP to test the feasibility of collecting recidivism rates for youths who exited juvenile corrections systems (Krisberg, DeComo, and Wordes 1997). This preliminary research effort was gathered data from forty states and employed a very conservative metric on failure rates. NCCD took a list of youths who were released from forty state juvenile corrections systems. Next, researchers examined whether any of the youths who were released—and still under the jurisdiction of the juvenile court after one year of release—had been readmitted to the state youth corrections system. Left out of this measure were youths who were subsequently arrested but not incarcerated, those held in local facilities such as detention centers, and those locked up in jails or prisons. Even this very limited definition of juvenile recidivism produced results showing that 27% of released youths were returned to state youth corrections facilities within the first year of their first release.

This pilot also revealed substantial variation among states in these rates of reincarceration. The OJJDP discontinued the pilot study in the late 1990s. However, there is still no national-level measure of the success or failure of various juvenile correctional programs. This absence of data is unfortunate, given the strong public interest in reforming juvenile offenders and the large taxpayer investments in juvenile corrections.

Although the national-level data are absent, isolated research studies have examined the post-release results of various juvenile corrections programs. These studies are merely suggestive, because they all suffer from significant limitations in terms of research design or complex measurement issues. For example, there are no studies that employ classic experimental designs with random assignment of clients into various kinds of correctional settings. Most of the available research has inadequate or nonexistent comparison or control groups. Data collection in these studies is rudimentary.

Florida's DJJ followed about 1,700 youths released from various juvenile corrections programs (Tollett 1987). Approximately 44% of youths were arrested for a new juvenile or adult offense within a year of release. Thirty percent were incarcerated during the one-year follow-up period. The Florida study found that youths who were released from secure juvenile facilities and those who had the most prior incarcerations possessed the highest recidivism rates. These youths had other personal attributes that may have accounted for these results, such as disorganized families, school failure, and drug abuse issues.

A Pennsylvania study of ten juvenile residential programs reported that 48% of released youths were rearrested within twelve months, and 55% were arrested within eighteen months (Goodstein and Sontheimer 1987). Like the Florida results, the Pennsylvania youths who had been confined at the youngest ages and those who had experienced multiple prior incarcerations showed the highest recidivism rates.

Studies of youths released from Utah juvenile corrections programs had a 79% re-arrest rate within one year of release (Austin and Krisberg 1988). Researcher Christopher Baird found a one-year, 70% re-arrest rate of youths released from California state youth facilities (Baird et al. 1999), and Haapanen (1988) found that 96% of California Youth Authority clients were later arrested as adults. A study of the Massachusetts training schools that were closed by Dr. Jerome Miller revealed a failure rate of 66% after one year (Coates et al. 1978). Every one of these research efforts found that the highest recidivism rates belonged to those youths who were locked up at younger ages and who had multiple episodes of confinement.

A number of meta-analyses of many juvenile corrections programs were compiled by Mark Lipsey (1992), Peter Greenwood et al. (1996), and Steve Aos and colleagues (1999). Each of these literature reviews found that intensive home-based services produced lower recidivism rates than locked institutional programs. There is virtually no evidence that juvenile facilities produce positive results in reducing future law-breaking behavior. Moreover, there is growing evidence that youths who more deeply penetrate the juvenile justice system, especially those who are securely confined, have the worst long-term public safety outcomes (Gatti, Tremblay, and Vitaro 2009). One explanation is that incarceration creates negative labeling and encourages youths to embrace a criminal self image. It is also true that adolescence is a particularly vulnerable time of life, and the pressures and challenges of group residential settings are especially disruptive. Vulnerable youths are confronted daily with drug use, violence, and abuse from other inmates and from staff. Moreover, the extensive use of isolation and seclusion does not help young people develop healthy communication skills. There is little evidence that the enormous investments in juvenile corrections are cost-effective.

VI. Juvenile Boot Camps—The Latest Juvenile Correctional Fad

The field of juvenile justice has been dominated by the search for "magic bullets." Elected officials and the public are often swayed by media-driven panaceas. One such program, "Scared Straight," was based on an award-winning documentary that claimed that exposing delinquent youths to prisoners would deter them from crime. Scores of jurisdictions took youth groups into maximum security prisons where they toured the facility and had group meetings with selected inmates who yelled at them and threatened to assault and rape them. The documentary claimed extraordinary success, but more careful and objective research showed no positive results from Scared Straight programs and even quite negative results (Finckenauer et al. 1999).

Another media-generated phenomenon was "Tough Love," in which parents were encouraged to have their wayward youngsters arrested and incarcerated. The proponents of Tough Love even trumpeted the value of putting juveniles in jails— despite all of the evidence about the harmful effects of this practice. There was no research to support the claims of Tough Love, but it appealed to the instincts of some parents to pass their problems on to state and local corrections facilities. By far the most influential fad was to put delinquent youths in correctional boot camps, which pretended to replicate the military experience. It was a very old and a very bad idea.

Zebulon Brockway introduced military drill as part of the regimen of the Elmira Reformatory at the close of the nineteenth century. In the 1990s, juvenile boot camps that supposedly mimicked military boot camps remerged as the latest panacea for youth crime. The United States Congress and many state and local officials invested hundreds of millions of dollars to open boot camps for juvenile offenders. Some of these emphasized the supposed deterrent value of harsh correctional environments;

others argued that military drill and physical challenges would assist the rehabilitation process. Some claimed that boot camps were cheaper than traditional juvenile training schools, since the average stays of youths in these programs were shorter.

The government-funded boot camps were supplemented by private programs that accepted volunteer placements from parents of troubled youngsters. The private boot camps promised miracle cures for teens who were involved with drugs, were rebellious and failing in school, or were sexually promiscuous. The private programs sometimes provided inducements to school officials or counselors to make referrals to their programs.

Research on the results of juvenile boot camps was not encouraging. Many boot camps collected no data on their outcomes. The programs that *were* subject to some rigorous study were not impressive. University of Maryland researchers reported that boot camps were largely ineffective in reducing recidivism (Sherman et al. 1997). OJJDP attempted to test the results of an ideal model of juvenile boot camps; however, the research showed that the OJJDP boot camps produced no better results than traditional juvenile correctional programs (Peters, Thomas, and Zamberlan 1997). The boot camps were often used for juvenile offenders who had historically been placed on probation rather than those who were headed to secure residential programs. The added costs of these programs were substantial.

Even more troubling, boot camps produced terrible tragedies. Although there is no system-wide national data on the death rates in boot camps compared to conventional youth corrections programs, there were several reports in Maryland, Florida, South Dakota, Nevada, and Texas of staff at boot camps employing excessive physical force, requiring youths to engage in extreme physical exertion, or denying youths medical attention. Staff in boot camps typically received little or no training and lacked clinical backgrounds. They attributed the behavior of mentally ill youth to "malingering" or "playing possum." Some juvenile courts sent youths to boot camps in other states, and there was essentially no oversight or regulation of these programs.

The boot camp movement is in retreat. Although there are still several boot camp programs across the nation, federal and local funding for boot camps has abated. Lawsuits charging wrongful deaths of youths in these programs have slowed the growth of this dangerous juvenile corrections fad. Research has continued to show little or no positive results in terms of reducing juvenile recidivism (Aos, Phipps, and Korinek 1999).

VII. Policy Considerations

The history of juvenile corrections has been plagued with a legacy of abuse, tragedies, and limited positive results. The legacy of juvenile corrections has been one of excessive use of incarceration for young women, for youth of color, and for youth charged with minor crimes. The trend to "get tough" with juveniles has led to the most serious young offenders being sent to the adult criminal justice system and confined in adult prisons and jails. Many states such as Illinois and California turned over the administration of their juvenile facilities to state prison officials. As a result, the mentality of managing adult felony offenders has come to dominate juvenile corrections. For the past decade, OJJDP has played a hands-off role in terms of training and advising juvenile correctional agencies. State budget problems and the increasing demands to fund adult prisons have diverted some funding from juvenile facilities. The conditions of many juvenile correctional facilities have deteriorated, and standards for professional practices have also declined. As we approach the 185th anniversary of the founding of the New York House of Refuge, the enterprise of juvenile corrections seems to be in big trouble.

The era of the large-scale congregate youth correctional facility appears to be ending. States and localities continue to reduce the populations of these facilities, and it is unlikely that any large institutions will be built in the near term. Legal oversight of existing juvenile facilities, especially by the Civil Rights Division of the U.S. Department of Justice, continues to expand. Discussions are taking place about strengthening federal laws that prohibit "dangerous practices such as isolation and seclusion, harsh physical punishments, and the excessive use of psychotropic medications. As the courts have demanded greater scrutiny of juvenile facilities—especially in terms of mental health services, basic education, and meeting the needs of disabled children—the costs of secure incarceration have increased significantly. Moreover, cutbacks in state mental health and drug treatment services for youths have resulted in additional responsibilities and fiscal burdens on juvenile corrections. There is some renewed interest at the national, state, and local levels in exploring the value of alternatives to incarceration for juvenile offenders.

The reforms ushered in by Dr. Jerome Miller in Massachusetts in the early 1970s seem to be experiencing a comeback. The Missouri DYS is often put forward as a model for juvenile corrections in terms of humane care of delinquent youths. The progressive direction of current reforms is supported by a generally declining juvenile arrest rate. But we cannot know if another "moral panic" about juvenile gangs and street violence will reverse that trend. Recall the way in which the hysteria over "super predators" stopped the deinstitutionalization trends in the 1980s. This "get tough" political movement and the unwillingness of public officials to invest in reform efforts have led to a nationwide crisis in juvenile corrections. The current status of juvenile corrections is deeply troubled; the future of this enterprise is uncertain.

REFERENCES

Acoca, Leslie. 2000. *Educate Don't Incarcerate: Girls in the Florida and Duval County Juvenile Justice Systems.* San Francisco: National Council on Crime and Delinquency.

Acoca, Leslie, and Kelly Dedel. 1998. *No Place to Hide: Understanding and Meeting the Needs of Girls in the California Juvenile Justice System*, San Francisco, CA: National Council on Crime and Delinquency.

Aos, Steve, Polly Phipps, and Kim Korinek. 1999. *Research Findings on Adult Corrections' Programs: A Review*. Olympia, WA: Washington State Institute for Public Policy.

Austin, James F., and Barry Krisberg. 1988. *Reinventing Juvenile Justice*. Thousand Oaks, CA: Sage.

Baird, Christopher, Dennis Wagner, Theresa Healy, and Kristen Johnson. 1999. "Risk Assessment in Child Protective Services: Consensus and Actuarial Model Reliability." *Child Welfare* 78(6): 723–48.

Bakal, Yitzhak. 1973. *Closing Correctional Institutions*. Lexington, MA: Lexington Books.

Bartollas, Clemens, and Stuart J. Miller. 1997. *Juvenile Justice in America*. Englewood Cliffs, NJ: Prentice-Hall.

Beck, Allen J., Paul Guerino, Paige M. Harrison. 2010. *Sexual Victimization in Juvenile Facilities Reported by Youth, 2008–09*. Bureau of Justice Statistics NCJ 228416. Washington, DC: U.S. Department of Justice, Office of Justice Programs.

Behan, Brendan. 1958. *Borstal Boy*. New York: Samuel French.

Bishop, Donna, and Charles Frazier. 1992. "Gender Bias in the Juvenile Justice System: Implications of the JJDP Act." *Journal of Criminal Law and Criminology* 82: 1162–86.

Brace, Charles Loring. 1872. *The Dangerous Classes of New York*. New York: Wynkoop and Hallenbeck.

Bremner, Robert, John Barnard, Tamara K. Hareven, and Robert M. Mennel. 1970. *Children and Youth in America: A Documentary History*, vol. 1. Cambridge, MA: Harvard University Press.

California Department of Corrections and Rehabilitation. 2009. Juvenile recidivism statistics in California (unpublished raw data).

Carson, Sonny. 1972. *The Education of Sonny Carson*. New York: Norton.

Chesney-Lind, Meda. 1997. *The Female Offender: Girls, Women and Crime*. Thousand Oaks, CA: Sage Publications.

Chesney-Lind, Meda, and Randall Shelden. 1992. *Girls, Delinquency, and Juvenile Justice*. Florence, KY: Cengage Learning.

Coates, Robert B., Alden D. Miller, and Lloyd B. Ohlin. 1978. *Diversity in a Youth Correctional System: Handling Delinquents in Massachusetts*. Cambridge, MA: Ballinger.

Davis, Antoinette, Chris Tsukida, Susan Marchionna, and Barry Krisberg. 2008. *The Declining Number of Youth in Custody in the Juvenile Justice System*. Oakland, CA: National Council on Crime and Delinquency.

Dedel, Kelly. 1998. "National Profile of the Organization of State Juvenile Corrections Systems." *Crime and Delinquency* 44: 507–25.

DiIulio, John J. 1995. "Crime in America: It's Going to Get Worse." *Reader's Digest*. August: 55–60.

Empey, Lamar T., and Maynard L. Erickson. 1972. *The Provo Experiment: Evaluating Community Control of Delinquency*. Lexington, MA: Lexington Books.

Empey, Lamar T., and Steven G. Lubeck. 1971. *The Silverlake Experiment; Testing Delinquency Theory and Community Intervention*. Chicago: Aldine.

Feld, Barry. 1977. *Neutralizing Inmate Violence: Juvenile Offenders in Institutions*. Cambridge, MA: Ballinger.

Finckenauer, James, Patricia Gavin, Arlid Hovland, and Elisabet Storvoll. 1999. *Scared Straight: The Panacea Phenomenon Revisited*. Prospect Heights, IL: Waveland Press.

Fisher, Sethard. 1961. "Social Organization in a Corrections Residence." *Pacific Sociological Review* 5: 89–99.

Freitag, Raelene, and Madeline Wordes. 2001. "Improved Decision Making in Child Maltreatment Cases." *Journal of the Center for Families, Children & the Courts.* 3: 75–85.

Friedman, Lawrence. 1993. *Crime and Punishment in American History.* New York: BasicBooks.

Gatti, Uberto, Richard E. Tremblay, and Frank Vitaro. 2009. "Iatrogenic Effect on Juvenile Justice." *Journal of Child Psychology and Psychiatry.* 50: 991–98.

Giallombardo, Rose. 1974. *The Social World of Imprisoned Girls; A Comparative Study of Institutions for Juvenile Delinquents.* New York: Wiley.

Goodstein, Lynne, and Henry Sontheimer. 1987. *A Study of the Impact of Ten Pennsylvania Residential Treatment Placements on Juvenile Recidivism.* Shippensburg, PA: Center for Juvenile Justice Training and Research.

Greenwood, Peter, Karyn Model, Peter Rydell, and James Chiesa. 1996. *Diverting Children from a Life of Crime: Measuring Costs and Benefits,* rev. ed. Santa Monica, CA: Rand.

Haapanen, Rudy A. 1988. *Selective Incapacitation and the Serious Offender: A Longitudinal Study of Criminal Career Patterns.* Sacramento, CA: California Department of Youth Authority, Program Research and Review Division.

Haley, Alex. 1964. *The Autobiography of Malcolm X.* New York: Ballantine.

Hartney, Chris. 2006. *Youth Under Age 18 in the Adult Criminal Justice System.* Oakland, CA: National Council on Crime and Delinquency.

Hartney, Chris, and Linh Vuong. 2009. *Created Equal: Racial and Ethnic Disparities in the U.S. Criminal Justice System.* Oakland, CA: National Council on Crime and Delinquency.

Holt, Marilyn. 1992. *The Orphan Trains: Placing Out in America.* Lincoln, NE: University of Nebraska Press.

Howell, James C., ed. 1995. *Implementation Guide for the Comprehensive Strategy for Serious, Violent, and Chronic Juvenile Offenders.* Washington, DC: Office of Justice Programs, Office of Juvenile Justice and Delinquency Prevention.

Howell, James C. 1997. *Juvenile Justice and Youth Violence.* Thousand Oaks, CA: Sage.

Hoyt, Stephanie, and David G. Scherer. 1998. "Female Juvenile Delinquency: Misunderstood by the Juvenile Justice System, Neglected by Social Science." *Law and Human Behavior* 22(1): 81–107.

Hurtibise, Ron. 2002. "Juvenile Detainees' Abuse Reports Spike." *Daytona Beach News Journal* (June 30).

Krisberg, Barry. 1975. *Crime and Privilege.* Englewood Cliffs, NJ: Prentice Hall.

Krisberg, Barry. 2003. "Safety and Welfare Review of the California Youth Authority." In *Continuing the Struggle for Justice,* edited by Barry Krisberg, Susan Marchionna, and Christopher Baird. 2007. Thousand Oaks, CA: Sage.

Krisberg, Barry. 2005. *Juvenile Justice: Redeeming Our Children.* Thousand Oaks, CA: Sage.

Krisberg, Barry. 2009. *Breaking the Cycle of Abuse in Juvenile Facilities.* NCCD Focus. Oakland, CA: National Council on Crime and Delinquency.

Krisberg, Barry, James Austin, and Patricia Steele. 1991. *Unlocking Juvenile Corrections.* San Francisco: National Council on Crime and Delinquency.

Krisberg, Barry, Bob DeComo, and Madeline Wordes. 1997. *Juveniles Taken into Custody.* Washington, DC: U.S. Department of Justice. Office of Juvenile Justice and Delinquency Prevention.

Lemert, Edwin M. 1972. *Social Action and Legal Change: Revolution within the Juvenile Court.* Chicago: Aldine.

Lerman, Paul. 1975. *Community Treatment and Social Control: A Critical Analysis of Juvenile Correctional Policy*. Chicago: University of Chicago Press.

Lipsey, Mark. 1992. "The Effect of Treatment on Juvenile Delinquents: Results from Meta-Analysis." In *Psychology and Law: International Perspectives*, edited by F. Loesel, D. Bender, & T. Bliesener. Berlin, NY: Walter de Gruyter.

Mayer, Judith. 1994. "Girls in the Maryland Juvenile Justice System: Findings of the Female Population Taskforce." Paper presented at the Gender Specifics Services Training. Minneapolis, MN.

Mennel, Robert. 1973. *Thorns and Thistles*. Hanover: University of New Hampshire Press.

Miller, Jerome. 1991. *Last One Over the Wall*. Columbus, OH: Ohio State University Press.

Montgomery, Ben, and Waveney Ann Moore. 2009. "Details Buried with Dozier's Dead." *St. Petersburg Times* (December 20).

Murray, Charles A., and Louis Cox. 1979. *Beyond Probation: Juvenile Corrections and the Chronic Delinquent*. Beverly Hills, CA: Sage.

NCCD. 2007. *And Justice for Some: Differential Treatment of Youth of Color in the Justice System*. Oakland, CA: National Council on Crime and Delinquency.

Obeidallah, Dawn A., and Felton J. Earls. 1999. *Adolescent Girls: The Role of Depression in the Development of Delinquency*. Washington, DC: U.S. Department of Justice, Office of Justice Programs, National Institute of Justice Research Preview.

O'Connor, Stephen. 2001. *Orphan Trains: The Story of Charles Loring Brace and the Children He Saved and Failed*. New York: Houghton Mifflin.

Office of Inspector General. 2000. *Management Audit of the Heman G. Stark Youth Corrections Facility*. Sacramento, CA: Office of Inspector General.

Peters, Michael, David Thomas, and Christopher Zamberlan. 1997. *Boot Camps for Juvenile Offenders: Program Summary*. Washington, DC: U.S. Department of Justice. Office of Juvenile Justice and Delinquency Prevention.

Pickett, Robert. 1969. *House of Refuge: Origins of Juvenile Justice Reform in New York, 1815–1857*. Syracuse, NY: Syracuse University Press.

Platt, Anthony. 1968. *The Child Savers: The Invention of Delinquency*. Chicago: Chicago University Press.

Polsky, Howard. 1962. *Cottage Six: The Social System of Delinquent Boys in Residential Treatment*. New York: Russell Sage Foundation.

Rhine, Edward. 1996. "Something Works: Recent Research on Effective Correctional Programming." In *The State of Corrections: 1995 Proceedings*. Lanham, MD: American Correctional Association.

Rothman, David. 1971. *The Discovery of the Asylum*. Philadelphia: Little Brown Company.

Sherman, Lawrence, Denise Gottfredson, Doris McKenzie, John Eck, Peter Reuter, and Shawn Bushway. 1997. *Preventing Crime: What Works, What Doesn't, What's Promising. Report to the U.S. Congress*. Washington, DC: U.S. Department of Justice, Office of Justice Programs, National Institute of Justice.

Sickmund, Melissa, T. J. Sladky, and Wei Kang. 2008. *Census of Juveniles in Residential Placement Data Book*. http://www.ojjdp.ncjrs.gov/ojstatbb/cjrp/.

Street, David, Robert D. Vinter, and Charles Perrow. 1966. *Organization for Treatment: A Comparative Study of Institutions for Delinquents*. Foreword by Morris Janowitz. New York: Free Press.

Swanson, Doug. 2007a. "Sex Abuse Reported at Youth Jail." *The Dallas News* (February 18), accessed January 8, 2009, http://www.dallasnews.com/sharedcontent/dws/news/texassouthwest/stories/021807dntextycsex.1bd0f05.html.

Swanson, Doug. 2007b. "Complaints Filed Against Guards at all 13 Youth Prisons, Documents Show." *The Dallas News* (March 6), accessed January 8, 2009, http://www.dallasnews.com/sharedcontent/dws/dn/latestnews/stories/030707dnpronutyc.39129f4.html.

Tappan, Paul W. 1947. *Delinquent Girls in Court: A Study of the Wayward Minor Court of New York*. New York: Columbia University Press.

Thomas, Piri. 1967. *Down These Mean Streets*. New York: Knopf.

Tollett, Ted. 1987. *A Comparative Study of Florida Delinquency Commitment Programs*. Tallahassee, FL: Florida Department of Health and Rehabilitative Services.

Wilson, James Q. 1995. "Crime and Public Policy." In *Crime*, edited by J. Q. Wilson and Joan Petersilia. San Francisco: Institute for Contemporary Studies Press.

Wooden, Kenneth. 1976. *Weeping in the Playtime of Others: America's Incarcerated Children*. New York: McGraw Hill.

CHAPTER 31

EXAMINING THE EFFECTIVENESS OF JUVENILE RESIDENTIAL PROGRAMS

DORIS LAYTON MACKENZIE AND RACHEL FREELAND

CONTROVERSIES exist about the use of residential facilities for juvenile delinquents. Some believe incarceration in such facilities is inherently detrimental, while others believe they are necessary to deter juveniles from future criminal behavior. Still others argue that such facilities should be used only when the juvenile is a danger to self or others and that appropriate programming can be successfully provided in institutions. This chapter reviews the literature on the effectiveness of juvenile residential programs with an emphasis on the impact on later criminal or delinquent behavior. The research does not support the perspective that incarceration is successful in deterring juveniles, nor do all facilities have detrimental impacts. Appropriate correctional programming focusing on positive changes in behavior, thinking, and attitudes can be successfully delivered within residential facilities. Successful programs appear to be those that use cognitive-behavioral and behavioral models of change and, are skill-based and multimodel. Programming that brings about cognitive transformations may be the most effective in reducing recidivism.

In the United States, many juveniles are sent to residential facilities either because they are detained while awaiting placement or adjudication, or they are committed by the juvenile court for involvement in delinquent activities. A debate continues about how the experience of incarceration in a residential facility influences later behavior. In particular, questions arise about whether spending time in a residential facility leads to a corresponding increase or decrease in future delinquent or criminal activities. Furthermore, there is interest in determining what programs or type of facilities influence (either positively or negatively) future criminal or delinquent behavior for those confined in institutions. This chapter reviews the research literature examining such questions.

I. The Juvenile Court and Disposition of Cases

The juvenile court in the United States was developed as a way to separate youth from adult offenders. Prior to this, children as young as 7 were processed identically to adults and, similar to adults, they could stand trial in criminal court and be sentenced to prison or death. With a focus on rehabilitation, the juvenile court reflected a change in philosophy toward juveniles. Dependent, neglected, and delinquent minors were sent to the juvenile court, and in most states juvenile courts had exclusive jurisdiction over all youths under age 18 who were charged with violating criminal laws.

In most states, disposition of juvenile cases is supposed to be tailored to the individual needs and circumstances of each juvenile, and as a result, a wide variety of programs has been developed to address their needs. Juveniles whose crimes or records are not very serious and who have supportive families often continue to reside at home. For these youths, various programs exist, including informal or formal probation, intensive supervision, in-home supervision, mentoring, after-school or all-day programs, and community service.

Youths who are placed out of their homes and who are low-risk may be sent to community group homes, foster care, or other community living situations. Most states provide a continuum of increasingly restrictive settings ranging from isolated wilderness camps and ranches to securely fenced and locked facilities. Juveniles may be committed to a residential facility as part of a court-ordered disposition (e.g., court-committed), or they may be detained prior to adjudication or after adjudication while awaiting disposition or placement elsewhere.

II. Juvenile Residential Facilities

Some juvenile correctional facilities are similar to adult prisons. Others are more like a home environment. In contrast to the adult system, private facilities play a substantial role in the custody and care of juveniles. In the United States there are more than twice as many privately operated juvenile facilities as there are publicly operated facilities, although the private facilities hold fewer juveniles. For example, in 2003, 41% of the residential facilities were publicly operated (18% state-run and 23% local-run) while 59% were privately run facilities; however, 62% of the juveniles were in the public operated facilities, and only 38% were in private facilities (Godwin and Helms 2002).

In 2006, 92,854 juveniles were in public and private residential custody facilities (Sickmund, Sladky, and Kang 2008).[1] This is a rate of 295 in custody for every 100,000 juveniles in the population. Of these 4,717, or a little less than 5%, were status offenders who were being held for behavior such as running away, truancy or incorrigibility—activities that would not be a law violation for adults. The other youths in residential facilities were held for person (34%) or property (25%) offenses, fewer were in for drugs (9%), public order (11%), or technical violations (17%).

As in the adult system, more males (85%) than females were in juvenile residential facilities (Sickmund, Sladky, and Kang 2008). Thirty-five percent of the youths were white (non-Hispanic), 40% were black (non-Hispanic), 21% were Hispanic, and relatively few were American Indian, Asian, or other (4%).

Court-committed juveniles spend longer in residential facilities when compared to detained youths. The median number of days in facilities for committed juveniles varies between 105 (public facilities) and 121 days (private) facilities, while detained youths spend a median of 15 days in the facilities. While almost all of the detained youth are in detention centers (91%), few of the committed juveniles (13%) are; many of the committed juveniles are in long-term secure facilities (45%). Detained and committed youths may also be in shelters, reception/diagnostic centers, group homes, and boot camps (Snyder and Sickmund 2006).

III. CONDITIONS OF CONFINEMENT

Since its inception, the Office of Juvenile Justice and Delinquency Prevention has gathered and reported data on youths held in pubic and private juvenile custody facilities. The concern has been with both the numbers held in facilities and the conditions of that confinement. In its 1988 Amendments to the Juvenile Justice and Delinquency Prevention (OJJDP) Act, Congress required OJJDP to conduct a nationwide investigation of conditions in secure juvenile detention and correctional facilities. In response, OJJDP requested Abt Associates to conduct a study of conditions of confinement in U.S. juvenile detention and correctional facilities (Parent 1993).

The study examined juveniles in traditional types of confinement facilities— detention centers, reception centers, training schools, ranches, camps, and farms— operated by private organizations, as well as state and local governments. Included in the study were 984 facilities with just under 65,000 juveniles, or 69% of all juveniles in custody. The goals of the study were to examine the conditions of confinement and to determine the extent to which the conditions were consistent with national standards. The researchers used data from the biennial Census of Juveniles in Residential Placement conducted by the U.S. Census Bureau, a mail survey of the facilities, and site visits to a representative sample of 95 facilities.

Overall the study revealed serious problems with the conditions of confinement of many juveniles. The researchers concluded that serious and widespread problems existed in the areas of living space, health care, institutional security and safety, and control of suicidal behavior. Evaluators went on to propose that in important areas of treatment, rehabilitation, and education, there was a demonstrated need for more rigorous assessment of how facilities are meeting juveniles' needs in these areas. In only three areas were the conditions deemed generally adequate: (a) food, clothing, and hygiene; (2) recreation; and (3) living accommodations.

One major problem identified in the study was that standards only require the existence of policies, procedures, or programs without stipulating evidence of outcomes or performance measures. For example, a facility may offer an educational program and meet the standards, but there is no assessment of the impact of the program on the juveniles' educational level or future behavior. Standards do not stipulate performance measures or desired outcomes. Therefore, interpretation of the conformance to standards is problematic.

More recent surveys continue to find problems with the conditions in residential facilities. Crowding is a problem in a significant number of residential facilities. For example, the OJJDP 2002 Juvenile Residential Facility Census found 30% of the surveyed facilities reported residential populations at the limit of available standard beds, and 6% had more residents than standard beds (Sickmund 2006). Many youths were held in secure facilities and were locked in their sleeping rooms. More than 25% were held in large facilities with two hundred to one thousand residents. Facility crowding affects a substantial proportion of youths in custody—6% of the facilities are over their standard bed capacity, and 30% are at standard bed capacity. While most facilities evaluate all youths for suicide risk, 17% evaluate only some youths, and 15% do not screen them. In 56% of the facilities, this screening was done by professional mental health staff. Similarly, not all youths are assessed by mental health professionals for mental health needs. Fifty-three percent of the facilities have in-house mental health professional evaluate all youths, in 34% some are evaluated, but not all youths are assessed by professionals, and in 13% of the facilities there is no in-house mental health professional to evaluate youths. Limited information exists about the type and quality of programs offered to youths. Moreover, there is little detailed information about their experiences while incarcerated.

One concern has been whether risk of death is greater for youths in custody than for youths in general (Sickmund 2006). In the twelve months before the 2002 census, there were twenty-six deaths while in custody. Ten of these were for suicide, six each were accidents and illness/natural causes, two were homicide, and two were for other reasons. A comparison of death rates by demographics indicated more than sixty deaths would be expected in the custody population if they were similar to the general population. This is more than double the number of deaths occurring in the facilities in the census.

IV. Changing Opinions about Treatment and Residential Placements

People in the field of juvenile justice have differed in their opinions about the extent to which residential placements are necessary and desirable. The primary criticisms leveled against traditional long-term secure facilities are that (1) they are sterile and unimaginative programs, (2) they are inappropriate places to rehabilitate, and (3) they foster abuse and mistreatment of their charges (Bartollas, Miller, and Dinitz 1976; Feld 1977). Many people consider residential facilities to be training grounds for delinquent and criminal behavior, where lower-risk juveniles learn from more delinquent youths (Greenwood 2002).

Until the early 1970s, in most states the typical residential placement for juvenile delinquents consisted of small community group homes or large congregate training schools. Reports of the dismal situation in juvenile institutions led many to argue against incarceration of youths. Furthermore, theorists argued that labeling youths as criminal had a self-fulfilling prophecy. Those labeled as criminal were believed to begin to view themselves as such and act accordingly. The experience of incarceration was expected to have a negative influence on youths because their treatment within the facility was often abusive, they would view themselves as delinquents, and they would be negatively influenced by others more delinquent than themselves. Taken as a whole, these influences led to a call for deinstitutionalization of juveniles.

During this time, many states began to attempt to reduce the number of juveniles held in large facilities. For example, when he was head of the Massachusetts Department of Youth Services (DYS), Jerry Miller abruptly removed most of the youths from the state's training schools and placed them in a variety of small community-based institutions and programs. A relatively small number of youths who were judged to require more secure care were placed in small twenty- to thirty-bed facilities. Studies examining the impact of these changes found mixed results. The largest impacts on post-reform recidivism were found in the areas of the state where the new programs were most successfully implemented (Coates, Miller, and Ohlin 1982). These results indicated the importance of program integrity and implementation.

Many states used the results of the Massachusetts studies as a basis for shifting more of their youths to privately run, community-based programs. Between 1975 and 1986, the number of commitments to public programs declined by 7%, while commitments to private programs increased by 122%; however, these changes varied greatly by state (Krisberg, DeComo, and Herrera 1992). In general, the number of juveniles committed to public and private facilities increased from approximately 74,270 in 1975 to approximately 108,746 in 1995, an increase of over 46% (Flanagan and Maguire 1990; Moone 1997a, 1997b).

In part, Jerry Miller's actions reflected the opinions of President Johnson's Commission on Law Enforcement and the Administration of Justice (1967) Task Force Report: Juvenile Delinquency and Youth Crime. This report reflected the optimism of the times and the hope that the recommended changes would solve the problems of the juvenile justice system. The focus was on "benevolent reform" of delinquents. One important recommendation in the proposal was the need for the deinstitutionalization of juveniles. Congress subsequently passed the Act that established the Office of Juvenile Justice and Delinquency Prevention (OJJDP) with a mandate to discourage the use of secure incarceration and detention and promote community-based alternatives (Pisciotta 1994); although later the focus of OJJDP changed away from deincarceration of juveniles.

One of the most visible influences for the change in attitudes toward offenders and delinquents was the seminal piece by Martinson summarizing the work he and his colleagues completed for the State of New York (Lipton, Martinson, and Wilkes 1975). They were asked to determine what was effective in reducing the recidivism of delinquents and offenders. They assessed 231 studies of different types of programs conducted from 1947 to 1967. They concluded "with few and isolated exceptions the rehabilitative efforts that have been reported so far have had no appreciable effect on recidivism" (Martinson 1974, p. 25). This report was widely interpreted as demonstrating "nothing works" in the rehabilitation of delinquents and offenders. "Nothing works" became a mantra for many policy makers and correctional staff and administrators.

Later, critics pointed out two major flaws in the conclusions of the Martinson et al. report (Cullen and Gilbert 1982; Cullen and Gendreau 2000; Palmer 1992). First, the methodology used in most of the research was so inadequate that only a few studies warranted any unequivocal interpretations, and second, the majority of studies examined such poorly implemented programs that they could hardly be expected to have an impact on behavior. Yet these criticisms did not stop the general acceptance of the perspective that no correctional programming was effective in reducing recidivism.

Several factors helped to explain why Martinson's conclusion became so widely accepted. The historical times were ripe for a full-scale attack on rehabilitation (Cullen and Gendreau 2000; MacKenzie 2006). Prior to the publication of the Martinson article, there had been a decade of social turbulence. Inequities based on gender, race, and class were exposed, issues such as civil rights and the Vietnam War caused protests, riots, and bombings, and riots occurred in prisons. The public began to doubt whether social institutions could be trusted to solve social problems.

A second major factor that influenced the management and treatment of juveniles was the growth of the conservative era during the late seventies and eighties. In the two decades after President Johnson's Commission, attitudes toward juvenile delinquents changed dramatically, becoming much more punitive (MacKenzie 2006; Cullen and Gendreau 2000). In general, the public and policy makers were less supportive of benevolent reform and rehabilitation. They argued for more punitive case dispositions for juveniles. This "get tough" movement was part of a moral panic. As a result, the philosophy of corrections leaned toward more use of incapacitation and deterrence.

In part, the change in public opinion was due to the increase in crime rates during the seventies and eighties. Serious juvenile crime was increasing, and the justice system was perceived by many as too lenient with juvenile delinquents. In reaction, many states passed more punitive laws. Some of these laws removed young lawbreakers from the juvenile system and required them to be tried in adult criminal courts. During the 1990s, all states passed laws designed to crack down on juvenile crime. The change in public attitudes toward more punitiveness had a major impact on the institutionalization of juveniles. The number of juveniles committed to public and private facilities increased from approximately 74,270 in 1975 to approximately 108,746 in 1995, an increase of over 46% (Flanagan and Maguire 1990; Moone 1997a, 1997b). This increase worries many who believe institutionalization will negatively influence juveniles.

V. Theoretical Perspectives

Many theories propose that criminal justice system involvement has a negative impact on juveniles and that the greater the involvement of the child with the system, the more negative the impact. For example, labeling theory posits that juveniles who become involved with the justice system will begin to view themselves as criminal, and in turn, this self-concept will influence their behavior (Kubrin, Stucky, and Krohn 2009). As a result, they will have a greater chance of continuing their delinquency and becoming adult offenders. Others argue in support of the idea that residential facilities are "criminogenic." In particular, the facilities are expected to be "schools of crime" where many children meet and interact with peers who are more delinquent than they are (Steinberg, Chung, and Little 2004; Dodge, Dishion, and Lansford 2006). Thus, according to Sutherland's differential association theory (Sutherland, 1939), the child learns attitudes favorable to crime and/or how to commit crimes through the symbolic interaction with other adjudicated peers (Kubrin, Stucky, and Krohn 2009). Those with this perspective believe every chance should be given to juveniles to keep them out of the juvenile justice system and particularly out of any residential placement.

From the opposite perspective, some people argue that residential facilities are not necessarily criminogenic—in their opinions, it depends upon the facility (Gordon, Moriarty, and Grant 2000). Some children involved in delinquency come from particularly destructive homes where they have been neglected or physically, emotionally, or sexually abused. They often live in communities where many of their peers are involved with gangs or are delinquents. From this point of view, a residential placement removes them from these negative influences. In well-run residential facilities youths interact with positive, caring adults and are required to attend educational classes, counseling, or other constructive activities. From the perspective of these theorists a range of options should be available, the child's needs should be assessed, and decisions should be made with a focus on rehabilitation. The state acts according to the legal doctrine of *parens patriae*, or acting as parent, and legitimately intervenes in the life of the child. One option is institutional placement, but this should only be used if it is in the best interest of the child or for those who present a danger to themselves or others. Theoretically, at least, the decision is not offense-driven but rather is based on the assessed rehabilitative needs of the juvenile.

Others have very different reasons for being supportive of the use of residential facilities. They support residential placement of juveniles for deterrence and incapacitation purposes (Fass and Pi 2002; Altschuler 1994). Deterrence theory posits that youths who are or might become involved in delinquent activities should be threatened with the possibility of incarceration in a facility; such threats are expected to deter delinquent behavior. Furthermore, for those who commit delinquent acts, incarceration in a facility will incapacitate them. They will not be able to continue their delinquency while in a facility, and thus crime in the community will be reduced. This perspective became particularly important during the time when people accepted the faulty "nothing works" philosophy.

Another group argued for more selective use of incapacitation based on the influential cohort study, Delinquency in a Birth cohort, conducted by Wolfgang and his colleagues (Wolfgang, Figlio, and Sellin 1972). The study consisted of all males born in 1945 who resided in the city of Philadelphia from their 10th through their 18th birthdays. Of the nearly ten thousand subjects Wolfgang and colleagues found a relatively small percent (6.3%) of the total cohort were responsible for 51% of the total number of delinquent acts. The people in support of selective incapacitation argued that if these chronic delinquents could be identified and incapacitated, the number of crimes could be dramatically reduced.

Thus, large differences exist in the opinions of theorists about the impact of institutions on juveniles. Some expect institutions to reduce the later delinquent and criminal activities, but they differ in their opinions about why this is expected. According to some, the reduction will occur due to the positive influence of rehabilitation obtained while incarcerated; others believe it is because the onerousness of the experience will deter juveniles from committing crimes in the future. Another group of theorists believe the experience of being in an institution will negatively influence the juveniles and will lead to increased delinquency and criminal behavior. One way to inform these different theoretical perspectives is to review the research examining the impact of residential placements on the later behavior of juveniles.

VI. The Impact of Residential Placements

Effectiveness can be and has been measured in many different ways. Some studies focus on system-level effectiveness, asking questions about the costs of different types of placements and programs. System-level effectiveness is clearly a major interest of correctional administrators. Researchers have also focused on individual-level impacts of residential facilities. From this perspective, studies have examined attitudes of youths toward different types of facilities, their experiences in the facilities, and changes youths make during their time in the facilities (e.g., antisocial attitudes, educational gains, etc). Perhaps the primary measure of the juvenile justice system is its effectiveness in decreasing the likelihood of youths committing future delinquent or criminal acts. This is the outcome most often discussed by policy makers and the public. While other outcomes may be important, recidivism is the one that seems to be discussed most consistently. Many of the other individual level outcomes are viewed as proxies for recidivism. That is, antisocial attitudes are correlated with delinquent and criminal activity; therefore, if antisocial attitudes are reduced during incarceration, we would expect to see concomitant decreases in recidivism. In this chapter we emphasize studies examining the impact of residential programs on recidivism. While other outcomes are important, recidivism is the outcome of most interest to policy makers.

Researchers have used various methods to attempt to evaluate the effectiveness of programs for juveniles. Martinson and his colleagues (1975) did a literature review of the research. Since that time, several other methods have been developed to determine effectiveness. For example, my colleagues and I developed a two-stage quantitative method, often referred to as the Maryland Scoring Method, for reviewing studies (MacKenzie 2006; Sherman et al. 2002; Sherman et al. 1997). We began by identifying all studies of a particular program or intervention, and in stage one of the scoring we assessed each study for the quality of the research methodology and the direction and significance of results. Scientific quality was judged on a five-point scale with five being the most rigorous design, a randomized trial, and one being too poor a design to consider in evaluating a program. In stage two we assessed the group of studies to determine whether there was sufficient evidence to classify the program as effective, promising, ineffective, or whether there was insufficient evidence. We used decision rules to make the decisions about the classification categories. For instance, a program area like drug treatment during incarceration was considered effective if there were two studies classified as a three or higher in research methodology and showing significant differences in favor of the drug treatment.

Another relatively new method for determining whether programs are effective is the use of systematic reviews and meta-analyses (Lipsey and Wilson 2001; Campbell Collaboration 2009). Meta-analysis is a statistical technique examining a group of studies. The outcomes from independent samples, called "effect sizes," are analyzed to determine whether the program produces the desired outcome.

VII. An Assessment of the Quality of the Research and Outcome of Residential Placement

In one systematic review I identified eight evaluations of residential programs for juveniles (MacKenzie 2006). The question was: can specialized treatment in residential facilities have a more positive impact than traditional options for juveniles? Most facilities were some type of wilderness program (n=6). The comparison groups in most cases were in other types of facilities. Using the Maryland Scoring System, I assessed each program for scientific quality and the significance of the results. Six of the studies were assessed as three or above on scientific method. Two were rated as two or as a methodology too poor to permit conclusions about effectiveness. For the six well-designed studies, I used meta-analysis to examine the differences in recidivism between those who had the program and the comparison group. The meta-analysis compared the recidivism of those who were in the special residential programs with those who were in alternative programs. The results were so mixed that no conclusions could be drawn about the programs. Most likely this is because the specialized programs differed dramatically.

In two studies, the experimental groups had higher recidivism than the control groups. Both studies examined wilderness programs, and both were rated a four in research methods, indicating a relatively rigorous design. Deschenes and her colleagues studied the Nokomis Challenge program (Deschenes, Greenwood, and Marshall 1996). The group who attended the wilderness adventure and aftercare program had significantly higher recidivism than the comparisons. The second study finding higher recidivism for the control group was a study of the Spectrum Wilderness program by Castellano and Soderstrom (1992). The sample size was small, and this probably explains why the large difference in recidivism between the groups was not significant.

In contrast, three other studies found the group who received the treatment had lower recidivism upon release. These studies examined youths in the VisionQuest wilderness program (Greenwood and Turner 1987), the Paint Creek Youth Center (Greenwood and Turner 1993), and Outward Bound (Kelly and Baer 1971).

Perhaps the most interesting of the studies I reviewed was the Gottfredson and Barton (1993) study examining the recidivism of juveniles placed in a training school compared to community placement. Surprisingly, the residential placement group had significantly lower recidivism rates. The researchers suggest that the design of the intervention, rather than its location, appears to be important. It appears juveniles in the facility received more therapeutic treatment, while those released to the community did not. Thus, the researchers concluded that the important component was the treatment and not whether the youths were in a facility or in the community. Neither institutional programs nor community-based programs are uniformly effective or ineffective. To be effective, they require well-designed therapeutic programming that addresses the needs of the participants. The juveniles in the study had relatively serious needs and therefore required treatment if they were going to change. Treatment could be provided in either a facility or in the community, but in this situation, the juveniles in the facility received more treatment, and, hence, their recidivism was lower than those who were in the community. It is unclear if the same results would have been found for youths in the community if they also had received therapeutic treatment. This would support the perspective that treatment is important for these youths and that treatment can be successful when delivered in a facility.

The recidivism results varied greatly for this group of studies of residential facilities. Some studies found reduced recidivism for those released from residential programs, while others found the exact opposite. Many evaluations examined wilderness programs, and the results appear to vary. The most interesting study was the Gottfredson and Barton study finding juveniles released from a training school had lower recidivism than those who remained in the community. These results suggest that juvenile residential programs are not always detrimental to residents and can have a positive impact on youths in comparison to just letting the youths remain in the community without treatment. That is, many delinquent youths have treatment needs that must be addressed if their delinquent activities are to be reduced, and treatment can be provided in an institution or the community.

VIII. Wilderness Programs

Wilderness programs are usually residential treatment facilities where juvenile delinquents are challenged with a series of physical activities, such as backpacking or rock climbing, in an outdoor setting (Wilson and Lipsey 2000). Although programs vary, their treatment concepts are based on the construct of "learning by doing" (Gass 1993). Thus, youths participate in activities that challenge their skills and self-concepts. The goal of wilderness programs is to modify antisocial behavior in two ways. First, by successfully completing a series of incrementally challenging physical activities, the youth builds confidence and self-esteem (Wilson and Lipsey 2000). This newfound success should empower the youth to discontinue his or her previous pattern of inappropriate or illegal behavior. Second, by working together with other participants to solve challenging problems, youths are expected to learn prosocial interpersonal skills that will extend to situations outside the program (Wilson and Lipsey 2000)

Wilson and Lipsey (2000) completed a meta-analysis examining juvenile wilderness and challenge programs with therapeutic components. The programs they included in the analyses had to be designed to reduce or prevent antisocial or delinquent behavior using physical challenge, and, significantly, the programs had to have an interpersonal component. Outcomes included both recidivism and antisocial behavior, and participating youths were not all delinquents (at-risk juveniles were included). Most of the participants were white boys. There were insufficient numbers of girls, minorities, or nondelinquent youths to separately examine the impact of the programs on these groups.

Wilson and Lipsey (2000) identified twenty-eight studies with sixty independent comparisons (sixty effect sizes). Overall, the programs were effective in reducing the antisocial and delinquent behavior of those who participated in the programs. Ten of the studies measured recidivism as the outcome. In these studies, approximately 37% of the comparison group recidivated. In comparison, according to the analysis, only 29% of the group who went to the wilderness camp recidivated. The authors conclude: "This reduction, though modest, is not trivial, and could represent a considerable number of juveniles" (Wilson and Lipsey 2000, p. 5).

They did follow-up analyses to examine whether the results differed depending upon the study methods, subject characteristics (age, risk), or treatment components. Significant differences were found for the treatment components. High-intensity wilderness challenge programs with strenuous solo and group expeditions and other difficult physical activities lowered antisocial and delinquent behavior more than less rigorous programs. Therapy also made a difference. Challenge programs incorporating a distinct therapy enhancement resulted in lower antisocial and delinquent behavior than those without such enhancements. Therapeutic enhancements such as individual counseling, family therapy and therapeutic group sessions appeared to be particularly effective.

The one finding they could not explain was a dose or duration effect. They expected that more exposure and involvement in the programs would produce greater effects on recidivism and antisocial behavior. When the programs were less than six weeks in duration, program length was not related to the magnitude of the impact on the behaviors. Surprisingly, for programs more than six weeks, the longer juveniles were in the programs the less impact the program had on their recidivism. According to the authors, longer programs may differ from the shorter programs in ways not controlled in the analyses. There were only five programs longer than six weeks, and in these programs, youths were usually institutionalized and the challenge portion was only a part of their activities.

Consistent with other literature is the finding that stronger therapeutic enhancements led to the largest reduction in delinquent and antisocial behavior (Cullen and Gendreau 2000; MacKenzie 2006; Andrews et al. 1990; Gass1993). The finding that intense physical activity is also associated with a reduction in these behaviors is surprising. Other research examining physical activity has not found this result. It may be that the difference is in either the outcomes measured (both antisocial behavior and delinquency) or the characteristics of the participants (at-risk, white). Therefore, when comparing these results to other studies, it is important to keep in mind the fact that the meta-analysis included both delinquents and at-risk youths, and also, the outcomes studied were antisocial behavior as well as recidivism.

IX. Boot Camp Facilities

Boot camps, a residential alternative to traditional detention centers and training schools for juveniles, were popular during the 1990s. They appeared to reflect the more punitive attitudes of the public and policy makers that developed toward juveniles during the 1980s. Correctional boot camps began in adult systems in 1983 in Oklahoma and Georgia and rapidly spread throughout the nation. Boot camps for juveniles did not develop until the late 1980s but then became very popular during the nineties. By 2000 there were seventy juvenile camps in the United States for juveniles. State and local jurisdictions as well as private and not-for-profit companies developed boot camps.

Most correctional boot camps are short-term residential programs designed to be similar to military basic training. Participants are required to follow a rigorous daily schedule of activities involving drill and ceremony and physical training. There is often an elaborate intake ceremony where those who are entering are told the rules, stand at attention, and have their heads shaved. Staff is addressed by military titles. Participants in the camps must arise early each morning and are kept busy most of the day. Punishments for misbehavior are swift and usually involve some type of physical activity such as push-ups or running a track. Some programs punish the whole squad of juveniles if one person misbehaves. A graduation ceremony marks successful completion of the program, and government officials and family members may be invited to the graduation.

Camps differ in the amount of time devoted to therapeutic activities in the daily schedule (MacKenzie and Hebert 1996; MacKenzie and Rosay 1996; MacKenzie and Armstrong 2004). In some camps, juveniles spend a great deal of time in education, counseling, and drug treatment, while in other camps, they spend a limited amount of time in these therapeutic activities and more time in physical activities such as physical training and drill and ceremony. Camps also differ in whether they provide aftercare and reentry programs to assist participants with adjustment in the community. Large differences exist in the type of aftercare and reentry programs when these programs are provided by the camps.

Perhaps the most interesting research from the perspective of policy makers and the public are the studies examining participants' behavior upon release from the camps. Wilson, MacKenzie, and Mitchell (2005) completed a meta-analysis examining the impact of boot camps on the criminal behavior of convicted adults and adjudicated juveniles. They did an intensive search of databases in order to locate eligible studies of boot camps or boot camp-like programs (alternatively called shock incarceration, intensive incarceration). Studies included in the meta-analysis had to have used a control group design, participants must have been under the supervision of corrections or juvenile justice systems, and the study must have reported some outcome measure of criminal behavior such as arrests, convictions, or reincarceration.

The researchers identified forty-three independent studies comparing boot camp participants with a control group. Of these, seventeen studied juvenile camps.

The authors examined whether the programs differed depending upon the characteristics of (1) the research design, (2) the participants, or (3) the program.

Overall, the meta-analysis of the programs showed no significant differences
between those who went to the boot camps and the comparison groups. According
to the results, the odds of recidivating were approximately the same for those who
participated in a boot camp and those who did not. While the overall results showed
no differences between the recidivism rates of the boot camp releases and the comparisons, there were some studies demonstrating differences between the groups.
The researchers investigated whether some particular aspects of the participants or
the program lead to differences in outcomes. They found boot camps with a strong
treatment emphasis had more of an impact on recidivism than those with a weak
treatment focus (with treatment identified as therapeutic activities), but the difference in recidivism between the boot camp participants and the comparisons was
still not very great. The authors concluded that there is no evidence that correctional boot camps reduce the recidivism of participants. Insufficient evidence exists
to examine the impact of combining a rehabilitative focus with the camps, nor is it
possible to examine the impact of the programs on different types of delinquents
and offenders (higher risk, genders, races, etc.).

X. Deterrence versus Rehabilitation

The focus on punishment and deterrence increased greatly during the 1980s and
1990s. Boot camp facilities reflect the type of specific deterrence programs that were
particularly popular at this time, when attitudes toward delinquents became more
punitive. Many believed the major goal of correctional interventions was to deter
future criminal behavior. In a review of meta-analyses, Lipsey and Cullen (2007)
examined what types of programs were effective in reducing criminal activities.
They located all meta-analyses examining correctional programs and summarized
the findings. One issue they explored was the impact of sanctions and surveillance
on later delinquent and criminal behavior. Sanctions and surveillance programs
were those based on deterrence-oriented correctional policies such as boot camps,
community supervision, intensive supervision, or electronic monitoring. In general, the meta-analyses they reviewed did not find much of an impact for these
types of programs. Similar to the research findings for boot camps, also a deterrence-based program, the recidivism of the comparison groups in the deterrence-
oriented correctional programs was almost the same as the group who received the
studied sanction. In fact, in some cases, the sanctioned offenders and delinquents
had higher recidivism.

In addition, Lipsey and Cullen (2007) were interested in the impact of imprisonment on recidivism. The studies of the impact of imprisonment they included in
the meta-analyses review were of limited methodological rigor because random

assignment to a facility versus a noncustodial alternative is generally not considered ethically viable. However, several meta-analyses of studies using quasi-experimental studies examined whether incarceration had an impact on the later behavior of juveniles and adults (Smith, Goggin, and Gendreau 2002). In the meta-analyses, they compared the impact of those who had (1) longer verses shorter imprisonment sentences and (2) incarceration versus a community sentence. Adults and juveniles with longer sentences or who were sentenced to a facility rather than the community had increased recidivism. According to their review, correction programs relying on sanctions and deterrence such as boot camps, imprisonment versus a community sanction, or longer terms of imprisonment are not effective in reducing the future criminal activities of adults and juveniles. In fact, such programs may lead to an increase in recidivism.

Lipsey and Cullen's findings are consistent with a more recent study by Loughran and his colleagues examining the impact of incarceration on subsequent behavior (Loughran et al. 2009). In comparison to community placement, they found there was no benefit to incarceration, nor were longer periods of incarceration effective in reducing recidivism. This provides more support for the conclusion that deterrence and punishment-based programs are not effective in reducing delinquent and criminal behavior.

In contrast to the deterrence-based programs, according to Lipsey and Cullen's review of meta-analyses, rehabilitation programs are effective in reducing recidivism. Rehabilitation programs were distinguished from sanctions because they were designed to motivate and guide offenders and delinquents and support constructive change in whatever characteristics or circumstances engendered their delinquent or criminal behavior. Hundreds of studies have been conducted on these programs, and the findings have been examined in numerous meta-analyses. More meta-analyses have been conducted on rehabilitation programs for juveniles than adults. In all of the meta-analyses Lipsey and Cullen (2007) studied, they found rehabilitation reduced the recidivism. Most of the studies found recidivism reductions between 20% to 30%. That is, if 50% of the comparison group recidivated, then only 20% to 30% of the treated group would recidivate, a substantial reduction.

Two of the meta-analyses looked at rehabilitation in residential facilities versus the community. In both environments, rehabilitation reduced recidivism. However, treatment had a greater impact when delivered in the community. In other words, the effect sizes for community-based rehabilitation treatment were greater than if the program was provided in a residential facility. Neither study examined whether this was due to differences in the nature or quality of the treatment, characteristics of participants, or the influence of the context. One meta-analysis (Andrews et al. 1990) included both adults and juveniles in the comparison of community versus residential treatment. The other meta-analysis included only juveniles in the sample of studies examined (Lipsey and Wilson 1998). In the later study, they found treatment for juveniles resulted in a substantial reduction in recidivism rates—an estimated 24% of the juveniles treated in the community recidivated compared to 50% of the control. In comparison, recidivism estimates were higher for those treated in a facility, but still lower than the comparison group. Thirty-six percent of the residentially treated group would be expected to recidivate when compared with 50% recidivism for the comparisons. However, it is important to keep in mind that despite the fact that treatment was not as effective in a facility as it was when given in the community, it was still better than no treatment at all.

Hundred of studies have been conducted examining the impact of correctional interventions on recidivism, some investigating punitive approaches and some investigating rehabilitative treatment. There is amazing consistency in the results of systematic reviews (meta-analyses) despite the differences in the techniques and coverage. Supervision and sanctions based on a deterrence model of corrections find only moderate reductions in recidivism, and, in fact, in some instances these interventions increase recidivism. In comparison, the effects of rehabilitation programs consistently show a reduction in recidivism and, at times, this reduction is substantial.

XI. Impact of Treatment Provided in Facilities

In another meta-analysis, Lipsey (2009) focused on the identification of the correlates of recidivism. He was interested in identifying the characteristics of the study methods, programs, delinquents, and intervention circumstances most strongly associated with a reduction in recidivism. He found a considerable amount of the variability in recidivism outcomes in the studies was due to the study design, and these results often made it difficult to disentangle the program effects. That is, it was often difficult to tell whether differences in recidivism rates between those who had the treatment and those who did not could have been due to some characteristic of the research design and not to the impact of the program.

Once the study design was controlled, three factors were more strongly associated with intervention effects: (1) the intervention approach or type of treatment; (2) the quantity and quality of treatment provided or the implementation; and (3) the characteristics of the juveniles themselves. According to Lipsey (2009), interventions using a cognitive-behavioral and skill-building approach are more effective than other approaches. Second, a well-implemented program has a stronger impact than a poorly implemented program, even if the intervention used a cognitive-behavioral approach. However, quality of implementation is not well documented in most of the studies, so as a proxy variable, Lipsey used involvement of the researcher/developer in the program delivery. If the researcher or developer was involved in the delivery of the program, the program had a larger impact on recidivism. In comparison, the characteristics of the juveniles do not seem to have a strong impact on recidivism. That is, the impact of the programs was similar for participants of different ages, genders, or ethnicities. The one exception to this finding is that programs are more effective for juveniles who are at higher risk of recidivism.

Lipsey added to the above findings by examining the following questions: What treatment programs are most effective in reducing the recidivism of delinquents? And what impact does the level of juvenile justice supervision have on recidivism? That is, does a particular type of treatment given within a facility have the same impact as the identical treatment given during probation supervision? Finally, they contrast programs with a therapeutic approach, which attempts to engage the youths in supportive, constructive processes of change, with those relying more on external control and coercion (discipline or surveillance).

Particularly interesting was their analysis of the effectiveness of various types of programs delivered to juveniles in different levels of justice supervision. In regard to juvenile justice supervision, they classified programs as: (1) no supervision—mostly prevention programs; (2) diversion—diverted to community treatment after law enforcement or juvenile court contact; (3) probation or parole—juveniles in the community but under the supervision of the juvenile court or parole officers; and (4) incarceration in juvenile correctional institutions. Interestingly, they found no significant relationship in the analysis between recidivism outcome and the level of juvenile justice supervision. That is, for juveniles of similar risk, age, gender, and ethnicity (these were controlled in the analysis) who were given similar interventions, there were no differences in recidivism. Said in another way, if youths were given the same interventions, it did not matter if these interventions were given in the community, after diversion, while on probation or parole, or while incarcerated. More high-risk juveniles were incarcerated, however, if they were given an effective program while in the facility, it was as effective as a similar program given to lower-risk juveniles in the community. Thus, good programs can be effective even when given within an institutional environment where there is more potential for adverse effects through, for instance, association with antisocial peers.

Lipsey examined the impact of therapeutic interventions compared with non-therapeutic interventions. Restorative programs, counseling, skill-building programs, and multiple coordinated services were classified as therapeutic, while surveillance, deterrence, and discipline programs were considered non-therapeutic. Therapeutic programs were more effective in reducing recidivism than non-therapeutic programs. Deterrence and discipline programs increased recidivism, but the impact was not significant.

XII. Institutionalized Serious Juvenile Offenders

In another systematic review and meta-analysis, Lipsey and Wilson identified eighty-three studies of institutionalized serious juvenile offenders, and they studied the impact of programs on their recidivism. Most of the studies included males of

Anglo or mixed ethnicity between 14 and 17 years of age. A majority of the juveniles had prior offenses, and for approximately 66% there was an indication of a history of aggressive behavior. In seventy-four of the studies, the juveniles were in juvenile justice institutions, and in nine, they were in residential facilities under private or mental health administration. Typically, the study compared juveniles who received a specialized service versus a control group. Both groups were in institutions.

Overall, they found therapeutic programs provided within institutions were effective in reducing later recidivism. However, the impact differed depending upon how the program was implemented. For example, recidivism was lower if youths spent more time in the program and if the program was monitored to ensure juveniles received the expected treatment. More established programs had larger impacts on recidivism as did programs delivered by mental health personnel. As with the previous meta-analysis, characteristics of the juveniles did not make a difference in the results. That is, the impact of treatment does not change for juveniles of different ages, genders, ethnic mixes, or with histories of prior offenses.

In regard to the impact of residential placement, the most important finding from this study was that the most effective treatment had a relatively strong impact on recidivism. The results indicated that if 50% of the control group recidivated, then the treated group's recidivism would be in the 30% to 35% range—a substantial reduction considering these are institutionalized delinquents. The effective programs taught interpersonal skills, used teaching family homes, were community-based residential facilities (mostly non-juvenile justice), or provided multiple services.

In contrast, Milieu Therapy programs did not reduce recidivism. Six programs—individual counseling, group counseling, guided group interactions, drug abstinence, wilderness/challenge, and employment related—had mixed results. Some of these were effective, others were not. Overall, they did not demonstrate a significant impact on recidivism.

In summary, the meta-analyses conducted by Lipsey and his colleagues provide strong evidence that therapeutic programs with certain characteristics provided in institutions are effective in reducing later criminal and delinquent behavior. This appears to be true even when the participants are serious delinquents.

It is important to note that Wilson and Lipsey studied therapeutic programs offered within facilities, therefore the results are not similar to other studies of residential placement versus community placement. For example, Loughran and colleagues compared (1) the recidivism of juveniles placed in facilities versus similar youths placed on probation and (2) the impact of length of stay on recidivism (Loughran et al. 2009). They found no differences in recidivism between youths placed in residential facilities and those on probation (they rigorously controlled for selection effects). Furthermore, length of stay (dosage) in a facility also did not have an impact on recidivism. In their opinions, this raises questions about the rehabilitative mission of the juvenile justice system. There was no indication of the type of rehabilitative programming youths received in the community or facilities in the Loughran study, whereas Lipsey and Wilson were studying therapeutic programs provided to youths in facilities.

XIII. Effective Programs

The results of the theoretical meta-analyses provide evidence that effective programs may be delivered either within a facility or in the community. Although the impact of programs provided in the community may be greater than those given in residential facilities, if the programs in residential facilities have the appropriate characteristics, recidivism is reduced and, at times, the reduction is substantial. Therapeutic programs focusing on positively changing juveniles are effective, while deterrence-based interventions are not. Furthermore, therapeutic programs incorporating cognitive-behavioral and behavior therapy models, skill-based training, and multimodal approaches are more effective than other types of therapeutic programs.

In contrast to the more theoretical meta-analyses, a relatively large number of meta-analyses have focused on the effects of specific interventions or programs such as cognitive-behavioral therapy, drug treatment, or education. In a review of this literature, MacKenzie (2006) examined correctional interventions, management strategies, and rehabilitation programs in order to identify which were effective in reducing the recidivism of offenders and delinquents. She found 284 evaluations of sufficient research quality to be used to assess effectiveness. According to her systematic reviews and the Maryland Scoring Methods, she found academic education, vocation education, cognitive skills programs, cognitive-behavior treatment and behavioral treatment for sex offenders, Multisystemic therapy (see next section of chapter), drug courts, drug treatment in the community, and incarceration-based drug treatment to be effective in reducing recidivism. Ineffective programs were those with poor or no theoretical basis, were poorly implemented, focused on punishment, deterrence, or control instead of rehabilitation, and emphasized the formation of ties or bonds without first changing the individual's thought process.

After examining the results of these systematic reviews, MacKenzie (2006) proposed that effective programs are those that bring about a change within the individual (MacKenzie 2006; see also Giordano, Cernkovich, and Rudolph, 2002; Farrington 1998). Such cognitive transformations are necessary before the individual is ready to take advantage of opportunities within the environment. Some individuals may be particularly difficult to change, and this may be why domestic violence treatment has not been found to be effective in reducing later criminal activity (MacKenzie 2006). Similarly, programs designed to give people opportunities such as work or employment services may not be effective because they don't focus on changing individuals so that they are ready to take advantage of the opportunities (MacKenzie 2006).

In summary, this research gives some examples of the types of programs that can be provided to juveniles in residential facilities to reduce their later recidivism. Drug treatment, cognitive skills programs, sex offender treatment using cognitive-behavioral or behavioral methods, and academic and vocation education may be particularly important programs to offer to juveniles. These programs appear to assist juveniles in making a cognitive transformation of the type that will enable them to move away from criminal and delinquent activities in the future. However, as noted in studies of the impact of programs and the theoretical meta-analyses, the implementation of the programs will have a major impact on the outcomes.

XIV. Blueprint Programs

In support of evidence-based practices, several groups have put forward lists of model programs based on the specific criteria they have developed. These lists make use of the opinions of experts who are knowledgeable about programs and research design. One of these lists is the Blueprints for Violence Prevention, a project of the Center for the Study and Prevention of Violence at the University of Colorado (Blueprints for Violence Prevention n.d.). The Blueprints identify exemplary violence and drug prevention programs that meet a high standard of effectiveness based on research. Program effectiveness is first evaluated by the Blueprints staff and is sent for a final review from an advisory board consisting of experts in the field of violence prevention. The Blueprints staff has assessed more than eight hundred programs and has designated eleven model programs and nineteen promising programs. These programs have been found to be effective in reducing adolescent violent crime, aggression, delinquency, and substance abuse. The programs are evaluated based on three criteria: (1) evidence of a deterrent effect with a strong research design, (2) sustained effect, and (3) multiple site replications. In order to be labeled as a model program, the program must meet all three criteria. However, promising programs only have to meet the first criterion.

Of the eleven model programs and nineteen promising programs identified, there were no specific residential programs selected. Additionally, most of the Blueprint programs are directed at preventing juveniles from becoming involved in criminal behavior and therefore are not directly relevant to the population of juveniles examined in this chapter. Only one program focuses on juvenile delinquents—Multisystemic Therapy (MST). However, it may be possible to adapt many of the model and promising programs so that they can be conducted in residential facilities. The prior research by Lipsey and his colleagues suggests programs with proven effectiveness can be successfully delivered within facilities.

MST is the one Blueprint program that addresses the needs of juvenile delinquents, and it has recently garnered a great deal of attention because preliminary data indicated it successfully reduced criminal activities (MacKenzie 2006). It is designed to provide cost-effective, community-based treatment for youths with serious behavior disorders who are at high risk for out-of-home placement. A recent systematic review determined that there is inconclusive evidence of the effectiveness of MST compared with other interventions for youth (Littell, Popa, and Forsythe

2005). While there is no evidence that MST has harmful effects, there is also no evidence that it is effective in reducing delinquent and criminal activities. In one of the studies in the meta-analysis by Littell and colleagues—a rigorous (intent-to-treat) study—no significant differences in arrests and convictions were found when MST was compared to usual services in restrictive out-of-home placements. From one perspective, it is disappointing that MST is not effective. However, the results again lend support to the perspective that facility placement is not inherently detrimental. That is, juveniles who were in out-of-home placements did no worse than those given the very intensive MST treatment in the community. It is not an issue of community or facility, but rather what is done in each environment that makes a difference.

Another example of expert system-based lists is the model programs identified by The Office of Juvenile Justice and Delinquency Prevention (OJJDP). A variety of topics, including substance abuse, mental health, and education are induced in the model programs list. The OJJDP model program database consists of programs that comprise the complete range of youth services, including preventions, sanctions, residential placements, and reentry. These model programs lists are designed to be utilized to aid juvenile justice practitioners, administrators, and researchers to increase accountability, ensure public safety, and reduce recidivism.

All programs considered by OJJDP to be model programs are evaluated using a specific rating system. The model program guide ratings are derived from four measures of program effectiveness: (1) conceptual framework of the program; (2) program fidelity; (3) evaluation design; and (3) empirical evidence demonstrating the prevention or reduction of problem behavior, the reduction of risk factors related to problem behavior, or the enhancement of protective factors related to problem behavior.

Programs are classified into three categories (exemplary, effective, and promising), which supply the reader with a summary of the research supporting a particular program. Exemplary programs are implemented with a high degree of fidelity, and high quality research demonstrates strong empirical findings. Effective programs are implemented with sufficient fidelity and have adequate empirical findings demonstrating effectiveness. Promising programs are implemented with minimal fidelity, and empirical findings are reasonable strong. Although the model program database contains summary information on 209 evidence-based delinquency intervention and prevention programs, only 7 of those programs are residential programs (Residential Student Assistance Program; Phoenix House Academy; Sexual Abuse, Family Education, and Treatment; Aggression Replacement Training; Mendota Juvenile Treatment Center; VisionQuest; and Boys Town). Furthermore, of the seven programs, all but Boys Town are rated by OJJDP as effective. Boys Town is rated as promising, but none are rated exemplary.

In contrast to the earlier reported meta-analyses, the model program lists (Blueprints and OJJDP model programs) focus on specific programs (e.g., "brand name") with the assumption that effectiveness depends upon following one of a relatively few recipes. The meta-analyses indicate that a large range of generic programs may be effective if they incorporate specific components demonstrated to be effective (Lipsey 2009). Well-implemented programs targeting high-risk offenders can successfully reduce later criminal and delinquent behavior, and these successful programs are not limited to the "brand name" programs.

XV. AFTERCARE SERVICES

Most juveniles placed in residential facilities will ultimately reenter the community. However, many of these juveniles are released into the same communities where they were initially arrested, and any gains made while incarcerated are forgotten. It is estimated that re-arrest rates reach as high as 55% in the first twelve months after release from incarceration (Synder and Sickmund 2006). Therefore, juvenile justice practitioners have begun to explore ways to provide transitional and reintegrative supervision and services to serious juvenile delinquents.

Aftercare programs, as they have traditionally been called, or the recently popular label reentry programs, are designed to help individuals make the transition back to the community after a period of incarceration. Those working in the field of juvenile justice emphasize the importance of starting the preparation for release at the very beginning of the period of incarceration (Gies 2003; Altschuler and Armstrong 1994a, 1994b, 1994c). The research on effective programs supports this proposal. This period can be used to help bring about the cognitive transformation that will be necessary if the juvenile is going to be able to take advantage of opportunities provided in the community after release.

Similar to MST, aftercare programs are designed to provide assistance in various areas of the juveniles' lives including family, peers, schooling, and work. Preliminary findings from studies of an aftercare model developed with support from OJJDP have been positive (Altschuler and Armstrong 2001; Weibush, McNulty, and Le 2000). However, Atlschuler and Armstrong (2001), the designers of the OJJDP model, conclude that it is too early to know the exact impact of intensive aftercare programs on juvenile offenders. One problem that arises is the link between facility staff and the outside world. Frequently, staff has little contact with individuals who will be involved with the juveniles once they are released. In one study my colleagues and I completed, we visited more than forty juvenile facilities (MacKenzie et al. 2001). As part of the study, we interviewed administrators and staff about their work. One question we asked was what they knew about what would happen to the juveniles after they left the facility. Disappointingly, they knew very little—the majority did not know if the juveniles returned home or to some other placement, or if the juveniles returned to school, worked on a GED, or were employed. They did not know if the juveniles were re-arrested or returned to a facility. One wonders how they can design an appropriate program enabling juveniles to succeed in the community if they do not know what happens to the juveniles upon release.

Obviously, their ability to prepare the juveniles for eventual release is severely limited.

XVI. Conclusions

Debate and controversy exist over whether the use of residential facilities for juveniles is reasonable. People differ in their opinions about the impact of residential programs on juveniles. Some believe they are inherently detrimental, others assert they are necessary to deter youths from future problem behavior, while others argue they are necessary in some instances, and in certain situations they can have a positive impact on youths. In this chapter we have reviewed the research examining the impact of residential placement. We focused on the impact such placement has on the later delinquent and criminal behavior. The answer to the question of whether residential placement is effective is not easy to determine.

One concern is whether residential placement has a negative influence on juveniles. There are few studies of residential placement versus community placement. In part, this is because of the difficulties and ethical dilemmas in designing studies that compare juveniles sent to facilities with others who are given community sanctions. Few people would agree that randomly assigning juveniles to these options is ethically justified despite the fact that this would be the strongest research design to answer the question. A few quasi-experimental research designs found juveniles incarcerated in a facility had higher recidivism rates when compared to those given a community alternative. In addition, juveniles given longer sentences in a facility had higher recidivism rates than those with shorter sentences. These results suggest a negative influence of residential placement.

However, the finding of a negative influence from residential placement is not consistent. What appears to be important is what happens to the juveniles in the facility. Treatment within a facility can reduce the later recidivism of juveniles. For instance, juveniles who spent time in a facility had lower recidivism than those who were in the community, and the effect is most likely due to the fact that juveniles in the facility received treatment while those in the community received little or no treatment (Gottfredson and Barton 1993). Furthermore, effectiveness of interventions does not depend on the level of juvenile justice supervision. With risk and other characteristics of juveniles controlled, interventions are about equally effective whether the youths were in a custodial facility or in the community (Lipsey 2009).

Further support for the finding that treatment can be effectively given in residential facilities comes from the meta-analysis by Lipsey (2009). He found the level of criminal justice supervision did not make a difference in outcomes. An effective program given to youths in either a facility or in the community reduced recidivism. An effective program provided to juveniles in facilities can successfully reduce recidivism despite the fact that these juveniles may be at more high risk for recidivism, that they may be institutionalized serious delinquents, and that there may be negative impacts on them while they are in facilities. While treatment in either the community or a residential facility can successfully reduce recidivism, treatment in the community may have a greater impact. However, it is unclear whether this is due to differences in the quality of treatment, characteristics of participants, or the context (e.g., community versus residential). These results would seem to argue against the assertion that all residential placements have negative impacts on juveniles. At times, with appropriate programs, the impact can be positive and reduce later criminal and delinquent behavior.

Not all interventions are effective. Effective interventions have particular characteristics. Ineffective programs emphasize a deterrent or punishment philosophy. Boot camps, intensive supervision, and electronic monitoring are programs that are not effective in reducing recidivism, and some of these may actually increase criminal or delinquent activity. Just sending a juvenile to a residential facility will not deter the youth from later misbehavior. To be effective, the intervention must have a therapeutic focus emphasizing constructive change in the characteristics or circumstances engendering the delinquent or criminal behavior. Such programs can have a substantial impact on later recidivism. Programs that bring about a cognitive transformation in thinking and attitudes may be particularly important in changing juveniles so their criminal and delinquent activities are reduced. As noted above, such programs can be successfully provided within residential facilities or in the community.

In general, the impact of programs is similar for different races, ethnicities, genders, or ages. Studies have not demonstrated differences between these groups in the impact on recidivism. An effective, or conversely, ineffective program has a similar effect on the recidivism for these different groups. However, information given in the reports of the studies of various programs used in the meta-analyses was limited, and, additionally, there were often small numbers (e.g., few girls) participating in the studies, so the results are certainly not definitive. More work needs to be done to discover any possible differences in the impacts of programs delivered to these different groups. Recently, there has been interest in identifying the success of gender- and race/ethnic-sensitive programming and how such programs may be more successful for some groups.

The one consistent finding of differences in groups is for high-risk groups versus low-risk groups. Programs delivered to high-risk groups have a greater impact on reducing recidivism. Possibly this is because there is little room for recidivism to be reduced by even effective programs if the juveniles are at low risk for recidivism to begin with. Since many high-risk juveniles are in facilities, this provides further support for the need for well-implemented, therapeutic programming residential facilities.

Residential facilities are not inherently detrimental to youths. The impact of the experience is dependent upon what is offered to the juveniles while they are in custody. On the other hand, it is important to note that programs offered in the community have a greater impact on recidivism. Furthermore, incarceration alone will not deter juveniles from future criminal and delinquent activities. Juveniles must have positive experiences while they are in the facility. Given these results, it appears the most sensible decision about whether to incarcerate should be based on a decision about how much danger the youths pose to themselves or the community. And once the decision is made to incarcerate, it is important to provide well-implemented programs that are effective in bring about a cognitive transformation.

NOTES

1. The numbers and rates include secure and nonsecure facilities that hold alleged or adjudicated juvenile delinquents or status offenders who were under 21 years of age.

REFERENCES

Altschuler, David. 1994. "Tough and Smart Juvenile Incarceration: Reintegrating Punishment, Deterrence, and Rehabilitation." *Saint Louis University Public Law Review* 14: 217–37.

Altschuler, David, and Troy Armstrong. 1994a. *Intensive Aftercare of High-Risk Juveniles: An Assessment.* Report. Washington, DC: Office of Juvenile Justice and Delinquency Prevention, U.S. Department of Justice.

———. 1994b. *Intensive Aftercare for High-Risk Juvenile Offenders: A Community Care Model.* Summary. Washington, DC: Office of Juvenile Justice and Delinquency Prevention, U.S. Department of Justice.

———. 1994c. *Intensive Aftercare for High-Risk Juvenile Offenders: Polices and Procedures.* Summary. Washington, DC: Office of Juvenile Justice and Delinquency Prevention, U.S. Department of Justice.

———. 2001. "Reintegrating High-Risk Juvenile Offenders into Communities: Experiences and Prospects." *Corrections Management Quarterly* 5(1): 79–95.

Andrews, Donald, Ivan Zinger, Robert Hoge, James Bonta, Paul Gendreau, and Francis Cullen. 1990. "Does Correctional Treatment Work? A Clinically Relevant and Psychologically Informed Meta-analysis." *Criminology* 28(3): 369–404.

Bartollas, Clemens, Stuart Miller, and Simon Dinitz, 1976. *Juvenile Victimization: The Institutional Paradox.* New York: Wiley.

Blueprints for Violence Prevention. n.d. Center for the Study and Prevention of Violence. Boulder: Institute of Behavioral Science, University of Boulder. http://www.colorado.edu/cspv/blueprints/index.html.

Campbell Collaboration. 2009. www.campbellcollaboration.org.

Castellano, Thomas, and Irina Sodertrom. 1992. "Therapeutic Wilderness Programs and Juvenile Recidivism: A Program Evaluation." *Journal of Offender Rehabilitation* 17(34): 19–46.

Coates, Robert, Alden Miller, and Lloyd Ohlin. 1982. *Diversity in a Youth Correctional System.* Cambridge, MA: Ballinger.

Cullen, Francis and Paul Gendreau. 2000. "Assessing Correctional Rehabilitation: Policy, Practice, and Prospects." In *Policies, Processes, and Decisions of the Criminal Justice System*, edited by J. Horney, J. Martin, D. L. MacKenzie, R. Peterson and D. Rosenbaum. Washington, DC: National Institute of Justice.

Cullen, Francis, and Karen Gilbert. 1982. *Reaffirming Rehabilitation*. Ohio: Anderson Publishing Co.

Deschenes, Elizabeth, Peter Greenwood, and Grant Marshall. 1996. *The Nokomis Challenge Program Evaluation*. Santa Monica, CA: The RAND Corporation.

Dodge, Kenneth, Thomas Dishion, and Jennifer Lansford. 2006. *Deviant Peer Influences in Programs for Youth: Problems and Solutions*. New York: Guilford.

Farrington, David. 1998. "Individual Differences and Offending." In *Handbook of Crime and Punishment*, edited by M. Tonry. Oxford: Oxford University Press.

Fass, Simon, and Chung-Ron Pi. 2002. "Getting Tough on Juvenile Crime: An Analysis of Costs and Benefits." *Journal of Research in Crime and Delinquency* 39(4): 363–99.

Feld, Barry. 1977. *Neutralizing Inmate Violence*. Cambridge, MA: Ballinger.

Flanagan, Timothy, and Kathleen Maguire. 1990. *Sourcebook of Criminal Justice Statistics: 1989*. Washington, DC: U.S. Government Printing Office.

Gass, Michael. 1993. "Foundations of Adventure Therapy." In *Adventure Therapy: Therapeutic Applications of Adventure Programming*, edited by M. Gass. Dubuque, IA: Kendall Hunt Publishing Co.

Gies, Steve. 2003. *Aftercare Services Bulletin*. Washington, DC: Office of Juvenile Justice and Delinquency Prevention, U.S. Department of Justice.

Giordano, Peggy, Stephen Cernkovich, and Jennifer Rudolph. 2002. "Gender, Crime and Desistance: Toward a Theory of Cognitive Transformation." *American Journal of Sociology* 107(4): 990–1064.

Godwin, C. Draven, and Jeffery Helms. 2002. "Statistics and Trends in Juvenile Justice and Forensic Psychology." In *Handbook of Juvenile Forensic Psychology*, edited by N. Ribner. San Francisco, CA: John Wiley & Sons Inc.

Gordon, Jill, Laura Moriarty, and Patricia Grant. 2000. "The Impact of a Juvenile Residential Treatment Center on Minority Offenders." *Journal of Contemporary Criminal Justice* 16: 194–208.

Gottfredson, Denise, and William Barton. 1993. "Deinstitutionalization of Juvenile Offenders." *Criminology* 31: 591–611.

Greenwood, Peter. 2002. "Juvenile Crime and Juvenile Justice." In *Crime: Public Policies for Crime Control*, edited by J. Q. Wilson and J. Petersilia. Oakland, CA: ICS Press.

Greenwood, Peter, and Susan Turner. 1993. "Evaluation of the Paint Creek Youth Center: A Residential Program for Serious Delinquents." *Criminology* 31: 263–79.

———. 1987. *The VisionQuest Program: An Evaluation*. Santa Monica, CA: The RAND Corporation.

Kelly, Francis, and Daniel Baer. 1971. "Physical Challenge as a Treatment for Delinquency." *Crime and Delinquency* 17: 437–45.

Krisberg, Barry, Robert DeComo, and Norma Herrera. 1992. *National Juvenile Custody Trends 1978–1989*. Washington, DC: Office of Juvenile Justice and Delinquency Prevention, U.S. Department of Justice.

Kubrin, Charis, Thomas Stucky, and Marvin Krohn. 2009. *Researching Theories of Crime and Deviance*. New York: Oxford University Press Inc.

Lipsey, Mark. 2009. "The Primary Factors That Characterize Effective Interventions with Juvenile Offenders: A Meta-analytic Overview." *Victims and Offenders* 4: 124–47.

Lipsey, Mark, and Francis Cullen. 2007. "The Effectiveness of Correctional Rehabilitation: A Review of Systematic Reviews." *Annual Review of Law and Social Science* 3: 297–320.

Lipsey, Mark, and David Wilson. 1998. "Effective Intervention for Serious Juvenile Offenders." In *Serious and Violent Juvenile Offenders: Risk Factors and Successful Interventions*, edited by R. Loeber and D. Farrington. Thousand Oaks, CA: Sage.

Lipsey, Mark, and David Wilson. 2001. *Practical Meta-analysis*. Thousand Oaks, CA: Sage.

Lipton, Douglas, Robert Martinson, and Judith Wilkes. 1975. *The Effectiveness of Correctional Treatment: A Survey of Treatment Evaluation Studies*. New York: Praeger.

Littell, Julia, Melanie Popa, and Burnee Forsythe. 2005. "Multisystemic Therapy for Social, Emotional, and Behavioral Problems in Youth Aged 10–17." http://www.campbellcollaboration.org/artman2/uploads/1/Multisystemic_therapy_Littell_2005.pdf.

Loughran, Thomas, Edward Mulvey, Carol Schubert, Jeffery Fagan, Alex Piquero, and Sandra Losoya. 2009. "Estimating a Dose-Response Relationship between Length of Stay and Future Recidivism in Serious Juvenile Offenders." *Criminology* 47: 699–740.

MacKenzie, Doris. 2006. *What Works in Corrections: Reducing the Criminal Activities of Offenders and Delinquents*. New York: Cambridge University Press.

MacKenzie, Doris and Gaylene Armstrong, eds. 2004. *Correctional Boot Camps: Military Basic Training as a Model for Corrections*. Sage Publications: Thousand Oaks, CA.

MacKenzie, Doris, and Eugene Herbert, eds. 1996. *Correctional Boot Camps: A Tough Intermediate Sanction*. Washington DC: National Institute of Justice, U.S. Department of Justice.

MacKenzie, Doris, and Andre Rosay. 1996. *Juvenile Boot Camps in the United States. Boot Camps: What Works for Whom? A Practitioners' Guide*. Maryland: American Correctional Association.

Mackenzie, Doris, David Wilson, Gaylene Armstrong, and Angela Grover. 2001. "The Impact of Boot Camps and Traditional Institutions on Juvenile Residents: Adjustment, Perception of the Environment and Changes in Social Bonds, Impulsivity, and Antisocial Attitudes." *Journal of Research in Crime and Delinquency* 38: 279–313.

Martinson, Robert. 1974. "What Works? Questions and Answers about Prison Reform." *Public Interest* 35: 22–54.

Moone, Joseph. 1997a. *Juveniles in Private Facilities, 1991–1995. Fact Sheet*. Washington, DC: Office of Juvenile Justice and Delinquency Prevention.

———. 1997b. *States at a Glance: Juveniles in Public Facilities, 1995. Fact Sheet*. Washington, DC: Office of Juvenile Justice and Delinquency Prevention.

OJJDP Model Programs Guide. n.d. http://www2.dsgonline.com/mpg/Default.aspx.

Palmer, T. 1992. *Re-emergence of Correctional Intervention*. Thousand Oaks, CA: Sage Publications Inc.

Parent, Dale. 1993. *Conditions of Confinement*. Washington, DC: U.S. Department of Justice, Office of Juvenile Justice and Delinquency Prevention.

Pisciotta, Alexander. 1994. "A Retrospective Look at the Task Force Report on Juvenile Delinquency and Youth Crime." In *1967 President's Crime commission Report: Its Impact 25 Years Later*, edited by J. A. Conley. Cincinnati, OH: Anderson Publishing Co.

President's Commission on Law Enforcement and the Administration of Justice. 1967. *Task Force Report: Juvenile Delinquency and Youth Crime*. Washington, DC: U.S. Government Printing Office.

Sherman, Lawrence, David Farring, Brandon Welsh, and Doris MacKenzie, eds. 2002. *Evidence Based Crime Prevention*. New York: Routledge.

Sherman, Lawrence, Denise Gottfredson, Doris MacKenzie, John Eck, Peter Reuter, Shawn
    Bushway. 1997. *Preventing Crime: What Works, What Doesn't Work, What's Promising.*
    Washington, DC: National Institutes of Justice.
Sickmund, Melissa. 2006. *Juvenile Residential Facility Census, 2002: Selected Findings.*
    Washington, DC: Office of Justice Programs, U.S. Department of Justice.
Sickmund, Melissa, Thomas Sladky, and Wei Kang. 2008. "Census of Juveniles in
    Residential Placement Databook." Washington, DC: National Center for Juvenile
    Justice, Office of Juvenile Justice and Delinquency Prevention. http:www.ojjdp.ncjrs.
    org/ojstatbb/cjrp.
Smith, Paula, Claire Goggin, and Paul Gendreau. 2002. *The Effects of Prison Sentences and
    Intermediate Sanctions on Recidivism: General Effects and Individual Differences.*
    Ottawa, Canada: Correctional Services of Canada.
Snyder, Howard, and Melissa Sickmund. 2006. *Juvenile Offenders and Victims: 2006
    National Report.* Washington, DC: U.S. Department of Justice, Office of Justice
    Programs, Office of Juvenile Justice and Delinquency Prevention.
Steinberg, Laurence, He Len Chung, and Michelle Little. 2004. "Reentry of Young
    Offenders from the Justice System: A Developmental Perspective." *Youth Violence and
    Juvenile Justice* 2: 21–38.
Sutherland, Edwin H. 1939. *Principles of Criminology*, 3rd ed. Philadelphia: J. B. Lippincott
    Company.
Weibush, Richard, Betsie McNulty, and Thao Le. 2000. *Implementation of the Intensive
    Community-Based Aftercare Program.* Bulletin. Washington, DC: U.S. Department of
    Justice, Office of Justice Programs, Office of Juvenile Justice and Delinquency
    Prevention.
Wilson, Sandra, and Mark Lipsey. 2000. "Wilderness Challenge Programs for Delinquent
    Youth: A Meta-analysis of Outcome Evaluations." *Evaluation and Program Planning* 23:
    1–12.
Wilson, David, Doris MacKenzie, and Fawn Mitchell. 2005. "Effects of Correctional Boot
    Camps on Offending." http://nicic.gov/Library/022761.
Wolfgang, Marvin, Robert Figlio, and Thorsten Sellin. 1972. *Delinquency in a birth cohort.*
    Chicago: University of Chicago Press.

PART IX

YOUTH IN CRIMINAL COURT

CHAPTER 32

TRANSFER OF JUVENILES TO CRIMINAL COURT

BARRY C. FELD AND DONNA M. BISHOP

TRANSFER of juvenile offenders for adult prosecution provides the nexus between the deterministic, rehabilitative premises of juvenile justice and the free-will, punishment assumptions of criminal justice. Although juvenile courts theoretically attempt to rehabilitate all young offenders, for a small but significant number, juvenile court intervention is deemed inappropriate. These typically are youths charged with very serious crimes, for which the public demands sanctions that exceed those that juvenile courts can impose; older youths near the maximum age of juvenile court jurisdiction, for whom the window of eligibility for treatment is very short; and/or recidivists who, because they have not responded to prior intervention, appear resistant to treatment (Podkopacz and Feld 1995, 1996; United States General Accounting Office 1995). During the "get tough" era of the 1980s and early 1990s, dramatic increases in juvenile gun violence and homicide evoked community outrage to which politicians responded with promises to "crack down" on youths with punitive adult sanctions (White et al. 1999; Feld 2003a, 2003b). What ensued was a fundamental transformation of the jurisprudence and practice of transfer, change in the legal and cultural construction of adolescence, and a dramatic increase in the numbers of youths convicted and sentenced as adults.

Transfer of jurisdiction constitutes a type of *sentencing* decision. Juvenile courts traditionally focused on an offender's "best interests" and assigned primary importance to individualized treatment. Criminal courts accord greater significance to the seriousness of the offense and attempt to deliver proportionate punishments. All of the differences between juvenile and criminal courts' sentencing philosophies and practices emerge in debates about transfer policies (Zimring and Fagan 2000). Transfer laws attempt to resolve both fundamental crime control issues and the ambivalence embedded in our cultural construction of youth—immature and dependent versus responsible and almost adult-like. Even as research on adolescent culpability (Scott and Steinberg 2008) and the Supreme Court's decisions in *Roper v. Simmons* (543 U.S. 551 [2005]) and *Graham v. Florida* (No. 08-7412,—U.S.— [2010]) emphasize youths' diminished criminal responsibility, transfer laws emphasize punitive policies—"adult crime, adult time"—that ignore developmental differences between youths and adults. Transfer laws reflect tensions in penal objectives—rehabilitation, deterrence, incapacitation, and retribution—and differ in emphases on offender and offense, discretion and rules, indeterminacy and determinacy, and appropriate decision makers—judges, legislatures, and prosecutors.

This chapter analyzes the history, implementation and consequences of changes in transfer laws over the past few decades. The first part of the chapter places transfer decisions in a broader sentencing policy context, examines alternative transfer strategies, and reviews evaluations of their implementation. It analyzes the legislative approaches and the characteristics of youths transferred under each regime. The second section of the chapter considers the sentencing policy goals of transfer and assays to what extent transfers of jurisdiction achieve goals of retribution, general deterrence, incapacitation, specific deterrence, or recognition of youths' diminished criminal responsibility. The final part of the chapters ends with a prescriptive conclusion about appropriate waiver policies for juvenile courts.

I. Transfer Statutes: Policy, Practice, and Problems

Every jurisdiction uses one or more statutory approaches to prosecute some juveniles as adults (Snyder and Sickmund 2006; Griffin 2008). Although the details of states' transfer laws vary considerably, the three generic approaches are judicial waiver, legislative offense exclusion, and prosecutorial direct-file (see Table 32.1). The three strategies emphasize different sentencing policies, rely on different organizational actors, and elicit different information for deciding whether to sentence young offenders as adults or children. They allocate the decision to different branches of government: judicial, executive, and legislative.

Judicial waiver represents the oldest and most numerically prevalent transfer strategy, although it may account for the fewest number of youths transferred (Bishop and Frazier 2000). Statutes in forty-five states specify the minimum age of eligibility and the types of offenses a judge may transfer (see Table 32.2). A juvenile court judge may waive jurisdiction after conducting a hearing to determine whether a youth is "amenable to treatment" or poses a threat to public safety. These indi-

Table 32.1. Transfer Mechanisms

| State | Judicial Waiver | | | Prosecutorial | Statutory | Reverse | Once an Adult |
	Discretionary	Presumptive	Mandatory	Discretion	Exclusion	Waiver	Always an Adult
Number of states	45	15	15	15	29	25	34
Alabama	■				■		■
Alaska	■	■			■		
Arizona	■			■	■	■	■
Arkansas	■			■		■	
California	■	■		■	■	■	■
Colorado	■	■		■		■	
Connecticut			■			■	
Delaware	■		■	■	■	■	■
Dist. Of Columbia	■	■		■			■
Florida	■				■		■
Georgia	■		■	■	■	■	
Hawaii	■						
Idaho	■				■		■
Illinois	■	■	■		■	■	■
Indiana	■		■		■		■
Iowa	■				■		■
Kansas	■	■					■
Kentucky			■			■	
Louisiana	■		■	■	■		■

(continued)

Table 32.1. (continued)

State	Judicial Waiver			Prosecutorial Discretion	Statutory Exclusion	Reverse Waiver	Once an Adult / Always an Adult
	Discretionary	Presumptive	Mandatory				
Maine	■	■					■
Maryland	■				■	■	■
Massachusetts					■		
Michigan	■			■			■
Minnesota	■	■			■		■
Mississippi	■				■	■	■
Missouri	■						■
Montana				■	■	■	
Nebraska				■		■	
Nevada	■	■			■	■	■
New Hampshire	■	■					■
New Jersey	■	■	■				
New Mexico					■		
New York					■	■	
North Carolina	■	■	■				■
North Dakota	■		■				■
Ohio	■		■				■
Oklahoma	■				■	■	■
Oregon	■			■	■	■	■
Pennsylvania	■	■			■	■	■
Rhode Island	■	■	■		■		■

South Carolina	■				■
South Dakota	■	■		■	■
Tennessee	■				■
Texas	■				■
Utah	■	■			■
Vermont	■	■	■		■
Virginia	■	■	■	■	■
Washington	■		■		■
West Virginia	■	■			
Wisconsin	■			■	■
Wyoming	■	■		■	

Note: Table information is as of the end of the 2008 legislative session.

vidualized assessments reflect the traditional discretion exercised by juvenile courts (Feld 1987; Fagan 2008).

Legislative offense exclusion frequently supplements judicial waiver, emphasizes serious offenses, and reflects the criminal law's retributive values (Snyder and Sickmund 2006). Legislatures create juvenile courts, and they may define their jurisdiction to exclude youths based on age and offense. For example, a number of states exclude from juvenile court jurisdiction youths 16 or older and charged with first-degree murder, and others exclude offenses more extensively (Griffin 2008; Table 32.3). Legislative line drawing that sets the maximum age of juvenile court jurisdiction at 15 or 16 years of age, below the general 18-year-old age of majority, results in the adult prosecution of the largest numbers of chronological juveniles (United States General Accounting Office 1995; Snyder and Sickmund 2006).

Prosecutorial waiver or direct-file constitutes a third method by which fifteen states transfer some youths to the criminal justice system (Snyder and Sickmund 2006; Griffin 2008; Table 32.4). In these states, juvenile and criminal courts share concurrent jurisdiction over certain categories of ages and offenses—typically older youths and serious crimes—and the prosecutor decides in which forum the case will be heard (Bishop, Frazier, and Henretta 1989). For example, in some states prosecutors may select either juvenile or criminal processing for youths 14 or older and charged with murder or other serious offenses (Snyder and Sickmund 2006; Griffin 2008).

Blended sentencing represents another juvenile-criminal court sentencing option (Snyder and Sickmund 2006; Griffin 2008). Based on age, offense, and prior record, some states extend the dispositional jurisdiction of juvenile courts to enable judges to impose delinquency sentences as well as a stayed adult criminal sentence (Table 32.5). In other states, a criminal court judge may impose a delinquency disposition backed up by the threat of a criminal sentence (Snyder and Sickmund 2006; Table 32.6). Blended sentences attempt to give youths "one last chance at rehabilitation," and if juveniles successfully complete their delinquency dispositions, then courts need not execute their criminal sentences. Because blended sentences expose youths to the possibility of a criminal sentence, they are entitled to receive all criminal procedural safeguards, including a jury trial, prior to imposition of these mixed sanctions.

The Supreme Court in *Kent v. United States*, 383 U.S. 541 (1966), required juvenile courts to provide procedural due process in waiver hearings—including a full investigation and specific findings of fact—and thereby encumbered the informality, flexibility, and ease of judges' transfer decisions. Although a few states always had excluded serious crimes, such as capital offenses, from juvenile court jurisdiction (Feld 1987), many more states adopted offense exclusion and prosecutor direct-file laws in reaction to *Kent's* requirement of procedural formality as law makers sought simple and efficient alternatives to waiver hearings (White et al. 1999; Feld 2000; Fagan 2008). In the 1970s, proponents of "just deserts" sentencing policies advocated determinate and proportional offense-based sentences as an alternative to judicial discretion and provided a rationale for offense exclusion (von Hirsch

Table 32.2. Judicial Waiver Age and Offense Thresholds

State	Any Criminal Offense	Certain Felonies	Capital Crimes	Murder	Certain Person Offenses	Certain Property Offenses	Certain Drug Offenses	Certain Weapon Offenses
Alabama	14							
Alaska	NS							
Arizona		NS						
Arkansas		14	14	14	14			14
California	16							
Colorado		12		12	12			
Delaware	NS							NS
Dist. of Columbia	16	15						
Florida	14							
Georgia	15		13		13			
Hawaii		14		NS				
Idaho	14	NS		NS	NS	NS	NS	
Illinois	13							
Indiana		14		10			16	
Iowa	14							
Kansas	10							
Kentucky		14	14					
Louisiana				14	14			
Maine		NS						
Maryland	15		NS					
Michigan		14						
Minnesota		14						
Mississippi	13							

(continued)

Table 32.2. (continued)

State	Any Criminal Offense	Certain Felonies	Capital Crimes	Murder	Certain Person Offenses	Certain Property Offenses	Certain Drug Offenses	Certain Weapon Offenses
Missouri		12						
Nevada		14						
New Hampshire		15		13	13			
New Jersey	14			14	14	14	14	14
North Carolina		13						
North Dakota	16				14			
Ohio		14						
Oklahoma		NS						
Oregon		15		NS	NS	15		
Pennsylvania		14						
Rhode Island		16	NS					
South Carolina	16	14		NS	NS		14	14
South Dakota		NS						
Tennessee	16			NS	NS			
Texas		14	14				14	
Utah		14						
Vermont				10	10	10		
Virginia		14						
Washington	NS							
West Virginia		NS		NS	NS	NS	NS	
Wisconsin	15	14		14	14	14	14	
Wyoming	13							

Notes: An entry in the column below an offense category means that there is some offense or offenses in that category for which a juvenile may be waived for criminal prosecution. The number indicates the youngest possible age at which a juvenile accused of an offense in that category may be waived. "NS" means no age restriction is specified for an offense in that category. Table information is as of the end of the 2008 legislative session.

Table 32.3. Statutory Exclusion Thresholds

State	Any Criminal Offense	Certain Felonies	Capital Crimes	Murder	Certain Person Offenses	Certain Property Offenses	Certain Drug Offenses	Certain Weapon Offenses
Alabama		16	16				16	
Alaska					16	16		
Arizona		15		15	15			
California				14	14			
Delaware		15						
Florida				16	NS	16	16	
Georgia				13	13			
Idaho				14	14	14	14	
Illinois		15		13	15			15
Indiana		16		16	16		16	16
Iowa		16					16	16
Louisiana				15	15			
Maryland			14	16	16			16
Massachusetts				14				
Minnesota				16				
Mississippi		13	13					
Montana				17	17	17	17	17
Nevada	16*	NS		NS	16			
New Mexico				15				
New York				13	13	14		14
Oklahoma				13				
Oregon				15	15			

(continued)

Table 32.3. (continued)

State	Any Criminal Offense	Certain Felonies	Capital Crimes	Murder	Certain Person Offenses	Certain Property Offenses	Certain Drug Offenses	Certain Weapon Offenses
Pennsylvania				NS	15			
South Carolina		16						
South Dakota		16						
Utah		16		16				
Vermont				14	14	14		
Washington				16	16	16		
Wisconsin				10	10			

Note: An entry in the column below an offense category means that there is some offense or offenses in that category that are excluded from juvenile court jurisdiction. The number indicates the youngest possible age at which a juvenile accused of an offense in that category is subject to exclusion. "NS" means no age restriction is specified for an offense in that category. Table information is as of the end of the 2008 legislative session.

* In Nevada, the exclusion applies to any juvenile with a previous felony adjudication, regardless of the current offense charged, if the current offense involves the use or threatened use of a firearm.

Table 32.4. Prosecutorial Discretion Thresholds

State	Any Criminal Offense	Certain Felonies	Capital Crimes	Murder	Certain Person Offenses	Certain Property Offenses	Certain Drug Offenses	Certain Weapon Offenses
Arizona		14						
Arkansas	16	16	14	14	14			
California		14	14	14	14	14	14	
Colorado		14		14	14	14		14
Dist. of Columbia				16	16	16		
Florida	16	16	NS	14	14	14		14
Georgia			NS					
Louisiana				15	15	15	15	
Michigan		14		14	14	14	14	
Montana				12	12	16	16	16
Nebraska	16	NS						
Oklahoma		16		15	15	15	16	15
Vermont	16							
Virginia				14	14			
Wyoming		14		14	14	14		

Notes: An entry in the column below an offense category means that there is some offense or offenses in that category that are subject to criminal prosecution at the option of the prosecutor. The number indicates the youngest possible age at which a juvenile accused of an offense in that category is subject to criminal prosecution. "NS" means no age restriction is specified for an offense in that category. Table information is as of the end of the 2008 legislative session.

Table 32.5. Juvenile Blended Sentencing Thresholds

State	Any Criminal Offense	Certain Felonies	Capital Crimes	Murder	Certain Person Offenses	Certain Property Offenses	Certain Drug Offenses	Certain Weapon Offenses
Alaska					16			14
Arkansas		14		NS	14			
Colorado		NS			NS			
Connecticut		14			NS			
Illinois		13						
Kansas	10							
Massachusetts		14			14			14
Michigan	NS	NS		NS	NS	NS	NS	
Minnesota		14						
Montana		12		NS	NS	NS	NS	NS
New Mexico		14		14	14	14		
Ohio		10		10				
Rhode Island		NS						
Texas		NS		NS	NS		NS	

Notes: Ages in the columns under the offenses may not apply to all offense restrictions, but represent the youngest possible age at which a blended sentence may be imposed by a juvenile court. "NS" indicates that in at least one of the offense restrictions indicated, no minimum age is specified. Table information is as of the end of the 2008 legislative session

Table 32.6. Individualized Judicial Corrective Mechanisms

State	Automatic/ Prosecutor-Controlled Transfer	Reverse Waiver Available	Criminal Blended Sentencing Available	Not Available in All Cases	No Judicial Corrective Available
Number of States	44	25	18	15	14
Alabama	■				■
Alaska	■				■
Arizona	■	■		■	
Arkansas	■	■	■		
California	■	■	■	■	
Colorado	■	■	■		
Connecticut	■	■		■	
Delaware	■	■			
Dist. of Columbia	■				■
Florida	■	■	■	■	
Georgia	■		■	■	
Idaho	■		■		
Illinois	■	■	■	■	■
Indiana	■				
Iowa	■	■	■		
Kentucky	■	■	■	■	
Louisiana	■				■
Maryland	■	■		■	
Massachusetts	■		■	■	
Michigan	■		■	■	■
Minnesota	■				
Mississippi	■	■			

(continued)

Table 32.6. (continued)

State	Automatic/ Prosecutor-Controlled Transfer	Reverse Waiver Available	Criminal Blended Sentencing Available	Not Available in All Cases	No Judicial Corrective Available
Missouri			■		
Montana	■		■		
Nebraska	■	■			
Nevada	■	■		■	
New Jersey	■				■
New Mexico	■			■	
New York	■	■	■	■	
North Carolina	■				■
North Dakota	■	■			■
Ohio	■	■			■
Oklahoma	■	■	■		
Oregon	■			■	
Pennsylvania	■				
Rhode Island	■	■			■
South Carolina	■	■			■
South Dakota	■	■			
Tennessee		■			
Utah	■	■			
Vermont	■		■		■
Virginia	■	■	■	■	
Washington	■				
West Virginia	■		■		
Wisconsin	■	■	■		■
Wyoming	■	■			

Note: Table information is as of the end of the 2008 legislative session.

1976, 1986; Feld 1978; Tonry 1995; Garland 2001). Research on criminal careers in the 1970s and 1980s provided an empirical rationale for selective incapacitation strategies, including waivers contingent on youths' prior records (Wolfgang, Figlio, and Sellin 1972; Blumstein et al. 1986). These rationales—retribution and incapacitation—proved attractive for politicians who proposed to "crack down" on "baby boom" increases in youth crime that peaked in the late 1970s (Feld 1987, 2003a, 2003b). In addition, legislators expected that increased certainty and severity of sentences would deter young offenders.

During the early 1990s, increases in urban youth violence and gun-homicide associated with a crack-cocaine epidemic fueled the desire to "get tough" and provided political impetus to prosecute larger numbers of youths as adults (Blumstein 1995; Feld 1999, 2003a, 2003b). Legislators augmented lists of excluded offenses, lowered the ages at which states could criminally prosecute youths, and expanded prosecutors' authority to direct-file them in criminal court (Snyder and Sickmund 2006; Torbet et al. 1996). Get tough amendments shifted the focus of transfer policies and practices from the offender to the offense and moved discretion from judges to prosecutors.

Analysts estimate that states criminally prosecute about 250,000 youths under 18 annually (Bishop 2000; Snyder and Sickmund 2006; Fagan 2008). States that set their maximum juvenile court jurisdiction at 15 or 16 years of age account for the majority of youths tried as adults (Snyder and Sickmund 2006). Judges waive about 7,500 cases annually, prosecutors direct-file about 27,000 youths in criminal courts, and youths charged with excluded offenses account for the remainder (Campaign for Youth Justice 2007).

Table 32.1 summarizes the diversity of transfer statutes. States use one or more different and overlapping strategies to select youths for criminal prosecution. Forty-five states have judicial waiver provisions, twenty-nine exclude certain categories of offenses from juvenile court jurisdiction, fifteen allow prosecutors to make the jurisdictional determination, and more than two dozen have some type of juvenile or criminal court blended sentencing option or reverse waiver provision. Tables 32.2–32.5, discussed *infra*, provide additional details about each of these alternatives, including the ages and types of offenses for which judges or prosecutors may transfer jurisdiction. The following sections analyze each transfer strategy—judicial waiver, legislative offense exclusion, and prosecutorial direct-file—and assess the costs, benefits, and consequences of different types of transfer laws.

A. Judicial Waiver and Individualized Sentencing: The Impetus for Alternatives

From the inception of juvenile courts, judges could transfer some young offenders to criminal courts (Rothman 1980; Tanenhaus 2000). In *Kent v. United States* (1966), the Supreme Court formalized judicial waiver hearings and required juvenile courts to provide youths with some procedural protections before making a waiver decision (Feld 1978). *Kent* concluded that the loss of juvenile court protections was a critically important action that required a hearing, assistance of counsel, access to probation reports, and written findings for appellate courts to review. *Kent* anticipated many of the procedural safeguards that the Court mandated for delinquency adjudications in *In re Gault*, 387 U.S. 1 (1967). Later, in *Breed v. Jones*, 421 U.S. 519 (1975), the Court applied the double jeopardy clause of the Fifth Amendment to delinquency convictions and required states to determine juvenile or court jurisdiction before proceeding to trial so that transferred youths would not be twice tried for the same offense.

Until "get tough" amendments in the 1990s (Torbet et al. 1996), most states allowed judges to transfer jurisdiction based on assessments of a youth's "amenability to treatment" or "threat to public safety." For example, *Kent*, 383 U.S. at 566–67, included in its opinion a list of substantive criteria that juvenile court judges should consider:

> An offense falling within the statutory limitations...will be waived if it has prosecutive merit and if it is heinous or of an aggravated character, or—even though less serious—if it represents a pattern of repeated offenses which indicate that the juvenile may be beyond rehabilitation under Juvenile Court procedures, or if the public needs the protection afforded by such action.
>
> The determinative factors which will be considered by the Judge in deciding whether the Juvenile Court's jurisdiction over such offenses will be waived are the following:
>
> 1. The seriousness of the alleged offense to the community and whether the protection of the community requires waiver.
> 2. Whether the alleged offense was committed in an aggressive, violent, premeditated or willful manner.
> 3. Whether the alleged offense was against persons or against property, greater weight being given to offenses against persons especially if personal injury resulted.
> 4. The prosecutive merit of the complaint, i.e., whether there is evidence upon which a Grand Jury may be expected to return an indictment....
> 5. The desirability of trial and disposition of the entire offense in one court when the juvenile's associates in the alleged offense are adults....
> 6. The sophistication and maturity of the juvenile as determined by consideration of his home, environmental situation, emotional attitude and pattern of living.
> 7. The record and previous history of the juvenile, including previous contacts with the Youth Aid Division, other law enforcement agencies, juvenile courts and other jurisdictions, prior periods of probation to this Court, or prior commitments to juvenile institutions.
> 8. The prospects for adequate protection of the public and the likelihood of reasonable rehabilitation of the juvenile (if he is found to have committed the alleged offense) by the use of procedures, services and facilities currently available to the Juvenile Court.

State court decisions and statutes detail waiver criteria with varying degrees of precision and frequently incorporate the *Kent* criteria. As Table 32.2 indicates, some states limit judicial waiver to felony offenses and establish a minimum age for adult prosecution—typically 16, 15, or 14. Other jurisdictions prescribe no minimum offense or age restrictions and remit waiver decisions to each judge's discretion (Feld 1987; Snyder and Sickmund 2006). In 15 states, a prosecutor's allegation of certain crimes creates a presumption for transfer and shifts the burden of proof to the youth to prove amenability to treatment in juvenile courts. In 15 other states, if a prosecutor shows probable cause that a youth committed the alleged crime, then transfer is mandatory and a judge must waive the youth. Both presumptive and mandatory provisions limit judges' broad waiver discretion.

In practice, judges focus on three sets of factors when they assess a youth's "amenability to treatment" and threat to public safety. A youth's age and the length of time remaining within juvenile court jurisdiction provide impetus for judges to waive older youths more readily than younger ones (Fagan and Deschenes 1990; Podkopacz and Feld 1995; 1996; United States General Accounting Office 1995). Limits on the upper end of the juvenile court's disposition jurisdiction preclude proportional sentences for older juveniles charged with serious crimes, and impel judges to waive them to criminal courts for longer sentences. Second, judges focus on youths' "amenability to treatment," as evidenced by clinical evaluations and prior interventions. Once youths receive several correctional interventions—i.e., exhaust available juvenile treatments—transfer becomes more likely (Podkopacz and Feld 1995, 1996). Finally, judges assess youths' threat to public safety based on multiple factors, including present offense, prior record, whether the youth used a weapon, and whether the youth is gang-involved (Fagan and Deschenes 1990; Podkopacz and Feld 1995, 1996; Howell 1996; Lanza-Kaduce et al. 2005). Judges balance a crime's seriousness, a youth's pattern of offending, and her prospects for successful juvenile treatment.

Despite those factors' seeming rationality and applicability, criteria like "amenability to treatment" and "threat to public safety" are open to interpretation and, consequently, give judges broad discretion. Lists of substantive factors, such as those set forth in *Kent*, allow them selectively to emphasize one criterion or another to justify any decision. Zimring (1981) described judicial waiver laws as the juvenile equivalent of the standardless capital punishment statute condemned by the Supreme Court in *Furman v. Georgia*, 408 U.S. 238 (1972). The subjective nature of decisions, the absence of guidelines, and the dearth of clinical tools with which to assess amenability to treatment or to predict dangerousness allow judges to make inconsistent rulings without procedural or appellate checks.

Liberal critics of judicial waiver complain that judges' discretion leads to inconsistent and disparate outcomes in similar cases, to racial disparities, and to geographic disparities across counties and between urban and rural courts (Feld 1978, 1990). During the 1990s, conservative critics charged judges with being too reluctant to waive cases to criminal courts: their "soft on crime" attitudes were said to contribute to rising adolescent crime rates (Fagan 2008). Empirical research clearly documents inconsistent decisions and over-representation of racial minorities.

States' rates of judicial waiver for similar offenders vary considerably (Hamparian et al. 1982; United States General Accounting Office 1995). Even within a single jurisdiction, judges do not apply waiver statutes consistently from county to county or from court to court (Feld 1990). Research in several states reports a contextual pattern of "justice by geography" in which where youths live, rather than what they did, determines their juvenile or adult status (Hamparian et al. 1982; Heuser 1985; Feld 1990). In some states, for example, rural judges waive jurisdiction more readily than do urban judges confronted with similarly charged juveniles (Feld 1990; Lemmon, Sontheimer, and Saylor 1991; Poulos and Orchowsky 1994). Within a single urban county, different judges in the same court decide cases of similarly situated offenders differently (Podkopacz and Feld 1995, 1996). To avoid unproductive litigation, prosecutors attempt to anticipate judges' waiver decisions and only file transfer motions in a small proportion of eligible cases (Dawson 1992).[1] These practices affect the characteristics of youths waived and the subsequent criminal sentences they receive.

Examinations of judicial waiver proceedings consistently report that minority juveniles are more likely to be transferred than similar white offenders (Eigen 1981a, 1981b; Hamparian et al. 1982; Fagan, Forst, and Vivona 1987; United States General Accounting Office 1995; Bortner, Zatz, and Hawkins 2000; Amnesty International 2005). Recent "get tough" law reforms that target violent and drug offenders have exacerbated racial disparities (Poe-Yamagata and Jones 2007; Campaign for Youth Justice 2007; Snyder and Sickmund 2006). As a result of successive screenings, differential processing, and cumulative disadvantage, minority youths comprise the majority of juveniles transferred to criminal court and three-quarters of youths under age 18 who enter prison (Bortner, Zatz, and Hawkins 2000; Juszkiewicz 2000; Males and MacAllair 2000; McCord, Widom, and Crowell 2001).

B. Legislative Offense Exclusion and Prosecutorial Direct File: Criminal Responsibility without a Hearing

Legislative offense exclusion simply removes from juvenile court jurisdiction youths charged with certain offenses (Feld 1987; Snyder and Sickmund 2006). Concurrent jurisdiction or direct-file laws give prosecutors the power to charge youths of specified age with certain offenses in either juvenile or criminal court (Bishop and Frazier 1991; McCarthy 1994). State laws define juvenile courts' jurisdiction, powers, and purposes in different ways. For example, they may set juvenile courts' maximum age limits at 17, 16, or 15 years of age (Snyder and Sickmund 2006). If a legislature defines juvenile court jurisdiction to include only those persons below a jurisdictional age and whom prosecutors charge with a nonexcluded offense, then, by statutory definition, all other chronological juveniles are adults and subject to criminal prosecution. Table 32.3 summarizes the twenty-nine states that exclude some offenses from juvenile court jurisdiction. Most of these jurisdictions exclude murder by youths 14 years of age or older and many exclude broader ranges of offenses—crimes against the person, property, drugs, or weapons offenses as well.

1. *Legislative Offense Exclusion*

Analysts long have criticized offense exclusion and prosecutorial direct file laws because they conflict with juvenile courts' rehabilitative philosophy and focus exclusively on offenses (Mylniec 1976; Zimring 1981, 1991; Fagan 1990; Guttman 1995; Sabo 1996; Klein 1998). Youths have claimed that allowing prosecutors to charge them directly in criminal courts violates the Constitution because they do not receive *Kent's* procedural safeguards. Appellate courts uniformly reject these claims and grant legislators and prosecutors broad discretion to exclude or charge youths as adults.[2]

Sometimes, a single, highly visible case inflames public fears and political passions and provides the impetus to lower the criminal court's jurisdictional age and/ or to exclude additional offenses. One dramatic case that produced an excluded offense law occurred in New York in the mid-1970s. At that time, juvenile court jurisdiction ended at age 16 and did not allow for transfer of younger offenders. After 15-year-old Willie Bosket robbed and murdered two subway passengers within months of his release from a secure juvenile facility (Butterfield 1995; Singer 1996), New York passed the Juvenile Offender (JO) Act, which excluded from juvenile court jurisdiction youths 13 years of age or older and charged with murder, and those 14 or 15 and charged with kidnapping, arson, assault, manslaughter, rape, burglary, or robbery.

In *Recriminalizing Delinquency* (1996), Singer analyzed the New York laws' genesis and implementation and concluded that the JO-excluded offenses and prosecutorial and judicial transfer-back provisions simply shifted discretion to prosecutors rather than eliminated it. More recently, Kupchik (2006) reported that youths tried in New York's criminal courts were much more likely to be incarcerated and for longer periods of time than comparable youths tried as juveniles. Despite the increased punitiveness in New York's law, he observed that the courtroom work groups attempted to ameliorate its harshness, tried to provide rehabilitative measures, and sought to recognize youthfulness as a mitigating factor, but failed to achieve those goals (Kupchik 2006).

2. *Concurrent Jurisdiction and Prosecutorial Direct-File Laws*

Direct-file statutes create concurrent jurisdiction in both juvenile and criminal courts for categories of offenses and give prosecutors authority to charge youths with those crimes in either forum. Direct-file laws give prosecutors more authority to choose the forum than do offense exclusion laws, which require certain serious offenses to be tried only in criminal court. As Table 32.4 indicates, in fifteen jurisdictions, juvenile and criminal courts share concurrent jurisdiction over youths 16 years or older charged with any felony and over youths 14 years or older charged with enumerated violent crimes or who have prior felony convictions (Feld 2000). Essentially, prosecutors makes two types of decisions: charge and forum. They first decide whether probable cause exists to believe that the youth committed an offense and, if it is one that falls within concurrent jurisdiction, whether to charge the youth in juvenile or criminal court.

In most direct-file states, statutes provide no guidelines, standards, or criteria to control the prosecutor's choice of forum (Feld 2000). While judges in waiver hearings typically receive information from clinicians and court services personnel about a youth's maturity, sophistication, or amenability to treatment, prosecutors lack access to personal information and rely primarily on police reports (Bishop and Frazier 1991; Kupchik 2006). While prosecutors possess expertise to evaluate the sufficiency of evidence and to select charges, they bring no professional insight or offender-related information to the decision to try a youth as a juvenile or as an adult (Sabo 1996).

Critics of the direct-file approach contend that locally elected prosecutors readily succumb to political pressures, symbolically posture on crime issues just like "get tough" legislators, exercise their discretion just as subjectively and idiosyncratically as do judges but without an opportunity for appellate review, and introduce substantial geographic variability into the administration of justice (Bishop, Frazier, and Henretta 1989; Bishop and Frazier 1991). Young prosecutors typically work in juvenile court as their first assignment and often lack the experience or maturity that judges possess. It makes little sense to give recent law school graduates with limited life experience the authority to make such consequential sentencing decisions (Bishop and Frazier 1991; Kupchik 2006). Moreover, the paucity of guidelines to direct prosecutors' discretion and their lack of access to personal or clinical information about juveniles make it unlikely that prosecutors will identify only the worst youths better than judges (Guttman 1995).

Most states' direct-file statutes do not provide any formal criteria, although prosecutors administratively could adopt informal guidelines. However, interviews with prosecutors in one state revealed that relatively few did so and of those who did, guidelines provided minimal control over jurisdiction selection decisions (Bishop and Frazier 1991). For example, prosecutors' juvenile justice philosophy— just deserts, public safety, rehabilitation—had little impact on their charging or waiver practices; most youths whom they transferred were not especially violent or dangerous (Bishop and Frazier 1991). The failure to provide any review procedures or to specify the waiver criteria results almost inevitably in arbitrary, idiosyncratic, and inconsistent decisions.

An evaluation of a prosecutorial direct-file law in Virginia reported that prosecutors only charged about one-quarter of those youths statutorily eligible for transfer and used seemingly rational factors like offense seriousness, weapon use, and injury to victim (Sridharan et al. 2004). However, prosecutors' emphasized offense seriousness to the exclusion of assessments of youths' culpability or criminal responsibility. Compared with judges in juvenile court waiver hearings, prosecutors deemphasized offenders' social history or prior record. The paucity of guidelines to direct prosecutors' discretion and the lack of access to personal or clinical information about juveniles made it unlikely that they would identify only the worst youths to direct file from among eligible offenders (Bishop 2004). Without formal criteria to guide their exercise of discretion, prosecutors made idiosyncratic decisions that resulted in a pattern of justice by geography—where youths lived, as well as what they did, affected the outcome of the cases (Sridharan, Greenfield, and Blakley 2004). Moreover, Virginia's criminal sentencing laws perversely treat youthfulness as an aggravating, rather than mitigating factor, and judges sentenced youths tried as adults more harshly than adults convicted of the same crimes (Tonry 2004).

Even though most states formally have judicial waiver statutes (see Table 32.1), prosecutors actually transfer the vast majority of youths without a hearing (Amnesty International 2005; Snyder and Sickmund 2006). Prosecutors in some states charged about 10% of chronological juveniles as adults (United States General Accounting Office 1995; Feld 1998). In the 1990s, Florida prosecutors alone transferred as many juveniles to criminal courts as did juvenile court judges via waiver hearings in the entire country (Bishop and Frazier 1991; Frazier et al. 1999; Schiraldi and Zeidenberg 2000). Recent statutory changes have made judicial waiver hearings the exception rather than the rule (Torbet et al. 1996). In one study, prosecutors determined the adult status of 85% of youths tried as adults based solely on age and the offense charged (Juszkiewicz 2000). As a result, states do not assess juveniles' "amenability to treatment" or culpability before they prosecute them in criminal courts (Torbet et al. 1996; Feld 2000).

State laws that exclude long lists of offenses or that give prosecutors authority to direct-file charges in criminal court simply shift sentencing discretion from judges in a waiver hearing to prosecutors making charging decisions. Because offense categories are necessarily crude and imprecise indicators of the seriousness of any offense, prosecutors exercise enormous sentencing discretion when they decide whether to charge a youth with an excluded offense rather than a lesser included offense, or to select the forum in a direct-file jurisdiction. Despite extensive lists of excluded offenses and the ascendance of "get tough" policies, it seems unlikely that legislators intend prosecutors to charge every potentially eligible youth in criminal court. For example, assaults and robberies account for more than 90% of youth violence arrests and vary widely in seriousness: generic crime categories provide a poor basis by which to decide the majority of cases (Dawson 1992; Zimring 1998b). The heterogeneity of offenses within each category requires some decision maker, either a judge or a prosecutor, qualitatively to evaluate both the seriousness of that crime and the degree of the actor's participation. Youths' degrees of criminal participation vary as much as do offenses within generic legal categories. Young offenders commit crimes in groups to a much greater extent than do adults (Zimring 1981, 1998a; Snyder and Sickmund 2006). While criminal law treats all participants as equally responsible and may sentence principals and accessories alike, young people's susceptibility to peer group influence requires some individualized assessment of their degree of participation, personal responsibility, and culpability.

The heterogeneity of offenses, the variability of youths' participation in crimes, and prosecutors' idiosyncrasies have important implications for implementing offense exclusion and direct-file laws. Such statutes enable prosecutors covertly to manipulate charges or to select a juvenile or criminal forum in a low-visibility, discretionary setting with minimal information or record, and without providing any legal justification, accountability, or review. In terms of institutional competencies and the allocation of authority, judicial waiver statutes vest discretion in more experienced, better informed, and less politicized judges, whereas offense exclusion and direct-file laws place the adulthood determination in the hands of less experienced, less knowledgeable, and more political decision makers (Bishop and Frazier 1991; Kupchik 2006).

C. Blended Sentencing: Procedural and Substantive Convergence of Juvenile and Criminal Courts

Juvenile courts lose authority over youths when they attain the age of majority or some statutory limit. As a result, they cannot achieve proportional sentencing when confronted with older chronic offenders or youths convicted of very serious offenses (Allen 2000). Limits on dispositions heighten public and political concerns that juvenile courts inadequately punish or control these youths and provide impetus either to transfer them to criminal courts or to increase juvenile courts' sanctions.

Statutes that increase juvenile courts' punitive capacity may provide judges with an alternative to waiver (Redding and Howell 2000). Blended sentencing laws attempt to meld the rehabilitative sentences of juvenile courts with the threat of criminal sanctions and to provide longer sentences for serious crimes than otherwise would be available to the juvenile court (Feld 1995). Blended sentences give juvenile courts the option to punish as well as to treat youths of certain ages charged with serious or repeated offenses.

As Table 32.5 indicates, states use several variants of blended sentencing, some of which lodge initial authority in juvenile court judges to impose extended sentences and others of which give criminal court judges authority to impose a juvenile or young offender disposition in lieu of adult imprisonment (Snyder and Sickmund 2006; Torbet et al. 1996). States base eligibility for blended sentences on combinations of age and offense, and judges impose both juvenile and criminal sentences. With juvenile blended sentences, the juvenile court tries the case, imposes both a juvenile and criminal sentence and stays execution of the latter pending successful completion of the juvenile disposition (Torbet et al. 1996; Redding and Howell 2000). In other jurisdictions, the youth's sentence may continue beyond the age of juvenile court jurisdiction and a court reviews the sentence when a youth turns 18 or 21 to decide whether he should serve the remainder of the sentence in the adult correctional system. In other states, a criminal court imposes a juvenile and adult sentence with the latter stayed while the youth completes the delinquency disposition (Snyder and Sickmund 2006). Although states use several different versions of these enhanced sanctions, they share several common features. Because the laws provide juvenile offenders with adult criminal procedural safeguards, including the right to a jury trial, juvenile courts can acknowledge that many delinquency sanctions are punitive (Feld 1995). Once a state gives a juvenile the right to a jury trial and other criminal procedural safeguards, it retains the option to punish without apology and thereby gains greater flexibility to treat a youth as well.

These various enhanced sentencing strategies recognize that age jurisdictional limits of juvenile courts create binary forced-choices—either juvenile or adult and either treatment or punishment. Trying juveniles with criminal procedural rights preserves the option to extend jurisdiction for several years beyond that available for ordinary delinquents. Blended sentences embody the procedural and substantive convergence between juvenile and criminal courts, provide an alternative to binary waiver statutes, and recognize that adolescence constitutes a developmental continuum that requires an increasing array of graduated sanctions (Feld 1995).

Blended sentences increase the punitive powers of juvenile courts (Redding and Howell 2000). However, increasing the sentence lengths available in juvenile courts may make them as disfiguring and debilitating as the sentences criminal courts impose (Zimring and Fagan 2000). Critics charge that endorsing punishment blurs and confuses the purpose and functions of rehabilitative juvenile courts (Zimring 1998a). It intrudes criminal sanctions into juvenile courts, places juvenile judges in the role of imposing criminal sentences, and erodes courts' rehabilitative mission with spillover effects on other delinquents (Redding and Howell 2000). Blended sentences also increase prosecutors' plea bargaining leverage by enabling them to coerce pleas to extended sentences in lieu of outright transfer. Finally, blended sentencing exacerbates the manifold procedural deficiencies of juvenile courts, such as lack of access to and performance of defense counsel (Feld 2003b).

Although some analysts endorse blended sentences as an alternative to waiver, critics note that juvenile court judges do not use them in lieu of transfer, but instead impose them on less serious offenders, which results in "net widening" (Redding and Howell 2000; Podkopacz and Feld 2001). Net-widening occurs when reformers introduce a new sanction to be used in lieu of another, more severe sanction—e.g. blended sentencing in lieu of transfer—but which judges then use on offenders whom they previously treated less severely than the new sanction permits (Podkopacz and Feld 2001). An evaluation of changes in waiver practices after Minnesota adopted a blended sentencing law reported that judges continued to transfer the same numbers and types of youths whom they previously waived and that they imposed blended sentences with a stayed criminal sentence on many younger delinquents with less extensive prior records. Judges used the new option to sentence more severely youths whom they previously dealt with as ordinary delinquents, rather than youths whom they previously waived and sentenced to prison. More than one-third of youths who received blended sentences subsequently failed during their juvenile probation, primarily for probation violations rather than for serious new offenses. Subject to probation revocation proceedings, youths shifted into the adult correctional system nearly doubled in number, and most were younger and less serious offenders than those whom judges transferred through waiver hearings (Podkopacz and Feld 2001). Additionally, prosecutors used the threat of transfer as leverage to coerce youths to plead to blended sentences, to waive their procedural rights, and to risk exposure to criminal sanctions.

D. Relocating Judicial Discretion: Reverse Waiver, Transfer Back, and Sentencing Adults as Juveniles

Progressive reformers created separate juvenile courts and institutions to avoid confining vulnerable youths in prisons with adults (Schlossman 1977; Rothman 1980). Legislative policies to transfer more juveniles to criminal courts also expose more youths to adult correctional consequences. Because many excluded offenses carry mandatory minimum prison sentences, juveniles charged and convicted as adults face greater prospects of incarceration (Feld 1998). Juveniles confined in adult prisons are more likely to be victims of violent attacks, to experience sexual assaults, and to commit suicide than those confined in juvenile facilities (Fagan, Forst, and Vivona 1987; Klein 1998). And despite the legislative desire to increase the sentences imposed on juveniles tried as adults, many youths receive shorter sentences as adults than juvenile court judges could have imposed on them as delinquents (Noon 1994; Podkopacz and Feld 1995, 1996).

Many states allow criminal court judges to reverse-waive or transfer-back to juvenile court cases that originated in criminal court either as a result of excluded-offense or prosecutorial direct-file decisions. These provisions help to restore some flexibility to a prosecutor-dominated waiver process and to allow for the application of traditional juvenile sanctions to offenders believed to be amenable to treatment. As Table 32.6 indicates, about half of the direct-file and excluded-offenses jurisdictions allow a criminal court judge either to return a youth to juvenile court for trial or sentencing or to impose a juvenile or youthful offender sentence in lieu of an adult criminal sentence (United States General Accounting Office 1995; Snyder and Sickmund 2006). In some states, offense exclusion or direct-file laws that place a youth initially in criminal court create a presumption of "unfitness" and shift the burden of proof to the juvenile to demonstrate why he should be returned to juvenile court for trial or disposition (Feld 2000). In other states, the criminal court has exclusive jurisdiction over youths 13 to 17 years of age and charged with murder, rape, or armed robbery, but the prosecutor may make a reverse-waiver motion and prosecute the youth in juvenile court instead (Feld 2000). In most states, however, a criminal court judge makes the reverse-waiver, transfer-back, or juvenile sentencing decision. Unfortunately, because records are seldom maintained on criminal court decisions to apply these options to underage offenders, we know very little about the numbers of youths who are returned to the juvenile system following transfer.

Although *Kent* provided impetus for states to expedite transfer via offense exclusion and direct-file laws, reverse waiver provisions frequently relocate *Kent*-type proceedings to the criminal court. When criminal court judges decide whether to impose a juvenile or adult sentence, they review a pre-sentence investigation report, conduct a sentencing hearing, and consider statutory criteria—seriousness of offense, prior record, sophistication and maturity, previous correctional dispositions—in a process that closely mirrors the *Kent* framework. In short, reverse-waiver provisions mandate the equivalent of a judicial waiver hearing with written findings and conclusions of law, albeit in the context of an adult criminal-sentencing decision rather than a juvenile court hearing (Feld 2000). We have no evidence that criminal court judges possess any greater expertise to decide whether a youth is "suitable for treatment" as a juvenile than a juvenile court judge does to decide that a juvenile is not "amenable to treatment" (Kupchik 2006). Criminal court judges may lack knowledge of juvenile disposition options, and may be more predisposed to impose punitive sanctions to ratify prosecutors' decisions.

II. POLICY JUSTIFICATIONS FOR WAIVER— INCAPACITATION, DETERRENCE, AND RETRIBUTION

Although states should prosecute and sentence some serious young offenders in criminal courts, law makers seldom articulate their sentencing policy goals. Most justifications for waiver rest on utilitarian grounds: to increase the likelihood of criminal sanctions; to deter waived youths or other would-be offenders; or to reduce recidivism through incapacitation. Purely retributive justifications—"old enough to do the crime, old enough to do the time"—seek simply to punish youths for their offenses. However, all of these rationales fail adequately to consider how the reduced culpability and diminished criminal responsibility of youths conflict with these goals. For example, both retributive and deterrent justifications presume a degree of culpability and rationality on the part of juvenile offenders that the Supreme Court in *Roper* and *Graham* found most adolescents lack.

A. Waiver and the Punishment Gap

Until recent "get tough" amendments that focus on drug and violent crimes, criminal courts often sentenced chronic juvenile property offenders more leniently than they did nonviolent adult offenders and those with prior criminal records. If waiver criteria and criminal sentencing practices are not congruent, then some offenders fall between the cracks of the two justice systems in a "punishment gap" (Feld 1987, 1995; Podkopacz and Feld 1995, 1996). Judges in waiver hearings confront two somewhat different but overlapping populations of juvenile offenders: older chronic offenders currently charged with a property crime *and* violent youths, some of whom also may be persistent offenders. Criminal court judges sentence waived property offenders more leniently than they do youths charged with violent offenses.

Prior to the "get tough" amendments of the mid-1990s, juvenile court judges transferred the largest plurality of youths for property offenses, rather than for violent crimes (Sickmund, Snyder, and Poe-Yamagata 1997). Although substantial jurisdictional variation existed in sentencing of youths tried as adults, a policy of leniency often prevailed. Early studies report that urban criminal courts incarcerated younger waived offenders at a lower rate than they did adult offenders, younger violent offenders received shorter sentences than did older offenders, and for about two years after becoming adults, youths benefited from leniency in criminal courts (Greenwood, Abrahamse, and Zimring 1984; Twentieth Century Fund Task Force 1978). A nationwide study of judicially waived youths sentenced as adults in the 1980s found that criminal courts fined or placed the majority on probation. Even among those confined, 40% received sentences of one year or less—dispositions within the range of juvenile courts—and only about one-quarter received sentences of five years or more (Hamparian et al. 1982). Until the 1990s, juvenile court judges continued to waive primarily older chronic offenders charged with property crimes rather than violent offenders, and criminal court judges fined them or placed most of them on probation (Gillespie and Norman 1984; Heuser 1985; Feld 1995). Moreover, criminal court judges typically treated chronic juvenile property offenders as if they were adult first-time offenders, sentencing them more leniently than adult chronic offenders (Gillespie and Norman 1984; Heuser 1985; Bortner 1986; Feld 1995). Although states transfer youths so that they can receive more severe sentences, they will not achieve greater severity unless both systems use similar waiver and sentencing criteria.

More recent research indicates that when states' waiver policies target violent youths, they increase the likelihood and severity of adult criminal sentences. Studies in several jurisdictions indicate that youths charged with violent crimes and convicted in criminal court have a greater likelihood of incarceration than do their nonwaived juvenile counterparts and that they receive significantly longer sentences (Bishop et al. 1996; Kupchik, Fagan, and Lieberman 2003).

B. General Deterrence

During the "get tough" era, legislators assumed that increasing the number of youths exposed to criminal sanctions would deter them and other youths from offending. Researchers have analyzed juvenile crime rates before and after passage of laws that lowered the age or increased the categories of offenses that could lead to criminal prosecution. Most studies find that "get tough" changes in laws have little or no general deterrent effect. Despite extensive publicity, after New York passed its Juvenile Offender law, it had minimal impact on juveniles' arrest rates for excluded offenses, especially for youths in urban high-crime areas (Singer and McDowall 1988). Researchers compared juvenile arrest rates for several years before and after Idaho adopted a tough exclusion law with those in adjacent Washington and reported that they declined in the latter and actually rose in Idaho (Jensen and Metsger 1994). An analysis of juvenile arrest rates spanning a decade during which

Washington adopted "get tough" waiver laws reported no difference between the state's rates and national trends over the same period (Barnoski 2003). A comparison of juvenile arrest rates in states in which juvenile court jurisdiction ended at 16 rather than 17 years of age suggests that juvenile incarceration rates have a greater impact on crime rates than did the criminal court age of majority (Levitt 1998). Finally, analysts examined juvenile arrest rates for violent crimes and homicide for five-year periods before and after states adopted legislative offense-exclusion and direct-file laws (Steiner, Hemmens, and Bell 2006; Steiner and Wright 2006). Despite the enormous amount of legislative activity, they report that neither type of get tough response to youth violence had any significant or consistent impact on juvenile arrest rates.

C. Specific Deterrence: Juvenile or Criminal Confinement and Recidivism

Other studies have explored the specific deterrent effects of transfer by comparing the recidivism rates of youths tried and sentenced in juvenile and in criminal courts. A follow-up comparison of youths waived by the juvenile court in Hennepin County (Minneapolis), Minnesota, with those who were referenced for waiver but retained in the juvenile system, reported that transferred youths had higher recidivism rates than did youths sentenced in juvenile courts (Podkopacz and Feld 1995, 1996). A similar study was conducted by Myers (2005) in Pennsylvania, who obtained very similar results. This kind of research has been criticized for the nonequivalence of the comparison groups. Although the researchers in both of these studies controlled for a number of variables, including offense seriousness and prior record, given the number of factors for which they were unable to control, the results are at best suggestive.

Fagan (1995) conducted a more scientifically robust evaluation of the specific deterrent effects of juvenile versus criminal court processing. He drew a random sample of four hundred 15- and 16-year-old boys charged with first- and second-degree robbery and first-degree burglary in New York, and a sample of four hundred boys charged with the same offenses from neighboring New Jersey. The boys hailed from adjacent counties in the two states (separated only by the Hudson River) that had very similar demographic, socioeconomic, and youth crime patterns. In New York, the state prosecuted all 15- and 16-year-old youths charged with these offenses in criminal courts, whereas juvenile courts retained jurisdiction over similarly charged youths in New Jersey. These differences in law allowed Fagan to analyze a somewhat unusual "natural experiment." Although he found no significant differences in recidivism for youths charged with burglary, Fagan reported that youths prosecuted for robbery in criminal courts were more likely to reoffend than robbers prosecuted in juvenile courts. Robbers who were tried in criminal courts also had higher rates of recidivism and reoffended more quickly than robbers prosecuted in juvenile courts. These differences held up for the most part irrespective of the type of sanction that the courts imposed. Police re-arrested 81% of those sen-

tenced to adult probation, compared with 64% of those sentenced to juvenile probation. Police re-arrested 91% of those incarcerated by the criminal court, compared
to 73% of those incarcerated by the juvenile court.

More recently, Fagan and his colleagues conducted a replication and extension
of their earlier research, this time including 2,400 juveniles charged with robbery,
burglary, and assault in adjacent counties from New York and New Jersey (Fagan,
Kupchik, and Liberman 2003). They examined recidivism during a follow-up period
that ranged from two years (for those incarcerated) to seven years (for those who
received probation). After controlling for prior record and other variables related to
possible selection effects, they found that adolescents prosecuted in criminal courts
were rearrested more quickly and more often for violent, property, and weapons
offenses than those processed in juvenile courts. Processing in criminal court was
associated with a 50% increase in the likelihood of being arrested for a violent crime,
a 67% increase in the likelihood of being arrested for a felony property crime, and
an 80% increase in the likelihood of being arrested for a weapons offense.

Studies conducted by a team of researchers in Florida reinforce Fagan's findings
(Bishop et al. 1996; Winner et al. 1997). Unlike New York, Florida transfers juveniles
to criminal court almost exclusively via prosecutorial direct-file. While thousands
of juveniles are transferred to Florida's criminal courts each year, because the state's
transfer law is so broad, thousands of equally serious offenders are retained in the
juvenile system. This situation provided an opportunity to carry out a series of
policy studies in which the researchers compared the recidivism of youths prosecuted as adults to matched youths who were not transferred. In an initial study, a
total of 2,738 pairs were matched on seven criteria, including the most serious
offense, the number of counts, the number of prior delinquency referrals, the most
serious prior referral, age, gender, and race. The researchers assessed recidivism
after twenty-four months, and again after seven years, in terms of the prevalence of
re-arrest, the incidence of re-arrest, the severity of the first re-arrest offense, and
time to failure. Over every measure of recidivism in the short term, and over most
comparisons in the long term, the transferred juveniles fared worse than their
matches in the juvenile system. Over the short term, arrest was more prevalent
among the transfers, and transferred youths were more often re-arrested for a more
serious offense. Among those who reoffended in both groups, the transfers reoffended more quickly and more often. Over the long term, the researchers found that
the transfers were more likely to reoffend in six of seven offense categories. Moreover,
rates of re-arrest were significantly higher for the transfers in all offense categories.

A more recent study by the same Florida research group extended and improved
on their earlier research with more precise matching, using a seriousness index to
increase the equivalence of the comparison groups (Lanza-Kaduce et al. 2005). The
index was made up of twelve factors over and above the seven criteria used initially
to match the pairs. It included such details as weapon involvement, victim injury,
property damage or loss, whether the offender was a gang member, and the presence of juvenile or adult accomplices. Using this index, the researchers identified a
subset of 315 "best matched pairs." When the analysis was restricted to these closely

comparable cases, the difference in recidivism was still substantial and in the same direction as before. Further, they reported that transferred youths were significantly more likely than those retained in the juvenile system to be re-arrested for a violent felony offense.

The Task Force on Community Preventive Services (CDC 2007) recently reviewed all studies that have compared the recidivism of youths transferred to criminal courts and those retained in juvenile courts. Although these studies were carried out in different jurisdictions, at different times, using different methodologies, and analyzed the effects of different transfer strategies, the results were strikingly similar. The Task Force concluded that after their return to the community, youths tried in criminal courts had higher and faster rates of recidivism, especially for violent crimes, than did youths tried in juvenile courts. "[T]ransfer policies have generally resulted in increased arrests for subsequent crimes, including violent crime, among juveniles who were transferred compared with those retained in the juvenile justice system. To the extent that transfer policies are implemented to reduce violent or other criminal behavior, available evidence indicates that they do more harm than good" (CDC 2007, p. 13).

D. Retribution, Culpability, and Youthfulness as Aggravating or Mitigating Factors

States also transfer youths to achieve retributive goals—"adult crime, adult time"— and some sentence waived youths more harshly than they do young adults convicted of similar crimes (Snyder and Sickmund 2006; Levin, Langan, and Brown 1996; Tanenhaus and Drizin 2004; Kurlychek and Johnson 2004, 2010). Despite the historical leniency theoretically and practically accorded children, in some jurisdictions, youthfulness appears to be an aggravating rather than a mitigating factor. For example, Virginia has adopted a "youth-as-an-aggravating circumstance sentencing policy that has nothing to do with moral ideas about offenders' culpability or the seriousness of their crimes" (Tonry 2004, p. 155). In Florida, judges are more likely to sentence direct-filed youths to longer terms than they are young adults convicted of the same crimes (Bishop and Frazier 1991). Nationwide, more youths convicted of murder receive life-without-parole sentences than do their adult counterparts sentenced for murder (Snyder and Sickmund 2006; Feld 2008). A study of sentences in thirty-nine urban counties in nineteen states reported that courts were as likely to convict juveniles as adult offenders and more likely to incarcerate them (Rainville and Smith 2003). A comparison in Pennsylvania of juveniles sentenced as adults with young adult offenders sentenced for the same crimes reported that judges sentenced the juveniles more harshly than their adult counterparts (Kurlychek and Johnson 2004). Kurlychek and Johnson (2010) compared juveniles sentenced as adults to a matched sample of young adult offenders in Maryland and reported that judges sentenced all types of juvenile offenders more severely than they did adults. The differences were most pronounced for drug offenders: juvenile drug offenders received sentences that were more than six times more severe than those imposed on comparable adult offenders. Steiner (2009) compared the bail and incarceration outcomes for transferred juveniles and young adults (aged 29 years or younger) in a sample drawn from thirty-seven urban counties. He found that judges were somewhat more likely to deny bail and substantially more likely to imprison transferred juveniles compared with young adult offenders. In short, judges treat youthfulness as an aggravating factor and attach a penalty to juvenile status, quite apart from the offense, prior record, and other legally relevant variables.

Treating youthfulness as an aggravating, rather than a mitigating, factor in sentencing is fundamentally at odds with how law, morality, and justice do and should view the crimes of children. The Supreme Court in *Roper v. Simmons* conducted a proportionality analysis of adolescents' culpability to decide whether the death penalty ever could be an appropriate punishment for juveniles (Feld 2008). More recently, the Court in *Graham v. Florida* extended *Roper's* proportionality analyses and held that imposition of a life-without-parole sentence on a nonhomicide young offender violated the Eighth Amendment. *Roper* and *Graham* offered three reasons that states could not punish youths whom they found to be criminally responsible as severely as adults. First, juveniles immature judgment and lesser self-control caused them to act impulsively and without full appreciation of consequences and reduced their culpability (*Roper* 2005). Second, juveniles are more susceptible than adults to negative peer influence, which further diminishes their criminal responsibility (*Roper* 2005). Youths' greater dependence on parents and peers extends some responsibility for their crimes to others. Third, juveniles' personalities are more transitory and not as well formed as those of adults, and their crimes provide less reliable evidence of "depraved character." The Court's rationale recognized both adolescents' reduced moral culpability and their greater capacity for growth and change—i.e., their diminished responsibility for past offenses, and their unformed and perhaps redeemable character. Juveniles' immature judgment, susceptibility to negative influence, and transitory character also negated the retributive and deterrent justifications for the death penalty (*Roper* 2005). The *Roper* Court concluded that juveniles' reduced culpability warranted a categorical prohibition of execution and the *Graham* Court applied that diminished responsibility prohibition to sentences of life-without-parole for nonhomicide offenders (Feld 2008).

Roper and *Graham* focused on adolescents' immature judgment, rather than the narrower criminal law inquiry into the ability to distinguish right from wrong, and concluded that their immaturity reduced culpability (Cauffman and Steinberg 1995; Scott et al. 1995; Scott and Grisso 1997). Youths' immature judgment in several areas—perceptions of risk, appreciation of future consequences (especially negative ones), self-regulation, and ability to make autonomous choices—distinguishes them from adults (Scott and Steinberg 2003; Morse 1997). Youths' characteristically bad choices are categorically less blameworthy than those of adults because inexperience, short-term time perspective, susceptibility to external influence, emotionality, preference for risk, and impulsivity are features of normal adolescent development (Scott et al. 1995; Scott and Grisso 1997; Scott and Steinberg 2003; Morse 1997).

Youths engage in risky behavior because it provides heightened sensations, excitement, and an "adrenaline rush" (Scott and Grisso 1997; Spear 2000). The widest divergence between the perception of and the preference for risk occurs during mid-adolescence when youths' criminal activity also increases. Youths' feelings of invulnerability and immortality heighten these risk proclivities.

Many of these differences between adolescents' and adults' thinking and behaving reflect basic developmental differences in the human brain which does not fully mature until the early twenties (Scott and Steinberg 2003, 2008; Dahl 2001; Sowell et al. 1999; Sowell et al. 2001; Paus 1999; NIMH 2008). Adolescents simply do not have the physiological capacity of adults to exercise judgment or control impulses. The prefrontal cortex (PFC) operates as the "control center" of the brain (Kandel et al. 2000; Gruber and Yurgelun-Todd 2006) and is responsible for reasoning, abstract thinking, planning, anticipating consequences, and impulse control (Sowell et al. 1999; Sowell et al. 2001; Aronson 2007). By contrast, the limbic system, located at the base of the brain, controls instinctual behavior, such as the "fight or flight" response (Kandel 2000). In adolescence the PFC grows, and a complex circuitry that connects it to and enables it to control the limbic system develops, but this process is generally not complete until the early twenties. Consequently, adolescents rely more heavily on the limbic system than do adults, especially during times of stress (Baird et al. 1999; NIMH 2008). Their impulsive behavior reflects "gut reaction" rather than sober reflection. Novel circumstances and emotional arousal challenge youths' exercise of self-control. Neuroscientific research provides a hard-science explanation for social scientists' observations about adolescent behavior and self-control. It enhances our understanding of how and why juveniles think and behave differently than adults and furnishes a basis for mitigating punishment (Morse 2006; Scott and Steinberg 2008).

III. Implications of Transfer Research for Juvenile Justice Policy: Toward a Rationale for Waiver

Waiver policies adopted over the past few decades fail to advance any legitimate penal goals. Policies that equate juveniles with adults in the name of retribution—"old enough to do the crime, old enough to do the time"—ignore fundamental differences between adolescents and adults. As much as we might wish it were otherwise, the fact remains that the commission of a serious crime does not transform a juvenile into a fully responsible adult. Anglo-American law has a long history of recognizing degrees of culpability based on the offender's capacity to reason and to control his behavior. Because adolescent judgment and self-control are impaired relative to adults, it follows that desert-based retributive principles that ignore adolescent developmental immaturity impose disproportionately harsh, unjust penalties on less blameworthy young people. As a general deterrent, waiver policies also fail. There is not a scintilla of evidence that the threat of waiver deters young people from offending. Juveniles' immature judgment, short-term perspective, and susceptibility to negative peer influence reduce their responsiveness to the abstract threat of sanctions. As we have seen above, the empirical evidence further indicates that waiver laws fail to secure any specific deterrent benefits. Indeed, they appear to be iatrogenic: youths tried as adults, rather than as juveniles, tend to reoffend more often, more quickly and more seriously, negating any incapacitative benefit of incarceration that might be achieved in the short term. In the longer term, transfer seems only to increase the risk to public safety. The simple fact of being tried as an adult, regardless of the criminal sentence, appears to aggravate youths' recidivism. Policies of selective incapacitation can succeed only if they identify high base-rate career offenders who are very likely to recidivate. However, offense-driven transfer statutes do not systematically target these career offenders. In the section that follows, we examine why states adopted and retain transfer policies that were destined to fail, and what they should do to improve them.

During the 1970s, Progressives' optimistic assumptions about human malleability and the promise of rehabilitation foundered on empirical evaluations that questioned the effectiveness of correctional programs and the scientific expertise of those who administered them (Martinson 1974; Allen 1981). Coincidental with other jurisprudential and criminological developments taking place at the same time (Feld 1999; Garland 2001; Tonry 2004), retributive and just deserts philosophies enjoyed a renaissance. Just deserts and retribution displaced rehabilitation as the dominant rationales for criminal sentencing, and indeterminate sentencing gave way to determinate sentences for adults (Cullen and Gilbert 1982; Tonry 1996; Garland 2001). Subsequently, increases in violent youth crime in the mid-1980s, especially by black urban males, encouraged politicians to demagogue on crime as a symbolic issue and provided political impetus to crack down on young offenders (Beckett 1997). The just deserts rationale for offense-based criminal sentencing soon altered juvenile transfer laws and practices as well (Feld 1987, 1988, 1998, 2003a; Sheffer 1995).

Historically, judges made waiver decisions based on assessments of amenability to treatment and dangerousness that were often informed by little more than hunch or intuition (Feld 1987, 1998). Critics objected that both amenability to treatment and dangerousness were vague concepts and that judges' efforts to assess them, especially without objective standards, produced inconsistent, arbitrary, and discriminatory outcomes (Feld 1978, 1995). By contrast, legislative offense exclusion offered a tidier, offense-based, just deserts framework.

Early empirical research on criminal careers offered the prospect that decision makers could predict recidivism and selectively incapacitate chronic offenders (Wolfgang, Figlio, and Sellin 1972), providing a second criminological rationale and intellectual legitimacy for offense-focused legislation (Blumstein et al. 1986). While a just deserts rationale might exclude older youths who committed heinous offenses simply because they deserved more punishment, waiver laws to selectively incapacitate high-base-rate career offenders would focus on a prior record of persistent offending Youths who begin their delinquent careers early and become chronic offenders as juveniles are more likely to continue offending into adulthood (Blumstein, Farrington, and Moitra 1985; Farrington 1998). Waiver laws attempt to differentiate between adolescent-limited offenders and life-course persistent offenders, but confront a frustrating trade-off between serious and chronic offenders. Significant differences in delinquent careers occur between adolescent-limited delinquents who desist after one or two misdeeds and life-course persistent offenders who begin earlier, record multiple justice system contacts, and persist into adult criminality (see, e.g., Moffitt 1993, 2003, 2007; Patterson, Capaldi, and Blank 1991; Patterson and Yoerger 2004; Simons et al. 1994). A serious offense alone has very little probative value as an indicator of career criminality (Wolfgang, Figlio, and Sellin 1972; Langan and Levin 2002; Elliott, Huizinga, and Morse 1986).

Despite the legislative frenzy to adopt get tough provisions, virtual consensus exists among juvenile justice scholars in support of a carefully structured judicial waiver process (e.g., Zimring 1998a, 1998b; Feld 1999, 2008; Bishop 2004; Fagan 2008; Scott and Steinberg 2008). They conclude that a state only should waive youths whose serious and persistent offenses require minimum lengths of confinement in excess of the maximum sanctions available in juvenile courts (Zimring 1981, 1991, 1998a, 1998b; Feld 1987, 1995, 1999; Bishop 2004; Fagan 2008; Scott and Steinberg 2008). Retributive waiver rationale limits severe sanctions to the most culpable youths, imposes a degree of proportionality and determinacy on decisions, and restricts eligibility to the most serious crimes. However, punishing all youths who commit serious crimes may be overly inclusive and may inflict harm without any offsetting utilitarian gain because violent offenders desist at higher rates than other delinquents (Langan and Levin 2002). A small group of chronic offenders may deserve minimum sentences longer than those available in juvenile court because of their persistent criminality and exhaustion of rehabilitative services. We can identify chronic offenders based on their past conduct without trying to predict future criminality—e.g., "danger to public safety"—and thereby avoid legitimate civil liberties concerns about overprediction, false positives, and preventive incarceration (Zimring and Hawkins 1995).

Waiver policy reflects value choices applied to empirical research. What criteria and evidence will best enable us to distinguish between the few persistent and serious young offenders whom states could prosecute as adults and the vast majority of youths who should remain in juvenile courts? The principal values of waiver are the imposition of deserved punishment on the most serious offenders and incapacitation of serious and chronic offenders in more secure adult facilities. States do not need to incarcerate most young offenders, and waiver policies should focus on those youths who deserve longer periods of confinement than juvenile courts can impose. Except in rare instances, these will be older adolescents who have demonstrated by the severity and chronicity of their offending that they deserve to be incarcerated for lengthy periods and that the public needs to be protected from them.

To meet these waiver policy goals, transfer criteria should focus initially on a very serious offense—e.g., homicide, rape, armed robbery, assault with a firearm or assault that produces substantial injury. Incapacitative criteria would require an extensive record of recidivism or prior unsuccessful treatment, rather than just an isolated serious present offense.

A legislature also must prescribe a minimum age of eligibility for criminal prosecution. At what age should states hold youths who commit serious crimes responsible for their offenses and to what degree? "Adult crime, adult time" does not constitute a sufficiently nuanced policy. *Roper* and *Graham* recognized adolescents' diminished criminal responsibility, and sentencing laws should formally recognize youthfulness as a mitigating factor when judges sentence youths in criminal court (Feld 1997, 2008). If the rationale for waiver is that youths who commit serious offenses deserve more severe punishment than delinquents, then regardless of the prosecutor's initial charge, if a judge or jury does not convict the youth of one of those serious offenses, then the criminal court should return him to juvenile court for sentencing. Although *Bland* declined to review a prosecutor's charging decision before a trial, nothing precludes reassessing the jurisdiction for disposition after a trial determines that the prosecutor's charges were erroneous. A legislature can adopt these sentencing factors—seriousness, persistence, prior treatment intervention, minimum age of criminal responsibility, youthfulness as a mitigating factor, and transfer back—as waiver criteria.

The only process by which to make sensible decisions about serious and chronic adolescent offenders is a juvenile court waiver hearing guided by substantive offense criteria and clinical considerations, and subject to rigorous appellate review (e.g., Feld 1998, 1999, 2003a; Zimring 1998a, 2000; Bishop 2000a, 2004; Kupchik 2006; Tonry 2007; Scott and Steinberg 2008). Although waiver hearings are less administratively efficient than prosecutorial charging decisions, states should not impose the "capital punishment" of the juvenile court easily, readily, or generally (Zimring 1981). An adversarial hearing at which both the state and defense can present relevant evidence about the offense, culpability, and clinical responsivity will produce more accurate and fair decisions than prosecutors will make in their offices without access to critical information and subject to political considerations.

Defining the substantive criteria constitutes the crucial question of any waiver process. The amorphous *Kent* criteria invite judicial subjectivity, idiosyncrasy, and disparity without any effective recourse. So which chronological juveniles should a state prosecute as adults? States should waive youths only when their serious offenses, persistent offending, heightened culpability, active criminal participation, and clinical evaluations indicate a need for minimum sentences that exceed the maximum sanctions available in juvenile court. To define the boundary of juvenile court jurisdiction, policy makers should work backward from the sentence that a criminal court judge likely would impose on a youth with that record of offending and clinical assessment.

In light of *Roper*'s and *Graham*'s categorical recognition of adolescents' diminished criminal responsibility, states should also formally recognize youthfulness as a mitigating factor that further reduces the expected duration of adult confinement (Feld 1997, 2008). Juvenile court judges may impose dispositions for delinquents of two or three, or even five years or more, depending on a youth's age at the time of the offense. Waiver criteria should identify those combinations of serious present offenses, offense histories, offender culpability, criminal participation, clinical evaluations, and other aggravating and mitigating factors that deserve "real time" sentences substantially longer than those available in juvenile court. States could use current offense and prior record criteria to create a presumption for waiver or to allocate the burdens of proof between the juvenile and the state to balance the private and public interests and the risks of errors that inhere in any discretionary process (McCarthy 1994; Feld 1995). Finally, appellate courts should closely review judges' waiver decisions and develop general sentencing principles to define a consistent boundary of adulthood.

NOTES

1. Under the then applicable Texas law, prosecutors could file a judicial waiver motion against any youths 15 or 16 years of age charged with *any felony*. During the period of the study, juvenile courts received 14,150 felony referrals against youths aged 15 and 16, but prosecutors filed transfer motions against only 112 youths. Prosecutors filed motions primarily for serious offenses like those listed in excluded-offense and some direct-file statutes. Significantly, however, prosecutors filed transfer motions against less than 2% of felony offenders, including only 31% of eligible youths referred for homicide, only 3% of those charged with sexual assault, only 6% of those charged with robbery, and only 0.5% of those charged with aggravated assault. While prosecutors filed nearly two-thirds of all waiver motions for youths charged with murder, robbery, and rape, they did *not* file transfer motions against the vast majority of youths referred to juvenile court for those offenses (Dawson 1992).

2. *See, e.g.*, United States v. Bland, 472 F.2d 1329 (D.C. Cir. 1972), *cert. denied*, 412 U.S. 909 (1973) (leading case upholding offense-exclusion and direct-file statutes). *See also* Manduley v. Superior Court of San Diego County, 41 P.3d 3, (Cal. 2002) (holding that eliminating judicial waiver hearing did not violate due process and that expanding prosecutors' authority to directly charge cases in criminal court did not violate equal protection, notwithstanding absence of statutory guidelines to channel their discretion).

REFERENCES

Allen, Francis A. 1981. *The Decline of the Rehabilitative Ideal: Penal Policy and Social Purpose*. New Haven, CT: Yale University Press.

———. 2000. The Changing Borders of Juvenile Justice: Transfer of Adolescents to the Criminal Court In *The Changing Borders of Juvenile Justice: Transfer of Adolescents to* the Criminal Court, edited by Jeffrey Fagan and Franklin Zimring. Chicago: University of Chicago Press.

Amnesty International. 2005. The Rest of Their Lives: Life Without Parole for Child Offenders in the United States. New York: Human Rights Watch, Amnesty International. http://www.amnestyusa.org/countries/usa/clwop/report.pdf.

Aronson, Jay D. 2007. "Brain Imaging, Culpability and Juvenile Death Penalty." Psychology, Public Policy, & Law 13:115–138.

Baird, Abigail A., Staci A. Gruber, Fein, D.A.; Mass, L.C.; et al. (1999). Functional magnetic resonance imaging of facial affect recognition in children and adolescents. Journal of American Academy of Child & Adolescent Psychiatry 38:195–212.

Barnoski, Robert. 2003. "Changes in Washington State's Jurisdiction of Juvenile Offenders: Examining the Impact." Olympia, WA: Washington State Institute for Public Policy. www.wsipp.wa.gov./rptfiles/JuvJurisChange.pdf.

Beckett, Katherine. 1997. Making Crime Pay: Law and Order in Contemporary American Politics. New York: Oxford University Press.

Bishop, Donna M. 2000. "Juvenile Offenders in the Adult Criminal Justice System." In Crime and Justice: A Review of Research, vol. 27, edited by Michael Tonry. Chicago: University of Chicago Press.

Bishop, Donna. 2004. Injustice and Irrationality in Contemporary Youth Policy. Criminology and Public Policy 3: 633–44.

Bishop, Donna M., and Charles E. Frazier. 1991. "Transfer of Juveniles to Criminal Court: A Case Study and Analysis of Prosecutorial Waiver." Notre Dame Journal of Law, Ethics, and Public Policy 5: 281–302.

Bishop, Donna M., and Charles E. Frazier. 2000. "Consequences of Transfer." In The Changing Borders of Juvenile Justice: Transfer of Adolescents to the Criminal Court, edited by Jeffrey Fagan and Franklin Zimring. Chicago: University of Chicago Press.

Bishop, Donna M., Charles E. Frazier, and John C. Henretta. 1989. "Prosecutorial Waiver: Case Study of a Questionable Reform." Crime and Delinquency 35: 179–201.

Bishop, Donna M., Charles E. Frazier, Lonn Lanza-Kaduce, and Lawrence Winner. 1996. "The Transfer of Juveniles to Criminal Court: Does It Make a Difference?" Crime and Delinquency 42: 171–91.

Blumstein, Alfred. 1995. "Youth Violence, Guns, and the Illicit-Drug Industry." Journal of Criminal Law and Criminology 86: 10–36.

Blumstein, Alfred, Jacqueline Cohen, Jeffrey A. Roth, and Christy A. Visher, eds. 1986. Criminal Careers and "Career Criminals." Washington, DC: National Academy Press.

Blumstein, Alfred, David P. Farrington, and Soumyo Moitra. 1985. "Delinquency Careers: Innocents, Desisters, and Persisters." In Crime and Justice: An Annual Review, vol. 6, edited by Michael Tonry and Norval Morris. Chicago: University of Chicago Press.

Bortner, M. A. 1986. "Traditional Rhetoric, Organizational Realities: Remand of Juveniles to Adult Court." Crime and Delinquency 32: 53–73.

Bortner, M. A., Marjorie S. Zatz, and Darnell F. Hawkins. 2000. "Race and Transfer: Empirical Research and Social Context." In The Changing Borders of Juvenile Justice: Transfer of Adolescents to the Criminal Court, edited by Jeffrey Fagan and Franklin Zimring. Chicago: University of Chicago Press.

Butterfield, Fox. 1995. All God's Children: The Bosket Family and the American Tradition of Violence. New York: Avon Books.

Campaign for Youth Justice. 2007. The Consequences Aren't Minor: The Impact of Trying Youth as Adults and Strategies for Reform. Washington, DC: Campaign for Youth Justice.

Cauffman, Elizabeth and Laurence Steinberg. 1995. "The Cognitive and Affective Influences on Adolescent Decision-Making." Temple Law Review 68:1763–1789.

Centers for Disease Control. 2007. "Effects on Violence of Laws and Policies Facilitating the Transfer of Youth from the Juvenile to the Adult Justice System." Morbidity and Mortality Weekly Report 56: 1–11. http://www.cdc.gov/mmwr/preview/mmwrhtml/rr5609a1.htm.

Cullen, Francis T., and Karen E. Gilbert. 1982. Reaffirming Rehabilitation. Cincinnati, OH: Anderson Publishing.

Dahl, Ronald E. 2001. "Affect Regulation, Brain Development, and Behavioral/Emotional Health in Adolescence." CNS Spectrums 6:60–82.

Dawson, Robert O. 1992. "An Empirical Study of Kent Style Juvenile Transfers to Criminal Court." St. Mary's Law Journal 23: 975–1048.

Eigen, Joel. 1981a. "The Determinants and Impact of Jurisdictional Transfer in Philadelphia." In Readings in Public Policy, edited by John Hall, Donna Hamparian, John Pettibone, and Joe White. Columbus, OH: Academy for Contemporary Problems.

———. 1981b. "Punishing Youth Homicide Offenders in Philadelphia." Journal of Criminal Law and Criminology 72: 1072–1093.

Elliott, Delbert S., David Huizinga, and Barbara J. Morse. 1986. "Self-Reported Violent Offending: A Descriptive Analysis of Juvenile Offenders and Their Offending Careers." Journal of Interpersonal Violence 1(4): 472–514.

Fagan, Jeffrey. 1990. "Social and Legal Policy Dimensions of Violent Juvenile Crime." Criminal Justice and Behavior 17: 93–133.

Fagan, Jeffrey. 1995. "Separating the Men from the Boys: The Comparative Advantage of Juvenile versus Criminal Court Sanctions on Recidivism among Adolescent Felony Offenders." In A Sourcebook: Serious, Violent and Chronic Juvenile Offenders, edited by James C. Howell, Barry Krisberg, J. David Hawkins, and John J. Wilson. Thousand Oaks, CA: Sage.

Fagan, Jeffrey. 1996. "The Comparative Impacts of Juvenile and Criminal Court Sanctions on Adolescent Felony Offenders." Law and Policy 18: 77–119.

Fagan, Jeffrey. 2008. "Juvenile Crime and Criminal Justice: Resolving Border Disputes." Future of Children 18: 81–118.

Fagan, Jeffrey, Martin Forst, and Scott Vivona. 1987. "Racial Determinants of the Judicial Transfer Decision: Prosecuting Violent Youth in Criminal Court" Crime and Delinquency 33: 259–286.

Fagan, Jeffrey, Aaron Kupchik, and Akiva Liberman. 2003. "Be Careful What You Wish for: The Comparative Impacts of Juvenile versus Criminal Court Sanctions on Recidivism among Adolescent Felony Offenders." Columbia Law School Working Paper No. 03–62. http://ssrn.com/abstract=491202.

Fagan, Jeffrey, and Elizabeth Piper Deschenes. 1990. "Determinants of Judicial Waiver Decisions for Violent Juvenile Offenders." Journal of Criminal Law and Criminology 81: 314–X.

Farrington, David P. ———. 1998. "Causes and Correlates of Male Youth Violence." Crime and Justice: A Review of Research 24: 421–475.

Feld, Barry C. 1978. "Reference of Juvenile Offenders for Adult Prosecution: The Legislative Alternative to Asking Unanswerable Questions." Minnesota Law Review 62: 515–X.

———. 1987. "Juvenile Court Meets the Principle of Offense: Legislative Changes in Juvenile Waiver Statutes." Journal of Criminal Law and Criminology 78: 471–533.

———. 1988. "Juvenile Court Meets the Principle of Offense: Punishment, Treatment, and the Difference It Makes." Boston University Law Review 68: 821–915.

———. 1990. "Bad Law Makes Hard Cases: Reflections on Teen-Aged Axe Murderers, Judicial Activism, and Legislative Default." *Law and Inequality* 8: 1–101.

———. 1995. "Violent Youth and Public Policy: A Case Study of Juvenile Justice Law Reform." *Minnesota Law Review* 79: 965–1128.

———. 1997. "Abolish the Juvenile Court: Youthfulness, Criminal Responsibility, and Sentencing Policy." *Journal of Criminal Law and Criminology* 88: 68–136.

———. 1998. "Juvenile and Criminal Justice Systems' Responses to Youth Violence." *Crime and Justice: An Annual Review* 24: 189–261.

———. 1999. *Bad Kids: Race and the Transformation of the Juvenile Court*. New York: Oxford University Press.

———. 2000. "Legislative Exclusion of Offenses from Juvenile Court Jurisdiction: A History and Critique." In *The Changing Borders of Juvenile Justice: Transfer of Adolescents to the Criminal Court*, edited by Jeffrey Fagan and Franklin Zimring. Chicago: University of Chicago Press.

———. 2003a. "The Politics of Race and Juvenile Justice: The 'Due Process Revolution' and the Conservative Reaction." *Justice Quarterly* 20: 765–800.

———. 2003b. "Race, Politics, and Juvenile Justice: The Warren Court and the Conservative 'Backlash.'" *Minnesota Law Review* 87: 1447–578.

———. 2008. "A Slower Form of Death: Implications of *Roper v. Simmons* for Juveniles Sentenced to Life without Parole." *Notre Dame Journal of Law, Ethics & Public Policy* 22:9–65.

Frazier, Charles E. et al. 1999. "Juveniles in Criminal Court: Past and Current Research in Florida." *Quinnipiac Law Review* 18: 573–X.

Garland, David. 2001. *The Culture of Control: Crime and Social Order in Contemporary Society*. Chicago: University of Chicago Press.

Gillespie, L. Kay, and Michael D. Norman. 1984. "Does Certification Mean Prison: Some Preliminary Findings from Utah." *Juvenile and Family Court Journal* 35: 23–X.

Greenwood, Peter, Allan Abrahamse, and Franklin Zimring. 1984. *Factors Affecting Sentence Severity for Young Adult Offenders*. Santa Monica, Calif.: RAND.

Griffin, Patrick. (2008). Different from adults: An updated analysis of juvenile transfer and blended sentencing laws, with recommendations for reform. Pittsburgh, PA: National Center for Juvenile Justice and John D. and Catherine T. MacArthur Foundation.

Gruber, Staci A. and Deborah A. Yurgelun-Todd. 2006. "Neurobiology and the Law: A Role in Juvenile Justice." *Ohio State Journal of Criminal Law* 3:321–348.

Guttman, Catherine R. 1995. "Listen to the Children: The Decision to Transfer Juveniles to Adult Court." *Harvard Civil Rights-Civil Liberties Law Review* 30: 507–548.

Hamparian, Donna, Linda Estep, Susan Muntean, Ramon Priestino, Robert Swisher, Paul Wallace, and Joseph White. 1982. *Youth in Adult Courts: Between Two Worlds*. Washington, DC: Office of Juvenile Justice and Delinquency Prevention.

Heuser, James Paul. 1985. *Juveniles Arrested for Serious Felony Crimes in Oregon and "Remanded" to Adult Criminal Courts: A Statistical Study*. Salem, OR: Department of Justice Crime Analysis Center.

Howell, James C. 1996. "Juvenile Transfers to the Criminal Justice System: State of the Art." *Law and Policy* 18: 17–60.

Jensen, Eric, and Linda Metsger. 1994. "A Test of the Deterrent Effect of Legislative Waiver on Violent Juvenile Crime." *Crime and Delinquency* 40: 96–114.

Juszkiewicz, Jolanta. 2000. "Youth Crime/Adult Time: Is Justice Served?" Washington, DC: Pretrial Services Resource Center, Building Blocks for Youth. http://www.cclp.org/documents/BBY/Youth_Crime_Adult_Time.pdf.

Eric Kandel, James Schwartz, and Thomas Jessell. 2000. Principles of Neural Science 4th Ed. New York: McGraw Hill

Klein, Eric K. 1998. "Dennis the Menace or Billy the Kid: An Analysis of the Role of Transfer to Criminal Court in Juvenile Justice." American Criminal Law Review 35: 371–412.

Kupchik, Aaron. 2006. Judging Juveniles: Procesuting Adolscents in Adult and Juvenile Courts. New York: New York University Press.

Kupchik, Aaron, Jeffrey Fagan, and Akiva Liberman. (2003). Punishment, proportionality, and jurisdictional transfer of adolescent offenders: A test of the leniency gap hypothesis. Stanford Law & Policy Review, 14, 57–83.

Kurlychek, Megan, and Brian D. Johnson. 2004. "The Juvenile Penalty: A Comparison of Juvenile and Young Adult Sentencing Outcomes in Criminal Court." Criminology 42: 485–517.

Kurlycheck, Megan, and Brian D. Johnson. 2010. "Juvenility and Punishment: Sentencing Juveniles in Adult Criminal Court." Criminology 48: 725–757.

Langan, Patrick, and David J. Levin. 2002. Recidivism of Prisoners Released in 1994. Washington, DC: U.S. Department of Justice, Bureau of Justice Statistics.

Lanza-Kaduce, Lonn, Jodi Lane, Donna M. Bishop, and Charles E. Frazier. 2005. "Juvenile Offenders and Adult Felony Recidivism: The Impact of Transfer." Journal of Crime and Justice 28: 59–77.

Lemmon, John H., Henry Sontheimer, and Keith A. Saylor. 1991. A Study of Pennsylvania Juveniles Transferred to Criminal Court in 1986. Harrisburg, PA: Pennsylvania Juvenile Court Judges' Commission.

Levin, David J., Patrick A. Langan, and Jodi M. Brown. 1996. "State Court Sentencing of Convicted Felons, 1996." Washington DC: U.S. Department of Justice, Bureau of Justice Statistics, Office of Justice Programs.

Levitt, Steven D. 1998. "Juvenile Crime and Punishment." Journal of Political Economy 106: 1156–85.

Males, Mike, and Daniel Macallair. 2000. "The Color of Justice: An Analysis of Juvenile Court Transfers in California." Washington, DC: U.S. Department of Justice, Building Blocks for Youth.

Martinson, Robert. (1974). What Works? Questions and answers about prison reform. Public Interest 35:22–54.

McCarthy, Francis Barry. 1994. "The Serious Offender and Juvenile Court Reform: The Case for Prosecutorial Waiver of Juvenile Court Jurisdiction," St. Louis University Law Journal 389: 629–671.

McCord, Joan, Kathy Spatz Widom, and Nancy A. Crowell. 2001. Juvenile Crime, Juvenile Justice. Washington DC: National Research Council.

Moffitt, Terrie E. 2007. A Review of Research on the Taxonomy of Life-Course Persistent and Adolescence-Limited Offending. In The Cambridge Handbook of Violent Behavior, edited by Daniel Flannery, Alexander Vazonsyi, and Irwin Waldman. New York: Cambridge University Press.

Moffitt, Terrie E. 2003. "Life-course Persistent and Adolescence-Limited Antisocial Behaviour: A 10- year Research Review and a Research Agenda. In The Causes of Conduct Disorder and Serious Juvenile Delinquency, edited by Benjamin Lahey, Terrie Moffitt, and Avshalom Caspi. New York: Guilford.

Moffitt, Terrie E. 1993. "Adolescence-Limited and Life-Course-Persistent Delinquent Behavior: A Developmental Taxonomy." Psychological Review 100: 674–701.

Morse, Stephen J. 1997. "Immaturity and Irresponsibility." Journal of Criminal Law & Criminology 88:15–59.

————. 2006. "Brain Overclaim Syndrome and Criminal Responsibility: A Diagnostic Note." Ohio State Journal of Criminal Law 3:397–423.

Myers, David L. 2005 *Boys among Men: Trying and Sentencing Juveniles as Adults*. Westport, CT: Praeger Publishing.

Mylniec, Wallace. 1976. "Juvenile Delinquent or Adult Convict: Prosecutor's Choice." *American Criminal Law Review* 14: 29–52.

National Institute of Mental Health. (2001). Teenage Brain, http://www.nimh.nih.gov/ health/publications/teenage-brain-a-work-in-progress.shtml (accessed March 6, 2010)

Noon, Cynthia R. 1994. "'Waiving' Goodbye to Jvenile Defendants, Getting Smart vs. Getting Tough." *University of Miami Law Review* 49: 431–477.

Patterson, Gerald R., D. Capaldi, and L. Blank. 1991. "An Early Starter Model for Predicting Delinquency." In *The Development and Treatment of Childhood Aggression*, edited by Debra J. Pepler and Kenneth H. Rubin. Hillsdale, NJ: Earlbaum.

Patterson, Gerald R., and Karen Yoerger. 2002. "A Developmental Model for Early- and Late-Onset Delinquency." In *Antisocial Behavior in Children and Adolescents: A Developmental Analysis and Model for Intervention*, edited by J. B. Reid, G. R. Patterson, and J. Snyder. Washington, DC: American Psychological Association.

Paus, Tomaz, Zijdenbos, A., Worsley, K., Collins, D.L., Blumenthal, J., Giedd, J.N., Rapoport, J.L., Evans, A.C. (1999). "Structural maturation of neural pathways in children and adolescents: In vivo study." *Science* 283,1908–1911.

Podkopacz, Marcy Rasmussen, and Barry C. Feld. 1995. "Judicial Waiver Policy and Practice: Persistence, Seriousness, and Race." *Law and Inequality Journal* 14: 73–178.

————. 1996. "The End of the Line: An Empirical Study of Judicial Waiver." *Journal of Criminal Law and Criminology* 86: 449–492.

————. 2001. "The Back-Door to Prison: Waiver Reform, 'Blended Sentencing,' and the Law of Unintended Consequences." *Journal of Criminal Law and Criminology* 91:997–1071.

Poe-Yamagata, Eileen and Michael A. Jones. 2007. And Justice for Some, *available at* http:// www.buildingblocksforyouth.org/justiceforsome/jfs.pdf.

Poulos, Tammy Meredith, and Stan Orchowsky. 1994. "Serious Juvenile Offenders: Predicting the Probability of Transfer to Criminal Court." *Crime and Delinquency* 40: 3–17.

Rainville, G. A., and Steven K. Smith. 2003. "Juvenile Felony Defendants in Criminal Courts." Washington, DC: Bureau of Justice Statistics, Office of Justice Programs, U.S. Department of Justice.

Richard E. Redding and James C. Howell. 2000. "Blended Sentencing in American Juvenile Courts" In *The Changing Borders of Juvenile Justice: Transfer of Adolescents to the Criminal Court*, edited by Jeffrey Fagan and Franklin Zimring. Chicago: University of Chicago Press.

Rothman, David. 1980. *Conscience and Convenience: The Asylum and Its Alternatives in Progressive America*. Boston: Little, Brown.

Sabo, Stacey. 1996. "Rights of Passage: An Analysis of Waiver of Juvenile Court Jurisdiction." *Fordham Law Review* 64: 2425–2467.

Scott, Elizabeth S. and Thomas Grisso. 1997. "The Evolution of Adolescne: A Developmental Perspective on Juvenile Justice Reform." Journal of Criminal Law and Criminology 88:137–189.

Scott, Elizabeth S., N. Dickon Reppucci, and Jennifer L. Woolard. (1995). "Evaluating adolescent decision making in legal contexts." Law & Human Behavior 19, 221–244.

Scott, Elizabeth S., and Laurence Steinberg. 2008. *Rethinking Juvenile Justice*. Cambridge, MA: Harvard University Press.

Scott, Elizabeth S. and Laurence Steinberg. (2003). "Blaming youth." *Texas Law Review*, 81, 799–840.

Schiraldi, Vincent, and Jason Ziedenberg. 2000. "The Florida Experiment: Transferring Power From Judges to Prosecutors." *Criminal Justice* 15: 46–62.

Schlossman, Steven. 1977. *Love and the American Delinquent: The Theory and Practice of "Progressive" Juvenile Justice, 1825–1920*. Chicago: University of Chicago Press.

Sheffer, Julianne. 1995. "Serious and Habitual Juvenile Offender Statutes: Reconciling Punishment and Rehabilitation within the Juvenile Justice System." *Vanderbilt Law Review* 48: 479–512.

Sickmund, Melissa, Snyder, Howard N., and Poe-Yamagata, Eileen. (1997). *Juvenile offenders and victims: 1997 update on violence*. Washington, DC: Office of Juvenile Justice and Delinquency Prevention.

Simons, Ronald L., Chyi I. Wu, Rand D. Conger, and Frederick O. Lorenz. 1994. "Two Routes to Delinquency: Differences Between Early and Late Starters in the Impact of Parenting and Deviant Peers." *Criminology* 32: 247–76.

Singer, Simon I. 1996. *Recriminalizing Delinquency: Violent Juvenile Crime and Juvenile Justice Reform*. New York: Cambridge University Press.

Singer, Simon I., and D. McDowell. 1988. "Criminalizing Delinquency: The Deterrent Effects of the New York Juvenile Offender Law." *Law and Society Review* 22: 521–35.

Snyder, Howard N., and Melissa Sickmund. 2006. *Juvenile Offenders and Victims: A National Report 2006*. Washington, DC: Office of Juvenile Justice and Delinquency Prevention.

Sowell, Elizabeth R., Thompson, H. C. J., Jernigan, T. L., & Toga, A. W. (1999). "In vivo evidence for post-adolescent brain maturation in frontal and striatal regions." *Nature Neuroscience* 2(10):859–861.

Sowell, Elizabeth R., Thompson, P. M., Tessner, K. D., & Toga, A. W. (2001). "Mapping continued brain growth and gray matter density reduction in dorsal frontal cortex: Inverse relationships during postadolescent brain maturation." *Journal of Neuroscience* 21(22):8819–8829.

Spear, P. (2000). "The adolescent brain and age-related behavioral manifestations." *Neuroscience and Biobehavioral Reviews*, 24(4), 417–463.

Sridharan, Sanjeev, Lynette Greenfield, and Baron Blakley. 2004. "A Study of Prosecutorial Certification Practice in Virginia." *Criminology and Public Policy* 4: 605–32.

Steiner, Benjamin. 2009. "The Effects of Juvenile Transfer to Criminal Court on Incarceration Decisions." *Justice Quarterly* 26(1): 77–106.

Steiner, Benjamin, Craig Hemmens, and Valerie Bell. 2006. "Legislative Waiver Reconsidered: General Deterrent Effects of Statutory Exclusion Laws Enacted Post 1979." *Justice Quarterly* 23: 34–59.

Steiner, Benjamin, and Emily Wright. 2006. "Assessing the Relative Effects of State Direct File Waiver Laws on Violent Juvenile Crime: Deterrence or Irrelevance?" *Journal of Criminal Law and Criminology* 96: 1451–77.

Tanenhaus, David S. 2000. "The Evolution of Transfer out of the Juvenile Court," In *The Changing Borders of Juvenile Justice: Transfer of Adolescents to the Criminal Court*, edited by Jeffrey Fagan and Franklin Zimring. Chicago: University of Chicago Press.

Tanenhaus, David S., and Steven A. Drizin. 2003. "Owing to the Extreme Youth of the Accused: The Changing Legal Response to Juvenile Homicide." *Journal of Criminal Law and Criminology* 92:641–705.

Tonry, Michael. 1995. *Malign Neglect: Race, Crime, and Punishment in America*. New York: Oxford University Press.

———. 1996. *Sentencing Matters*. New York: Oxford University Press.

———. 2004. *Thinking About Crime: Sense and Sensibility in American Penal Culture.* New York: Oxford University Press.

———. 2007. "Treating Juveniles as Adult Criminals: An Iatrogenic Violence Prevention Strategy if Ever There Was One." *American Journal of Preventive Medicine* 32: 3–4.

Torbet, Patricia, Richard Gable, Hunter Hurst IV, Imogene Montgomery, Linda Szymanski, and Douglas Thomas. 1996. *State Responses to Serious and Violent Juvenile Crime: Research Report.* Washington, DC: Office of Juvenile Justice and Delinquency Prevention, National Center for Juvenile Justice.

Twentieth Century Fund Task Force on Sentencing Policy toward Young Offenders. 1978. *Confronting Youth Crime.* New York: Holmes & Meier.

United States General Accounting Office. 1995. *Juvenile Justice: Juveniles Processed in Criminal Court and Case Dispositions.* Washington, DC: United States General Accounting Office.

von Hirsch, Andrew. 1976. *Doing Justice.* New York: Hill & Wang.

———. 1986. *Past vs. Future Crimes.* New Brunswick, NJ: Rutgers University Press.

White, Henry George, Charles E. Fraizer, Lonn Lanza-Kaduce, and Donna M. Bishop. 1999. "A Socio-Legal History of Florida's Transfer Reforms." *University of Florida Journal of Law and Public Policy* 10: 249–76.

Winner, L., Lonn Lanza-Kaduce, Donna Bishop, and Charles Frazier. 1997. "The Transfer of Juveniles to Criminal Court: Reexamining Recidivism over the Long Term." *Crime and Delinquency* 43: 548–63.

Wolfgang, Marvin E., Robert W. Figlio, and Thorsten Sellin. 1972. *Delinquency in a Birth Cohort.* Chicago: University of Chicago Press.

Zimring, Franklin E. ———. 1981. "Notes toward a Jurisprudence of Waiver." In *Major Issues in Juvenile Justice Information and Training: Readings in Public Policy*, edited by John C. Hall, Donna Martin Hamparian, John M. Pettibone, and Joseph L. White. Columbus, OH: Academy for Contemporary Problems.

———. 1991. "The Treatment of Hard Cases in American Juvenile Justice: In Defense of Discretionary Waiver." *Notre Dame Journal of Law, Ethics, and Public Policy* 5: 267–280.

———. 1998a. *American Youth Violence.* New York: Oxford University Press.

———. 1998b. "Toward Jurisprudence of Youth Violence." *Crime and Justice: A Review of Research* 24: 477–501.

———. 2000. "The Punitive Necessity of Waiver." In *The Changing Borders of Juvenile Justice: Transfer of Adolescents to the Criminal Court*, edited by Jeffrey Fagan and Franklin Zimring. Chicago: University of Chicago Press.

Zimring, Franklin E., and Jeffrey Fagan. 2000. "Transfer Policy and Law Reform." In *The Changing Borders of Juvenile Justice: Transfer of Adolescents to the Criminal Court*, edited by Jeffrey Fagan and Franklin Zimring. Chicago: University of Chicago Press.

Zimring, Franklin E., and Gordon Hawkins. 1995. *Incapacitation: Penal Confinement and Restraint of Crime.* New York: Oxford University Press.

CHAPTER 33

YOUTH IN PRISON
AND BEYOND

EDWARD P. MULVEY AND
CAROL A. SCHUBERT

I. INTRODUCTION

THE juvenile court started as an effort to separate adolescent offenders from the potentially harmful effects of involvement in the adult criminal justice system and to capitalize on the possibility of turning adolescents away from crime while there was still hope of success from such efforts. There has always been a glitch in this plan, however. Some juvenile offenders hurt people severely or threaten community safety substantially, and treating them separately and less harshly offends the sensibilities of many community members about the need for just retribution (Feld 1999). As a result, there has always been a mechanism for transferring particular adolescents to the adult criminal justice system and punishing them accordingly. The debate endures about when it is sound and just policy to incarcerate these adolescents in adult facilities.

Youth incarcerated in the adult system have usually committed a very serious (often "heinous") crime and/or they have a history of chronic offending and failed treatment involvements. There are, of course, stunning exceptions to this pattern, where a youth has been subjected to severe punishment as the result of ill-conceived exertions of judicial authority or illogically punitive and poorly written statutes, e.g., *Wilson v. State of Georgia*, 631 S.E.2d 391 (Ga. Ct. App. 2006). In general, though, sending an adolescent to the adult correctional system is—and has always been (Tanenhaus 2004)—a dramatic statement from the court that an adolescent, by virtue of his or her acts, will no longer be sheltered from the just harshness of the criminal justice system. With the incarceration of an adolescent in the adult system, the demand for penal proportionality (Zimring 2005) trumps the goal of individualized rehabilitation.

Arguments about whether an adolescent should be subjected to incarceration in an adult facility revolve around a number of issues, including the culpability of adolescents, the utility of deterrence, the symbolic importance of retribution, and the amount worth investing in rehabilitation. In *Roper v. Simmons*, 543 U.S. 551 (2005), the Supreme Court banned capital punishment for adolescent offenders, coming to the conclusion that adolescents, by their nature, are more immature, malleable, and subject to the influence of others, and thus do not deserve the ultimate punishment of death for their actions. The court's decision rested on the distinct nature and immature quality of adolescent judgment as well as the transitory, developmental nature of this type of decision-making, making it less indicative of depraved character. Following similar logic, the Supreme Court also ruled that life without parole was unconstitutional for juveniles convicted of non-homicide offenses (Graham V. Florida, 560 U.S.—2010).

Policy regarding the imprisonment of juveniles, although ultimately a matter of normative social principles, could be informed by research findings about the effects of such a practice. There is, however, very little data on this question (Bishop 2000). Little is known about how adolescents incarcerated in adult facilities fare, either during their stay or after.

In this chapter, we explore how the fundamental orientation and the operational realities of the adult versus juvenile system appear to affect young offenders in terms of both their prison experience and their life after this experience.[1] We frame this examination in terms of the "fit" between the needs of adolescents and the adult prison or jail environment. Adult prisons and jails face unique issues when dealing with adolescents (e.g., safety or programming needs), and we identify some areas that are particularly salient when considering the impact of the experience on adolescents. Finally, we consider the reentry issues associated with young prison releasees.

II. Person-Environment Fit

The notion of "person-environment fit" has long been an orienting framework for psychologists interested in how settings affect behavior. In early field theory in psychology, understanding a person's behavior was seen as requiring an analysis of the interaction between an individual's capacity and the demands of the setting (Lewin 1938, 1951). Behavioral expressions change with the demands of the environment, and an individual's capacities are more or less likely to be expressed and adaptive, depending on these demands. In personality psychology, the influence of setting characteristics was termed "environmental press" (Murray 1938), and included both the objective aspects (the concrete features or the normative or consensual judg-ments of the environment) and the subjective judgments about the environment. In both formulations and their associated research, it is clear that (a) the objective and perceived aspects of an environment delimit the range of behaviors that will be appropriate and useful, and (b) an individual's capacities and limitations may be particularly well- or ill-suited to a given setting's demands. Also in both formula-tions, the power of the "fit" between the individual and the setting is seen as deter-mining the long-term adjustment of an individual and self-representations over time.

The idea of person-environment fit has been adapted to developmental psychology as a way of explaining the inadequacies of theories that posited an inevitable unfolding of capacities and skills within children and adolescents. Bronfennbrener 1979 introduced the idea of a child's ecosystem and the poten-tial influences on development from environments with different levels of prox-imity to the everyday life of the child. Others (e.g., Eccles et al. 1993) presented the idea of "stage-environment" fit when discussing the interaction of capacities and settings for adolescents, expanding the work of Hunt (1975a, 1975b), dem-onstrating that different development demands of childhood required different setting features to promote positive outcomes. In this formulation, developing children and adolescents will flourish most productively when the demands of the environment present challenges and supports for mastery of the skills needed to move on to the next developmental phase.

These general theoretical formulations are useful for framing a consideration of the effects of adult incarceration on adolescents. The idea of an adolescent offender in adult prison or jail facilities presents a rather stark picture of an indi-vidual with fluid, and potentially rather limited, capacities, interacting with a pow-erful setting. Although many aspects of cognitive decision-making are rather well formed by mid-adolescence, there is considerable evidence that this time period is still one in which individuals are undergoing marked change in capacities regarding the assessment of risk, impulse control, future orientation, and susceptibility to peer influence (Steinberg 2007). Adolescent offenders can be assumed to be particu-larly diverse, and potentially delayed, in many of these aspects of social develop-ment (Monahan et al. 2009). There is also considerable evidence that prison and jail environments present challenges to one's sense of self and identity that even rather hardened criminals find disorienting, upsetting, and traumatic. Particularly suscep-tible or limited adolescents are thus taking the next steps of their developmental journey in an environment that is not only far from promotive of their next devel-opmental stage, but also potentially harmful for that progress.

There are numerous ways that being in a prison or jail environment can pres-ent particular risks to adolescents, and several of these are reviewed below. Many of the risks of incarceration differ for adolescents compared to adults, either in their intensity, form, or impact. As we will see, we have very little definitive knowl-edge about how an adult incarceration experience affects an adolescent offender. Weaving together what we know about the "person" of an adolescent and the "environment" of adult prison/jail facilities, though, we can make some reasonable assumptions about the potential harms and outcomes associated with this type of experience.

III. Potential Harms from Incarceration

A. Victimization

Being physically, sexually, or psychologically victimized by other inmates is one of the stereotypic features of doing time in an adult prison. It is so much an expectation of incarceration in America that late-night comedians make reference to it as a possible, well-deserved outcome for particularly disliked public figures facing criminal sanctions. The idea of adolescent offenders being subjected to such treatment as a consequence of their confinement in adult facilities, however, gives pause to even the most ardent supporters of retribution. It just does not seem fair to expose juvenile offenders to an increased likelihood of being raped, infected with HIV/AIDS, beaten up, or terrorized while serving their punishment for a serious offense. Doing the time for doing the crime might be seen as fair, but doing much worse time because the crime was done while an adolescent seems to tip the balance beyond even-handed justice.

There is little dispute that physical and sexual violence are an integral part of prison life for adult offenders. Personal accounts, ethnographies, and observational studies of adult offenders all document the occurrence and utility of physical encounters, forced sexual activities, and an atmosphere of watching one's back against such incidents (Irwin 1980; Toch, Adams, and Grant 2002; Gillespie 2003; Johnson 1987; McCorkle 1992). Official statistics report that about 2.8% of inmates are physically assaulted by other inmates annually (Stephen and Karsberg 2003), but self-report studies find rates about ten times those seen in official figures (Bowker 1980). A recent study by Wolff and her colleagues (2007), for example, reported a 20% prevalence rate of involvement in violence over six months. This disparity in estimates is not surprising, given the lack of official reporting of staff-on-inmate violence and the lack of incentive for official reporting systems to document all incidents (Camp 1999). Sexual violence, although less prevalent, is nonetheless disturbingly high (Gaes et al. 2004), with a recent survey conducted by the Bureau of Justice Statistics (Beck and Harrison 2008) finding that 4.5% of a large jail and prison inmate sample reporting experiencing sexual abuse at least once during the last twelve months.

There is also little dispute that adolescents housed in adult facilities are at greater risk for involvement in these incidents. As one might expect, age is one of the most consistent predictors of being victimized in a prison setting (MacKenzie 1987; Flanagan 1983). Moreover, because of their relative lack of experience in these settings, their smaller size and strength, and their potential lack of interpersonal sophistication, it is just commonsensical that adolescents in adult facilities are easy potential targets for a variety of forms of victimization (Ziedenberg and Schiraldi 1998 (citing J. Fagan); Lerner 1984). Simply considering the realities of life in jails and prisons and the apparent differences between adolescents and adults, one can easily come to the conclusion that adolescents are readily identifiable prey in these settings.

Conclusive empirical evidence about the extent to which adolescents might experience a markedly higher rate of victimization than adults in these facilities, however, is sparse. Ideally, an adolescent victimization rate could be calculated by simply putting the number of officially or self-reported victimization incidents involving an adolescent over the number of adolescents in the facilities surveyed. Unfortunately, there are few solid estimates of either figure. For instance, there is no systematic national count of the number of youths who are transferred or waived to criminal court (Fagan 2008), and there are inconsistent sources for estimating the number of adolescents in prisons or jails on any given day or during any given period of time (Woolard et al. 2005). The best estimates indicate that the number and proportion of adolescents in adult prisons appears to have peaked in the mid-1990s (about five thousand prisoners, or 2.3%, according to Snyder and Sickmund 2006) and have fallen since then (less than three thousand or 1.2% in 2004; Snyder and Sickmund 2006; see Austin, Johnson, and Gregoriou, 2000 for somewhat higher estimates for the previous time period). Estimates of the number of adolescents in jails on any given day are considerably higher, somewhere around nineteen thousand (Austin, Johnson and Gregoriou 2000). Given the low representation of juveniles in these populations, it is then striking that in 2005 and 2006, 21% and 13%, respectively, of all victims of substantiated incidents of inmate-on-inmate sexual violence in jails were juveniles under the age of 18 (Beck and Harrison 2008). Although the numbers in the literature are variable and of dubious quality, it is reasonable to conclude that the risk of assault for a juvenile in these settings is substantial and higher than that for an adult.

Some analysts maintain that there is a sizable increase in risk to an adolescent in an adult prison or jail compared to placement in a juvenile facility. Beyer (1997), for instance, states that juveniles in adult facilities are five times more likely to be sexually assaulted and two times more likely to be beaten by staff than youth held in juvenile facilities (see also Feld 1977 for a discussion of violence in juvenile settings). These estimates, however, are based on limited data and are probably high. Interviews conducted by researchers at the Bureau of Justice Statistics indicate that the annual prevalence of sexual assaults in juvenile facilities may range between 12% (Beck, Harrison, and Guerino 2010) and 20% (cited in National Prison Rape Elimination Commission Report 2009, p. 17), and other survey data by Fagan and Kupchik (cited in Fagan, 2008, p. 100) indicate that the rates of reported physical violence in the juvenile facilities examined was higher than that reported by adolescents in adult facilities.

In probably the most widely cited study regarding adolescent victimization, Forst, Fagan, and Vivona (1989) found marked differences between the reported experiences of adolescents in juvenile (training school) and adult (prison) facilities. These researchers interviewed fifty-nine adolescents who had been sent to an institution in the juvenile system and eighty-one who spent time in an adult facility as an adolescent. Each youth had spent several years in their respective facilities. Victimization for violence ranged from 36.7% in training schools to 45.7% in prisons. Sexual assault was tapped by single question, and 1.7% of the training school group (N=1) and 8.6% of the prison group (N=7) answered positively to this question. The statistical analyses contained no controls for background differences between the groups, and none of the tests of statistical differences between the two groups were significant regarding the victimization questions. Nonetheless, this study has been presented in numerous forums (e.g., Ziedenberg and Schiraldi 1998; Kurlycheck and Johnson 2004) as indicating clear evidence that physical and sexual victimization is several times more prevalent in the adult versus the juvenile system. This study certainly shows trends toward more victimization in the adult system rather than the juvenile system, but the data from this study do not provide solid indicators of the magnitude of any differences.

The available evidence all points toward the conclusion that adolescents are at increased risk of being physically or sexually victimized from being housed in adult facilities. This is not a surprising conclusion, since placements in prisons and jails put less mature, less experienced adolescents into a social environment that stresses survival and toughness. Such an arrangement seems to inevitably increase an adolescent's chances of being involved in a physical confrontation, either through efforts to establish a reputation or to resist assaults or sexual advances (Lane et al. 2002; McShane and Williams 1989). The exact amount of increased risk of victimization is difficult to estimate, however, because of the inadequacies of the data available and the tenuous validity of comparing data sets collected in different ways. Given the consistency and magnitude of the documented rates, though, it seems reasonable to conclude that the risk of physical and sexual assault in the adult system is elevated several times over what would be experienced in the juvenile system.

B. Interruption of Normative Life Experiences

Adolescents may be harmed from an adult incarceration in other, more subtle and involved, ways related to the "opportunity cost" associated with a period of incarceration. There is a price paid by an individual in terms of what he or she might have accumulated or achieved if he or she had not been incarcerated for a given period. For adolescents, this price is considerable, and considerably different from what it is for an adult.

When incarcerated in an adult facility, adolescents are being locked up in a harsh environment during a period of rapid and influential development changes. The experiences of late adolescence and emerging adulthood present numerous "turning points" (Abbott 1997), and the adjustments in lifestyle and habits made during this period either limit or expand the possibilities for future adult life (Arnett 2000). Thus, although an adolescent and an adult might be given what is on the surface an equivalent sentence for a similar crime (e.g., three years for a felony assault), adolescents are paying in a different currency; and the adolescent's currency is worth a lot more in terms of life consequences. Because the "person" aspect of the person-environment fit in this situation is in great flux, the experience of incarceration during late adolescence can dramatically increase the chances of negative outcomes and limit the likelihood of more positive ones.

1. Identity Formation

One of the most salient processes of adolescent development that might be affected by incarceration is identity formation. Fashioning a sense of self—figuring out who one is in relation to family and others as well as what life might hold—has long been considered the central psychological task of adolescence (Erikson 1968). Most adolescents follow a pattern of individuating from parents, orienting toward peers, and integrating components of attitudes and behavior into an autonomous self-identity (Collins and Steinberg 2006). The last part of this process involves choosing the identity that really fits from the many that might have been "tried on," as well as reconciling and consolidating what you might want to be (the idealized self) with who you might worry about being (the feared self) (Oyserman and Fryberg 2006). Navigating this developmental period successfully requires supportive adults, healthy relationships with peers, and opportunities to make autonomous decisions (Scott and Steinberg 2008; Steinberg and Scott 2003).

Adolescents in adult facilities try to accomplish this developmental task in a demanding environment (see Woolard, et al. 2005) where there is little exploration of positive possibilities (Lane et al. 2002). As mentioned earlier, jail and prison environments present very real dangers to one's safety, hardly the environment where experimentation with a wide range of self-presentations or alternative viewpoints can be pursued with impunity. Acting "out of line" in terms of the strict rules of the setting or voicing radical views of the way the world should operate can have extremely uncomfortable, or even life-threatening, consequences. Moreover, the ongoing process of "prisonization"—adaptation to prison through identification with the role of being a criminal among criminals—has been described and characterized by many authors (Clemmer 1958; Gillespie 2003; Thomas 1977), and is a pervasive influence in these environments that would undermine healthy identity development. Being behind bars introduces a stark contrast between a closed environment in prison and the outside world (Toch 1996), and becoming a "criminal" serves an immediate and compelling purpose, with little opportunity or benefit from exploring alternative identities.

The likelihood of receiving positive support for identity development from either peers or adults in these settings certainly seems low. Peer relationships often offer little more than "schooling" that is useful for later criminality (Maruna and Toch 2005). Adult relationships, meanwhile, are not likely to be positive. Jails and prisons have appreciably lower ratios of guards to residents than do juvenile facilities

(Snyder and Sickmund 2006), and the orientation of these staff is toward security rather than developmental concerns. In addition, it is unlikely that relationships with adult residents in these facilities will provide reasoned guidance about future possibilities.

Talbott's (2000) account of one adolescent girl's circumstances in an adult facility provides a vivid illustration of being taken under the wing of an adult in such a facility.

> In October of last year, however, Jessica was transferred to Dade County Correctional Institution, near Miami. Her "family" at Dade is larger and more elaborate than it was in Tallahassee—it includes women whom Jessica calls her grandparents, great-grandparents, uncles, cousins, sisters, brothers. It is also considerably rougher, and for this reason, it is easy to see how a girl could settle into a life not just of crime but of truly depraved crime. The woman Jessica now refers to as Mommy, a beautiful, blue-eyed, heavily tattooed 29-year-old with the nickname Blackie, is serving a life sentence for murder. She and a male accomplice robbed two elderly people and cut their throats with a machete. The other Dade prisoner who wanted to be Jessica's mommy—they staged a sort of custody battle—stole an elderly man's checks with an accomplice, who then beat the man to death.

Alignment with adult figures and peers in these settings may be more a matter of survival than support.

In the end, prisons and jails are primarily designed to break down identities, not foster new, resilient ones adaptive to the world outside the facility walls, and they do this effectively even with adults who have a rather clear sense of who they are. Adolescents in these settings are forming a sense of who they are in an environment that tells them they shouldn't trust, and they shouldn't try to be different. Instead, the predominant daily message is to be a compliant inmate, and the long-term message is that a criminal identity is a reasonable one.

2. Lost Opportunities for Learning in Late Adolescence

By definition, adolescence marks the transition period between childhood and adulthood during which an individual progresses toward adult levels of responsibility and adult roles. Individuals pass through early, mid, and late adolescence, acquiring different developmental skills during each period (Berger 1994), but always moving toward the development of autonomy. Adolescents gradually take greater control over an expanding range of life decisions, making mistakes, picking up pointers, and learning lessons along the way. In the terms of Frank Zimring (Zimring 2005), they are operating during this period with a "learners permit" for developing maturity, generally under the watchful eye of caring individuals and afforded more tolerance from society for bad choices. This practice takes place primarily in the context of work, dating relationships, and independent living as youth "try out" various forms of each of these in search of a relaxed and more permanent lifestyle fit.

Spending time in prison or jail, however, curtails the amount of practice time that an individual has to freely develop skills and competencies in each of these areas. Learning job-related expectations, gaining actual resume-building skills, discovering qualities in a life-partner that are a good match, learning what to do with unstructured time, and learning to manage a household are not easily acquired behavioral repertoires—they require some trial and error. The regimented and highly structured schedules and restrictions in jail/prison environments, however, eliminate opportunities to develop lasting romantic relationships, identify career interests, or develop work skills. Even the most progressive jail and prison environments (e.g. specialized young adult offender programs) cannot provide experiences as broad as those provided to nonconfined youths.

While many adolescents can catch up when they return to the community, the longer they are out of the normal, developmental pattern, the more difficult this becomes. Starting to learn how to act on a job site or how to treat a member of the opposite sex in social situations in one's mid- or late twenties is a different type of challenge than it is at age 16 or 18. Society extends little forgiveness to adults who cannot negotiate the basic aspects of adult roles, and the same behavior displayed by an adult may be interpreted differently than if the actor is an adolescent. For example, an adolescent who has many short-term relationships is displaying typical behavior that is seen as part of learning about relationships (Furman, Brown, and Feiring 1999); an adult who moves from one relationship to another may be seen as "unable to commit," cunning, or shallow by nature. There is simply less room for experimentation and error when developing these skills for the first time as an adult, and more need for fortitude in developing these skills in the face of adversity.

C. Development of Human/Social Capital

Positive movement into adult status is more than simply accumulating and learning from experiences. Making a successful transition to adulthood also requires the establishment of skills and relationships that will open up new opportunities and allow an individual to weather inevitable setbacks. Adolescence is the period during which, for the first time, youths accumulate "human and social capital" (Coleman 1988; Putnam 2000) independent of their parents (Furstenberg and Hughes 1995). Human and social capital refer to commodities that human beings acquire throughout life and that can be used to acquire other goods. Human capital generally refers to skills or material possessions, while social capital usually refers to relationships, although the distinctions between these forms of capital are fluid and symbiotic (Caspi et al. 1998; Rose and Clear 1998). Family relationships, for example, may be viewed as both human and social capital, since these resources may help an individual find a job that subsequently alters both human and social capital.

In adolescence, the central tasks associated with developing capital are entry into the labor force and the development of peer networks independent of parental social relationships, and the assets built during this period (e.g., a job accreditation, supportive friends) are often the springboard for later life accomplishments or complications (Boyce et al. 2008; Wright and Fitzpatrick 2006; VanDerGeest, Blokland, and Bijleveld 2009). For a "typical" adolescent, the transmission of human and social capital takes place in the context of family, school, and neighborhood relationships (Wright and Fitzpatrick 2006; Caspi et al. 1998), with considerable variability in the relative importance of these contexts. For example, familial or neighborhood relationships might be most prominent for a youth who does not have much attachment to school, while an adolescent who is very tied into his school friends may find opportunities through those connections.

Removal from the community during adolescence in and of itself has a profound effect on both present and future human and social capital. Every person entering prison has a net of social connections, and there is some "cost" (e.g. weakened bonds) to the social capital of the community that is associated with the removal of that individual (Rose and Clear 1998). From the perspective of the adolescent, removal from the community means loss of access to positive social relationships in the context of school settings or supportive work environments in the community and an erosion of previously established positive relationships from restricted contact (in person and by phone) with individuals on the "outside." While prison environments may attempt to develop human capital through vocational training programs, the possible training options are very limited and often do not match either the interest of the individual or the employment opportunities of the individual's home community. For an adolescent, simply being incarcerated limits the range of opportunities for development of human and social capital during a period when the foundation of these assets are being built by adolescents in the community.

It is also very difficult to "make up for lost time" in this process once an adolescent returns to the community. Upon return to the community, now with a criminal record, there are often barriers to family and social reintegration, civil penalties (e.g. loss of voting rights), barriers to education and housing, and obstacles to employment (see Mauer and Chesney-Lind 2002). These new limitations are now usually compounding a set of already existing problems (i.e., early risk factors for delinquency), putting these individuals at a pronounced level of disadvantage (Laub and Sampson 2003; Uggen and Wakefield 2006).

The difficulties encountered from an adult incarceration become apparent when one considers the issue of employment. The amount of time served in prison by youths aged 17 to 25 is negatively related to continuity of employment and work commitment at ages 25 to 32 (Sampson and Laub 1993). In addition, prison experience has been linked to a lower likelihood of being hired (because of requirements to report felony convictions on a job application) and reduced wages over time (Freeman 1992; Kuzma 1996). A prison experience appears to create a reduction in wages (possibly about 30%) across subsequent employment experiences, through a variety of mechanisms like the stigma of criminal conviction limiting job opportunities to less skilled types of employment, the loss of opportunities to maintain or acquire new job skills, and the erosion of social contacts that provide information about job opportunities (Western 2002).

Despite these clear costs from incarceration, a key question is whether incarceration in an adult facility creates any more of a disruption in the accumulation of human and social capital than does placement in a juvenile facility. If the critical mechanism for these effects is time spent out of a developmental process, then it would seem to matter little where the individual was during this disruption of development. We and others (Chung, Little, and Steinberg 2005) suggest that many of the costs to the development of human and social capital noted above do exist when an adolescent serves time in the juvenile system, although the cost may be limited somewhat by generally shorter stays. More important though, some costs of incarceration are avoided in the juvenile system (e.g., there is no criminal record that follows the individual), and there are deliberate attempts to avert or reduce some of the negative impact of time out of the community.

Unlike the adult system, the juvenile system makes an attempt to mirror some of the development of human and social capital that might otherwise occur in the community for this age group. Indeed, many of the stated core values for juvenile correction systems include the promotion of productive lives, positive change, and the acquisition of competencies (e.g., see Arizona Department of Juvenile Corrections mission and values—www.azdjc.gov; and the Pennsylvania Balanced and Restorative Justice philosophy—www.jcjc.state.pa.us/portal/server.pt/community/balanced_and_restorative_justice/5032), but this type of language and emphasis is not found in reference to the adult corrections system. Rehabilitation is given at least as much (if not more) emphasis as punishment in the juvenile system, and juvenile institutions make resolute attempts to continue the education of the youth (mandated by law), focus on skill development (e.g., anger management, life-skill development, vocational programs), and provide positive role models (Mulvey, Schubert, and Chung 2007). While the effectiveness of these efforts may be limited in many situations (Lipsey 2009), there is still a qualitative difference in the orientation between these two systems regarding the development of human and social capital.

IV. COMMUNITY REENTRY

Over the past few years, policy makers and researchers have increasingly focused on how offenders (both adults and juveniles) make the adjustment back into society after incarceration, prompted at least partially by the dismal rates of successful community reintegration (Heide et al. 2001). In 2002, the Office of Justice Programs directed significant funds toward the support of the Serious and Violent Offender Reentry Initiative (SVORI), and Congress passed the Second Chance Act of 2007 (Pub. L. No. 110–199) to help state and local governments develop reentry initiatives aimed at reducing recidivism. These efforts have produced numerous program models to promote successful reentry, all with different names, but most with basically the same approaches, e.g., the Intensive Aftercare program popular in the juvenile system (see Altschuler and Armstrong 1994) and Critical Time Intervention, recently applied to persons with mental illness emerging from the adult system (see Draine and Herman 2007). Across models, there is an emphasis on prerelease planning, the recognition of a critical time period for re-engaging the individual, and a focus on services that will delay or prevent return to a facility, e.g., housing, social supports and employment (Draine et al. 2005). Models for juveniles include many of these components, but usually take a more individualized, developmental perspective and place a greater emphasis on family engagement.

The reentry process is an especially relevant issue for juvenile offenders serving time in the adult system because these offenders are likely to return to the community during a critical transition period in their development (Mears and Travis 2004). Both "get tough" policies promoting long sentences for youths transferred to the adult system, and reformist rhetoric opposing adult sentences for juveniles imply that transfer to adult court produces long confinement in an adult facility. The evidence, however, indicates that adolescents who are processed in the adult court do not necessarily go away for extended periods, but instead come back to the community while they are still young adults. For example, Redding (1999), citing a 1996 Texas study, reports that although 87% of a sample of 946 juveniles received longer sentences in criminal court than they would have received in juvenile court, the average prison time actually served was only 3.5 years (an average of about 27% of the imposed sentence). Additionally, Steiner (2005) found that the median amount of time served was 188 days for youths waived to criminal court in a rural northwestern state, shorter than the average time served in the juvenile system, and Males (2008), tracking thirty-five thousand releasees from the California Department of Juvenile Justice, reported that juveniles were released from the adult system after a shorter time served than youths sentenced for the same offenses in the juvenile system. Finally, the Bureau of Justice Statistics estimates that 78% of person under the age of 18 when admitted to a state prison in 1997 would be released by age 21 (Strom 2000). In terms of raw numbers, some have estimated that more than a hundred thousand young adults, aged 18–24, will be released from federal or state prisons each year (Uggen et al. 2005), and that these releasees will be overwhelming male (94%) and minority (40% Black, 23% Hispanic, 8% Other Non-Caucasian, 29% Caucasian) (West and Sabol 2008).

Many of these young released offenders will be enrolled in adult aftercare programs, most of which take a "one size fits all" approach, unlike the more individualized efforts in juvenile justice (Altschuler and Brash 2004; for an exception, see Visher and Travis 2003). In this section, we describe the range of characteristics and needs of young offenders who are being released after adult incarceration and discuss some of the unique challenges faced by this group as they reenter the community. Unfortunately, we do this without the benefit of much solid empirical evidence about how these factors actually relate to community adjustment in this group.

A. Physical and Mental Health Needs

Young offenders present a range of needs for physical and mental health care. Individuals who engage in criminal behavior are often risk takers in other areas, such as drug use and sexual activity, and the physical health problems related to infectious diseases thus often exist at higher rates in groups of incarcerated adolescent and young adult offenders than in their comparable nonincarcerated peers (New York City Health Department. 1998. Report on HIV Seroprevalences in New York City in 1998. New York: NY: New York City Department of Health, 1999, cited in Freudenberg et al. 2005). In addition, offenders have disproportionately high rates of mental health disorders compared to the general population (Petersilia 2003; James and Glaze 2006; Abram et al. 2003), with younger inmates (age 24 years or younger) having the highest rates. Bureau of Justice Statistics surveys indicate that at least two-thirds of younger inmates had a mental health problem and rates of substance use disorders were highest among inmates with mental health problems (approximately 70% of the group with a mental health problem also had a substance use disorder, reported in Psychiatric Services 2006).

The high rates of physical and mental health issues within the reentry population point toward the need for ongoing care in the community. Ironically, while health care is constitutionally required during the prison term (Estelle v. Gamble, 429 U.S. 97 [1976]), most individuals lose access to health care when they are released. Many states, as a matter of policy, terminate Medicaid coverage for incarcerated individuals upon release (Gupta et al. 2005), and correctional facilities generally do not assist discharged offenders in obtaining health care in the community (Maruschak and Beck 2001). As a result, a large percentage of individuals returning to the community following a jail or prison stay are uninsured (Mallik-Kane 2005), since private insurance is rare in this group. The lapse in Medicaid, SSI, and/or SSDI coverage means that many of these individuals must go through a lengthy eligibility-determination process, remaining without care and/or medication in the interim. These issues may disproportionately affect the youngest group of releasees since this group is most likely to have the highest rates of mental health problems and substance use disorders, as well as the least experience in navigating the complicated process for enrolling in Medicaid. These barriers to continued care would seem to not only have health consequences for these individuals, but also increase their risk for a return to jail or prison (Draine, Solomon, and Meyerson 1994; Morrissey et al. 2007).

B. Education and Employment

Young adults are more likely to adjust successfully in the community and avoid re-arrest if they have stable employment (Sampson and Laub 1993; Bushway and Reuter 2002). Working regularly potentially provides legitimate income, more structured use of one's time, an opportunity to develop friendships with less antisocial peers, and a new identity in the community (Staff and Uggen 2003). Yet getting a respectable job that can fulfill this potential often rests on having a high school diploma or certificate, and young offenders returning to the community start from behind in this race.

Overall, inmate populations, younger inmates included, are less educated than their counterparts in the general population. Approximately 18% of the general population had less than a high school diploma in 1997, while 27% to

47% of inmates (depending on the setting type) and 31% of probationers did not have a high school degree (Harlow 2003). Deviations from the general population figures are particularly evident among young inmates age 24 or younger. Bureau of Justice Statistics (Harlow 2003) indicate that over half (52%) of inmates in this age group have not completed high school and do not have a GED, and that these younger inmates are also less likely to have pursued a post-secondary education.

Rates of employment prior to incarceration are also lower for prison inmates compared to the general population during a concurrent time period, and employment rates increase as education levels increase in both populations. Harlow (2003) reports that approximately 38% of those with less than a high school diploma had not worked in the month prior to their arrest, while 32% of those with a GED, 25% with a high school education, and 21% of those with some post-secondary/some college education report not working during this time period. While these data are not broken down by age, we can presume that unemployment rates are high among inmates age 24 or younger, given the previous information that the younger inmates are less likely to have finished high school or to have obtained a GED. This link is critical in an era when tight state budgets are producing cuts in prison educational programs. Young offenders will be affected most in terms of their long-term ability to find stable employment at a living wage if their chance to earn at least a GED is taken away.

The potential for individuals returning from prison to find employment is closely linked to their prior work history and their newly obtained work skills. Unfortunately, these individuals now also have a criminal conviction on their record, a factor with significant negative consequences on the likelihood of future employment (Freeman 1992), as well as obtaining some types of professional or occupational licenses (Kuzma 1996). Given that about one-fifth of the reentry population have a health or mental health condition that limits their ability to work, coupled with lower educational attainment (also linked to lower rates of employment), the challenges of finding meaningful employment with a future are immense for young offender reentering the community.

C. Housing

Perhaps the most immediate issue confronting releasees is finding and keeping a place to live. The majority of returning offenders return to family or friends, and this may be especially true for younger offenders who have not irreparably harmed too many of the relationships in their lives. For those young returning prisoners who do not live with family members, loved ones, or friends upon release, housing options may be severely limited by the higher likelihood of physical or mental health issues noted above (e.g., infectious disease, substance use problems). In fact, for the general population of prison releasees, the issue of housing for mentally ill releasees is so dire that federal and state governments often provide subsidized housing options with treatment attendance as a leverage for maintaining access (Monahan

2008). Housing options are further limited by federal housing laws that, for a period of time defined only as "reasonable," exclude all individuals with a criminal record from eligibility for Section 8 and other federally assisted housing (Rubenstein and Mukamal 2002). Also, it has been observed that prisoners are generally released back into a "small number of urban core counties," giving these locales a high concentration of releasees and the individuals in them a higher likelihood of associations with individuals with similar problems (Lynch and Sabol 2001). The cumulative effect of these realities is not surprising; about a tenth of those who leave prisons end up homeless, for at least a while (Roman and Travis 2004).

D. Relationships

Reestablishing ties with family and friends is one of the primary tasks for an individual during reentry after prison or jail. Families—either parents or partners—often provide one of the only ongoing sources of support for an offender coming back to the community; they are often the only place that offenders have to go to while trying to get their lives back in order. Moreover, approximately 16% of individuals in state prisons who were age 24 and younger have children of their own (Mumola 2000), and about 45% of those individuals live with their child prior to incarceration. Even young offenders are often returning to a nuclear family where they are one of the heads of the household, but the dynamics of daily life have changed from what they remember. In addition, offenders returning to the community must also reestablish or renegotiate ties with friends, and this process can have a strong influence on their community adjustment. Many studies have demonstrated the link between negative peer influences and crime (Loeber and Farrington 1998; Fergusson, Swain-Campbell, and Horwood 2002), and this connection holds for offenders' involvement in antisocial activities during the reentry process (Schubert et al. 2010).

    This trying process of making positive connections with family and friends is, unfortunately, often made more difficult by existing policies. Many prisons have set limits on the number of visits to prisoners from families (including their own children) and have required that phone calls be made "collect," thus creating a cost burden for families (Petersilia 2003, p. 45), decreased contact, and increased alienation from loved ones when the offender returns to the community. The irony, of course, is that strong family support has been linked to lower recidivism (Nelson, Deess, and Allen 1999), and men who assumed husband and parenting roles upon release had higher rates of success than those who did not (Hairston 2002). Similarly, policies related to peer relations rarely promote positive influences. Parole supervision is usually concerned only with monitoring egregious cases of fraternization with negative peers, rather than carefully assessing and promoting positive peer relationships, which are important for forming a prosocial identity (Laub and Sampson 2001; Maruna 2001).

    The issue of establishing positive emotional supports in the community is especially consequential for the youngest group of releasees. As noted by several commentators (Steinberg, Chung, and Little 2004; Altschuler and Brash 2004), having positive guidance and support is a key factor promoting successful transition to adulthood. Receiving sound advice and a sense of emotional security from one's family members and friends provides the grounding necessary for withstanding the frustrations and insecurities connected to the new roles of early adulthood. Many individuals incarcerated as juveniles will have missed many learning opportunities in earlier years and may have an even greater need for this support upon release.

E. Access to Public Assistance

If, as noted in the previous paragraphs, educational achievement is stifled, employment limited, housing assistance curtailed, and supportive relationships damaged, it follows that young prison releasees will be in dire need of assistance from somewhere. Once again, however, we see policies that create barriers to program participation. Welfare reforms introduced in 1996 included the Temporary Assistance for Needy Families (TANF) program, which was designed to end lifetime entitlement to welfare. The TANF program imposed a lifetime cap on benefits and required recipients to work to receive benefits. This provision alone puts prison releasees at a disadvantage (given barriers to employment), but the program further imposes a lifetime ban on eligibility for individuals with a drug felony conviction (although this latter provision is implemented with various degrees of severity across states) (Rubinstein and Mukamal 2002). Clearly, the cards are stacked against prison releasees who might aspire to a crime-free life. It is hardly a wonder that recidivism rates are high.

V. Conclusion

Probably the most striking conclusion from the above review is how much we do not know about adolescents who are incarcerated in adult facilities. There is a body of work on adolescents in the juvenile justice system and on adults in the criminal justice system, but we found very little empirically based information about juveniles in adult settings. We do not have firm estimates of the number of adolescents in these types of facilities, the experiences of adolescents while in these facilities, or the effects of incarceration on future life chances. Policy choices in this area seem to be rooted in unsubstantiated assumptions about who these adolescents are and who they might become. At this point, informed opinion seems to be educated speculation regarding literature about adults in prison settings integrated with general findings from developmental psychology.

It does seem valid to say, however, that most adolescents are bound to be worse off for their experience in an adult facility—both while they are still in the facility and when they leave. Adolescents are more likely to be victimized while in adult facilities. How much more likely is still an open question, but there is no consistent evidence that points toward adolescents being at reduced likelihood of harm in these settings. Also, the likelihood of receiving high-quality, individualized services in prisons or jails is lower than it would be in juvenile facilities. Adolescents who might benefit from a particular form of intervention are not likely to get a chance to do so while in an adult facility. Given the higher needs of many of these adolescents and the chances of higher amenability to these interventions, time in an adult facility is at least a lost opportunity to head off the long-lasting negative effects of certain disorders.

We also know that some effects of incarceration are different for adolescents than for adults. Serious adolescent offenders in adult facilities are incarcerated during a particularly influential period of their lives, when their patterns of social relationships and their adult roles are just being solidified. The primary developmental activities of identity building and the accumulation of independent human and social capital can clearly be disrupted—and potentially permanently sidetracked—by a period of incarceration. Moreover, once disrupted, it is not simply a matter of "catching up" at some later date. Opportunities shift, societal demands stiffen, and one's notion of self can be set in a negative direction, with the long-term trajectory of development unalterably shifting at this point of early adulthood.

Given these realities, one can question why we would incarcerate adolescents in adult facilities, since the most predictable outcomes are negative ones, both in the short and long term. The obvious answer is that incarceration in these facilities accomplishes other important goals of the justice system, i.e., retribution, deterrence, and incapacitation, and these accomplishments are worth the negative outcomes. Such sentences send an appropriate message of societal outrage at the serious acts committed by these adolescents, the most serious adolescents are incapacitated during their prime crime committing years, and the individual adolescent and others learn that there are severe consequences for serious crime.

Certainly, in this chapter, we cannot provide the type of in-depth discussion that these assumptions warrant, and other authors in this collection address these issues. What we have addressed are simply the logical outcomes of this practice on the life course of the adolescents involved. As mentioned at the beginning of the chapter, this is just one aspect of the larger debate about normative social principles that ultimately determine the outcome of the debate about the suitability of policies aimed at incarcerating adolescent offenders in adult facilities.

For the purposes of this debate, however, it is also important to recognize that the degree of disruption and the resulting harm to development has not been demonstrated conclusively and is difficult to assess accurately. As highlighted above, the numbers of adolescents affected is not available, and there is very little, if any, consistent information on the outcomes for these adolescents after incarceration. Perhaps more important, though, it is difficult to determine the appropriate comparison for assessing the magnitude of any observed negative impacts.

Youths who are transferred to the adult system and incarcerated are generally atypical, not only in comparison to their age mates in the community, but also to other juvenile offenders. The prevalence of serious developmental problems, early traumatic events, early onset of disorders, substance use, and other problems are higher in these youths as a group (Loughran et al. 2010). This does not mean, however, that all of these adolescents are the same; there is considerable variability within the group of transferred adolescents that could contribute to positive and negative outcomes (Schubert et al. 2010). The question of determining the possible negative effects of adult incarceration is thus not an absolute determination. It instead is one of gauging the relative impact of this experience while considering the effects of other risk factors present in the group of affected adolescents. The policy question is really whether or how much an adolescent is worse off than he or she might have been if not incarcerated in an adult facility, even if the set of likely outcomes are not as favorable as we might have wanted.

Framed this way, it then seems that a consideration of the likelihood of achieving normal adolescent experiences and outcomes (upon which most developmental literature is based) may not provide the appropriate comparisons for assessing the likely outcomes for this group. The chances of these youths for successfully mastering the developmental challenges of late adolescence and young adulthood may have been lower than we would like even without an incarceration experience. These youths were at high risk for veering off the general "normal" life course, and our notions of what might have been in store for them might be idealized. Until more controlled approaches (see Loughran and Mulvey 2010) are taken to assessing the likely impact of this experience on these adolescents in particular, the question of just how damaging adult incarceration is remains an open question.

Where do we go from here in light of these conclusions? At the very least, it is clear that there is a critical need for the justice system to systematically track transferred youths from the point of the transfer decision or criminal conviction through their probation/parole period. We cannot fully understand the impact, benefit, or detriment of transfer policies for youthful offenders without knowing this basic information about this policy relevant group. This type of information gathering would be especially useful for assessing the possible alternatives to adult incarceration. Once we begin tracking the experiences of transferred youths in the adult system, there will be information available regarding the specific programs in which these youths participate and an opportunity to evaluate the effects of particular program components on outcomes. There are some prison programs that make clear attempts to mirror selected features of the juvenile system (see, e.g., Pennsylvania Department of Corrections Young Adult Offender program—www.portal.state.pa.us/portal/server. pt/community/hide_pine_grove/11402) by meeting the educational and developmental needs of the individual. On the surface, these programs show promise for meeting the demands of deterrence, retribution, and incapacitation while still responding to the realities of adolescence. It would be useful to document the differential outcomes for youths experiencing these facilities compared to those in other types of prison programs. More broadly, systematic assessments of the fidelity of prison programs and their outcomes (e.g., the effect of anger management or substance use treatment) for adolescents could promote more cost-effective practices.

Addressing the issue of what to do with serious adolescent offenders requires more than simple political posturing. While these adolescents have done serious harm to others and the community, they are still adolescents. Treating these offenders with harsh punishment without consideration of their distinct status as adolescents oversimplifies that issue and sells the justice system short. It can do better.

NOTES

1. Due to space limitations, we will not distinguish between prison and jail experiences in this chapter; however, the reader should be aware that these two environments do present some distinct challenges. Prison stays are longer, and the social structure of prisons can be more established than jail environments. In addition, availability of services and the impact of the experience on an individual's life routines can vary widely across these two types of facilities.

REFERENCES

Abbott, Andrew. 1997. "On the Concept of the Turning Point." *Comparative Social Research* 16: 85–105.

Abram, Karen M., Linda A. Teplin, Gary M. McClelland, and Mina K. Dulcan, 2003. "Comorbid Psychiatric Disorder in Youth in Juvenile Detention." *Archives of General Psychiatry* 60(11): 1097–108.

Altschuler, David M., and Troy L. Armstrong. 1994. "Reintegrating High-Risk Juvenile Offenders into Communities: Experiences and Prospects." *Correction Management Quarterly* 5: 72–88.

Altschuler, David M., and Rachel Brash. 2004. "Adolescent and Teenage Offenders Confronting the Challenges and Opportunities of Reentry." *Youth Violence and Juvenile Justice* 2(1): 72–87.

Arnett, Jeffrey. 2000. "Emerging Adulthood." *American Psychologist* 55: 469–80.

Austin, James, Kelly Johnson, and Maria Gregoriou. 2000. "Juveniles in Adult Prisons and Jails: A National Assessment." Washington, DC: U.S. Department of Justice, Office of Justice Programs, Bureau of Justice Assistance.

Beck, Allen, and Paige M. Harrison. 2008. "Sexual Victimization in State and Federal Prisons Reported by Inmates." 2007: Washington, DC: U.S. Department of Justice, Office of Justice Programs, Bureau of Justice Statistics.

Beck, Allen, Paige M. Harrison, and Paul Guerino. 2010. "Sexual Victimization in Juvenile Facilities Reported by Youth. 2008–09. Washington, DC: U.S. Department of Justice, Office of Justice Programs, Bureau of Justice Statistics.

Berger, Kathleen S. 1994. *The Developing Person through the Life Span*, 3rd ed. New York: Worth.

Beyer, Martin. 1997. "Experts for Juveniles at Risk of Adult Sentences." In *More Than Meets the Eye: Rethinking Assessment, Competency and Sentencing for a Harsher Era of Juvenile Justice*, edited by P. Puritz, A. Capozello, and W. Shang. Washington, DC: American Bar Association Juvenile Justice Center.

Bishop, Donna. 2000. "Juvenile Offenders in the Adult Criminal Justice System." In *Crime and Justice: A Review of Research*, vol. 27, edited by Michael Tonry. Chicago: University of Chicago Press.

Bowker, Lee H. 1980. *Prison Victimization*. New York: Elsevier North Holland.

Boyce, William F., Diane Davies, Owen Gallupe, and Danielle Shelly. 2008. "Adolescent Risk Taking, Neighborhood Social Capital and Health." *Journal of Adolescent Health* 43: 246–52.

Bronfennbrenner, Urie. 1979. *The Ecology of Human Development: Experiments by Nature and Design*. Cambridge, MA: Harvard University Press.

Bushway, Shawn, and Peter Reuter. 2002. "Labor Markets and Crime." In *Crime: Public Policies for Crime Control*, edited by James Q. Wilson and Joan Petersilia. San Francisco, CA: ICS Press.

Camp, Scott D. 1999. "Does Inmate Survey Data Reflect Inmate Conditions? Using Surveys to Assess Prison Conditions of Confinement." *The Prison Journal* 79: 250–68.

Caspi, Avshalom, Terrie E. Moffitt, Bradley R. Entner Wright, and Phil A. Silva. 1998. "Early Failure in the Labor Market: Childhood and Adolescent Predictors of Unemployment in the Transition to Adulthood." *American Sociological Review* 63: 424–51.

Chung, He Len, Michelle Little, Laurence Steinberg. 2005. "The Transition to Adulthood for Adolescents in the Juvenile Justice System; A Development Perspective." In *On Your Own Without a Net: The Transition to Adulthood for Vulnerable Populations*, edited by D. Wayne Osgood, E. Michael Foster, Constance Flanagan, and Gretchen R. Ruth. Chicago, IL: University of Chicago Press.

Clemmer, Donald. 1958. *The Prison Community*. New York: Holt, Rinehart and Winston.

Coleman, James S. 1988. "Social Capital in the Creation of Human Capital." *American Journal of Sociology* 94, Supplement S95–S120, Organizations and Institutions: Sociological and Economic Approaches to the Analysis of Social Structure.

Collins, W. Andrew, and Laurence Steinberg. 2006. "Adolescent Development in Interpersonal Context." In *Handbook of Child Psychology: Socioemotional Processes*, edited by William Damon and Nancy Eisenberg. New York: Wiley

Draine, Jeffrey, and Daniel B. Herman. 2007. "Critical Time Intervention for Reentry from Prison for Persons with Mental Illness." *Psychiatric Services* 58(12): 1577–81.

Draine, Jeffrey, Phyllis Solomon, and Arthur Meyerson. 1994. "Predictors of Reincarceration among Patients Who Received Psychiatric Services in Jail." *Hospital Community Psychiatry* 45: 163–67.

Draine, Jeffrey, Nancy Wolff, Joseph E. Jacoby, Stephanie Hartwell, and Christine Duclos. 2005. "Understanding Community Reentry of Former Prisoners with Mental Illness: A Conceptual Model to Guide New Research." *Behavioral Sciences and the Law* 23: 689–707.

Eccles, Jacqulynne S., Carol Midgley, Allan Wigfield, Christy M. Buchanan, David Reuman, Constance Flanagan, and Douglas M. MacIver. 1993. "Development during Adolescence: The Impact of Stage-Environment Fit on Young Adolescents' Experiences in Schools and in Families." *American Psychologist* 48(2): 90–101.

Erikson, Erik. 1968. *Identity: Youth and Crisis*. New York: Harcourt, Brace.

Fagan, Jeffrey. 2008. "Juvenile Crime and Criminal Justice: Resolving Border Disputes." *Future of the Children* 18: 81–118.

Feld, Barry. 1977. *Neutralizing Inmate Violence: Juvenile Offenders in Institutions*. Massachusetts: Ballinger Publishing Company.

———. 1999. *Bad Kids: Race and the Transformation of Juvenile Court*. New York: Oxford University Press.

Fergusson, David M., Nicola R. Swain-Campbell, and L. John Horwood. 2002. "Deviant Peer Affiliation, Crime and Substance Use: A Fixed Effects Regression Analysis." *Journal of Abnormal Child Psychology* 30(4): 419–30.

Flanagan, Timothy. 1983. "Correlates of Misconduct among State Prisoners." *Criminology* 21: 29–39.

Forst, Martin, Jeffrey Fagan, and T. Scott Vivona. 1989. "Youth in Prisons and Training Schools: Perceptions and Consequences of the Treatment-Custody Dichotomy." *Juvenile and Family Court Journal* 40: 1–14.

Freeman, Richard B. 1992. *Urban Labor Markets and Job Opportunity*. Washington, DC: The Urban Institute.

Freudenberg, Nicholas, Jessie Daniels, Martha Crum, Tiffany Pekins, and Beth E. Richie. 2005. "Coming Home from Jail: The Social and Health Consequences of Community Reentry for Woman, Male Adolescents and Their Families and Communities." *American Journal of Public Health* 95(10): 1725–36.

Furman, Wyndol, B. Bradford Brown, and Candice Feiring, eds. 1999. *The Development of Romantic Relationships in Adolescence*. New York: Cambridge University Press.

Furstenberg, Frank, and Mary Elizabeth Hughes. 1995. "Social Capital and Successful Development among At-Risk Youth." *Journal of Marriage and the Family* 57: 580–92.

Gaes, Gerald G., and Andrew L. Goldberg. 2004. *Prison Rape: A Critical Review of the Literature* (National Institute of Justice, Working Paper).

Gillespie, Wayne. 2003. *Prisonization: Individual and Institutional Factors Affecting Inmate Conduct*. New York: LFB Scholarly Publishing LLC.

Gupta, Ravindra A., Kelly J. Kelleher, Kathleen Pajer, Jack Stevens, and Alison Cuellar. 2005. "Delinquent Youth in Corrections: Medicaid and Reentry Into the Community." *Pediatrics* 115: 1077–83.

Hairston, J. Creasie Finney. 2002. "Prisoners and Families: Parenting Issues during Incarceration." Paper read at "From Prison to Home." January 30–31.

Harlow, Caroline W. 2003. *Education and Correctional Populations*. Washington, DC: Bureau of Justice Statistics.

Heide, Kathleen M., Erin Spencer, Andrea Thompson, and Eldra P. Solomon. 2001. "Who's In, Who's Out, and Who's Back: Follow-Up Data on 59 Juveniles Incarcerated in Adult Prison for Murder or Attempted Murder in the Early 1980s." *Behavioral Sciences and the Law* 19: 97–108.

Hunt, David E. 1975a. "Person-Environment Interaction: A Challenge Found Wanting before It Was Tried." *Review of Educational Research* 45: 209–30.

———. 1975b. "The B-P-E Paradigm for Theory, Research, and Practice." *Canadian Psychological Review* 16: 185–97.

Irwin, John. 1980. *Prisons in Turmoil*. Boston: Little, Brown.

James, Doris J., and Lauren Glaze, E. 2006. *Mental Health Problems of Prison and Jail Inmates*. Washington, DC: Bureau of Justice Statistics.

Johnson, Robert. 1987. *Hard Time: Understanding and Reforming the Prison*. Monterey, CA: Brooks/Cole.

Kurlycheck, Megan C., and Brian D. Johnson. 2004. "The Juvenile Penalty: A Comparison of Juvenile and Young Adult Sentence Outcomes in Criminal Court." *Criminology* 42(2): 485–517.

Kuzma, Susan M. 1996. *Civic Disabilities of Convicted Felons: A State-by-State Survey*. Washington, DC: U.S. Department of Justice, Office of the Pardon Attorney.

Lane, Jodi, Lonn Lanza-Kaduce, Charles E. Frazier, and Donna M. Bishop. 2002. "Adult versus Juvenile Sanctions: Voices of Incarcerated Youths." *Crime and Delinquency* 48: 431–55.

Laub, John, and Robert Sampson. 2001. "Understanding Desistance from Crime." In *Crime and Justice: An Annual Review of Research*. Chicago, IL: University of Chicago Press.

———. 2003. *Shared Beginnings, Divergent Lives: Delinquent Boys to Age 70*. Cambridge, MA: Harvard University Press.

Lerner, Steve. 1984. "The Rule of the Cruel." *The New Republic*, Oct. 15.

Lewin, Kurt. 1938. *The Conceptual Representation and the Measurement of Psychological Forces*. Durham, NC: Duke University Press.

———. 1951. *Field Theory in Social Science*. New York: Harper.

Lipsey, Mark W. 2009. "The Primary Factors that Characterize Effective Interventions with Juvenile Offenders: A Meta-analytic Overview." *Victims and Offenders* 4: 124–47.

Loeber, Rolf, and David P. Farrington, eds. 1998. *Serious and Violent Juvenile Offenders: Risk Factors and Successful Interventions*. Thousand Oaks, CA: Sage.

Loughran, Thomas, and Edward. P. Mulvey. 2010. "Estimating Treatment Effects: Matching Quantification to the Question." In *Handbook of Quantitative Criminology*, edited by Alex Piquero and David Weisburd. New York: Springer.

Loughran, Thomas, Edward P. Mulvey, Carol A. Schubert, Laurie Chassin, Laurence Steinberg, Alex Piquero, Jeffrey Fagan, Sonya Cota-Robles, Elizabeth Cauffman, and Sandy Losoya. 2010. "Differential Effects of Adult Court Transfer on Juvenile Offender Recidivism." *Law & Human Behavior* 34(6): 476–88.

Lynch, James P., and William J. Sabol. 2001. "Prisoner Reentry in Perspective." Washington, DC: The Urban Institute/Justice Policy Center.

MacKenzie, Doris. 1987. "Age and Adjustment to Prison." *Criminal Justice and Behavior* 14: 427–47.

Males, Mike A. 2008. *Myths and Facts About "Direct File," Minorities, and Adult-Court Sentencing*. Accessed May 8, 2009. http://www.cjcj.org/post/juvenile/justice/myths/and/facts/about/direct/file/minorities/and/adult/court/sentencing/0.

Mallik-Kane, Kamala. 2005. "Returning Home Illinois Policy Brief: Health and Prisoner Reentry." Washington, DC: The Urban Institute, Justice Policy Center. Illinois Criminal Justice Information Authority. August.

Maruna, Shadd. 2001. *How Ex-Convicts Reform and Rebuild Their Lives*. Washington, DC: American Psychological Association.

Maruna, Shadd, and Hans Toch. 2005. "The Impact of Imprisonment on the Desistance Process." In *Prisoner Reentry and Crime in America*, edited by Jeremy Travis and Christy Visher. New York: Cambridge University Press.

Maruschak, Laura M., and Allen J. Beck. 2001. "Medical Problems of Inmates, 1997." Washington, D.C: Bureau of Justice Statistics, Special Report. Bureau of Justice Statistics, NCJ 181644.

Mauer, Marc, and Meda Chesney-Lind. 2002 *Invisible Punishment: The Collateral Consequences of Mass Imprisonment*. New York: New Press.

McCorkle, Richard C. 1992. "Personal Precautions to Violence in Prison." *Criminal Justice and Behavior* 19: 160–73.

McShane, Marylin D., and Frank P. Williams. 1989. "The Prison Adjustment of Juvenile Offenders." *Crime and Delinquency* 35(2): 254–69.

Mears, Daniel P., and Jeremy Travis. 2004. "Youth Development and Reentry." *Youth Violence and Juvenile Justice* 2: 3–20.

Monahan, John. 2008. "Mandated Community Treatment: Applying Leverage to Achieve Adherence" *Journal of the American Academy of Psychiatry and Law* 36: 282–85.

Monahan, Kathryn C., Laurence Steinberg, Elizabeth Cauffman, and Edward P. Mulvey. 2009. "Trajectories of Antisocial Behavior and Psychosocial Maturity from Adolescence to Young Adulthood." *Developmental Psychology* 45(6): 1654–68.

Morrissey, Joseph P., Gary S. Cuddeback, Alison E. Cuellar, and Henry J. Steadman. 2007. "The Role of Medicaid Enrollment and Outpatient Service Use in Jail Recidivism Among Persons with Severe Mental Illness." *Psychiatric Services* 58: 794–801.

Mulvey, Edward P., Carol A. Schubert, and He Len Chung. 2007. "Service Use after Court Involvement in a Sample of Serious Adolescent Offenders." *Children and Youth Services Review* 29: 518–44.

Mumola, Christopher J. 2000. *Incarcerated Parents and Their Children*. Washington, DC: Bureau of Justice Statistics, Special Report.

Murray, Henry A. 1938. *Explorations in Personality*. New York: Oxford University Press.

National Prison Rape Elimination Commission Report. 2009. Accessed December 16, 2009. http://www.cybercemetery.unt.edu/archive/nprec/20090820155502/http://nprec.us/files/pdfs/NPREC_FinalReport.PDF.

Nelson, Marta, Perry Deess, and Charlotte Allen. 1999. *The First Month Out: Post-Incarceration Experiences in New York City*. New York: Vera Institute of Justice.

New York City Health Department. 1998. Report on HIV Seroprevalences in New York City in 1998. New York: NY: New York City Department of Health, 1999.

Oyserman, Daphna, and Stephanie A. Fryberg. 2006. "The Possible Selves of Diverse Adolescents: Content and Function across Gender, Race and National Origin." In *Possible Selves: Theory, Research, and Application*, edited by Curtis Dunkel and Jennifer Kerpelman. Huntington, NY: Nova Science Publishers.

Petersilia, Joan. 2003. *When Prisoners Come Home: Parole and Prisoner Reentry*. New York: Oxford University Press.

Psychiatric Services. October 2006. "Federal Surveys Document High Rates of Mental Health Problems Among Prison and Jail Inmates." *Psychiatric Services Online*. 57(10): 1540–41. ps.psychiatryonline.org.

Putnam, Robert. 2000. *Bowling Alone: The Collapse and Revival of American Democracy*. New York: Simon & Shuster.

Redding, Richard E. 1999. "Examining Legal Issues: Juvenile Offenders in Criminal Court and Adult Prison." *Corrections Today* 92–123.

Roman, Caterina J., and Jeremy Travis. 2004. *Taking Stock: Housing, Homelessness and Prisoner Reentry*. Washington, DC: The Urban Institute.

Rose, Dina, and Todd R. Clear. 1998. "Incarceration, Social Capital, and Crime: Implications for Social Disorganization Theory." *Criminology* 36(3): 441–79.

Rubinstein, Gwen, and Debbie Mukamal. 2002. "Welfare and Housing: Denial of Benefits to Drug Offenders." In *Invisible Punishment: The Collateral Consequences of Mass Imprisonment*, edited by Marc Mauer and Meda Chesney-Lind. New York: New Press.

Sampson, Robert J., and John H. Laub. 1993. *Crime in the Making: Pathways and Turning Points through Life*. Cambridge, MA: Harvard University Press.

Schubert, Carol A., Edward P. Mulvey, Thomas Loughran, Jeffrey Fagan, Laurie Chassin, Alex Piquero, Sandy Losoya, Laurence Steinberg, and Elizabeth Cauffman. 2010. "Predicting Outcomes for Transferred Youth: Implications for Policy and Practice." *Law and Human Behavior* 34(6): 460–75.

Scott, Elizabeth, and Laurence Steinberg. 2008. *Rethinking Juvenile Justice*. Cambridge, MA: Harvard University Press.

Snyder, Howard N., and Melissa Sickmund. 2006. *Juvenile Offenders and Victims: 2006 National Report*. Washington, DC: U.S. Department of Justice, Office of Justice Programs, Office of Juvenile Justice and Delinquency Prevention. Accessed April 2, 2006. http://www.ojjdp.ncjrs.gov/ojstatbb/nr2006.

Staff, Jeremy, and Christopher Uggen. 2003. "The Fruits of Good Work: Early Work Experiences and Adolescent Deviance." *Journal of Research in Crime and Delinquency* 40(3): 263–90.

Steinberg, Laurence. 2007. *Adolescence*. New York: McGraw-Hill.

Steinberg, Laurence, He Len Chung, and Michelle Little. 2004. "Reentry of Young Offenders from the Justice System: A Developmental Perspective." *Youth Violence and Juvenile Justice* 1: 21–38.

Steinberg, Laurence, and Elizabeth Scott. 2003. "Less Guilty by Reason of Adolescence: Developmental Immaturity, Diminished Responsibility and the Juvenile Death Penalty." *American Psychologist* 58(12): 1009–18.

Steiner, Benjamin. 2005. "Predicting Sentencing Outcomes and Time Served for Juveniles Transferred to Criminal Court in a Rural Northwestern State." *Journal of Criminal Justice* 33: 601–10.

Stephan, James J., and Jennifer C. Karsberg. 2003. *Census of State and Federal Correctional Facilities 2000 (No. NCJ 198272)*. Washington, DC: U.S. Department of Justice, Bureau of Justice Statistics.

Strom, Kevin J. 2000. *Profile of State Prisoners under Age 18, 1985–97*. Washington, DC: Bureau of Justice Statistics.

Talbott, Margaret. 2000. "What's Become of the Juvenile Delinquent?" *New York Times Magazine*. September 10.

Tanenhaus, David S. 2004. *Juvenile Justice in the Making*. New York: Oxford University Press.

Thomas, Charles W. 1977. "Theoretical Perspectives on Prisonization: A Comparison of the Importation and Deprivation Models." *Journal of Criminal Law and Criminology* 68(1): 135–45.

Toch, Hans. 1996. *Living in Prison*. New York: Free Press.

Toch, Hans, Kenneth Adams, and J. Douglas Grant. 2002. *Acting Out: Maladaptive Behavior in Confinement*, 1st ed. Washington, DC: American Psychological Association.

Uggen, Christopher, and Sara Wakefield. 2006. "Young Adults Reentering the Community from the Criminal Justice System: The Challenge of Becoming an Adult." In *On Your Own Without A Net: The Transition to Adulthood for Vulnerable Populations*, edited by D. Wayne Osgood, E. Michael Foster, Constance Flanagan, and Gretchen R. Ruth. Chicago: University of Chicago Press.

Uggen, Christopher, Sara Wakefield, Jeremy Travis, and Christy Visher. 2005. "Weaving Young Ex-Offenders Back into the Fabric of Society." MacArthur Foundation Research Network on Transitions to Adulthood and Public Policy. Issue 22 (February).

VanDerGeest, Victor, Arjan Blokland, and Catrien Bijleveld. 2009. "Delinquent Development in a Sample of High-Risk Youth: Shape, Content and Predictors of Delinquency Trajectories from Age 12–32." *Journal of Research in Crime and Delinquency* 46(2): 111–43.

Visher, Christy, and Jeremy Travis. 2003. "Transitions from Prison to Community: Understanding Individual Pathways." *Annual Review of Sociology* 29: 89–113.

West, Heather C., and William J. Sabol. 2008. "Prisoners in 2007." Washington, DC: Bureau of Justice Statistics Bulletin. December 11. http://bjs.ojp.usdoj.gov/index.cfm?ty=pbdetail&iid=903.

Western, Bruce. 2002. "The Impact of Incarceration on Wage Mobility and Inequality." *American Sociological Review* 67: 526–46.

Wolff, Nancy, Cynthia L. Blitz, Jing Shi, Jane Siegel, and Ronet Bachman. 2007. "Physical Violence Inside Prisons: Rates of Victimization." *Criminal Justice and Behavior* 34: 588–99.

Woolard, Jennifer L., Candice Odgers, Lonn Lanza-Kaduce, and Hayley Daglis. 2005. "Juveniles within Adult Correctional Settings: Legal Pathways and Developmental Considerations." *International Journal of Forensic Mental Health* 4: 1–18.

Wright, Darlene R., and Kevin M. Fitzpatrick. 2006. "Social Capital and Adolescent Violent Behavior; Correlates of Fighting and Weapon Use among Secondary School Students." *Social Forces* 84(3): 1435–53.

Ziedenberg, Jason, and Vincent Schiraldi. 1998. "The Risks Juveniles Face: Housing Juveniles in Adult Institutions Is Self-Destructive and Self-Defeating." *Corrections Today* 60(5). August 1.

Zimring, Frank E. 2005. *American Juvenile Justice*. New York: Oxford University Press.

PART X

JUVENILE JUSTICE POLICY

CHAPTER 34

JUVENILE JUSTICE CROSS-NATIONALLY CONSIDERED

MICHAEL TONRY AND COLLEEN CHAMBERS

JUVENILE justice systems vary much more widely between countries than do criminal justice systems. Adult systems vary in many details, and they vary dramatically in how punitive they are, but at heart they are much the same. Defendants, at least in principle, are mentally competent, developmentally mature people who have been charged with crimes they are believed to have committed. The business of the courts is to determine whether they are guilty, and of what, and to impose a sentence that is proportionate to the gravity of the offense. Community and institutional corrections systems administer the sentence. The influence of rehabilitative and crime-preventive considerations on sentences in individual cases varies between countries (and, of course, between individual judges), but everywhere the overriding aim is to determine whether people are guilty of committing designated crimes and to impose appropriate punishments.

It is a different story with juvenile systems. In the United States and England and Wales, for example, the juvenile justice system has at its center a juvenile court that strongly resembles the adult court in its formal procedures and its emphasis on punishing wrongdoing. Denmark, Sweden, and Finland, by contrast, do not have special courts for juvenile offenders: the child welfare system deals with the actions of people under age 15; the adult courts handle alleged offenses of those aged 15 and over. Scotland has not juvenile courts but "children's hearings," which are not headed by judges and in which, under section 16 of the Children (Scotland) Act 1995, the welfare of the child is the "paramount consideration." Belgium has a "youth court" but in principle it may not impose criminal punishments; it is restricted to measures "in the best interest of the child." In New Zealand, every case referred to the court by the police involves a "family group conference," the offender, the victim, family members of both, a policeman, and sometimes a social worker or a defense lawyer or both. Depending on the circumstances, the aim of the conference is to decide what should be done or to recommend to the judge what should be done. The system is not officially based on ideas about restorative justice, but it is largely consistent with them. Germany, to give one last variant approach, has specialized juvenile criminal courts, in principle focused primarily on the welfare of the child, for offenses committed by people aged 17 and under. Adult courts have jurisdiction over offenses committed by those older than 17. In practice, nearly all 18-, 19-, and 20-year-olds are dealt with in adult courts but are sentenced as if they were juveniles.

Countries also vary considerably in how they define the jurisdiction of adult and juvenile courts and where they draw the lines between them. The starkest differences concern jurisdictional ages. The age of criminal responsibility, that is, the age below which an individual is deemed insufficiently responsible to commit a crime, varies from 7 in Switzerland and 8 in Scotland, to 18 in Belgium (with the exception of homicide, for which the age is 16).

Ages of responsibility vary widely. The most common in the United States are 10 and 12. In other developed Western countries, the most common ages are 14 and 15. This means that people below those ages who steal, assault, rape, or kill cannot be charged with crimes. It does not mean that nothing will happen when young people cause serious harms, but it does mean that neither juvenile nor adult courts will be involved. Social welfare, child welfare, school, mental health, or medical professionals may be mobilized.

The existence of minimum ages of responsibility produces a conceptual conundrum: the victim in an assault, rape, or killing by an individual below the age of responsibility has experienced something that the law defines as a crime, and which will be recorded by the police as a crime. At the same time, the law defines underage people as incapable of being criminals; they cannot be convicted or even charged for committing a crime. Similar conundrums occur elsewhere in the criminal law— the insanity defense, for example, also presupposes that people will sometimes be victimized by crimes at the hands of people who are legally defined as incapable of committing them. The examples illustrate the normative importance in particular cultures of recognizing reasons to exempt some people from criminal responsibility. We return to this topic in the conclusions. The ages which countries set as the age of responsibility constitute an important indicator—and consequence—of their political and legal cultures.

The other important jurisdictional limit is the minimum age of adult court jurisdiction. Traditionally in the United States, the juvenile court's jurisdiction covered offenses committed before the 18th birthday, after which adult courts took over. Eighteen remains the norm for adult court jurisdiction; all the others are 17 except New York and North Carolina where the juvenile court's jurisdiction ends at the 16th birthday. Outside the United States, age 18 is the norm, though it is age 15 in the Scandinavian countries and 16 in a few others (e.g., Scotland, Portugal).

The preceding paragraphs were much easier to write than they would have been in earlier times. The world is a smaller place, and the increasing use (for good and ill) of English as the international language of scholarship makes communication across national boundaries much easier. In the 1990s, there were only a handful of English-language collections of descriptive case studies of national juvenile justice systems; most were published by low-profile publishers and had modest sales and distribution (Klein 1984; Winterdyk 1997; Mehlbye and Walgrave 1998). As the second decade of the twenty-first century unfolds, there are many such collections on Western countries (e.g., Winterdyk 2002; Tonry and Doob 2004; Jensen and Jepsen 2006; Junger-Tas and Decker 2006; Muncie and Goldson 2006; and at least one on non-Western systems (Friday and Ren 2006).

Some of those books are better than others, in some cases much better; but taken together, they provide a rich array of writings that make it possible to trace developments in particular countries over time. Some countries—Canada, England and Wales, the Netherlands, Germany, various Scandinavian countries, the United States—appear in Klein (1984) and reappear again and again. Other countries—Australia, France, Italy, New Zealand—are featured in several collections. A few—Portugal, Switzerland, Austria—appear seldom or not at all.

Even with so many sources on which to draw, however, it is not easy to compare justice systems of different countries, for three primary reasons. The first is that no country can serve as a pure case of anything. An inevitable human ambivalence exists everywhere about how to reconcile concerns for providing compassionate treatment for troubled young people with concerns about punishing seriously wrongful conduct and protecting public safety. Political pressures for severe punishments and public anxiety about youth crime are ubiquitous, and manifest themselves in different ways.

The second is that justice systems continuously changes in laws, policies, or practices. Each case study is like a fly in amber. However good it is, it depicts a system, as seen by an individual writer, at a particular time. Case studies are inevitably partial and idiosyncratic and out-of-date when they are written. They depend on the writer's personal knowledge, which can never be complete, and on published sources which were written years earlier.

The third problem, and the most important, is the inherent difficulty of comparative work. As David Nelken (e.g., 2006), a British scholar based in Italy and probably the leading active criminal and juvenile justice comparativist, has observed, no one is optimally placed to describe or explain a country's justice system. There is no "view from nowhere." Everyone sees things through his or her own eyes in light of his or her own knowledge and experience. Nationals necessarily make cultural assumptions and take things for granted that foreigners cannot know, and so their accounts inevitably are incomplete. Foreigners necessarily observe a country's institutions and processes in reference to their own country's system, and so their frame of reference is distorted.

Even so, it is much easier than in earlier times to learn about differences in the structure and ostensible philosophies of countries' juvenile justice systems. That is a good thing. Unfortunately, we still know relatively little about how differences in structure and philosophy affect outcomes. There are three important sets of outcomes: what processes occur, what dispositions are made, and whether, overall, different systems are more or less effective at preventing later crime and enhancing young offenders' life chances. We briefly illustrate each.

Processes. In countries with relatively high ages of criminal responsibility, social and public institutions other than courts and prosecutors must take charge. If a 14-year-old is alleged in Sweden or Belgium to have committed a rape or serious assault, for example, the police may be called in the immediate aftermath but must promptly hand the case over to other public authorities. In principle, it should be easy to learn what happens then, but in practice it is not. Child welfare, mental health, educational, and medical systems are managed by their own bureaucracies, and are each mostly studied by specialized groups of scholars other than criminologists and criminal lawyers. Because data systems are based on individual case records and files of separate agencies, they are not easy to aggregate into statistics for an entire country. As a result, little is known about, for example, whether a 14-year-old in Sweden who commits a serious assault is more or less likely than a similar 14-year-old in England to wind up in confinement. In Sweden, the confinement will be in an educational, mental health, or medical facility rather than a youth prison. In England, confinement might be in such facilities, but it is likely to be in a youth prison. To the young person looking at passing traffic through a barred window, secure confinement in a residential educational or mental health facility compared with secure confinement in a youth prison may be a distinction without a difference. Almost nothing is known about the effects of case processing differences between juvenile systems of different types. For example, it would be interesting to have cross-national data on the percentage of 14-year-old boys in some kind of secure confinement, or to know what percentage of 14-year-olds who commit particular crimes wind up in some kind of secure confinement. Such data do not exist in any reliable form.

Short-term outcomes. More is known about national differences in short-term juvenile justice system outcomes. Young offenders are much more likely in some countries than in others to be diverted away from the juvenile justice system or, conversely, to end up in youth prisons. It is much more probable, for example, that young American and English offenders dealt with by juvenile courts will end up in confinement than are young offenders dealt with by French of German juvenile courts or older adolescent offenders dealt with by Finnish or Swedish courts.

Broad comparative statements are difficult to make, however, because of structural differences between systems. Because every young offender over age 14 in the Scandinavian countries is dealt with in the adult courts, 15- to 17-year-olds are included in descriptive data about adult sentences (however, data disaggregated by age are available). Young offenders age 16 and over in Scotland likewise are handled only in adult courts. In countries in which nearly all offenders younger than 18 are dealt with in juvenile courts, they do not appear in adult court data. Differences like these make many comparative statistical statements, such as "the adult imprisonment rate for offenders under age 18 in country X compared with country Y," suspect. The numerators of those fractions will vary between jurisdictions: in Scandinavia, they will include all young offenders over age 14; in Scotland and New York, all young offenders over age 15; in England and most American states, only those young offenders under 18 who were transferred to adult courts.

Though generalizations must be carefully offered, some things can be said about outcomes. Young offenders are much likelier to be put behind bars in some countries than others. Young offenders are likely to receive longer terms of confinement in some countries than in others. Young offenders are more likely to be transferred to adult courts in some countries than in others.

Long-term outcomes. Least is known about what, in policy terms, may be the most important set of questions. Are some juvenile justice approaches more successful than others at helping troubled children—as indicated by their antisocial and criminal behavior—successfully complete their developmental passages through troubled adolescence to successful adulthoods? More mundane, but not unimportant in policy terms, are some approaches more successful than others at altering the subsequent antisocial and criminal behavior of young people? All of the standard questions about criminal careers arise. Do some approaches lead young offenders to desist earlier, to reduce the frequency of their misbehavior, or to shift from more to less serious misbehavior?

There are plausible theoretical bases for hypothesizing that some systems are more effective than others at achieving preferable outcomes, and some data from comparative surveys offers hints at answers, but in truth little is known. The overriding problem is that the effects of the different natures and patterns of operation of youth justice systems are impossible to separate out from the effects of differing social welfare systems, political systems, and national cultures. If it were true, as there appears to be some basis for believing, that young people in Scandinavian countries are less involved in antisocial behavior than young people in many other countries, is that because the age of criminal responsibility is 15, because there is no juvenile court, because Sweden has well-funded and well-organized child welfare programs, because Sweden has a social democratic political culture, or because extended families remain closely integrated? All those claims may be true, or only some of them. It may be that Sweden has the approach to juvenile offending that it does because the other claims are true, and that juvenile offending outcomes would be the same if there were some other form of juvenile justice system.

This chapter provides an overview of current knowledge about national differences in juvenile justice systems. It has four sections. The first provides descriptive information on formal structural differences between systems. The second provides brief depictions of systems representing importantly different models: the English juvenile court model with its heavy emphasis on crime reduction, the German

youth criminal court model with its emphasis on social integration of young offenders, the Scandinavian non-juvenile-court model, and the New Zealand conferencing model. The third section discusses immediate outcomes in terms of the use of
confinement and the frequency of transfers to adult courts. In the fourth section, we
step back and offer a number of observations about comparative advantages and
disadvantages of different approaches.

I. STRUCTURAL DIFFERENCES

Systems for dealing with serious misconduct by young people differ in a number of
interacting respects. The first concerns institutional arrangements: are there special
institutions for young offenders and if so, what are they? Two concern age limits: the
age of criminal responsibility and the minimum age of adult court jurisdiction.
A fourth concerns the permeability of the adult and any juvenile system: may individuals legally defined as juveniles be transferred to adult courts, or dealt with by
special systems for juveniles, but sentenced as if they were adults and, conversely,
may people otherwise handled by adult courts be referred back to juvenile systems
or sentenced as if they were juveniles? We briefly discuss these questions below.

There is a fifth structural issue we do not discuss further that is salient mostly
in the United States: whether juvenile justice systems have jurisdiction over "status"
offenders. American juvenile courts traditionally had jurisdiction over three groups
of young people: delinquents, victims of abuse or neglect, and children (or people
or minors) "in need of supervision" (referred to acronymically as CHINS, PINS, or
MINS). In most other countries, juvenile justice systems do not deal with status
offenders. They and victims of abuse and neglect are dealt with by social welfare
agencies or sometimes by family courts that do not also have criminal jurisdiction.

A. Institutional Arrangements

The structural forms of national systems for dealing with juvenile misconduct vary
substantially and interact in diverse ways with the ages of criminal responsibility
and of adult court jurisdiction. In one model, exemplified by the United States and
other English-speaking countries, a juvenile court has authority over juveniles above
the age of responsibility until they reach the age of adult court jurisdiction (usually
18 but sometimes younger), with some possibilities for transfer between systems,
usually from the juvenile to the adult courts. In a second model, exemplified by the
Scandinavian countries and Belgium, there is no juvenile criminal court, and child
welfare agencies have jurisdiction until a young person reaches the age of adult
court jurisdiction. In a third model, exemplified uniquely by Scotland, a child welfare institution, the children's hearing, has jurisdiction over juvenile misconduct
and crime before the age of criminal court jurisdiction, but also has authority to

refer selected cases to the adult court. In a fourth model, unique to New Zealand, a restorative justice-like conferencing system has been superimposed over a conventional juvenile court model.

Those four "models" understate the differences between systems. The Germans, the French, and the Dutch, for example, have systems that look like the conventional juvenile court model, but they diverge from each other and from Anglo-Saxon systems in important ways.

B. Age of Responsibility

Ages of responsibility range much more widely outside the United States than inside. The minimum age of responsibility and the minimum age of juvenile court jurisdiction are not necessarily the same, though in most countries they are. New Zealand, however, is the exception that proves the rule. The age of criminal responsibility is ten, but the minimum age of juvenile justice jurisdiction is 14. Below that age, only child welfare agencies have authority over children (Morris 2007).

Most American states adopted age 7 from English common law as the minimum age of criminal responsibility (Meijers and Grisso 2009, tables 4.1, 4.3). A few have adopted higher ages, usually 8 or 10. Juvenile courts in some states observe the same minimum jurisdictional age, though a majority have established no minimum age. This should not be surprising, because child abuse and neglect can affect children of any age and it would be odd if the institution with authority to deal with them lacked jurisdiction over them (National Center for Juvenile Justice 2008).

There is much wider variation in minimum ages of responsibility outside the United States. The Beijing Rules recommend that decisions about criminal responsibility take into account emotional, mental, and intellectual maturity. In 2008, the United Nations Convention on the Rights of the Child called for a minimum age of 12 and specified that nations should establish an age of criminal responsibility "below which children shall be presumed not to have the capacity to infringe the penal law" (Weijers and Grisso 2009, p. 45). The European Rules for Juvenile Offenders Subject to Sanctions or Measures recommends a minimum age of 14 (Junger-Tas and Dünkel 2009).

Table 34.1 shows minimum ages of criminal responsibility in a number of developed states. Belgium has the highest at 18 (except for murder and manslaughter, for which 16 is the age), and the Nordic countries of Denmark, Finland, Iceland, Norway, and Sweden are not far behind at 15.[1] The countries with the highest ages of criminal responsibility tend to be those with the most welfare-oriented juvenile justice programs. The Scandinavian states have similar systems of juvenile justice with a tradition of humane and welfare-oriented approaches to justice. This tradition is reflected in their high age of criminal responsibility. Belgium, similarly, has worked to incorporate welfare and interventionist policies into its system, also reflected in its high age of criminal responsibility.

Most European countries have set the ages of criminal responsibility at 12 or 14. The countries with lower ages are mostly part of the United Kingdom (England and

Table 34.1. Minimum Age of Criminal Responsibility

MINIMUM AGE	COUNTRY
8	Scotland
10	Australia (Australian Capital Territory, South Australia, Western Australia), England and Wales, Ireland, New Zealand, Northern Ireland, Switzerland
12	Canada, Netherlands, Portugal, Turkey
13	France, Greece, Poland
14	Austria, Bulgaria, Germany, Italy, Japan, Spain
15	Denmark, Finland, Iceland, Norway, Sweden
16	Belgium

Source: Weijers and Grisso (2009)

Wales, Scotland, Northern Ireland) or are former British colonies (Ireland, Canada, Australia, New Zealand). Scotland's age 8 is the lowest. Except for Canada (age 12), the others set the age at ten. The United States falls into this group.

Scotland's low age might be thought anomalous because the children's hearing system places great emphasis on child welfare. The Commissioner of Human Rights of the Council of Europe has criticized Scotland's law, but it has remained in effect (Gil-Robles 2004). The Scottish Law Commission recently rejected a change in the statute (Weijers and Grisso 2009).

C. Age of Adult Court Jurisdiction

There is substantially less variation internationally (and within the United States) in the minimum ages of adult court jurisdiction. Age 18 is by far the most common.

Within the United States, three-fourths of states and the District of Columbia in 2007 used age 18. Two states, New York and North Carolina, used age 16, and eleven used age 17 (National Center for Juvenile Justice 2008).

Table 34.2 shows ages of adult court jurisdiction for eighteen Western European Countries plus Canada, New Zealand, and Australia. A large majority set 18 as their minimum age of responsibility. Except for the Scandinavian countries, only three countries use other ages: Portugal and Scotland, both 16, and New Zealand, 17. Denmark, Finland, Norway, and Sweden set the age of adult court jurisdiction of 15. This low age may result from the absence of a judicial system for dealing with juvenile offenders; the welfare system only handles those under age 15. As noted above, they also set the age of responsibility at 15 and have no specialized judicial institutions for handling young offenders.

It is difficult not to conclude that—with the possible exception of the Scandinavian countries—the countries and American states that set ages below 18 have adopted unsound policies.[2] Every country has some distinct system for dealing with juvenile misconduct and crime, which compellingly implies that there is almost universal recognition that young people are importantly different from adults, and

Table 34.2. Adult Court Age Jurisdiction

AGE OF CRIMINAL COURT JURISDICTION	COUNTRY
15	Denmark
	Finland
	Norway
	Sweden
16	Portugal
	Scotland
17	Poland, New Zealand
18	Australia, Austria, Belgium, Bulgaria, Canada, England, France, Germany, Greece, Hungary, Italy, Ireland, Netherlands, Spain, Switzerland

Source: Weijers and Grisso (2009)

accordingly that their misconduct and crimes should be dealt with in other ways. Different arguments can be made, and different empirical data deployed, concerning whether the basis of those views is best described in terms of emotional or cognitive maturity, or of normal developmental processes. Whatever the best argument is, the near universal adoption of age 18 suggests that it is the optimal age and that lower ages inevitably result in unjust treatment and punishment—as adults—of young people who are in a meaningful sense not yet adults.

D. Transfer

How countries handle transfers of young offenders between adult and juvenile systems may be the best indicator of, put gently, a country's willingness to acknowledge that young offenders are importantly different from older ones, or, put a bit more harshly, a country's (or state's) willingness to let public emotion and politics trump sound policy considerations. By a large margin, the United States is the extreme case of a country that ignores or denies that young offenders should be treated differently than adult criminals. This is expressed in the frequently heard sound bite: "Do the crime, do the time." It is generally estimated that 250,000 young offenders are dealt with by adult American courts for acts occurring before their 18th birthday (Bishop 2009, p. 90).

The United States has the most diverse and baroque set of transfer provisions (see Chapter 32 by Feld and Bishop, this volume). Most states long had systems by which judges could choose to transfer some cases, usually of older juveniles or involving especially serious crimes, or prosecutors for a designated set of usually serious crimes could elect to file particular charges in adult courts, or both. Since the 1970s, however, many states have adopted policies making transfers a more common occurrence or creating simpler, less restrictive procedures and policies. The most extreme laws—New York's and North Carolina's are by far the worst—simply reduced the age of adult court jurisdiction. Accordingly, in these states, every 16- and 17-year-old has effectively been transferred to the adult courts (and even younger juveniles charged with serious crimes are also transferred one-by-one). Other laws simplified the procedures and loosened the criteria for judicially authorized transfers, gave prosecutors broader authority to file charges directly in adult courts, and required adult court prosecutions for people charged with designated serious charges. As a result of these changes, compared with the 1960s, tens of thousands more people who are chronologically and developmentally children are prosecuted, and punished, as if they were adults.

The only other country that has closely emulated the United States, England and Wales, where children as young as age 10 are prosecuted from the outset in adult courts, and many others are transferred. In Germany, Austria, and Switzerland, transfer is impossible; adult courts lack jurisdiction over minors. In the Scandinavian countries, young offenders cannot by definition be transferred to adult courts as there are no juvenile courts. In Canada (Doob and Sprott 2004) and the Netherlands (Junger-Tas 2004), policy makers in the 1990s loosened the criteria governing transfers, but the numbers of young people transferred declined. In most European countries, only small absolute numbers of young offenders are transferred (Weijers, Nuytiens, and Christiaens 2009).

Many American states have "blended jurisdiction" laws in which some juvenile court offenders may be sentenced as adults, some adult court offenders may be sentenced as juveniles, or adult court offenders may be "transferred back" to juvenile courts for sentencing (Griffin 2003). German courts authorize judges to sentence 18 to 20-year-olds as if they were juveniles, and in most cases that is what they do (Albrecht 2004). In most European countries, transfers to adult courts are rare, and the jurisprudence of sentencing in adult courts authorizes less burdensome sentences for younger offenders (see the articles in Tonry and Doob [2004] and Junger-Tas and Decker [2006] for detailed discussions of many countries).

II. Models of Juvenile Justice

We refer often in this article to features of different countries' processes, institutions, and practices for dealing with young people who commit criminal offenses or engage in behaviors that would be criminal if committed by adults. Necessarily, those allusions provide only fragmentary images of particular systems. In this section, in order to give a fuller picture of how national approaches differ, we provide thumbnail descriptions of the English, German, Scandinavian, and New Zealand systems.

A. England and Wales

Since Labour Governments took power in England and Wales in 1997 the English (and Welsh: hereafter with apologies to the Welsh, we simply say English) juvenile justice system has become the most punitive in Europe. The proportion of young people in custody is the highest in Europe (though not much different from Scotland or Northern Ireland). The imprisonment custody rate in 2004 was twenty-five times higher than in the Scandinavian countries; five to twelve times higher than in Belgium, the Netherlands, Italy, or Spain; and three to four times higher than in Hungary, France, the Netherlands, or Belgium (Graham and Moore 2006, table 3.2).

The age of responsibility is 10. Alleged offenses by young people aged 10 or over can be brought before a Youth Court, which is essentially a criminal court for young people but with less formal procedures. Proceedings are partly private: the general public may not attend proceedings, though members of the press may, subject to a general prohibition against identifying young offenders. After conviction, however, that prohibition can be lifted on the basis that "naming and shaming" will "encourage young offenders to face up to the consequences of their offending behaviour and thus deter future offending" (Graham and Moore 2006, p. 71).

Anyone aged 10 or over can, however, be prosecuted from the outset in adult criminal courts, as notoriously happened in the killing by two 10-year-olds of the toddler William Bulger. Even children younger than 10 can be brought before the Family Proceedings Court and made subject to a "child safety order," which is in effect a form of community corrections supervision.

Before the effectuation of Labour Government changes, the English system was a more traditional juvenile justice system, which gave emphasis to child welfare and to the "best interests of the child." Since then, the first principles governing sentencing in the Youth Court are that primacy be given to the seriousness of the current offense and, for violent or sexual offenses, the need to protect the public from serious harm from the offender. Only subject to those priorities is the welfare of the child a priority. For children not immediately bound for confinement, a remarkably complex system of YIPs, (youth inclusion programs), YOTs (youth offending teams), YOPs (youth offender panels), and "youth offender" contracts is triggered. Bottoms and Dignan (2004), though out-of-date in some details, is the most comprehensive and detailed discussion and analysis of the English system (and also of the Scottish).

B. Germany

The age of criminal responsibility in Germany is 14. Young offenders are dealt with in a specialized youth criminal court which, as in England, is in effect a criminal court for juveniles, but with simper procedures. Proceedings are confidential and may not as in England be made public.

The jurisdiction of the youth criminal court over 14- to17-year-old offenders is exclusive. In no case, however serious, may young offenders be prosecuted in adult courts, and in no case may a young offender's case be transferred to an adult court.

The first principle of the German youth criminal court is the "education" of the child, by which is meant the socialization of the child into prosocial values which will enhance his or her prospects of becoming a responsible adult capable of living a productive and satisfying life. However, this principle coexists with the German criminal law tradition of basing sentences primarily on the seriousness of the offense, which means that youth criminal court judges attempt to achieve proportionality in the sentence imposed. In practice, however, two-thirds of the—usually short—prison sentences imposed are immediately suspended.

Jurisdictional ages are inevitably arbitrary. Different people develop in different patterns and reach cognitive, emotional, and social maturity at different rates and at different times. Recognizing this, German law authorizes judges to sentence 18- to 20-year olds as if they were young offenders under age 18. Hans-Jörg Albrecht reports that "virtually all adolescent offenders adjudicated for serious offenses [in adult courts] are sentenced under the Youth Court Law" (2004, p. 474). Albrecht's article and one by Frieder Dünkel (2006) are among the most exhaustive and informative on the German system.

C. The Scandinavian Countries

There are considerable similarities among the juvenile justice systems of the four large Scandinavian countries, and there are literatures on each. As of 2009, 15 was the age of responsibility in each. Below that age, serious misbehavior by children must be dealt with by child welfare authorities or, in appropriate cases, by medical or mental health authorities. Children younger than 15 may be taken into custody by police in the immediate aftermath of actions that would constitute crimes if committed by older people, but under strict limitations concerning questioning and subject to requirements that parents and child welfare authorities be contacted immediately.

The Scandinavian countries do not have anything named or resembling a juvenile court, and transfer to an adult court is impossible. Alleged offenses by individuals 15 and older are dealt with in the adult criminal court; such young offenders, however, are also subject to oversight by child welfare authorities. and dispositions often involve programs run by welfare agencies.

Sentencing principles direct judges to sentence offenders under age 18 less severely than if they were adults. In practice, as in Germany, most offenders between 18 and 20 receive less severe punishments than do older people. For all adults, including young ones, use of community-based punishments is common, prison is used sparingly, and prison sentences are short (but shorter still for young offenders). Imprisonment of offenders under age 21 is rare (Lappi-Seppälä 2007).

The only comprehensive treatment of all four systems can be found in Lappi-Seppälä (2011). Among the most ambitious and comprehensive articles on individual countries are Janson (2004) and Sarnecki and Estrada (2006) on Sweden; Kyvsgaard (2004) on Denmark; and Lappi-Seppälä (2006) on Finland.

D. New Zealand

New Zealand's youth justice system has attracted substantial international attention in recent decades. The principal reason is that the Children, Young Persons, and Their Families Act 1989 established a requirement that family group conferences become an integral element of almost every juvenile case that the police decide to refer to court processing. Although Allison Morris, the leading scholar of the New Zealand system, observed that "the phrase 'restorative justice' did not feature in the New Zealand debates about youth justice at this time" (2004, p. 259), New Zealand is "widely hailed as the principal exemplar of a fully fledged restorative justice model" (Cavadino and Dignan 2006, p. 233).

The second—perhaps[m1] in part a consequence of the first—is that throughout the 1990s, New Zealand's system became markedly less punitive in relation to young offenders. The rates at which young people were brought to the youth court, and the absolute number of young people receiving prison sentences in adult courts, fell by two-thirds in 1990 compared with the mid-1980s, and remained at those levels through the early years of the twenty-first century.

The third however, is that in other respects, the New Zealand system is among the more punitive of the developed countries (Pratt 2006, 2007), and the special provisions for young people end at age 16. This in some ways parallels the Scottish system in which the child-welfare-centered children's hearing system ends at the 16th birthday after which young people are dealt with by the adult court.

There are three critical ages in New Zealand. The age of criminal responsibility is 10, but this is subject to the important caveat that a system of noncriminal "children's boards" has jurisdiction over young people for offenses committed before the 14th birthday. For the ensuing three years, offenses are dealt with by a specialized court that has authority to refer the most serious cases to the adult courts. For offenses committed from the 17th birthday onward, young offenders are dealt with solely by the adult courts.

Police themselves deal informally with a large percentage of offenses committed by 14- to 16-year-olds, without referring the affected cases to the youth justice system. For the cases police do refer, a family group conference must be held. The participants include the young person and his family, the victim, victim support personnel, a police officer, the young person's lawyer, and sometimes a social worker. The decision on what should happen must be unanimous and, for less serious cases, is binding on all participants. For the most serious cases, the decision constitutes a recommendation to the judge. Importantly, police cannot refer to the court young offenders who have not been arrested without first convening a conference, and judges may not sentence young offenders without convening a conference and considering its recommendations.

III. Short-Term Outcomes

There are lots of things it would be nice to know about the effects of various national approaches, ranging from what actually happens to young offenders in the aftermath of formal proceedings to whether, as a result of those proceedings, young offenders reoffend less often, or less frequently, or in different ways, whether and when and why they desist from offending, and whether their subsequent life chances are enhanced or diminished. Unfortunately we know next to nothing about these things in relation to different juvenile justice approaches or cross-nationally. We know a bit about national differences in the use of imprisonment and have glimmers of insight into national differences in offending by young people.

A. Imprisonment

The differences in age limits and in the structure of national juvenile justice systems make cross-national comparisons of outcomes almost impossible. That is not to say that methods are unavailable for making some useful comparisons, but they would require use of original research designs, measures, and data collection, which, so far, researchers have not been sufficiently motivated to undertake and funding agencies have not been inspired to support—or most likely a combination of both.

The only available sources of cross-national data are ongoing efforts by international organizations such as the United Nations, the Council of Europe, and the International Prison Centre at King's College, London. Of these, the Council of Europe data are probably the most believable and the United Nations data the least. The overriding problem is that countries organize their data systems in different ways, partly reflecting distinctive structural features of their justice systems. As a result, data delivered to an international organization may present apples and oranges problems when numbers are compared. For example, concerning adult prison population statistics, countries may or may not include in their totals people held in juvenile institutions, illegal aliens held in administrative detention, and individuals held in mental health institutions. Sensible comparisons cannot be made unless the compositions of the prison population are made consistent. UN data contain few controls for consistency. The International Prison Centre does its best, but with a tiny staff. The Council of Europe's SPACE 1 data are year-by-year being improved and made more consistent, but careful reading of any report will reveal anomalies (Aebi and Delgrande 2009). If particular data found in any of these sources seem to well-informed people to be wildly implausible, they probably are.

The cross-national data on imprisonment of young people must therefore be taken with a grain of salt. They do, however, suggest some patterns that are consistent with other sources of knowledge about particular countries. Tables 34.3 and 34.4, showing comparative data on imprisonment of young offenders, are based respectively on the latest available data at the time of writing from the International

Prison Centre and from the Council of Europe's latest SPACE 1 report on prison populations in Europe (Aebi and Delgrande 2009).

Three patterns stand out. First, percentages of people under 18 and between 18 and 20 among prisoners are typically low in Scandinavian countries, and among the lowest of the included countries. This is consistent with case studies that emphasize a Scandinavian reluctance to use imprisonment for young people and a preference for short prison sentences (fifty-two people sentenced for two weeks each in Sweden take up as many prison beds as one person sentenced for two years in England or Scotland). It is also consistent with a widespread belief in Scandinavian countries that child welfare approaches should take precedence over repressive approaches when dealing with young people.

Second, jurisdictions in the British Isles (Ireland, Scotland, England and Wales) typically have high percentages of young people within their prison populations, and among the highest of the included countries. For Scotland, this is not surprising because all offenders over age 15 are dealt with in the adult system. For all three jurisdictions, as case studies (e.g., Bottoms and Dignan 2004) show, it is not surprising because all exhibit the moralistic and punitive approaches to crime that characterize most Anglo-Saxon countries and all have less well-developed social welfare and child welfare systems than exist in many other European countries.

Third, the data from some other European countries are broadly consistent with the structural characteristics of their youth justice systems and with case studies. Belgium, for example, has an age of responsibility of 18 except for murder and manslaughter, so large numbers of prisoners under 18 would be surprising. In the Netherlands, case studies describe a strong preference for diversionary and alternative dispositions for young offenders, which is consistent with a low percentage of people in prison younger than 18, but an almost Anglo-Saxon moralism in sentencing of adults, which is consistent with the relatively high percentage of 18- to 20 year-olds. France fits a similar pattern.

Fourth, to a considerable extent, the approaches of tables 34.3 and 34.4 (used in the original sources) understate differences between countries because their uses of prison generally differ. The Scandinavian countries, for example, have total imprisonment rates, including pretrial confinement ("remand" outside the United States) that fluctuate between 60 and 75 per 100,000 population. Scotland and England and Wales have imprisonment rates that in recent years are at least twice as high, around 150 to 160 per 100,000. Table 34.3 shows an English and Welsh prison population of 83,378, of whom 2.2 percent were 18 and younger. Multiplied, that means that nearly 1800 prisoners were under age 18. The total prison population shown for Norway is 3,369, of whom 0.5 percent were under 18. That's sixteen or seventeen prisoners under age 18. England's population is approximately fourteen times Norway's. If Norway's population numbers are projected upward to be comparable to England's, Norway would have 200 to 225 young prisoners, a sixth of the English number. Put differently, these rough calculations show that, expressed as rates, England imprisons five to seven times as many young people as Norway.

Table 34.3. Prisoners under Age 18 as Percentage of Total Prisoners, Selected
           Countries, Recent Years

COUNTRY	PRISON TOTAL	PERCENT JUVENILE
Australia	29,327	.1%
	(6/30/2008)	(6.30.2009)—under 18
Austria	8,308	2.5%
	(5/1/2009)	(5/1/2009)—under 18
Belgium	10,159	.3%
	(3/1/2009)	(6/17/2008)—under 18
Canada	38,348	5.7%
	(3/31/2008)	(3/31/2006)—under 18
Denmark	3,645	.5%
	(5/20/2009)	(5/20/2009)—under 18
England and Wales	83,378	2.2%
	(1/29/2010)	(12/18/2009)—under 18[3]
Finland	3,583	.1%
	(5/16/2009)[4]	(5/16/2009)
France	59,655	1.1%
	(7/1/2008)	(9/1/2007)—under 18
Germany	72,043	4.0%
	(3/31/2009)	(of pretrial prisoners only, 8/31/2009)—under 18
Greece	12,300	3.5%
	(November 2008)	(6/30/2007)—under 18
Hungary	15,373	3.0%
	(12/31/2009)	(of convicted prisoners—12/31/2009)—under 18
Iceland	175	1.1%
	(9/1/2009)	(9/1/2009)—under 18
Republic of Ireland	3,895	1.7%
	(6/5/2009)	(10/26/2007)—under 18
Italy	64,595	.5%
	(9/30/2009)	(12/31/2008)—under 18[5]
Netherlands	16,416	7.6%
	(8/31/2008)[6]	(8/31/2008)—under 18
New Zealand	8,509	1.1.%
	(9/21/2009)	(5/31/2009)—under 18
Northern Ireland	1,456	.7%
	(9/28/2009)	(6/16/2009)
Norway	3,369	.5%
	(5/1/2009)	(5/1/2009)—under 18
Poland	84,003	1.3%
	(1/4/2010)	(12/9/2004)—under 18
Portugal	11,238	.8%
	(2/1/2010)[7]	(4/1/2009)—under 18

COUNTRY	PRISON TOTAL	PERCENT JUVENILE
Scotland	7,630	12.2%
	(1/22/2010)	(12/18/2009)—under 18
Spain	76,455	0%
	(1/29/2010)[8]	(November 2009)—under 18[9]
Sweden	6,853	0%
	(10/1/2008)	(10/1/2008)—under 18
Switzerland	5,780	1.2%
	(9/3/2008)	(9/3/2008)—under 18
Turkey	116,340	2.3%
	(12/31/2009)	(12/31/2009)—minors
USA	2,304,115	.4%
	(12/31/2008)	(6/30/2007)

Source: King's College London. 2010. "World Prison Brief." http://www.kcl.ac.uk/depsta/law/research/icps/worldbrief/?search=europe&x=Europe.

Fifth, for many countries, the data shown in table 34.3 are not reliable. This is not surprising since the International Prison Centre numbers typically come from national prison administrations and, especially for federal countries, may provide noncomparable numbers. In Canada, for example, federal prisons hold people serving terms of two years or longer, provincial prisons hold pretrial detainees and those serving sentences less than two years, and provincial youth institutions hold some but not all young offenders. In the United States, prisoners are distributed among federal, state, and county institutions, and among state and county juvenile institutions. The U.S. data in table 34.3 are simply not believable. If only 0.4 percent of 2,304,115 prisoners are under age 18, they would total 9200 for the entire United States, a surprisingly small number, especially since all 16- and 17-year-old offenders in New York are dealt with in the adult justice system. In 2007, there were 89,000 young people in U.S. *juvenile* institutions (that is, ignoring juveniles in adult institutions, and people in adult institutions for offenses committed as juveniles) (OJJDP 2010). We left the United States in table 34.3 because that is what the data show and in order to emphasize that all these numbers need to be considered skeptically. They are more likely to be reasonably reliable when they come from countries with unitary rather than federal political systems, when the numbers in tables 34.3 and 34.4 for a particular country are broadly consistent, and when they are reconcilable with the narrative case study literature.

B. Effects on Offending Levels

For reasons spelled out in the introduction—that offending patterns and the nature of juvenile justice policies may both be consequences of fundamental social and political differences between countries—there is little that can usefully be said about the effects of different juvenile justice approaches on offending and reoffending patterns. Findings from the second International Self-Reported Delinquency study, however, offer the tantalizing finding that levels of self-reported delinquency are lowest in Scandinavian countries, second lowest in Western Europe, third lowest in Southern Europe, and highest in the English-speaking Anglo-Saxon countries (Junger-Tas 2009). Assuming that those findings capture something real, they do not answer the chicken-and-egg problem of what mechanism produces those results. Do strong social welfare policies deserve the credit, or child-welfare-oriented juvenile justice approaches, or both?

IV. COMPARATIVE ADVANTAGES AND DISADVANTAGES

In this section, we discuss a number of generalizations that can be offered about the operations and effects of different juvenile justice approaches: English-speaking countries are typically more punitive toward young offenders than are most other developed countries; there are stark national differences in how youth crime is conceptualized legally and morally; it may be difficult to establish and operate youth justice institutions successfully if they differ significantly in their values and aims from a country's adult justice system; and there are stark differences between countries in the juvenile justice philosophies of practitioners.

So, which approaches are better? That is hard to answer for two reasons. What is best depends on the criteria according to which that label is awarded, and those criteria necessarily implicate normative ideas that vary between people, and cultural values that vary between countries. People who believe that the aim of juvenile justice should be to punish bad behavior will differ in their evaluations and preferences from people who believe the aim should be to help as many young people as possible complete the passage from childhood through the troubled waters of adolescence to adulthood. People in countries characterized by highly individualistic and moralistic cultural values are more likely to view youthful crime as signs of individual moral failures, to favor formal juvenile court processes and low age limits of criminal responsibility, and to place greater emphasis on punishment. People in countries characterized by less individualistic and more welfarist cultural values are more likely to see young offenders as troubled, to attribute wrongdoing to social and economic influences, to favor greater reliance on child welfare and higher ages of criminal responsibility, and to place less emphasis on punishment. We believe, nonetheless, that some approaches are better—welfarist rather than criminal court approaches, high ages of responsibility rather than low ones, retention of young offenders in institutions tailored to youth rather than transfer to adult courts—and explain why.

A. Generalizations

A number of generalizations leap out from the preceding discussion. First, English-speaking countries using the juvenile court model have lower ages of criminal responsibility than most other developed countries, reflect more moralistic attitudes toward youthful wrongdoing, and rely much more heavily on imprisonment. This is true even of New Zealand, which operates a juvenile justice system that incorporates restorative elements that might be expected to produce less punitive results.

Second, countries vary enormously in their implicit attitudes toward juvenile offending and appropriate responses to it. Many European countries appear to regard crime by young people as a mixture of developmentally expected adolescent behavior, which most will put behind them as they mature, or as signs of psychological, social, and educational problems that must be addressed if troubled young peoples' chances of becoming successful adults are to be increased. The absence of juvenile courts in Sweden, Finland, and Denmark requires governments to develop social welfare approaches for dealing with troubled young people, and the distinctively less punitive sanctions for young people in adult courts demonstrate an emphasis on treating young people differently from adults. The German practice of sentencing most 18- to 20-year-old offenders as if they were juveniles shows a preference for treating crimes by young people differently from crimes by older people. So—dramatically—does Belgium's setting the age of criminal responsibility at age 18.

Conversely, English-speaking countries appear to have great difficulty breaking away from moralistic attitudes symbolized by their adoption of a criminal-court-for-young-people model for juvenile justice, and by the appeal to many people of such slogans as "adult time for adult crime." All the major countries—the United States, Canada, England and Wales, Scotland, Australia, New Zealand—rely more heavily on criminal sanctions than most European countries and lock up young people at higher rates. Even when, as in Scotland and New Zealand, juvenile justice approaches are adopted that appear to represent less moralistic values, the overall pattern of punitive outcomes does not much change.

Third, reform approaches that challenge prevailing cultural values have a steep hill to climb if they are to alter the experiences of young people significantly. Before the children's hearings system was adopted in Scotland in 1968, the Scottish juvenile system did not differ greatly from England's. More than forty years later, the children's hearing system continues to exist, but its jurisdiction stops at the 16th birthday, the age of criminal responsibility at age 8 is the lowest of any Western country, sizable numbers of children are transferred to adult courts, and imprisonment rates for young offenders sentenced in adult courts are high by international standards. Although New Zealand is often extolled as a country that has taken restorative justice (or equivalent) ideas seriously, at day's end, it locks up young offenders at high rates. The moral may be that it is difficult to establish and operate youth justice institutions that reflect significantly different values and goals than the adult system does.

Fourth, the attitudes and beliefs of practitioners vary widely between countries, and this has a strong effect on how systems operate. Good examples come from Canada (Doob and Sprott 2004) and the Netherlands (Junger-Tas 2004). In both, in response to public anxieties about apparently rising rates of serious juvenile crime, laws were enacted that were described by their sponsors as making transfers easier to accomplish. The sponsors presumably hoped or expected that transfers would become more common. In both they became less common. A similar story can be told about France where new legislation encouraged increased use of confinement sentences for young offenders; instead, use of confinement decreased (Roché 2007).

Practitioners in most countries—the United States and England and Wales are the most conspicuous exceptions—tend to be career civil servants and tend to be insulated from direct political pressures from politicians and indirect political pressures from public opinion and emotion. In the United States, where most judges and prosecutors are elected, and in England, where the Crown Prosecution Service is controlled by politically selected officials and the judges have a strong tradition of deference to politically elected officials, practitioners are subject to political influences they have difficulty resisting. When elected officials wish to make the justice system more severe, they meet less resistance than occurs in nonpolitical justice systems. This is a major reason American and English juvenile justice systems became much more punitive after the early 1990s (Feld 1999; Bottoms and Dignan 2004). As the Canadian, Dutch, and French examples just given demonstrate, practitioners are often likely to resist politically motivated changes that in their view make the juvenile justice system less just or less effective.

B. Reflections

In no country are major changes in legal or governmental institutions easy to accomplish. Partly, this is because they reflect traditional understandings of how things should be. Partly, it is because proposals for change are often premised on new ideas about values or aims, or new understandings or conceptualizations of problems. Not unexpectedly, people who subscribe to conventional ideas often resist new ones. Partly, it is because of inertia: most people are more comfortable doing what they know how to do than taking on something different. Partly, it is because of the inter-connectedness of government. Major changes in a juvenile justice system imply—or will require or precipitate—changes in the operations (and budgets) of police, child welfare agencies, educational authorities, treatment providers, and correctional agencies. It is all very complicated, and resistance can be expected whenever budgets or usual ways of doing business are threatened. We recognize that changes are not easy to achieve. Nonetheless, we discuss four subjects concerning which a look at juvenile justice systems across national boundaries suggests that some national approaches are markedly better than others.

1. *Conceptualization*

The threshold issue is: why should there be juvenile justice systems? The polar answers are "to punish wrongdoing by young people" and "to help young people successfully navigate adolescence." The second is the right answer, and it is one that American and English policy makers have offered less often than they should have in recent decades. Wrongdoing by young people often should be punished, or at least dealt with in a solemn and responsible way, but not as a primary aim of the system. Diverse rationales have been offered for why juvenile justice systems exist (Bishop 2009). One is that young people are cognitively immature and don't adequately understand why some behaviors are wrongful. Another is that young people are emotionally immature; even if in cognitive terms they understand why behaviors are wrongful, in emotional terms they lack a sufficiently nuanced, empathic, and mature understanding to justify punishing them as adults. A third is that young people are socially immature and that adolescence is a time of risk-taking and experimentation. That is why age-crime curves peak in the mid- and late-teens and then fall rapidly (e.g., a classic source: Farrington 1986). Most people grow out of adolescent excesses, and the primary function of the juvenile justice system should be to help them do it.

A number of the major structural differences in youth justice systems are related to different conceptions of the juvenile justice system's purpose. High ages of responsibility, for example, as in Scandinavia or Germany, eliminate the possibility of punitive responses and effectively require countries to develop strong child welfare systems aimed at helping children. Germany's system of sentencing young adults as if they were juveniles is expressly predicated on the idea that many young adults lack the emotional maturity that is imputed to older adults. A system like Scotland's children's hearings with express purposes of supporting child welfare, or the official German view that successful maturation is the youth criminal court's primary aim, reflect an overriding child welfare purpose.

2. *Age of Responsibility*

High ages of responsibility are preferable to low ones for three reasons. One is structural—societies must respond in some way to serious juvenile misconduct from concerns both to minimize it and resulting victimization, and to respond to the warning flags it embodies about children at risk. If the criminal justice system is categorically unavailable to respond to children's misconduct, other state agencies will have to be developed to do it. Conversely, if the justice system is available, other agencies are let off the hook. Perversely, in countries with low ages of responsibility, other agencies can shift the most difficult children to the justice system. This has happened often in recent years in the United States when, for example, schools develop "zero-tolerance" policies toward violence and possession of weapons in and around schools and refer increasing numbers of troubled and troublesome children to the police. School administration is made easier, but at the cost of excluding troubled children and reducing their life chances.

A second reason high ages of responsibility are preferable to younger ages is political. When public attitudes become harsher, or particular crimes or types of crimes provoke strong emotional responses, a low age of responsibility creates formidable pressures to treat young offenders as if they are adult criminals. Countries with ages of responsibility of 14 or 15 or higher cannot transfer controversial cases to adult courts. The English phenomenon illustrated by the infamous William Bulger case of 10- and 11-year-olds being tried for murder in an adult court is a legal impossibility. So are life sentences without possibility of parole for offenders in their early teens.

A third reason is normative. If young people are believed to be developmentally immature, as most adults most of the time recognize they are, and nearly always when their own children misbehave, it is simply unjust to ignore that reality and treat some children as if they were adults.

3. Age of Adult Court Jurisdiction

Likewise ages of minimum adult court jurisdiction. Most countries, and most American states, have adopted the 18th birthday as the minimum age of general adult court jurisdiction. Even despite this bright line, many people above it remain developmentally immature in some respect and deserve to have that taken into account. As a result, recognizing this, many U.S. jurisdictions in the 1960s had separate laws and facilities for young adults, often to age 24 or 25. The German practice of sentencing most young adults under 21 as if they were juveniles acknowledges this.

There must, however, be some bright line. The 18th birthday is not a prima facie implausible one, especially if youth is generally recognized as a mitigating factor in sentencing and a basis for diverting young "adults" to programs and resources that can contribute in positive ways to their maturation.

Jurisdictional ages lower than 18 are, however, difficult to justify. The younger the age limit, the larger the number of people processed in criminal court who are developmentally immature in one or another sense and should more appropriately be considered troubled young people rather than adult criminals. Assigning such people under 18 to adult courts in the first instance gets the priorities wrong and effectively makes conventional criminal processes the norm and constructive responses the exception, rather than the other way round, as it should be. Having age 16 as the bright line, as New York and North Carolina do, means that tens of thousands of young people are each year processed in those states as criminals— rather than as the troubled young people that most are. We earlier noted that high ages of responsibility create structural pressures on governments to devise social, educational, and welfare solutions for troubled children. A low age of adult court jurisdiction does the opposite: it removes structural pressures to create constructive approaches for dealing with troubled young people. It is reasonable to hypothesize that New York and North Carolina have less well-developed and less well-funded programs for addressing their special needs than do states that set the adult court's jurisdiction at age 18. Similarly, it is reasonable to hypothesize that Scotland's children's hearings would do more good than it now does were the age of adult court jurisdiction raised from 16 to 18. The Scandinavian courts' age 15 threshold, however, are at least partly a different story because child welfare agencies also play roles to age 18, and there are well-established traditions of special (i.e., much less punitive) policies for sentencing younger offenders.

There has long been good reason to believe that processing young people through juvenile courts, much less adult criminal courts, does more harm than good. Most young offenders will, as a natural part of normal patterns of adolescent development, desist from offending in their middle or late teenage years. The juvenile and criminal justice systems can create impediments to that happening. These include the labeling of children as delinquents or criminals that court procedures cause, and the resulting stigmatization that may affect how other people deal with young people. They also include disruption of schooling, reinforcement of delinquent self-identity, and the obstacles to employment that often result from convictions and sometimes even from arrests. That is why the great German reformer Franz von Liszt in his Marburg Program observed: "If a juvenile commits a criminal offense and we let him get away with it, then the risk of relapse is lower than the risk we face after having him punished" (von Liszt 1905, p. 346). That is a timeless idea that Edwin Schur reiterated in the title and the contents of his 1973 book, *Radical Non-Intervention: Rethinking the Delinquency Problem*. For all but the most troubled teenagers, less is generally more. Low ages of adult court jurisdiction in general means more damage to young people and less healthy development.

4. *Waiver and Blended Jurisdiction*

Outside the United States and England and Wales, transfers to adult court are relatively uncommon, but blended jurisdiction (which in various combinations allows sentencing juveniles as if they were adults and adults as if they were juveniles) in only one direction is common. Germany's policy and practice of sentencing most young adults as if they were juveniles is the best example. The special sentencing polices for both juvenile (15–17) and young adult (18–20) offenders in Scandinavia is effectively another.

It is true both that many countries could improve the humanity and, probably, the crime-preventive effectiveness of their juvenile justice system by importing practices and policies from elsewhere, and that transfer of policies across national boundaries is difficult to do. However, successful transfers have been made in other times. Many European countries, for example, have been influenced by American developments. Early twentieth century developments in Denmark (Kyvsgaard 2004) and Germany (Albrecht 2004) were influenced by the child-saving and juvenile court movements in the United States. And others were influenced by the U.S. movement in the 1960s, symbolized by the U.S. Supreme Court decison *In re Gault*, to establish stronger procedural protections in juvenile courts. It is clear that American practices and policies for dealing with juvenile misconduct could be improved greatly if efforts were made to emulate many practices in other lands.

Policy makers can learn from looking across national boundaries to see what is going on elsewhere. It is fair to conclude that officials in Anglo-Saxon countries have much more to learn than to teach. "Youth" and "juvenile" justice systems have those names for reasons; countries in which officials forget what those reasons are do so to their detriment and to the detriment of their young people.

The English-speaking countries have much to learn from continental Europe. There is no evidence-based reason to believe that treating young offenders as adults (as the Scots and New Zealanders also do once the low age limits for their programs for younger offenders are reached) is an effective way to reduce crime rates or to reduce reoffending by young offenders. There are evidence-based reasons to believe that treating young offenders as if they were adults does harm to many. If American and English policy makers in particular wished to do less harm, they would raise the age of criminal responsibility to 14 or 15, set the minimum age of adult court jurisdiction at 18, forbid transfer of young offenders to adult courts, and create special policies for dealing with young adults.

Table 34.4. Juvenile (under age 18) and Young Adult (18 to 20 years old) Prisoners as Percentage of Total, Selected Countries, September 1, 2007

Country	Percentage under age 18	Percentage ages 18–20
Austria	3.4 percent	12.7 percent
Belgium	0.2	4.9
Denmark	0.7	9.7
England and Wales	2.4	8.3
Finland	0.3	2.3
France	1.0	7.5
Germany	1.0	5.2
Ireland	3.2	11.2
Italy	Not available	3.2
Netherlands	0.1	7.0
Norway	0.1	3.0
Portugal	0.2	3.3
Scotland	6.2	18.3
Spain	Not available	2.3
Sweden	0.0	2.6
Switzerland	0.9	0.0

Source: Aebi and Delgrande 2009, table 2.1.

NOTES

1. Information on ages of responsibility is available as of September 1 each year for the forty-seven Council of Europe member states in the Council's annual SPACE 1 statistical report on prison populations (see Aebi and Delgrande (2009) for information as of September 1, 2007).

2. The case for the Scandinavian countries is that policies and a jurisprudence exist concerning special, less severe treatment of 15- to 17-year-old juveniles and 18- to 20-year-old young adult offenders, thereby providing a rational, gradual shift from no criminal responsibility before age 15 to full responsibility at 21.

3. In addition to these 1,873 juveniles, an additional 248 were being held in Secure Training Centres and 157 in Local Authority Secure Children's Homes.

4. This does not include eighty-six remand prisoners in police establishments.

5. 271 of those in institutions for minors.

6. This includes 1,679 illegal aliens,1,750 in juvenile institutions, and 1,893 in TBS clinics.

7. This includes 155 in psychiatric institutions.

8. This includes 10,574 in Catalonia.

9. 2.2% under age 21.

REFERENCES

Aebi, Marcelo F., and Natalia Delgrande. 2009. *Council of Europe Annual Penal Statistics, SPACE 1, Survey 2007.* Strasburg: Council of Europe.

Albrecht, Hans-Jörg. 2004. "Youth Justice in Germany." In *Youth Crime and Youth Justice,* edited by Michael Tonry and Anthony Doob. Vol. 31 of *Crime and Justice: A Review of Research,* edited by Michael Tonry. Chicago: University of Chicago Press.

Bishop, Donna M. 2009. "Juvenile Transfer in the United States." In *Reforming Juvenile Justice,* edited by Josine Junger-Tas and Frieder Dünkel. Dordrecht, the Netherlands: Springer.

Bottoms, Anthony, and James Dignan. 2004. "Youth Justice in Great Britain." In *Youth Crime and Youth Justice,* edited by Michael Tonry and Anthony Doob. Vol. 31 of *Crime and Justice: A Review of Research,* edited by Michael Tonry. Chicago: University of Chicago Press.

Cavadino, Michael, and James Dignan. 2006. *Penal Systems: A Comparative Approach.* London: Sage.

Doob, Anthony R., and Jane Sprott. 2004. "Youth Justice in Canada." In *Youth Crime and Youth Justice,* edited by Michael Tonry and Anthony Doob. Vol. 31 of *Crime and Justice: A Review of Research,* edited by Michael Tonry. Chicago: University of Chicago Press.

Dünkel, Frieder. 2006. "Juvenile Justice in Germany: Between Welfare and Justice." In *International Handbook of Juvenile Justice,* edited by Josine Junger-Tas and Scott Decker. Dordrecht, the Netherlands: Springer.

Farrington, David P. 1986. "Age and Crime." In *Crime and Justice: An Annual Review of Research,* edited by Michael Tonry and Norval Morris. Vol. 7 of *Crime and Justice: A Review of Research,* edited by Michael Tonry. Chicago: University of Chicago Press.

Feld, Barry. 1999. *Bad Kids: Race and the Transformation of the Juvenile Court.* New York: Oxford University Press.

Friday, Paul, and Xin Ren, eds. 2006. *Delinquency and Juvenile Justice Systems in the Non-Western World.* Monsey, NY: Criminal Justice Press.

Gil-Robles, Alvaro. 2004. "Report by Mr. Alvaro Gil-Robles, Commissioner for Human Rights, on his Visit to the United Kingdom 4th–12th November 2004 for the Attention of the Committee of Ministers and the Parliamentary Assembly." Council of Europe, Strasbourg.

Graham, John, and Colleen Moore. 2006. "Beyond Welfare Versus Justice: Juvenile Justice in England and Wales." In *International Handbook of Juvenile Justice*, edited by J. Junger-Tas and S. H. Decker. Dordrecht, the Netherlands: Springer.

Janson, Carl-Gunnar. 2004. "Youth Justice in Sweden." In *Youth Crime and Youth Justice*, edited by Michael Tonry and Anthony Doob. Vol. 31 of *Crime and Justice: A Review of Research*, edited by Michael Tonry. Chicago: University of Chicago Press.

Jensen, Eric L., and Jørgen Jepsen. 2006. *Juvenile Law Violators, Human Rights, and the Development of New Juvenile Justice Systems.* Oxford: Hart.

Junger-Tas, Josine. 2004 "Youth Justice in the Netherlands." In *Youth Crime and Youth Justice*, edited by Michael Tonry and Anthony Doob. Vol. 31 of *Crime and Justice: A Review of Research*, edited by Michael Tonry. Chicago: University of Chicago Press.

———. 2009. "Challenges to Criminology in the 21st Century." *Criminology in Europe* 8(3): 3, 13–16.

Junger-Tas, Josine, and Scott Decker, eds. 2006. *International Handbook of Juvenile Justice.* Dordrecht, the Netherlands: Springer.

Junger-Tas, Josine, and Frieder Dünkel. 2009. "Reforming Juvenile Justice: European Perspectives." In *Reforming Juvenile Justice*, edited by Josine Junger-Tas and Frieder Dünkel. Dordrecht, the Netherlands: Springer.

King's College London. 2010. "World Prison Brief." http://www.kcl.ac.uk/depsta/law/research/icps/worldbrief/?search=europe&x=Europe.

Klein, Malcolm. 1984. *Western Systems of Juvenile Justice.* Beverly Hills, CA: Sage.

Kyvsgaard, Britta. 2004. "Youth Justice in Denmark." In *Youth Crime and Youth Justice*, edited by Michael Tonry and Anthony Doob. Vol. 31 of *Crime and Justice: A Review of Research*, edited by Michael Tonry. Chicago: University of Chicago Press.

Lappi-Seppälä, Tapio. 2006. "Finland: A Model of Tolerance." In *Comparative Youth Justice*, edited by John Muncie and Barry Goldson. London: Sage.

———. 2007. "Penal Policy in Scandinavia." In *Crime, Punishment, and Politics in Comparative Perspective*, edited by Michael Tonry. Vol. 36 of *Crime and Justice: A Review of Research*, edited by Michael Tonry. Chicago: University of Chicago Press.

———. 2011. "Youth Justice in Scandinavia." In *Crime and Justice in Scandinavia*, edited by Michael Tonry and Tapio Lappi-Seppälä. Volume 40 of *Crime and Justice: A Review of Research*, edited by Michael Tonry. Chicago: University of Chicago Press.

Mehlbye, Jill, and Lode Walgrave, eds. 1998. *Confronting Youth in Europe: Juvenile Crime and Juvenile Justice.* Copenhagen: AKF Forlaget.

Meijers, Ido, and Thomas Grisso. 2009. "Criminal Responsibility of Adolescents: Youth as Junior Citizenship." In *Reforming Juvenile Justice*, edited by Josine Junger-Tas and Frieder Dünkel. Dordrecht, the Netherlands: Springer.

Morris, Allison. 2004. "Youth Justice in New Zealand." In *Youth Crime and Youth Justice*, edited by Michael Tonry and Anthony Doob. Vol. 31 of *Crime and Justice: A Review of Research*, edited by Michael Tonry. Chicago: University of Chicago Press.

Muncie, John, and Barry Goldson, eds. 2006. *Comparative Youth Justice.* London: Sage.

National Center for Juvenile Justice. 2008. "State Juvenile Justice Profiles." www.ncjj.org/stateprofiles.

Nelken, David. 2006. "Italy: A Lessen in Tolerance?" In *Comparative Juvenile Justice*, edited by John Muncie and Barry Goldson. London: Sage.

OJJDP (Office of Juvenile Justice and Delinquency Prevention). 2010. *Juveniles in Residential Placement, 1997–2008*. Washington, DC: U.S. Department of Justice, Office of Juvenile Justice and Delinquency Prevention.

Pratt, John. 2006. "The Dark Side of Paradise: Explaining New Zealand's History of High Imprisonment." *British Journal of Criminology* 46(4): 541–60.

———. 2007. *Penal Populism*. London: Routledge.

Roché, Sebastian. 2007. "Criminal Justice Policy in France: Illusions of Severity." In *Crime, Punishment, and Politics in Comparative Perspective*, edited by Michael Tonry. Vol. 36 of *Crime and Justice: A Review of Research*, edited by Michael Tonry. Chicago: University of Chicago Press.

Sarnecki, Jerzy, and Felipe Estrada. 2006. "Keeping the Balance between Humanism and Penal Punitivism: Recent Trends in Juvenile Delinquency and Juvenile Justice in Sweden." In *International Handbook of Juvenile Justice*, edited by J. Junger-Tas and S. H. Decker. The Netherlands: Springer.

Schur, Edwin M. 1973. *Radical Non-Intervention: Rethinking the Delinquency Problem*. Englewood Cliffs, NJ: Prentice-Hall.

Tonry, Michael, and Anthony E. Doob, eds. 2004. *Youth Crime and Youth Justice: Comparative and Cross-National Perspectives*. Chicago: University of Chicago Press.

Weijers, Ido, and Thomas Grisso. 2009. "Criminal Responsibility of Adolescents: Youth as Junior Citizenship." In *Reforming Juvenile Justice*, edited by Josine Junger-Tas and Frieder Dunkel. Dordrecht, the Netherlands: Springer.

Weijers, Ido, An Nuytiens, and Jenneke Christiaens. 2009. "Transfer of Minors to the Criminal Court in Europe: Belgium and the Netherlands." In *Reforming Juvenile Justice*, edited by Josine Junger-Tas and Frieder Dünkel. Dordrecht, the Netherlands: Springer.

Winterdyk, John, ed. 1997. *Juvenile Justice Systems: International Perspectives*, 2d ed. Toronto: Canadian Scholars Press.

———. 2002. *Juvenile Justice Systems: International Perspectives*, 2d ed. Toronto: Canadian Scholars Press.

CHAPTER 35

TRENDS IN JUVENILE JUSTICE POLICY AND PRACTICE

DONNA M. BISHOP AND BARRY C. FELD

INTRODUCTION

PROGRESSIVE reformers embraced a view of young people as immature, dependent, and exceptionally vulnerable to external influence. They created a separate justice system for children in an effort to shield them from the stigmatizing punishments of criminal courts and the corrupting influence of adult jails and prisons, and to intervene in a positive way where parents and others had failed, in order to promote youth development. They replaced the criminal-punitive model of justice with a civil-therapeutic one: the juvenile court would identify the sources of youths' problem behaviors and, acting *in loco parentis*, provide guidance, care, and supervision to help them mature into responsible and law-abiding adults (Zimring 2000).

Over the last century, at different times and for multiple reasons, the juvenile justice system has strayed far afield of its foundational ideals. Attentiveness to children's needs has given way to concentration on the offense. The social welfare model has been overshadowed by one that emphasizes punishment and accountability. Images of juvenile offenders as adult-like and responsible rival traditional conceptions of delinquents as immature kids who deserve "room to reform" (Zimring 1998b). The juvenile court's tradition of inclusiveness (of delinquent, status offending, and even pre-delinquent youths) has yielded to "front end" diversion policies and overreaching, exclusionary "back end" transfer policies (Bernard 1992; Feld

2003). Moreover, juvenile justice practices "in action" often have differed starkly from juvenile law and policy "on the books." Indeed, the disjuncture between rhetoric and reality has prompted some of the most profound systemic reforms.

In this chapter, we examine trends in juvenile justice policy and practice with a special emphasis on changes occurring over the last thirty years that have both challenged and reasserted the juvenile court's founding principles. We organize the discussion in four parts. In the first part, we provide a brief overview of the early juvenile court—its philosophical underpinnings and historic mission. The second part examines the due process revolution of the 1960s and 1970s and assesses its intended and unintended consequences. The third section focuses on punitive shifts in the 1980s and 1990s, their structural and political origins, and their impact on the juvenile justice landscape. Finally, in the last section, we examine a number of policies and programs that have emerged in the past decade in response both to juvenile courts' historical deficiencies and the punitive overreaction of the "get tough" era. We conclude with cautious optimism that the penal pendulum has begun to swing in a direction that may provide a much-needed correction to the punitive excesses that have characterized the previous two decades.

I. 1899–1960s: *Parens Patriae* Set Loose

Many scholars have analyzed the social history of the Progressive Era and the founding of a separate juvenile court (e.g., Feld 1999; Tanenhaus 2004; Platt 2009; Tanenhaus, Chapter 19 this volume), so we offer only a brief summary here. Macro-structural changes in the nineteenth century—most notably, industrialization, immigration, and urbanization—transformed the nature of everyday American life. Factories sprang up in northeastern and midwestern cities, causing the demand for labor to soar. Internal migrants from rural areas and Western and Eastern European immigrants flocked to the nation's burgeoning cities, settling in the poorest and most densely populated areas around the new manufacturing centers. The new factories employed men, women, and children for twelve or more hours per day, and separated home from work. In impoverished urban neighborhoods, children teemed out of crowded ghetto tenements into city streets to play, to scavenge, and to work—as newsboys, shoe shiners, flower sellers, beggars, and thieves. The presence of destitute children in the streets, unsupervised and exposed to drunkards, gamblers, prostitutes, and other perceived evils of urban life, unsettled upper- and middle-class Child Savers. They exercised strict social control over their own offspring, and made urgent appeals to save these endangered (and possibly dangerous) children whose lower-class parents they alternately described as beleaguered, ignorant, neglectful, and abusive (Gish 2004).

Progressive reformers drew from the fledgling discipline of developmental psychology and the child study movement to promote a nascent image of children as fragile, dependent, and vulnerable innocents who require special protection and supervision. They successfully pressed for the enactment of a number of child-centered reforms: juvenile courts, child labor laws, compulsory school attendance laws, mothers' pensions, and social welfare laws, each of which reflected and enhanced the changing imagery of childhood (Feld 1999).

The emergence of positive criminology coincided with the founding of the juvenile court and was influential in its design. Criminological positivism challenged the classical view of crime as a rational, calculated act of free will that could be deterred by legal sanction threats, replacing it with a conceptual framework that viewed offending as caused by external factors (e.g., a corrupting environment, exposure to older offenders, or lack of parental supervision) whose influence might be removed or mitigated by appropriate treatment and rehabilitation. These ideas—that children are immature and vulnerable, that offending is determined by external influences, and that positive intervention is the best cure—formed the philosophical foundations for the juvenile court.

From its inception in 1899 and for the next seventy years, the juvenile court remained firmly grounded in the doctrine of *parens patriae*—the State as parent and arbiter of child rearing. The court was conceived as a benign, nonpunitive, and therapeutic institution. The juvenile courts' founders closed proceedings to public scrutiny, substituted euphemisms for the stigma-producing terminology (e.g., charge, conviction) used in criminal courts, excluded lawyers and juries, and afforded judges maximum flexibility to administer their courts and choose how to treat and supervise children (Ryerson 1978; Tanenhaus 2004).

The juvenile court's rehabilitative ideal envisioned a specialized judge trained in social work and child development whose empathy and insight would enable him to make individualized and therapeutic dispositions in the "best interests" of the child. Proof of the offense—which today is a logical and necessary predicate to an inquiry into the child's needs and circumstances—was of secondary importance: Reformers viewed a child's offense primarily as a symptom of unmet needs. Reformers exhibited little concern about protecting children from erroneous adjudications of delinquency because they believed the court would deliver benign treatment from which children would profit in any event. Progressives' belief in the benign nature of juvenile court intervention also gave no cause to circumscribe narrowly the scope of the state's authority; they defined juvenile court jurisdiction expansively to include youths accused of crimes, status offenders, dependent and neglected children, and those merely "at risk" for delinquency.

Juvenile courts imposed indeterminate sentences (dispositions), primarily probation and residential placement, which they characterized as "individualized treatment." Judge Julian Mack, who in 1904 became the presiding judge of the Cook County juvenile court, eloquently explained the distinctiveness of his approach:

> [The criminal court] put but one question, "Has he committed this crime?"
> It did not inquire, "What is the best thing to do for this lad?" It did not even
> punish him in a manner that would tend to improve him; the punishment
> was visited in proportion to the degree of wrongdoing evidenced by the single
> act.... Why is it not just and proper to treat these juvenile offenders, as we deal

with the neglected children, as a wise and merciful father handles his own child whose errors are not discovered by the authorities? Why is it not the duty of the state, instead of asking merely whether a boy or a girl has committed a specific offense, to find out what he is, physically, mentally, morally, and then if it learns that he is treading the path that leads to criminality, to take him in charge, not so much to punish as to reform, not to degrade but to uplift, not to crush but to develop, not to make him a criminal but a worthy citizen (Mack 1909, p. 107).

Mack believed that developing a warm, avuncular relationship with a child and encouraging him to talk freely were essential both to understanding the child's problems and needs and to planning an appropriate course of treatment. In the service of those ends, juvenile court proceedings were closed and informal—held in chambers or around a table. Procedural safeguards, such as representation by defense counsel, were lacking, as they would obstruct open communication between judge and child.

At its inception, the juvenile court was a fragile innovation whose continued existence depended on garnering public and political support (Tanenhaus 2004). The behavior of some young offenders—especially violent and chronic offenders— threatened to erode that support (Tanenhaus 2004). While commission of a serious violent act neither transformed a young person into a fully responsible adult nor rendered him a poor candidate for juvenile court intervention, the public tended to view violent offenders not as immature children, but as sophisticated and adult-like, and to press for lengthy sentences that were beyond the juvenile court's capacity to provide.

Persistent recidivists posed an equally great challenge for the court. Their failure to respond to the court's interventions suggested that young people might be more intractable than juvenile court advocates assumed. One solution, used from the start, was to transfer serious and persistent problem cases to the criminal court. Although waiver of jurisdiction conflicted with the juvenile court's founding principles, it was politically expedient. By relinquishing authority over a few chronic and serious offenders, judges could placate public fear and political clamor and preserve the juvenile court's rehabilitative role for the vast majority of young offenders.

Although the boundaries of juvenile court jurisdiction were permeable from the start, by the mid-1920s, the court had shored up its perimeter and strengthened its institutional legitimacy in a number of ways. In some jurisdictions, juvenile court proceedings were opened to the public so that the community might see the good that the court did on behalf of young people. Judges and probation officers used these proceedings to educate the public and also to underscore the plight of poor and immigrant children (Tanenhaus 2004). Juvenile court advocates had great faith that education would energize the public to improve the conditions in which impoverished children lived (Breckenridge and Abbott 1912).

The Progressives' pursuit of the Rehabilitative Ideal situated the juvenile court on several cultural, legal, and criminological fault lines. They created binary distinctions between the juvenile and criminal justice systems: either child or adult; either immature or fully responsible; either treatment or punishment; either devoid of rules and informal, or formal and adversarial. Beginning in the 1960s, a rise in serious youth crime and startling revelations about abuses of power in the adjudicatory process and the reality of "rehabilitation" in the juvenile correctional system presaged a shift from the former to the latter of each binary pair.

II. 1960s–1980s: Crisis and Change

Juvenile courts' idealistic vision of individualized assessment and benign and effective treatments often fell far short of realization, but for nearly seventy years, systemic institutional failures remained shielded from public view. Judges' broad authority over delinquent and pre-delinquent youths and the virtual absence of procedural safeguards—viewed as essential to the child-saving mission—fostered judicial arbitrariness, discriminatory decisions, and abuses of power. Almost all youths appeared in juvenile court without lawyers. Probation caseloads were commonly extraordinarily high, and probation officers were frequently political appointees who lacked appropriate qualifications or training for their positions (Ryerson 1978). Further, conditions in juvenile correctional institutions were often horrific (see, e.g., Miller 1991; President's Commission on Law Enforcement and the Administration of Justice 1967). Detention centers and training schools were large, chronically overcrowded, and unsanitary. Personnel were poorly trained and underpaid. Staff-inmate and inmate-inmate brutality was rampant (Feld 1977). In many institutions, silence was the norm, and recalcitrant inmates spent lengthy periods in dark and dank isolation rooms (e.g., Miller 1991). In the 1960s, a series of reports—the most influential of which was the *Task Force Report on Juvenile Delinquency and Youth Crime* prepared by the President's Commission on Law Enforcement and the Administration of Justice (1967)—exposed the deficiencies of juvenile court and correctional systems and the plight of juvenile offenders.

Beginning with *In re Gault* (1967), the Supreme Court set out to correct some of these deficiencies and, in the process, began to transform the juvenile court into a very different institution than contemplated by the Progressives. *Gault* highlighted the disjunction between the rhetoric of juvenile "rehabilitation"—which had long been the justification for differences between the procedural safeguards afforded criminal defendants and those available to delinquents—and the reality of juvenile corrections in practice. The Court in *Gault* engrafted some formal procedures at trial onto the juvenile court's individualized treatment approach with the admonition that "[u]nder our Constitution, the condition of being a boy does not justify a kangaroo court" (at 27–28)." The Court concluded that, despite juvenile courts' therapeutic rhetoric, the punitive reality of institutional confinement required procedural safeguards that would guarantee "fundamental fairness"—i.e., advance notice of charges, a fair hearing, assistance of counsel, an opportunity to confront and cross-examine witnesses, and the protection against compelled self-incrimination. The Court asserted that adversarial procedural safeguards were essential both to determine the factual accuracy of the allegations and to prevent governmental oppression, but averred that their introduction would not impair the juvenile court's ability to pursue its rehabilitative mission.

Several subsequent Supreme Court decisions further "criminalized" juvenile court proceedings. *In re Winship* (397 U.S. 358 [1970]) required states to prove juveniles' guilt by the criminal law's "beyond a reasonable doubt" standard. *Breed v. Jones* (421 U.S. 519 [1971]) applied the constitutional ban on double jeopardy to juvenile proceedings based on their functional equivalence to criminal trials. However, in *McKeiver v. Pennsylvania* (403 U.S. 528 [1971]), the Court declined to grant juvenile defendants the right to a jury trial. The Court in *McKeiver* concluded that jury trials would adversely affect the informality and flexibility of juvenile proceedings and might lead to the demise of a separate juvenile justice system. Despite the juvenile court's failings, the Court insisted that its therapeutic mission was worth pursuing.

Notwithstanding the Court's reaffirmation of the rehabilitative ideal, in the aftermath of these due process reforms, judicial, legislative, and administrative changes fostered both procedural and substantive convergence of juvenile and criminal courts. *Gault* and *Winship* unintentionally, but inevitably, transformed the juvenile court from its original conception as a social welfare agency into a scaled-down version of the criminal court (Feld 1988). By emphasizing criminal procedural regularity in the adjudicatory process, the Supreme Court shifted the focus of the juvenile court's inquiry from assessment of a youth's "real needs" to proof of commission of a crime. By formalizing the connection between law violations and coercive intervention, the Court made explicit a relationship previously implicit, unacknowledged, and deliberately obscured. Ironically, *Gault*'s and *Winship*'s insistence on greater procedural safeguards seems to have legitimated more punitive dispositions for young offenders. The newfound right to counsel made it imperative that prosecutors participate in juvenile proceedings for the first time and transformed the court's organizational structure. Prosecutors established juvenile divisions, staffed them with traditionally trained attorneys, and infused the juvenile court with a criminal law orientation and expectations of proportionality.

Critics from both the left and right identified two serious problems with the rehabilitative model: it was grossly unfair and it was ineffectual. In its influential publication, *Struggle for Justice* (1971), the American Friends Service Committee exhorted courts to rein in judicial discretion and called for a return to "just deserts" as a remedy for the irregularities (now defined as "injustices") of indeterminate sentencing. Almost simultaneously, negative appraisals of the effectiveness of treatment programs (e.g., Lipton, Martinson, and Wilks 1975; Wright and Dixon 1977; Sechrest, White, and Brown 1979)—highlighted by Martinson's (1974) celebrated conclusion that "nothing works"—raised substantial doubts about clinicians' abilities to coerce behavioral change. Although other researchers subsequently challenged these negative assessments—attributing the lack of positive results to methodological flaws in the research, weak evaluation designs, and poor program implementation, rather than the absence of viable treatment methods (e.g., Palmer 1991; Lipsey 1992; Fagan and Forst 1996)—those responses drew little attention. In the wake of these criticisms, juvenile penal policy moved steadily toward determinacy and proportionality.

III. 1980s–1990s: The "Get Tough" Era

Macro-structural, economic, and racial demographic changes, and an escalation in youth gun violence, provided the backdrop for the adoption of a rash of hard-line juvenile justice policies beginning in the 1980s (Feld 1999). Between 1916 and 1970, an estimated seven million blacks moved from the rural South to the urban North, pushed by Jim Crow and pulled by the promise of greater employment opportunities. This Great Migration produced large concentrations of African Americans in inner-city ghettoes (Massey and Denton 1993). Beginning in the 1970s, the transition from an industrial and manufacturing to an information and service economy reduced job prospects for poor and unskilled urban dwellers. Meanwhile, private and governmental highway, housing, and mortgage policies encouraged suburban expansion and contributed to the growth of middle-class, predominantly white suburbs around increasingly poor and minority urban cores (Feld 1999; Massey and Denton 1993; Garland 2001). By the 1980s, an impoverished black underclass was trapped in the inner cities (Wilson 1987). The introduction of crack cocaine combined with the proliferation of guns set off turf wars in inner-city neighborhoods over control of lucrative new drug markets, and rates of black youth homicide escalated sharply (Blumstein 1996; Feld 1999; Zimring 1998a).

The upsurge in juvenile gun violence provided the political impetus to transform juvenile justice policies. The media responded to the urban, predominantly black youth gun violence with heavy and sensationalized coverage (Feld 2003). Media portrayals of juvenile offenders shifted from the traditionally rather benign images of puerile and corrigible delinquents to menacing portraits of savvy, cruel, and morally impoverished "superpredators" who were forecast to number 270,000 by the year 2010 (Dilulio 1995). Political scientist John Dilulio (1995, p. 23) famously claimed that "Americans are sitting atop a demographic crime bomb," and others warned of a coming "blood-bath" of youth violence (Fox 1996).

A moral panic ensued as politicians fueled public fears for electoral advantage (Chiricos 2004; Feld 1999, 2003). Conservative politicians and the mass media pushed crime to the top of the political agenda, focusing on violent gun crime to promote "get tough" policies (McCollum 1996[1]). Wary of being labeled "soft on crime," politicians vied to outdo their opponents in the race to take a hard line on juvenile offending. They sharply challenged the underlying assumptions about youths that had animated the earlier juvenile court movement. Depictions of young offenders as responsible, autonomous, and adult-like (Garland 2001) gave traction to a new sound bite—"adult crime, adult time." For offenders who did not even approach "worst cases," legislators touted the utility of punishment as a deterrent and as a means to protect public safety (Bishop, Frazier, and Lanza-Kaduce 1999; Lanza-Kaduce, Frazier, and Bishop 1999; Bishop 2006).

Legislatures in nearly every state responded by amending their juvenile code purpose clauses to endorse "punishment," "holding youth accountable," and "protecting the public safety" (Bishop 2006). Although rehabilitation remained a goal, it was eclipsed by these other objectives. Legislatures in nearly half the states adopted desert-based sentencing. Some states adopted sentencing guidelines to impose presumptive, determinate, and proportional sentences based on age, offense seriousness, and prior record (Feld 1998). Others enacted mandatory minimum sentencing provisions that prescribed either a minimum period of confinement or a minimum level of secure placement commensurate with the seriousness of the offense. Each of these sentencing methodologies applied principles of proportionality to rationalize sentencing decisions, increase the penal bite of juvenile sanctions, and demonstrate symbolically legislators' toughness.

Other changes chipped away at special protections that youths had traditionally enjoyed. Juvenile court proceedings had historically been closed to the public, juvenile records were confidential and subject to later expungement, and at least nonserious juvenile offenders were exempt from a "booking process" that included mug shots and fingerprints. During the "get tough" era, the vast majority of states opened juvenile proceedings to the public, allowed juveniles to be photographed and fingerprinted (all, with some age and offense restrictions), and required them to give DNA samples (Szymanski 2007, 2008, 2009a). Especially controversial were decisions to make juvenile sex offenders subject to "Megan's Law"—requiring them to register with police and, for more serious offenders, providing for community notification of their identities, whereabouts, and offenses (Zimring 2004). By the turn of the century, most states permitted or required juveniles convicted of sex crimes to register as sex offenders. In about half of the states, sex offenders adjudicated in juvenile court faced a possible lifetime of registration (Szymanski 2009b, 2009c, 2009d).

States also took steps to facilitate the transfer of greater numbers of juvenile defendants to criminal court for prosecution and punishment as adults (see Feld and Bishop, Chapter 32 this volume). Historically, juvenile court judges could waive a youth to criminal court only if, following an investigation and an adversarial hearing, they determined that the child was too dangerous to remain in the juvenile system or was not amenable to treatment. Believing that juvenile court judges were loath to waive even serious offenders, legislators created alternative, expedited transfer methods that circumvented the juvenile court or that sharply constrained juvenile court judges' discretion to retain youths in the juvenile system (Bishop and Frazier 2000).

In many states, law makers shifted authority to choose the forum in which a youth would be tried from the juvenile judge to the prosecutor, who could "direct file" a case in criminal court without either a hearing or judicial review. In addition, most states statutorily excluded certain (mostly violent) crimes or offense/

prior record combinations from juvenile court jurisdiction—often without regard to the offender's age. Other statutes tied juvenile court judges' hands by making waiver mandatory or presumptive. The adoption of "once an adult, always an adult" provisions amplified the effects of these other changes. Finally, some states lowered the maximum age of juvenile court jurisdiction, creating criminals out of all delinquents above a new (lower) age threshold. By the turn of the century, analysts estimate that upwards of two hundred thousand offenders under age 18 were being tried annually in American criminal courts. Many were neither particularly serious nor particularly chronic offenders, and some had not yet reached their teens (Bishop 2000).

In the criminal courts, judges did not treat youthfulness as a mitigating factor in sentencing transferred youths. Indeed, they imposed harsher sentences than those imposed on comparable adult defendants (see Feld and Bishop, Chapter 32 this volume). Even extreme punishments were not deemed inconsistent with youth. Until the Supreme Court's decision in *Roper v. Simmons* (543 U.S. 551 [2005]) to ban capital punishment for offenders under age 18, judges in several states sentenced teens to death. Moreover, by the turn of the century, nearly ten thousand inmates were serving life sentences for crimes committed before they were 18; over two thousand of these had been sentenced to life without possibility of parole (LWOP) in contravention of the United Nations Convention on the Rights of the Child (1989, Article 37a) (Human Rights Watch/Amnesty International 2005). In the rest of the world, only three other countries had imposed LWOP sentences on a total of twelve juvenile offenders (Human Rights Watch/Amnesty International 2005, p. 5).

The frenzy to "get tough" on juveniles reflected a broader climate of fear of young people—especially other people's children—and a simplistic view of "punishment as panacea" that was soon adopted in other arenas. In response to escalating youth violence, Congress passed the Gun Free Schools Act of 1994 (20 U.S.C. § 7151 [2003]), which required states receiving federal funding to enact policies of expulsion for a minimum of one year for any student found in possession of a firearm on school grounds. States and schools responded by adopting zero tolerance policies, often expanding the prohibition beyond possession of firearms to include all manner of weapons or drugs, as well as other violations (Pinard 2003). In some jurisdictions, school administrators applied these draconian policies broadly and senselessly to children who made innocent mistakes, such as bringing scissors, table knives, or over-the-counter medications to school (see, e.g., Blumenson and Nilsen 2003). Zero tolerance policies have not proven beneficial. Analysts link them to increased dropout rates and referrals to juvenile court for behaviors that school officials have traditionally handled informally (American Psychological Association Zero Tolerance Task Force 2008). Further, because these policies have more often been implemented in urban schools, they have had a disproportionate impact on minority youths (Fenning and Rose 2007).

In the 1980s, school departments also began hiring sworn police officers as School Resource Officers (SROs) to combat drugs, enforce school rules, and teach anti-drug and anti-gang curricula in middle and high schools, and, in the 1990s, to provide heightened security following some high-profile school shootings (Redding and Shalf 2001). Expanded use of metal detectors and drug sniffing dogs accompanied the heightened police presence (Pinard 2003; Redding and Shalf 2001). Increasingly, police arrested young violators not for drug and weapons offenses, but for disorderly conduct, disturbing the peace, and disruption of school assembly—based on normative adolescent acting-out behaviors like cursing, clowning, and taking part in cafeteria food fights that used to be handled informally by school officials (with detention or intervention with the youth's parents). The combination of zero tolerance policies and SRO programs resulted in the removal of thousands of youths from mainstream educational environments and produced a dramatic escalation in arrests and referrals to juvenile courts—a phenomenon that has aptly come to be known as the School-to-Prison Pipeline.

In sum, as the twentieth century came to a close, the United States embraced policies that increased the punitive powers of juvenile courts, expanded the reach and bite of transfer laws, and criminalized much ordinary adolescent misbehavior. The harshness with which the United States responded to youthful misconduct was unparalleled, and the punitive fervor showed few signs of abating.

IV. 2000–2010: Finding a New Balance?

It is difficult to characterize juvenile justice trends in the past decade because of the admixture of opposing strategies that are underway. Some states continue to expand punitive measures with respect to some issues, while other jurisdictions have adopted new policies and practices that represent a retrenchment of punitive reforms and a renewed focus on prevention, diversion, and rehabilitation. These latter innovations provide some basis for optimism that the punitive excesses of the previous two decades have begun to wane, and that we may be on the cusp of a new cycle (Bernard 1992) that will usher in more inclusionary, protectionist, and treatment-oriented reforms.

Several recent and significant developments seem to be driving a shift in the tone and direction of American juvenile justice policy. These include a dramatic drop in juvenile violence, evidence of broad public support for delinquency prevention and offender treatment, advances in developmental psychology and the neuroscience of the human brain, the proliferation of sophisticated youth advocacy groups, and cost pressures. We briefly discuss each of these below.

A. Factors Driving Reform

1. *The Crime Drop*

Beginning in 1994, rates of youth crime—especially serious and violent crime—declined dramatically. The number of murders attributed to juveniles rose 146%

between 1985 and 1993—to the highest levels ever recorded—then dropped off precipitously to pre-1985 levels—indeed, to levels not seen since the 1970s. Rates of
other serious forms of youth violence also declined sharply, while property crime
rates slowed more gradually (See Snyder, Chapter 1 this volume.). Because the factors responsible for the sharp drop in violent offenses are not well understood, there
is considerable uncertainty as to whether low rates are likely to continue. Nevertheless,
the crime drop seems to have alleviated the moral panic that sparked the unprecedented spate of punitive legislation, allowing for consideration of more moderate,
humane, and sensible policies.

2. *Public Support for Non-Punitive Approaches*

Opinion polls indicate that the American public strongly supports treatment for
juvenile offenders. It has for a very long time. Although legislators have frequently
claimed to be fulfilling a public mandate to get tough on juvenile crime, in truth,
they often fueled public fears with alarmist rhetoric, hired pollsters to survey public
opinion with questions designed to ensure a punitive response—e.g., "What penalty is appropriate for a juvenile who uses a gun to commit robbery?"—then touted
the false promise of simplistic repressive solutions for which they were rewarded at
the ballot box (Beckett and Sasson 2000). In recent years, the "accepted wisdom"
(Matthews 2005) that the public broadly and single-mindedly demands punishment of juvenile offenders is increasingly being exposed as a myth (Nagin et al.
2006; Bishop 2006).

Despite major fluctuations in crime over the past thirty years, public opinion
polls show strong and unwavering support for rehabilitation as a response to all but
the most violent juvenile offenders (Cullen et al. 2000; Moon et al. 2000). According
to a national poll conducted in 1981, when juvenile crime rates were relatively low, 75%
of the public favored rehabilitation over punishment (Opinion Research Corporation
1982). A decade later, at the height of the surge in youth violence, a national survey
queried the public about whether the main purpose of the juvenile court should be to
"treat and rehabilitate" or "punish." Over three quarters chose "treat and rehabilitate"
(Schwartz et al. 1992). Support for rehabilitation continued unabated after juvenile
crime rates began their precipitous decline. Another national survey conducted in
1999 showed that 90% of the public supported prevention and rehabilitation of juvenile offenders (Soler 2001). Most recently, over 80% of survey respondents in Florida
supported rehabilitation for a wide range of juvenile offenders—young and old, first
offenders and repeaters, and violent and nonviolent youths (Applegate and Davis
2005), while in Pennsylvania, 72% of citizens surveyed not only endorsed rehabilitation for serious juvenile offenders but also expressed a willingness to pay additional
taxes to support rehabilitative programming (Nagin et al. 2006).

Solid public support for rehabilitation coupled with social science evidence of
effective treatment methodologies (see MacKenzie and Freeland, Chapter 31 this
volume; Greenwood and Turner, Chapter 29 this volume) together bode well for a
return to more traditional, treatment-oriented juvenile justice systems.

3. *Advances in Neuroscience*

Neuroscientists long believed that the brain changed little after the first few years of life; however, with the advent of sophisticated magnetic resonance imaging techniques, scientists have discovered substantial changes in brain structure and circuitry that do not begin until the onset of puberty and that continue into the early adult years. Although neuroscientists have not established the precise causal mechanisms linking changes in brain structure and circuitry to changes in behavior (Aronson 2009), it seems clear that the neurobiological immaturity of the adolescent brain is at least partially responsible for the poor judgment and impulsive behavior associated with the teen years.

In the past decade, the popular press has prominently featured stories linking adolescent brain development and behavior. As well, some youth advocates have taken the position that brain science and developmental psychological research should guide juvenile law and policy (e.g., Scott and Steinberg 2008). It is noteworthy that the Supreme Court in *Graham v. Florida* (560 U.S.—[2010]) cited neuropsychological research in reaching its decision that, on account of their lesser culpability, persons under age 18 convicted of nonhomicide offenses can no longer receive LWOP sentences (see below).

4. *Advances in Developmental Psychology*

In the past two decades, psychologists have made significant advances in the understanding of adolescent development. Especially relevant is the body of research on changes in qualities of decision-making and judgment as youths make their way from early adolescence to the early adult years. Breakthroughs have been made in our understanding of cognitive differences (in reasoning and understanding) between adolescents and adults, as well as psychosocial differences (in social and emotional functioning) that affect the exercise of cognitive capacities (Cauffman and Steinberg 1995, 2000; see also Woolard, Chapter 5 this volume). Although, to be sure, there is wide variation among individuals, adolescents as a class tend to process information differently than adults, and their judgments reflect preferences and orientations that tend to be characteristic of this developmental period (Scott and Grisso 1997).

A considerable amount of experimental research conducted in laboratory settings indicates that by mid-adolescence, most youths have capacities for reasoning and understanding that are roughly equivalent to those of adults. But the laboratory setting is artificial: All subjects are supplied identical information relevant to the decisions they are asked to make, and the research setting is most often relaxed, quiet, and free of distractions. Consequently, the laboratory yields information about cognitive performance under optimal conditions that may bear little relation to decision-making under more natural conditions (Scott and Steinberg 2003, pp. 812–13).

In the real world, people base decisions and judgments on experience and on the information they possess. Decision-making is generally better when the kinds of decisions individuals are called on to make are ones they have made before. As Zimring (2005, p. 17) has observed: "Being mature takes practice." Thus, although youths' cognitive *capacities* for understanding and reasoning may be equal to adults, mid- to late-adolescents' decision-making is frequently impaired. By virtue of their inexperience, teens are less likely than adults to consider all of their options, to recognize or appreciate all of the ramifications of behavioral alternatives, and to weigh the alternatives in a way that produces favorable and desired outcomes.

Psychosocial factors also play an important role in decision-making. They are often referred to as "judgment" factors because they refer to things like risk perceptions, self perceptions, emotions, motivations, time perspective, and responsiveness to others that influence preferences and, ultimately, judgments and decisions. Researchers have identified multiple psychosocial factors that are especially salient during the teen years and that contribute to the adolescent immaturity, impetuosity, and vulnerability noted by the Supreme Court in *Roper* and *Graham*. These include greater susceptibility to peer influence, shortened time perspective, less capacity for self regulation, and differentially greater attention to anticipated benefits and lesser attention to potential losses (the "personal fable"). (For a full discussion, see Woolard, Chapter 5 this volume.) Important to note here is that these insights reaffirm critical differences between juveniles and adults, are consistent with foundational principles of the juvenile court, call for less punitive responses to juvenile misbehavior than those that have characterized the recent past, and have begun to influence juvenile law and policy.

5. *Youth Advocacy*

Youth advocacy groups have proliferated and flourished in the past decade. The contemporary youth advocacy movement comprises more than fifty groups; they have opposed the sound-bite politics of punitive sentencing, encouraged state legislatures fully to implement the right to counsel, lobbied to raise the age of juvenile court jurisdiction in states that define adulthood at ages lower than 18, worked to reform expansive transfer policies, and mounted legal attacks against abuses of power in juvenile courts and abominable conditions in juvenile correctional institutions. Although it is difficult to gauge the impact of these groups with any degree of precision, they have had numerous high profile successes[2] and have been influential in shaping reforms in juvenile law and policy.[3]

B. Recent Trends in Juvenile Justice Policy and Practice

In this section, we explore substantive developments in juvenile justice policy and practice that have occurred over the past decade. While some policies are decidedly punitive and maintain the course of the past few decades, others indicate a softening of attitudes—an acknowledgement that juvenile offending is more often transitory than prophetic and deserving of responses that are solicitous and ameliorative.

To gauge current trends, we consulted a number of sources, including annual state-by-state inventories of juvenile justice legislation through May 2010, compiled by the National Conference of State Legislatures and by the National Juvenile Defender Center. We also reviewed updates on policies and trends prepared by the National Center for Juvenile Justice, and conducted Internet and article searches to obtain more detailed information, especially regarding two major multistate reform initiatives: Models for Change, sponsored by the John B. and Catherine T. MacArthur Foundation, and the Juvenile Detention Alternatives Initiative (JDAI), sponsored by the Annie E. Casey Foundation. In the sections below, we explore trends in several areas: (1) delinquency prevention and early intervention; (2) juvenile court processing; (3) juvenile transfer and sentencing; (4) juvenile corrections; and (5) major foundation-supported reform initiatives. Discussion of trends in each of these areas is not intended to be comprehensive, but to survey and highlight recent developments.

1. *Trends in Prevention and Early Intervention*

Delinquency prevention recently has taken on significant new dimensions and, equally important, become increasingly research-based. Funding of large-scale cohort studies, such as the Office of Juvenile Justice & Delinquency Prevention's (OJJDP) Research Program on Causes and Correlates of Delinquency, has led to the identification of early childhood risk factors and protective factors for delinquency (e.g., Loeber et al. 2008). Theoretical and research advances in developmental criminology have made planners and policy makers more cognizant of the connections between the family, school, and neighborhood contexts in which young children live and their risk of later delinquency and crime. Simultaneously, a push within criminology—and the social sciences generally—for scientifically rigorous program evaluations (reflected, for example, in the emergence of The Campbell Collaboration in 2000) has advanced both the development and dissemination of evidence-based programming (See Welsh, Chapter 18 this volume).

To an unprecedented degree, research is playing a role in shaping the nation's delinquency prevention policy agenda. For example, the reauthorization of the Juvenile Justice and Delinquency Prevention Act in 1992 created the Title V Community Prevention Grants Program, which was further amended in 2002 to provide financial incentives to localities that submitted proposals for "data-driven evidence-based prevention" programs (42 U.S.C. §§ 5781–5784 [2002]). Especially noteworthy aspects of this effort are its reliance on (1) findings of criminal careers research and epidemiological criminology regarding individual, family, school, and community factors that put children at risk for serious delinquency as well as protective factors that buffer the exposure to risk, and (2) findings from evaluation research regarding the comparative efficacy of various prevention/intervention strategies.

The Communities That Care (CTC) program, which has been adopted in several hundred localities, illustrates the new emphasis on risk-focused and evidence-based prevention. Under CTC, entire communities receive funding and technical assistance to implement a systematic, multistep process leading to coordinated systems of delinquency prevention. CTC brings together community leaders, representatives of business and industry, police, courts, and correctional agencies, and public and private youth-serving organizations. Together they conduct an assessment of risks and protective factors in the community, inventory existing community resources, and identify resource needs. With that empirical foundation, they prioritize risks to be reduced and protectors to be strengthened, then select programs from a portfolio of research-based "best practices" in designing a multifaceted prevention plan (Hawkins and Catalano 2005).

Another important area of prevention and early intervention involves school-based programs. Since the 1980s, ties between schools and law enforcement have become increasingly strong. Police have maintained a continuing presence in grades K–12—first with Drug Abuse Resistance Education (DARE), then with Gang Resistance Education and Training (GREAT) and, most recently, with SRO programs. Each of these programs has tried to motivate students to refrain from inappropriate behaviors through a combination of education, counseling, and threats of legal sanctions. They have also endured irrespective of their effectiveness. Evaluations of DARE have consistently been disappointing. GREAT has produced somewhat more promising, but far from stellar, results (Esbensen et al. 2001). And the federal government has heavily invested in SRO programs in advance of any evidence of their efficacy. Between 1999 and 2005, the federal Community Oriented Policing Services (COPS) office awarded more than $750 million to more than three thousand agencies to fund SRO programs (Office of Community Oriented Policing Services 2008). Although there are now approximately seventeen thousand SROs in schools nationwide (Wald and Thurau 2010), there has not yet been a single published evaluation of their actual (as opposed to perceived) impact on school safety.

In the past decade, SRO programs and zero tolerance policies have begun to receive some pushback at the grassroots level. Concern about the overreach and inflexibility of zero tolerance policies has prompted some school districts (e.g., Los Angeles) and states (e.g., Rhode Island, Connecticut, Louisiana) recently to replace them with alternatives to suspension and expulsion that are applied on a case-by-case basis. Similarly, because SROs tend to criminalize normative behaviors that used to be handled informally within the schools,[4] school officials are reclaiming more of their disciplinary functions, either abandoning SRO programs altogether or restricting the scope of SROs' authority to carry out responsibilities traditionally vested in school administrators (see, e.g., Wald and Thurau 2010; Advancement Project 2010).

2. *Trends in Juvenile Court Processing*

The number of youths referred to the juvenile courts rose significantly from 1990 to —the year that juvenile arrests peaked—but, unlike arrests, which declined dramatically in the years that followed, referrals continued to rise through 1997, then declined only slightly. Thus, although the juvenile arrest rate in 2005 was 10% *below* its 1985 level, the rate of referrals to juvenile court in 2005 was 22% *above* its 1985 level (See Snyder, Chapter 1 this volume). In 1980, 58% of juvenile arrests were referred to juvenile court. By 2005, 71% were referred to juvenile court. The trend signals a widening net of control around youths who previously would have been handled outside of the formal juvenile court system. The increase in court referrals is especially marked for public order offenses, particularly those involving black youths; this pattern may reflect a police-induced crime wave (Pinard 2003) associated with zero tolerance policies and SRO programs in urban schools.

Also reflective of net widening, juvenile court intake refers a greater proportion of cases for formal processing than in years past, rather than diverting them or simply closing them without action. In 1985, 45% of cases referred to intake were formally petitioned; by 1993, 53% were petitioned. By 1998, despite precipitous declines in serious youth crime, 58% were referred for formal processing. In 2005, the rate of petitioned cases had leveled off at 56% (Puzzanchera and Kang 2008). In sum, over the twenty year period 1985–2005, states referred higher proportions of arrestees to the juvenile court and prosecuted greater proportions of them.

The movement toward greater formal control is also apparent in responses to status offenders. The number of petitioned status offenses processed in juvenile courts nationwide more than doubled between 1985 and 2004, especially for truancy and curfew violations (Puzzanchera, 2007). In Washington State, after the murder of a 13-year-old habitual runaway, the legislature passed the "Becca Bill" permitting the secure detention of status offenders in contravention of a core principle of the JJDP Act. In the wake of this change, detention of status offenders in the state increased by 835% (Arthur 2008). However, offsetting the pattern in Washington were changes in the laws in Connecticut, New Hampshire, and New York that repealed the JJDP Act's "valid court order" exception to secure detention of repeat status offenders.

3. Diversion

In the area of intervention with first-time and low-risk offenders, policy makers have long preferred brief, inexpensive, short-term interventions that can show fairly immediate and quantifiable results (Lab 2004). Policy makers' quest for a panacea has led them frequently to adopt ill-conceived programs based in "common sense" that often lack either theoretical or empirical foundation. Consider, for example, the tremendous popularity and eventual demise of Scared Straight programs and juvenile boot camps, both quick-fix, deterrence-based strategies adopted during the "get tough" era.

Teen court represents one of the most popular new innovations for first-time and low-risk offenders (See Butts, Roman, and Lynn-Whaley, Chapter 25 this volume). With ongoing financial support from OJJDP, teen courts have spread rapidly—from 50 programs in 1991 to about 1,200 in 2010, in forty-nine states and the District of Columbia (OJJDP 2010)—and represent the fastest growing alternative to formal court intervention. Like Scared Straight and juvenile boot camps, teen courts have a "common sense" pedigree. The idea is that every youth who violates the law should be held accountable, and that being sanctioned by one's peers—who serve as jurors and sometimes as judges in teen court—can have a more powerful impact than sanctioning by an adult. Typical sanctions include community work service, letters of apology, teen court jury service, and fines and restitution. Because offenders typically appear in teen court only once, and because teen courts rely heavily on student volunteers, these programs are brief and inexpensive. Whether they succeed in preventing recidivism is unknown: Evaluation results have been mixed (See Butts et al., this volume).

Other recent reforms flow out of the restorative justice movement, which was "virtually unknown to all but a small group of academics at the beginning of the 1990s" (Bazemore and Walgrave 1999, p. 1). Restorative justice programs take a variety of forms—including victim-offender mediation, community reparation boards, family group conferencing, and circle sentencing—and have assumed an important place in schools as well as in the juvenile justice system (Bazemore and Umbreit 2001; see also Bazemore, Chapter 28 this volume). These programs focus on the offense; on its impact on the victim and the community; and on offender apology, forgiveness, and reparation of harm. Broadly stated, restorative justice goals include educating participants about the harms—especially the emotional harms and fracturing of relationships—caused by the offense; holding offenders accountable for active participation in the reparation of harm; and rebuilding relationships and strengthening systems of informal social control. Although the establishment of restorative justice programs in the United States has not kept pace with similar developments in Western Europe, Australia, New Zealand, and Canada, some jurisdictions have made substantial progress. Minnesota and Pennsylvania have emerged as leaders in the use of family group conferencing, and Vermont has made community reparation boards a centerpiece of its juvenile justice system. Indications are that these programs are likely to grow in the years ahead.

4. *Juvenile Court Orientation*

Over the last two decades, legislatures in most states have revised their juvenile codes. In preparing this chapter, we reviewed them to assess their compatibility with the juvenile court's traditional mission. We looked for indications that the system is expected to provide offenders with rehabilitation and/or treatment,[5] or is expected to act in the "best interests of the child." We found that forty jurisdictions continue to identify treatment or rehabilitation as a goal. An additional five instruct their juvenile courts to act in the child's best interest. Of the remainder, one uses the language of rehabilitation, but appears to redefine punishment as treatment,[6] while the other four endorse objectives that are limited to some combination of punishment, accountability, protection of victim rights/victim reparation, and protection of public safety. In sum, although state legislatures have rewritten their juvenile codes to endorse punitive objectives, forty-five maintain allegiance to the juvenile court's traditional benevolent mission. While few identify that mission as its sole purpose, most feature rehabilitation prominently alongside the goals of protecting the public and holding youths accountable. Several states explicitly reject the goal of retribution as inappropriate for children.

5. *Specialized Juvenile Courts*

Signs of a revitalized treatment orientation are apparent in two specialized courts that have recently emerged on the current scene, and which harken back in many respects to juvenile courts of a century ago. These are drug courts and mental health courts. Drug courts began in the mid-1990s and, with much federal funding, have rapidly proliferated to about five hundred today. Butts et al. (this volume) describe the atmosphere and dynamics of contemporary drug courts:

> Instead of the bureaucratic, sometimes impersonal atmosphere of the contemporary juvenile courtroom, juvenile drug courts employ a more personal, team-oriented courtroom where procedures are highly interactive, even theatrical. Practitioners place great value on the dynamic interaction between offenders and judges in drug court proceedings. Juvenile drug court judges motivate participants by maintaining close and frequent communication with each youth and by keeping track of each offender's personal situation from one hearing to the next. A judge may confront a young offender with the results of a failed drug test and apply a sanction in one hearing, and then praise the youth for a clean drug test and provide a reward in the next hearing. During court hearings, the judge plays the role of a concerned authority figure, compassionate when possible but always ready to impose sanctions (including detention) so that offenders understand their actions have consequences.

An even more recent development, and smaller in number, are juvenile mental health courts, specialized courts that apply a multidisciplinary team approach to address the needs of offenders with serious mental illnesses. According to Butts et al. (this volume) the court is offender- rather than offense-based: judges, attorneys, probation staff, and mental health practitioners in these courts treat the offense as symptomatic of mental illness and work together to devise and implement appropriate treatment plans involving the youth, his family, and community health providers. As is the case with drug courts, juveniles in mental health courts remain in regular contact with a single judge who establishes a supportive relationship with each youngster, monitors the youth's progress in treatment, applies sanctions for noncompliance, and provides positive reinforcement for desired behaviors. Mental health courts, like drug courts, are strongly reminiscent of the Progressives' vision of juvenile courts. That the modern juvenile court is being "reinvented" in these new forms speaks volumes about the court's departure from its historical mission and the move to return it to its original form, at least for youths with conditions (substance abuse, mental health disorders) that are easily medicalized and made targets of treatment rather than punishment.

6. *The Right to Counsel*

More than forty years after *Gault* granted delinquents a constitutional right to counsel, the delivery of quality legal services in juvenile courts remains problematic (see Feld, Chapter 27 this volume). Recently there has been a stepped-up effort to preserve the right by disallowing or dissuading waivers. Currently, a handful of states flatly prohibit some or all juvenile defendants from waiving the right to counsel,[7] while many more have tried to better protect the right, e.g., by permitting waiver only after consultation with an attorney.[8] Nevertheless, most states afford juveniles no special protections. Many juveniles—including those charged with serious crimes—continue to waive their rights and to navigate the court process without any legal assistance at all (Feld 1993; Feld and Schaefer 2010). In the last decade, the American Bar Association and the National Juvenile Defender Center have completed assessments of access to counsel and quality of defense representation in juvenile court proceedings in nineteen states (http://www.njdc.info). They report that most juveniles are not represented by counsel and, even when they are, their lawyers often provide substandard representation due to structural impediments to effective advocacy such as inadequate support services, heavy caseloads, and lack of investigators or dispositional advisors. In some jurisdictions, attorneys rarely file motions, advocate for alternate dispositions, or provide post-dispositional representation. Moreover, regardless of how poorly lawyers perform, juvenile courts seem incapable of correcting their own errors. Defense attorneys rarely appeal adverse decisions and often lack a record with which to challenge legal errors (Feld and Schaefer 2010).

The collateral consequences of a delinquency adjudication amplify the procedural deficiencies of juvenile courts. In most states, an offender of any age tried in criminal court is liable to have prior uncounseled juvenile felony adjudications counted as prior convictions for the purpose of sentence enhancements (e.g., in California, under its "three strikes" law). As noted above, juvenile sex offense adjudications may trigger requirements for lifelong reporting to a sex offender registry. Adjudications for drug offenses often disqualify youths and their families from public housing and, under the federal Higher Education Act of 1998, routinely bar them from student loans, grants, and work-study programs.

7. Juvenile Transfer and Sentencing

Juvenile court jurisdiction has been a "hot button" issue for nearly three decades. In the 1980s and 1990s, as juvenile violence increased, legislatures in every jurisdiction except Nebraska expanded the number and types of youths eligible for transfer to criminal court and/or expedited the process of getting them there (see Feld and Bishop, Chapter 32 this volume). In the last decade, in view of mounting evidence that transfer has iatrogenic effects, and considering the moral culpability implications of adolescent brain research, states' expansion of transfer policies has slowed almost to a halt; in some instances, legislatures retrenched and modified some of the harshest laws. Most dramatically, the Connecticut legislature in 2008 raised the lower bound of the criminal court's jurisdiction, from 16 to 18.[9] Only two other states—New York and North Carolina—continue to define 16- and 17-year-olds as adults. North Carolina may soon go the way of Connecticut: after considering bills to raise the age of juvenile court jurisdiction in each of its past two terms, the legislature in 2009 ordered a feasibility study to assess the costs of the proposed reform.

In 2005, the Illinois legislature voted unanimously to repeal a law mandating transfer of youths accused of drug offenses in or around schools or low-income housing after it was revealed that the law had been applied almost exclusively to youths of color from disadvantaged neighborhoods. Three year later, the Illinois legislature shifted the lower bound of juvenile court jurisdiction from 17 to 18 for youths charged with misdemeanors. A Task Force has been charged with preparing a plan for similar change for youths charged with felonies. In 2008, the voters of California defeated Proposition 6, which would have created a presumption that 14-year-olds charged with gang-related felonies are unfit for juvenile court. In the same year, legislation that would have raised the age of criminal responsibility from 17 to 18 was introduced in the Wisconsin legislature. A Juvenile Justice Commission established by Governor Jim Doyle to examine the issue returned a unanimous rec-ommendation to approve the change conditional upon the provision of sufficient additional fiscal resources. A bill consistent with that recommendation was intro-duced in the legislature in the spring of 2010, but had not been acted on as of this writing.

Several other notable changes in transfer law have been made in the past decade. Although some states (e.g., California, Alabama, Oklahoma) expanded the offense or offender criteria for transfer, at least as many restricted them (e.g., Arizona, Connecticut, Delaware, Mississippi, Virginia) or mitigated the criminal sentences to which transferred youths might be subject (e.g., Pennsylvania, Colorado, Maine, Oklahoma, Virginia). Others took steps to rein in prosecutorial discretion either by severely restricting the scope of offenses subject to direct file (Colorado, Nevada) or by requiring prosecutors to provide criteria and assessment procedures for choos-ing the forum in which youths will be tried (Colorado, Wyoming). In addition, some states repealed "once an adult, always an adult" provisions (e.g., Indiana) with respect to certain offenders.

8. *Sentencing in Adult Court*

As mentioned above, in a watershed reform, the Court in *Roper v. Simmons* (2005) abolished the death penalty for persons convicted of crimes committed before they were 18 years of age. The *Roper* Court's Eighth Amendment assessment of "evolving standards of decency" relied on objective indicators such as state statutes and jury decisions, and found that a national consensus existed against executing adoles-cents. The Court also conducted an analysis of youths' criminal responsibility and concluded that their reduced culpability warranted a categorical prohibition of execution (Feld 2008).

In *Graham v. Florida* (2010), the Court extended *Roper's* diminished responsi-bility rationale to youths convicted of nonhomicide crimes who are sentenced to life without possibility of parole. Historically, the Court's Eighth Amendment proportionality analysis had distinguished between capital sentences and long terms of imprisonment and, reasoning that "death is different," deferred to legislative decisions about noncapital punishments. *Graham* (2010) concluded that nonhomicide offenders are "categorically less deserving of the most serious forms of punishment than are murderers." Moreover, because of juveniles' diminished responsibility, those convicted of nonhomicide offenses have "twice diminished moral culpability." The Court concluded that the age of the offender and the nature of the crime categorically precluded the penultimate penalty for nonhomicide crimes. *Graham* emphasized youths' immature judgment, reduced self-control, susceptibility to negative peer influences, and ongoing character development, and found that new research in developmental psychology and neuroscience bolstered *Roper*'s conclusion that adolescents' reduced culpability required somewhat mitigated sentences.

Although *Graham* extended *Roper*'s rationale of youths' diminished moral culpability, it granted the 129 youths convicted of nonhomicide crimes and serving LWOP sentences very limited relief. The Court only required states to "give defendants like Graham some meaningful opportunity to obtain release based on demonstrated maturity and rehabilitation." And even the opportunity for parole review "does not require the State to release the offender during his natural life." Because *Graham* distinguished the seriousness of nonhomicide crimes and murder, its holding does not affect the more than two thousand youths convicted of murder and serving LWOP sentences nor the tens of thousands of youths convicted of other crimes and serving very lengthy prison terms.

At the time of the Court's decision in *Graham*, there were more than 2,250 prisoners serving sentences of life without possibility of parole for offenses committed when they were juveniles (Human Rights Watch 2005). Their best hope for release is legislative repeal of LWOP provisions. In 2009, Texas (one of the toughest "tough on crime" states) became the seventh state to place an absolute ban on LWOP sentences for juveniles, a step that the Colorado legislature had taken the year before. It remains to be seen whether other states will also follow suit.

9. *Juvenile Corrections*

Recent developments in juvenile corrections suggest a softening of the punishment agenda. The 1980s saw the establishment of boot camps, first in the adult system (1983), then in the juvenile system (1985). OJJDP supported the boot camp initiative and funded an evaluation of three programs in three different states, which showed that boot camp participants had higher recidivism rates than controls (See MacKenzie and Freeland, Chapter 31 this volume). Despite the negative results and allegations of staff abuse, boot camps "caught on" in the same way that other deterrence-based programs have. At least two states (Texas and Virginia) incorporated them into the continuum of graduated sanctions (Howell 2003, p. 134). However, the tide is beginning to turn. Several states have eliminated juvenile boot camps, and a comparison of OJJDP's Juvenile Residential Facility Census for 2006 with that for 2002 shows that the number of boot camps declined by nearly 50% over that period.

In addition, several states have closed (or been forced by the courts to close) training schools following the disclosure of terrible conditions of confinement (California, New York, Mississippi, Texas, Louisiana). Under court order, California shut down training schools and reduced its incarcerated juvenile population by more than half (See Krisberg, Chapter 30 this volume). Texas also shut down four maximum security juvenile facilities and reduced its juvenile institutional population by more than half. Florida not only shut down all of its boot camps, but also downsized its training schools and youth development centers and placed a cap of 165 beds on all residential placements. In 2009 Arizona Governor Jan Brewer recommended that, due to budgetary constraints, the Arizona Department of Juvenile Corrections be eliminated in July, 2010. In a move reminiscent of the closing of all state correctional institutions for juveniles in Massachusetts in the 1970s, youths in Arizona's state correctional system would be transferred to the custody of smaller programs in local counties, where they might also maintain closer contact with families. The Arizona legislature recently voted to continue the state system through July 2011. As of this writing, it is unclear whether the state correctional system will exist after that date. The downsizing that we are witnessing across the nation is motivated in part by external pressures to close large institutions where conditions of confinement are most problematic, and in part by budgetary constraints. These pressures open the door for greater use of smaller institutions and community-based programs, where rehabilitative aims are more likely to be realized.

There are also signs of a revitalization of rehabilitation in juvenile corrections. In the last fifteen years, both private foundations and the federal government have invested significant funds to assess the effectiveness of various forms of treatment. This research has produced fairly consistent evidence that treatment-oriented programs, especially those that focus on interpersonal skills development and parent/family interventions, are considerably more effective than punishment-oriented ones (See Greenwood, this volume; MacKenzie and Freeland, this volume). Research has identified effective nonresidential treatment programs for minor and first-time offenders as well as effective residential interventions for serious and chronic offenders. Some show very substantial reductions in recidivism, especially when programs are well designed and faithfully implemented (Lipsey 1999a, 1999b, 2009). It is possible that, at the local level, thousands (or even tens of thousands) of rehabilitation programs are currently operating. Unfortunately, because most states and the federal jurisdiction do not maintain detailed inventories of juvenile correctional programs, it is impossible to determine the extent to which rehabilitative programming has taken hold.

10. *Major Reform Initiatives*

One major reform effort, underway in sixteen states, is Models for Change, an initiative funded by the MacArthur Foundation (www.modelsforchange.net). This initiative began in 1996, when the Foundation established the interdisciplinary

Research Network on Adolescent Development and Juvenile Justice, which supported research on adolescent culpability, juvenile competence, transfer/waiver, as well as policy analysis and advocacy. This effort gave birth to a second initiative in 2001 to help states develop model juvenile justice systems. The Foundation selected four states—Pennsylvania, Washington, Illinois, and Louisiana—based on their commitment to reform and the likelihood that other states would emulate them. Models for Change focuses on five key outcomes: reducing racial disparities, reducing transfer to criminal court, increasing youth participation in treatment programs aimed at prosocial development, reducing recidivism, and reducing reliance on incarceration/increasing use of community-based alternatives. The Foundation is also supporting evaluation research throughout the change process and has undertaken a major initiative to disseminate results. In 2007–2008, the Foundation created three "action networks" to support the development of reform models. One aims to reduce minority contact, another to find better ways to respond to offenders with mental health needs, and another to improve indigent defense policy and practice. Each of them is active in eight states.

Another major reform initiative is the Juvenile Detention Alternatives Initiative (JDAI), funded by the Annie E. Casey Foundation (www.aecf.org). The Casey Foundation launched JDAI in Broward County, Florida, in 1992—at a time when two-thirds of detention facilities were overcrowded, many departments of juvenile justice faced lawsuits, and most detained youths were held for nonviolent offenses. JDAI is an effort to reduce the use of secure detention by (1) encouraging the adoption of risk assessment instruments and objective detention criteria to reduce detention admissions without increasing risk to public safety; (2) expediting the removal from secure detention of youths who can, with careful treatment planning, safely return to their home communities; and (3) generating nonsecure alternatives, including shelter care and day treatment programs, that can be used in lieu of secure detention facilities. JDAI currently has programs in over one hundred sites, in nineteen states and the District of Columbia. Although the inappropriate use of secure detention remains a national problem, the JDAI sites have substantially reduced detention populations in the localities in which the program has been implemented.

V. CONCLUSION

At the dawn of the twentieth century—a time when cultural conceptions of young people held them to be immature, vulnerable, and dependent, and when trust in government to reform all manner of social ills was at its height—the juvenile court was founded as a social welfare institution and afforded extraordinary latitude to intervene in the best interests of juvenile offenders and at-risk youths. By mid-century, however, it had become apparent that giving juvenile courts and correctional systems virtually unlimited discretionary authority was a terrible mistake. The Supreme Court attempted to correct this in a series of decisions that provided procedural safeguards for children in delinquency proceedings. The constitutional domestication of the juvenile court altered not only its procedure but also its substance, shifting its focus from the offender to the offense. As juvenile courts took on the look and feel of criminal courts, notions of punishment and proportionality gained ascendancy.

In the 1980s, rates of urban black youth gun violence took a dramatic upward turn, drawing sensationalized media coverage and triggering a moral panic. Cultural conceptions of delinquents rapidly shifted from the benign images of the past to menacing portraits of sophisticated and remorseless "superpredators." Politicians touted harsh punishment as a solution, which struck a responsive chord with a fearful public. Legislatures expanded the range of offenses for which young people could be tried in criminal court, created presumptive and mandatory transfer, and adopted determinate and mandatory minimum sentencing in juvenile courts. Furthered by claims that rehabilitation was an unattainable goal, the punitive trend caused detention centers and training schools to swell past capacity.

At the start of the twenty-first century, the future of juvenile justice looked bleak. But a decline in youth violence nearly as precipitous as the surge that preceded it assuaged public fears. Important new discoveries in the social and natural sciences affirmed the Progressives' belief that adolescents are by nature immature, vulnerable, and prone to poor and impulsive decision-making. The Supreme Court has recently given its imprimatur to notions of adolescent immaturity, impetuosity, and vulnerability and to their legal corollary—lesser culpability—the linchpin of two decisions limiting the punishments to which even the most serious young offenders can be subject. Simultaneously, research on the efficacy of various treatment approaches showed that some strategies are effective when implemented well. These findings revitalized an interest in the rehabilitation of juvenile offenders and animated widespread endorsement of evidence-based practices.

This is not to say that the punitive approaches of the 1980s and 1990s have disappeared. They have not. It is likely that their legacy will continue for some time. But they cannot be long sustained given the renewed focus on children perceived much more in line with the views that animated the Progressives. In the softening of criminal punishments, the introduction of specialized treatment-oriented courts, the extension of the upper bounds of juvenile court jurisdiction, and the retrenchment of transfer laws in various jurisdictions, we see signs of a counterbalance to the repressive policies of the recent past. The investment of major private foundations in better models of doing juvenile justice and the proliferation of sophisticated youth advocacy groups dedicated to protecting young offenders in courts and correctional systems raise hope for continuing shifts toward more sensible and humane practices.

NOTES

1. U.S. Representative Bill McCollum (R-Fla.) dubbed legislation he introduced in Congress the "Violent Youth Predator Act of 1996." The bill would have automatically transferred young chronic violent offenders to criminal court and imposed lengthy mandatory prison terms if a firearm was used in the commission of an offense. McCollum argued that these offenders "should be thrown in jail, the key should be thrown away and there should be very little or no effort to rehabilitate them."

2. One of the best examples is Juvenile Law Center's success in exposing and successfully challenging massive abuses of judicial power in Luzerne County, Pennsylvania.

3. Consider that more than fifty youth advocacy groups filed amicus briefs in *Roper v. Simmons*.

4. One recent study documented how school-based arrests in Pennsylvania tripled in a seven-year period after the implementation of these programs (Advancement Project 2010).

5. Jurisdictions that described rehabilitation as optional were not considered to have met this criterion.

6. The Texas juvenile code endorses "rehabilitation that emphasizes the accountability and responsibility of both the parent and the child for the child's conduct."

7. These include Iowa, Illinois, Louisiana, Montana, New Mexico, Texas, and Vermont.

8. These include Arizona, Connecticut, Colorado, Florida, Georgia, Indiana, Minnesota, New Jersey, West Virginia, and Virginia. Requiring consultation with an attorney by no means insures that juvenile defendants receive counsel, as Feld and Schaefer's recent (2010) analysis of practices in Minnesota has shown.

9. The "Raise the Age" movement in Connecticut was a highly organized effort by law makers, youth advocacy groups, and the families of youths prosecuted in the adult system to raise a line of demarcation between juvenile and adult courts that had been in place since 1949 (Conn. Gen Stat., ch. 815, § 46b-120). It involved a three-pronged approach of (1) educating the public and policymakers about consequentialists' misplaced belief in the deterrent effects of transfer, (2) building a normative case for the lesser culpability of 16- and 17-year-olds based on evidence from neuroscience and developmental psychology, and (3) demonstrating cost effectiveness.

REFERENCES

Advancement Project. 2010. *Test, Punish, and Push Out: How "Zero Tolerance" and High-Stakes Testing Funnel Youth into the School-to-Prison Pipeline*. http://www.advancementproject.org.

American Friends Service Committee. 1971. *Struggle for Justice*. New York: Hill and Wang.

American Psychological Association Zero Tolerance Task Force. 2008. "Are Zero Tolerance Policies Effective in Schools? An Evidentiary Review and Recommendations." *American Psychologist* 63: 852–62.

Applegate, Brandon K., and Robin King Davis. 2005. "Examining Public Support for 'Correcting' Offenders." *Corrections Today* 67(3) (June): 94–102.

Aronson, Jay D. 2009. "Neuroscience and Juvenile Justice." *Akron Law Review* 42: 917–29.

Arthur, Pat. 2008. "The Incarceration of Status Offenders under the Valid Court Order Exception to the Juvenile Justice and Delinquency Prevention Act." Paper presented at the First National Conference on Homeless Youth and the Law. June 18. http://www.youthlaw. org/fileadmin/ncyl/youthlaw/juv_justice/Homeless_Youth_Presentation_2_.pdf.

Bazemore, Gordon, and Mark Umbreit. 2001. "A Comparison of Four Restorative Justice Conferencing Models." *Juvenile Justice Bulletin* February. 1–18.

Bazemore, Gordon, and Lode Walgrave. 1999. "Restorative Juvenile Justice: In Search of Fundamentals and an Outline for Systemic Reform." In *Restorative Juvenile Justice: Repairing the Harm of Youth Crime*, edited by Gordon Bazemore and Lode Walgrave. Monsey, NY: Criminal Justice Press.

Beckett, Katherine, and Theodore Sasson. 2000. *The Politics of Injustice: Crime and Punishment in America*. Thousand Oaks, CA: Pine Forge Press.

Bernard, Thomas. 1992. *The Cycle of Juvenile Justice*. New York: Oxford University Press.

Bishop, Donna M. 2000. "Juvenile Offenders in the Criminal Justice System: An Examination of Trends and Consequences." In *Crime and Justice: A Review of Research*, vol. 23, edited by Michael Tonry. Chicago: University of Chicago Press.

Bishop, Donna M. 2006. "Public Opinion and Juvenile Justice Policy: Myths and Misconceptions." *Criminology and Public Policy* 5: 653–64.

Bishop, Donna M., and Charles E. Frazier. 2000. "The Consequences of Transfer." In *The Changing Borders of Juvenile Justice: Transfer of Adolescents to the Criminal Court*, edited by Jeffrey Fagan and Franklin Zimring. Chicago: University of Chicago Press.

Bishop, Donna M., Charles E. Frazier, and Lonn Lanza-Kaduce. 1999. "Juvenile Under Attack: An Analysis of Causes and Impacts of Recent Reforms." *University of Florida Journal of Law and Public Policy* 10: 129–56.

Blumenson, Eric, and Eva S. Nilsen. 2003. "One Strike and You're Out? Constitutional Constraints on Zero Tolerance in Public Education." *Washington University Law Quarterly* 81: 65–117.

Blumstein, Alfred C. 1996. "Youth Violence, Guns and the Illicit-Drug Industry." *Journal of Criminal Law and Criminology* 86: 10–36.

Breckenridge, Sophonisba Preston, and Edith Abbott. 1912. *The Delinquent Child and the Home*. New York: Charities Publication Dahl Committee.

Butts, Jeffrey A., Dean Hoffman, and Janeen Buck 1999. *Teen Courts in the United States: A Profile of Current Programs* (OJJDP Fact Sheet #118). Washington, DC: U.S. Department of Justice, Office of Juvenile Justice and Delinquency Prevention.

Campbell Collaboration. http://www.campbellcollaboration.org/.

Cauffman, Elizabeth, and Laurence Steinberg. 1995. "The Cognitive and Affective Influences on Adolescent Decision-Making," *Temple Law Review* 68: 1763–89.

———. 2000. "(Im)maturity of Judgment in Adolescence: Why Adolescents May Be Less Culpable than Adults." *Behavioral Sciences and the Law* 18: 741–60.

Chiricos, Ted. 2004. "The Media, Moral Panic & the Politics of Crime Control." In *Criminal Justice: Law & Politics*, 9th ed., edited by George F. Cole, Marc G. Gertz, and Amy Bunger. Belmont, CA: Wadsworth.

Cullen, Francis T., Bonnie S. Fischer, and Brandon K. Applegate. 2000. "Public Opinion about Punishment and Corrections." In *Crime and Justice: A Review of Research*, vol. 27, edited by Michael Tonry. Chicago: University of Chicago Press.

Dilulio, John. 1995. "The Coming of the Super-Predators." *The Weekly Standard* 1(11) (November 19): 23–29.

Esbensen, Finn-Aage, D. Wayne Osgood, Terrence J. Taylor, Dana Peterson, and Adrienne Freng. 2001. "How Great is G.R.E.A.T? Results from a Longitudinal Quasi-Experimental Design." *Criminology and Public Policy* 1: 87–118.

Fagan, Jeffrey, and Brian Forst. 1996. "Risks, Fixers, and Zeal: Implementing Experimental Treatments for Violent Juvenile Offenders." *The Prison Journal* 76: 22–59.

Feld, Barry C. 1977. *Neutralizing Inmate Violence: Juvenile Offenders in Institutions*. Cambridge, MA: Ballinger.

———. 1988. "The Juvenile Court Meets the Principle of Offense: Punishment, Treatment, and the Difference it Makes." *Boston University Law Review* 68: 821–915.

———. 1993. *Justice for Children: The Right to Counsel and the Juvenile Courts*. Boston, MA: Northeastern University Press.

———. 1998. "Juvenile and Criminal Justice Systems' Responses to Youth Violence." *Crime and Justice* 24: 189–261.

———. 1999. *Bad Kids: Race and the Transformation of the Juvenile Court*. New York: Oxford University Press.

———. 2003. "Race, Politics and Juvenile Justice: The Warren Court and the Conservative 'Backlash.'" *Minnesota Law Review* 87: 1447–577.

———. 2008. "A Slower Form of Death: Implications of *Roper v. Simmons* for Juveniles Sentence to Life Without Parole." *Notre Dame Journal of Law, Ethics, and Public Policy* 22: 9–65.

Feld, Barry C., and Shelly Schaefer. 2010. "The Right to Counsel in Juvenile Court: Law Reform to Deliver Legal Services and Reduce Justice by Geography." *Criminology and Public Policy* 9: 327–56.

Fenning, Pamela, and Jennifer Rose. 2007. "Overrepresentation of African American Students in Exclusionary Discipline: The Role of School Policy." *Urban Education* 42: 536–59.

Fox, James Alan. 1996. *Trends in Juvenile Violence: A Report to the United States Attorney General on Current and Future Rates of Juvenile Offending*. Washington, DC: U.S. Department of Justice.

Garland, David. 2001. *The Culture of Control: Crime and Social Order in Contemporary Society*. Chicago: University of Chicago Press.

Gish, Clay. 2004. "Street Arabs and Street Urchins." In *Encyclopedia of Children and Childhood in History and Society*, edited by Paula S. Fass. New York: Macmillan.

Hawkins, J. David, and Richard F. Catalano. 2005. *Investing in Your Community's Youth: An Introduction to the Communities That Care System*. http://download.ncadi.samhsa.gov/Prevline/pdfs/ctc/Investing%20in%20Your%20Community's%20Youth.pd.

Howell, James C. 2003. *Preventing and Reducing Juvenile Delinquency: A Comprehensive Framework*. Thousand Oaks, CA: Sage.

Human Rights Watch/Amnesty International. 2005. *The Rest of Their Lives: Life without Parole for Child Offenders in the United States*. New York: Amnesty International. http://hrw.org/reports/2005/us1005/.

Lab, Steven. 2004. "Crime Prevention, Politics, and the Art of Going Nowhere Fast." *Justice Quarterly* 21: 681–92.

Lanza-Kaduce, Lonn, Charles E. Frazier, and Donna M. Bishop. 1999. "Juvenile Transfers in Florida: The Worst of the Worst?" *University of Florida Journal of Law and Public Policy* 10: 277–312.

Lipsey, Mark W. 1992. "Juvenile Delinquency Treatment: A Meta-analytic Inquiry into the Variability of Effects." In *Meta-analysis for Explanation: A Casebook*, edited by Thomas D. Cook, Harris Cooper, David S. Cordray, Heidi Hartmann, Larry V. Hedges, Richard J. Light, Thomas A. Louis, and Frederick Mosteller. New York: Russell Sage Foundation.

———. 1999a. "Can Rehabilitative Programs Reduce the Recidivism of Juvenile Offenders? An Inquiry into the Effectiveness of Practical Programs." *Virginia Journal of Social Policy and the Law* 6: 611–41.

————. 1999b. "Can Intervention Rehabilitate Serious Delinquents?" *The Annals of the American Academy of Political and Social Science* 564: 142–66.

————. 2009. "The Primary Factors that Characterize Effective Interventions with Juvenile Offenders: A Meta-analytic Overview." *Victims and Offenders* 4: 124–47.

Lipton, Douglas, Robert Martinson, and Judith Wilks. 1975. *The Effectiveness of Correctional Intervention: A Survey of Treatment Evaluation Studies*. New York: Praeger.

Loeber, Rolf, David P. Farrington, Magda Stouthamer-Loeber, and Helene Raskin White. 2008. *Violence and Serious Theft: Development and Prediction from Childhood to Adulthood*. New York: Routledge.

Mack, Julian W. 1909. "The Juvenile Court," *Harvard Law Review* 23: 104–22.

Martinson, Robert. 1974. "What Works? Questions and Answers about Prison Reform." *The Public Interest* 35: 22–54.

Massey, Douglas, and Nancy Denton. 1993. *American Apartheid: Segregation and the Making of the Underclass*. Cambridge, MA: Harvard University Press.

Matthews, Roger. 2005. "The Myth of Punitiveness." *Theoretical Criminology* 9: 175–201.

McCollum, Bill. 1996. Comments made in support of the Violent Youth Predator Act, introduced in the U.S. House of Representatives. April.

Miller, Jerome G. 1991. *Last One Over the Wall*. Columbus, OH: The Ohio State University Press.

Moon, Melissa M., Jody L. Sundt, Francis T. Cullen, and John Paul Wright. 2000. "Is Child Saving Dead? Support for Juvenile Rehabilitation." *Crime and Delinquency* 46: 38–60.

Nagin, Daniel S., Alex R. Piquero, Elizabeth S. Scott, and Laurence Steinberg. 2006. "Public Preference for Rehabilitation versus Incarceration of Juvenile Offenders: Evidence from a Contingent Valuation Study." *Criminology and Public Policy* 5: 627–52.

Office of Community Oriented Policing Services. 2008. *Cops in Schools*. http://www.cops.usdoj.gov/Default.asp?Item=54.

Office of Juvenile Justice and Delinquency Prevention. 2010. Overview of Youth Court Program. http://www.ojjdp.ncjrs.gov/programs/ProgSummary.asp?pi=23&ti=&si=&kw=&PreviousPage=ProgResults.

Opinion Research Corporation. 1982. *Public Attitudes toward Youth Crime*. Minneapolis: Hubert H. Humphrey Institute of Public Affairs.

Palmer, Ted B. 1991. "The Effectiveness of Intervention: Recent Trends and Current Issues." *Crime and Delinquency* 37: 330–46.

Pinard, Michael. 2003. "From the Classroom to the Courtroom: Reassessing Fourth Amendment Standards in Public School Searches Involving Law Enforcement Authorities." *Arizona Law Review* 45: 1067–124.

Platt, Anthony M. 2009. *The Childsavers: The Invention of Delinquency*. New Brunswick, NJ: Rutgers University Press.

President's Commission on Law Enforcement and the Administration of Justice. 1967. *Task Force Report on Juvenile Delinquency and Youth Crime*. Washington, DC: U.S. Government Printing Office.

Puzzanchera, Charles. 2007. "Trends in Justice System's Response to Status Offending: OJJDP Briefing Paper." Pittsburgh, PA: National Center on Juvenile Justice. http://www.new/abanet.org/child/PublicDocuments/adolescent-15.pdf.

Puzzanchera, Charles, and W. Kang. 2008. "Easy Access to Juvenile Court Statistics: 1985–2005." http://ojjdp.ncjrs.gov/ojstatbb/ezajcs.

Redding, Richard E., and Sarah M. Shalf. 2001. "The Legal Context of School Violence: The Effectiveness of Federal, State, and Local Law Enforcement Efforts to Reduce Gun Violence in Schools." *Law and Policy* 23: 297–343.

Ryerson, Ellen. 1978. *The Best Laid Plans: America's Juvenile Court Experiment*. New York: Hill and Wang.

Schwartz, Ira M., John Johnson Kerbs, Danielle M. Hogston, and Cindy L. Guillean. 1992. *Combating Youth Crime: What the Public Really Wants*. Ann Arbor, MI: Center for the Study of Youth Policy.

Scott, Elizabeth S., and Thomas Grisso. 1997. "The Evolution of Adolescence: A Developmental Perspective on Juvenile Justice Reform." *Journal of Criminal Law and Criminology* 88: 137–89.

Scott, Elizabeth S., and Laurence Steinberg. 2003. "Blaming Youth." *Texas Law Review* 81: 799–840.

———. 2008. *Rethinking Juvenile Justice*. Cambridge, MA: Harvard University Press.

Sechrest, Lee B., Susan O. White, and Elizabeth D. Brown, eds. 1979. *The Rehabilitation of Criminal Offenders*. Washington, DC: National Academy of Sciences.

Soler, Marc. 2001. *Public Opinion on Youth, Crime, and Race: A Guide for Advocates*. http://www.buildingblocksforyouth.org/advocacyguide.html.

Szymanski, Linda A. 2007. "Fingerprinting of Alleged or Adjudicated Juvenile Delinquents (2007 Update)." *NCCJ Snapshot*. 12(8) (August). Pittsburgh: National Center for Juvenile Justice.

———. 2008. "Confidentiality of Juvenile Delinquency Hearings (2008 Update)." *NCCJ Snapshot*. 13(5) (May). Pittsburgh: National Center for Juvenile Justice.

———. 2009a. "DNA Registration of Juvenile Offenders (2008 Update)." *NCCJ Snapshot*. 14(1) (January). Pittsburgh: National Center for Juvenile Justice.

———. 2009b. "Megan's Law: Juvenile Sex Offender Registration (2009 Update)." *NCCJ Snapshot*. 14(7) (July). Pittsburgh: National Center for Juvenile Justice.

———. 2009c. "Megan's Law: Juvenile Sex Offender Lower Age Limits (2009 Update)." *NCCJ Snapshot*. 14(8) (August). Pittsburgh: National Center for Juvenile Justice.

———. 2009d. "Megan's Law: Termination of Registration Requirement (2009 Update)." *NCCJ Snapshot*. 14(9) (September). Pittsburgh: National Center for Juvenile Justice.

Tanenhaus, David S. 2004. *Juvenile Justice in the Making*. New York: Oxford University Press.

Wald, Johanna, and Lisa Thurau. 2010. *First, Do No Harm: How Educators and Police Can Work Together More Effectively to Preserve School Safety and Protect Vulnerable Students. Policy Brief*. Cambridge, MA: Institute for Race and Justice, Harvard University.

Wilson, William Julius. 1987. *The Truly Disadvantaged: The Inner City, the Underclass, and Public Policy*. Chicago: University of Chicago Press.

Wright, William F., and Michael C. Dixon. 1977. "Community Treatment of Juvenile Delinquency: A Review of Evaluation Studies." *Journal of Research in Crime and Delinquency* 19: 35–67.

Zimring, Franklin E. 1998a. *American Youth Violence*. New York: Oxford University Press.

———. 1998b. "Toward a Jurisprudence of Youth Violence." *Crime and Justice* 24: 477–501.

———. 2000. "The Punitive Necessity of Waiver." In *The Changing Borders of Juvenile Justice: Transfer of Adolescents to the Criminal Court*, edited by Jeffrey Fagan and Franklin E. Zimring. Chicago: University of Chicago Press.

———. 2004. *An American Travesty: Legal Responses to Adolescent Sexual Offending*. Chicago: University of Chicago Press.

———. 2005. *American Juvenile Justice*. New York: Oxford.

Index

CPSIA information can be obtained at www.ICGtesting.com
Printed in the USA
BVOW06s1549290813

329752BV00004B/11/P